MASTER RECIPES

MASTER RECIPES

Stephen Schmidt

FAWCETT COLUMBINE • NEW YORK

A Fawcett Columbine Book
Published by Ballantine Books

LIBRARY OF CONGRESS CATALOGING-IN-PUBLICATION DATA
Schmidt, Stephen, 1952–
Master recipes.
Includes index.
1. Cookery, American. I. Title.
TX715.S29695 1987 641.5 86-47805
ISBN 0-449-90259-5

Text design by Mary A. Wirth

Manufactured in the United States of America
First Edition: November 1987
10 9 8 7 6 5 4

For Sally and Herk

CONTENTS

Acknowledgments ix
Introduction xi
The Master Kitchen 3
The Master Herb and Spice Shelf 15
Stocks 23
Three Master Sauces and Their Variations 31
A Venerable Art: Deep-Frying 59
Hors d'Oeuvre Inspirations 67
Soups and Chowders 75
Salads, Tossed and Other 107
Eggs 131
The Italian Influence: Pasta and Pizza 177
The Basic American Casserole 199
From Burgers to Pâtés: Ground Meat 203
Fish 217
Shellfish, Snails, and Squid 279
About Meat and Poultry 329
Roasted Meat and Poultry 345
Broiled Meat and Poultry 383
Sautéed Meat and Poultry 393
Braised Poultry and Meat 425
Stewed Poultry and Meat 455
Fresh Vegetables 467
Rice and Dried Beans and Peas 615

The Honest Loaf: Yeast Breads 631
Quick Breads and Pancakes 663
About Chocolate, Coconut, and Various Nuts 695
Puddings, Chilled Desserts, and Sweet Soufflés 705
Bars and Cookies 727
Pies and Other Pastries 749
The Classic American Sweet: Cakes 801
The Finishing Touch: Cake Fillings and Frostings, Pastry Creams, and Dessert Sauces 843
Fresh Fruit and Fruit Desserts 863
Index 903

ACKNOWLEDGMENTS

Foremost and very special thanks are due to my two editors, Marilyn Abraham and Virginia Faber. Never doubting my abilities, Marilyn supported me as I expanded what was originally a book of modest length into the present tome. Ginny saw the book through to completion, painstakingly piecing together a marked-up manuscript as we groped toward a final draft. My thanks also to Pat Connell and Jane Mollman, who copy edited the manuscript at two different stages; Gloria Greaves, who typed the final draft from very messy copy; and Phyllis Wender, my agent, whose kindness, generosity, and hard work helped to make the book happen.

Finally, this being a cookbook, my family and friends, treasured guests at my table, are its music and life. To all of them, and especially to my sister Leah, whose support has always meant so much, my great gratitude and love.

INTRODUCTION

The last twenty years have been an exciting time for people who love to eat and cook. New cuisines of various ethnic persuasions—French, Italian, Chinese, Thai, and Mexican, among others—have spilled across our shores, and culinary movements ranging from classic European to nouvelle European to nouvelle American have swept like fires across the collective cooking consciousness. Every major city boasts its share of chic, ambitious restaurants, run by a new breed of chefs who believe in cooking as a serious, significant art. Hardly a week passes without the appearance of another food or wine magazine, the publication of a new cookbook, the introduction of a novel foodstuff or a new line of cookware. Having grown up in the fifties and sixties, when the notion of glamorous innovation was confined to adding a splash of wine to a stew or topping a tuna casserole with shredded cheese, I find the new atmosphere heady and stimulating. America has come of age culinarily speaking, and to the blaring of a legion of trumpets.

Among many of my friends, cooking has become a major recreational pastime, supplanting reading, gardening, and even television sports watching. My friends follow the trends and clip the recipes—the incredible number of fresh, exciting, innovative, and sometimes perhaps a bit outlandish recipes that are published in magazines, newspapers, and cookbooks, broadcast on radio and television, printed on food packages, and now even demonstrated on video cassette. Over the years, as I have cooked with friends and fielded their panicked questions over my informally dubbed "cooking hotline," I have diagnosed a certain malaise underlying the contemporary food fascination. The truth is that while many people have become adept at following recipes and turning out creditable dishes, they don't really know how to cook. Raised on canned soups, hamburger helpers, frozen vegetables, supermarket bread, and cakes made from out of a box, many of the cooks of my generation stand in relation to recipes as worshippers before a shrine, humble readers of a sacred text, slaves to an inscrutable, all-knowing master. Lacking a familiarity with basic techniques, they cannot expand upon the letter of a recipe's instructions, adding those little touches that make all the difference between a pedestrian and a grand dish. Lacking an instinctive knowledge of their ingredients, they are afraid to make substitutions to suit their own preferences or to stand in for some item they happen not to have on hand. And if disaster should strike, as too often it does, many fledgling cooks have no notion how the dish might be rescued. In short, though many of today's cooks would like to view cooking as a relaxing and satisfying recreational experience rather than as merely another household chore, they are beset with anxiety about the whole enterprise, dimly aware that they just don't know how cooking works.

In *Master Recipes,* my aim is to lay bare the fundamentals of cooking and thereby to give readers a sense of mastery, purpose, and expertise. What cooking professionals know—and what our grandmothers, or perhaps great-grandmothers, also knew—is that cooking, like all other arts and sciences, is built on the relationship between the general and the specific, the major pattern and its various spin-offs—the master formula, or recipe, and its variations. On one level, *Master Recipes* is a collection of recipes for favorite American dishes, an American cookbook. But, unlike other cookbooks, its central ambition is not simply to collect good recipes but rather to organize these recipes in such a way as to make their similarities, in ingredients, in techniques, or in both, readily apparent. A knowledge of the basic patterns that run through cooking leads to the development of cooking instinct, and from this flows the capacity to embellish, invent, and, when necessary, to rescue.

Master Recipes, however, aims to do more than merely provide a conceptual framework for cooking. This book is meant to be cooked from, to be of immediate use to those struggling to master the repertoire of American cooking. One of the most obvious advantages of learning recipe sets rather than single, isolated recipes is that you can increase your culinary range and flexibility in rapid order. Once you've gotten down pat the making of, say, cream of broccoli soup, you are ready to make over two dozen other cream soups. You become a "master" of cream soups, even though you have learned only one basic recipe. Another major advantage of cooking the master recipes way is that each time you prepare a new variation you repeat the same steps you used in preparing the last. This repetition reenforces your knowledge and skill, but, because each variation produces a new dish, you are not liable to the boredom that often sets in when you make the same recipe repeatedly. Finally, it is simply a lot of fun to cook according to the master/variation recipe format, creating entirely new dishes simply by making small changes in ingredients and/or technique in a familiar recipe.

About the Recipes

Master Recipes presents the favorite dishes of traditional American cuisine, the classics. I grew up on these dishes and have, over the years, developed my own special ways with them. And even amidst the ferment of today's many gastronomic revolutions, people of my generation most frequently ask me for recipes for the standard dishes, not the new-fangled ones. Among these are vegetable soup, bean soup, corn and clam chowder; deviled eggs, pizza, and casseroles based on cream sauces; pan-fried fish, baked stuffed clams, and boiled lobster; hamburgers, broiled steak, fried chicken, and beef pot roasts and stews; white bread, corn bread, muffins, and baking powder biscuits; buttered green vegetables, mashed potatoes, and baked beans; chocolate chip, oatmeal, and peanut butter cookies; covered fruit pies, cream pies, and layer cakes. You will also find a number of relatively recent imports: bouillabaisse, soufflés, quiches, and frittatas; pasta in sauces based on heavy cream; fish in white wine sauce; snails in garlic butter and tempura shrimp and oysters; sautéed meat and poultry served with deglazing sauces made with wine, butter, and cream; guacamole; fruit tarts, chocolate ganache cake, and Italian rum cake. Although of foreign influence, these dishes are now so common that no truly comprehensive book of American cooking could fail to include them. It is interesting to note, though perhaps not terribly surprising, that the majority of these imported dishes turn out to be borrowed from French cuisine. Always an important source of inspiration, French cooking, in the sixties and early seventies, practically supplanted American cuisine under the redoubtable sponsorship of Julia Child, whose works taught me and thousands of others what serious cooking means.

Master Recipes also contains recipes—as well as shopping tips and other sorts of basic information—for many of the new varieties of fruits, vegetables, fish, and shellfish that are beginning to appear in our markets. Most of these new foods can be prepared in ways similar to more familiar foods—that is, they can be used in variation recipes—which demonstrates yet another benefit of the master/variation recipe concept, namely the flexibility it provides by enabling you to work easily with new ingredients. For those few newly popular foods that are so anomalous as to require special treatment—fresh tuna, rabe broccoli, and squid spring to mind—I have developed recipes that are straightforward, uncomplicated, and generally within the spirit of the rest of the book.

Finally, scattered here and there you will find recipes that are neither traditional, nor well known, nor based on a recently available fresh food. Most of these are variations of my own devising. Corn and bacon soufflé; ham, bleu cheese, and parsley quiche; anchovy-chili pizza; pork and caper casserole; pan-fried salmon steaks with tomato cream sauce; sautéed ham steaks with apples, curry, and cream; puréed winter squash with Parmesan cheese; honey-ginger bars; orange cream pie; and whole wheat layer cake are just a few of these. These recipes gained a place in this book not only because they are good, fun to make, and a nice change from the usual, but also because they concretely suggest one of the main advantages of thinking in terms of theme and variation: the capacity to invent.

HOW TO USE THIS BOOK

The great majority of individual recipes in this book are variations—on either a Master Recipe or a Master Technique—and thus, in order to complete a dish, you will have to look in two places: first at the variation recipe and then back to the Master formula on which it is based.

If you are working with a variation of a Master Recipe, the ingredients list of the variation will give the title of the Master Recipe and, directly under it, any changes in ingredients that you need to make: "ADD: 2 tablespoons sugar" or "SUBSTITUTE: ½ cup red wine for water." The instruction text of the variation will then explain how the ingredient changes are to be implemented. The majority of variation recipes directly follow the Master Recipe from which they are derived. In those few instances—primarily in the shellfish and dessert chapters—where a variation appears apart from its Master Recipe, a page reference to the appropriate Master Recipe is provided.

The Master Techniques and their variations are set up differently from the Master and variation recipes, but they are used in a similar manner. Most of the variations for Master Techniques are found in long charts which list specific foods and explain how they are to be prepared using the instructions given in the preceding Master Technique. Thus, if you want to prepare baked stuffed codfish, you turn to the cod entry in the chart following the master technique for baked stuffed fish. The entry will tell how much cod you need, which cut to choose, and any other necessary information for preparing cod according to the basic method.

When you are working directly with a Master Recipe (rather than with one of its variations) or with one of the autonomous recipes (that is, recipes that are presented on their own, neither master formulas nor variations), no special procedures are required.

MASTER RECIPES

THE MASTER KITCHEN

Above all, you must feel comfortable in your kitchen. Cleanliness is essential, for it is impossible to feel good about cooking in a dreary, grease-bespattered cubicle.

About counter space. Many of us who live in small apartments or in homes with badly designed kitchens content ourselves with the poorest sorts of counters—a rickety, shallow ledge that has been bracketed to the wall, or a two- or three-foot square patch of counter next to the sink. But cutting and mixing and rolling and all the other movements involved in cooking require that the cook have elbow room, and that he feel comfortable with the surface he is working on. A wobbly counter won't do, nor will a surface that is so narrow that bowls are in danger of sliding off and smashing to the floor. And don't forget that a counter must be of adequate height. Thirty-six inches is standard, and persons six feet tall or more may prefer thirty-eight- or forty-inch counters.

If you cannot replace inadequate counter space entirely, you still owe it to yourself to make a second-best choice. Structurally weak surfaces can often be reinforced, sometimes just with hammer and nails. And certainly you can strip off old contact paper, scour off lingering glue, and give the counter a new surface.

Bright light is essential. Some eschew it, but I love fluorescent light for kitchen work. In my small kitchen I have a four-foot fluorescent fixture over the counter, in addition to three conventional fixtures that I fit with 100-watt bulbs. White- or light-painted walls also help to make a kitchen seem well lit.

In short, what you need is good work space, good light, and, in general, an atmosphere of cleanliness and order. If you are lucky enough also to have a good ventilating fan, all the better, but lacking one, you can keep the air fresh in your kitchen by opening a window.

STORAGE SPACE: Storage space is a real problem in many kitchens. But it is not, as many people suppose, a problem that has no remedy. In dealing with a storage-space shortage, the first thing to do is to throw out whatever food and equipment you really don't need. Discard anything that you cannot remember having used within the past year. (If you can't bring yourself to toss out a certain piece of culinary equipment, an expensive wedding gift, say, store it in some underused closet in another part of your home, or present it to a neighbor or friend as an indefinite "loan." Either way, if you should decide that you need the piece after all [though you never will, of course!] it will be easy to retrieve.)

Before you begin putting things away again, it is a wise idea to transfer some food staples from their original packages to storage containers. Particularly in need of transfer are those products, like flour and sugar, that come in paper bags or unsealable cardboard boxes. Besides blotting up moisture and odors, such packages tear and puncture easily, causing their contents to spill all over your newly cleaned cupboards. For items that are stored in relatively small quantities—rice, dried fruits, pasta shells—I prefer to use glass canning jars, which are inexpensive and have a nice look. If you have small children around, you may prefer containers made of unbreakable plastic; although plastic does absorb food odors, if washed thoroughly in hot water and detergent before each use it can be an acceptable material. There are also those very handsome and practical metal tins, similar to the ones that fruitcakes come in, that are sold in cookware shops and department stores. You don't need to get too fancy. Even empty peanut butter jars, coffee cans, and plastic tubs from the delicatessen can enjoy long and glorious afterlives as food containers.

In organizing your storage space, bear two things in mind. First, food and equipment should be stored separately. Second, the more often you use something the handier it should be. I keep oils, vinegar, garlic, salt, and pepper on an open shelf directly over the counter because these are items I use nearly every day. Similarly, I have the pots and pans that I use regularly hanging right over my stove, while I store those less often called for—the stock pot, the turkey roaster, the large casserole—in out-of-the-way places where I will not keep bumping into them. Remember that all frequently used items should be stored with room to spare so that you can get at them easily.

Here follow my subjective, but I hope useful, notions of what the master kitchen absolutely must have, as well as what it might have, budget permitting. The tour begins with pots and pans.

COOKWARE: Numerous factors must be taken into consideration when buying cookware, which should be thought of as a lifetime investment. Design and color are a consideration, especially if you plan to hang pots and pans on the wall. Each piece must also feel right in your hand, being of a weight that you can manage without strain, with a handle that is the right size and shape for your grasp. Beyond these personal considerations are several equally important matters having to do with the way in which cookware is made and what it is made out of. It is not an exaggeration to say that the pleasure you will take in cooking as well as the success you will enjoy are largely dependent on a proper match of cooking vessel and the culinary task at hand.

WEIGHT: Good-quality cookware always has a certain heft in the hand and a thick bottom so that the heat will be conducted slowly and distributed evenly, thus helping to prevent scorching, sticking, or uneven cooking. Saucepans and casseroles used for general purposes should be of this good-quality, heavy-bottomed type. However, some pieces of cookware need not be. A small saucepan used to hard-cook eggs or warm milk may be made of a light material. Stock pots, spaghetti pots, and turkey roasters may also be lightweight.

CHEMICAL REACTIVITY OF COOKWARE: When shopping for pots and pans it is crucial to consider whether they are made of or lined with a noncorroding material that will not react chemically with foods containing acid (wine, lemon juice, or vinegar, for example), milk, or eggs. Nonreacting materials include ceramic, stainless steel, enamel, and tin. Corrodable metals include aluminum, cast iron, and copper. When a chemically vulnerable food is prepared in an unsuitable pot or pan the results can be disastrous. For example, a deglazing sauce containing wine or vinegar will pick up an extremely unpleasant metallic taste if prepared in a skillet made of unlined cast iron. Similarly, a hollandaise sauce will turn gray if made in an unlined aluminum saucepan and green if prepared in a bare-metal copper pan. Of course, some cooking vessels are rarely used in the preparation of chemically sensitive foods, and these vessels need not be constructed of nonreacting materials. Stock pots, spaghetti pots, and turkey roasters do not have to be chemically nonreacting.

MATERIALS: As a quick tour of a good cookware shop will demonstrate, pots and pans are available in an almost endless variety of materials. A discussion of the advantages and disadvantages of the four most common types of cookware follows. It omits reference to unusual or specialized pots and pans—those made of copper, silver, or various exotic alloys, for example—which are hard to find and generally outrageously expensive.

Lightweight aluminum: This is not an acceptable material for saucepans and casseroles because it conducts heat unevenly and thus causes foods to scorch, stick, and curdle. However, spaghetti pots, stock pots, and turkey roasters made of lightweight aluminum are quite usable, especially if they are coated with enamel, which not only adds weight but also prevents chemically sensitive foods from reacting with the pan.

Stainless steel: Cookware made of stainless steel and reinforced on the bottom with copper or aluminum is excellent for all cooking tasks. However, only the expensive brands will prove heavy enough on the bottom to protect delicate egg yolk sauces such as hollandaise or to maintain dishes such as stews and pot roasts at a slow but steady simmer over several hours without scorching.

Cast aluminum: Most restaurant professionals work with heavy (1/8 inch thick or more) die-cast aluminum cookware, which distributes heat evenly and holds heat well. Since aluminum can react with acidic foods and egg yolks, best-quality cast aluminum pans are lined with stainless steel. Until recently, cast aluminum cookware was a rarity at retail outlets, but it is now generally available.

Cast iron: Like cast aluminum, cast iron heats foods slowly and evenly and thus has always been a favored material for cookware. Since iron is very prone to reacting with chemically sensitive foods, most cast iron cookware, except for skillets, is lined with enamel. Enamel-lined cast iron is a particularly good material for casseroles, because it can maintain stews and similar recipes at a simmer over a period of many hours. Unlined (or "bare") cast iron also makes excellent skillets, for it promotes the browning of foods. However, I find saucepans made of enameled cast iron too heavy for easy maneuverability and too prone to developing hot spots.

POTS AND PANS: First, *saucepans.* You need at least three of them: a small one (about 1 quart) for melting butter or simmering a couple of eggs; a medium-sized one (about 2 quarts) for sauces and the like; and a rather large one (say, 3½ to 4½ quarts) for general cooking purposes. All should have lids.

Second, *frypans* and *skillets.* A small skillet 4 or 5 inches in diameter is handy for toasting a handful of sesame seeds or for frying a hamburger for lunch. A sturdy heavy-gauge aluminum skillet, 9 to 10 inches across and coated with nonstick Teflon or Silverstone, is essential. Though you cannot brown meat in this skillet, it is terrific for making braised vegetables, fried eggs, and, of course, omelets. I could not survive without mine. For browning meat, frying chicken, and preparing meat or poultry sautés, you need at least one large skillet 10 or more inches in diameter (measured across the bottom) and 2 to 3 inches deep (so that fat won't spatter all over the kitchen). For certain sautés, an even larger skillet—12 inches in diameter—is handy. If you are investing in only one skillet, it should be made of cast aluminum lined with stainless steel, so that it can be used to prepare chemically sensitive foods. You should have lids for your large skillets—you may be able to use the lids that come with your casseroles.

You need two enamel-lined cast iron *casseroles,* with lids, a 1½- to 2½-quart casserole for preparing rice and baked vegetable dishes, and one with a capacity of 5 or 6 quarts for braising whole chickens or preparing baked beans for a crowd.

The standard *roasting pan* is about 10 inches wide, 14 to 15 inches long, and 2 or 3 inches deep. Heavy aluminum and enameled cast iron are the materials of choice for roasters, because these materials can be placed over direct heat to make gravy. (Even quite large turkeys will fit inside a conventional roasting pan, so you don't really need one of those oval-shaped, lidded turkey roasters. However, if you do own a turkey roaster, you will find it very handy for poaching fish and boiling lobsters.)

A good *broiling pan* is essential. I own two: a large pan (17×12 inches) that will accommodate a whole cut-up chicken or two large T-bone steaks, and a smaller one (10×7 inches) that is useful for broiling a few chicken pieces or a couple of chops. A broiling pan consists of a slotted or perforated broiling tray on which the food is placed, and a pan that fits underneath to catch the drippings. Even in a pinch, you should think twice before following the common practice of fashioning an impromptu broiling apparatus by setting a cake rack atop a baking tray: Fat drippings may catch fire when meat or, especially, chicken is broiled.

A *fish poacher* is a marvelous thing to own, but quite expensive. If you decide to invest in a poacher, buy one that measures 4 to 5 inches deep and 16 to 18 inches long. Such a poacher will accommodate a 4- to 5-pound whole dressed fish serving 4 to 6 persons and is adequate for most other uses. Stainless steel or enamel-lined poachers are preferable to those made of unlined aluminum, which may react with the wine, lemon juice, or vinegar often used in fish-poaching broths.

For boiling vegetables and making pasta you need a nice, roomy *pot*—8 quarts at least, and 10, 12, or 14 quarts if possible. My vegetable pot comes with a slotted basket that fits snugly inside, reaching down to within a couple of inches of the bottom of the pot. This basket makes the draining of pasta and vegetables a snap—you simply lift the food out of the pot and over the sink—and I highly recommend that you consider purchasing a pot of this type.

MEASURES: You should have at least two full sets of cup measures (1 cup, ½ cup, ⅓ cup, ¼ cup) and of spoon measures (1 tablespoon, 1 teaspoon, ½ teaspoon, ¼ teaspoon). It is helpful also to have a 2-tablespoon (that is, ⅛-cup) measure—I use a plastic scoop that came in a can of coffee—and both a 2-cup and a 4-cup (1-quart) measure. Measuring cups and spoons should be made of stainless steel—not plastic (which melts and picks up grease and odors), not tin (which bends and dents) and not glass (which shatters when placed directly on a burner). With the exceptions of the 2-cup and 4-cup containers, cup measures should be the type that are filled to the brim, not those with a lip extending beyond their maximum measured capacity. Brim-type cups are called "dry measures," while the lip type are often referred to as "liquid measures." Dry measures can be used to hold liquids as long as you are careful not to jostle the brimming cup, but liquid measures are not suitable for measuring dry ingredients such as flour. Flour should always be measured by dipping a cup into a large container of flour and sweeping off the excess with the back of a knife. A lipped cup makes this impossible.

BOWLS: You need five at least, and more if you can afford them. They should be made of stainless steel or heat-proof ceramic or glass, and have deep, steep-sloping sides, so that food does not spill out of them when mixed. For a starter set, I recommend one 4-quart, one 3-quart, one 2-quart, and two 1-quart bowls. When you want to expand your collection, get a 5- to 6-quart bowl, plus additional bowls in 3- and 2-quart sizes.

KNIVES: In my view, there are three essentials: a small *paring knife*, 3 to 3½ inches long, for peeling, paring, and slicing; a medium-sized all-purpose *chopping* (or "*utility*") *knife* about 7 or 8 inches long, for cutting up vegetables, slicing meat, and so on; and a medium-sized *serrated knife* for slicing bread, tomatoes (though any sharp knife can do this), frozen cake, frozen vegetables, and the like. Once you've got these essential knives, you can expand your collection by purchasing a good, sturdy *cleaver* (for cutting poultry bones and frozen meats); a large *chef's knife* (for chopping onions or parsley); and perhaps a small serrated knife. Though not strictly a knife, a *vegetable peeler*—the inexpensive, lightweight kind with a swivel blade—is surely a must in any kitchen for the peeling of potatoes, carrots, cucumbers, asparagus, and various fruits. And don't forget to invest in an effective *knife sharpener*—either a rod type or, if you can stand the noise, the type that you scrape the blade through—and to use it frequently. (Always chop on a relatively soft surface such as wood or plastic, or you may damage your knife beyond repair.)

Professional-quality knives are made either of carbon steel or so-called "high-carbon" stainless steel. Many professional cooks work with carbon steel knives because they are able to take an extremely sharp edge and are also lightweight and easy to maneuver for delicate tasks. However, carbon steel knives dull quickly—they have to be sharpened with every use—and they tend to nick and dent easily. Worse, they blacken and rust upon exposure to moisture, which means that they must be washed and dried immediately after they are used. By contrast, high-carbon stainless steel knives are tough and rust-resistant (because they are "stainless") while at the same time soft enough to take a good edge (because they contain a high amount of carbon). Thus, I think high-carbon stainless steel knives are the practical choice for the home cook.

Another critical consideration in buying a knife is the size, shape, and weight of the handle. In the best knives, the blade runs all the way through the handle rather than merely being attached to it. Never buy a knife without holding it in your hand to make sure that it has the right feel or "fit" for you. Some people, myself included, feel more masterly and in control of the task at hand when working with a heavy-handled knife; many others feel exactly the opposite way.

COOKING TOOLS, WOODEN SPOONS, SPATULAS, TONGS, WIRE WHIPS: I think it essential to have two *metal spatulas* (one large and one small), a *slotted skimmer* or *slotted spoon*, and a large *ladle*. A *large metal spoon* for skimming stocks and a *large fork* for turning meats are also nice to have, but not crucial. Try to find cooking tools made of heavy-gauge stainless steel—not lightweight stainless (it will bend), or copper (it is handsome, but it bends, tarnishes, and even turns some foods green). I very much like to hang my large cooking tools over the stove.

Wooden spoons are a kitchen necessity. They are very inexpensive, so get fistfuls of them in different sizes and lengths, and buy a few straight-ended *wooden spatulas* while you're at it, as these are perfect for stirring scorchable sauces. *Rubber spatulas* are indispensable for scraping out bowls, smoothing dips, and folding beaten egg whites and whipped cream into cake batters, soufflés, chiffon pies, and such. You can also use them for frosting cakes, if you do not own a long-bladed metal frosting spatula. Buy at least two rubber spatulas, a medium-sized and a large one. Finally, a sturdy pair of tongs is a must for deep-frying and for turning those sautéed foods that should not be punctured with a fork.

The *wire whip*, sometimes called balloon whip or wire whisk, does almost any kind of beating or aerating work quickly and efficiently, and you may find that you begin to use it even for such tasks as beating egg whites and whipping cream, instead of lugging out the electric mixer. Be sure to buy a good, professional-quality whip constructed of multiple layers of wire coil with a wide, sturdy handle that can be grasped comfortably. If you are investing in only one whip, buy one measuring 2½ to 3 inches across at the widest point and 12 inches long. Such a whip will fit into a bowl as small as 1½ quarts but can also be used to beat up to a dozen large egg whites or whip 2 to 3 cups of cream. Remember to keep your whip immaculately clean.

GRATERS, GRINDERS, SQUEEZERS, CHOPPERS, PRESSERS: Buy a *grater* with at least four sides, each side having perforations of different sizes and shapes for doing different jobs. The grater should include a slicing plate (mainly for coleslaw), a shredding plate (for Swiss cheese or for apples, zucchini, or carrots that are destined for bread), a small-hole grating plate (for citrus zest, onions, and Parmesan cheese), and a very small-hole grating plate (for nutmeg). Look for one that is made of stainless steel and has a handle on the top. Wash the grater carefully after every use, scrubbing the small-hole plates with an old toothbrush if necessary.

Although some people consider pressed garlic inferior in taste to garlic that has been finely minced with a knife, my palate cannot detect the difference between the two in most dishes, and pressing is often more convenient than mincing. But you must shop carefully for a *garlic press* if you want to be sure of getting one that actually works, as there are many inferior models on the market. Look for one that is made of heavy-gauge metal, with a deep barrel and a swinging plunger that fits into the barrel tightly.

A *potato ricer* is specifically designed for pressing potatoes into ricelike strands; this preliminary operation insures smooth, lump-free mashed potatoes. You can also rice potatoes by forcing them through a colander or sieve with the back of a spoon, so a ricer is not a mandatory item unless you happen to eat lots of mashed potatoes.

Both the old-fashioned *meat grinder* and the *food mill* are rapidly taking on the look of nineteenth-century curiosity pieces in this age of food processors and superefficient blenders, mixers, and nut grinders. If you happen not to own a food processor, you will need a meat grinder if you wish to make croquettes, pâtés, or soufflés that are flavored with fish or meat. (Blenders do not have motors powerful enough to handle the work that these recipes require.) As for the food mill, its main function is to purée solid foods.

Peppercorns should be ground just prior to use because the volatile oils in pepper quickly evaporate and the flavor dissipates once the berries are broken. Thus you need at least two *peppermills*, one for black and another for white peppercorns, and you may wish to invest in a third peppermill for black pepper that is used at the table. A particularly useful kind of peppermill has recently appeared on the market. This has a mechanism for regulating the fineness of the pepper and a detachable cup on the bottom that catches the pepper as it is ground so that it may be easily measured for a recipe.

The difference between ground nutmeg that comes in a tin and nutmeg that has been freshly grated from a whole berry is dramatic. The former has very little taste because nutmeg, like pepper, loses its volatile flavor oils to the atmosphere soon after being grated or ground. A serious cook, therefore, will always grate nutmeg fresh for each use. The tiny *nutmeg grater* that does the job costs only a dollar or two, and it takes up little space in a cluttered kitchen. Whole nutmegs, which are sold in supermarkets, last for years.

If you find yourself needing to pulverize or mash a small amount of herbs or spices a *mortar and pestle* are handy, as a blender generally will not dispatch small amounts of anything very efficiently. Purchase a mortar and pestle large enough to do a job without ejecting mashed matter all over the countertop.

Marble and brass are both good materials; wood is too soft and porous and will soak up liquid and odors.

BASKETS, COLANDERS, STRAINERS: The collapsible *steaming basket*, which comes in several sizes, is indispensable in cooking a variety of vegetables, and it may also be used to steam chicken and fish and to remoisturize stale rolls. A *deep-frying basket* is convenient for frying small pieces of food—french-fried potatoes, shellfish, or miniature cocktail croquettes, for example—because it allows you to lower and raise the food in and out of the fat all at one time, insuring that the pieces cook evenly. For draining cooked foods a *colander* is essential. Buy a large one—6 quarts at least—so that you will be able to toss a large quantity of food without worrying that it will spill out. Stainless steel is an attractive and durable material, but aluminum colanders are cheaper and do the job just as well.

Most kitchens can use several *strainers* of various capacities and mesh sizes. Buy a small, very fine-mesh tea strainer for preparing tea, filtering small amounts of highly reduced stocks, or straining the residue out of a béarnaise sauce. A 2- or 3-cup medium-mesh all-purpose strainer is handy for sifting flour, cocoa, and confectioner's sugar (a strainer is actually faster and easier to use than a sifter), for sieving out pieces of ground nuts that need to be ground again, and for the straining of stocks, broths, soups and such. If you have a 1½- to 2-quart strainer with a medium or coarse mesh you can rice potatoes, remove the skins and seeds from cooked tomatoes, or mash fruits and vegetables by pushing the food against the mesh basket with the back of a spoon. A large strainer can also double as a colander for draining small amounts of vegetables and pasta, and can be used to filter the impurities out of stocks and broths if it is lined with cheesecloth.

THERMOMETERS: A set of accurate thermometers is essential to serious cooking. First, you'll need a good-quality *meat thermometer*. Look for the professional needle-stemmed vest-pocket type, also known as an "instant reading" thermometer, which gives readings all the way from 0°F to 220°F and is accurate to within just a few degrees. It can be used not only for meat but for taking the temperature of delicate egg-yolk sauces or of liquids in which yeast is to be dissolved for breadmaking.

A *candy/deep-fry thermometer* takes all the guesswork out of sugar cookery and deep-frying. When shopping for a candy/deep-fry thermometer, look for a sturdy model that can be entirely immersed in water for washing. You get what you pay for. A dimestore brand is likely to be way off.

Last, *oven* and *freezer thermometers* will reveal your appliances' idiosyncrasies and allow you to compensate for them. These thermometers are reasonably priced and, if of good quality, durable. I think everyone should use them.

Small Appliances: An *electric mixer* is a necessity but you need not invest in a large, expensive, stationary model unless you frequently prepare large quantities of heavy batters. A lightweight hand-held mixer is easy to maneuver, and because you can push the beaters all through the batter and around the edges of the bowl, you actually get a more thorough blending than you do using a stationary mixer.

A well-equipped kitchen should have both a blender and a food processor, but if you must make a choice between the two appliances, start with a blender. Buy a sturdy, powerful *blender* that has controls both for pulsing and for sustained blending. The pulse speed is used for grating cheese, grinding nuts, and crumbing bread—all of which tend to cake at the bottom of the blender jar unless the motor is switched on and off. Invest a little extra to get a blender with a glass jar; plastic jars tend to warp and crack and they also pick up odors and gradually become filmed with unremovable grease. Some types of blenders come with miniature blending jars (about 1 cup capacity), which are very convenient for making a small amount of bread crumbs or chopping a handful of parsley.

A good *food processor* can do many tricks that a blender cannot. It can slice and shred vegetables and cheese, knead bread dough, and, most crucially, it can chop or reduce to a fine silken paste any meat or fish, whether raw or cooked. But with food processors too, you get what you pay for. It is far wiser to do without one entirely than to buy a bargain-basement model, for the recipes you are most likely to prepare in the processor—breads, pâtés, cream puff pastry, and the like—cannot be made efficiently in the cheaper machines, no matter what the company may claim. Models with large containers and wide feed tubes have recently appeared on the market. These models are much more versatile than smaller machines and are worth their hefty price.

A *toaster oven* comes in handy for toasting bread, reheating leftovers, and baking potatoes, but I don't consider it satisfactory for any other kind of cooking or baking.

If you have the space, you might consider investing in a *microwave* oven. It doesn't do much, but what it does do it does very well. Specifically, it reheats foods, especially liquidy ones, quickly and evenly; it makes terrific bacon; it melts butter and chocolate and softens refrigerated cheese; and it recrisps soggy potato chips and crackers. It also does a spectacular job of cooking fresh fish. But don't try to roast meat, cook vegetables, or bake breads or cakes in a microwave oven; your regular oven will do a much better job.

BAKING EQUIPMENT: To roll out pastry evenly, you need a *rolling pin* that is at least 12 inches long, not counting the handles, but that is not too heavy for you to manipulate easily. If your work surface is large enough you might want to invest in a pin 14, 16, or even 18 inches long. Such a pin will allow you to dispatch even triple recipes of pie crust in a flash. I like to work with a pin made of heavy, unvarnished wood; some prefer lacquered wood, heavy-weight plastic, or marble. I also prefer to use a pin with handles (preferably constructed with a ball-bearing mechanism), but others are more comfortable using a one-piece, handleless pin.

You should have either a *sifter* or a medium-capacity, medium-mesh sieve or strainer that can be used as a sifter. You need *racks* for cooling cakes and cookies—racks are one of those things that no cook ever seems to have quite enough of—as well as a large, soft, thick *pastry brush* for painting on glazes and for brushing unwanted crumbs off cakes and pastry crusts. (A soft-bristle paint-brush bought at a hardware store is every bit as efficient as an "official" pastry brush; also useful are tied-together chicken feathers, which are the Middle European version of the pastry brush.) If you dislike blending pastry doughs with your fingertips, by all means invest in a *pastry blender.* This is a tool fitted with bow-shaped blades or wires that cut butter and shortening into dry ingredients; as a substitute for this tool you can also use two knives, one held in each hand.

A *pastry bag* and various different decorating tips will help to give your confections a professional look. The bag itself—and you really ought to have several in various sizes—should be made of nylon (like a windbreaker), not canvas or rubber, both of which become smelly no matter how well they are washed.

BAKING PANS, MOLDS, AND SHEETS: Baking pans and sheets that look very similar to one another are often subtly different in size and/or shape. Make sure of the exact dimension you need before you buy. Avoid cake pans whose sides slope outward, pie pans with small holes punched in the bottom, or a tart mold whose bottom turns out not to be removable. Read the label also to ascertain that the pan is the size you want. If the label does not provide complete measurement information, ask a salesperson to measure the pan for you, or do it yourself. Always choose bakeware made of a durable, nonrusting material.

The yeast bread recipes in this book and in many other standard American cookbooks yield enough dough to fill one standard *loaf pan* measuring 9 inches by 5 inches across and 2½ inches high, with a capacity of about 7½ cups. These same recipes may be prepared using two smaller loaf pans, with a capacity of about 4 cups each. Many tea loaf recipes require medium-sized loaf pans, with a capacity of approximately 6 cups. Loaf pans may be made of ordinary polished aluminum, the most usual material; black-finished aluminum, which some people feel promotes a good, brown crust; or glass, which conducts heat very efficiently.

A standard *pie pan* measures 9 inches across (the measurement is taken from inside the lip of the pan) and 1½ inches deep. Unless you are a prolific baker, one or perhaps two pie pans are all you will need. Like loaf pans, pie pans may be made of ordinary aluminum, black-finished aluminum, or glass. Both ordinary aluminum and black-finished aluminum are satisfactory, the latter perhaps imparting a deeper brown to the finished crust, but I find that glass browns pie crusts unevenly and sometimes causes them to burn.

For baking quiches and fruit tarts you need a *French tart mold* made of ordinary or black-finished aluminum, with a removable bottom. These molds come in a variety of sizes: those measuring about 9½ inches across and 1½ inches deep have roughly the same capacity as standard pie pans. When shopping for *tartlet molds,* whether individual dessert size or bite-sized (for hors d'oeuvre), choose relatively shallow molds with broad bottoms. Tartlets made in deep, narrow-bottomed molds are likely to crack when unmolded, and, because their base is so small, they are apt to wobble and even fall over after they are filled.

If you have just two round *cake pans* measuring 9 inches across and 2 inches deep you can make most cakes. If you also buy three 9×1½-inch round pans, an 8-inch square pan, a tube pan (for angel cakes), and a Bundt pan (a tube pan with a fancy fluted bottom), you will have even more flexibility. For more information on cake pans, see the cake chapter. Cake pans are also available in fancy shapes—stars, hearts, flowers, bunnies, venison saddles, and numerals, to name just a few. Aluminum is the only acceptable material for cake pans. Cakes made in glass pans rise unevenly and tend to become crusty and/or tough on the outside.

A *springform pan* has hinged and detachable sides so that a delicate baked good—most commonly cheesecake—can be partially unmolded for cutting without being removed from the bottom of the pan. Springform pans range in size from 7 to 12 inches across; all are about 3 inches deep. The best all-purpose size is about 10 inches in diameter. This can often be used in recipes specifying a pan of a slightly different size.

To make cookies you need two large, rimless *baking sheets.* (More information on cookie sheets appears in the cookie chapter.) Biscuits and the like may be baked on the same rimless baking sheets or on a *jelly roll pan.* Jelly roll pans come in two sizes: 17 inches long and 11 inches wide, and 15 inches long and about 10 inches wide. I think it is a good idea to have as many as half a dozen rimless baking sheets and jelly roll pans around for such uses as holding batches of fried or sautéed foods in a warm oven, catching chocolate glaze that drips off a cake, and so on. Be sure that your baking sheets and jelly roll pans are made of top-quality aluminum and not that other aluminum alloy that has a dull, blackish sheen and that rusts easily.

If you make soufflés you will want to have a nice porcelain *soufflé mold.* It should have straight sides and hold 6 cups. Molds holding 4, 5, and 8 cups are also available. If you want to make muffins or cupcakes, you should have a 12-cup *muffin tin.*

THE MASTER HERB and SPICE SHELF

Early Americans were mad for highly seasoned foods. They grew in home gardens whatever herbs and spices they could, and the ones they could not grow—cinnamon, cloves, and pepper, for example—they were willing to buy at exorbitant prices. By the late nineteenth century the pendulum had swung the other way. American cooks began using fewer herbs and spices, and used them very sparingly. Recipes typically called for mere pinches and 1⁄16 teaspoons of seasonings that had once been added liberally. Today, the proverbial pendulum is swinging back the other way once again. Influenced by the cuisines of China, India, and southern Europe, American cooks are conducting bold experiments with a variety of herbs and spices. In addition to adding the usual seasonings in the usual dishes—thyme in stews, oregano on pizza, bay leaf in tomato sauce, ginger in gingerbread—creative cooks are coming up with new and provocative combinations, such as mint and cold beef, coriander seed and pastry, turmeric and fish broth, cinnamon and root vegetables. My own feeling about "unusual" seasonings is that they can do nothing to rescue a badly or indifferently prepared dish and that they can ruin a perfectly good dish if they are ill-chosen or used too freely. On the other hand, if added thoughtfully and with panache, unusual seasonings can make an already good dish spectacular.

Horticulturally speaking, an herb consists of leaves and/or stems of an aromatic plant, while a spice is derived from seeds, roots, bark, or buds. Thus basil, mint, parsley, and tarragon are considered herbs, while cinnamon, cloves, nutmeg, and ginger are spices. Although all bottled seasonings are commonly referred to as "spices," spices and herbs have somewhat different properties.

HERBS: Since dried herbs deteriorate in the presence of heat, light, and moisture, you should, whenever possible, buy them in metal tins rather than bottles; store them tightly lidded in a cool, dry, dark place. You will find that whole-leaf dried herbs lose their savor within six to twelve months and that crushed or ground herbs go stale even more quickly. There are, however, certain rather potent herbs, thyme and rosemary among them, that retain their taste for somewhat longer. Use your nose to determine if a dried herb is still good. If the scent is faint or nonexistent, the herb has lost its flavoring power.

Fresh herbs always are more complex and interesting in taste than dried herbs, and fortunately fresh herbs are becoming an increasingly common sight at markets. As a general rule of thumb, use fresh herbs in a quantity two to three times greater than you would use dried herbs.

SPICES: With the exceptions of ginger and horseradish, spices are available only in dried form. Like herbs, spices should be purchased in metal tins and stored away from heat, moisture, and light. However, spices retain their flavor much longer than herbs, and even when they are quite old they are often still usable. Simply double or triple the amount called for in the recipe.

GRINDING HERBS AND SPICES: Special herb and spice grinders, most of which can also be used to grind coffee, are especially handy and efficient. However, a blender will also do an adequate job, especially if fitted with a small blending jar, which can be purchased as a special attachment for some models. Those who like to work with their hands and muscles can make short work of herbs and spices using a marble or metal mortar and pestle.

COMMON HERBS AND SPICES

I know that the huge selection of herbs and spices in supermarkets can look daunting to the uninitiated. Therefore, I have marked with an asterisk (*) those seasonings that I think no kitchen should be without. Others can be purchased as needed.

ALLSPICE: Available both whole and ground, allspice tastes like a mixture of cinnamon, nutmeg, and cloves, with cloves predominating. You can substitute it for the cloves in many recipes. It is frequently used in Swedish-influenced dishes.

ANISE: This spice, which comes both whole and ground, has a mild but definite licorice taste that one either abhors or loves. Whole anise seeds are most commonly sprinkled on top of cookies. Ground anise is used to flavor various baked goods and may be substituted for star anise in Chinese cooking.

*BASIL: This is an extremely important herb in all Mediterranean and Mediterranean-influenced cooking. When fresh, basil is a rather pungent aromatic, with licorice undertones; when dried, the herb loses much of its potency and complexity, and a certain buttery flavor comes to the fore. Basil goes particularly well with tomato-based dishes, but it also gives zip to fish, soups, and creamed dishes.

*BAY LEAF: Domestic bay (from California) is stronger and more resinous than imported bay (usually from Turkey). Bay provides an indispensable background flavor in dark soups, stews, sauces, and tomato mixtures, and in ground form it gives a spicy, woodsy bite to pork dishes, sausages, and pâtés. Use bay with discretion; it is potent.

CARAWAY SEED: Generally used whole, this resinous-tasting seed is best known as a flavoring for rye bread, but it also goes well with cabbage and sauerkraut. Caraway can also be used as a seasoning for roast veal, pork, or duck.

CARDAMOM: Whether you buy it in large whole seeds or ground, cardamom is always very expensive. With its distinctly sweet taste and a pungent nutmeg-like bouquet, cardamom is most commonly used in coffeecakes and Christmas cookies. It is often used in Indian cooking as well.

CAYENNE PEPPER: Consisting of the ground pods and seeds of a chililike pepper, cayenne is perhaps the hottest spice available, so use it sparingly. Egg and cheese dishes and creamed foods are often seasoned with cayenne.

CELERY SEED: Taken from the wild celery plant, celery seed has a spicier flavor than stalks of fresh celery. It is generally added to potato salad, cole slaw, and pickles. Do not substitute celery seed for fresh celery in a soup, stock, sauce, or stew.

CHERVIL: This very mild herb is similar in taste to parsley, with slight licorice undertones. Unfortunately, it is nearly tasteless when dried.

*CHILI POWDER: The main ingredient of most chili powders is ground dried chili peppers. Other herbs, spices, and flavorings such as oregano, garlic, cumin, turmeric, coriander seed, and cloves are added in varying proportions. All chili powders are hot; some, particularly those labelled "Mexican," are downright incendiary.

CHIVES: See page 555.

*CINNAMON: One of the most widely used of all spices, cinnamon comes both ground and in stick form. In addition to its common use as a flavoring for baked goods, ground cinnamon is a prevalent seasoning in Middle Eastern meat dishes. Stick cinnamon is added to hot drinks, syrups, and dessert sauces.

*CLOVE: Sold both whole and ground, clove is a very potent spice and should be used with discretion. It is most often used in breads, spice cakes, and cookies. One or at most two cloves stuck in a small onion or wrapped in a cheesecloth bag will impart a pleasant, sweetish, but not overly spicy flavor to soups, stews, and tomato sauces. Under proper storage conditions, cloves will keep for several years without losing their flavor.

CORIANDER(CILANTRO): Sometimes called Chinese parsley, this plant provides both a spice and an herb. The spice, coriander seed, is the more familiar to Western cooks. Coriander seed has a citrusy, tart-bitter taste; it is used whole in pickling solutions and ground as a component of curry powder. The leaves, strangely enough, do not resemble the seeds in taste but rather harbor suggestions of lemon, lavender, black pepper, and parsley. Seviche, guacamole, and a number of Chinese and Southeast Asian dishes are traditionally prepared with coriander leaves, and they are also used to brighten salads and deviled eggs. Be sure to add chopped coriander leaves to a dish just before serving, as they lose most of their flavor within fifteen or twenty minutes if the dish is cold, just two or three minutes if hot. Coriander leaves lose all flavor if dried. Fresh coriander can be found at Spanish and Asian vegetable markets (and some supermarkets) in large cities, and it is very easy to grow in a home garden.

CRUSHED RED PEPPER: Made from the pods and seeds of dried chili peppers, crushed red pepper is reliably hot and a little usually goes a long way. It can be sprinkled on pizza and is often called for in Spanish, Italian, and Latin American soups, stews, sauces, and egg dishes. To substitute crushed red pepper for whole dried chilis, use 1/4 teaspoon for each dried chili called for. Further information on chili peppers appears on page 569.

CUMIN: An essential ingredient in both curry and chili powders, cumin has an exotic flavor suggestive of cedar but is not hot. It complements many different sorts of foods, including eggs, fish, meat, and poultry, and it can be offered plain as a dip for barbecued or broiled lamb or beef. It is generally used ground, though whole seeds are also available.

*CURRY POWDER: Many spices go into curry powder, though the kinds and proportions vary from one brand to the next. The four major components of curry are usually coriander seed, cumin, turmeric, and cayenne pepper; fenugreek, cardamom, mustard seed, ginger, and black pepper are other common additions. Curry powders differ greatly with respect to hotness, with those labeled "Madras" (after the Indian province) being the most explosive. A variety of savory dishes can be curried or given a curry accent.

*DILL: Seeds of dill are used to make pickles, while the leaves, either fresh or dried, add a distinctive taste to salads, cream sauces, cream soups, and fish. When using fresh dill, discard the stems, which are tough and fibrous.

FENNEL SEED: Generally used whole rather than ground, fennel seed has a pronounced licorice flavor and is always added in modest amounts. It is particularly identified with the cooking of southern France and Italy, but is also used in Indian curries and in American cucumber pickles. A few fennel seeds may be included in an herb bag used to flavor a Mediterranean-style soup, stew, or tomato sauce.

FINES HERBES: This is a classic French combination of equal proportions of fresh parsley, tarragon, chervil, and chives. To make a substitute for 1 tablespoon of fines herbes, combine 2 teaspoons minced fresh parsley, 1 teaspoon snipped chives, and ½ teaspoon dried tarragon.

*GARLIC: See page 556.

*GINGER: This very popular spice is available in several forms and finds its way into a wide range of dishes. The familiar ground dried ginger was once reserved for use in cakes, cookies, and pies, but nowadays it is added to vegetable, fish, and meat dishes as well. Fresh ginger root is becoming an increasingly common sight in American supermarkets. It is primarily used in Asian cooking, but you can substitute 2 parts finely grated fresh ginger for 1 part ground ginger in American recipes. To preserve fresh ginger root, peel it, cover it with dry sherry or vodka in a glass jar, and store it, covered, in the refrigerator. It will keep for a year or more. Candied or crystallized ginger can be substituted for fresh ginger root in recipes if you wash off the sugar. It can also be eaten like candy.

HORSERADISH: This wonderful root is most commonly available "prepared" in jars, but in the late fall and winter check your market for fresh horseradish root, which resembles a large knobby carrot in appearance. Freshly grated horseradish is tastier and more pungent than prepared horseradish. To use the fresh root, peel it deeply, grate it, and use as you would prepared horseradish. Cover any leftovers with lemon juice or vinegar to prevent discoloration, and refrigerate.

JUNIPER: Juniper berries are not always available at the market, but you can pick them yourself from wild juniper bushes, which grow in wooded areas in many parts of the country. Juniper is the evergreenlike flavor in gin; its chief culinary use is in marinades for pork and game.

MACE: This spice is ground from the fleshy shell that covers a nutmeg, and it is similar to nutmeg in taste, only somewhat more pungent. It has traditionally been added to pound cakes, fruit pies, and certain chocolate desserts. Unlike nutmeg, it retains its flavor for a good while after it is ground.

MARJORAM: This term denotes a family of herbs, the best known member of which is oregano. The type of marjoram commonly available at supermarkets has an oreganolike taste with suggestions of evergreen and mint. It is used in many egg, fish, poultry, and meat recipes.

MINT: This refreshing herb can be put in the accustomed places—iced drinks, candies, and chocolate desserts—or in more unexpected places, such as cold salads, cold soups, steamed fish, and any number of vegetable dishes. Fresh mint has infinitely more flavor than the dried herb, but the latter is useful in an emergency.

*MUSTARD: This highly versatile spice comes in three forms: whole mustard seed, dry mustard, and prepared mustard. The whole seed is used chiefly in making pickles. Dry mustard, which is ground mustard seed, is prized as a flavoring for sauces, egg dishes, and shellfish, and can also be mixed with a cold liquid to produce an extremely pungent condiment. After being blended with a liquid, mustard must be allowed to stand, uncovered, for at least 15 minutes so that it will lose any harsh, bitter taste.

Prepared mustards are a whole world unto themselves. Americans are most familiar with so-called "ballpark" mustard, the very bright yellow stuff with the brash, vinegary taste that goes so well with hot dogs. For most cooking purposes, Dijon-style mustards are preferred. These are much hotter than ballpark mustard and, because they are prepared with wine and herbs and matured in wooden casks, they are exceptionally rich and flavorful. True Dijon mustard must come from the Dijon region of France, but excellent Dijon-style mustards are made in Germany, Great Britain, and the United States. Asian cuisines also make use of various prepared mustards, most of which are, by occidental standards, exceedingly hot—so beware.

*NUTMEG: This is one of the few spices that is equally at home in savory and sweet dishes. Nutmeg has a natural affinity for veal, spinach, onions, and potatoes, and a goodly grating of the spice is crucial to a well-made cream sauce. It is also used to flavor cakes, pies, cookies, and hot and cold drinks. Nutmeg does not keep well in its ground form, so it is a good idea to buy only whole nutmegs and grate them as needed. Special nutmeg graters are available at gourmet cookware shops, or you can simply use the smallest holes of an ordinary grater.

ORANGE PEEL: Dried orange peel may be purchased either in strips or ground, and has nearly as much flavor as the fresh zest. It is used to impart a sunny Mediterranean flavor to tomato sauces and fish soups and stews.

*OREGANO: This rather strong herb complements tomatoes and tomato sauces especially well, and it brings out a sweet, buttery taste in fish. Some people like to use the seasoning with eggs and cheese as well, but I find it overpowering with these foods. The herb becomes bitter and flat when it is stale. Generally sold in whole-leaf form, oregano may be ground or crushed with a mortar and pestle before it is added to salads or other dishes in which the spiky, gritty texture of the whole dried leaves would be inappropriate.

PAPRIKA: The paprika sold at the supermarket is fine to use as a decorative dusting on deviled eggs and sauced foods, but if you want it as a flavoring you should buy imported paprika in bulk at a gourmet foods shop. Made from a type of capsicum pepper, paprika is available both "sweet" (that is, mild) and hot. Most recipes call for sweet paprika. Since it is vulnerable to heat, paprika should be stored in a covered container in the refrigerator.

*PARSLEY: Perhaps the most widely used of all herbs, parsley adds a fresh, verdurous taste to virtually any savory food, and it certainly should not be thought of solely as a garnish. Fresh parsley is available in most supermarkets all year, and it will keep for several weeks in a lidded container in the refrigerator. There is no reason, therefore, to rely on dried parsley, which has about as much taste as lawn clippings. There are two varieties—curly-leaf, the more familiar, and flat-leaf, sometimes called Italian parsley. The assertive flavor of Italian parsley makes it good for cooking, but curly-leaf parsley makes a more attractive garnish.

*PEPPER: Black, white, and green peppercorns are the berry of the pepper plant, *Piper nigrum,* at various stages of maturity. Black peppercorns are slightly underripe berries. White peppercorns are fully matured berries from which the black outer coating has been rubbed off. Green peppercorns are berries picked very young, while they are still green and soft. Both black and white pepper should be ground just before use, as the aromatic oils in peppercorns dissipate quickly after grinding. White pepper is often called for in light-colored dishes (cream sauces, for example), where specks of black pepper might be distracting, but its appeal is not limited to its visual unobtrusiveness. White pepper has a distinctive musty taste and a subdued but lingering heat that are just what is wanted in many dishes made with eggs, cheese, or dairy products. Green peppercorns taste like black pepper with undertones of mustard. They are most commonly used in deglazing sauces for meat and poultry. Buy those that are packed in water or brine rather than the freeze-dried kind, which have little flavor. Mash green peppercorns using a mortar and pestle or with the back of a spoon or fork just before use.

A spice known as pink peppercorns is available at some gourmet food shops. The name is misleading, for these are not derived from the true pepper plant but are rather the berries of a bush that grows in Madagascar. Generally packed in brine, pink peppercorns are mashed and added to creamy sauces. They impart a mild heat and a taste that might be described as woody, but I suspect their main appeal is the rosy tint they give a sauce.

POPPYSEED: Whole poppyseed is used as a topping for breads or as a filling for certain Middle Eastern pastries. The seeds are mild and nutlike in taste.

POULTRY SEASONING: The dominant herbs in most commercial poultry seasonings are sage and thyme. You may substitute two parts ground or rubbed sage and one part ground thyme for the poultry seasoning called for in any recipe.

*ROSEMARY: This resinous, pungent, and slightly bitter herb is a delicious seasoning for roast lamb, spinach, boiled potatoes, and poultry stuffing. But it should be used sparingly or it will overwhelm the taste of the food it is added to. Rosemary is always sold in whole-leaf form because it loses its flavor very quickly after grinding. Before use, it should be powdered using a mortar and pestle or moistened with a few drops of water and minced fine, as the pine-needlelike texture of the whole leaves can be quite unpleasant.

SAFFRON: This seasoning is derived from the hand-picked stigmas of a special variety of crocus, so its costliness should come as no surprise. The taste of saffron hits the palate in two waves, the first wave pungent, musty, and slightly oniony, and the second distinctly mentholated and almost medicinal. Saffron is probably as much valued for the bright yellow color that it gives to food—especially rice and broths—as for its taste. A dash of turmeric can be used to tint food a saffronlike color.

*SAGE: This highly aromatic, woodsy herb can be purchased ground, rubbed (crushed), or in whole-leaf form. It is particularly popular as a seasoning for pork, pork sausages, and bread stuffings for fish and poultry.

*SALT: Salt is a mineral that can either be mined from the earth or crystallized out of sea water. It is commonly available in either of two forms: ordinary finely ground table salt and various large-grained coarse salts, among them kosher salt and sea salt. Shop carefully for table salt. Some brands are loaded with additives and have a poor taste; others are not ground fine enough and are reluctant to dissolve. Coarse salts may be sprinkled on food "whole," or they may be ground in a salt grinder. Because coarse salts melt less quickly than regular table salt, they provide a crunchy coating for meats and breads, and are less apt to draw the moisture out of fresh salad greens.

SAVORY: The kind of savory available at supermarkets is summer savory. More pungent winter savory can be bought at some specialty stores. Summer savory has an oreganolike taste with peppery undertones. It is a traditional seasoning for green beans and legumes and is also used in poultry stuffings.

SESAME SEED(BENNE SEED): This seed has a nutlike yet sharp flavor all its own. It can be sprinkled on fish just before it is removed from the broiler, used with bread or cracker crumbs to coat fish, meat, or poultry before frying, toasted lightly in a 350°F oven and tossed with salads or vegetables, or added to cookies, cakes, and breads. Sesame paste, or tahini, is the basis for numerous Middle Eastern sauces and dips and is also made into a delicious candy called halva.

*TARRAGON: Among the most sophisticated of all herbs, tarragon has a mild anise taste complicated by subtle hints of parsley, pepper, and menthol. It is classic and delectable with creamed fish, chicken, and egg dishes, and it is one of the basic flavorings of béarnaise sauce.

*THYME: Available in both whole-leaf and ground form, thyme is an indispensable herb that imparts a rich, savory taste to chowders, meat broths, stews, stuffings, and gravies. Like bay leaf, parsley, salt, and pepper, thyme is typically used as a background seasoning in dishes that may or may not be flavored with additional herbs or spices.

TURMERIC: This pungent, musty, deep yellow spice is an ingredient in all curry powders. Use it in judicious amounts wherever you would use curry.

STOCKS

In former times, many householders kept at a perpetual simmer on the back of the stove a big pot into which they would toss whatever scraps of poultry, meat, or vegetables that might be produced during a day's culinary labors. Thus there was always flavorful fresh stock on hand that could serve as a soup or be used as the base of a braising medium, gravy, or sauce. Few of us today spend enough time in our kitchens to emulate the stock-making practices of our ancestors, but we can still make excellent stocks from scratch. The recipes in this chapter have been specially tailored for modern cooks and streamlined to eliminate some of the messy, time-consuming steps that make people shy away from making stocks. Unlike our forebears, we are blessed with refrigerators and freezers, so we can stop the stock-making process at any number of points as suits our schedules, and can also freeze the finished stocks for up to six months.

Often, of course, we must rely on canned broths. These are decent enough, and can be made even better if simmered briefly with fresh ingredients. Recipes for rescuing canned broths or even those made with bouillon cubes appear on page 28.

MASTER RECIPE

Beef Stock

Makes about 3 quarts all-purpose or 2 quarts rich stock

❦ *Many classic stock recipes are tedious, messy, and seemingly wasteful affairs, requiring a preliminary browning of the meat and vegetables, and, finally, one or more strainings, the by-product of which is an unappealing mass of spent stock ingredients that are discarded. All that for just a few quarts of stock!*

This recipe and its variations will serve, I hope, the needs of contemporary home cooks. The brown color of the stock is achieved by the addition of caramelized onions, eliminating the smoky business of browning, and a whole piece of meat rather than scraps and bones is used, making it unnecessary to strain the stock. You will find that a whole stewing cut makes better-flavored stock then scraps, and it does not turn out to be appreciably more expensive. Best of all, the meat can be eaten, either cold with horseradish mayonnaise or green goddess dressing, or hot with tomato sauce or a cup or two of the stock, thickened, if you wish, with cornstarch or arrowroot.

Although you can use any cut of stewing beef—round, rump, chuck, or neck, for example—beef shank, sometimes called beef shin, seems to me the best overall choice in terms of flavor and economy. Supermarkets do not always display beef shank, but they can usually get it for you from the back if you ask.

STEP 1: CARAMEL COLORING TO MAKE THE STOCK BROWN

½ cup chopped onion
1 tablespoon sugar
Water

Place the onions in a small heavy-bottomed saucepan or skillet; do not add oil or butter. Place over moderately high heat and, stirring frequently, roast the onions until they are dry and crispy around the edges and the bottom of the pan is dark brown. Add the sugar and, stirring constantly, cook until the onions clump together and the sugar has darkened and begun to smoke. You want to cook the sugar enough to darken it and remove most of its sweetness, but you must not burn it, or it will impart a bitter taste to the stock. Remove the pan from the heat, let cool a moment, and then slowly pour in about ½ cup water, standing back in case the caramel bubbles up. Return the pan to moderate heat and, stirring, simmer the mixture for a minute or two, scraping the bottom of the pan. Strain the caramel into a bowl. Pour a little additional water over the onions in strainer to dissolve the last of the caramel, then discard the onions. (The caramel can be prepared months ahead, and refrigerated in a covered jar.)

Step 2: Making the Stock

A whole beef shank, weighing 4 to 5 pounds
3 medium onions, peeled and left whole
2 medium carrots, peeled, trimmed, and cut in half
2 small celery ribs, cut in half
The following, tied together in a cheesecloth bag:
1 teaspoon whole dried thyme; 1 teaspoon whole black peppercorns; 1 large bay leaf; 1 whole clove; 4 large parsley sprigs
2 teaspoons salt

Tie the meat securely with white string. Place meat, vegetables, and herb bag in an 8- to 10-quart stock pot; add enough cold water to cover the meat by 1 inch, and add the salt. Place over high heat and bring to a simmer, skimming off fat and scum as they accumulate. Turn heat down to the point where the stock barely simmers, pour in the caramel mixture from Step 1, and partially cover the pot. Simmer for about 8 hours, skimming frequently and adding hot water whenever the meat becomes exposed.

Ahead of Time: The cooking process may be stopped at any point. Remove stock from heat, refrigerating it if the delay is longer than 5 hours; resume cooking within 5 days. Also, fully simmered stock may be allowed to cool to room temperature, then refrigerated for up to 5 days before being reduced. In this case, you can scrape the solidified fat off the top with a spoon and skip the first part of the next step.

Step 3: Removing Meat and Vegetables; Degreasing and Reducing Stock

Salt, if needed

Remove the vegetables and herb bag with a slotted spoon and discard. Skim the clear, yellowish fat and any impurities from the surface of the stock with a wide shallow spoon; blot up remaining specks of fat by trailing strips of paper toweling over the surface. Unless you are serving it immediately, transfer the meat to a deep bowl just wide enough to hold it and add enough stock to cover; this prevents the meat from drying out. Set aside in a cool place.

At this point you will have 4 to 5 quarts of light stock. Place stock over moderate heat and simmer until reduced to about 3 quarts. Add the stock covering the meat and reduce again to 3 quarts. (Wrap meat and refrigerate.)

Taste. If the stock seems weak, or if you are planning to use it for a consommé or aspic, reduce further, to 2 to 2½ quarts. Salt lightly if necessary.

The stock is now ready for use.

AHEAD OF TIME: Let stock cool to room temperature, then cover and refrigerate for up to 5 days. If you wish to store stock for a longer period, proceed to Step 4.

STEP 4: REDUCING STOCK TO A GLAZE FOR FREEZING (OPTIONAL) Simmer the stock down to about 1 quart, then strain through a fine sieve into a heavy-bottomed 1½-quart saucepan. Bring to a slow boil, skimming off any scum that accumulates. When the stock has reduced to about 2½ cups, lower the heat so that it barely simmers and begin to keep a close watch over it. When the froth of large bubbles on top begins to subside and the liquid seems to shudder and rock in the saucepan, the glaze is almost ready. Set the heat as low as possible to prevent burning, and stir constantly until the glaze is thick enough to coat the spoon lightly. Pour into a bread pan or ice cube tray and refrigerate until hard; cut into 12 equal-sized cubes. Layer the cubes between sheets of waxed paper, place them in a tightly covered container, and freeze for up to 6 months. To reconstitute each cube, add 1 cup boiling water to make all-purpose stock, about ¾ cup to make rich stock.

Variation: CHICKEN STOCK

Makes about 3 quarts all-purpose or 2 quarts rich stock

❦ *Use the cooked chicken to make chicken salad or croquettes.*

Beef Stock

OMIT: Step 1

SUBSTITUTE: 1 4- to 5-pound whole stewing hen or roasting chicken for beef shank

Omit Step 1; for most purposes, chicken stock should be "white." Using sturdy white twine, tie the drumsticks together, then wrap chicken in a double layer of well-rinsed cheesecloth, tying it securely at the ends. Proceed according to the Master Recipe, but simmer the stock 5 hours if made with a stewing hen, 3½ if made with a roasting chicken.

Variation: VEAL STOCK

Makes about 3 quarts all-purpose or 2 quarts rich stock

❦ *Though rarely called for in American home cooking, veal stock is the base of many classic sauces and also, when brown, makes excellent consommé.*

Traditional recipes call for a preliminary blanching and rinsing of the veal in order to rid it of scum, which might cloud the stock. I have found, however, that the veal available in today's markets does not tend to release scum in great quantities, and thus I think this step can be supplanted by careful skimming of the stock as it simmers.

Beef Stock

OMIT: Step 1, if you wish

SUBSTITUTE: A veal shoulder roast, preferably bone-in, weighing 4 to 6 pounds, for beef shank

Unless you are using the stock to make consommé, stew, or some other recipe that is supposed to be brown in appearance, you may omit Step 1. Tie the veal roast securely with loops of sturdy white twine and use it in place of beef in the Master Recipe. Skim the stock frequently, particularly at the outset of cooking, to remove any grayish scum, and simmer the stock just 5 to 6 hours rather than 8.

FISH STOCK

Makes about 3 quarts all-purpose or 2 quarts rich stock

❦ *It would be terribly expensive to use a whole fish or pieces of fish to make stock, so meaty fish heads and skeletons are used instead. Ask for them at your fishmonger's; you will usually get them free. Dark-fleshed, strong-tasting, or oily fish such as bluefish, mackerel, and whitefish are not suitable for stock; choose instead bass, snapper, sole, flounder, halibut, cod, or tilefish. To give the stock a shellfish flavor, add also the chopped shells of one or two lobsters or a handful of shrimp shells. If you use fish heads that are more than a day or two old (as heads sold at a fish market are bound to be), pull out and discard the reddish pink gills, which are apt to be off-tasting.*

5 quarts meaty fish heads and skeletons (about 5 pounds)
1 cup thinly sliced onions
The following, tied together in a cheesecloth bag:
8 large parsley stems, without leaves; 3/4 teaspoon whole black or white peppercorns; 1 small bay leaf
2 cups dry white wine
1 to 2 teaspoons salt

Choose an 8- to 12-quart stock pot, preferably not one made of unlined aluminum, which will darken the stock slightly. Combine fish, onions, herb bag, and wine in the pot, add enough water to cover by 1 inch, and bring to a boil. Immediately turn down the heat to the point where the stock barely simmers, cover partially, and cook 40 minutes—no longer, or the stock may turn bitter. Strain, discarding solids, and taste. If the stock seems weak, reduce it by simmering over moderate heat. Salt to taste.

AHEAD OF TIME: Stock may be stored in the refrigerator for several days or frozen for 3 months. You may also boil down the stock to a glaze to facilitate storage. See Step 4 of the recipe for Beef Stock, page 26.

RESCUED CANNED BEEF (OR CHICKEN) BROTH

Makes 1 quart

❦ *When you do not have time to make stock from scratch, you can rescue canned broth or even, in a pinch, broth from bouillon cubes by simmering it with fresh ingredients plus a bit of wine.*

1 quart undiluted canned beef (or chicken) broth or 1 quart water and 4 beef (or chicken) bouillon cubes
1/3 cup dry white wine
1/3 cup minced lean beef (or chicken) (about 3 ounces; optional)
1/4 cup finely chopped onion
3 tablespoons finely chopped peeled carrot
2 tablespoons finely chopped celery
1 tablespoon finely chopped tomato, fresh or canned (optional)
1 tablespoon finely chopped mushroom stems (optional)
The following, tied in a cheesecloth bag:
2 large parsley sprigs; 1/2-inch piece bay leaf; 1/2 teaspoon whole black peppercorns; 1/4 teaspoon dried whole thyme

Combine all ingredients in a 2½-quart saucepan and simmer, partially covered, for 40 minutes to an hour. Strain into a bowl. Add enough water to make 1 quart.

RESCUED BOTTLED CLAM JUICE

Makes 1 quart

❦ *This makes an excellent substitute for fish stock.*

3 cups bottled clam juice
1 cup water
⅔ cup dry white wine
½ cup thinly sliced or chopped onion
2 parsley stems, without leaves
¼ teaspoon whole black or white peppercorns

Combine all ingredients in a 2½-quart saucepan and simmer, partially covered, for 30 minutes. Strain into a bowl. Add enough water to make 1 quart.

THREE
MASTER SAUCES and THEIR VARIATIONS

Sauces are fun to make and they make any dish special and exciting, even a dish made with leftovers. Care and discretion are the golden rules that govern the preparation and use of sauces. A sauce should be made with the best stock, the freshest butter and eggs, the finest oil, and the most flavorful herbs and spices you can muster. And you must remember to taste a sauce before serving and to season it carefully. Just a drop or two of fresh lemon juice or Worcestershire sauce, a pinch of salt, or a grinding of fresh pepper can make an enormous difference. A sauce must always be chosen according to its compatibility with the food it is to accompany. A sauce should enhance the taste of the food, not clash with or smother it. In general, poultry and meat may be sauced in a variety of ways, while for fish and vegetables, which are subtle in taste, the possibilities are more limited. When planning a meal, remember not to repeat sauce ingredients in other foods or to serve two or more sauces that are similar in their basic nature. For example, if you are including a cream sauce in one part of the meal, do not begin the meal with a cream soup or conclude it with a dessert that is custardy or creamy. Similarly, a meal that includes a hollandaise or mayonnaise sauce should contain at most only one other dish that is rich in butter, oil, or egg yolks. Finally, the presentation of a sauce is important. If the sauce is to be used as a dip or passed with a food, present it in an attractive bowl or sauceboat just large enough to hold it comfortably. When saucing a food prior to serving, spoon the sauce onto the plate or platter and place the food on top of it, perhaps also laying a ribbon of sauce down the center of the food; pass remaining sauce separately. You want the food to be plainly visible and the sauce to seem a discreetly and thoughtfully added accompaniment, not a camouflage or a smothering blanket.

An Invitation to Cream Sauces

Many contemporary chefs scorn them because they are thickened with flour. Dieters reject them as fattening. Inexperienced cooks won't even attempt to prepare them because they have heard that they are liable to become lumpy or scorched in the cooking. And countless others, having found them in one form or another on their plates at school cafeterias and roadside restaurants, think they are a dull camouflage for overcooked, stale, or otherwise badly prepared food. In short, cream sauces—also known as white sauces, béchamel sauces, or, when made with stock, veloutés—have so lost favor with American cooks and diners that many dishes based on them have been all but dropped from our culinary repertory. I think this most unfortunate, for cream sauces are delicious if carefully prepared, and they bring glamour to the simplest foods with little expenditure of effort, time, or money.

CREAM SAUCE NOTES

Flouriness: Although they are thickened with a paste made of butter and flour, cream sauces do not taste floury if properly made. To insure a smooth, silky texture, allow a cream sauce to simmer for several minutes after the milk or stock is added. If you have the time and inclination, you may simmer a cream sauce for a half hour or longer to further refine its texture, but for the purposes of everyday cooking such prolonged simmering strikes me as unwarranted. Thinning the sauce with additional liquid also serves to undercut any floury taste. Finally, careful flavoring is crucial. A bland or gracelessly flavored cream sauce is likely to seem floury on the palate, while a well-flavored sauce will not.

The antiflouriness strategy used in classic French cooking is to cook the roux (the flour and butter thickening) slowly for several minutes before adding the liquid (milk or stock). Out of respect for tradition I always follow this procedure, and the Master Recipe includes this step in the instructions. However, I must confess that my tongue cannot detect any difference between a sauce made with a cooked roux and one made with a raw roux.

CONSISTENCY: For most purposes, a cream sauce should be just a bit thicker than heavy cream. It should coat a spoon fairly heavily and should fall from the spoon in a satiny, instantly dissolving ribbon. A too thick cream sauce is unappetizing; a too thin sauce will run off the food and make the dish seem soupy.

The plain cream sauce outlined in the Master Recipe is very thick. This is because it is generally used as a base to which other flavorings are added, and these flavorings are either moist (fresh herbs, cheese, horseradish) or acidic (grapes, tomato paste, lemon juice) and thus will thin the sauce out. Do not thin the sauce until such flavorings have been incorporated. If a sauce is still too thick after additions have been made—or if you are serving the sauce plain—simply thin the sauce with additional cream, milk, or stock.

Rescue for a too thin cream sauce: The best thing to do is to simmer the sauce slowly, stirring often, until it thickens by reduction. If the sauce is quite thin and will need a long simmering, strain out flavorings such as hard-cooked egg, grapes, or olives that will not stand up to cooking. You can also thicken a too thin sauce by making a smooth paste of 1 to 1½ tablespoons each of butter and flour and then beating this paste bit by bit into the simmering sauce, stirring constantly. Simmer the sauce for several minutes after the last of the paste has gone in, to cook the flour. Finally, you can thicken a runny sauce with egg yolks. Beat 1 to 3 egg yolks—depending on how thin the sauce is—with several tablespoons of cream. Beat ½ cup of the *hot* sauce, a teaspoon or two at a time, into the yolks, then beat the yolk sauce mixture into the rest of the sauce and, stirring constantly, bring just to the simmer. Cheese sauces that turn out too thin should be thickened with egg yolks.

LUMPS: Beating is the key to a lump-free sauce. Beat constantly while adding the hot liquid to the flour and butter paste; beat again, scraping up any unblended roux from the corners of the saucepan, before setting the sauce over heat; and beat the sauce constantly during cooking.

Rescue: If lumps do occur, whirl the sauce in a blender or food processor until smooth. Strain through a very fine-meshed sieve into a clean saucepan and simmer over low heat for several minutes to cook any raw flour that may have been protected inside the lumps. If the sauce is too thin, continue to simmer it until it reduces and thickens.

SCORCHING: The thicker and heavier the saucepan, the more slowly and evenly the sauce will heat and the less likely it will be to scorch or turn lumpy. Pans made of enameled cast iron, heavy-gauge stainless steel, or stainless steel-lined aluminum are all good choices. (Avoid using unlined cast iron or aluminum pans, as the sauce may react with the metal and darken or take on a metallic taste.)

Rescue: If the sauce does scorch, strain it through a fine-meshed strainer, leaving the scorched parts on the bottom of the saucepan. Taste, discarding the sauce if it has a burnt flavor.

MILK-BASED VS. STOCK-BASED CREAM SAUCES: Cream sauces are made either with milk or with a combination of stock and cream. Stock-based cream sauces are generally made with chicken stock or canned chicken broth. Veal stock can also be used, and cream sauces that are to accompany a fish dish can be prepared with fish stock or bottled clam juice.

MASTER RECIPE

Basic Cream Sauce

Makes about 2 cups; 4 to 6 servings or enough to sauce 3 to 4 cups of food

❦ *This simple and quickly made sauce is most often used as a base for one of the flavored cream sauces that are outlined in the variation recipes. However, if made with stock or broth, it may be used plain as an accompaniment to poached or sautéed chicken, veal, or fish.*

2 cups liquid: *either* 2 cups milk *or* ½ cup heavy cream *plus* 1½ cups stock (Chicken Stock, page 26, or canned chicken broth; Veal Stock, page 27; Fish Stock, page 27, or bottled clam juice; or other liquid indicated in a recipe)
4 tablespoons butter
¼ cup all-purpose flour
⅛ teaspoon nutmeg, preferably freshly grated
¼ teaspoon salt (omit if you are using stock, broth, or clam juice)
⅛ teaspoon pepper, preferably white and freshly ground
1 to 6 tablespoons additional milk, cream, stock, or broth, as needed
Fresh lemon juice and other seasonings, as needed

Place the liquid in a saucepan or heatproof measure and set over low heat to warm up. Melt the butter over low heat in a heavy 1½- to 2-quart saucepan. Remove from heat, add the flour, and stir with a wooden spatula or wire whip until the paste is perfectly smooth. Return this paste, or roux, to low heat and cook for 3 minutes, stirring constantly, being sure that the mixture does not color in the slightest. Remove from heat.

Immediately turn up the heat under the liquid, bringing it almost to the simmer. Pour the hot liquid into the roux all at once, beating constantly with the wire whip. Using a spatula, scrape up any roux that may be stuck on the bottom and sides of the pan. Beat again with the wire whip, adding the nutmeg, salt, and pepper.

Place saucepan over moderate heat and beat the sauce constantly with the whip until it comes to a *full boil;* it will be quite thick. Turn heat down to low and, stirring frequently with the whip and scraping periodically with a spatula, let the sauce simmer very slowly for about 5 minutes to cook the flour.

Remove saucepan from heat. The sauce is now ready to be flavored (if you are following a variation recipe), then thinned and seasoned as necessary. To thin, beat in tablespoons of milk, cream, stock, or broth until the sauce is just a bit thicker than heavy cream and flows from the spoon in a satiny, instantly dissolving ribbon. If you have added a moist flavoring, the sauce will require little or no thinning; otherwise, up to 6 tablespoons additional liquid may be necessary. Taste the sauce and season carefully, starting with a few drops of fresh lemon juice and adding salt, pepper, and other seasonings as you see fit.

AHEAD OF TIME: Place the bottom of the saucepan in cold water and stir the sauce until it cools to tepid. Turn it into a storage container, place a piece of plastic wrap or waxed paper directly on top of the sauce to prevent a skin from forming, and seal the container tightly. The sauce will keep for 4 or 5 days in the refrigerator or several months in the freezer. Reheat sauce in a heavy pan over low flame, beating with a wire whip to smooth.

Variation: BACON-HORSERADISH CREAM SAUCE

Makes about 2½ cups

❦ *Good with boiled potatoes served as an accompaniment to pork chops, ham, or poached fish.*

Basic Cream Sauce made with milk, unthinned

ADD: 6 to 8 slices bacon, crisply fried, drained, and crumbled
1½ to 3 tablespoons freshly grated horseradish or 2 to 4 tablespoons well-drained prepared horseradish
Sugar

Using milk as the liquid, prepare basic cream sauce, but do not yet thin the sauce or adjust the seasoning. Stir in bacon and horseradish and simmer sauce for a couple of minutes to allow flavors to blend. Thin if necessary, season highly with enough fresh lemon juice to make the sauce slightly tangy, and add a bit of sugar.

Variation: CALIFORNIA CREAM SAUCE WITH OLIVES AND ALMONDS

Makes about 2½ cups

❦ *This sauce, which turns a lovely pink from the pimientos in the olives, is nice with full-flavored fish such as bluefish and mackerel, as well as with poultry.*

Basic Cream Sauce made with cream and chicken or fish stock, unthinned

ADD: ½ cup pimiento-stuffed green olives
⅓ cup (about 1½ ounces) sliced almonds, lightly toasted

Slice olives thin and press firmly between sheets of paper toweling to blot up excess brine. Using cream and chicken or fish stock as the liquid, prepare basic cream sauce, but do not yet thin the sauce or adjust the seasoning. Stir olives into sauce and simmer for a few minutes to blend flavors. Thin as necessary. Correct seasoning. Just before serving, stir almonds into the sauce, or sprinkle them as a garnish over the sauced food.

Variation: CAPER CREAM SAUCE

Makes about 2 cups

❦ *The classic use for this sauce is as an accompaniment to roast lamb, but it is also very good with hard-cooked eggs or poached or baked fish.*

Basic Cream Sauce made with milk, unthinned

ADD: 3 to 4 tablespoons well-drained capers
2 to 3 teaspoons caper bottling liquid

Using milk as the liquid, prepare basic cream sauce, but do not yet thin the sauce or adjust the seasoning. Stir capers into sauce and simmer for about 5 minutes to blend flavors. Thin as necessary and correct the seasoning with caper bottling liquid.

Variation: CHAMPAGNE CREAM SAUCE

Makes about 2 cups

❦ *This is an elegant sauce and should be reserved for such elegant foods as sole fillets, sautéed chicken breast cutlets, sautéed scallops of turkey breast or veal, sautéed veal chops, or a chicken or seafood soufflé. If dressed up with a handful of wine-soaked dried currants, the sauce may also be used with a baked ham.*

Basic Cream Sauce made with cream and chicken or fish stock, unthinned

ADD: 1½ cups sweet Champagne or other sparkling wine (it can be flat)
2 tablespoons finely chopped shallots or scallions (white part only)
2 tablespoons finely chopped mushrooms (optional)
2 tablespoons soft butter

Combine Champagne, shallots or scallions, and mushrooms in a saucepan made of or lined with a noncorroding material. Simmer briskly until liquid has reduced to about 2 tablespoons. Meanwhile, using cream and stock (chicken for general purposes; fish for fish dishes), prepare basic cream sauce, but do not yet thin the sauce or adjust the seasoning. Strain the Champagne reduction into the sauce, pressing the solids in the sieve with the back of a spoon to extract the last drops of liquid before discarding. If necessary, simmer the sauce for several minutes to thicken it. Off heat, beat in soft butter a teaspoon at a time and correct the seasoning, adding pinches of sugar if the sauce seems sour.

Variation: CHEESE SAUCE

Makes about 2½ cups

❦ *Cheese sauce is good with many foods, particularly poached and hard-cooked eggs, soufflés flavored with cheese or spinach, and boiled or steamed vegetables.*

Basic Cream Sauce made with milk, unthinned

ADD: 1 cup (about 4 ounces) shredded flavorful Swiss cheese (preferably imported Gruyère) or Cheddar cheese
Cayenne pepper or hot pepper sauce (optional)

Using milk as the liquid, prepare basic cream sauce, but do not yet thin the sauce or adjust the seasoning.

Off heat, beat in the cheese. Return the sauce to *very low* heat and stir just until the cheese has melted and the sauce is completely smooth; if sauce reaches the simmer stage, the cheese may become stringy. Remove from heat, thin as necessary, and correct seasoning, adding, if you wish, sprinklings of cayenne or drops of hot pepper sauce.

Variation: CHEESE SAUCE WITH WINE

Makes about 2½ cups

❦ *This rich and savory sauce is excellent with hard-cooked eggs served on buttered toast, and with poached and baked fish.*

Basic Cream Sauce made with cream and chicken stock, unthinned

ADD: 1 cup (about 4 ounces) shredded Swiss cheese, preferably imported Gruyère

1 cup dry white vermouth

1 large garlic clove, crushed with the side of a knife

Using cream and chicken stock as the liquid, prepare basic cream sauce, but do not yet thin the sauce or adjust the seasoning. Slowly boil down the wine with the crushed garlic clove in a noncorroding saucepan until reduced to less than 2 tablespoons. Remove garlic and pour the wine into the sauce. With the sauce off the heat, beat in cheese, then return sauce to *very low* heat and stir, without bringing to a simmer, just until cheese has melted. Thin if necessary and correct the seasoning.

Variation: CREAM SAUCE WITH HARD-COOKED EGGS AND FRESH HERBS

Makes about 2½ cups

❦ *This sauce is sumptuous over boiled potatoes and, when made with parsley, is a traditional accompaniment to baked and poached fish and chicken croquettes.*

Basic Cream Sauce made with milk, unthinned

ADD: 2 hard-cooked eggs, sliced or coarsely chopped

2 tablespoons finely chopped fresh parsley *or* dill (feathery leaves only) *or* 1 tablespoon finely chopped fresh tarragon

Using milk as the liquid, prepare basic cream sauce, but do not yet thin the sauce or adjust the seasoning. Off heat, stir in eggs and herbs, then return to low heat and, stirring gently, bring to just below the simmer. Remove from heat and thin with cream or milk if necessary. Correct the seasoning.

Variation: CREAM SAUCE WITH WHITE GRAPES

Makes about 2¾ cups

❦ *This lovely, slightly sweet sauce particularly suits delicate foods such as poached or baked white-fleshed fish, poached chicken breasts, and roast veal. It is a nice idea to serve rice with any meal that includes this sauce.*

Basic Cream Sauce made with milk, unthinned
ADD: 1 cup white grapes, preferably seedless

First peel the grapes by stripping off their skins a piece at a time, starting at the stem end. Cut grapes in half lengthwise and, if necessary, remove seeds with the point of a paring knife. Bring 2 quarts water to a rapid boil, drop in grapes, and let stand for exactly 15 seconds. Immediately drain in a sieve and rinse under cold water until the grapes are cool. (This blanching procedure neutralizes the acid in the grapes and thus insures that the sauce will not curdle.)

Using milk as the liquid, prepare basic cream sauce, but do not yet thin the sauce or adjust the seasoning. Stir in grapes and simmer very slowly for about 5 minutes, stirring frequently, to blend flavors. Thin as necessary and correct the seasoning.

Variation: CURRIED CREAM SAUCE

Makes about 2 cups

❦ *This rich, mellow curry sauce is compatible with a variety of foods, including poached and hard-cooked eggs, baked and poached fish, sautéed chicken, pork, and baked ham. Although the coconut flavoring may be considered optional, it does add a delicious sweetness and softens the harsh bite of the spices. If you omit the coconut, add pinches of sugar to the finished sauce. Many of the traditional curries of Southeast Asia, by the way, are made with coconut milk.*

Basic Cream Sauce made with cream and chicken stock, unthinned

ADD: ½ cup grated fresh or desiccated coconut (available at health-food stores) (optional)
¼ cup minced onion
½ teaspoon mashed, pressed, or very finely minced garlic
1½ to 2 teaspoons mild curry powder or 1¼ to 1½ teaspoons hot (Madras) curry powder

DECREASE: Flour to 3 tablespoons

Using cream and chicken stock as the liquid called for in the Master Recipe, combine liquid and coconut in a saucepan and set over low heat to warm.

Melt butter called for in the Master Recipe in a saucepan, add the onion and garlic, and sauté over moderate heat for about 10 minutes, or until the onion has turned yellow and begun to brown very faintly around the edges. Lower the heat, stir in the curry powder, and cook slowly for 2 minutes. Add 3 tablespoons flour and cook briefly, as indicated in the Master Recipe. Add the almost-simmering liquid and coconut to the sauce and simmer for about 10 minutes to blend the flavors. Strain the sauce through a fine sieve, pressing down hard on the coconut with the back of a spoon to extract the last drops of liquid. Reheat the sauce and thin if necessary. Be sure to add a few drops of fresh lemon juice to brighten the flavor.

Variation: DEVILED CREAM SAUCE

Makes about 2¼ cups

❦ *This is made to order for deep-fried foods, especially fish, shellfish, and chicken, and it's less cloying and fattening than the usual tartar sauce. It is also delicious with roast pork, ham, and calves' liver.*

Basic Cream Sauce made with milk, unthinned

ADD: 2 tablespoons Dijon mustard
2 tablespoons well-drained capers
¼ teaspoon mashed, pressed, or very finely minced garlic
¼ teaspoon anchovy paste (optional)
Worcestershire sauce and hot pepper sauce

Using milk as the liquid, prepare basic cream sauce, but do not yet thin the sauce or make a final adjustment in the seasoning. Beat mustard, capers, garlic, and anchovy paste into sauce and simmer for about 10 minutes to blend flavors, thinning sauce with milk as necessary. Season to taste, adding drops of Worcestershire and hot pepper sauce.

Variation: DILLED OR PARSLEYED CREAM SAUCE

Makes about 2 cups

❦ *Good with hard-cooked eggs, boiled potatoes, poached or baked fish, chicken, and ham.*

Basic Cream Sauce made with milk, unthinned
ADD: 2 tablespoons finely chopped fresh dill (feathery leaves only) *or*
1/4 cup finely chopped fresh parsley

Using milk, prepare basic cream sauce, stirring in the herbs before proceeding to thin the sauce and make final adjustments in the seasoning.

Variation: HORSERADISH CREAM SAUCE

Makes about 2 1/3 cups

❦ *This lovely sauce is for poached and baked fish. Use fresh rather than prepared horseradish for the best flavor.*

Basic Cream Sauce made with milk, unthinned
ADD: About 3 tablespoons grated fresh horseradish or about 4 tablespoons well-drained prepared horseradish
1/4 cup sour cream

Using milk as the base, prepare basic cream sauce, but do not thin the sauce or make a final adjustment in the seasoning. Stir in horseradish and sour cream and simmer the sauce for several minutes to blend the flavors and, if necessary, to thicken sauce to proper consistency. Season with fresh lemon juice, and add salt and white pepper if needed.

Variation: LEMON CREAM SAUCE

Makes about 2 1/3 cups

❦ *Delicious with both fish and vegetables, this sauce suggests hollandaise but is easier to make and far less fattening.*

Basic Cream Sauce made with milk, unthinned

ADD: 2 egg yolks
¼ cup milk or cream
About 2 tablespoons strained fresh lemon juice
3 to 5 tablespoons soft butter

Using milk as the liquid, prepare basic cream sauce, but do not yet thin the sauce or make a final adjustment in the seasoning.

Beat egg yolks and milk or cream together in small bowl until well blended. Using a wire whip, beat about ½ cup of the hot sauce, a tablespoon at a time, into the egg yolk mixture, then beat the yolk mixture into the rest of the sauce off heat. Return sauce to moderate heat and, stirring constantly, bring sauce just to the simmer. Immediately remove from heat and beat in lemon juice, then add soft butter 2 teaspoons at a time, beating constantly. Thin the sauce if necessary and adjust the seasoning. If reheated, the sauce will thin out—the butter emulsion breaks down—but it will rethicken if simmered over low heat for several minutes.

Variation: LOBSTER OR CRAB CREAM SAUCE

Makes about 2 cups

❦*A nifty use for the lobster or crab shells and bodies left after a feast, this sauce is delicious with lobster, crab, or shrimp (serve over rice or in patty shells) or with poached or baked fish. Should you have more than 2 quarts of shells, make extra stock, freeze it, and use it later.*

STEP 1: PREPARING THE SHELLFISH STOCK

2 quarts lobster or crab shells and other scraps chopped into 1½-inch pieces
½ cup chopped onion
A small bay leaf
½ teaspoon peppercorns

Place shells and scraps, onion, bay leaf, and peppercorns in a 4-quart pot, cover with water, and simmer slowly for about an hour. Strain, discarding solids, and turn stock into a saucepan. Simmer stock until reduced to about 1½ cups.

STEP 2: PREPARING THE SAUCE

Basic Cream Sauce made with cream and the shellfish stock from Step 1

ADD: 1 teaspoon tomato paste (optional)

Prepare cream sauce according to the Master Recipe, using ½ cup cream and 1½ cups shellfish stock as the liquid. If you wish, add a teaspoon of tomato paste to the finished sauce to tint it a rosy pink.

Variation: MUSHROOM CREAM SAUCE

Makes about 2½ cups

❦ *This excellent sauce has a far better flavor than canned mushroom soup and thus is a better base for the all-American favorite, tuna-noodle casserole. Use it also as an accompaniment to hard-cooked eggs, fish, poultry, pork, or veal.*

Basic Cream Sauce made with cream and chicken stock, unthinned

INCREASE: butter to 6 tablespoons

ADD: 2 tablespoons minced shallots or scallions (white part only)
2 cups (8 ounces) packed chopped mushrooms
Sherry (optional)

Melt 6 tablespoons of butter in a heavy 3-quart saucepan and sauté the shallots for a minute to soften. Add mushrooms and, stirring frequently over moderate heat, sauté for about 7 minutes, or until all the liquid in the pan has evaporated and the mushrooms are beginning to brown.

Proceed according to the Master Recipe, stirring the flour into the mushrooms to make the roux and using cream and chicken stock as the liquid. Simmer for 10 minutes to blend flavors, thin if necessary, and season, adding, if you wish, a few drops of Sherry.

Variation: ONION CREAM SAUCE

Makes about 2¾ cups

❦ *A simplified version of the famous French* sauce soubise, *this sumptuous sauce is heavenly with roast veal or turkey and good as well with soufflés, boiled potatoes, poached fish, and sautéed calves' liver.*

Basic Cream Sauce made with cream and chicken stock, unthinned

INCREASE: Butter to 6 tablespoons

ADD: 3 cups chopped onions

Melt 6 tablespoons butter in a heavy-bottomed 3-quart saucepan. Stir in onions, turn heat down to its lowest point, and cook very slowly, stirring frequently, for 20 to 30 minutes, or until onions have reduced to soft, small, nearly transparent flecks without browning at all.

Proceed according to the Master Recipe, stirring the flour into the onion mixture to make the roux and using cream and chicken stock as the liquid. Simmer sauce for 10 minutes to blend flavors, then purée in blender or food processor. Return sauce to a clean saucepan and reheat. Thin, if necessary, with teaspoons of heavy cream and correct the seasoning. Sprinkle the sauced food with chopped fresh parsley.

Variation: SHERRIED CREAM SAUCE

Makes about 2 cups

❦ *Use this old-fashioned sauce with hard-cooked eggs, chicken soufflé, poached or baked fish, chicken, turkey, or ham.*

Basic Cream Sauce made with cream and chicken or fish stock, unthinned
ADD: 1 to 2 tablespoons medium-dry Sherry, preferably Manzanilla

Using cream and chicken stock, prepare basic cream sauce, but do not yet thin the sauce or make a final adjustment in the seasoning. Stir in the Sherry, return sauce to heat, and simmer for a few minutes to evaporate the alcohol. Thin the sauce if necessary and correct the seasoning.

Variation: SOUR CREAM SAUCE

Makes about 2⅔ cups

❦ *This fine, subtle sauce is nice with poached or baked fish and with boiled vegetables.*

Basic Cream Sauce made with milk unthinned
INCREASE: Flour to 5 tablespoons
ADD: ⅔ cup sour cream

Using milk as the liquid and adding an extra tablespoon of flour in making the roux, prepare basic cream sauce, but do not yet thin the sauce or make a final adjustment in the seasoning. The sauce will seem quite thick until the sour cream is added. Beat in the sour cream and, stirring constantly, bring the sauce to a simmer. Thin if necessary and season with drops of lemon juice.

Variation: TOMATO-BASIL CREAM SAUCE

Makes about 2 cups

❦ *This sauce is delicious with poached and baked fish, hard-cooked eggs, and, of course, with pasta.*

Basic Cream Sauce made with milk, unthinned
ADD: 3 tablespoons tomato paste
1½ tablespoons chopped fresh basil or 1½ teaspoons crumbled dried
½ cup heavy cream

Prepare basic cream sauce according to Master Recipe, using milk. Beat in the tomato paste and basil, then stir in the heavy cream. Simmer sauce slowly for about 10 minutes, or until it thickens to serving consistency. Season to taste.

HOLLANDAISE NOTES: Hollandaise is notorious for its trickiness. Egg yolks are warmed over a low flame until they thicken; then melted butter is slowly beaten in to make a thick, creamy sauce. If the yolks are warmed too quickly or get too hot they will scramble. (Some people prepare hollandaise in a double boiler, which lowers the risk of scrambling the egg yolks, but this is a slow, tedious procedure.) If the butter is added to the yolks too much at a time or in too great a quantity, the sauce will break down and separate. But don't be put off by hollandaise sauce. Paying close attention to the work at hand virtually guarantees success, and you can always chalk a mistake up to experience.

Rescue: If the sauce starts to separate, immediately beat in 1 tablespoon cold water or milk. If the sauce curdles anyway, or if it refuses to thicken, proceed as follows. Warm a mixing bowl in hot water and dry thoroughly. Place 1 teaspoon lemon juice and 1 tablespoon of sauce in the mixing bowl and beat until thick and creamy. Beat in the remaining sauce a tablespoon at a time, waiting for each addition to emulsify before adding the next. This is guaranteed to work unless you have scrambled the egg yolks in the initial step and thereby ruined their capacity to absorb butter. If this is the case, throw out the sauce and start over.

BLENDER OR FOOD PROCESSOR HOLLANDAISE: Machine-made hollandaise is similar but not identical to hand-mixed hollandaise. When hollandaise is made with a machine, the egg yolks are not cooked, which gives the sauce a thick mayonnaiselike consistency rather than the puffy consistency typical of hollandaise.

Place 3 egg yolks, 1 tablespoon fresh lemon juice, 1 tablespoon warm water, 1/4 teaspoon salt, and 1/8 teaspoon white pepper in container of blender or food processor. Blend for 5 seconds. With the motor still running, pour in 10 tablespoons (1 1/4 sticks) sizzling-hot melted butter in a very thin stream. (To prevent spattering, pour the butter through the small opening in the cover of the blender.) The sauce will thicken at once. Taste and adjust seasoning.

A NOTE ON CONSISTENCY: Hollandaise sauces vary in consistency from stiff and glistening, almost like mayonnaise, to soft and foamy, reminiscent of beaten egg white. To make a stiff hollandaise, warm the egg yolks to the point that they become thick enough to hold the furrows left by the wire whip for several seconds. Admittedly, this is a very risky procedure—you are just a few degrees away from scrambled eggs—but if you are serving the hollandaise on a steak or chop and you want the sauce to stand in a dollop, this really is the way to do it. To make a loose, foamy hollandaise, especially good with vegetables, warm the egg yolks only to the point where they show—but do not retain for more than a second—the grooves made by the whisk. For an especially frothy hollandaise, add a tablespoon or two of water along with the lemon juice. This will make the egg yolks puff and mount as they warm.

MASTER RECIPE

Hollandaise Sauce

Makes about 1 1/4 cups

Satiny, thick, and buttery-rich yet at the same time lemony and light on the palate, hollandaise is surely among the most glorious of all sauces. Though it has primarily earned its reputation as an accompaniment to vegetables such as artichokes, asparagus, and broccoli, hollandaise is also excellent with poached or baked fish and almost any kind of deep-fried food. Hollandaise may be turned into a number of other related and equally delicious egg-and-butter sauces by substituting concentrated wine or fish broth for lemon juice or by incorporating minced fresh herbs, mustard, or even whipped cream; the variation recipes beginning on page 48 show how such magical transformations are accomplished.

12 tablespoons (1½ sticks) butter
3 large egg yolks
1 tablespoon strained fresh lemon juice
¼ teaspoon salt
⅛ teaspoon white pepper, preferably freshly ground

Melt the butter and set aside. Have handy a bowl of ice water (or fill the sink with very cold water) so that you can quickly cool the bottom of the pan should the yolks seem on the verge of scrambling.

In a heavy 1½-quart saucepan made of or lined with a noncorroding material (see page 5), beat egg yolks, lemon juice, salt, and pepper with a wire whip for just a minute or two, until the mixture thickens and lightens in color. Place saucepan over lowest possible heat. Being sure to reach all parts of the saucepan bottom, stir yolks constantly as they foam, mount, and begin to resemble a thick lather. As soon as you can glimpse the bottom of the saucepan between the strokes of the whip, the yolk mixture is sufficiently cooked to make a medium-thick sauce. For a very thick sauce, warm the yolks slightly beyond this point, allowing them to become heavy, glistening, and mayonnaiselike, but do not heat the yolks beyond this point or they will scramble. If there are any signs of lumping, immediately set the saucepan in cold water and beat the sauce hard; if necessary, resume warming the yolk mixture over very low heat.

With saucepan off the heat, pour in the warm melted butter by drops while beating constantly with a wire whip, until the sauce thickens and resembles softly whipped cream. From here on you may add the butter by teaspoons, still beating constantly, until all the butter is incorporated. Add the milky liquid at the bottom of the butter saucepan only if you wish to thin the sauce. Taste and adjust seasoning with salt, white pepper, and drops of lemon juice. The sauce will be warm, not hot.

It is best to use hollandaise soon after it is prepared, but the sauce can be held for 20 minutes in a pan of tepid—but *not* warm or hot—water. If held longer, the sauce is likely to separate. Hollandaise can be refrigerated in a covered container for several days. To serve, bring sauce to room temperature, then beat it in a bowl set in barely warm water until it is just tepid. If the sauce separates—and it may—rescue according to the instructions on page 45.

Variation: BÉARNAISE SAUCE

Makes about 1¼ cups

❦ *This is perhaps my favorite sauce. It is sublime on charcoal-broiled beef and lamb steaks, and is also good with beef, lamb, and pork roasts, ham, eggs, and dark-fleshed fish such as bluefish, salmon, and swordfish. It also makes a rapturous combination with french-fried potatoes.*

I think the egg-yolk base of this sauce should be warmed thoroughly, so the sauce will stand stiffly. Béarnaise can be made quite successfully in a blender or food processor simply by substituting the wine/tarragon reduction indicated below for both the lemon juice and water called for in the recipe for machine-made hollandaise on page 45.

STEP 1: PREPARING THE WINE/TARRAGON REDUCTION

½ cup dry white wine
2 tablespoons wine vinegar
1½ tablespoons minced shallots or scallions (white part only)
1½ tablespoons finely chopped fresh tarragon or 2 teaspoons dried
½-inch square of bay leaf
4 white or black peppercorns

Combine wine, vinegar, shallots or scallions, tarragon, bay leaf, and peppercorns in a small saucepan made of or lined with a noncorroding material (see page 5). Simmer slowly for 10 to 12 minutes, or until reduced to 1½ tablespoons liquid. Let cool to tepid.

STEP 2: PREPARING THE SAUCE

Hollandaise Sauce
SUBSTITUTE: The wine/tarragon reduction from Step 1 for lemon juice
ADD: 1 teaspoon finely chopped fresh tarragon (optional)

Proceed according to the Master Recipe, but *strain* the wine/tarragon reduction into the egg yolks in place of lemon juice and fold fresh tarragon into the sauce if you wish.

Variation: DILLED HOLLANDAISE

Makes about 1¼ cups

❦ *This is for poached or baked fish.*

Hollandaise Sauce
1 tablespoon finely chopped fresh dill (feathery leaves only)

Stir dill into hollandaise.

Variation: MOUSSELINE SAUCE

Makes about 1½ cups

❦ *This room-temperature sauce is a devilishly good contradiction of creamy, buttery richness and frothy lightness. It is wonderful with poached fish, soufflés, and asparagus.*

Hollandaise Sauce
⅓ cup cold heavy cream, whipped soft (see page 857)
Salt, pepper, and lemon juice

Leave hollandaise sauce at room temperature for 10 to 20 minutes, or until cooled to tepid. Fold the whipped cream into the cooled hollandaise, correct the seasoning with salt, white pepper, and drops of fresh lemon juice, and serve at once.

Variation: MUSTARD HOLLANDAISE

Makes about 1¼ cups

❦ *This sauce is particularly nice with ham, broccoli, and deep-fried fish.*

Hollandaise Sauce
2 to 3 tablespoons Dijon mustard
¼ to ½ teaspoon anchovy paste (optional; only if serving with fish)

Stir mustard and optional anchovy paste into hollandaise.

Variation: SEAFOOD HOLLANDAISE

Makes about 1¼ cups

❦*Any fish or shellfish can be napped with this heavenly sauce. If the fish stock you use contains white wine, you may call the sauce by its French name,* sauce vin blanc.

Hollandaise Sauce

SUBSTITUTE: 1 cup Fish Stock, page 27 *or* ⅔ cup bottled clam juice and ⅓ cup dry white wine for lemon juice

OMIT: Salt

In a small saucepan, boil down stock or clam juice plus wine over moderate heat until reduced to 1½ tablespoons. Let cool to tepid. Proceed according to Master Recipe, substituting the fish reduction for the lemon juice and omitting salt. Be sure to season the finished sauce with drops of fresh lemon juice.

MAYONNAISE NOTES

Whether plain or flavored, mayonnaise is basically an emulsion of eggs and oil and should be made with the freshest eggs you can find and the finest oil you can afford. What kind of oil to use is a mildly controversial matter. Many contend that only a highly refined olive oil or perhaps a combination of olive and vegetable oils should be used. However, I find that mayonnaise made with a large proportion of olive oil can have an unpleasantly acrid flavor. Thus, I make mayonnaise with a pure, fresh, neutral oil—safflower is my favorite—sometimes adding a tablespoon of olive or walnut oil for extra favor.

MAYONNAISE PROBLEMS AND RESCUES: You will have no trouble whatsoever with your mayonnaise if you remember these three simple rules:

1. All the ingredients must be at room temperature.
2. The oil must be added to the egg yolks very slowly; otherwise, the sauce will separate.
3. A single large egg yolk will emulsify with a maximum of ¾ cup oil—and in fact things become risky after just ½ cup oil is added. If the yolks are force-fed more oil than they can handle, they will have a breakdown—and so will your sauce.

Luckily, mayonnaise is easy to rescue. If at any point it begins to look grainy, quickly beat in 2 teaspoons boiling water to prevent the sauce from separating; add any remaining oil by drops. If the mayonnaise separates, or refuses to thicken, proceed as follows: In a separate bowl, beat a fresh egg yolk until it is thick and lemon yellow in color. Beating constantly, add the separated sauce 1/4 teaspoon at a time, completely incorporating each addition before adding the next. When you have about 1/4 cup of thickened sauce, begin beating in the rest of the turned mayonnaise by teaspoonfuls.

To Make Mayonnaise in a Blender or Food Processor: Machine-made mayonnaise does not have quite the same unctuous, satiny consistency as hand-mixed mayonnaise, because the machine-made version must contain a whole egg to lighten the sauce enough to keep it flowing over the blades as the oil is added. On the other hand, machine-made mayonnaise has the advantage of being simple and virtually foolproof.

Place a whole egg, an egg yolk, and the lemon juice or vinegar, mustard, salt, and pepper called for in the Master Recipe in the container of a blender or food processor fitted with either the metal or plastic blade. Blend at medium-high speed or process for 15 seconds. With the machine running constantly, pour the oil into the egg mixture in a thin, steady stream.

MASTER RECIPE

Mayonnaise

Makes about 1 cup

Invented in 18th century France, mayonnaise has long been one of America's favorite all-purpose condiments. Homemade mayonnaise is fresher, eggier, and less sweet-tasting than its commercial counterparts, which are made with low-grade oil, a paucity of eggs, and lots of sugar, all bound together with a variety of thickeners, stabilizers, and preservatives. It is well worth the extra effort to make mayonnaise from scratch. Homemade mayonnaise is a treat with cold chicken or roast beef and it raises such dishes as chicken salad and potato salad to unexpected heights of gourmandise. When flavored with herbs, cucumbers, chili sauce, or pickles, mayonnaise takes on numerous delicious identities, becoming sauces and dressings that complement a wide range of cold and hot foods. Finally, as the variation recipes indicate, many types of mayonnaise dressings are easily transformed into tasty salad dressings simply by adding small amounts of liquid.

2 large egg yolks, at room temperature
1 teaspoon strained fresh lemon juice or white wine vinegar
1/4 teaspoon Dijon mustard
1/4 teaspoon salt
1/8 teaspoon white pepper, preferably freshly ground
1 cup neutral vegetable oil, preferably safflower oil, at room temperature

Mayonnaise can be made either with a wire whip or a hand-held electric mixer. You can use any fairly deep 2½-quart mixing bowl, but if you are working with a whip, it is a good idea to prepare mayonnaise in a small heavy-gauge saucepan that will not wobble all over the counter as you beat.

Place yolks, lemon juice or vinegar, mustard, salt, and white pepper in bowl and beat until the mixture becomes lemon-colored and thick enough to cling to the whip or beaters; this will take a minute or two. Measure out a tablespoon of oil and, beating constantly, add it to the yolks drop by drop. Repeat this procedure 3 or 4 times more, or until the sauce has begun to thicken, then add remaining oil a tablespoon at a time, beating constantly and incorporating each addition of oil before adding the next. If the mayonnaise becomes too stiff, thin with drops of water. Taste and correct the seasoning.

STORAGE: To store mayonnaise, place a sheet of plastic wrap directly on the surface, then cover the bowl and refrigerate. It will keep for about a week.

Variation: BUTTERMILK, SOUR CREAM, OR YOGURT DRESSING

Makes about 1⅓ cups

❦ *This is for cold poached fish.*

Mayonnaise
4 to 6 tablespoons buttermilk, sour cream, or yogurt
Salt, pepper, and lemon juice

Stir buttermilk, sour cream, or yogurt into the mayonnaise by tablespoons until a saucelike consistency is reached. Season, if necessary, with additional salt, white pepper, and fresh lemon juice.

Variation: CUCUMBER MAYONNAISE AND CUCUMBER SALAD DRESSING

Makes about 2 cups

❦ *Cucumber mayonnaise is particularly good with cold fish or veal.*

Mayonnaise
1 large or 2 to 3 small farm-type cucumbers
½ cup sour cream or yogurt

Peel, cut in half lengthwise, and scoop the seeds out of the cucumbers. Shred cucumbers on the large holes of a grater and measure out about ⅔ cup. A small handful at a time, squeeze cucumbers firmly to extract as much moisture as possible.

Fold the shredded cucumbers and sour cream or yogurt into the mayonnaise. Refrigerate for several hours or overnight before serving.

Variation: GREEN GODDESS MAYONNAISE AND GREEN GODDESS SALAD DRESSING

Makes about 1½ cups

❦ *Green goddess mayonnaise is very nice with cold meats, poultry, and fish. It also makes a superb dip for raw vegetables.*

Mayonnaise
3 tablespoons finely chopped onion
3 tablespoons finely chopped fresh parsley
1 teaspoon anchovy paste or 1½ teaspoons mashed drained anchovies
½ teaspoon mashed, pressed, or very finely minced garlic
1 teaspoon wine vinegar
¼ teaspoon pepper, preferably freshly ground
½ cup sour cream

Combine mayonnaise and flavorings, then fold in sour cream. Refrigerate for several hours before serving.

For salad dressing: Stir in milk, buttermilk, or cream by tablespoonfuls until desired consistency is reached.

Variation: HERB MAYONNAISE (GREEN MAYONNAISE)

Makes about 1¼ cups

❦ *Herb mayonnaise can be used in almost any way that plain mayonnaise can. It is particularly suited to cold fish.*

Mayonnaise
4 4- to 5-inch lengths scallions (white and tender green parts), cut into ½-inch pieces
½ cup tightly packed tender spinach and/or watercress leaves, stems removed
1 large parsley sprig
2 tablespoons olive oil
2 teaspoons chopped fresh tarragon or ¾ teaspoon dried
½ teaspoon fresh lemon juice

Combine scallions, spinach and/or watercress leaves, and parsley in a small saucepan and add just enough water to cover (about 1 cup). Bring to a full boil over high heat, then drain at once in strainer and rinse under cold water until cold. Turn vegetables out onto a triple layer of paper towels and press firmly with additional towels to blot up as much moisture as possible. Purée vegetables with olive oil, tarragon, and lemon juice in blender (a food processor does not purée small amounts like this efficiently) or pound to a paste in a mortar. Stir into mayonnaise. Herb mayonnaise will have more character if it is refrigerated for several hours. Taste and adjust seasoning with drops of fresh lemon juice before serving.

Variation: HORSERADISH MAYONNAISE

Makes about 1½ cups

❦ *This is for cold meats or fish or for a salad platter containing cold beets and hard-cooked eggs.*

Mayonnaise
2 to 3 tablespoons grated fresh horseradish or about ¼ cup well-drained prepared horseradish
¼ cup sour cream

Fold horseradish and sour cream into the mayonnaise.

Variation: MUSTARD MAYONNAISE

Makes about 1 cup

❦ *Very good with cold pork.*

Mayonnaise
2 to 3 tablespoons Dijon mustard
Drops of fresh lemon juice

Stir mustard into the mayonnaise and correct the seasoning with drops of fresh lemon juice.

Variation: RÉMOULADE SAUCE

Makes about 1½ cups

❦ *This is for cold meat, chicken, or shrimp, or for deep-fried shellfish.*

Mayonnaise
¼ cup well-drained minced sour pickles
2 tablespoons well-drained small capers or minced larger capers
2 tablespoons finely chopped fresh parsley
1½ tablespoons snipped chives or minced tender green parts of scallion
1 tablespoon Dijon mustard
½ teaspoon anchovy paste or mashed drained anchovies
1 hard-cooked egg, forced through a sieve or finely chopped

Stir flavorings into the mayonnaise, then fold in sieved hard-cooked egg. Refrigerate for several hours before serving.

Variation: RUSSIAN DRESSING AND RUSSIAN SALAD DRESSING

Makes about 1¼ cups

❦ *This sauce is terrific with cold chicken or turkey, cheese, or hard-cooked eggs, and it is often the dressing of choice for a chef's salad.*

Mayonnaise
3 tablespoons chili sauce (or ketchup plus 1/4 teaspoon chili powder)
2 tablespoons minced onion
1 tablespoon grated fresh or well-drained prepared horseradish
Worcestershire sauce, vinegar, and fresh lemon juice, as needed

Fold the chili sauce, onion, and horseradish into the mayonnaise, then correct the seasoning with drops of Worcestershire sauce, vinegar, and lemon juice. Refrigerate for several hours before serving.

For salad dressing: Add a tablespoon or two of water or tomato juice to thin to desired consistency.

Variation: TARTAR SAUCE

Makes about 1 1/4 cups

❦ *The ever-popular sauce that is so good with deep-fried seafood.*

Mayonnaise
2 1/2 tablespoons minced well-drained sour pickles
2 1/2 tablespoons minced well-drained sweet gherkins
2 tablespoons minced onion
1 1/2 teaspoons Dijon mustard
Worcestershire sauce
Cayenne pepper

Stir the pickles, onion, and mustard into the mayonnaise. Add about 4 drops Worcestershire sauce and a pinch or two of cayenne. Refrigerate for several hours before serving. Bring sauce to room temperature before offering it with a hot food such as deep-fried fish.

Variation: WHIPPED CREAM MAYONNAISE

Makes about 1 1/2 cups

❦ *This is my favorite accompaniment for cold poached fish. When serving the sauce with cold trout, I generally add a tablespoon of grated fresh horseradish.*

Mayonnaise
1/4 cup cold heavy cream, whipped soft (see page 857)

Stir several tablespoons of the whipped cream into the mayonnaise to lighten it, then gently fold in the rest using a rubber spatula. Refrigerate sauce for several hours or for up to a day to firm it.

CLARIFIED BUTTER

Makes about 6 tablespoons

❦ *To clarify butter means to remove the whitish, opaque whey and milk solids, leaving only the clear, yellow butterfat. Once the milk components have been removed, the butter can be heated to a much higher temperature without darkening or burning, making it more suitable for frying. There are many methods of clarifying butter; I find the following traditional one the least prone to difficulties.*

8 tablespoons (1 stick) butter

Cut the butter up and melt it slowly, without stirring or otherwise disturbing, in a small heavy saucepan. Remove from heat, tilt the pan, and skim the foam off the top with a large, shallow spoon. Let the butter settle for 2 minutes. Tilt the pan and spoon out the clear yellow butterfat, discarding the milky liquid left in the bottom of the pan.

STORAGE: Stored in a sealed container, clarified butter will keep for several weeks in the refrigerator.

A VENERABLE ART: DEEP-FRYING

Foods that have been deep-fried with care and attention are incomparably delicious—crisp and crunchy on the outside, moist, meltingly tender, and intensely flavorful within. Doughnuts, pastry turnovers, and various batter-dipped (or "frittered") foods are but a few of the deep-fried delicacies that eighteenth and nineteenth century Americans regularly prepared at home. But in these health-conscious times, the whole idea of deep-frying seems to put people off, and my guess is that when a recipe says "fry in deep fat," most cooks pass it by. Yet the current aversion to deep-frying is largely undue. Deep-frying is not as messy or difficult a procedure as some people believe: One need only clear an adequate area of counter space and lay out the necessary ingredients and equipment in advance so that things can proceed in an orderly and relaxed manner. Nor is deep-frying dangerous, so long as one works with the right equipment and concentrates on the process. And, above all, deep-fried foods need not be either greasy or fattening. Greasiness is invariably the result of faulty technique (usually the oil is not hot enough). By my admittedly rough calculations, a 1-inch morsel of food, properly deep-fried, will have absorbed no more than 1/4 teaspoon of oil, or about 10 calories' worth.

The Master Technique for deep-frying contained in this chapter is to be used in conjunction with the recipes for deep-fried foods that appear throughout this book. The instructions are extremely detailed, so the timid, the skeptical, and the just plain inexperienced will feel that nothing has been left to chance.

HOW TO MAKE FINE FRESH BREAD CRUMBS: Because they are soft, tender, and somewhat moist, fresh bread crumbs behave quite differently from the dry type, which are hard, crisp, and tend to soak up a great deal of liquid. Though prepackaged dry bread crumbs have a place in many dishes and are certainly convenient, they cannot be considered a proper substitute when fresh bread crumbs are called for.

To make bread crumbs, use either homemade bread or the sort of store-bought bread that is sometimes called "homemade-type"—that is, firm, fairly dense, and only minimally sweetened. The bread should be at least a day old, so that the crumbs will not be so moist and soft that they clump together. By the way, I see no need whatsoever to trim off the crust before making bread crumbs.

TIP: If the bread that you wish to make into crumbs is very fresh and moist, either spread the slices out on a wire rack and let stand uncovered for about an hour, or arrange the slices over an oven rack and dry them in a 200°F oven for 10 minutes.

Five to 6 slices of bread (or about 4 ounces) will make 1 cup of crumbs. Here are several ways to make bread crumbs:

- The food processor makes quick work of bread crumbs. Simply cut the bread into cubes and, using the metal chopping blade, process the cubes for 10 to 20 seconds. A large-capacity processor can do a whole 1-pound loaf in one batch.
- Lacking a food processor, you can make bread crumbs in a blender. Cut the bread into smallish pieces and blend a handful at a time, flicking the motor on and off.
- Bread crumbs can also be made by rubbing slices of bread against the small holes of a hand-held grater. The problem here is that part of the bread slice always wads up in your hand rather than turning into crumbs, and thus there is a lot of waste.
- An old-fashioned way of making bread crumbs is to shred slices of bread between two forks. This is a good technique when you need just a few slices' worth of crumbs.

Leftover bread crumbs can be stored in the freezer for 6 months. Use crumbs as needed, and return the rest to the freezer. Let crumbs that are to be used to coat a deep-fried food come to room temperature.

MASTER TECHNIQUE

Deep-fried Food in Simple Breading
Deep-fried Food in Bound Breading
Batter-Dipped Deep-fried Food
Tempura

❦ *This Master Technique is to be used in conjunction with the recipes for deep-frying that appear throughout this book. Prepare the food as directed in the recipe. Choose one of the coatings described in Steps 1a, 1b, 1c, and 1d below, then fry the food as directed in Step 2.*

STEP 1A: TO COAT THE FOOD IN SIMPLE BREADING: Simple breading is the tenderest and least heavy of all coatings. It is used with firm foods (squid, certain fish) that require a minimum of protection against the hot oil and are not prone to leaking. For a light coating the food can be dipped in milk; for a heavier one half-and-half or light cream can be used. The character of the fried food is determined by the coating that you choose: dry bread crumbs, cracker crumbs, cornmeal or flour.

½ cup milk, half-and-half, or light cream
1 cup fine dry bread crumbs, cracker crumbs, or cornmeal *or* ⅔ cup all-purpose flour
1 teaspoon salt
½ teaspoon pepper, preferably freshly ground

Before you begin, lay everything out in an assembly-line fashion. Place the food to be deep-fried on a dinner plate or a sheet of waxed paper and set a soup plate containing the liquid next to it. In a bowl combine crumbs or other coating, salt, and pepper, and toss with a fork to blend thoroughly. Pour ⅓ of the seasoned coating onto a dinner plate or sheet of waxed paper and place it next to the milk. Set remaining coating aside for later use. Fit a rack inside a large rimmed baking sheet and place it next to the plate of seasoned coating.

Moisten the food in the liquid. One piece at a time, grasp food between two forks (not between your fingers, which would soon become caked with coating) and transfer it to the coating mixture. Roll it around until completely covered, pressing crumb or meal coatings lightly with the back of a fork to make sure they adhere. Still using the forks, shake the food lightly to remove excess coating and transfer it to the rack.

Repeat this procedure until all the food has been coated, replenishing coating mixture as necessary. Should the crumbs become caked together, wipe the plate or waxed paper clean before adding fresh coating.

You are now ready to fry the food; proceed to Step 2 of this Master Technique. If you wish, you may cover coated food loosely with waxed paper or plastic wrap and let it stand for up to 30 minutes at room temperature or 3 hours in the refrigerator prior to frying. Let chilled food stand at room temperature at least 20 minutes before frying, as cold foods tend to absorb oil.

STEP 1B: TO COAT FOOD IN BOUND BREADING: Bound breading is a crunchy, substantial coating, akin to a light crust. It is used with delicate foods such as shrimp and veal scallops, which need protection from the hot oil, and with very moist foods such as croquettes, which need a sturdy outer wall in order to retain their shape and not to leak. Foods in bound breading are dipped in flour, then in egg, and finally in bread crumbs, cracker crumbs, cornmeal, or even coconut, depending on the effect one wishes to create.

½ cup all-purpose flour
2 large eggs
2 tablespoons neutral vegetable oil
1 teaspoon salt
½ teaspoon pepper, preferably freshly ground
1½ to 2 cups fine fresh bread crumbs, dry bread crumbs, cracker crumbs, cornmeal, or finely grated fresh coconut or desiccated coconut

Before you begin, lay everything out in an assembly-line fashion. Place the food to be deep-fried on a dinner plate or on a sheet of waxed paper. Distribute flour over a dinner plate or sheet of waxed paper and set it next to the food. Combine eggs, oil, and salt and pepper in a soup plate and beat thoroughly with a fork. Set the mixture next to the flour. Pour ⅓ of the crumbs or other coating onto a dinner plate or sheet of waxed paper and place next to the beaten egg; set the remaining coating aside for later use. Fit a rack inside a large rimmed baking sheet (for croquettes, line baking sheet with waxed paper) and place it next to the plate of coating.

Place a piece of food in the flour and, using two forks (not your fingers, which would soon become caked with flour), toss until uniformly dusted. (Form croquettes with your fingers as indicated in recipes.) Grasp the food between the forks, shaking it lightly to remove excess flour, and place the food in the egg mixture. Turn with a fork until well coated, then transfer it to the crumbs. Roll food in the crumbs to coat completely, pressing with the back of a fork to make sure the coating adheres. Pick the food up between the forks, shake it lightly or rap it against the plate or waxed paper to remove excess crumbs, and transfer it to the rack.

Repeat this procedure until all the food has been coated, replenishing crumbs as necessary. Should the crumbs become caked together, wipe the plate or waxed paper clean, and add fresh coating.

The food should rest briefly before frying to give the coating time to dry and set. Cover the food loosely with waxed paper and let stand at room temperature for about 30 minutes or refrigerate for 3 to 4 hours. Let chilled food stand at room temperature at least 20 minutes before frying, as cold foods tend to absorb oil.

To fry the food, proceed to Step 2 of this Master Technique.

STEP 1C: TO COAT FOOD WITH FRITTER BATTER: A food dipped in batter emerges with a light, tender, puffy, crispy outer crust after frying; it becomes, in effect, a kind of fried pastry, or fritter. Fish and shellfish are often batter-dipped, as are various fruits. Fritter batter may be either salted or sweetened, depending on the food with which it is to be used.

2 large eggs
3/4 cup beer
2 tablespoons neutral vegetable oil or melted butter
1 cup unbleached all-purpose flour
For savory foods:
1 teaspoon salt and 1/4 teaspoon pepper, preferably freshly ground
For fruit fritters:
1 1/2 tablespoons sugar and 1/8 teaspoon salt

First, mix the batter. Carefully separate eggs. Place the whites in a clean 1-quart mixing bowl, cover, and set aside. Combine the flour and the savory or sweet flavorings in a 3-quart mixing bowl, tossing with a wire whip until well blended. Make a well in the center of the dry ingredients and add the egg yolks, beer, and oil or melted butter. Beat with a wire whip until perfectly smooth, then cover.

The batter may be used immediately but will make a more tender coating if allowed to rest for 2 to 24 hours in the refrigerator (refrigerate egg whites also if there is to be a delay of more than 8 hours between mixing the batter and frying). If the batter has been chilled, be sure to bring it (and egg whites) to room temperature before frying, or it will absorb the oil.

TIP: Chilled batter and egg whites may be warmed in a jiffy if you set the bowls in a sink filled with warm—not hot—water for a few minutes, stirring once or twice.

Shortly before frying, beat the reserved egg whites until they form soft, rounded peaks. Using a rubber spatula, gently fold the whites into the batter, then add the prepared food—well dried with paper toweling—and gently fold it in also, coating it completely.

To fry the food, proceed to Step 2 of this Master Technique.

STEP 1D: TO MAKE TEMPURA: Tempura is batter-dipped deep-fried food, Japanese-style. The foods most commonly used for tempura are oysters, shrimp, chicken, and raw or blanched vegetables, including green beans, onion rings, and sweet potatoes. A tempura coating is thin, nearly translucent, crackling crisp, and in general much lighter and more delicate than the usual fritter coating.

1 cup ice water
1 large egg yolk
1 cup unbleached all-purpose flour or cake flour (not self-rising)
½ teaspoon ground ginger (optional)
½ teaspoon salt

Beat ice water and egg yolk in a 3-quart bowl until thoroughly blended. Add all remaining ingredients and beat with the whip just until the flour is barely moistened; there are supposed to be lumps. *Use at once.*

Dry the food to be deep-fried well with paper toweling and, with a rubber spatula, fold it into the tempura batter. Fry according to instructions in Step 2 of this Technique.

STEP 2: TO DEEP-FRY THE FOOD

PRELIMINARIES:

Select a heavy pot or casserole 9 to 10 inches across and 5 to 6 inches deep. The pot must be heavy so that it will retain heat and so that it will not tip during frying. It should be wide so that a fair quantity of food can be fried in a single layer, and it should be deep enough so that oil will not spill over the lip of the pot and possibly catch fire.

Pour into the pot 3 quarts fresh neutral vegetable oil, or enough to cover the bottom to a depth of about 3 inches. There must be enough oil in the pot to cover the food completely and to allow the pieces of food to expand as they cook and move around in the pot. And, unless there is a quantity of oil in the pot, the temperature of the oil will plummet as soon as each batch of food is added, making the food greasy.

One can deep-fry in lard or solid vegetable shortening (6 pounds of either will be needed), but foods fried in solid fats tend to be greasy and heavy. Avoid stale oils—they will give your deep-fried foods an off taste. And don't use olive oil, butter, or margarine—they'll burn.

Attach a deep-fry thermometer to the side of the pot, being sure that the thermometer stem reaches at least 1 inch into the oil but does not touch either the side or bottom of the pot. The temperature of the oil should be somewhere between 360°F and 390°F. If the oil is not hot enough, the food lolls around in the pot, barely cooking—and all the while soaking up grease like a sponge. If the oil is too hot, the outside coating will turn leathery and burn before the food has a chance to cook through.

A reliable deep-fry/candy thermometer is an absolutely essential piece of equipment for anyone who is serious about deep-frying. Lacking a thermometer, one can roughly gauge the temperature of the oil using the bread-cube test:

- Heat the oil until you guess that it has reached the proper temperature—a shimmer or haze over the top is a crucial sign.
- Drop in a 1-inch cube of bread.
- If the fat is at the proper temperature, the bread will brown nicely in a minute.
- Rerun the above test each time you add a new batch of food to the pot.

Set the pot of oil over a moderate flame and heat to a temperature of about 380°F. This will take 10 minutes or longer. If you are using a frying basket, heat it in the oil. Never heat oil over high flame. You may cause it to smoke (thus destroying its flavor) or to catch fire.

If the pot you are using has a long handle, be sure that it is turned toward the back of the stove, away from you, so that you won't accidentally brush the handle and tip over the oil.

While the oil is heating, set the oven at 150°F (or "warm"). Line a 17×11-inch baking sheet with a triple layer of paper toweling and set it in the oven. Set the breaded or batter-dipped food adjacent to the pot of hot oil. Have ready a pair of tongs and, if you are not using a deep-frying basket, either a skimmer or a slotted spoon. Always cook fried foods in small batches. Transfer cooked food to a towel-lined baking sheet to drain, and keep it warm in a slow oven (150°F).

TO FRY BREADED FOODS: If you are using a deep-frying basket, lift the heated basket from the pot of oil, hold it over the pot, and, using tongs, arrange the food in a single layer on the bottom of the basket, spacing the pieces at least ½ inch apart. Lower the basket back into the oil. If you are not using a basket, quickly drop the pieces of food into the oil using tongs, leaving a good ½ inch between the pieces.

As the food cooks, turn it periodically with the tongs to make sure it browns evenly. Try to keep the temperature of the fat at around 370°F, adjusting the flame as necessary. As each batch of food is done, remove it from the oil by lifting the basket (or by straining it out with a skimmer or slotted spoon) and then scatter the pieces over the towel-lined baking sheet. Keep it warm in the preheated oven. Before frying the next batch, check the temperature of the fat and adjust the heat as necessary.

TO FRY BATTER-DIPPED FOODS: Raise the deep-frying basket out of the hot oil and hold it over the pot. One at a time, grasp battered pieces of food with tongs, allowing excess batter to drip off, then place in the basket. Add no more than 6 or 8 pieces of food at one time—there should be about an inch of space around each piece—as batter-dipped foods expand considerably as they cook. If you are not using a basket, transfer the pieces of food directly from bowl to pot using tongs.

Cook until the bottoms of the pieces have browned nicely, gently turn the pieces over with tongs or a slotted spoon, and fry until nicely browned on the other side. Try to keep the temperature of the oil at around 370°F, adjusting the flame as necessary. As each batch of food is done, remove it from the oil by lifting the basket (or by straining it out with a skimmer or slotted spoon) and then scatter the pieces over the towel-lined baking sheet. Keep warm in the preheated oven. Before adding the next batch, check the temperature of the fat and adjust the heat as necessary.

REUSING OIL (OR FAT): If you have used the oil exclusively for making french fries, you may strain it through a triple layer of cheesecloth, return it to its original container, store it (preferably in the refrigerator) for several months, and use it again (or several more times, if you fry potatoes in it each time). Discard the oil as soon as it begins to look dark or thick or when it foams or smokes when reheated. When frying foods other than potatoes, I prefer not to reuse the oil, for I find that the tastes of strong foods—fish, onions—permeate frying oil and that crumbs and batter bits dislodged from coated foods turn frying oil dark and smelly.

HORS D'OEUVRE INSPIRATIONS

For many people, hors d'oeuvre are the best part of a meal, and many cooks, myself included, tremendously enjoy the handwork involved in crafting handsome hors d'oeuvre and presenting them attractively. Some hosts feel they must offer expensive foods as hors d'oeuvre—smoked salmon, macadamia nuts, caviar, and so on—but in fact many of the same foods that are enjoyed as main dishes will also do very nicely at cocktail time. This is the philosophy that underlies the hors d'oeuvre "inspirations" in this chapter. Most of the inspirations consist simply of notes on how to adapt recipes appearing elsewhere in this book for cocktail service.

When planning hors d'oeuvre, remember not to overdo things. Hors d'oeuvre are meant to excite the eye and stimulate the palate—to lead into, but not to upstage or overwhelm, the main part of the meal that is to follow. Never offer hors d'oeuvre that are so piquant or salty that they burn out the palate before the meal has begun. And if your meal is rather heavy—say, a cream soup, a roast, and then a rich dessert—start with only a few light hors d'oeuvre. As a general rule, I think that two kinds—perhaps one hot and one cold—are quite sufficient, and I typically offer only one.

Please consult the index to locate the recipes referred to in the Inspirations.

Inspiration 1: Breads and Spreads

Setting out one or two kinds of breads and a couple of things to put on them is a simple yet always appealing way of putting together a cocktail party. If you add dishes of pickles, olives, and raw vegetables, you have a light buffet.

Breads

- Baking powder biscuits or one of the variations—buttermilk, bacon-chive, Cheddar, garden herb, Little Italy savory biscuits, or Virginia ham—are a good base for spreads. If you want to be especially fancy, try baking the biscuits in 1-inch miniature sizes. One recipe will make at least 50 miniature biscuits, which will only need about 10 minutes in the oven to bake.
- Basic American white bread, or one of its variations—light or dark rye, whole wheat, Cheddar cheese, or herb bread—can be baked in three or four miniature loaf pans (2- to 3-cup capacity) and sliced thinly to make small elegant canapés. Bread dough can also be fashioned into cloverleaf dinner rolls according to the instructions on page 643–44.
- Hard rolls, perhaps flavored with ham and cheese, or with olives and garlic, are always welcome. Here again you might consider baking miniature rolls, or make hero rolls and then slice the bread before serving it.

Spreads

- Prepare any of the mayonnaise salads on pages 119–23, cutting the salad ingredients into small pieces so that the salad can be used as a spread. Mold it into a dome or cone on a platter and garnish it with chopped parsley and/or toasted almonds. A crab, lobster, or shrimp salad is elegant, but expensive—and you might find that a more affordable salad made with pork or leftover veal will arouse more interest because it is unusual.
- Party-type egg salad is one of my favorite hors d'oeuvre. Press 3 or 4 hard-cooked eggs through a fine sieve with the back of a spoon. Beat in half a stick of soft, fresh, unsalted butter, a teaspoon of minced shallot or scallion bulb, another teaspoon or two of well-drained minced capers, several dabs of Dijon mustard, and a tad of anchovy paste. Season with salt, freshly ground pepper, and a few drops of lemon juice. Form the mixture, which should be quite stiff, into a pyramid or cone and cover it with finely chopped fresh parsley. Melba toast, is a nice base for the spread, and dry Sherry—the type of cocktail I like best—goes with it very well.

- Pâtés are perennial favorites. Prepare either the rich, unctuous chicken liver pâté or the country-type pâté, slicing at least part of it beforehand.
- For a very substantial hors d'oeuvre, put out a platter of sliced cold roast chicken or turkey, rare roast beef or lamb, or baked ham. Of course the platter can include several meats instead of just one, and you might also set out sliced Swiss cheese or a wheel of Brie. Several spreads should also be offered—mustard (perhaps two or three kinds of varying degrees of hotness), soft butter, or a mayonnaise (plain mayonnaise, herb mayonnaise, horseradish mayonnaise, rémoulade sauce, or Russian dressing).

Inspiration 2: Eggs

Savory egg preparations go well with drinks, can be made ahead of time, and are inexpensive to put together. Here are a few ideas:

- Plain or flavored deviled eggs and baked stuffed eggs all make nice hors d'oeuvre. For an elegant presentation, consider using very small chicken eggs, sometimes called peewee eggs (these are hard to find at the supermarket, but easy to get at any egg farm). The proportions given in the recipe are sufficient for a dozen or more peewees.
- Prepare any of the frittatas on pages 151–54. Let the frittata cool to room temperature, then unmold it upside down onto a serving platter or tray. Cut it into small slices or cubes and pass it with picks or perhaps just cocktail napkins.
- Quiches of all types (see pages 162–67) make delightful hors d'oeuvre fare. Although you can cut a regular-size quiche into small squares to serve as an hors d'oeuvre, pieces of quiche are messy to eat without a fork, so for cocktails I am inclined to make tiny individual quiches instead of a single larger one. For these, prepare a half recipe of any of the quiche mixtures and turn it into fully baked tiny tartlet shells (page 759) that have been arranged on a baking sheet. Bake the miniature quiches in a 375°F oven for 7 to 10 minutes, or until puffed and set. Assuming that your tartlet shells hold about 1 tablespoon filling each, a half recipe of one of the quiche mixtures will be sufficient to make 28 to 32 hors d'oeuvre.

Inspiration 3: Deep-Fried Tidbits

Deep-fried foods are perhaps the classiest and most highly appreciated of all hors d'oeuvre. Although the actual frying needs to be performed close to serving time (it helps here to have a friend working with you in the kitchen), the cutting up and coating of the food can be done several hours in advance. Deep-fried foods should always be offered with a sauce for dipping (see suggestions below); if possible, pass the foods on serving trays, with bowls of sauce set in the middle. If you set them out on a cocktail table they may get cold before anyone takes notice of them.

- Deep-fried shellfish are sure to be a success at any gathering. Choose clams, oysters, scallops, or shrimp, following any of the deep-frying recipes in the shellfish chapter. Offer two dips—a mayonnaise type such as rémoulade or tartar sauce, and a nonoily condiment such as hot mustard, finely chopped mustard fruits or sweet chutney, or, for tempura shellfish, soy sauce (which may be lightly flavored with grated orange zest, grated fresh ginger, chopped scallions, a bit of honey, drops of sesame oil, and so on).
- Miniature croquettes, either fish or poultry, and miniature crab cakes (made according to the crab cake recipe on page 290 but deep-fried rather than sautéed) make fine hors d'oeuvre. Form the croquette or crab cake mixture into small balls that can be picked up with the fingers or speared with picks, coat them as indicated in the recipe, and then deep-fry for just a couple of minutes, or until golden. Pass fish croquettes and crab cakes with tartar sauce, poultry croquettes with béarnaise sauce.
- To make deep-fried chicken wings or chicken, turkey, or pork fingers, consult the chart on page 423. Sauce/dip suggestions are on page 422.
- Tempura vegetables make an hors d'oeuvre that is both light and satisfying. Start with a firm, flavorful vegetable such as asparagus, green beans, broccoli, mushrooms, onions, peppers, sweet potatoes, or summer or winter squash. Cut vegetable into sticks about the same size as whole green beans (or break broccoli into small florets, halve or quarter large mushrooms, and so on). Following the procedures in the chapter on deep-frying, coat the vegetables in tempura batter (page 66) and deep-fry (page 64) for 2 to 3 minutes. One recipe of tempura batter will coat about one quart of fresh vegetables.

Inspiration 4: Shellfish

Shellfish make fine hors d'oeuvre, not only because they are so tasty but also because they happen to be a perfect size and shape for eating with the fingers or with little spears. For deep-fried shellfish see Inspiration #3, above. Here is a rundown of other ways you might present various shellfish as hors d'oeuvre:

- *Clams:* Serve raw on the half-shell or prepare clams casino, oreganato, or in garlic butter. Broil or bake the clams on the half-shell and pass with picks.
- *Crab:* Bake deviled crab in clam shells. Set out with seafood forks.
- *Mussels:* Pass mussel salad or mussels broiled in garlic butter with picks.
- *Oysters:* Serve oysters raw on the half-shell or prepare oysters Rockefeller, oysters casino, or oysters broiled in garlic butter.
- *Scallops:* Raw scallops served with rémoulade sauce are a treat. Scallops sautéed with garlic and lemon also make excellent hors d'oeuvre.
- *Shrimp:* Plain cold steamed shrimp never fail to please; offer them with green goddess dressing, horseradish mayonnaise, or rémoulade sauce and let guests pick them up with their fingers. Baked in a handsome oven-to-table dish and set out with picks and cocktail napkins, the crumbled shrimp recipe on page 318 makes a fine hors d'oeuvre.

Inspiration 5: Poultry and Meats

Poultry and meats are usually reserved for the body of the meal, but a few recipes have become classic hors d'oeuvre fare:

- *Broiled chicken livers:* After broiling, remove livers from skewers and impale on picks. Half a recipe makes about 24 pieces.
- *Sautéed chicken livers:* One of my standard hors d'oeuvre; pass with toothpicks. A half recipe yields about two dozen liver halves.
- *Meatballs in parsley cream sauce and Swedish meatballs:* These recipes will make about 72 ¾-inch meatballs. The classic way to serve these, especially Swedish meatballs, is in a chafing dish; however, you may also mound them in a serving dish, nap them with their sauce, and sprinkle them with chopped fresh parsley. Have a bowl of picks nearby.
- *Cannibal balls:* These are miniature balls of steak tartare that are rolled in finely chopped parsley, passed with picks, and sometimes served with mustard. A half recipe of steak tartare will make about thirty 1-inch balls.

Inspiration 6: Vegetables

Tempura vegetables as an hors d'oeuvre are discussed on page 70. Here are two other vegetable ideas:

- *Raw vegetables (crudités):* It's hard to imagine a cocktail party that does not include a platter of raw vegetables plus a dipping sauce. Be inventive about the vegetables. The usual carrots and celery are fine, but try also raw mushrooms, broccoli florets, or, my personal favorites, pencil-thin raw asparagus stalks (these need not be peeled) and leaves of endive. The dip I always choose is green goddess mayonnaise, but herb mayonnaise and Russian dressing are also good.

- *Boiled new potatoes* make a delicious hors d'oeuvre when cut in half or sliced and topped with sour cream and caviar. Serve with Champagne or ice-cold vodka.

HOT FILLED HORS D'OEUVRE
Using Tartlet Shells, Miniature Cream Puff Shells, Miniature Crêpes, and Bread Cases

Tiny hors d'oeuvre made with bread, pastry, or crêpes and filled with a hot, savory mixture of one sort or another always add elegance and sophistication to a party. Be forewarned, however, that such hors d'oeuvre take some time to put together and are not to be tackled by those who do not enjoy working with their hands.

A Master Recipe for three hors d'oeuvre fillings is given on page 73. But first, here's how to do the hors d'oeuvre cases and shells.

- *Tartlet shells:* Prepare according to the recipe on page 759.
- *Bite-size cream puff shells:* Prepare according to Step 1 of the recipe on page 795, using salt rather than sugar.
- *Crêpes:* Prepare a half recipe of the crêpe batter on page 690 and use it to make 24 to 30 3-inch crêpes. Spread with hors d'oeuvre filling and either roll cigarwise or fold into small envelopes.

BREAD CASES

Makes 20 to 24

PRELIMINARIES

1. Adjust rack to middle level of oven.
2. Preheat oven to 300°F 20 minutes before baking.
3. Select a 17×11-inch rimmed baking tray; butter lightly.

20 to 24 3/8-inch slices firm, unsweet bread (about 1½ pounds)
1 large egg beaten with ½ teaspoon water
4 to 6 tablespoons butter

Using a 2-inch round cookie or biscuit cutter, cut 2 crustless circles from each slice of bread, making 40 to 48 circles altogether. Arrange half the circles on the prepared baking tray. With a 1½-inch cutter, cut a hole out of the centers of remaining bread circles. Lightly dip one side of the open circles in beaten egg. Press these on top of the whole circles, egg side down. Brush cases lightly with melted butter and bake about 15 minutes, or until golden. If you wish, you may butter and toast the cut-out bread "holes" and use these as lids or caps for the filled bread cases.

MASTER RECIPE

Hot Cheese, Chicken, or Seafood Hors D'oeuvre

Makes about 1¼ cups filling, or enough for 20 to 30 hors d'oeuvre

Here shredded cheese or ground chicken or seafood is beaten into a very thick cream sauce, which is then spooned into miniature pastry shells, puffs, crêpes, or bread cases, and baked in a hot oven just long enough to warm through. The procedure is very simple, and the hors d'oeuvre may be completely assembled several hours in advance and baked just before serving.

Basic Cream Sauce, page 34, made with milk
DECREASE: Milk to 1 cup
ADD: 2 teaspoons grated onion
One of the followings flavorings:

- ¾ cup (about 3 ounces) shredded Swiss or Cheddar, or crumbled Roquefort or bleu cheese, and sprinklings cayenne pepper
- ⅓ cup ground cooked chicken, 2 tablespoons freshly grated Parmesan cheese, and 1 teaspoon dried tarragon
- ¼ cup ground cooked shrimp, crab, or lobster and ½ teaspoon dry mustard

20 to 30 miniature tartlet shells, bite-size cream puff shells, 3-inch crêpes, or bread cases

Prepare basic cream sauce according to the Master Recipe, using only 1 cup milk. Do not thin; this sauce should be very thick. Remove sauce from heat and add grated onion and *one* of the flavorings, beating until mixture is smooth. Taste carefully and correct the seasoning, remembering that an hors d'oeuvre filling should be rather piquant.

Spoon about 2 teaspoons filling into each hors d'oeuvre case and arrange on a lightly buttered baking sheet. The assembled hors d'oeuvre may be covered with plastic wrap and refrigerated for several hours. Just before serving, pop hors d'oeuvre into preheated 400°F oven and bake 3 to 5 minutes, or until hot.

AHEAD OF TIME: You can turn the filling into a plastic container, cover the surface directly with plastic wrap, seal, and refrigerate for several days or freeze for 3 months.

SOUPS and CHOWDERS

Soup can be hearty and comforting, to be craved during illness or distress, or decidedly elegant, meant to pique and excite the palate. Some soups and chowders are creamy; others have a brothlike base. Some soups are puréed smooth, while others are so laden with chunks of meat, vegetables, pasta, or beans that they are less to be sipped than chewed. Given their great diversity, it is no surprise that soups play dissimilar roles. Consommé, a clear, amber broth flavored with Sherry or Madeira, is most at home as the opening of an elegant three- or four-course dinner. The vegetable cream soups, though they may also be served as a first course, have come to be favored as lunchtime soups, accompanied by sandwiches. The various home-style soups, including chicken noodle, gumbo, split pea, and Manhattan clam chowder, can be fitted into almost any meal plan. In small portions they make fine first courses. Accompanied by crusty rolls or bread and perhaps a plate of raw vegetables, they constitute a highly satisfying lunch. Such soups can become a supper hearty enough to get one through the coldest winter night when they are augmented by sandwiches, cheese, and a salad, and followed by a slice of pie or some other substantial dessert. The last soups presented in this chapter, the chowders and bean soups, are practically meals by themselves. Only bread or crackers and, perhaps, a salad need be added.

All soups are simple and nearly failproof to make, and most

fit neatly into the Master Recipe concept. Once you understand the basic technique of making each type of soup, endless variations are possible. Soups are also a wonderful use for leftover meats, pasta, and vegetables. As a final word, it must be said that the very best soups start with a homemade stock. Still, because the ingredients added to a soup will impart their own flavors, canned broth or even, in a pinch, bouillon cubes, will do.

CONSOMMÉ

Makes about 1½ quarts; 5 to 6 servings

❦ *Often served as the first course of a formal dinner, consommé is a crystal clear, amber soup that is made by clarifying a concentrated meat or poultry stock with raw egg whites and shells. Generally flavored with a dash of Sherry and a sprinkling of parsley, consommé can also be lightly thickened with tapioca and, when the occasion demands, dressed up with such elegant additions as blanched julienned vegetables or diced fresh tomato, or strips of crêpe.*

It goes without saying that a consommé will only be as good as the stock it is made from. If you can, use a homemade stock; otherwise, start with canned beef or chicken broth, adding the enrichments, including the meat or poultry, indicated in the rescue recipe on page 28.

A NOTE ON CLARIFYING STOCKS: The clarification process is one of the most amazing of all culinary spectacles, but if it is to work there must be no grease anywhere. The stock must be thoroughly degreased, the egg whites and shells must be completely free of yolk, and all bowls and utensils must be sparkling clean.

Either 4 quarts Beef Stock, page 24, or Chicken Stock, page 26 *or* 2 quarts Rescued Canned Beef or Chicken Broth, page 28
5 large egg whites, free of all yolk, and their shells, finely crushed
⅓ cup quick-cooking *granulated* (not small pearl) tapioca (optional; only if you want to thicken the consommé)
1 to 2 tablespoons dry Sherry or Madeira (optional)
Salt and/or fresh lemon juice (optional)
2 to 3 tablespoons finely chopped fresh parsley

If you are using homemade stock, gently boil it down until reduced by half, about 2 quarts. Blot up any specks of grease on stock or rescued canned broth with pieces of paper towel. Let stock or broth cool to room temperature.

Combine stock and egg whites and shells in a 4-quart saucepan and set over moderate heat. Slowly and continually—do not stop for a moment—circulate a wire whip around the inside wall of the saucepan, so that a shallow whirlpool is constantly maintained in the center of the consommé. As the consommé heats, the egg whites will clot in small specks and begin to rise to the top, forming a whitish cap. At the first sign of a bubble, indicating that the simmer has been reached, turn the heat down to its lowest point (if your stove is electric, very gently slide the saucepan to the side of the burner as the heating element cools), and let the broth stand for 10 minutes. The consommé must not simmer during this time—briefly turn off heat if you see a bubble—and the saucepan must not be jostled or moved.

While consommé is standing, cut a 3- to 4-foot length of cheesecloth, rinse it thoroughly under cold water, wring dry, and then fold it into a triple or quadruple layer and use it to line sides and bottom of a sieve, letting excess drape over the sides. Place cheesecloth-lined sieve over a deep 4-quart mixing bowl.

Very gently ladle consommé into the sieve and let it drip undisturbed into the bowl; this may take as long as 10 minutes. The resulting consommé should be crystal clear. Discard residue in strainer.

Rinse out saucepan thoroughly, return consommé to it, and bring to a simmer. If you wish to thicken the consommé, sprinkle in the tapioca and, stirring frequently, simmer for about 5 minutes or until the tapioca granules are swollen and completely transparent. Remove consommé from heat and, if you wish, stir in Sherry or Madeira. Taste and add salt or a few drops of lemon juice if necessary. Turn consommé into a warmed tureen or individual soup cups and garnish each portion with chopped fresh parsley.

STORAGE: Consommé may be tightly covered and refrigerated for several days or frozen up to 6 months. Thicken with tapioca and flavor with Sherry just before serving.

MASTER RECIPE

Cream of Broccoli Soup

Makes about 1½ quarts; 4 main-course or 6 to 8 first-course servings

❦ *Few dishes are both so elegant and so simple, so soothing and yet so exciting to the palate, as a well-made vegetable cream soup. This Master Recipe is prepared with broccoli, but virtually any vegetable may be used as the soup base, as the 31 variation recipes that follow attest. Equally good hot and chilled, a vegetable cream soup may be served as the main course of a lunch or light supper or as the first course of an important dinner.*

1 to 1½ pounds broccoli
6 tablespoons butter
⅔ cup minced onions
¼ teaspoon salt
⅛ teaspoon pepper, preferably white, freshly ground
¼ cup all-purpose flour
1 quart Chicken Stock, page 26, or canned broth
½ to ¾ cup heavy cream
2 large egg yolks
Additional salt and pepper, freshly grated nutmeg, and lemon juice, as needed
2 to 3 tablespoons minced fresh parsley
1 to 2 tablespoons additional butter (optional; if serving the soup hot)
⅓ cup heavy cream, whipped, or ½ cup sour cream (optional; if serving the soup cold)

Peel and trim the broccoli (see page 493), then cut it into ½-inch pieces. You should have 2½ to 3 cups. Set aside.

Melt 6 tablespoons butter in a 3- to 4-quart saucepan or casserole made of or lined with a noncorroding material. Sauté the onions in the butter over low heat until soft but not brown, about 10 minutes. Add the broccoli, sprinkle with salt and pepper, and stir to coat with butter. Cover pan and, stirring occasionally, cook the broccoli slowly for about 5 minutes, or until slightly softened. Sprinkle on the flour, stirring thoroughly to prevent any lumps from forming, and cook slowly for another 3 minutes, stirring frequently. In the meantime, heat the stock or broth to just below the simmer in a small saucepan. Remove the broccoli mixture from heat, add the hot stock or broth, and beat thoroughly with a wire whip to combine. Bring soup to a rapid simmer over moderately high heat and cook for 1 minute, stirring constantly. Reduce heat to low, partially cover the pan, and simmer the soup slowly for 25 minutes, stirring occasionally and adding a bit of water or additional stock or broth if the soup appears to be reducing.

Using a food mill, blender, or food processor, purée the soup in small batches. If using an electric machine, blend only briefly; the soup will have more character if the texture is slightly coarse. Turn batches into a clean 3-quart mixing bowl. In the rinsed-out soup pot beat together the heavy cream and egg yolks using a wire whip. Slowly add 2 cups of the hot soup, beating constantly, then add the remaining soup all at once, blending thoroughly.

Place soup over moderately low heat and, stirring constantly with a wooden spoon, heat it just until it begins to steam. The soup should become smooth and thicken slightly. Do not let the soup reach the simmer, or the egg yolks will overcook and the soup will be grainy. Remove soup from heat and thin, if necessary, with additional tablespoons of cream.

Season the soup carefully to bring out the flavor of the broccoli. Add salt and/or pepper as necessary, then a grating or two of nutmeg to give the soup a nutlike savor, and finally a few drops of fresh lemon juice to sharpen the taste.

To serve hot: Stir in half the chopped parsley, then ladle the soup into warmed soup plates. Sprinkle each portion with some of the remaining parsley and garnish with a pat of butter, if desired.

To serve chilled: Let soup cool slightly, then turn into a lidded storage container and chill for at least 4 hours or up to 3 days. Just before serving, correct the seasoning (it will probably need salt and possibly other seasonings as well) and stir in half the parsley, reserving the rest for garnish. Serve either in chilled mugs or soup plates and top with a dollop of whipped cream or sour cream, if you wish.

AHEAD OF TIME *(to serve the soup hot)*: If you plan to serve the soup within 24 hours, blend the puréed broccoli mixture with the cream and egg yolks but do not heat to thicken. Let soup cool slightly, then cover and refrigerate. Just before serving, reheat to just below the simmer and season.

For longer storage, prepare soup only through the puréeing of the broccoli mixture. Turn soup into a lidded storage container and refrigerate for up to 5 days or freeze for several months. To serve, combine soup with cream and egg yolks and proceed with the Master Recipe.

Variation: CREAM OF ALMOND SOUP

Makes about 1½ quarts; 6 to 8 first-course servings

❦ *Deliciously subtle in taste, this is a good holiday soup.*

Cream of Broccoli Soup

SUBSTITUTE: 1 cup (about 4 ounces) blanched slivered almonds for broccoli
INCREASE: Onions to 1½ cups
OMIT: Egg yolks

Substituting almonds for broccoli and increasing the onions, prepare the soup base; purée very thoroughly, using a blender or food processor. Combine with cream (no egg yolks are needed) and heat to just below the simmer. Season generously with nutmeg, but go easy on the lemon juice, just a drop or two. Serve hot.

Variation: CREAM OF ARTICHOKE SOUP

Makes about 1½ quarts; 4 main-course or 6 to 8 first-course servings

Cream of Broccoli Soup

SUBSTITUTE: 6 large artichokes for broccoli

Following the instructions on page 470, trim the artichokes and boil until the bottoms are just tender enough to be pierced with a sharp knife. Pull off the leaves and scrape off the edible portion with a teaspoon. Remove and discard the chokes. Use the scraped-off parts of the leaves and the bottoms, quartered, in place of the broccoli and proceed with the Master Recipe. Serve hot or chilled.

Variation: CREAM OF ASPARAGUS SOUP

Makes about 1½ quarts; 4 main-course or 6 to 8 first-course servings

Cream of Broccoli Soup

SUBSTITUTE: 1¼ pounds asparagus for broccoli
OMIT: Nutmeg

Peel and trim the asparagus (see page 475), then cut it into ½-inch pieces. Proceed according to the Master Recipe, substituting the asparagus for the broccoli. Omit nutmeg. Serve hot or chilled.

Variation: CREAM OF CABBAGE AND POTATO SOUP

Makes about 1½ quarts; 4 main-course or 6 to 8 first-course servings

Cream of Broccoli Soup

SUBSTITUTE: 2 small to medium baking potatoes (about 12 ounces) *and* 2 packed cups shredded green cabbage for broccoli

OMIT: Egg yolks

ADD: ½ teaspoon caraway seed, ground or moistened with a few drops of water and minced fine (optional)

Peel and dice the potatoes, making about 1½ cups. Proceed according to the Master Recipe, substituting potatoes and cabbage for broccoli and omitting the egg yolks. Season with caraway, if desired, and serve hot.

Variation: CREAM OF CARROT SOUP

Makes about 1½ quarts; 4 main-course or 6 to 8 first-course servings

❦ *One of my personal favorites, this soup is especially good as a first course preceding roast turkey, beef, or lamb.*

Cream of Broccoli Soup

SUBSTITUTE: 1 pound carrots for broccoli

OMIT: Egg yolks

ADD: ⅛ teaspoon ground cloves *or* ⅛ teaspoon dried rosemary, ground or moistened with a few drops of water and minced fine (optional)

Peel, trim, and slice the carrots. Proceed according to the Master Recipe, substituting the carrots for the broccoli and omitting the egg yolks. Season with cloves or rosemary, if desired, and serve hot.

Variation: CREAM OF CAULIFLOWER SOUP

Makes about 1½ quarts; 4 main-course or 6 to 8 first-course servings

Cream of Broccoli Soup

SUBSTITUTE: 1 small head cauliflower for broccoli

Quarter the cauliflower lengthwise and chop three of the quarters into ½-inch pieces. You should have about 3 cups; if not, chop the remaining quarter. Proceed according to the Master Recipe, substituting the cauliflower for the broccoli. Season the soup with a very light hand to avoid overpowering the delicate taste of the cauliflower. Serve hot or chilled.

Variation: CREAM OF CELERY SOUP

Makes about 1½ quarts; 4 main-course or 6 to 8 first-course servings

Cream of Broccoli Soup
SUBSTITUTE: 6 to 8 ribs celery for broccoli
ADD: ½ to 2 teaspoons dry Sherry

Slice enough celery into ½-inch pieces to make 2½ to 3 cups. Proceed according to the Master Recipe, substituting celery for broccoli. Season with Sherry, added by half teaspoons. Serve hot or chilled.

Variation: CREAM OF CELERY ROOT SOUP

Makes about 1½ quarts; 4 main-course or 6 to 8 first-course servings

Cream of Broccoli Soup
SUBSTITUTE: about 1 pound celery root for broccoli
OMIT: Egg yolks
ADD: ½ to 2 teaspoons dry Sherry

Scrub and peel the celery root (see page 515), then cut into ½-inch cubes. Proceed according to the Master Recipe, substituting the celery root for broccoli. Season with Sherry, added by half teaspoons. Serve hot.

Variation: CREAM OF CHESTNUT SOUP

Makes about 1½ quarts; 6 to 8 first-course servings

❦ *This very special soup might precede a Thanksgiving turkey.*

Cream of Broccoli Soup
SUBSTITUTE: 1 pound fresh chestnuts for broccoli
ADD: ⅓ cup minced celery
OMIT: Egg yolks

Shell and peel the chestnuts (see page 519), then chop coarsely. Proceed according to the Master Recipe, substituting the chestnuts for the broccoli, sautéing the minced celery along with the onions, and omitting the egg yolks. Season generously with nutmeg but sparingly with lemon juice. Serve hot.

Variation: CREAM OF CORN SOUP

Makes about 1½ quarts; 4 main-course or 6 to 8 first-course servings

❦ *Only fresh corn will produce the right results here. If you use fairly mature corn, you may find, after puréeing and straining, that the soup is quite thick; in this case you may omit the egg yolks or add only one.*

To give the soup a provocative Latin touch, spice it with cayenne pepper and substitute chopped fresh basil for parsley.

Cream of Broccoli Soup

SUBSTITUTE:	5 to 6 large ears fresh corn for broccoli
DECREASE OR OMIT:	Egg yolks (as necessary)
ADD:	Sugar, if needed

Cut the ears of corn into kernels (see page 522), making about 3 cups kernels and pulp. Substituting corn for broccoli, prepare the soup base; either force the soup through a food mill or purée in blender or food processor and then strain through a very fine sieve to eliminate all tough bits and pieces. Use only 1 egg yolk or none at all if the soup appears thick. Season with pinches of sugar to sweeten slightly, if necessary. Serve hot.

Variation: CREAM OF CUCUMBER SOUP

Makes about 1½ quarts; 4 main-course or 6 to 8 first-course servings

❦ *Though delicious warm, this soup is more often served chilled, with a dollop of sour cream on top. Finely chopped fresh dill (feathery leaves only) or fresh tarragon may be used in addition to or in place of chopped parsley.*

Cream of Broccoli Soup

SUBSTITUTE:	2 pounds cucumbers (4 to 7 large or 12 to 15 small kirby) for broccoli

Following Step 1 of the recipe on page 529, peel, seed, and slice the cucumbers (about 3 cups), macerate in 1 teaspoon salt, and squeeze well to eliminate excess moisture. Proceed with the Master Recipe, substituting the cucumbers for broccoli.

Variation: CREAM OF FENNEL SOUP

Makes about 1½ quarts; 4 main-course or 6 to 8 first-course servings

Cream of Broccoli Soup
SUBSTITUTE: 1 pound fennel for broccoli

Slice fennel into ½-inch pieces, making about 3 cups. Proceed according to the Master Recipe, substituting the fennel for broccoli. Season the soup with a delicate hand so as not to overwhelm the subtle taste of the fennel. Serve hot.

Variation: CREAM OF GREEN PEA SOUP

Makes about 1½ quarts; 4 main-course or 6 to 8 first-course servings

❦ *This is a good way to make use of starchy, mature peas. If the soup is to be served chilled—and it's very good this way—consider using fresh mint rather than parsley as a garnish.*

Cream of Broccoli Soup
SUBSTITUTE: 2 pounds peas in the shell or 2½ to 3 cups frozen peas for broccoli
DECREASE OR OMIT: Egg yolks (as necessary)

Shell fresh peas; thaw frozen peas at room temperature. Substituting peas for broccoli, prepare the soup base; purée very thoroughly in a blender or food processor to pulverize any tough pieces of skin. Use egg yolks only if the soup needs to be thickened; generally it will be thick enough without them.

Variation: CREAM OF JERUSALEM ARTICHOKE SOUP

Makes about 1½ quarts; 4 main-course or 6 to 8 first-course servings

Cream of Broccoli Soup
SUBSTITUTE: 1 pound Jerusalem artichokes for broccoli
OMIT: Egg yolks

Following Step 1 of the recipe on page 542, peel and slice the Jerusalem artichokes, dropping them into cold water, lemon juice, and salt as you go to prevent discoloration. You should have 2½ to 3 cups. Proceed according to the Master Recipe, substituting the Jerusalem artichokes for broccoli and omitting the egg yolks. Serve hot.

Variation: CREAM OF KOHLRABI SOUP

Makes about 1½ quarts; 4 main-course or 6 to 8 first-course servings

Cream of Broccoli Soup
SUBSTITUTE: 1 pound kohlrabi bulbs for broccoli

Peel the kohlrabi deeply and cut into ½-inch cubes; you should have 2½ to 3 cups. Proceed according to the Master Recipe, substituting the kohlrabi for broccoli. Serve hot or chilled.

Variation: CREAM OF LETTUCE SOUP

Makes about 1½ quarts; 4 main-course or 6 to 8 first-course servings

❦*Lettuce makes a lovely soup indeed, with a distinctive, subtly bitter flavor. Either hot or chilled, the soup makes an elegant first course preceding a roast.*

Cream of Broccoli Soup
SUBSTITUTE: 1 pound (3 to 6 heads) Boston or Bibb lettuce for broccoli

Wash the lettuce well and cut into thin strips; you may use both the large outer leaves that are unsuitable for salad and the core. You should have 4 tightly packed cups. Proceed according to the Master Recipe, substituting the lettuce for broccoli. Season liberally with fresh lemon juice.

Variation: CREAM OF MUSHROOM SOUP

Makes about 1½ quarts; 4 main-course or 6 to 8 first-course servings

Cream of Broccoli Soup
SUBSTITUTE: 12 ounces fresh mushrooms for broccoli

Wipe the mushrooms clean and slice thinly; you should have 4 to 5 cups. Substituting mushrooms for broccoli, prepare the soup base, but *do not purée.* To thicken the soup, beat the cream and egg yolks together in a bowl, then slowly beat in about 2 cups of the hot soup; pour this mixture into the soup remaining in the pot and heat until thickened. Season liberally with fresh lemon juice. Serve hot.

Variation: CREAM OF MUSHROOM-POTATO SOUP WITH DILL

Makes about 1½ quarts; 4 main-course or 6 to 8 first-course servings

Cream of Broccoli Soup

SUBSTITUTE: 2 large baking potatoes (about 1¼ pounds) *and* 4 ounces mushrooms for broccoli

OMIT: Egg yolks

SUBSTITUTE: 2 tablespoons finely chopped fresh dill (feathery leaves only) for parsley

Peel the potatoes and cut into ½-inch cubes. You should have about 2½ cups. Wipe the mushrooms clean and slice thinly, making about 1½ cups. Proceed according to the Master Recipe, substituting potatoes and mushrooms for broccoli and omitting the egg yolks. Season, and garnish with dill instead of parsley. Serve hot.

Variation: CREAM OF ONION SOUP

Makes about 1½ quarts; 6 to 8 first-course servings

Cream of Broccoli Soup

OMIT: Broccoli

INCREASE: Minced onions to 4 cups (about 1¼ pounds)

Proceed according to the Master Recipe, omitting the broccoli and increasing the onions to 4 cups. Season with lots of freshly grated nutmeg and garnish liberally with chopped fresh parsley. Serve hot.

Variation: CREAM OF PARSNIP SOUP

Makes about 1½ quarts; 6 to 8 first-course servings

Cream of Broccoli Soup

SUBSTITUTE: 1 pound parsnips for broccoli

OMIT: Egg yolks

ADD: 1 to 2 teaspoons dry Sherry (optional)

Peel and slice the parsnips, dropping the pieces into cold water as you go to prevent discoloration. You should have about 2½ cups. Proceed according to the Master Recipe, substituting the parsnips, drained, for broccoli and omitting the egg yolks. Stir a bit of Sherry into the soup just before serving, if you wish. Serve hot.

Variation: CREAM OF POTATO SOUP

Makes about 1½ quarts; 4 main-course or 6 to 8 first-course servings

❦ *A simple and soul-satisfying soup for a cold winter day.*

Cream of Broccoli Soup
SUBSTITUTE: 2 large baking potatoes (about 1¼ pounds) for broccoli
ADD: ⅓ cup minced celery
OMIT: Egg yolks

Peel the potatoes and cut into ½-inch cubes; you should have about 2½ cups. Proceed according to the Master Recipe, substituting the potatoes for broccoli, sautéing the celery along with the onions, and omitting the egg yolks. Season liberally with freshly grated nutmeg. Serve hot.

Variation: CREAM OF SALSIFY SOUP

Makes about 1½ quarts; 6 to 8 first-course servings

❦ *This was much favored in the nineteenth century, when salsify was a popular vegetable. The soup deserves a comeback; it is spectacular.*

Cream of Broccoli Soup
SUBSTITUTE: About 2 pounds salsify for broccoli
OMIT: Egg yolks

Wash the salsify thoroughly. Peel each root, cut into 1-inch pieces, and immediately drop into cold water to prevent discoloration. You should have 2½ to 3 cups. Proceed according to the Master Recipe, substituting the salsify, drained just before using, for broccoli and omitting the egg yolks. Serve hot.

Variation: CREAM OF SORREL SOUP

Makes about 1½ quarts; 6 to 8 first-course servings

Cream of Broccoli Soup
SUBSTITUTE: ½ pound *each* sorrel and Boston or Bibb lettuce (2 to 3 heads) for broccoli

Remove and discard all but the smallest, tenderest stems, and cut sorrel leaves into thin strips; cut the lettuce into thin strips and combine with the sorrel. You should have about 4 packed cups of greens. Proceed according to the Master Recipe, substituting the sorrel and lettuce for broccoli. Serve hot or chilled.

Variation: CREAM OF SPINACH SOUP

Makes about 1½ quarts; 4 main-course or 6 to 8 first-course servings

Cream of Broccoli Soup
SUBSTITUTE: 1 pound spinach for broccoli
ADD: ⅛ teaspoon dried rosemary, ground or moistened with a few drops of water and minced fine (optional)

Wash the spinach well, remove any especially large stems, and cut into thin strips; you should have about 4 packed cups. Proceed according to the Master Recipe, substituting the spinach for broccoli. If you wish, add rosemary along with the nutmeg and lemon juice. Serve hot or chilled.

Variation: CREAM OF SWISS CHARD SOUP

Makes about 1½ quarts; 4 main-course or 6 to 8 first-course servings

❦ *With its fresh, distinctive flavor, Swiss chard makes a particularly good cold soup that is even more refreshing when served with dollops of sour cream.*

Cream of Broccoli Soup
SUBSTITUTE: About 1 pound Swiss chard, both leaves and stems, for broccoli

Cut the chard leaves into strips and the stems into ½-inch lengths; you should have about 3½ cups. Proceed according to the Master Recipe, substituting the chard for broccoli.

Variation: CREAM OF TOMATO SOUP

Makes about 1½ quarts; 4 main-course or 6 to 8 first-course servings

❦ *Chopped fresh basil or fresh dill (the fine, feathery leaves only) may be substituted for parsley here. If you serve the soup iced—and it's excellent this way—consider flavoring it with dill and topping each portion with a mound of horseradish-spiked whipped cream.*

Cream of Broccoli Soup
SUBSTITUTE: 4 large very ripe fresh tomatoes (about 2 pounds) for broccoli
OMIT: Egg yolks
ADD: Sugar, if needed

Peel and seed the tomatoes (see page 607), then chop them coarsely, making about 3 cups. Proceed according to the Master Recipe, substituting the tomatoes for broccoli and omitting the egg yolks. If the soup seems acidic after the cream is added, correct the seasoning with pinches of sugar.

Variation: CREAM OF TURNIP OR RUTABAGA SOUP

Makes about 1½ quarts; 4 main-course or 6 to 8 first-course servings

Cream of Broccoli Soup
SUBSTITUTE: 1 pound turnips or rutabagas for broccoli
OMIT: Egg yolks
ADD: Sugar and dry Sherry (optional)

Peel the turnips or rutabagas and cut into ½-inch cubes; you should have about 3 cups. Proceed according to the Master Recipe, substituting the turnips or rutabagas for broccoli and omitting the egg yolks. Season the soup with pinches of sugar and drops of dry Sherry, if you wish.

Variation: VICHYSSOISE

Makes about 1½ quarts; 6 to 8 first-course servings

❦ *Vichyssoise is a classic cold soup, typically served before beef or lamb. It may also be served hot.*

Cream of Broccoli Soup
SUBSTITUTE: 2 medium-large baking potatoes (about 1 pound) for broccoli
3 to 4 medium-sized leeks for onions
OMIT: Egg yolks
SUBSTITUTE: 2 to 3 tablespoons snipped fresh chives for parsley (optional)

Peel the potatoes and cut into ½-inch cubes; you should have about 2 cups. Cut away and discard the green tops and the roots of the leeks. Cut a lengthwise cross in the leaf ends of the leeks going halfway to the root ends and, spreading the layers, rinse the leeks under a strong stream of water to remove all traces of sand. Chop the leeks coarsely; you should have about 2 cups.

Proceed according to the Master Recipe, substituting the potatoes for broccoli and the leeks for onions and omitting the egg yolks. Garnish the soup with chives instead of parsley, if you wish.

Variation: CREAM OF WATERCRESS SOUP

Makes about 1½ quarts; 6 to 8 first-course servings

❦ *This classic and very elegant soup is as good cold as it is hot.*

Cream of Broccoli Soup
SUBSTITUTE: About 1¼ pounds watercress for broccoli

Remove any especially large stems and chop the watercress coarsely, to make about 4 tightly packed cups. Proceed according to the Master Recipe, substituting the watercress for broccoli.

Variation: CREAM OF WINTER SQUASH OR PUMPKIN SOUP

Makes about 1½ quarts; 6 to 8 first-course servings

❦ *There are several ways of seasoning and garnishing a cream soup made with winter squash or pumpkin. The simplest is to follow the procedure outlined in the Master Recipe, adding freshly grated nutmeg, drops of lemon juice, salt and pepper, if needed, plus a few pinches of white or brown sugar if sweetness seems lacking; parsley or a mixture of parsley and snipped chives could be used as the garnish. A racier alternative is to season the soup with 1 to 2 teaspoons of ground ginger and drops of dry Sherry. Use lemon juice and pinches of sugar to round out the flavor and garnish the soup with chopped pecans or walnuts. Finally, a delicious soup may be made by sweetening the soup slightly with half teaspoons of maple syrup and adding ¼ teaspoon* each *cinnamon, ground cloves, and freshly grated nutmeg. Correct the seasoning with salt, pepper, and drops of fresh lemon juice and garnish with either chopped fresh parsley or chopped walnuts or pecans.*

Cream of Broccoli Soup
SUBSTITUTE: About 1¼ pounds winter squash (butternut, banana, turban, or Hubbard) or pumpkin for broccoli
OMIT: Egg yolks

Peel the squash or pumpkin and cut into ½-inch cubes; you should have about 3 cups. Proceed according to the Master Recipe, substituting the squash or pumpkin for broccoli and omitting the egg yolks. Serve piping hot.

Variation: CREAM OF ZUCCHINI SOUP

Makes about 1½ quarts; 4 main-course or 6 to 8 first-course servings

❦ *Home gardeners finding themselves with a surplus of zucchini on their hands will appreciate this soup, which is delicious both hot and chilled.*

Cream of Broccoli Soup
SUBSTITUTE: About 1½ pounds zucchini for broccoli

Trim the ends of the zucchini, then split lengthwise and scoop out and discard the seeds. Shred on the large holes of a grater or in a food processor fitted with a grating disc. A handful at a time, firmly squeeze the zucchini to extract as much moisture as possible. You should have 2½ to 3 cups shredded, squeezed zucchini.

Proceed according to the Master Recipe, substituting the zucchini for broccoli. Season the soup lightly to avoid overpowering the delicate taste of the zucchini.

MASTER TECHNIQUE

For Home-style Soups

Makes about 2 quarts; 4 to 6 servings

❦ *Hot, savory soup made with a rich broth and lots of flavorful ingredients—meat, vegetables, pasta, and the like—is a wonderful solace on a cold winter day and yet so simple to make that one hardly needs a recipe at all.*

The basic procedure for making any home-style soup is outlined below; nine different soups made according to this Master Technique follow.

The ingredients specified in the soup variation you have chosen: fat, vegetable flavoring, seasoning, stock, soup ingredients, final seasoning, garnish

In a 4-quart saucepan made of or lined with a noncorroding material, melt the *fat* over low heat. Stir in the *vegetable flavoring* and cook very slowly over low heat, stirring occasionally, until the vegetables are soft but not brown, about 10 minutes. Stir the *seasoning* into the vegetables, including any herb bundle that might be called for, then slowly pour in the *stock*, stirring. Raise the heat, bring the soup to a simmer, and cook 10 minutes, partially covered. Add the *soup ingredients* sequentially as indicated in the variation you are using, maintaining the soup at a gentle simmer. Partially cover the saucepan and simmer the soup just until all the ingredients are tender. Add the *final seasoning,* taste and correct. Remove bay leaf or herb bundle, if any. Ladle soup into warmed tureen or soup plates and sprinkle on the *garnish.*

STORAGE: Soup may be turned into a lidded storage container and refrigerated for several days or frozen for several months. Especially if the soup contains rice or pasta, it is preferable to undercook it slightly before storing.

Variation: BEEF-MUSHROOM-NOODLE SOUP

Makes about 2 quarts; 4 to 6 servings

❦ *This hearty soup is a lunchtime favorite. To make it, use the ingredients listed below in the preceding Master Technique.*

FAT: 4 tablespoons butter

VEGETABLE FLAVORING: ½ cup chopped onion
½ cup chopped celery

SEASONING: ½ teaspoon mashed, pressed, or very finely minced garlic
¼ teaspoon whole or ground thyme
¼ teaspoon dried rosemary, ground or moistened with a few drops of water and minced fine
1 small bay leaf
⅛ teaspoon pepper, preferably freshly ground

STOCK: 1½ quarts Beef Stock, page 24, or canned broth

SOUP INGREDIENTS: *Add and simmer until tender, about 1 hour:*
1½ (about 12 ounces) cups raw beef stew meat, cut into ⅜-inch cubes
Add and simmer about 10 minutes longer:
2½ cups (about 4 ounces) uncooked egg noodles
2 cups (about 6 ounces) cleaned and sliced mushrooms

FINAL SEASONING: Salt and pepper, preferably freshly ground

GARNISH: 2 to 3 tablespoons finely chopped fresh parsley

Variation: BOUILLABAISSE

Makes about 2 quarts; 4 to 6 servings

❦ *This classic soup from the French Mediterranean makes a fine lunch or supper dish when accompanied by toasted French bread; a fruit tart might follow for dessert. To make this soup, use the ingredients listed below in the Master Technique on page 91.*

FAT: ⅓ cup olive oil

VEGETABLE FLAVORING: 1 cup chopped onions
½ cup chopped white part of leek, or additional onion
¼ cup chopped fennel or celery

SEASONING: 1 teaspoon mashed, pressed, or very finely minced garlic
1½ teaspoons chopped fresh basil or ½ teaspoon dried
⅛ teaspoon pepper, preferably freshly ground
The following, tied together with twine: 6 parsley stems, without leaves; 3-inch strip orange zest; 1 small bay leaf

STOCK: *Either* 1½ quarts Fish Stock, page 27, *or* 1 quart clam juice, ⅔ cup dry white wine, and 2 cups water

SOUP INGREDIENTS: *Add and simmer 5 minutes:*
1½ cups peeled, seeded, diced tomatoes, fresh or canned (see page 607)

	Add and simmer 1 minute longer:
	1½ pounds boneless, skinless, lean, white-fleshed, firm-textured raw fish, cut into 1-inch chunks
	Add and simmer 2 minutes longer, or until they open:
	16 well-scrubbed steamer clams
	Add and simmer 30 seconds longer, or until they curl:
	12 medium-sized raw shrimp, unshelled
FINAL SEASONING:	Salt, freshly ground pepper, cayenne pepper (optional)
GARNISH:	½ cup coarsely chopped fresh parsley

Variation: CABBAGE-POTATO SOUP

Makes about 2 quarts; 4 to 6 servings

❦ *This satisfying soup is based on the classic Middle European combination of cabbage, potato, and caraway. To make the soup, use the ingredients listed below in the Master Technique on page 91.*

FAT:	5 tablespoons butter
VEGETABLE FLAVORING:	1½ cups chopped onions
SEASONING:	½ teaspoon mashed, pressed, or very finely minced garlic
	¼ teaspoon caraway seed, ground or moistened with a few drops of water and minced fine
STOCK:	1½ quarts Chicken Stock, page 26, or canned broth
SOUP INGREDIENTS:	*Add and simmer about 10 minutes:*
	2 to 3 cups very thinly sliced cabbage
	Add and simmer about 10 minutes longer, or until tender:
	2 small to medium baking potatoes (about 12 ounces), peeled and cut in ¼-inch dice
FINAL SEASONING:	Additional ground or minced caraway, salt, and freshly ground pepper
GARNISH:	None

Variation: CHICKEN-NOODLE SOUP WITH CORN

Makes about 2 quarts; 4 to 6 servings

❦ *Variations on the classic American chicken-noodle soup abound. The corn, green pepper, and basil used here give this version a provocative Latin American accent. To make this soup, use the ingredients listed below in the Master Technique on page 91.*

FAT:	5 tablespoons butter
VEGETABLE FLAVORING:	⅔ cup chopped onions
	⅓ cup chopped green bell pepper
SEASONING:	2 teaspoons paprika
	1 tablespoon chopped fresh basil or 1 teaspoon dried
	¼ teaspoon whole or ground thyme
STOCK:	1½ quarts Chicken Stock, page 26, or canned broth
SOUP INGREDIENTS:	*Add and simmer 10 minutes:*
	1 cup (about 8 ounces) diced skinless, boneless raw chicken
	Add and simmer 7 minutes longer, or until noodles are done:
	2½ cups (about 4 ounces) uncooked egg noodles
	1 cup corn kernels, preferably freshly cut (see page 522)
FINAL SEASONING:	Salt and freshly ground pepper
GARNISH:	None

Variation: CHICKEN GUMBO

Makes about 2 quarts; 4 to 6 servings

❦*Gumbo is a classic dish of the Cajun South. The one ingredient that any gumbo must contain is okra—gumbo is the Creole word for okra—but otherwise there is considerable variation on the theme, some gumbos being made with shrimp or oysters and some with a combination of poultry and shellfish. Because it contains many solid ingredients and because the okra acts as a thickening agent, gumbo is a substantial dish, as much a stew as it is a soup. Traditionally it is ladled over rice in individual soup plates, and you may wish to serve it this way if it is to be a main course.*

To make this soup, use the ingredients listed below in the Master Technique on page 91.

FAT:	5 tablespoons butter or bacon drippings
VEGETABLE FLAVORING:	⅔ cup chopped onions
	½ cup chopped green bell pepper
SEASONING:	1½ teaspoons mashed, pressed, or very finely minced garlic
	1 teaspoon paprika
	1 teaspoon whole dried thyme
	⅛ teaspoon cayenne pepper
	½ teaspoon salt
	4 parsley sprigs and 1 bay leaf, tied together with twine
STOCK:	1 quart Chicken Stock, page 26, or canned broth
SOUP INGREDIENTS:	*Add and simmer 20 minutes:*
	1½ cups peeled, seeded, diced tomatoes, fresh or canned (see page 607)
	1½ cups sliced fresh okra or 10 ounces frozen
	½ cup freshly cut, canned, or frozen corn
	Add and simmer 2 minutes longer:
	1½ cups (about 12 ounces) diced skinless, boneless raw chicken
FINAL SEASONING:	1½ teaspoons fresh lemon juice
	1 teaspoon Worcestershire sauce
	1 teaspoon hot pepper sauce
	Salt
GARNISH:	None

Variation: CURRIED CHICKEN SOUP WITH RICE

Makes about 2 quarts; 4 to 6 servings

❦ *This mild, aromatic soup goes well with sandwiches at lunch. To make it, use the ingredients listed below in the Master Technique on page 91.*

FAT:	6 tablespoons butter
VEGETABLE FLAVORING:	½ cup finely chopped onion ½ cup finely chopped celery ½ cup finely chopped green bell pepper ½ cup peeled and shredded green apple
SEASONING:	1 tablespoon mild curry powder or 2 teaspoons hot (Madras) curry powder ⅛ teaspoon ground cloves or allspice
STOCK:	1½ quarts Chicken Stock, page 26, or canned broth
SOUP INGREDIENTS:	*Add and simmer about 10 minutes:* ½ cup peeled, seeded, diced tomatoes, fresh or canned (see page 607) ⅓ cup raw white rice *Add and simmer about 10 minutes longer, or until rice is tender:* 1 cup (about 8 ounces) diced skinless, boneless raw chicken
FINAL SEASONING:	1 to 1½ tablespoons dry Sherry (optional) Salt and pepper, preferably freshly ground
GARNISH:	A bit of chopped fresh parsley

Variation: MANHATTAN CLAM CHOWDER

Makes about 2 quarts; 4 to 6 servings

❦ *Manhattan-style clam chowder is made with a tomato-flavored broth. To make it, use the ingredients listed below in the Master Technique on page 91.*

FAT: 5 tablespoons butter

VEGETABLE FLAVORING: 1½ cups chopped onions
⅔ cup chopped celery

SEASONING: ½ teaspoon whole or ground thyme
6 parsley sprigs and 1 small bay leaf tied together with twine

STOCK: Juice from 16 quahogs (see below), 2 cups bottled clam juice, and enough water to make 1½ quarts liquid

SOUP INGREDIENTS: *Add and simmer about 15 minutes:*
1½ cups peeled, seeded, diced tomatoes, fresh or canned (see page 607)
2 cups (about 1 pound) peeled diced boiling potatoes
Add and simmer exactly 1 minute longer:
16 quahogs (largest size hard-shell clam), shelled according to the instructions on pages 280–81 and coarsely chopped

FINAL SEASONING: Salt and freshly ground pepper
Fresh lemon juice to taste

GARNISH: ⅓ cup coarsely chopped fresh parsley

Variation: SPLIT PEA SOUP

Makes about 2 quarts; 4 to 6 servings

❦*Accompanied by buttered black bread, this makes a delicious winter night supper. To make this soup, use the ingredients listed below in the Master Technique on page 91.*

FAT: 5 tablespoons bacon drippings or butter

VEGETABLE FLAVORING: 1½ cups chopped onions
⅔ cup chopped carrot

SEASONING: ¾ teaspoon mashed, pressed, or very finely minced garlic
1 bay leaf

STOCK: 1½ quarts Chicken Stock, page 26, or canned broth, or broth left from poaching a ham

SOUP INGREDIENTS: *Add and simmer about 1 hour, or until the peas are falling apart:*
1 cup (about 8 ounces) dried green split peas
1 cup (about 8 ounces) diced smoked ham (optional)

FINAL SEASONING: Salt and freshly ground pepper
Drops of fresh lemon juice and/or dry Sherry

GARNISH: Finely chopped fresh parsley
Pats of butter (optional)

Variation: TOMATO-RICE SOUP WITH DILL

Makes about 2 quarts; 4 to 6 servings

To make this soup, use the ingredients listed below in the Master Technique on page 91.

FAT: 6 tablespoons butter

VEGETABLE FLAVORING: 2 cups chopped onions

SEASONING: ¾ teaspoon salt
¼ teaspoon pepper, preferably freshly ground
8 large dill sprigs, tied together with twine

STOCK: 5 cups Chicken Stock, page 26, or canned broth

SOUP INGREDIENTS: *Add and simmer about 20 minutes:*
3 cups peeled, seeded, and finely chopped tomatoes, fresh or canned (see page 607)
Add and simmer 20 minutes longer, or until tender:
½ cup raw white rice

FINAL SEASONING: Salt and freshly ground pepper
Sugar

GARNISH: 2 tablespoons finely chopped fresh dill (feathery leaves only)

Variation: VEGETABLE SOUP

Makes about 2 quarts; 4 to 6 servings

❦ *Garlic, basil, and orange zest give this vegetable soup a Mediterranean flavor. The vegetable combination suggested here may certainly be varied according to one's taste and the season. To make this soup, use the ingredients listed below in the Master Technique on page 91.*

FAT:	4 tablespoons butter
VEGETABLE FLAVORING:	1 cup thinly sliced onions
	½ cup celery, cut in sticks ¼ inch wide and 1 inch long
SEASONING:	1 teaspoon mashed, pressed, or very finely minced garlic
	1 tablespoon finely chopped fresh basil or 1 teaspoon dried
	¼ teaspoon dried rosemary, ground or moistened with a few drops of water and minced fine
	½ teaspoon salt
	The following, tied together with twine: 5 parsley sprigs; 3-inch strip orange zest; 1 medium bay leaf
STOCK:	2 cups water and *either* 3 cups Chicken Stock, page 26, or canned broth, *or* 3 cups Beef Stock, page 24, or canned broth
SOUP INGREDIENTS:	*Add and simmer 5 minutes:*
	1 cup peeled, seeded, diced tomatoes, fresh or canned (see page 607)
	⅔ cup diced peeled turnip or rutabaga
	⅔ cup sliced carrot
	Add and simmer 5 minutes longer:
	1 cup fresh green beans, sliced in 1-inch pieces
	Add and simmer 5 minutes longer:
	1 cup small whole cauliflower or broccoli florets, or fresh shelled peas
FINAL SEASONING:	Salt and freshly ground pepper
GARNISH:	3 tablespoons finely chopped fresh parsley or other herb(s)

MASTER RECIPE

Corn Chowder

Makes about 2 quarts; 4 to 5 main-course servings

❦ *A savory, rib-sticking chowder, accompanied by homemade bread and butter and a dish of raw cut up vegetables and followed by a warm apple pie or tart, makes a wonderful winter night supper.*

- 3 ounces salt pork, rinsed and diced, or 6 slices bacon, chopped, or 4 tablespoons butter
- 1 cup finely chopped onions
- 1/4 cup finely chopped celery
- 3 tablespoons all-purpose flour
- 2 cups milk
- 2 cups liquid: corn canning liquid, if any, and/or water
- 1 pound boiling potatoes, peeled and cut in 1/2-inch cubes (about 2 cups)
- *The following, tied in a cheesecloth bag:*
  - 4 parsley sprigs; 1 bay leaf; 1/4 teaspoon whole thyme; 1 small whole clove (optional)
- 1/4 teaspoon salt
- 1/4 teaspoon pepper, preferably white, freshly ground
- 1 1/2 cups corn kernels, freshly cut (page 522), frozen, or canned
- 1/2 to 1 cup heavy cream
- 1/4 cup finely chopped fresh parsley
- 2 to 3 tablespoons butter (optional)

Select a heavy-bottomed 3 1/2- to 4-quart saucepan or pot. If you are using salt pork or bacon, cook it slowly in the saucepan or pot until it has rendered most of its fat and become browned. If you are using butter, simply melt it over moderate heat.

Add onion and celery and cook gently for 8 minutes, or until the vegetables are soft but not brown. Sprinkle on the flour, stir until thoroughly blended, and cook a minute or two longer. Remove from heat and blend in milk and corn liquid or water. Return to heat and bring to simmer, stirring. Add potatoes, herb bag, salt, and pepper, cover the saucepan partially, and cook soup at the barest simmer, stirring occasionally, for about 30 minutes, or until potatoes are very tender.

Add corn and heavy cream and, regulating the heat so that soup remains just below the simmer, cook for about 5 minutes, stirring. Taste and adjust seasoning, adding salt, pepper, and, if the corn was not young, a few pinches of sugar. Ladle soup into a hot tureen or individual soup plates and garnish liberally with fresh parsley and, if you wish, pats of butter.

STORAGE: The soup may be turned into a lidded storage container and refrigerated for 4 or 5 days; it will actually improve in flavor with standing. To serve, reheat the soup at just below the simmer, so that it doesn't lose its silky smooth consistency. The chowder may also be frozen for several months, though the potatoes will get a bit soggy upon thawing.

Variation: CLAM CHOWDER

Makes about 2 quarts; 4 to 5 main-course or 6 to 8 first-course servings

❦ *My preference here is to use butter rather than either salt pork or bacon, though this will undoubtedly strike some as heretical.*

Corn Chowder

USE: Clam liquor and water as the liquid

SUBSTITUTE: 16 quahogs (largest size hard-shell clams) for corn

Scrub the clams with a stiff brush under warm running water, then arrange in a single layer on a rimmed baking sheet. Set clams in a preheated 450°F oven for about 1 minute, or until they open just a crack; don't let the flesh begin to cook. When they are cool enough to handle, open clams by cutting through the muscle that holds the shell together, being sure to reserve clam liquor (work over a bowl). Scrape meat out of the clams and chop coarsely. When you are through, you should have about 1½ cups each clam liquor and chopped clam meat.

Proceed according to Master Recipe, using clam liquor and water as the liquid and substituting chopped clams for corn. Be sure not to let chowder simmer after adding the clams, or they will become rubbery.

Variation: CHICKEN CHOWDER

Makes about 2 quarts; 4 to 5 main-course servings

Corn Chowder

USE: 1 cup Chicken Stock, page 26, or canned broth and 1 cup water as the liquid

SUBSTITUTE: 1½ cups (about 12 ounces) diced skinless, boneless raw chicken, or about 2 cups diced cooked chicken, for corn

Proceed according to Master Recipe, using chicken stock or broth and water as the liquid and substituting chicken for corn.

Variation: FISH CHOWDER

Makes about 2 quarts; 4 to 5 main-course or 6 to 8 first-course servings

Corn Chowder

USE: 1 cup Fish Stock, page 27, or clam juice, and 1 cup water as the liquid

SUBSTITUTE: About 1 pound boneless, skinless, lean, white-fleshed, firm-textured raw fish, cut into ¾-inch cubes, or 2 cups flaked cooked fish, for corn

Proceed according to Master Recipe, using fish stock or clam juice and water as the liquid and substituting fish for corn. Poach the fish at below the simmer for no longer than 5 minutes; do not stir the chowder hard after adding fish, or the fish will fall apart.

NAVY BEAN OR BLACK BEAN SOUP

Makes about 2 quarts; 4 main-course or 8 first-course servings

❦*Accompany bean soup with a hearty black bread and butter.*

1 cup (about 8 ounces) dried navy beans or dried black beans
6 cups water
4 ounces salt pork, rinsed
1 cup chopped onions
2 to 4 cloves garlic, crushed with the side of a knife and peeled
½ teaspoon freshly ground pepper
The following, tied in a cheesecloth bag: 4 parsley sprigs; 1 large bay leaf; 2 whole cloves or allspice berries
1 cup chopped carrots
1 cup coarsely chopped onions
1 cup chopped celery
1⅓ cups (about 10 ounces) smoked pork or ham cut in ¼-inch dice
½ teaspoon salt, or to taste
⅓ cup chopped parsley (optional)
½ to 1 cup shredded Cheddar or Monterey Jack cheese (optional)

Turn beans into a strainer or colander, rinse thoroughly under running water, and pick over carefully to remove pebbles and any other foreign matter. Turn beans into a 3½- to 4-quart saucepan, cover with water, bring to a boil, and boil rapidly for 2 minutes. Remove beans from heat, cover tightly, and let stand for 1 hour. (As an alternative, you can simply cover the beans with cold water and let them stand overnight.)

Drain beans in strainer or colander, discarding the soaking liquid. Return beans to saucepan and add 6 cups fresh water, the salt pork, 1 cup chopped onions, the crushed garlic, pepper, and the herb bag. Simmer, partially covered, for about 1½ hours, or until beans are tender, adding water if soup becomes too thick. Discard herb bag; strain out and reserve ½ cup beans. Remove salt pork, cut it into small cubes, and set aside. Using a food mill, blender, or food processor, purée the rest of the soup in small batches, turning puréed batches into a large mixing bowl. Return puréed soup to saucepan and stir in reserved beans, diced salt pork, chopped carrots, coarsely chopped onions, and celery, and the diced smoked pork or ham. Simmer the soup about 30 minutes longer, or until vegetables are tender but not mushy. Season to taste with salt. Garnish each portion with a bit of chopped fresh parsley and/or a handful of shredded Cheddar or Monterey Jack cheese.

STORAGE: The soup may be refrigerated for 4 days in a lidded storage container or frozen for several months.

MINESTRONE

Makes about 2 quarts; 4 main-course or 6 to 8 first-course servings

❦ *Serve this with freshly grated Parmesan cheese and rounds of hard-toasted Italian bread.*

½ cup (about 4 ounces) Great Northern or other dried white beans
3 tablespoons olive oil
4 ounces salt pork, rinsed and diced
1 cup coarsely chopped onions
1½ teaspoons mashed, pressed, or very finely minced garlic
6 cups water
1 tablespoon finely chopped fresh basil or 1 teaspoon dried
4 parsley sprigs and 1 small bay leaf, tied together with twine
½ teaspoon pepper, preferably freshly ground
1½ cups shredded cabbage
1 cup sliced carrots
1 cup diced celery
½ cup peeled, seeded, diced tomatoes, fresh or canned (see page 607)
1 large handful of spinach or escarole leaves, roughly torn
½ cup diced zucchini or sliced green beans
½ cup fresh or frozen peas (optional)
½ to 1 cup cooked small pasta (optional)
About ½ teaspoon salt
⅓ cup coarsely chopped fresh parsley or parsley mixed with chopped fresh basil

Turn beans into a strainer or colander, rinse thoroughly under running water, and pick over carefully to remove pebbles and any other foreign matter. Place beans in small saucepan, cover with water, bring to boil, and boil rapidly for 2 minutes. Remove beans from heat, cover tightly, and let stand 1 hour. (As an alternative, you can simply cover the beans with cold water and let them soak overnight.) Drain beans in strainer or colander, discarding the soaking water. Set beans aside.

Combine olive oil and diced salt pork in a 3½- to 4-quart saucepan and sauté over moderate heat until pork is crisp and brown. Add chopped onions and continue to cook over moderate heat until onions color lightly around the edges. Add garlic and cook a minute longer. Add 6 cups water, the beans, basil, herb bundle, and pepper. Partially cover the saucepan and simmer about 1 hour, or until beans are almost tender.

Add cabbage, carrot, and celery and simmer the soup, partially covered, for about 15 minutes. Add remaining vegetables and simmer 10 minutes longer. If you are using it, stir in the pasta just before serving, letting it heat through. Discard the parsley/bay leaf bundle and season soup to taste with salt. Garnish each portion of soup liberally with chopped fresh parsley or a combination of parsley and basil.

STORAGE: The soup may be stored in a tightly lidded container in the refrigerator for several days; if you are using pasta, add it just before serving. Soup may also be frozen for several months, though the vegetables will become a bit mushy upon thawing.

SALADS, TOSSED and OTHER

An ancient dish that derives its name from *salum,* the Latin word for salt, salad has been enjoyed in America since colonial times. Although Americans of the seventeenth and eighteenth centuries had to forego salad during the winter months, records show that the greens grown in their gardens and sold in their markets during the summer were actually more diverse than those that are generally available to us today. Watercress, for example, has not always been an exotic plant that summons forth rarefied associations with crustless tea sandwiches. According to John and Karen Hess in their book *The Taste of America,* a type of watercress was grown by Thomas Jefferson in his Washington garden at the dawn of the nineteenth century—along with corn salad, sorrel, and endive, leafy vegetables that are difficult to find in American supermarkets today. Thus the current vogue for sophisticated salads should not be considered a new fad; rather, it is a renaissance.

THE ART OF THE GREEN SALAD

A green salad may be quite simple—a single kind of lettuce tossed with a vinaigrette dressing—or it may be complex, containing several different greens and one or more extras such as tomatoes, bacon, or cheese. The nature of the salad is largely determined by the role it is intended to play within a meal.

A salad that accompanies the main course should have enough character to be interesting yet not be so substantial as to upstage the other dishes. Separate salad plates or bowls are nearly always called for so that the dressing does not mix with the other foods on the plate. It should be kept in mind that some main courses are not complemented by a green salad at all. As a general rule, simple, hearty, informal main courses invite a green salad, while complex, delicate dishes discourage one. Steaks, chops, and fried, roast, or broiled chicken, for example, all go well with salad—often no other accompaniment is needed. But the slightly acidic taste of salad dressing and the moist, crunchy texture of salad greens do little to enhance most fish and egg dishes, cooked vegetables, creamed foods, and the like.

TIP: Remember that wine and salad are basically antipathetic, as the taste of wine is distorted by the flavors of salad greens and vinegar. If you plan to serve a fine wine with your meal, serve the salad as a separate course, unaccompanied by wine.

A first- or main-course salad should be especially enticing and should contain, in addition to greens and a few vegetables, at least one or two special ingredients—marinated mushrooms, strips of ham or cheese, olives, and so on. In salads of this type, it is preferable to arrange the greens in a "bed" on a large platter and place the other ingredients artfully on top, in the manner of an antipasto or chef's salad, rather than tossing them together. The salad is then divided at the table onto dinner plates and passed with cruets of dressing; it is a nice touch to offer two dressings, one a plain vinaigrette and the other a mayonnaise-based dressing. A salad that is served after the main course to cleanse and refresh the palate must always be plain: greens plus a vinaigrette dressing. Such a salad is often accompanied by bread or crackers; butter and soft cheese may be offered as well.

NOTES ON VARIOUS SALAD GREENS: There are many types of salad greens, each with its own taste and texture. Different combinations of greens produce various effects in a salad. The most familiar combination is that of mild greens (Boston or Bibb lettuce, for example) and bitter, pungent types such as dandelion or chicory, with the latter always used sparingly. One can also pair relatively dry greens like leaf lettuce with juicy ones (endive or romaine), or soft, delicate lettuces with harder, crunchier varieties such as iceberg or escarole. The possibilities are limited only by the availability of greens. And nowadays, with the ever-growing popularity of salads, supermarkets are stocking an increasingly large variety of suitable vegetables. In the summer, fragile, hard-to-ship leaf lettuces are sold at roadside stands.

Here is a brief discussion of various salad greens.

TIP: Allow six to eight cups of torn greens for a salad for four persons. This roughly translates into one large or two small heads or bunches of greens.

Sometimes called rocket, *arugula* has long been popular in England and is becoming increasingly available in the United States. The arugula plant has dark green, spearlike leaves, at their best when fairly small and immature. In taste, arugula is smoky, with a horseradishlike bite. You can make a tossed salad entirely of arugula, but most often it is combined with milder greens.

Belgian endive, with its silken yet crunchy texture and slightly bitter savor, adds spark to a tossed salad. Mixed with other greens, one head of this expensive vegetable is enough for a salad for four persons. Endive leaves may be added whole to a salad or they may be cut or torn. Be sure to add cut or torn endive to the salad just before serving, as it discolors rapidly. See page 539 for more information on endive.

Roughly the size of a navel orange and slightly elongated, a head of *Bibb lettuce* resembles a miniature head of escarole. The small, stiffly curled leaves have a mild yet faintly bitter taste and a marvelously tender crunch. Though it is among the choicest of all salad greens, Bibb lettuce is relatively scarce in most markets.

Boston lettuce is a small, floppy head lettuce with soft, pale green leaves. It has a mild, pleasant taste but is a bit limp and crepey in texture unless very fresh, and it does not hold up well under salad dressing. Be sure to select a heavy, dense head, which will contain more usable inner leaves than a lightweight, flimsy one.

Chicory is a wild-looking plant, its long, whitish ribbed leaves fringed with feathery, spiky points of green. It is definitely on the bitter side, and can best be described as chewy—or perhaps springy—in texture. I was introduced to chicory by my Italian grandparents when I was a small child, and I remain very fond of it, especially in salads accompanying breaded and fried veal and chicken. However, it is not to everyone's taste. Use chicory in combination with other greens.

Dandelion greens—the very ones that bedevil one's lawn—are puckery and slightly bitter in taste. A few in a salad go a long way. The greens are less bitter when small and harvested in the spring from plants that have not yet flowered.

A head of *escarole* is dark green and thick-leafed. Only the pale inner heart of escarole is used for salads; the tough outer leaves are cooked as for spinach. Mildly bitter, escarole may be used by itself or with other greens in a tossed salad.

Iceberg lettuce is held in low repute by many who object to its bland taste and wet, mulchy texture. Nonetheless, this green continues to be the favorite American lettuce both because of the crunch it brings to salads and because of its excellent keeping qualities. If you are an iceberg fan, choose heads by weight rather than by size. A large head may well be nothing more than a ball of rubbery, withered leaves, while a small head that feels heavy in the hand will likely be juicy and full of crunch.

There are many varieties of *leaf lettuce*—some have flat leaves, some have crinkly leaves, some are red, some are green, and some are golden. Leaf lettuces are prized for their delicate, fresh flavor and exceptional tenderness. Look for the smallest plants you can find as the larger ones are apt to be tough and bitter. Pass over also any plants whose leaves sprout from a thick central core, like sprays of water from a fountain. Such lettuces have "bolted" due to unfavorable weather conditions, and they will have an off taste.

Radicchio is a small, ruby red lettuce with a cabbagelike texture and a very bitter taste. It is imported and expensive, but only a small amount is needed in a salad. Radicchio will remain fresh for two to three weeks if kept in a closed plastic container in the refrigerator.

Romaine, a long, elegant, spear-shaped lettuce, has made its reputation as the main ingredient of Caesar salad. It is also good in an ordinary tossed salad, where it adds a slightly bitter taste and crunchy texture. Small heads of romaine are the best buy, as the outer leaves of large heads are likely to be tough, dry, and bitter.

Sorrel was once widely used in this country's cuisine but is difficult to find in today's markets. It has a sharp, lemony taste that can be pleasant in a salad if added in modest quantities. More information on this green can be found on page 589.

Spinach adds color, texture, and flavor to a tossed salad. Use only small, tender leaves—well washed, please! More information on spinach appears on page 589.

Last, there is *watercress,* one of my favorite salad greens. I often use watercress alone in a salad, but many people like to blunt its spicy edge by mixing it with blander greens. Pull off and discard the larger stems, which are tough and stringy. Don't trim watercress for a salad more than an hour or so in advance, for it wilts very quickly. More information on watercress appears on page 613.

STORING GREENS: Place greens, unwashed and still attached to the head or bunch, either in a plastic bag or in a lidded plastic container. Sprinkle with a tablespoon or two of water and leave bag or container partially open. Store in the refrigerator. Iceberg lettuce will keep for up to two weeks, while most other lettuces may be held for five to seven days. Do plan, though, to consume fragile greens—leaf lettuces, for example—promptly. Watercress requires special storage procedures: see page 613.

Greens that are to be used within two or three days can be washed and dried before being put away in the refrigerator. Just be sure to handle them as gently as possible so as not to bruise them. Store the greens in a sealed plastic bag or container or—if you're feeling lazy—still in the salad spinner.

RESCUING WILTED GREENS: Greens that are somewhat soft and withered but not yet brown at the edges will often perk up if soaked for an hour or more in a large bowl or a sink filled with ice water.

WASHING AND DRYING SALAD GREENS: This step is often performed indifferently, yet it is the one that spells the success or failure of a salad. Salads containing gritty, bruised, or soggy wet greens are ruined from the start, no matter what is added to them in the way of other vegetables, seasonings, or dressings.

To wash greens, place them in a sink or large bowl filled with cool water. Gently swish the greens around in the water to dislodge grit and pesticides, then allow greens to stand in the water for several minutes so that soil can sink to the bottom. Skim the greens from the water with your hands, taking care not to crush them together and bruise them. If the water seems especially dirty, repeat using fresh water.

Greens must be dried *thoroughly.* Salad dressing will not properly coat wet greens, and in any case a damp, limp salad is quite unappetizing. There are several ways to dry greens, of which the salad spinner is the easiest and most effective. Hand-drying is another option. Place greens convex side down in a single layer on a triple thickness of paper toweling and gently blot the moisture from the leaves with additional paper toweling. To dry greens in the refrigerator, place washed greens in a salad bowl lined with a dish towel or several thicknesses of paper toweling and refrigerate for two to three hours. The towel will soak up the water, leaving the greens dry—or at least this is what is supposed to happen; I always find that further hand-drying is necessary.

CHOOSING A SALAD BOWL: I prefer glass bowls for salads because they allow you to view the salad from all angles. Bowls made of porcelain, pottery, stainless steel, or enameled metal are also fine, but never mix a salad in a bowl made of unlined copper, aluminum, tin, or cast iron, for these metals will react with the acid in the dressing and cause the salad to taste metallic. Wooden salad bowls tend to develop an unpleasant smell after a time because they blot up salad dressing, which eventually turns rancid.

Remember that the bowl you choose should be roomy enough to allow you to toss the salad without spilling any of it. As a rule of thumb, I would suggest that a salad bowl be 50 percent larger than the volume of salad greens.

TEARING OR CUTTING SALAD GREENS: Torn greens are considered to be more elegant and pleasing to the eye than cut greens in a tossed salad. When tearing greens, hold them gently between your fingertips and rip them as though you were ripping a sheet of paper. In my view, the pieces should be about two inches across, so that they will fold up as they go into the mouth and make a pleasant chew. Pieces larger than that are awkward to eat.

By the way, if you do want to cut greens—say, for a chiffonade salad—be sure to use a very sharp knife, or the greens will turn brown at the edges.

SERVING A SALAD: Allow about ½ cup of a vinaigrette-type dressing or ¾ cup or more of a mayonnaise-based dressing for 8 cups of salad, serving 4 persons. To toss the salad, pour the dressing evenly over the top of the salad, then give the salad as many light, brief, upward tosses with salad spoons as are necessary to coat the greens evenly. Never stir the salad or you will bruise the greens. Serve the salad as soon as it is dressed, or the salt and vinegar in the dressing will begin to draw the moisture out of the greens and leave you with a limp, soggy mess.

NONGREEN ADDITIONS TO GREEN SALADS: An almost endless variety of vegetables and other foods may be added to a green salad. Some of these foods—marinated artichoke hearts, ham, cheese—are so substantial and assertive in character that they can be used appropriately only in first- or main-course salads. For a salad that is to accompany a main course, the choice of ingredients generally depends on their compatibility with the main dish. Here is a list of some possible additions to a green salad, complete with my quite subjective feelings about each:

Two or three minced *anchovies* will impart a definite but not overpowering taste of anchovy to a salad; of course, if you are an anchovy fan, you may want to use more. Anchovies are particularly nice in a salad containing crunchy, slightly bitter greens such as romaine, chicory, or escarole. An anchovy-flavored salad goes well with fried chicken or veal cutlets.

Artichoke hearts, whether marinated in oil or packed in acidulated water, can be added to a first- or main-course salad, perhaps along with ham or cheese. However, I wouldn't use them in a salad that accompanies a meal; they are too assertive. Always blot canned artichokes thoroughly with paper towels before using them; tips for cutting back their acidic taste are on page 469.

Avocados add to salads a pleasant nutlike taste that is particularly good with steaks. Avoid cutting avocados until just before serving, as they discolor easily. I prefer to place slices of avocado on top of an already tossed salad rather than tossing them into the salad; this way, the slices remain whole and do not make the rest of the salad slimy.

Bacon is compatible with many salad ingredients—greens, tomatoes, hard-cooked egg, or cheese, just to name a few—but its pronounced flavor can overwhelm the rest of a meal. Use it in first- or main-course salads only. Bacon must be crisply fried and finely crumbled so that it will stick to the greens and not sink to the bottom of the bowl.

Shredded *cabbage,* either red or green, lends a pleasant crunch to a salad. Don't use too much, and add it just before the salad is served, as cabbage can take on a stale taste if it sits.

One of my pet dislikes is finding slices or chunks of *carrot* in a salad that are so large and hard that a fork can hardly spear them. If you want to add carrots, either grate them or shave them with a vegetable peeler.

Rather than slicing or chopping *celery,* I prefer to mince it very fine, so that it will cling to the other ingredients in the salad like an herb. Celery leaves may also be added, either whole or chopped. Celery, remember, is a potently aromatic vegetable and should generally be used sparingly. It is particularly nice in salads accompanying chicken or veal.

Cheese tends to take on a dominating role when added to a salad. Strips or shavings of Swiss or Cheddar cheese can be added when you want a very substantial first- or main-course salad. Feta, bleu, or Roquefort cheese are good crumbled over first- or main-course salads or tossed with a salad that is to accompany a broiled or grilled red meat. Salads made with crunchy, slightly bitter greens—preferably chicory, escarole, or romaine—and freshly grated Parmesan cheese are nice with broiled, grilled, and roasted poultry or veal. Toss the salad first with vinaigrette dressing, then sprinkle on the Parmesan cheese and toss again.

Cooked *chickpeas* and other legumes are best used in first- or main-course salads. Canned chickpeas will taste better if drained of their canning liquid, rinsed, and marinated for 2 to 24 hours in vinaigrette.

Croutons must be added to a salad at the very last moment before serving. Leave the croutons out of any salad that is being served with a pasta, rice, or potato dish. To make garlic-flavored croutons, see the recipe for Caesar salad on page 127.

Small farm-type *cucumbers,* such as kirbys, are preferable to the supermarket behemoths, which are often watery, full of hard seeds, and lacking in taste. If supermarket cucumbers are all that you can find, peel them, halve them lengthwise, scoop out the seeds, and slice the halves into crescents.

Hard-cooked egg is nice in first- or main-course salads, especially those containing ham and/or cheese. It is common practice to slice or quarter the eggs and to arrange them on top of the salad, but they may also be pressed through a sieve with the back of a spoon and tossed with the salad when it is dressed.

Strips or slices of boiled *ham* can turn a salad into a meal. When ham is used with hard-cooked egg and Swiss cheese, you have what is commonly called a chef's salad.

Used discreetly, *herbs* can give a salad distinction; used wantonly, they overwhelm it and become unpleasant. It is my view that a salad can tolerate only a single herbal flavoring; thus I am opposed to anything that comes in a bottle labeled "salad seasoning." Fresh herbs are always preferable to dried. Be sure to match up whatever herb you are using with the foods that are to be served with or after the salad. For example, a salad containing fresh dill might be delicious preceding a broiled salmon steak, but it would not go well with roast beef. Italian meals are complemented by salads containing basil or oregano. An herbal flavoring can also be introduced by means of an herb vinegar; see page 117.

Sliced fresh *mushrooms* are a treat in a salad, but be sure to add them at the last minute, as they quickly wilt and discolor after being cut. Marinated mushrooms may be added to first- and main-course salads.

Olives are salty, strong in taste, and sometimes juicy, and should be added sparingly to most salads. They are frequently found in Greek salads, where two or three whole olives are allotted for each portion; other ingredients include feta cheese, pickled hot peppers, greens, and an oregano-flavored vinaigrette.

Rings of mild, sweet *onions* or sliced scallions are welcome in salads that are to be served with steaks, chops, broiled or fried chicken, or some other plain, straightforward main course. If you put onion in your salad, leave the garlic out of the salad dressing.

Green bell *peppers* go well only with certain foods and should not be added to a salad unthinkingly. Because they have so pronounced a character, a small one cut into thin rings or strips is plenty for a salad serving four. Red bell peppers, on the other hand, which are mild and sweet, complement a wide variety of foods and can be added to a salad fairly liberally. Roasted and marinated red peppers might be served along with or placed on top of a salad, in the manner of an antipasto ingredient. Blot roasted and marinated peppers with paper toweling before using. Pickled hot peppers may be added to salad as a garnish.

Radishes add a pleasant bite to any salad. Slice them in very thin rounds.

Sprouts, bean, alfalfa, and other, have many devotees because, while they are juicy and crunchy, they do not leak or weep, diluting the salad dressing. However, they certainly do wilt—in a flash—so dress any salad that contains them at the last possible moment. Sprouts have a certain musty bitterness that can be overwhelming in a salad; use them with discretion.

Some people think that sliced *tomatoes* are a poor idea in salads because they are juicy and thus dilute the dressing. However, when tomatoes are in season I can't resist using them. Whole cherry tomatoes do not water down a salad, but I find them a bit awkward to eat.

NOTES ON SALAD DRESSINGS, OILS, AND VINEGARS:

It seems a great pity to me to go to the trouble of preparing a salad carefully and then to drown out its fresh, delicate taste with a bottled salad dressing. Bottled dressings are made with low-grade oils, harsh vinegars, artificial flavorings and colors, and a horrifying assortment of chemical gums, thickeners, stabilizers, and preservatives. Worst of all, many of them are nearly half sugar.

Two types of salad dressings are included in this book—oil and vinegar mixtures, and mayonnaise salad dressings. Most of the time you'll want a simple oil and vinegar dressing, which can be prepared in just a couple of minutes. When, however, you are serving as a main course a salad that includes all sorts of extras—ham, cheese, olives, and so on—you might want to offer a creamy mayonnaise dressing.

OILS: Most salad dressings consist primarily of oil, with just enough vinegar mixed in to give the dressing flavor and a pleasant bite. It goes without saying, then, that the oil used in a salad dressing should be of the best possible quality. It must also be very fresh. To determine freshness, open the bottle and sniff. Neutral vegetable oils should have no scent; olive, nut, and sesame oils should be mildly and pleasantly fragrant of the raw material from which they were pressed. All oils should be stored in the refrigerator. Kept on a shelf, they deteriorate within just two to three weeks of opening, developing the bitter, metallic taste characteristic of rancidity.

Oils divide into two groups, the more or less neutrally flavored vegetable oils derived from peanuts, corn, soybeans, cottonseeds, sunflower seeds, or safflower seeds, and the flavorful oils pressed from olives, sesame seeds, or nuts such as almonds, walnuts, or hazelnuts.

Neutral vegetable oils differ widely in quality. Those offered at bargain prices have often been pressed from inferior seeds or have been mishandled at some point in their production. As a result, they may taste rancid, smoky, bitter, or in some other way "off," and they may even taste overpoweringly of the raw material they were extracted from. Always choose an oil that has been extracted from a specific seed or vegetable—safflower oil seems to me the lightest and most delicate—rather than a nameless blended oil, whose flavor will invariably be inferior. Finally, resist advertising claims that make a correlation between "light" taste and the lightness of color. Taste has nothing whatsoever to do with color but is a function of purity and freshness.

All European olive oils are graded with respect to quality; domestic olive oils are not required by law to be graded, but many of them are. There are three grades of olive oil: "extra virgin," made from the finest olives and often pressed by hand in cold stone presses; "virgin," machine-pressed from second-grade olives; and "pure," extracted from the pulp and pits of olives initially pressed to make extra virgin and virgin oils. In addition, some very fine European extra virgin olive oils are, like wines, labeled with respect to the region in which they were produced—and a few are even vintage-dated!

While you can count on any extra virgin or virgin olive oil to be pure and pleasant—as well as expensive—there is no way of knowing how strongly the oil will taste of the fruit until you have sampled it. Olive oils with a greenish cast often have more flavor than golden colored (and often more expensive) ones, but some green oils are quite flat. An olive oil from Italy, Spain, Greece, or California is likely to be stronger than one from France, but some French olive oils are assertive. It is often helpful to ask a salesperson for advice before making a purchase. You may find that some olive oils are too potent for your taste.

Oils pressed from nuts and strongly flavored seeds are expensive and sometimes hard to find, but they are lovely indeed. Among the nut oils, my favorites are walnut and hazelnut, both of which have a rich, roasted-nut flavor that is particularly good in salads containing assertive vegetables such as peppers or blanched broccoli. Pressed from sesame seeds, sesame oil comes in two forms—so-called "light" sesame oil, with a deep gold color and a mild taste, and "dark" sesame oil, with the hue of very dark caramel and a pronounced flavor. Dark sesame oil is the one to choose if both kinds are available. Sesame oil is never used alone in a salad dressing—nor in a fried dish, for that matter—but is added to a neutral oil in small quantities, as vanilla extract is added to a dessert. If your grocery store does not stock nut or seed oils, try a specialty store, a health-food store, or, for sesame oil, a shop that specializes in Asian foodstuffs.

VINEGARS: There are three types of vinegars commonly available in this country: cider vinegar, made from apples; so-called "white vinegar," distilled from grains; and wine vinegar, derived from grapes. Cider and white vinegars have only limited uses in salads, as the former tends to taste slightly sweet and appley and the latter has no intrinsic flavor and can be very harsh. Wine vinegars are of several types. First there are the standard red and white wine vinegars sold at supermarkets. Among these I prefer those that have a maximum of winy flavor and a minimum of acidic bite. Unfortunately, there is no way to tell in advance what a vinegar is going to taste like—the acid content printed on the label, by the way, does not provide any clue as to the vinegar's harshness—so all you can do is shop around, trying different brands. Sherry vinegars, which must generally be sought out at specialty stores, constitute a second major type of wine vinegar. They have a more assertive taste than ordinary red or white wine vinegars but are rarely bitingly harsh. Finally, in a class by itself is balsamic vinegar, a special kind of wine vinegar produced only in the Modena province of Italy. Balsamic vinegar is aged over a period of years in a series of specially designed wooden casks. The end result is spectacular—a dark, rich, faintly sweet, and almost completely nonacidic-tasting liquid that should perhaps more properly be called a sauce than a vinegar. Indeed, in Italy balsamic vinegar is often used straight as a dressing for meat and poultry, just as we use Worcestershire sauce. Balsamic vinegar is available at specialty shops.

Flavored vinegars—generally made with herbs or berries using a wine vinegar base—are becoming increasingly popular. These have their place in salad-making and cooking, but they should be used sparingly as their flavor tends to be strong. It is possible, by the way, to make one's own flavored vinegar simply by steeping sprigs of tarragon, rosemary, or other herbs, or a handful of raspberries or blueberries, in a bottle of ordinary wine vinegar.

LOW-CALORIE DRESSING: For each two-cup serving, sprinkle 1½ teaspoons olive oil over salad and toss until well coated. Add drops of vinegar and salt and freshly ground pepper to taste and toss again. Note: Always add the oil first; if you add the vinegar and salt first, you will make the greens wet and the oil will not adhere to them.

MASTER RECIPE

Oil and Vinegar Salad Dressing (Vinaigrette Dressing)

Makes about ½ cup, or enough to dress 2 quarts of salad serving 4

A small clove garlic (optional)
⅜ teaspoon salt
⅛ teaspoon pepper, preferably freshly ground
⅛ teaspoon Dijon mustard
4 to 5 teaspoons vinegar
½ cup oil, preferably olive

If you are using garlic, either press the clove into a shallow, flat-bottomed 1-quart mixing bowl or peel the garlic and slice it thinly into the bowl; add the salt and, using a fork, mash to form a smooth paste.

Add to the garlic paste (or to the salt alone) the pepper, mustard, and 4 teaspoons vinegar and beat with fork to blend. Beat in oil a little at a time. The dressing should emulsify and thicken, but if it doesn't, or if it should separate before serving, simply continue to beat it until the vinegar and oil finally mix. Taste the dressing, adding a bit more vinegar or other seasonings as necessary. If you wish, strain to remove the small pieces of garlic.

The dressing may be covered with plastic wrap and left for a couple of hours at room temperature before being added to the salad. Remember that the salad should not be dressed until you are ready to bring it to the table, or it will become soggy.

Variation: ITALIAN SALAD DRESSING

Makes about ½ cup, or enough to dress 2 quarts of salad serving 4

Oil and Vinegar Salad Dressing

ADD: ¼ teaspoon dried oregano, crumbled
2 tablespoons very finely minced red bell pepper

Proceed according to Master Recipe, beating in oregano and red pepper after all the oil has been added.

Variation: MUSTARD-TARRAGON SALAD DRESSING

Makes about ¾ cup, or enough to dress 2 quarts of salad serving 4

❦ *This piquant, delicious dressing is different from other oil and vinegar salad dressings because it is made with egg and so is thick and creamy.*

Oil and Vinegar Salad Dressing

INCREASE: Mustard to 1 tablespoon
ADD: 1 large egg
¼ teaspoon dried tarragon
Anchovy paste (optional)

Add to the garlic paste (or to the salt alone) a full tablespoon of mustard and a whole egg in addition to the pepper and vinegar called for in Master Recipe. Beat with wire whip or fork until mixture is thoroughly combined and frothy. Just as though you were making a mayonnaise, add oil in a slow, steady stream while beating constantly with whip or fork; the dressing will become thick. Beat in the tarragon, taste, and adjust seasoning, adding a dab or two of anchovy paste if you wish. The dressing will have more character if allowed to stand, covered with plastic wrap, for about 20 minutes before serving.

Variation: SOUR CREAM SALAD DRESSING

Makes about ⅔ cup, or enough to dress 2 quarts of salad serving 4

Oil and Vinegar Salad Dressing
ADD: 2 to 3 tablespoons sour cream

Proceed according to Master Recipe, beating in sour cream after the last of the oil has gone in.

ROQUEFORT OR BLEU CHEESE SALAD DRESSING

Makes 1½ cups, or enough to dress 2 quarts of salad serving 4

4 ounces (about 1 cup) Roquefort or bleu cheese, crumbled
1 cup plain whole-milk yogurt or sour cream
1 tablespoon olive oil
½ teaspoon fresh lemon juice
⅛ teaspoon pepper, preferably freshly ground

Crumble cheese into a 2-quart mixing bowl, add yogurt or sour cream, and mash mixture lightly with a fork, leaving the cheese in fairly large lumps. Beat in remaining ingredients; taste and correct seasoning. The dressing will have more flavor if allowed to stand in the refrigerator, covered, for several hours before use.

MASTER RECIPE

Chicken Salad

Makes about 1 quart, serving 4 to 5 as a main course

Chicken salad and all of the variations that follow make a terrific one-course summer lunch or supper. Serve on lettuce and garnish with tomato wedges, quartered hard-cooked eggs, cooked beets, or perhaps blanched green beans tossed in vinaigrette. Pass French bread, rye bread, or dark pumpernickel, and offer a light white wine, nicely chilled.

3 cups skinless, boneless cooked chicken cut or torn into strips about 1/4-inch wide (more or less the meat of a 4-pound chicken)
1 tablespoon strained fresh lemon juice
1/2 teaspoon salt
1/4 teaspoon pepper, preferably freshly ground
1 cup diced celery
1/4 cup finely chopped onion
3 tablespoons drained small capers or chopped large capers
3/4 to 1 cup mayonnaise, preferably homemade, page 51
1/2 cup (about 2 ounces) slivered almonds, toasted, or coarsely chopped walnuts (optional)

Combine chicken, lemon juice, salt, and pepper in a 3-quart mixing bowl and toss to blend. Add celery, onions, and capers, then fold in 2/3 cup of mayonnaise. Cover and chill several hours or overnight to blend flavors. Just before serving, pour off any watery juices that may have accumulated and fold in additional mayonnaise—just enough to give the salad body and a moist, creamy look. Correct the seasoning, and garnish with nuts, if you wish.

Variation: BEEF OR LAMB SALAD

Makes about 1 quart, serving 4 to 5 as a main course

❦ *In addition to being delicious in its own right, a beef or lamb salad is a terrific way to use up leftovers. Accompany the salad with tomatoes, cold beets, and cold blanched green beans.*

Chicken Salad

SUBSTITUTE: 3 cups cubed or sliced cooked beef or lamb, trimmed of all fat, for chicken

ADD: 4 teaspoons grated fresh horseradish or 2 tablespoons well-drained prepared horseradish

Proceed according to the Master Recipe, substituting the beef or lamb for chicken and adding the horseradish along with the capers.

Variation: CRAB SALAD

Makes about 1 quart, serving 4 to 6 as a main course

❦ *You might want to garnish this with slices of ripe avocado or a few oil-cured black olives.*

Chicken Salad

SUBSTITUTE: 2½ to 3 cups diced crabmeat, fresh cooked or well-drained canned, for chicken

ADD: ½ teaspoon dry mustard

Pick over crabmeat carefully, removing any bits of shell or cartilage. Proceed according to the Master Recipe, substituting crab for chicken and adding the mustard along with the salt and pepper.

Variation: RUTH HOBERMAN'S FISH SALAD

Makes about 1 quart, serving 4 to 5 as a main course

❦*My friend Ruth introduced me to this wonderful summertime salad. Ruth makes hers with bluefish, but salmon or virtually any other fish, including a mild-flavored, light-fleshed variety, can be used.*

Chicken Salad

SUBSTITUTE: 3 cups cubed or coarsely flaked cooked boneless, skinless fish for chicken

Proceed according to the Master Recipe, substituting fish for chicken. You may wish to add a bit of extra lemon juice when giving the salad its final seasoning.

Variation: HAM SALAD

Makes about 1 quart, serving 4 to 5 as a main course

❦*This salad can be made with either very mild ham—the baked or boiled types bought at a deli, or even canned ham—or with brine-cured, lightly smoked ham that has been fully cooked.*

Chicken Salad

SUBSTITUTE: 3 cups cubed ham, trimmed of all rind and fat, for chicken

OMIT OR DECREASE: Salt

ADD: 3 tablespoons minced parsley
1 to 3 teaspoons Dijon mustard

Proceed according to the Master Recipe, substituting ham for chicken, omitting or decreasing the salt depending on the saltiness of the ham, and adding parsley along with the celery. Add mustard to taste along with the mayonnaise.

Variation: LOBSTER SALAD

Makes about 1 quart, serving 4 to 6 as a main course

Chicken Salad

SUBSTITUTE: 2½ to 3 cups cubed cooked lobster meat (more or less the meat of two 2-pound lobsters) for chicken

ADD: ½ teaspoon dry mustard

Proceed according to Master Recipe, substituting lobster for chicken and stirring in mustard along with the salt and pepper.

Variation: PORK SALAD

Makes about 1 quart, serving 4 to 5 as a main course

❦ *Most people think of pork as a meat that must be eaten hot, but cold pork, such as leftovers from a roast, is delicious in a salad.*

Chicken Salad

SUBSTITUTE: 3 cups cubed cooked pork, trimmed of all fat, for chicken

ADD: 2 tablespoons minced well-drained sour pickles
2 teaspoons grated fresh horseradish or 1 tablespoon well-drained prepared horseradish
Wine vinegar

Proceed according to Master Recipe, substituting pork for chicken and stirring in the pickles and horseradish along with the capers. Correct the seasoning with drops of vinegar.

Variation: SHRIMP SALAD

Makes about 1 quart, serving 4 to 6 as a main course

❦ *Slices of sweet red onion and orange segments (seeds and membrane removed) are excellent garnishes for a shrimp salad.*

Chicken Salad

SUBSTITUTE: 3 cups diced cooked peeled shrimp for chicken

Proceed according to the Master Recipe, substituting shrimp for chicken. (The recipe for steamed shrimp, page 317, makes enough for this salad.)

Variation: TURKEY SALAD

Makes about 1 quart, serving 4 to 5 as a main course

Chicken Salad
SUBSTITUTE: 3 cups cubed cooked turkey for chicken

Proceed according to the Master Recipe, substituting turkey for chicken.

Variation: VEAL SALAD

Makes about 1 quart, serving 4 to 5 as a main course

❦*A veal salad is so unusual and such a nice surprise that you might consider specially cooking up a small roast of veal (about 1½ pounds before cooking) rather than waiting for the unlikely day when you have leftovers.*

Chicken Salad
SUBSTITUTE: 3 cups cubed cooked veal for chicken
ADD: ½ to 1 teaspoon anchovy paste or 1 to 2 teaspoons mashed drained anchovies
2 to 3 tablespoons minced fresh parsley

Squeeze the lemon juice called for in the Master Recipe into a small bowl. Add anchovy paste and stir until dissolved. Proceed from there with Master Recipe, substituting veal for chicken, adding the anchovy-flavored lemon juice, and stirring in the parsley along with the capers.

COLE SLAW

Makes about 1 quart, to serve 6 to 8

1½ pounds cabbage
½ cup shredded or finely chopped carrot
½ cup shredded or finely chopped green bell pepper
½ cup shredded or finely chopped peeled green apple
¼ cup finely chopped scallion, including tender green parts
⅔ to 1 cup mayonnaise, preferably homemade, page 51
⅓ to ½ cup sour cream
1½ tablespoons grated fresh horseradish or 2 tablespoons well-drained prepared horseradish
½ teaspoon sugar
Wine vinegar or cider vinegar, if needed
½ teaspoon salt
¼ teaspoon white pepper, preferably freshly ground

Quarter a 1½-pound cabbage lengthwise (or use part of a larger cabbage) and remove the tough, whitish core. Using a sharp utility knife, the slicing plate of a grater, or the slicing disc of a food processor, cut the cabbage quarters lengthwise in long, very thin slices. You should have 1 quart, tightly packed. A handful at a time, squeeze the cabbage firmly so that it will better absorb the dressing. Combine cabbage with carrot, green pepper, apple, and scallion in 3-quart bowl. Add remaining ingredients and stir thoroughly. Taste and correct the seasoning. Cover cole slaw and refrigerate for at least 1 hour—overnight is better—to blend flavors.

MY MOTHER'S POTATO SALAD

Makes about 1 quart, to serve 6

❦ *This unusually simple recipe allows the subtle but definite flavor of the potatoes to come through.*

2 pounds boiling potatoes
1 tablespoon salt
3 tablespoons red wine vinegar
1 cup mayonnaise, preferably homemade, page 51
⅓ cup very finely minced onion
⅓ cup minced fresh parsley
Salt and freshly ground pepper, to taste

Place unpeeled potatoes in a 3½- to 4-quart saucepan, cover with cold water, and add 1 tablespoon salt. Bring to a boil, turn heat down to low, cover partially, and simmer for 20 to 35 minutes, or until potatoes feel tender but not mushy when pierced with a fork. Drain off water. Let potatoes cool to room temperature, then refrigerate for at least 1 and preferably 2 to 3 hours so that they will be firm and will hold their shape when cut.

Peel potatoes, cut into ¾-inch dice, and place in a 3-quart mixing bowl. Sprinkle vinegar over potatoes 1 tablespoon at a time, stirring gently after each addition. Fold in mayonnaise, onion, and parsley, and season to taste with salt and pepper. Cover and chill for at least 2 hours, preferably 12 to 24. Serve very cold.

CUCUMBER SALAD

Makes about 2 cups, to serve 4

❦ *This is a superb accompaniment to cold poached fish.*

1½ pounds cucumbers: 3 to 5 large or 9 to 12 kirby
1 teaspoon salt
1 teaspoon sugar
⅔ cup sour cream
2 tablespoons minced scallion (including tender green parts)
2 teaspoons finely chopped fresh dill (feathery leaves only) or ½ teaspoon dried dillweed
White pepper, preferably freshly ground, vinegar, and sugar, as needed

Peel cucumbers, cut in half lengthwise, scoop out the seeds with a spoon, and cut into slices about ¼ inch thick. You want about 2 cups. Place cucumbers in colander and toss with 1 teaspoon each salt and sugar. Set colander in sink and let cucumbers drain for at least 1 hour. A handful at a time, very firmly press cucumbers between sheets of paper toweling to squeeze out moisture (cucumbers should look translucent and ice green after pressing). Turn cucumbers into mixing bowl. Fold in sour cream, scallion, and dill. Taste and adjust seasoning with white pepper, drops of vinegar, and pinches of sugar. Refrigerate, covered, for at least an hour before serving.

SPINACH, MUSHROOM, AND BACON SALAD

4 main-course or 8 side-dish servings

❦ *This classic American salad combines the unique tastes and textures of fresh spinach, marinated mushrooms, and crisply fried bacon in one highly satisfying whole. The salad may be presented either as the main course of a lunch or supper, in which case it would be accompanied by bread and butter, or as a side dish or separate course within a meal featuring roasted or broiled meat.*

Initially, this salad has an enormous volume, but after the hot bacon fat and marinated mushrooms are added and the salad is tossed briefly, the spinach wilts and the salad shrinks to a manageable size. Combine ingredients in a very large mixing bowl or pot, such as a spaghetti pot, and then, after the salad has wilted, transfer it to a salad bowl for serving.

STEP 1: PREPARING MARINATED MUSHROOMS

1 pound mushrooms
½ teaspoon salt
¼ teaspoon pepper, preferably freshly ground
1½ tablespoons wine vinegar
1½ tablespoons strained fresh lemon juice
3 tablespoons very finely minced scallions
⅛ teaspoon dried rosemary, ground or moistened with a few drops of water and minced fine

Either wipe the mushrooms clean with damp paper towels or, if they are very dirty, turn them into a colander and rinse quickly under cool running water. Dry them quickly in paper towels; the mushrooms must not become waterlogged. Trim the stem ends, then slice mushrooms rather thickly. Turn mushrooms into a 3-quart noncorroding bowl, sprinkle evenly with salt and pepper, and toss. Add vinegar and lemon juice and toss a second time. Finally, add the scallions and rosemary and toss once more. Cover bowl with plastic wrap and, stirring once or twice, let mushrooms marinate for 1 to 3 hours at room temperature or in the refrigerator.

STEP 2: PREPARING SPINACH AND BACON; ASSEMBLING SALAD

2 pounds spinach
8 to 10 slices (8 ounces) bacon
1 tablespoon wine vinegar
1 tablespoon strained fresh lemon juice
2 to 4 hard-cooked eggs, sieved or chopped (optional)

Wash spinach well in one or more changes of cold water (see page 111). Pull away and discard any stems that seem especially large or tough and dry spinach thoroughly using either a salad spinner or paper towels. Turn dried spinach into a large bowl or pot.

Just before serving the salad, fry bacon until crisp in a 10-inch skillet. Drape the slices of bacon over the spinach, let cool for a few minutes, then crumble over the top. Return skillet containing bacon fat to low heat, add vinegar and lemon juice, and stir briefly until liquid is thick and glistening. Immediately pour hot fat mixture evenly over the spinach and crumbled bacon and toss several times. Add marinated mushrooms with their liquid and toss again. Taste the salad, add salt, pepper, additional lemon juice or vinegar (or anything else you deem necessary), and toss once more. Transfer to a serving bowl and serve immediately, decorating the top with hard-cooked egg if you wish.

CAESAR SALAD

4 to 5 main-course or 6 first-course servings

❦ *This delicious and grandly festive salad can be the mainstay of a brunch, lunch, or summertime supper or it can be the prelude to a meal featuring steamed or baked fish, fried chicken, roast beef, pork, or lamb, or perhaps something done on the outdoor grill. To serve Caesar salad in the manner that befits it, all of its components should be made ready beforehand in the kitchen, and the salad itself assembled and tossed before the delighted eyes of your guests.*

Step 1: Preparing Salad Ingredients

1 cup olive oil
1 teaspoon mashed, pressed, or very finely minced garlic
About 8 ounces French, Italian, or firm, unsweet white bread
2 large heads romaine lettuce
2 large eggs, at room temperature
1 to 2 large lemons
4 or more anchovy fillets, drained (optional)
¾ cup (about 3 ounces) freshly grated Parmesan cheese
Salt
Pepper in a peppermill

The garlic-flavored oil: Combine oil and garlic in a small saucepan and place over very low heat just until oil is warm. Remove from heat and let stand at least 30 minutes (several hours if possible) to let the flavor of the garlic permeate the oil. Pour about ⅔ cup of the flavored oil into a pitcher suitable for bringing to the table, filtering it through a tea strainer if you wish to remove the bits of garlic. Reserve remaining oil for preparing croutons.

The croutons: Using a serrated knife, remove crusts from bread and cut bread into ½-inch croutons, making about 1½ cups. Turn croutons into a 10-inch skillet and slowly drizzle with remaining ⅓ cup garlic-flavored oil, tossing with a spoon. Set skillet over moderately high heat and, tossing constantly with the spoon, sauté croutons until they turn a deep golden brown. Drain croutons on paper towels if they seem very oily, then turn into a bowl suitable for bringing to the table.

The lettuce: Gently break whole leaves one at a time from the bunch; reserve the tough, dark green outer leaves and any that are blemished or wilted for some other use. Wash the leaves in cold water, shake, and arrange in a single layer on paper towels or on a cloth towel. Using additional toweling, blot exposed surfaces of the leaves dry. (Since the leaves must remain whole and unbruised, you cannot use a salad spinner here.) In a very wide and roomy salad bowl, arrange lettuce leaves to resemble the petals of a giant flower. Drape the lettuce with a well wrung out towel or with damp paper towels and refrigerate until just before serving.

The eggs: Lower the eggs, their large, rounded ends pricked with a pin, into 2 quarts rapidly simmering water, and cook for exactly *15 seconds.* The whites are to be coddled—that is, barely thickened and opaque—but not set. Lift eggs out of the water with a slotted spoon and set on a small plate suitable for bringing to the table.

The lemons: Slice each lemon in half and remove the seeds using the point of a small knife or the tines of a fork. Set lemon halves on a small plate suitable for bringing to the table, and set a fork beside them.

TIP: Roll lemons over a flat surface, pressing them firmly with the palms of your hands; this will help them to yield more juice when squeezed.

The anchovies: Chop anchovies into small pieces and set on a small plate suitable for bringing to the table.

The cheese: Turn cheese into a small bowl suitable for bringing to the table.

Place pitcher of oil, croutons, coddled eggs, rolled and seeded lemon halves, chopped anchovies, grated cheese, salt, and a peppermill on a serving tray.

AHEAD OF TIME: After you have assembled all the ingredients, you may cover the tray loosely with plastic wrap and, with the lettuce refrigerated, wait for a couple of hours before assembling and serving the salad.

STEP 2: ASSEMBLING AND TOSSING THE SALAD: Drizzle about half the oil evenly over the lettuce and toss gently until the leaves become coated with the oil. Sprinkle liberally with salt, grind in pepper to taste, and strew anchovy pieces over all. Drizzle on remaining oil and again toss briefly. Using a fork, squeeze the juice from two of the lemon halves over the greens. Break eggs over the salad and toss just enough to break up and blend in the eggs. Taste a small leaf and add more lemon juice if necessary. (You may not need the juice from the remaining halves.) Finally, sprinkle cheese and croutons over the salad and toss just until leaves are coated with cheese.

Arrange 6 to 8 lettuce leaves side by side on each plate, being sure to include an ample helping of croutons with each portion. Guests should be encouraged to eat the salad with their fingers, scooping up croutons with the lettuce leaves.

EGGS

For a long time eggs were thought of solely as a breakfast food and were accordingly given simple and routine culinary treatments. But with the rise of the institution of brunch, people began looking for new things to do with eggs; they discovered that eggs are a delicious and unusually versatile food that can be cooked and served in a variety of interesting ways. Even the most ordinary and basic egg recipes—fried, scrambled, poached, or hard-cooked eggs—can be turned into elegant dishes if such compatible additions as cheese, ham, seafood, or vegetables are introduced in one way or another. And if a clever conceit is employed as well—if a pastry shell or popover is used as a receptacle for scrambled eggs, or if deviled eggs are flavored with smoked salmon and then baked under a blanket of cream sauce—commonplace egg dishes achieve elegance. Also included in this chapter are a number of egg recipes that are not based on everyday egg-cooking techniques and that are unlikely ever to be set on a breakfast table. Still, even these recipes—such "gourmet"-sounding and impressive concoctions as frittatas, quiches, and soufflés—turn out to be fairly easy to make and, because they are based on eggs, very easy on the wallet.

About Eggs

BUYING AND STORING EGGS: Though there are four grades of eggs—AA, A, B, and C, in order of descending quality—most supermarkets only stock grades AA and A. The difference between them is negligible. In theory, grade AA eggs have firmer whites and larger, better-rounded yolks than do grade A eggs, but in practice, whatever advantages grade AA eggs might have had when they were first laid will likely have disappeared by the time they are purchased at the supermarket days later. There is no difference between white-shelled and brown-shelled eggs, except that the latter sometimes cost more.

Always store eggs in the refrigerator. Since eggshells are porous and will absorb odors, it is wise to keep strongly flavored food tightly covered and away from eggs. According to the United States Department of Agriculture, storing eggs with the wider end up will help to keep the yolks centered, making for more attractive hard-cooked eggs.

EGG SIZES: There are five commercially available sizes of eggs: jumbo, extra-large, large, medium, and small. Most modern recipes, including all of the recipes in this book, are based on large eggs, which weigh 2 ounces and contain approximately 2 tablespoons white and 4 teaspoons yolk. The chart on the next page presents the weights and approximate volume measurements of the five egg sizes. When substituting one size for another in recipes, place in a bowl as many whole eggs, egg whites, or yolks as you think you'll need and beat with a fork just until loose and pourable but not frothy, then measure.

TESTING FOR FRESHNESS: Eggs used in the preparation of a recipe that contains other strong flavors—chocolate cake, for example—can be a month or more old and no one will know the difference. But you should use the freshest eggs possible when making a subtly flavored, egg-intensive recipe such as custard or egg bread, or when serving the eggs for breakfast. If you suspect your eggs are past their prime, put them in a bowl of cold water. Fresh eggs will sink, but stale eggs will float because the shell membranes have shrunk back, forming air pockets beneath the shells.

TIP: Before preparing especially delicate egg recipes, very choosy cooks are advised to subject eggs to a further test. One at a time, break eggs into a small bowl, then sniff. Fresh eggs will be virtually scentless, or perhaps mildly eggy in smell, but stale eggs will smell exactly like wet straw—or *à la paille,* as the French expression goes.

SEPARATING EGGS: Crack the egg across the middle against the rim of a bowl. Working over a small, clean bowl, pass the yolk back and forth between the shell halves, letting the white drop down into the bowl underneath. If a last, ropelike bit of white (the chalaza) clings to the yolk, tip the shell half so that the yolk is on the verge of spilling over the edge, then scrape and nudge the chalaza from the yolk using the other half of the shell. By the way, it is a good idea to transfer each egg white as it is separated from the small bowl you are working over to a larger bowl; this way, if you get yolk in an egg white, you will spoil only that white, not the whole batch.

STORING EGG WHITES AND YOLKS: To store egg whites, turn them into a clean container, preferably *not* of plastic. Cover and refrigerate for up to a week or freeze for 6 months or more. Egg yolks, which tend to dry out or coagulate when stored, require special attention. To keep yolks for 1 or 2 days in the refrigerator, place them—unbroken if possible—in a small container and cover tightly. To freeze, stir ½ teaspoon sugar *or* ¼ teaspoon salt into every 3 yolks to prevent coagulation; cover tightly. Try to use the yolks within a month or so. Use the sweetened yolks in desserts and the salted yolks in savory dishes.

EGG SIZES

EGG SIZE	APPROXIMATE NUMBER OF WHOLE EGGS PER CUP	APPROXIMATE NUMBER OF EGG WHITES PER CUP	APPROXIMATE NUMBER OF EGG YOLKS PER CUP	WEIGHT PER DOZEN EGGS
Jumbo	3	5	8	30 ounces
Extra Large	4	6	10	27 ounces
Large	4½	7 to 8	12	24 ounces
Medium	5	9	14	21 ounces
Small	6	10	16	18 ounces

BEATING EGG WHITES

1. *Select a deep, steep-sided bowl, preferably with a rounded bottom.* Shallow, flat-bottomed bowls permit the egg whites to expand laterally, escaping the strokes of the beater, and thus the whites do not rise as high as they should. Be sure to use a bowl large enough to accommodate the beaten volume of the whites—about 1 quart for every 2 large eggs. The bowl should be made of glass, stainless steel, or copper. Plastic, which may harbor particles of grease, and unlined tin or aluminum, which may discolor the egg whites, are not good for beating egg whites.

2. *Everything—your fingers, the bowl, beaters, and the egg whites themselves—must be completely dry and free of grease or egg yolk.* Even a drop of grease or yolk will weigh down the air cells in the whites as they form, or prevent them from forming altogether. If you haven't used your bowl or your beaters for a while, it is a good idea to wash them before using them—just to be on the safe side.

3. *Egg whites must be at room temperature or slightly warmer in order to mount to their fullest glory.* If the eggs have just come out of the refrigerator, separate the whites into the bowl in which you will beat them and set in a basin filled with very warm, but not hot, water; stir with a clean spoon or clean finger until the whites are warmed through. If the water is too hot, the whites will set and you will have to throw the entire batch away and start over. Never immerse whole eggs in the shell in hot water to warm them; the whites will become water-logged and will not mount properly.

4. *For best results, stabilize the egg whites by adding ¼ teaspoon cream of tartar for every 4 egg whites during the beating process.* A product of grapes, cream of tartar is the acid compound potassium bitartrate ($C_4H_5KO_6$). It stiffens the protein in egg whites so that the whites can absorb and retain a greater quantity of air without breaking down, separating, or turning granular. If in the past your beaten egg whites have been brittle or soupy, or if they have slipped down the sides of the bowl and deflated, you probably forgot to add the cream of tartar. Or perhaps your cream of tartar was past its prime and no longer worked. To be on the safe side I would recommend buying a new bottle of cream of tartar once a year.

TIP: Did people use cream of tartar in the eighteenth century, when (more or less) soufflés were invented? No, they used bowls made of unlined copper, a metal that reacts with egg whites in the same way that cream of tartar does. If you happen to have an unlined and unlacquered copper bowl on hand in which to beat egg whites, you can dispense with the cream of tartar.

5. *The best device for beating egg whites is a small, hand-held electric mixer.* If you do not own one, you can use a stationary electric mixer instead, but you will find that the egg whites will not rise to the fullest possible height. Of course egg whites can also be beaten by hand, using a balloon-wire whip, but most people find this procedure hard on the arm muscles.

With the hand-held mixer set at low speed, beat the egg whites until they have become a loose, foamy mass, then add salt and cream of tartar (1). Increase speed to medium and begin moving the beaters all around the circumference of the bowl (try to disregard the clattering sounds!) and up through the middle of the whites. The more energetic you are in pushing the beaters around in the bowl, the more air you will incorporate into the egg whites. In a couple of minutes the whites will have quadrupled in volume and become opaque, fluffy, and stiff enough to stand in small, soft peaks when the beaters are lifted out of the bowl (2). Increase speed to high and beat the whites until they have increased six to eight times their original volume and are thick and glossy, very much resembling aerosol shaving cream. At this point the whites will stand in tall, stiff peaks when the beaters are lifted from the bowl and will swath the beaters thickly (3). This is the stage referred to as "stiff but not dry," and the whites should not be beaten further. Use immediately in the recipe.

RESCUING OVERBEATEN EGG WHITES: If your egg whites become brittle, watery, grainy, dry, dull, or deflated due to overbeating, add a fresh egg white and beat just until the sheen and body return. Use rescued egg whites at once; their longevity is precarious.

FOLDING IN EGG WHITES: The purpose of folding is to incorporate an aerated substance—usually stiffly beaten egg whites or whipped cream—into a heavy batter without rupturing the air cells in the aerated food. A soufflé, chiffon pie filling, or cake made from a skillfully folded batter will be light and delicate; the end product of a clumsily folded batter will be dense, flat, rubbery, wet, or worse. Be sure to fold mixtures in a large, roomy bowl, and use the largest rubber spatula you own.

Stir a quarter (or the amount specified in the recipe) of the beaten egg whites into the heavier batter to lighten it. Scoop remaining whites in a mound in the center of the heavier batter. Holding the spatula perpendicular to the mixture (curved edge down), cut through the middle of the egg whites and down through the batter (1). When you reach the bottom of the bowl, rotate the spatula toward you, then bring it up along the side of the bowl and over the top of the egg whites in an arc (2). With the first downward cut of the spatula you will have brought a bit of the egg whites down into the batter; with the arc-sweep of the spatula from the bottom of the bowl over the top you will have scooped a trail of batter over the whites (3). *Rotating the bowl a quarter turn each time,* repeat these two movements until batter and whites are fairly well blended (4). Scrape the sides of the bowl occasionally. As a general rule, it is preferable to leave a few patches of egg whites unblended than to fold so thoroughly that you risk deflating the mixture.

MASTER RECIPE

Fried Eggs

2 to 4 servings

Fried eggs are usually eaten at breakfast, but if seasoned with capers, blanketed with melted cheese, or cooked with a savory vegetable such as red peppers or zucchini, they are suitable as the main offering for brunch or lunch. Fried potatoes or toasted French bread round out the meal nicely.

Although fried eggs are seemingly a simple dish to make, arguments abound over which cooking procedure is best. I present here one of the less usual and more controversial of the many techniques. When prepared in this manner, fried eggs are very soft and delicate, with no crispy, fried edges. The layer of white that covers the yolk sets and turns opaque, eliminating the need to turn the egg and risk breaking the yolk. In truth, these eggs are more "butter-poached" than "fried."

Use the freshest eggs possible for fried eggs. Stale eggs taste "off" and tend to spread out in the pan.

1½ tablespoons butter
4 large, extra-large, or jumbo eggs
Salt and pepper, preferably freshly ground, to taste

Melt the butter in a 10-inch skillet (preferably nonstick) over moderate heat. When the foam starts to subside, indicating that the butter is hot, break the eggs into the skillet. Immediately turn heat to low and cover the skillet tightly. Cook the eggs in the butter for 3 to 5 minutes. The eggs should make low murmuring noises in the pan; if you hear crackling and sizzling, turn the heat down still more. The eggs are done when the white covering the yolk has become an opaque white veil; don't overcook or the yolk will begin to harden.

Season to taste with salt and freshly ground pepper and transfer to warm plates or a warm serving platter. Serve immediately.

Variation: FRIED EGGS WITH BROWNED BUTTER AND CAPERS

2 to 4 servings

❦*A classic dish. Serve with hash browns or lacy potato pancakes for a hearty yet elegant brunch.*

Fried Eggs
4 tablespoons butter
1½ tablespoons drained small capers
½ teaspoon caper bottling liquid
A few grindings fresh pepper

Remove the cooked eggs to warmed plates or platters and cover loosely with a sheet of waxed paper. Add 4 tablespoons butter to the skillet and turn heat to high. Swirl skillet by the handle and heat the butter until it turns a light nut-brown, being sure not to let it burn and turn black. Remove skillet from heat and stir in capers and caper liquid. Spoon the caper sauce over the eggs, sprinkle with pepper, and serve at once.

Variation: CHEESE-BLANKETED FRIED EGGS

2 to 4 servings

Fried Eggs
ADD: ½ cup (about 2 ounces) shredded Monterey Jack or Gouda cheese

When the eggs are almost set, sprinkle them evenly with cheese, return cover to skillet, and continue to cook until eggs are done and cheese has begun to melt. Season with salt and pepper to taste.

Variation: FRIED EGGS WITH RED PEPPERS

2 to 4 servings

Fried Eggs

ADD:	2 medium-size red bell peppers
	¼ teaspoon mashed, pressed, or very finely minced garlic
SUBSTITUTE:	3 tablespoons olive oil for butter
ADD:	Chopped fresh parsley (optional)

If you wish to peel the peppers, follow the procedure outlined on page 570. Core the peppers, remove the seeds and ribs, and cut them lengthwise into ½-inch strips. Heat the olive oil until fragrant in the same skillet you will use to fry the eggs, and add pepper strips and garlic. Stirring frequently, sauté the peppers over moderate heat for 10 to 15 minutes, or until soft.

Push the cooked peppers to the edges of the skillet, forming a ring, and turn heat to low. Break the eggs into center of the skillet and cook according to the Master Recipe. To serve, slide the eggs and peppers, which will more or less have amalgamated into a cake, onto a warm serving platter and, if you wish, sprinkle with chopped fresh parsley.

Variation: FRIED EGGS WITH ZUCCHINI

2 to 4 servings

❦ *This recipe is inspired by a dish that my grandmother used to make at her winter home in Sicily, using just-laid eggs and zucchini that were barely larger than carrots. If topped with freshly grated Parmesan cheese and accompanied by home fries or Italian bread, this will easily serve four as a lunch or light supper.*

Fried Eggs

ADD:	2 small zucchini (about 12 ounces)
SUBSTITUTE:	3 tablespoons olive oil for butter
ADD:	½ cup peeled, seeded, diced tomatoes, fresh or canned (see page 607)
	¼ teaspoon mashed, pressed, or very finely minced garlic

Wash the zucchini thoroughly, trim ends, and cut into ½ inch cubes. Heat the olive oil until fragrant in the same skillet you will use to fry the eggs. Add the zucchini and toss over moderately high heat for several minutes, or until it has begun to soften and turn golden. Add the tomatoes and garlic and continue to cook, stirring frequently, until the juice from the tomatoes has evaporated and the zucchini is very soft.

Push cooked zucchini to the edges of the skillet and turn heat to low. Break eggs into the center of the skillet and cook according to the Master Recipe. Serve each portion of eggs with some of the zucchini on the side.

MASTER RECIPE

Scrambled Eggs

4 servings

In former times, scrambled eggs were prepared as a soft, buttery-rich custard with a consistency akin to small-curd, cream-style cottage cheese. To achieve this result, the eggs were cooked slowly over low heat. No liquid was added, since liquid tends to make scrambled eggs tough and watery. I like this old-fashioned type of scrambled eggs best, and I have adapted the old cooking method here with one significant adjustment: I use considerably less butter. One recipe from Colonial Virginia suggests equal *quantities of butter and eggs—or 1 pound of butter for every 8 large eggs. Sounds delicious, but whose waistline could afford it?*

Sophisticated scrambled eggs deserve to be treated in a sophisticated manner. Spoon them over hot toast or into tartlet shells or popovers and sprinkle with chopped fresh herbs, grated cheese, or crumbled bacon. If you're serving the eggs for brunch, lunch, or supper, broccoli, asparagus, or creamed spinach make nice vegetable accompaniments.

8 large eggs
1/4 teaspoon salt
1/8 teaspoon pepper, preferably freshly ground
4 to 6 tablespoons butter

In a 3-quart mixing bowl, beat the eggs with the salt and pepper until the whites and yolks are completely blended. Set a heavy-bottomed 10-inch skillet (preferably nonstick) over very low heat and melt the butter in it. Pour in the beaten eggs. Slowly and continually stir the eggs with a wooden spoon or spatula, reaching all parts of the bottom and sides of the skillet. In about 5 minutes the eggs will thicken and begin to break into small curds. Stirring more briskly now to keep the curds small and creamy, cook the eggs 7 to 10 minutes longer, or until they are just firm enough to hold their shape on the spoon. Remove the skillet from the heat and immediately transfer the eggs to plates or a platter to prevent them from cooking further. Serve at once.

Variation: BACON AND ONION SCRAMBLE

4 servings

Scrambled Eggs
SUBSTITUTE: 6 slices bacon for butter
ADD: ½ cup finely chopped onions

In the same skillet you will use to cook the eggs, fry the bacon until crisp. Drain the bacon on paper towels; crumble when cool enough to handle. Over moderately high heat sauté the onions in bacon drippings until soft and very lightly browned.

Remove the skillet from the heat and let cool to just lukewarm. Proceeding according to the Master Recipe but omitting the butter, prepare scrambled eggs in the skillet. Stir reserved crumbled bacon into the eggs just before you remove them from the heat.

Variation: CHEESE SCRAMBLE

4 servings

Scrambled Eggs
ADD: ½ to ¾ cup (about 2 to 3 ounces), shredded Swiss, Cheddar, or Monterey Jack cheese *or* ⅓ cup (about 1½ ounces) freshly grated Parmesan cheese

When the eggs are nearly cooked, remove the skillet from the heat and gently stir in the cheese. Wait a moment for the cheese to begin to melt and then again stir gently. Transfer to plates or platter and serve.

Variation: CURRIED CRAB SCRAMBLE

4 servings

Scrambled Eggs
1½ tablespoons butter
½ teaspoon mild curry powder or ⅜ teaspoon hot (Madras) curry powder
¼ to ⅓ cup minced well-cleaned crabmeat, fresh cooked or well-drained canned

Melt 1½ tablespoons butter in a small skillet or saucepan, stir in curry powder, and cook slowly for 3 minutes. Add crabmeat and warm in the curry-butter mixture for a minute or so, stirring occasionally. Remove from heat and set aside.

Prepare scrambled eggs according to the Master Recipe. Just before removing eggs from the heat, stir in the curried crab mixture.

Variation: GEORGIA SCRAMBLE WITH HAM AND GREEN PEPPERS

4 servings

Scrambled Eggs

INCREASE: Butter to 6 to 8 tablespoons

ADD: 1/3 cup finely diced green bell pepper
1/3 cup finely diced smoked ham

In the same skillet you will use to prepare the eggs, gently sauté green pepper in 2 tablespoons butter until soft. Stir in ham and sauté 1 or 2 minutes longer. Adding remaining butter, proceed to make scrambled eggs in the skillet according to the Master Recipe.

Variation: HAM AND SWISS SCRAMBLE

4 servings

Scrambled Eggs

ADD: 1/2 cup (about 2 ounces) shredded Swiss cheese
1/3 cup (about 2 ounces) diced boiled ham

Prepare the eggs according to the Master Recipe removing them from the heat when they are almost as firm as you like them. Gently stir in cheese and ham. Wait a moment for the cheese to begin to melt and then gently stir again. Serve at once.

Variation: HERB SCRAMBLE

4 servings

Scrambled Eggs

ADD: 1 to 2 tablespoons chopped fresh herbs (parsley, chives, feathery leaves of dill, or a combination)

Prepare the eggs according to the Master Recipe, stirring in herbs just before removing eggs from heat.

Variation: LOX (OR CAVIAR) AND CREAM CHEESE SCRAMBLE

4 servings

❦ *These eggs could be served for brunch or as an elegant midnight supper after theater or the opera. Accompany with toast points or spoon the eggs into individual tartlet shells. A dry champagne or other sparkling wine will add further elegance to the occasion.*

Scrambled Eggs

ADD: 3 ounces cream cheese (preferably "natural" cream cheese, made without gums or thickeners, available at health-food stores and gourmet food shops)
2 to 3 tablespoons finely chopped smoked salmon or caviar

About 20 minutes before serving, cut cream cheese into 1/4-inch cubes and bring to room temperature.

Prepare scrambled eggs according to the Master Recipe. When the eggs are almost as firm as you like them, remove skillet from heat and gently fold in cream cheese and salmon or caviar. Serve at once, before the cream cheese becomes runny.

Variation: WILD MUSHROOM SCRAMBLE

4 servings

❦ *An old family friend, Helen Reschovsky, used to take my sister and me on mushroom-gathering hikes through the Connecticut woods when we were children. When we got back to Helen's with our treasure, we would sauté the mushrooms in butter and then proceed to scramble eggs using the same skillet. The taste of pungent, woodsy mushrooms and creamy scrambled eggs remains in my memory to this day. If you do not know a mushroom expert who can act as your field guide—some species of mushrooms are* deadly *poisonous—you will have to buy your "wild" mushrooms at a specialty store.*

Scrambled Eggs

INCREASE: Butter to 6 to 8 tablespoons
ADD: 4 ounces wild mushrooms (shiitake mushrooms, chanterelles, cèpes, or some other firm, meaty type)
ADD: Salt and pepper, preferably freshly ground, to taste

Clean the mushrooms and cut them into ½-inch strips. In the same skillet you will use to prepare the eggs, melt 2 tablespoons butter, add mushrooms, and toss over moderately high heat until they are cooked through. Season lightly with salt and pepper. Transfer the mushrooms to a plate, add remaining butter to the skillet, and prepare scrambled eggs following the Master Recipe. When the eggs are nearly cooked, stir in the mushrooms and continue to cook for a moment longer, or until the eggs are as firm as you like them. Serve immediately with buttered toast.

MASTER RECIPE

Soft- and Hard-Cooked Eggs

❦ *Soft- and hard-cooked eggs are both cooked in the same manner; the difference between the two is simply how long they are cooked. A perfectly executed soft-cooked egg has a solid but tender white and a warm, liquid yolk. A perfect hard-cooked egg has a tender, not rubbery, white and a yolk that is soft, moist, and pale yellow—never hard, crumbly, dry, or discolored. To ensure success, you must conscientiously perform three simple procedures: measure the water, regulate the heat carefully, and time the eggs exactly.*

If you are fortunate enough to be using eggs that have been laid within the previous 48 hours, let them stand at room temperature for a day or so before cooking them. This allows an air space to develop between the egg and the shell, thus facilitating peeling.

3 to 6 servings

2 quarts water
6 eggs, cold from the refrigerator

Pour the water into a saucepan and bring to a simmer over moderately high heat.

Using either an ordinary pushpin or an egg pricker, prick the eggs ¼ to ⅜ inch deep at the wider end. Pricking allows air to escape from the eggs as they cook and prevents them from leaking too much, even if they do crack. Lower eggs into the simmering water, immediately raise heat to high and begin timing. When water returns to the simmer, lower heat so that the water bubbles just enough to cause the eggs to bounce occasionally on the bottom of the pan. You may have to adjust the flame several times during cooking, especially if you are making hard-cooked eggs. If the heat is too high, the eggs will toughen and a dark gray-green ring may appear around the yolks of hard-cooked eggs. Six large eggs will take 4 minutes to soft-cook, 14 minutes to hard-cook. Prepare eggs of other sizes according to the Timing Chart below.

TIMING CHART—FOR SIX EGGS*

EGG SIZE:	MINUTES TO SOFT-COOK	MINUTES TO HARD-COOK
Jumbo	4½	15
Extra Large	4	15
Large	4	14
Medium	3½	13
Small	3	12

*Cooking times remain constant no matter how many eggs you are preparing, as long as you use 1 quart water for every 3 eggs that you are cooking.

PEELING AND STORING SOFT-COOKED EGGS: As soon as eggs are done, drain, crack the shells lightly with the back of a spoon, and peel under a stream of cool water. Blot with paper towels. Serve soft-cooked eggs on buttered toast or use in any of the variation recipes for poached eggs, pages 149–51. Peeled soft-cooked eggs may be submerged in a bowl of water, covered, and refrigerated for several days. To reheat, bring 1 quart water just to a simmer, remove from heat, add the eggs, and let warm for 1 minute before draining, drying, and serving.

PEELING AND STORING HARD-COOKED EGGS: When the eggs are done, drain and submerge at once in a large bowl or sink filled with very cold water and let stand until thoroughly chilled. To peel, gently roll the eggs over a countertop to crack the shells and remove the shells under a stream of cool water. Hard-cooked eggs may be stored in the refrigerator for several days. I always leave them in the shells until I am ready to use them, but they may also be stored peeled. Simply cover them with damp paper towels and store in a container with a tight lid until ready to use.

MASTER RECIPE

Deviled Eggs

Makes 12 hors d'oeuvre

If proof of the versatility of eggs were needed, this recipe and the variation that follows certainly provide it. The starting point is that long-time favorite of picnickers, the humble deviled egg, made by halving hard-cooked eggs, mashing the yolks with mayonnaise, butter, or cream cheese, and refilling the whites with the yolk mixture. Add a flavoring such as seafood, ham, or puréed vegetables to the yolk mixture and your deviled eggs become even grander. Finally, deviled eggs may be covered with a cream sauce and baked until piping hot to produce baked stuffed eggs, an easy and economical but very beguiling luncheon, supper, or buffet dish that may be served with toast or on a bed of spinach or fried potatoes. A few twists on one simple idea produce a wealth of different dishes!

Hard-cooked Eggs, using 6 large or extra-large eggs
2 teaspoons finely grated onion
1 tablespoon finely chopped fresh parsley (optional)
½ teaspoon Dijon mustard
One of the Following Flavorings (optional):
- ⅓ cup minced ham
- Mushroom Stuffing, page 553
- ⅓ cup minced well-cleaned shrimp, crab, or lobster, fresh cooked or well-drained canned
- 3 to 4 tablespoons mashed, drained canned tuna or salmon and 1 tablespoon finely chopped well-drained capers or green olives
- 2 to 3 tablespoons minced smoked salmon
- 3 to 4 tablespoons puréed cooked spinach or asparagus, firmly squeezed dry in a square of cheesecloth

3 to 4 tablespoons mayonnaise or soft butter or soft cream cheese
Salt and pepper, preferably freshly ground, to taste
Drops of fresh lemon juice

Cut the eggs in half lengthwise with a sharp, thin-bladed knife dipped in cold water. Holding each egg half upside down over a sieve, gently pinch egg underneath the yolk to release yolk into the sieve. Set aside emptied whites.

Using the back of a wooden spoon, force the yolks through the sieve into a 3-quart mixing bowl. Stir in grated onion, optional parsley, and mustard. If you wish, beat in one of the flavorings listed above as well. Mash the yolk mixture with 3 to 4 tablespoons mayonnaise, soft butter, or cream cheese, using just enough to form a stiff but moist paste. Taste and season carefully with salt, pepper, and lemon juice. Mound yolk mixture into the reserved egg-white halves, or pipe through a pastry bag fitted with a ½-inch star tip.

Cover with plastic wrap and allow to stand in a cool place for about 20 minutes before serving, or refrigerate for up to 36 hours. Let refrigerated eggs stand at room temperature for 30 minutes before serving.

Variation: BAKED STUFFED EGGS

4 to 6 main-course servings

❦*An almost infinite variety of baked stuffed egg dishes may be prepared by baking flavored deviled eggs with a cream sauce. Before proceeding with this recipe, select one of the deviled egg flavorings from the Master Recipe and then use the Chart on page 148 to choose a compatible cream sauce.*

PRELIMINARIES

1. Set rack in upper level of oven.
2. Preheat oven to 400°F 20 minutes before baking.
3. Select a shallow 9-by-7-inch "oven-to-table" dish. Grease with 1 tablespoon soft butter.

Basic Cream Sauce page 34, made with milk, or one of the variations, pages 35–45
Deviled Eggs, prepared with one of the optional flavorings
⅓ cup bread crumbs, preferably fresh (see page 60)
2 tablespoons butter cut into small pieces

Prepare the flavored deviled eggs plus a compatible cream sauce (see Chart below). Ladle a thin layer of cream sauce onto the bottom of the prepared baking dish and arrange the eggs on top. Cover the eggs with the remaining sauce, sprinkle evenly with bread crumbs, and dot with butter. Bake in preheated oven for about 25 minutes, or until the sauce is bubbling around the edges of the baking dish and the crumbs have browned lightly. Be careful not to overbake or the whites of the eggs will toughen. Serve at once.

AHEAD OF TIME: The entire dish may be assembled as long as 1½ days in advance, covered with plastic wrap, and stored in the refrigerator. If baked right out of the refrigerator, add about 5 minutes to the baking time.

FLAVORING *and* SAUCING CHART *for* BAKED STUFFED EGGS

DEVILED-EGG FLAVORING

CREAM SAUCE	HAM	MUSHROOM	SHELLFISH	TUNA/SALMON	SMOKED SALMON	VEGETABLE
Basic	X	X	X	X	X	X
California	X			X	X	
Caper	X			X	X	
Cheese	X					X
Cheese/Wine	X	X		X		X
Onion	X	X	X	X	X	X
Curried	X	X	X	X		X
Dilled or Parsleyed	X	X		X	X	
Lobster/Crab			X			
Mushroom	X	X		X		X
Sherried	X	X	X	X		
Tomato-Basil	X		X	X		

MASTER RECIPE

Poached Eggs

2 to 4 servings

I have done more than a few experiments with poached eggs, and the method that follows works best for me. But no matter what method you choose, the eggs will spread out and look quite messy unless they are fairly fresh—certainly no more than 1 week old.

Serve poached eggs on buttered toast or on a bed of cooked vegetables. If you wish to poach more than 4 eggs prepare them in two or more batches, keeping the cooked eggs warm in a bowl of hot water while you make more. It is difficult to time accurately the poaching of a large number of eggs.

Vinegar
4 eggs, preferably large or extra-large

Select a noncorroding pot measuring about 8 inches across and 3 to 4 inches deep. Pour in enough water to reach a depth of about 2 inches and stir in 2 tablespoons vinegar per quart of water used. Bring to just below the simmer over low heat.

Break each egg into a heatproof ⅓-cup measuring cup or small teacup. Plunge each cup at a 45° angle into the simmering water. *Hold the cup in the water for 2 seconds,* then tip to release the egg. Add eggs to the pot in a clockwise circle so that you can remember which have cooked the longest.

Maintaining the water at just below the simmer, poach eggs for about 4 minutes, or until the whites are solidly set. Using a slotted spoon or skimmer, remove eggs from the water in the same order in which you added them.

Transfer cooked eggs to a 3-quart bowl of hot water (this helps to wash off the vinegar). Before serving, remove eggs from bowl of water with a slotted spoon or skimmer and drain on paper towels. Cut away any unsightly wisps of egg white, or "streamers."

AHEAD OF TIME: You may keep poached eggs warm for 30 minutes or longer—while you prepare more poached eggs or other parts of the meal—simply by replenishing the hot water in the bowl. To store poached eggs, leave them in the bowl of water, cover, and refrigerate. They will keep for at least 3 days. To reheat, simply bring 1 quart of water to the simmer, remove from heat, and drop in the eggs for a minute or so.

Variation: EGGS BENEDICT

2 to 4 servings

Poached Eggs
2 English muffins, split, toasted, and buttered
4 slices warm ham (each about 3⁄16 inch thick)
½ to 1 cup Hollandaise Sauce, page 46

Arrange English muffins on a warmed serving platter. Top each half with a slice of ham and a poached egg, then cover with 2 tablespoons of hollandaise. Serve immediately, passing additional hollandaise on the side if you wish.

Variation: EGGS FLORENTINE

2 to 4 servings

Poached Eggs
Steamed Spinach, page 590, squeezed to remove liquid
Cheese Sauce with Wine, page 38

Arrange spinach in an even layer on lightly buttered heat-proof serving platter. Place poached eggs on top of spinach and cover eggs completely with sauce. Place dish briefly under a very hot broiler to lightly brown the top.

Variation: EGGS "BENETINE"

2 to 4 servings

❦ *That's right—a cross between Eggs Benedict and Eggs Florentine, and my personal favorite way with poached eggs.*

Poached Eggs
4 slices warm ham (each about 3⁄16 inch thick)
Steamed Spinach, page 590, squeezed to remove liquid
½ to 1 cup Hollandaise Sauce, page 46

Arrange ham slices on a warmed serving platter. Divide the spinach equally over the ham slices, top with a poached egg, and cover each portion with 2 tablespoons hollandaise. Serve at once, passing additional hollandaise on the side, if you wish.

Variation: HUEVOS RANCHEROS (COWBOY EGGS)

2 to 4 servings

Poached Eggs
3 tablespoons olive oil
⅓ cup minced onion
¼ cup minced green bell pepper
¾ cup canned tomato purée
2 to 3 teaspoons chili powder, or to taste (the sauce is supposed to be very spicy)
½ teaspoon oregano
½ teaspoon salt
¼ teaspoon pepper, preferably freshly ground
½ cup (about 2 ounces) shredded Monterey Jack or other mild cheese

SPECIAL EQUIPMENT: 2 or 4 individual-serving gratin dishes

Heat the olive oil in a 10-inch skillet, add the onion and green pepper, and cook over moderate heat for 5 minutes, or until vegetables are nearly soft. Stir in all remaining ingredients except eggs and cheese. Cover skillet and simmer slowly for 10 minutes to blend flavors.

Spoon a thin layer of sauce into each gratin dish. Place 1 or 2 poached eggs in each dish, cover with remaining sauce, and sprinkle with shredded cheese. Place 2 to 3 inches under a hot broiler for about 20 seconds, just until cheese melts. Serve immediately.

MASTER RECIPE

Potato Frittata

6 servings

❦*A frittata is a kind of giant egg cake that you cook in a skillet. Easy to make and practically fail-safe, it is a great dish for entertaining since it can be prepared in advance and reheated, or served at room temperature (which is the Italian way), or served cold. If you plan to refrigerate then reheat the frittata do not cook it in a cast-iron pan, which will impart a slightly metallic taste on reheating. A tossed salad or tomato salad is an appropriate accompaniment.*

½ cup olive oil
1½ cups chopped onions
2 medium boiling potatoes, peeled and cut into ½-inch cubes (about 1½ cups)
1 tablespoon mashed, pressed, or very finely minced garlic
½ teaspoon salt
¾ teaspoon pepper, preferably freshly ground
8 large eggs
½ cup (about 2 ounces) freshly grated Parmesan cheese
⅓ cup chopped fresh parsley, preferably flat-leaf Italian parsley

Pour the olive oil into a heavy 10-inch skillet at least 3 inches deep and set the skillet over moderately high heat. When the oil is shimmery and fragrant, add onions and potatoes and cook, tossing frequently with a spatula, for 10 to 15 minutes, or until the vegetables are soft and just beginning to brown. Add garlic, season with half the salt and pepper, and cook 1 minute longer.

Beat the eggs in a 3-quart mixing bowl just enough to combine the yolks and whites, then blend in 6 tablespoons Parmesan cheese, parsley, and the remaining salt and pepper. Scrape the bottom of the skillet with the spatula to loosen vegetables and immediately pour in egg mixture. Reduce heat to moderately low and cook frittata undisturbed for about 15 minutes, or until it has solidified, with just a few shallow pools of uncooked egg remaining on top.

Sprinkle frittata with the remaining 2 tablespoons cheese and place it about 3 inches under a hot broiler for a minute or so, just long enough to cook the loose egg on top and brown the cheese very lightly. To serve the frittata, loosen edges with a knife and cut into wedges.

AHEAD OF TIME: Let the frittata cool to room temperature in the skillet, then cover the skillet with aluminum foil and refrigerate for up to 2 days. To reheat, place the skillet, still covered with foil, in a 300°F oven for about 20 minutes, or until the frittata is warmed through.

Variation: FRITTATA WITH ARTICHOKES

6 servings

Potato Frittata

ADD: 3 to 4 cooked artichoke bottoms, cut into ½-inch cubes

Add the artichoke bottoms along with the garlic; proceed according to the Master Recipe.

Variation: FRITTATA WITH HAM

6 servings

Potato Frittata
ADD: 8 ounces ham, cut into ¼-inch cubes (about 1 cup)

Add the ham with the garlic; proceed according to the Master Recipe.

Variation: FRITTATA WITH GREEN OR RED PEPPERS

6 servings

Potato Frittata
ADD: 2 medium-size green or red bell peppers

Cut the peppers in half lengthwise, remove cores, seeds, and ribs, and cut into ½-inch squares. Add to the skillet along with the onions and potatoes; proceed according to the Master Recipe.

Variation: FRITTATA WITH SAUSAGE

6 servings

Potato Frittata
ADD: 8 ounces sweet or hot sausage

Squeeze the sausage out of its casings (you should have about 1 cup) and crumble into the skillet you plan to use for cooking the frittata. Sauté the sausage over moderately high heat, stirring frequently, until lightly browned. With a slotted spoon, transfer the sausage to a plate; pour off and discard all fat remaining in skillet.

Add olive oil to the skillet and proceed with the Master Recipe, adding cooked sausage along with the garlic.

Variation: FRITTATA WITH SPINACH

6 servings

Potato Frittata
SUBSTITUTE: ½ recipe Steamed Spinach, page 590, squeezed dry and finely chopped (about 1 cup), for parsley

Proceed according to the Master Recipe, substituting spinach for parsley.

Variation: FRITTATA WITH TOMATO

6 servings

Potato Frittata
ADD: 2 medium fresh tomatoes, or 1 large (about ½ pound)

Peel and seed the tomatoes (see page 607), then cut into ½-inch cubes. You should have about 1 cup. When the onions and potatoes are almost tender, add the tomatoes, raise heat to high, and cook, tossing frequently, until tomato liquid has evaporated. Proceed according to the Master Recipe.

Variation: FRITTATA WITH ZUCCHINI

6 servings

Potato Frittata
ADD: 1 small zucchini cut into ½-inch cubes (about 1 cup)

When the onions and potatoes have cooked for about 5 minutes, add the zucchini and continue to cook until all the vegetables are tender and lightly browned. Proceed with the Master Recipe.

MASTER RECIPE

French Omelet

Makes a 1-serving omelet

❦*A true French omelet is puffy and oval in shape, the outside lightly browned and firmly set (never tough or rubbery), and the inside creamy, soft, and custardlike, similar to good scrambled eggs. In both taste and texture a*

French omelet is superior to the more familiar flat version, which is made by allowing beaten egg to solidify in a skillet and then rolling the egg cake up like a rug. The problem is that a French omelet is tricky to make—the entire procedure is accomplished in less than 30 seconds; to become adept you must practice, practice, practice. The Master Recipe is intended as a lesson in omelet making; before you begin read it through several times. Then go ahead and make several omelets. The process is akin to learning to ride a bike: You keep getting on and falling off until, finally, some vital connection is made between eye, mind, and body and suddenly you have acquired a new skill that you will never forget.

No matter how misshapen or otherwise imperfect they may be, your practice omelets can be put to other uses. A cold leftover omelet makes a good sandwich with mayonnaise, tomato, and lettuce. If you have several leftover omelets, dice them and use them as you would hard-cooked eggs to make egg salad; or cut them into cubes, fold into a cream sauce, and serve them on toast. Finally, you can use leftover omelets to make a delicious supper dish of Chinese Shredded Eggs (page 161).

NOTES ON OMELET PANS: A French omelet should be made in a moderately heavy-bottomed pan that measures 6 to 7 inches across the bottom and has sides 2 to 3 inches deep. To my mind, the most practical choice is an ordinary 10-inch skillet that is lined with a nonstick material. Special omelet pans of cast iron and heavy aluminum are available, but they must be used for omelet-making only, or else omelets subsequently made in the pans will stick. Special omelet pans must be seasoned before use; follow the manufacturer's instructions.

PRELIMINARIES

**Bring the eggs to room temperature.* Remove the eggs from the refrigerator at least 2 hours before using. (For breakfast omelets, leave the eggs out overnight.) This step is not optional but essential, especially if you are a beginner. Omelets made with cold eggs tend to cook unevenly, becoming rubbery on the outside while remaining watery and underdone within.

**Warm the oven.* If you are making more than 2 or 3 omelets and wish to serve them all at once, set your oven at the lowest temperature possible (under 150°F) and place a heat-proof serving platter in the oven. As you make each omelet, transfer it to the platter until ready to serve.

**Select an appropriate omelet pan according to the preceding notes.*

1 tablespoon butter
3 large eggs
Salt and pepper to taste

1. *Beating the eggs.* Using a fork, beat the eggs with a pinch each of salt and pepper until the whites and yolks are combined, about 40 to 50 strokes. Do not overbeat; the eggs must remain in a cohesive mass and must not become aerated if the omelet is to have the proper shape and texture.

2. *Heating the pan.* It is crucial that the pan be at the temperature where the butter is just beginning to brown, or around 325°F. If the pan is too hot, the eggs become shocked and the omelet will be rubbery; if the pan is not hot enough, the inside of the omelet will be heavy and overcooked. Place 1 tablespoon butter in the pan, set over moderately high heat, and swirl the pan to melt the butter. When the butter has stopped foaming and is on the verge of coloring—it will have a pronounced fragrance at this point—pour in the eggs.

3. *Stirring the eggs.* Holding the back of a fork parallel to, but not quite touching, the bottom of the pan, rapidly stir the eggs in a circular motion. Holding the handle of the pan in your other hand, at the same time briskly shake the pan back and forth over the flame. In about 10 seconds the eggs will become a broken-looking custard, creamy but no longer liquid, and you are ready to fill the omelet if you wish (but stick with plain omelets until you've mastered the technique).

4. *Forming the omelet.* Quickly gather up the egg mass with the back of the fork and push it over to the half of the pan opposite the handle. Tilt the pan at a 45° angle and continue pushing the omelet until half of it is resting on the wall of the pan. Hold the pan over the flame at the same angle for 3 or 4 seconds to solidify the omelet.

5. *Folding the omelet.* Rap the pan sharply against the burner (or, if you have an electric stove with a damageable heating element, against the bottom of a cast-iron skillet that you have set nearby). Now give the pan a quick upward flip, as though you were flipping a pancake. This should cause the half of the omelet that is resting against the wall of the pan to detach itself and to fold over the other half of the omelet. If it refuses to fold over, loosen the omelet with a fork and fold it in half.

6. *Browning the omelet.* Holding the pan nearly perpendicular to the burner, push the folded omelet against the wall of the pan with the back of the fork. The seam side of the omelet should be facing you. The other side, which will be the top when the omelet is served, should be resting against the wall of the pan. Hold the pan in this position for a few seconds to brown the top of the omelet lightly.

7. *Turning the omelet onto a plate.* In one quick movement, invert the pan over a plate or serving platter while, at the same time, giving the pan a sharp jerk to the side. The omelet should fall onto the plate seam-side down, with its brown top showing. You may rub the top of the omelet with 1 or 2 teaspoons of soft butter, or slit the omelet lengthwise and ladle on a filling. (If you are preparing additional omelets and are not serving them immediately, set each one in a warm oven and butter or fill it just before bringing it to the table.)

Holding the fork parallel to, but not touching, the bottom of the pan, rapidly stir the eggs in a circular motion. At the same time, briskly shake the pan back and forth over the flame.

Tilt the pan at a 45° angle and push the omelet until half of it is resting on the wall of the pan.

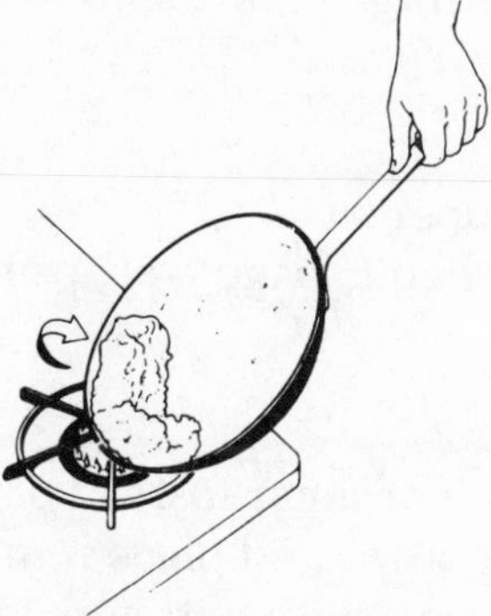

To fold the omelet, rap the pan sharply against the burner, give the pan a quick upward flip, then . . .

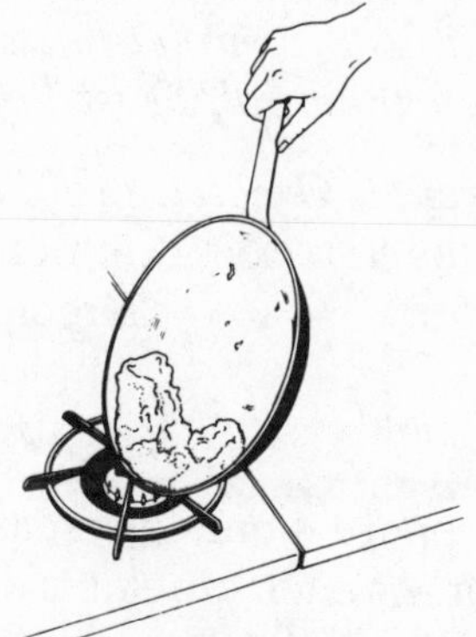

Hold the pan nearly perpendicular to the burner for a few seconds to brown the top of the omelet.

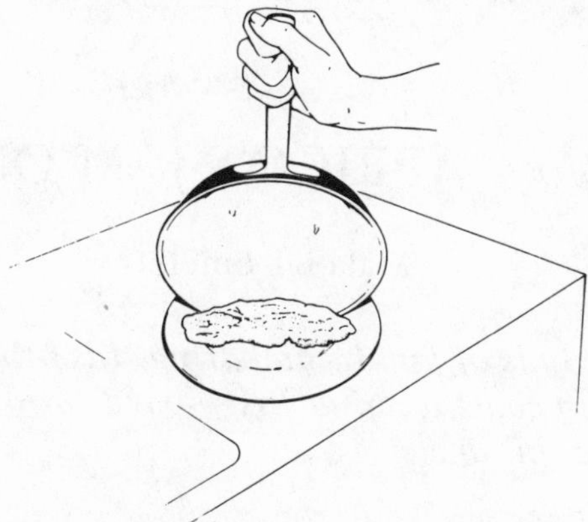

Invert the pan over a plate or serving platter, giving it a sharp jerk to the side as you do so.

To make additional omelets, remove the pan from the heat to cool. Beat 3 eggs, add fresh butter to the cooled skillet, and begin again. (If the butter sizzles and colors rapidly when added to the pan, the pan is still too hot. Wipe out the burnt butter, let the pan cool a little longer, and try again.)

Variation: APPLE OMELET

Makes 4 omelets

❦ *Half sweet and half savory, an apple omelet is just about the perfect brunch dish. If you are a skilled omelet-maker, you can stuff the omelets with the apple mixture before forming them (step 3 of the Master Recipe), but it is less anxiety-provoking to complete the omelets without the filling, then to slit them and ladle on the apples just before serving.*

French Omelet; prepare 4 omelets
SUBSTITUTE: A pinch sugar for salt and pepper
ADD: ½ recipe Sautéed, Flambéed Fruit, page 871, using apples, page 872
¼ cup confectioner's sugar

Prepare 4 omelets, seasoning each with a pinch of sugar instead of salt and pepper. As each omelet is done set it on a serving platter and place it in a warm oven. When all the omelets are ready, slit them lengthwise with a sharp knife, cutting to within ½ inch of the ends and bottom. Fill the slits with the apple mixture and dust the omelets heavily with confectioner's sugar. If you wish, very briefly place the omelets about 1 inch under a hot broiler to melt and lightly caramelize the sugar. Be careful, though, not to overheat the omelets, or they will toughen.

Variation: APRICOT JAM OMELET

Makes 1 omelet

❦ *You can use other kinds of jam in preparing this brunch or dessert omelet—cherry and strawberry come to mind first—but I think apricot jam makes the richest and most elegant omelet.*

French Omelet
SUBSTITUTE: 1 teaspoon sugar for salt and pepper
ADD: 2 to 3 tablespoons apricot jam
Confectioner's sugar in a sieve or shaker

Beat the eggs with the sugar instead of salt and pepper and proceed according to the Master Recipe, dotting the omelet with apricot jam just before forming it (end of step 3). Turn the omelet onto a plate and dust with confectioner's sugar.

Variation: CHEESE OMELET

French Omelet

ADD: 3 to 4 tablespoons shredded Swiss or Cheddar or freshly grated Parmesan cheese (about 1 ounce)

Proceed according to the Master Recipe, sprinkling the omelet with cheese just before forming it (end of step 3).

Variation: CHICKEN LIVER OMELET

Makes 4 omelets

French Omelet; prepare 4 omelets
½ recipe Sherried Sautéed Chicken Livers, page 399

Prepare 4 omelets, removing each to a warm oven as it is done. When all the omelets are ready, slit them lengthwise with a sharp knife, cutting to within ½ inch of the ends and bottom. Fill the slits with the chicken livers and their sauce.

Variation: CREAMED CHICKEN AND MUSHROOM OMELET

Makes 4 omelets

❦ *This takes the omelet about as far as it can go.*

Mushroom Cream Sauce, page 43
1 cup (about 8 ounces) boneless, skinless cooked white meat of chicken, cut in ¼-inch shreds
French Omelet; prepare 4 omelets
¼ cup (about 1 ounce) freshly grated Parmesan cheese

Fold 1 cup of the sauce into the chicken and set over low flame to keep warm. Prepare 4 omelets, removing each to a warm oven as it is done. When the omelets are ready, slit them lengthwise with a sharp knife, cutting to within

½ inch of the ends and bottom. Fill slits with the creamed mixture. Cover the tops of the omelets with the remaining cream sauce, sprinkle with Parmesan cheese, and place about 4 inches beneath a hot broiler for a minute or so, just long enough to brown lightly. Be careful, though, not to overheat the omelets or they will toughen. Serve immediately.

Variation: PARSLEY-CHIVE OMELET

Makes 1 omelet

French Omelet

ADD: 1 tablespoon *each* finely chopped fresh parsley and snipped chives

Beat the herbs with the eggs, salt, and pepper and proceed with the master recipe.

Variation: SPANISH OMELET

Makes 4 omelets

❦ *Serve this classic dish with French or Italian bread.*

French Omelet*; prepare 4 omelets through step 4*
⅓ cup olive oil
1 large boiling potato, peeled and diced (about 1 cup)
½ cup thinly sliced onion
½ cup diced green bell pepper
⅔ cup peeled, seeded, diced tomatoes, fresh or canned (see page 607)
½ teaspoon mashed, pressed, or very finely minced garlic
¼ teaspoon salt
¼ teaspoon pepper, preferably freshly ground
Chopped fresh parsley (optional)

In a heavy 10-inch skillet, heat the olive oil until fragrant, then add the potatoes, onion, and green pepper and sauté over moderate heat, stirring frequently, until the vegetables are tender and just beginning to brown. Stir in the tomatoes, garlic, salt, and pepper, raise heat to moderately high, and, stirring constantly, cook until all liquid from the tomatoes has evaporated. Remove from heat and set aside.

Prepare each omelet only through step 4 of the Master Recipe; push the unfolded omelet out of the skillet and onto a serving platter or plate. Place cooked omelets in a warm oven while you prepare the rest. When all the omelets are done, cover them with the vegetable mixture and, if you wish, sprinkle with chopped fresh parsley.

Rescue Recipe: CHINESE SHREDDED EGGS

2 servings

❦ *A botched omelet can be wrapped in plastic and kept in the refrigerator for several days before being used in this recipe.*

2 tablespoons peanut or vegetable oil
4 small slices fresh ginger, peeled
½ cup chicken stock, page 26, or canned broth
1 tablespoon soy sauce
2 teaspoons cornstarch
⅛ teaspoon salt
½ cup raw or cooked pork cut into ⅛-inch shreds (4 to 5 ounces)
2 to 4 tablespoons chopped green bell pepper
3 medium scallions, including tender green parts, chopped
1 cup fresh or canned bean sprouts, rinsed and well drained
French omelet, shredded

Heat the oil in a wok or 10-inch skillet until it shimmers. Add the ginger and sauté for 3 minutes, stirring occasionally. In the meantime, combine the chicken broth, soy sauce, cornstarch, and salt in a small bowl and stir to blend thoroughly. Set broth mixture aside.

Remove ginger from oil and discard. Add pork to wok and stir-fry over high heat for 1 minute if cooked (or for 3 minutes if raw, or until stiffened and lightly browned). Add green pepper and stir-fry 2 minutes longer. Add scallions and cook for 30 seconds, then add bean sprouts and shredded omelet and cook, stirring constantly, until sprouts and egg are thoroughly heated.

Stir up broth mixture and pour it into wok. Heat, stirring constantly, until sauce is thick and translucent, about 30 seconds. Serve at once, accompanied by rice.

❦

MASTER RECIPE

Ham and Swiss Quiche

❦ *Although it is nothing more than a savory custard pie, a skillfully made quiche is a handsome sight indeed. Accompanied by a tossed salad and a chilled white wine, it is a delicious and elegant offering for brunch or lunch.*

SPECIAL CRUST NOTES: The downfall of many quiches is a soggy crust. To avoid this disaster, prepare quiche with a *fully baked,* rather than a partially baked, butter pie-crust shell. The baked shell will not burn when returned to the oven with the quiche filling because the baking time for quiche is relatively short—only 25 to 30 minutes. Be sure to brush the inside of the baked pie shell with beaten egg yolks as directed in the recipe. The egg glaze acts as a waterproofing agent that prevents the crust from becoming soggy.

The crispest-crusted and most authentic-looking quiches are those made in a French tart shell.

4 to 6 servings

PRELIMINARIES

1. Prepare a fully baked, egg-glazed 9-inch pie shell, page 753, or tart shell, page 758.
2. Bring all ingredients to room temperature. This is essential; if the ingredients are chilled, the filling will be slow to set and the crust may burn or become soggy during baking.
3. Set rack in lower-middle level of oven.
4. Preheat oven to 375°F 20 minutes before baking.

1 cup (about 8 ounces) boiled or baked ham cut into ¼-inch cubes
¾ cup shredded Swiss cheese (about 3 ounces)
3 large eggs
1 cup heavy cream
2 teaspoons finely grated onion
⅛ teaspoon nutmeg, preferably freshly grated
½ teaspoon salt
¼ teaspoon pepper, preferably white and freshly ground

Distribute the ham and cheese evenly over bottom of pie or tart shell. Beat all remaining ingredients in a 3-quart mixing bowl until thoroughly combined.

If using a pie shell, pour enough of the egg mixture into the shell to reach to within 1/4 inch of the rim, set the quiche on a baking sheet, and place in the preheated oven. (If using a tart shell, place the baking sheet containing the shell on the pulled-out rack of the preheated oven. Ladle in as much of the egg mixture as the shell will hold. (If a part of the shell threatens to give away, stop.) Then sprinkle on the ham and cheese. Carefully slide in the oven rack. Do not be alarmed if the shell leaks a bit when it first goes into the oven; the filling will soon begin to set and the leaking will stop.) Bake the quiche for 25 to 30 minutes, or until the sides have puffed and the center quivers only slightly when lightly shaken. A knife inserted into the center should come out nearly clean with just a few small curds adhering to it. Do not overbake the quiche or it may curdle and turn watery.

If you are serving the quiche hot, bring it to the table as soon as it is baked so that everyone can admire its puffy top, but wait a few minutes before cutting it to give the filling a chance to firm up a bit. You may also serve the quiche at room temperature or chilled.

AHEAD OF TIME: You can prepare the component parts of the quiche—the baked pie shell, the diced ham and shredded cheese, the egg filling—a day or so ahead. Refrigerate the perishable items, and then assemble and bake the quiche just before serving. Remember to bring the ingredients to room temperature before baking. You may also wrap a fully baked and cooled quiche in foil and store it in the refrigerator for several days or in the freezer for several months. To reheat, place the uncovered quiche (thawed, if previously frozen) in a 350°F oven for about 15 minutes.

Variation: CHEDDAR AND JALAPEÑO QUICHE

4 to 6 servings

Ham and Swiss Quiche

SUBSTITUTE: Two (4-ounce) cans jalapeño peppers, drained and chopped, for ham
Cheddar cheese for Swiss

Distribute peppers and Cheddar cheese over the bottom of the pastry shell and proceed according to the Master Recipe.

Variation: CHICKEN OR TURKEY QUICHE

4 to 6 servings

Ham and Swiss Quiche

SUBSTITUTE: 1 cup cooked chicken or turkey cut into ¼-inch cubes for ham

ADD: 1 teaspoon dried tarragon

Proceed according to the Master Recipe, substituting poultry for ham and adding tarragon to the egg/cream mixture.

Variation: CRAB OR LOBSTER QUICHE

4 to 6 servings

Ham and Swiss Quiche

SUBSTITUTE: 8 ounces crab or lobster, cooked fresh or canned, for ham

1 tablespoon medium-dry sherry, preferably Manzanilla, for nutmeg

If you are using canned shellfish, drain it thoroughly and pick over to remove any cartilage or shell bits. Cut fresh crab or lobster into ¼-inch cubes. You should end up with about 1 cup. Distribute shellfish over bottom of pastry shell and proceed with the Master Recipe, flavoring the quiche filling with Sherry instead of nutmeg.

Variation: CLASSIC QUICHE LORRAINE

4 to 6 servings

❦ *Classic quiche Lorraine is made with lightly browned slab bacon and contains no cheese. You might expect it to taste bland, but the flavor is subtly rich and delicious.*

Ham and Swiss Quiche

SUBSTITUTE: 8 ounces slab bacon, preferably a mild, unsweetened type, for ham

OMIT: Cheese

Cut the bacon into strips ½ inch long and ¼ inch wide and sauté slowly in a skillet, until lightly browned but not yet crisp. Using a slotted spoon, remove bacon from skillet and distribute evenly over bottom of pastry shell. Proceed with the Master Recipe, omitting Swiss cheese.

Variation: MUSHROOM QUICHE

4 to 6 servings

Ham and Swiss Quiche

ADD: 2 tablespoons butter

SUBSTITUTE: 8 ounces mushrooms, coarsely chopped (about 2 cups) for ham

Melt the butter in a 10-inch skillet, add the mushrooms, and toss to coat with butter. Stirring frequently, sauté the mushrooms over moderate heat for about 10 minutes, or until all their liquid has evaporated and they have started to brown. Distribute the mushrooms over bottom of pastry shell, cover with Swiss cheese, and proceed according to the Master Recipe.

Variation: HAM, BLEU CHEESE AND PARSLEY QUICHE

4 to 6 servings

Ham and Swiss Quiche

SUBSTITUTE: ½ cup (about 2 ounces) crumbled bleu cheese for Swiss cheese

ADD: ¼ cup minced fresh parsley

Substitute bleu cheese for Swiss, beat parsley into the egg mixture, and proceed according to the Master Recipe.

Variation: QUICHE MOIRA (ONION AND CHEESE QUICHE)

4 to 6 servings

Ham and Swiss Quiche

ADD: 3 tablespoons butter

SUBSTITUTE: 2 cups thinly sliced onions for ham

Melt the butter in a heavy-bottomed skillet over fairly low heat. Add the onions, toss to coat with butter, and cook slowly for about 20 minutes, stirring frequently. The onions should be very tender but not mushy and should not brown at all during cooking. Scatter cooked onions over bottom of pastry shell, cover with Swiss cheese, and proceed according to the Master Recipe.

Variation: SALMON QUICHE

4 to 6 servings

❦ *Other cooked or canned fish, including tuna, may be substituted for the salmon here.*

Ham and Swiss Quiche

SUBSTITUTE: 7 ounces cooked or canned salmon for ham

ADD: 1 tablespoon fresh lemon juice

If you are using canned salmon, drain it thoroughly and pick over to remove bits of skin and bone. Remove any small bones from freshly cooked salmon and flake with a fork. You will have about 1 cup. Place salmon in a bowl, sprinkle with lemon juice, and toss lightly with a fork, breaking up the fish as little as possible. Distribute the salmon and Swiss cheese over bottom of pastry shell and proceed with the Master Recipe.

Variation: SHRIMP-CHILI QUICHE

4 to 6 servings

❦ *This piquant and very American-tasting quiche is particularly well suited to being cut into small pieces and served as an hors d'oeuvre with cocktails.*

Ham and Swiss Quiche

SUBSTITUTE: 1 cup chopped cooked shrimp for ham
Cheddar cheese for Swiss cheese

ADD: 1 tablespoon tomato paste
1 teaspoon chili powder
½ teaspoon hot pepper sauce

Distribute the chopped shrimp and shredded Cheddar cheese over bottom of pastry shell. Prepare the filling, adding tomato paste, chili powder, and hot pepper sauce. Proceed according to the Master Recipe.

Variation: SPINACH QUICHE

4 to 6 servings

Ham and Swiss Quiche
SUBSTITUTE: ½ recipe Steamed Spinach, page 590, squeezed dry and finely chopped (about 1 cup), for ham
ADD: 1 tablespoon fresh lemon juice

Toss the spinach with the lemon juice. Distribute the spinach and Swiss cheese evenly over bottom of pastry shell, and proceed according to the Master Recipe.

Variation: ZUCCHINI QUICHE

4 to 6 servings

Ham and Swiss Quiche
SUBSTITUTE: ¾ pound zucchini (2 to 3 small) for ham
ADD: 3 tablespoons butter

Wash the zucchini thoroughly, trim ends, and shred using coarse holes of a grater or in a food processor fitted with the shredding blade. A handful at a time, firmly squeeze the zucchini to press out as much of its juice as possible. Measure out 1½ lightly packed cups. Melt the butter in a 10-inch skillet, add the zucchini, and cook over moderately high heat, tossing frequently, for 5 to 7 minutes, or until it is tender but not brown. Distribute the cooked zucchini evenly over bottom of pastry shell, sprinkle with the Swiss cheese, and proceed according to the Master Recipe.

Variation: MUSHROOM, SPINACH, OR ZUCCHINI TIMBALE

4 main course or 6 to 8 side-dish servings

❦*A timbale is simply a quiche filling that is baked in a dish or an individual-serving custard cup rather than a pastry shell. It may be presented as the main offering of a brunch or light lunch—in which case it is accompanied by tomato sauce or hollandaise—but is more usually served as a side dish with poultry, meat, or fish.*

PRELIMINARIES

1. Place rack in the center of oven.
2. Preheat oven to 375°F 20 minutes before baking.
3. Select either a single large mold with a capacity of 5 to 6 cups—this can be a ring mold, a soufflé dish, or an aluminum or glass cake pan—or 4 to 8 individual molds. Butter the mold(s) generously (you will need 1 tablespoon butter for a large mold, 2 to 3 tablespoons for individual molds).

Filling for Mushroom Quiche, page 165, Spinach Quiche, page 167, or Zucchini Quiche, page 167

2 cups Tomato Sauce, preferably homemade, page 183, or 1 cup Hollandaise Sauce, page 46

Prepare a quiche filling, combining both the solid ingredients (cheese, vegetables) and the liquid ingredients in a blender or food processor. Puree thoroughly. Ladle the custard into the prepared mold(s).

Set the mold(s) in a roasting pan and place on the pulled-out rack of preheated oven. Add enough boiling water to the roasting pan to come halfway up the sides of the custard. Bake a single large timbale for 35 to 50 minutes (a deep mold will require a long baking time, a shallow mold a shorter one); bake individual molds 20 to 25 minutes. The custard is done when a knife inserted in the center comes out almost clean, with just a tiny curd or two of custard adhering to it. Allow a large timbale to stand 10 to 15 minutes, small timbales about 5 minutes, to firm up. Run a knife around the edge and invert the custard onto a platter. Surround with a bit of the sauce that you are serving, and pass the rest of the sauce separately.

ABOUT SOUFFLÉS

A lot of people are frightened by soufflés. Part of their anxiety-inducing mystique has to do with the fact that they are French and, therefore, fancy in origin and pedigree. Furthermore, many cooks think of soufflés as being fantastically temperamental creations that are loath to rise in the oven and, once risen, malevolently eager to collapse into a shriveled wad. (One friend even asked me, in all seriousness, what precautions I recommended taking against the possibility that a soufflé might explode during baking!) In truth, the reputation with which soufflés are burdened is ill-deserved. Soufflés are not all that tricky to put together—all one really has to know is how to beat and fold egg whites properly—and most of them can be made from scratch in less than an hour, using the most commonplace ingredients. Best of all, soufflés are *fun:*

fun to play around with (one Master Recipe leads to a host of great variations), fun to make, fun to watch puff up in the oven (if your oven has a window), and fun to serve—as a first course, main course, or dessert—to delighted guests.

If you are new to soufflé making or if the prospect of making one makes you nervous, read through the following notes before embarking on a soufflé recipe.

NOTES ON EGG WHITES: A soufflé consists of nothing more than stiffly beaten egg whites folded into a thick cream sauce. When the soufflé is baked, the air molecules trapped in the beaten egg whites expand, causing the soufflé to rise and puff to nearly twice its original size. Because the proper beating and folding of egg whites is such a crucially important technique, not only in the making of soufflés but also in the preparation of cakes, meringues, chiffon pies, and other familiar recipes, the matter is taken up in some detail in the beginning of this chapter on pages 133–36. It is a good idea to read through this material before preparing a soufflé.

SOUFFLÉ BAKING DISHES: Soufflés are usually baked in straight-sided white porcelain molds, with a capacity of either 6 cups (to serve 4) or 8 cups (to serve 6). Such molds, most of which are imported from France, are available in all cookware shops, and if you become a frequent soufflé-maker you will certainly want to own one. However, you can bake a soufflé in any baking dish with a 6-to-7-cup or 8-to-10-cup capacity. Just be sure that your substitute dish is deep rather than wide and shallow (about 6 inches across for a 4-serving soufflé; 8 inches across for a 6-serving soufflé) and that it has fairly straight sides. Soufflés do not rise well in shallow molds or in molds that have pronouncedly outward-sloping sides.

SOUFFLÉ PROPORTIONS: The master and variation recipes are all based on a soufflé baked in a 6-cup dish, serving 4. To prepare a 6-serving soufflé, simply increase all the ingredients except the extra egg white by half and bake the soufflé 10 to 15 minutes longer (40 to 45 minutes total in most cases). In case you forget this rule, the chart below gives the proportions of ingredients for medium and large cheese soufflés.

SERVING AND SAUCING SOUFFLÉS: Savory soufflés may be served as a first course, perhaps followed by something important, like a baked stuffed fish or a roast, or they may be the main dish of a brunch, lunch, or supper if accompanied or followed by a tossed salad. Except when served with a salad, savory soufflés may be accompanied by a sauce—a cream sauce, hollandaise or one of its variations, or a light tomato sauce. A dry white wine is appropriate with a savory soufflé.

RESCUING A FALLEN SOUFFLÉ: If you remove the soufflé from the oven before it is quite ready—or if it is ready before you and your guests are—you can serve the fallen soufflé by unmolding it, bottom-side up, onto a serving plate

	6-CUP SOUFFLE (4 SERVINGS)	8-CUP SOUFFLE (6 SERVINGS)
Butter	4 tablespoons	6 tablespoons
Flour	4 tablespoons	6 tablespoons
Milk	1 cup	1½ cups
Cheese	1 cup (about 4 ounces)	1½ cups (about 6 ounces)
Salt	½ teaspoon	¾ teaspoon
Pepper	⅛ teaspoon	heaping ⅛ teaspoon
Nutmeg	1 large pinch	1/16 teaspoon
Eggs	4	6
Egg Whites	1	1
Cream of Tartar	¼ teaspoon	heaping ¼ teaspoon
Baking Time	about 30 minutes	about 45 minutes

and cutting it into wedges like a pie. If you happen to have some tomato sauce or flavorful cream sauce on hand to ladle around the edges of the soufflé, so much the better.

TO PREPARE AHEAD OF TIME: Though soufflés must be served as soon as they come out of the oven, much of the preparation can be done in advance. The cream sauce base can be made as much as 2 days ahead of time, and the mold can be buttered and crumbed and the eggs separated into bowls several hours before the soufflé is baked. Thus you do not have to be locked away in the kitchen for long periods of time after the guests have arrived. A soufflé may also be assembled in its entirety and covered with an inverted bowl for an hour or so before being baked. Even a fully baked soufflé can be held—for a few minutes—in the oven while your guests rush to their seats.

NOTES ON FLAVORING VARIATIONS: I have chosen a cheese soufflé for the Master Recipe because it is perhaps the easiest of all soufflés to make and is certainly the kind most familiar to American cooks. But many flavorings other than cheese are possible. Various entree soufflés can be made by substituting puréed fish, meat, poultry, or vegetables for all or part of the cheese, and dessert soufflés are put together simply by flavoring the cream sauce base with sugar and a sweet (chocolate, fruit, coconut, and so on) instead of with cheese, salt, and pepper. You will find that soufflés containing a chopped or puréed solid food do not rise as high as those made with cheese. Dessert soufflés, on the other hand, tend to rise even higher.

RESCUING A SOUFFLÉ THAT NEVER ROSE: If the soufflé does not rise something probably went wrong with the beating or the folding of the egg whites, but don't despair, for it is still edible. Unmold the soufflé onto a cutting board and let it cool slightly. Prepare Cheese Sauce; if you have any cooked diced vegetables or ham on hand, fold them into the sauce. Butter a shallow glass or ceramic baking dish measuring about 9 inches by 7 inches and dust it with dry bread crumbs. Spoon a thin layer of the sauce mixture into the baking dish. Cut the soufflé into ½-inch-thick slices and arrange them on top of the sauce. Cover the soufflé slices with the remaining sauce and top with a few spoonfuls of dry bread crumbs or grated cheese and 1 tablespoon of butter, cut into bits. Place the dish about 4 or 5 inches under a hot broiler until the top has browned, 2 to 4 minutes. (If the assembled dish becomes cold, bake it for 15 to 20 minutes in a 400°F oven before browning the top under the broiler.)

MASTER RECIPE

Cheese Soufflé

4 servings

❦ *If your soufflé is to be flavorful, you must start with a flavorful cheese. Classic French soufflés are made either with Swiss cheese or with a mixture of Swiss and Parmesan. Avoid supermarket Swiss cheeses, which generally are underaged and have little taste, and use instead either imported Emmenthal or Gruyère, hard, dark-yellow Swiss cheeses with a sharp, nutlike flavor. Likewise, reject packaged grated Parmesan in favor of freshly grated aged Parmesan. Sharp Cheddar and bleu cheese also make excellent soufflés.*

PRELIMINARIES

1. Remove top rack in oven so that soufflé will have room to rise. Set rack in lower-middle level of oven.
2. Preheat oven to 375°F 20 minutes before baking.
3. Select a 6-cup porcelain soufflé dish or other tall, deep, straight-sided baking dish with a capacity of 6 to 7 cups (see page 169). Smear the inside of the mold with 1 tablespoon soft butter and dust with 2 tablespoons freshly grated Parmesan cheese or dry bread crumbs. Set the prepared mold on a shallow-rimmed baking sheet. *(If your baking dish is slightly too small for your soufflé, you can increase its capacity by tying a sheet of aluminum foil, folded in half lengthwise for extra*

strength, around the top. It should make a "collar" that extends about 3 inches above the rim of the dish. Butter and crumb the inside of the collar as well as the inside of the mold. Remove the collar just before serving.)

Step 1: Preparing The Cream Sauce Base

1 cup milk
4 tablespoons butter
¼ cup all-purpose flour (measure by scooping cup into large container of flour and sweeping off excess with the back of a knife)
1 cup lightly packed shredded Swiss cheese, shredded Cheddar, crumbled bleu cheese, or a mixture of half shredded Swiss and half freshly grated Parmesan (about 4 ounces)
½ teaspoon salt
⅛ teaspoon pepper, preferably freshly ground
A generous pinch of nutmeg, preferably freshly grated

Warm the milk over a low flame. Melt the butter in a heavy-bottomed 1½-quart saucepan, remove from heat, and stir in flour, using a wire whip, to make a smooth paste. Gradually add warmed milk, scraping the corners of the saucepan with a spatula or spoon to get up all of the flour-butter paste, and beat hard until the mixture is perfectly smooth. Place saucepan over moderate heat and, stirring constantly, bring the sauce to a full boil; it will be as thick as paste. Turn heat down to low and continue to cook the sauce, stirring, for 1 minute. Remove saucepan from heat, add cheese, and stir until it is melted and the sauce is smooth. Stir in the salt, pepper, and nutmeg.

Ahead of Time: At this point you may cover the top of the sauce directly with a sheet of plastic wrap to prevent a skin from forming, cover the saucepan, and set it aside at room temperature for several hours, or refrigerate it for 2 to 3 days before continuing with the recipe. *Be sure to warm the sauce over low heat until it is just on the verge of simmering before going on to the next step.*

Step 2: Beating Sauce Base into Egg Yolks; Folding in Beaten Egg Whites

4 large egg yolks
5 large egg whites
¼ teaspoon cream of tartar
A pinch of salt

Place the yolks in a 4-quart mixing bowl and gradually add the hot cream sauce base, beating steadily. Set aside.

Turn the egg whites into a grease-free 3-quart mixing bowl and beat at low speed with an electric mixer until foamy. Add cream of tartar and salt, increase speed to medium, and beat until the whites are frothy, opaque, and stiff enough to retain furrows made by the beaters. Turn mixer to high speed and beat the whites until they are thick and glossy and will stand firmly at the end of the uplifted beaters. Be careful not to overbeat the whites or they will become dry and grainy and will lose much of their puffing capability.

Stir a quarter of the beaten egg whites into the sauce base to lighten it. Scoop remaining egg whites on top of the sauce mixture and gently fold in with a rubber spatula. It should take less than half a minute to fold the batter; it is better to have a few patches of uncombined egg whites than to overfold and deflate the whites.

Turn the soufflé mixture into the prepared baking dish, gently smoothing the top with the spatula. The baking dish should be nearly full, but be sure to leave at least ½ inch space between the top of the soufflé and the rim of the dish; leave out a couple of spoonfuls of the soufflé mixture if necessary.

AHEAD OF TIME: At this point you may cover the soufflé with an inverted bowl and let it stand at room temperature for an hour or so before baking. If the soufflé sits for longer than an hour, the sauce base will begin to sink and the bottom part of the soufflé will be heavy and wet.

STEP 3: BAKING THE SOUFFLÉ

Place the soufflé, set on a baking sheet, in the preheated oven. Do not open the oven door for 20 minutes, and discourage wrestling or other jostling activities in the kitchen while the soufflé is rising. Bake the soufflé for a total of about 30 minutes, or until it has puffed 3 to 4 inches above the rim of the dish and a cake needle comes out nearly clean, with just a few curds of custard adhering to it, when inserted into the side of the puff and down toward the bottom of the baking dish. Another way to test for doneness is by nudging the side of the puff with your finger: if the puff holds firmly, rather than jiggling back and forth, the soufflé should be done. It is better to overbake a soufflé by a few minutes than to underbake it, because an underdone soufflé will collapse almost at once when removed from the oven. However, be sure not to leave a soufflé for too long in the oven once it is cooked through, or the egg white bubbles will turn brittle and break and the whole thing will begin to sag.

Bring the soufflé to the table and give everyone a few seconds to admire it. Then quickly divide the soufflé into serving portions by plunging a broad, shallow serving spoon through the top and straight down to the bottom. Make sure that each serving includes a piece of the frothy puff, a spoonful of the creamier bottom section, and a piece of the crusty outside layer. If you have a sauce, spoon a bit of it around—not over—each helping of soufflé, and pass the rest of the sauce separately.

Variation: CHICKEN SOUFFLÉ

4 servings

❦ *This delicious and substantial soufflé makes a terrific lunch dish, especially when served with hollandaise or béarnaise sauce.*

Cheese Soufflé

ADD: 1 cup (about 8 ounces) ground raw skinless chicken
2 teaspoons finely grated onion
1 teaspoon dried tarragon

DECREASE: Cheese to ½ cup (about 2 ounces) and use Swiss

In step 1, before adding the cheese, beat the ground chicken, grated onion, and tarragon into the finished cream sauce base, add the salt, pepper, and nutmeg, and then return the sauce base to moderate heat and simmer for 3 minutes, stirring, to cook the chicken. Remove the saucepan from heat and add the cheese, decreased by half, stirring until it melts. Proceed with the Master Recipe. This will not rise quite as high as a cheese soufflé.

Note: You may also make this soufflé with ground cooked chicken. Add 1 tablespoon chicken broth or white wine with the chicken and do not simmer as called for above.

Variation: CORN-BACON SOUFFLÉ

4 servings

❦ *This is a good soufflé for a winter supper.*

Cheese Soufflé

DECREASE: Cheese to ½ cup (about 2 ounces) and use Cheddar or Monterey Jack

ADD: 1 cup finely chopped cooked corn
5 slices bacon, crisply fried, drained, and crumbled
1 tablespoon finely grated onion

Proceed according to the Master Recipe, decreasing the cheese and adding the corn, crumbled bacon, and grated onion to the sauce base along with the salt, pepper, and nutmeg. This will not rise quite as high as a cheese soufflé.

Variation: HAM AND CHEESE SOUFFLÉ

4 servings

Cheese Soufflé

DECREASE: Cheese to 3/4 cup (about 3 ounces) and use Cheddar or Swiss

ADD: 3/4 cup (about 6 ounces) ground baked ham, preferably lightly smoked
2 teaspoons finely grated onion

Proceed according to the Master Recipe, decreasing the cheese and adding the ham and grated onion to the sauce base along with the salt, pepper, and nutmeg. This will not rise quite as high as a cheese soufflé.

Variation: PIZZA SOUFFLÉ

4 servings

❦*Accompany this blasphemous but fine-tasting soufflé with tomato sauce.*

Cheese Soufflé

USE: 1/2 cup *each* shredded Swiss cheese and freshly grated Parmesan

ADD: 3 tablespoons tomato paste
1 teaspoon dried basil
1 teaspoon mashed, pressed, or very finely minced garlic

Proceed according to the Master Recipe, using a mixture of Swiss and Parmesan for the cheese and adding tomato paste, oregano, and garlic to the sauce base with the salt, pepper, and nutmeg.

Variation: SEAFOOD SOUFFLÉ

4 servings

❦*I prefer to use mild-tasting, white-fleshed fish or shellfish in making a seafood soufflé, but dark-fleshed fish or canned salmon or tuna may also be used. See the note at the end of this recipe if you are using canned or cooked fish.*

A sauce is almost mandatory with a seafood soufflé. Choose a hollandaise-type sauce or any cream sauce that is compatible with the fish you have used in the soufflé.

Cheese Soufflé

ADD: 1 cup ground skinless fish
2 teaspoons finely grated onion
1 tablespoon fresh lemon juice

DECREASE: Cheese to ½ cup (about 2 ounces) and use Swiss

In Step 1, before adding the cheese, beat the ground fish, grated onion, and lemon juice into the finished cream sauce base, add salt, pepper, and nutmeg, and then return sauce base to moderate heat and simmer for 3 minutes, stirring, to cook the fish. Remove the saucepan from the heat and add the cheese, stirring until it melts. Proceed with the Master Recipe. This will not rise quite as high as a cheese soufflé.

Note: You may also use cooked or canned fish. Drain it thoroughly and pick over to remove any bones or bits of shell and cartilage. Grind the fish and beat it into the finished cream sauce, also adding 1 tablespoon fish broth, white wine, or clam juice. Do not simmer the sauce as is called for above.

Variation: SPINACH SOUFFLÉ

4 servings

Cheese Soufflé

DECREASE: Cheese to ¾ cup (about 3 ounces) and use shredded Swiss, freshly grated Parmesan, or a mixture of both

ADD: ½ recipe Steamed Spinach, page 590, squeezed dry and finely chopped (about 1 cup)
2 teaspoons finely grated onion

INCREASE: Nutmeg to ⅛ teaspoon

Proceed according to the Master Recipe, decreasing the cheese and adding chopped spinach and grated onion to the sauce base along with the salt, pepper, and ⅛ teaspoon nutmeg. This will not rise quite as high as a cheese soufflé.

THE ITALIAN INFLUENCE: PASTA and PIZZA

Being of partly Italian ancestry and having grown up eating Italian foods, I never suffered from the common misconception that Italian cooking consists solely of pizza and pasta dishes. However, when it comes to what might be termed Italian-*American* cuisine, pasta and pizza indisputably reign supreme. In this country, pasta noodles and pizza have traditionally been bought outside the home, but both are fun to make in your own kitchen, and the results are well worth the extra effort involved.

Because Italian cooking is simple and straightforward, the quality of the ingredients is important. Always use the freshest and best of everything—freshly grated aged Parmesan cheese, fresh herbs, fresh garlic, flavorful, fruity olive oil, and so on. This way, your Italian-American dish will taste of the sun and the earth, and no matter how idiosyncratic the recipe variation, it will be within the spirit of *la cucina Italiana.*

PASTA

PASTA SAUCES AND SHAPES: Tomato sauce, sometimes containing meat or shellfish, is the most familiar pasta sauce in this country, but there are many other possibilities. Pasta is delicious when sauced with a reduction of butter and cream to which various flavorings such as herbs, wine, vegetables, meat, or seafood can be added, and then tossed with a liberal quantity of freshly grated Parmesan cheese. Another possible dressing is pesto, a marvelous purée of basil, olive oil, cheese, garlic, and nuts. And then, of course, there are your own pasta sauce creations, which can be anything from butter or olive oil plus grated cheese to extra gravy left over from a pot roast or stew.

What kind of pasta to serve with which sauce is always a subjective issue, but there are some generally accepted guidelines. Thin spaghetti, including spaghettini and capelli d'angelo (angel hair pasta), needs a light, thin sauce—melted butter or olive oil, for example—that will coat individual strands without weighing them down and matting them together. Thicker spaghetti, fettuccine noodles, and regular egg noodles have more body and can take a heavier sauce such as a cream or tomato sauce. Sauces that contain small pieces of meat or seafood are best served with shell-shaped, tubular, or grooved macaroni such as penne, ziti, or fusilli, as the macaroni provides hollows or crevices that hold the sauce.

SERVING PASTA: In this country we most often eat pasta as a main course or perhaps as a side dish with fried clams or a veal cutlet. In Italy, however, pasta is most often served as a second course after the antipasto. If you serve pasta as a first course, be sure not to overload your guests' plates, or they will be too full to enjoy the main dish. A pound of pasta will serve 8 as a first course.

Pasta neither needs nor wants much in the way of accompaniments. Grated Parmesan cheese is often considered obligatory, but pasta dishes containing meat may be served without it and those with a seafood sauce become cloying if cheese is added. If you do use cheese, choose only freshly grated Parmesan of the best quality you can find. Though not essential, bread can be offered with either a first- or main-course pasta. Salad as an accompaniment can be problematic. Personally, I find the acidic taste of salad dressing incompatible with most pasta sauces, and so I usually serve salad either before or after the pasta. However, in this country, it is customary to serve a tossed green salad with pasta, especially when it has a tomato sauce, and it seems to me that one should do as one wishes.

A final note. Italians and many other pasta lovers insist that pasta should be served in broad, shallow soup plates, not on dinner plates, where it tends to slide and slosh about. In Italy, no one winds spaghetti against a soup spoon; the curve of the soup plate is used instead.

HOW TO COOK DRIED PASTA: For every pound of pasta, bring 1 gallon of water and 2 to 3 tablespoons salt (depending on the saltiness of the sauce) to a rapid boil in a 2-gallon pot. Stir in 1 tablespoon oil, which helps to prevent the pasta from sticking together, then add the pasta all at once. Do not break up long spaghetti that will not fit into the pot; simply push it down into the water as it softens.

Begin testing pasta for doneness when it has cooked about half as long as the instructions on the package direct. Pasta should be al dente, that is, firm and springy to the bite, but without any suggestion of rawness. As soon as it is done, drain the pasta in a large colander (do not rinse with cold water, or you will cool the pasta). Then turn it into a serving bowl or return to the thoroughly dried cooking pot. Toss with some grated cheese if cheese is being offered with the pasta; this helps the sauce to cling and gives the dish a nice creaminess. Add the sauce and toss again. Serve immediately.

LEFTOVER PASTA: Cooked, drained pasta that has not been sauced may be tossed with 2 or 3 tablespoons of oil and refrigerated, covered, for several days. To reheat, drop pasta into simmering water for a minute or less, just long enough to warm, then drain and serve at once. If the pasta was not overcooked to begin with, it should be quite acceptable reheated. Leftover sauced pasta can be reheated over gentle flame, though it will inevitably be soft and a bit matted together.

HOMEMADE EGG NOODLES

Initially, the most compelling reason to make pasta at home is that it is simply so much fun to do. As one gains practice, the pasta itself is justification enough for the effort that is required to produce it. Homemade pasta is fresh and eggy in taste, firmer to the bite and less pasty than the dried version. For those who have never had it before, it is a whole new eating experience.

USING MACHINES: In the recipe that follows the pasta is mixed, kneaded, rolled, and cut, completely by hand. If you prefer, however, these tasks may be done by machine. To mix and knead the dough in a food processor, place 1 cup plus 2 tablespoons flour and two large eggs in the container of the machine fitted with the metal blade and process for about 15 seconds or until the dough has gathered into a ball. Remove dough from machine, wrap in plastic, and let rest 5 minutes. If the dough is still sticky, knead in a tablespoon or so additional flour. To roll and cut the dough using a pasta machine, simply follow the manufacturer's instructions. The disadvantage of the pasta machines is that they roll and cut the dough so evenly that the finished product lacks the charm and character of hand-cut pasta.

THE PASTA ROLLING PIN: An ordinary household rolling pin is both too short and too thick to be of any use in rolling pasta dough. Use either an imported Italian pasta pin 1½ inches in diameter and 2½ feet long (see the illustration on page 181) or a perfectly straight, smooth, unvarnished hardwood pole of the same dimensions. Wash and dry the pin or pole before the first use and rub lightly with vegetable oil; thereafter it should only be wiped clean, never washed. To be sure that the pin remains unwarped, store it flat or hang it on the wall (the Italian pins have a little hole in the top for hanging on a hook).

THE ROLLING SURFACE: You need a work surface that is at least 2½ feet square. Unvarnished wood and rough-finished plastic work best. Smoother surfaces such as Plexiglas, marble, or linoleum result in a pasta that is slick and slippery when cooked, suggestive of the factory-made product.

Note: If you double this recipe, roll the dough out in two or more batches rather than trying to roll it all at once.

HAND-MADE EGG NOODLES

Makes about 8 ounces fresh pasta, or enough for 2 main-course or 4 first-course servings

1 cup plus 2 to 4 tablespoons unbleached all-purpose flour
2 large eggs, at room temperature

SPECIAL EQUIPMENT: a pasta rolling pin (see above)

STEP 1: PREPARING THE DOUGH: Place 1 cup plus 2 tablespoons flour on work surface, form a crater in the center, and break in eggs. Using a fork, gently beat eggs while gradually incorporating flour into them. Shore up the progressively thinning walls of the crater with your free hand, cupped, so that the egg does not run out. When mixture has become too stiff to beat, work in any unblended flour with your fingertips. Gather dough into a ball, scrape the work surface clean, and wash and dry your hands well (1).

Knead dough by pushing it out with the heel of your hand, then gathering it up and pushing it out again. The dough will be soft and sticky at first, but will soon firm up. If, after several minutes of kneading, the dough still sticks to your hand, slowly work in 1 to 2 tablespoons additional flour; take care, though, not to make the dough too stiff, or you will have trouble rolling it out. Knead the dough for 8 to 10 minutes altogether, or until it is smooth and very satiny. Wrap dough in plastic—it must be covered tightly or a ruinous crust will form—and let it rest for at least 15 minutes so that it will relax slightly and become easier to work with. If you wish, you may let the dough stand at room temperature for several hours before proceeding to the next step (2).

STEP 2: ROLLING OUT THE DOUGH: Lightly dust the work surface, the rolling pin, the dough, and your hands with flour. Rolling from the center to the edge, flatten the dough into a 10- to 12-inch circle, turning it 45° after each stroke (3).

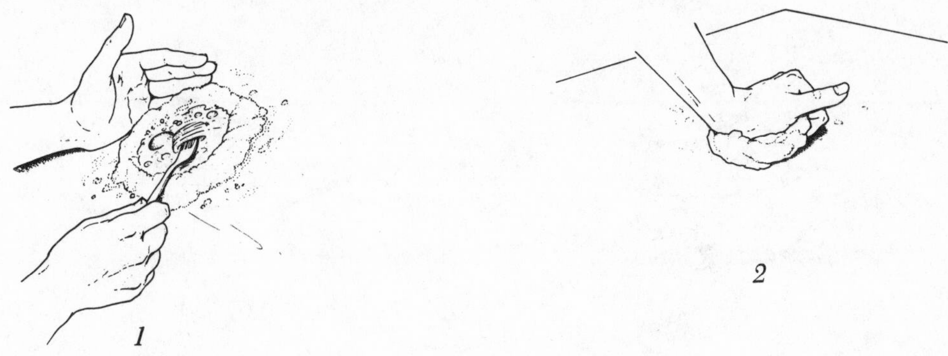

Sprinkle the work surface and the dough with additional flour as necessary to prevent sticking.

Pasta dough requires a unique rolling procedure in order to become sufficiently thin. Work as quickly as you can so that the dough does not dry out and become unmalleable.

Lightly flour the dough circle. Wrap the edge nearest you *one turn* around the pin. Place the palms of your hands, your fingers outspread, on top. Bearing down lightly, push your hands back and forth, so that the pin rolls from the heels of your hands to the tips of your fingers and back again; at the same time, gradually move your hands apart, toward the ends of the pin. You will feel the dough loosen from the pin as it thins out and elongates (4). Now, unwrap the dough from the pin, then wrap it around the pin again, but this time take up *two turns* instead of one. Again roll the dough backward and forward while stretching it sideways (5). Flour the dough well and repeat the procedure a third time, this time taking up *three turns* of the dough. Unwrap. Especially in the third rolling, you may find that the dough sticks to itself a bit when you try to unwrap it. Gently pull it apart, and patch any tears by pressing the edges of the dough together. Smooth out puckers and flatten creases by rolling with the pin. Don't worry about slight imperfections, as they are not noticeable once the pasta is cut and cooked.

Turn the sheet of dough 90° and repeat the entire process from the opposite side. If necessary, repeat the process one, two, or three additional times, taking up the dough from various angles. When you are through, the sheet of dough should be 24 to 28 inches in diameter. It will be nearly, but not quite, translucent and about as thick as the cover of a paperbound book. While it is possible to roll pasta dough too thin—very thin pasta tends to be tough—it is much worse to roll the dough too thick, for the cooked pasta will then be both tough and pasty. If you are a beginner, err on the side of thinness.

Let dough dry on the work surface for 10 to 20 minutes, or until it looks and feels like soft glove leather. Don't let it become too dry, or it will crack when you cut it.

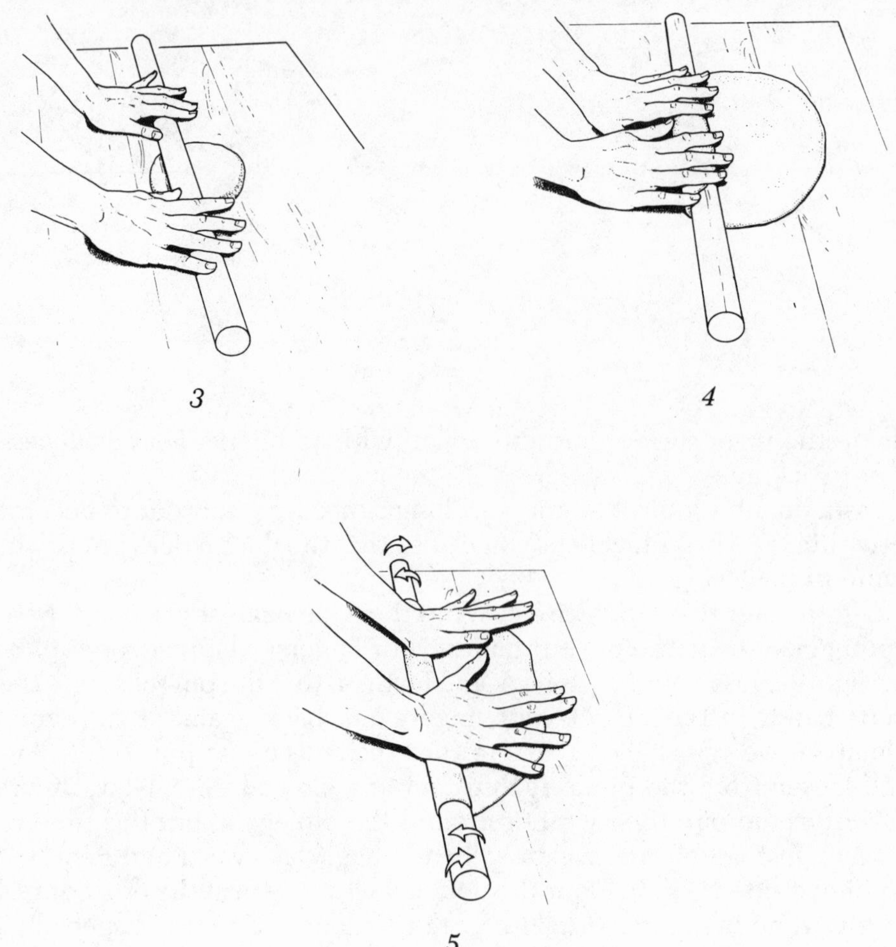

STEP 3: CUTTING AND COOKING THE PASTA: Lightly fold the dough into a flat roll about 3 inches wide. Using a very sharp heavy knife or a cleaver, cut the roll into slices about 1/4 inch wide, or a bit wider if you will be serving the pasta with a sauce that contains chunks of meat or vegetable (6). When the entire sheet has been cut, lightly shake the noodles to separate them. Sprinkle them with a touch of flour, toss lightly, and allow to dry for 5 minutes before cooking.

To cook fresh pasta, bring 3 quarts water, 1½ tablespoons salt, and 1 tablespoon oil to a rapid boil in a 6- to 8-quart pot. Drop in the pasta. As soon as the water returns to the boil, begin tasting the pasta at 10-second intervals; the pasta will be cooked al dente in just 1 to 3 minutes after the boil has returned. Do not overcook. Drain and sauce at once.

Note: If you wish to dry the pasta for later use, cut and shake out the noodles as outlined above, then wrap small batches of noodles around your fingers to form small "nests." Arrange nests on a floured tray and let dry, uncovered, for 2 days. Gently transfer nests to a roomy container, cover, and store for up to a month. Dried pasta will take longer to cook than fresh (7).

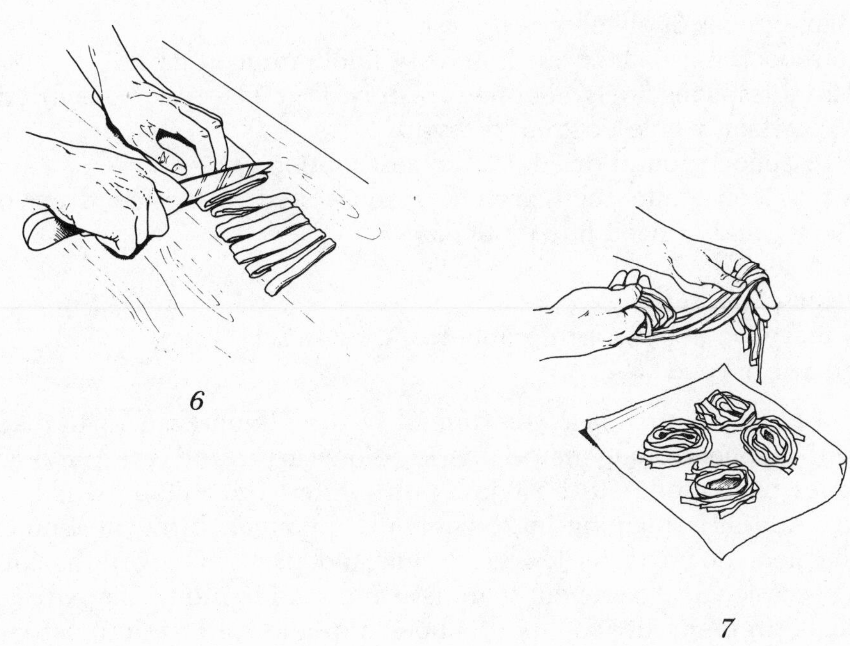

6

7

MASTER RECIPE

Tomato Sauce

Makes 2½ cups, or enough for 1 pound pasta

This is the classic Italian tomato sauce—long-simmered, rich, and very thick. Though it is customary to put the cooked sauce through a food mill to remove the tomato seeds and skins, it is much easier to simply purée it in a blender or food processor, and the results are quite satisfactory. Make this sauce up in big batches in the late summer, when tomatoes are in season, and freeze it in single-recipe-size storage containers. It will keep for up to a year!

⅓ cup olive oil
½ cup chopped onion
2 tablespoons finely chopped peeled carrot
2 tablespoons finely chopped celery
Either one 35- to 40-ounce can tomatoes, preferably Italian plum tomatoes, *or* 3 pounds very ripe fresh tomatoes, cored and cut into wedges
2 tablespoons tomato paste
2 tablespoons finely chopped fresh parsley
1 teaspoon mashed, pressed, or very finely minced garlic
1½ tablespoons finely chopped fresh basil or 1½ teaspoons dried
⅛ teaspoon whole or ground thyme
⅛ teaspoon ground dried orange zest (optional)
⅛ teaspoon fennel seed, ground or moistened with a few drops of water and minced fine (optional)
1 bay leaf
½ teaspoon salt
¼ teaspoon pepper, preferably freshly ground
Sugar if needed

Pour olive oil into a heavy-bottomed 2½- to 3-quart saucepan made of or lined with a noncorroding material. Add onion, carrot, and celery and sauté the vegetables over moderate heat just until wilted but not browned, about 3 minutes. Add all remaining ingredients except sugar, bring to simmer, then turn the heat down to its lowest setting and partially cover the saucepan. Stirring occasionally to prevent scorching and mashing tomatoes with the back of a spoon, simmer sauce for about 4 hours if made with fresh tomatoes, about 2 hours if made with canned tomatoes. (You may simmer the sauce even longer if you want it to be especially rich and thick.)

Purée in blender or food processor or force through a food mill. Taste for seasoning. Do *not* salt if you plan to add clams or sausage; otherwise, add up to ½ teaspoon additional salt plus any other seasoning that is needed, including a pinch or two of sugar if the sauce is bitter or acidic.

STORAGE: Placed in a lidded storage container, tomato sauce may be refrigerated for up to a week or frozen for a year.

Variation: MEAT SAUCE

Makes about 3 cups, or enough for 1 pound pasta

Tomato Sauce
1½ cups (about 12 ounces) ground beef, pork, or lamb, or crumbled sausage meat
Olive oil, if needed

Turn meat into a heavy-bottomed saucepan made of or lined with a noncorroding material and brown it lightly over moderately high heat, adding a tablespoon or two of olive oil if the meat seems dry. Pour off most of the fat, then add tomato sauce. Simmer for an hour or longer.

Variation: MEAT SAUCE BOLOGNESE

Makes about 2 cups, or enough for 1 pound pasta

❦ *This creamy tomato-meat sauce equals in delicacy and subtlety the fine sauces of French haute cuisine, and may in fact be an ancestor of béchamel sauce. Bolognese sauce may be served with either noodles or penne; try also substituting a double recipe for both the meat and cream sauce called for in the lasagna recipe on page 192.*

Tomato Sauce
4 tablespoons butter
¾ cup (about 6 ounces) finely ground lean veal
⅔ cup dry white wine
1 cup milk
½ cup Chicken Stock, page 26, or canned chicken broth
⅛ teaspoon nutmeg, preferably freshly grated

Melt 3 tablespoons of the butter in a heavy-bottomed saucepan made of or lined with a noncorroding material. Add veal and cook slowly, stirring, until it looks crumbly and cooked through; the veal must not brown. Add wine, raise the heat slightly, and simmer until wine has completely evaporated. Pour in milk and chicken stock and simmer until liquid is reduced to about ¾ cup of thick, creamy sauce. Add nutmeg and blend in tomato sauce. Simmer very, very slowly, stirring occasionally to prevent scorching, for about 3 hours. At the end of this time the veal will have nearly disintegrated and the sauce will have reduced to about 2 cups and be very thick. Just before serving, stir in remaining tablespoon butter.

Variation: RED CLAM SAUCE

Makes 2½ to 3 cups, or enough for 1 pound pasta

❦ *Serve this with linguine or very thin spaghetti.*

Tomato Sauce
½ cup bottled clam juice, clam liquor, or broth from steamed clams
½ cup chopped canned, cooked, or raw clams
1 teaspoon mashed, pressed, or very finely minced garlic
⅔ cup coarsely chopped fresh parsley, preferably flat-leaf Italian parsley

Bring tomato sauce to a simmer, add clam juice, and cook sauce down over moderately high heat until it returns to previous thickness. Stir in chopped clams and garlic and simmer sauce very slowly for a couple of minutes. Remove from heat, stir in parsley, and serve at once.

MASTER RECIPE

Pasta in Cream

4 main-course or 8 first-course servings

❦ *This or one of its variations is often served as a first course. Use either commercial noodles or your own homemade pasta.*

4 tablespoons butter
2 large unpeeled garlic cloves, crushed with the side of a knife
2 cups heavy cream
½ teaspoon salt
1 pound pasta, freshly cooked and hot
¾ to 1 cup (3 to 4 ounces) freshly grated Parmesan cheese
Pepper

Heat butter in 2-quart saucepan or 10-inch skillet (*not* cast iron) until melted and foamy. Add garlic and sauté slowly for several minutes, then remove garlic and discard. Add cream, raise heat to moderately high, and cook until sauce is reduced by about ¼ and is as thick as a cream soup. Stir in salt.

Return drained pasta to the dried cooking pot (or turn it into a bowl), add cheese, and toss. Add the simmering hot sauce and toss again until pasta is coated. Season to taste with grindings of fresh black pepper. Serve immediately, with additional grated Parmesan cheese on the side.

Variation: FETTUCCINE ALFREDO

4 main-course or 8 first-course servings

Pasta in Cream
OMIT: Garlic
USE: Fettuccine noodles or homemade noodles cut 1/8 inch wide

Follow the Master Recipe, omitting garlic and using fettuccine noodles as the pasta. Since fettuccine Alfredo is customarily very rich, you may also increase the butter by a tablespoon or two or add an additional ounce of cheese.

Variation: PASTA IN CREAM WITH GARLIC AND WALNUTS

4 main-course or 8 first-course servings

Pasta in Cream
SUBSTITUTE: 1 teaspoon mashed, pressed, or very finely minced garlic for the 2 crushed garlic cloves
ADD: 1 cup (4 ounces) finely chopped walnuts

Proceed according to the Master Recipe, ubstituting mashed, pressed, or very finely minced garlic for crushed garlic; do not strain garlic out of the sauce. Add chopped nuts along with completed cream sauce when tossing the pasta.

Variation: PASTA IN CREAM WITH GORGONZOLA, COGNAC, AND WALNUTS

4 main-course or 8 first-course servings

If you can't find Gorgonzola (you want the soft, creamy kind sometimes called "sweet"), substitute crumbled Roquefort or bleu cheese. Serve this on noodles—your own or store-bought—instead of spaghetti or macaroni.

Pasta in Cream

ADD: ⅓ cup Cognac or good brandy
SUBSTITUTE: 1 cup (4 ounces) finely diced Gorgonzola cheese for Parmesan cheese
ADD: ¾ cup (3 ounces) finely chopped walnuts

After removing garlic from saucepan or skillet, add Cognac or brandy, averting your face in case it should flame up. Boil liquor off almost entirely. Add cream and proceed with the Master Recipe, substituting Gorgonzola for Parmesan. Toss sauced pasta briefly with the nuts just before serving.

Variation: PASTA IN CREAM WITH BASIL

4 main-course or 8 first-course servings

Pasta in Cream

ADD: ½ cup finely chopped fresh basil

Proceed according to the Master Recipe, adding basil after the cream has reduced and thickened. Simmer about 1 minute.

Variation: PASTA PRIMAVERA

4 main-course or 8 first-course servings

❦ *This is a very simple, fresh-tasting version of the famous dish. The vegetable combination suggested here is one that appeals to me, but it may be altered to suit your own tastes. When I have not made my own pasta, medium-sized tubular macaroni is my choice here.*

Pasta in Cream

ADD: ⅔ cup peeled ½-inch asparagus pieces
⅔ cup green beans, cut into ½-inch pieces
⅔ cup small broccoli florets

After removing garlic from saucepan or skillet, add vegetables and cook over moderate heat, stirring frequently, for several minutes, or until they have begun to soften. Add cream and proceed according to the Master Recipe. By the time the cream has reduced and thickened, the vegetables will be tender.

Variation: PASTA IN CREAM WITH PROSCIUTTO OR PEPPERONI AND PEAS

4 main-course or 8 first-course servings

❦ *Use small shells or elbows as the pasta here if you have not made your own noodles.*

Pasta in Cream

ADD:	4 ounces prosciutto or pepperoni, very thinly sliced and cut into ½-inch pieces 1 cup peas—if frozen, uncooked; if fresh, cooked if large, raw if small and new
OMIT OR DECREASE:	Salt

Proceed according to the Master Recipe, adding meat and peas after the cream has reduced and thickened. Simmer gently for 2 minutes, taste, and add salt only if the sauce needs it. Do not simmer longer and do not make the sauce wait before serving, or the meat will toughen and the peas will shrivel.

Variation: PASTA IN CREAM WITH SAUSAGE

4 main-course or 8 first-course servings

❦ *If you do not make pasta from scratch, use either small shells or corkscrews, whose surfaces will attract and hold the small crumbles of meat.*

Pasta in Cream

ADD:	1½ cups (about 12 ounces) sweet or hot Italian sausage meat, squeezed out of casings and finely crumbled
OMIT OR DECREASE:	Salt

In the same skillet you will use to prepare the sauce, cook the sausage over moderate heat, stirring, just until it is cooked through; do not brown. Turn sausage into a sieve, set over a bowl, and let drain. Pour fat out of skillet, add butter, and proceed with Master Recipe, returning the sausage to the skillet when you add the cream. Taste the sauce before adding salt, as the sausage is likely to be salty.

Variation: PASTA IN CREAM WITH SEAFOOD

4 main-course or 8 first-course servings

❦ *It is traditional to serve seafood sauces on very narrow noodles—angel hair (very thin spaghetti) or linguine, for example. If you make your own pasta, cut the noodles about 1/8 inch wide.*

Pasta in Cream

ADD: ½ cup Fish Stock, page 27, or bottled clam juice
¼ cup dry white wine
About ¾ cup diced cooked lobster meat or crabmeat, or diced *raw* peeled shrimp

OMIT OR DECREASE: Salt

OMIT: Parmesan cheese

After removing garlic from the saucepan or skillet, add the clam juice and white wine and simmer until liquid is almost completely evaporated. Add cream, reduce and thicken, then stir in shellfish and simmer gently for just a minute or so. Taste and add salt only if needed. Do not add Parmesan cheese.

Variation: PASTA WITH VODKA AND HOT PEPPER

4 main-course or 8 first-course servings

❦ *The flavoring may sound peculiar, but it's quite delicious. Use either commercially prepared fettuccine or your own homemade noodles, cut 1/8 inch wide.*

Pasta in Cream

ADD: ¼ cup vodka (the better the vodka, the better the sauce)
¼ to ½ teaspoon crushed red pepper (½ teaspoon will make the sauce distinctly spicy)
2 tablespoons finely chopped fresh parsley, preferably flat-leaf Italian parsley
1 tablespoon tomato paste

After removing garlic from saucepan or skillet, add vodka and hot pepper flakes and simmer until the vodka is almost completely evaporated. Proceed according to the Master Recipe, stirring in parsley and tomato paste after the cream has reduced and thickened. Simmer for 1 minute.

PESTO

Makes 1½ to 2 cups, or enough for 1 pound pasta

❦ *Pesto, a delicious fresh basil sauce, is best known in this country as a sauce for pasta. However, pesto is also superb on broiled, steamed, and baked fish, and it turns boiled and baked vegetables, particularly potatoes, into sumptuous side dishes.*

Fresh basil is in season only in the summer, but you can enjoy pesto year-round. Buy quantities of fresh basil when it is plentiful and cheap. Following the proportions listed below, blend basil and olive oil to a thick paste, then freeze. When you want to have pesto, thaw the paste overnight in the refrigerator; just before serving add the remaining ingredients. Basil, by the way, is very easy to cultivate outdoors, and can also be grown successfully as a houseplant. If basil is unavailable, you can substitute parsley, preferably the flat-leaf Italian variety. The final result will be quite different, but still a delicious sauce in its own right.

2½ cups firmly packed fresh basil leaves
⅔ cup olive oil
½ cup (2 ounces) pine nuts or walnuts
1 teaspoon mashed, pressed, or very finely minced garlic
1 teaspoon fresh lemon juice
1 teaspoon salt
½ cup freshly grated Parmesan cheese
3 tablespoons soft butter

Combine basil, olive oil, pine nuts, garlic, lemon juice, and salt in blender or food processor and purée thoroughly, flicking machine on and off and scraping the sides of the container with a rubber spatula. The paste will be quite thick.

Turn the paste into a bowl and beat in first the cheese, then the butter. (The texture of the pesto is creamier if these ingredients are beaten in by hand than if they are added to the blender or processor.) Before tossing the pasta with pesto, thin the sauce with a tablespoon or two of hot pasta cooking water.

AHEAD OF TIME: Pesto is best when freshly made. However, it can be refrigerated for a day or so in a tightly covered container. Spoonfuls of leftover pesto can be frozen and used in soups or tomato sauces.

LASAGNA

6 to 8 servings

❦ *What? No ricotta? That is the reaction I often get from people when I give them my recipe for lasagna. In fact, lasagna is a much tastier, firmer, and better-textured dish when made with good meat sauce and a cream sauce rather than with plain tomato sauce and ricotta, and I urge you to suspend your skepticism and give this recipe a try. The Italians have been making lasagna this way for centuries. Ricotta did not enter the picture until the dish emigrated to this country.*

PRELIMINARIES

1. Set rack in upper third of oven.
2. Preheat oven to 425°F 20 minutes before baking.
3. Select an 8×14- or 10×12-inch baking dish between 2 and 3 inches deep. Oil the pan with olive oil.

12 ounces lasagna noodles
1 gallon water
2 tablespoons salt
1 tablespoon oil
Meat Sauce, page 185, preferably made with sausage
3 cups (1½ recipes) Basic Cream Sauce, page 34, made with milk and thick enough to coat a spoon heavily
3 cups (about 12 ounces) shredded mozzarella cheese
1 cup (about 4 ounces) freshly grated Parmesan cheese
2 tablespoons butter

Boil the lasagna noodles in 1 gallon water mixed with 2 tablespoons salt and 1 tablespoon oil. Begin testing for doneness several minutes before the minimum time given on the package. The noodles should be cooked just until they are no longer crunchy at the center; they must remain firm, or the baked lasagna will be mushy and pasty. Drain noodles in a colander and rinse with cold water. Pat dry with paper towels.

Spoon a thin layer of meat sauce into prepared baking dish. Add a layer of lasagna noodles, overlapping them slightly and folding them back at the ends if they are too long for the dish. Cover with half of the remaining meat sauce and ⅓ of the cream sauce, then sprinkle on half of the mozzarella and ⅓ cup Parmesan cheese. Repeat with a second layer of noodles, using up all the meat sauce and mozzarella. Top with a third and final layer of noodles. Completely cover with the remaining cream sauce, sprinkle with remaining ⅓ cup Parmesan, and dot with butter. Bake for about 25 minutes, or until the edges are bubbling and the top is lightly browned. Let lasagna rest for 10 minutes after removing from the oven so that it can firm up, then cut into squares and serve from the pan.

AHEAD OF TIME: The lasagna may be covered with foil and set aside at room temperature for several hours before baking. It can also be refrigerated for a day or so, though the pasta tends to soften and turn the dish pasty. Freezing has the same effect and is not advisable.

MASTER RECIPE

Cheese Pizza

Makes two 12-inch pizzas, serving 4 to 8

Pizza is tremendously fun to make at home, and there is nothing at all difficult about the procedure. The crust can be rolled out on a table or countertop using an ordinary rolling pin. And while an especially crispy crust can be obtained by baking pizza on special tiles or a pizza stone—both available at specialty cookware shops—you can get excellent results using an ordinary baking sheet.

This Master Recipe makes pizzas with a thin and crispy—rather than breadlike—crust and a creamy, piquant topping that consists of a thin layer of garlicky tomato sauce and lots of mozzarella cheese. Variations can be made by topping the pizzas with anything from anchovies and chilis to eggplant and lamb, to onions, anchovies, and oil-cured black olives. In this country we think of pizza as an informal meal, sometimes accompanied by a tossed green salad, but homemade pizza, which tends to be lighter than the restaurant variety, also makes a marvelous appetizer or first course.

PRELIMINARIES

1. Set a rack in the lowest level of the oven.
2. Preheat oven to 450°F 20 minutes before baking.
3. Have ready two large baking sheets that are rimless on the long sides.

1 cup tomato sauce, preferably homemade, page 183
1 teaspoon mashed, pressed, or very finely minced garlic
4 cups (1 pound) shredded mozzarella cheese
½ cup (about 2 ounces) freshly grated Parmesan cheese
⅓ cup olive oil
½ teaspoon oregano
¼ teaspoon salt
¼ teaspoon pepper, preferably freshly ground
The dough for Hard Rolls, page 654, prepared through Step 5

Combine tomato sauce and garlic in a 1-quart bowl and set aside. Toss cheeses with olive oil, oregano, salt, and pepper in a 3-quart bowl and set aside.

Divide dough in half and place one half in the refrigerator. On a lightly floured work surface roll remaining dough into a circle about 8 inches across. Place your closed fists underneath the dough and raise the dough to eye level. Jerking your arms lightly to twirl the dough, gently tug outward with your fists to stretch the dough thinly at the center while leaving the edges a bit thicker (1). When you're finished, the disk should be about 12 inches in diameter. Turn the dough onto an ungreased baking sheet and pinch and pat the edges to form a small rim (2). Repeat with the other half of the dough.

Cover both pizza crusts with a thin layer of tomato sauce and sprinkle evenly with the cheese mixture. Set the pizza whose crust you formed *last* in a cool place—in the refrigerator if the kitchen is warm—so that the crust will not begin to rise. Place the other pizza in the preheated oven and bake for 12 to 15 minutes, or until the crust is nicely browned and the cheese is melted and bubbly. Remove from the oven and serve at once; bake the second pizza immediately.

AHEAD OF TIME: The pizza dough can be made ahead and refrigerated or frozen; see the instructions on page 657. Both the sauce and the cheese mixture can be assembled several hours in advance and set aside at room temperature, covered.

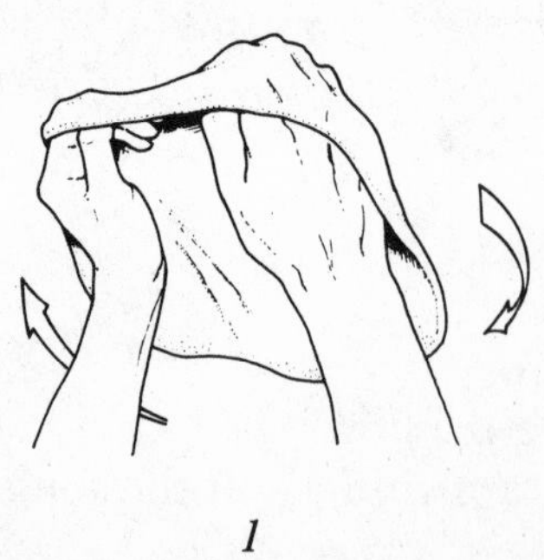
1

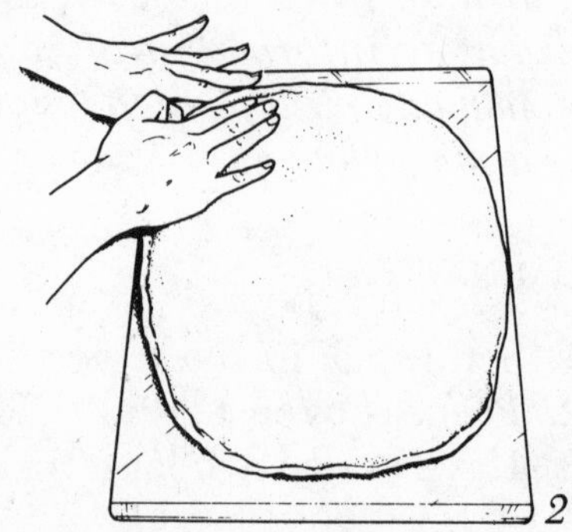
2

Variation: ANCHOVY PIZZA

Makes two 12-inch pizzas, serving 4 to 8

Cheese Pizza
ADD: 1 to 2 cans flat anchovy fillets, well drained

Arrange the anchovies over the pizzas after ladling on the tomato sauce; sprinkle with the cheese mixture.

Variation: ANCHOVY-JALAPEÑO PIZZA

Makes two 12-inch pizzas, serving 4 to 8

Cheese Pizza
ADD: 1 to 2 cans flat anchovy fillets, well drained
4 to 8 fresh or well-drained canned jalapeño peppers, seeded and cut lengthwise into very thin shreds

Arrange the anchovies and jalapeño peppers over the pizzas after ladling on the tomato sauce; sprinkle with the cheese mixture.

Variation: EGGPLANT PIZZA

Makes two 12-inch pizzas, serving 4 to 8

Cheese Pizza
ADD: Broiled Eggplant Slices, page 535

Cover pizza crusts with tomato sauce, arrange eggplant on top, and sprinkle with the cheese mixture.

Variation: "MOUSSAKA" PIZZA

Makes two 12-inch pizzas, serving 4 to 8

❦ *This is a spectacular treat.*

Cheese Pizza
ADD: Broiled Eggplant Slices, page 535
1 pound ground lamb

Crumble the ground lamb into a skillet, brown lightly, and drain off all the fat.

Cover the pizza dough with tomato sauce. Top first with the browned lamb, then with the eggplant, and finally with the cheese mixture.

Variation: MUSHROOM PIZZA

Makes two 12-inch pizzas, serving 4 to 8

Cheese Pizza

ADD: Sautéed Mushrooms, page 550; halve small mushrooms and quarter larger ones before cooking

Cover pizza crusts with tomato sauce, then add the mushrooms and sprinkle with the cheese mixture.

Variation: ONION PIZZA

Makes two 12-inch pizzas, serving 4 to 8

Cheese Pizza

ADD: 4 to 5 cups thinly sliced onions
6 tablespoons olive oil

In a heavy-bottomed skillet or large saucepan, cook the onions in olive oil over very low heat, stirring frequently, until they are dark yellow and very soft. This will take 15 to 20 minutes.

Cover pizza dough with tomato sauce, strew cooked onions on top, and sprinkle with the cheese mixture.

Variation: ONION-ANCHOVY-OLIVE PIZZA

Makes two 12-inch pizzas, serving 4 to 8

❦ *This marvelous combination of flavors is similar to that of the famous French pizza,* pissaladière. *This is particularly recommended as an appetizer or first course, though it is also good as a main course.*

Cheese Pizza

ADD: 4 cups thinly sliced onions
6 tablespoons olive oil
1 can flat anchovy fillets, well drained
⅔ cup oil-cured black olives, pitted and cut into slivers

In a heavy-bottomed skillet or large saucepan, cook the onions in olive oil over very low heat, stirring frequently, until they are dark yellow and very soft. This will take 15 to 20 minutes.

Cover pizza dough with tomato sauce. Strew the onions on top, arrange the anchovies in a spokelike fashion, and sprinkle with the slivers of olive and the cheese mixture from the Master Recipe.

Variation: PEPPER OR PEPPER-ANCHOVY PIZZA

Makes two 12-inch pizzas, serving 4 to 8

Cheese Pizza

ADD: 3 to 4 large green or red bell peppers
3 to 4 tablespoons olive oil
1 can flat anchovy fillets, well drained (optional)

If you wish, peel the peppers according to the instructions on page 570, then seed, remove the membranes, and cut into lengthwise slices ¾ inch wide. Sauté slowly with olive oil in a heavy skillet until fairly soft but still firm enough to hold their shape.

Cover pizza dough with tomato sauce, then with sautéed peppers and optional anchovies. Sprinkle on the cheese mixture.

Variation: PEPPERONI PIZZA

Makes two 12-inch pizzas, serving 4 to 8

Cheese Pizza

ADD: 6 to 8 ounces thinly sliced pepperoni

Arrange the pepperoni over the pizzas after covering with tomato sauce; sprinkle on the cheese mixture.

Variation: SAUSAGE PIZZA

Makes two 12-inch pizzas, serving 4 to 8

Cheese Pizza

ADD: 1 pound sweet or hot Italian sausage

Remove sausage from casings and crumble into a skillet. Cook until lightly browned, then drain off all fat.

Cover pizza crusts with tomato sauce, top with sausage, and sprinkle with the cheese mixture.

THE BASIC AMERICAN CASSEROLE

The classic American casserole is a simple mixture of cooked foods—meat, fish, poultry, eggs, pasta, vegetables—bound together with a flavorful cream sauce, covered with a topping of bread crumbs, grated cheese, and dots of butter, and baked until piping hot. The casserole's merits are almost too numerous to list. It is one of the quickest and simplest of all dishes to put together, and because it may be composed partially or entirely of leftovers, it is economical too. A casserole recipe may be doubled, tripled, quadrupled, and so on to feed a big gathering and because it may be assembled entirely in advance, your nerves remain calm when your guests arrive. Finally, a casserole can provide an opportunity for you to exercise your imagination and ingenuity to the fullest. A carefully prepared casserole, even one made with leftovers, can be a spectacularly good dish that appeals to practically everyone.

MASTER TECHNIQUE

Basic Casserole

4 to 6 servings

This Master Technique is to be used in conjunction with the Casserole Variation Chart that follows. Although the technique gives specific measurements and the chart lists specific ingredients for the making of casseroles, both measurements and ingredients may certainly be varied, depending on what you have on hand or what sounds good to you. Simply bear the following guidelines in mind:

- There should be a total of about 1 quart solid food and 2 to 2½ cups cream sauce.
- If your casserole is unusually heavy in pasta or rice, thin the sauce enough to make it slightly runny, as pasta and rice absorb moisture.
- Highly season any casserole that is skimpy on flavorful meat or vegetables or that is made with a plain cream sauce.
- If you are preparing the casserole from scratch, rather than using leftovers, slightly undercook all of the solid components. This way, the foods will be firm and full of character, rather than soft and mushy, once the casserole is baked.
- Casseroles are best baked in fairly shallow dishes, which promote rapid heating (thus avoiding overcooking and pastiness) and which have enough surface area for a generous topping of buttery crumbs.

PRELIMINARIES

1. Set the rack in upper-middle level of oven.
2. Preheat oven to 400°F 20 minutes before baking.
3. Select either an 8×2-inch square or a 9×2-inch round baking dish. Smear the inside of the dish with 2 tablespoons (¼ stick) soft butter and dust with 2 to 3 tablespoons bread crumbs or grated cheese, tapping out the excess.

1½ cups primary ingredient, cut into bite-size pieces: cooked meat, poultry, fish, or egg
1½ cups starch ingredient: cooked small pasta, rice, or cubed or sliced potatoes
1 cup chopped cooked vegetable
2 to 2½ cups cream sauce, thinned to serving consistency
Any of the following seasonings: Salt and pepper, preferably freshly ground; herbs and spices; or wine, fresh lemon juice, hot pepper sauce, or Worcestershire sauce
Either ½ cup Fine Fresh Bread Crumbs (see page 60) *or* ⅓ cup Fine Fresh Bread Crumbs and ¼ cup (1 ounce) freshly grated Parmesan cheese
2 tablespoons butter, cut into bits or thin pats

Combine the primary ingredient, starch ingredient, vegetable, and cream sauce in a 3-quart mixing bowl and fold gently together with a wooden spoon. Taste and adjust seasoning, folding in whatever flavors seem appropriate. It is better to overseason slightly than to underseason, as the heat of the oven tends to mute the casserole's flavor.

Turn casserole mixture into prepared baking dish. Gently smooth the top, and sprinkle evenly with crumbs or crumbs and cheese. Dot with butter. Bake the casserole for 25 to 30 minutes, or until top is richly browned and you can see juices bubbling around the edges of the dish. Serve promptly, as the casserole may dry out or become heavy and pasty if it sits too long.

AHEAD OF TIME: A casserole may be entirely assembled in advance, covered with aluminum foil, and held in the refrigerator for a day or so before being baked; add about 5 extra minutes to the baking time. It is better not to freeze a casserole before baking, but it can be done. Cover the dish with foil and protect with a plastic bag; freeze no longer than 2 months. Take the casserole directly from the freezer, remove the foil covering, and bake in a 350°F oven for 45 minutes to an hour.

CASSEROLE VARIATION CHART

	CUBED COOKED MEAT, POULTRY, FISH, OR EGG 1½ CUPS	COOKED PASTA, RICE, OR POTATO 1½ CUPS	CHOPPED COOKED VEGETABLE 1 CUP	CREAM SAUCE 2 TO 2½ CUPS
Chicken and olive casserole	Boned chicken	Elbow macaroni or rice	Green beans	California, page 36
Curried casserole	Chicken, pork, beef, or lamb	Rice	Broccoli or any other green vegetable	Curried, page 39
Day-after-Thanks-giving-casserole	Boned turkey	Rice or noodles	Spinach, green beans, and/or broccoli	Onion, page 43
Egg casserole	Sliced hard-cooked egg	Potatoes	Any green vegetable or mushrooms	Dilled or Parsleyed, page 41
Macaroni and cheese	—	Small elbow macaroni, 4 full cups	—	Cheese, page 37, using Cheddar, and almost runny
Macaroni and ham	Diced ham	Elbow macaroni or corkscrews	Broccoli or asparagus	Cheese, page 37, using Cheddar
New England fish casserole	Codfish or other firm white fish or salmon	Potatoes	Broccoli, green beans, or peas	Dilled or Parsleyed, page 41, using parsley
Party casserole with grapes	Veal, or boned duck or chicken	Rice	Mushrooms	Grape, page 39
Pork and caper casserole	Pork or ham	Potatoes or sweet potatoes	Green or wax beans	Caper, page 36
Shellfish casserole	Shelled lobster, crab, or shrimp	Rice	Peas or green beans	Sherried, page 44, or Lobster or Crab, page 42
Spaghetti casserole	Crumbled sausage or ground meat	Spaghetti	Bell peppers, eggplant, or mushrooms	Tomato-basil, page 45
Tuna-noodle casserole	Canned tuna, drained and flaked (two 7-ounce cans)	Noodles	Peas	Mushroom, page 43

FROM BURGERS TO PÂTÉS: GROUND MEAT

Traditionally, we Americans have tended to think of ground meat primarily in connection with informal dishes such as hamburgers and meat loaf. But in recent years, as European influences have pervaded our cooking, we have begun to use ground meat in more sophisticated ways. Reflecting this change, supermarkets now commonly stock ground veal, lamb, and sometimes pork, as well as ground beef. This chapter presents an eclectic collection of ground-meat recipes.

Food processor: The food processor will grind meat much more conveniently than an old fashioned hand-cranked grinder. Fit your processor with the metal chopping blade or with whatever blade the manufacturer recommends. Trim all gristle and much of the fat from the meat. Take care not to grind too finely, since pulverized meat tends to be crumbly and dry when cooked. Food processors vary in their efficiency, but as a general rule, assume that your processor will not need longer than 20 seconds to dispatch a moderate load of trimmed and diced poultry or meat, and it may take less time than that. Check on the meat every 5 seconds or so during processing, and use the pulse switch if your processor is equipped with one.

SOME TIPS ON HAMBURGERS

- Calculate the amount of meat to buy based on the appetites of the people you are serving. Four ounces of ground meat makes a small, child-size burger; 5 to 6 ounces makes a regular-size burger; 8 ounces of ground meat makes a jumbo burger.
- Use moderately lean ground beef, such as ground sirloin or lean ground chuck. If the meat is too lean, the burgers will be hard and dry; if too fatty, the burgers will shrink too much during cooking.
- Season the meat with about ½ teaspoon *each* salt and freshly ground pepper per pound of meat before shaping. You may also add a tablespoon or two of finely chopped onion or fresh parsley, a teaspoon of fresh lemon juice, or ½ teaspoon of Worcestershire sauce or hot pepper sauce per pound of meat.
- Do not overwork the meat or be too fussy about molding the burgers into a perfect circle, or you will compact the meat and make the burgers coarse and heavy.
- Burgers should be about ¾ inch thick. Thinner burgers dry out during cooking; thicker ones do not cook evenly.
- Fry rather than broil the burgers, as broiled burgers tend to dry out. Use a high-sided skillet so that grease does not spatter. An old-fashioned cast iron frying pan is ideal.
- Sprinkle the bottom of the skillet lightly with salt. (Do not add fat or oil.)
- Fry hamburgers over as high a heat as possible without causing the drippings to smoke. The pan should be hot enough to make drops of water "dance" before you add the burgers. Cook about 2 minutes on each side for rare, 2½ minutes for medium rare, and 3 to 4 minutes for medium to well done.
- *Never* bear down on burgers with a spatula during cooking. This compacts the meat and squeezes out the juices.
- To make cheeseburgers, after flipping the patties, top the cooked side with cheese—perhaps a good bleu cheese or Cheddar or Swiss. During the last minute or so of cooking, cover the skillet to help the cheese melt.

Burgers may be served on a bun or in the traditional European way, also called "chopped steak." To give burgers a continental flair, prepare a deglazing sauce, following the Master Recipe for sautéed beef steaks or one of the variation recipes on pages 412–16. Remember that you must use a skillet made of or lined with a metal that does not react with wine if you are preparing a deglazing sauce. Accompany with rice and a green vegetable such as asparagus or broccoli.

MOTHER'S MEAT LOAF, CIRCA 1958

8 servings

❦ *Sophisticated meat loaves that approach pâtés certainly have their place, but what I often crave is my mother's old-fashioned, fifties-style meat loaf, made with ground beef and flavored with such homey, simple things as onions, rolled oats, and ketchup. It is hearty, simple, savory—just plain good. Mashed potatoes are almost obligatory here; a green vegetable—steamed zucchini is very good—or a tossed salad should be offered as well. This meat loaf also makes terrific cold sandwiches.*

PRELIMINARIES

1. Set rack in the middle of oven.
2. Preheat oven to 350°F 20 minutes before baking.
3. Select an 8-cup loaf pan.

2½ pounds moderately lean ground beef (half ground chuck and half ground round is an ideal combination)
1½ cups minced onions
1 cup rolled oats
⅔ cup ketchup (preferably Heinz brand)
⅔ cup chopped fresh parsley
3 large eggs
1 teaspoon ground thyme
1 teaspoon salt
½ teaspoon pepper, preferably freshly ground

Mix all ingredients together with your hands in a 4-quart bowl. Pat into loaf pan and bake about 1½ hours, basting the top occasionally with the fat collecting in the pan. The meat loaf is done when it feels firm to the touch and has shrunk noticeably from the sides of the pan; the internal temperature should be around 165°F on a meat thermometer. Remove from the oven, pour most of the fat out of the pan, and allow to stand at room temperature for about 15 minutes before slicing.

❦

STEAK TARTARE

4 to 6 main-course or 8 first-course servings

❦ *Steak tartare is raw ground beef subtly flavored with onions, capers, chopped fresh parsley, and lemon juice.*

The beef tenderloin, trimmed of all fat and filament, is the only acceptable cut for this dish. Buy the meat from a first-rate butcher, as supermarket meat too frequently is stale and tastes of its wrappings.

Steak tartare should be light, almost fluffy, in texture—never heavy or compacted. In the past, it was frequently recommended that the meat be chopped very finely with a knife in order to achieve this effect, as the meat grinder does not really do the job properly. Luckily for us, the food processor produces fine results.

I generally serve steak tartare as a first course preceding a richly sauced fish dish or as an after-theater supper, accompanied by buttered black bread and a well-chilled dry white wine. When serving it as a supper dish, I top each serving with a raw egg yolk and garnish with anchovy fillets.

1½ pounds beef tenderloin, trimmed of all fat and filament
¼ cup minced onion
¼ cup minced fresh parsley
2 tablespoons minced well-drained capers
1 tablespoon strained fresh lemon juice
¾ teaspoon salt
½ teaspoon freshly ground pepper
Optional garnishes:
    3 tablespoons minced fresh parsley
    4 to 6 egg yolks
    8 to 12 drained anchovy fillets

Cut the beef into ½-inch cubes and place it in the container of a food processor fitted with the metal chopping blade. Flicking the motor on and off, process for 7 to 10 seconds, or until the meat is chopped into ⅛-inch pieces. Do not overdo it; the steak tartare will be pasty if the beef is too finely ground. Mince the onions, parsley, and capers—this should be done by hand—and add them to the meat. Sprinkle on the lemon juice, salt, and pepper. Process 1 to 2 seconds, just long enough to blend.

It is important now to handle the meat as little as possible to avoid compacting it. Using a fork, transfer the meat directly from the container of the food processor to a platter or individual plates and gently form into serving-size pyramid or mound shapes. If you wish, sprinkle with additional minced parsley. Each portion may also be topped with an unbroken raw egg yolk (form a small depression with a spoon to hold the yolk) and garnished with anchovies.

AHEAD OF TIME: Steak tartare may be covered loosely with waxed paper and refrigerated for about an hour before serving—but not longer, or the dish will discolor, become watery, and lose its fresh taste. Garnish and top with yolks and anchovies just before serving. Leftover steak tartare can be formed into patties and sautéed.

CHICKEN LIVER PÂTÉ

6 to 8 first-course or 10 to 15 hors d'oeuvre servings

❦ *Technically speaking this is a mousse, not a pâté, because it is not baked after being assembled. But no matter what one chooses to call it, this preparation is wonderfully smooth, rich, and flavorful—and quite simple to make.*

- 4 tablespoons (½ stick) butter, plus 12 tablespoons (1½ sticks) butter at room temperature
- ⅓ cup very finely minced onion
- 8 ounces chicken livers, trimmed of large strings and any green spots
- ¼ teaspoon ground thyme
- Ground allspice or cloves
- ¼ teaspoon salt
- ¼ teaspoon white or black pepper, preferably freshly ground
- ⅓ cup Madeira, Port, or medium-dry Sherry

Melt 4 tablespoons butter in a 10-inch skillet, add onion, and cook over very low heat until soft but not brown, about 10 minutes. Stir in trimmed livers, thyme, a generous pinch of allspice or cloves, salt, and pepper. Cover skillet and cook livers slowly for 10 minutes, stirring several times; the livers must be well done, with no trace of pink in the middle, or the pâté will be too soft. When the livers have finished cooking, pour in the wine, raise heat to high, and boil until the liquid has evaporated and livers are sizzling in butter. Remove livers from heat and cool to room temperature. Combine contents of skillet with the 1½ sticks softened butter in blender or food processor and purée very thoroughly. Taste carefully and adjust seasoning; oversalt slightly, since the pâté will be served cold and cold diminishes the flavoring power of salt.

If the pâté is to be served as an hors d'oeuvre, pack it into an attractive bowl from which it can be scooped up with a knife and spread on crackers or bread. If it is to be presented as a first course, turn it into a small loaf pan or similar container so that it can be cut into thin, neat slices. Cover pâté with plastic wrap and refrigerate for several hours, or until solid; the flavor will improve if the pâté matures in the refrigerator for 2 or 3 days. Let stand at room temperature for 30 minutes before serving.

MASTER RECIPE

Veal, Chicken, and Pork Patties

4 to 6 servings

❦ *These tender, savory patties make a welcome change from hamburgers, and, if accompanied by the mustard-caper sauce outlined at the end of the recipe, they are elegant enough to serve to guests. Sauced or not, the patties go exceptionally well with a tossed salad, preferably one containing a few bitter or spicy greens such as dandelion, chicory, or arugula. Baked or mashed potatoes might also be offered.*

The proportions of veal, poultry, and pork can be varied depending on your preferences and what you have on hand. Some pork should always be included—it adds flavor—but the chicken may be replaced by turkey or additional veal or the veal by poultry. You may be dismayed to see that the recipe calls for the addition of ground pork fat, or, as a second choice, butter. Remember, though, that veal and poultry are lean; the patties will be dry and tough if prepared without added fat.

This recipe is written for use with a food processor. However, the meats may also be ground, either by the butcher or at home, and combined with the other ingredients in a mixing bowl.

STEP 1: THE GROUND MEAT MIXTURE

8 ounces lean boneless pork
8 ounces lean boneless veal
8 ounces skinless, boneless chicken or turkey
2 ounces fresh pork fat or 4 tablespoons butter
½ cup finely chopped onion
2 tablespoons butter

- 1/3 cup Fine Fresh Bread Crumbs (see page 60)
- 1 large egg
- 2 tablespoons finely chopped fresh parsley
- 1 teaspoon mashed, pressed, or very finely minced garlic
- 1/2 teaspoon dried rosemary, ground or moistened with a few drops of water and minced fine
- 1/4 teaspoon ground thyme
- 1/8 teaspoon ground allspice
- 1 1/4 teaspoons salt
- 3/4 teaspoon pepper, preferably freshly ground

One at a time, chop the pork, veal, and poultry medium-fine in a food processor fitted with the metal chopping blade; you will have about 1 cup of each. (The meat should look slightly rough, as though finely ground, not smooth or puréed.) Mince the pork fat fine by hand (it becomes overblended in the machine), or cut the 4 tablespoons butter into small pieces. Return the meats and poultry to the processor, add the pork fat or butter, and process 2 to 3 seconds, or just long enough to blend.

In a small, heavy skillet, sauté the onion in 2 tablespoons butter over low heat for about 8 minutes, or until the onion is soft but not brown. Scrape the onion into the processor, add all remaining ingredients, and process for about 5 seconds, or until blended. Do not overblend, or you will pulverize the mixture and the patties will be tough. Sauté a small amount of the mixture in the skillet you used to cook the onions, taste, and adjust the seasoning as necessary.

AHEAD OF TIME: The mixture may be wrapped securely in foil and refrigerated for a day or frozen for several months.

STEP 2: FORMING AND COOKING THE PATTIES

- 2 tablespoons butter
- 1 tablespoon vegetable oil

Form meat mixture into 4 large or 6 medium patties about 3/4 inch thick. Over moderately high heat, heat butter and oil in a heavy 10- to 12-inch skillet (do not use unlined cast iron if you plan to make the deglazing sauce in Step 3) until the mixture just begins to color. Brown the patties lightly on each side, then turn the heat down to moderately low and cook the patties 2 to 3 minutes longer on each side, or until they feel firm when pressed lightly with a spatula and have begun to spill juices into the skillet. Remove to a warm serving platter and serve at once or cover with foil and proceed to make the deglazing sauce outlined in the next step.

STEP 3: THE MUSTARD-CAPER DEGLAZING SAUCE (OPTIONAL)

⅔ cup Beef Stock, page 24, or canned broth
½ cup dry white wine or ⅓ cup dry vermouth
3 tablespoons well-drained small capers or chopped large capers
1½ tablespoons Dijon mustard
2 to 3 tablespoons soft butter

Spoon off most of the fat from the skillet, being careful not to discard the juices. Add the stock and wine, raise heat to moderately high, and boil until reduced to about ¼ cup, stirring continuously with a wooden spoon to scrape up the browned bits from the bottom of the skillet. Stir in the capers and mustard, bring to just below the simmer, and remove from heat. Add the soft butter, cut into bits, and swirl the skillet by the handle until the butter melts and the sauce thickens. (Do not stir; stirring liquefies the butter and the sauce does not thicken properly.) Taste for seasoning, adding drops of the caper pickling solution if the sauce needs more piquancy. Dress each patty with a spoonful of sauce and serve immediately.

Variation: VEAL, CHICKEN, AND PORK MEATBALLS IN PARSLEY CREAM SAUCE

4 to 6 servings

❦ *Here the meat mixture from the Master Recipe is formed into meatballs, which are then poached in chicken stock and served with a parsley cream sauce made from the poaching liquid. Serve the meatballs with noodles or rice and a green vegetable.*

Veal, Chicken, and Pork Patties, prepared through Step 1
3 to 4 cups Chicken Stock, page 26, or canned broth
Basic Cream Sauce, page 34, made with ½ cup heavy cream and 1½ cups of the poaching broth from this recipe
3 to 4 tablespoons minced fresh parsley
Fresh lemon juice
Salt and white pepper, preferably freshly ground

Form meat mixture from Step 1 of the Master Recipe into 36 1-inch balls. Bring 3 cups chicken stock or broth to a simmer in a large saucepan or dutch oven. Drop in meatballs, adding more stock if necessary to cover them completely. Poach meatballs at just below the simmer for about 10 minutes, or until they feel firm when pressed with the back of a spoon. Remove meatballs to a plate with a slotted spoon and cover tightly with aluminum foil to keep them from drying out.

Prepare cream sauce, using ½ cup heavy cream and 1½ cups of the poaching broth, strained and degreased, as the sauce base. (Save poaching broth remaining in the pot for a sauce or a soup.) Gently fold meatballs into finished sauce along with the chopped parsley. Warm over very low heat, without simmering, for 5 minutes. Correct the seasoning, adding drops of lemon juice, salt, and white pepper. Dribble in a bit of cream or stock if the sauce is too thick.

AHEAD OF TIME: The sauced meatballs can be refrigerated for a day or two in a tightly covered container.

Variation: SWEDISH MEATBALLS

4 to 6 main-course or about 25 hors d'oeuvre servings

❦ *Standard fare at cocktail parties in the fifties and sixties, Swedish meatballs are utterly delicious if seasoned and sauced with care. The trick is to add enough allspice and freshly grated nutmeg to give the meatballs a pleasantly spicy flavor but not so much as to overwhelm the taste of the meats. As a main course Swedish meatballs may be served with buttered noodles or riced potatoes plus steamed cabbage or boiled green beans, broccoli, or brussels sprouts. Cocktail meatballs are customarily presented in a chafing dish, to be speared with toothpicks.*

Veal, Chicken, and Pork Patties, prepared through Step 1
OMIT: Rosemary
INCREASE: Ground allspice to ¾ teaspoon
ADD: ¼ teaspoon freshly grated nutmeg
⅓ cup all-purpose flour
2 tablespoons butter
1 tablespoon vegetable oil
1 cup Beef Stock, page 24, or canned broth
½ cup medium-dry Sherry, preferably Manzanilla
1 cup heavy cream
¼ teaspoon freshly grated nutmeg
Fresh lemon juice
2 to 3 tablespoons minced fresh parsley

Prepare the meat mixture as indicated in Step 1 of the Master Recipe, but omit the rosemary, increase the allspice to 3/4 teaspoon, and add 1/4 teaspoon nutmeg. Sauté a small amount of the mixture and taste. Adjust the seasoning carefully.

Form the meat mixture into 36 1-inch meatballs or 72 1/2-inch cocktail meatballs. Roll in the flour, spread on a sheet of waxed paper. Over moderately high heat, heat the butter and oil in a 10- to 12-inch heavy-bottomed skillet (do not use unlined cast iron) until the mixture has just begun to color. Add as many meatballs as will fit comfortably in a single layer and brown well on all sides; remove with a slotted spoon and brown remaining meatballs. Spoon as much fat from the skillet as possible without discarding any of the meat juices. Return all meatballs to the skillet (it doesn't matter if they won't fit in one layer), reduce heat to low, cover, and cook slowly for 3 to 6 minutes, or until the meatballs feel firm when pressed with the back of a spoon.

Transfer meatballs to a platter, using a slotted spoon, and cover closely with foil or plastic wrap. Pour the stock and Sherry into the skillet, raise the heat to high, and boil down until reduced by half, stirring continuously with a wooden spoon to scrape up the browned bits from the bottom of the skillet. Add the cream and 1/4 teaspoon nutmeg and, stirring, simmer the sauce for a minute or so, or until it just begins to thicken. Gently fold the meatballs into the sauce and simmer very slowly for 2 or 3 minutes, or just long enough to reheat the meatballs and thicken the sauce. Taste and correct the seasoning, adding drops of lemon juice plus a few additional gratings of nutmeg, if needed. Sprinkle with parsley and serve.

AHEAD OF TIME: The sauced meatballs can be refrigerated for a day or two in a tightly covered container. Sprinkle with parsley just before serving.

Variation: COUNTRY PÂTÉ

12 first-course servings

❦ *Although a certain rarefied aura still surrounds them, pâtés were originally rather humble creations invented as a means for using up meat scraps, and they are, in fact, simple to make and do not require expensive or exotic ingredients. Their special characteristic is their fine, smooth texture, their quality of melting in the mouth as they are chewed. This texture is achieved by grinding the meats fine and adding a hefty quantity of pork fat, and by weighting the pâté down after it is baked so that air pockets do not develop.*

The usual way to serve pâtés is as a first course, accompanied by French bread or melba toast and the tiny French sour pickles known as cornichons. However, they also make a fine supper or lunch main course when served with a tossed salad, and they are a welcome addition to a picnic basket.

A NOTE ON FRESH PORK FAT FOR LINING THE PÂTÉ MOLD: Pâtés are always baked in a protective wrapping of fresh pork fat or bacon, which serves to hold in the meat's juices and prevent the pâté from drying out and developing a coarse texture. Most butchers can get fresh pork fatback—the large, solid piece of fat from the animal's back—if you ask for it. Have your butcher slice fat into ⅛-inch sheets using his slicing machine; it is a nuisance to do it by hand. If you cannot get fresh pork fat, you can substitute bacon, but the various flavors that are added to bacon during the curing process—spices, smoke, sugar—tend to overwhelm the delicate taste of the pâté.

PRELIMINARIES

1. Place rack in the center of the oven.
2. Preheat oven to 350°F 20 minutes before baking.
3. Select a 4- to 5-cup rectangular loaf pan or covered pâté mold. Have ready a shallow baking dish large enough to hold the pan or mold, plus a kettle of boiling water.

Veal, Chicken, and Pork Patties, prepared through Step 1
INCREASE: Pork fat to 6 to 8 ounces (do not use butter)
ADD: ⅓ cup Madeira, Port, Cognac, or brandy
1 pound fresh pork fatback, cut into sheets ⅛ inch thick, or, as a second choice, 1 pound unsmoked bacon, thoroughly rinsed under hot water and patted dry
6 chicken livers, halved, or 4 ounces boiled ham cut into ¼-inch sticks
⅓ to ½ cup (1⅓ to 2 ounces) shelled pistachios

Prepare the meat mixture from Step 1 of the Master Recipe, making the following modifications. Triple or quadruple the quantity of pork fat. When the onion is tender, add the wine or spirits, standing back in case the alcohol should flame, and gently boil down until reduced by half. Add onion and other ingredients from the Master Recipe to meat and process for 10 to 15 seconds rather than 5 as specified in Master Recipe, or until the mixture is well blended but retains small white specks from the pork fat. A suggestion of fluffiness is a signal that you are on the verge of overprocessing the mixture.

Line the inside of the pan or mold with sheets of pork fat or slices of bacon. The pieces should overlap by about 1/4 inch and hang over the sides of the pan by 1/2 inch or more. Spread 1/3 of the meat mixture evenly over the bottom of the pan or mold. Arrange over it half the chicken livers or ham sticks and half the pistachios, leaving a 1-inch border on all sides. Cover with another third of the meat mixture, pressing down gently, and arrange remaining livers or ham and pistachios on top, again leaving a 1-inch border. Smooth the remaining meat mixture over the top, forming a flat loaf. Cover the top of the pâté completely with a sheet of pork fat or strips of bacon, then bring up the overhanging fat or bacon and press the ends over the top of the loaf. Press a sheet of aluminum foil over the top of the pâté, extending it straight across to the sides of the pan; if the pâté doesn't fill the mold completely, flatten the foil against the inner walls of the pan between the top of the pâté and rim. Cover the pan with a lid or with a second sheet of foil, stretching it over the top of the pan and pinching at the edges to seal.

Set the pâté in a shallow baking dish and pour enough boiling water into the dish to reach about 1/3 of the way up the sides of the pâté. Bake for 1 1/4 to 1 1/2 hours. The easiest way to test for doneness is to insert a meat thermometer through the foil into the center of the loaf; 165°F is done. Otherwise, peel back the foil and press the pâté with your finger. If it is done, it will feel firm and will have shrunk noticeably from the sides of the pan.

Remove the lid or top sheet of foil—but not the lower sheet—from the pâté. Place on top of the pâté a pan or mold just large enough to cover it, then weight down the pan or mold with a 5-pound object, such as a brick or stone. (Do not use a heavier weight, or you will squeeze the fat and juices out of the pâté and make it dry and crumbly.) Let the pâté cool to room temperature, then refrigerate, still weighted down, for at least 24 hours. Remove the weight, cover the pâté with lid or foil, and allow to mature in the refrigerator for 1 to 5 days.

Let pâté stand at room temperature for about an hour before serving. To serve, either cut thin slices directly from the pan or dip the pan briefly in boiling water and unmold the pâté onto a platter.

CHICKEN OR TURKEY CROQUETTES

4 servings

❦ *In addition to being a delicious way of using up leftover chicken or turkey, croquettes are fun to make, culinary marvels. Ground or very finely minced poultry is mixed with a thick cream sauce and other ingredients, then chilled until stiff enough to handle. The mixture is then formed into balls or other shapes, coated with a bound breading, and deep-fried. The result is a firm, crunchy, golden-brown exterior and a moist, creamy inside. Croquettes have been traditionally considered a luncheon dish. They should always be served with a cream sauce and with a green vegetable such as peas or green beans.*

For the filling:

6 tablespoons butter
½ cup finely chopped onion
½ cup finely chopped celery
¼ cup all-purpose flour
1 cup Chicken Stock, page 26, or canned broth
2 cups ground or very finely minced skinless, boneless cooked chicken or turkey
½ cup diced boiled ham or additional chicken or turkey
¼ cup (1 ounce) chopped walnuts or toasted, sliced almonds
¼ cup finely chopped fresh parsley
2 teaspoons fresh lemon juice
1 teaspoon Dijon mustard
¼ teaspoon ground thyme
⅛ teaspoon nutmeg, preferably freshly grated
¼ teaspoon salt
¼ teaspoon black or white pepper, preferably freshly ground

For breading and frying:

½ cup all-purpose flour
2 large eggs, beaten
1½ to 2 cups Fine Fresh Bread Crumbs (see page 60)
3 quarts vegetable oil for deep-frying

Dilled or Parsleyed Cream Sauce, page 41, or Curried Cream Sauce, page 39

Melt the butter in a 1½ quart saucepan, add the onion and celery, and sauté over low heat for about 5 minutes, or until the vegetables are softened but retain a slight crunchiness. Add ¼ cup flour, stir to combine thoroughly, and cook over low heat for 1 minute. Do not allow the mixture to color. Remove from heat. Bring the chicken stock to a boil, add it all at once to the vegetable/

flour mixture, and beat with a wire whip until completely smooth. Place over moderately high heat and, stirring constantly, bring to a simmer and cook 1 minute. The sauce will be very thick.

Turn sauce into a 4-quart mixing bowl. Add the ground poultry, diced ham, nuts, and parsley and stir until blended. Beat in the lemon juice, mustard, thyme, nutmeg, salt, and pepper. Taste and adjust the seasoning. Cover the bowl with plastic wrap and refrigerate for 2 to 3 hours, or until the mixture is very cold and firm.

Spread ½ cup flour over a large sheet of waxed paper. One at a time, drop ¼-cup gobs of the croquette mixture onto the flour and gently roll until evenly coated; push each one to a corner of the paper while you prepare the next. You should end up with 8 pieces. Using your fingers, roll each croquette in beaten egg until coated, then drop into bread crumbs spread out on waxed paper. Roll in crumbs to coat, all the while coaxing the croquette into the shape you desire—a ball, cylinder, pyramid, or whatever. The croquette mixture is soft and rather tricky to handle, but you may be assured that no matter how lumpy the croquettes may appear at this stage, they will be a handsome sight once they are fried. Just be sure that the entire exterior is covered with crumbs so that the inside will not leak out during cooking.

Arrange the formed croquettes on a fresh sheet of waxed paper, cover loosely with a second sheet of waxed paper, and let stand at room temperature for 30 minutes or in the refrigerator for several hours. Let refrigerated croquettes stand at room temperature for 30 minutes before frying. Following Step 2 of the Master Technique for deep-frying, page 64, deep-fry in 3 quarts oil heated to 370°F for 3 to 4 minutes, or until deep brown, adding no more than 4 croquettes to the pot at once. Serve immediately, accompanied by cream sauce.

FISH

Throughout the eighteenth and nineteenth centuries Americans ate fish and shellfish regularly and with great enthusiasm; it was common practice, for example, to consume several dozen oysters as a first course. But due to a number of factors—among them overfishing, pollution, and the increasing availability of good-quality, affordable meat—fish consumption declined in the early part of this century, with the result that to many Americans seafood came to seem a strange food full of bones, shells, and other nasty surprises that no one knew how to cook and that no one ate—except perhaps at restaurants.

Americans are now rediscovering the many advantages of this food. Fish is relatively low in saturated fat and calories. It is light but satisfying, and does not leave one with a feeling of being overfull. And best of all, at least from a cook's point of view, most types of fish respond well to very similar cooking techniques, so one need only master a handful of recipes to be able to cook a wide variety of fish, ranging from cod to halibut to sole to salmon. The Master Techniques in this chapter tell how to broil, broiler-grill, oven-broil, braise, bake, sauce, poach, pan-fry, and french-fry fish in general. At the end of each Master Technique appears a chart listing specific fish that are especially well suited to the particular cooking method; following the charts are some variations on the basic techniques that are good with individual fish.

For those interested in learning more about various fish there is a glossary at the end of the chapter. Twenty-nine of the most common American market fish are entered in the glossary, and information on weights and sizes, usual market cuts, availability and seasonality, and special cooking needs are given on each.

Before proceeding to the Master Techniques and the glossary, here are some tips on choosing and storing fish and on dealing with one of the creatures' least attractive features, their bones.

About Fish

Choosing Fresh Fish: Perhaps the best advice that can be given about choosing fresh fish is to evaluate the place in which you purchase it. A first-rate market will keep fish on ice or on refrigerated trays made especially for displaying fish. The colder the temperature at which the fish is stored, the fresher it will be. Preferably, the market will also cover the fish with glass or clear plastic to protect it from dirt and bacteria. Freshly caught fish is odorless; it only takes on a scent when it begins to decay. A fish market, like the product it sells, should smell fresh and pleasant, maybe a bit briny, but never foul or "fishy."

The realities of transportation and distribution dictate that virtually any fish you see at the market will be at least 48 hours out of the water, and probably 72 hours or more. But how long ago the fish was caught matters less than how it has been handled. If kept cold and clean, most fish will remain relatively fresh for five days or even longer after harvesting. But if allowed to lie around—in a fishing boat, at the fish monger's, or in your car on the way home from the market, for instance—all fish will deteriorate significantly in a matter of hours.

As a general rule of thumb, whole fish remain fresh longer than pieces do, and large whole fish and large pieces will be in better condition than smaller whole fish and smaller pieces. Whole fish have been handled less than fish pieces, and thus they have not been held as long between hot human fingers or exposed to as many bacteria as have fish steaks and fillets. Similarly, large whole fish and large pieces retain the cold as they are moved from boat to truck to distribution center to truck to market to shopping bag to refrigerator to pot, and thus they are more resistant to spoilage than are tiny fish, fillets, and steaks.

Therefore, if you have a choice, it is always wise either to buy whole fish or to have steaks or fillets custom-cut for you from a whole fish right before your eyes at the market.

To judge the freshness of a whole fish, look it in the eyes: they should be clear, bright, and protruding—never murky, bloody, glassy, or sunken. The scales should glisten and lie flat against the body, and the underside of the gills should be red and moist. The fish should be virtually odorless.

The signs of freshness in fish steaks and fillets are more subtle. The flesh should look moist, translucent, and pearly—never spongy, glassy, or dry—and should range in color from pink to light rose to bluish gray, depending on the type of fish (if you look closely, even flounder and sole will appear pinkish, provided the fish is fresh). Whiteness or a chalky appearance are definite signs of a downhill trend. In texture, the fish should appear dense and solid, the natural grain of the flesh closely packed. If the fish appears flaky, crumbly, or chunky-looking, it is spoiled or dried out or both. And here too, you can always trust your nose: Reject any piece of fish that smells like iodine or ammonia, or just plain fishy.

People living in inland states must often settle for frozen fish. This is not necessarily a bad thing, provided that the fish has been handled with care and held *consistently* at a temperature of around 0°F or below. If the thermometer in your grocer's freezer reads much higher than 0°F, pass the fish by. And reject any packages that are bulging, dented, or covered with ice, as these may have been allowed to thaw partially during handling, and the fish inside will probably have turned to mush.

PURCHASING FISH: Most fish are mild and pleasant-tasting, but some have pronounced personalities that offend less gung-ho fish eaters. But even if the fish stocked by your market are all complete strangers to you, you need not run the risk of bringing home a fish you will not enjoy eating. You only need to know what to look for—and what to ask the fish man about.

Flesh color is very revealing. So-called "dark-fleshed" fish—whether the color is reddish (tuna), orangey (salmon), or, most commonly, blue gray (bluefish, mackerel, trout, and others)—usually have a strong flavor. By contrast, "light-fleshed" fish, which range in hue from grayish white (halibut, cod) to pearly pink (most other varieties such as snapper and most flounder), tend to be mild in flavor.

Though you cannot see the *fat content* of fish, you can ask your fish man about it. You can also assume, as a general rule of thumb, that most dark-fleshed fish will be moderately fatty to fatty and that most light-fleshed fish will be fairly lean. Few fish are either so lean or so fatty as to be unpleasant.

All fish vary slightly with respect to *texture* and *moistness,* but, unlike meat, fish are seldom tough or dry unless they have been abused during cooking. You can make some good guesses about the texture of a fish just by looking at it. The small, fine graining of sole and flounder belies the softness and delicacy of the flesh. By contrast, the striated appearance of raw cod steaks indicates the chewy flakiness of this fish, just as the densely packed appearance of swordfish suggests its firmness. Texture is a point of interest with regard to fish, but it is rarely a make-or-break matter. The only fish I can think of to whose texture I definitely object are sturgeon, which strikes me as cartilagenous, weakfish, which I find too soft, and a few off-beat species of shark, which tend to be tough.

CHOOSING AMONG CUTS OF FISH: Since nearly all the major cuts of fish can be used in almost any recipe, you should shop with the willingness to buy whichever fish looks freshest and best that day. But suppose you should find yourself in the enviable position of being able to choose among various cuts of equally prime fish? Which cut should you choose?

a) *Whole dressed fish* have been eviscerated, scaled, and clipped of their dorsal and ventral fins but otherwise left intact. Whole dressed fish tend to be in better condition at the market than fish steaks or fillets, and it is easy to judge their freshness. They also retain their flavor and juiciness better during cooking, provided that the heads are left attached. I very much like the dramatic look of a whole dressed fish on a plate or platter. However, if you object to the head, have the fish decapitated at the market and save the head for fish stock.

b) *Pan-dressed fish* are small fish from which the heads, fins, scales, and viscera have been removed. Because they are headless, they are easier to maneuver in a skillet than whole dressed fish.

c) *Fillets* are made by cutting away the flesh of a fish from either side of the backbone to produce two (or four, in the case of flat fish) tapering pieces. As a general rule, only fish weighing under 10 pounds are filleted. Long, thick fillets of such fish as salmon or cod are often sliced crosswise into manageable chunks. The popularity of fillets is undoubtedly due to the fact that they are boneless. But, on the negative side, they are prone to spoilage, and they are liable to dry out or fall apart during cooking.

Fillets may be sold with the skin still attached. To remove skin, lay each fillet skin side down on a work surface and cut and scrape the flesh off the skin with a very sharp, curve-tipped knife, holding the skin down flat with your free hand.

d) *Fish steaks,* sometimes called *darnes,* are made by slicing a large, thick fish into crosswise sections, generally about 1 inch thick. Unlike fillets, fish steaks always contain some bone, which is why some people object to them. However, the largest bone, the spine, is prominent and very easy to remove so that even the most bone-phobic of eaters has nothing to fear from it. The few smaller bones that may be embedded in the flesh can be easily removed before the fish is cooked. Run your index finger firmly over the steak until it snags on a bone, then pull the bone out with tweezers.

STORING FRESH FISH: Tightly wrapped in a plastic bag and placed on a bed of crushed ice at a temperature near freezing, fish can be kept in good condition for three to five days. The problem is that the melting beds of ice need constant replenishing, and few refrigerators, even in their coldest parts, maintain a temperature that is anywhere near the freezing mark. Thus it is best to eat fish the day of purchase or freeze for longer storage. To freeze fish, wrap first in plastic, then in foil, and seal in an airtight plastic bag. Whole dressed fish may also be placed in a milk carton or other flexible container, covered with water, and then frozen in a solid block of ice. Frozen fish will deteriorate if held too long, especially if the freezer temperature is higher than 0°F. Fillets should be consumed within a month, whole fish and fish steaks within three months. Frozen fish should be thawed slowly, preferably in the refrigerator. Otherwise, sharp ice crystals will rupture the flesh and leave the fish mushy, fibrous, or dry in texture.

COPING WITH FISH BONES: Anatomically speaking, fish fall into two groups: flat fish and round fish. Sole, flounder, fluke, and halibut fall into the first group; most other fish belong to the second. If you know how to fillet one flat fish, you can fillet them all. If you know how to fillet one round fish, you can fillet almost all of them. A few unusually bony species of round fish, such as shad and pickerel, should be filleted by a skilled fishmonger.

The *flat fish* have a skeleton that consists of a single central bone shaped like a double comb. To fillet, first cut along the quite visible line in the skin that delineates the top and bottom fillets on each side of the fish (there are four fillets on a flat fish). Next, make a cut around the head and gently scrape the two fillets on one side free from the central bone. Turn the fish over and repeat on the other side.

The top, or dorsal, half of the backbone of a *round fish* is flat, like the backbone of a flat fish; but the bottom, or ventral, half of a round fish's backbone divides into an overlapping cage of bones at the abdominal cavity, to enclose the viscera. To fillet round fish, cut around the gills, up along the spine, and then down along the tail. To free the fillet, scrape the flesh off the bone at the tail end, where the backbone is flat; when you reach the abdominal cavity, where the backbone divides, scrape the knife along the abdominal bones until you reach the bottom of the fillet. Leave behind the flesh that is intertwined with the bones of the ventral cavity. Turn the fish over and repeat on the other side.

BONING A FLAT FISH

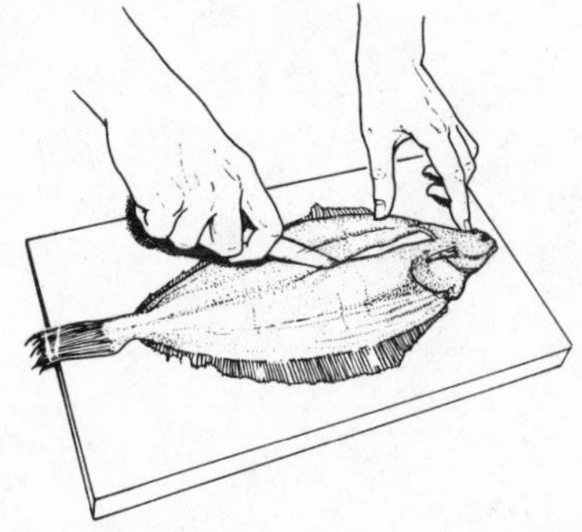

Cut along the visible line of skin that delineates the top and bottom fillets.

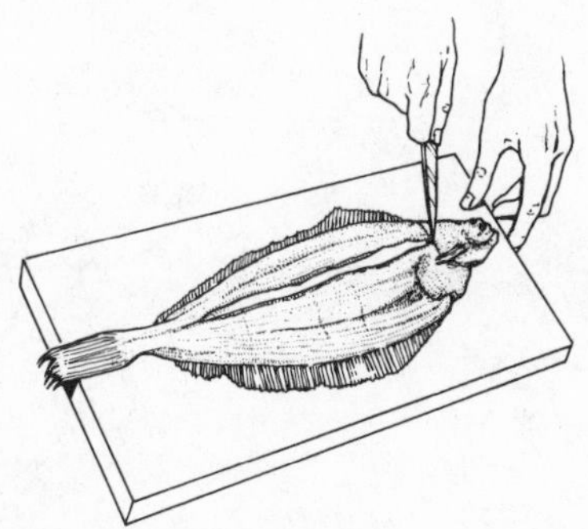

Make a cut around the head.

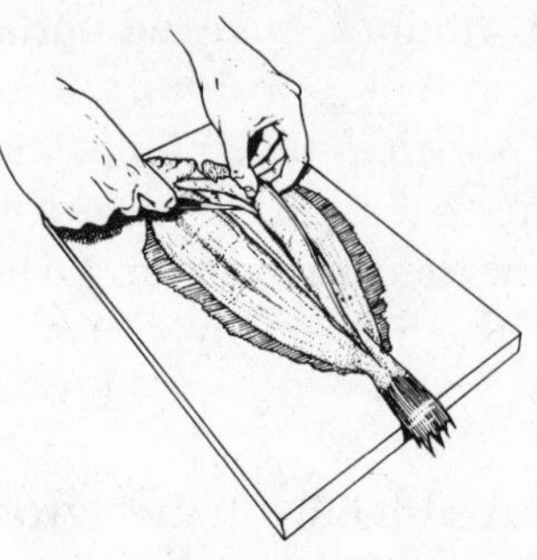

Gently scrape each fillet free from the central bone.

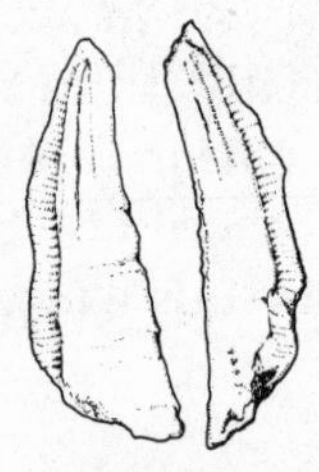

Finished fillets.

Boning a Round Fish

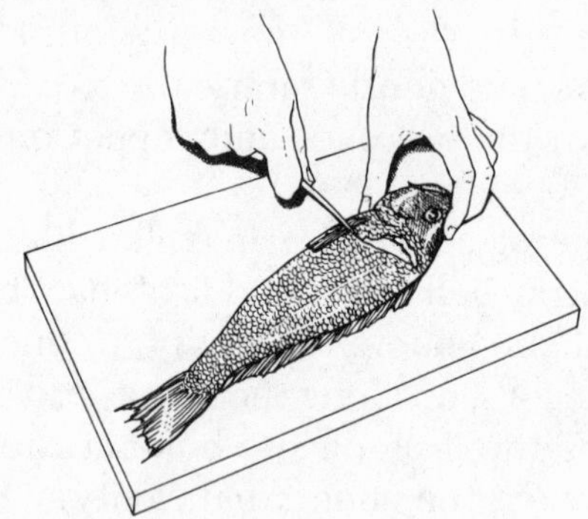

Cut around the gills . . .

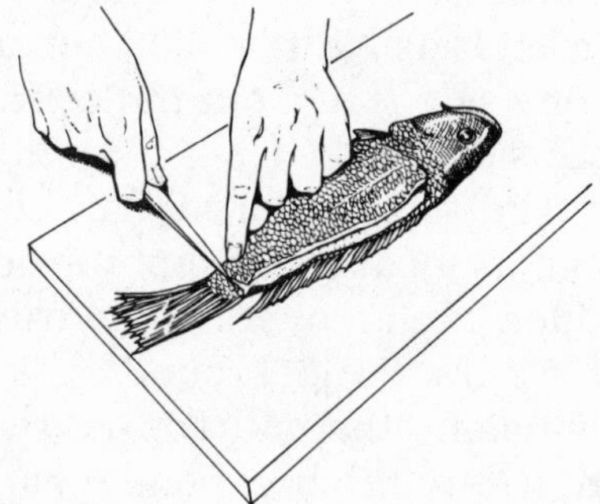

. . . up along the spine and down across the tail.

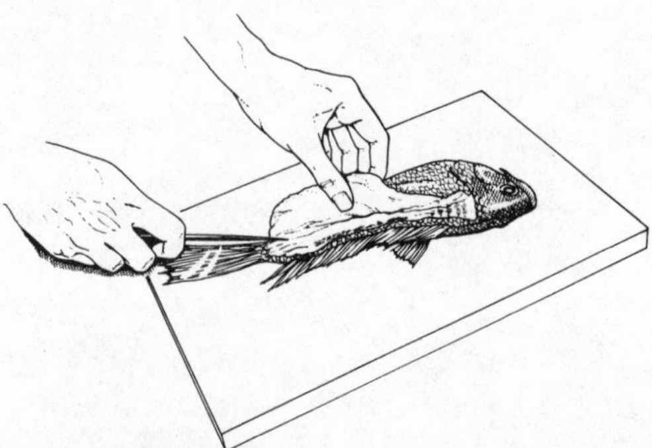

Scrape the flesh free from the bone at the tail end until you reach the rounded bones of the abdominal cavity.

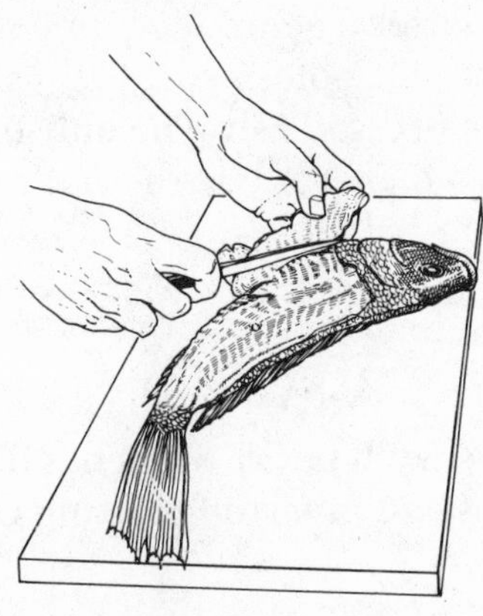

Scrape the knife along the abdominal bones to free the fillet.

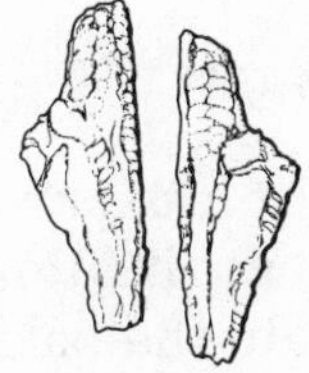

Finished fillets.

MASTER TECHNIQUE

Broiled Fish

4 servings

In addition to being quick and simple to do, broiling is a cooking method perfectly suited to fish, for the brief, intense heat renders the flesh extremely tender and concentrates the natural flavors into a buttery, briny essence. Do remember, though, that broiled fish cannot tolerate overcooking; it becomes dry, coarse, and tasteless. Calculate the cooking time carefully as indicated in the instructions, check frequently for doneness, and serve the cooked fish immediately, for it will continue to cook on its stored heat as it sits.

Subtle and simple, broiled fish does not need elaborate accompaniments. A boiled or steamed vegetable such as green beans, broccoli, or zucchini is sufficient; steamed white or brown rice might be added. Lemon wedges should be offered, but no sauce is necessary; the delicious pan juices are sauce enough. A chilled dry white wine is always welcome.

Choosing a Fish to Broil: At the end of the Master Technique you will find tips on how to broil specific kinds of fish. As you will note, nearly all fish can be broiled, and in any cut—fillets, steaks, or whole dressed fish. The only exception is fish measuring more than 1¼ inches thick, which tends to dry out or char on the outside when broiled. Thick fish should be baked.

Preliminaries

1. Adjust broiler rack so that the top of the fish will be 3 to 4 inches distant from the heating element. (If necessary, use an inverted roasting pan to elevate the baking dish.)
2. Preheat the broiler 10 minutes before proceeding.
3. Select a shallow baking dish or baking sheet large enough to hold the fish in a single layer with at least ¼ inch but not more than 1 inch of space between the pieces.

8 tablespoons (1 stick) butter, at room temperature
4 teaspoons strained fresh lemon juice
¼ teaspoon salt
¼ teaspoon pepper, preferably freshly ground
One of the following (see chart, page 225, for specific fish):
- 2 pounds fish fillets or fillet sections less than 1¼ inches thick
- 2 pounds fish steaks less than 1¼ inches thick
- 4 whole dressed fish weighing about 12 ounces each and less than 1¼ inches thick

½ to 1 cup dry white wine, Fish Stock, page 27, or water, if needed

Place the butter in a small bowl and beat with a wooden spoon until very soft and glistening; it should have the appearance and consistency of mayonnaise. Add the lemon juice, salt, and pepper and blend well.

Pat the fish dry with paper toweling. Brush one side of the fish (the skin or skin side of fillets) with half the butter mixture, then place it buttered side down on the baking dish. Brush the top of the fish with the remaining butter mixture.

Broil the fish for 8 to 10 minutes per inch of thickness measured at the thickest part, basting every 3 to 4 minutes with the pan juices. Do not turn the fish during cooking. If the pan begins to smoke, pour a ⅛-inch film of wine, stock, or water around the fish; this will be necessary only if the fish is thick and requires a relatively long cooking time. The fish is done as soon as the flesh at the thickest part is opaque, flaky, and juicy—rather than translucent, solid, and sticky—when separated with a fork. Transfer the fish to a warmed platter with a spatula and spoon the cooking juices over it. Serve immediately.

FISH BROILING CHART

BASS See Sea Bass; Striped Bass.

BLOWFISH (SEA SQUAB) Coat 2 pounds of blowfish tails with the butter mixture and arrange on a baking sheet; they may take as little as 5 minutes to cook. If you wish, sprinkle with parsley just before serving.

BLUEFISH Both fillets and small whole dressed fish, sometimes called baby blues, may be broiled, though whole fish are perhaps better when broiler-grilled. A teaspoon of dark soy sauce added to the creamed butter mixture is a great complement. Curried, fruited, or Middle Eastern steamed rice go well with this full-flavored fish.

BUTTERFISH Butterfish are always cooked and served whole. Broil according to the Master Technique.

CATFISH Broil skinned catfish fillets, catfish steaks, or small skinned whole dressed fish as in Master Technique.

COD AND SCROD Broil fillets, steaks, and small split scrod according to the Master Technique. Be very careful not to overcook. Scrod is decidedly more delicate in taste and texture than mature cod when broiled.

CROAKER Treat as for porgy.

FLOUNDER See Sole and Flounder.

GROUPER Broil fillets or steaks according to the Master Technique.

HADDOCK Broil fillets or steaks according to the Master Technique. Take care not to overcook.

HALIBUT Choose fillet sections or steaks under 1 inch thick. Thick pieces may cook unevenly, partially drying out. Broil according to Master Technique.

KINGFISH See Mackerel.

MACKEREL Atlantic and small Spanish mackerel, both fillets and small whole dressed fish, and steaks of king mackerel and large Spanish mackerel are excellent. Broil according to the Master Technique, adding, if you wish, a teaspoon of soy sauce to the creamed butter mixture.

MONKFISH Broil fillets according to the Master Technique. This is a dry, firm-textured fish that needs to be basted conscientiously and is especially intolerant of overcooking.

OCEAN PERCH Treat as for Sole and Flounder.

POMPANO Broil fillets or whole dressed fish according to the Master Technique.

PORGY Porgy fillets as well as whole dressed fish may be broiled according to the Master Technique, although I am more inclined to broiler-grill whole porgy.

RED SNAPPER Broil fillets according to the Master Technique. Be careful not to overcook.

SALMON If possible, choose fillet sections or steaks cut from near the head, where the flesh is fattest; broil according to the Master Technique.

SEA BASS Broil fillets or small whole dressed fish according to the Master Technique. Be careful not to overcook.

SHAD In my view, broiling is the cooking method of choice for shad fillets. Proceed according to Master Technique.

SHARK Treat as for Swordfish.

SMELTS Whole dressed or split smelts may be broiled according to the Master Technique, but I personally prefer to broiler-grill or fry this fish. Smelts are variable in size; allow 3 to 4 pounds of whole-dressed fish for 4 persons.

SOLE AND FLOUNDER Broil fillets according to the Master Technique. Since fillets can measure a mere ¼ inch in thickness, they may cook in as little as 2 to 3 minutes. If you wish, sprinkle with chopped fresh parsley or toasted sliced almonds just before serving.

STRIPED BASS Broil fillets and small whole dressed fish according to the Master Technique.

SWORDFISH Broil swordfish steaks according to the Master Technique.

TILEFISH Broil tilefish steaks according to the Master Technique, being careful not to overcook.

TROUT Broil fillets and small whole dressed fish according to the Master Technique.

WEAKFISH (SEA TROUT) Broil fillets or small whole dressed fish according to the Master Technique.

WHITEFISH Broil fillets according to the Master Technique.

WHITING Broil fillets or small whole dressed fish according to the Master Technique.

MASTER TECHNIQUE

Broiler-Grilled Fish

4 servings

❦ *Broiling fish on a pan that has been thoroughly preheated—a technique I call broiler-grilling—is an excellent treatment for whole dressed fish, whose skins come out deliciously crispy, and for steaks of very firm fish such as swordfish and tuna, which emerge beautifully browned on both sides and exceptionally tender. The one caveat that must be mentioned is that this procedure generates a great deal of smoke, making it problematic for those whose kitchens are not well ventilated. If this is the case with your kitchen, you may prefer to broil by the conventional method.*

Serve broiler-grilled fish with a tossed salad and, if you wish, steamed white or brown rice (one of the variations containing parsley or pine nuts would be lovely). A hearty white table wine, well chilled, could also be offered.

CHOOSING A FISH TO BROILER-GRILL: At the end of the Master Technique you will find a listing of fish particularly suitable for this cooking method. This method works best with whole dressed fish and steaks of firm, dark-fleshed fish. Fish fillets and steaks of delicately flavored fish are not enhanced by being seared and browned.

PRELIMINARIES

1. Adjust broiler rack so that the top of the fish will be 3 to 4 inches from the heating element. (If necessary, use an inverted roasting pan to elevate the baking dish.)
2. Select a two-piece broiling pan, preferably one with indented slits, rather than simple perforations, in the top tray. *Do not* use a disposable aluminum foil pan or a cake rack set on a baking sheet.
3. Place the broiling pan in the broiler compartment and preheat for 10 minutes before cooking.

One of the following (see chart, page 228, for specific fish):
 2 pounds fish steaks, preferably about 1 inch thick
 4 whole dressed fish weighing about 12 ounces each
1 teaspoon salt
½ teaspoon pepper, preferably freshly ground
12 tablespoons (double recipe) Clarified Butter, page 57
2 tablespoons strained fresh lemon juice
2 tablespoons neutral vegetable oil

Rinse the fish quickly under cool running water and blot well with paper toweling. Dry the cavities of whole fish thoroughly. Sprinkle the fish, inside and out, with salt and pepper.

Combine the clarified butter and lemon juice in a 10-inch skillet; if the butter has congealed, set mixture over a low flame until the butter is melted. Brush the hot broiling pan with oil, then dip the fish on both sides in the butter/lemon mixture and place on the pan. Cook the fish for 7 to 8 minutes per inch of thickness measured at the thickest part, basting every 2 to 3 minutes with more of the lemon butter. Do not turn the fish during cooking. The fish is done as soon as the flesh at the thickest part is opaque, flaky, and juicy—rather than translucent, solid, and sticky—when separated with a fork. Transfer the fish to a warmed platter using a large spatula (if the fish is of a manageable size and shape, you may wish to flip it over, so that the browner bottom side shows). Heat the remaining lemon butter to sizzling and pour it over the fish. Serve immediately.

FISH BROILER-GRILLING CHART

BASS See Sea Bass; Striped Bass.

BLUEFISH Whole baby bluefish are excellent cooked according to the Master Technique.

BUTTERFISH Broil whole dressed butterfish according to the Master Technique.

CROAKER Prepare as for porgy.

KINGFISH See Mackerel.

MACKEREL Whole Atlantic mackerel or small Spanish mackerel and steaks of king or large Spanish mackerel are excellent prepared according to the Master Technique. To make any of these fish milder and more succulent, arrange in a container just large enough to hold them, cover with about 2 cups of buttermilk, and let stand in the refrigerator, covered, for 1 to 2 hours. Drain and blot dry, discarding buttermilk, and proceed with the Master Technique.

POMPANO Broiler-grill whole dressed pompano according to Master Technique.

PORGY Whole dressed porgy are excellent when prepared according to the Master Technique or the Mediterranean variation suggested for swordfish steaks, page 229.

RED SNAPPER Broiler-grill whole dressed red snapper according to the Master Technique, or use the Mediterranean variation suggested for swordfish, page 229.

SALMON Broiler-grill salmon steaks and small whole dressed salmon according to the Master Technique.

SEA BASS Broiler-grill small whole dressed sea bass according to the Master Technique.

SHARK Treat as for swordfish.

SMELTS Whole dressed smelts are excellent prepared according to the Master Technique. Choose 3 to 4 pounds of smelts of any size. Allow several per serving if the fish are small.

STRIPED BASS Small whole dressed striped bass may be prepared according to the Master Technique.

SWORDFISH Broiler-grilling is, in my view, the cooking method of choice for swordfish (and shark) steaks. Proceed according to the Master Technique, or use the excellent variation on page 229.

TROUT Whole dressed trout are excellent when prepared according to the Master Technique. If you wish, substitute about ¾ cup well-strained bacon fat for the clarified butter called for in the Master Technique.

TUNA Broiler-grilling is one of the best methods for cooking tuna steaks. Proceed according to the Master Technique, but cook the tuna for only about 5 minutes per inch of thickness measured at the thickest part. The interior of the tuna should remain solid, red, and uncooked, like the center of a rare beef steak.

WEAKFISH (SEA TROUT) Broiler-grill small whole dressed weakfish according to the Master Technique.

Variation: BROILER-GRILLED BLUEFISH TERIYAKI

4 servings

Broiler-Grilled Fish, using 4 whole baby bluefish

ADD: 1/4 cup orange juice
3 tablespoons dark soy sauce
2 teaspoons dark sesame oil
2 teaspoons mashed, pressed, or very finely minced garlic
2 teaspoons grated or very finely minced fresh ginger
Grated zest of 1 orange

In a glass, stainless steel, or enameled dish just large enough to hold the fish, combine the 2 tablespoons lemon juice called for in the Master Technique plus all ingredients listed above. Add fish, spooning some of the marinade in the cavities and turning once to coat. Cover and refrigerate for 2 to 4 hours, turning once. Drain fish, scraping off marinade ingredients from exterior, and blot with paper toweling. Strain 3 tablespoons of the marinade mixture into the clarified butter called for in the Master Technique and proceed according to the Master Technique.

Variation: MEDITERRANEAN BROILER-GRILLED SWORDFISH

4 servings

Broiler-Grilled Fish, using swordfish steaks

ADD: 2 tablespoons mashed, pressed, or very finely minced garlic
2 tablespoons olive oil
3 tablespoons chopped fresh parsley

Combine garlic and olive oil and spread mixture as evenly as possible on both sides of steaks. Arrange on a plate, cover, and refrigerate 2 hours. Scrape off garlic, blot with paper toweling, and proceed with Master Technique, adding parsley to the lemon/butter mixture remaining in the skillet after the fish has been cooked.

MASTER TECHNIQUE

Oven-Broiled Fish

4 servings

❦ *Oven-broiling entails coating fish, generally fillets or steaks, with a flavored butter and baking it at high heat in the uppermost level of the oven. The method is similar to broiling, but has several distinct advantages. First, because the heat of the oven is less direct than that of the broiling compartment, there is less danger of the fish drying out or becoming tough. Thus it need not be watched so carefully or timed with such precision. Greater flavoring variations are possible, because ingredients that would burn under the broiler, such as fresh or dried herbs, mustard, green peppercorns, and others, may be added. Finally, oven-broiling does not cause fish to brown—it would be more accurate to say that the fish steams in its own juices—and this is a plus when you are cooking cod, halibut, sea bass, or other lean, white-fleshed fish with a delicate flavor.*

Accompany oven-broiled fish with boiled potatoes or steamed white or brown rice plus a green vegetable. The pan juices provide a delicious sauce. Chilled dry white wine is always appropriate.

CHOOSING A FISH TO OVEN-BROIL: At the end of this Master Technique you will find a chart listing fish particularly suitable for this cooking method. Following the chart are a handful of recipe variations. As you will note, a wide variety of fish may be oven-broiled, with lean, white-fleshed fish being particularly prime candidates. The only fish that are not desirable for oven-broiling are oily varieties such as mackerel and smelts, largish whole fish such as pompano and porgy, and very firm fish such as shark and swordfish. All such fish are better broiled or broiler-grilled.

PRELIMINARIES

1. Set a rack in the uppermost level of the oven.
2. Preheat oven to 475°F a full 20 minutes before baking; the fish may toughen if the oven isn't hot enough.
3. Select a shallow baking dish, preferably oven-to-table, just large enough to hold the fish pieces without their touching. (If the dish is too wide and roomy, the juices will tend to burn.)

8 tablespoons (1 stick) butter, at room temperature
4 teaspoons strained fresh lemon juice
1/4 teaspoon salt
1/4 teaspoon pepper, preferably freshly ground
One of the following (see chart, below, for specific fish):
2 pounds fish fillets
2 pounds fish steaks
4 whole dressed fish, preferably weighing under 10 ounces each

In a small bowl, beat the butter with a wooden spoon until fluffy. Add lemon juice, salt, and pepper and beat until all ingredients are thoroughly combined.

Dry the fish well with paper toweling. Using a pastry brush, spread both sides of the fish with the creamed butter mixture, and put a little inside the cavities of whole dressed fish also. Arrange fish in the baking dish, placing fillets skin side down. Bake in preheated oven for 10 to 12 minutes per inch of thickness measured at the thickest part: thin fillets, like sole or flounder, will take just 3 to 4 minutes, while thick fish steaks and whole fish will take about 10 minutes or a little longer. The fish is done when it has exuded juices into the baking dish and the flesh is white and opaque rather than pinkish and translucent when flaked at the thickest point with a fork. Serve at once, spooning some of the juices in the baking dish over each helping.

FISH OVEN-BROILING CHART

BASS See Sea Bass; Striped Bass.

BLOWFISH (SEA SQUAB) Coat 2 pounds blowfish tails with the butter mixture indicated in the Master Technique and bake 5 to 8 minutes, depending on size. Broccoli is a good accompaniment. See also the variation on page 232.

BLUEFISH Oven-broil fillets according to the Master Technique, adding a few drops of soy sauce and/or a bit of finely minced garlic to the butter mixture, if you wish.

BUTTERFISH Small whole butterfish may be prepared as in the Master Technique, though I would be more inclined to broil them. Accompany with boiled new potatoes rather than rice.

CATFISH Oven-broil skinned fillets according to the Master Technique.

COD AND SCROD Oven-broil either fillets or steaks according to the Master Technique, or follow one of the variations on page 233. For cod steaks there is no better cooking method than oven-broiling.

FLOUNDER See Sole and Flounder.

GROUPER Oven-broiling is a particularly good cooking method for grouper. Prepare fillets or steaks as indicated in the Master Technique.

HADDOCK Prepare as for Cod and Scrod.

HALIBUT Oven-broiling is the method of choice for halibut. Prepare steaks according to the Master Technique; asparagus or snow peas make excellent vegetable accompaniments.

MONKFISH Oven-broil fillets according to the Master Technique.

OCEAN PERCH Prepare as for Sole and Flounder.

POMPANO Oven-broil large pompano fillets according to the Master Technique.

RED SNAPPER Oven-broil fillets according to the Master Technique.

SALMON If possible, select fillet sections or steaks cut from the middle or tail section of the body, where the flesh is leanest. Oven-broil according to the Master Technique, or use one of the variations on pages 233–34.

SEA BASS Oven-broil fillets, steaks, or small whole fish according to the Master Technique. Sea bass responds very well to oven-broiling.

SHAD Oven-broil fillets according to the Master Technique or see the variation on page 234. Serve with parsleyed boiled potatoes and asparagus.

SOLE AND FLOUNDER Oven-broil fillets according to the Master Technique. Steamed white or brown rice with mushrooms and steamed spinach are delicious accompaniments.

STRIPED BASS Oven-broil fillets according to the Master Technique.

TILEFISH Oven-broil steaks according to the Master Technique or use the green peppercorn variation suggested for salmon, page 234. Oven-broiling is one of the best cooking methods for tilefish.

TROUT Oven-broil fillets or small whole fish according to the Master Technique. Serve with boiled potatoes and green beans.

WHITEFISH Oven-broil fillets according to the Master Technique.

WHITING Oven-broil fillets, steaks, or small whole-dressed fish according to the Master Technique.

Variation: OVEN-BROILED BLOWFISH TAILS WITH ROSEMARY

4 servings

Oven-broiled Fish, using 2 pounds blowfish tails

ADD: 1/2 teaspoon dried rosemary

Crush rosemary in a mortar or moisten with a few drops of water and mince fine. Add to butter mixture and proceed according to Master Technique, cooking the tails for 5 to 8 minutes, depending on size.

Variation: OVEN-BROILED COD WITH MUSTARD

4 servings

Oven-broiled Fish, using cod steaks

ADD: 2 tablespoons Dijon mustard
2 teaspoons anchovy paste or 1 tablespoon mashed drained anchovies
1 teaspoon mashed, pressed, or very finely minced garlic

Add mustard, anchovy paste or mashed anchovies, and garlic to the butter mixture, then proceed with Master Technique.

Variation: OVEN-BROILED COD WITH PARSLEY AND GARLIC

4 servings

Oven-broiled Fish, using cod steaks

ADD: 3 tablespoons minced fresh parsley
2 teaspoons mashed, pressed, or very finely minced garlic

Add parsley and garlic to butter mixture, then proceed according to the Master Technique.

Variation: OVEN-BROILED SALMON WITH DILL

4 servings

Oven-broiled Fish, using salmon fillet sections or steaks

ADD: 2 teaspoons distilled white vinegar
DECREASE: Lemon juice to 2 teaspoons
ADD: 1½ tablespoons finely chopped fresh dill (feathery leaves only) or 1½ teaspoons dried dillweed

Proceed according to the Master Technique, but in preparing the creamed butter mixture, substitute vinegar for half the lemon juice and add dill.

Variation: OVEN-BROILED SALMON WITH LIME BUTTER

4 servings

Oven-broiled Fish, using salmon fillet sections or steaks
SUBSTITUTE: 4 teaspoons strained fresh lime juice for lemon juice

Proceed according to the Master Technique, but use lime juice instead of lemon.

Variation: OVEN-BROILED SALMON WITH GREEN PEPPERCORNS

4 servings

Oven-broiled Fish, using salmon fillet sections or steaks
ADD: 2 teaspoons drained brine-packed green peppercorns

Mash peppercorns to a paste using a mortar and pestle or the back of a fork. Add to the creamed butter mixture and proceed according to the Master Technique.

Variation: OVEN-BROILED SHAD WITH ANCHOVY BUTTER

4 servings

Oven-broiled Fish, using shad fillets
ADD: 1 tablespoon anchovy paste or 1½ tablespoons mashed drained anchovies
2 tablespoons finely chopped fresh parsley

Proceed according to the Master Technique, adding the anchovy paste or mashed anchovies to butter mixture and sprinkling the cooked fish with parsley just before serving.

MASTER TECHNIQUE

Braised Fish with Vegetables

4 servings

Braising entails baking fish slowly on a bed of flavorful vegetables. In this Master Technique the vegetables are cut in julienne sticks and steamed in butter until crisp-tender; then the fish is laid in the dish and baked, covered, for about 25 minutes per inch of thickness, measured at the thickest part. The procedure is as simple as it sounds, and yet the results are quite special, the fish emerging moist and tender and its juices commingling with the vegetables and butter to produce a light but intensely flavorful sauce. In addition, the fish with its colorful vegetable garnish makes a particularly handsome sight on the plate. Several variations can be wrought on the braising theme, making Thai-style, Mediterranean-style, and sweet-and-sour braised fish dishes, among others; consult the variation recipes that begin on page 238 for instructions.

Braised fish is at its best when accompanied only by plain steamed white rice, though small servings of steamed snow peas or broccoli might be included.

CHOOSING A FISH TO BRAISE: At the end of this Master Technique you will find a listing of fish that may be braised. Lean, meaty, chunky-fleshed fish such as bass, cod, grouper, and monkfish are particularly recommended for braising, as they can withstand the relatively prolonged cooking period without drying out or disintegrating. Thick pieces of fish—thick fillets or steaks or whole fish—work best. Thin fillets may be used if they are folded in half first, to give them greater durability.

PRELIMINARIES

1. Set rack in the center of the oven.
2. Preheat oven to 325°F 20 minutes before baking.
3. Select a lidded baking dish or fish poacher just large enough to hold the fish in a single layer. The baking dish or poacher should be made of or lined with a noncorroding material and, if possible, be able to withstand being used on a burner.

3 to 4 medium carrots
3 to 4 medium celery stalks
2 medium onions
6 tablespoons butter
One of the following (see chart, page 237, for specific fish):
- 2 pounds fish fillets or fillet sections, preferably 3/4 inch thick or more
- 2 pounds fish steaks, 3/4 inch thick or more
- 2 to 4 small whole dressed fish of equal size, weighing 3 to 4 pounds altogether
- 1 large whole dressed fish weighing 3 to 4 pounds

1/2 teaspoon salt
1/4 teaspoon pepper, preferably white and freshly ground

Peel the carrots and cut into julienne sticks about 1 1/2 inches wide and 1/8 inch thick, making about 1 cup altogether. Cut celery into the same size pieces as the carrots, again making about 1 cup. Peel the onions and cut in half from top to bottom. Slice each half into crescents about 1/8 inch thick, then separate into half-rings, making 1 cup or a little more.

In the baking dish or poacher (or in a 10-inch skillet if the dish cannot tolerate direct heat) melt the butter over moderate heat. Add the julienned vegetables, toss to coat with butter, and cover. Stirring once or twice, steam the vegetables in butter for about 5 minutes, or until crisp-tender. Remove from heat and set aside.

Blot the fish with paper toweling. Sprinkle on all sides with salt and pepper. Lay the fish on the bed of vegetables, then spoon some of the vegetables and butter on top of the fish. Cover and bake about 25 to 30 minutes per inch of thickness, measured at the thickest part of the fish. The fish is done when the flesh looks white, opaque, and juicy rather than pink, translucent, and sticky when a fork is inserted into the center of the thickest part of the fish. Serve at once, accompanying each portion of fish with vegetables and a spoonful of the juices in the dish.

FISH BRAISING CHART

BASS See Sea Bass; Striped Bass.

CATFISH Braise skinned catfish fillets, folded in half lengthwise, or catfish steaks as in Master Technique.

COD AND SCROD Braise thick fillet pieces or, better, steaks as in the Master Technique. Cod and scrod may also be braised with coconut milk or sweet-and-sour flavorings (see Sea Bass and Sole and Flounder respectively) or prepared according to the variation on p. 238.

FLOUNDER See Sole and Flounder.

GROUPER Braise thick fillet pieces or steaks as in Master Technique or use the coconut milk variation suggested for Sea Bass, page 238.

HADDOCK Treat as for Cod and Scrod.

KINGFISH See Mackerel.

MACKEREL Atlantic mackerel seems to me too fine-fleshed and oily to braise, but thick steaks of king mackerel or large Spanish mackerel are good choices. Proceed as in Master Technique or use the coconut milk variation suggested for Sea Bass.

MONKFISH Braise thick fillet pieces as in Master Technique.

OCEAN PERCH Braise fillets, preferably skinless, as for Sole and Flounder.

RED SNAPPER Braise thick fillet pieces or a whole fish as in Master Technique. Also delicious is the coconut milk variation suggested for Sea Bass, page 238.

SEA BASS Braise thick fillet pieces or a whole fish as in Master Technique. Sea Bass is also very good when braised with sweet-and-sour flavorings (see page 239) or with coconut milk, page 238.

SHAD Braise fillets as in Master Technique.

SOLE AND FLOUNDER Sole and flounder are delicious braised, either according to the Master Technique or the sweet-and-sour variation given on page 239. Choose the thickest fillets possible and fold them in half (or even in thirds if very long and thin), with the skin side in.

STRIPED BASS Braise thick fillet pieces or whole fish as in Master Technique or use the coconut milk or sweet-and-sour variations suggested for Sea Bass or Sole and Flounder respectively, page 238 and page 239.

SWORDFISH Braise steaks as in Master Technique.

TILEFISH Braise steaks as in Master Technique.

TROUT Braise whole trout as in Master Technique, or, for an especially elegant dish, use the variation with tarragon and cream on page 239.

WHITEFISH Braise thick fillet pieces or whole fish as in Master Technique.

WHITING Braise small whole whiting as in Master Technique. Be careful in handling the fish after cooking, as it is apt to break apart.

Variation: MEDITERRANEAN BRAISED COD OR SCROD

4 servings

Braised Fish, using thick cod or scrod fillet pieces or steaks

SUBSTITUTE: 1/4 cup olive oil for butter

ADD: 1 cup peeled, seeded, diced tomatoes, fresh or canned (see page 607)
1/4 cup dry white wine
3 tablespoons finely chopped fresh parsley
3 tablespoons drained sliced green olives
1 teaspoon tomato paste
3/4 teaspoon mashed, pressed, or very finely minced garlic

Prepare vegetables as in Master Technique, but use olive oil instead of butter. When vegetables are tender, add all ingredients listed above and simmer 3 minutes. Proceed from there according to Master Technique. If, after the fish is cooked, the braising juices seem watery, remove the fish to a platter and boil down the juices to reduce. Serve with boiled potatoes.

Variation: SEA BASS BRAISED IN COCONUT MILK

4 servings

❦ *This is a variant of a traditional Thai method of cooking fish. Use a whole sea bass if you can find one.*

Braised Fish, using a whole sea bass or thick fillet pieces

SUBSTITUTE: 1/4 cup neutral vegetable oil for butter

ADD: 1 1/4 cups coconut milk (see page 698)
1 tablespoon finely chopped fresh basil or 1 teaspoon dried
2 teaspoons fresh lime juice
Cayenne pepper

Prepare vegetables as in Master Technique, but use oil instead of butter. When the vegetables are crisp-tender, add coconut milk, basil, lime juice, and a few shakes of cayenne pepper. Bring to a simmer, then remove from heat and proceed according to the Master Technique.

Variation: SWEET-AND-SOUR BRAISED SOLE OR FLOUNDER

4 servings

❦ *This is a sweet-and-sour recipe with a very mild flavor; it makes no pretense to authenticity of any kind.*

Braised Fish, using sole or flounder fillets

ADD: 1 small red bell pepper, cored, seeded, and cut into julienne strips (optional)
½ cup fresh or canned pineapple, cut into ¼-inch dice
½ cup pineapple juice
1 tablespoon distilled white vinegar
2 teaspoons cornstarch mixed to a smooth paste with 2 tablespoons additional pineapple juice

Steam vegetables in butter as in the Master Technique, adding, if you wish, red pepper strips. Just before removing vegetables from heat, stir in pineapple, pineapple juice, and vinegar. Lay in the fish fillets, seasoned and, if thin, folded in halves or thirds. Cook as in Master Technique. When the fish is done, remove it to a platter with a slotted spatula. Bring braising juices to a boil, stir in cornstarch paste, and cook until lightly thickened. Season with drops of vinegar, pinches of sugar, or a bit of salt if necessary. Spoon sauce and vegetables over fish and serve at once.

Variation: BRAISED TROUT WITH TARRAGON AND CREAM

4 servings

❦ *Serve this with rice and a green vegetable and accompany with a chilled white wine.*

Braised Fish, using 4 whole trout

ADD: 2 teaspoons chopped fresh tarragon or 1 teaspoon dried
1 cup heavy cream
Salt, white pepper, preferably freshly ground, and lemon juice, as needed

Proceed according to the Master Technique, but rub the trout with tarragon before cooking. When the trout are done, carefully remove them to a platter using spatulas. Add cream to the juices in the pan and boil down until reduced by 1/3 and lightly thickened. Season with salt, white pepper, and drops of lemon juice. Carefully remove the skin from the bodies—but not the heads—of the exposed sides of the trout. Spoon a ribbon of sauce and vegetables over the trout, surround with remaining sauce and vegetables, and serve at once, accompanied by a chilled white wine.

MASTER TECHNIQUE

Baked Stuffed Fish

4 servings

❦ *Fish takes particularly well to being stuffed and baked. The brief intense heat of the hot oven renders the flesh tender and moist, and the buttery stuffing blots up the delicious juices that are often lost when fish is cooked in other ways. Although whole dressed fish make for the more spectacular presentation at the table, fish fillets and steaks can also be stuffed and baked.*

Baked stuffed fish should always be served with lemon wedges; with fillets and steaks of lean fish such as cod or sole I generally offer pots of melted butter as well. Accompany with a green vegetable, or, for a real treat, consider serving a vegetable cooked in heavy cream—green beans, broccoli, cucumbers, peas, spinach, or summer squash, for example. Boiled potatoes are not necessary, as the rich bread-crumb stuffing can fill the role of starch accompaniment.

CHOOSING A FISH TO STUFF AND BAKE: The chart at the end of this Master Technique gives a list of fish particularly suitable for this cooking method, as well as a few tips on preparing each; a handful of recipe variations follows the chart. Virtually all fish can be stuffed and baked, the only exceptions being very oily varieties such as smelts.

PRELIMINARIES

1. Set rack in the upper-middle level of the oven.
2. Preheat the oven to 400°F 20 minutes before baking.
3. Select a shallow baking dish, preferably oven-to-table, large enough to hold the fish comfortably. A heat-resistant ceramic fish platter is ideal, especially for a single whole dressed fish.

STEP 1: PREPARING THE STUFFING

6 tablespoons butter
½ cup chopped onion
½ cup diced celery
1⅓ cups Fine Fresh Bread Crumbs (see page 60)
3 tablespoons finely chopped fresh parsley
½ teaspoon fresh lemon juice
¼ teaspoon salt
¼ teaspoon pepper, preferably freshly ground

Melt the butter in a 10-inch skillet, add the onion and celery, and sauté over gentle heat for about 5 minutes, or until the vegetables are fairly soft but not at all brown. Remove skillet from heat, add bread crumbs and parsley, and toss to blend. Sprinkle on the lemon juice, salt, and pepper, and toss again. Set aside.

STEP 2: STUFFING AND BAKING THE FISH

6 tablespoons butter
2 tablespoons neutral vegetable oil
½ lemon
½ teaspoon salt
¼ teaspoon pepper, preferably freshly ground
One of the following (see chart, page 243, for specific fish):
- 8 small fish fillets, weighing about 4 ounces each (2 pounds total)
- 4 medium fish fillets, weighing about 8 ounces each (2 pounds total)
- 2 large fish fillets or fillet sections, weighing about 1 pound each (2 pounds total)
- 4 fish steaks, at least 1 inch thick and weighing about 8 ounces each (2 pounds total)
- 4 small whole dressed fish, weighing 10 to 14 ounces each
- 1 large whole dressed fish, weighing 3 to 4 pounds

Combine butter and oil in a small saucepan and stir over gentle heat until the butter is melted. Slather the bottom and sides of the baking dish with about 2½ tablespoons of the butter/oil mixture; set baking dish and remaining butter/oil aside.

Depending on the cut of fish you are preparing, proceed as follows:

Small fillets: Lightly score the skin or skin side of the fillets, as though scoring a ham. Cut a single gash, widthwise, in the middle of the skin side of each fillet, going about ⅓ of the way through the flesh. Rub the fillets on both sides with the cut lemon and sprinkle on both sides with salt and pepper. Spread ½ of the skinless sides of each of the fillets with the reserved stuffing, then fold over the other half at the slash mark to enclose the stuffing. Arrange in the baking dish and brush liberally with the reserved butter/oil mixture. Basting once or twice with the remaining butter/oil or with the pan juices, bake the fish, uncovered, for 8 to 12 minutes, or until the flesh is white and opaque, rather than pinkish and translucent, when flaked with a fork. Serve at once.

Medium fillets: Prepare as for small fillets, above, increasing the baking time slightly if the fillets are thick rather than elongated.

Large fillets: Lightly score the skin or skin side of the fillets, as though scoring a ham. Turn the fillets skin side up and run your finger up and down the flesh; if you snag on a bone, remove it with tweezers or your fingers. Rub both sides of the fillets with the cut lemon and sprinkle on both sides with salt and pepper. Place one of the fillets skin side down in the prepared baking dish. Cover with the stuffing and place the second fillet, skin side up, on top, pressing it down lightly. Brush liberally with the reserved butter/oil mixture. Basting two or three times with the remaining butter/oil or with the pan juices, bake the fish, uncovered, for 15 to 20 minutes, or until the flesh is white and opaque, rather than pinkish and translucent, when flaked with a fork. Serve at once.

Fish steaks: Leave the central spine bone in place, but locate and remove smaller bones by running your finger over the flesh and pulling out with tweezers or with your fingers any bones you snag on. Using a pointed paring knife, cut a deep sideways pocket on both sides of the spine bone of each of the steaks. Rub the steaks on both sides and inside the pockets with the cut lemon and sprinkle inside and out with salt and pepper. Poke the stuffing into the pockets, arrange the steaks on the prepared baking dish, and brush liberally with the reserved butter/oil mixture. Basting two or three times with the remaining butter/oil or with the pan juices, bake the fish, uncovered, for 12 to 16 minutes, or until the flesh is white and opaque, rather than pinkish and translucent, when flaked with a fork. Serve at once.

Small whole dressed fish: Quickly rinse fish under cool running water and pat dry inside and out with paper towels. Cut two diagonal gashes reaching almost to the bone on each side of the fish. Rub fish inside and out with the cut lemon and sprinkle inside and out with salt and pepper. Gently pack the stuffing into the stomach and head cavities; there is no need to sew or truss the openings. Arrange the fish on the prepared baking dish and brush liberally with the reserved butter/oil mixture. Basting 2 or 3 times with the remaining butter/oil or with the pan juices, bake fish, uncovered, 12 to 16 minutes, or until the flesh near the backbone looks white and opaque, rather than pinkish and translucent, when flaked with a fork. Serve at once.

Large whole dressed fish: Proceed as for small whole dressed fish, above, but cut 3 gashes on each side of the fish and bake fish 8 to 10 minutes *per pound.*

BAKED STUFFED FISH CHART

BASS See Sea Bass; Striped Bass.

BLUEFISH Four medium or two large fillets or 4 small or 1 large whole dressed bluefish may be prepared according to the Master Technique. The bacon stuffing suggested for trout, page 247, is also terrific with bluefish.

BUTTERFISH Four whole dressed butterfish are delicious and make a charming presentation when prepared according to the Master Technique.

CATFISH Prepare 8 small or 4 medium skinned fillets or 4 small or 1 large skinned whole dressed fish according to the Master Technique.

COD AND SCROD Two large cod fillets, 4 cod steaks, or 1 large whole dressed scrod or cod may be prepared according to the Master Technique or one of the variations on pages 244 to 245. Members of the cod family take especially well to being baked and stuffed.

CROAKER Four whole dressed croaker may be prepared according to the Master Technique.

FLOUNDER See Sole and Flounder.

GROUPER Two large grouper fillets or fillet sections or 4 grouper steaks may be prepared according to the Master Technique.

HADDOCK Prepare as for Cod.

HALIBUT Four halibut steaks may be prepared according to the Master Technique; be sure to baste the fish frequently during cooking to prevent it from becoming dry. The crab and mushroom stuffing variations suggested for sole and flounder, page 246, are also good with halibut.

KINGFISH See Mackerel.

MACKEREL Eight small or 4 medium Atlantic or Spanish mackerel fillets, 4 small whole dressed Atlantic or Spanish mackerel, or 4 steaks of king mackerel or large Spanish mackerel may all be prepared according to the Master Technique.

MONKFISH Monkfish fillets are tricky to stuff, for they tend to be rather thick and irregular in shape, making it difficult either to fold them over or to sandwich them. However, should you be able to find stuffable pieces, you may prepare monkfish fillets according to the Master Technique, folding or sandwiching them, depending on their size. Be sure to baste the fish frequently during cooking, as it is very lean.

OCEAN PERCH Prepare as for Sole and Flounder.

POMPANO Eight small fillets or 4 small whole dressed fish may be prepared according to the Master Technique.

PORGY Four small whole dressed fish may be prepared according to the Master Technique.

RED SNAPPER Two large fillets or, if you are lucky enough to find one, a large whole dressed fish may be prepared according to the Master Technique. Snapper is a particularly tasty and eye-pleasing dish when stuffed and baked.

SALMON Any cut of salmon—2 large fillets or fillet sections, 4 steaks, 4 whole dressed baby fish, or a single large whole dressed fish—is delicious stuffed and baked according to the Master Technique. Boiled potatoes and spinach, perhaps creamed, puréed, or butter-braised, are excellent vegetable accompaniments.

SEA BASS Eight small or 2 large fillets, 4 steaks, and 4 small or 1 large whole dressed fish may all be prepared according to the Master Technique.

SHAD Select 2 pounds of boned shad fillets. Pack the stuffing in the pockets left by the removal of the bones, and bake the fillets flat, stuffed side up, for 8 to 12 minutes, otherwise following the general procedure for small fish fillets in Step 2 of the Master Technique.

SOLE AND FLOUNDER Eight small or 4 medium fillets of any of the various flatfish are excellent stuffed and baked. Proceed according to the Master Technique, or use one of the variations on pages 246.

STRIPED BASS Two large fillets or 1 large whole dressed fish may be prepared according to the Master Technique. Also good with this fish are the crabmeat and mushroom stuffing variations indicated for Sole and Flounder, page 246.

TILEFISH Four tilefish steaks may be prepared according to the Master Technique. Baste this lean fish frequently during cooking.

TROUT Eight small or 4 medium fillets or 4 small whole dressed trout may be prepared according to the Master Technique. Also excellent with trout is the variation on page 247 using a bacon-flavored stuffing.

WHITEFISH Four medium or two large fillets or a single large whole dressed fish can be prepared according to the Master Technique.

WHITING Small whole dressed whiting are excellent prepared according to the Master Technique.

Variation: BAKED COD WITH TOMATO STUFFING

4 servings

Baked Stuffed Fish, using 2 large cod fillets, 4 cod steaks, or 1 whole dressed cod or scrod

ADD: ½ cup peeled, seeded, diced tomatoes, fresh or canned (see page 607)

½ teaspoon mashed, pressed, or very finely minced garlic

1½ cups Tomato Sauce, page 183 (optional)

In Step 1 of the Master Technique, add tomatoes and garlic to the onion and celery after the vegetables have been sautéed. Raise heat to high and cook, stirring, until all liquid from the tomatoes has boiled away. Proceed according to the Master Technique, serving the fish with tomato sauce, if you wish.

Variation: NEW ENGLAND BAKED STUFFED WHOLE COD

4 servings

❦ *The traditional accompaniments for this dish are peas and boiled potatoes.*

Baked Stuffed Fish, using a whole dressed cod

ADD: ½ pint raw oysters or clams, drained and quartered

Cream Sauce with Hard-cooked Eggs and Fresh Herbs, page 38, made with parsley

Prepare cod according to Master Technique, adding oysters or clams to the finished stuffing. Serve with cream sauce.

Variation: BAKED SALMON WITH DILL AND CUCUMBER STUFFING

4 servings

Baked Stuffed Fish, using salmon (any cut listed in the chart on page 243)

SUBSTITUTE: 1 medium-large cucumber for celery
1½ tablespoons finely chopped fresh dill (feathery leaves only) or 1½ teaspoons dried dillweed for parsley

Sour Cream Sauce, page 44 (optional)

Peel cucumber, halve it lengthwise, scoop out the seeds with a spoon, and cut the halves into ¼-inch dice; you should have about ¾ cup. In Step 1 of the Master Technique, substitute diced cucumber for celery, and sauté the onion and cucumber for about 10 minutes, or until quite soft. Flavor stuffing with dill rather than parsley, then proceed with Master Technique, serving the fish with sour cream sauce, if you wish.

Variation: BAKED SOLE OR FLOUNDER FILLETS WITH CRABMEAT STUFFING

4 servings

❦ *Serve this elegant dish with asparagus, sautéed cucumbers, or peas.*

Baked Stuffed Fish, using 8 small or 4 large sole or flounder fillets
ADD: 1/4 cup finely diced green pepper
INCREASE: Lemon juice to 1 teaspoon
ADD: 1/4 teaspoon dry mustard
1/2 cup chopped crabmeat, fresh cooked or well-drained canned
Lobster or Crab Cream Sauce, page 42, or Sherried Cream Sauce, page 44, or melted butter

In Step 1 of the Master Technique, sauté green pepper along with the onion and celery. Increase lemon juice to 1 teaspoon, add dry mustard along with the salt and pepper, and fold crabmeat into stuffing. Proceed from there according to the Master Technique, serving the fish with a cream sauce or with melted butter.

Variation: BAKED SOLE OR FLOUNDER FILLETS WITH MUSHROOM STUFFING

4 servings

Baked Stuffed Fish, using 8 small or 4 large sole or flounder fillets
ADD: Mushroom Stuffing, page 553
Sherried Cream Sauce, page 44, or melted butter

Prepare mushroom stuffing, scrape it out of the skillet, and set aside. Use the same skillet to prepare the stuffing outlined in Step 1 of the Master Technique; fold the reserved mushroom mixture into the stuffing. Proceed from there according to the Master Technique. Serve with sherried cream sauce or melted butter.

Variation: WHOLE BAKED TROUT WITH BACON STUFFING

4 servings

Baked Stuffed Fish, using 4 whole dressed trout

ADD: 12 slices bacon
OMIT: Butter called for in Step 1
ADD: 2 to 4 tablespoons (½ to 1 ounce) chopped pecans (optional)

Fry 8 slices bacon until crisp, drain on paper toweling, crumble, and set aside. Prepare the stuffing as indicated in Step 1 of the Master Technique, but use the drippings from the bacon in lieu of butter and add the reserved crumbled bacon to the finished stuffing. You may also add a few tablespoons of chopped pecans to the stuffing if you like. Proceed according to Step 2 of the Master Technique, stuffing the trout with the bacon mixture and wrapping each in a slice of bacon just before baking.

MASTER TECHNIQUE

Fish in White Wine Sauce

4 servings

❦ *Classic French cuisine boasts numerous splendid fish dishes in which fish is poached in white wine and fish stock and then served with a cream sauce made with the concentrated poaching broth and enriched with egg yolks, heavy cream, and butter. Fine though the classic recipes are, however, they seem to me to require some modification for modern cooks. For one thing, fish poached in the classical manner picks up a rather strong taste of wine, and its inherent flavor is barely able to squeak through. Furthermore, as there is quite a lot of diluted poaching broth left at the end of cooking, a prolonged boiling down is required to concentrate the broth and make the sauce, and during this time the fish tends to dry out and even get cold. And thus, with apologies to Escoffier and other great shades of the past, I offer the following* à la moderne *recipe for fish in white wine sauce. The sauce itself is basically the same as that dictated by tradition, but the fish, rather than being poached, is arranged on a bed of onions, mostened with a bit of wine, and baked—or, really, steamed—in a very hot oven. The fish emerges from the oven tasting like itself. Since only a rather small and already concentrated quantity of delicious fish juices is produced, the sauce-making can proceed rapidly and the fish is not subjected to a long wait before serving.*

This is an elegant dish and should be served with elegantly simple accompaniments. Plain steamed white rice is definitely called for. My favorite vegetable accompaniment is sautéed cucumbers; asparagus, snow peas, or ordinary peas are other possibilities. Unless you should happen to be oenophobic, you will want to serve this dish with a dry white wine. A French white Burgundy or a California Chardonnay are particularly nice choices.

Choosing a Fish to Serve in White Wine Sauce: The chart at the end of this Master Technique gives a list of fish particularly suitable for preparation in this manner, as well as a few tips on preparing each. In general, lean, white-fleshed fish respond better to this treatment than oily, dark-fleshed fish, and small, thin fillets, preferably skinless, have a more elegant look on the plate than fish steaks or whole fish.

Preliminaries

1. Set rack in the middle of the oven.
2. Preheat oven to 475°F 20 minutes before baking.
3. Select a covered casserole or a non-aluminum baking dish, with a sheet of foil to cover, just large enough to hold the fish in one layer. (Thin fillets will be folded in halves or thirds; see below.) Using 1 to 2 tablespoons soft butter, grease the dish lavishly.
4. Cut a sheet of waxed paper to fit snugly inside the baking dish. Grease one side of the paper with 1 tablespoon soft butter.

Step 1: Baking the Fish

2 large parsley stems, without leaves
1 medium-large onion, peeled, sliced, and separated into rings
Ground thyme
One of the following (see chart, page 251, for specific fish):
  2 pounds fish fillets or fillet sections, preferably skinless
  2 pounds fish steaks
½ teaspoon salt
¼ teaspoon white pepper, preferably freshly ground
⅔ cup excellent dry white wine, preferably the same wine that will be drunk with the fish
¼ to ½ cup Fish Stock, page 27, clam juice, or water

Lay parsley stems on the bottom of the prepared baking dish, then cover the bottom of the dish with a bed of onion rings, jumbled. Add a pinch of thyme. Lightly score the skin or skin side of fish fillets with a sharp knife, as though scoring a ham. Run your index finger over fish steaks, pulling out with tweezers any bones that your finger snags on, but leaving the central spine bone in place. Season the fish with salt and white pepper. Fillets that are ¼ inch thick or less should be folded in half if 5 to 6 inches long, in thirds if more than 6 inches in length. The skin side should be in the middle.

Arrange fish in a single layer in the baking dish. Slowly drizzle the wine over the fish, then pour into the dish—but not over the fish—enough clam juice, fish stock, or water to film the bottom of the dish to a depth of about 3⁄16 inch. Place the prepared waxed paper, buttered side down, directly over the fish, then cover the dish with lid or foil. Place in preheated oven and bake 10 to 12 minutes per inch of thickness measured at the thickest part; the thickness of fillets should be based on the total height after folding. The fish is done when the flesh is white and opaque when flaked with a fork, rather than pink and translucent.

(While the fish is in the oven, you should proceed to the next step of this recipe.)

Step 2: Preparing the White Wine Cream Sauce

½ cup heavy cream
2 large egg yolks
3 tablespoons butter, plus 2 to 3 tablespoons to enrich the sauce
2½ tablespoons all-purpose flour
¾ cup milk, more if needed
Salt and white pepper, preferably freshly ground, as needed
Fresh lemon juice

Beat the cream and egg yolks together in a 2-quart bowl until thoroughly blended; set aside.

Melt 3 tablespoons butter over low flame in a heavy-bottomed 1½- to 2-quart saucepan made of or lined with a noncorroding material. Remove from heat, add the flour, and stir with a wire whip until perfectly smooth. Return to low flame and, stirring constantly, let the flour-butter paste, or roux, bubble for 2 to 3 minutes without coloring. Remove from heat and set aside.

Remove cooked fish from oven, uncover, and remove waxed paper. Tilt the baking dish and, using a bulb baster or small ladle, remove all the cooking liquid from the bottom of the dish, transferring it to a noncorroding saucepan. Replace the waxed paper and lid on the fish; set aside. Set the saucepan of cooking liquid over high heat and boil down until reduced to ½ cup or slightly less. Pour into a measure and add enough milk to make 1¼ cups liquid. Return liquid to the saucepan and bring to just below the simmer; warm the reserved flour/butter paste over low heat to the point where it just begins to bubble. Remove flour/butter paste from heat and pour the hot liquid into it all at once, beating with a whip as you do so. The sauce will begin to thicken at once. Set sauce over moderate heat, bring to a simmer, then lower heat and cook very slowly, stirring, for 2 to 3 minutes.

Beating constantly, slowly pour the hot sauce into the reserved cream/yolk mixture, then pour the sauce back into the saucepan. Set sauce over moderately low heat and, stirring constantly, heat just until the sauce thickens and trembles on the verge of simmering. Remove from heat and season to taste with salt and white pepper; little salt will be needed if you baked the fish using fish stock or clam juice. If you wish a deliciously rich sauce, add soft butter ½ tablespoon at a time, beating constantly with a whip, as though making hollandaise. (If the butter is added too quickly—or if you happen to have overheated the egg yolks—the sauce may thin out at this point; stop adding butter if the sauce is becoming runny.) If the sauce needs to be thinned, dribble in any juices that may have accumulated around the fish or add teaspoons of milk. Make a final correction in the seasoning using drops of fresh lemon juice.

Spoon some of the sauce over the bottom of a serving platter or individual plates, preferably slightly warmed, and arrange the fish on top. Place a small dollop or ribbon of sauce over each piece of fish and decorate with a tiny sprig of parsley, if you wish. Serve at once, passing any remaining sauce separately.

FISH IN WHITE WINE SAUCE CHART

BASS See Sea Bass; Striped Bass.

COD AND SCROD Prepare fillet sections or steaks according to the Master Technique.

FLOUNDER See Sole and Flounder.

GROUPER Prepare fillet sections or steaks according to the Master Technique.

HADDOCK Prepare fillet sections or steaks according to the Master Technique.

HALIBUT This fish is particularly choice with a white wine sauce; prepare steaks according to the Master Technique.

MONKFISH Prepare fillets according to the Master Technique; this is one of the best treatments for this lean, subtly flavored fish.

OCEAN PERCH Prepare fillets, preferably skinless, as for Sole and Flounder.

POMPANO Prepare fillets according to the Master Technique.

RED SNAPPER Prepare fillets or steaks according to the Master Technique.

SALMON Prepare fillet sections or steaks according to the Master Technique. Do not skin fillets before cooking, but scrape off both skin and the grayish fat underneath after cooking.

SEA BASS Prepare fillets or steaks according to the Master Technique.

SHAD Prepare fillets according to the Master Technique.

SOLE AND FLOUNDER These are classic fish for serving with a white wine sauce. Folding the fillets in halves or thirds, prepare according to the Master Technique or, for an especially fancy dish, try the variation with a shrimp stuffing on page 252.

STRIPED BASS Prepare fillets, preferably skinless, according to the Master Technique.

TILEFISH Prepare steaks according to the Master Technique.

TROUT Prepare fillets according to the Master Technique, laying the fillets flat in the baking dish and removing the skin after cooking.

Variation: SOLE OR FLOUNDER FILLETS STUFFED WITH SHRIMP MOUSSE

4 servings

Fish in White Wine Sauce, using sole or flounder fillets
ADD: 8 ounces raw shrimp in the shells, peeled (see page 316)
½ cup heavy cream
½ teaspoon tomato paste (optional)
½ teaspoon salt
¼ teaspoon white pepper, preferably freshly ground
1 teaspoon strained fresh lemon juice

Combine shrimp, cream, tomato paste, salt, and white pepper in blender or food processor and purée until very smooth. Add 1 teaspoon lemon juice and blend again briefly. Divide the stuffing among the fillets, spreading it on the skin side and folding the fillets in halves or thirds, depending on their length. Proceed according to the Master Technique, basing the cooking time on the thickness of the folded fillets plus stuffing.

MASTER TECHNIQUE

Poached Fish

4 servings

❦ *The simplest and most "natural" of all fish-cooking methods, poaching entails cooking fish at just below the simmer in a flavored broth. Although poached fish is most commonly served hot, it is equally good cold with mayonnaise, and it can also be used to make a fish casserole, fish salad, or fish croquettes. The classic cuisine boasts numerous poaching broths, some of them made with wine, fish stock, aromatic vegetables, or herbs, but these tend, I think, to impart a stronger and more intrusive flavor to fish than most people want these days. In this recipe, the broth is lighter and much easier to make, consisting merely of water mixed with enough lemon juice and salt to ensure a fresh taste. The inherent flavor of the fish comes through without interference.*

A judicious choice of accompaniments is important here since, unadorned, poached fish can seem rather bland and uninteresting. The fish poaching chart at the end of this Master Technique suggests accompaniments particularly appropriate to specific kinds of fish. In general, hot poached fish needs a sauce of some sort. I am partial to those from the hollandaise family, though dieters can get by with just a squirt of lemon juice and perhaps a slim pat of butter. Boiled potatoes, preferably small new potatoes, are a traditionally favored accompaniment, and a green vegetable is definitely called for, asparagus and broccoli being almost ubiquitously appropriate. Cold poached fish, which is most frequently found on lunch menus, should always be served with mayonnaise or one of its variants containing herbs or horseradish. For accompaniments, choose among the usual cold-platter garnishes—sliced fresh tomatoes, quartered hard-cooked eggs, and cold cooked vegetables such as asparagus, broccoli, green beans, beets, or potatoes.

CHOOSING A FISH TO POACH: The chart at the end of this Master Technique gives tips on how to poach specific kinds of fish. As you will note from the chart, lean, firm, flavorful fish such as cod, grouper, sea bass, and snapper are best for poaching, although delicate and mild-tasting fish such as halibut, porgy, and sole are also amenable to poaching if they are handled carefully during cooking and are served with sauces and accompaniments that enhance rather than overwhelm their subtle qualities. With the important exceptions of salmon and trout, dark-fleshed or oily fish are not good candidates for poaching, as they tend to come out tasting fishy.

NOTES ON THE FISH POACHER: Although a fish poacher equipped with a removable rack for lifting the cooked fish out of the pot is convenient and fun to use, it is not essential. Fish fillets and steaks as well as small whole fish can be prepared in any noncorroding pot or deep skillet large enough to hold the pieces in a single layer; use a large slotted spatula to remove the cooked fish from the pot. Large whole fish are most easily prepared in a poacher, but here too you can improvise. Before cooking, wrap the fish in several layers of rinsed cheesecloth and tie securely at both ends, leaving protruding tufts of cloth at the head and tail by which the fish can be lifted out of the pot when it is done. Cut away the cheesecloth after setting the fish on its serving platter. A turkey roaster or other deep roasting pan can be used as a poaching vessel.

One of the following (see chart, page 254, for specific fish):
- 2 pounds fish fillets or fillet sections, preferably 3/4 inch thick or more
- 2 pounds fish steaks, preferably 3/4 inch thick or more
- 2 to 4 small whole dressed fish of equal size, weighing 3 to 4 pounds altogether
- 1 large whole dressed fish weighing 3 to 4 pounds

1 quart water, more if needed
Fresh lemon juice
Salt

Laying fillets or fillet sections skin side down, arrange fish in a single layer in an 18×6×4-inch fish poacher or in a deep skillet or wide pot made of or lined with a noncorroding material. Keeping track of how much you are adding, pour enough water over the fish to cover it by ½ inch, then add 3 tablespoons lemon juice and 1 tablespoon salt per quart of water used. Cover and set over high heat. As soon as the poaching broth begins to steam and quiver gently, indicating that it is on the verge of simmering, turn the heat down to low. Begin timing at this point, poaching the fish approximately 8 minutes per inch of thickness measured at the thickest part; regulate the heat so that the broth remains continuously at just below the simmer. The fish is cooked when the flesh looks white, opaque, and juicy rather than pink, translucent, and sticky when flaked with a fork at the thickest part.

If the fish is to be served hot, lift the rack out of the poacher, hold the rack for a few moments over the poacher to drain the fish, then slide fish onto a platter. (If you are working without a poacher, follow the same procedure using a slotted spatula.) If the fish is to be served cold, set the poacher or pot, uncovered, in a sink filled with ice water (in the winter, set it outside). When the poaching broth has cooled to tepid, cover and refrigerate for up to 24 hours, draining the fish just before serving.

FISH POACHING CHART

BASS See Sea Bass; Striped Bass.

CATFISH Poach skinned catfish fillets, folded in half lengthwise, catfish steaks, or small whole skinned catfish according to the Master Technique. Serve hot with caper cream sauce or tartar sauce; accompany with boiled potatoes and a green vegetable.

COD AND SCROD Cod is a fine poaching fish. Thick fillets may be used, but steaks or whole fish are even better; proceed as in Master Technique. Cod may be served hot with a number of different cream sauces—caper cream sauce, cheese sauce, cream sauce with hard-cooked eggs and fresh herbs, curried cream sauce, or dilled or parsleyed cream sauce. Accompany with boiled potatoes and a green vegetable. Poached cod is also delicious cold with green goddess dressing or herb mayonnaise, and it is excellent to use in a fish salad, a fish casserole, or fish croquettes.

FLOUNDER See Sole and Flounder.

GROUPER Treat as for Sea Bass.

HADDOCK Treat as for Cod and Scrod.

HALIBUT Poach steaks according to Master Technique. Serve hot with hollandaise sauce plus steamed rice and a green vegetable, or cold with plain mayonnaise.

MONKFISH Poach thick fillets according to Master Technique. Serve hot with hollandaise or seafood hollandaise plus steamed rice and a green vegetable. Cold poached monkfish is thought by some to resemble cold lobster both in taste and texture. Serve with mayonnaise, use to make a fish salad, or substitute for lobster in lobster salad.

OCEAN PERCH Score the skin of fillets in a diamond pattern (as though scoring a ham), then fold in half, the skin side in the middle. Poach according to the Master Technique and serve with hollandaise sauce plus boiled potatoes and a green vegetable.

RED SNAPPER A whole poached snapper makes a beautiful sight on a platter, and fillets may also be poached. Proceed according to the Master Technique. Serve hot with hollandaise sauce plus either boiled potatoes or steamed rice and broccoli, asparagus, or snow peas. Cold snapper is as good as hot; serve with plain mayonnaise or cucumber dressing.

SALMON A classic fish for poaching. Choose thick-cut pieces from the center of the fillet, center-cut steaks, or, for a real treat, a single whole fish. Proceed according to the Master Technique. Especially when you are serving the salmon cold, it is an attractive touch to scrape off the skin and the underlying gray fat before serving. (The skin covering the head of a whole fish should be left intact.) Serve hot poached salmon with hollandaise or dilled hollandaise sauce and accompany with boiled potatoes and asparagus, sautéed cucumbers, or peas. Serve cold poached salmon with mayonnaise, cucumber dressing, or whipped cream mayonnaise.

SEA BASS Poach thick fillet sections or whole fish according to the Master Technique. Serve hot with hollandaise or seafood hollandaise and accompany with boiled potatoes or steamed rice and a green vegetable. Also good cold with mayonnaise.

SOLE AND FLOUNDER I prefer to oven-poach these delicate fish and serve with a white wine sauce, but they may also be poached plain. Lightly score the skin side of the fillets as though scoring a ham. Fold the fillets in half, or, if very long and thin, in thirds, with the skin side in the middle. Serve hot with Champagne cream sauce, cream sauce with white grapes, lemon cream sauce, or hollandaise sauce. Accompany with steamed rice and a green vegetable. Sole and flounder are also good cold with mayonnaise or rémoulade sauce.

STRIPED BASS Treat as for Sea Bass.

TILEFISH Poach steaks according to Master Technique. Serve hot with hollandaise sauce plus steamed rice and a green vegetable, or cold with mayonnaise.

TROUT Like salmon, trout is a classic fish for poaching. Choose whole fish, preferably small ones suitable for single servings, and prepare according to the Master Technique. Serve hot with hollandaise or melted butter, accompanied by boiled potatoes and green beans, or serve cold with horseradish mayonnaise or whipped cream mayonnaise flavored with a tad of horseradish. See also variation on page 256.

WHITEFISH Poach fillets or whole fish according to the Master Technique. Serve hot with caper cream sauce or tartar sauce, accompanied by boiled potatoes and a green vegetable. Also good cold with mayonnaise or rémoulade sauce.

WHITING Poach small whole whiting according to the Master Technique. Take care in removing from the poacher or pot, as the fish are apt to break apart. Serve hot with hollandaise sauce, accompanied by boiled potatoes and a green vegetable, or cold with mayonnaise.

Variation: TROUT "AU BLEU"

4 servings

❦ *The natural slime and tiny scales covering trout turn a dazzling metallic blue when the fish are cooked in a vinegary poaching broth. However, for this chemical reaction to take place, the trout must be freshly taken from a stream or tank, handled as little as possible during cleaning, and neither scaled nor rinsed.*

Poached Fish, using 4 whole dressed trout
SUBSTITUTE: ¾ cup distilled white vinegar for lemon juice

Proceed according to the Master Technique, but substitute vinegar for the lemon juice called for, adding ¾ cup vinegar for each quart of water. Serve hot or cold, with the sauces and accompaniments listed in the chart on page 255.

MASTER TECHNIQUE

Pan-fried Fish

4 servings

❦ *Pan-fried fish is lightly dredged in flour, or sometimes fine cornmeal, and skillet-fried in a small amount of butter and oil or other fat until browned and crispy. Properly speaking, the method should be called sautéing, frying implying the use of a quantity of fat, but pan-frying has come to be the usual American term: southern-sautéed catfish just does not have the right ring. However it is named, pan-frying is a lovely and quite simple way to cook fish that is classic not only in this country but throughout the world. The recipes beginning on page 260 present pan-frying variations with French, Italian, Indian, and Vietnamese undertones.*

Except when sauced according to one of the variation recipes, pan-fried fish should be served with lemon wedges. It is nice to offer a flavored butter (butter creamed with anchovy paste, or shallot vinegar, or parsley and lemon juice, or the like), tartar sauce, or rémoulade sauce as well. As accompaniments, I most frequently find myself serving boiled green beans and boiled potatoes. However, virtually any green vegetable will do, and steamed rice or one of its variations may stand in for potatoes.

CHOOSING A FISH TO PAN-FRY: The chart at the end of this Master Technique gives a list of fish particularly suitable for pan-frying, as well as a few tips on preparing each. As you will note, virtually all fish are amenable to this cooking method. You will find that small, thin fillets and small whole-dressed or pan-dressed fish are easier to handle during cooking and less apt to turn soggy than are thick fillets or fish steaks. However, large fish pieces can also be pan-fried. Stand well back when turning them to prevent being spattered by hot fat, and use a roomy skillet and lively heat so that the fish does not steam in its own juices and become limp.

One of the following (see chart, page 258, for specific fish):

2 pounds fish fillets or sections of fillets, preferably no more than 6 inches long and 1/4 inch thick

2 pounds fish steaks, no more than 3/4 inch thick and preferably thinner

4 small whole dressed or pan-dressed fish weighing 10 to 12 ounces each

1 1/2 teaspoons salt

1/4 teaspoon pepper, preferably freshly ground

1/2 cup all-purpose flour

8 tablespoons (1 stick) butter

1/4 cup neutral vegetable oil

Set oven to "warm" (about 150°F) and place a heat-proof platter in the oven.

Rinse fish quickly under cold running water and pat lightly with paper toweling, leaving the fish slightly moist. Using a very sharp knife, cut two or three diagonal gashes through the skin of skin-on fish fillets; cut three gashes almost to the bone on each side of whole dressed or pan-dressed fish. (The gashes help keep the fish from curling up during cooking.) Sprinkle all surfaces of the fish with salt and pepper. Dip both sides of the fish in flour, pressing lightly to make the flour adhere, then shake gently to remove the excess. Place the fish on a rack and let rest 5 to 10 minutes to set the coating.

Select either a very large skillet (about 12 inches across the bottom) or two smaller skillets (8 to 10 inches across the bottom) and add the butter and oil. Set skillet(s) over moderately high heat, and when the fat is very hot and has just begun to color, add the fish. Regulating the heat so that the fat continues to bubble vigorously but does not smoke or blacken, fry the fish 8 to 10 minutes per inch of thickness measured at the thickest part, turning the fish once with a spatula midway through the estimated cooking time. Fillets are done as soon as they are brown and crispy and feel firm when pressed with your finger. A sign of doneness for steaks is the emergence of juices into the pan; remove at once. To test whole fish for doneness, pry open the belly flap with a fork and examine the backbone; the flesh around the bones should look milky, opaque, and juicy, rather than pink, translucent, and sticky-dry.

Remove fish with a spatula to the heated serving platter and bring to the table at once.

FISH PAN-FRYING CHART

BASS See Sea Bass; Striped Bass.

BLOWFISH (SEA SQUAB) Prepare 2 pounds blowfish tails according to the Master Technique; tongs may be more useful than a spatula in turning them. The tails will take about 5 minutes to cook.

BLUEFISH Fillets, the smaller the better, or whole baby bluefish are delicious pan-fried. Proceed according to the Master Technique or use the meunière variation suggested for sole and flounder, page 264.

BUTTERFISH For whole dressed butterfish pan-frying is perhaps the cooking method of choice. Proceed according to the Master Technique. Pan-fried butterfish are especially nice with Maître d'Hôtel butter: Cream 4 tablespoons butter with 1 tablespoon minced fresh parsley, 2 teaspoons strained fresh lemon juice, and a few grindings pepper. Turn out onto a sheet of waxed paper, roll into a cylinder, and chill until firm. Top each butterfish with a slice of the butter just before serving.

CATFISH Skinned catfish fillets or small skinned whole dressed or pan-dressed fish are classic pan-fried. Serving the fish with tartar sauce or rémoulade sauce, prepare according to the Master Technique or the classic Southern variation on page 260.

COD AND SCROD Choose the smallest, thinnest fillets possible, and cut them into serving pieces before cooking. Proceed as in the Master Technique; serve with tartar sauce. Cod steaks are too juicy and too prone to breaking apart to be pan-fried.

CROAKER Treat as for Porgy.

GROUPER Treat as for Cod and Scrod.

HADDOCK Treat as for Cod and Scrod.

HALIBUT This fish has the right taste and texture for pan-frying, but it is generally available only in large and often odd-shaped steaks that are difficult to maneuver in the skillet. Choose the smallest, thinnest, and most compactly shaped steaks possible, or cut large or floppy steaks into manageable pieces, removing the bones in the process. Proceed as in the Master Technique, perhaps serving the fish with tartar sauce, or follow the meunière variation suggested for sole and flounder, see page 264.

KINGFISH See Mackerel.

MACKEREL Fillets of either Atlantic mackerel or small Spanish mackerel, small whole dressed or pan-dressed mackerel, or king mackerel steaks may all be pan-fried. Proceed according to the Master Technique, or follow the Southeast Asian or meunière variations suggested for porgy or sole and flounder respectively (page 261 and 264), or prepare with rosemary (page 261).

MONKFISH Pan-fry thin fillet pieces according to the Master Technique or follow the meunière variation suggested for sole and flounder, page 264.

OCEAN PERCH Treat as for sole and flounder.

POMPANO Prepare fillets or whole dressed fish according to the Master Technique or follow the meunière variation suggested for sole and flounder, page 264.

PORGY Pan-frying is an excellent cooking technique for porgy or other small fish that are usually served whole dressed or pan-dressed. Proceed according to the Master Technique or coat in cornmeal as suggested for catfish, page 260. For an unusual dish, try the sweet-and-sour version on page 261.

RED SNAPPER Prepare fillets or small whole dressed or pan-dressed fish according to the Master Technique, or use the Southeast Asian variation suggested for porgy, page 261.

SALMON Fillet sections or steaks may be prepared according to the Master Technique or the variation on page 262. If using steaks, try to choose those from the tail end of the fish, which are leaner and more compact than those from the head or stomach sections.

SEA BASS Fillets and small whole fish may be prepared according to the Master Technique; serve with tartar sauce. Small whole sea bass are also excellent done in the Southeast Asian style suggested for porgy, page 261.

SHAD Prepare boned shad fillets according to the Master Technique; serve with tartar sauce or rémoulade sauce.

SHARK Steaks may be prepared according to the Master Technique. Tartar sauce or rémoulade sauce should be offered.

SMELTS Smelts are very well suited to pan-frying. Fillets may be pan-fried, but it is more usual to choose small whole fish. Allow 2 to 4 whole fish per serving, depending on their size. A fatty and richly flavored fish, smelts also take well to the spicy-sweet variation on page 263.

SOLE AND FLOUNDER These are among the most favored of all fish for pan-frying. Since these fillets are very lean, they are enhanced by a sauce of some kind. Prepare according to the Master Technique and serve with tartar sauce, rémoulade sauce, or, my personal favorite, anchovy butter (prepare maître d'hotel butter, page 258, adding 2 teaspoons anchovy paste or 1 tablespoon mashed anchovies). Or prepare one of the classic recipes on pages 263 and 264, each of which includes a butter sauce.

STRIPED BASS Prepare fillets or small whole dressed or pan-fressed fish according to the Master Technique.

SWORDFISH If large, cut swordfish steaks into manageable, serving-size pieces; prepare as in Master Technique. Also excellent are the rosemary variation suggested for mackerel, page 261, and the meunière variation for Sole and flounder, page 264.

TILEFISH Small, compact steaks may be prepared according to the Master Technique. Serve with tartar sauce.

TROUT This is a classic fish for pan-frying. Choose either fillets or small whole dressed or pan-dressed fish. Prepare according to the Master Technique, substituting well-strained bacon fat for the oil and butter if you wish, or use the meunière variation suggested for sole and flounder, page 264. Speaking personally, I simply must have boiled potatoes with trout. Accompany also with green beans or follow with a salad.

TUNA A slightly anomalous fish, tuna is pan-fried—or perhaps a more accurate term would be pan-grilled—according to a procedure somewhat different from that presented in the Master Technique. Wipe tuna steaks with paper toweling, rub on both sides with a lemon half, and season with salt and pepper, peppering the steaks rather heavily. Heat a thin film of vegetable oil or olive oil in a skillet or skillets large enough to hold the tuna with room to spare. When the oil is on the verge of smoking, add the tuna and sauté just 2 to 3 minutes on each side, depending on the thickness of the steaks. The idea is to sear the outside while keeping the interior quite underdone—it should be red and translucent, like rare steak. Serve with lemon wedges. Good accompaniments are spinach sautéed Chinese-style and steamed brown rice.

WEAKFISH (SEA TROUT) Fillets or small whole fish may be prepared according to the Master Technique.

WHITEFISH Fillets or small whole fish may be prepared according to the Master Technique. Serve with tartar sauce.

WHITING Small whole whiting are excellent pan-fried according to the Master Technique. Serve with tartar sauce.

Variation: SOUTHERN-FRIED CATFISH

4 servings

Pan-fried fish, using skinned catfish fillets or skinned whole dressed or pan-dressed fish

SUBSTITUTE: ¾ cup white or yellow cornmeal for flour

½ cup additional neutral vegetable oil for butter or ¾ cup well-strained bacon fat for both butter and vegetable oil

Proceed according to the Master Technique, but coat catfish in cornmeal rather than flour and fry in vegetable oil or bacon fat.

Variation: PAN-FRIED MACKEREL WITH ROSEMARY

4 servings

Pan-fried fish, using small mackerel fillets or whole dressed or pan-dressed mackerel

ADD:	1 teaspoon dried rosemary, ground or moistened with a few drops of water and minced fine
	½ teaspoon mashed, pressed, or very finely minced garlic
SUBSTITUTE:	¾ cup olive oil for butter and neutral vegetable oil
ADD:	½ lemon

Proceed according to the Master Technique, but rub fish with rosemary and garlic before sprinkling with salt and pepper, and fry in olive oil. Squeeze lemon over fish after removing from the pan.

Variation: SWEET-AND-SOUR FRIED PORGY SOUTHEAST ASIAN STYLE

4 servings

❦*Accompany this with steamed rice and sliced raw cucumbers.*

Pan-fried Fish, using whole dressed or pan-dressed porgies
SUBSTITUTE: An additional ½ cup neutral vegetable oil for butter
1 tablespoon minced garlic
1½ teaspoons minced ginger
½ teaspoon crushed red pepper (optional)
¼ cup packed dark brown sugar
¼ cup distilled vinegar
2 tablespoons dark soy sauce
½ teaspoon anchovy paste or Thai fish sauce *(nam pla)*
1 bunch scallions

Prepare the fish as indicated in the Master Technique, but fry in vegetable oil only rather than in butter and oil. Remove to heated platter, cover loosely, and place in warm oven. Pour off all but 3 tablespoons of the fat in the skillet. Add to the fat the garlic, ginger, and, if you wish, red pepper (minced with either the garlic or ginger). Fry gently for 1 minute, then add brown sugar, vinegar, soy sauce, and anchovy paste or Thai fish sauce *(nam pla).* Raise heat to high and boil hard for 30 seconds, stirring. Remove from heat and stir in 1 bunch scallions sliced on the diagonal into 3⁄8-inch pieces (including the tender green parts). Pour sauce over the fish and serve at once.

Variation: PAN-FRIED SALMON STEAKS WITH TOMATO CREAM SAUCE

4 servings

❦ *Serve this with peas or asparagus and steamed rice.*

Pan-fried Fish, using salmon steaks (see page 259)
3 tablespoons butter
1 tablespoon minced shallots or scallion (white parts only)
1⁄3 cup peeled, seeded, diced tomatoes, fresh or canned (see page 607)
1 cup heavy cream
Salt and white pepper, preferably freshly ground, to taste
1⁄2 to 1 teaspoon Cognac or brandy

Prepare salmon steaks according to the Master Technique, then remove to warmed serving platter, cover loosely, and place in warm oven. Pour the fat out of the skillet and wipe with paper towels. Melt butter in the skillet, add shallots or scallions, and sauté over low heat for 2 minutes, or until soft but not brown. Add tomatoes, raise heat to high, and cook until all the liquid from the tomatoes has evaporated. Add the cream and simmer over moderate heat until reduced by one quarter and lightly thickened. Season with salt and white pepper, then add Cognac to taste. Surround salmon steaks with sauce and serve at once.

Variation: CURRIED PAN-FRIED SMELTS

4 servings

❦ *Serve this with steamed rice and a plain green vegetable.*

Pan-fried Fish, using 8 to 16 whole dressed smelts (depending on size)
SUBSTITUTE: An additional ½ cup neutral vegetable oil for butter
¼ cup finely chopped onion
2 teaspoons mild curry powder or 1½ teaspoons hot (Madras) curry powder
1 teaspoon ground ginger
½ teaspoon dry mustard
¼ teaspoon ground allspice
¼ cup packed dark brown sugar
3 tablespoons water
2 tablespoons distilled vinegar
¼ teaspoon salt
¼ teaspoon pepper, preferably freshly ground

Prepare fish according to the Master Technique, but fry in oil only rather than in butter and oil. Place smelts on heated serving platter, cover loosely, and place in warm oven. Pour all but 3 tablespoons of fat out of the skillet, add the onion, and fry over moderate heat for 3 minutes, or until wilted. Stir in curry powder, ginger, mustard, and allspice, and cook slowly, stirring, for 2 minutes. Add brown sugar, water, vinegar, salt, and pepper. Raise heat to high and boil the sauce for 30 seconds, then pour over fish and serve at once.

Variation: SAUTÉED SOLE OR FLOUNDER FILLETS AMANDINE

4 servings

Pan-fried Fish, using sole or flounder fillets
12 tablespoons (1½ sticks) butter
½ cup (2 ounces) sliced almonds
1 teaspoon lemon juice

Prepare sole or flounder fillets according to the Master Technique. Remove to a warmed serving platter, cover loosely, and set in warm oven. Pour the fat out of the skillet and wipe with paper towels. Add 12 tablespoons butter to the skillet and set over moderate heat. When the butter foam begins to subside, stir in sliced almonds. Without letting the butter color more than a very pale gold, sauté the almonds until deep tan. Remove from heat, stir in lemon juice, and pour over the fish.

Variation: SOLE OR FLOUNDER MEUNIÈRE

4 servings

❦*A simple but classic treatment for fish. Be sure to serve boiled potatoes as an accompaniment here.*

Pan-fried Fish, using sole or flounder fillets
12 tablespoons (1½ sticks) butter
1 tablespoon strained fresh lemon juice
3 tablespoons minced fresh parsley

Prepare sole or flounder fillets according to the Master Technique. Remove to a warmed serving platter, cover loosely, and set in warm oven. Pour the fat out of the skillet and wipe with paper towels. Add 12 tablespoons butter to the skillet and stir over moderate heat until it turns a light nut-brown; watch what you're doing here, or the butter will burn. Remove skillet from heat and stir the butter for a few moments to cool it, then add lemon juice. Pour the butter sauce over the fish and sprinkle evenly with minced fresh parsley. Serve at once.

MASTER TECHNIQUE

French-Fried Fish

4 servings

❦*In former times, when Americans were less concerned about calories and fat consumption than they are today, deep-frying was one of the most popular cooking methods for fish. The reason is not hard to discover. The hot oil cooks fish very rapidly and evenly—the way, generally speaking, that fish likes to be cooked—while the coating surrounding the fish seals in the juices. The result is moist, meltingly tender fish surrounded by a deliciously contrasting crunchy exterior. In this recipe, fish is french-fried—that is, dipped in flour, then in beaten egg, and finally in fresh or dry bread crumbs or cornmeal—rather than frittered, which entails coating fish in a batter before frying. In my view, a batter coating is too heavy and overwhelming, and no matter how expeditiously one serves batter-dipped fish, it seems that the coating is always slightly soggy by the time the fish reaches the table.*

You will never go wrong if you serve French-fried fish with tartar sauce or rémoulade sauce plus lemon wedges and accompany it with french fries and cole slaw. Hollandaise is another sauce possibility, and for small whole fish boiled potatoes and green beans or peas are good accompaniments.

CHOOSING A FISH TO FRENCH-FRY: With the notable exceptions of catfish, smelt, and trout, fish that are to be french-fried should be white-fleshed, lean, mild-tasting, firm and dense in texture, and not too moist. The chart at the end of this Master Technique gives a list of fish particularly suitable for this cooking method, as well as some tips on preparing each.

One of the following (see chart, page 266, for specific fish):

1½ to 2 pounds fish fillets, skinned and cut into pieces no more than 1 inch thick or 6 inches in length

1½ to 2 pounds skinned and boned fish steaks, none more than 8 ounces in weight or more than 1 inch thick

4 whole dressed or pan-dressed fish, none more than 1 pound in weight or more than 8 inches in length

For breading and deep-frying:

½ cup all-purpose flour

2 large eggs beaten with 2 tablespoons neutral vegetable oil, 1 teaspoon salt, and ½ teaspoon pepper, preferably freshly ground

1½ to 2 cups Fine Fresh Bread Crumbs (see page 60), dry bread crumbs, or fine cornmeal

3 quarts very fresh vegetable oil

Before beginning you may wish to consult the Master Technique for Deep-frying. Step 1b, page 62, details the process of coating a food in bound breading; Step 2, page 64, explains how to fry.

Dip the fish in flour, then in the beaten egg mixture, and finally in fresh or dry bread crumbs or cornmeal. Heat oil to around 375°F. Cooking the fish in small batches, fry about 6 minutes per inch of thickness measured at the thickest part, or until golden brown on the outside and milky and flaky—rather than translucent and solid—within. Drain on paper towels and keep cooked fish in a warm oven (150°F) while you prepare the rest. Serve at once.

FISH FRENCH-FRYING CHART

CATFISH French-fried catfish is a classic American treat. Choose either skinned fillets or skinned whole dressed fish; coat in cornmeal. For a spicy, Cajun-style dish, beat the eggs with 2 teaspoons salt, 1 teaspoon pepper, and ½ to 1 teaspoon cayenne pepper.

COD AND SCROD I prefer scrod fillets here to cod fillets or steaks, which are chunky in texture and rather juicy; however, the latter may be used. Proceed according to the Master Technique, trimming fillets as indicated and using fresh or dry bread crumbs as the coating.

CROAKER French-fry small whole dressed croaker according to the Master Technique, using cornmeal as the coating.

FLOUNDER See Sole and Flounder.

GROUPER Proceed according to the Master Technique, trimming fillets as indicated and using fresh or dry bread crumbs as the coating.

HADDOCK Proceed according to the Master Technique, trimming fillets as indicated and using fresh or dry bread crumbs as the coating.

HALIBUT A very good fish for french-frying. Proceed according to the Master Technique, skinning and boning and using a coating of fresh bread crumbs. Hollandaise is as good a sauce accompaniment as tartar sauce here.

OCEAN PERCH Proceed as for Sole and Flounder.

PORGY Small whole dressed or pan-dressed porgy may be prepared according to the Master Technique. Use cornmeal as the coating and serve with tartar sauce.

SEA BASS Another fish that takes especially well to french-frying. Trim fillets as indicated in the Master Technique or use small whole dressed or pan-dressed fish. Coat with fresh or dry bread crumbs.

SMELTS Deep-frying is the usual and perhaps the best way of preparing these small fish. If possible, select small-medium fish—3 or more to the pound—and have them dressed whole. Proceed according to the Master Technique, coating the fish with fresh bread crumbs. If your smelts are very small and you fry them rather dark, you may eat them in their entirety—head, bones, and all. Always serve french-fried smelts with tartar sauce.

SOLE AND FLOUNDER Sole fillets may be left whole; large flounder fillets should be cut in half. Proceed according to the Master Technique, coating the fish with fresh or dry bread crumbs. It cannot be overemphasized how important it is not to overcook these fish. Fry just a minute or two.

TROUT Both skinned fillets and whole dressed or pan-dressed small fish (skinned or not, as you prefer) may be french-fried according to the Master Technique. I prefer a coating of fresh bread crumbs, but many like cornmeal.

RESCUING LEFTOVER FISH: A cold fish need not be unlovable. In addition to being usable in delicious old-fashioned fish cakes and croquettes, cold leftover fish—or fish that has suffered a disaster during cooking—may find a home in the following recipes:

Fish chowder: After removing skin, bones, and any coating, use fish in the chowder recipe, page 103.

Fish casserole: This is one of the handiest and most versatile of fish rescues. Remove skin, bones, and any coating, then combine fish with other ingredients indicated for New England fish casserole in the Casserole Variation Chart, page 202.

Fish salad: This is a particularly good rescue for leftover poached fish. Remove skin, bones, and any coating, flake the flesh, and combine with other ingredients according to the recipe on page 121.

Seafood soufflé: Use any fish here other than strongly flavored or oily types such as mackerel or bluefish. Remove skin, bones, and any coating, and grind the fish in a blender or food processor. Proceed with the recipe on page 175.

MASTER TECHNIQUE AND RESCUE: FISH CAKES OR CROQUETTES

4 to 6 servings

❦ *Mixed with riced potatoes and seasonings, shredded cooked fish is ready to be formed into patties and sautéed in butter, making fish cakes, or rolled into balls or other shapes, coated in bound breading, and deep-fried as croquettes. Step 1 of this recipe gives instructions on preparing the basic fish mixture; Step 2a shows how to make fish cakes, step 2b croquettes.*

Fish cakes and croquettes make fine brunch, lunch, or supper fare. Fish cakes may be served with tartar sauce or mayonnaise or simply with lemon wedges. Traditional New England accompaniments are baked beans and cole slaw; mashed potatoes and a green vegetable, perhaps cooked in cream or served with a cream sauce, are also good. Fish croquettes are best, in my view, when served in the style of the traditional ladies' luncheon. Offer them with a cream sauce flavored with capers, hard-cooked eggs and parsley, parsley, or mushrooms, and accompany with asparagus, green beans, or peas, and warm rolls.

CHOOSING A FISH FOR FISH CAKES OR CROQUETTES: You will find that codfish, the traditional choice, and other mild-tasting, white-fleshed fish such as grouper, haddock, halibut, sea bass, and tilefish work best here. Salmon, either freshly cooked or canned, is also very good.

STEP 1: PREPARING THE FISH MIXTURE

2 medium baking potato or 3 medium all-purpose potatoes (about 12 ounces)
6 tablespoons butter
3 tablespoons minced shallots or scallions (white parts only)
3 tablespoons minced green bell pepper (optional)
1½ cups finely shredded cooked skinless, boneless fish
1 large egg, lightly beaten
2 tablespoons minced fresh parsley
1 teaspoon Dijon mustard
¼ teaspoon salt
¼ teaspoon pepper, preferably white and freshly ground
Fresh lemon juice and/or Worcestershire sauce

Peel and quarter potatoes, turn into a 2-quart saucepan, cover with salted water, and boil until tender but not mushy; it is imperative that the potatoes not be waterlogged, or the fish cakes or croquettes will not hold their shape. Drain potatoes thoroughly and force through a ricer or press through a sieve with the back of a wooden spoon into a 2-quart mixing bowl; you should have about 1½ cups. Set aside.

Melt butter in a small skillet, add shallots or scallions and green pepper, and sauté slowly for 3 minutes. Scrape vegetables and butter into the reserved potatoes, add egg, parsley, mustard, salt, and pepper, and beat to blend well. Season with additional salt and white pepper if necessary, adding also drops of lemon juice and/or Worcestershire sauce to taste. Proceed either to Step 2a or Step 2b.

AHEAD OF TIME: The mixture may be made 24 hours in advance. Cover tightly and refrigerate.

STEP 2A: TO MAKE FISH CAKES

All-purpose flour
8 to 12 tablespoons (1 to 1½ sticks) butter

Preheat oven to warm (about 150°F) and place a serving platter in oven.

Lightly dusting your hands with flour, pat ¼-cup gobs of the fish mixture into cakes about 2½ inches in diameter, setting the cakes on a sheet of waxed paper. You will have about 12 altogether. Melt enough butter in a heavy-bottomed 10- to 12-inch skillet to cover the bottom to a depth of about ⅛ inch. Heat the butter to the point where the foam subsides, then add 4 to 6 cakes, or however many will fit comfortably in the skillet. Regulating the heat so that the butter remains hot but does not color more than a deep tan, sauté the cakes about 3 minutes on each side, or until golden brown, turning once with a spatula. Transfer fish cakes to the heated platter and keep warm in the oven while you prepare additional batches, adding a bit more butter to the skillet if necessary.

STEP 2B: TO MAKE FISH CROQUETTES

½ cup all-purpose flour
2 large eggs beaten with 2 tablespoons neutral vegetable oil, 1 teaspoon salt, and ½ teaspoon pepper, preferably freshly ground
2 cups Fine Fresh Bread Crumbs (see page 60)
3 quarts very fresh vegetable oil

Before forming and frying the croquettes, you may wish to consult the Master Technique for Deep-frying. Step 1b, page 62, covers the breading process, and Step 2, page 64, covers frying.

Chill the fish mixture thoroughly, at least 2 hours. Set oven at very slow temperature (about 150°F) and set a serving platter inside.

Drop ¼-cup gobs of the fish mixture into the flour, gently roll between your hands to coat, then pat into balls, cylinders, or, for special elegance, pyramids. Using your hands, dip the floured shapes in the egg mixture, then roll in crumbs, patting with your fingertips to make the crumbs stick and to mold the croquettes into perfect shapes. Let croquettes stand at room temperature on a sheet of waxed paper for 5 to 15 minutes to firm the coating. Heat oil to around 375°F. Fry the croquettes 3 or 4 at a time for about 3 minutes, or until golden brown. Drain on paper towels and keep cooked croquettes in warm oven while you prepare the rest. Serve at once.

FISH GLOSSARY

BASS: See Sea Bass; Striped Bass.

BLOWFISH (SEA SQUAB): This odd fish puffs up when it senses danger; hence its name. Only the tails, skinned, are edible; the rest is actually poisonous. At the market, the tails may at first glance be mistaken for large shrimp. Buy about 2 pounds of tails, five or six per serving, for four people. Blowfish, which is usually sautéed, is a mild-tasting, white-fleshed fish with firm, close-grained flesh. It becomes rather dry and fibrous if overcooked.

BLUEFISH: Bluefish can attain a weight of 10 pounds or more, though most of those caught range between 3 and 5 pounds. They are sold both as fillets and as whole fish. Bluefish weighing under 1 pound are often referred to as "baby blues"; they are dressed whole and are especially good pan-fried. Fillets are generally broiled, large whole fish baked. Bluefish is a fat, dark-fleshed, fine-textured fish with a sweet musty flavor reminiscent of, but somewhat milder than, mackerel. It is at its best when very fresh. Bluefish is regularly available along the East and Gulf Coasts, especially during the summer months, but is less common elsewhere.

BUTTERFISH: Butterfish are small, usually no more than 10 ounces, and are always dressed whole. Generally they are broiled or pan-fried, though they may also be baked. The flesh is fat, dark, soft, and rich without being at all strong or fishy. Butterfish are regularly available on the East Coast at all times of the year, less frequently seen on the West Coast, where they are sometimes called Pacific pompano.

CATFISH: There are numerous types of this freshwater fish, including the spotted cat, the goujon, and the various bullheads caught by sport fishermen throughout the country. Since the fish is so popular, particularly in southern and central regions of the country, it is now raised on fish farms. Catfish come to the market as small whole fish, fillets, and occasionally steaks. The usual treatments are pan-frying and deep-frying. The flesh is moderately firm, beige in color, oily, and sweet. Wild catfish caught in muddy or stagnant waters are prone to having an off taste, but commercially raised catfish are reliable in flavor. The fish is easy to find in the areas in which it is well loved, but is less available elsewhere. Urban dwellers might scout their local Chinatown, where the fish may be carried live in tanks.

Skinning catfish: All catfish must be skinned before cooking. Generally, this will have been done before the fish is marketed, but, if not, it is quite easy to do yourself. Make an incision through the skin around the neck, grip the head of the fish, and pull the skin back, using pliers if necessary to get a grip.

COD AND SCROD: Among the world's most important food fish, cod and related fish are available fresh in markets throughout the United States at all times of the year, and are often the mystery fish contained in packages of frozen "deep-sea fillets." Cod is also smoked, salted, and air-dried. Young cod weighing under 3 pounds are called scrod; they are sold whole or filleted. Mature cod are sold either as fillets or steaks at most markets, though sometimes large whole fish can be found. Cod is lean, white-fleshed, juicy, and fairly mild in taste. Its distinctive characteristic is the chunky texture of the flesh, which mandates that the fish be handled carefully during cooking, lest it break apart. The skin of fillets is best left on during cooking to keep the fish intact. Nearly any cooking method may be employed with this fish, though I find it rather apt to dry out and toughen when pan-fried.

Cod's close relatives include haddock, pollack, cusk, hake, and whiting.

Although cusk, hake, and whiting have a softer, finer, and more delicate texture than the others, the fish are otherwise similar and may be used interchangeably in recipes.

CROAKER: The Atlantic croaker is part of a family of fish that includes the various drums and numerous other fish. The name is derived from the odd noise the fish make when they collect in groups during spawning. These fish generally come to market whole, in weights ranging from 12 ounces to just over a pound. They are instantly recognizable by their lovely red skins. White-fleshed, lean, and sweet, croakers are best broiled, oven-grilled, or baked. Any recipe for porgy may be used for croaker as well.

FLOUNDER: See Sole and Flounder.

GROUPER: There are several types of groupers, some of which, such as the jewfish, can attain weights of 500 pounds or more. Small specimens sometimes come to the market whole, but it is more common to see fillets or steaks. Groupers are lean, mild-tasting, white-fleshed fish similar to the sea bass, to which they are related. They take well to virtually any cooking method, though care must be exercised in broiling these fish, for they are liable to become dry. Groupers are caught in the southern Atlantic and in the Gulf and are more frequently seen in eastern and southern markets than elsewhere.

HADDOCK: Haddock is a close relative of cod, which it closely resembles in taste and texture. It generally runs under 5 pounds and comes to the market whole or filleted. Almost any cooking method may be used with haddock; I am particularly partial to braising it with tomatoes. Haddock is available throughout the country, both fresh and in its famous smoked form, finnan haddie.

HALIBUT: Halibut is actually a flat fish like flounder, but it is much larger than other flat fish, routinely weighing 10 to 50 pounds and sometimes attaining monstrous weights of a quarter ton or more. Almost always sold as steaks, halibut is available at well-stocked fish markets in all parts of the country. The flesh is lean, snow white when cooked, and slightly nutlike in flavor. Its texture is especially agreeable, being at once firm and meaty, yet also flaky. Halibut responds well to a wide range of cooking techniques, though it is perhaps at its very best when poached or served with a white wine cream sauce. This is a fish that nearly everyone can love, even those who generally shun fish entirely.

KINGFISH: See Mackerel.

MACKEREL (INCLUDING KINGFISH AND SPANISH MACKEREL): The Irish poet William Butler Yeats wrote of the "mackerel-crowded seas," and indeed the seas do brim with varieties of this fine fish. The two types most prevalent at markets are the Atlantic (or Boston) mackerel and the Spanish mackerel. The Atlantic mackerel is a fairly small fish that is sometimes filleted but more commonly sold whole; one fish is perfect for a single serving. Though the Spanish mackerel can attain a weight of 50 pounds or more, specimens weighing just a pound or two are more usual at the market. Small Spanish mackerel are often sold whole; larger ones are filleted or sometimes cut into steaks. The giant cousin in this family is the king mackerel, sometimes called kingfish, which often reaches a weight of 75 pounds or more. King mackerel is almost invariably marketed as steaks. The Atlantic, Spanish, and king mackerels are Atlantic and Caribbean fish and are widely available along the East Coast, somewhat less commonly elsewhere. There is also a West Coast species, the Pacific mackerel, which is similar to the Atlantic mackerel and may be cooked in the same ways.

Mackerel is definitely a fish lover's fish—dark-fleshed, oily, rich, and pronounced in flavor. The smaller species are softer and more buttery than the king mackerel, which has a firm, meaty texture reminiscent of swordfish. Dry-heat methods—broiling, oven-grilling, and baking—work especially well with mackerel; small mackerel are also good pan-fried. Some who find mackerel too "fishy" like to soak the fish in milk, buttermilk, or a lemon-based marinade for an hour prior to cooking in order to tame the flavor.

MONKFISH: Also known as anglerfish, rockfish, and lotte (its French name), monkfish has only recently become popular in this country, though it has always been avidly appreciated in Europe. The reason for the fish's obscurity is perhaps its ugliness—it suggests a monstrous, bumpy-skinned tadpole and has a mouth large enough to swallow a duck whole, which on occasion it does. Luckily, fish eaters need never encounter this beast face to face, as only the edible tail section reaches the market. The tail is skinned and cut into pieces that are advertised as monkfish fillets, though these fillets might more accurately be termed boneless chunks, as they tend to be thick and quite irregular in shape. Try to buy pieces of more or less similar size and shape so that they will cook at the same rate.

There are many who compare monkfish in taste and texture to lobster, and while this comparison eludes me, I would agree that the fish is exceptionally sweet and succulent. The flesh is pinkish in color, firm, and quite lean. Broiling and other dry-heat cooking methods are possible, but the fish is perhaps best poached, served with a white wine cream sauce, or sautéed meunière.

OCEAN PERCH: Tons of this fish are caught each year, but relatively little of it reaches the market fresh, as most of the catch is processed as frozen fillets, fish cakes, and fish sticks. Sometimes the fillets sold at the market as fresh turn out to have been frozen and thawed; chalkiness, graininess, and a wet appearance are telltale signs of this. Ocean perch is very lean and has a mild, unfishlike flavor, which may account for its wide appeal. It suggests flounder and may be used in any flounder or sole recipe.

POMPANO: This thin, wide, oval-shaped fish, with arrowy fins, forked tail, and lovely iridescent skin, is found along much of the Atlantic coast, though it is most abundant in the waters around Florida. A small fish that is usually sold whole though sometimes also filleted, pompano is shipped to all parts of the country. However, it is highly perishable, and by the time it comes to market it is often not worth the high price that it always commands. When in peak condition, pompano is a real treat, its dark, rich meat having a silky-firm texture suggestive of trout and a sweet, nutlike taste. I like the fish best broiled or broiler-grilled, though it is also good stuffed and baked.

PORGY (SCUP): This small fish is loved throughout the world. There are both East and West Coast varieties, and porgy is widely available in all American markets. Because porgies generally weigh a pound or less, the fish is usually sold whole, though sometimes you will see fillets. With its white, moderately fatty, sweet-tasting flesh, porgy is excellent broiled or pan-fried.

RED SNAPPER: Its flesh firm, white, lean, juicy, and sweet, red snapper is one of the most delicious of all American fish. It is also one of the most versatile, taking well to virtually all cooking methods and to a wide range of different flavorings. Snappers can weigh 25 pounds or more, but the usual market weight is 1 to 3 pounds. There is a great demand for whole snapper, as the handsome red skin of the fish makes a spectacular sight on plate or platter. The fish is also sold as fillets and, occasionally, steaks. Red snapper is particularly prevalent in markets in Florida and the Gulf Coast states, where most of the catch is taken, but it is available in all other regions of the country as well.

SALMON: Anadromous fish, salmon are born in rivers, spend most of their adult lives in salt water, and then return to the rivers of their birth when they are mature, where they spawn and then immediately die. The Atlantic and Pacific salmon are two distinct species, and each in turn encompasses several varieties. All of the salmon sold frozen or in cans and most fresh salmon is from the Pacific, as overfishing has made Atlantic salmon extremely scarce. Salmon has traditionally been associated with the Fourth of July, and it used to be difficult to find in the winter months. Nowadays, however, due mostly to improved stocking and conservation methods, salmon is available in markets throughout the country all year round.

The most prevalent variety of Pacific salmon, the chinook, can attain a weight of 20 pounds or more, but the usual market weight is between 5 and 10 pounds. The coho salmon is smaller, rarely weighing more than 8 pounds and sometimes reaching the market as a pan fish weighing just a pound or so. Other varieties are generally in the 5- to 8-pound range at the market. Salmon is sold in a variety of cuts: fillets, fillet sections, steaks, whole fish, and even cheeks, which can be cooked in the same ways as the other cuts. Nearly all basic cooking methods can be used. Since salmon tend to be fatter around the head than around the tail, some people request steaks from near the head when they plan to broil the fish, center-cut and tail steaks for other purposes.

Removing salmon skin: When preparing fillets or whole salmon, it is a nice touch to scrape off both the skin and the underlying layer of grayish fat with a teaspoon or butter knife after the fish is cooked, thus exposing the lovely orange-pink flesh underneath. Do not, however, remove the skin before cooking, for it holds the flesh together and the fat provides lubrication.

SEA BASS (SEE ALSO STRIPED BASS): On the East Coast, the term "sea bass" generally refers to the black sea bass, a black-skinned fish, normally weighing 5 pounds or less, whose flesh is white, moderately firm, moist, and deliciously sweet and mild in taste. A number of other fish, all closely related to each other and to the black sea bass, are caught on the West Coast. These taste similar to the East Coast black sea bass, but they run slightly larger and their skins are colorful rather than black; Pacific sea bass are commonly referred to as "rockfish." Sea bass are sold whole, filleted, and sometimes as steaks. They are amenable to almost all cooking methods.

SHAD (INCLUDING SHAD ROE): Shad and shad roe are specialties of the spring and early summer, when shad enter the rivers of both the East and West Coasts to spawn. The fish is delectable—firm yet silky in texture and buttery-rich in taste, vaguely suggesting trout. Since the skeletal structure is quite complicated, the fish is almost always boned before being offered for sale. The fillets produced run rather large and have lateral pockets left from the removal of the bones. I think shad is at its best when broiled, oven-broiled, or baked (the pockets form natural spaces for stuffing), but it may also be braised or served with a white wine cream sauce.

Shad roe—the egg sac of the female shad—comes by the pair and looks something like an orangey red Valentine heart. A large pair will serve two, a smaller pair one. Shad roe has a briny and somewhat fishy taste. I think it tends to dry out when broiled or sautéed, so I prefer the butter-poaching method on page 275.

BUTTER-POACHED SHAD ROE

4 servings

❦ *You can also prepare this recipe by sautéing 8 ounces bacon until crisp and poaching the roe in the bacon drippings instead of in butter; the bacon is then served with the roe.*

Good accompaniments for shad roe are boiled new potatoes and either boiled green beans or a simple tossed salad.

2 large or 4 small pair shad roe (1½ to 2 pounds)
8 to 10 tablespoons (1 to 1¼ sticks) butter
Salt and pepper, preferably freshly ground
2 tablespoons finely chopped fresh parsley (optional)

Divide large roe in half; leave small roe whole. Using an egg pricker or straight pin, prick membrane of roe in a half dozen places on each side. Melt 1 stick of butter in a 10-inch skillet over low heat and lay in the roe. The butter should come nearly to the top of the roe; if it doesn't, add more. Keeping the heat very low—the butter should "tremble" rather than bubble, like water at just below the simmer—poach the roe, covered, for 4 to 6 minutes on each side, or until it has stiffened (in much the way liver does as it cooks). Transfer cooked roe to a heated serving platter, pour the butter sauce over it, sprinkle with salt and pepper, and decorate with chopped parsley. Serve at once, very hot, with lemon wedges.

Shark: Shark appears periodically in my market, often under the euphemistic name "chicken of the sea." There are quite a number of different varieties, but the most common one, at least on the East Coast, is mako, which tastes so much like swordfish that it is hard to tell the difference. Always sold as steaks, shark is best broiler-grilled, broiled, or sautéed.

Smelts: These small fish are fatty and dark-fleshed, yet surprisingly mild in taste, suggesting trout or salmon. Though they can grow somewhat larger, their usual market length is 6 inches or less, which means that three or more fish may be required for each serving, depending on appetites. The most suitable cooking methods are pan-frying and deep-frying. If your market does not carry fresh smelts, you may be able to find them, usually whole dressed, in the frozen food bin of your supermarket.

Sole and Flounder: Restaurants and even some fish markets commonly refer to all of the American flat fish as "sole." Other establishments reserve that term for small, elegant fish such as gray sole and lemon sole, while calling the larger, meatier flat fish such as winter flounder, plaice, and brill "flounder." However, to be absolutely accurate, all of the American flat fish should be called flounder. True or Dover sole is a European fish that does not grow in American waters, although it is available here in frozen form and is flown in fresh to a few large cities during the summer.

Although all of the flat fish respond similarly in cooking and can be used interchangeably in recipes, there are definite differences between them in taste and texture. The choicest of the flounder are gray sole (actually witch flounder) and lemon sole (sometimes called English sole). These small fillets have a subtle, extremely nonfishy taste and a soft, fine, curdlike texture. They are sometimes scarce and always expensive. By contrast, winter flounder and other fish that are sold as flounder have a slightly sharper flavor (though they are still quite mild) and a coarser, drier texture. Flounder fillets are larger and thicker than sole fillets and are generally available at more reasonable prices.

Because sole and flounder are very lean, very mild-tasting fish, they can be cooked in almost any way, though care must be taken not to overseason them, and thus overwhelm their natural taste. Be sure also not to overcook these fish, as they dry out easily.

STRIPED BASS: This fine fish has firm, sweet, moist flesh with a taste suggesting shad or perhaps whitefish; strangely, it does not taste at all like the other sea basses, which are blander and less rich. Though striped bass can attain a weight of 75 or even 100 pounds, the usual market weight is between 1 and 8 pounds. The fish is sold whole, filleted, and sometimes as steaks. It is more readily available on the East Coast than elsewhere. Almost any cooking method can be used, though my favorites are broiling, oven-broiling, and baking.

SWORDFISH: This giant fish—specimens weighing over 1,000 pounds have been caught—is much prized for its firm, meatlike texture and assertive yet nonfishy taste. Always expensive and often scarce, swordfish steaks have a moist, meaty look when fresh and at their peak but take on a glassy appearance as they become stale. Broiling and broiler-grilling are the cooking methods of choice.

TILEFISH: A rather large fish that is nearly always sold as steaks, tilefish has lovely green iridescent skin and firm, sweet, juicy flesh that reminds some people of lobster. It is generally available only in the East, though a Pacific variety sometimes appears in Western markets. I like tilefish best when poached, oven-broiled, or served with a white wine cream sauce. If broiled or baked, the fish must be basted frequently during cooking, or it will dry out.

TROUT: Wild trout are in season only in the spring, but trout farms produce a year-round harvest. Fish markets almost always have fresh trout on hand, and some even keep live trout in tanks. Frozen whole trout and trout fillets are stocked by most supermarkets. There are a fair number of varieties of this freshwater fish. All are similarly rich, dark-meated, and delicious, but there are differences in size, most trout weighing just a pound or so but some lake trout attaining weights of several pounds. Smaller trout are generally dressed whole and either broiled or pan-fried, though they are also delicious baked or poached. Larger trout may be dressed whole or filleted; they are particularly good baked or poached.

TUNA: Fresh red tuna is becoming increasingly available in American markets. It is not to be confused with white tuna, or albacore, most of which goes into cans, with only a tiny fraction of the catch sold fresh, mainly in California markets. Always sold as steaks, red tuna is a fairly oily and assertively flavored fish. I think it is at its best when broiler-grilled or sautéed just to the point of medium-rare, with a band of translucent, uncooked flesh in the center, like a rare beef steak. Overcooked, it has all the charm of light tuna in the can. You can also eat red tuna raw, in a Japanese sushi or sashimi, or cut in very thin slices and dressed with olive oil, lemon juice, and garlic.

WEAKFISH (SEA TROUT): Sea trout generally weigh around 5 pounds. Smaller specimens are sometimes sold whole, but it is more usual to encounter this fish in fillets. Sea trout is widely available along the East Coast, but is less obtainable elsewhere. The flesh is dark in color and musty-sweet in taste, reminiscent of bluefish. Like bluefish, it responds best to dry-heat cooking methods—broiling, oven-broiling, and baking. The unusual—and perhaps regrettable—feature of sea trout is its very soft, fine, almost flimsy texture. In *The Fish-Lovers' Cookbook,* Sheryl and Mel London suggest freezing sea trout for a day or more before cooking in order to firm up the flesh.

WHITEFISH: The whitefish family includes a large number of freshwater fish, but it is the lake whitefish that one usually encounters at the market. This fish generally runs between 1½ and 4 pounds and is most commonly sold whole, though it is quite easy to fillet. The whole fish represents an uncommonly good buy because the head is tiny, and most of what one is paying for is flesh. Whitefish is fatty, soft-textured, and has that certain freshwater taste one associates with trout, though whitefish is a bit milder and sweeter than trout. I prefer the fish stuffed and baked, though it may also be poached and fillets are good broiled.

WHITING: A member of the cod family, whiting resembles its relatives closely in taste but is considerably softer and more delicate in texture. It is also smaller than most cod-type fish, generally coming to market at a pound or less, though it can reach a weight of several pounds. The small fish are sold whole, the larger fish whole or filleted. It is most prevalent at East Coast markets. Braising, baking, and pan-frying are my favorite cooking methods for this fish.

SHELLFISH, SNAILS, and SQUID

I like fish, but I love shellfish so much that I think I could eat it every day of the week were it not so expensive and so hard to find in prime condition. If you live in an area where good-quality fresh shellfish is in short supply, think in terms of second-best alternatives. The mollusks—clams, mussels, and oysters—are all available in cans, and the canned variety, while not suitable for sautéing or deep-frying, can be broiled or used in baked dishes. Fresh cooked crab is sold in many markets that never carry live crabs in the shell; it's expensive, but worth the price if you are a crab lover. Rock lobster tails, scallops, and shrimp are all available frozen. The quality of frozen shellfish depends primarily on how carefully it has been handled. Avoid packages that are dented, bulging, or filled with ice crystals, as these are telltale signs that the shellfish has been on a roller-coaster ride of thawing and refreezing, which will have ruined its taste and texture. Thaw frozen shellfish slowly, preferably overnight in the refrigerator, to best preserve its texture.

Shellfish are assertive in flavor and toothsomely firm, though they should never be tough and rubbery—the deplorable result of the crime of overcooking. Because shellfish have so much character, shellfish recipes are typically chock full of piquant flavorings that make the taste of the fish even richer and racier. You will find recipes for shellfish containing such ingredients as bacon, oregano, garlic, fresh herbs, mustard, green peppers, tomato, lemon, curry, and soy sauce. And these are just a few of the flavorings that complement shellfish. Today innovative cooks are doing such things as broiling scallops with chicken livers and saucing lobster meat with vinegar and shallots. You should definitely feel free to run your own experiments.

Clams

Clams were among the foods that saved the early settlers from starvation, and they have been an important part of American cooking ever since. Commercially available clams are classified according to two major types: the oval-shaped soft-shell clams, often called "steamers," and the round hard-shell clams, which subdivide according to size into the small "littlenecks," the medium-sized "cherrystones," and the large "quahogs." Technically, all hard-shelled clams are "quahogs," but fish markets label only the big ones by that name. On the Pacific Coast are found soft- and hard-shelled clams similar to the East Coast types, plus a wide variety of specialties such as the pismo clam and the strange-looking, very large geoduck. Many of the more offbeat West Coast clams are either scarce or limited to small breeding areas, and thus they rarely make it to the market.

Recipes usually specify either soft- or hard-shell clams. If not, use the tender soft-shelled variety in recipes where the clams are to remain whole or are briefly cooked, as in steamed or fried clams. Use the chewier, more strongly flavored hard-shelled clams for chowders, stews, fritters, hashes, and other recipes that call for the clams to be minced and/or cooked for a prolonged period. Small hard-shelled clams—littlenecks or cherrystones—can also be served raw on the half shell.

PURCHASING AND STORING: Clams should be tightly closed, or opened no more than 1/4 inch or so, when you buy them; the slightly opened ones are "breathing," and they should immediately snap shut if you tap them. If they don't, discard them. They are defunct. Placed in a perforated plastic bag in the refrigerator, clams will keep for three to seven days, depending on how fresh they were to begin with. Sprinkle with water daily. Do not eat any clam that has died before being cooked; it can make you sick.

CLEANING: Scrub clams with a stiff brush under cool running water to remove mud and grit, then soak the clams for 40 minutes in several changes of cold water.

OPENING AND SHUCKING CLAMS: *(1) Professional method:* Clams are easiest to open when they are very cold, as the shell muscle relaxes at low temperatures. With your hand protected by a potholder, hold the clam in your palm with the hinge abutting the heel of your hand. Working over a bowl to catch dripping juices, force the blade of a thin, sturdy knife sideways between the shells fairly close to the hinge; then twist the blade to make the shells part. If you are dealing with a particularly large, strong clam, you may have to root around with the knife inside the shell to locate and sever the muscle that holds the shells together.

(2) Lazy man's method: This is the way I do it. Preheat oven to 550°F. Place clams in a single layer on a baking sheet. Set in the oven for a minute or two or three, just until the shells open a crack, indicating that the creatures have breathed their last. Remove clams at once before the flesh becomes heated.

To remove clam meat from the shells (this is called shucking), simply scrape the meat free with the point of a knife.

RAW CLAMS ON THE HALF SHELL: to serve 4 persons as an appetizer, open 16 to 24 small hard-shell clams (littlenecks or cherrystones) using either of the methods outlined above. Discard one of the shells, leaving the clams attached to the other. Arrange in plates and serve very cold with lemon or lime quarters, pepper in a peppermill, and cocktail sauce if you wish. Accompany with black bread and unsalted butter.

STEAMED CLAMS

4 main-course or 6 first-course servings

❦ *The most important thing to remember when steaming clams is not to overcook them. They are done as soon as their shells have opened just a half inch or so; if cooked beyond this point, the clams will shrivel up and toughen.*

3 to 4 quarts soft-shell clams, cleaned
About 2 cups water or 1½ cups water and ½ cup dry white wine

Pour ½ inch of water or water mixed with wine into the bottom of an 8- to 10-quart pot. Add clams, cover, and place over high heat. As soon as you hear boiling noises and see steam escaping from the pot—in about 2 minutes—stir up the clams with a spoon to redistribute them. Cover the pot, lower heat slightly, and steam the clams for 3 to 5 minutes longer, or until most have opened just ½ inch or so, stirring once. Transfer clams to serving bowls with skimmer or saucepan. You may simmer any clams that do not open a bit longer until they finally relent, but discard any that remain tightly closed after this second simmering, as they may be sick.

Once all clams have been removed from the pot, let broth settle off heat for a half minute so that sand and sediment can sink to the bottom. Carefully ladle broth over the clams or into small bowls to accompany clams. Serve with melted butter.

CLAMS MARINER-STYLE

4 main-course or 6 first-course servings

Mussels Mariner-style, page 301
SUBSTITUTE: 3 to 4 quarts soft-shell clams, cleaned, for mussels

Proceed according to the recipe for mussels mariner-style, using clams instead of mussels.

CLAMS CASINO

4 main-course, 6 to 8 first-course servings

❦ *A classic recipe, clams casino makes a fine appetizer or first course preceding Italian dishes of any sort. If you are serving the clams as a main course, accompany them with crusty bread for sopping up the juices, and a tossed salad that includes a few bitter greens such as escarole, chicory, or dandelion.*

PRELIMINARIES

1. Set broiling rack 3 to 4 inches beneath heating element.
2. Preheat broiler at highest setting.
3. Select a 17×11-inch rimmed baking sheet.

8 slices (about 8 ounces) bacon
½ cup finely chopped onion
½ cup finely chopped celery
½ cup finely chopped green bell pepper
¼ teaspoon salt
¼ teaspoon pepper, preferably freshly ground
½ cup Fine Fresh Bread Crumbs (see page 60)
3 tablespoons finely chopped fresh parsley
12 tablespoons (1½ sticks) butter, at room temperature
1½ tablespoons strained fresh lemon juice
40 littleneck or cherrystone clams, cleaned and opened

Sauté bacon slices in a 9-inch skillet until they are curled at the edges and lightly browned but still quite soft. Remove bacon and cut each slice into 5 pieces; set aside. Add onion, celery, and green pepper to bacon drippings in the skillet, raise heat to moderately high, and, stirring frequently, cook vegetables for 3 to 4 minutes, or until partially softened and beginning to brown very lightly. Remove skillet from heat, season the mixture with salt and pepper, and add bread crumbs and parsley, tossing to blend. Set mixture aside and let cool to tepid.

Place butter in a mixing bowl and beat with a wooden spoon until very soft and creamy. Add lemon juice a little bit at a time, beating constantly. Add cooled crumb mixture and beat until thoroughly blended.

Remove the top shells from the clams, then arrange clams on the half shell in a single, close layer on the 17×11-inch rimmed baking sheet. Spread the clams with the butter mixture and top with pieces of the partially cooked bacon. Broil for 2 to 4 minutes, or just until heated through. Serve immediately.

Ahead of Time: The butter/crumb mixture can be turned into a lidded storage container and refrigerated for several days; wrap partially cooked bacon in foil and refrigerate also. The entire dish can be assembled several hours in advance and held in the refrigerator, covered with plastic wrap. Broil just before serving.

CLAMS OREGANATO

4 main-course, 6 to 8 first-course servings

❦ *Pungent and savory, clams oreganato is generally served either as an hors d'oeuvre or a first course.*

Preliminaries

1. Set broiling rack 3 to 4 inches beneath heating element.
2. Preheat broiler at highest setting.
3. Select a 17×11-inch rimmed baking sheet.

1½ cups Fine Fresh Bread Crumbs (page 60)
2 teaspoons oregano
1 teaspoon mashed, pressed, or very finely minced garlic
1 teaspoon salt
½ teaspoon pepper, preferably freshly ground
⅔ cup olive oil
1 tablespoon strained fresh lemon juice
40 littleneck or cherrystone clams, cleaned and opened

Combine crumbs, oregano, garlic, salt, and pepper in a small mixing bowl and toss with a fork to blend. Add olive oil and lemon juice and toss again.

Remove the top shells from the clams, then arrange clams on the half shell in a single, close layer on the 17×11-inch rimmed baking sheet. Top with the crumb mixture and broil 2 to 4 minutes, or until the crumbs are lightly browned and the clams heated through. Serve immediately.

AHEAD OF TIME: The crumb mixture may be made several days in advance and stored in a covered container in the refrigerator. The dish may be entirely assembled several hours in advance and held in the refrigerator, covered.

CLAMS BROILED IN GARLIC BUTTER

4 main-course, 6 to 8 first-course servings

Mussels Broiled in Garlic Butter, page 303
SUBSTITUTE: 48 soft-shell clams *or* littleneck or cherrystone clams for mussels

Clean the clams and open by either of the methods outlined on page 280. Discard the top shells; if using soft-shell clams, pull away and discard the neck sheaths. Lay clams on the half shell in a single layer on the baking sheet and proceed as for mussels broiled in garlic butter.

BAKED STUFFED CLAMS

3 to 4 main-course, 8 first-course servings

❦ *This classic American favorite is always better when made at home than when ordered at a restaurant, for you can be generous with the clam meat, butter, and other ingredients, while a restaurant must skimp. If the dish is to be a main course, accompany it with a tossed green salad.*

PRELIMINARIES

1. Set rack in upper third of oven.
2. Preheat oven to 425°F 20 minutes before baking.
3. Select a 17×11-inch rimmed baking sheet.

The bread crumb mixture for ***Scalloped Oysters,*** page 308
ADD: 2 teaspoons mashed, pressed, or very finely minced garlic
16 large hard-shell clams (quahogs), cleaned and opened
½ cup (2 ounces) freshly grated Parmesan cheese
⅓ cup additional Fine Fresh Bread Crumbs (see page 60)
4 tablespoons butter

Prepare bread crumb mixture as described in the first paragraph of the recipe for scalloped oysters, stirring in garlic just before adding the bread crumbs. Set aside.

Shuck the clams over a bowl, reserving their liquor. Set aside 16 shell halves, discarding the rest. Chop the clams coarsely (you should end up with 1½ to 2 cups), and combine with the reserved bread crumb mixture in the skillet. Add just enough of the reserved clam liquor to bind the mixture—2 to 4 tablespoons will probably be enough; freeze the remaining liquor for future use. Divide the stuffing among the reserved shell halves and arrange clams on the baking sheet. Combine the cheese and crumbs in a small bowl, then top the clams with this mixture. Dot with butter. Bake 15 to 20 minutes, or until the clams are lightly browned and crusty-looking. Serve immediately.

AHEAD OF TIME: Dish may be entirely assembled several hours in advance. Cover loosely with plastic wrap and refrigerate.

FRIED CLAMS

4 to 6 servings

❦ *Serve fried clams with lemon wedges and tartar sauce, and accompany with either french fries or potato salad and, of course, cole slaw.*

Refer to the chapter on deep-frying, pages 59–66, for guidance.

3 quarts soft-shell clams (about 60)
For breading and deep-frying:
½ cup all-purpose flour
2 large eggs
2 tablespoons neutral vegetable oil
1 teaspoon salt
½ teaspoon pepper, preferably freshly ground
1½ to 2 cups fine cracker crumbs or cornmeal
3 quarts very fresh vegetable oil

Clean the clams and open by either of the methods outlined on page 280. Remove the meat from the shells, and pull away and discard the neck sheaths. Following the Master Technique for Deep-frying, dredge the clams in flour, dip in eggs beaten with 2 tablespoons oil, salt, and pepper, and coat with either fine cracker crumbs or cornmeal (Step 1b, page 62); deep-fry in 3 quarts oil heated to 370°F (Step 2, page 64) for just a minute or two, or until puffy and lightly browned, adding the clams to the pot in batches of about a dozen. Serve immediately.

CRABS

When Easterners hear the word "crab," they think of the blue crab, a creature weighing 4 to 5 ounces that is occasionally sold in the shell, either live or cooked, but is more commonly processed for crabmeat. When a blue crab molts, that is, sheds its old shell and begins to form another slightly larger shell, it becomes a soft-shell crab. Soft-shell crabs are available at the market only during the spring and early summer, when the molting process occurs.

People living on the West Coast most likely think of the Dungeness crab when the word "crab" is spoken. The Dungeness may weigh 3 pounds or more and has a great deal of meat in the claws, legs, and body. It is often sold whole and precooked.

Two other important species dwell in the extreme southern and extreme northern parts of the United States. In Florida waters are harvested the claws of stone crabs: just the claws, and, in fact, only one claw per crab. The rest of the crab is thrown back to produce another claw. The colorful claws of stone crabs are available cooked in many markets throughout the country. Alaska's pride is the gigantic king crab, a creature that can weigh up to 20 pounds and measure 9 feet across with the claws spread. Its legs, claws, and shoulders are edible, and these parts are available in frozen form at the market. If kept at the proper freezing temperature and thawed slowly, frozen king crab can be quite good. Unfortunately, this species is now endangered due to overfishing.

There are of course differences in taste and texture between various kinds of crabs, but all may be used interchangeably in recipes. You may also substitute crab in most lobster dishes and vice versa.

PREPARED CRABMEAT: Crabmeat comes in four forms: canned, frozen, fresh, and "fresh pasteurized." All should be carefully picked over before use to remove bits of shell and cartilage.

Canned crabmeat is not nearly as good as fresh, but if canned is all that is available, buy a quality brand. Inferior brands contain a lot of tendon and mere shreds of flesh. The meat is also likely to be brownish, waterlogged, and slightly metallic in taste.

Frozen crabmeat can be quite good—or completely tasteless. Don't buy a package of frozen crab that looks as though it has been in the freezer compartment for some time; frozen crab loses its taste quickly. And pass over any package that contains frozen liquid, for this may indicate that the crab was thawed and then refrozen, a process that will have ruined it. Be sure to thaw frozen crab slowly, in the refrigerator; otherwise sharp ice crystals will pierce the flesh and make it mushy.

Fresh crabmeat should be snowy white and should smell clean and fresh, not fishy or ammoniac. Fresh crabmeat is classified as follows: lump meat (large, white chunks taken from the body); backfin meat (smaller chunks, also from the body); flaked meat (from any part of the crab; it may include tendon); and claw meat (which tends to be a bit limp, though very good-tasting). Lump meat is, obviously, the choicest—and the most expensive. Although backfin meat doesn't look as nice as lump meat, it is perfectly acceptable for all purposes, including a fancy crab cocktail. When you are going to use the crab for crab cakes, stuffings, and the like, flake meat or claw meat is the most economical choice, but remember to pick it over to remove bits of shell and tendon.

Fresh pasteurized crabmeat has been sealed in a tin and then heated to kill off contaminants. It is classified in the same way as regular fresh crabmeat ("lump," "backfin," and so on). It is generally just as expensive, but the flavor is not as good. The pasteurization process imparts a distinctly canned flavor. It is acceptable in cooked crab dishes, but should not be used in salads or crab cocktails. It must be stored under refrigeration.

SHELLING COOKED BLUE CRABS: Shelling crabs can be a messy and tedious business, especially if they are small. (You need close to a dozen blue crabs to produce just a pound of crabmeat.) To shell crab, first break off the two claws and crack them with a mallet or nutcracker. Tug at the meat by grasping the movable pincer; if you're lucky, the meat will come out in one piece. Next, pull off the small legs. If the crab is large enough, you may be able to press a bit of meat out of the legs using the back of a wooden spoon, but don't bother with the legs at all if the crabs are small. (If you're shelling the crab for your own on-the-spot consumption, the best way to get at the leg meat is by sucking it out.) Last comes the body. Turn the crab on its back. Lift up the flap—or "apron"—on the underside of the crab and twist it off. In the process of removing the apron, you will also loosen the top shell; to remove the top shell completely, pry it apart from the body using your thumbs or a spoon. Turn the body of the crab on its back and peel off the whitish, fan-shaped gills, sometimes called "dead men's fingers." Finally break the body in half lengthwise, and pull out the meat with your fingers.

STEAMED BLUE CRABS

6 servings; about 2 pounds crabmeat

❦ *The traditional—and most fun—way to serve steamed crabs is to dump them onto the center of a newspaper-covered table and let everyone have a go at them with mallets, nutcrackers, and nut picks. Bibs and napkins should also be provided. Cold beer is almost a requirement, and cole slaw might be offered as well.*

2 cups cider vinegar
24 live blue crabs (about 8 pounds)
⅓ cup coarse (kosher) salt
⅓ cup commercially prepared seafood seasoning or crab boil (optional; only when serving crabs in the shell)

SPECIAL EQUIPMENT: A spaghetti pot or stockpot with a capacity of at least 8 gallons; a tall-footed rack or slotted lift-out basket to fit into the bottom of the pot

Pour the vinegar plus enough water into the pot to come ⅔ of the way up to the bottom of the rack or basket. Rinse crabs quickly under cold water and arrange in six layers on the rack, sprinkling each layer with about 1 tablespoon coarse salt and, if the crabs are to be served in the shell, 1 tablespoon seafood seasoning.

Bring vinegar and water to a rapid simmer, cover the pot tightly, and steam the crabs for 20 minutes, or until they turn bright pink and their legs can be pulled from the sockets fairly easily.

CRAB LOUIS

4 main-course or 6 to 8 first-course servings

❦ *Crab Louis is a sophisticated kind of crab cocktail that makes a lovely summer lunch dish or a good first course preceding a simple meal featuring a roast. Accompany the crab with crusty French bread, hard rolls, or sourdough bread and serve with a dry white California wine.*

1 cup mayonnaise, preferably homemade, page 51
3 tablespoons chili sauce or cocktail sauce
2 tablespoons very finely minced onion
1 tablespoon grated fresh horseradish or well-drained prepared horseradish
⅓ cup cold heavy cream, whipped soft (see page 857)
1 to 2 teaspoons fresh lemon juice
Worcestershire sauce
1 large head romaine lettuce, washed and dried
1 pound cooked fresh crabmeat, preferably lump or backfin
2 to 3 hard-cooked eggs, quartered lengthwise
2 ripe tomatoes, cut into eighths
1 ripe avocado, peeled, pitted, and cut into wedges (optional)
2 tablespoons finely chopped fresh parsley

In a small bowl, stir chili or cocktail sauce, onion, and horseradish into mayonnaise. Fold whipped cream into mayonnaise mixture and season to taste with lemon juice and drops of Worcestershire sauce. Cover and refrigerate for at least 30 minutes, but not longer than 24 hours, before serving.

Gather lettuce leaves together in a single sheaf (as though you were reconstructing the head) and slice crosswise into shreds 1/8 inch wide or less. Pick over crabmeat, removing shell bits and tendon, but leave in large lumps. Line a platter or individual plates with shredded lettuce, top with crabmeat, and garnish with hard-cooked eggs, tomatoes, and avocado. Mound prepared dressing on crab and sprinkle with parsley. Serve immediately.

SAUTÉED SOFT-SHELL CRABS AMANDINE OR MEUNIÈRE

4 servings

❦ *Serve these with steamed white or brown rice and either asparagus or green beans.*

- 8 large or 12 small soft-shell crabs, cleaned and ready for cooking
- Salt and pepper, preferably freshly ground
- 1/2 cup all-purpose flour
- 8 tablespoons (1 stick) butter
- 3 tablespoons neutral vegetable oil
- *Either* 1/2 cup (2 ounces) slivered or sliced almonds *or* 1/4 cup finely chopped fresh parsley
- 2 to 3 tablespoons strained fresh lemon juice

Quickly rinse crabs under cool running water and blot up excess moisture with paper toweling. Using a pin or egg pricker, pierce both sides of the crabs, both bodies and claws, in 6 to 8 places; the little holes will allow steam to escape and prevent the crabs from bursting and spattering hot butter all over you as they cook. Sprinkle crabs with salt and pepper, then dredge in flour, coating completely and shaking off excess.

Heat butter and oil in a heavy-bottomed 10- to 12-inch skillet over moderately high heat until foam subsides and the mixture has just begun to turn a very pale gold. Sauté crabs 3 to 4 minutes on each side, or until golden brown, turning them with tongs and regulating heat so that the fat remains very hot but does not darken beyond a pale nut brown. Remove cooked crabs to a heated serving platter.

To prepare crabs amandine: Add almonds to the hot fat and sauté until lightly browned. Remove skillet from heat, stir in lemon juice, and pour sauce over the crabs. Serve immediately.

To make crabs meunière: Remove skillet from heat, add lemon juice, and stir for half a minute or so to cool slightly. Then add parsley and immediately pour sauce over the crabs. Serve immediately.

MARYLAND CRAB CAKES

4 main-course or 8 first-course servings

❦ *Serve these with cole slaw and french fries or potato salad.*

1 egg white
2 tablespoons strained fresh lemon juice
1½ teaspoons dry mustard
½ teaspoon Worcestershire sauce
⅛ teaspoon cayenne pepper, or to taste
¼ teaspoon salt
¼ teaspoon pepper, preferably white and freshly ground
⅔ cup mayonnaise, preferably homemade, page 51
2 tablespoons very finely minced scallions, including tender green parts
1 tablespoon very finely minced fresh parsley
1 pound fresh cooked crabmeat, preferably lump or backfin, carefully picked over
1½ to 2 cups fine dry bread crumbs
2 large eggs
½ teaspoon water
4 to 8 tablespoons (½ to 1 stick) butter

Combine egg white, lemon juice, dry mustard, Worcestershire sauce, cayenne pepper, salt, and pepper in a 3-quart mixing bowl and beat with a fork until blended. Using a rubber spatula, stir in mayonnaise, minced scallions, and parsley, then gently fold in the crabmeat and 3 tablespoons of the bread crumbs, breaking up lumps of crabmeat as little as possible.

Sprinkle about ⅔ cup of the remaining bread crumbs on a 16-inch sheet of waxed paper. To form each cake, drop a ⅓-cup gob of crabmeat mixture onto the crumb-strewn waxed paper, flipping it once to coat both sides with crumbs and gently patting it into a disk about 3 inches wide and ¾ inch thick. (The crab mixture will be quite soft, so work quickly to prevent it from sticking to your hands or to the waxed paper. Don't worry if the cakes look messy at this point—they will have a final shaping later.) As each cake is formed, transfer it to a waxed paper-lined baking sheet using a spatula; you should have 8 cakes altogether. When all the cakes are done, cover loosely with waxed paper and refrigerate for at least an hour—several hours would be better—to firm.

Sprinkle about ⅔ cup of the remaining bread crumbs on a fresh sheet of waxed paper. Beat eggs and water in a soup plate until foamy. One at a time roll cakes in the beaten egg, then roll cakes in a second coating of crumbs, pressing the crumbs in and gently patting the cakes into shape. Add more crumbs to the waxed paper if needed. At this point, the cakes may rest for 30 minutes on the waxed paper before frying.

Add enough butter to cover the bottom of a heavy-bottomed 10- to 12-inch skillet by ⅛ inch and heat until foam subsides and the butter is fragrant and on the verge of coloring. Add cakes, a few at a time, to the skillet and fry 4 to 5 minutes on each side, or until lightly browned, lowering the heat if the butter threatens to burn. (Flip the cakes over carefully, as they are delicate.) Keep finished cakes warm in a 150°F oven while you prepare more. Serve immediately.

DEVILED CRAB

4 main-course or 6 to 8 first-course servings

❦ *Deviling—baking in a spicy, rich cream sauce—is a traditional treatment for crab. Serve this with a tossed salad.*

PRELIMINARIES

1. Set rack in the upper level of oven.
2. Preheat oven to 450°F 20 minutes before baking.
3. Select a shallow baking dish measuring about 9 inches across or 6 to 8 individual crab or scallop shells or ramekins. Butter generously.

6 tablespoons butter
1 cup Fine Fresh Bread Crumbs (see page 60)
2½ tablespoons all-purpose flour
1 cup milk
2 hard-cooked eggs, forced through a fine sieve with the back of a spoon
2 tablespoons minced green bell pepper
2 tablespoons minced onion
2 tablespoons minced celery
1 tablespoon minced well-drained capers (optional)

(*Ingredients list continues on next page*)

1 tablespoon strained fresh lemon juice
1½ teaspoons dry mustard
1 teaspoon Worcestershire sauce
⅛ to ¼ teaspoon cayenne pepper, to taste
¼ teaspoon salt
White pepper, preferably freshly ground
1 pound fresh cooked crabmeat, carefully picked over

In a deep, heavy-bottomed 10- to 12-inch skillet made of or lined with a noncorroding material, melt 3 tablespoons of the butter over moderately high heat. Add the bread crumbs and toss them in the butter until lightly browned. Scrape into a bowl and set aside.

Melt remaining 3 tablespoons butter in the same skillet. Remove from heat, stir in the flour, and blend until smooth. Bring milk almost to the simmer in a small saucepan, then add all at once to the butter/flour paste, beating constantly. When mixture is completely smooth, return the skillet to heat and, stirring constantly, bring to a boil and cook 1 minute; the sauce will be thick. Again remove skillet from heat and stir in hard-cooked eggs, minced vegetables, capers, and seasonings. Taste and adjust seasoning, adding enough additional salt and cayenne or white pepper to make the mixture very piquant and spicy. Fold in the crabmeat.

Turn mixture into buttered dish or individual shells and top with reserved crumbs. Bake in preheated oven for 12 to 18 minutes, or until bubbling and nicely browned on top. Serve immediately.

AHEAD OF TIME: The dish may be completely prepared in advance. Cover with plastic wrap and refrigerate for up to 24 hours; add 3 to 5 minutes to the baking time if taken straight from refrigerator to oven.

CRAYFISH

Crayfish are small freshwater crustaceans that look like miniature lobsters; they taste quite a bit like lobster, too. Except in the South and in cities with large Scandinavian populations, crayfish are an uncommon sight at fish markets. There exists, however, a burgeoning crayfish-farming industry, so perhaps this situation will eventually change. If you are using a French recipe that calls for crayfish *(écrevisses)* tails as a garnish, you may substitute large-medium shrimp.

Preparing crayfish: Like most other shellfish, crayfish must be alive when they are cooked. To prepare for cooking, grasp the crayfish at the midsection and sharply pull on the *middle* tail fin (it looks like a small wing and is flanked by two somewhat larger fins) to release both the fin and the intestinal vein. Wash the crayfish under running water.

Drop cleaned crayfish a handful at a time into a large kettle of well-salted rapidly boiling water. Cook for 4 minutes after the water returns to the boil. Drain and serve with melted butter. To prepare crayfish in the Scandinavian manner, add several bunches of fresh dill to the boiling water and let the crayfish stand in their stock for several hours after cooking. Serve either at room temperature or chilled, accompanied by buttered black bread and white wine or beer.

LOBSTER

There are two basic types of lobsters. The most familiar and best loved is the "homard," the lobster with claws, which dwells in northern waters off both the American and European coasts. The second is the spiny or rock lobster; it has no claws and lives in the southern Pacific, the Gulf of Mexico, the Mediterranean, and in other warm-water seas off the coasts of South Africa, Australia, and elsewhere. The homard is available live at fish markets throughout the country; the spiny lobster is only available regionally. However, you can buy the tails of Australian or South African spiny lobsters frozen.

PURCHASING A LIVE ATLANTIC LOBSTER: As soon as a lobster dies, its flesh begins to deliquesce into a nightmarish bacterial jelly that can make you very sick or even kill you if you eat it. To insure that your lobster remains alive until the moment it hits the pot, be certain that it is full of vim and vigor when you buy it. Pick it up at the midsection (or ask the fish man to do it for you) and see how it behaves. If the lobster is in good health, it will respond by stretching out its claws, arching its back, and flapping its tail angrily.

Lobsters from colder northern waters are generally sweeter and firmer in texture than those which have been harvested off the coast of southern New England. You can tell northern from southern lobsters by the color of the shells. The shells of cold-water lobsters are very dark green-blue, almost black, while those of warmer-water lobsters are forest green with dabs of pale blue and sometimes yellow.

STORING LIVE LOBSTERS: A live lobster will remain alive and well for at least a day, possibly two, if kept in the bottom of the refrigerator in a brown paper bag punched with small holes.

HOW TO EXTRACT MEAT FROM A LOBSTER: As lobster lovers know, the largest part of the lobster's meat lies in the tail, claws, and arms. To extract the tail meat, bend the tail back and detach it from the body, then pry out the meat in one piece with a fork. The shells of the claws and arms must be cracked with a nutcracker or mallet before the meat can be removed. Though often neglected, choice, tasty morsels are found elsewhere in the lobster. First, the legs, though spindly, often contain a great deal of sweet meat, especially if the lobster is large. If it's your own lobster you're working on, get at the meat by drawing the legs between your teeth. If you're removing the meat to make a lobster dish for others, press the meat out of the legs with the back of a wooden spoon. Next, there's the delicious chest. Whenever I go to a lobster eatery, I am always sorry to see untouched lobster chests being cleared away from tables. What a waste! To get at the chest meat, first pry off the top shell with your fingers. Clinging to the underside of the shell will be whitish clots of lobster juices and parts of the greenish tomalley (the liver). All of this is delicious and should be spooned up or mopped up with a piece of bread and eaten. Next turn the chest upside down, so that the head is facing away from you. Gripping the chest between your hands, break it in half lengthwise. Near the head you will see a brownish ball called the sand sac. Pull this out and discard it. The lobster chest is now ready for your consumption. After eating any roe (it is reddish) and tomalley that may be present, pull apart the spongy whitish gills segment by segment and extract the very sweet meat that is hidden in the crevices. In larger lobsters, the amount of chest meat will be substantial.

And when there's nothing left of your lobster but a heap of shells, put the debris in a pot, add a sliced onion and a bay leaf, cover with water (and perhaps some white wine), and simmer the shells for an hour or longer to produce a delicious lobster broth. Serve it as a soup or use it as the base of a cream sauce.

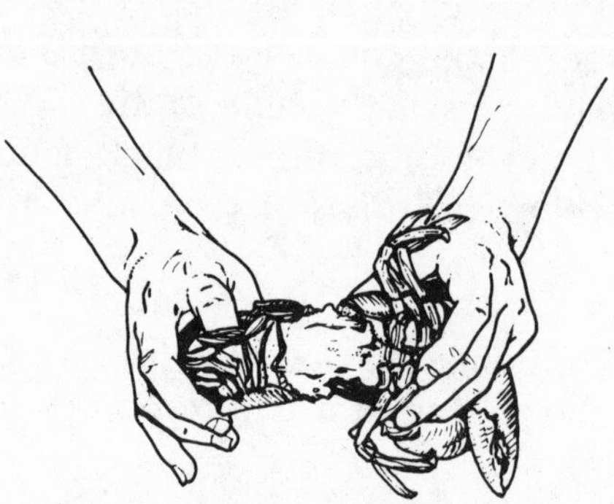

Bend the tail back and detach it from the body, then pry out the meat in one piece with a fork.

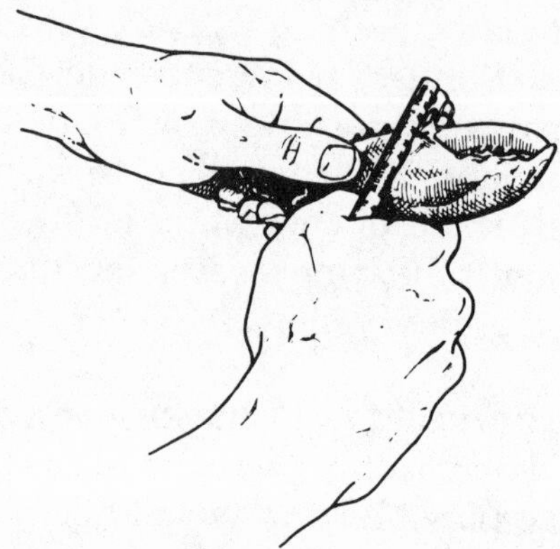

Crack the claws with a nutcracker or mallet.

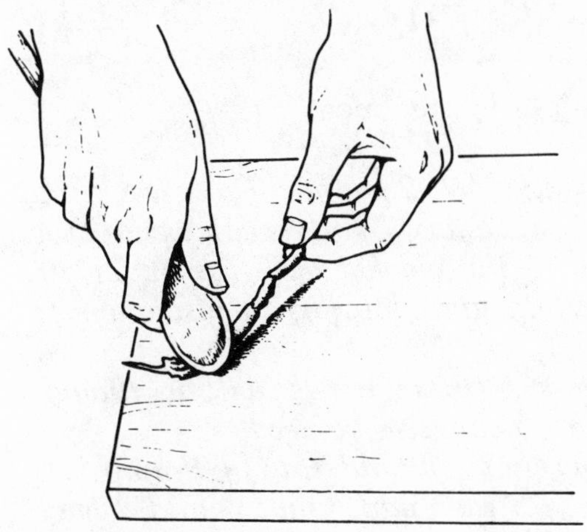

Remove meat from the legs with a wooden spoon.

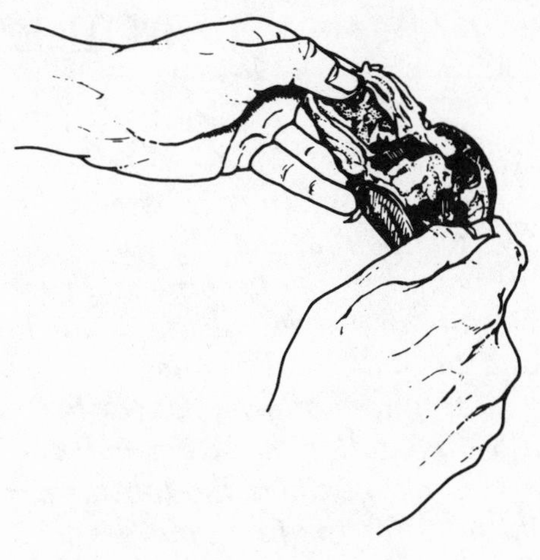

To remove the chest meat, first pry off the top shell with your fingers, then . . .

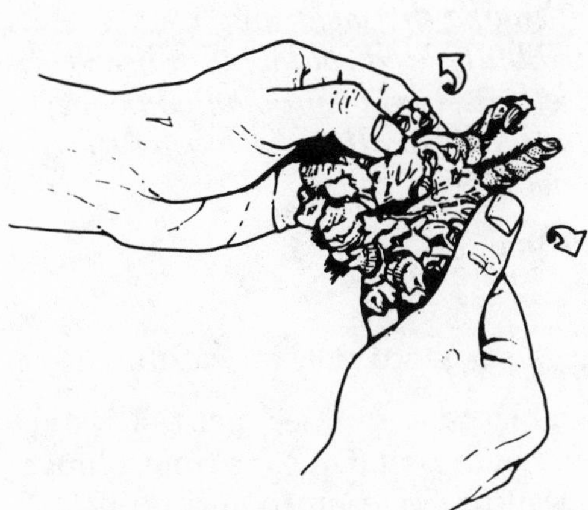

break the chest in half lengthwise.

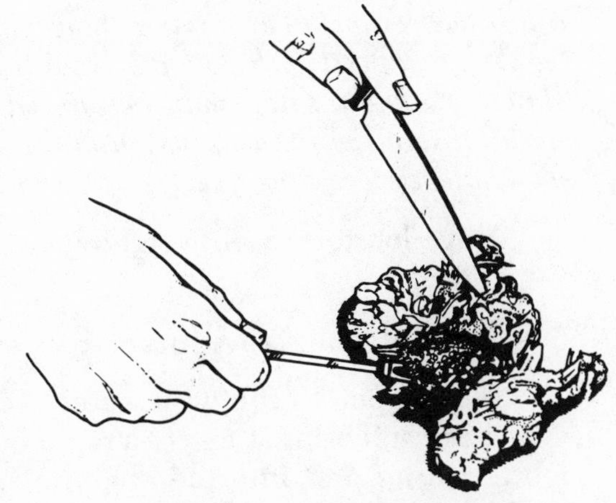

Remove the brown sand sac. The chest meat, including the reddish roe, and the greenish tomalley, is ready for your consumption.

BOILED LOBSTERS

4 servings; 1½ to 2 pounds lobster meat

❦ *For single servings, choose lobsters weighing 1¼ to 2 pounds. Those weighing 2½ to 5 pounds may be split lengthwise to serve two. Lobsters can weigh over 50 pounds, but the largest I've ever seen in the market was just under 20. Despite any wives' tales you may have been told, giant lobsters are just as tender and tasty as smaller ones.*

You need a large pot for boiling lobsters. A turkey roaster will do, though a 5- to 8-gallon stock pot is better; a washtub can also be used.

Cooking times for lobster are controversial. The old rule of thumb is 5 minutes for the first pound and 3 minutes for each additional pound. I have found, however, that this is sometimes not adequate to set the tomalley (green matter), so I prefer a slightly longer cooking time of about 6 minutes for the first pound and 4 minutes for each additional pound. Remember that lobsters, like turkeys or rib roasts, are bound to differ slightly in shape, density of flesh, and so on, and so any cooking time suggested by a recipe must be considered only approximate. Luckily, an extra minute or two in the pot will not damage a lobster; serious overcooking, however, will make the meat tough.

All you need with boiled lobster is melted butter and cold wine or beer; cole slaw and potato salad may be offered as well. Be sure to provide your guests with bibs and napkins, plus nutcrackers, nut picks, small forks, lobster shears, or whatever weapons you like to do battle with.

4 live lobsters, each weighing 1¼ to 2 pounds
Salt

Special Equipment: A turkey roaster, large spaghetti pot, or washtub

Fill the pot ¾ full with water. Add 1 tablespoon salt per quart of water. Cover pot and bring water to a rapid boil over high heat. One at a time, plunge lobsters *head first* into the boiling water, waiting for each to curl up its tail before adding the next. (Do not feel guilty about the lobsters wriggling and shifting in the pot just after they are added. They expire almost instantly, and their movements are merely a reflex response.)

When all the lobsters have been added, cover the pot and bring the water back to a boil, then uncover and reduce heat so that the boil subsides to a fast simmer. Begin timing from this moment, cooking 1¼- to 1½-pound lobsters about 8 minutes, 2-pound lobsters about 10 minutes. If you want to be doubly sure that a lobster is done, pry up the chest shell where it overlaps the tail and insert a meat thermometer deep into the chest. The thermometer should register between 160°F and 170°F.

Remove cooked lobsters from the pot with tongs.

Storing Cooked Lobsters: Wrap cooled lobsters individually in foil, seal in a plastic bag, and refrigerate for up to 3 days. In a pinch, cooked lobsters may also be frozen, still in their shells, for about a month; thaw slowly, preferably overnight in the refrigerator.

MASTER RECIPE

Lobster Newburg

4 main-course or 6 to 8 first-course servings

A classic American dish, lobster Newburg consists of slices of lobster meat warmed in butter and Sherry or Madeira and then swathed in a rich sauce of heavy cream and egg yolks. Shrimp is almost as delicious as lobster when given the Newburg treatment. Serve lobster Newburg over rice, on buttered toast, or in patty shells. Peas or asparagus are good accompaniments.

- 4 tablespoons butter
- 1 pound fresh cooked lobster meat cut in ½-inch cubes (the approximate yield of two 2-pound cooked lobsters)
- ¼ teaspoon salt
- ⅛ teaspoon white pepper, preferably freshly ground
- ¼ cup medium-dry Madeira or Sherry, preferably Manzanilla
- 1 cup heavy cream
- 3 large egg yolks

In a deep, heavy-bottomed 10- to 12-inch skillet made of or lined with a noncorroding material, melt the butter over moderate heat. Add the lobster and stir to coat with butter. Sprinkle with salt and pepper, then add the wine. Simmer slowly, stirring continuously, for several minutes, or until the juices in the pan have thickened slightly and reduced to about ¼ cup. Avoid overcooking the lobster at this point, or it will toughen. Remove from heat.

Beat the cream and egg yolks together in a small bowl until thoroughly blended. Beat the lobster juices by tablespoons into the cream/yolk mixture. When all the juices have been added, pour the cream/yolk mixture over the lobster and stir briefly. Place the skillet over very low heat and, stirring constantly, cook only until the sauce begins to give off steam and thickens enough to coat the spoon. Do not overheat the sauce or the egg yolks will curdle.

AHEAD OF TIME: It is best to make this dish just before serving. However, it may be refrigerated in a covered container for several days. Reheat in a double boiler over barely simmering water. Take care not to overheat the sauce and cause it to curdle.

Variation: CURRIED LOBSTER

4 main-course or 6 to 8 first-course servings

Lobster Newburg

ADD: 1/4 cup finely diced well-drained roasted sweet red peppers
3/4 teaspoon mild curry powder or 1/2 teaspoon hot (Madras) curry powder

Proceed according to the Master Recipe, but cook the peppers and curry powder in the butter over low heat for about 3 minutes, stirring, before adding the lobster.

MY MOTHER'S BAKED STUFFED LOBSTER

4 servings

❦ *Baking is a better treatment for lobster than broiling, for broiling tends to make the meat tough and dry. If you think all lobster stuffings are pasty and bland, try this one. Accompany the lobster with chilled white wine and, if you wish, a green salad. The rich stuffing makes melted butter unnecessary.*

PRELIMINARIES

1. Set rack in the upper third of oven.
2. Preheat oven to 375°F 20 minutes before baking.
3. Select a 17×11-inch shallow-rimmed baking sheet or broiling pan (without its tray).

3 cups Fine Fresh Bread Crumbs (see page 60)
1/2 cup chopped fresh parsley, preferably flat-leaf Italian parsley
1 tablespoon mashed, pressed, or very finely minced garlic
1 teaspoon salt
1 teaspoon freshly ground pepper
4 1 1/2- to 2-pound live lobsters
1 cup olive oil
1 1/2 cups dry white wine

Spread the bread crumbs over the baking sheet and place in the preheated oven. Stirring the bread crumbs up every minute or so, toast for 2 to 5 minutes, or until they have just begun to color. Scrape crumbs into a 2-quart mixing bowl and toss with garlic, parsley, salt, and pepper. Set aside.

Now you must split the live lobsters in half lengthwise. Set a large cutting board inside the baking sheet (the sheet will catch the juices) and lay a lobster on its back on the board. Plunge the point of a sharp, sturdy knife into the lobster's chest between the pair of legs closest to the head, then make a deep incision lengthwise to the end of the tail section, reaching almost to the lobster's top shell, which lies against the cutting board. Gripping the lobster's chest between your hands, break it open. Your object is to expose the chest meat and the flesh of the tail without detaching the two halves. Pull out and discard the brownish round sand sac in the head. Remove wooden pegs or elastic bands from claws. Set aside while you prepare the other lobsters. When all the lobsters are split, take the cutting board out of the baking sheet and arrange the lobsters on the sheet in a single layer (it's okay if the claws overlap).

Lightly press the reserved crumb mixture into the chest cavities and tails of the lobsters. Using a fork, bring some of the tomalley, which is very flavorful, up into the stuffing, then moisten the stuffing of each lobster with 1 tablespoon of the juices in the baking sheet. Drizzle 1/4 cup olive oil onto each lobster, using about 1 teaspoon to coat the claws and the rest to moisten the stuffing. Pour the wine into the bottom of the baking sheet.

Bake lobsters for 25 to 30 minutes, basting the claws two or three times with pan juices. If the stuffing looks dry, moisten it with pan juices, but don't add more than a teaspoon or two, or the stuffing will become soggy. The lobsters are done when the stuffing is very hot and browned on top and the tail meat feels firm when pressed with your finger. Serve immediately.

LOBSTER BAKED IN MUSTARD CRUMBS

4 servings

❦ *Lobster baked with mustardy, buttery bread crumbs is a real treat. Serve a tossed green salad or a tomato salad as an accompaniment.*

Preliminaries

1. Set rack in upper-middle level of oven.
2. Preheat oven to 425°F 20 minutes before baking.
3. Select a shallow baking dish measuring about 9 inches across or 4 empty lobster shell halves. Butter generously.

Two 2-pound lobsters or 1 pound cooked lobster meat, cubed
The bread crumb mixture for ***Scalloped Oysters***, page 308
ADD: ½ cup finely chopped green pepper
¾ teaspoon dry mustard
Cayenne pepper, to taste
Salt and pepper, preferably freshly ground
2 tablespoons butter

If you are using live lobsters, cook according to the recipe for boiled lobsters on page 296. When cool enough to handle, cut the lobsters in half lengthwise using a sharp knife, reserving the shell halves, and cut the meat in cubes.

Prepare bread crumb mixture as indicated in the first paragraph of the Master Recipe for scalloped oysters, sautéing the green pepper along with the onion and celery and adding dry mustard and cayenne pepper along with the salt and pepper. Combine the lobster with about ⅔ of the crumb mixture in a 3-quart bowl and season to taste with salt and pepper. Place the mixture in prepared baking dish or reserved lobster shells, distribute the remaining bread crumbs over the top, and dot with butter. Bake about 20 minutes, or until the top is lightly browned.

AHEAD OF TIME: The dish may be entirely assembled 24 hours in advance. Cover the top with plastic wrap and refrigerate.

MUSSELS

Mussels have always been relished by the peoples of the Mediterranean, and they play a crucial role in French haute cuisine. But until recently mussels were ignored in the United States, despite the fact that they are plentiful along both the Atlantic and Pacific coasts. This is a pity. Often dubbed the poor man's oysters, mussels are tender and pleasantly briny in flavor, and their plump, orange-pink bodies make a very handsome sight on the plate.

STORING LIVE MUSSELS: Rinse the mussels under cold water, but do not scrub or pull out the beard (see below) until you are ready to cook. Discard any mussels that are especially heavy (the shells will contain only mud), especially light (the occupants are likely moribund), or partially open (the occupants are probably ill). If a mussel that is slightly opened snaps shut when tapped, it is okay. Place mussels in a plastic bag along with a few pieces of damp paper towel, tie the bag loosely, and keep in the bottom of the refrigerator. Plan to eat the mussels within a day or two. Never consume mussels that have died before being cooked.

Cleaning and Soaking Mussels: First, scrub the mussels with a stiff brush. Most of the barnacles and vegetation clinging to the shells will come away easily; use a paring knife to scrape off stubborn barnacles. Next, feel around along the flat side of the shells to locate the hairy piece of vegetation (called the "beard") by which the mussel clings to the rocks. Holding the beard between the knife blade and your thumb, pull it out and discard. Rinse mussels. Last, cover the mussels with water and soak for at least 40 minutes; 2 or 3 hours is preferable. This allows the mussels to expel whatever sand they may harbor.

MASTER RECIPE

Mussels Mariner-Style

4 main-course or 6 first-course servings

Serve these delicious wine-steamed mussels in soup plates. The mussel meat is most efficiently picked out of the shells with the fingers, though some fastidious gourmets prefer to pluck it out with a pair of empty shells. The broth should be sipped using a soup spoon and/or sopped up with crusty rolls or bread.

1 cup dry white wine
1 cup water
4 tablespoons butter
⅓ cup finely chopped onion
3 parsley sprigs
½ teaspoon mashed, pressed, or very finely minced garlic
½ teaspoon whole thyme
⅛ teaspoon pepper, preferably freshly ground
3 to 4 quarts mussels, cleaned and soaked
⅓ cup coarsely chopped fresh parsley

Place all ingredients except mussels and chopped parsley in a 6- to 8-quart pot and simmer slowly for 5 minutes to blend flavors. Add mussels, cover, and raise heat to moderately high. Steam mussels for 4 to 5 minutes, or until they are swollen and just barely open, stirring twice so that they cook evenly; do not overcook, or the mussels will shrink and become tough and dry.

Transfer mussels to serving bowls with slotted spoon. Let broth stand a few moments so that any sand can settle to the bottom, then ladle broth over the mussels. Sprinkle with chopped parsley and serve at once.

Variation: MUSSEL SALAD

4 to 6 main-course, 6 to 8 first-course servings

❦ *The idea of eating mussels cold in a salad may sound odd, but in fact there is nothing that suits these particular mollusks any better. Mussel salad can either be passed as an hors d'oeuvre to be eaten with toothpicks or it can be a lunch dish or the first course of a meal; it should always be presented on a bed of leafy lettuce. As part of a meal, serve the salad with crusty bread. Grated carrots, cold boiled potatoes tossed in an oil-and-vinegar dressing, tomato wedges, or wedges of hard-cooked egg might all be used as garnishes.*

Mussels Mariner-style
OMIT: Butter
½ cup olive oil or walnut oil
¼ cup minced scallions, including tender green parts
¼ cup minced fresh parsley
1 teaspoon fresh lemon juice
Salt and pepper, preferably freshly ground

Prepare mussels mariner-style according to the Master Recipe, omitting the butter. Shell the mussels, then toss with olive oil or walnut oil, scallions, parsley, 2 tablespoons of the mussel cooking liquid, and lemon juice. Season to taste with salt and freshly ground pepper. Cover the mussels with plastic wrap and let stand at room temperature for at least 20 minutes before serving.

AHEAD OF TIME: Mussel salad can be stored, covered, for several days in the refrigerator; let stand at room temperature for 1 hour before serving.

MASTER RECIPE

Mussels Broiled in Garlic Butter

4 main-course, 6 to 8 first-course servings

Mussels broiled with a pungent butter sauce flavored with garlic, shallots, and parsley is a famous French recipe whose popularity is now worldwide. The same cooking method also works very well with clams and oysters and is, of course, the classic treatment for snails. Accompany this dish with plenty of crusty bread or rolls for mopping up the ambrosial sauce; a tossed salad might be served along with the mussels or might follow.

PRELIMINARIES

1. Set broiling rack 3 to 4 inches beneath heating element.
2. Preheat broiler at highest setting.
3. Select a 17×11-inch rimmed baking sheet.

16 tablespoons (2 sticks) butter, at room temperature
2 tablespoons dry white wine
2 teaspoons fresh lemon juice
3 tablespoons very finely minced shallots or scallions (white part only)
4 teaspoons mashed, pressed, or very finely minced garlic
¼ cup minced fresh parsley
40 mussels, scrubbed and soaked
¾ cup Fine Fresh Bread Crumbs (see page 60)

Place butter in a small mixing bowl and cream with the back of a wooden spoon until very soft and fluffy. Add the wine and lemon juice by drops, beating constantly, then beat in the shallots, garlic, and parsley.

Pry open the mussels with a knife, discard the empty shell halves, and arrange the mussels on the half shell in a single close layer on a 17×11-inch rimmed baking sheet. Spread with the garlic butter and sprinkle evenly with bread crumbs. Broil 2 to 3 minutes, or until the crumbs are browned and the mussels heated through. Serve immediately.

AHEAD OF TIME: The dish may be assembled several hours in advance. Cover with plastic wrap and refrigerate.

OYSTERS

There are three species of American oysters: the miniature Olympia, harvested in the Pacific; the giant-size Pacific oyster; and the various Atlantic types, including the blue point and the Chincoteague. While each species and type of oyster has its own distinctive flavor, all can be used interchangeably in recipes.

Shucked fresh oysters are sold at quite reasonable prices at most fish markets. They are usually packed in half-pint containers. Store them in the coldest part of the refrigerator and plan to use them promptly. I must say that I am not enthusiastic about shucked oysters—they never have the clean, briny taste of live oysters—but they can be quite convenient.

PURCHASING AND STORING OYSTERS IN THE SHELL: Oysters are available year-round, but they do taste better in the cooler months—the months spelled with the letter "r," as the old rule goes—than in spring and summer, when they spawn. Choose oysters with moist-looking, tightly closed, completely unbroken and unchipped shells. Oysters can be stored at home for quite a long time, provided that they are fresh to begin with and are treated with care. Scrub the oysters with a stiff brush under cool running water to remove dirt and bacteria. Then layer the oysters in a plastic bag, with the curved side of their shells *facing down,* and intersperse the layers with sheets of damp paper toweling (or wet seaweed, if you happen to have it). Tie the bag loosely and refrigerate at about 37°F. The oysters will remain alive and well for at least 5 days, possibly for 2 or 3 weeks—but why push your luck?

OPENING AND SHUCKING FRESH OYSTERS: Any fish market that sells oysters in the shell will open them for you. However, since oysters are best when they are opened just before serving, and since you cannot count on the market to take the necessary pains not to spill the precious oyster liquor out of the shells, it is useful to know how to open and shuck oysters yourself.

First set the rack in the middle of the oven and preheat the oven to 550°F, or to its highest setting. Scrub oysters with a stiff brush and arrange them in a single layer on a large baking sheet with the rounded, bottom shell facing down. Place in the hot oven for just a minute or two, or until their shells open a crack. Immediately take them out; they should still be chilled inside. A few recalcitrant oysters may not open along with the rest. Return them to the oven for another half minute or so after removing the others.

One at a time, hold the oysters over a bowl, the rounded, bottom half of the shell facing down, and scrape along the roof of the flat top shell with a sharp paring knife until you sever the muscle. Lift off and discard the top shell, then, using the paring knife, scrape beneath the oyster to detach it. If you are serving the oysters raw or broiled, leave them on the half shell; otherwise, tip them into a bowl.

SERVING RAW OYSTERS ON THE HALF SHELL: Raw oysters on the half shell are an ambrosial food, and the chances of their being contaminated are virtually nil if you purchase the oysters from a good fish market. Be sure to serve the oysters in the rounded, bottom shell half so that all the delicious juices will be retained. They are at their glorious best served with only a sprinkling of lemon or lime juice and a few grindings of black pepper. Both dry and rather sweet white wines go well with oysters, and of course Champagne is always a possibility. Thin slices of rye bread or pumpernickel spread with unsalted butter and/or a bit of anchovy paste are an elegant and delicious accompaniment.

THE LAW OF OYSTER COOKERY: Oysters must always be cooked gently and briefly, just until they are plump and swollen-looking and their edges (or "skirts") have curled and turned frilly. If overcooked, oysters will shrink and toughen. Think in terms of seconds, not minutes, when cooking oysters.

OYSTERS STEAMED IN SOY AND GINGER

4 servings

❦ *Some years ago, in a Japanese restaurant in New York City, I was served a plate of fine plump oysters in a soy-flavored broth that tasted as good as anything I had ever eaten. The dish seeming quite simple, I immediately set out to duplicate it at home, but it took more than a few tries before I arrived at a close approximation of the restaurant's masterpiece.*

Plain steamed rice, either white or brown, is mandatory here. For a vegetable accompaniment, choose either spinach or sautéed or steamed summer squash; or simply pass a plate of fresh, small farm-type cucumbers quartered lengthwise.

1 tablespoon neutral vegetable oil
1 tablespoon dark sesame oil
2 teaspoons grated or very finely minced fresh ginger
1 teaspoon mashed, pressed, or very finely minced garlic
⅓ cup dark soy sauce
⅓ cup dry Sherry, preferably Fino
2½ teaspoons sugar
2 to 3 pinches of cayenne pepper
32 freshly shucked oysters, the liquor reserved

Combine the oils in a lidded 10- to 12-inch skillet made of or lined with a noncorroding material. Set over moderate heat, add ginger and garlic, and sauté for about a minute, stirring, without letting the garlic color. Add ⅓ cup of the reserved oyster liquor, soy sauce, Sherry, sugar, and cayenne pepper, bring to a simmer, then turn heat down to its lowest point and let broth stand for about 10 minutes, steaming but not quite simmering. Without raising the heat, add the oysters, stirring once to coat with broth. Cover the skillet and, stirring once or twice, steam oysters in the broth for 3 to 5 minutes, or just until they swell and their edges curl. *At no time should the liquid in the skillet reach the simmer;* in fact, until near the end of the cooking time, the broth will barely be hot enough to steam. Serve the oysters at once, accompanied by spoonfuls of the broth.

OYSTER STEW

4 to 6 servings

❦ *I don't know how this venerable recipe got its name, for it's not a stew at all but rather a rich, creamy, oystery broth containing a trove of oysters, plump and just barely poached. There is nothing more comforting and revivifying than oyster stew on a cold winter evening.*

24 to 36 freshly shucked oysters, with their liquor, *or* 1 to 1½ pints packaged raw oysters
1 quart half-and-half *or* 1 cup heavy cream and 3 cups milk
8 tablespoons (1 stick) butter, cut up
Salt and white pepper, preferably freshly ground
2 tablespoons finely chopped fresh parsley and/or celery leaves, *or* sprinklings of paprika

Combine oyster liquor, half-and-half, and butter in a 3- to 4-quart saucepan and heat until liquid begins to steam. Add oysters and poach at just below the simmer for 2 to 3 minutes, or until they are plump and their edges curl. Season to taste with salt and pepper and ladle at once into serving bowls. Dust each serving with minced parsley and/or celery leaves, or paprika. Accompany with oyster crackers.

OYSTERS ROCKEFELLER

4 to 6 first-course servings

❦ *The unique blend of flavors in this famous dish—spinach, anise, lime juice—suits oysters in a particularly delicious and satisfying way. There are numerous versions of Oysters Rockefeller, so feel free to experiment with proportions, adding a bit of celery or a little more or less Pernod, if you like. Because the dish is so assertive in taste, Oysters Rockefeller is always served as a first course; wine does not really complement it. Follow the oysters with something simple like steak or a roast of beef or lamb.*

PRELIMINARIES

1. Set broiling rack 3 to 4 inches beneath heating element.
2. Preheat broiler at highest setting.
3. Select a 17×11-inch rimmed baking sheet

16 tablespoons (2 sticks) butter, at room temperature
½ cup finely chopped shallots or, as a second choice, scallions (white part only)
2 packed cups fresh raw spinach or ½ cup cooked or thawed frozen spinach (about 5 ounces)
½ teaspoon dried tarragon
1½ tablespoons strained fresh lime or lemon juice
3 tablespoons Pernod
¼ teaspoon salt
¼ teaspoon pepper, preferably freshly ground
Hot pepper sauce
24 freshly opened oysters on the half shell
¾ cup Fine Fresh Bread Crumbs (see page 60)

Melt 4 tablespoons of the butter in a 9-inch skillet, add chopped shallots or scallions, and cook over moderate heat for a minute or two, or until wilted. Add spinach and cook, stirring, for several minutes, or until fresh spinach wilts. Raise heat to moderately high and cook the mixture, stirring frequently, until all moisture has evaporated and the spinach is sautéing in butter. Add tarragon, lime or lemon juice, Pernod, salt, pepper, and a few drops of hot pepper sauce and continue to cook until the liquid has evaporated. Using a blender, food processor, or a large mortar, purée the mixture until it is reduced to a paste. Let cool to tepid, then blend thoroughly with remaining 12 tablespoons (1½ sticks) butter, either adding the butter to the machine and processing or, if you puréed the spinach mixture in a mortar, combining the spinach and butter in a mixing bowl.

Arrange oysters on the half shell on the baking sheet and spread each with 2 teaspoons of the spinach mixture. Sprinkle with bread crumbs and broil for 2 to 3 minutes, or just long enough to heat the oysters through. Serve at once.

AHEAD OF TIME: The spinach butter may be turned into a lidded storage container and refrigerated for several days or frozen for a month. The dish may be assembled in its entirety several hours in advance and held in the refrigerator, covered with plastic wrap. Broil just before serving.

OYSTERS BROILED IN GARLIC BUTTER

4 main-course, 6 to 8 first-course servings

Mussels Broiled in Garlic Butter, page 303
SUBSTITUTE: 24 freshly opened large oysters on the half shell for mussels

Proceed according to the recipe for mussels, substituting oysters for mussels.

MASTER RECIPE

Scalloped Oysters

4 servings

❦ *An old-fashioned and uniquely satisfying procedure, scalloping entails sandwiching a layer of oysters (or other shellfish) between two layers of heavily buttered and flavored crumbs and baking the dish briefly in a very hot oven. Traditionally, crushed cracker crumbs are used here, but I prefer fresh bread crumbs. Accompany with a tossed salad or cole slaw.*

PRELIMINARIES

1. Set the rack in upper-middle level of oven.
2. Preheat oven to 450°F 20 minutes before baking.
3. Select a shallow baking dish measuring about 9 inches across.

10 tablespoons (1¼ sticks) butter
½ cup finely chopped onion
¼ cup finely chopped celery
2 cups Fine Fresh Bread Crumbs (see page 60)
3 tablespoons finely chopped fresh parsley
¼ to ½ teaspoon salt, to taste
¼ teaspoon pepper, preferably freshly ground
24 to 32 freshly shucked oysters or 1½ pints packaged raw oysters

Melt butter in a 10-inch skillet. Add the onion and celery and sauté slowly until fairly soft but not brown, about 7 minutes. Add bread crumbs, stirring to moisten them uniformly with butter, then raise heat to moderately high and, tossing constantly with a wooden spoon, sauté crumbs for a minute or two to toast them lightly. Remove from heat and stir in parsley, salt, and pepper.

Spread ½ of the crumb mixture evenly over bottom of baking dish. Arrange the oysters in a single layer over the crumbs and top evenly with remaining crumbs. Bake 12 to 15 minutes, or until the oysters are heated through and the top of the dish is lightly browned.

AHEAD OF TIME: The dish may be assembled entirely several hours in advance and stored in the refrigerator, covered.

FRIED OYSTERS

4 servings

❦ *These are a treat. Serve with lemon wedges and tartar sauce. Cole slaw and french fries make nice accompaniments.*

Before you embark on the recipe, see the chapter on deep-frying, pages 59–66.

24 to 32 freshly shucked large oysters or 1½ pints packaged raw oysters
For breading and deep-frying:
½ cup all-purpose flour
2 large eggs
2 tablespoons neutral vegetable oil
1 teaspoon salt
½ teaspoon pepper, preferably freshly ground
1½ to 2 cups Fine Fresh Bread Crumbs (see page 60) or fine cracker crumbs
3 quarts very fresh vegetable oil

Following the Master Technique for deep-frying, dredge the oysters in flour, dip in eggs beaten with 2 tablespoons oil, salt, and pepper, and coat with either bread crumbs or fine cracker crumbs (Step 1b, page 62); deep-fry (Step 2, page 64) in 3 quarts of oil heated to 370°F in batches of 8 to 10 for about 1½ minutes, or until swollen and lightly browned. Serve immediately.

OYSTER FRITTERS

4 servings

❦ *Serve these with lemon wedges and tartar sauce and accompany with cole slaw.*

Consult the chapter on deep-frying, pages 59–66, for procedural details. Note especially that fritter batter is better if allowed to rest at least 2 hours before egg whites are folded in.

24 to 32 freshly shucked large oysters or 1½ pints packaged raw oysters
½ cup all-purpose flour
For fritter batter and deep-frying:
- 2 large eggs, separated
- ¾ cup beer
- 2 tablespoons neutral vegetable oil or melted butter
- 1 cup unbleached all-purpose flour
- 1 teaspoon salt
- ¼ teaspoon pepper, preferably freshly ground
- 3 quarts very fresh vegetable oil

Blot the oysters with paper toweling, then roll in flour, shaking off the excess. Prepare fritter batter according to instructions on page 63. Following the Master Technique for deep-frying, fold the oysters into the fritter batter and deep-fry in 3 quarts oil heated to 370°F (see page 64) for 1½ to 2 minutes, or until swollen, puffy, and lightly browned; fry only 6 to 8 oysters at a time, as they expand during cooking. Serve at once.

OYSTERS TEMPURA

4 main-course, 6 to 8 first-course servings

❦ *Oysters tempura is often served as an hors d'oeuvre or first course but it is also good as the main course, perhaps accompanied by tempura vegetables such as sweet potato, broccoli, or onion rings. Always serve these oysters with soy sauce. The chapter on deep-frying, pages 59–66, will be a helpful resource on tempura batter and frying techniques.*

24 to 32 freshly shucked large oysters or 1½ pints packaged raw oysters
½ cup all-purpose flour or cake flour
For tempura batter and deep-frying:
- 1 cup ice water
- 1 large egg yolk
- 1 cup unbleached all-purpose flour or cake flour
- ½ teaspoon ground ginger (optional)
- ½ teaspoon salt
- 3 quarts very fresh vegetable oil

Blot the oysters with paper toweling, then roll in flour, shaking off the excess. Prepare tempura batter as instructed on page 64. Following the Master Technique for deep-frying, fold the oysters into the tempura batter and deep-fry in 3 quarts oil heated to 370°F (see page 64) for 1½ to 2 minutes, or until the coating is crisp and lightly browned; fry only 6 to 8 oysters at a time, as the coating puffs up during cooking. Serve as soon as possible; the tempura coating softens quickly.

SCALLOPS

The part of the scallop that we Americans eat is the muscle holding the two lovely shells together. The body and the delicious roe, both of which are eaten in Europe, are either thrown away by fishermen out at sea or used to make pet food or fertilizer.

There are two types of American scallops: bay scallops, the size of grapes, and deep-sea scallops, the size and shape of marshmallows. Bay scallops are tenderer and arguably more elegant in appearance than sea scallops, but they are also more expensive, and, in my opinion, not necessarily worth their higher price. When quartered lengthwise, sea scallops make worthy stand-ins for their posher cousins.

PURCHASING FRESH SCALLOPS: Raw scallops should be sweet-smelling and pearly-translucent. Whiteness, chalkiness, and a grainy or fibrous appearance are signs that the scallops are old.

THE LAW OF SCALLOP COOKERY: Never overcook scallops, or they will be coarse, shriveled, dried out, and rubbery. When broiled, sautéed, or deep-fried, scallops must be served as soon as they are cooked, for they will weep their juice and toughen if they wait.

RAW SCALLOPS RÉMOULADE OR VINAIGRETTE

6 to 8 first-course servings

❦ *Raw scallops make a delicious and unusual summertime first course, perhaps preceding a charcoal-broiled steak. The thing to remember here is that the scallops must be very fresh. Rolls or crackers are a necessary accompaniment.*

1½ pounds very fresh bay scallops or quartered sea scallops
Rémoulade Sauce, page 55, or Vinaigrette Dressing, page 117
1 large bunch leaf lettuce, washed and dried
2 large or 3 medium tomatoes, cut in wedges
2 to 3 tablespoons chopped fresh parsley

About 30 minutes before serving, combine scallops with rémoulade sauce or vinaigrette dressing; cover and chill. Arrange scallops on lettuce, garnish with tomato wedges, and sprinkle with chopped parsley.

MASTER RECIPE

Scallops Sautéed with Garlic and Lemon

4 main-course or 6 to 8 first-course servings

❦ *Here is yet another shellfish recipe in which garlic, lemon juice, and fresh parsley make an appearance. This makes a fine first course or, with a salad, a main course. Scallops or other shellfish prepared in this manner also make a nice hors d'oeuvre. The whole sautéing procedure is simplicity itself and takes but a few minutes to do, but you must take care not to overcook the scallops. Serve this dish the minute it is done.*

1½ pounds bay scallops or quartered sea scallops
½ cup all-purpose flour
2 tablespoons olive oil
4 tablespoons butter
2 tablespoons strained fresh lemon juice
2 teaspoons mashed, pressed, or very finely minced garlic
½ teaspoon salt
¼ teaspoon pepper, preferably freshly ground
¼ cup minced fresh parsley

Pat scallops dry with paper towels, then roll in flour, shaking off the excess. Over a high flame, heat olive oil and butter in a heavy-bottomed 10- to 12-inch skillet made of or lined with a noncorroding material until the mixture is fragrant and on the verge of coloring. Add scallops all at once, toss to coat with fat, and keeping the heat high, toss scallops continually with spatula or wooden spoon for 2 to 3 minutes, or just until they have stiffened and begun to brown very lightly. Stir in lemon juice, garlic, salt, and pepper, and sauté a few moments longer. Remove from heat, sprinkle with parsley, and serve at once.

BROILED SCALLOPS

4 servings

❦ *Broiled scallops are exceedingly simple to prepare and quite delicious, but care must be taken not to overcook them. The nutty flavor of brown rice goes well with broiled scallops; scalloped potatoes are another possibility. Green beans or broccoli are good accompaniments. And don't forget to pass lemon wedges.*

PRELIMINARIES

1. Set broiler rack 3 to 4 inches beneath heating element.
2. Preheat broiler at its highest setting.
3. Select a 17×11-inch rimmed baking sheet or other large, shallow dish.

1½ to 2 pounds bay or sea scallops
8 tablespoons (1 stick) butter
½ teaspoon salt
¼ teaspoon pepper, preferably white and freshly ground
2 to 3 tablespoons finely chopped parsley

Spread scallops out on baking sheet. Melt the butter and pour it over the scallops, tossing with a spoon to coat them evenly. Sprinkle with salt and pepper. Broil bay scallops 2 to 4 minutes, sea scallops 5 to 6 minutes, without turning or stirring. The scallops are done as soon as they are heated through and have whitened; sea scallops will turn a delicate brown around the edges. Serve immediately, sprinkled with parsley.

SCALLOPS BAKED IN GARLIC CRUMBS

4 main-course or 6 to 8 first-course servings

Scalloped Oysters, page 308

SUBSTITUTE: 1½ pounds bay scallops or quartered sea scallops for oysters

ADD: 1 tablespoon mashed, pressed, or very finely minced garlic

Proceed according to the Master Recipe, substituting scallops for oysters and stirring the garlic into the onion and celery just before adding the bread crumbs. If you wish, bake the scallops in individual scallop shells, arranged on a baking sheet, rather than in a dish; in this case decrease baking time to 10 to 12 minutes.

DEEP-FRIED BREADED SCALLOPS

4 main-course or 6 to 8 first-course servings

❦ *Serve with lemon wedges and tartar sauce or the classic rémoulade sauce. French fries and cole slaw are good accompaniments.*

Look over the chapter on deep-frying, pages 59–66, for full information on breading and frying.

1½ pounds sea scallops

For breading and deep-frying:

- ½ cup all-purpose flour
- 2 large eggs
- 2 tablespoons neutral vegetable oil
- 1 teaspoon salt
- ½ teaspoon pepper, preferably freshly ground
- 2 cups Fine Fresh Bread Crumbs (see page 60)
- 3 quarts very fresh vegetable oil

Following the Master Technique, dredge the scallops in flour, dip in eggs beaten with 2 tablespoons oil, salt, and pepper, and coat with bread crumbs (see page 62); deep-fry (see page 64) in 3 quarts oil heated to 370°F in batches of 8 to 10 for 2 to 3 minutes, or until nicely browned. Serve at once.

Shrimp

Shrimp are a delicious shellfish. They also cost a great deal, and too often what you get for your money is a mass of little rubberized truncheons—not good shellfish. Almost all the shrimp that arrive in markets outside the Gulf Coast area have been frozen. In and of itself, freezing is not a problem; rather, it is the various forms of mishandling that shrimp are sometimes subjected to during the freezing process that cause disaster. For example, sometimes the freezing temperature at which shrimp are stored is not cold enough, permitting unchecked bacterial and enzymatic deterioration; sometimes shrimp are repeatedly thawed and refrozen, causing the flesh to turn to mush; and sometimes frozen shrimp are thawed and then left for a week or so in a refrigerator before finally being sold at the market. Any of these cavalier treatments will ruin shrimp, and some batches of shrimp that I have bought seem to have been subjected to all of them. Still, even if buying good shrimp is a difficult and chancy business, there are some things you can do.

Purchasing Shrimp: First, and most important, smell the shrimp. A faint iodine scent is okay, but avoid those shrimp with a fishy, rotten, or ammoniac odor. Next, look at the shrimp closely. Color is not an indicator of freshness, for some varieties are naturally greenish, grayish, or even brown, but all shrimp should be glistening and pearly-translucent. Pass over any that seem slimy, opaque, or chalky, or that give off hints of oily iridescence.

TIP: Another test of shrimp freshness is one that you may have difficulty performing in the fish market—unless the fish man's back is turned. Pick up a shrimp by the tail end and see if it holds its curled shape fairly firmly. If it flattens out, or if it feels very soft and limp, it is a sick shrimp and belongs in the garbage can, not on your dinner plate.

Finally, resist the temptation to buy preshelled raw shrimp at the market. They will have been handled a great deal during peeling, picking up bacteria that will cause them to spoil faster.

Shrimp Sizes and Servings: Shrimp range in size from tiny to colossal (as few as 6 to a pound). Tiny shrimp are usually canned; colossal shrimp are delicious baked and stuffed. In between are several middle sizes, which tend to be designated by different names depending on the market. Most markets carry at least two of the middle sizes, sometimes three. For most purposes, I prefer the large-medium size (24 to 30 to a pound) because they are less of a chore to peel than smaller shrimp; however, they are also more expensive than medium or small-medium shrimp.

Two pounds raw shrimp in the shell make 1½ to 1¾ pounds raw peeled shrimp and about 3 cups cooked peeled shrimp. Allow ⅓ to ½ pound raw shrimp in the shell per serving.

Peeling and Deveining Shrimp: To peel a shrimp, whether raw or cooked, grasp the shell on the underside between your thumbs and gently tear. The shell will peel right off except perhaps for a small piece around the tail, which you can pull free with one sharp tug. (When preparing plain steamed shrimp-(say, for a shrimp cocktail), I always shell shrimp after cooking, not because I think that the shells impart any flavor during cooking, as some people claim, but rather because I think peeling is easier when the shrimp have been firmed up a bit by cooking.) If, after peeling, you wish to remove the intestinal vein that runs along the back of the shrimp, slit the flesh that covers it with a small knife, and scrape the vein out. I must confess that I find deveining a nuisance, and I don't bother with it unless I have shrimp whose veins are especially dark and messy-looking. There is, by the way, nothing in the veins that will harm the diner or adversely affect the flavor of the dish.

The Law of Shrimp Cookery: Never, never overcook shrimp or they will turn rubbery and lose their flavor. If you should happen to overcook shrimp, the only thing that can be done with them is to grind them up and mix them with cream cheese, grated onion, chopped parsley, and a bit of Worcestershire sauce to make a dip.

STEAMED SHRIMP

4 main-course or 6 to 8 first-course servings

❦ *Treat hot steamed shrimp like steamed crabs or boiled lobster. Serve them in their shells with lemon wedges and melted butter and allow your guests, provided with bibs, napkins, and perhaps fingerbowls, to eat them with their hands. Cole slaw and rolls or french fries are good accompaniments; beer is the drink of choice. Cold steamed shrimp are generally peeled, arranged on lettuce, and served as a first-course shrimp cocktail. Appropriate dressings for a shrimp cocktail include green goddess dressing, horseradish mayonnaise, rémoulade sauce, or even commercial cocktail sauce.*

2 pounds raw large-medium shrimp (24 to 30 per pound), unpeeled
2 tablespoons salt
1 teaspoon whole black or white peppercorns

Place shrimp in a colander, rinse under cold water, drain, and turn into a heavy, lidded 10- to 12-inch skillet or pot. Sprinkle with salt and peppercorns and add just enough cold water to cover the shrimp. Place over high heat. As soon as the water comes to a brisk boil, cover the skillet or pot tightly and remove from heat. Let stand for 2 minutes exactly, then drain in a colander. Serve immediately or cover and chill for at least 2 hours (or up to 2 days) and use for shrimp cocktail. To peel and devein, see page 316.

SHRIMP SAUTÉED WITH GARLIC AND LEMON

4 main-course or 6 to 8 first-course servings

Scallops Sautéed with Garlic and Lemon, page 312
SUBSTITUTE: 2 pounds raw large-medium shrimp (24 to 30 per pound), peeled and, if you wish, deveined, for scallops

Proceed according to the Master Recipe, substituting shrimp for scallops. As soon as the shrimp begin to curl and turn pinkish and opaque, add the lemon juice,garlic, salt, and pepper, and sauté just until the shrimps are firm.

SHRIMP NEWBURG

4 main-course or 6 to 8 first-course servings

Lobster Newburg, page 297
SUBSTITUTE: 1½ pounds raw large-medium shrimp (24 to 30 per pound), peeled and, if you wish, deveined, for lobster

Proceed according to the Master Recipe, substituting *raw* shrimp for lobster. After combining the shrimp and wine in the skillet, simmer gently just until the shrimp have curled and turned opaque. Turn the shrimp frequently with a spoon.

CURRIED SHRIMP

4 servings

❦ *Serve this classic dish over rice or in patty shells, accompanied by peas.*

Curried Cream Sauce, page 39
1½ to 2 pounds raw large-medium shrimp (24 to 30 per pound), peeled and, if you wish, deveined

Bring sauce to a simmer in a 3-quart saucepan and fold in *raw* shrimp. Stirring frequently, cook at the barest simmer for 2 to 3 minutes, or just until the shrimp curl and turn pink. Do not overcook, or the shrimp will toughen. Serve at once.

SHRIMP BAKED IN CRUMBS LOUISIANA-STYLE

4 servings

❦ *Shrimp, green peppers, garlic, and herbs make a particularly felicitous combination. Serve cole slaw, a tossed salad, or tomato salad as an accompaniment.*

Scalloped Oysters, page 308
ADD: ½ cup finely chopped green pepper
2 teaspoons mashed, pressed, or very finely minced garlic
¾ teaspoon dry mustard
¼ teaspoon ground thyme
⅛ to ¼ teaspoon cayenne pepper, to taste
SUBSTITUTE: 1½ pounds raw large-medium shrimp (24 to 30 per pound), peeled and, if you wish, deveined, for oysters

Proceed according to the Master Recipe, but sauté green pepper along with onion and celery, stir in garlic just before adding the bread crumbs, and season with mustard, thyme, and cayenne pepper in addition to salt and pepper; substitute shrimp for oysters.

BAKED STUFFED GIANT SHRIMP

4 servings

❦ *These are delicious with a dry white wine and a tomato salad.*

Preliminaries

1. Set rack in upper level of oven.
2. Preheat oven to 450°F 20 minutes before baking.
3. Select a baking dish measuring about 11 inches long and 8 inches wide.

14 raw colossal shrimp (2 pounds or more), unpeeled
¼ teaspoon salt
¼ teaspoon pepper, preferably freshly ground
1½ cups Fine Fresh Bread Crumbs (see page 60)
6 tablespoons butter, melted
¼ cup finely chopped fresh parsley, preferably flat-leaf Italian parsley
2 teaspoons mashed, pressed, or very finely minced garlic
¾ to 1 cup dry white wine

Make an incision in the bellies of 12 of the shrimp, reaching from the neck to the tail and almost going through the back. Open the shrimp up so that they lie almost flat on their backs; season flesh lightly with salt and pepper. Peel the remaining 2 shrimp, chop coarsely, and combine with bread crumbs, melted butter, parsley, garlic, salt, and pepper in a 3-quart bowl. Arrange shrimp in a single layer in the baking dish and fill the slits with stuffing mixture, pressing it in lightly. Pour just enough wine into the baking dish to film the bottom. Bake shrimp for 10 to 12 minutes, or until piping hot; be careful not to overcook. Spoon a bit of the juices in the baking dish over each shrimp, and serve immediately.

❦

DEEP-FRIED BREADED SHRIMP

4 main-course or 6 to 8 first-course servings

❦ *These are a real treat. Serve with lemon wedges and a mayonnaise-based sauce such as mustard mayonnaise, rémoulade sauce, or tartar sauce. French fries and cole slaw are the classic accompaniments.*

For information on procedures and techniques, see the chapter on deep-frying, pages 59–66.

1½ pounds raw large-medium shrimp (24 to 30 per pound)
For breading and frying:
- ½ cup all-purpose flour
- 2 large eggs
- 2 tablespoons neutral vegetable oil
- 1 teaspoon salt
- ½ teaspoon pepper, preferably freshly ground
- 1½ to 2 cups Fine Fresh Bread Crumbs (see page 60)
- 3 quarts very fresh vegetable oil

Peel and, if you wish, devein the shrimp but leave the tails and the band of shell adjacent to the tails attached. Following Step 1b (page 62) of the Master Technique for deep-frying, dredge the shrimp in flour, dip in eggs beaten with 2 tablespoons oil, salt, and pepper, and coat with fine fresh bread crumbs. (Hold the shrimp by their tails instead of using forks when coating them to avoid covering the tails with breading.) Deep-fry (Step 2, page 64) in batches of 6 to 8 in 3 quarts oil heated to 370°F for 2 to 3 minutes, or until nicely browned. Serve immediately.

LEAH'S STUFFED COCONUT-FRIED SHRIMP

4 main-course or 6 to 8 first-course servings

❦ *These take the idea of deep-fried shrimp about as far as it can go. The shrimp are slit down the front and stuffed with finely chopped mango chutney or ginger preserves, then dipped in flour and beaten egg, and finally rolled in coconut. Serve these with a dip of reconstituted dry mustard or Japanese mustard. If you offer them as a main course, accompany the shrimp with a plate of raw vegetables—cucumbers, celery, carrots, and the like.*

The chapter on deep-frying, pages 59–66, gives many pointers you will find useful.

1½ pounds raw large-medium shrimp (24 to 30 per pound)
½ cup sweet mango chutney or ginger preserves, chopped fine
For breading and frying:
- ½ cup all-purpose flour
- 2 large eggs
- 2 tablespoons neutral vegetable oil
- 1 teaspoon salt
- ½ teaspoon pepper, preferably freshly ground
- 1½ to 2 cups finely grated fresh coconut or desiccated coconut (available at health food stores)
- 3 quarts very fresh vegetable oil

Peel the shrimp but leave the tails and the band of shell adjacent to the tails attached. Cut a deep pocket in the belly of each shrimp going from the tail to within ¼ inch of the head end and reaching almost through to the opposite side. Stuff each shrimp with about ½ teaspoon chutney or preserves, then press closed with your fingers; it doesn't matter if some of the stuffing bulges out as the coating will cover it up. Following Step 1b, page 62, of the Master Technique for deep-frying, dredge shrimp in flour, dip in eggs beaten with 2 tablespoons oil, salt, and pepper, and coat with coconut. (Hold the shrimp by their tails instead of using forks when coating them to avoid covering the tails with coconut.) In 3 quarts oil heated to 370°F, deep-fry (Step 2, page 64) in batches of 6 to 8 for 2 to 3 minutes, or until nicely browned. Serve immediately.

DEEP-FRIED BATTER-DIPPED SHRIMP

4 main-course or 6 to 8 first-course servings

❦*I like these best as an hors d'oeuvre, accompanied by a dip of reconstituted dry mustard lightly sweetened with honey, but they may of course be the main offering of a meal. In the latter case, the usual deep-fried seafood accompaniments—tartar sauce, lemon wedges, cole slaw, french fries—are appropriate.*

All details are covered in the chapter on deep-frying, pages 59–66. Note particularly that fritter batter is better if allowed to rest at least 2 hours before egg whites are folded in.

1½ pounds raw large-medium shrimp (24 to 30 per pound)
For fritter batter and deep-frying:
2 large eggs, separated
¾ cup beer
2 tablespoons neutral vegetable oil or melted butter
1 cup unbleached all-purpose flour
1 teaspoon salt
¼ teaspoon pepper, preferably freshly ground
3 quarts very fresh vegetable oil

Peel and, if you wish, devein the shrimp, but leave the tails and the band of shell adjacent to the tails attached. Prepare the fritter batter as instructed in Step 1c, page 63, of the Master Technique for deep-frying, but instead of folding the shrimp into the batter as directed in the Master Technique, one at a time dip them up to their tails in the batter and drop them at once into 3 quarts oil heated to 370°F (Step 2, page 64), adding no more than 6 or 8 to the pot at one time. Fry each batch for 2 to 3 minutes, or until the coating is lightly browned. Serve immediately.

SHRIMP TEMPURA

4 main-course or 6 to 8 first-course servings

❦ *Shrimp tempura should be accompanied by soy sauce and either reconstituted dry mustard or Japanese mustard. Tempura vegetables make a nice side dish.*

The chapter on deep-frying, pages 59–66, gives guidelines on tempura batter as well as frying.

1½ pounds raw large-medium shrimp (24 to 30 per pound)
For tempura batter and deep-frying:
1 cup ice water
1 large egg yolk
1 cup unbleached all-purpose flour or cake flour
½ teaspoon ground ginger (optional)
½ teaspoon salt
3 quarts very fresh vegetable oil

Peel and, if you wish, devein the shrimp but leave the tails and the band of shell adjacent to the tails attached to serve as handles. Prepare the tempura batter as described in Step 1d, page 64 of the Master Technique for deep-frying, but instead of folding the shrimp into the batter as directed in the Master Technique, one at a time dip them up to their tails in the batter and drop them at once into 3 quarts oil heated to 370°F (Step 2, page 64), adding no more than 6 or 8 to the pot at one time. Fry each batch for 2 to 3 minutes, or until the coating has just begun to brown. Serve immediately.

Snails

Fresh land snails require time-consuming precooking procedures, including a purgative diet of several days' duration, traditionally on grape leaves. Canned snails, which are imported to this country from France, do not have the flavor of fresh, but they are much more convenient.

Canned snails are generally sold with a separate package of empty snail shells. Snail shells may certainly be reused, but you must make sure to clean them thoroughly. Soak them for several hours in hot, soapy water, scrub inside and out with a small brush, and rinse thoroughly in several changes of hot water. To be certain they are sterile, you might also boil them for 1 minute in water to cover. Arrange on racks, the open side down, and allow to dry 24 hours before storing in a covered container.

If you eat snails frequently, you may want to invest in snail plates, tongs, and forks, all of which are available at specialty cookware shops. The plates are made of metal or ceramic and contain individual depressions to hold each snail, so that they do not spill their lovely juices. The tongs facilitate the picking up of the hot snail shells, and the forks are just the right size for getting at the meat.

Though snails may be prepared in a number of ways, the most famous recipe and the one most familiar to Americans is *Escargots Bourguignonne,* or snails in garlic butter. Indeed, the association between snails and garlic butter is so entrenched that the French have come to call garlic butter *beurre pour escargots*—or "butter for snails"—even when the butter is used with beef steaks or some other food.

SNAILS IN GARLIC BUTTER

4 to 6 main-course or 8 first-course servings

Preliminaries

1. Set rack in upper third of oven.
2. Preheat oven to 450°F 20 minutes before baking.
3. Select a rimmed baking sheet just large enough to hold the snail shells in a single tight layer. (Arrange snail plates, if you are using them, on one or two baking sheets.)

Mussels Broiled in Garlic Butter, page 303

SUBSTITUTE: 48 canned land snails (plus shells) for mussels
ADD: ¾ to 1 cup additional dry white wine

Drain and rinse the snails, then pat dry with paper toweling. Prepare garlic butter as indicated in the Master Recipe. Place a dab of the butter in each snail shell, fill with a snail, and cover the entrance to the shell with more butter. Press the butter-filled openings into the bread crumbs called for in the Master Recipe and arrange the snails open side up in a single close layer on baking sheet (or place on snail plates). Pour enough wine into the bottom of the baking sheet to make a depth of 1⁄16 inch. (If using snail plates, sprinkle the depressions with a bit of wine.)

Instead of broiling, as indicated in the Master Recipe, bake the snails in preheated oven for 10 to 12 minutes, or until they are piping hot. Serve immediately.

SQUID

Squid is extremely popular all along the Mediterranean, but until recently, Americans have not been much interested in it. I suspect that one of the reasons may be that many people in this country have sampled badly prepared squid. Squid reacts to mistreatment by turning as tough and hard as a rubber band (and just about as tasteless). But when cooked properly—that is, either briefly or very slowly—squid has a nice shrimplike taste and is pleasantly chewy. No doubt because it remains something of an undiscovered item, squid is a terrific bargain at the fish market. Buy 3 to 4 pounds of uncleaned squid, 1½ to 2 pounds of cleaned squid, for 4 people.

CLEANING SQUID: First pull off the head (1). Cut the tentacles off the head, pop the stony beak (if attached) out of the center of the tentacle cluster, and set the tentacles aside (2)(3). Discard the head itself and any viscera attached to it. Next, reach inside the body and pull out the transparent backbone; discard (4). Now hold the body upside down and squeeze it from the tail down to the neck (as though you were squeezing a tube of toothpaste) to release the jellylike entrails, and discard them (5). Last, strip off the thin, purplish skin that covers the body of the squid, along with the two fins; discard (6). Rinse squid body and tentacles.

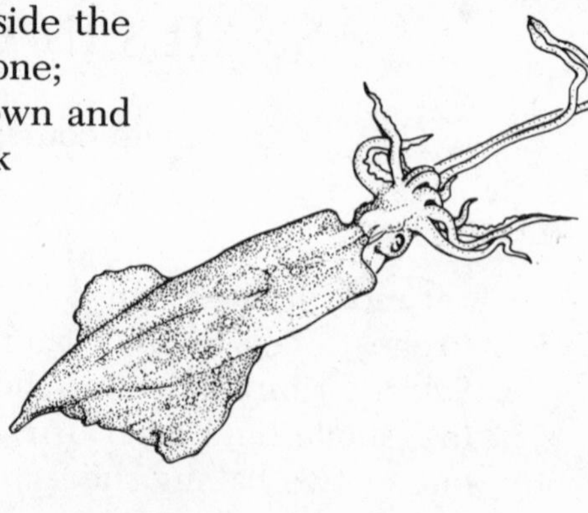

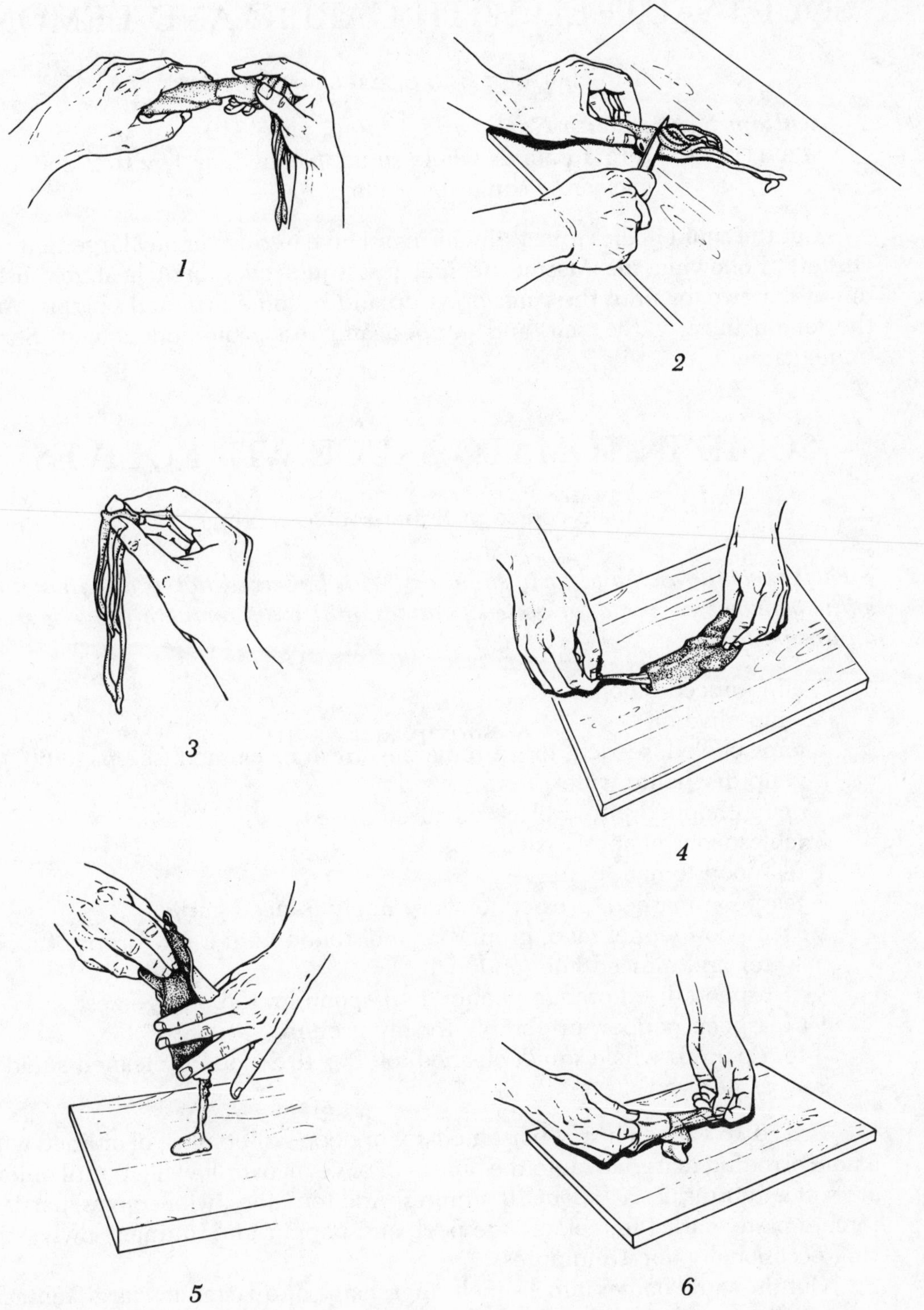
1
2
3
4
5
6

SQUID SAUTÉED WITH GARLIC AND LEMON

4 main-course or 6 to 8 first-course servings

Scallops Sautéed with Garlic and Lemon, page 312
SUBSTITUTE: 3 to 4 pounds whole squid, cleaned, or 1½ to 2 pounds cleaned squid for scallops

Cut the squid bodies into ⅜-inch rings; halve or quarter any large tentacle clusters. Following the Master Recipe, toss squid over high heat for just a minute or two, or until the rings open up and become firm and opaque. Add the lemon juice, garlic, salt, and pepper, and toss a moment longer. Serve immediately.

SQUID IN TOMATO SAUCE WITH OLIVES

4 main-course or 8 first-course servings

❦ *This especially rich and tasty squid dish can be served hot as a main course with steamed rice, pasta, or boiled potatoes or at room temperature as part of an antipasto.*

1 cup minced onions
⅓ cup olive oil
2 cups peeled, seeded, diced tomatoes, fresh or canned (see page 607)
½ cup dry white wine
¼ cup chopped pitted black oil-cured olives
3 tablespoons chopped parsley
1 teaspoon tomato paste
1 teaspoon mashed, pressed, or very finely minced garlic
¼ teaspoon fennel seed, ground or moistened with a few drops of water and minced fine (optional)
¼ teaspoon dried orange peel or 1 teaspoon grated orange zest
¼ teaspoon pepper, preferably freshly ground
3 to 4 pounds whole squid, cleaned, or 1½ to 2 pounds cleaned squid
Salt, as necessary

In a 10- to 12-inch heavy-bottomed pot or deep skillet made of or lined with a noncorroding material, sauté the onions in olive oil over low heat until onions are soft and translucent, about 10 minutes. Add tomatoes, wine, olives, parsley, tomato paste, garlic, fennel, orange peel, and pepper and simmer slowly, stirring occasionally, for 15 minutes.

Cut the squid bodies into ⅜-inch rings; halve or quarter any large tentacle clusters. Add the squid to the tomato mixture and bring to just below the simmer over gentle heat. Turn heat down to its lowest point and cook very slowly—the liquid should barely bubble—for about 1 hour, or until the squid is fork-tender. Never let the tomato mixture boil, or the squid will become rubbery. Remove squid with a slotted spoon and set aside. Turn heat to high and boil down the braising juices until reduced to about 1 cup of thick sauce. Remove from heat, fold in the squid, and season with salt as necessary. Set over very low heat and reheat to just below the simmer.

AHEAD OF TIME: This dish may be prepared several days ahead and stored in the refrigerator, covered.

FRIED SQUID

4 main-course or 6 to 8 first-course servings

❦ *This is a very popular way of preparing squid along the Mediterranean, and it is undoubtedly one of the best. Pass the squid with lemon wedges and accompany with a tossed salad.*

Check the chapter on deep-frying, pages 59–66, for guidance on simple breading and tips on frying.

3 to 4 pounds whole squid, cleaned, or 1½ to 2 pounds cleaned squid
For coating and deep-frying:
- ½ cup milk, half-and-half, or light cream
- ⅔ cup all-purpose flour
- 1 teaspoon salt
- ½ teaspoon pepper, preferably freshly ground
- 3 quarts very fresh vegetable oil

Cut the squid bodies into rings about ⅜-inch thick; leave the tentacle clusters whole. Following Step 1a, page 61, of the Master Technique for deep-frying, dip the squid in milk, then coat lightly with flour seasoned with salt and pepper. Adding the squid to the pot in 2 or 3 batches (a deep-fry basket is helpful here), deep-fry (Step 2, page 64) in 3 quarts oil heated to 370°F for 2 to 3 minutes, or until delicately browned. Serve at once, as fried squid softens quickly.

ABOUT POULTRY and MEAT

Chicken and Rock Cornish Hen

It is customary to classify chickens according to their size, small chickens being labeled "broilers," middle-sized chickens "fryers," and large chickens "roasters." In fact, the boundaries between the various classifications are elastic and subjective, and a chicken that one supermarket considers a "broiler" may be considered a "fryer" (or, sneakily, a "broiler-fryer") by another supermarket. It is my view that chickens for broiling should weigh no more than 3 pounds and that 1- to 1½-pound chickens are preferable; chickens for frying should weigh around 3½ pounds; and chickens for roasting may be any size, though those weighing 4 pounds or more will have a higher proportion of meat to bone than smaller birds. The important general rule to remember is that the quicker the cooking method, the smaller the chicken should be.

Several special types of chicken have led to confusion in some people's minds. *Rock Cornish game hens,* which generally weigh between 1 and 1½ pounds, are a hybrid of a chicken and a smaller wild bird called a Rock Cornish hen. Despite the word "game" that crops up in their name, Rock Cornish hens taste very much like chicken. They may be roasted, and they are excellent birds for broiling. A *capon* is a castrated rooster that is carefully fed and then slaughtered while still fairly young; it must be ordered specially from a butcher. Weighing between 5 and 9 pounds, tender, and well meated, capon is reserved exclusively for roasting. *Stewing hens,* also called stewing fowls, are hens that have reached the end of their productive lives as egg layers. Unlike other types of chicken, which are tender and do not require prolonged cooking, stewing hens are tough and must be stewed slowly in liquid.

CHICKEN GIBLETS

Chicken Livers: Buy moist, dark red livers, not ones that look dried out, grayish, or spongy; plan to eat the livers promptly after purchasing, or freeze them in their original container for future use. Before cooking, separate the livers into two lobes, removing any particularly large strings and any green spots (bile) that may be present. Rinse livers very quickly under cold water and blot with paper toweling.

Allow about ⅓ pound of chicken livers per person.

Chicken Gizzards and Hearts: The gizzards and hearts of chickens make excellent—and very economical—eating if allowed to stew slowly for a sufficient time to become fully tender. Rinse the giblets under cold water, then pat dry with paper toweling. Peel off the mantle of tough skin that covers the top of gizzards, thus separating the gizzards into two lobes roughly the same size as hearts. (The skin may be saved for making stock.)

Allow about ½ pound of giblets per person.

HOW TO CUT UP CHICKEN IN VARIOUS WAYS: Cut-up chickens and chicken breast cutlets are available at supermarkets, but you can save money and get handsomer pieces than the supermarket will give you if you do the cutting yourself.

To perform surgery on chickens, you need the right tools. Absolutely indispensable are a sharp utility knife and a sharp, pointed paring knife. Poultry shears are not essential, but they make the process quicker, neater, and a lot more fun.

Chicken Parts and How to Prepare Them: The following is the European method for cutting a whole chicken into parts. You will immediately see its virtues. First, it results in eight serving pieces of more or less equal size. Second, none of the pieces includes any part of the chicken's backbone, as the chicken is cut up in such a way as to leave the back meat attached to the thigh pieces.

1. Using a very sharp utility knife, make a deep slit down the backbone from one end of the chicken to the other (A).

2. Bend one leg away from the body at a 45° angle. Again using the utility

knife, make a deep cut through the skin down to the leg joint, holding the knife fairly close to the inside of the thigh (B). (If you make a cut too close to the breast, the thigh will end up with most of the skin and the breast practically none.) Continue to bend the leg outward and, if need be, make small slashes with the point of the knife into the leg joint, until the joint is severed.

3. Now comes the delicate part of the operation. The thigh is attached to two delicious lobes of meat buried next to the backbone, and you want to be sure to include those two pieces of meat as part of the thigh. Using a sharp-pointed knife, dig out the piece of meat, the "oyster," that is nestled at the base of the wide part of the backbone (C). Then, with the knife pressed against the backbone, cut down toward the tail and carve free the small strip of meat that lies parallel to the backbone just in back of the tail. The tail itself may also be included as part of the thigh piece if you like it (I certainly do). Proceed to remove the chicken's other leg in the same manner.

4. Using the utility knife, cut through the joint that connects the drumstick and thigh of each leg to make four pieces (D).

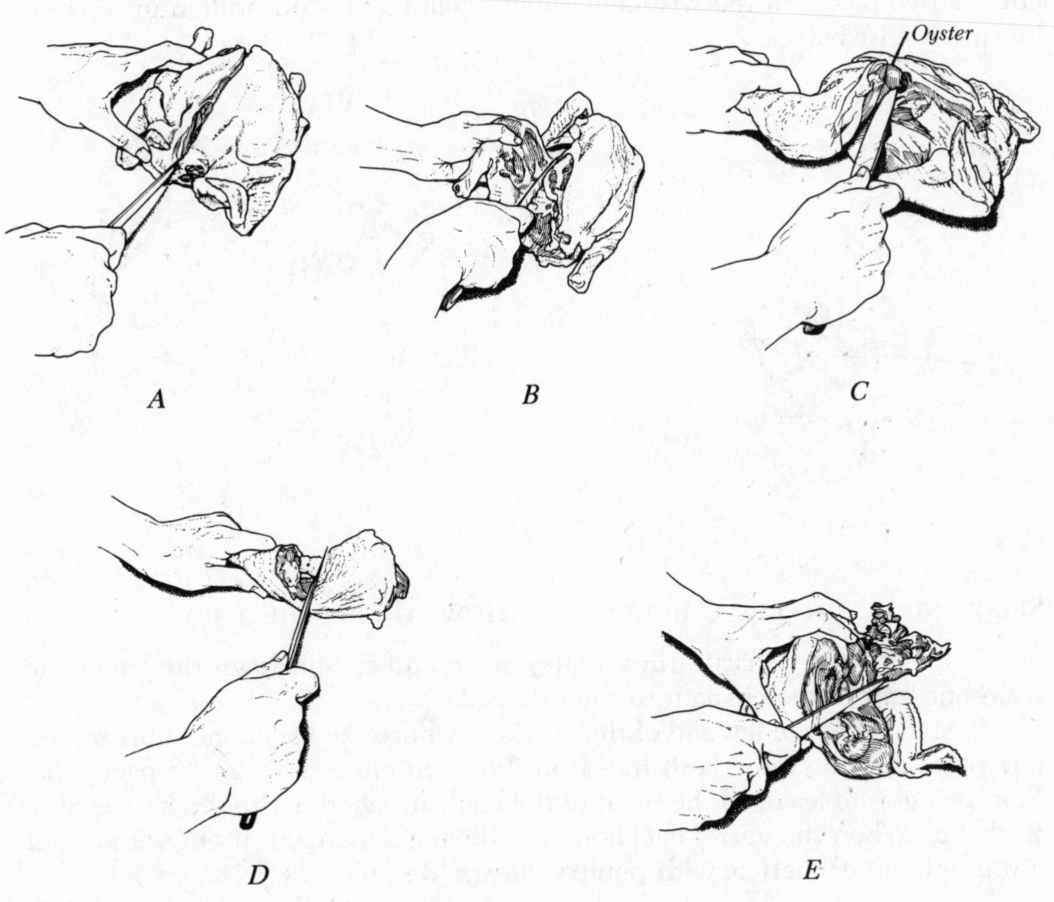

5. Turn the legless chicken on its back. Holding the utility knife more or less parallel to the rib cage, make a diagonal cut through the breast about two-thirds of the way toward the wing. Continue to cut down through the breast meat until you get to the wing joint (E). Bend the wing out from the body and slice through the joint. You now have a serving piece composed of both breast meat and wing. Carve the wing on the other side of the body in the same manner.

6. Using either the utility knife or, better, poultry shears, cut through the rib cage at the point where it meets the breast meat, thus detaching the backbone and most of the rib bones from the carcass. Discard the backbone and ribs or save them for the stockpot.

7. All that is left of the chicken now is the breast. Set the breast right side up on your work surface and press down on it with the heel of your hand to crack it down the middle. Bend it back and turn it over. Slit through the membrane covering the breast bone and its cartilaginous tip (the breast bone may already have popped through the membrane) and pull the breast bone free, discarding it or saving it for the stock pot (F). Using the utility knife or poultry shears, separate the two halves of the breast; if you wish, dig out the two pieces of the wishbone, which will have been broken in separating the breast halves.

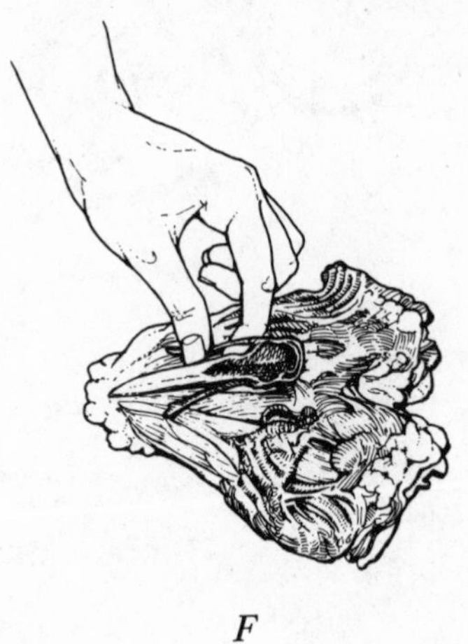

F

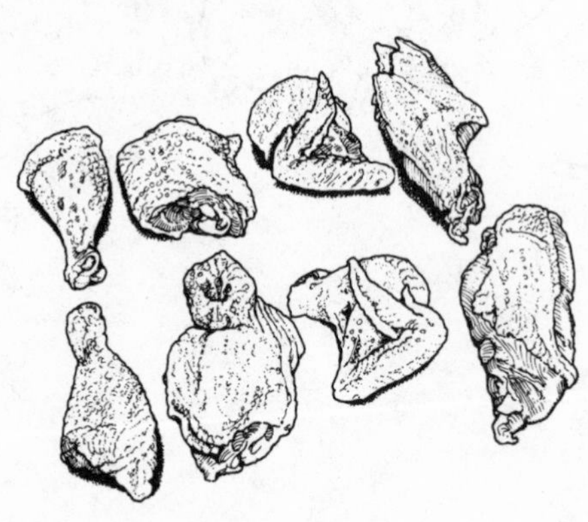

Split and Quartered Chickens and How to Prepare Them

1. Using a very sharp utility knife, make a deep slit down the backbone from one end of the chicken to the other (A).

2. Starting at the tail end of the chicken, where the backbone is broad, use a paring knife to scrape flesh free from bone on either side of the backbone. Your object is to leave all the meat of the back attached to the thighs (see Step 2, above). When the entire backbone has been exposed, cut it out with either a utility knife or, better, with poultry shears (B).

3. Turn the chicken breast side up and press down on it with the heel of your hand to crack the breast (C). Turn the chicken over and bend the breast back. Slit through the membrane covering the breast bone and its cartilaginous tip (D) (the breast bone may already have popped through the membrane) and pull the breast bone free. Using the utility knife or poultry shears, separate the breast down the middle, into halves, thus splitting the chicken (E). You may dig out the pieces of wishbone embedded in the breast halves if you wish.

4. To quarter the chicken, bend the leg away from the breast and slice through the leg joint, holding the knife fairly close to the inside of the thigh so as to avoid stripping the breast of its skin (F). Repeat procedure with the other half of the chicken.

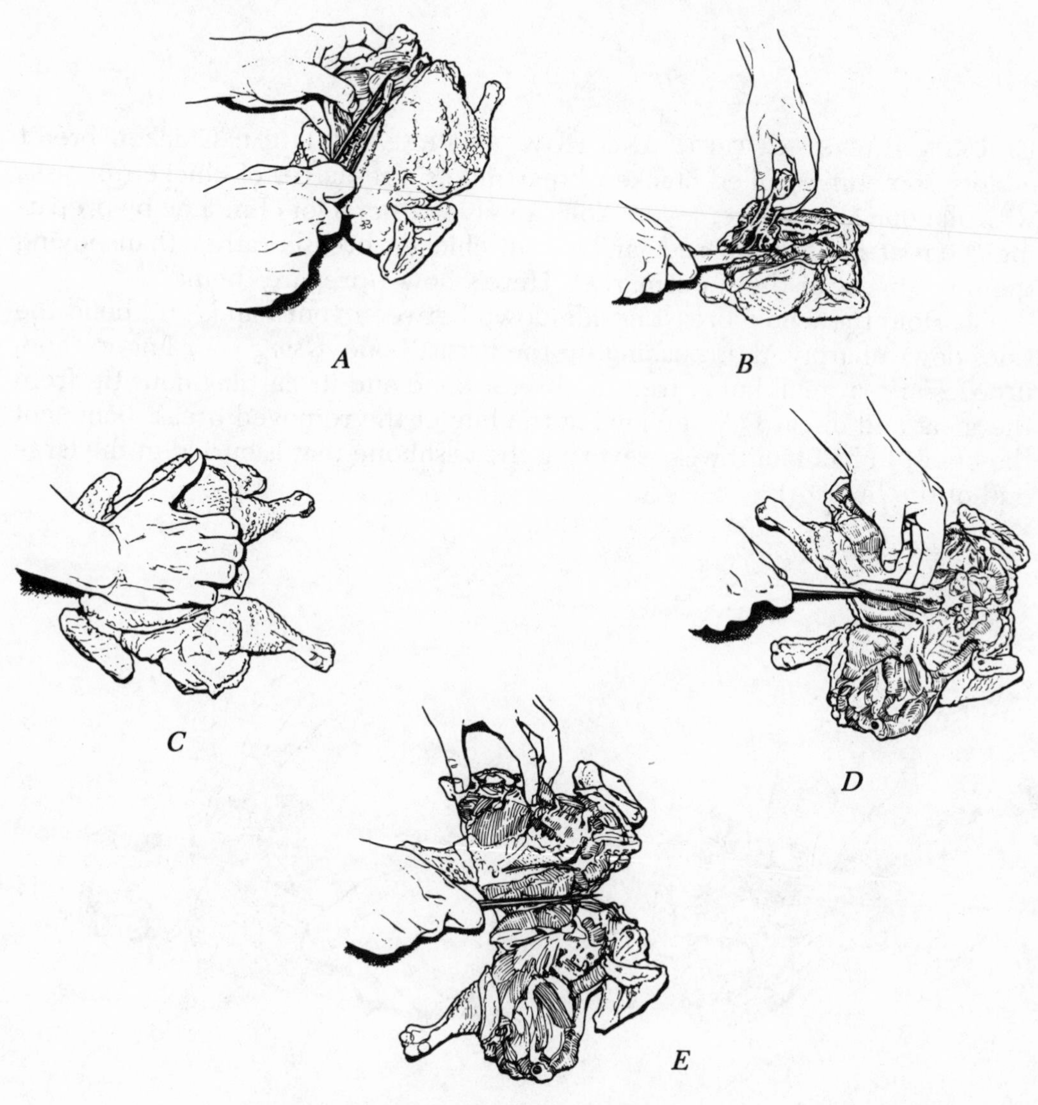

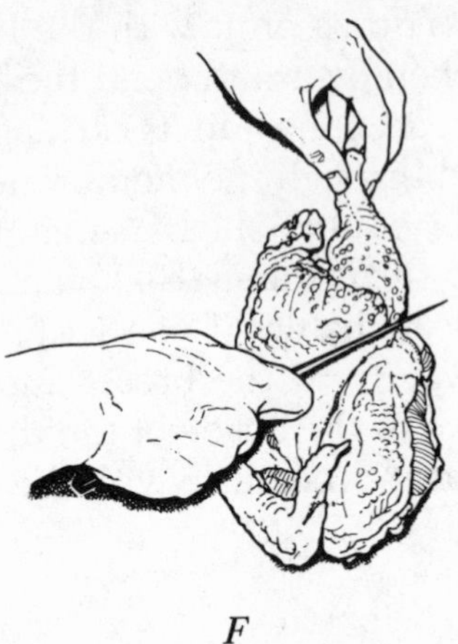

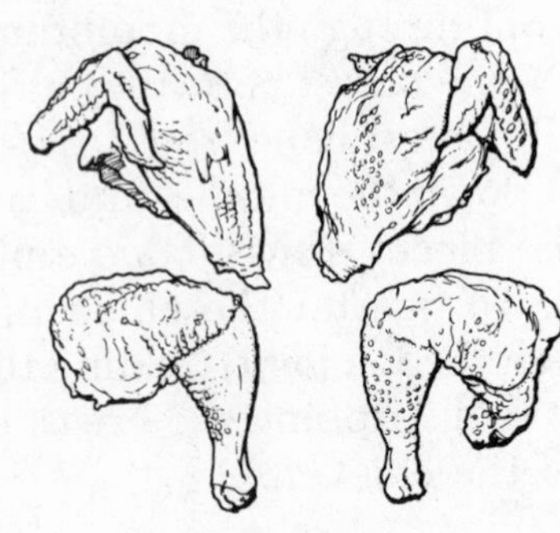

F

Chicken Breast Cutlets and How to Prepare Them: Chicken breast cutlets, sometimes called chicken breast fillets, are halves of chicken breasts, with all bone and skin removed. You can save rather a lot of money by preparing them at home from regular bone-in chicken breasts rather than buying them ready-cut at the supermarket. Here's how I prepare them:

1. Hold the whole breast upside down between your hands and bend the sides down sharply, thus pushing up the breast bone. Using your fingers, and, if necessary, a small knife, free the breast bone and its cartilaginous tip from the meat and discard (A). Following the line of the removed breast bone, cut the breast in half lengthwise, severing the wishbone that is buried in the large end of the breast (B).

A

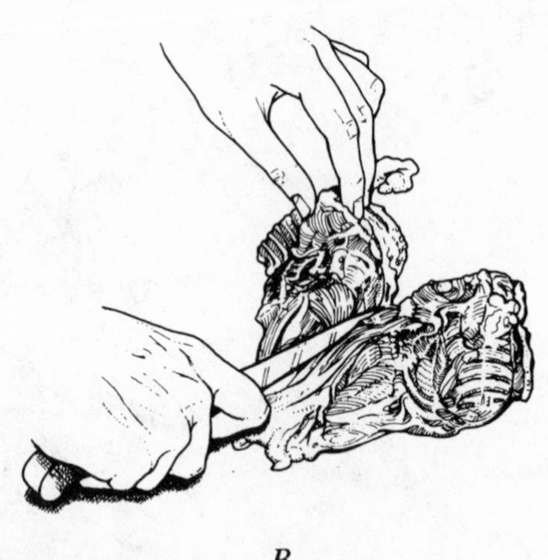

B

2. Insert your fingers between the rib bones and the flesh and pull the bones free of the flesh in one piece (C). You may find it useful to scrape flesh from the bones with a knife if bones and flesh are strongly fused, as sometimes is the case. Dig or cut out the embedded piece of wishbone. Cut and pull away the white tendon that runs down the center of the small conical piece of flesh on the underside of the breast (D). (If this small piece becomes separated from the rest of the breast, simply press it firmly back into place. It will become reattached during cooking.)

3. Turn the fillets skin side up and pull away the skin with your fingers (E). Use the knife to scrape and cut away any large specks of fat and to trim any messy edges. You now have two fillets. Some people like to flatten breast fillets slightly by placing them between sheets of wax paper and pounding lightly with a mallet, the flat side of a cleaver, or the bottom of a drinking glass.

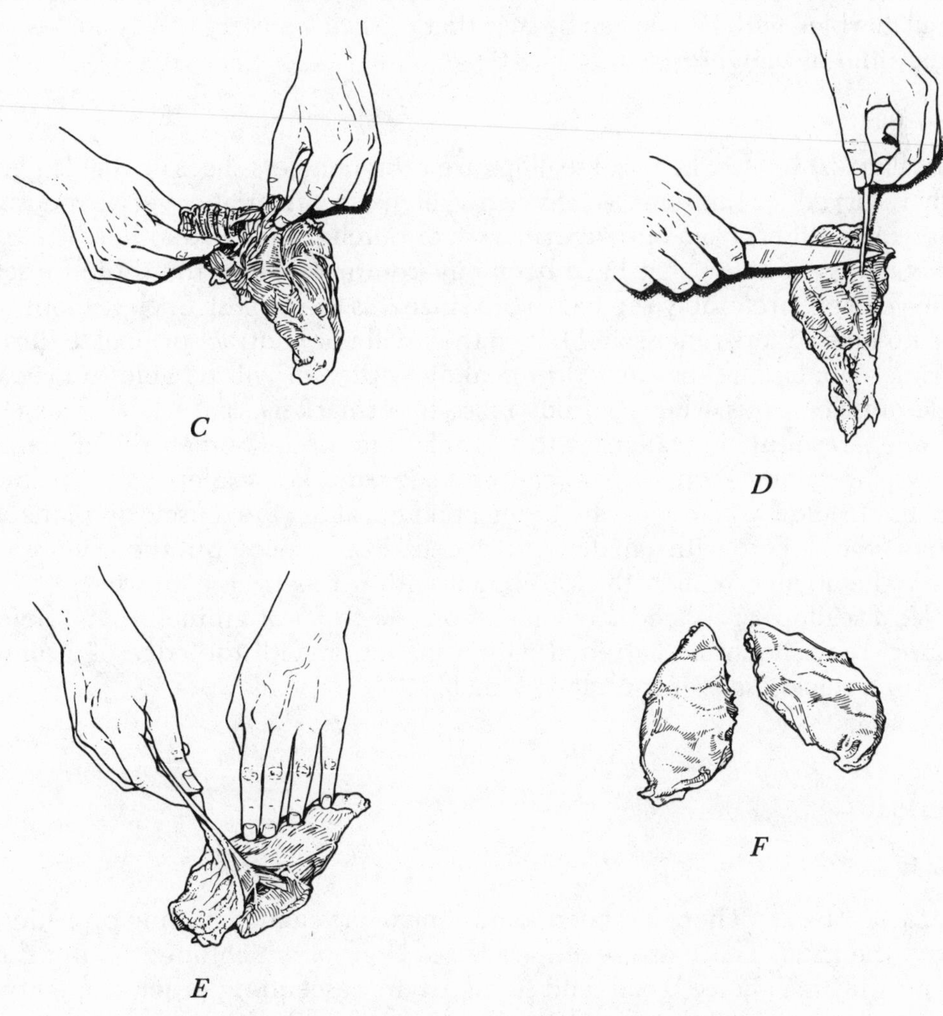

Veal

The choicest veal comes from calves that are about three months old at the time of slaughter and that have been raised exclusively on a diet of milk and milk by-products. The muscles of animals younger than three months are small and underdeveloped and therefore cannot be cut into decent-sized roasts, chops, scallops, and the like. The meat of older animals is coarse and fatty. And calves of any age that have been allowed to graze do not really produce veal—they produce a meat that is a hybrid of beef and veal but that lacks the best qualities of either. The major clue as to the age and dietary history of the calf from which veal has been cut is the color of the meat. The meat of young, milk-fed calves is a very pale pink, almost white, while the meat of older or grass-fed calves is dark pink or even reddish. Note too how fatty the meat is. A small rim of fat around the outside of a chop or roast is fine, but if the meat is at all marbled with fat you can be sure that the calf was very nearly adolescent by the time of slaughter.

VEAL SCALLOPS: Veal scallops are thin, boneless slices of veal leg generally reserved for sautéing. While veal scallops are invariably very expensive, their quality differs from one supermarket or butcher shop to another. The best veal scallops are those that have been cut from just *one* of the three muscles of the veal leg, preferably the top round since it is the largest. Such scallops will have no muscle separations and hence they will not contract or buckle during cooking. A butcher experienced in dealing with veal will be able to prepare single-muscle scallops for you, but most supermarkets, alas, slice across the *entire* leg, resulting in scallops with several separations. (Sometimes, if you are a very painstaking shopper, you can find supermarket scallops of a thickness sufficient to allow you to separate them, at home, along the muscle divisions and then to pound them with a mallet into decent-sized pieces. But the scallops will have to be about 3⁄16 inch thick to begin with if this trick is to work.)

Veal scallops are sliced anywhere from 1⁄8 to 1⁄4 of an inch thick. Before cooking, they should be flattened with a mallet or with the edge of a dinner plate to a thickness of just under 1⁄8 inch.

Beef

GRADES OF BEEF: There has been some controversy about grading procedures. Here's the issue. There are seven grades of beef, of which only the top three or four—prime, choice, good, and standard (in descending order of quality)—

commonly appear at the market. A number of factors are taken into account when assigning a grade to beef, but the most important, and most controversial, one continues to be the amount of marbling, or internal fat, that the beef displays. The more marbling in the meat, the more tender and juicy the steak or roast will be—or such has been the prevailing wisdom in the past. Now, however, there are those who dispute this. Some, for example, claim that modern-day cattle, bred and fed according to new methods and slaughtered at a younger age than cattle used to be, need not be fat to produce tender meat. Others, whether or not they believe that fattiness can be equated with tenderness, argue that excessively marbled meat is bad for one's health or waistline and wastefully expensive to boot. And many, but by no means all, cattlemen are also lined up against fat-laden meat, because fattening up cattle is an expensive proposition for a number of diverse reasons.

In 1976, the antimarbling people won a major battle when the United States Department of Agriculture, which conducts beef grading, relaxed marbling requirements all the way down the line. Only a bit of the beef that had once been "choice" got booted up into the "prime" zone, but quite a hunk of what had once been only "good" got upgraded to "choice." Choice is, and always has been, the most common supermarket grade, especially for roasts and steaks. So the upshot of the revision in grading has been that there is now a far greater variation in the degree of marbling in beef—and, in my view, in the quality of beef—sold at the supermarket than was formerly the case.

CHOOSING BEEF: Since beef graded "choice" does vary so much in quality, the buyer must choose carefully. Judge the extent of marbling yourself by noting the amount of white streaking in the eye or center portions of the cut of beef. Check, too, to see if the bones are white and blotched with bright red, which are good signs, or if the bones are grayish or dingy, indicating that the steer was elderly when slaughtered. If you buy beef graded lower than choice—good or standard—you must proceed at your own risk. The meat may be fine, but then it may also be tough as nails. "Lean," a new and nonofficial grade used by some supermarkets, designates choice, good, or sometimes even standard grades of beef that are exceptionally low in fat. Again, proceed at your own risk.

You may have wondered why beef is sometimes not graded at all. Although the United States Department of Agriculture provides the grading service, the whole process is strictly voluntary, and meat packers must actually pay for it themselves. Packers handling up-scale cuts of beef will usually decide that it is a good investment to have the meat graded, a kind of advertising, but packers dealing in bargain-basement beef may see no reason to have the low quality of their meat certified in purple ink. Furthermore, supermarkets are free to remove the grade stamp from meat if they wish. But you need not worry that gradeless beef (or any other meat, for that matter) may be *unsafe* to eat. All American meat must be inspected either by a federal or a state agency, and it will not pass unless it has been packed under sanitary conditions and is free of disease.

Some people are very fond of well-aged beef; others find it unpleasantly strong, almost gamy, in flavor. I myself like aged beef very much, but I have not specified it in any recipe because it is so scarce and so terrifically expensive. If you are a lover of aged beef, the best place to find it is at a wholesale butcher's specializing in high-quality meats. You may have to buy an entire wholesale or "primal" cut—the entire T-bone and porterhouse steak section, for example—but extra meat can be frozen for six months or so without damage.

Pork

Like veal, pork should be a very pale pink rather than rosy red, as reddishness indicates that the animal was old at the time of slaughter and that the meat, therefore, may be tough. Avoid pork that contains white streaks. These streaks are not marbling, as one might suppose, but rather connective tissue, and the presence of streaks is also a sign of toughness.

Unfortunately, it sometimes happens that pork that looks very good at the supermarket or at the butcher's turns out to be dry, tough, or stringy when cooked. Certain factors may account for these problems in a piece of pork—an insufficient amount of fat in the meat, a hormonal imbalance in the animal at the time of slaughter—but since the shortcomings cannot be seen in advance, the only course of action that one can follow is to cook pork with particular care, thus minimizing any bad characteristics that a given piece might have. As general rules, remember to cook pork covered, at a slow, steady temperature, and, except in the case of stewing cuts, to cease cooking when the meat reaches an internal temperature of between 155°F and 160°F. Letting the meat stand in salt for several hours prior to cooking, as suggested in the recipes for roast pork and sautéed pork chops, is another good safeguard against toughness.

Lamb

As an avid eater of lamb—it ties with pork as my favorite meat—I have found the quality of supermarket lamb both more consistent and consistently better than the quality of either beef or pork. Look for lamb with bright red, satiny-textured meat, dense, white fat, and small, pearly bones. The term "spring lamb" generally means only that the lamb was slaughtered between the months of March and October; since lambs nowadays are birthed throughout the year, the particular month when slaughtering occurs is irrelevant, and thus "spring lamb" is not worth its premium price. Lamb is graded according to a system very similar to the one used in the grading of beef. "Prime" lamb, the top grade, can be bought at some butcher shops. At supermarkets, only "choice" lamb is generally available, and since it is as flavorful and very nearly as tender as prime lamb, the matter of lamb grades does not seem to me to be of major consequence.

On Not Overcooking Poultry and Meat

To each his own, of course, and if you are of the mind that meat should be thoroughly cooked, then you should probably just skip over these remarks. I intend to address here all those people who, out of habit rather than out of conviction, have been eating their poultry and meat on the well done side and have not ever thought much about it. My very strong feeling is that poultry and meat, especially the tender, nonstewing cuts, are much tastier when, by conventional standards, they are somewhat undercooked. Here are my admittedly subjective views. (Internal temperatures for cooked poultry and meat are correlated with various stages of doneness in the "Cooking Temperature Table for Poultry and Meat" on page 344.)

Chicken: Chicken is done as soon as it begins to exude its juices into the pan or skillet, or at an internal temperature of between 160°F and 165°F. If the thickest part of the thigh is pricked deeply with a fork, the last drops of juice that come gushing out will be tinged with pink, and there will be some redness (probably) around the joint connecting the thigh to the body. If you cook chicken until you get rid of every trace of pink and red in the carcass, you inevitably dry out the meat, and I am certainly against that. Chicken should be veritably *dripping* with flavorful juices.

Turkey: Turkey is best when the breast is cooked to an internal temperature of around 155°F, the legs 160°F to 165°F. The roast turkey recipe in this book entails roasting the turkey on its sides, so that the thighs rest directly on the roasting pan—which is very hot—while the breast is turned away from the glaring heat of the oven roof. Prepared this way, the thighs lose all trace of pink, while the breast remains tinged with pink juices.

Duck: An extremely subjective and tricky matter. If you've never tried very rare-roasted duck breast, you owe it to yourself to have the experience. However, the dark meat should, I think, be cooked to medium. The roast duck recipe in this book attempts a compromise solution.

Poultry Livers: Cook poultry livers only until they have stiffened into a shape. They should be dark pink and quite soft inside, like an unctuous pâté.

VEAL: Shoulder veal and some leg cuts are best treated as stew meat, which means that they should be cooked for a fairly long time, though not so long as to cause the meat to fall apart. But other cuts—especially those choice morsels from the rack and loin, as well as veal scallops—are at their juicy best when cooked only until the juices pass from dark pink to rosy yellow and the flesh solidifies slightly but is not yet stiff. The internal temperature to shoot for is around 160°F.

PORK: Here we have a major issue of major importance. Like most other people, I grew up with the idea that pork had to be cooked until the meat virtually fell from the bones in order to kill off any trichinae parasites that might be present. Well, this just isn't so. The parasites are effectively killed off at an internal temperature of 140°F—or when pork is on the threshold between rare and medium. The question, then, is at what temperature does pork *taste* best—remembering, of course, that one must cook it past the 140°F mark.

A few parts of the pork animal must be treated as stew meat (the hocks, for example) and other parts may be stewed if one wishes (the arm and shoulder and perhaps the leg). Otherwise, the pork animal is made up of tender cuts, all of which should be cooked, in my view, to a temperature no higher than 155°F to 160°F. At such temperatures, the meat remains very juicy, slightly pink, and, above all, tender—tender, that is, if other procedures necessary in cooking pork are closely followed. If you associate pork with dryness, stringiness, and the whole host of other conditions to which overcooked meat is prone, I hope you will give this delicious meat another try, cooking it only until "medium."

BEEF: Everyone's mind is probably made up on this one already, so I won't belabor the point. Personally, I prefer beef—including ground beef—seared on the outside but very rare on the inside. At this stage of doneness, the thermometer will read between 115°F and 120°F when the cooking is stopped and in the case of roasts, will rise some 5°F as the meat rests.

LAMB: When cooked to rare, medium rare, or medium, lamb is savory, juicy, and tender—and it has absolutely none of the gamy, tallowy taste that people frequently cite as their reason for disliking the meat. I personally like most cuts of lamb the exact same way that I like beef—quite rare, or cooked to an internal remove-from-oven temperature of 120°F (which, in the case of roasts, rises to 125°F to 130°F after a 10-minute counter top rest). If you are not a rare-meat type, you can certainly roast lamb to a higher internal temperature without destroying it. But don't cook lamb any more than you would cook beef, or you will be disappointed.

The Essential Facts about Cooking Poultry and Meat

If, as the author of this cookbook, I could be granted one wish, I might wish that all those who set out to prepare a recipe using poultry or meat would read this brief essay first. The essential facts about cooking poultry and meat are simple and few, yet crucial.

The Overview: Tough Versus Tender Cuts: All cuts of poultry and meat can be divided into two groups: the cuts that are relatively tough (braising and stewing meat) and the cuts that are relatively tender (oven roasts and poultry and meat for broiling and sautéing). It is important to remember this distinction because the purposes and methods of cooking poultry and meat of each type are different. In the case of tough cuts, the aim of cooking is to break down the muscle fibers sufficiently to render the poultry or meat chewable. Usually this aim is accomplished by partially or completely covering the poultry or meat with liquid and maintaining the liquid at or near the simmer (about 190°F) for a fairly prolonged period. By contrast, the purpose of cooking the tender cuts is to heat them to some specific temperature, generally between 120°F and 160°F, at which they will attain the flavor and texture that the cook desires.

In this book recipes involving the roasting or broiling of tender cuts of poultry and meat give not only estimated cooking *times* (for example, in minutes per pound) but also final cooking *temperatures.* The cooking times are estimates of *how long it will take the poultry or meat to reach certain internal temperatures,* and thus certain degrees of doneness. Because different birds and pieces of meat vary significantly in size, shape, and density, and because ovens vary in temperature and efficiency, cooking-time estimates given in recipes for tender cuts of poultry and meat are always very rough. *You can never rely on cooking-time estimates exclusively.* Rather, you must determine doneness either by examining the poultry or meat as it cooks or—better—by actually taking its temperature as it nears the completion of the estimated cooking time.

Inspecting Tender Cuts of Poultry and Meat for Doneness: As poultry and meat cook, the flesh shrinks slightly, stiffens, and assumes an increasingly rigid and defined shape. Experienced and rather clever people—and I'm afraid that I can't count myself among this select group—are able to tell how well done a piece of meat is simply by pressing it with the fingertips: The more resisting the meat feels, the more thoroughly it is cooked. Another way of estimating the doneness of poultry or meat is by noting how much juice has been wept into the skillet or pan. Poultry begins to weep juice when it has nearly finished cooking (about 160°F). Meat begins to exude liquid as soon as it enters the "medium" stage (about 140°F), and continues to pour forth until it reaches "well done" (about 170°F). Juice-watching is thus very useful in the cooking of poultry and in the cooking of meats such as pork and veal, which should be done to the medium-well stage. But it isn't of much help in the cooking of rare beef or lamb, which are done at an internal temperature of between 120°F and 130°F. Finally, you can always cut into a piece of poultry or meat and see what's going on, but this tactic is somewhat destructive because the cut will cause precious juices to gush out of the bird or joint and drain into the pan. Furthermore, in the roasting of rare beef or lamb, the meat does not finish cooking until after it has been removed from the oven and allowed to rest for 15 minutes or more.

MEAT THERMOMETERS AND HOW TO USE THEM: While chops and steaks may be tested for doneness by visual and tactile examination alone, I feel that the only way to judge the doneness of a whole bird or a meat roast is by taking its temperature with an accurate meat thermometer. There are two types of meat thermometers. The most sensitive and accurate thermometers are so-called "instant-reading" or "vest-pocket" thermometers, which are only inserted in the meat long enough to obtain a reading and are then removed. Less dependable, but better than guessing, are the traditional dial-type meat thermometers, which remain in the poultry or meat during the entire cooking period. The "Cooking Temperature Table for Poultry and Meat" on page 344 correlates remove-from-oven temperatures as indicated on a thermometer with degrees of doneness. If you happen to have an old-fashioned dial-type thermometer, you will note that the temperatures suggested on the face of the dial for poultry and meat cooked to various stages of doneness are much higher than those suggested in the table. Unless you have a decided preference for well-done poultry and meat, you will be wise to follow the table's notion of rare, medium rare, and so on—not the thermometer's.

TIP: To test the accuracy of your meat thermometer place it in a pan of warm water, then bring the water gradually to the boil over moderate heat. If the thermometer is working properly, it will register 140°F or so when the water feels distinctly hot to your fingers, 165°F or so when the first steam is visible, 190°F when the water begins to simmer, and 212°F when the water is at a rolling boil.

There are three very important things to remember when taking the temperature of poultry or meat with a thermometer.

- First, never let the stem of the thermometer touch bone, for bone is likely to be either somewhat hotter or somewhat cooler than the flesh.
- Second, thicker parts of a roast will always cook more slowly than thinner parts, and this is why, as recipes always direct, the thermometer should be inserted in the thickest part of the poultry or meat. Actually, it is wisest to take the temperature of a roast in two or three places; this way, you can take the roast out of the oven when the largest section, be it thick or thin, is done to perfection, rather than, for example, allowing a thin, and perhaps substantial, part of the roast to overcook while a thick little nub piece takes its sweet time.
- Third—and this is the most crucial consideration of all—roasts must always be removed from the oven when they are 5°F to 10°F short of their final desired internal temperature and allowed to rest for 15 minutes or so prior to carving. During the rest, the juices are reabsorbed by the flesh and the meat firms up and becomes uniformly cooked in the center, rather than remaining red and soft, as when raw.

Those meat thermometers that give 130°F as the correct temperature for rare beef are right in the sense that beef is indeed rare (or at least medium rare) at that temperature. However, if a roast beef—or even a London broil—is left in the oven until the thermometer registers 130°F, by the time the meat is carved it will be 135°F to 140°F—medium and, in my view, ruined.

The cooking temperature table that follows presents both the remove-from-oven temperatures and the final temperatures for meat and poultry cooked to various degrees of doneness.

COOKING TEMPERATURE TABLE FOR POULTRY AND MEAT

VERY RARE (BLUE RARE):	REMOVE FROM OVEN: 110°F–115°F	FINAL TEMPERATURE: 115°F–120°F

Only beef and lamb are served at this degree of doneness. In the very center, the meat will be soft and red, as when raw; the rest of the meat will be bright pink, and juicy.

RARE	REMOVE FROM OVEN: 120°F	FINAL TEMPERATURE: 125°F–130°F

This is the degree of doneness that people usually have in mind when they specify "rare" as their preference in beef. Lamb, but not pork or veal, may also be considered done at this temperature. Cooked to this internal temperature, the meat will be fairly soft, bright pink, and very juicy, but it will no longer be pulpy-soft or blood-red, as in the raw state. A few traces of blue-rare meat may remain in the very center of a large cut or around deep bones.

MEDIUM RARE	REMOVE FROM OVEN: 125°F	FINAL TEMPERATURE: 130°F–135°F

Medium-rare meat—again only beef and lamb are served at this degree of doneness—is quite pink in the center, but it will have begun to turn grayish around the periphery. Meat cooked to this point is discernibly firmer than rare meat but still very juicy. When one orders lamb "rare" at a restaurant, this is the way one often gets it.

MEDIUM	REMOVE FROM OVEN: 135°F–140°F	FINAL TEMPERATURE: 140°F–150°F

This is a no-man's land. Most bacteria and the trichinae parasite in pork are considered killed at a remove-from-oven temperature of 140°F. However, to develop their best flavor pork and veal cuts should be cooked further and beef and lamb, in my view, should be cooked less. Medium-cooked beef and lamb are blushed with pink but gray is fast gaining. The meat will have become quite stiff and the grain of the muscle will appear close and compact. Though not dried out, medium-cooked beef and lamb are considerably less juicy than rare and medium-rare meat.

MEDIUM WELL	REMOVE FROM OVEN: 155°F–165°F	FINAL TEMPERATURE: 160°F–175°F

This is the ideal point of doneness for chicken, turkey, pork, and veal. At this temperature, poultry and white meats are ivory-colored, juicy, and firm but not hard. There may be traces of pinkish flesh and pinkish juices in the very interior and near the bones, but this will only be discernible if the light is strong. There will be no suggestion of fibrousness or of a hemp-ropelike dryness.

RUINED	REMOVE FROM OVEN: 170°F–190°F	FINAL TEMPERATURE: 175°F–200°F

These are the temperatures recommended on the dials of old-fashioned meat thermometers for virtually all poultry and meat except beef cooked to rare or medium. IGNORE these silly recommendations, unless you like your poultry and meat cooked to the consistency of a cardboard packing crate.

ROASTED POULTRY and MEAT

About Roast Chicken

Roast chicken is a one of those simple everyday dishes that can be either sublime or dreadful depending on the care taken in its preparation. I do not find it necessary to bard the bird or to give it a full-dress trussing or to turn it frequently during cooking, but I also do not think it possible to obtain the best results simply by plopping the chicken in the oven, setting the timer, and letting it cook. The bird will brown unevenly, overcook, and dry out. This recipe requires a bit of effort on the part of the cook, but not so much as to make roasting a chicken a daunting task for someone coming home from a long day at work. The crucial thing to remember is to watch over the bird closely toward the end of the roasting so that it does not overcook.

Roasting Chickens of Other Sizes: This recipe is based on a chicken weighing about 4 pounds. My rule of thumb for roasting chicken is 14 minutes per pound for the first 4 pounds, 10 minutes for each additional pound. For a 3- or 5-pound bird, proceed according to the Master Recipe, subtracting 14 minutes from the cooking time for a 3-pound chicken, adding about 10 minutes for a 5-pound bird. Birds weighing 6, 7, or 8 pounds will require about 75, 85, and 95 minutes' total cooking time respectively, and these larger birds should be given two extra 15-minute turns on their sides (the oven at 350°F) before being turned breast up. Also, increase other ingredients in the recipe proportionately when roasting large chickens.

For each person you are serving, allow about 1 pound of chicken.

Choosing a Chicken for Roasting: Avoid chickens that seem bony, scrawny, or misshapen or that exhibit reddish bruises, blemishes, or dry, leathery, greasy, scaly patches on the skin. Check also for the presence of hairs or embedded feather follicles, particularly at the ends of the drumsticks of wings; should you buy such a carelessly plucked chicken, you will have to singe off the hairs and pull out the follicles with a tweezer, which is a lot of extra work. Finally, always sniff packages of chicken, and reject any that have even the slightest odor of decay or gaminess.

One factor to which you should pay no attention whatsoever when selecting a chicken is its skin color. In some parts of the country, people prefer chickens with ivory skins; in other areas, consumers go for yellow birds. Producers get the profitable colors by feeding chickens special foods—marigold petals are fed to chickens to make their skin more yellow—but these foods have no effect on the taste.

MASTER RECIPE

Roast Chicken

4 servings

For a light, informal supper, the chicken need be accompanied only by a tossed green salad. Steamed brown rice, perhaps mixed with pine nuts or toasted almonds, might be served as well. When I am offering roast chicken as the centerpiece of a more formal meal, my favorite accompaniments are carrots in heavy cream, green beans, and mashed potatoes. Creamed spinach and scalloped potatoes, or sautéed summer squash and steamed rice, or creamed corn and boiled brussels sprouts are other good combinations with roast chicken.

Preliminaries

1. Set rack in the middle of the oven.
2. Preheat oven to 425°F 20 minutes before roasting.
3. Select a 9×12×2-inch roasting pan or other oven-safe dish large enough to hold the chicken comfortably. It is preferable to use a pan made of

enameled cast iron; nonstick-coated, heavy-gauge aluminum; or glass. The chicken may stick, ripping the skin, if an ordinary aluminum roasting pan is used.

4-pound chicken
½ teaspoon dried whole thyme
Salt
Pepper, preferably freshly ground
6 tablespoons soft butter
1 tablespoon vegetable oil
¾ cup Chicken Stock, page 26, or canned broth

Pull away the lumps of fat from both sides of the chicken's stomach cavity, rinse the chicken inside and out under tepid water, and pat dry inside and out with paper towels. Rub the cavity with ½ teaspoon each thyme, salt, and pepper, then smear the inside of the cavity with about 1½ tablespoons of the soft butter. Gently loosen the skin covering the breast and the tops of the thighs with your fingers, and smear an additional 1½ tablespoons of the butter over the breast and thigh meat. Press and smooth the skin back into place.

Using a piece of heavy white twine about 12 inches long, tie the drumsticks together at the ankles, then bring one end of the string around the tail piece and tie securely with the other end, thus bringing the drumsticks and tail piece together and closing the vent. Using a second piece of twine about 24 inches long, tie a loop around the wings, then tie a second loop around the bird from front to back, as though tying a package. Massage the remaining 3 tablespoons of butter evenly over the skin of the chicken.

Coat the bottom of the roasting pan with the vegetable oil and lay the chicken on its side in the pan. Place in preheated 425°F oven and roast for 15 minutes, basting once with a pastry brush midway through. Remove chicken from oven, baste quickly, then grip the drumsticks with your hands protected by paper towels and flip the chicken onto its other side. Baste, and roast for 15 minutes longer, again basting midway through.

Turn the oven down to 350°F.

Remove chicken from the oven, set breast side up, baste quickly, and return to oven. Roast 15 minutes longer, basting once midway through, then remove chicken from oven, baste again, and sprinkle to taste with salt and pepper. Return chicken to oven and roast 10 to 15 minutes longer, or 55 to 60 minutes altogether. Be ever watchful during this last part of the cooking period, as just a few minutes too long in the oven can dry out the bird. The signs of doneness are a swollen, puffy look around the drumsticks and thighs and a sudden increase of juices in the roasting pan, which is sometimes announced by a noisy showering in the oven. If you prick the thickest part of the thigh to the bone with a fork, the juices should run yellow, with just a trace of pink at the end of the trickle. A meat thermometer—your most reliable guide—should read 165°F when inserted sideways into the thickest part of the thigh.

Remove the chicken to a platter or cutting board, cover loosely with aluminum foil, and let rest 10 minutes before carving, so that the flesh can reabsorb the juices. In the meantime, allow the juices in the roasting pan to settle, then spoon off most of the fat (there will be far more fat than juice), add the chicken broth, and bring to a simmer on top of the stove, scraping up the browned roasting particles with a wooden spoon. Pour the juices into a warmed gravy bowl or boat, to accompany the chicken.

Untie the chicken and carve one side at a time. Holding the bird steady with a fork, first slice through the skin connecting the thigh and breast and then down through the thigh joint, severing the leg from the rest of the chicken. Detach thigh from drumstick by cutting through the joint. Next, with the knife blade tilted toward the rib cage, slice off the hindmost third of the breast and then down through the joint that connects the wing to the body, making a portion of breast and wing meat large enough for a whole serving. Last, cut against the ribcage to release the remaining breast meat in one piece; it may be sliced if you wish. And don't forget the two delicious nuggets of meat, the "oysters," that are lodged on either side of the chicken's back. Carve these out with the point of the knife.

Variation: ROAST CHICKEN WITH GIBLET CREAM GRAVY

4 servings

❦ *This is a rich, important roast chicken dish, suitable for Sunday dinner. I like it with green beans amandine, mashed potatoes, and sautéed cherry tomatoes.*

Roast Chicken

ADD: The neck, gizzard, heart, and liver from the chicken
1 cup heavy cream
Salt, freshly ground pepper, and lemon juice
1 tablespoon minced fresh parsley (optional)

Chop the neck into ½-inch pieces and set aside. Cut off the flap of skin on top of the gizzard and add to the neck pieces. Cut the gizzard, heart, and liver into fine dice, setting aside the liver for the time being. As soon as the chicken has gone into the oven, combine the neck pieces, gizzard skin, diced gizzard, and heart with the ¾ cup stock or broth called for in the Master Recipe in a 1½-quart saucepan. Simmer, partially covered, while the chicken roasts. Once the chicken is cooked and has been removed to a platter for its rest, pick out and discard the neck pieces and gizzard skin, then pour the broth and diced giblets into the degreased roasting pan and bring to a simmer, scraping up browned roasting particles with a spoon. Return mixture to the saucepan, add the cream, and boil down over high heat, stirring frequently to prevent boiling over. Reduce gravy to about 1 cup—it should thicken lightly—then lower the heat, add the reserved diced liver, and poach the liver at just below the simmer for about 30 seconds. Season to taste with salt, pepper, and drops of lemon juice, and stir in parsley if you wish. Pour into warmed sauce boat and pass with the chicken.

Variation: ROAST CHICKEN WITH GARLIC AND ROSEMARY

4 servings

❦ *Garlic and rosemary give an unusual but thoroughly delicious flavoring twist to roast chicken. Good accompaniments here are broccoli or broiled tomatoes plus scalloped or baked potatoes.*

Roast Chicken

ADD: 2 teaspoons mashed, pressed, or very finely minced garlic
1 tablespoon fresh rosemary leaves or 1 teaspoon dried

OMIT: Thyme

Combine garlic and fresh or dried rosemary on a chopping board and mince to a paste. Beat paste into the 6 tablespoons soft butter required in the Master Recipe.

Proceed as in the Master Recipe, but omit the thyme and coat the cavity, breast and thigh meat, and skin with the flavored butter. If you have the time, you may cover the chicken loosely with waxed paper and refrigerate for 1 to 2 hours prior to roasting so that the garlic and rosemary can permeate the flesh. This, however, is not essential.

About Roast Duck

Roast duck can be problematic for the cook. The breast meat is best when bloody rare, the wings and legs need to be cooked to medium, and the skin, many people's favorite part, has to be well done if it is to be properly crispy and rendered of fat. Some recipes suggest carving off the breast of a partially roasted bird and serving it separately, while the rest of the duck goes back into the oven to finish cooking; others direct that the skin be removed after roasting and fried until crisp. These are good strategies, but they entail extra work, and the duck must be served in pieces. Here the duck is steamed very slowly for several hours in the oven. During this time it renders much of its fat (the long, slow steaming keeps the meat from drying out). Then the duck is removed from the oven, patted dry, glazed with a bit of sugar, and allowed to cool. Finally, it is popped into a hot oven in order to glaze and crisp the skin; because the meat has been cooled, it does not overcook during its brief sojourn in the oven.

CHOOSING A DUCK FOR ROASTING: Frozen ducks make good eating, but freshly killed birds are of course preferable. Check to see that the skin is moist, uniform in color rather than mottled with red or blue, and free of feather follicles. Unfortunately, most ducks sold at supermarkets are packaged in opaque plastic, making it impossible to see what you are buying. At the very least, though, you can check the expiration date to be sure that the duck is not spoiled.

MASTER RECIPE

Roast Duck with Orange Sauce

2 to 4 servings

Included in this recipe is a delicious mildly sweet-and-sour orange sauce for roast duck. Duck, however, is so flavorful that the sauce is not absolutely mandatory. Among the traditional accompaniments for duck are braised red cabbage, peas, celery root purée, turnips, braised chestnuts, and lacy potato pancakes. A stuffing is not a good idea, as it will end up tasting greasy. A 5-pound duck makes two generous or three adequate servings. If the duck is to be stretched to feed four, be sure that the accompaniments are hearty.

PRELIMINARIES

1. Set rack in the center of oven.
2. Preheat the oven to 225°F 20 minutes before proceeding.
3. Select a turkey roaster or lidded casserole large enough to hold the duck with room to spare. Fit roaster or casserole with a rack that has an elevation of at least 1 inch.

Step 1: Preliminary Cooking of the Duck; Preparing a Duck Stock for the Sauce

A duck weighing about 5 pounds
½ lemon
3 tablespoons vegetable oil
½ cup chopped onion
¼ cup chopped peeled carrot
3 tablespoons sugar
2 cups water
1 cup Chicken Stock, page 26, or canned broth
1 tablespoon wine vinegar or cider vinegar
Zest of 1 orange (remove with swivel-blade vegetable peeler)
2 parsley sprigs
1 small bay leaf
¼ teaspoon peppercorns

Pull away large lumps of fat from around the tail vent of the duck and from the underside of the large flap of skin at the neck end. Snip or cut off the last joint of the wings and reserve along with the giblets for making the sauce. Rinse duck quickly under tepid water, pat dry with paper toweling, and rub inside and out with cut lemon. Using an egg pricker or push pin, gently prick the duck skin in about 30 places over the breast and legs to facilitate the draining of the subcutaneous fat. Do not penetrate more than ⅛ inch into the duck or you will go through to the flesh and cause juices to seep out and stain the skin.

Place duck on its back on the rack, cover tightly, and bake 3½ hours, removing some of the accumulated fat about halfway through cooking if it threatens to come up to the top of the rack. While the duck is baking, proceed to make the duck stock for the sauce as follows:

Cut the duck heart and gizzard into small chunks; chop the neck and wing tips into ½-inch pieces. Dry well with paper toweling. Heat oil in a 3-quart saucepan until on the verge of smoking, then add duck pieces and brown thoroughly over moderately high heat, stirring frequently. Remove duck pieces with slotted spoon and set aside. Pour all but a ⅛-inch film of oil out of the saucepan, add onion and carrot, and cook, stirring occasionally, over moderately high heat for about 10 minutes, or until lightly browned. Mix in reserved duck pieces and sprinkle on the sugar. Stir constantly over moderately high heat until the sugar caramelizes: You will see wisps of brownish syrup floating amid the oil, the duck pieces and vegetables will wad into a brownish red mass, and the pot will just begin to smoke. Standing back a bit to avoid spatters, add the water, stock or broth, and vinegar, then stir until the caramel dissolves and the duck and vegetable pieces separate. Add orange zest, parsley sprigs, bay leaf, and peppercorns, cover partially, and simmer for 2 to 3 hours, adding more water if the liquid reduces to less than 1 cup, exposing the solids.

STEP 2: ALLOWING THE DUCK TO REST, THEN ROASTING; FINISHING THE SAUCE

Salt and pepper, preferably freshly ground
1½ tablespoons boiling water
1½ teaspoons sugar
1 large or 2 small oranges
1 tablespoon cornstarch mixed to a smooth paste with 1½ tablespoons medium-dry Sherry, preferably Manzanilla
Salt, pepper, and vinegar if needed

Remove duck from oven and reset oven thermostat to 375°F.

Insert a wooden spoon into the tail cavity of duck, tip the duck up, and drain the juices into the roaster or casserole; set juices aside. Let the duck cool briefly, then dry the skin as thoroughly as possible with paper toweling. Sprinkle the duck inside and out with salt and pepper. Place on its back on a rack (this can be the same rack that was used before), then arrange in a shallow baking dish. Combine boiling water and sugar and stir until sugar is completely dissolved. Brush this glaze over the top and sides of the duck, then set duck aside at room temperature for 20 to 30 minutes.

While the duck is resting, spoon off all fat from the juices in the roaster or casserole and pour the juices into the duck stock. Bring to a boil and reduce liquid to about 1 cup. Strain stock through a fine-mesh sieve into an 8- to 9-inch skillet made of or lined with a noncorroding material; discard duck pieces and vegetables in sieve and set stock aside. Peel the orange(s) and cut off both the filament and pith from the outside. Cut in crosswise slices about ¼ inch thick, pick out the seeds, and set aside.

Roast cooled duck in 375°F oven for 35 to 45 minutes, or until the skin is nicely browned and crisp. Don't be too fanatical about achieving perfect skin because if the duck roasts too long the meat will dry out and be ruined. Remove duck from oven, place on a serving platter or carving board, and set aside for about 5 minutes to rest, while you finish the sauce.

Bring reserved duck stock to a simmer over moderate heat, add the reserved orange slices, and simmer slowly, basting, for about 2 minutes, or until the oranges are softened but not mushy. Remove oranges with slotted spoon and arrange attractively over and around the duck. Raise heat to high, bring stock to a boil, and slowly add as much of the cornstarch paste as you need to make a light, transparent sauce with the consistency of warm honey. Cook the sauce 1 minute, then spoon a bit of it over the duck to glaze it and pour the rest into a sauceboat.

If you are serving 2, simply divide the duck in half through the breast bone and back bone using a sharp, sturdy knife or poultry shears; the bones give way easily. If you are serving four, remove the legs and divide at the thigh-drumstick joint to make 4 pieces, then slice the breast meat on both sides into four roughly equal portions, being sure to give each diner some of the skin.

Variation: ROAST DUCK WITH CHERRIES

4 servings

Roast Duck

SUBSTITUTE: 1½ cups pitted sweet cherries, fresh or drained canned, for oranges
1½ tablespoons Port or cherry liqueur for Sherry

Proceed according to the Master Recipe, but substitute cherries for oranges, poaching fresh cherries 3 to 4 minutes, or until softened, canned cherries about 1 minute, or until warmed through. Use Port or cherry liqueur in making the cornstarch paste to thicken the sauce.

Variation: ROAST DUCK WITH PEACHES

4 servings

Roast Duck

SUBSTITUTE: 1½ cups sliced fresh or drained canned peaches for oranges
1½ tablespoons brandy for Sherry

Proceed according to the Master Recipe, but substitute peaches for oranges, poaching fresh peaches about 4 minutes, or until slightly softened, canned peaches about 1 minute, or until warmed through. Use brandy rather than Sherry in making the cornstarch paste to thicken the sauce.

NOTES ON ACHIEVING A PERFECT ROAST TURKEY

In this recipe, inspired by John and Karen Hess's suggestions in their book *The Taste of America,* the turkey begins its roast at a high temperature and is turned frequently during cooking. The high temperature hastens the cooking process—a 12- to 14-pound turkey needs just a little more than 2 hours in the oven!—and thus the bird spends its time cooking, not desiccating. Turning the turkey during roasting not only prevents the juices from sinking to the bottom of the bird and flowing into the roasting pan, but it also serves to cook the thighs (they need extra heat) at a faster rate than the breast (it dries out if it overcooks) because the thighs end up resting on the sizzling-hot roasting pan.

Since it is rather difficult to truss a big bird without assistance, and since the idea of flipping a hot turkey during cooking may at first seem rather daunting (though it is in fact quite easy to do), it is a good idea to work with a willing friend. Luckily, there are always people around at holiday time, so this shouldn't be a problem. Here are a couple of other tips:

- Start with the right equipment. You need a 10×14×3-inch roasting pan, preferably one made of enameled cast iron or nonstick-coated, heavy-gauge aluminum. Disposable foil pans and turkey roasters will not do: The bird will stick and burn. Also necessary are a trussing needle at least 10 inches long (try a specialty cookware shop for this), sturdy white twine, a bulb baster, and an old, clean dish towel or a good supply of paper towels. Finally, I would not undertake to roast a turkey—or anything else, for that matter—without an absolutely accurate meat thermometer, preferably the excellent instant-reading, vest-pocket type.
- To ensure that the cook is calm and composed on the day of the feast, it is a good idea to make the stuffing for the bird the day before: Refrigerate, then reheat the stuffing just before using. The turkey stock and giblets that are the base of the gravy may also be made a day ahead.
- There's nothing especially difficult about trussing a turkey, but the job must be done right if the turkey is to rest on its thighs, rather than toppling over onto its back, when turned. If you are not an experienced trusser, read the instructions over carefully before beginning and allow yourself plenty of time. (It is helpful to have somebody nearby to hold the string while you make the ties.)
- Once the bird is in the oven, be prepared to give it full-time attention, basting every 10 minutes, turning every 20 minutes, and taking the turkey's temperature frequently toward the end of cooking.

ROASTING LARGER TURKEYS: I have always disliked larger turkeys (say, over 15 pounds) because both the skin and dark meat tend to be tough. Still, if you're feeding a crowd and have no other choice, make the following changes in the Master Recipe: For turkeys weighing about 20 pounds, increase all ingredients, including those for the stuffing, by half; for turkeys weighing close to 25 pounds, double all ingredients. You will need a roasting pan 12 to 14 inches wide, 16 to 18 inches long, and 3 inches deep; enameled and nonstick pans this large are hard to come by, so you may have to make do with another sort of pan. In lieu of a trussing needle, which will prove too short to go through the bird, use a long knitting needle with a hole drilled in the end to hold the string. In turning the turkey, grip both the drumsticks and the neck end, your hands protected by towels; enlist the aid of a helper to steady the pan if necessary. (I don't want to mislead you here: turning a piping hot 25-pound turkey in a pan full of spattering drippings is not an easy task.) Assume the cooking time for the turkey to be 10 to 12 minutes per pound. Give a 20-pound turkey two extra turns on its thighs (40 minutes) and 10 to 20 minutes' extra time after turning breast side up. Give a 25-pound turkey four extra turns on its thighs (1 hour and 20 minutes) and allow a total cooking time of about 45 minutes to 1 hour after the turkey is turned breast side up.

CHOOSING A TURKEY FOR ROASTING: Fresh turkeys, widely available at holiday time, have a better flavor and texture than frozen turkeys, but frozen turkeys can be quite good if they have been kept at a constant temperature of 0°F or lower and have not been lying around in the freezer bin for months. (Thaw a frozen turkey over a two-day period in the refrigerator or for 6 to 8 hours in cold water to cover; roast as soon as it is thawed.) Avoid any turkey advertised as "self-basting"—the fat shot under the skins of such turkeys is invariably artificial and rancid-tasting.

While I cannot discern a taste difference between tom and hen turkeys, I do feel that toms, which are tallish and narrow-breasted, are easier to truss and maneuver during cooking than squat, broad-breasted hens. If you have the choice, choose a tom; otherwise, don't worry about it. (By the way, if you happen to be buying a bird weighing 20 pounds or more, you can be sure it is a tom, as only the males attain such weights.)

If you are buying a fresh turkey from a butcher or poulterer, check to see that the skin is moist and fresh-looking, not dry or glassy, and make sure the bird smells fresh and clean. Like ducks, supermarket turkeys, whether fresh or frozen, are generally packaged in opaque plastic, making it impossible to know what you're getting until you've unwrapped the bird at home. I have never bought a bad turkey at the supermarket, but I have heard stories about people who have. If your turkey proves to have a spoiled smell or slimy feel, don't even think of eating it, as it could make you very sick.

ROAST TURKEY WITH BREAD AND OYSTER STUFFING AND GIBLET GRAVY

About 12 servings

❦ *This unusual and perhaps rather exacting method of roasting a turkey produces what many consider the perfect bird: uniformly golden brown skin, moist, juicy breast meat, and tender, succulent dark meat. And with the perfect bird, my favorite stuffing—a buttery, herbal blend of sautéed aromatic vegetables, bread cubes, and plump oysters—plus a dark, rich giblet gravy flavored with Port or Madeira and lightly thickened with cornstarch, not with a flour and butter roux, which, in my view, tends to make gravies cloying and pasty. For a holiday meal, start with a cream soup—carrot or winter squash are my perennial choices, but almond, celery, or chestnut will do just as nicely—and accompany the bird with brussels sprouts or broccoli, mashed potatoes, creamed onions, and homemade cranberry-orange relish. Some also like to sneak in a small serving of candied yams, and almost everyone agrees that hot breads are required, cloverleaf dinner rolls, baking powder biscuits, and cornbread being the usual options. For dessert it must be pie, but it needn't be the usual pumpkin or apple, though both are nice. Coconut custard and pecan are fine choices, and lemon meringue pie makes a particularly tart and satisfying finish.*

PRELIMINARIES

1. Set rack in the lowest level of the oven.
2. Preheat the oven to 425°F 20 minutes before roasting.
3. Select a 10×14×3-inch roasting pan, preferably one made of enameled cast iron or nonstick-coated heavy-gauge aluminum. (The turkey may stick to pans made of other materials.)

STEP 1: ROASTING THE TURKEY

12- to 14-pound turkey, preferably a fresh tom
Bread and Oyster Stuffing, page 361, or one of its variations
½ cup vegetable oil
Salt and pepper, preferably freshly ground

SPECIAL EQUIPMENT: A 10- to 12-inch trussing needle; heavy white twine; a bulb baster; paper towels or a dish towel; aluminum foil, if needed; a meat thermometer, preferably the instant-reading, vest-pocket type (optional but handy)

Rinse turkey under tepid water and pat dry inside and out with paper toweling. Pull away any lumps of fat that may lie just inside the stomach cavity.

Fill the stomach cavity completely with *hot* stuffing, gently but firmly packing in the stuffing with the back of a spoon. (The stuffing must be hot when it goes into the bird, or the cooking will be slowed. If you made it a day ahead and refrigerated it, reheat it.) Tie an 18-inch length of twine to the trussing needle. Sew the cavity shut, suturing flaps to the turkey's tail piece. (If the tail piece is partially severed at the spine, which is often the case, reattach with a few stitches.) When you are through, the end of the turkey should look something like a protruding tongue (1).

Turn the turkey around and pack the remainder of the stuffing into the neck cavity. With the string remaining on the needle, sew the neck cavity shut (2).

Attach a 36-inch length of twine to the trussing needle. Press one wing so that it lies flush against the side of the bird and molds itself to the contour of the thigh and drumstick. Insert the trussing needle into the middle of the second joint of the wing (that is, between the wrist and elbow) and into the body. Press the wing on the other side into the same position as the first wing and, holding it in place, push the trussing needle through. (Hopefully, the needle will come out through the middle of the second joint of the second wing, but, if it doesn't, simply withdraw it and try again.) (3) Now, push the needle through a thigh just below the thigh-drumstick joint, then through the front of the breast, and then through the other thigh (4). Cut the string free of the needle. Pull the ends of the string firmly to draw the bird together, then tie securely; snip off any loose twine (5).

Attach an 18-inch length of twine to the needle. Push the needle through the drumsticks about 1 inch from the ends, then push it through one side of the back and out the other (6). Cut the string free of the needle and tie the loop securely, drawing the drumsticks slightly downward. Snip off loose twine (7).

A stuffed and trussed bird must be roasted immediately, or the stuffing may begin to spoil.

Place turkey in roasting pan, pour oil over it, and rub with your hands to coat turkey completely with oil. Turn turkey so that it rests on one of its thighs; should the bird be inclined to topple over, prop it up with crumpled balls of aluminum foil. Place in thoroughly preheated 425°F oven and roast for 20 minutes, basting midway through with pan drippings.* Working as quickly as possible, remove the turkey from oven and, protecting your hands with dish towels or paper towels, lift it by the drumsticks and set it on its other side, again

*As soon as the turkey goes into the oven, begin to prepare the turkey stock and giblets that are to be the base of the gravy (Step 2).

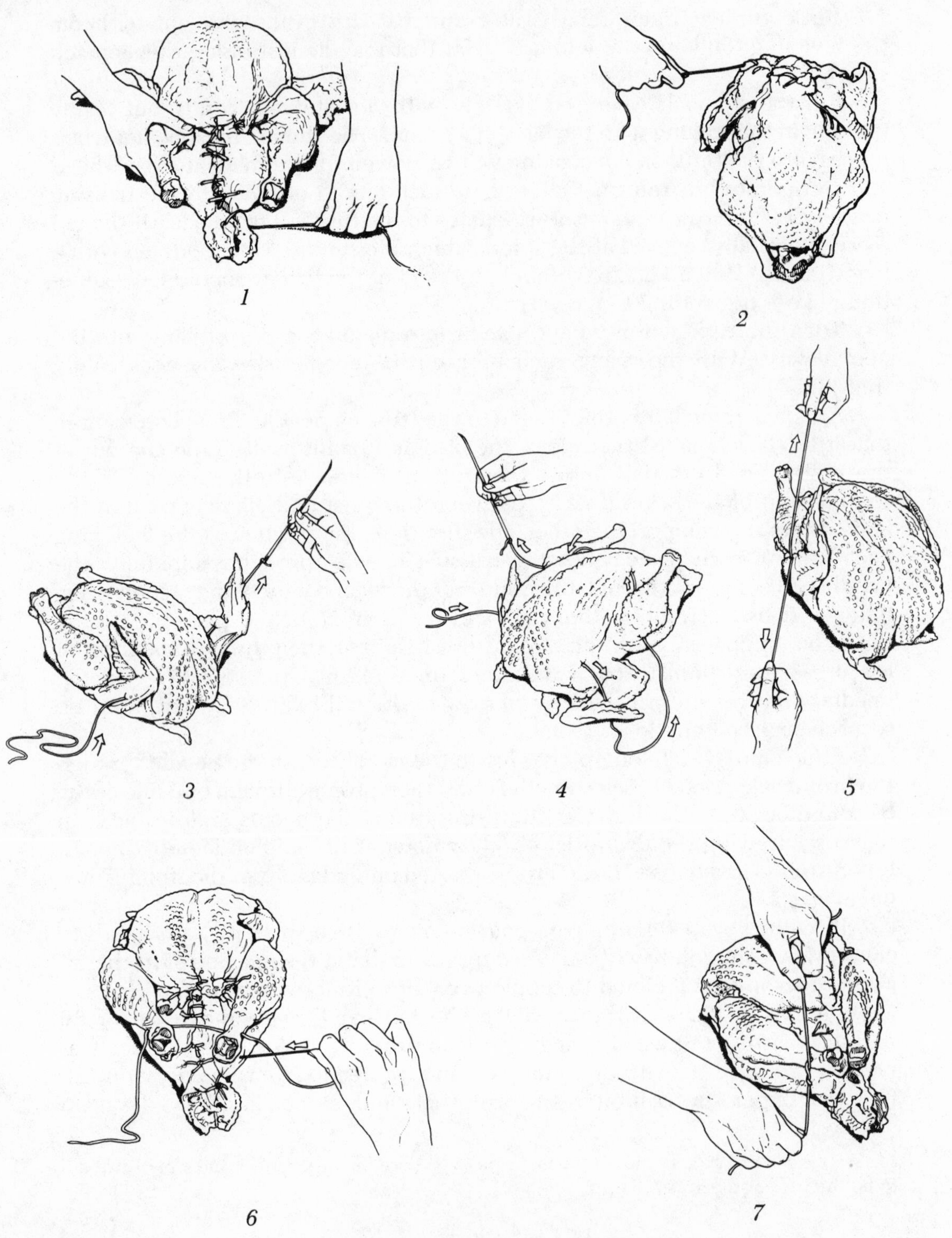
1
2
3
4
5
6
7

propping it up with balls of foil if necessary. Baste, then return to the oven and roast for 20 minutes longer, basting after 10 minutes. (The oven is likely to begin to smoke during the end of this initial roasting period, but the smoking will cease as soon as the thermostat is turned down.)

Turn the oven down to 350°F.

Remove the turkey from the oven, baste, and once again flip it over, propping it up if necessary, and roast 20 minutes, basting midway through. Repeat this same procedure three more times—that is, at the 60-, 80-, and 100-minute marks—roasting the turkey on its sides for a total of 120 minutes, or 2 hours.

At the 2-hour mark, remove the turkey from the oven, turn breast side up, baste, and sprinkle lightly with salt and pepper. Return to the oven and roast 10 minutes longer, then remove from the oven and test for doneness. The best way to do this is with a meat thermometer. It should read:

- 155°F when inserted sideways into the thickest part of the breast (at the back, just over the wing).
- 165°F when inserted sideways into the thickest part of the thigh.

If you are not using a meat thermometer, test for doneness by pricking the thickest part of the thigh deeply with a fork. The juices should run yellow, without a trace of pink.

If the turkey is not completely cooked, return it to the oven, still breast up, and cook for another 10 to 20 minutes, basting every 10 minutes.

Remove the cooked turkey to a platter or carving board with sides (it will exude juices as it stands), cover loosely with a tent of aluminum foil, and let stand for 20 minutes before carving, so that the flesh can reabsorb the juices. While the turkey is resting, proceed to complete the giblet gravy according to Step 2.

A turkey is carved one side at a time. Holding the bird steady with a large fork, first cut through the joint connecting the thigh to the rest of the turkey, detaching a leg. Transfer leg to a small platter and carve thigh and drumstick into pieces. Tilting the turkey on its side so that the back is partially exposed, cut through the joint that connects the wing to the carcass. Transfer wing to plate with dark meat. Last, cut breast meat into thin parallel slices.

STEP 2: THE GIBLET GRAVY

Neck, heart, and gizzard from the turkey (the liver may be added to the gravy at the end of this step, or used in the liver stuffing variation, or saved for some other purpose)
2 tablespoons neutral vegetable oil
⅔ cup chopped onion
⅓ cup chopped peeled carrot
⅓ cup chopped celery
3 tablespoons chopped peeled parsnip or white turnip (optional)
1 quart Chicken Stock, page 26, or canned broth
1 cup water
½ cup dry white wine (optional)
The following, tied together in a cheesecloth bag:
6 large parsley sprigs; 1 large bay leaf; 1 teaspoon whole dried thyme; ½ teaspoon whole peppercorns; 1 whole clove or allspice berry
⅔ cup medium-dry Madeira or Port
2 tablespoons cornstarch
Liver from the turkey cut into fine dice (optional)
Salt and pepper, preferably freshly ground, as necessary

Using a heavy knife or cleaver, chop the neck into 1-inch pieces. Heat the oil in a heavy-bottomed 3- to 4-quart saucepan until it is on the verge of smoking, add the neck pieces, gizzard, and heart, and brown well over moderately high heat, stirring frequently. Add the vegetables to the saucepan and continue to cook, stirring frequently, until they are lightly browned around the edges. Pour in the stock or broth, water, and optional wine, and add the herb bag. Bring to a very slow simmer, cover partially, and simmer over low heat for about 2 hours, adding water if the stock cooks down below the level of the solid ingredients. Skim off fat or scum as they accumulate.

Strain the stock into a heavy 1½-quart saucepan, and boil it down to about 2½ cups, if necessary. Retrieve the gizzard and heart from the strainer, discarding the other ingredients. Remove and discard the flap of skin covering the top of the gizzard, then cut both the gizzard and heart into fine dice and add to the reduced stock.

Note: While it is customary to prepare the turkey stock and giblets while the turkey is roasting, this work may be done a day ahead. Cover the stock and refrigerate.

With the turkey removed to a platter or cutting board, spoon all of the fat out of the roasting pan, leaving behind any juices and the coagulated clumps clinging to the bottom of the pan. Pour the wine into the roasting pan, set over moderate heat, and bring to a simmer, scraping up and mashing the browned bits with a wooden spoon. Pour this deglazing liquid into the reserved stock and giblets. Pour about 1/4 cup of the stock mixture into a small bowl, stir briefly to cool, then add the cornstatch and mix until a perfectly smooth paste forms. Bring stock mixture to a simmer, beat in the cornstarch paste, and simmer slowly, stirring, for 1 minute, or until the gravy thickens and clears. If you are using it, stir the diced liver into the gravy and poach at just below the simmer for 1 to 2 minutes longer. Taste the gravy and season with salt and pepper if necessary. Pour into a warmed gravy boat or bowl.

MASTER RECIPE

Bread Stuffing With Oysters

Makes about 4 cups, or enough to stuff a 12- to 15-pound turkey

❦ *This savory, buttery mixture is the classic American stuffing for turkey and, if the ingredients are decreased by half, may be used with roast chicken as well. If the idea of putting oysters inside poultry sounds odd to you, be assured that the taste combination is anything but disquieting. The oysters seem almost to melt away during cooking, leaving behind only a rich and thoroughly agreeable flavor that has nothing to do with fish and that is considerably milder than, say, liver.*

STUFFING POULTRY: Here are some points to bear in mind when stuffing poultry:

- Always fill the bird with a hot stuffing. Cold stuffings slow down the cooking process, causing the outside of the bird to dry out by the time the interior is heated through. (If you wish, you can make the stuffing a day in advance and reheat it in the oven just before use.)
- Never, ever, stuff a bird and then refrigerate it for later roasting. Bacterial growth may begin in the stuffing, and the temperature inside the bird may not climb sufficiently high during roasting to kill the bacteria off.
- Fill the stomach cavity of the bird completely, gently packing in the stuffing with the back of a spoon; use any leftover stuffing in the neck cavity. The old rule that a turkey should be stuffed only 3/4 full applies only when the bird is cooked for a very long time, in which case the stuffing becomes soaked with leaking juices and expands considerably.

- If you find yourself with more stuffing than will fit inside your turkey, simply turn the extra into a well-buttered baking dish, moisten it with a bit of stock, cover, and bake until piping hot.
- Increase the stuffing ingredients by half for a 20-pound turkey; double ingredients for a 25-pound bird.

PRELIMINARIES

1. Set rack in the middle level of oven.
2. Preheat oven to 400°F 20 minutes before toasting the bread cubes.
3. Select a 17×11-inch rimmed baking sheet.

12 ounces day-old firm, homemade-type bread, either all white or 8 ounces white and 4 ounces whole wheat
16 tablespoons (2 sticks) butter
1½ cups chopped onions
¾ cup chopped celery
¼ cup finely chopped fresh parsley
¾ teaspoon rubbed or ground dried sage
¾ teaspoon whole or ground dried thyme
⅛ teaspoon nutmeg, preferably freshly grated
Ground allspice
½ teaspoon salt
½ teaspoon pepper, preferably freshly ground
1 pint shucked oysters, drained

Trim the crusts from the bread and cut into ½-inch cubes. You should have about 4 lightly packed cups of bread. Spread bread out on the baking sheet and toast in the preheated oven for about 10 minutes, stirring once or twice. The bread should dry out and the edges just begin to color but the bread should still seem soft and chewy if pressed between your fingers. Turn bread cubes into a 4-quart mixing bowl and set aside.

Melt butter in a 10-inch skillet, add the onions and celery, and sauté the vegetables over low heat for about 8 minutes, or until tender but not mushy. Remove from heat and stir in the parsley, sage, thyme, nutmeg, big pinch of allspice, salt, and pepper. Pour mixture over the bread cubes and toss to blend. Add the oysters and toss again. Taste and adjust the seasoning if necessary.

AHEAD OF TIME: The stuffing may be covered and refrigerated for up to 24 hours. Before using, turn into a shallow dish and bake in a 425°F oven for about 5 minutes, or until heated through, stirring once.

Variation: BREAD STUFFING WITH APPLES AND PRUNES

Makes about 4 cups, or enough to stuff a 12- to 15-pound turkey

Bread Stuffing with Oysters

ADD: 2 large tart, firm apples, preferably Granny Smiths
3/4 cup chopped pitted tenderized prunes

OMIT: Oysters

Toast the bread cubes as indicated in the Master Recipe.

Peel and core the apples and cut into 1/2-inch cubes; you should have 1 1/2 to 2 cups. In the same skillet you will use to cook the vegetables, heat 4 tablespoons of the butter called for in the Master Recipe to the verge of coloring. Add the apples and sauté over moderately high heat for 2 to 3 minutes, stirring constantly; the apples should brown very lightly around the edges but remain fairly firm. Scrape apples into the toasted bread cubes, then proceed according to the Master Recipe, sautéing the vegetables in the remaining 12 tablespoons butter and adding prunes, rather than oysters, at the end.

Variation: BREAD STUFFING WITH CHESTNUTS AND APPLES

Makes about 4 cups, or enough to stuff a 12- to 15-pound turkey

Bread Stuffing with Oysters

ADD: 1 1/2 cups chopped cooked chestnuts

DECREASE: Bread to 8 ounces

ADD: 2 medium-sized tart, firm apples, preferably Granny Smiths

OMIT: Oysters

Deal with the chestnuts first. You may use commercially prepared chestnuts, but you will obtain better results if you start from scratch. Prepare 1/2 recipe braised chestnuts, page 519. Instead of glazing the chestnuts as indicated at the end of Step 2, drain off their cooking liquid and then chop coarsely.

Toast the bread cubes as indicated in the Master Recipe, but use only 8 ounces bread (3 cups bread cubes). Turn into the mixing bowl and add the chestnuts, tossing to blend.

Peel and core the apples and cut into 1/2-inch cubes. Sauté the vegetables as indicated in the Master Recipe, adding the apples 3 to 4 minutes before removing the mixture from heat; the apples should remain slightly crisp and firm. Add parsley and seasonings to the vegetables and apples and combine with the bread and chestnuts, omitting the oysters.

Variation: BREAD STUFFING WITH DRIED FRUITS

Makes about 4 cups, or enough to stuff a 12- to 15-pound turkey

Bread Stuffing with Oysters

ADD: 2⁄3 cup chopped dried apricots
2⁄3 cup chopped dried prunes
2⁄3 to 3⁄4 cup dry Sherry, Port, or Madeira

OMIT: Oysters

Place dried fruits in a small bowl, cover with wine, and soak overnight. Drain fruits in a sieve, lightly pressing with the back of a wooden spoon. Discard unabsorbed wine, if any.

Proceed according to the Master Recipe, substituting the wine-soaked fruits for the oysters.

Variation: BREAD STUFFING WITH OYSTERS AND PECANS

Makes about 4 cups, or enough to stuff a 12- to 15-pound turkey

Bread Stuffing with Oysters

ADD: 1⁄2 to 1 cup (2 to 4 ounces) very coarsely chopped pecans

Proceed according to the Master Recipe, adding the pecans along with the oysters.

Variation: BREAD STUFFING WITH SAUSAGE

Makes about 4 cups, or enough to stuff a 12- to 15-pound turkey

❦ *This is a very substantial stuffing, and you may wish to go a bit lighter than usual with the other traditional "trimmings."*

Bread Stuffing with Oysters

ADD: 1½ cups (about 12 ounces) mild sausage meat

DECREASE: Butter to 12 tablespoons (1½ sticks)

OMIT: Oysters

Toast the bread as indicated in the Master Recipe.

Crumble the sausage into the same skillet you will use to sauté the vegetables. Brown lightly over moderate heat, stirring frequently. Drain in a sieve, discarding the fat, and add to the bread cubes. Proceed from here according to the Master Recipe, but sauté the vegetables in only 12 tablespoons of butter and omit the oysters.

Variation: BREAD STUFFING WITH TURKEY AND CHICKEN LIVERS

Makes about 4 cups, or enough to stuff a 12- to 15-pound turkey

Bread Stuffing with Oysters

ADD: 8 ounces chicken livers plus, if you wish, the turkey liver

OMIT: Oysters

Toast bread cubes as indicated in the Master Recipe.

After removing strings and any green spots, cut the chicken livers and optional turkey liver into ¼-inch dice. In the same skillet you will use to cook the vegetables, heat 4 tablespoons of the butter called for in the Master Recipe until it is on the verge of coloring. Add the diced livers and sauté for about 30 seconds, or until the livers just stiffen, stirring constantly. Scrape livers into the bread cubes and proceed with the Master Recipe, sautéing the vegetables in the remaining 12 tablespoons butter and omitting the oysters.

Variation: CORN BREAD STUFFING WITH OYSTERS

Makes about 4 cups, or enough to stuff a 12- to 15-pound turkey

❦ *Corn bread may be substituted for yeast bread not only in the Master Recipe, but also in the variations using apples and prunes, oysters and pecans, and sausage. Store-bought and mix-made corn breads will not do here, as they are apt to be too crumbly and too sweet.*

Bread Stuffing with Oysters

SUBSTITUTE: Corn bread, page 668, for white (and whole wheat) bread

Bake the corn bread several hours in advance, allowing it to cool completely, or use leftovers from a day-old loaf. Cut about 2⁄3 of a loaf into 1⁄2-inch cubes, making 4 lightly packed cups, and toast as indicated in the Master Recipe, letting the cubes take on a nice golden color. Proceed according to the Master Recipe, substituting the toasted corn bread for yeast bread and mixing the stuffing gently so as not to break the corn bread up.

About Pork Loin Roasts

The pork loin is the back between the shoulder and the rump. The choicest cut for roasting is the pork loin center rib roast, which consists of one solid piece of meat, the loin eye muscle, plus the rib bones. Be sure to buy a roast containing at least one rib for each person you are serving; have the bottoms of the rib bones sawed at the rib intervals so that you can cut straight through the roast, making perfect slices. A second-best alternative is the pork loin center loin roast. This contains rib eye and tenderloin muscles separated by T-shaped bones, plus the rib bones. The T-bones make this roast a bit tricky to carve; the bottoms of the rib bones should be sawed at the rib intervals. Less desirable cuts for roasting are the pork loin blade roast, from the shoulder end of the loin, and the pork loin sirloin roast, from the hip end. Both of these contain numerous muscle separations and bones, making carving difficult; both should weigh close to 4 pounds to serve 4 to 5, as the bones make for considerable waste.

Small pork loin roasts make very good eating, but they require a bit of special treatment if they are to turn out as tender, juicy, and flavorful as they should. A marination in salt, herbs, and spices makes pork tender and gives it the flavor boost it often seems to need. Roasting pork in a *covered* casserole and cooking it only to the end of the "medium" stage (around 155°F) prevents it from drying out and losing its fresh texture. (Pork, by the way, is safe to eat at any temperature over 140°F; see page 340.)

MASTER RECIPE

Roast Pork (or Veal or Turkey Breast)

4 to 5 servings

❦ *Potatoes and other root vegetables go especially well with roast pork. Try mashed potatoes, either white or sweet, scalloped potatoes, or glazed parsnips or turnips. Spinach, especially creamed or butter-braised, cabbage or red cabbage prepared in almost any way, braised collards, kale, or mustard greens, or plain buttered broccoli all make excellent vegetable accompaniments.*

Notes on preparing veal roast and turkey breast according to this recipe appear on page 369.

Step 1: Flavoring and Tying the Roast

A bone-in pork loin roast weighing 3 to 4 pounds
2 teaspoons salt
1 teaspoon whole dried thyme
1 teaspoon dried rosemary
1 teaspoon whole black or white peppercorns
1/8 teaspoon ground cloves or 1 whole clove
2 juniper berries (optional)
1 2-inch bay leaf, broken up
1 1/2 teaspoons mashed, pressed, or very finely minced garlic

If necessary, trim excess fat off the roast with a sharp utility knife, leaving a layer about 1/4 inch thick. Blot all surfaces of the meat lightly with paper toweling.

Combine salt, thyme, rosemary, peppercorns, cloves, juniper berries, and broken-up bay leaf in a blender jar (preferably a small one) or spice grinder and grind to a fairly fine powder. Rub all surfaces of the meat with garlic then carefully sprinkle all the surfaces with ground spice mixture, gently pressing it into the meat with your hands to make sure it sticks. There will seem to be a lot of ground spice, but do not worry: the meat will not be overpowered.

Using sturdy white twine, tightly tie the roast lengthwise as though tying a ribbon around a package. This will fuse the backbone, which has presumably been split between the ribs to facilitate carving, and prevent the roast from sagging or bulging during cooking.

Wrap the roast first in plastic and then in foil, or seal it in a heavy-gauge plastic bag. Either let the meat stand at room temperature for about 3 hours or refrigerate it for at least 8 hours or up to several days. The longer the meat marinates, the more strongly it will be flavored; you needn't worry about spoilage because the salt in the marinade acts as a preservative.

STEP 2: BROWNING AND ROASTING THE MEAT

3 tablespoons neutral vegetable oil
1 medium onion, chopped
1 small carrot, peeled and chopped
1 small celery rib, chopped

SPECIAL EQUIPMENT: Meat thermometer, preferably an instant-reading, vest-pocket type

If the roast has been refrigerated, let it stand for 1 hour at room temperature before cooking it. Set the rack in middle or lower-middle level of oven and preheat to 325°F 20 minutes before the roast goes in.

Scrape off the flavoring mixture with a knife and gently blot meat dry with paper toweling. Pour oil into a heavy, lidded 5- to 6-quart casserole just large enough to hold the meat, and heat over a moderately high flame until oil looks shimmery. Add roast and brown on all sides, including the bone sides; this may take as long as 20 minutes. Keep heat high, but not so high as to darken the oil or cause the meat to scorch; turn the meat with two wooden spoons or spatulas (or by gripping the loops of twine) rather than by spearing it with a fork, which causes juices to run out.

When the roast is browned, transfer it to a plate and cover loosely with a sheet of aluminum foil. Add onion, carrot, and celery to oil in the casserole and sauté over moderately high heat, stirring frequently, until vegetables are softened and lightly browned around the edges (you must cook the vegetables at least halfway through at this point, or they will still be hard by the time the roast is done). Return the roast and any juices that may have pooled around it to the casserole. Arrange meat with its fat side up and its bone side resting on the bottom of the casserole. If you are using the kind of thermometer that stays in the meat during cooking, insert it into the center of the thickest part of the roast, not touching bone.

Cover the casserole tightly and place meat in the preheated oven. Cook for 23 minutes per pound, then check the temperature with a meat thermometer. (If using the instant-reading type, insert it deeply into the thickest part of the roast, being sure the stem is not touching bone at any point, and wait 15 seconds.) Done is 155°F to 160°F. When cooked to this temperature, the meat will feel firm but not hard when pressed with a finger and the juices will run faintly red when the roast is pricked to the bone with a long fork. If the roast is not quite done return it to the oven, but be careful not to overcook.

Step 3: Preparing Sauce; Carving and Serving the Roast

¼ to ½ cup Chicken Stock, page 26, or canned broth, *or* 1 cup heavy cream

Transfer roast to a carving board and cover snugly with aluminum foil. Let roast stand for 10 to 15 minutes so that the juices can be reabsorbed by the flesh.

If pan juices appear especially oily, you may skim some of the fat off with a spoon; however, since loin pork tends to be dry, I rarely bother to do this. Using a table fork, mash the vegetables in the casserole until reduced to a lumpy purée. You may now complete the sauce in one of two ways. For a light sauce, add just enough chicken stock or broth to bring the vegetable mixture to spooning consistency, then bring to a rapid boil and stir for about 30 seconds to amalgamate solids and liquid. For a creamy sauce, add heavy cream and boil, stirring, for about 3 minutes, or until the sauce is the consistency of a heavy cream soup. Taste and adjust the seasoning.

Carve the roast between the ribs and arrange slices on a warmed serving platter. Pour any juices exuded by the roast into your sauce and serve the sauce separately.

Ahead of Time: The sooner the roast is served, the better, as the meat will tend to dry out as it sits. If there is an unavoidable delay, prepare the sauce in the casserole and add the roast, uncarved and bone side down. Cover and place in a very slow oven (120°F); the sauce should barely steam, let alone come near a simmer. Hold no longer than 1 hour.

To prepare a veal roast: Veal reacts similarly to pork in cooking and should be roasted in the same way. Choose a 4- or 5-rib veal rib roast or a 3- to 4-pound bone-in veal loin roast. Proceed according to the Master Recipe, but omit Step 1 (the maceration in spices and salt) and instead season the veal with salt, pepper, and ½ teaspoon whole dried thyme after it is browned (Step 2).

To prepare turkey breast: Choose a small bone-in breast half weighing about 4 pounds, or a boned and rolled turkey breast roast weighing about 2 pounds. Proceed according to the Master Recipe, but omit Step 1 (the maceration in spices and salt) and instead season the turkey with salt, pepper, and ¼ teaspoon *each* whole dried thyme and rubbed or ground sage after it is browned (Step 2); roast only 15 minutes per pound, rather than 23, before testing for doneness.

Variation: ROAST PORK WITH APPLES

4 to 5 servings

❦ *Serve this classic autumnal dish with mashed or roasted potatoes and a green vegetable from the cabbage family such as braised red cabbage, boiled brussels sprouts, or braised collard greens or kale.*

Roast Pork (or Veal or Turkey Breast), using a pork roast
ADD: 4 to 5 very firm apples (Granny Smiths or other baking apples)
2 to 3 tablespoons applejack or calvados (optional)
2 tablespoons white or packed brown sugar (optional)

Prepare a pork roast according to Steps 1 and 2 of the Master Recipe. About 20 minutes before end of cooking time, arrange apples, halved and cored but unpeeled, cut side down in an overlapping layer around the roast. By the time the meat is done the apples will be tender. Remove both apples and meat from the casserole and set aside.

To prepare sauce (Step 3), after mashing vegetables into the pan juices as indicated in the Master Recipe, add, if you wish, some applejack or calvados and bring sauce to a boil. Finally, stir in 1 cup heavy cream and cook down until the sauce thickens.

To give the dish a bit of added glamour, place the apples cut side up in a shallow broilerproof pan, sprinkle with sugar, and run briefly under a very hot broiler to brown and glaze them lightly. Arrange the sliced pork and the apples, glazed or not, in an attractive manner on a platter.

Variation: ROAST PORK STUFFED WITH WINE-SOAKED DRIED FRUITS

4 to 5 servings

❦ *Serve this clever and delicious dish with puréed winter squash or corn pudding, and a green vegetable.*

To make this dish successfully you need a roast composed primarily of a long, solid piece of meat. A loin center rib roast is ideal; a center loin roast will also do, though it has a T-bone at one end.

Roast Pork (or Veal or Turkey Breast), using a pork roast
ADD: About 8 ounces dried fruit (apricots, pitted prunes, pears, apples, or a combination)
⅔ cup sweetish Sherry, Port, or Madeira

Rub pork roast with seasonings and tie up as indicated in Step 1 of the Master Recipe. Set aside for several hours or refrigerate up to several days.

At least 2 hours before you plan to roast the meat and preferably 4 to 6 hours in advance, turn dried fruit into a small bowl and cover with wine. Set aside, covered with plastic wrap, and let the fruit marinate; stir up once or twice. Drain fruit well in a sieve, reserving wine marinade.

Using a long utility knife, cut a 1-inch-wide tunnel lengthwise all through the meat. (If necessary, pierce the roast from both ends with the knife, to make sure that the tunnel is sufficiently wide at all points.) Stuff fruit into the tunnel, pushing it into the roast with the handle of a wooden spoon.

Proceed to brown, roast, and sauce the pork as indicated in Steps 2 and 3 of the Master Recipe, adding reserved wine marinade to the pan juices after mashing the vegetables, and finishing sauce with heavy cream.

Variation: ROAST PORK OR VEAL WITH POTATOES AND ONIONS

4 to 5 servings

❦*All you need to make this dish into a complete dinner is a green vegetable such as asparagus, broccoli, or spinach. Pork and veal are equally good prepared in this manner.*

Roast Pork (or Veal or Turkey Breast), using a pork or veal roast

ADD: 12 small white onions (about 1 pound), peeled

12 small new potatoes (about 1 pound), peeled

Drop onions and potatoes into 2 to 3 quarts of well-salted rapidly boiling water and parboil for 5 minutes after water returns to the simmer. Drain.

Prepare a pork or veal roast according to the Master Recipe, adding small onions to the casserole along with the meat at the outset of cooking and adding potatoes about 20 minutes before the end of the estimated cooking time. Gently stir up vegetables several times during cooking so that they will absorb the juices from the meat. Finish the sauce with either stock or heavy cream, as you wish.

Variation: ROAST PORK WITH TURNIPS

4 to 5 servings

❦ *Turnips and pork are a fine and classic combination. A leafy green vegetable is my choice for an accompaniment here.*

Roast Pork (or Veal or Turkey Breast), using a pork roast
ADD: 12 small white turnips (about 1 pound), peeled

Prepare pork roast according to the Master Recipe, adding turnips to the casserole along with the meat when the roast goes into the oven. Turn the turnips once to coat with fat and gently stir them up every 20 minutes or so during cooking. Finish the sauce with stock or cream, as you wish.

Variation: PROVENÇAL ROAST PORK OR VEAL

4 to 5 servings

❦ *This variation is prepared by stirring a piquant tomato sauce into the pan juices left by the roasted meat; the resulting sauce is then served with the roast. Rice is perhaps a better accompaniment here than potatoes. Sautéed spinach, sautéed eggplant, or perhaps oil-braised peppers might also be served.*

Roast Pork (or Veal or Turkey Breast); use a pork or veal roast and prepare through Step 2
3 tablespoons olive oil
½ cup chopped onion
3 tablespoons chopped pitted oil-cured black olives
2 tablespoons well-drained small capers
1 teaspoon mashed, pressed, or very finely minced garlic
¼ teaspoon oregano
¼ teaspoon ground dried orange peel
⅛ teaspoon fennel seed, ground or moistened with a few drops of water and minced fine
⅛ teaspoon pepper, preferably freshly ground
¼ cup dry white wine
1 cup peeled, seeded, diced tomatoes, fresh or canned (see page 607)
2 tablespoons finely chopped fresh parsley

Prepare a pork or veal roast through Step 2 of the Master Recipe, and make the following sauce base while the roast is in the oven. Pour olive oil into a 10-inch skillet and heat until fragrant. Add chopped onion and cook over moderate heat, stirring frequently, for about 7 minutes, or until onion is soft but not at all brown. Add olives, capers, garlic, oregano, orange peel, fennel seed, pepper, and white wine and simmer, stirring, until wine is nearly evaporated. Stir in tomatoes, turn heat down to low, and cook slowly for 15 to 20 minutes, stirring occasionally, or until sauce is very thick and oily looking. Add parsley and cook a minute longer. Remove from heat and set aside.

To prepare sauce (Step 3), mash the roasting vegetables into the pan juices, add chicken stock, and bring to a boil. Stir in tomato mixture (above), and continue to boil, stirring, until sauce is thick. Taste and adjust seasoning. Spoon a bit of the sauce around the carved meat on the platter and pass the rest separately.

Variation: VEAL, PORK, OR TURKEY TONNATO

4 to 5 servings

❦*A classic Italian dish, veal tonnato is cold veal that is covered with a tuna-flavored mayonnaise and kept a while in the refrigerator to absorb the flavor of the tuna. Though it sounds odd at first, the combination of veal and tuna is both subtle and delicious. Pork and turkey may also be used. The dish is most commonly served as the main course of a summertime luncheon or supper, and is best accompanied by a tossed green salad, crusty bread, and a chilled white wine.*

Roast Pork (or Veal or Turkey Breast); use a veal, pork, or turkey-breast roast, and prepare through Step 2
⅓ cup dry white wine
A 7-ounce can of oil-packed white tuna fish, undrained
4 anchovy fillets
½ teaspoon mashed, pressed, or very finely minced garlic
1 cup mayonnaise, preferably homemade, page 51, using ¼ cup olive oil and ¾ cup neutral vegetable oil
3 tablespoons well-drained small capers
2 to 3 tablespoons finely chopped fresh parsley
Fresh lemon juice or vinegar, if needed
Additional capers and chopped parsley, and strips of pimiento (optional)

Prepare a veal, pork, or turkey-breast roast as indicated in Steps 1 and 2 of the Master Recipe. When the roast is done, remove it from the casserole, wrap it in foil, and refrigerate it until thoroughly chilled. Add wine to pan juices and roasting vegetables in the casserole and boil sauce down until it returns to its original volume. Cover and refrigerate until the roast is chilled and you are ready to complete the recipe.

Turn pan juices and vegetables into blender or food processor. Add the tuna fish and its packing oil, anchovy fillets, and garlic and purée thoroughly. With the motor running, add 4 to 6 tablespoons of the mayonnaise 1 tablespoon at a time; the sauce should now look smooth. Turn sauce into a bowl and fold in the remaining mayonnaise along with the capers and chopped parsley. Taste and carefully correct the seasoning, adding drops of lemon juice or vinegar if the sauce seems to need some spark.

Thinly slice the cold roast. Arrange the least attractive half of the slices in a slightly overlapping layer on a serving platter and mask with half of the tuna sauce. Arrange remaining slices of meat or turkey on top and cover with remaining sauce. Cover the dish loosely with plastic wrap and then seal with foil. Refrigerate for several hours at least, preferably 12 hours or longer, so that the flavors will meld. If you wish, just before serving, decorate with additional capers and chopped parsley and perhaps with a few strips of pimiento.

ROASTED SPARERIBS

4 servings

❦ *The following recipe produces a savory sort of spareribs rather than the sweet, sticky kind. French fries, cole slaw, and cold beer are good accompaniments.*

CHOOSING SPARERIBS: Sparerib terminology can be quite confusing. Genuine *spareribs* are the hog's breast. One side of spareribs—that is, one half of the breast—weighs about 2 pounds and will serve 2 or 3 people. When sold at the supermarket, a side is generally cut into pieces. *Pork loin back ribs,* often labeled *pork ribs for barbecue,* are the bones of the rib loin, removed in one piece. These may be prepared like spareribs, but their meat is drier and, I think, less delectable. There is also a cut variously called *country-style spareribs, country ribs,* or *blade end country spareribs.* This is actually part of the blade end of the pork loin, a nice cut, but quite unlike true spareribs in texture and flavor.

PRELIMINARIES

1. Set rack in center of oven.
2. Preheat oven to 350°F 20 minutes before roasting.
3. Select a roasting pan fitted with a rack, or a broiling pan equipped with slotted broiling tray large enough to hold the spareribs in one layer

4 pounds pork spareribs
2 teaspoons rubbed or ground sage
2 teaspoons mashed, pressed, or very finely minced garlic
4 or 5 juniper berries, crushed (optional)
1½ teaspoons salt
1 teaspoon pepper, preferably freshly ground

Rub both sides of the spareribs with all remaining ingredients. Cover ribs loosely with plastic wrap and let stand at room temperature for 1 hour (or in the refrigerator for several hours) so that flavorings can penetrate the meat.

Arrange ribs on rack or broiling tray and roast about 1½ hours, or until very tender and nicely browned, turning once. Carve ribs into serving pieces with a sharp knife or cleaver.

About Ham

In former times, when slaughtering was a seasonal event and refrigerators and freezers were undreamt-of inventions, most of the meat that people ate was cured—that is dried, salted, smoked, or pickled (corned)—rather than fresh. But today, other than bacon and various delicatessen-type items, ham is virtually the only cured meat regularly served in American homes.

Choosing a Ham: There are numerous types of hams. The recipe that follows is not intended for use with a canned ham or a specialty country ham but rather with a so-called "tenderized" brine-cured ham. A tenderized ham has been precooked in order to soften the flesh and remove any danger of parasitic infection. The purpose of baking a tenderized ham is to warm it up and give it a handsome glazed exterior. It doesn't actually need to be cooked.

Tenderized hams, which are available both at supermarkets and butcher shops, vary widely in taste. Factors influencing the final flavor include the quality of the meat, the amount of salt added, the spices and other flavorings introduced during curing, and whether or not the ham has been smoked. Because of these variables, buying a ham is always something of a gamble. Most supermarkets buy hams from a variety of sources and change suppliers frequently; thus you could enjoy one ham but dislike another bought at the same supermarket a week later. Perhaps you are best advised to seek the counsel of someone behind the counter, who may know the history of a given ham and what it is like. You could also pick a ham produced by a national supplier whose other products are to your liking.

If possible, choose a ham with the skin (or "rind") still attached, as skinned hams often have too thin a layer of protective fat to be glazed properly.

MASTER RECIPE

Baked Glazed Ham (and Roasted Fresh Ham)

15 to 20 servings

Ham may be dressed up or dressed down, depending on what it is served with. Formal accompaniments might include a creamed vegetable (broccoli is particularly good) and mashed potatoes, while for an informal down-home-style dinner, baked ham might be served with mashed potatoes and greens (collards or kale); biscuits or corn bread are a must. Favorite holiday meal trimmings for ham are sweet potatoes, candied or mashed, puréed winter squash, braised celery, either plain or creamed and/or nutted, and peas. Biscuits or corn bread are always welcome here too.

Ham is also delicious when served at room temperature or chilled. The traditional and best accompaniments are cole slaw and either potato salad or baked beans. If a cold ham is part of a buffet, it is nice to surround it with different types of rolls (say, hard rolls and rye rolls) and with pots of mustard and mayonnaise.

Notes on preparing fresh ham according to this recipe appear on page 377.

PRELIMINARIES

1. Set rack in the lowest level of the oven.
2. Preheat oven to 325°F 20 minutes before baking.
3. Select a turkey roaster or other oven-safe pan large enough to hold the ham; fit with a rack. Also have at the ready a large shallow roasting pan or sturdy rimmed baking sheet, fitted with a rack.

A 14- to 16-pound tenderized ("ready-to-eat") ham, preferably with the skin attached
2 cups sweet white wine or sparkling wine
1 cup packed dark brown sugar
3 tablespoons dry mustard
2 teaspoons ground cloves or allspice
1 teaspoon freshly ground black pepper (omit if not freshly ground)
1½ to 2 cups Fine Fresh Bread Crumbs (see page 60)

Place ham with the skin (or fat) side up on a rack in turkey roaster or roasting pan and pour the wine over it. Cover with lid or foil and bake in preheated oven for about 3½ hours, basting every 30 minutes with the pan juices. At this point, the ham should have reached an internal temperature of around 140°F on a meat thermometer, and the meat will have shrunk slightly from the ends of the bone.

Remove ham from oven and reset oven thermostat to 375°F.

Transfer ham, still set on rack, to roasting pan or baking sheet, and set aside to cool slightly. Pour drippings out of roasting pan, reserving about ¼ cup.

Combine brown sugar, mustard, cloves or allspice, and pepper in a small bowl. Add just enough of the reserved drippings to make a thick, barely spreadable paste; blend thoroughly. Using a sharp utility knife, cut away the rind of the ham (if still attached) and shave off the excess fat underneath, leaving a ¼- to ⅜-inch layer of fat all around. Score the fat in a diamond pattern, cutting almost through to the meat. Spread the brown sugar mixture over the fat sides of the ham with a knife or the back of a spoon, and lightly brush the wide bone end of the ham with the mixture as well. Press the bread crumbs gently but firmly over the entire exposed surface of the ham, coating the fat sides particularly thickly.

Return ham to oven and bake about 1 hour longer, or until the crumbs are nicely browned and the internal temperature of the meat is around 160°F. Remove from oven and let rest about 20 minutes before serving. To carve, cut thin slices perpendicular to the bone, freeing the slices by cutting parallel to the bone. Divide the larger slices in half crosswise if you wish. When the top of the ham, which produces the most attractive slices, has been carved, turn the ham on its side and cut off the meat in long, thin slices parallel to the bone. Repeat this procedure with the bottom and opposite side.

AHEAD OF TIME: Ham can be held for about 1 hour at room temperature or for 3 to 4 hours in a warm oven (120°F). Leftovers can be wrapped in foil and refrigerated for 4 to 5 days. Reheat in a 350°F oven or slice and sauté according to the recipe on page 409.

PREPARING A FRESH HAM: A fresh ham is simply an uncured—that is, fresh—leg of pork. It may be prepared exactly as for ham according to this Master Recipe. Resembling other pork roasts in taste and texture, a pork leg roast makes a dramatic and delicious main course for a large party, and it is generally quite reasonable in price.

About Roast Beef

Even today, when many people are cutting back on their consumption of meat, there remains something undeniably grand and festive about a perfectly roasted joint of beef. Although a variety of beef cuts may be used, the Master Recipe calls for beef rib roast, the traditional favorite.

A complete beef rib roast consists of seven ribs. Of these, the two that are from the so-called large end, that is, adjacent to the shoulder, are the less choice, for they are fatty, coarse, and contain muscle separations. The remaining five ribs, which make up the beef rib roast small end, contain the solid, lovely center muscle, or eye, of the rib. It is from among these five ribs that you wish your roast to be cut. Since the rib is so tender, either prime or choice beef will do, though a prime roast will have more flavor.

To make a rib roast oven-ready, the backbone or chine bone (pronounced "shine") should be sawed off so that the ribs will be easy to cut apart. Also, the flap of fatty meat covering the eye of the roast—the cap meat—should be removed, and the ends of the ribs—the short ribs—should be cut off. Most butchers trim rib roasts in this manner as a matter of course. Supermarkets generally remove the backbone and short ribs but often leave the cap meat attached, inflating the weight, and thus the price, of the roast.

MASTER RECIPE

Roast Beef (or Lamb) au Jus

6 servings

❦ *Roast beef is most often served with potatoes—roasted, mashed, scalloped, or baked—though glazed chestnuts or Yorkshire pudding also make delicious accompaniments. Green beans, broccoli, brussels sprouts, or spinach are the green vegetables of choice; the vegetable might be creamed, crumbed, or given some other fancy treatment if the starch is on the simple side. An additional vegetable garniture of glazed carrots or turnips, sautéed mushrooms, or sautéed cherry tomatoes will add grandeur to the menu.*

Notes on preparing other cuts of beef, as well as lamb, according to this recipe appear on page 380.

TEMPERATURE CONSIDERATIONS: Rib roasts can be relied on to require a minimum roasting time of 10 minutes per pound for very rare (110°F to 115°F), 12 minutes for rare (120°F), and 14 minutes for medium-rare (125°F to 130°F). Very often, though, a roast will take somewhat longer, perhaps because the meat was rather cold going into the oven, or the roast was unusually fatty, dense in texture, or squat and thick in shape. In short, you cannot accurately predict in advance the cooking time for a roast by calculating a certain number of minutes per pound. You must test the roast for doneness toward the end of the estimated cooking time. A meat thermometer, preferably the instant-reading, vest-pocket type rather than the less accurate type that is inserted into the roast at the outset of cooking, is essential here. (Cutting into the nearly cooked meat tells you little because roasts continue to cook and to firm up after they are removed from the oven.) See pages 342–44 for further discussion of the relationship between meat temperature and various stages of doneness and notes on meat thermometers.

PRELIMINARIES

1. Set the rack in the middle or upper-middle level of the oven. When laid fat side up, the roast should be about 8 inches from the oven roof.
2. Preheat the oven to 500°F 20 minutes before roasting.
3. Select a roasting pan large enough to hold the meat comfortably. Fit the pan with a slotted broiling tray or with a rack.

A fully trimmed prime or choice beef 3-rib roast small end, weighing 6½ to 7½ pounds
3 tablespoons soft butter
1 cup Beef Stock, page 24, or Rescued Canned Beef Broth, page 28
1½ teaspoons cornstarch mixed to a smooth paste with 1 tablespoon Madeira or Port (optional)
Salt and pepper, preferably freshly ground

SPECIAL EQUIPMENT: A meat thermometer, preferably the instant-reading vest-pocket type

Trim away excess fat, leaving a layer about ½ inch thick. Dry all surfaces of the meat thoroughly with paper toweling (wet meat will not brown properly) and massage with soft butter any meaty surfaces of the roast that are not covered with fat. Arrange the roast fat side up on the slotted tray or rack in the roasting pan. If you are using the kind of meat thermometer that remains in the roast throughout cooking, insert it into the thickest part of the meat, not touching bone.

Place the roast in the oven, close the oven door, and immediately reset the thermostat to 350°F.

Basting the fatless sides of the meat every 30 minutes with the pan drippings, roast the meat 10 minutes per pound for very rare, 12 minutes per pound for rare, and 14 minutes per pound for medium rare, then test for doneness using a meat thermometer. (If using an instant-reading thermometer, insert into the thickest part of the meat, being sure that it does not touch bone, and wait 15 seconds.) The correct temperatures at which to remove the meat from the oven are 110°F to 115°F for very rare; 120°F for rare; and 125°F for medium rare. If the meat is not quite done, roast 1 additional minute for each 1-degree increase in temperature, then test again. Remember that the more thoroughly cooked the meat becomes, the faster its internal temperature rises. Thus, while it may take 15 or more minutes for a roast to go from 90°F to 100°F, it may only take about 10 minutes for the meat to pass from 120°F—rare—to 130°F—the very end of the medium-rare stage. In other words, a few minutes too long in the oven may spell ruin, so be vigilant!

Lift the cooked roast on its rack out of the roasting pan. Cover the roast loosely with foil and allow to rest about 15 minutes. During this time the juices will be reabsorbed by the flesh, improving the texture of the meat, and the internal temperature of the roast will rise another 5°F to 10°F, thus completing the cooking.

Pour most of the fat out of the roasting pan and add to it stock or rescued broth. Set the roasting pan over a low flame on top of the stove and scrape up browned bits with a wooden spoon to dissolve them in the hot stock. (If your roast is quite rare, there will be little juice and few roasting particles in the pan.) Boil down the liquid slightly to concentrate the flavor; season to taste. You now have *jus,* as in roast beef *au jus.* If you want a lightly thickened gravy, stir into the *jus* the cornstarch/wine paste and simmer, stirring, for 1 minute or so to cook the starch.

To carve the roast, cut down along the ribs and then across along the backbone to free the eye of the roast in one piece, then cut the eye vertically into slices about 3/8 inch thick. Cut between the rib bones to separate them and serve the ribs along with meat, if you wish. Sprinkle with salt and fresh pepper and serve at once.

Ahead of Time: Covered with foil, the roast will remain warm enough to serve for 30 minutes at least. If the wait is longer, return the roast to the turned-off oven, leaving the oven door open until the oven temperature lowers to around 100°F. Thereafter, turn the oven on for a few seconds at 10-minute intervals to retain the temperature at about 100°F. Kept warm in this manner, the roast may be held 1 additional hour before serving.

To Prepare a Beef Loin Top Loin Roast: Also called beef shell, the beef top loin is the top section (or "saddle") of the steer's back between the rib and the rump (T-bone and porterhouse steaks consist of vertical slices of the top loin, plus, on the opposite side of the T-bone, a nugget of the softer tenderloin). To serve 6, choose a 3-pound section of the top loin. Proceed according to the

Master Recipe—the total cooking time will be short because the roast is small—and carve in vertical slices about 3/8 inch thick.

To Prepare a Beef Top Round Roast: Cut from the steer's leg, the top round is not a particularly tender or juicy cut, but it is lean, boneless, without muscle separations, and much less expensive than beef rib or loin roasts. It is widely available at supermarkets. To serve 6, choose a 3-pound roast, preferably one that is fairly uniform in thickness and has some protective fat on at least one side. Proceed according to the Master Recipe, but roast 22 minutes per pound for rare, 28 minutes per pound for medium rare. Carve vertically, slightly on the bias, in the thinnest slices possible.

To prepare leg of lamb: A whole leg of lamb roast consists of two parts: the sirloin section, which includes the hip bone, and the shank, which includes the round shank bone. You can also buy a leg of lamb roast with part of the sirloin sliced off and the hip bone removed—this is sometimes called lamb leg short cut—or one with the entire sirloin removed, which is called a lamb leg shank half. To serve 6, you need a 5- to 6-pound whole leg, lamb leg short cut, or lamb leg shank half.

To prepare a leg of lamb for roasting, trim off any silvery, papery layers of skin, or fell, that may be covering the leg, and, if you wish, poke small slits in the lamb with the point of a paring knife and stuff with slivers of garlic and/or pinches of dried rosemary and bits of anchovy. Proceed according to the Master Recipe, but roast the leg only 10 to 12 minutes per pound for medium rare. To carve, hold the roast by the shank bone (your hand protected by a towel, of course) and cut thin slices parallel to the bone. Serve on heated plates as lamb fat congeals at room temperature. Accompany as for beef, or serve with sautéed eggplant or summer squash, broiled tomatoes, or puréed dried beans.

BROILED POULTRY and MEAT

Because it is quick and requires a minimum of added fat, broiling is a highly favored cooking method for poultry and meat. It is not, however, foolproof. First-rate results can only be obtained if a very good cut is used, and attention must be paid to such details as the placement of the broiler rack, the preheating of the broiler, and, of course, the cooking process itself. The greatest danger is overcooking; the best preventive action is vigilance.

A NOTE ON THE BROILING PAN: The best sort of broiling apparatus is an inch-deep (or so) pan fitted with a tray that is both corrugated and slotted to allow grease to run off and drip through into the pan underneath. It must be large enough to hold the poultry or meat in a single layer without crowding, or the food will not brown properly. Except when broiling chicken, it is possible to improvise by setting a sturdy cake rack atop a shallow-rimmed baking sheet.

OUTDOOR AND INDOOR GRILLING: All of the recipes in this chapter may be adapted for an indoor grill or an outdoor barbecue. Adjust the grill rack so that the food will be the distance indicated in the recipes from the hot coals or other heat source. When cooking outdoors remember that food will take longer to cook on cool or breezy days.

MASTER RECIPE

Broiled Chicken

4 servings

I generally serve broiled chicken with a tossed green salad, tomato salad, or cole slaw, but, for dressier occasions, it can also be accompanied by a green vegetable and pasta in cream or scalloped or baked stuffed potatoes.

CHOOSING CHICKEN FOR BROILING: Choose the smallest possible chickens for broiling, as these will be tender and will cook quickly; large chickens tend to char on the outside by the time they are cooked through to the bone. Squab chickens, weighing about 1 pound, and broiling chickens, weighing about 1½ pounds, were once common at markets, but they are now scarce. Should you be able to find either, allow 1 squab chicken, split, or ½ broiling chicken for each serving. Rock Cornish game hens, hybrid birds that taste much like chicken, are an excellent alternative to squab and broiling chickens. Game hens weighing around 1 pound make a single generous serving; those weighing around 1½ pounds make 2 servings. As a last resort, a small frying chicken weighing about 3 pounds may be used for broiling. The chicken, which should be quartered, serves 4.

PRELIMINARIES

1. Select a broiling pan covered with a slotted tray that is large enough to hold the chicken pieces in a single comfortable layer. (Do not use either a one-piece disposable foil broiling pan or a baking sheet with a rack set on it. Both of these contrivances will allow accumulating fat to smoke or even catch fire.)
2. Adjust the rack in your broiler so that the tops of the tallest pieces of chicken will be about 5 inches away from the heating element.
3. Preheat broiler—with the broiling pan outside—for a full 5 minutes before proceeding to cook the chicken.

4 1-pound squab chickens or Rock Cornish game hens *or* two 1½-pound broiling chickens or game hens *or* one 3-pound frying chicken
6 tablespoons butter, melted
Salt and pepper, preferably freshly ground

Remove giblets and save for some other use. Using poultry shears or a sharp, sturdy utility knife, cut through the ribs along one side of the backbone and open the chicken flat on your work surface, with the inside facing up. Dig out the wish bone, reddish breast bone, and piece of attached cartilage with your fingers; discard. Cut through the breast, thus separating the chicken into halves; if you wish, cut off and discard the backbone from the half of the bird to which it is attached. If you are using a frying chicken, quarter it by cutting each half in two diagonally, separating wing and breast from drumstick and thigh. Rinse chicken under tepid water and pat as dry as possible with paper toweling. Arrange pieces bone side up on broiling tray, brush liberally with melted butter, and sprinkle with salt and pepper.

Watch chicken closely during cooking; be prepared to move the chicken farther from or closer to the heat, if necessary. Broil chicken about 12 to 14 minutes on the bone side, or until dark brown and just beginning to char, brushing midway through with additional melted butter. Turn chicken with tongs and brush the skin side with more melted butter and sprinkle with salt and pepper. Broil 8 to 10 minutes longer, basting once with butter. The chicken is done when it is browned and has begun to drip juices into the broiling tray. To be doubly sure the chicken is cooked, you can make a deep cut into a thick piece adjacent to the bone; there may be a tinge of pink in the juices, but the flesh itself should look firm and yellow, with no sign of dark red.

Broiled chicken must be served as soon as it is done. It cannot be kept warm—it dries out and overcooks as it sits—nor can it be reheated.

TIP: If, as sometimes happens, the skin of the chicken becomes as brown as you would like it to be but the inside is not yet fully cooked, transfer the chicken to a very hot oven (about 450°F) and bake until done, usually no more than 5 minutes. Unless the broiling compartment of your stove is totally independent of the oven, the oven will already be quite hot by the time you realize the need for baking the chicken.

Variation: MARINATED BROILED CHICKEN WITH CHILI, SOY SAUCE, OR LEMON

4 servings

I think of marinated broiled chicken, regardless of what flavorings are used, as an informal, eat-with-your-hands dish that is best accompanied by cole slaw and potato salad. It also makes excellent picnic food.

Broiled Chicken

OMIT: Butter
Salt and pepper

One of the following marinades:

Chili marinade:

- ¾ cup ketchup
- ⅓ cup neutral vegetable oil
- 3 tablespoons cider vinegar
- 3 tablespoons packed dark brown sugar
- 2 tablespoons strained fresh lemon juice
- 2 tablespoons hot chili powder, or to taste
- 1½ teaspoons mashed, pressed, or very finely minced garlic
- 1 teaspoon oregano
- 1 teaspoon salt

Soy sauce marinade:

- ½ cup dark soy sauce
- ⅓ cup honey
- ¼ cup neutral vegetable oil
- 3 tablespoons distilled vinegar
- 2 tablespoons dry Sherry or rice wine
- 1½ tablespoons grated or very finely minced fresh ginger or 2 teaspoons ground
- 1 tablespoon dark sesame oil (optional)
- 1 teaspoon mashed, pressed, or very finely minced garlic
- ½ teaspoon crushed red pepper (optional)

Lemon marinade:

- ½ cup olive oil
- ⅓ cup strained fresh lemon juice
- 1 teaspoon mashed, pressed, or very finely minced garlic
- 1 teaspoon dried rosemary, ground or moistened with a few drops of water and minced fine
- 1 teaspoon salt
- ½ teaspoon pepper, preferably freshly ground

Rinse chicken and pat dry with paper towels. To marinate chicken in a plastic bag—a very effective and convenient method—mix marinade ingredients in 3-quart mixing bowl with a fork, add chicken pieces, turning them to coat with the marinade, and then turn chicken and marinade into a plastic bag and seal tightly, squeezing out as much air as possible. Turn the bag from one side to the other periodically as chicken marinates. To marinate the chicken by more conventional means, mix marinade ingredients in a ceramic, glass, or stainless steel pan, lay in the chicken pieces, turn them once to coat, and cover tightly with plastic wrap. Turn chicken occasionally.

The longer chicken marinates, the more strongly flavored it will become. If you are pressed for time, marinate the chicken for 2 hours at room temperature. For longer marination—up to 2 days—refrigerate.

When you are ready to cook the chicken, remove the pieces from the marinade and shake lightly to remove excess. Broil according to the Master Recipe, omitting salt and pepper and brushing chicken with additional marinade rather than melted butter. If the chicken has been marinated in a mixture containing sugar or honey, be especially watchful to be sure that it doesn't burn.

BROILED CHICKEN LIVERS ON SKEWERS

4 servings

❦ *Mashed or baked potatoes are very satisfying accompaniments; broccoli, green beans, peas, or oil-braised red peppers would do nicely as vegetable side dishes.*

PRELIMINARIES

1. Select a broiling pan covered with a slotted tray that is large enough to hold the skewers in one layer.
2. Adjust broiler rack so that livers will be about 2 inches below the heating element.
3. Preheat broiler—with broiling pan outside—for 5 minutes before cooking the livers.

1½ pounds chicken livers
½ cup dark soy sauce
¼ cup neutral vegetable oil
1 tablespoon honey or sugar
1 tablespoon strained fresh lemon juice
1 tablespoon medium-dry Sherry, preferably Manzanilla
½ teaspoon mashed, pressed, or very finely minced garlic
¼ teaspoon ground dried thyme
¼ teaspoon ground or very finely crushed bay leaf
½ teaspoon pepper, preferably freshly ground

SPECIAL EQUIPMENT: Eight 10- to 12-inch skewers or 16 shorter skewers

Turn livers into a colander and rinse briefly under cool water. One at a time, cut livers in half, removing any large strings or green spots, and transfer to a 3-quart mixing bowl. Add all remaining ingredients, stir to blend, and cover bowl with plastic wrap. Let livers marinate for 30 minutes to 1 hour at room temperature or for 2 to 24 hours in the refrigerator.

Divide livers into four or eight batches, depending on the number of skewers you are using. Thread each batch onto *two* parallel skewers; impaling them on two skewers instead of one allows you to turn the livers during cooking without their twisting or flipping about. (This works for other kinds of kabobs and brochettes, too.)

Arrange skewers on broiling tray, brush or dribble with some of the marinade, and place 2 inches beneath the preheated broiling element. Broil about 2 minutes, moistening once with reserved marinade. Turn skewers and broil about 2 minutes longer, spooning or brushing on all remaining marinade shortly before the livers are done. The livers are done when they have gone from dark red to bright pink inside and feel spongy-firm to the touch. Be careful not to overcook. (Do not expect livers to get brown and sizzling-looking on the outside—they won't.)

Either transfer skewers to a serving platter or dinner plates or unthread livers from skewers before serving. Moisten livers with some of the juices in the broiling pan and turn remaining juices into a gravy boat or bowl and pass separately.

MASTER RECIPE

Broiled Veal Chops

4 servings

❦ *Broiled veal chops are a real treat. Serve with a plain green vegetable and scalloped potatoes, or with broccoli purée or gratin, creamed spinach, or cucumbers in heavy cream plus baked potatoes.*

CHOOSING VEAL CHOPS FOR BROILING: Only rib or loin veal chops, cut about 1 inch thick, will do for broiling. Other cuts do not brown properly, and become leathery.

PRELIMINARIES

1. Select a broiling pan covered with a slotted tray that is large enough to hold the chops in one roomy layer.
2. Adjust broiler rack so that the top surface of the chops will be about 3 inches from the heating element.
3. Preheat broiler—with broiling pan *inside*—for a full 10 minutes before cooking the chops.

4 rib or loin veal chops about 1 inch thick (about 2½ pounds)
1 tablespoon neutral vegetable oil
3 tablespoons butter, melted
Salt and pepper, preferably freshly ground

Pat chops dry with paper toweling; trim off excess fat, leaving a layer about ¼ inch thick all around. Brush hot broiling tray with oil, lay on the chops, brush exposed surface with melted butter, and sprinkle with salt and pepper. Broil 4 minutes. Turn chops with tongs, brush with remaining butter, and sprinkle with more salt and pepper. Broil 3 to 5 minutes longer, or until the chops are lightly browned and have begun to exude juices into the broiling pan. To be sure the meat is done, you can test by cutting into one chop adjacent to the bone. The meat should look solid, rather than rare and squashy, but the juices should still be distinctly pink. Veal chops become hard and dry when overcooked. Serve immediately.

Variation: BROILED VEAL CHOPS WITH CHEESE, GARLIC, AND SAGE

4 servings

Broiled Veal Chops

ADD: 1 teaspoon mashed, pressed, or very finely minced garlic
1 teaspoon rubbed or ground sage
½ cup (2 ounces) freshly grated Parmesan cheese
2 to 3 tablespoons heavy cream

Two hours before cooking, rub veal chops with garlic and sage, arrange on a plate, cover tightly with plastic wrap, and set aside at room temperature. After 2 hours scrape off garlic and sage, dry meat, and broil according to the Master Recipe, undercooking the chops ever so slightly. Mix Parmesan cheese with just enough cream to form a thick paste. Spread paste thinly over the chops and return to the broiler for 30 to 60 seconds, or just until the cheese turns a very pale golden. Serve at once.

MASTER RECIPE

Broiled Beef Steaks (Including London Broil)

4 servings

For an informal dinner, choose a tossed salad with Roquefort dressing and a baked potato, or peas and mashed potatoes, as accompaniments. For a dressier presentation, consider serving the steaks with creamed spinach, a gratin of green beans or broccoli, broccoli purée, sautéed eggplant or mushrooms, broiled tomatoes, or scalloped potatoes. If a fine red wine is part of the meal plan, the steaks are best served with french-fried potatoes and béarnaise sauce; a salad and bread could follow.

CHOOSING BEEF STEAKS FOR BROILING: Prime beef, preferably aged, is better for broiling than choice, which tends to be dry, lacking in flavor, and distinctly tough. For the best results, choose steaks cut from the loin, that is, the part of the steer's back between the rib and the hip. These include T-bone steaks, consisting of a large section of top loin and, on the other side of the bone, a small piece of the choicer tenderloin; porterhouse steaks, similar to T-bone steaks but cut from further back on the loin and including a larger piece of tenderloin; and shell steaks, which are, in effect, T-bone or porterhouse steaks from which the tenderloin nugget has been removed. Sirloin steaks, which are cut from the hip, are less expensive than loin steaks but also bonier and tougher; however, they can be used as well.

PREPARING LONDON BROIL: To serve 4, choose either of the following: a beef chuck shoulder steak (also called honey cut), cut 1 to 1½ inches thick and weighing about 1½ pounds; or a beef top round steak, cut 1 to 1½ inches thick and weighing about 1½ pounds. Of the two cuts, my personal favorite is chuck shoulder.

If you wish, marinate the steak for several hours at room temperature in one of the mixtures suggested for chicken, page 386, then proceed according to the Master Recipe; broil 1¼-inch steaks 1 extra minute on each side, 1½-inch steaks 2 extra minutes on each side. To carve, slice thinly against the grain.

PRELIMINARIES

1. Select a broiling pan covered with a slotted tray that is large enough to hold the steaks in a single roomy layer.
2. Adjust broiler rack so that the top surface of the meat will be about 2 inches from the heating element.
3. Preheat broiler—with broiling pan *inside*—for a full 10 minutes before cooking the steaks.

2 T-bone, porterhouse, or sirloin steaks, each about 1 inch thick and weighing 1½ to 2 pounds, *or* 4 shell loin steaks, each about 1 inch thick and weighing 12 to 16 ounces
2 tablespoons neutral vegetable oil or olive oil
Salt and pepper, preferably freshly ground

SPECIAL EQUIPMENT: A vest-pocket instant-reading meat thermometer (optional but convenient)

Dry steaks as thoroughly as possible with paper toweling; trim off excess fat, leaving a layer about ½ inch thick all around. Brush hot broiling tray with oil, lay on the steaks, and broil for 3 minutes *exactly.* Sprinkle cooked side liberally with salt and pepper, turn meat with tongs, and broil about 3 minutes longer for very rare, 4 minutes for rare, and 5 minutes for medium rare, seasoning with salt and pepper when done. An instant-reading meat thermometer is your most reliable guide to doneness: Inserted *sideways* at least 2 inches into the steak, it will read 115°F when the meat is very rare, 120°F when rare, and 125°F to 130°F when medium rare. Otherwise, determine doneness by cutting into a steak near the bone. Remove steaks to platter, preferably warmed, and let rest 1 minute before serving.

BROILED LAMB CHOPS

4 servings

❦ *My favorite accompaniments for broiled lamb chops are green beans, broiled tomatoes or sautéed cherry tomatoes, and scalloped potatoes. Other possibilities include sautéed eggplant, broccoli purée, cucumbers or green beans in heavy cream, and puréed winter squash.*

CHOOSING LAMB CHOPS FOR BROILING: The best choices here are rib or loin chops cut about 1 inch thick. Though tougher and less flavorful, shoulder or arm chops may also be broiled.

Preliminaries

1. Select a broiling pan covered with a slotted tray that is large enough to hold the chops in a single roomy layer.
2. Adjust broiler rack so that the top surface of the chops will be about 2 inches from the heating element.
3. Preheat broiler—with broiling pan *inside*—for a full 10 minutes before cooking the chops.

8 lamb loin chops or 12 lamb rib chops cut about 1 inch thick *or* 8 lamb shoulder or arm chops cut about ½ inch thick (about 2½ pounds altogether)
2 tablespoons neutral vegetable oil or olive oil
Salt and pepper, preferably freshly ground

Dry chops with paper toweling, and trim off excess fat, leaving a layer about ¼ inch all around. Brush hot broiling tray with oil and lay on the chops. Lamb chops are best when broiled to the beginning of the medium-rare stage (125°F); the meat should be very red and juicy but not raw-looking. Broil 1-inch rib and loin chops about 3 minutes per side, ½-inch shoulder or arm chops about 2 minutes per side. The meat is done when it feels slightly resistant, rather than soft, when pressed firmly with a finger. Serve at once, preferably on heated platter or plates.

SAUTÉED POULTRY and MEAT

With the introduction to American kitchens of classic French cooking and, more recently, of the so-called nouvelle cuisine, sautéing has become second nature to many American cooks.

The procedure is exceedingly simple. Poultry or meat—anything from chicken to veal scallops to pork chops to beef or lamb steaks to beef liver—is sautéed on all sides in hot fat until done. The object is to give the meat a nice brown exterior while keeping it juicy and tender within. Some types of poultry or meat are dusted with flour prior to sautéing, some are given a preliminary browning over high heat, some are cooked in a covered skillet, and each, of course, requires a somewhat different cooking time. But the basic procedure is similar for all sautés.

Once the poultry or meat is done, you can either serve it plain or with a "deglazing" sauce. This is made by adding a flavorful liquid—typically stock and/or wine—to the sautéing skillet to dissolve (or "deglaze") the delicious browned bits of coagulated poultry or meat juices left in the bottom. The liquid is boiled down until there is just an intensely flavored spoonful or two of lightly thickened sauce for each serving of poultry or meat. Cream may also be added, as well as such flavorings as capers or mustard. Off heat, bits of butter are swirled in to give the sauce body, richness, and finesse. No matter what particular deglazing sauce you decide to make, the fundamental procedure is the same and does not take longer than three or four minutes to accomplish.

SKILLET NOTES: Foods brown better in a bare-metal skillet than in a ceramic or enamel-lined skillet. Nonstick skillets do not allow foods to brown at all and so are unacceptable for sautéing. Avoid also light-bottomed, flimsy skillets, which cause foods to burn.

Since foods must be sautéed in a single layer, you need a wide skillet, preferably one that measures 12 inches across the bottom. If you do not have such a large skillet, use two smaller skillets or, if you are sautéing a food that cooks quickly, such as veal or turkey scallops, ham steaks, or slices of calves' liver, sauté the food in two or more batches, keeping successive batches warm in a 120°F oven as they are done.

If you plan to make a deglazing sauce that includes an acidic liquid such as wine, lemon juice, or vinegar, it is crucial that you use a skillet made of or lined with a material that does not react with the acid. Skillets made of stainless steel or lined with stainless steel, enamel, or tin are all nonreacting. But do not use an unlined cast iron or aluminum skillet. Iron and aluminum will react chemically with acidic ingredients and your sauce will pick up a strong metallic taste.

MASTER RECIPE

Sautéed Chicken (with Lemon)

4 servings

❦ *Plain sautéed chicken can be served with scalloped or mashed potatoes and a green vegetable or, for a light, informal meal, simply with a tossed salad. When accompanied by the optional sauces outlined in Step 2 of this recipe and in the variations, the chicken is best accompanied with a green vegetable and rice.*

CHOOSING CHICKEN FOR SAUTÉING: Smallish chicken parts work best here. If you are cutting the parts yourself, choose either one 3½-pound chicken or, better, two 2-pound chickens. The thighs and drumsticks should be separated at the joint and the breast split in half lengthwise.

Step 1: Sautéing the Chicken

3½ to 4 pounds frying-chicken parts
Salt and pepper, preferably freshly ground
2 to 3 tablespoons *each* butter and neutral vegetable oil

Set oven thermostat at 120°F (or lowest possible temperature) and place a heat-proof serving platter in the oven. Select a heavy-bottomed 12-inch skillet or two 9- to 10-inch skillets (see Skillet Notes, page 394).

Rinse chicken pieces under tepid water and pat very dry with paper towels. Sprinkle lightly with salt and pepper. Over moderately high flame, heat 2 tablespoons *each* butter and oil in skillet. When foam has subsided, indicating that the fat is hot enough, add as many of the chicken pieces to the skillet as will fit comfortably. Regulating heat so that fat remains very hot but does not burn, brown chicken pieces on all sides. Remove browned chicken pieces to a plate and proceed to brown remaining chicken in the same manner, adding more fat if necessary. When all chicken has been browned, return dark meat (drumsticks and thighs) to the skillet, cover, and cook for 8 minutes, keeping the flame just hot enough to maintain chicken at a quiet sizzle. Turn thighs and drumsticks and bury the white meat among the pieces of dark meat. Cover the skillet and continue to cook chicken about 15 minutes longer, or until the juices run clear when the thick parts of the pieces are pierced deeply with a fork; turn chicken once during the last 15 minutes of cooking. Transfer cooked chicken to warmed serving platter and either serve at once or place in warm oven and proceed to make a deglazing sauce.

Step 2: Preparing Lemon Deglazing Sauce (Optional)

1 cup Chicken Stock, page 26, or canned broth
¼ cup strained fresh lemon juice
2 tablespoons minced fresh parsley
Pepper, preferably freshly ground

Spoon most of the fat out of the sautéing skillet, taking care not to discard any of the juices. Set skillet over moderately high heat and pour in the stock or broth. Scraping up the browned particles on the bottom of the skillet with a wooden spoon or spatula, boil the mixture down until reduced by half. Add the lemon juice and continue to boil until you have about ½ cup of very lightly thickened sauce. Remove from heat and stir in the parsley. Taste, adding more lemon juice if necessary; the sauce should have a pronounced lemony flavor. Spoon the sauce evenly over the chicken and sprinkle to taste with pepper. Serve immediately.

Variation: SAUTÉED CHICKEN WITH LEMON AND GARLIC

4 servings

Sautéed Chicken (with Lemon)
ADD: 1½ tablespoons mashed, pressed, or very finely minced garlic

Proceed according to the Master Recipe, but add garlic to the skillet at the beginning of Step 2, after removing most of the fat. Set skillet over low heat and cook the garlic, stirring, for about 1 minute, making sure that it does not brown. Raise heat to moderately high, immediately add stock or broth, and continue with recipe.

Variation: SAUTÉED CHICKEN WITH VINEGAR

4 servings

Sautéed Chicken (with Lemon)
SUBSTITUTE: ¼ cup wine vinegar for lemon juice

Proceed according to the Master Recipe, substituting vinegar for lemon juice in preparing the sauce in Step 2.

Variation: SAUTÉED CHICKEN WITH WHITE WINE

4 servings

Sautéed Chicken (with Lemon)
SUBSTITUTE: ⅓ cup dry white wine or dry vermouth for lemon juice
ADD: 3 to 4 tablespoons soft butter, preferably unsalted, cut into pieces

Proceed according to the Master Recipe, substituting wine for lemon juice and boiling the sauce down to just ¼ cup (Step 2). When the sauce has reduced and thickened, remove skillet from heat, add the butter, and swirl the skillet by the handle until the butter has melted into the sauce, thickening it lightly. Do not stir, or you may cause the sauce to separate. Swirl in parsley. Pour the sauce over chicken and serve.

MASTER RECIPE

Sautéed Chicken Breast Cutlets (with White Wine and Herbs)

4 servings

Sautéed chicken breast cutlets can be served plain, with lemon wedges on the side, or with the white wine deglazing sauce outlined in Step 2 of this recipe. In either case, they are particularly good when accompanied by a green vegetable cooked in heavy cream—green beans, broccoli, or spinach, for example—and rice.

CHOOSING CHICKEN BREAST CUTLETS: Chicken breast cutlets are boneless, skinless halves of chicken breasts. They are sold ready-cut at most supermarkets, but you can save yourself some money by preparing them yourself. Instructions are on page 334.

STEP 1: SAUTÉING THE CUTLETS

8 small-medium chicken breast cutlets (1½ to 2 pounds)
Salt and pepper, preferably freshly ground
½ cup all-purpose flour
2 to 4 tablespoons *each* butter and neutral vegetable oil

Set oven thermostat at 120°F (or lowest possible temperature) and place a heat-proof serving platter in the oven. Select either a heavy-bottomed 12-inch skillet or two 9- to 10-inch skillets (see Skillet Notes, page 394).

Pat chicken dry with paper toweling. Sprinkle cutlets lightly with salt and pepper and dredge in flour, shaking off excess. Over moderately high flame, heat 2 tablespoons *each* of the butter and oil in each skillet you are using. When foam has subsided, indicating that the fat is hot enough, add cutlets to the skillet in one uncrowded layer. Cook, uncovered, over moderate heat for 3 to 4 minutes on each side, or until cutlets feel firm when pressed with a finger. Transfer to warmed serving platter and either serve at once or place in warm oven and proceed to prepare a deglazing sauce.

Step 2: Preparing a White Wine Deglazing Sauce (Optional)

2 tablespoons minced shallots or scallions (white part only)
⅓ cup dry white wine or dry vermouth
⅔ cup Chicken Stock, page 26, or canned broth
3 to 4 tablespoons soft butter, preferably unsalted, cut into pieces
Fresh lemon juice, if necessary
2 tablespoons minced fresh parsley or a mixture of parsley and fresh tarragon (optional)

Spoon all but 2 tablespoons of fat out of the skillet, taking care not to discard any of the juices. Over low heat, sauté shallots or scallion in the fat for 1 minute, or until wilted, then raise heat to high and pour in wine. Scraping up the browned particles on the bottom of the skillet with a wooden spoon or spatula, boil down the wine until it has reduced to just a couple of tablespoons. Pour stock or broth into skillet and bring to a rapid boil, stirring constantly. Reduce liquid to about ⅓ cup of syrupy sauce. Add to the sauce any juices that have accumulated on the serving platter around the chicken and again reduce sauce by boiling if necessary. Remove skillet from heat and strew the pieces of butter over the sauce. Swirl skillet by the handle until the butter melts into the sauce, thickening it lightly. Do not stir, or you may cause sauce to separate. Taste for seasoning and gently swirl in drops of lemon juice if necessary. Spoon the sauce over the chicken and sprinkle herbs on top. Serve immediately.

Variation: BREADED SAUTÉED CHICKEN CUTLETS (WITH WHITE WINE SAUCE)

4 servings

❦ *Breaded sautéed chicken cutlets are typically served with lemon wedges, béarnaise sauce, or a cream sauce, though a deglazing sauce is nice too. A tossed green salad is a good accompaniment. For tips on how to apply breading see the deep-frying chapter, pages 59–66.*

Sautéed Chicken Breast Cutlets (with White Wine Sauce)

ADD: 2 large eggs beaten well with 1 tablespoon neutral vegetable oil
1½ to 2 cups Fine Fresh Bread Crumbs (see page 60)

After dredging the chicken in flour as indicated in the Master Recipe, dip in beaten eggs, then coat with crumbs. Place chicken on a rack and let stand 15 minutes at room temperature to set the coating. Sauté according to Step 1 of the Master Recipe. If you prepare the deglazing sauce in Step 2, remove any large pieces of breading that may be stuck to the skillet before proceeding.

Variation: SAUTÉED CHICKEN BREASTS WITH CREAM AND PORT

4 servings

❦ *Serve this sumptuous, classic dish with rice, a green vegetable, and, as a special touch, sautéed mushrooms.*

Sautéed Chicken Breast Cutlets (with White Wine Sauce)

SUBSTITUTE: ⅓ cup sweet Port (or Madeira or cream Sherry) for white wine
ADD: ¾ cup heavy cream
OMIT: Butter in Step 2

Sauté chicken according to Step 1 of the Master Recipe. In Step 2, substitute Port for white wine, boil down to ½ cup and add the cream along with the accumulated poultry juices. Continue to boil down until reduced to ¾ cup of sauce thick enough to coat a spoon. Omit the butter, and correct the seasoning.

MASTER RECIPE

Sherried Sautéed Chicken Livers

4 servings

❦ *Sautéed chicken livers, which are always served in a sauce, are particularly good with boiled or mashed potatoes and green beans or peas. The important thing to remember here is not to overcook the livers; they should be firm but still quite pink within.*

STEP 1: SAUTÉING THE CHICKEN LIVERS

1½ pounds chicken livers
Salt and pepper, preferably freshly ground
2 to 4 tablespoons *each* butter and neutral vegetable oil

Set oven thermostat at 120°F (or lowest possible temperature) and place a heat-proof serving platter in the oven. Select a heavy-bottomed 10- to 12-inch skillet made of or lined with a noncorroding material.

Cut livers in half and remove any strings or bits of green bile. Turn livers into a colander and rinse under cool water; pat as dry as possible with paper toweling. Heat 2 tablespoons *each* butter and oil in the skillet over moderately high flame. When butter foam has subsided, indicating that the fat is hot enough, add as many pieces of liver as will fit in one somewhat sparse layer. Keeping the skillet as hot as possible without causing fat to burn, gently stir-fry the livers for about 2 minutes, or until they have darkened uniformly on the outside and stiffened into a firm shape; they should remain moist and bright pink inside. Immediately remove livers to warmed serving platter with a slotted spoon, cover with foil, and place in oven. Adding more butter and oil to the skillet if necessary, sauté remaining livers in the same manner, then proceed to make the deglazing sauce.

Step 2: Preparing the Deglazing Sauce

2 tablespoons minced shallots or scallions (white part only)
1/4 cup medium-dry Sherry, preferably Manzanilla
2/3 cup Beef Stock, page 24, or canned broth
3 to 4 tablespoons soft butter, preferably unsalted, cut into pieces
Lemon juice, if necessary
2 tablespoons minced fresh parsley

Spoon all but 2 tablespoons of fat out of the sautéing skillet, taking care not to discard any of the juices. Over low heat, sauté shallots or scallions in the fat for 1 minute, or until wilted. Raise heat to high and pour in Sherry. Scraping up the browned particles on the bottom of the skillet with a wooden spoon or spatula, boil until the Sherry is reduced by half. Pour stock or broth into skillet and bring to a rapid boil, stirring constantly. Reduce liquid to about 1/4 cup sauce. Add to the sauce any juices that have accumulated on the serving platter around the livers and again reduce sauce by boiling, if necessary. Remove skillet from heat and strew bits of butter over the sauce. Swirl skillet by the handle until the butter melts into the sauce, thickening it lightly. Do not stir, or you may cause sauce to separate. Taste for seasoning and gently swirl in drops of lemon juice if needed. Spoon sauce over livers and sprinkle with herbs. Serve at once.

Variation: SAUTÉED CHICKEN LIVERS WITH WHITE WINE AND MUSTARD

4 servings

Sherried Sautéed Chicken Livers

SUBSTITUTE: 1/3 cup dry white wine or dry vermouth for Sherry
ADD: 1 tablespoon Dijon mustard

Sauté livers according to Step 1 of the Master Recipe. In preparing the deglazing sauce, substitute wine for Sherry and, after the sauce has been reduced, beat in the mustard, then immediately remove skillet from the heat. Swirl in butter and correct seasoning.

MASTER RECIPE

Sautéed Veal Scallops or Turkey Breast Scallops (with Lemon-Butter Sauce)

4 servings

❦ *Sautéed veal and turkey breast scallops, which taste so similar to each other as to be nearly indistinguishable, can be served plain or with a sauce. Pass lemon wedges and accompany with a tossed salad and crusty bread if you are serving them plain. Accompany sauced scallops with a green vegetable and rice.*

CHOOSING VEAL SCALLOPS AND TURKEY BREAST SCALLOPS FOR SAUTÉING: Veal scallops are thin slices of veal leg. The best ones are cut from a single muscle but scallops with muscle separations will certainly do if they are all you can find. They should be cut about 1/8 inch thick, but slightly thicker ones can be used if they are flattened with a mallet before cooking. Turkey breast scallops are not generally sold ready-cut at supermarkets or butcher shops and must be prepared at home. Buy raw turkey breast cutlets (the thicker the better) or whole turkey breast. Place in the freezer until icy-firm, then cut in the widest and longest slices possible, making the scallops about 1/8 inch thick.

STEP 1: SAUTÉING THE SCALLOPS

1½ pounds veal scallops or turkey breast scallops
Salt and pepper, preferably freshly ground
½ cup all-purpose flour
2 to 5 tablespoons *each* butter and neutral vegetable oil or olive oil

Before proceeding, set oven at 150°F and place an oven-proof serving platter inside. Select a heavy-bottomed 12-inch skillet or 2 smaller skillets (see Skillet Notes, page 394).

Pound scallops gently with the edge of a meat mallet or dinner plate to help prevent shrinking and curling. Dry with paper toweling, sprinkle lightly with salt and pepper, and dredge in flour, shaking off excess. Heat over moderately high flame 1½ tablespoons *each* butter and oil in each skillet you are using. When butter foam has subsided, indicating that the fat is hot enough, add as many scallops as will fit in one layer. Keeping flame as hot as possible without allowing the fat to burn, sauté scallops, uncovered, 1½ to 2 minutes per side, or until lightly browned and firm to the touch. Remove scallops as they are cooked to warmed serving platter and place in oven. Cook remaining scallops in the same manner, adding more butter and oil to the skillet if necessary. Serve at once or proceed to make a deglazing sauce.

STEP 2: PREPARING A LEMON-BUTTER DEGLAZING SAUCE (OPTIONAL)

1 cup Chicken Stock, page 26, or canned broth
3 tablespoons strained fresh lemon juice
3 to 4 tablespoons soft butter, preferably unsalted, cut into pieces
Pepper, preferably freshly ground, if needed

Spoon most of the fat out of the sautéing skillet, taking care not to discard any of the juices. Set skillet over moderately high heat and pour in stock or broth. Scraping up the browned particles on the bottom of the skillet with a wooden spoon or spatula, boil the mixture down until reduced by half. Add the lemon juice and any juices that may have accumulated around the scallops and continue to boil until you have about ⅓ cup sauce. Remove from heat and scatter the pieces of butter over the sauce. Swirl skillet by the handle until the butter melts into the sauce, thickening it lightly. Do not stir, or you may cause sauce to separate. Taste for seasoning and gently swirl in pepper if needed. Pour sauce over scallops and serve immediately.

Variation: SAUTEED VEAL SCALLOPS OR TURKEY BREAST SCALLOPS WITH LEMON, GARLIC, AND CAPERS

4 servings

Sautéed Veal Scallops or Turkey Breast Scallops (with Lemon-butter Sauce)

ADD: 2 teaspoons mashed, pressed, or very finely minced garlic
2 tablespoons well-drained small capers
1 to 2 tablespoons minced fresh parsley (optional)

Sauté scallops as indicated in Step 1 of the Master Recipe. In Step 2, reserve a little of the sautéing fat in the skillet, add the garlic, and stir over low heat for about 1 minute, or until garlic is softened but not at all browned. Proceed according to the Master Recipe, adding the capers just before removing the sauce from heat and swirling in the butter; sprinkle sauced scallops with parsley if you wish.

Variation: SAUTÉED VEAL SCALLOPS OR TURKEY BREAST SCALLOPS WITH MARSALA

4 servings

❦ *Veal (or turkey) and marsala, a sweet Italian wine, is a classic combination of flavors. Good accompaniments here are creamed spinach, sautéed mushrooms, and rice.*

Sautéed Veal Scallops or Turkey Breast Scallops (with Lemon-butter Sauce)

SUBSTITUTE: ⅓ cup sweet Marsala for lemon juice

Proceed according to the Master Recipe, substituting marsala for lemon juice in Step 2. If the sauce seems too sweet after the butter is added, swirl in a few drops of lemon juice.

Variation: BREADED SAUTÉED VEAL SCALLOPS OR TURKEY BREAST SCALLOPS (WITH LEMON-BUTTER SAUCE)

4 servings

❦ *Breaded sautéed veal or turkey breast scallops can be served with a deglazing sauce, but it is more usual to serve them with lemon wedges or tomato sauce. A tossed green salad, perhaps one containing chicory or dandelion greens, a few chopped anchovies, and a sprinkling of Parmesan cheese, makes a good accompaniment.*

Tips on applying breading appear in the deep-frying chapter, pages 59–66.

Sautéed Veal Scallops or Turkey Breast Scallops (with Lemon-butter Sauce)

ADD: 2 large eggs beaten well with 1 tablespoon neutral vegetable oil or olive oil
2 cups Fine Fresh Bread Crumbs (see page 60)

After dredging the scallops in flour as directed in the Master Recipe, dip in beaten eggs, then coat with crumbs. Place scallops on a rack and let stand 15 minutes at room temperature to set the coating. Sauté according to Step 1 of the Master Recipe, but cook the scallops about 3 minutes per side to brown the coating. If you prepare a deglazing sauce, remove any large pieces of breading that may be stuck to the skillet before proceeding.

MASTER RECIPE

Sautéed Veal Chops (with White Wine and Cream)

4 servings

❦ *Sautéeing is a particularly good cooking method for veal chops, as it keeps the meat moist. If you serve the chops without a sauce, accompany them with a vegetable cooked in heavy cream—green beans, broccoli, cucumbers, or spinach would be good—and scalloped or mashed potatoes. Sauced veal chops are best with a plain green vegetable and rice.*

Choosing Veal Chops for Sautéing: Veal loin chops are the first choice here. Rib chops can also be used, but they are rather large and thus are difficult to fit into a skillet. Veal loin and rib chops must usually be bought at a butcher shop, and they will cost you plenty.

Step 1: Sautéing the Veal Chops

4 veal loin chops cut about 1 inch thick or 4 veal rib chops cut about 3/4 inch thick (about 2 1/2 pounds)
Salt and pepper, preferably freshly ground
1 1/2 to 3 tablespoons *each* butter and neutral vegetable oil

Set oven thermostat at 150°F and place a heat-proof serving platter in oven. Select a heavy-bottomed 12-inch skillet or 2 smaller skillets (see Skillet Notes, page 394).

Trim excess fat from around circumference of chops, leaving a layer about 1/4 inch thick. Dry chops well with paper toweling and sprinkle lightly with salt and pepper. Heat 1 1/2 tablespoons *each* butter and oil over moderately high flame in each skillet you're using. When butter foam has subsided, indicating that the fat is hot enough, add chops and sauté uncovered for about 5 minutes per side over lively—but not scorching—heat. The chops are done when pale pink juices appear on the top surface of the meat as second side is being cooked. Don't overcook; chops should remain slightly pink inside. Remove cooked veal chops to warmed serving platter. Either serve at once or place in oven and proceed to prepare a deglazing sauce.

STEP 2: PREPARING THE WINE AND CREAM DEGLAZING SAUCE (OPTIONAL)

2 tablespoons minced shallots or scallions (white part only)
1/4 cup dry white wine
1/2 cup Veal Stock, page 27, or Chicken Stock, page 26, or canned broth
1 cup heavy cream
Salt and pepper, preferably white and freshly ground
Fresh lemon juice and/or Sherry
1 to 2 tablespoons minced fresh parsley (optional)

Spoon all but 2 tablespoons of fat out of the sautéing skillet, taking care not to discard any of the juices. Over low heat, sauté the shallots or scallions in the fat for 1 minute, or until wilted. Raise heat to high and pour in wine and stock or broth. Scraping up the browned particles on the bottom of the skillet with a wooden spoon or spatula, boil the mixture down to a few tablespoons of syrupy glaze. Add the cream and again boil down, reducing the sauce to about 3/4 cup. Pour in any juices that may have accumulated in the serving platter around the veal and again reduce by boiling if necessary. The sauce should be thick enough to coat a spoon. Remove from heat and season to taste with salt, pepper, and drops of lemon juice and/or Sherry. Spoon some of the sauce over each chop and, if you wish, sprinkle with parsley. Serve immediately.

Variation: SAUTÉED VEAL CHOPS WITH MADEIRA AND CREAM

4 servings

Sautéed Veal Chops (with White Wine and Cream)
SUBSTITUTE: 1/4 cup dry (Sercial) Madeira for white wine

Proceed according to the Master Recipe, substituting Madeira for white wine in Step 2.

Variation: SAUTÉED VEAL CHOPS WITH WILD MUSHROOMS

4 servings

❦ *This is a sumptuous treat. Serve with spinach or asparagus and rice.*

Sautéed Veal Chops (with White Wine and Cream)

ADD: 4 to 8 ounces cèpes (porcini mushrooms), chanterelles, morels, or other wild mushrooms

Clean the mushrooms, trim off any withered or tough pieces, and cut into ½-inch strips. Set aside. Sauté the veal chops as indicated in Step 1 of the Master Recipe. In Step 2, reserve the sautéing fat and set skillet over moderately high heat. When fat begins to sizzle, add the mushrooms and stir-fry for 2 to 5 minutes, or until cooked through, lowering the heat a bit if the skillet starts to smoke. Remove mushrooms from skillet with slotted spoon and set aside. Add shallots or scallions to skillet and prepare sauce as indicated in the Master Recipe. When the cream has reduced and thickened, return mushrooms and their juices to skillet and simmer slowly for 1 to 2 minutes. Correct the seasoning and spoon sauce over chops. Sprinkle with parsley and serve immediately.

MASTER RECIPE

Sautéed Pork Chops (with Mustard, Capers, and Cream)

4 servings

❦ *Sautéing is, in my view, the cooking method of choice for pork chops. The trick is to sauté the pork rather slowly in a covered skillet, being careful not to overcook it. This way the meat will be juicy and tender. To further ensure tenderness, the pork can be steeped in salt for several hours before cooking. See below.*

Plain pork chops make a delicious, homey meal; when sauced, pork chops assume an elegance not usually associated with them. Favorite accompaniments for plain pork chops include apple sauce, scalloped or mashed potatoes, puréed winter squash, steamed green or braised red cabbage, and green beans. Serve sauced pork chops with a plain green vegetable and rice.

CHOOSING PORK CHOPS FOR SAUTÉING: For an especially elegant dish, choose 4 rib or loin chops cut 1 inch thick. For everyday fare, 6 to 8 thinner chops—½ to ¾ inch thick—will do. These can be rib or loin or a less expensive blade or sirloin cut.

STEP 1: SAUTÉING THE PORK CHOPS

4 thick or 6 to 8 thin pork chops (about 2½ pounds)
Salt and pepper, preferably freshly ground
1½ to 4½ tablespoons *each* butter and neutral vegetable oil

Although you may omit the following step in the interest of time, you will find that pork chops are markedly more tender when they are steeped in salt before cooking. If the meat looks wet, dab it lightly with paper toweling, then rub on both sides with salt, using about 2 teaspoons altogether. Arrange in an overlapping layer on a plate, cover securely with plastic wrap, and let stand at room temperature for 2 to 3 hours or in the refrigerator for 4 to 6 hours. Before proceeding to cook the chops, scrape as much of the salt as you can off the meat with a knife.

Set oven thermostat at 150°F and place a heat-proof serving platter in the oven. To prepare 4 thick chops you will need a heavy, lidded 12-inch skillet or 2 smaller skillets; to prepare 6 to 8 thin chops, you will likely need two 10- to 12-inch skillets or 3 smaller skillets. (See Skillet Notes, page 394.)

Trim excess fat from around circumference of the chops, leaving a layer about ¼ inch thick all around. Dry well with paper toweling, and sprinkle lightly with salt and pepper (season only with pepper if chops stood in salt as suggested above). Heat over moderately high flame 1½ tablespoons *each* butter and oil in each skillet you are using. When butter foam has subsided, indicating that the fat is hot enough, add meat and brown lightly about 1 minute on each side, with skillet(s) uncovered; regulate heat so that the fat remains hot but does not burn. Turn heat down to low, cover skillet(s) tightly, and cook 6 minutes *on each side per inch of thickness*—that is, about 6 minutes total for ½-inch chops, 9 minutes total for ¾-inch chops, and 12 minutes total for 1-inch chops. Throughout cooking, it is imperative that the flame be kept just high enough to maintain the pork at a quiet sizzle; if cooked too quickly the meat will toughen. The pork is done when pale pink juices appear on the top surface of the meat as the second side is being cooked. To double-check for doneness, make a cut between flesh and bone: the meat should be solid and ivory-colored but tinged with pink juices. Do not overcook the pork or you will ruin it. Transfer the chops to warmed serving platter and either serve at once or place in oven and proceed to prepare a deglazing sauce.

STEP 2: PREPARING THE CREAM DEGLAZING SAUCE (OPTIONAL)

2 tablespoons minced shallots or scallions (white part only)
1/4 cup dry white wine
1/2 cup Chicken Stock, page 26, or canned broth
1 cup heavy cream
2 tablespoons well-drained small capers
2 tablespoons Dijon mustard
Salt, pepper, and fresh lemon juice, if needed

Spoon all but 2 tablespoons of fat out of the sautéing skillet, taking care not to discard any of the juices. Over low heat, sauté the shallots or scallions in the fat for 1 minute, or until wilted. Raise heat to high and pour in wine and stock or broth. Scraping up the browned particles on the bottom of the skillet with a wooden spoon or spatula, boil the mixture down to a few tablespoons of syrupy glaze. Add the cream and again boil down, reducing the sauce to about 3/4 cup. Add to the sauce any juices that have accumulated on the serving platter around the pork and again reduce by boiling, if necessary. The sauce should be thick enough to coat a spoon. Beat in the capers and mustard, then remove from heat. Season as necessary with salt, pepper, and drops of lemon juice. Spoon sauce over the chops and serve at once.

Variation: SAUTÉED PORK CHOPS WITH APPLEJACK AND CREAM

4 servings

❦ *Serve this perhaps with cabbage and a purée of winter squash.*

Sautéed Pork Chops (with Mustard, Capers, and Cream)
SUBSTITUTE: 1/3 cup applejack or calvados for white wine
OMIT: Capers
Mustard

Proceed according to the Master Recipe, substituting applejack for white wine and omitting capers and mustard when making the sauce in Step 2.

Variation: SAUTÉED PORK CHOPS WITH TOMATOES AND FRESH HERBS

4 servings

❦ *This piquant, fresh-tasting sauce takes pork chops in a rather unaccustomed but welcome direction. Serve this with green beans or peas and rice.*

Sautéed Pork Chops (with Mustard, Capers, and Cream)

ADD: ½ cup peeled, seeded, diced tomatoes, fresh or canned (see page 607)

SUBSTITUTE: 2 tablespoons minced fresh parsley or basil *or* 1 tablespoon minced fresh tarragon, thyme, or rosemary for capers and mustard

Sauté pork chops according to Step 1 of the Master Recipe. In Step 2, add the tomatoes to the skillet after you have sautéed the shallots or scallions. Raise heat to moderate and cook, stirring, for several minutes, or until the juice has evaporated. Proceed from there according to the recipe, but omit capers and mustard and instead add fresh herbs.

MASTER RECIPE

Sautéed Ham Steaks (with Apples and Cream)

4 servings

❦ *Ham steaks are especially delicious when served with the apple and cream sauce suggested in this recipe or one of the other sauces outlined in the variations. However, they are also good plain.*

Good accompaniments include broccoli, cabbage, spinach, creamed corn, puréed winter squash, sweet potatoes, mashed or scalloped potatoes, baked beans, biscuits, and corn bread.

CHOOSING HAM STEAKS FOR SAUTÉING: Use slices of tenderized (or "ready-to-eat") ham here. You can buy these ready-cut at most supermarkets, or you can cut them yourself from a whole ham or from the leftovers of a baked ham. If possible, select 4 small end-cut steaks, each of which will make an attractive single serving, rather than 2 large center-cut steaks, which will have to be divided in half.

It is also possible to sauté slices of canned ham, though these will not have much taste.

Step 1: Sautéing the Ham Steaks

2 large or 4 small ham steaks between 3/8 and 1/2 inch thick (about 2 1/2 pounds altogether)
Pepper, preferably freshly ground
1 to 2 tablespoons *each* butter and neutral vegetable oil

Before proceeding, set oven at 150°F and place an ovenproof serving platter inside. Select a heavy-bottomed skillet large enough to hold half the ham steaks at a time. If you plan to make a deglazing sauce (Step 2), the skillet must be made of or lined with a noncorroding material.

Trim excess fat from around circumference of ham steaks, leaving a layer about 1/4 inch thick all around. Blot steaks with paper toweling and season lightly with pepper. Heat 1 tablespoon *each* of butter and oil in the skillet until the butter stops foaming, indicating that the fat is hot enough. Lay a single layer of ham steaks in the skillet and, over fairly lively heat, sauté steaks uncovered for 2 to 4 minutes on each side, or until lightly browned and warmed through. Remove steaks as they are cooked to the warmed serving platter and place in oven; cook remaining ham in the same manner, adding more butter and oil to skillet if necessary. Serve at once or proceed to make a deglazing sauce.

Step 2: Preparing the Apple and Cream Deglazing Sauce (Optional)

2 medium tart green apples, preferably Granny Smiths
1/2 cup unsweetened apple juice
1 cup heavy cream
White pepper, preferably freshly ground, and fresh lemon juice, if needed

Peel and core the apples, then cut into rings about 3/8 inch thick. Set sautéing skillet over moderately high heat, bringing the fat and juices to a sizzle, then add the apple rings in a single close layer (leave out a ring or two if they won't all fit). Sauté the apples for 2 to 3 minutes on each side, or until lightly browned and just tender enough to be pierced easily with a fork. Arrange apple slices in an attractive manner over the ham, then return to the warm oven. Pour apple juice into skillet and boil it down, over high heat, to a few tablespoons, scraping the bottom of the skillet with a wooden spoon or spatula to get up the browned particles. Add the cream and boil down until the sauce is reduced to about ⅔ cup and is just thick enough to coat a spoon lightly. Season as necessary with white pepper and drops of lemon juice, then spoon over the ham and apples and serve at once.

Variation: SAUTÉED HAM STEAKS WITH APPLES, CURRY, AND CREAM

4 servings

❦ *Serve this with a green vegetable and rice.*

Sautéed Ham Steaks (with Apples and Cream)
ADD: 1 teaspoon mild curry powder or ¾ teaspoon hot (Madras) curry powder

Proceed according to the Master Recipe, adding the curry powder to the skillet after removing the apples and stirring it over low heat for 2 minutes before adding the apple juice.

Variation: SAUTÉED HAM STEAKS WITH PINEAPPLE

4 servings

❦ *This is an especially light and fresh way of combining the highly compatible flavors of ham and pineapple. Accompany with broccoli and puréed winter squash or mashed sweet potatoes.*

Sautéed Ham Steaks (with Apples and Cream), page 409, prepared through Step 1
4 to 8 pineapple rings, fresh or unsweetened canned
¾ cup unsweetened pineapple juice (all or part may be canning juice)

Set the sautéing skillet over moderately high heat, bringing the fat and juices to a sizzle, then add as many of the pineapple rings as will fit in a single close layer. Sauté canned pineapple rings for 1 to 2 minutes on each side, or until very lightly browned, fresh rings 2 to 3 minutes per side, or until lightly browned and softened. Arrange pineapple over the ham in an attractive manner, then return to warm oven; sauté remaining pineapple, if any, in the same way. Pour pineapple juice into skillet and bring to a rapid boil over high heat, scraping up the browned particles on the bottom of the skillet with a wooden spoon or spatula. Cook the juice down until it has reduced to about ⅓ cup of very lightly thickened sauce, then pour over the ham and pineapple and serve at once.

MASTER RECIPE

Sautéed Beef Steaks (with Cognac and Parsley)

4 servings

For an informal meal, accompany the steaks, sauced or not, with a green or tomato salad plus baked potatoes or rolls. For a fancier presentation, serve the steaks with creamed spinach, broccoli purée, sautéed mushrooms, broiled tomatoes, or sautéed cherry tomatoes, plus scalloped, mashed, or french-fried potatoes.

CHOOSING BEEF STEAKS FOR SAUTÉING: Choose boneless cuts ¾ inch to 1 inch for sautéing. Bone-in and/or very thick steaks tend to cook unevenly; thin steaks too easily become overcooked. Allow 1 steak weighing between 8 and 12 ounces for each person. The choicest steaks for sautéing are rib-eye, top loin (or "shell") and center-cut tenderloin (or "fillet"). Rib-eye steaks are, in effect, slices of boned rib roast. Top loin steaks can be tough unless prime; they are T-bone or porterhouse steaks minus the bone and nugget of tenderloin. Tenderloin steaks, which also sometimes go by the names filet mignon and chateaubriand, are crosswise slices of the tenderloin. All of these cuts, especially rib-eye and tenderloin steaks, are expensive. Chuck eye (also called chuck fillet) steaks may be chosen as a more economical alternative, but these must be cooked very rare or they are likely to be tough.

STEP 1: SAUTÉING THE STEAKS

4 boneless beef steaks between ¾ inch and 1 inch thick (about 8 to 12 ounces each)
Salt and pepper, preferably freshly ground
1½ to 3 tablespoons *each* butter and vegetable oil

Set oven thermostat at 120°F (or lowest possible temperature) and place a heat-proof serving platter in the oven. Select a heavy 12-inch skillet or 2 smaller skillets (see Skillet Notes, page 394).

Trim excess fat from around circumference of the steaks, leaving a layer about ½ inch thick all around. Blot meat dry with paper toweling; season with salt and pepper. Place 1½ tablespoons *each* butter and oil in each skillet you are using and heat over moderately high flame until butter has stopped foaming and is just beginning to color. Immediately lay steaks in the skillet(s) in a single uncrowded layer. Regulating heat so that the fat remains very hot but does not burn, sauté the steaks about 3 to 4 minutes per side (depending on thickness) for rare or 4 to 5 minutes per side for medium rare, turning with tongs. When steaks are in the rare to medium-rare range they will look slightly swollen in the center and feel springy—rather than soft and raw—when pressed with your finger. Transfer steaks to a warmed serving platter and either serve at once or place in oven and proceed to prepare a deglazing sauce.

Step 2: Preparing the Cognac Deglazing Sauce (Optional)

2 tablespoons minced shallots or scallions (white part only)
⅓ cup Cognac or brandy
¾ cup Beef Stock, page 24, or canned broth
3 to 4 tablespoons soft butter, preferably unsalted, cut into pieces
Salt, pepper, and fresh lemon juice, if necessary
2 to 3 tablespoons minced fresh parsley

Spoon all but 2 tablespoons of fat out of the sautéing skillet, taking care not to discard any of the juices. Over low heat, sauté the shallots or scallions in the fat for 1 minute, or until wilted. Raise heat to high and pour in Cognac, standing back in case the alcohol ignites. Scraping up the browned particles on the bottom of the skillet with a wooden spoon or spatula, boil down the Cognac until it has reduced to just a couple of tablespoons. Pour in stock or broth, bring to a rapid boil, and reduce liquid to about ¼ cup of syrupy sauce. Add to the sauce any juices that have accumulated on the serving platter around the steak and reduce again if necessary. Remove skillet from heat and strew the pieces of butter over the sauce. Swirl the skillet by the handle until the butter melts into the sauce, thickening it lightly. Do not stir, or you may cause the sauce to separate. Taste for seasoning and gently swirl in salt, pepper, or drops of lemon juice if necessary. Spoon the sauce over the steaks, sprinkle with parsley, and serve at once.

Variation: SAUTÉED BEEF STEAKS WITH MUSTARD AND GREEN PEPPERCORNS

4 servings

Sautéed Beef Steaks (with Cognac and Parsley)

ADD: 1½ tablespoons brine-packed green peppercorns, drained and mashed to a paste with the back of a fork

1½ tablespoons Dijon mustard

Proceed according to the Master Recipe, beating the peppercorns and mustard into the sauce just before removing the skillet from the heat, and swirling in the butter.

Variation: SAUTÉED BEEF STEAKS WITH RED WINE AND MUSHROOMS

4 servings

❦ *This rather grand twist on the sautéing theme is best served with green beans or peas and mashed potatoes.*

Sautéed Beef Steaks (with Cognac and Parsley)

SUBSTITUTE: ¾ cup dry red wine for Cognac

ADD: 2 teaspoons tomato paste

⅓ recipe Sautéed Mushrooms, page 550

In preparing the sauce (Step 2), substitute red wine for Cognac and boil it down by half. Beat in the tomato paste, then add the stock or broth and reduce to ½ cup of very lightly thickened sauce. Add meat juices and boil down again if necessary. Add the mushrooms and stir. As soon as the sauce reaches the barest simmer, remove from heat and swirl in the butter, using a full 4 tablespoons. Adjust seasoning, then spoon the sauce over the steaks and sprinkle with parsley.

Variation: SAUTÉED BEEF STEAKS WITH COLBERT SAUCE

4 servings

❦ *Colbert sauce, a béarnaise sauce flavored with the deglazed juices of the sautéing skillet, is a traditional French accompaniment for beef steaks. Especially if the steaks are well aged, the combination of flavors is nothing short of sumptuous. For a chic little supper for four, serve the steaks with french-fried potatoes and either a green vegetable or a few sprigs of watercress; finish the meal with sherbet or ice cream.*

Sautéed Beef Steaks, prepared through Step 1
3 tablespoons dry white wine
3 tablespoons Beef Stock, page 24, or canned broth
Warm Béarnaise Sauce, page 48

Spoon out of the steak sautéing skillet as much fat as you can without discarding any of the juices. Pour in wine and stock or broth and, over high heat, boil down to just 1½ tablespoons of very syrupy liquid, all the while scraping the bottom of the skillet with a wooden spoon to dislodge browned bits. Remove skillet from heat and cool for a moment or two, then beat liquid by teaspoonfuls into the béarnaise sauce. Spoon a small dollop of the sauce over each steak and pass the rest of the sauce separately.

Variation: PEPPERED SAUTÉED BEEF STEAKS WITH COGNAC AND CREAM

4 servings

❦ *This is the famous French recipe* steak au poivre, *which is traditionally served with french-fried potatoes and garnished with watercress. Use beef top loin steaks here.*

Sautéed Beef Steaks (with Cognac and Parsley)
ADD: 2 tablespoons peppercorns (black, white, or a mixture)
1 cup heavy cream
OMIT: butter in Step 2

Coarsely crush the peppercorns, either using a mortar and pestle or by placing the peppercorns in a sturdy plastic bag and cracking them with a rolling pin. Blot steaks dry with paper toweling and press peppercorns into the meat with your fingers. Arrange steaks on a dinner plate, cover tightly with plastic wrap, and let stand for 2 hours at room temperature or up to 8 hours in the refrigerator. Without removing the peppercorns, proceed to sauté as indicated in Step 1 of the Master Recipe.

In Step 2, after adding the stock or broth and boiling the sauce down to 1/4 cup, pour in the cream and again boil down until the sauce is reduced to a little less than 1 cup and is thick enough to coat the spoon lightly. Pour in any meat juices, boil down again if necessary, and season, omitting the butter enrichment. Spoon sauce over steaks, sprinkle with parsley, and serve at once.

MASTER RECIPE

Sautéed Lamb Chops or Steaks (with Mustard and Capers)

4 servings

Plain sautéed lamb chops are excellent with creamed spinach, oil-braised peppers, broccoli purée, sautéed summer squash or eggplant, or scalloped potatoes. Sauced lamb chops are best served with green beans, broccoli, or some other green vegetable and either scalloped or baked potatoes.

CHOOSING LAMB FOR SAUTÉING: Most cuts of lamb are tender enough to be sautéed, though some are naturally choicer—and more expensive—than others. The most exquisitely tender and flavorful chops are from the rib and loin. Both rib and loin chops should be cut about 1 inch thick. You will need 3 of the tiny rib chops for each serving, or 2 loin chops. Though a bit chewy and gristly, arm and shoulder lamb chops are also acceptable for sautéing. These are customarily cut about 1/2 inch thick; 2 make an adequate serving. Finally, lamb leg steaks make an excellent alternative to lamb chops, as they are more reasonably priced than rib and loin cuts and make better eating than chops from the shoulder area. Lamb steaks are crosswise slices of the shank end of the leg. They should be cut about 3/4 inch thick and, for single servings, should weigh 8 to 12 ounces each.

Step 1: Sautéing the Chops or Steaks

8 lamb loin chops about 1 inch thick; or 12 lamb rib chops about 1 inch thick; or 8 lamb shoulder or arm chops about ½ inch thick; or 4 lamb leg steaks about ¾ inch thick (2 to 3 pounds altogether)
Salt and pepper, preferably freshly ground
2 to 6 tablespoons neutral vegetable oil

Set oven thermostat at 120°F (or lowest possible temperature) and place a heat-proof serving platter in the oven. Select one or two 10- to 12-inch skillets or 3 smaller skillets; the lamb must cook in one uncrowded layer. (See Skillet Notes, page 394.)

Trim excess fat from around circumference of the chops or steaks, leaving a layer about ¼ inch thick all around. Blot meat dry with paper toweling; season with salt and pepper. Place 2 tablespoons oil in each skillet you are using and heat over moderately high flame until oil shimmers and just begins to smoke. Immediately lay in the lamb in a single uncrowded layer. For rare chops or steaks sauté about 3 minutes *on each side per inch of thickness*; for medium rare, sauté 4 minutes on each side per inch. Throughout cooking, regulate the heat so that the oil remains very hot but does not burn. Turn the meat with tongs. When the lamb is in the rare to medium-rare range, it will look slightly swollen in the center and feel springy to the touch. If juices begin to bead on top of the meat while the second side is cooking, remove lamb from the skillet at once; the juices are a warning that the meat is entering the medium stage.

Transfer lamb to warmed platter and either serve at once, preferably on hot plates, or place in oven and proceed to prepare a deglazing sauce.

Step 2: Preparing the Mustard-Caper Deglazing Sauce (Optional)

2 tablespoons minced shallots or scallions (white part only)
1 teaspoon mashed, pressed, or very finely minced garlic
¼ cup dry white wine or dry vermouth
¾ cup Beef Stock, page 24, or canned broth
2 tablespoons well-drained small capers
1½ tablespoons Dijon mustard
3 to 4 tablespoons soft butter, preferably unsalted, cut into bits
Pepper and bottling liquid from the capers, if necessary
2 tablespoons minced fresh parsley (optional)

Spoon all but 2 tablespoons of fat out of the sautéing skillet, being careful not to discard any of the juices. Over low heat, sauté the shallots or scallions and garlic in the fat for 1 minute, or until wilted. Raise heat to high and pour in the wine. Scraping up the browned particles on the bottom of the skillet with a wooden spoon or spatula, boil down the wine until reduced to just a couple of tablespoons. Pour in stock or broth, again bring to a rapid boil, and reduce liquid to about ½ cup sauce with the consistency of warmed maple syrup. Add the capers and any juices that may have accumulated in the serving platter around the lamb and again reduce by boiling if necessary. Beat in mustard, then immediately remove skillet from heat. Strew the bits of butter over the sauce and swirl the skillet by the handle until the butter melts, thickening the sauce lightly. Do not stir, or you may cause the sauce to separate. Taste for seasoning and gently swirl in pepper or drops of caper bottling juice if necessary. Spoon sauce over the lamb and sprinkle with parsley if you wish. Serve at once, preferably on heated plates.

Variation: SAUTÉED LAMB CHOPS OR STEAKS WITH MADEIRA

4 servings

❦*Lamb and Madeira is another delicious flavor combination that crops up again and again in classic recipes. I like spinach, scalloped potatoes, and sautéed mushrooms as accompaniments here.*

Sautéed Lamb Chops or Steaks (with Mustard and Capers)

SUBSTITUTE: ⅓ cup dry (Sercial) Madeira for white wine
OMIT: Garlic
Capers
Mustard

Proceed according to the Master Recipe, but in making the sauce (Step 2), omit the garlic, capers, and mustard, and substitute Madeira for white wine. If the sauce needs sharpening, add a few drops of fresh lemon juice rather than caper bottling liquid.

Variation: SAUTÉED LAMB CHOPS OR STEAKS WITH COLBERT SAUCE

4 servings

❦ *Serve this with artichokes, green beans, or asparagus and french-fried or baked potatoes.*

Sautéed Lamb Chops or Steaks (with Mustard and Capers) prepared through Step 1
3 tablespoons dry white wine
3 tablespoons Beef Stock, page 24, or canned broth
Warm Béarnaise Sauce, page 48

Spoon out of the lamb sautéing skillet as much fat as you can without discarding any of the juices. Pour in wine and stock and, over high heat, boil down to just 1½ tablespoons of very syrupy liquid, all the while scraping the bottom of the skillet with a wooden spoon to dislodge browned bits. Remove skillet from heat and cool for a moment or two, then beat liquid by teaspoonfuls into the béarnaise sauce. Spoon a small dollop of the sauce over each chop or steak and pass the rest of the sauce separately.

SAUTÉED CALVES' LIVER WITH BACON AND ONIONS

4 servings

❦ *My friend Daphne Chapin, an excellent cook and charming hostess, quite rightly says that prime young calves' liver, if sliced thin and properly sautéed, is nearly indistinguishable from veal. My favorite accompaniments for this classic dish are green beans and mashed potatoes.*

CHOOSING CALVES' LIVER FOR SAUTÉING: Choose the palest pink calves' liver you can find; liver that is distinctly red is from a mature animal and is likely to have a strong taste. The liver should be sliced no more than 3/16 inch thick.

8 slices bacon
3 large onions (about 1 pound), thinly sliced
1½ pounds calves' liver, sliced 3/16 inch thick or less
Salt and pepper, preferably freshly ground
½ cup all-purpose flour
2 to 3 tablespoons neutral vegetable oil, if needed
½ cup dry white wine
2 tablespoons coarsely chopped fresh parsley

Before proceeding, set oven at 120°F (or lowest possible temperature) and place an ovenproof plate and a serving platter inside.

Fry bacon slices until nicely browned but still pliable in a 10- to 12-inch skillet made of or lined with a noncorroding material. Drain bacon on paper towels, then transfer to plate in oven. Pour about half of the bacon fat out of the skillet and reserve. Over moderate heat, sauté the onions in the remaining bacon fat for about 10 minutes, or until soft and just beginning to brown. Transfer onions to plate in oven.

Trim away from the liver any large tubes or prominent pieces of gristle and make ⅛-inch-deep cuts at 1-inch intervals around the edges of the liver slices (this helps prevent liver from curling as it cooks). Dry liver well with paper toweling, sprinkle with salt and pepper, and dredge in flour, shaking off excess. Heat 2 to 3 tablespoons of the reserved bacon fat in the skillet over moderately high flame. When the bacon fat is on the verge of smoking, add as many liver slices as will fit in one uncrowded layer. Keeping the flame as hot as possible without causing the fat to smoke, sauté the liver uncovered for about 1½ minutes per side, or just until it stiffens; the liver should remain quite pink inside. Remove liver as it is cooked to warmed serving platter and place in oven. Cook remaining slices in the same manner, adding more bacon fat or, if you run out of fat, oil to the skillet if necessary.

When all the liver has been cooked, pour the wine into the skillet and rapidly boil it down until reduced by half, all the while scraping the bottom of the skillet with a wooden spoon or spatula to get up the browned bits. Arrange the liver in an attractive manner in the serving platter and moisten lightly with the wine deglazing mixture. Place the onions and bacon slices on top, sprinkle with parsley, and serve at once.

FRIED CHICKEN (WITH CREAM GRAVY)

4 servings

❦*I like my fried chicken crispy-skinned but still very moist and pleasantly chewy within, not dry and falling from the bone. I have found that the best way to accomplish this is to fry the white and dark meat in separate batches in a great big skillet that gives the pieces room to spare. The two batches can of course be done simultaneously if you have two skillets, but such a procedure seems unnecessarily nerve-wracking to me, given the fact that the first frying can be dispatched in less than 15 minutes and the chicken kept warm in the oven. I cover fried chicken as it cooks in order to keep the flesh juicy and prevent the kitchen (and myself) from becoming spattered with fat. This does not have any adverse effect on the crispiness of the skin.*

The traditional and, I think, best accompaniments for plain fried chicken are french-fried or baked potatoes and cole slaw or a tossed salad. If the chicken is accompanied by cream gravy, it is delicious served with green beans or peas and mashed potatoes. Biscuits or corn bread are always welcome too.

STEP 1: FRYING THE CHICKEN

3½ to 4 pounds frying-chicken parts
1 cup all-purpose flour
1 tablespoon salt
1 tablespoon freshly ground black pepper
1 tablespoon chili powder (optional)
1½ to 2 cups (12 to 16 ounces) lard or vegetable shortening

Before proceeding, set oven at 120°F (or lowest possible temperature) and place a heat-proof serving platter, lined with paper toweling, inside.

Separate drumsticks and thighs at the joint. Divide the breast in half lengthwise, removing the reddish bone and attached cartilage, then cut each piece in half crosswise. Cut the back in half crosswise. Save the gizzard, heart, and liver for some other purpose.

Rinse chicken under tepid water and lightly shake off excess moisture; do *not* dry. Combine flour, salt, pepper, and optional chili powder in a sturdy plastic or paper bag, then add the chicken a few pieces at a time and shake to coat well. Arrange chicken pieces on a rack as they are coated, and let stand 20 to 30 minutes before frying.

Place a heavy 10- to 12-inch skillet (the larger size is preferable) over moderately high flame and add enough lard or shortening to make melted fat about 3⁄16 inch deep. Heat fat until it seems to shimmer and is on the verge of smoking.

Arrange the dark meat (drumsticks, thighs, and neck) skin side down in the skillet. Cover tightly and cook 7 minutes, turning the heat down slightly if the skillet begins to smoke. Turn with tongs, cover, and cook 6 to 7 minutes longer. Transfer dark meat to towel-lined platter and place in oven. Add the white meat (breast and back) to the skillet skin side down, and cook, covered, about 5 minutes on each side. Transfer to platter and either serve at once or return to the oven while you prepare the optional cream gravy.

Step 2: Preparing the Cream Gravy (Optional)

Basic Cream Sauce, page 34, made with cream and chicken stock, and *unthinned*
½ cup Chicken Stock, page 26, or canned broth
Salt and pepper, preferably white and freshly ground

Place cream sauce over low heat to keep warm. Pour all the fat out of the chicken frying skillet, then add ½ cup stock or broth to skillet and set over moderate heat. Simmer slowly for 1 to 2 minutes, all the while scraping the bottom of the skillet with a wooden spoon or spatula to get up the coagulated juices and bits of skin. As soon as the skillet seems fairly clean, pour contents into cream sauce. Bring gravy to a simmer and cook for 1 to 3 minutes, or until thick enough to coat a spoon fairly heavily. Add salt if necessary and season highly with pepper. Remove paper towels from under chicken and decorate with a few ribbons of gravy. Pass the rest separately.

DEEP-FRYING POULTRY AND MEAT: Deep-frying has always been one of the most popular methods for preparing poultry, veal, and pork, and no wonder. When deep-fried, poultry and white meats are crunchy on the outside and meltingly tender and juicy within. Indeed, deep-frying is virtually the only technique to choose if you want to prepare veal or pork that has a crisp crust and is juicy at the same time. This has inspired Austrian cooks to bread and deep-fry veal scallops to make the famous wiener schnitzel (see chart).

Deep-fried foods are excellent as a main course. Deep-fried breaded chicken breast cutlets or strips are delicious with béarnaise sauce; a simple green vegetable such as broccoli, asparagus, or green beans makes a good accompaniment. I like to serve breaded and deep-fried turkey breast scallops and veal scallops with lemon wedges, accompanied by a tangy tossed green salad made with anchovy and onion.

Deep-fried poultry and meat also make appealing hors d'oeuvre finger foods. With an hors d'oeuvre of breaded chicken wings or chicken or turkey breast strips, offer a dipping sauce of mustard-flavored hollandaise sauce or mustard- or herb-flavored mayonnaise. If you coat the wings or poultry breast strips in fritter or tempura batter, offer a dip of soy sauce, teriyaki sauce, finely chopped sweet chutney, or oriental peanut sauce. Breaded and deep-fried strips of pork loin are a provocative and delicious hors d'oeuvre too. Pass them with Chinese or French mustard, chopped sweet chutney, a sweet-and-sour sauce, or oriental peanut sauce.

DEEP-FRIED POULTRY OR MEAT VARIATION CHART

This chart is to be used in conjunction with the Master Technique for deep-frying on pages 61–66. Follow the Master Technique, choosing a coating and plugging in cooking procedures and times as indicated for various kinds of poultry and meat in the chart.

POULTRY OR MEAT	AMOUNT TO BUY		COATING	COOKING PROCEDURES	
	FOR DINNER SERVING 4 PERSONS	FOR HORS D'OEUVRE SERVING 4 TO 6 PERSONS	STEPS 1A, 1B, 1C, 1D FROM THE MASTER TECHNIQUE. NOTE: DOUBLE THE COATING IF PREPARING DINNER PORTIONS	HANDLING	MINUTES COOKING TIME (FAT AT 370°F)
Chicken parts: drumsticks and thighs	3½ pounds	—	Step 1a (use flour) OR Step 1b (use fresh bread crumbs) OR Step 1c (batter)	Fry 3 or 4 pieces at a time	9–12
Chicken parts: breast halves and wings	3½ pounds	2 pounds (wings)	As above	Fry 3 or 4 pieces at a time	4–6
Chicken breast cutlets, whole	8 small (1½–2 pounds)	—	Step 1b (use fresh bread crumbs) OR Step 1c (batter) OR Step 1d (tempura)	Fry 2 or 3 at a time	4–5

POULTRY OR MEAT	AMOUNT TO BUY		COATING	COOKING PROCEDURES	
	FOR DINNER SERVING 4 PERSONS	FOR HORS D'OEUVRE SERVING 4 TO 6 PERSONS	STEPS 1A, 1B, 1C, 1D FROM THE MASTER TECHNIQUE. NOTE: DOUBLE THE COATING IF PREPARING DINNER PORTIONS	HANDLING	MINUTES COOKING TIME (FAT AT 370°F)
Chicken breast fillets, in strips	1½–2 pounds	8–12 ounces	As above	Fry in small batches	1½–2½
Turkey breast scallops	8 (about 1½ pounds)	—	Step 1b (use fresh bread crumbs)	Fry 2 or 3 at a time	2–3
Turkey breast, in strips (boneless)	1½ pounds	8–12 ounces	Step 1b (use fresh bread crumbs) OR Step 1c (batter) OR Step 1d (tempura)	Fry in small batches	1½–2½
Veal scallops	8 (about 1½ pounds)	—	Step 1b (use fresh bread crumbs)	Fry 2 or 3 at a time	2–3
Pork loin, in strips (boneless)	—	8–12 ounces	Step 1b (use fresh bread crumbs)	Fry in small batches	1½–2½

BRAISED POULTRY and MEAT

To braise a food means to cook it slowly in a small amount of liquid. The fundamental cooking technique in most fricassees, stews, and ragouts and in many other recipes,* braising is a good treatment for tough or very lean cuts of meat, as the long slow cooking serves to break down tough connective tissues while keeping the flesh moist.

This chapter contains two Master Techniques, one for chicken and "white meats" such as giblets, pork, and veal, and the other for the red meats, beef and lamb. The Master Techniques show you how the basic braising procedure is done; the variations that follow list the ingredients needed to make various braised dishes according to the method outlined in the Master Techniques.

A wide range of different types and cuts of meat—boneless or bone-in stew meat, chops or steaks, pot roasts—can be used interchangeably in most braised dishes, and most of the other

*Some chicken and veal stews and fricassees are made by poaching unbrowned poultry or meat in enough liquid to cover it completely. This results in a somewhat different dish. What are the differences between fricassees, stews, and ragouts? The matter is controversial, and even dictionaries don't agree. In my private lexicon, a fricassee is a dish in which the poultry or meat plays the dominant role, with added vegetables, if there are any, acting mainly as a flavoring. In a stew, by contrast, the poultry or meat and the vegetables have equal importance. Ragout is a french word for a stew.

ingredients can be increased, decreased, or replaced entirely to suit your tastes and needs. Stews, fricassees, pot roasts, and their ilk are, at heart, homey and informal dishes, many of which were invented in the first place in order to make the most of tough meats and odds and ends that might be thrown into a stew pot. Experimentation is more likely to yield an unexpectedly good result than a disappointment.

MASTER TECHNIQUE

Braised Chicken (or Giblets or Pork or Veal Stew Meat, Chops, or Steaks)

4 servings

This Master Technique outlines the basic procedure for braising chicken; the notes on page 427, show how to braise giblets and various cuts of veal and pork according to the same method. The Master Technique gives general cooking instructions only. Use it in conjunction with the braising variations on pages 428–40, which list the specific ingredients needed to produce a variety of stews, fricassees, and ragouts.

3½ to 4 pounds frying chicken parts
The ingredients specified in the braising variation you have chosen: fat; vegetable flavoring; flour, curry, or paprika; liquid; seasoning; stew ingredients; thickening; liaison

If chicken pieces seem sticky, rinse them quickly under tepid water. Pat thoroughly dry with paper toweling; wet poultry or meat does not brown properly.

Select a heavy, lidded skillet or pot that is at least 10 inches wide across the bottom and that is made of or lined with a noncorroding material. (Poultry and meat brown best in a skillet or pot made of heavy-gauge aluminum lined with stainless steel, but an enamel-lined cast iron cooking vessel ensures more even heating.) Add the minimum amount of *fat* called for in the braising variation and heat over moderate flame until hot but not browned or smoking. Add as many chicken pieces as will fit without crowding and brown to a deep golden color on both sides, turning with tongs. Remove chicken to a plate and brown remaining pieces in the same manner, regulating the heat so that the fat does not burn. Add more fat if necessary.

When all the chicken is browned pour excess fat out of skillet or add more fat to make a depth of about 1/8 inch. Stirring now and then, sauté the *vegetable flavoring* in the fat for about 5 minutes, or until softened but not browned. Blend in *flour, curry,* or *paprika* and cook slowly, stirring, for 2 minutes. Add the *liquid,* using the minimum amount of stock or broth, raise heat to moderately high, and bring mixture to a simmer, scraping the bottom of the skillet with a wooden spoon or spatula to get up browned bits. Stir in the *seasoning.* Return the chicken pieces to the skillet, the breasts and thighs placed flesh side down; if necessary, add enough of the remaining stock or broth to bring the liquid about 1/3 of the way up the sides of the chicken. Baste the chicken with liquid.

Bring to a fast simmer, then turn heat down to the point where the liquid barely bubbles. Cover tightly and cook for 15 minutes, adding more stock or broth if the chicken becomes dry and threatens to scorch. Turn the chicken and scatter around it any *stew ingredients* that might be called for. Cook about 10 minutes longer, or until the chicken feels tender and exudes clear yellow—rather than reddish—juices when pricked deeply with a fork.

Transfer chicken to a plate and cover with foil to keep warm. Remove and discard bay leaf, if added. Tilt skillet and skim as much fat as you can from the pan gravy. There should be about 1 1/2 cups of gravy. If there is more, or if the gravy tastes weak, rapidly boil it down over high heat to reduce and concentrate it.

With the gravy at a fast simmer, beat in teaspoon by teaspoon as much of the *thickening* as is needed to make the gravy thick enough to coat the spoon heavily. You may not need all the paste. Simmer for 3 minutes. Stir in any *liaison* called for and continue to simmer, stirring occasionally, for 5 to 10 minutes, or until the gravy rethickens. Adjust seasoning as necessary. Return chicken to skillet and simmer slowly for a couple of minutes, basting with the gravy.

AHEAD OF TIME: Unlike other braised meats, which only improve upon standing and reheating, chicken is at its best when served at once. However, it can be refrigerated for several days or frozen for several months in a tightly covered container. Reheat over low flame; thaw frozen chicken beforehand.

PREPARING GIBLETS: My mother tells the story of how, in the days when my father was a struggling, penurious academic, she served a delicious giblet ragout to an equally penurious academic couple, who, in turn, politely but firmly informed her that they didn't feel giblets were suitable as the main dish of a human supper. This prejudice, which I have found to be widely shared, is truly regrettable, for giblets are not only delicious but also quite elegant when properly prepared. And they are extremely economical. To serve 4, choose 2 pounds chicken or turkey hearts or 2 1/2 pounds gizzards or a mixture of gizzards and hearts. Rinse; cut off and discard the mantle of tough skin that connects the two lobes of gizzards. Proceed according to the Master Technique, but cook the giblets 2 to 3 hours, or until very tender, stirring every 20 minutes and adding any stew ingredient called for in the braising variation 10 minutes before the end of cooking.

PREPARING PORK OR VEAL CHOPS, STEAKS OR STEW MEAT: To serve 4, choose 4 pork or veal chops cut ¾ to 1 inch thick (about 2½ pounds altogether), or 2 pork or veal steaks cut about ¾ inch thick and weighing 1 to 1½ pounds apiece, or 2 pounds boneless pork or veal stew meat. The best cuts for braising are pork shoulder arm, shoulder blade, and leg steaks, and veal shoulder arm, shoulder blade, sirloin, and round. The more expensive pork loin and veal rib and loin cuts make a handsome presentation but tend to be dry and hard when braised. Proceed according to the Master Technique, but cook the meat for 2 to 3 hours, or until tender but not falling apart, basting periodically with the pan gravy and turning every 40 minutes. Add any stew ingredients called for in the braising variation 10 minutes before the end of cooking.

Variation: COUNTRY CAPTAIN FRICASSEE OF CHICKEN OR GIBLETS

4 servings

❦ I grew up eating different versions of this very American dish without, somehow, ever hearing it called by its traditional name, "country captain." Most recipes call for currants or raisins, but I prefer mushrooms as the stew ingredient. Serve this with rice.

To prepare this dish, use chicken or giblets, plus the ingredients listed below, in the preceding Master Technique.

FAT:	¼ to ½ cup bacon fat, lard, or vegetable shortening
VEGETABLE FLAVORING:	1 cup chopped onions
	⅔ cup chopped green bell peppers
FLOUR, CURRY, OR PAPRIKA:	1½ tablespoons mild curry powder or 1 tablespoon hot (Madras) curry powder, or to taste
	1 tablespoon all-purpose flour
LIQUID:	1 14- to 16-ounce can tomatoes with their juice (break up the tomatoes with your hands)
	⅓ to 1⅓ cups Chicken Stock, page 26, or canned broth

3 tablespoons strained fresh lemon juice
1 tablespoon packed dark brown sugar

SEASONING: 1 teaspoon mashed, pressed, or very finely minced garlic
½ teaspoon whole dried thyme
½ teaspoon salt
¼ teaspoon pepper, preferably freshly ground

STEW INGREDIENTS: 2 cups (about 8 ounces) thinly sliced mushrooms or ⅔ cup dried currants or raisins

THICKENING: 2 tablespoons all-purpose flour mixed to a smooth paste with 2½ tablespoons soft butter

LIAISON: None

Variation: CREOLE CHICKEN OR GIBLET STEW

4 servings

❦ *Serve with rice and accompany with plenty of cold beer if you spice the stew liberally.*

To prepare this dish, use chicken or giblets, plus the ingredients listed below, in the Master Technique on page 426.

FAT: ¼ to ½ cup olive oil, bacon fat, or vegetable shortening

VEGETABLE FLAVORING: ⅔ cup chopped onions
⅔ cup chopped green bell peppers
⅔ cup chopped celery

FLOUR, CURRY, OR PAPRIKA: 1 tablespoon all-purpose flour

LIQUID: 1 14- to 16-ounce can tomatoes with their juice (break up the tomatoes with your hands)
½ to 1½ cups Chicken Stock, page 26, or canned broth

SEASONING: 1 teaspoon mashed, pressed, or very finely minced garlic
1 large bay leaf
½ teaspoon whole dried thyme
⅛ to ¼ teaspoon cayenne pepper, or to taste

(*Ingredients list continues on next page*)

	½ teaspoon salt
	½ teaspoon pepper, preferably freshly ground
STEW INGREDIENTS:	1 cup freshly cut, drained canned, or frozen corn
	½ cup sliced okra, frozen or fresh (optional)
THICKENING:	2 tablespoons all-purpose flour mixed to a smooth paste with 2½ tablespoons soft butter
LIAISON:	None

Variation: GREEN PEPPER RAGOUT OF CHICKEN, PORK, OR VEAL

4 servings

This is perhaps best when made with chicken or veal, but pork may also be used. If you wish, serve with noodles tossed with olive oil and freshly grated Parmesan cheese.

To prepare this dish, use chicken or veal or pork stew meat, plus the ingredients listed below, in the Master Technique on page 426.

FAT:	¼ to ½ cup olive oil
VEGETABLE FLAVORING:	1 large onion, thinly sliced
	2 large green bell peppers, cut into thin lengthwise strips
FLOUR, CURRY, OR PAPRIKA:	1 tablespoon all-purpose flour
LIQUID:	1 14- to 16-ounce can tomatoes with their juice (break up the tomatoes with your hands)
	½ cup dry red wine
	½ to 1 cup Beef Stock, page 24, or canned broth
SEASONING:	1 teaspoon mashed, pressed, or very finely minced garlic
	¾ teaspoon salt
	½ teaspoon pepper, preferably freshly ground
STEW INGREDIENTS:	None

THICKENING: 2 tablespoons all-purpose flour mixed to a smooth paste with 2½ tablespoons soft butter

LIAISON: None

Variation: HUNTER STEW (CHICKEN CACCIATORE AND VEAL CHASSEUR)

4 servings

❦ *This dish becomes chicken cacciatore if made with chicken and veal chasseur if made with veal. Serve either version with rice or noodles.*

To prepare this dish, use chicken or veal stew meat, plus the ingredients listed below, in the Master Technique on page 426.

FAT: ¼ to ½ cup olive oil

VEGETABLE FLAVORING: ⅔ cup chopped onions

FLOUR, CURRY, OR PAPRIKA: 1 tablespoon all-purpose flour

LIQUID:
- 1 14- to 16-ounce can tomatoes with their juice (break up the tomatoes with your hands)
- ½ cup dry white wine
- ½ to 1 cup Chicken Stock, page 26, or canned broth

SEASONING:
- 1 to 1½ teaspoons mashed, pressed, or very finely minced garlic
- 1 large bay leaf
- 1 2-inch strip orange zest or ¼ teaspoon ground dried orange peel
- 2 teaspoons finely chopped fresh basil or ½ teaspoon dried
- ½ teaspoon salt
- ¼ teaspoon pepper, preferably freshly ground

STEW INGREDIENTS: 2 cups (about 8 ounces) thinly sliced mushrooms

THICKENING: 2 tablespoons all-purpose flour mixed to a smooth paste with 2½ tablespoons soft butter

LIAISON: None

Variation: MEXICAN-STYLE CHICKEN OR PORK STEW WITH SPICES, FRUITS, AND OLIVES

4 servings

❦ *This delicious stew makes a most intriguing change from the ordinary, but there is nothing either unusual or difficult about its preparation. Serve with rice—that's a must—and, if you wish, a characteristically Mexican salad of sliced ripe tomatoes and avocadoes.*

To prepare this stew, use chicken or pork stew meat, plus the ingredients listed below, in the Master Technique on page 426.

FAT:	¼ to ½ cup lard or vegetable shortening
VEGETABLE FLAVORING:	1 cup chopped onions
	2 to 8 fresh jalapeño peppers or other chilis, seeded and cut into thin strips (if fresh chilis are not available, substitute all or part of a 4-ounce can of chilis, thoroughly drained and chopped; season stew with cayenne pepper to taste to compensate for the blandness of canned chilis)
FLOUR, CURRY, OR PAPRIKA:	1 tablespoon all-purpose flour
LIQUID:	1 14- to 16-ounce can tomatoes with their juice (break up the tomatoes with your hands)
	½ to 1½ cups Chicken Stock, page 26, or canned broth
SEASONING:	1 teaspoon mashed, pressed, or very finely minced garlic
	2 teaspoons cinnamon
	½ teaspoon ground cloves
	½ teaspoon oregano
	½ teaspoon salt
	½ teaspoon pepper, preferably freshly ground
STEW INGREDIENTS:	⅔ to 1 cup sliced pimiento-stuffed green olives
	½ cup chopped pineapple (use fresh pineapple or partially drained crushed

pineapple canned without added sugar)

½ cup prunes, snipped into ¼-inch pieces

THICKENING:	2 tablespoons all-purpose flour mixed to a smooth paste with 2½ tablespoons soft butter
LIAISON:	None

Variation: MUSHROOM FRICASSEE OF CHICKEN, GIBLETS, PORK, OR VEAL, OR SMOTHERED PORK OR VEAL CHOPS OR STEAKS

4 servings

❦*Sometimes this recipe and its numerous close cousins are simply called "smothered," with no reference in the title to the mushrooms that are always involved. By whatever name it goes, the dish is delicious, classically American, and very easy to do. Serve with rice and a plain green vegetable.*

To prepare this dish, use chicken, giblets, pork or veal stew meat, or pork or veal chops or steaks, plus the ingredients listed below, in the Master Technique on page 426.

FAT:	3 to 5 tablespoons butter and 1 to 3 tablespoons neutral vegetable oil
VEGETABLE FLAVORING:	1 cup chopped onions
FLOUR, CURRY, OR PAPRIKA:	1 tablespoon all-purpose flour
LIQUID:	1 to 2 cups Chicken Stock, page 26, or canned broth
SEASONING:	¼ teaspoon whole dried thyme
	¼ teaspoon salt
	¼ teaspoon black or white pepper, preferably freshly ground
STEW INGREDIENTS:	2 cups (about 8 ounces) thinly sliced mushrooms
THICKENING:	2 tablespoons all-purpose flour mixed to a smooth paste with 2½ tablespoons soft butter
LIAISON:	½ to 1 cup heavy cream

Variation: PAPRIKA FRICASSEE OF CHICKEN, GIBLETS, PORK, OR VEAL, OR SMOTHERED PORK OR VEAL CHOPS OR STEAKS

4 servings

❦ *Traditionally, chicken is the star ingredient in this dish. While chicken is indeed succulent when prepared in this manner—especially if you bind the pan gravy with lots and lots of sour cream—other white meats, too, are complemented by the flavor of paprika. By the way, it is worthwhile to shop around for a premium brand of imported sweet paprika, for supermarket types rarely seem to have much taste. Always serve this dish with noodles.*

This dish may be prepared using chicken, giblets, pork or veal stew meat, or pork or veal chops or steaks, plus the ingredients listed below, in the Master Technique on page 426.

FAT:	1/4 to 1/2 cup lard or vegetable shortening
VEGETABLE FLAVORING:	1 1/2 cups chopped onions
FLOUR, CURRY, OR PAPRIKA:	2 tablespoons sweet paprika
	1 tablespoon all-purpose flour
LIQUID:	1 to 2 cups Chicken Stock, page 26, or canned broth
SEASONING:	1 teaspoon mashed, pressed, or very finely minced garlic
	1/4 teaspoon salt
	1/4 teaspoon pepper, preferably freshly ground
STEW INGREDIENTS:	None
THICKENING:	2 tablespoons all-purpose flour mixed to a smooth paste with 2 1/2 tablespoons soft butter
LIAISON:	3/4 to 1 1/2 cups sour cream

❦

Variation: TARRAGON AND WHITE WINE FRICASSEE OF CHICKEN OR VEAL, OR SMOTHERED VEAL CHOPS OR STEAKS

4 servings

❦ *This is an elegant French-style dish that is best served with rice and a subtle fresh vegetable such as asparagus or tiny peas.*

To prepare this dish, use chicken or veal stew meat, chops, or steaks, plus the ingredients listed below, in the Master Technique on page 426.

FAT:	3 to 5 tablespoons butter and 1 to 3 tablespoons neutral vegetable oil
VEGETABLE FLAVORING:	2 tablespoons finely chopped onion
FLOUR, CURRY, OR PAPRIKA:	1 tablespoon all-purpose flour
LIQUID:	½ to 1 cup Chicken Stock, page 26, or canned broth
	⅔ cup dry white wine
SEASONING:	1½ teaspoons dried tarragon
	¼ teaspoon salt
	¼ teaspoon white or black pepper, preferably freshly ground
STEW INGREDIENTS:	None
THICKENING:	2 tablespoons all-purpose flour mixed to a smooth paste with 1½ tablespoons soft butter
LIAISON:	⅔ to 1 cup heavy cream

Variation: RED WINE FRICASSEE OF CHICKEN, GIBLETS, PORK, OR VEAL, OR SMOTHERED PORK OR VEAL CHOPS OR STEAKS

4 servings

❦ *When prepared with chicken, this variation is quite similar to* coq au vin rouge, *the French dish that has long been popular in this country. Chicken is, however, by no means the only poultry or meat that may be cooked in this fashion; veal and pork, especially the latter, are also delicious. Garnish the dish with additional chopped parsley, if you wish, and serve with boiled potatoes or noodles and a simple vegetable such as green beans or peas.*

This dish may be prepared by using chicken, giblets, pork or veal stew meat, or pork or veal chops or steaks, plus the ingredients listed below, in the Master Technique on page 426.

FAT:	¼ to ½ cup bacon fat or olive oil
VEGETABLE FLAVORING:	1 cup chopped onions
FLOUR, CURRY, OR PAPRIKA:	1 tablespoon all-purpose flour
LIQUID:	1½ cups dry red wine
	¼ to ½ cup Beef Stock, page 24, or canned broth
	2 tablespoons brandy or Cognac
	1½ tablespoons tomato paste
SEASONING:	2 tablespoons finely chopped fresh parsley
	1 teaspoon mashed, pressed, or very finely minced garlic
	1 large bay leaf
	½ teaspoon whole dried thyme
	¾ teaspoon salt
	½ teaspoon pepper, preferably freshly ground
STEW INGREDIENTS:	2 cups (about 8 ounces) thinly sliced mushrooms
THICKENING:	2 tablespoons all-purpose flour mixed to a smooth paste with 2½ tablespoons soft butter
LIAISON:	None

Variation: GEORGIA-STYLE STUFFED PORK CHOPS

4 servings

❦*An old-time favorite, stuffed pork chops are best served with braised collards or kale, sautéed broccoli rabe, steamed cabbage, or some other similarly assertive vegetable. For this dish to work, it is crucial that you use the right kind of pork chops. Tell your butcher that you want pork loin rib chops, also called center cut pork chops, and that you do* not *want regular pork loin chops, which have a T-bone and are therefore impossible to slice through for stuffing. The chops should be cut 1 to 1¼ inches thick.*

To prepare this dish, stuff the chops as indicated in Step 1 and then use the ingredients listed in Step 2 of this variation in the Master Technique on page 426.

STEP 1: PREPARING STUFFING AND STUFFING THE CHOPS

6 tablespoons butter
½ cup finely chopped onion
⅓ cup finely chopped celery
¼ cup finely chopped baked ham, preferably smoked
3 tablespoons bourbon
1 cup Fine Fresh Bread Crumbs (see page 60)
3 to 4 tablespoons (about 1 ounce) chopped pecans
¼ teaspoon ground thyme
¼ teaspoon fresh lemon juice
Salt, if necessary
¼ teaspoon pepper, preferably freshly ground
4 pork loin rib chops, 1 to 1¼ inches thick

SPECIAL EQUIPMENT: Four 4- to 5-inch metal skewers

Melt butter in small sauté pan over moderate heat. Add onion, celery, and ham and cook slowly, stirring, for about 10 minutes, or until vegetables are soft but not at all brown. Add bourbon to the pan, raise heat to high, and boil the liquor down, stirring, until it practically disappears. Remove from heat and stir in bread crumbs, pecans, thyme, and lemon juice. Taste and season carefully with salt and pepper; the stuffing should be strongly flavored and rather salty.

Trim off nearly all fat from circumference of chops. Cut a deep horizontal pocket in each chop, reaching all the way to the rib bone. Spoon into each of the chops about ⅓ cup stuffing (or as much as they can hold comfortably; extra stuffing may be frozen), and close up pockets with skewers.

STEP 2: BRAISING THE CHOPS

FAT: 3 to 5 tablespoons butter and 1 to 3 tablespoons neutral vegetable oil
VEGETABLE FLAVORING: 2/3 cup chopped onions
1/3 cup chopped celery
FLOUR, CURRY, OR PAPRIKA: 1 tablespoon all-purpose flour
LIQUID: 1 to 2 cups Chicken Stock, page 26, or canned broth
SEASONING: 1/4 teaspoon ground thyme
1/4 teaspoon salt
1/4 teaspoon pepper, preferably freshly ground
STEW INGREDIENTS: None
THICKENING: 2 tablespoons all-purpose flour mixed to a smooth paste with 2 1/2 tablespoons soft butter
LIAISON: 1/2 to 1 cup heavy cream

Cook the chops according to the Master Technique on page 426, using the ingredients listed above. Simmer the chops until they are very tender—2 to 3 hours—but don't overcook them to the point that they fall apart and the stuffing comes out. Baste periodically and turn every 40 minutes. Remember to remove the skewers before serving.

Variation: DILLED STUFFED VEAL OR TURKEY ROLLS

4 to 6 servings

❦ *For this dish, you need either 8 veal leg scallops or 8 raw turkey breast slices, 5 to 6 inches long, 4 to 5 inches wide, and about 1/8 inch thick. If you use veal, try to find scallops that have been sliced from a single muscle of the leg and that therefore contain no muscle separations. It is preferable that the scallops be cut across the muscle grain; scallops cut with the muscle grain may shrink or split during cooking. If you are using turkey breast, simply see that the slices are in one solid piece.*

Buttered noodles and peas or green beans make good accompaniments here.

To prepare this dish, stuff the rolls as indicated in Step 1, and then use the ingredients listed in Step 2 of this variation in the Master Technique on page 426.

Step 1: Preparing Stuffing and Making the Rolls

6 tablespoons butter
½ cup finely chopped onion
3 tablespoons vodka
1 cup Fine Fresh Bread Crumbs (see page 60)
4 anchovy fillets, drained and chopped
1 tablespoon finely chopped fresh dill (feathery leaves only) or 1 teaspoon dried dillweed
Salt, if necessary
¼ teaspoon pepper, preferably freshly ground
8 veal scallops or raw turkey breast slices, 5 to 6 inches long, 4 to 5 inches wide, and about 3⁄16 inch thick

Melt butter in small sauté pan over moderate heat. Add onion and cook slowly, stirring, for about 10 minutes, or until soft but not brown. Add vodka to the pan, raise heat to high, and boil the liquor down, stirring, until it practically disappears. Remove from heat and stir in bread crumbs, anchovy fillets, and dill. Taste and season carefully with salt and pepper as necessary.

One at a time, place veal scallops or turkey breast slices between sheets of waxed paper and gently pound with a meat mallet or some other implement (the bottom of a drinking glass, for instance) to a uniform thickness of about ⅛ inch. Spread about 2 tablespoons stuffing on each of the scallops or slices and roll up. Secure the rolls by tying them with twine at each end.

Step 2: Cooking the Rolls

FAT:	3 to 5 tablespoons butter and 1 to 3 tablespoons neutral vegetable oil
VEGETABLE FLAVORING:	⅔ cup chopped onions
FLOUR, CURRY, OR PAPRIKA:	1 tablespoon all-purpose flour
LIQUID:	1 to 1½ cups Chicken Stock, page 26, or canned broth
	⅓ cup vodka
SEASONING:	½ tablespoon finely chopped fresh dill (feathery leaves only) or ½ teaspoon dried dillweed
	¼ teaspoon salt
	¼ teaspoon pepper, preferably freshly ground
STEW INGREDIENTS:	None

(*Ingredients list continues on next page*)

THICKENING: 2 tablespoons all-purpose flour mixed to a smooth paste with 2½ tablespoons soft butter

LIAISON: ¾ to 1½ cups sour cream

Use the stuffed rolls and the ingredients listed above in the Master Technique on pages 426 to 427, simmering the rolls about 45 minutes, or until tender when pierced with a fork. Baste periodically and turn every 20 minutes during cooking. Untie before serving.

MASTER TECHNIQUE

Braised Beef Stew Meat (or Lamb Stew Meat, or Beef Pot Roast or Round Steak)

This Master Technique outlines the basic procedure for braising beef stew meat; the notes on page 442 show how to braise other cuts of beef, and lamb, according to the same method. The Master Technique gives general cooking instructions only. Use it in conjunction with the braising variations on pages 443–53, which list specific ingredients needed to produce a variety of stews, pot roasts, and other braised dishes.

CHOOSING BEEF STEW MEAT: My favorite types of beef stew meat are chuck, preferably boneless, short ribs, and oxtails (which are steer tails). Chuck tends to be fatty and to fall apart a bit during cooking, but the meat is succulent and full of flavor. Short ribs and oxtails are bony and therefore something of a nuisance to cook and eat, but they make for a very rich-tasting stew. Another frequently used cut for beef stew is round. Round is lean and boneless and holds its shape nicely during cooking, but it can be rather dry and lacking in flavor.

Boneless beef stew meat should be cut in chunks about 1 inch around; short ribs should be cut along the lines of the bones into manageable pieces for cooking and eating; oxtails should be cut in 1-inch sections.

Cut up beef stew meat, 2 pounds if boneless, 3 to 4 pounds if bone-in
The ingredients specified in the braising variation you have chosen:
coating; fat; vegetable flavoring; curry or paprika; liquid; seasoning; stew ingredients; thickening; liaison

Dab the meat with paper toweling to blot up excess moisture, then dredge in *coating,* shaking off the excess. Arrange in a single layer on a baking sheet or rack and let stand for 10 to 20 minutes.

Select a heavy, lidded skillet or pot at least 10 inches wide across the bottom and made of or lined with a noncorroding material. (The meat will brown best in a skillet or pot made of heavy-gauge aluminum lined with stainless steel, but an enamel-lined cast iron cooking vessel ensures more even heating.) Add the minimum amount of *fat* called for in the braising variation and heat over moderate flame until hot but not browned or smoking. Add as many pieces of meat as will fit without crowding and brown well on all sides, turning with tongs or a long-handled fork. Remove meat to a plate and brown remaining pieces in the same manner, regulating the heat so that the fat does not burn. Add more fat if necessary.

When all the meat is browned, pour excess fat out of skillet or add more fat to make a depth of about 1/8 inch. Stirring occasionally, sauté the *vegetable flavoring* in the fat for about 5 minutes, or until softened but not browned. Blend in *curry* or *paprika* and cook slowly, stirring, for 2 minutes. Add the *liquid,* using the minimum amount of stock, broth, water, or wine, raise heat to moderately high, and bring mixture to a simmer, scraping the bottom of the skillet with a wooden spoon or spatula to get up browned bits. Stir in *seasoning.* Scrape meat and accumulated juices into skillet; if the liquid does not reach at least 1/4 of the way up the sides of the meat, add a bit more stock, broth, or other liquid.

Bring to a fast simmer, then turn heat down to the point where the liquid barely bubbles. Cover tightly and cook for 2 to 4 hours, or until the meat is just tender enough to be pierced easily with a fork; don't overcook, or the meat will become dry and stringy and will begin to disintegrate. Stir up every 20 minutes or so during cooking, and add more stock or broth if the meat becomes dry and threatens to scorch; be careful not to add more liquid than is really needed, or you will give the dish a boiled taste and texture. About 15 minutes before the end of cooking, stir in any *stew ingredients* that may be called for, adding also a bit more stock or broth if necessary.

Transfer meat to a dinner plate, picking out and discarding any loose bones. Remove bay leaf, if used. Tilt the pot and skim as much fat as you can from the pan gravy. There should be about 1 1/2 cups of gravy. If there is more, or if the gravy tastes weak, rapidly boil it down over high heat to reduce and concentrate it.

With the gravy at a fast simmer, beat in teaspoon by teaspoon as much of the *thickening* as is needed to make the gravy thick enough to coat the spoon heavily. You may not need all the paste. Simmer for 3 minutes. Stir in any *liaison* called for and continue to simmer, stirring occasionally, for 5 to 10 minutes, or until the gravy rethickens. Adjust seasoning as necessary. Return meat to skillet and simmer slowly for a couple of minutes, basting with the gravy.

AHEAD OF TIME: The dish may be refrigerated for several days, which will actually improve its flavor, or frozen for several months. To reheat, thaw if necessary and place over a low flame or in a 300°F oven.

TO PREPARE LAMB STEW MEAT: To serve 4, choose 2 pounds boneless lamb shoulder, cut into 1-inch chunks. Proceed according to the Master Technique, but cook just 1½ to 2½ hours, or until fork-tender.

TO PREPARE A BEEF POT ROAST: Beef pot roasts may be cut from the chuck (or shoulder area), the rump, or the round (that is, the leg). The various chuck blade pot roasts, the most common supermarket cuts, are rich and flavorful, but because most are wide and flat (like steaks) and contain muscle separations, wide streaks of fat, and, in some cases, bones, they are difficult to maneuver during cooking and look messy when carved. The beef chuck shoulder, chuck eye, and chuck tender are better bets. Rump and round pot roasts are generally compact and contain few muscle separations or bones; however, they also tend to be dry and fibrous.

To serve 4, choose a 2-pound boneless or 3-pound bone-in pot roast and prepare according to the Master Technique, making the following modifications. Shave excess fat from the surface of the meat, leaving a layer ¼ inch thick all around, and tie the meat securely with loops of sturdy white twine, making it as tidy and uniform in shape as possible. Press the flour into the meat with the heels of your hands before browning well on all sides. Add just enough liquid to come ¼ of the way up the sides of the meat. Baste periodically during cooking; unless the meat is too awkward to maneuver, turn every 30 to 40 minutes. Braise a steak-shaped pot roast 2 to 3 hours, a more compact roast 3 to 5. The meat is done as soon as it can be cut easily with a knife; do not overcook. Remove to a plate and keep warm while you finish the gravy; instead of returning the roast to the pot, carve and arrange slices on a serving platter, spooning some of the gravy on top and passing the rest separately.

TO PREPARE A BEEF CHUCK OR ROUND STEAK: To serve 4, choose a 2- to 2½-pound chuck steak containing a minimum of muscle separations, internal fat, or bone (shoulder is preferable), or a 2-pound top round steak. Proceed according to the Master Technique, making the following modifications. Pound the flour into the meat with a mallet or the heel of your hand; brown well on both sides. Add enough liquid to come ½ of the way up the sides of the meat. Baste periodically during cooking and lift the corners of the steak with a spatula to allow gravy to run underneath. Turn every 30 minutes. Cook the steak for about 3 hours, or until tender, but be careful not to overcook or it will fall apart. Lift onto a serving platter with two large spatulas and keep warm while you finish the gravy; pour gravy over the top rather than returning steak to the skillet or pot.

Variation: OLD-FASHIONED BEEF OR LAMB STEW

4 servings

❦ *Traditionally this stew is made with beef, but being a lamb lover I always prepare it with lamb. Salad and hot biscuits go well here and apple pie makes a fine dessert.*

To prepare this stew, use beef or lamb stew meat, plus the ingredients listed below, in the preceding Master Technique.

COATING:	½ cup all-purpose flour
FAT:	¼ to ½ cup lard, vegetable shortening, or bacon fat
VEGETABLE FLAVORING:	1 cup thinly sliced onions
CURRY OR PAPRIKA:	None
LIQUID:	½ to 1½ cups Beef Stock, page 24, or canned broth
	1 14- to 16-ounce can tomatoes with their juice (break up the tomatoes with your hands)
	1 tablespoon tomato paste
SEASONING:	1 bay leaf
	½ teaspoon mashed, pressed, or very finely minced garlic
	½ teaspoon whole dried thyme
	½ teaspoon salt
	½ teaspoon pepper, preferably freshly ground
STEW INGREDIENTS:	2 to 3 small boiling potatoes, peeled, quartered, and parboiled until almost tender
	2 to 3 carrots, peeled, cut up, and parboiled until almost tender

(*Ingredients list continues on next page*)

	1 cup fresh or frozen peas (fresh may be raw; frozen need not be thawed)
THICKENING:	2 tablespoons all-purpose flour mixed to a smooth paste with 2½ tablespoons soft butter
LIAISON:	None

Variation: OLD-FASHIONED BEEF POT ROAST

4 servings

❦*Accompany your pot roast with mashed potatoes, boiled potatoes, or noodles, plus a green vegetable.*

To prepare this dish, use a beef pot roast, plus the ingredients listed below, in the Master Technique on page 440.

COATING:	½ cup all-purpose flour
FAT:	¼ to ½ cup lard or vegetable shortening
VEGETABLE FLAVORING:	½ cup chopped onion ⅓ cup finely diced peeled carrot ⅓ cup finely diced celery ¼ cup finely diced peeled parsnip or turnip
CURRY OR PAPRIKA:	None
LIQUID:	1½ to 2½ cups Beef Stock, page 24, or canned broth
SEASONING:	2 tablespoons chopped fresh parsley 1 bay leaf ½ teaspoon mashed, pressed, or very finely minced garlic ½ teaspoon whole dried thyme ⅛ teaspoon ground cloves or allspice ¼ teaspoon salt ½ teaspoon pepper, preferably freshly ground
STEW INGREDIENTS:	None
THICKENING:	2 tablespoons all-purpose flour blended to a smooth paste with 2½ tablespoons soft butter
LIAISON:	½ to ¾ cup sour cream (optional)

Variation: PENNSYLVANIA DUTCH SOURED BEEF POT ROAST WITH GINGER

4 servings

❦ *This is a bit like sauerbraten, only not as sour and with a provocative accent of ginger. Serve the pot roast with noodles and green beans or peas.*

To prepare this dish, use a beef pot roast, plus the ingredients listed below, in the Master Technique on page 440.

COATING:	½ cup all-purpose flour
FAT:	¼ to ½ cup lard, vegetable shortening, or bacon fat
VEGETABLE FLAVORING:	1 cup chopped onions
	½ cup chopped peeled carrot
CURRY OR PAPRIKA:	None
LIQUID:	1 to 1¾ cups Beef Stock, page 24, or canned broth
	⅔ cup cider vinegar
	¼ cup packed dark brown sugar
SEASONING:	4 teaspoons ground ginger or 2 tablespoons grated or very finely minced fresh ginger
	1 bay leaf
	¼ teaspoon ground cloves or allspice
	½ teaspoon salt
	¼ teaspoon pepper, preferably freshly ground
STEW INGREDIENTS:	⅔ cup raisins (optional)
THICKENING:	None
LIAISON:	½ cup heavy cream (optional)

Variation: FLEMISH BEEF STEW, POT ROAST, OR STEAK WITH ONIONS AND BEER

4 servings

❦ *Serve this famous dish with noodles or plain boiled potatoes. Homemade sherbet would be a nice dessert.*

To prepare this variation, use beef stew meat, pot roast, or chuck or round steak, plus the ingredients listed below, in the Master Technique on page 440.

COATING: 1/2 cup all-purpose flour
FAT: 1/4 to 1/2 cup lard, vegetable shortening, or bacon fat
VEGETABLE FLAVORING: 2 cups thinly sliced onions
CURRY OR PAPRIKA: None
LIQUID: 1 1/2 to 2 1/2 cups beer
1 tablespoon packed dark brown sugar
SEASONING: 1 teaspoon mashed, pressed, or very finely minced garlic
1/2 teaspoon whole dried thyme
1 teaspoon salt
1/2 teaspoon pepper, preferably freshly ground
STEW INGREDIENTS: None
THICKENING: 2 tablespoons all-purpose flour mixed to a smooth paste with 2 1/2 tablespoons soft butter
LIAISON: None

Variation: LAMB STEW WITH FLAGEOLETS OR LIMA BEANS

4 servings

❦*Flageolets are lovely little greenish beans that are much beloved by the French. Similar in taste and texture to lima beans but somewhat more delicate, flageolets are sold here in cans at some specialty stores. But don't pass up the recipe if you can't find them, for lima beans will do very nicely. Accompany the stew with crusty rolls or bread.*

To prepare this stew, use lamb stew meat, plus the ingredients listed below, in the Master Technique on page 440.

COATING: 1/2 cup all-purpose flour
FAT: 1/4 to 1/2 cup olive oil
VEGETABLE SEASONING: 1 cup chopped onions
1 carrot, peeled and sliced
CURRY OR PAPRIKA: None
LIQUID: 1/3 to 1 1/3 cups Beef Stock, page 24, or Chicken Stock, page 26, or canned broth
1 14- to 16-ounce can tomatoes with their juice (break up the tomatoes with your hands)

SEASONING: 1 teaspoon mashed, pressed, or very finely minced garlic
1 bay leaf
½ teaspoon dried rosemary, ground or moistened with a few drops of water and minced fine
½ teaspoon salt
¼ teaspoon pepper, preferably freshly ground

STEW INGREDIENTS: 1½ cups cooked fresh or drained canned flageolets or lima beans

THICKENING: 2 tablespoons all-purpose flour mixed to a smooth paste with 2½ tablespoons soft butter

LIAISON: None

Variation: LAMB OR BEEF CURRY

4 servings

❦ *Personally, I prefer lamb here, but beef is often used in curried dishes of this sort. Rice is an obligatory accompaniment; you might also offer green beans, okra, eggplant, or broiled tomatoes. It is customary and fun, though not necessary, to garnish curries with chopped cashews, dried currants, or grated fresh coconut.*

To prepare this curry, use beef or lamb stew meat, plus the ingredients listed below, in the Master Technique on page 440.

COATING: ½ cup all-purpose flour

FAT: ¼ to ½ cup neutral vegetable oil

VEGETABLE FLAVORING: 1 cup chopped onions

CURRY OR PAPRIKA: 3 tablespoons mild curry powder or 2½ tablespoons hot (Madras) curry powder

LIQUID: 1½ to 2½ cups Chicken Stock, page 26, or canned broth
2 tablespoons strained fresh lemon juice

SEASONING: 1 bay leaf
1 teaspoon mashed, pressed, or very finely minced garlic
½ teaspoon salt

(Ingredients list continues on next page)

STEW INGREDIENTS:	1 large tart green apple, peeled, cored, and shredded
THICKENING:	2 tablespoons all-purpose flour mixed to a smooth paste with 2½ tablespoons soft butter
LIAISON:	¾ to 1½ cups yogurt

Variation: SWEDISH-AMERICAN BEEF POT ROAST

4 servings

❦ *The combination of ingredients used here—coffee, allspice, anchovy paste—may seem unlikely, but the final result is marvelous, and none of the ingredients, except perhaps the spice, could ever be guessed by the unknowing. I like to serve this with noodles and an assertive green vegetable such as cabbage or brussels sprouts.*

To prepare this variation, use a beef pot roast, plus the ingredients listed below, in the Master Technique on page 440.

COATING:	½ cup all-purpose flour
FAT:	3 to 5 tablespoons butter and 1 to 3 tablespoons neutral vegetable oil
VEGETABLE FLAVORING:	1 cup chopped onions
CURRY OR PAPRIKA:	None
LIQUID:	1⅓ cups very strong freshly brewed coffee
	⅓ to 1⅓ cups Beef Stock, page 24, or canned broth
	2 tablespoons packed dark brown sugar
	2 teaspoons anchovy paste or 1 tablespoon drained mashed anchovy fillets
SEASONING:	½ teaspoon ground allspice
	⅛ teaspoon ground cardamom (optional)
	¾ teaspoon salt
	½ to 1 teaspoon pepper, preferably freshly ground, to taste
STEW INGREDIENTS:	None
THICKENING:	2 tablespoons all-purpose flour mixed to a smooth paste with 2½ tablespoons soft butter
LIAISON:	⅓ cup heavy cream (optional)

Variation: CHILI BEEF OR LAMB STEW, OR BEEF STEAK

4 servings

❦*Accompany this classic favorite with tortillas, a tossed green salad, and plenty of cold beer for putting out the fire. Beef is the traditional meat for chili, but lamb may also be used.*

To prepare this variation, use beef or lamb stew meat or a beef chuck or round steak, plus the ingredients listed below, in the Master Technique on page 440.

COATING:	1/4 cup all-purpose flour
	1/4 cup cornmeal
FAT:	1/4 to 1/2 cup lard or vegetable shortening
VEGETABLE FLAVORING:	1 cup chopped onions
CURRY OR PAPRIKA:	None
LIQUID:	1 14- to 16-ounce can tomatoes with their juice (break up the tomatoes with your hands)
	1/3 to 1 cup water
	3 tablespoons tomato paste
SEASONING:	2 to 3 tablespoons hot (Mexican-style) chili powder, to taste
	2 large bay leaves
	1 tablespoon mashed, pressed, or very finely minced garlic
	1 teaspoon oregano
	1 1/2 teaspoons salt
	1/2 teaspoon pepper, preferably freshly ground
STEW INGREDIENTS:	1 to 2 cups cooked red kidney beans (optional)
THICKENING:	None
LIAISON:	None

❦

Variation: NAPA VALLEY BRAISED BEEF OR LAMB

4 servings

❦ *This is my homage to the California countryside of vineyards, sun, and warm sage-scented winds. Serve simply, with just boiled potatoes, and follow with a tossed salad or a plate of cold asparagus or artichokes.*

To prepare this variation, use beef or lamb stew meat or a beef pot roast or chuck or round steak, plus the ingredients listed below, in the Master Technique on page 440.

COATING:	½ cup all-purpose flour
FAT:	¼ to ½ cup olive oil
VEGETABLE FLAVORING:	1½ cups chopped onions
CURRY OR PAPRIKA:	None
LIQUID:	1½ to 2½ cups dry red California wine (the better the wine, the better the dish)
	1 tablespoon tomato paste
SEASONING:	1 bay leaf
	1½ teaspoons dried rosemary, ground or moistened with a few drops of water and minced fine
	1 teaspoon mashed, pressed, or very finely minced garlic
	½ teaspoon rubbed or ground sage
	¼ teaspoon dried marjoram, crushed
	¾ teaspoon salt
	½ teaspoon pepper, preferably freshly ground
STEW INGREDIENTS:	1¼ cups pitted green olives, rinsed and drained
THICKENING:	2 tablespoons all-purpose flour mixed to a smooth paste with 2½ tablespoons soft butter
LIAISON:	None

Variation: GOULASH

4 servings

❦ *This simple and perennially popular stew may be made with beef or lamb stew meat, or with a combination of both. It is sometimes also prepared with veal and/or pork. Accompany with noodles or boiled potatoes and perhaps green beans, and, if you wish, top each portion with a healthy dollop of room-temperature sour cream.*

To prepare goulash, use beef or lamb stew meat, plus the ingredients listed below, in the Master Technique on page 440.

COATING:	½ cup all-purpose flour
FAT:	¼ to ½ cup lard or vegetable shortening
VEGETABLE FLAVORING:	1½ cups thinly sliced onions
	1 large green bell pepper, seeded, deribbed, and cut into thin lengthwise strips
CURRY OR PAPRIKA:	1 tablespoon sweet paprika
LIQUID:	1 14- to 16-ounce can tomatoes with their juice (break up the tomatoes with your hands)
	½ to 1½ cups water
SEASONING:	½ teaspoon caraway seeds, ground or moistened with a few drops of water and minced fine
	1 teaspoon salt
	½ teaspoon pepper, preferably freshly ground
STEW INGREDIENTS:	None
THICKENING:	2 tablespoons all-purpose flour mixed to a smooth paste with 2½ tablespoons soft butter
LIAISON:	None

❦

Variation: ITALIAN-STYLE BEEF ROLLS STUFFED WITH SAUSAGE AND EGGS

4 to 6 servings

❦ *This is a simplified adaptation of my grandmother Denaro's long-time family recipe. Only a tossed green salad and crusty rolls or bread are needed as accompaniments.*

Eight fairly large slices of beef top round are required here. It is possible to use slices cut with the grain of the muscle—these might be taken from a small top round roast bought at a supermarket—but slices cut across the grain have a better texture.

To prepare this dish, stuff the rolls as indicated in Step 1, and then use the ingredients listed in Step 2 of this variation in the Master Technique on page 440.

STEP 1: PREPARING STUFFING AND MAKING THE ROLLS

- 2⁄3 cup chopped onions
- 3 tablespoons olive oil
- 8 ounces sausage meat (preferably hot Italian sausage flavored with fennel), squeezed out of casings (about 1 cup)
- 1⁄2 cup Fine Fresh Bread Crumbs (see page 60)
- 2 tablespoons tomato paste
- 2 tablespoons finely chopped fresh parsley
- 1 teaspoon mashed, pressed, or very finely minced garlic
- 1⁄4 teaspoon fennel seed (1⁄2 teaspoon if sausage meat contains no fennel), ground or moistened with a few drops of water and minced fine
- 1⁄2 teaspoon oregano
- 1⁄4 to 1⁄2 teaspoon salt
- 1⁄4 to 1⁄2 teaspoon pepper (depending on spiciness of sausage)
- 1 large egg
- 8 slices beef top round, each about 6×4×1⁄4 inches
- 4 hard-cooked eggs, peeled and cut in slices 1⁄4 inch thick

In a small skillet, slowly sauté onions in olive oil for about 10 minutes, or until soft but not at all brown. Scrape into mixing bowl and blend in all remaining ingredients except beef and hard-cooked eggs. Sauté a small spoonful of the stuffing, taste, and adjust seasoning accordingly.

One at a time, place beef slices between sheets of waxed paper and gently pound with a meat mallet or other suitable implement until reduced to a thickness of about 3⁄16 inch. Spread about 3 tablespoons stuffing on each slice and top with a row of hard-cooked egg slices, pressing egg lightly into the stuffing. Roll up beef starting from a short end and tie securely at each end with white twine.

STEP 2: BRAISING THE ROLLS

COATING:	½ cup all-purpose flour
FAT:	¼ to ½ cup olive oil
VEGETABLE FLAVORING:	⅓ cup chopped onion
	⅓ cup chopped celery
CURRY OR PAPRIKA:	None
LIQUID:	1 14- to 16-ounce can tomatoes with their juice (break up the tomatoes with your hands)
	½ to 1 cup dry red wine
	3 tablespoons tomato paste
SEASONING:	1 bay leaf
	1 teaspoon mashed, pressed, or very finely minced garlic
	½ teaspoon oregano
	¾ teaspoon salt
	½ teaspoon pepper, preferably freshly ground
STEW INGREDIENTS:	None
THICKENING:	None
LIAISON:	None

Braise the stuffed beef rolls, using the ingredients listed above, as in the Master Technique, simmering the beef for about 1½ hours, or until tender enough to be cut with the side of a fork. Baste periodically and turn every 20 minutes during cooking. Untie before serving.

STEWED POULTRY and MEAT

If roasting was the first cooking technique to be invented, stewing must have been the second. Having learned to roast, early hominids must soon have discovered—and, while gathered around their roasting fires, perhaps discussed—how certain parts of their quarry were too tough to chew. A longer than usual roasting seemed to soften the interior of the meat, but it also had the unfortunate side effect of turning the outer parts of the meat to leather. Eventually, it must have occurred to someone that cooking the meat over a prolonged period in liquid might solve the problem. And thus stewing was born.

This chapter consists mainly of variations on stewed chicken. The preferred chicken for stewing is a geriatric hen—rich in flavor, but tough—but since stewing hens are often in short supply, the Master Recipe uses a roasting chicken; notes on stewing hen and other types of poultry and meat appear at the end of the recipe text. The chapter also includes two classic American recipes that were invented to make the most of spare, tough foods. These are New England boiled corned beef dinner, one of the dishes the early settlers ate when they had only preserved meat and a few winter vegetables on hand, and pork hocks and greens, a dish invented by southern slaves.

MASTER RECIPE

Old Fashioned Chicken (or Turkey, Giblet, or Veal) Stew With Vegetables and Cream Gravy

6 to 8 servings

❦ *In this recipe, chicken and vegetables are poached until tender in an aromatic stock; they are then removed from the pot and the poaching liquid is transformed into a rich cream gravy to accompany them. A true Master Recipe, this stew can be topped with dumplings, baked under a crust to make a pot pie, or, with a few simple modifications, turned into such classic party dishes as chicken à la king, chicken tetrazzini, or curried chicken. Of course it can also be served as is, accompanied by peas or green beans and mashed potatoes or rice.*

Notes on preparing a stewing hen, turkey, giblets, or veal according to this recipe appear on pages 457–58.

STEP 1: STEWING THE CHICKEN

A 6-pound roasting chicken
The following, tied in a cheesecloth bag: 4 large parsley sprigs; 1 large bay leaf; 1 clove garlic, unpeeled (optional); 1 teaspoon whole peppercorns; 1 teaspoon whole dried thyme; 1 whole clove or allspice berry
The following stew vegetables:
- 12 to 16 1-inch white onions, peeled
- 4 large carrots, peeled and cut into 3/4-inch lengths
- 2 large ribs celery, cut into 3/4-inch lengths
- 2 parsnips, peeled and cut into 3/4-inch lengths (optional)

1 quart Chicken Stock, page 26, or canned broth
2 to 4 cups water
Salt

Rinse the chicken under tepid water. Cut the chicken into serving pieces (drumsticks, thighs, wings, and breast halves); save backbone and giblets for future use in a stock. Place chicken, herb bag, and stew vegetables in a 6-quart lidded pot. Add stock or broth plus enough water to cover the ingredients by 1/2 inch. Sprinkle on 1/4 teaspoon salt for each cup of water used.

Bring stew to a fast simmer over high heat, then turn flame down to the point where the liquid is barely bubbling; partially cover the pot. Periodically skimming off any fat or scum and adding more water if the stew ingredients become exposed, cook at the barest simmer for 45 minutes to 1 hour, or until both the chicken and vegetables are tender when pierced with a fork.

STEP 2: PREPARING THE CREAM GRAVY

8 tablespoons (1 stick) butter
⅔ cup all-purpose flour
⅔ to 1 cup heavy cream
Salt, white pepper, preferably freshly ground, and fresh lemon juice

Using a slotted spoon or skimmer, carefully transfer chicken and vegetables to a 4-quart bowl and cover loosely with lightly buttered waxed paper. Set aside. Discard the herb bag. Skim fat from the surface of the poaching liquid, then pour broth into a large bowl. Return 5 cups of the liquid to the stew pot to make gravy. Refrigerate or freeze remainder of the broth for future use.

Melt butter in a heavy-bottomed 2½-quart saucepan, remove from heat, and stir in flour with a wooden spoon, blending until absolutely smooth. Return saucepan to low heat and cook the butter-flour paste very slowly, without letting it color, for 3 minutes, stirring constantly with a wooden spoon. Again remove saucepan from heat. Bring reserved poaching liquid to a boil, then beating hard with a wire whip, pour it all at once into the butter-flour paste. Stir the mixture with a wooden spoon, scraping up any butter-flour paste that may be lurking in the corners of the pan. Set saucepan over moderate heat and bring to a simmer, stirring frequently; the gravy will be quite thick. Blend in ⅔ cup or more heavy cream and lower flame to the point where the gravy barely simmers. Stirring frequently to prevent scorching, simmer gravy slowly for 10 minutes. If necessary, thin with additional cream or poaching liquid. Taste and correct seasoning with salt, white pepper, and drops of lemon juice. Return chicken and vegetables to pot and warm briefly in the gravy, basting occasionally.

AHEAD OF TIME: Stew may be refrigerated for several days or frozen for several months, though freezing will soften the vegetables and coarsen the texture of the chicken. To reheat cold stew, place it over a low flame or in a 300°F oven until hot.

PREPARING A STEWING HEN: This is the perfect sort of recipe in which to use a stewing hen, but since stewing hens are rare in many markets, I have featured a roasting chicken in the main recipe text.

Select a 6-pound stewing hen and cut into 8 serving pieces. Proceed according to the Master Recipe, but simmer the hen (with herb bag) for about 1½ hours before adding the vegetables (and, if necessary, additional water to cover). Simmer about 45 minutes longer, or until both the bird and vegetables are tender when pierced with a fork. Test the bird for doneness frequently toward the end of cooking. Should it become tender before the vegetables are cooked, remove it from the pot at once; if overcooked, it will become mushy.

PREPARING TURKEY PARTS: Choose 6 to 8 drumsticks and/or thighs (1 per serving); if using whole legs, separate drumsticks and thighs at the joint. Proceed according to the Master Recipe, but simmer the turkey parts (with herb bag) for about 1 hour before adding the vegetables (and, if necessary, additional water to cover). Simmer about 45 minutes longer, or until both the turkey and the vegetables are tender when pierced with a fork.

PREPARING CHICKEN OR TURKEY GIBLETS: Giblets make a very flavorful and elegant stew, and they can be had for very little money. To serve 6 to 8, choose about 3 pounds hearts or 3½ pounds gizzards or mixed hearts and gizzards. Rinse, then detach the two lobes of gizzards from the mantle of tough skin that connects them; discard the skin. Proceed according to the Master Recipe, but simmer the giblets for 1¼ to 1½ hours, or until almost tender, before adding the vegetables (and, if necessary, additional water to cover). Simmer about 45 minutes longer, or until the vegetables are tender and the giblets are very soft.

PREPARING VEAL STEW MEAT: To serve 6 to 8, choose about 3 pounds of boneless veal shoulder cut into strips roughly 1 inch long and ½ inch wide. Proceed according to the Master Recipe, but simmer the veal for about 1 hour before adding the vegetables (and, if necessary, additional water to cover). Simmer about 45 minutes longer, or until the vegetables and veal are tender when pierced with a fork. Veal throws off a considerable quantity of grayish scum as it cooks; skim the broth frequently to prevent the scum from mixing in with the broth and discoloring it.

Variation: CHICKEN À LA KING

8 servings

❦*Although this dish has suffered cruelly at the hands of cafeteria chefs and convenience food manufacturers, it is in fact first-rate when carefully prepared using the best ingredients. Serve chicken à la king in hot patty shells or over rice and accompany with green beans, peas, asparagus, or quartered artichoke bottoms. You can, by the way, make this dish with turkey or giblets, and, when prepared with veal and without pimiento, the dish becomes the famous French stew,* blanquette de veau.

Old-fashioned Chicken (or Turkey, Giblet, or Veal Stew) with Vegetables and Cream Gravy

ADD: 1 onion, peeled and chopped; 1 small carrot, peeled and sliced; and 1 small rib celery, sliced, to herb bag

OMIT: Stew vegetables

ADD: 2 cups (about 8 ounces) sliced mushrooms tossed with 2 teaspoons fresh lemon juice

⅔ cup pimientos cut into small strips

4 large egg yolks

Prepare a roasting chicken or stewing hen as indicated in Step 1 of the Master Recipe, adding onion, carrot, and celery to the herb bag and omitting the stew vegetables.

Following Step 2 of the Master Recipe, make a thick cream gravy using butter, flour, and 5 cups of the poaching liquid. However do not add the cream called for in the Master Recipe yet. Stir mushrooms and pimientos into the gravy and simmer slowly for 10 to 15 minutes, stirring occasionally. Thin the gravy, if necessary, with additional poaching broth. While gravy is simmering, proceed to remove all skin and bones from the chicken and cut meat into ½-inch dice.

Blend ¾ cup of the cream called for in the Master Recipe and the egg yolks in a 3-quart bowl. Remove gravy from heat and very slowly pour 3 cups hot gravy into the yolk mixture, beating constantly with a wire whip. Beat this mixture back into gravy remaining in the pot. Place over low heat and bring to the barest simmer, stirring constantly with a wooden spoon; the sauce will thicken. Fold diced chicken into the sauce and stir gently over low flame just until chicken is warmed through. Taste and adjust seasoning. It is best to serve this dish immediately, but it may be refrigerated for a day and reheated in a double boiler over gently simmering water.

Variation: CREAMED CHICKEN WITH OLIVES AND TOASTED ALMONDS

6 to 8 servings

❦ *This can be served in patty shells, but I prefer it over rice. A good accompaniment is cherry tomatoes sautéed in butter.*

Old-Fashioned Chicken (or Turkey, Giblet, or Veal) Stew with Vegetables and Cream Gravy

ADD: 1 onion, peeled and chopped; 1 small carrot, peeled and sliced; and 1 small rib celery, sliced, to herb bag

OMIT: Stew vegetables

ADD: 1 cup drained pimiento-stuffed green olives
½ cup (about 2 ounces) slivered or sliced almonds, lightly toasted (see page 699)

Prepare a roasting chicken or stewing hen as indicated in Step 1 of the Master Recipe, adding onion, carrot, and celery to the herb bag and omitting the stew vegetables. While the chicken is cooking, slice the olives thinly, scatter the slices over a double thickness of paper toweling, cover with another double thickness of toweling, and press firmly with your hands to squeeze out some of the brine.

Prepare cream gravy as indicated in the Master Recipe, folding in olives and then simmering the sauce slowly for 10 minutes. While the sauce is simmering, remove all skin and bones from chicken and cut meat into thin strips or ½-inch dice. Fold chicken into the sauce and warm briefly over low heat, stirring, just until chicken is heated through. Taste and adjust seasoning. Serve sprinkled with almonds.

Variation: CREAMED CHICKEN OR TURKEY WITH WHITE GRAPES (CHICKEN OR TURKEY VÉRONIQUE)

6 to 8 servings

❦ *Serve this over rice or in hot patty shells, accompanied by broccoli.*

Old-fashioned Chicken (or Turkey, Giblet, or Veal) Stew with Vegetables and Cream Gravy

ADD: 1 onion, peeled and chopped; 1 small carrot, peeled and sliced; and 1 small rib celery, sliced, to herb bag

OMIT: Stew vegetables

ADD: 2 cups white grapes, preferably seedless

Prepare a roasting chicken, stewing hen, or turkey legs as described in Step 1 of the Master Recipe, adding onion, carrot, and celery to herb bag and omitting the stew vegetables. While the chicken is cooking, drop the grapes into 2 quarts rapidly boiling water for 30 seconds, drain in a colander, and rinse with cold water until cool. Peel grapes if you wish, cut in half, and, if necessary, flick out seeds with the point of a paring knife.

Prepare cream gravy as indicated in Step 2 of the Master Recipe. While gravy is simmering, remove all skin and bones from the chicken or turkey and cut poultry into ½-inch dice. Fold grapes into the cream gravy and, without letting it return to a simmer, poach grapes in the gravy over very low heat for 3 minutes, stirring gently. Fold in chicken or turkey and stir over low heat, without simmering, until heated through. Taste and adjust seasoning. This dish is best if served immediately, but it may be refrigerated or frozen.

Variation: CURRIED CHICKEN, TURKEY, GIBLET, OR VEAL STEW WITH VEGETABLES

6 to 8 servings

❦ *Serve this soul-satisfying stew with rice and accompany with broccoli, peas, green beans, or okra.*

Old-Fashioned Chicken (or Turkey, Giblet, or Veal) Stew with Vegetables and Cream Gravy

ADD: 2 tablespoons mild curry powder or 1½ tablespoons hot (Madras) curry powder
Sugar, if needed

Prepare a roasting chicken, stewing hen, turkey legs, giblets, or veal as indicated in Step 1 of the Master Recipe. If you wish, remove the skin and bones from cooked poultry and cut the meat into ½-inch dice.

In Step 2 of the Master Recipe, melt butter in large saucepan, stir in curry powder, and cook slowly, stirring, for 3 minutes. Remove from heat, blend in flour, and proceed to make the gravy as indicated. Season gravy with drops of fresh lemon juice and, if needed, pinches of sugar.

Variation: CHICKEN, TURKEY, GIBLET, OR VEAL STEW WITH PARSLEY DUMPLINGS

6 to 8 servings

❦*Accompany this traditional favorite with peas or green beans.*

Old-Fashioned Chicken (or Turkey, Giblet, or Veal) Stew with Vegetables and Cream Gravy, made with the poultry or meat of your choice
1½ cups cake flour or, as a second choice, 1⅓ cups unbleached all-purpose flour (measure by scooping cup into large container of flour and sweeping off excess with the back of a knife)
1 tablespoon baking powder
¾ teaspoon salt
2 tablespoons cold butter
¼ cup finely chopped fresh parsley
½ cup *boiling* water

After you have prepared the cream gravy, combine it with the poultry either in the stew pot (as in the Master Recipe) or in an attractive 4-quart stove-to-table casserole. You may do this ahead of time. Before proceeding with recipe, set the stew over low-moderate heat so that it will be at or near the simmer by the time the dumplings are ready to be cooked.

To prepare the dumplings, combine the flour, baking powder, and salt in a 2-quart bowl and blend thoroughly with a fork or with your fingertips. Cut butter into bits and work it into the flour mixture with your fingertips, as though you were making pie pastry. Stir in chopped parsley. Pour in boiling water all at once and beat with a wooden spoon just until the dough gathers together. If the dough seems very stiff and dry, beat in an additional tablespoon of boiling water. Roll dough into 16 to 18 rough 1-inch balls between the palms of your hands.

When the stew has reached a lazy simmer, scatter dumplings evenly over the top and cover tightly. *Without lifting the lid for the first 3 minutes,* steam the dumplings for about 5 minutes, or until they have swelled and look cakelike rather than raw and doughy in the center when cut into. Serve the stew without delay, as the dumplings will begin to turn gooey within a matter of minutes.

Variation: CHICKEN OR TURKEY POT PIE

6 to 8 servings

❦ *This is yet another dish whose homemade and commercially manufactured versions bear little resemblance to each other. Serve with a green vegetable and/or cherry tomatoes sautéed in butter.*

PRELIMINARIES

1. Set rack in the upper-middle level of oven.
2. Preheat oven to 400°F 20 minutes before baking.
3. Select a 13×9×2-inch baking dish, preferably glass or ceramic. Butter lightly.

Old-Fashioned Chicken (or Turkey, Giblet, or Veal) Stew with Vegetables and Cream Gravy

Butter Pie Crust Dough, page 751, using proportions for a 9-inch pie shell

1 egg, beaten to blend with 1 teaspoon water

Prepare the Master Recipe for the stew using a roasting chicken, stewing hen, or turkey parts. While the cream gravy is simmering (Step 2) remove all skin and bones from the poultry and cut the flesh into ½-inch chunks. Do not recombine poultry and gravy.

Pour an inch of cream gravy into the baking dish. Distribute poultry and vegetables evenly in the dish, reaching nearly to the rim, then pour in enough additional gravy to almost—but not quite—cover the solid ingredients.

On a well-floured work surface roll the pie crust dough into a rectangle about 14×10 inches. Fold dough in thirds lengthwise, transfer to the baking dish, and unfold over the top of the dish, covering it completely. Tuck overhanging dough underneath itself to build up a rim. Press rim of dough firmly against edge of the baking dish to seal, then flute the rim decoratively. Brush top of the pie with a double coating of egg glaze. Cut three 1-inch-long slits in the crust to allow steam to escape.

Bake the pie for 30 to 40 minutes, or until the crust is nicely browned and the filling is steaming hot. The sooner the pie is served, the flakier the crust will be.

Variation: CHICKEN OR TURKEY TETRAZZINI

6 to 8 servings

❦ *The bad reputation of this dish is largely undeserved. The combination of flavors—chicken or turkey, Parmesan cheese, mushrooms, almonds, and wine—is excellent, and the dish makes a very attractive addition to a buffet table because it is easy to serve. My favorite accompaniment here is a tossed green salad, but a green vegetable can be offered instead.*

PRELIMINARIES

1. Set rack in the upper-middle level of oven.
2. Preheat oven to 425°F 20 minutes before baking.
3. Select a 13×9×2-inch baking dish, preferably glass or ceramic.

Old-Fashioned Chicken (or Turkey, Giblet, or Veal) Stew with Vegetables and Cream Gravy

ADD: 1 onion, peeled and chopped; 1 small carrot, peeled and sliced; and 1 small rib celery, sliced, to herb bag

OMIT: Stew vegetables

2 cups cooked small macaroni or egg noodles

½ recipe Sautéed Mushrooms, page 550

½ cup (2 ounces) slivered or sliced almonds, lightly toasted (see page 700)

2 tablespoons dry vermouth

2 tablespoons soft butter

¾ cup (3 ounces) freshly grated Parmesan cheese

Prepare the Master Recipe with a roasting chicken, stewing hen, or turkey parts, adding onion, carrot, and celery to the herb bag and omitting the stew vegetables. While the gravy is simmering (Step 2), remove all skin and bones from poultry and cut flesh into ½-inch chunks. Measure 3 cups of the diced poultry into a 2½-quart mixing bowl; save any remaining poultry for some other use. Fold 2 cups of the cream gravy into the diced poultry; set aside. Combine remaining gravy with cooked pasta, sautéed mushrooms, toasted almonds, and vermouth in a 3- to 4-quart mixing bowl.

Coat the inside of the baking dish with soft butter and sprinkle with ¼ cup of the Parmesan cheese, pressing any loose cheese lightly against the sides and bottom of the dish to make it adhere. Spoon pasta mixture into the dish, make a well in the center, and fill with the poultry and gravy mixture. Smooth the top of the casserole and sprinkle remaining ½ cup Parmesan cheese on top. Bake for 20 to 25 minutes, or just until the top is lightly browned and the casserole is bubbly around the edges. Don't overcook this dish, or it will turn pasty. Serve at once.

AHEAD OF TIME: Dish may be assembled several hours in advance of baking. Cover and set aside at room temperature.

NEW ENGLAND BOILED CORNED BEEF DINNER

6 servings

Serve boiled dinner with horseradish-flavored sour cream, plain grated horseradish, and/or English or Dijon mustard.

3½ pounds corned beef brisket
1 large onion stuck with 2 cloves
1 large bay leaf
12 small boiling potatoes, peeled
8 medium carrots, peeled and cut into 2-inch lengths
4 medium parsnips, peeled and cut into 2-inch lengths
3 to 4 white turnips, peeled and halved or quartered, or ½ small rutabaga, cut into pieces the same size as the carrots (1 to 1½ cups)
½ medium cabbage, cut lengthwise into 4 to 6 wedges

Rinse meat under cold running water and tie into a neat, compact shape with twine. Place meat, onion, and bay leaf in a large kettle and add enough water to cover meat by 2 inches. Bring to a simmer, cover partially, and cook very slowly for 2 to 2½ hours, or until brisket is nearly tender, removing scum from the surface as it accumulates. Add vegetables to the kettle; if necessary, pour in enough boiling water to allow vegetables to float. Simmer, partially covered, for 20 to 30 minutes longer, or until both meat and vegetables are fully cooked. Remove meat to carving board, cover loosely with foil, and let rest 5 minutes before untying and carving into thin slices. Arrange slices on platter and surround with vegetables. Pass with a small bowlful of the broth; save the rest of the broth, if not too salty, for a soup.

PORK HOCKS AND GREENS

4 servings

❦ *This classic American dish was devised by Southern slaves who had to make the best of tough meat scraps and greens. It is always served with corn bread.*

Pork hocks are the front shank of the hog, where the foot joins the arm. They are available either fresh or cured and require long, slow stewing in liquid to become tender. Sometimes you will also see hind hocks at the market. Consisting of the knuckle that connects the hind leg and hind hoof, hind hocks may be prepared in the same ways as pork hocks.

4 large or 8 medium-sized fresh or smoked pork hocks (3 to 4 pounds)
1 cup chopped onions
1 teaspoon salt (omit if you are using smoked meat)
½ teaspoon crushed red pepper
4 to 8 ounces salt pork
2 pounds collard, kale, turnip, or mustard greens (a combination of two or more is preferable), tough stems removed

Place meat, onions, salt, and red pepper in an 8-quart pot, pour on enough water to cover, and bring to a simmer. Meanwhile, cut salt pork into ¼-inch dice and brown in a skillet. When the meat has cooked 1 hour, add browned salt pork along with the fat it has rendered and simmer 30 minutes longer. Add greens to the pot and simmer for 45 minutes or longer, or until greens are very soft and meat is falling from the bones. Taste the broth and season as necessary. Serve meat and greens on a platter. Ladle some of the "pot likker" into a bowl, to be spooned onto plates by diners and sopped up with corn bread.

❦

FRESH VEGETABLES

The length and breadth of this chapter no doubt betrays my personal fondness for vegetables. I eat them in preference to fish, fowl, flesh, and most other foods as well. People often ask me what basic cooking method I prefer for vegetables, as if there were one correct way to prepare them all. This of course is not the case. The vegetable kingdom includes everything from artichokes to corn, lima beans to mushrooms, asparagus to beets, zucchini to chestnuts. Each vegetable requires its own special trimming and paring procedures, and each is better suited to some basic cooking methods (or Master Recipes) than to others.

About Cooking Vegetables

Basic Cooking Methods for Vegetables: Of the major vegetable cooking techniques, perhaps the simplest and most widely used is *boiling.* Because it preserves their color and texture, boiling is a particularly good way of cooking green vegetables, but only those that are flavorful enough to withstand being cooked in a quantity of water and sturdy enough not to break up when drained in a colander. These would include artichokes, green beans, broccoli, brussels sprouts, and okra. Root vegetables requiring prolonged cooking such as beets, celery root, Jerusalem artichokes, potatoes, sweet potatoes, and salsify are also generally boiled, preferably in their skins so that they do not become mushy or leached of taste.

In recent years *steaming* has become an increasingly popular vegetable cooking technique, partly because it is thought to protect vegetables' nutrients better than boiling. Vegetables can be steamed on a rack or collapsible basket over simmering water, the usual method, or directly in a small quantity of water. Particularly good candidates for steaming are those vegetables that would tend, if boiled, to lose their taste and texture in the cooking water (cabbage, kohlrabi, spinach), or to break up in the colander when drained (cauliflower), or both (the summer and winter squashes). Steaming, however, is not a good way to cook bright green vegetables. These release a chemical during cooking that, in reaction with condensed steam, forms a new compound that causes the color to fade.

Braising entails cooking vegetables slowly in butter or other fat and a small to moderate amount of water or stock; when the vegetables are tender, the cooking liquid is boiled down to form a light, syrupy glaze. Braising is particularly recommended for vegetables that need to stew in their own juices in order to develop their full flavor. Among these are the strongly flavored or slightly sweet root vegetables (carrots, parsnips, rutabagas, and turnips), the delicate stalk and head vegetables (celery, endive, fennel, lettuce), the tough greens (collards, kale, mustard), leeks and onions, and chestnuts.

Certain vegetables become mushy and flavorless when cooked in the presence of liquid, making boiling, steaming, and braising equally inappropriate. For some of these vegetables—cucumbers, eggplant, and mushrooms—*sautéing* is the best solution. Others are good *baked* (winter squash, onions), *stir-fried* (watercress, young mustard), or *deep-fried* (plantains), and a few such as asparagus, bell peppers, and freshly cut corn require their own specialized cooking procedures.

It goes without saying that there are, in the case of many vegetables, several right ways—onions can be braised as well as baked, summer squash can be both sautéed and steamed, and potatoes respond well to practically any cooking method. The wise course is not to seek out the one and only, the "best" cooking technique for each vegetable, but rather to become comfortable with all the ways so that no one method need be depended on exclusively.

VEGETABLE COOKING TIMES AND DONENESS: In the 1960s, when the current preference for fresh vegetables over frozen or canned was beginning to take shape, people looked to classic French cuisine for guidance and inspiration. The long-standing Anglo-American tradition of boiling most vegetables until they practically fell apart no longer seemed desirable; the French practice of cooking vegetables briefly, so that they emerged with all their colors, flavors, and textures still intact, was universally admired. Now, the movement favoring lightly cooked vegetables has progressed so far that vegetables prepared in the traditional French manner strike many as woefully overdone. The current practice, at least in many New York restaurants, is to blanch most vegetables very briefly, and some are served barely warmed through. I wonder if we are verging on excess. Overcooking destroys flavor; undercooking prevents it from developing. Careful, considered preparation of each vegetable according to its own particular characteristics and needs seems to me the solution.

ARTICHOKES

In addition to their fine, sweet, nutlike flavor, artichokes, the fruit of a species of thistle, make a beautiful sight on the plate and are tremendously fun to eat. In some specialty markets you may see very small artichokes, barely bigger than walnuts. These are generally sautéed rather than boiled and are eaten whole, petals, choke, stem, and all. More usually, though, artichokes are somewhere between oranges and small grapefruits in size. Grab the very large ones if you are lucky enough to find them as they are every bit as tender and tasty as smaller specimens and make a very dramatic presentation. When fresh and at their prime, artichokes are just a shade paler than leaf green, with tightly closed petals and a firm but not rock-hard feel in the hand. As they age, artichokes darken, open up, and begin to soften. Slightly elderly artichokes look better cooked than raw, and though they tend to be a bit dry and mealy, their flavor is acceptable. Very old artichokes that have become blackened and shriveled should be avoided as they are apt to be bitter.

CANNED ARTICHOKES: Often these might just as well be some other vegetable, so little resemblance do they bear to fresh artichokes. If you like canned artichokes in salads and cold dishes but wish to tone down their acidity, you can freshen them as follows: Drain the artichokes and drop into a quantity of boiling water for 1 minute. Drain, then rinse under cold water. Place the artichokes on paper toweling and pat dry with more toweling. Turn the artichokes into a bowl and spoon over them some flavorful nut or olive oil. Toss with fresh garlic, some fresh parsley perhaps, salt, and freshly ground black pepper. Cover loosely and marinate at room temperature. In an hour or two, they will develop a mild and pleasant savor.

RESCUING OVERCOOKED ARTICHOKES: It seems that overcooked artichokes become firmer and drier if they are served cold or at room temperature, preferably a day after the misfortune has occurred. If you must serve them warm, spoon out the chokes (they hold a great deal of water) and set the artichokes upside down on a rack for as long as possible, so that they can dry out. When you are ready to serve them, butter or oil the artichokes well, inside and out, and bake them in a 400°F oven until they are well heated.

Presenting and Eating Artichokes: Artichokes are best presented as a separate course preceding or following the main dish, rather than as an accompaniment. Be sure to serve them on plates large enough to hold the discarded leaves and chokes or to set out bowls, individual or communal, in which to cast the leavings.

The edible flesh of an artichoke is to be found at the base of the leaves and at the bottom of the vegetable. To eat an artichoke, pluck off the leaves one by one and draw them between your teeth, scraping off the flesh. When all the leaves have been removed, scrape the choke off the artichoke bottom (this may also be done in advance of serving); discard the choke and eat the bottom.

MASTER RECIPE

Boiled Artichokes

4 servings

❦*Artichokes are equally good hot and cold. Hot artichokes may be served with melted butter and lemon wedges or with hollandaise or béarnaise sauce. Cold artichokes are good with vinaigrette dressing, plain homemade mayonnaise, herb mayonnaise, or green goddess dressing. For an especially attractive presentation, remove the chokes before serving and fill the vegetables with a sauce.*

Step 1: Trimming the Artichokes

4 artichokes 3 to 4 inches in diameter
1 lemon, halved

Wash artichokes thoroughly under a strong stream of water, spreading the leaves to make sure that any sand is removed. Trim each artichoke as follows. First, cut off stem parallel to the base of the vegetable (1), pull away any small, leathery leaves at the base, and rub the cut with lemon to prevent discoloration. (If the stem is around ½ inch in diameter, it may be peeled and cooked along with the artichokes; if larger, it will prove tough and stringy when cooked and should be discarded.) (2) Next, lay artichoke on its side on a cutting board and slice off the top of the cone about 1 inch from the point. Rub cut with lemon (3). Last, snip off tops of leaves with kitchen shears to remove the prickers (4).

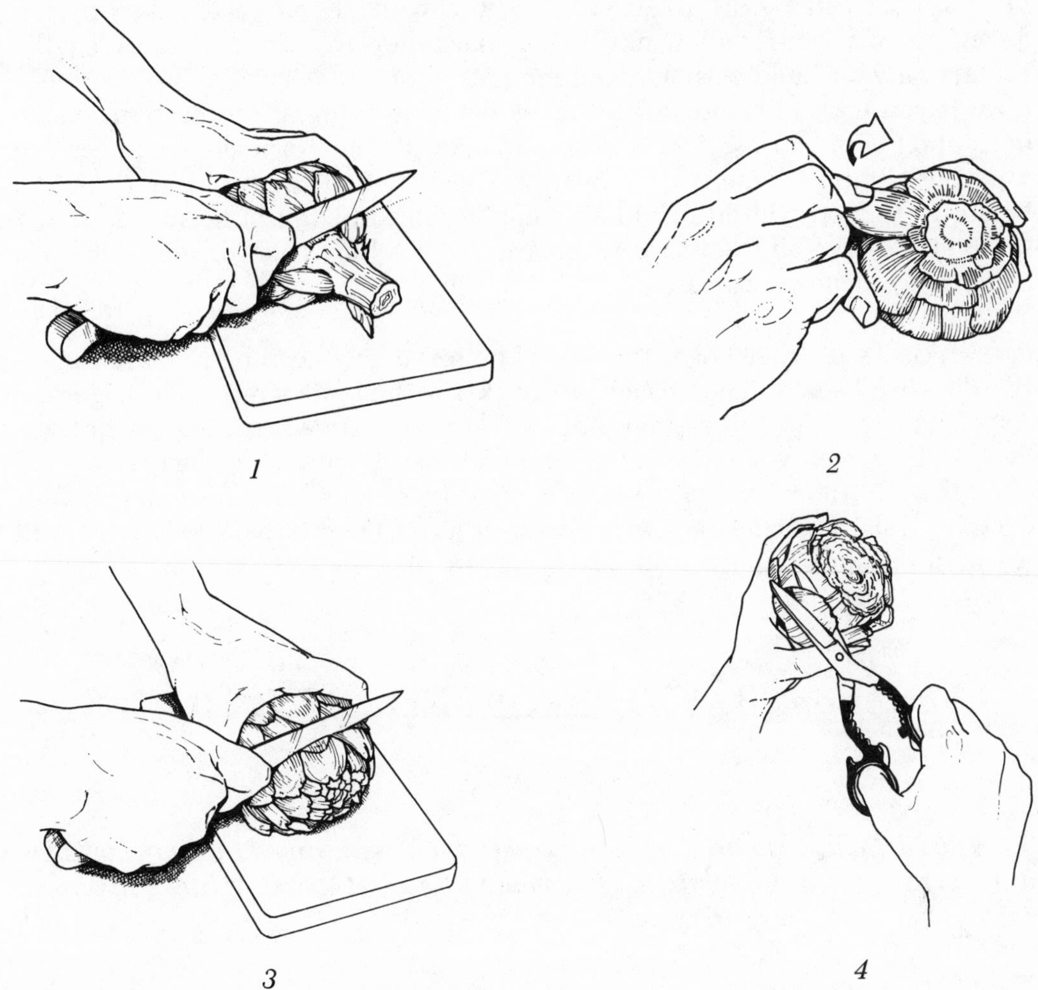

1 *2* *3* *4*

STEP 2: BOILING THE ARTICHOKES

4 quarts water
2 tablespoons salt

Bring salted water to a rapid boil in a 6- to 8-quart pot. Add artichokes and the remains of the cut lemon from Step 1, cover artichokes with cheesecloth to keep their exposed surfaces moist (the artichokes will float), and bring water back to the boil. Do not cover the pot. Cook for 25 to 45 minutes (depending on the size of the artichokes), replenishing water as necessary. To test for doneness, remove an artichoke from the pot and pierce the bottom deeply with a table fork. If it feels tender, the artichoke is cooked. Be sure to test each one, as some may cook more quickly than others.

STEP 3: DRAINING AND REMOVING THE CHOKE: Drain artichokes upside down in a colander for a few minutes, or until they are cool enough to handle. Protecting your hand with a towel, squeeze gently to extract additional moisture. If you wish to remove the chokes before serving, place each artichoke upright on your work surface and spread open the center leaves until you see a purplish, shiny, dome-shaped clump of leaves. Pull these out and discard. Underneath, you will find the hairy-looking choke. Using a teaspoon, gently scrape the choke off the heart. If the artichoke is fully cooked, the choke will come away cleanly and easily.

AHEAD OF TIME: Artichokes that are to be served cold can be prepared up to two days in advance. Cover cooled artichokes with plastic wrap and refrigerate. Artichokes that are to be presented hot are best served as soon as they are cooked. However, you may cook them beforehand, scrape out the chokes, and keep them in the refrigerator, each wrapped well in plastic, for a day or two. To reheat, slather artichokes with butter or oil and pop into a 400°F oven until warmed through.

Variation: BAKED STUFFED ARTICHOKES

4 servings

❦ Stuffed artichokes may be served hot, perhaps accompanied by lemon wedges, at room temperature, or chilled. They make a fine first course or lunch dish, and they are a marvelous—if somewhat messy—picnic food.

PRELIMINARIES

1. Set rack in middle of oven.
2. Preheat oven to 425°F 20 minutes before baking.
3. Select an 8-inch square baking dish or other dish just large enough to hold the artichokes snugly. An oven-to-table dish will prove convenient.

Boiled Artichokes; undercook slightly and remove chokes as indicated in Step 3
¾ cup olive oil
1 cup finely chopped onions
⅓ cup minced cooked ham (optional)
2 teaspoons mashed, pressed, or very finely minced garlic

1⅓ cups Fine Fresh Bread Crumbs (see page 60)
¼ cup finely chopped fresh parsley, preferably flat-leaf Italian parsley
½ teaspoon fresh lemon juice
¼ to ½ teaspoon salt
¼ teaspoon pepper, preferably freshly ground

Pour 3 tablespoons of the olive oil into the baking dish and either roll the artichokes in the oil until thoroughly coated on all sides or swab all surfaces of artichokes with oil using a pastry brush. Set artichokes upright in the dish and gently spread the leaves and center. Sprinkle lightly with salt and pepper.

Place 6 tablespoons of the olive oil in a 10-inch skillet, add onions, and sauté slowly until the onion is tender but not at all browned, about 10 minutes. Stir in the ham and garlic and cook slowly for about 1 minute longer. Remove from heat and stir in the crumbs, parsley, and lemon juice. Taste the stuffing and add salt to taste plus pepper.

Spoon some of the stuffing mixture between the leaves of the artichokes, then fill the cavities and cover tops of artichokes with remaining stuffing. Drizzle the remaining 3 tablespoons olive oil over tops of artichokes.

Basting once or twice with the olive oil in the baking dish, bake the artichokes for about 30 minutes, or until both stuffing and vegetables are hot and the crumbs on top are nicely browned.

AHEAD OF TIME: You may stuff the artichokes, cover loosely with plastic wrap, and leave them at room temperature for 3 to 4 hours before baking.

ASPARAGUS

The single most important determinant of freshness in cut asparagus is its moisture content. To keep it in prime condition, a good vegetable market will tie its asparagus in small bundles and stand the bundles upright in a shallow tray of water. Some markets will go one step further and keep the vegetable under refrigeration. Asparagus should be stored at home in the same manner—tied in bundles, resting upright in ½ inch or so of water, in the refrigerator. Plan to use asparagus soon after purchasing.

When choosing asparagus, look for stalks that are stiff, almost brittle, and that do not bend when held straight up. The skin should be smooth and bright green, the scales moist-looking, flat, and pointed, the head tight, hard, and compact. Provided asparagus is peeled (see instructions below), thick stalks are just as tender and tasty as thin ones, and thick stalks are easier to trim and more attractive to serve. However, stalks that are an inch or more wide at the base are overmature and should be avoided. Stalks with a long section of white skin at the base are not as choice as those that are green from top to bottom. However, most of the white part will prove to be edible if the asparagus is peeled.

CANNED AND FROZEN ASPARAGUS: A friend tells me that she considers canned and fresh asparagus two entirely different vegetables and likes both equally. While I do not share her love of canned asparagus, I have found it an acceptable ingredient in soufflés and other egg dishes. Frozen asparagus is not peeled and thus it is stringy on the outside, mushy within. The best way to use it is to thaw it partially, then to stir-fry it quickly in vegetable oil, adding, if you wish, a tablespoon of dark sesame oil.

RESCUING OVERCOOKED AND LEFTOVER ASPARAGUS: The flaws of overcooked asparagus are best camouflaged by baking the vegetable with a cream sauce or topping it with cheese and crumbs. See the variation recipes starting on page 476. Leftover asparagus is excellent served cold with vinaigrette dressing or mayonnaise.

PEELING ASPARAGUS: This is not nearly so time-consuming or laborious a job as might at first be supposed, and it makes an enormous difference in the final result. Consult the Master Recipe for details.

PRESENTING ASPARAGUS: Hot or cold, asparagus can be presented either as a separate course or as an accompaniment. Especially when served separately, it may quite properly be eaten with the fingers. Because asparagus is too fragile to drain in a colander and because it exudes a great deal of juice, it tends to come to the table a bit wet. I have never found this terribly troublesome, but some connoisseurs insist on the use of a special ridged asparagus platter on which the stalks are arranged across the ridges, allowing moisture to run off. As an alternative to the platter, you may serve asparagus on a heavy cloth napkin; of course you must then serve any sauce separately.

MASTER RECIPE

Skillet-boiled Asparagus

4 servings

❦ *My favorite way to serve hot asparagus is to brush it liberally with very soft butter, sprinkle it lightly with drops of fresh lemon juice, and then to season it with salt and a few grindings of white pepper. Hollandaise sauce and mousseline sauce are classic with asparagus but appropriate only when the rest of the meal is rather light. Cold asparagus is generally served with either mayonnaise or vinaigrette dressing.*

STEP 1: PEELING AND TRIMMING THE ASPARAGUS

24 to 32 asparagus stalks (2 pounds or more)

To peel a stalk of asparagus, lay it on a work surface and hold it in place at the tip. Using a swivel-blade vegetable peeler, strip off the skin starting just below the pointy tip, moving all the way down to the base of the stalk. Rotate the stalk until all skin is removed. The trick is to bear down rather lightly at the top of the stalk, where the skin is thin, and to exert greater pressure at the base, where the skin is thick and stringy. The stalk should be a very pale, uniform green. If the base is a dark mint green, you can be sure that you have not taken off all the skin; peel the base portion a second time.

Nearly all of a peeled stalk of asparagus will prove to be edible. Still, a small

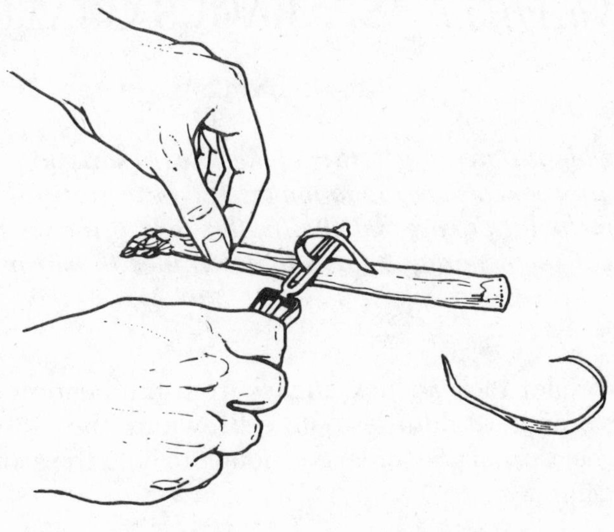

portion of the bottom may be woody and fibrous. To determine where to trim the stalk, gently press the sharp edge of a paring knife against the stalk about 1/4 inch up from the bottom. If the knife does not readily cut through the stalk, move it up another 1/4 inch and press again. After you have cut a few stalks, you will begin to get a feel for where to trim asparagus spears. It is better to trim asparagus with a knife than by "snapping," as the latter method often results in the waste of edible stalk.

Step 2: Skillet-boiling the Asparagus

2 quarts water
1 to 2 tablespoons salt

Bring water to boil in a kettle or saucepan. Arrange trimmed asparagus, preferably in a single layer, in a 10- to 12-inch skillet. Add just enough boiling water barely to cover, stir in 1 tablespoon salt per quart, and bring back to boil over high heat. Lower the heat so that the water is maintained at a moderate simmer and, timing from this point, cook uncovered for 5 to 8 minutes, or until a stalk droops slightly when lifted in the middle with a fork. Transfer asparagus to a platter using tongs or two forks.

Ahead of Time: Asparagus that has sat for even a minute or two before being served will weep a great deal of its succulent juice. Thus it is best to serve the vegetable as soon as possible. If delay is unavoidable, remove asparagus from the skillet and arrange in a single layer on a clean linen or cotton towel. Just before serving, reheat the water in the skillet to a simmer and drop in the asparagus for a few seconds—just long enough to heat through.

Variation: ASPARAGUS GRATIN

4 to 6 servings

❦*Accompanied by buttered toast, this makes a very satisfying lunch or supper dish. Hot, freshly cooked asparagus makes the best gratin, but leftovers may also be used. In the latter case, set the broiler rack 6 inches from the heating element and heat the asparagus for 3 to 4 minutes to warm it through.*

Preliminaries

1. Set the broiler rack about 3 inches from the heating element.
2. Preheat broiler 10 minutes before browning the gratin.
3. Select a heat-proof platter large enough to hold the asparagus in a single overlapping layer.

Skillet-boiled Asparagus
3 tablespoons soft butter
6 tablespoons Fine Fresh Bread Crumbs (see page 60)
Basic Cream Sauce, page 34, made with milk and a bit thicker than serving consistency
2 coarsely chopped hard-cooked eggs (optional)

Spread 1 tablespoon of the butter over the bottom of the platter and sprinkle evenly with 2 tablespoons of the crumbs. Arrange the asparagus in a neat overlapping layer on top. Bring the cream sauce to a simmer and gently stir in the hard-cooked eggs if you are using them. Mask the asparagus completely with the sauce, then sprinkle with the remaining crumbs and dot with the remaining butter. Place under the hot broiler for about 2 minutes, or just until the top browns lightly. Serve at once.

Variation: ASPARAGUS WITH CRUMBS AND PARMESAN CHEESE

4 servings

❦ *This is particularly delicious with veal or lamb.*

Skillet-boiled Asparagus
6 tablespoons butter
⅔ cup Fine Fresh Bread Crumbs (see page 60)
¼ cup (1 ounce) freshly grated Parmesan cheese
Salt and freshly ground pepper

Melt the butter in a skillet over medium heat. When the foam has subsided, indicating that the butter is hot enough, add the bread crumbs and sauté over moderately high heat until lightly browned. Arrange cooked asparagus in a serving dish. Spoon on the crumb mixture, then sprinkle with the Parmesan cheese. Season to taste with salt and freshly ground pepper. Serve at once.

Variation: ASPARAGUS WITH SESAME SEEDS (AND HARD-COOKED EGG)

4 servings

❦ *The addition of the egg garniture makes this dish substantial enough to constitute the main course of a lunch.*

Skillet-boiled Asparagus
4 tablespoons butter
1 tablespoon dark sesame oil
3 tablespoons sesame seeds
Salt and freshly ground pepper
Fresh lemon juice
1 to 2 hard-cooked eggs (optional)

Melt butter with the sesame oil in a small skillet. Add sesame seeds and sauté over moderately high heat until light golden. Arrange cooked asparagus in a serving platter and pour the sesame mixture over. Season with salt, pepper, and drops of fresh lemon juice. If you wish, you may also sprinkle the asparagus with 1 or 2 warm sieved hard-cooked eggs (press eggs through a fine sieve with the back of a spoon).

AVOCADOS

Although there are countless avocado varieties, you are most likely to find either the small, blackish green, rough-skinned Haas or the large, forest green, smooth-skinned Fuerte at the supermarket. The Haas has a decidedly richer flavor. To choose a ripe avocado, squeeze the fruit gently in the palm of the hand. It should feel soft but not mushy. If the skin feels loose or leathery, or if the fruit appears bloated, the avocado is overripe and will slice poorly and may also turn out to be quite bruised. To ripen a hard avocado, leave the fruit at room temperature, away from direct sunlight, for 1 to 3 days.

Once peeled and exposed to air, the flesh of avocado is highly prone to discoloration. Sprinkle avocado slices with lemon or lime juice as they are cut, and place a sheet of plastic wrap directly over avocados cut or puréed ahead of time, and refrigerate. Popular wisdom has it that keeping the pit in halved avocados or burying it in the middle of an avocado purée prevents blackening, but this is sheer myth.

GUACAMOLE

Makes about 2 cups

❦ *Not only is it delicious; this fiery Mexican cocktail dip is one of the best uses for overripe avocados. Pass with corn chips or tortilla chips.*

1 large or 2 small very ripe avocados
1 to 3 tablespoons finely shredded fresh chili peppers, or to taste
1 tablespoon strained fresh lime juice
2 teaspoons mashed, pressed, or very finely minced garlic
½ teaspoon ground cumin
½ teaspoon salt
¼ teaspoon freshly ground pepper
1 medium very ripe tomato, cut into small cubes
2 to 3 tablespoons finely chopped fresh coriander (cilantro) leaves (substitute parsley if coriander is unavailable)
Fresh lemon juice

Peel the avocados, remove the pits, and mash flesh with a fork, leaving some largish chunks; you should have about 1¼ cups. Stir in shredded chilis, lime juice, garlic, cumin, salt, and pepper, then fold in cubed tomato and coriander or parsley. Taste and adjust seasoning, adding drops of lemon juice and whatever else seems necessary. Cover the surface directly with a sheet of plastic wrap and let stand at room temperature for 15 to 20 minutes—but no longer—before serving.

AHEAD OF TIME: Prepare the basic guacamole purée, but do not add the tomato or coriander. Cover surface directly with a sheet of plastic wrap and refrigerate for up to 3 hours—but no longer, or the mixture may become runny, discolored, or bitter. About 15 minutes before serving, fold in tomato and coriander or parsley and let the guacamole stand, covered, at room temperature.

GREEN BEANS AND WAX BEANS

The most familiar member of this family is the *string bean* or *snap bean,* so called because old-fashioned varieties had a string running down the middle that could only be removed by snapping off the ends. Modern-day market snap beans, however, are stringless, unless they are quite overmature. The *Italian green bean* is broader and flatter than a regular green bean, and its seeds are larger, giving it a somewhat starchy quality. If you live in a large city, you may be able to find *haricots verts,* or French green beans, fresh at the market. These resemble American snap beans in shape but are thinner and darker in color and have bumpy skins. They have a piquant, beany flavor and a slightly gelatinous texture. The *Chinese green bean* is the exotic-looking member of the bean clan, for it can measure a foot or more in length. In taste and texture, though, it is much like an American snap bean. Yellow *wax beans* have a certain mild sourness of taste that other beans do not have. They are best when picked small and young, and may then be treated as for any other bean. When allowed to become large and mature, they require a longer cooking time and are best simmered in cream or in a tomato flavoring.

If your market sells beans loose in open bins, it is well worth your time to choose each one separately, as individual beans vary considerably in quality. Ordinary snap beans should be uniformly green, plump, smooth-skinned, and hard. Soft, shriveled, or puckered snap beans have been handled improperly or stored for too long and should be avoided. Pale, large snap beans whose seeds bulge beneath the skin are overmature and should also be passed over. With a few modifications, the same guidelines may be used in selecting other types of beans. The seeds of Italian green beans are visible beneath the skin even when the beans are very young, but the seeds should not seem to protrude sharply. The skins of haricots verts and Chinese green beans are naturally bumpy, and wax beans, of course, should have a nice yellow color, without pale patches or dark speckles.

FROZEN GREEN OR WAX BEANS: Thaw beans at room temperature until they have softened enough to be broken apart. Heat several tablespoons of oil in a wide skillet or wok and quickly stir-fry the beans over very high heat until they are heated through. Add salt, pepper, and drops of fresh lemon juice to taste.

RESCUING OVERCOOKED GREEN OR WAX BEANS: The best cure is the Greek-style tomato sauce recipe, page 483.

MASTER RECIPE

Boiled Green or Wax Beans

4 to 6 servings

I staunchly adhere to the continental method of boiling beans in a large kettle of salted water. I think this produces fresher-tasting and more brightly colored beans than steaming.

In my view, butter, drops of fresh lemon juice, salt, and freshly ground pepper constitute the best dressing for beans. Finely chopped parsley may also be added. Cold green beans are very nice in a garlic vinaigrette, but be sure to add the dressing just before serving or the beans will lose their color and texture.

Step 1: Trimming the Beans

2 pounds green beans or young wax beans

Immerse beans in sink filled with lukewarm water and rub them to remove soil and pesticides. Rinse by handfuls under the tap and shake off excess water.

To determine whether or not the beans you are cooking have strings (likely only in the case of wax beans), snap off one end of a bean and pull it along the lengthwise groove toward the other end. If a string comes up with the end, snap and pull the other end as well, and snap all remaining beans in this manner. If no string is present, line up a number of beans at a time on a cutting board and cut off the stem ends with a sharp knife. The blossom ends need not be snapped or cut. Do not slice the beans. Whole beans retain their flavor and texture better than do cut beans.

Step 2: Boiling the Beans

4 quarts water
2 tablespoons salt

Bring 4 quarts salted water to a fast boil in a 5- to 6-quart pot. Add beans a handful at a time, allowing the water to return to the verge of simmering before adding the next handful. Boil beans rapidly, uncovered, for 5 to 8 minutes, or until they are tender enough to be cut easily with the side of a fork and have lost any starchy raw taste but still retain their color and character. Drain thoroughly in a colander.

AHEAD OF TIME: Cook the beans a couple of minutes short of doneness. Drain in a colander, then run cold water over them until they are stone cold inside and out. Drain well, pat dry, and turn beans into a plastic bag or container; tie or cover securely. The beans will keep in the refrigerator for as long as a day and a half. To serve, toss beans in a skillet with plenty of hot butter until they are heated through.

Variation: GREEN OR WAX BEANS IN HEAVY CREAM

4 to 6 servings

❦ *This dish is especially delectable with roasts and chops.*

Boiled Green or Wax Beans; use snap beans, *haricots verts,* or young wax beans and boil only 5 minutes
1½ cups heavy cream
1 teaspoon cornstarch mixed to a smooth paste with 1 tablespoon additional heavy cream (optional)
Salt and white pepper, preferably freshly ground
Fresh lemon juice
1 to 2 tablespoons minced fresh parsley (optional)

Turn beans into a 10-inch skillet and pour the heavy cream over them. Simmer over moderately high heat, stirring occasionally, for 3 to 5 minutes, or until the cream has reduced by about ⅓ and thickened slightly. If you want the sauce to be thicker still, beat in the optional cornstarch paste and simmer, stirring, 30 seconds longer. Season to taste with salt and white pepper, plus drops of fresh lemon juice. If you wish, fold in minced parsley. Serve immediately.

Variation: GRATIN OF GREEN OR WAX BEANS WITH MUSHROOMS

4 to 6 servings

❦ *This may accompany a roast or chops or be the mainstay of a light lunch or supper.*

PRELIMINARIES

1. Set rack in the upper third of the oven.
2. Preheat oven to 425°F 20 minutes before baking.
3. Select a 9-inch baking dish attractive enough to be brought to the table.

Boiled Green or Wax Beans; use snap beans or young wax beans and boil only 5 minutes
Mushroom Cream Sauce, page 43, unthinned
3 tablespoons soft butter
6 tablespoons Fine Fresh Bread Crumbs (see page 60)

Once drained, return beans to dry cooking pot, fold in mushroom cream sauce, and bring to a simmer. Grease the baking dish with 1 tablespoon of the butter and sprinkle with 2 tablespoons of the bread crumbs. Turn sauced beans into the dish and cover with remaining crumbs and dot with 2 tablespoons additional butter. Bake for about 15 minutes, or until sauce is bubbly and the top of the gratin has browned lightly. Serve at once.

Variation: GREEN OR WAX BEANS IN GREEK-STYLE TOMATO SAUCE

4 to 6 servings

❦ *This dish may be served hot, at room temperature, or cold. It is a fine addition to a picnic basket, especially if you bring along some hard-cooked eggs.*

⅔ cup minced celery
⅔ cup minced onion
⅓ to ⅔ cup olive oil (the more oil the better, but you can use the lesser amount if you are watching calories)
2½ cups peeled, seeded, and diced tomatoes, fresh or 35 ounces canned (see page 607)
1 teaspoon mashed, pressed, or very finely minced garlic
1½ tablespoons chopped fresh basil or 1½ teaspoons dried
¾ teaspoon salt
¼ teaspoon pepper, preferably freshly ground
Boiled Green or Wax Beans; use snap beans, Italian green beans, or young wax beans and cook 1 to 2 minutes short of doneness
1 to 3 tablespoons finely chopped fresh parsley

Slowly sauté celery and onion in olive oil in a 10-inch skillet until the vegetables are quite tender but not brown, about 10 minutes. Stir in all remaining ingredients except beans and parsley and simmer uncovered for 15 to 20 minutes, stirring occasionally; the mixture should become thick and oily looking. Add beans, stir to coat with the tomato sauce, and cook uncovered over low heat for 5 minutes or so to blend flavors. Remove from heat; correct seasoning and stir in parsley.

Variation: GRANDMOTHER ROSALIND'S GREEN OR WAX BEANS WITH VINEGAR AND BACON

4 to 6 servings

6 slices bacon
½ cup chopped onion
¼ cup cider vinegar or distilled vinegar
1 teaspoon sugar
½ teaspoon dry mustard
Boiled Green or Wax Beans, using snap beans, Italian green beans, or wax beans
Salt and freshly ground pepper, if needed

In a heavy, large skillet made of or lined with a noncorroding material, fry bacon until very crisp. Remove from skillet and set aside. Add onion to bacon fat in skillet and sauté over moderately high heat for about 5 minutes, or until onion colors lightly around the edges. Add vinegar, sugar, and dry mustard and simmer until vinegar has nearly evaporated and the mixture has become thick and glistening. Turn beans into skillet and toss over moderate heat until hot. Crumble reserved bacon over the beans; season with salt and pepper. Serve immediately.

Fresh Shell Beans: Cranberry Beans, Fava Beans, Lima Beans

Unlike green and wax beans, which are eaten in their entirety, shell beans are cultivated for their large, starchy seeds only; the pods, being tough and stringy, are discarded. Although individual varieties of shell beans are distinctive in taste, texture, and appearance, they may all be cooked in similar ways. A long-time American favorite, *cranberry beans* have lovely pink streaks on the pods and seeds. When small and young, cranberry beans are thin-skinned, tender, and less starchy than other shell beans. The Italians love *fava beans,* which are available in this country for a few weeks in the spring. These beans, which have a robust, slightly acrid flavor, must be very small and young. If the beans are too mature, it becomes necessary to pop them individually out of their tough, shiny skins after cooking, which, needless to say, is quite a nuisance. More familiar in canned and frozen form (see below) than fresh, *lima beans,* though often slandered, make marvelous eating if prepared with care and attention. Choose limas with stiff, unspotted, dark green pods; pass up any that seem large and overmature.

Canned and Frozen Lima Beans: Processed lima beans make surprisingly acceptable substitutes for fresh. To perk up canned limas, drain off and discard their liquid, rinse under cold water, and stew slowly in butter for several minutes, adding drops of fresh lemon juice, salt, and freshly ground pepper to taste. Frozen limas should be thawed partially and boiled just until tender in a quantity of lightly salted water.

Rescuing Overcooked Shell Beans: Turn the overcooked beans into a purée, omitting or cutting down on the cream specified in the recipe on page 487 to compensate for the moisture that the beans will have absorbed.

MASTER RECIPE

Boiled Shell Beans

4 to 5 servings

I like shell beans best when dressed with a fairly copious amount of butter (4 or 5 tablespoons at least), salt, and freshly ground pepper. Fresh lemon juice and minced fresh parsley are nice with limas, and a bit of puréed or mashed garlic may be added to fava beans.

3 to 3½ pounds cranberry, fava, or lima beans
2 quarts water

Cranberry beans and, usually, fava and lima beans as well can be shelled in the same way as peas—that is, by opening the pods between your thumbs and scraping out the beans with a finger. Should you have older, tough pods that resist this method, open them by cutting a thin strip along the seam side with a sharp paring knife, then remove the beans.

Turn shelled beans into a colander and rinse thoroughly under cold running water. Combine beans and 2 quarts water in a 3½- to 4-quart pot and bring to a rapid boil. Boil beans uncovered just until tender—generally 15 to 20 minutes, but start testing after 10 minutes to be sure that you don't overcook them. Large, mature beans naturally take longer to cook than small, young beans. Drain well in a colander.

AHEAD OF TIME: Shell beans are best when served at once but may be cooked several days in advance and reheated. Add 2 teaspoons oil to the beans and toss to coat; store in a tightly lidded container in the refrigerator. To reheat, toss in hot butter in a skillet.

Variation: LIMA BEANS IN HEAVY CREAM

4 to 5 servings

❦ *This dish should be made with the smallest, youngest limas you can find. It is especially good with roast lamb or lamb chops.*

Boiled Shell Beans, using lima beans
1½ to 2 cups heavy cream
1½ tablespoons minced fresh parsley
1½ tablespoons snipped fresh chives (optional)
Salt and pepper, preferably white and freshly ground
Fresh lemon juice

Turn beans into a 10-inch skillet and cover with cream. Simmer over moderately high heat for 4 to 5 minutes, or until the cream thickens. Stir in herbs, then remove from heat and season to taste with salt, pepper, and drops of lemon juice. Serve at once.

Variation: PURÉE OF CRANBERRY OR LIMA BEANS

4 to 5 servings

❦ *This is an excellent and classic accompaniment for roast lamb.*

Boiled Shell Beans; use cranberry or lima beans and reserve cooking water
4 tablespoons soft butter
3 to 8 tablespoons cream or bean cooking water
Freshly grated nutmeg
Salt and pepper, preferably white and freshly ground
Fresh lemon juice

Purée beans thoroughly in a food processor or blender. (If you use a blender, you will have to do the beans in several batches, and it will probably be necessary to add some of the cream or cooking water to the blender jar to get the purée mixture started.) Warm purée in a 3-quart saucepan over low heat, gradually stirring in the soft butter. When the butter has been absorbed, stir in cream or bean cooking water a tablespoon at a time, using enough liquid to form a light, loose purée just stiff enough to hold its shape on a fork. Season to taste with pinches of nutmeg, salt, pepper, and drops of fresh lemon juice.

Variation: WARM SHELL BEAN SALAD WITH BACON

4 to 5 servings

❦ *This makes an excellent accompaniment for hamburgers.*

Boiled Shell Beans, using cranberry, fava, or lima beans
Vinaigrette Dressing, page 117, made with garlic
4 to 6 slices bacon, crisply fried, drained, and crumbled
2 tablespoons minced fresh parsley
Salt and pepper, preferably freshly ground

Toss freshly cooked, hot beans with vinaigrette dressing in a 2-quart bowl. Let stand at room temperature for 5 to 10 minutes, stirring once, then toss again with bacon and parsley. Season to taste with salt and pepper and serve immediately.

BEETS

Just a bit bigger than walnuts, baby beets, with their melting tenderness and complex, delicate flavor, are a favored treat of home gardeners but rather difficult for the rest of us, who must rely on supermarkets, to find. In any case, large mature beets, though coarser than baby beets, have their own appealing flavor and contain great stores of sugar.

When buying beets it is important to select specimens of relatively equal size, as large beets may take as long as an hour and a half to cook, while smaller beets may be tender in as little as 20 minutes. Good fresh beets are rock-hard to the touch. Avoid any that are soft, puckery-skinned, or dried out.

BEET GREENS: If you buy fresh beets with the greens still attached, cut off the greens and store them separately once you get home. The sap from the beets continues to rise into the leaves even after the beets are pulled from the ground, depleting the root of moisture and sweetness. Beet greens, especially when young and tender, are a delicious vegetable in their own right. Wash thoroughly, strip off any especially thick stems, and cook as for spinach. Serve with butter or olive oil; freshly grated Parmesan is also nice.

CANNED BEETS: Canned beets are remarkably good and may be substituted for freshly cooked beets in any recipe. To serve canned beets hot and plain, drain off their liquid and stew them for several minutes in butter in a covered skillet.

Rescuing Flavorless and/or Unsweet Beets: Pickle the beets, letting them stand in the pickle dressing for a day or more before serving.

MASTER RECIPE

Boiled Beets

4 servings

Particularly good with pork or beef, beets need only a simple dressing of soft butter plus a pinch or two of salt and freshly ground pepper. A half teaspoon or so of honey can also be added should the beets seem to lack sweetness. As a meatless main-course lunch or supper dish, I am also extremely fond of beets topped with a cream sauce, flavored with Cheddar cheese, curry, hard-cooked eggs and fresh dill, or onions. Finally, cold beets, a fine addition to any cold platter, may be dressed either with mayonnaise or with vinaigrette dressing and a few pinches of oregano.

Step 1: Trimming the Beets

1½ pounds fresh beets

Cut away green tops of beets but leave a 2-inch length of stem attached to the root. Do not remove root and do not peel the beets, or the color and flavor will leach out into the cooking water. Scrub beets under warm water with a stiff vegetable brush.

Step 2: Boiling the Beets

2 quarts water

Place beets in a 3½- to 4½-quart saucepan and cover with 2 quarts water. Cover saucepan and boil slowly for 20 minutes to 1½ hours or more, depending on their size, or until beets are tender when pierced with a fork. Be sure to replenish water if necessary, keeping the beets completely covered.

To peel, let beets cool slightly, then pinch off skins with your fingers; the skins will come away quite easily. Slice off tap root and cut the beets in wedges, slices, or cubes. By the way, beets that turn out to be yellowish rather than the usual beet red under their skins generally taste fine; don't discard them without tasting.

AHEAD OF TIME: Cooked beets will keep perfectly well in a covered container in the refrigerator for as long as a week, but don't peel and cut them up until just before serving. To reheat, toss beets in a skillet with several tablespoons of butter.

Variation: PICKLED BEETS

Makes about 3 cups, or 8 or more servings

❦ *Pickled beets go well with any cold meat or poultry and are also good as a side dish with sandwiches.*

½ cup cider vinegar
¼ cup sugar
½ teaspoon dry mustard
⅛ teaspoon ground cloves
½ teaspoon salt
Boiled Beets, cut into slices, cubes, or wedges (or 3 cups cut-up canned beets, drained)

Combine vinegar, sugar, and seasonings in a 10-inch skillet made of or lined with a noncorroding material and simmer slowly for 2 minutes. Add beets, cover skillet, and simmer 2 minutes longer. Remove from heat, let beets cool to room temperature, then cover and chill.

STORAGE: Pickled beets will keep for several weeks in a covered container in the refrigerator.

Variation: HARVARD BEETS (GLAZED BEETS)

4 to 6 servings

Prepare pickled beets as above, but instead of cooling the beets in their pickle, uncover the skillet and boil off the liquid, stirring frequently. When beets look shiny and nearly dry, remove skillet from heat and stir in 2 to 3 tablespoons soft butter.

Variation: RUSSIAN BEETS

4 servings

❦ *Serve this dish with pot roast or pork chops.*

Boiled Beets, cut into cubes (or 3 cups cubed canned beets, drained)
3/4 cup sour cream
1 tablespoon grated fresh horseradish or 1 1/2 tablespoons well-drained prepared horseradish
1 tablespoon snipped chives or minced scallion (including tender green part)
1/2 teaspoon grated lemon zest
1/4 teaspoon salt
1/4 teaspoon pepper, preferably freshly ground
1/4 to 1/2 cup (1 to 2 ounces) coarsely chopped walnuts (optional)

Combine all ingredients except walnuts in 2-quart heavy-bottomed saucepan and stir over very low heat just until thoroughly heated through; do not let sour cream come near the simmer or it will curdle. Fold in nuts and serve at once.

BROCCOLI

Look for the youngest and freshest broccoli you can find. The stalks should be pale green, smooth-skinned, slender, and hard to the touch, and the buds (or florets) should be uniformly dark green, stiff, and densely clustered. As broccoli verges on overmaturity the stalks become thick and knobby, covered by thick, dry, whitish skin; the buds loosen and become soft and yellowish, as though the vegetable were about to go to seed. Overmature broccoli must be peeled deeply, and much of it will prove to be too yellowed or tough to be eaten at all. It is a bad buy no matter how inexpensive it is at the supermarket.

PEELING BROCCOLI: The skin of broccoli, like that of asparagus, is thick, tough, and stringy. By the time it has softened to the point of palatability (and some of the skin, particularly that covering the main stalk, may never soften, no matter how long the broccoli is cooked), the rest of the vegetable will have become overcooked. Thus conscientious cooks always peel their broccoli. This takes extra time and energy, but the improvement in flavor is well worth it.

FROZEN BROCCOLI: Partially thaw the broccoli at room temperature so that you can break the stalks apart. Chop into 1/2-inch pieces and stir-fry in a small amount of oil over very high heat, just until the broccoli is heated through and slightly softened. Serve at once.

RESCUING OVERCOOKED BROCCOLI: Crumb it; chill it and serve with a strong vinaigrette and plenty of chopped fresh parsley; or purée it.

MASTER RECIPE

Boiled Broccoli

4 servings

Boiled broccoli can be dressed with melted butter, olive oil, walnut oil, bacon drippings, or a combination of dark sesame oil and melted butter; sprinkle with fresh lemon juice, salt, and pepper to taste. Finely chopped walnuts, crumbled cooked bacon, freshly grated Parmesan cheese, grated lemon or orange zest, sieved hard-cooked eggs, or toasted sesame seeds may all be used as toppings. Hollandaise and cheese sauce (I prefer Cheddar) are classic with hot broccoli, and cold broccoli is good with any sort of vinaigrette or mayonnaise dressing.

STEP 1: TRIMMING THE BROCCOLI

2 pounds broccoli

Break florets off the main stalk. Peel the stalk by wedging the skin between the blade of a paring knife and your thumb and stripping the skin off one piece at a time (1). Most of the skin will come away easily, but you may have to dig a bit with the point of the knife to remove the skin in the crevices where the florets branch off. Cut the stalk into pieces roughly the same size as the stems of the florets. Proceed to strip the skin off the floret stems using either the knife or your fingernails (2). Wash the broccoli thoroughly.

STEP 2: BOILING THE BROCCOLI

4 quarts water
2 tablespoons salt

Combine 4 quarts water and salt in a 5- to 6-quart pot and bring to a furious boil. Add broccoli pieces a handful at a time, allowing the water to return to a simmer before adding the next handful. Boil broccoli rapidly, uncovered, for 4 to 6 minutes or until it is crisp-tender but still bright green. Carefully tip the

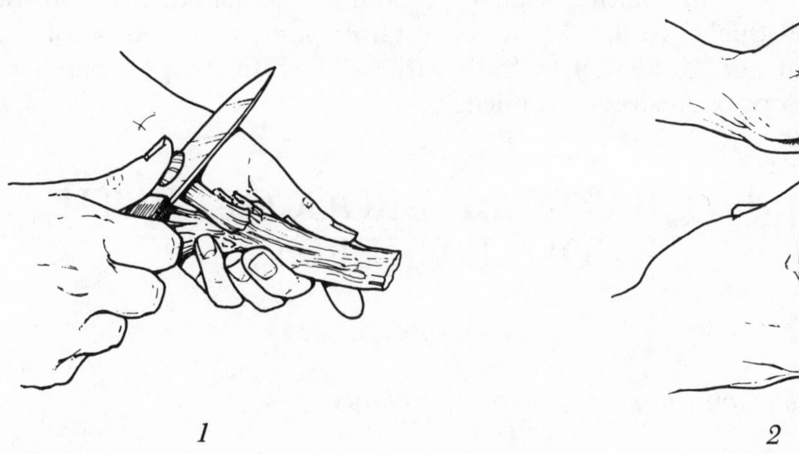

1 *2*

cooked broccoli into a colander—don't just dump it in, or you will mash the buds—and shake the colander very gently to drain.

AHEAD OF TIME: Boil the broccoli for only about 3 minutes. Drain in a colander and set colander in the refrigerator, uncovered. When the broccoli is completely cold, transfer it to a storage container, cover tightly, and refrigerate for up to 36 hours. To reheat, lay the broccoli piece by piece in a large skillet in which you have melted 3 to 4 tablespoons butter. Cover the skillet partially and steam the broccoli in the butter over very low heat, gently stirring once or twice, for 2 to 3 minutes, or until broccoli is completely tender and heated through.

Variation: BROCCOLI IN HEAVY CREAM

4 servings

❦ *This is particularly good with broiled or roast chicken or with fish.*

Boiled Broccoli, cooked only 3 minutes
1½ cups heavy cream
1 teaspoon cornstarch mixed to a smooth paste with 1 tablespoon additional heavy cream (optional)
Salt and white pepper, preferably freshly ground
Nutmeg, preferably freshly ground
Fresh lemon juice

Turn broccoli into a 10-inch skillet and add heavy cream. Bring to a simmer over moderate heat and cook gently for about 5 minutes, stirring occasionally;

cream should reduce in volume by about ⅓ and thicken slightly. If you want the sauce to be thicker still, add the cornstarch paste to the broccoli, and simmer a minute or so. Season to taste with salt, white pepper, pinches of nutmeg, and drops of fresh lemon juice.

Variation: GRATIN OF BROCCOLI WITH CHEDDAR CHEESE

4 to 6 servings

❦ *This is excellent with any sort of roast or chops.*

PRELIMINARIES

1. Set rack in the upper third of the oven.
2. Preheat oven to 425°F 20 minutes before baking.
3. Select a 9-inch baking dish attractive enough to be brought to the table.

Boiled Broccoli, cooked only 4 minutes
Cheese Sauce, page 37, made with Cheddar and a bit thicker than serving consistency
3 tablespoons soft butter
6 tablespoons Fine Fresh Bread Crumbs (see page 60)

Butter the baking dish with 1 tablespoon of the butter and sprinkle with 2 tablespoons bread crumbs. Return drained broccoli to dry cooking pot, gently fold in the sauce, and bring almost to the simmer. Turn into prepared baking dish and cover the top with the remaining bread crumbs and butter, cut into bits. Bake for about 20 minutes, or until bubbly and lightly browned on top.

Variation: BROCCOLI WITH CRUMBS, BACON, AND GARLIC

4 servings

Boiled Broccoli
6 slices bacon
⅔ cup Fine Fresh Bread Crumbs (see page 60)
1 teaspoon mashed, pressed, or very finely minced garlic
¼ to ½ teaspoon freshly ground pepper, or to taste
1 to 2 hard-cooked eggs (optional)

Cut bacon into bits and sauté until crisp in a 10-inch skillet. Add crumbs and toss over moderately high heat until lightly browned. Stir in the garlic and pepper and cook 30 seconds longer, stirring. Arrange broccoli in a serving dish and strew the crumb mixture over it. If you wish, press hard-cooked eggs through a fine sieve with the back of a spoon and sprinkle over the top. Serve immediately.

Variation: PURÉE OF BROCCOLI

4 servings

❦ *This is marvelous with roast chicken or turkey*

Martha Abraham's Bavarian Puréed Cabbage, page 503

SUBSTITUTE: ***Boiled Broccoli*** and broccoli cooking water for cabbage and cabbage cooking water

ADD: Nutmeg, preferably freshly ground (optional)

Drain the broccoli, reserving ⅓ cup of the cooking water. In a blender, food processor, or food mill, purée broccoli. Use the puréed broccoli and reserved cooking water in place of cabbage and cabbage cooking water in the recipe for Martha Abraham's Bavarian puréed cabbage. You may wish to season the purée with a bit of nutmeg.

Broccoli Rabe

Although related to ordinary broccoli, this is a leafy vegetable with rather tough stems and small yellowish buds. The flavor is reminiscent of broccoli, but it is more bitter.

SAUTÉED BROCCOLI RABE WITH GARLIC

4 servings

❦ *This recipe entails blanching the broccoli rabe before sautéing, a step that helps to remove some of its bitterness. Serve sautéed broccoli rabe with broiled chicken or pork chops or with ham.*

Step 1: Blanching the Broccoli Rabe

2 to 2½ pounds broccoli rabe
4 quarts water

Turn the broccoli rabe into a colander and rinse well. Pull off any leaves that appear dry and crepey and discard. Bring 4 quarts water to a fast boil, drop in the broccoli rabe, and, timing from the moment the water returns to a boil, cook for 3 minutes. Drain in the colander, pressing firmly with the back of a spoon to extract as much moisture as possible.

AHEAD OF TIME: After its preliminary blanching, the broccoli rabe may be left to cool at room temperature, then turned into a covered container and refrigerated for several days prior to sautéing and serving.

STEP 2: SAUTÉING THE BROCCOLI RABE

6 tablespoons olive oil
2 teaspoons mashed, pressed, or very finely minced garlic
Salt and pepper, preferably freshly ground, to taste

In a 10- to 12-inch skillet, heat the olive oil over moderately high heat until it takes on a shimmering appearance, then add both the blanched broccoli rabe and the garlic. Lowering the heat slightly if the vegetable threatens to scorch, cook for 5 to 7 minutes, stirring, or until the broccoli rabe is tender. Season with salt and pepper to taste and serve immediately.

BRUSSELS SPROUTS

Ideally, shoppers should have the opportunity to select brussels sprouts individually, but, alas, this vegetable nearly always comes packed in cellophane-covered paper tubs. Look for firm, uniformly green sprouts, with tightly closed leaves. Brussels sprouts that have turned yellowish, or whose outer leaves have become floppy and detached from the rest of the head, are overmature or stale and will taste bitter.

Some recipes suggest that brussels sprouts be soaked in salted water before cooking in order to drive out any hidden worms. However, commercially grown brussels sprouts are unlikely to have worms and need not be soaked.

FROZEN BRUSSELS SPROUTS: Freezing is not something that should ever happen to a brussels sprout, as mushiness inevitably sets in. If you must use frozen sprouts, thaw completely, pat dry, then stir-fry over high heat in a small amount of oil just long enough to heat through.

RESCUING OVERCOOKED BRUSSELS SPROUTS: Overcooking causes brussels sprouts to become bitter, odorous, mushy, and waterlogged and has given the vegetable a bad name. To redeem them you must allow the sprouts to absorb a flavoring that is strong enough to counteract the bitter cabbagey taste and odor that comes with overcooking. Your best bet is to prepare brussels sprouts with vinegar and garlic, page 499.

MASTER RECIPE

Boiled Brussels Sprouts

4 servings

Removed from the pot as soon as they are crisp-tender and crunchy at the core, brussels sprouts are a delicious and—yes—delicate vegetable.

Dress brussels sprouts with butter, salt, pepper, and drops of lemon juice and serve with red meats, pork, or ham.

STEP 1: TRIMMING THE BRUSSELS SPROUTS

1 quart brussels sprouts (about 1½ pounds)

Break off and discard any yellowed or withered outer leaves. Slice a thin section off bottom of the core and cut a deep cross in the core with the point of a paring knife; the cross promotes rapid and even cooking. Wash brussels sprouts thoroughly under running water.

STEP 2: BOILING THE BRUSSELS SPROUTS

4 quarts water
2 tablespoons salt

Bring 4 quarts salted water to a rapid boil in a 5- to 6-quart pot. Gradually add brussels sprouts, starting with the larger ones. If there is a substantial discrepancy in the sizes of the sprouts, give the large ones a 3- or 4-minute head start in the pot. Boil for 8 to 12 minutes, or until just tender. Drain in a colander.

AHEAD OF TIME: Boil the brussels sprouts only 6 to 8 minutes; drain in a colander and rinse under cold water for several minutes, or until sprouts are thoroughly chilled. Turn onto cloth or paper toweling and pat dry, then turn into a storage container or plastic bag, seal tightly, and refrigerate for up to 36 hours. Just before serving, melt 6 tablespoons (¾ stick) butter in a large, heavy-bottomed skillet over moderate heat. Add brussels sprouts and, stirring occasionally, cook gently until tender and heated through, 5 to 7 minutes. Serve at once.

Variation: GRATIN OF BRUSSELS SPROUTS WITH ONIONS AND CHEESE

4 to 6 servings

❦ *Baked with an onion cream sauce and a crusty topping of bread crumbs and Parmesan cheese, brussels sprouts assume a mild, savory character that will please almost anyone. Serve this special dish with roast beef, lamb, or turkey.*

PRELIMINARIES

1. Set rack in the upper third of oven.
2. Preheat oven to 425°F 20 minutes before baking.
3. Select a 9-inch baking dish attractive enough to be brought to the table.

Boiled Brussels Sprouts, cooked only 6 to 8 minutes
Onion Cream Sauce, page 43, thinned to serving consistency
3 tablespoons soft butter
3 tablespoons Fine Fresh Bread Crumbs (see page 60)
¼ cup (1 ounce) freshly grated Parmesan cheese

Return brussels sprouts to dry cooking pot, fold in the sauce, and bring to a simmer. Butter the baking dish with 1 tablespoon of the butter; mix together the cheese and crumbs and sprinkle 2 tablespoons of the mixture over the bottom of the baking dish. Add the sauced sprouts, top with the remaining cheese/crumb mixture, and dot with remaining butter. Bake about 20 minutes, or until bubbly and nicely browned. Serve at once.

Variation: BRUSSELS SPROUTS IN TOMATO SAUCE

4 servings

Green or Wax Beans in Greek-style Tomato Sauce, page 483
SUBSTITUTE: ***Boiled Brussels Sprouts***, cooked only 7 to 9 minutes, for beans

Halve the sprouts lengthwise (that is, through the core) and substitute for beans in the Greek-style tomato sauce recipe.

Variation: BRUSSELS SPROUTS WITH VINEGAR AND GARLIC

4 servings

❦ *Serve with broiled chicken or chill and add to a cold platter.*

6 tablespoons olive oil
1½ teaspoons mashed, pressed, or very finely minced garlic
½ cup red wine vinegar
½ teaspoon salt
⅛ teaspoon pepper, preferably freshly ground
Boiled Brussels Sprouts, cooked only 7 to 9 minutes and cut lengthwise into quarters

Heat olive oil until fragrant in a 10-inch skillet made of or lined with a noncorroding material. Add garlic and stir over moderate heat for 15 seconds. Remove skillet from heat. Standing back to avoid possible spattering, pour vinegar into skillet. Add salt and pepper, return skillet to moderate flame, and cook the vinegar sauce, stirring constantly, for a minute or two, or until it has reduced and thickened slightly. Add the quartered brussels sprouts, toss to coat with vinegar sauce, then reduce heat to very low and simmer sprouts for 5 minutes, or until tender. Raise heat and boil off nearly all liquid in the skillet so that sprouts are sizzling in olive oil. Taste and correct seasoning. Serve hot, at room temperature, or cold.

Cabbage

The three cabbages that one is most likely to find at the market are the ordinary green head cabbage, the slightly more exotic curly-leaf savoy, and the red cabbage. Head and savoy cabbage are similar in taste and texture and may be used interchangeably in recipes. Red cabbage, however, requires a longer cooking time than the other types and should always be cooked with an acid substance such as wine, apples, or vinegar, or its color will fade away.

Choose firm, compact, unwithered, unyellowed heads of cabbage. When preparing cabbage in quantity, it is better to select several small heads rather than one large one, as large cabbages—those over 2½ pounds—are likely to be tough and strong tasting.

Oriental Cabbages: *Chinese cabbage* much resembles a pale, elongated, frizzy head of romaine lettuce. It is similar to the more familiar Western cabbages in taste and may be cooked as they are. *Bok choy*, known in some markets as celery cabbage or Chinese chard, is a thick-stemmed, leafy vegetable that is, as its names imply, as much like celery or chard as it is like cabbage. If it is young—and it should be for best taste and texture—it may be steamed in the water that clings to the leaves as for spinach. The leaves and stems of mature bok choy should be cooked separately as for Swiss chard.

RESCUING OVERCOOKED CABBAGE: Use to prepare puréed cabbage, page 503.

MASTER RECIPE

Skillet-Braised Cabbage

4 servings

❦ *Old-fashioned recipes often say to boil cabbage for an hour or longer, a treatment that will render the vegetable limp and colorless and smell up the kitchen to boot. Tastes vary, of course, but unless the cabbage is quite old (and therefore tough), it will not need more than 10 minutes of cooking, probably less.*

Skillet-braised cabbage does not require extra seasonings, though minced or crushed caraway seeds, pinches of sugar, a few dashes of vinegar or hard cider, pressed garlic, or minced fresh herbs may be added. It is particularly good with duck, goose, turkey, pork, sausages, or ham.

STEP 1: TRIMMING THE CABBAGE

1 small head green cabbage (1½ to 2 pounds)

Pull away and discard any tough or withered outer leaves, then wash the cabbage well. Quarter the cabbage lengthwise and cut out the tough, whitish core from each wedge. Cut wedges crosswise into slices about ⅜ inch thick. You will have about 6 cups.

STEP 2: COOKING THE CABBAGE

6 tablespoons butter or bacon or goose fat
Salt and pepper, preferably freshly ground, to taste

Select a deep, heavy-bottomed 10- to 12-inch skillet with lid (do not choose an unlined cast iron skillet, which may darken the cabbage); add water to a depth of about ½ inch. Add cabbage to the skillet, cover, and bring to boil over a high flame. Cook the cabbage over moderately high heat for 4 to 7 minutes, or until nearly tender, then uncover skillet and boil off all cooking liquid, stirring. Add fat to the skillet and stir to coat the cabbage. Cook slowly, stirring, for several minutes, or until cabbage is completely tender but retains its shape and color. Season with salt and pepper.

AHEAD OF TIME: Steam cabbage, drain in a colander, and rinse under cold water until completely chilled. Drain well, then seal tightly and refrigerate, preferably not longer than a day. When ready to serve, braise cabbage in fat as indicated in Master Recipe.

Variation: CABBAGE IN HEAVY CREAM

4 servings

❦ *This is especially good with roast chicken or turkey.*

Skillet-braised Cabbage

SUBSTITUTE: 1½ cups heavy cream for butter or fat

ADD: ¼ teaspoon dried basil (optional)

1 teaspoon cornstarch mixed to a smooth paste with 1 tablespoon heavy cream (optional)

Salt and pepper, preferably white and freshly ground, to taste

Fresh lemon juice

After cabbage has been steamed and the cooking water boiled off, add cream in place of the butter or other fat called for in the Master Recipe. Season, if you wish, with basil and simmer slowly, uncovered, for about 5 minutes, or until cabbage has softened sufficiently to bend easily and cream has reduced and thickened slightly. If you wish, thicken the cream further by stirring in the cornstarch paste and simmering another minute to cook the starch. Season to taste with salt, pepper, and drops of fresh lemon juice.

Variation: SCALLOPED CABBAGE

4 servings

❦ *This goes well with almost any sort of broiled or roasted meat or poultry.*

PRELIMINARIES

1. Set rack in the upper third of the oven.
2. Preheat oven to 425°F 20 minutes before baking.
3. Select a shallow 10-inch baking dish attractive enough to be brought to the table. Butter or grease the dish lightly.

Skillet-braised Cabbage; omit final braising
Salt and pepper, preferably freshly ground, to taste
⅓ cup light cream or milk
½ cup Fine Fresh Bread Crumbs (see page 60)
3 tablespoons butter

Steam the cabbage, boil off cooking liquid, and add butter or other fat; season well with salt and pepper. Diverging from Master Recipe, do not braise the cabbage after adding the butter or other fat, but instead turn it into the baking dish. Pour cream or milk over the cabbage, sprinkle top with bread crumbs, and dot with butter. Bake about 20 minutes, or until cabbage is bubbling hot and crumbs are nicely browned. Serve at once.

Variation: CABBAGE WITH VINEGAR AND BACON

4 servings

❦ *Very, very good—especially with pork.*

Grandmother Rosalind's Green or Wax Beans with Vinegar and Bacon, page 484
SUBSTITUTE: ***Skillet-braised Cabbage***, the braising in butter or fat omitted, for beans

Steam cabbage and boil off the cooking liquid as in Master Recipe, but do not do the final braising in butter or other fat. Instead, proceed according to the recipe for beans with vinegar and bacon, substituting cabbage for beans.

STIR-FRIED CHINESE CABBAGE

4 servings

1½ pounds Chinese cabbage or celery cabbage (bok choy)—or substitute ordinary green cabbage
3 tablespoons peanut oil or other neutral vegetable oil
2 teaspoons sugar
1 teaspoon salt
⅛ teaspoon cayenne pepper
1½ tablespoons dark soy sauce
1½ tablespoons distilled vinegar or rice vinegar

Separate cabbage into leaves, discarding the core if you are using regular head cabbage. Wash the leaves, pat dry with paper toweling, and cut into 1-inch pieces.

Heat oil in a deep 10-inch skillet or wok over high heat until it shimmers, indicating that it is very hot. Add chopped cabbage and stir-fry for 3 minutes, turning down the heat slightly if pan begins to smoke. Add sugar, salt, and cayenne pepper and stir-fry 30 seconds longer. Add soy sauce and vinegar, stir briefly, then cover the skillet or wok and cook cabbage for a minute or two longer, or until crisp-tender. Uncover and boil off any remaining liquid over high heat, stirring. Serve the cabbage at once.

MARTHA ABRAHAM'S BAVARIAN PURÉED CABBAGE

4 servings

❦ *Martha Abraham, a fine cook of German-Jewish specialties, always prepares this dish with savoy cabbage, in the traditional fashion. Ordinary green head cabbage, however, may also be used, and puréed broccoli is excellent when made according to this formula.*

Puréed cabbage is an excellent accompaniment to chops, steaks, and roasts of all kinds. The night that Martha made this dish for us, I prepared dilled stuffed veal rolls and the combination turned out to be fine indeed.

1 small head savoy cabbage (1½ to 2 pounds)
2 tablespoons finely chopped onion
4 tablespoons butter
¼ cup all-purpose flour
1 cup Chicken Stock, page 26, or canned broth or 1 chicken bouillon cube dissolved in 1 cup hot water
Salt and pepper, preferably freshly ground, to taste

Following Step 1 of the Master Recipe on page 500, trim and cut up the cabbage. Proceeding to Step 2, boil the cabbage, covered, in water, but, diverging from the Master Recipe, cook the cabbage in the water until tender, about 10 minutes, omitting the braising in butter or fat. Drain the cabbage in a colander, reserving cooking liquid. Purée cabbage using a blender, food processor, or food mill; set aside.

In the same skillet you used to cook the cabbage, sauté chopped onion in butter over moderate heat until golden brown. Add flour and cook, stirring, for 1 minute. Remove from heat and add chicken stock or broth plus ⅓ cup reserved cabbage cooking liquid, stirring until mixture is perfectly smooth. Return to moderate heat and bring to a simmer, stirring constantly. Cook for 1 minute; the mixture will be quite thick.

Beat reserved puréed cabbage into the thickened broth and bring to a simmer, stirring. Turn heat down to low, cover partially, and cook very gently for about 20 minutes, adding more spoonfuls of reserved cooking liquid if the purée becomes too thick or threatens to scorch. Season to taste with salt and pepper.

AHEAD OF TIME: Turn purée into a lidded storage container, refrigerate for up to 3 days, and reheat just before serving by stirring over low heat in a heavy-bottomed saucepan.

BRAISED RED CABBAGE

4 to 5 servings

❦*Excellent with pork dishes, roast turkey, and pot roast.*

6 tablespoons butter
½ cup minced onion
1 head red cabbage (2 pounds), quartered, cored, and sliced
1 green apple, peeled, cored, and diced
¾ cup dry red wine
2 tablespoons cider vinegar

2 tablespoons packed brown sugar
½ teaspoon salt
¼ teaspoon pepper, preferably freshly ground
2 tablespoons red currant jelly (optional)

Melt butter in saucepan, add onion, and sauté over low heat for 8 to 10 minutes, or until tender but not brown. Add cabbage and cook slowly for 10 minutes, stirring frequently. Stir in all remaining ingredients, except jelly. Simmer, covered, over low heat for 1½ to 2 hours or until cabbage is very tender, stirring every 15 minutes to prevent scorching. Boil off any liquid remaining in saucepan at end of cooking time. Stir in optional jelly. Taste and adjust seasoning.

AHEAD OF TIME: This may be covered and refrigerated for nearly a week and actually improves in flavor upon standing. Reheat gently in a heavy saucepan, stirring frequently.

STUFFED CABBAGE ROLLS IN SWEET-AND-SOUR SAUCE

4 servings

❦ *The sour taste in this delicious main-dish lunch or supper recipe is provided by cocktail onions. Although gentled by cooking, the onions retain some of their original character. If you prefer not to use them, substitute 2 tablespoons vinegar and ¼ teaspoon salt.*

Serve stuffed cabbage rolls with boiled or mashed potatoes and a tossed green salad.

PRELIMINARIES

1. Set rack in upper third of oven.
2. Preheat oven to 375°F 20 minutes before baking.
3. Select a baking dish just large enough to hold the cabbage rolls. A dish measuring 13×9×2 inches is about right.

STEP 1: PREPARING THE CABBAGE

4 quarts water
2 tablespoons salt
12 to 14 large leaves from a 1½-pound head of green cabbage

Combine 4 quarts water and salt in a 6- to 8-quart pot and bring to boil. Meanwhile, remove leaves from cabbage in the following fashion: First, pull away and discard any tough-looking or floppy outer leaves. One leaf at a time, sever leaves at the base of the cabbage, where they are attached to the core, and gently peel them free from the head. Be careful when peeling; the leaves tear easily. You will need 12 large, untorn leaves—or perhaps 14, just to be on the safe side if any rip during stuffing.

Submerge leaves in rapidly boiling salted water and cook uncovered for 8 to 12 minutes; the leaves must be tender enough to bend easily when rolled around the stuffing. Drain in a colander and rinse lightly with cold water so that leaves will be comfortable to handle.

Step 2: Preparing Stuffing; Stuffing the Cabbage

3 tablespoons olive oil or bacon fat
1 cup minced onions
1 cup (about 8 ounces) hot sausage meat
1 cup (6 to 8 ounces) minced boiled ham
1 cup cooked rice
1 large egg
1 tablespoon Dijon mustard
½ teaspoon mashed, pressed, or very finely minced garlic
½ teaspoon caraway seed, ground or moistened with a few drops of water and minced fine
¼ teaspoon dried summer savory or rubbed or ground sage
¼ teaspoon whole dried thyme
½ teaspoon salt (use less if ham is salty)
¼ teaspoon pepper, preferably freshly ground

Heat olive oil or fat in a 10-inch skillet and sauté onions over low heat for about 10 minutes, or until quite tender. Turn onions into 3-quart mixing bowl, add all other ingredients, and blend thoroughly with a wooden spoon. At this point, it is a good idea—though not essential—to sauté a spoonful of the stuffing so that you can taste it and correct the seasoning.

Stuff the cabbage leaves as follows: Lay a leaf on a work surface, concave side up, with the stem end facing you. Drop ¼ cup or so of stuffing onto the leaf. Fold in sides of leaf, then roll the stem end up toward the tip, forming a neat little package. Proceed to stuff 12 leaves in this manner.

Step 3: Preparing Sauce and Cooking the Cabbage

3 cups Chicken Stock, page 26, or canned broth
1½ cups unsweetened apple juice
½ cup dry white wine

½ cup raisins or dried currants
½ cup cocktail onions (two 3-ounce jars), drained, rinsed in a colander, and patted dry with paper toweling
1 tablespoon cornstarch mixed to a smooth paste with 2 tablespoons stock, juice, or wine
½ to 1 teaspoon sugar
Salt and freshly ground pepper

Arrange cabbage rolls seam side down in baking dish. Combine all above ingredients except for cornstarch paste and sugar and bring to a simmer in a 2-quart saucepan. Pour over cabbage. If necessary, add enough water so that cabbage rolls are just barely covered. Cover dish with foil or lid and bake for about 40 minutes or until the rolls feel firm when pressed with the back of a fork.

Remove cooked cabbage rolls to a plate, cover with foil, and set aside. Pour cooking liquid into saucepan and boil down over high heat until reduced to about 3 cups (including solids). Stir in cornstarch paste and simmer 1 minute longer. Taste and season with sugar, salt, and pepper. Drain off any liquid that has accumulated around cabbage rolls and nap with sauce.

Carrots

Carrots range in size from giant iciclelike spears to tiny finger-size nubbins. Giant carrots are often woody and overpoweringly spicy, but you can tone down their taste a bit by slicing them in halves or quarters and prying out the strongly flavored yellowish cores. These behemoths belong in rich, long-simmering stews and soups. Normal-size carrots, the ones sold in plastic bags at the supermarket, are good for all uses. Baby carrots are handsome to look at, but they are often soft and lacking in flavor, turning to mush when they are cooked. If you want to serve small carrots, you are probably better off buying larger carrots and whittling them into the shape you want with a vegetable peeler.

No matter what their size, carrots should be stiff and hard to the touch. Sprouting tops and fuzzy roots protruding down the length of the carrots indicate old age or improper storage. Carrots should be whole, but the tinted plastic bags in which they are often packaged frequently hide from view the presence of mangled or broken carrots. Be on your guard.

Canned and Frozen Carrots: Both canned and frozen carrots will taste better if simmered until tender in chicken stock or broth flavored with pinches of thyme, pepper, and, if needed, sugar. If you wish, you can boil down the cooking broth until it turns into a glaze.

RESCUING OVERCOOKED CARROTS: It is unlikely that your braised carrots will overcook, since by the time they are tender the liquid in the saucepan should have completely evaporated. However, if your carrots do somehow become too soft, purée them.

MASTER RECIPE

Glazed Carrots

4 to 6 servings

Minced fresh herbs—parsley or mint in particular—are very nice with glazed carrots. Ground or minced dried rosemary or a hint of cinnamon or ground cloves are also good flavorings. Glazed carrots complement almost any kind of meat or poultry and go well with most fish dishes too.

STEP 1: TRIMMING THE CARROTS

2 pounds carrots

Peel carrots with a swivel-blade vegetable peeler, then slice off root and stem ends with a paring knife. You may cut the carrots into any shape you choose—rounds, inch-long pieces, or sticks. Naturally, smaller shapes will cook more quickly than larger ones.

STEP 2: COOKING THE CARROTS

2 cups water
3 tablespoons butter
2 teaspoons sugar
1 teaspoon salt

Combine carrots and all above ingredients in a 10-inch skillet and bring to a slow boil. Cover and cook over moderate heat for 7 to 12 minutes, or until carrots are almost tender. Uncover skillet, raise heat, and boil down the cooking liquid to a syrupy glaze that coats the carrots, stirring frequently. Be careful not to scorch the carrots.

AHEAD OF TIME: Carrots may be prepared a day ahead and kept in a tightly closed container in the refrigerator. Reheat slowly in a covered skillet or saucepan, adding a tablespoon of water to prevent scorching and stirring often.

Variation: CARROTS IN HEAVY CREAM

4 to 6 servings

❦ *Carrots in cream are sublime served with roasts, chops, steaks, or broiled chicken. Combined with some diced cooked chicken and gratinéed under a hot broiler with a topping of cheese and fresh bread crumbs, they may become the mainstay of a lunch or supper.*

Glazed Carrots, slightly undercooked (see below)
1½ cups heavy cream
1 teaspoon cornstarch mixed to a smooth paste with 1 tablespoon milk or additional cream (optional)
Salt and pepper, preferably white and freshly ground, to taste
Nutmeg, preferably freshly grated
Fresh lemon juice
2 tablespoons minced fresh parsley (optional)

Prepare carrots according to Master Recipe, but boil off their cooking liquid when they are still somewhat underdone—4 to 8 minutes, depending on the age of the carrots and how you have cut them. Pour heavy cream over the carrots and simmer slowly until cream has reduced and thickened and carrots are completely tender. If you wish, thicken with a paste of 1 teaspoon cornstarch mixed with milk or cream; cook a minute after adding starch mixture. Season carrots with salt, pepper, a pinch or two of nutmeg, and drops of fresh lemon juice. Fold in parsley if you'd like.

Variation: CARROT PURÉE

4 to 6 servings

❦ *Carrot purée is a very nice dish indeed, especially with roast chicken.*

Glazed Carrots, cooked very soft (see below)
1 to 2 tablespoons milk or cream
3 to 4 tablespoons soft butter
Salt and pepper, preferably white and freshly ground, to taste
Nutmeg, preferably freshly grated
Fresh lemon juice

Prepare carrots according to Master Recipe, but cook them until quite soft—15 to 20 minutes, or even longer—before boiling off the cooking liquid. Purée in food processor, blender, or food mill, adding a tablespoon or two of milk or cream and 3 to 4 tablespoons soft butter. Season to taste with salt, pepper, a pinch or two of nutmeg, and drops of lemon juice. If necessary, reheat purée over low heat, stirring.

Variation: GLAZED CARROTS IN MEAT STOCK

4 to 6 servings

❦*A perfect accompaniment for roast beef or lamb.*

Glazed carrots,

SUBSTITUTE:	Beef Stock, page 24, or canned broth for water
OMIT:	Salt
ADD:	2 tablespoons minced fresh parsley

Prepare carrots according to the Master Recipe but substitute stock or broth for water and omit the salt. Boil down the liquid in the skillet until it thickens enough to coat the carrots with a syrupy glaze. Should you reduce the liquid too much, causing it to separate, remove the skillet from heat, add 1 to 2 tablespoons water, and shake the skillet vigorously back and forth to reconstitute the glaze.

Just before serving, taste and adjust seasoning, and sprinkle with parsley.

CAULIFLOWER

A fresh, healthy head of cauliflower is stiff and snow white, its florets tightly compacted. Yellowish or blackish mottling is a sign of staleness, moldiness, or both, and may indicate an off taste. If there is a good deal of greenery attached to the base of a cauliflower, pull it back with your hand to determine the actual size of the head. It used to be common practice to soak cauliflower in salted water to rid it of worms, but today's cauliflowers are not likely to have worms and need not be soaked.

FROZEN CAULIFLOWER: An extremely delicate vegetable, cauliflower does not take well to being blanched and frozen at a processing plant, stored for months in a supermarket freezer, and then reheated at home. To salvage its taste and texture to the greatest extent possible, thaw the cauliflower just enough so that the pieces can be picked apart. Steam on a rack over an inch of water until heated through, and serve at once.

RESCUING OVERCOOKED CAULIFLOWER: Mushy and virtually tasteless, seriously overcooked cauliflower is not really rescuable as a vegetable, but it may be pressed in a sieve to eliminate some of its moisture and then used to make cream of cauliflower soup.

MASTER RECIPE

Steamed Cauliflower

4 servings

❦ *Though a very delicate vegetable, cauliflower takes well to rich, assertive sauces such as cheese sauce (made with either Cheddar or a combination of Swiss and Parmesan), lemon cream sauce, curried cream sauce, or even hollandaise. Of course it is also good when dressed simply with butter, salt, pepper, and lemon juice. Like its cousin, broccoli, cauliflower is a versatile vegetable that goes particularly well with poultry and fish, and it can also be served with beef and lamb. Perhaps the only meat it does not really complement is pork.*

Steaming is the cooking method that best preserves cauliflower's subtle flavor and texture. When boiled, the vegetable tends to become taste-leached and waterlogged.

STEP 1: TRIMMING THE CAULIFLOWER

1 medium-large head of cauliflower (1½ to 2 pounds)

Break the florets off the central stalk. Using a sharp paring knife, peel the central stalk thoroughly and cut into pieces roughly the same size as the stems of the larger florets. Cut or strip away with your fingers the skins of the floret stems and cut the larger florets in half lengthwise, making all the clusters more or less equal in size. Wash the cauliflower well.

STEP 2: STEAMING THE CAULIFLOWER

Select a pot or sauté pan at least 10 inches in diameter and 5 inches deep; add ½ inch water and bring to a rapid boil. Set a 9-inch steaming basket or rack in pot, cover with trimmed cauliflower, and clamp on the lid. Steam for 7 minutes, then test for doneness; cauliflower should be tender with just a suggestion of crunch. If it is undercooked, steam for a minute or two longer.

AHEAD OF TIME: Refrigerate cooked cauliflower, still on the steaming rack, until it is thoroughly cold, then pack in a plastic bag and refrigerate. Reheat by steaming in a basket, rack, or colander or by stewing slowly in butter in a covered skillet.

Variation: GRATIN OF CAULIFLOWER WITH CHEDDAR CHEESE

4 servings

Gratin of Broccoli with Cheddar Cheese, page 494
SUBSTITUTE: ***Steamed Cauliflower***, cooked only 5 minutes, for broccoli

Prepare gratin using cauliflower rather than broccoli.

Variation: CAULIFLOWER IN BROWNED BUTTER WITH CAPERS

4 servings

❦ *This is one of my favorite accompaniments for broiled or poached fish.*

Steamed Cauliflower
8 tablespoons (1 stick) butter
2 tablespoons drained small capers plus 1 teaspoon liquid from the caper bottle
1 teaspoon white or red wine vinegar
Pepper, preferably freshly ground, to taste

Melt butter in a small skillet over moderate heat. When foam has subsided, begin to swirl the skillet by the handle over the burner, heating butter until it turns a light nut brown; watch over this procedure carefully, as butter burns easily. Remove skillet from heat and add capers, the liquid from the caper bottle, and vinegar. Return skillet to heat and simmer briefly. Pour sauce over cauliflower, sprinkle with pepper, and serve at once.

Variation: CAULIFLOWER IN TOASTED CRUMBS

4 servings

❦ *This is lovely with almost any sort of fish or chicken dish.*

Steamed Cauliflower
1 cup Fine Fresh Bread Crumbs (see page 60)
6 tablespoons butter
2 tablespoons strained fresh lemon juice
Salt and pepper, preferably freshly ground, to taste

In a 10-inch skillet toss bread crumbs over moderate heat until golden brown. Scrape crumbs out of the skillet into a small bowl and set aside. In the same skillet melt the butter, then add the lemon juice. Lay in the cauliflower and stew slowly in the butter mixture for several minutes, stirring gently once or twice. Season highly with salt and pepper, then add reserved toasted bread crumbs and toss gently until cauliflower is evenly coated. Serve without delay.

CELERY

Most of the celery found in the market these days is unblanched, or pascal, celery, which is said to have a higher vitamin content than blanched celery. When buying celery packaged in plastic bags, check to make sure that none of the ribs is detached from the bunch. Celery should feel crisp and hard, and the leaves should be a sprightly green. If possible, select small bunches containing slender ribs, which are more tender and less stringy than large ribs.

RESCUING WILTED CELERY: You can refresh a whole bunch of celery that has wilted by detaching the ribs, covering them with ice water, and refrigerating them for several hours. Cut pieces that have gone limp may be wrapped in moist paper towels, placed in a plastic bag, and refrigerated until they regain their crispness, usually in about an hour.

MASTER RECIPE

Braised Celery

4 servings

❦*A homey, old-fashioned dish, braised celery is most commonly thought of as an accompaniment to the Thanksgiving turkey, though it is also delicious with veal roast or chops. A dusting of minced fresh parsley or, if you happen to have it, fresh chervil, may be added just before serving.*

STEP 1: TRIMMING THE CELERY

4 bunches celery, preferably small and young

Pull off (and save for some other purpose) the outer ribs of each bunch of celery, leaving a pale, tender heart 1½ to 2 inches in diameter at its thickest point. Trim each heart at the top, where the ribs tend to be stringy, so that you have a length of about 6 inches. Shave off a paper-thin disc from the root end, being careful not to detach any of the ribs. Wash celery hearts under a strong stream of water, gently parting the ribs.

STEP 2: BRAISING THE CELERY

½ cup Chicken Stock, page 26, or canned broth
4 tablespoons butter
1 tablespoon finely chopped shallots or scallion (optional)
Salt and pepper, preferably freshly ground, to taste

Select a 10- to 12-inch skillet, with lid (do not choose a skillet made of unlined cast iron, which may impart a metallic taste to the celery). Lay celery hearts in skillet, pour chicken stock over them, dot with butter, and sprinkle with optional shallots or scallion. Cover skillet and simmer celery slowly for 30 to 40 minutes, turning several times with spatulas or wooden spoons; when done, the celery should be soft enough to be pierced easily with a fork at the root end.

Transfer cooked celery to a dish. Raise heat and boil down cooking liquid until it becomes syrupy and has reduced to about ½ cup. Season with salt and pepper as necessary and pour over celery.

AHEAD OF TIME: Braised celery may be prepared entirely ahead of time and kept in a sealed container in the refrigerator for 4 to 5 days; it actually improves with standing. Reheat slowly in a covered skillet, adding a spoonful of water or stock if the celery threatens to scorch.

Variation: CELERY IN HEAVY CREAM

4 servings

❦ *This goes well with nearly any broiled or roasted poultry or meat.*

Braised Celery
1 cup heavy cream
Salt and pepper, preferably freshly ground, to taste
Fresh lemon juice
2 tablespoons minced fresh parsley

After boiling down the celery cooking liquid to ½ cup, add the cream and reduce over high heat to about 1 cup of sauce thick enough to coat a spoon lightly. Season to taste with salt, pepper, and drops of fresh lemon juice. Pour sauce over celery and sprinkle with minced parsley.

Variation: SHERRIED CELERY WITH WALNUTS

4 servings

❦ *This is a classic accompaniment to Thanksgiving turkey.*

Braised Celery
2 tablespoons medium-dry Sherry, preferably Manzanilla
3 tablespoons (less than 1 ounce) chopped black walnuts (substitute regular walnuts if black walnuts are not available)

After boiling down the celery cooking liquid to ½ cup, add Sherry and boil 1 to 2 minutes longer, or until sauce looks syrupy. Pour sauce over celery, then sprinkle with walnuts.

Celery Root (Celeriac)

Available in the fall and winter, celery root is an odd-looking vegetable indeed. The root, which is the edible portion, is dark brown, knobby, shaggy with small root hairs, and usually covered with dirt; the stems and leaves, if attached, suggest an immature celery plant.

Both the size and weight of celery root must be taken into account when making a purchase. The ideal celery root feels heavy in the hand, is no bigger than a tennis ball, and weighs ½ pound or less. Large celery roots are often dried out and pithy, and roots weighing over ¾ pound are apt to be tough and woody, with too strong a taste. Choose the smoothest, roundest roots you can find, as knobby specimens are a chore to peel.

RESCUING CANNED CELERY ROOT: To prepare canned celery root, turn it into a colander, rinse under cold water, pat dry, cut into cubes or slices, and warm in a skillet with butter. Serve as is, seasoned to taste with salt, pepper, drops of fresh lemon juice, and minced fresh parsley, or purée. Drained and rinsed canned celery root may also be combined with the sauce for celery root rémoulade, though the salad will not have as much character as when prepared with the fresh vegetable.

MASTER RECIPE

Boiled Celery Root

4 servings

Plain boiled celery root may be served with any dish that you would normally accompany with boiled potatoes. Toss the peeled, cut-up celery root in a serving bowl with 4 to 6 tablespoons soft butter, season to taste with salt, pepper, and drops of lemon juice, and fold in 2 tablespoons minced fresh parsley.

1½ to 2 pounds celery root, preferably 3 or 4 roots weighing about 8 ounces each
Salt

Pull off and discard stems and leaves if still attached. Using a stiff brush, scrub roots thoroughly under running water. Place roots in a pot, cover with cold water, and add about a tablespoon of salt per quart of water used. Bring to a boil, then reduce heat so that the water is maintained at a brisk simmer. Cover the pot and cook celery root for 25 to 40 minutes, depending on size; it is done when it feels just tender when pierced deeply with a fork.

Remove each root from the pot with a fork and let cool a moment. Then, with your hands protected by pot holders or towels if necessary, slip the skins off the roots, digging out any skin that remains in the crevices with a knife. Slice off both the stem and root ends, and cut the roots into cubes or slices.

AHEAD OF TIME: Remove celery root from the pot, let cool completely, and refrigerate, whole and unpeeled, in a covered storage container for up to 3 days. To serve, peel and cut up the celery root and warm it through in a skillet with 6 tablespoons butter. Season with salt, pepper, and fresh lemon juice and fold in minced fresh parsley.

Variation: CELERY ROOT PURÉE (WITH MUSHROOMS OR ONIONS)

4 servings

❦ *Puréed celery root, with or without a mushroom or onion flavoring, is particularly good with roast turkey, roast pork, or game. It may also be combined with another puréed winter root vegetable such as carrots, turnips, or potatoes. Be inventive and experimental here, using whatever proportion of each vegetable that strikes you as right—you really can't make a mistake.*

Boiled Celery Root, the cooking water reserved
4 to 6 tablespoons soft butter
Either Mushroom Stuffing, page 553, *or* 1 cup chopped onions sautéed until soft and very lightly browned in 2 tablespoons butter (optional)
Salt and pepper, preferably freshly ground, to taste
Fresh lemon juice
2 tablespoons minced fresh parsley

Proceed according to the Master Recipe, but purée the cooked, peeled, cut-up celery root using a food mill or processor, then beat in the soft butter. If the purée seems too thick add a spoonful of the cooking water. If you wish, fold in either mushroom stuffing or sautéed onions. Season to taste with salt, pepper, and drops of lemon juice and sprinkle with parsley.

CELERY ROOT RÉMOULADE

4 to 6 first-course or 6 side-dish servings

❦ *The French often serve this lovely, refreshing salad as a first course with crusty bread. It may also be used as an accompaniment for cold poached fish, a mayonnaise-dressed cold salad, or cold roast meat or fowl.*

1 pound celery root, preferably 2 small roots weighing about 8 ounces each
1/4 cup Dijon mustard
1 tablespoon strained fresh lemon juice
1 tablespoon white wine vinegar
3/8 teaspoon salt
1/4 teaspoon pepper, preferably freshly ground
1/2 cup olive oil
2 tablespoons finely chopped fresh parsley
1 tablespoon finely chopped scallion, including tender green parts

Pull off and discard stems and leaves of celery root if still attached. Wash the roots under running water, then peel with a very sharp knife and rinse again. Cut roots into 1/8-inch slices, then cut the slices into 1/8-inch matchsticks, dropping the pieces into a bowl of cold water to prevent discoloration. Drain, turn into a heat-proof 3-quart mixing bowl, and cover with rapidly boiling water. Let stand exactly 1 minute, then drain in a colander, and turn out onto paper toweling. Pat dry and set aside.

In the dried mixing bowl place the mustard, lemon juice, vinegar, salt, and pepper. Using a wire whip, beat the mustard mixture until blended, then add the olive oil a little at a time, beating constantly until a smooth, thick dressing forms. Fold prepared celery root, parsley, and scallion into the mustard dressing, cover with plastic wrap, and let stand at room temperature for several hours or refrigerate for 8 hours or longer. Let stand at room temperature 20 minutes before serving.

CHESTNUTS

Although more commonly thought of as a roasted snack or as an ingredient in certain classic desserts, chestnuts are also delicious braised in stock and served as a starchy vegetable. If possible, select chestnuts individually rather than buying them prepackaged, so that you'll know what you're getting. Good-quality chestnuts are firm, plump, and shiny. Reject any chestnuts that feel soft, puffy, or weightless, as these are likely to be rotted or dried up inside the shell.

BRAISED CHESTNUTS

4 to 6 servings

❦ *Braised chestnuts go particularly well with turkey, goose, duck, and pork, and are a delightful change from the usual potatoes or rice. The major drawback in preparing them is that they must be peeled before braising, a task that is rather hard on the fingers as it must be dispatched while the chestnuts are hot.*

STEP 1: PEELING THE CHESTNUTS

2 pounds whole chestnuts in the shell
4 quarts boiling water

Both the outer shell and the thin inner skin covering the nut must be removed before cooking. Cut a thin strip of shell ½ inch long off the edge of the flat side of each chestnut with a sharp paring knife. Drop the chestnuts in 4 quarts boiling water and boil rapidly for 2 minutes. Remove the pot from heat. A few at a time, skim chestnuts from their hot water bath and, using the paring knife, peel off the shell and the brownish inner skin. Return to the water any chestnuts that resist peeling and let them soak a few minutes longer before trying again. Keep in mind that chestnuts will not peel unless they are hot.

AHEAD OF TIME: Peeled chestnuts may be turned into a covered container and refrigerated for a day or so before being braised.

STEP 2: BRAISING THE CHESTNUTS

4 tablespoons butter
1 teaspoon sugar
¼ teaspoon salt
¼ teaspoon pepper, preferably freshly ground
2 to 3 cups Chicken Stock, page 26, or canned broth
2 large parsley sprigs
2 celery ribs, cut in half
1 large bay leaf, halved

In a 10- to 12-inch skillet (do not use unlined cast iron, which may impart an off taste), heat the butter over moderately high flame until the foam subsides. Add the peeled chestnuts, and stir to coat with butter. Lower the heat slightly and sauté the chestnuts for 3 to 4 minutes, shaking the pan or gently stirring several times. The chestnuts should brown lightly, but don't expect the color to be even.

Sprinkle chestnuts with sugar, salt, and pepper, add just enough stock or broth to cover, and lay the parsley sprigs, celery ribs, and bay leaf on top. Cook the chestnuts, uncovered, at the lowest possible simmer for 10 to 25 minutes, or until they are tender when pierced with a fork. You must watch that they don't overcook, or they will turn mushy and begin to break apart.

Remove and discard parsley, celery, and bay leaf and transfer chestnuts to a dish with a slotted spoon. Boil down the chestnut braising liquid over high heat until it is reduced to about ½ cup of syrupy sauce. Return chestnuts to skillet and, over low heat, gently roll them about until they are glazed and heated through.

AHEAD OF TIME: Chestnuts may be covered and refrigerated for 2 days. Reheat in a heavy skillet over low flame, adding a few tablespoons of stock or water if chestnuts look dry.

COLLARDS

A tall, olive-colored leafy vegetable, collard greens are much prized by Southerners for their assertive, pleasantly bitter savor. If the greens are very young, and if the stems (including the part that runs through the center of the leaves) are stripped away, collards may be cooked according to the recipes for spinach; the garlic sauté variation recipe is particularly good. Generally speaking, however, it is best to give collards a good long braising, as outlined in the Master Recipe below, or to cook them in the traditional Southern style with pork hocks.

MASTER RECIPE

Braised Collards with Bacon

4 servings

❦ *Other nontender greens such as mature turnip tops, mustard greens, and kale may be prepared according to this recipe. Braised collard greens go well with pork, ham, or roast chicken. If you wish, serve freshly baked hot corn bread.*

2½ pounds collard greens
6 slices bacon, cut into 1-inch pieces
⅔ cup chopped onions (optional)
½ teaspoon salt
Vinegar
Salt and pepper, preferably freshly ground, to taste
Sugar

Wash greens thoroughly and chop into 1-inch pieces; set aside. Fry bacon until lightly browned in a 5- to 6-quart pot suitable for cooking the greens. Add onions and chopped collards, stirring with a wooden spoon until greens are coated with fat. Cover greens with water, add salt, and bring to a boil. Cover the pot and lower the heat so that the greens simmer gently. Cook greens until tender, an hour or longer, stirring occasionally and adding water if they threaten to scorch. When greens are done, raise heat to moderately high and, stirring frequently, boil off nearly all of the cooking liquid. Add a dash or two of vinegar and correct seasoning with salt, pepper, and pinches of sugar. Serve very hot.

AHEAD OF TIME: Turn the cooked greens into a storage container, cover, and refrigerate for up to 5 days. Reheat before serving.

CORN

Corn is a tricky vegetable. If picked too early, it will be watery and short on flavor; if too mature when picked, it will likely be tough, dry, and lacking in sweetness. And corn doesn't like to sit around waiting to be eaten; its sugars begin to hydrolyze, or turn to starch, almost as soon as it is harvested.

Although it's hard to tell how mature corn is, it is a good bet that suspiciously short or slender ears are underripe. Similarly, large, fat ears, especially those with dull-looking or dried-out husks, are likely to be too old. As for sweetness, remember that the hydrolysis process is retarded if corn is chilled immediately after harvesting and held under refrigeration. Thus supermarket corn is sometimes sweeter than corn bought at a roadside stand if the latter has stood for some time under the hot sun. Partially husked corn may be dried out, so avoid it if you can. Avoid also any ear that appears to be bulging or whose tassel is blackened, stubby, or malformed. Such an ear may be infested by insects or blighted by mold.

I grew up hearing that dark yellow corn was sweeter and more flavorful than white corn; some people apparently hold the exact opposite opinion. Since there exist many different hybrids of corn in hues ranging from white to yellow to purple-black, the connoisseur is wise to pick corn according to what he knows about the varieties grown in his area rather than by color.

SHUCKING FRESH CORN: Strip off the green husk and break off and discard the stem. Pull away any strands of silk that adhere to the kernels. (Sometimes particularly stubborn pieces of silk can be rubbed off with a moist paper towel.) Wash ears thoroughly under running water.

PREPARING KERNEL CORN AND CORN PULP: Kernels of corn consist of two parts: the outer skin, which is tough and indigestible, and the inner pulp, which is creamy, soft, and flavorful. Frozen and canned cut corn come as whole kernels. When preparing fresh corn in home cooking, however, it is preferable to use either half kernels, omitting the very fibrous portion of the base, or just the pulp. Depending on how it is to be used in a recipe, corn is cut from the cob in one of the following two ways:

1. *Half kernels of corn:* Stand the husked corn cob on its base and, using a very sharp knife, slice down the length of cob, removing the bulbous ends of the kernels but leaving the bottom halves of the kernels embedded in the cob. When the ear is denuded, firmly press the stubs of the kernels still attached to the cob with the back of a knife to extract the pulp. Prepared in this manner, an ear of corn will yield ½ cup (or a little more) of corn kernels and a tablespoon or two of pulp.

2. *Corn pulp:* Using a very sharp knife, slash each row of corn kernels down the center to open the kernels up. Stand the ear of corn on its end and firmly press the back of a knife down the rows of kernels to extract the pulp. One ear of corn will yield between ¼ and ⅓ cup of pulp.

RESCUING CANNED AND FROZEN CORN: Canned corn is at its best when drained and poached briefly in butter in a covered skillet. Frozen corn should be defrosted, then treated as for canned corn. The starch in canned and frozen corn becomes cooked during processing, and thus these products cannot be substituted for fresh corn in creamed corn recipes.

RESCUING UNSWEET OR FLAVORLESS CORN: Sugar is often very helpful in small doses. Old, tough, starchy corn is probably best used in a mixed vegetable soup.

NOTES ON COOKING CORN ON THE COB: It is impossible for a recipe to give foolproof cooking times for corn on the cob because everything depends on the age and condition of the corn itself. Start with a big pot of unsalted boiling water (salt toughens the corn). If the corn is young, small, and tender, drop it into the boiling water, turn off the heat, and let the corn sit in the hot water for 3 minutes, or until the kernels have swelled and darkened slightly. Middle-aged corn should be given an extra minute or two in the hot water bath. Very old corn will probably need a minute or two of actual simmering, followed by a 3- to 5-minute off-the-heat bath. As in most things culinary, undercooking is preferable to overcooking.

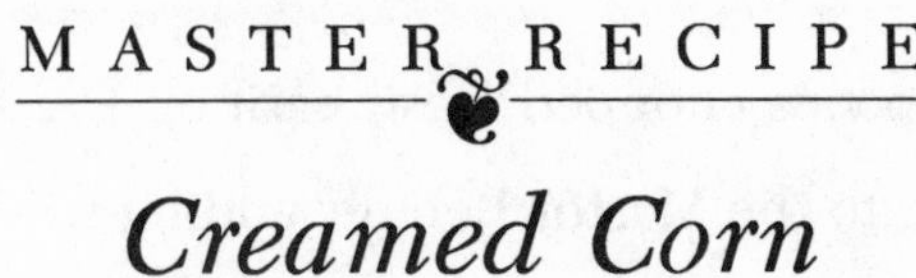

Creamed Corn

4 servings

❦ *Creamed corn is delicious with broiled chicken, pork chops, and beef steaks.*

3 tablespoons butter
5 to 6 ears fresh corn, shucked and cut into half kernels according to preceding instructions (2½ to 3 cups)
1 cup heavy cream
¼ teaspoon salt
⅛ teaspoon white pepper, preferably freshly ground
⅛ to ¼ teaspoon cayenne pepper (optional)

Melt butter in a 10-inch skillet; add corn and heavy cream. Bring mixture just to the simmer over medium heat. Reduce heat and poach corn at the simmer for 3 to 7 minutes, stirring. As soon as the corn is tender and the mixture thickens, it is done. Season with salt, white pepper, and also cayenne pepper if you like a spicy flavor. Serve at once.

Variation: CREAMED CORN WITH BACON

4 servings

❦ *This is particularly good with roast or broiled chicken or with ham.*

Creamed corn

SUBSTITUTE:	4 slices bacon for butter
ADD:	2 tablespoons minced fresh parsley (optional)

In the same skillet you will use to cook the corn, fry bacon until crisp; remove from skillet, drain, and crumble. Proceed according to the Master Recipe, substituting bacon drippings for butter. Garnish the finished dish with reserved crumbled bacon and, if you wish, fresh parsley.

Variation: CREAMED CORN WITH BASIL

4 servings

❦ *Latin American in inspiration, this makes an unusual and very satisfying accompaniment for fried fish.*

Creamed Corn

ADD: 1½ tablespoons chopped fresh basil or 1½ teaspoons dried

Proceed according to the Master Recipe, adding fresh or dried basil along with the cream.

Variation: CREAMED CORN WITH PARMESAN CHEESE

4 servings

❦ *This dish is good with any roast meat (rare roast beef, for example) or fowl.*

Creamed Corn

ADD: 3 tablespoons minced onion
3 to 4 tablespoons (about 1 ounce) freshly grated Parmesan cheese

OMIT: Salt

Slowly sauté minced onions in butter called for in the Master Recipe until soft but not at all brown. Add corn and cream and proceed with the Master Recipe, folding in grated Parmesan cheese when the corn is done and omitting salt (the cheese is quite salty). If cheese does not melt completely, briefly return skillet to heat.

Variation: CREAMED CORN WITH PEPPERS AND ONIONS

4 servings

❦*I particularly like this with ham and pork.*

Creamed Corn

ADD: ½ small green bell pepper, seeded, deribbed, and cut into ¼-inch dice (about ⅓ cup)
½ small red bell pepper, prepared as above
1 to 3 small chili peppers, cored, seeded, and cut into fine shreds (optional)
¼ cup chopped onion

Slowly sauté bell peppers, chili peppers, and chopped onion in the butter called for in the Master Recipe, cooking vegetables until tender but not at all brown. Add corn and cream and proceed according to the Master Recipe.

MARILYN'S TEX-MEX CORN QUICHE

4 main-dish or 4 to 6 side-dish servings

❦*Corn, chilis, and Monterey Jack cheese are a classic Tex-Mex combination, and this recipe makes excellent use of that combination. Make this as spicy or as mild as you like. What follows is a mild version and you can omit the cayenne pepper entirely if you don't like any heat at all. To make the dish hot in typical Tex-Mex fashion, double the cayenne, or use hot chilis in place of mild ones, or use Monterey Jack with chili peppers in it—or, if you dare, do all three.*

Serve the quiche for lunch, accompanied by a tossed green salad or perhaps cole slaw, or use as a side dish with chops, steaks, or chicken.

PRELIMINARIES

1. Set rack in upper-middle level of oven.
2. Preheat oven to 425°F 20 minutes before baking.
3. Select a 9-inch round pan—a cake pan, for example. Coat the pan with 1 tablespoon soft butter and dust with 2 tablespoons cornmeal, knocking out excess.

6 large ears fresh corn, shucked
2 cups (8 ounces) shredded Monterey Jack cheese; use, if possible, the low-moisture type rather than the less flavorful supermarket type
2⁄3 cup heavy cream
1 large egg
1 4-ounce can chopped mild chilis, thoroughly drained
1⁄4 teaspoon ground cumin
1⁄8 teaspoon cayenne pepper
1⁄4 teaspoon pepper, preferably freshly ground

Cut 3 of the corn ears into kernels and the other 3 into pulp (page 522). Combine with all remaining ingredients in a 3-quart mixing bowl and blend thoroughly. Turn into prepared pan and, if you wish, sprinkle top with a bit of cornmeal and/or additional shredded Monterey Jack. Bake for about 25 minutes, or until quiche is brown on top and does not quiver when lightly shaken. Let stand at room temperature about 5 minutes to firm before cutting into wedges and serving.

CORN PUDDING OR CUSTARD

4 servings

❦ *This recipe is admittedly a bit of work, but the rich, creamy dish that results justifies the effort. If you prepare the recipe with egg yolks you will end up with a soft pudding the consistency of very thick oatmeal; if you use whole eggs, the result will be a custard that can be cut with a knife. Both are delicious, particularly with ham and roast beef.*

PRELIMINARIES

1. Set rack in the center of oven.
2. Preheat oven to 325°F 20 minutes before baking.
3. Select a 5- to 6-cup baking dish that is 5 to 8 inches wide. Coat the dish with 1 tablespoon soft butter and sprinkle with 1 tablespoon dry bread crumbs.
4. Select a second pan at least 1 inch wider than the baking dish and at least 1 1⁄2 inches deep. Have ready a kettle of simmering water. (The baking dish will be set in a pan of simmering water to prevent pudding or custard from curdling.)

8 to 10 ears fresh corn
2 or 4 teaspoons cornstarch (see below)
⅔ cup heavy cream
2 large egg yolks (for pudding) or 3 large eggs (for custard)
¼ to ½ teaspoon sugar, if needed
⅛ teaspoon nutmeg, preferably freshly grated
½ teaspoon salt
⅛ teaspoon white pepper, preferably freshly ground
1 tablespoon butter
1 tablespoon dry bread crumbs

Shuck 8 ears of corn and prepare as pulp following the instructions on page 522. Force pulp through a fine sieve into a 1½-quart bowl using the back of a wooden spoon to eliminate all traces of fibrous matter. Measure the strained pulp; you should have 2 cups or a little more. If you do not have 2 cups, prepare an additional ear or two of corn.

Measure 2 or 4 teaspoons of cornstarch into a clean 1½-quart mixing bowl. (If the strained corn pulp is thick enough to hold its shape softly, somewhat like yogurt, use the lesser amount of starch; if corn pulp seems watery, use the greater amount of starch.) Slowly dribble into the starch 2 to 3 tablespoons cream and stir with wooden spoon until you have a perfectly smooth paste. Beat in remaining cream, the yolks or whole eggs, and the corn. Taste and add sugar if necessary; beat in seasonings, taste again, and correct seasoning if need be. Scrape mixture into prepared baking dish. Dot top with 1 tablespoon butter and sprinkle with 1 tablespoon dry breadcrumbs.

Set baking dish in larger pan and place in the oven. Pour simmering water into larger pan to a depth ⅔ that of the corn. Bake 40 to 50 minutes. When done, pudding will quiver slightly when shaken; custard will be firm. Remove from oven and let stand 2 minutes before serving.

CORN FRITTERS

Makes twenty 1½-inch fritters, serving 4 to 6

❦*A classic American treat, corn fritters are generally served with warmed maple syrup or honey. They are particularly congenial with pork or ham.*

- 3 to 4 ears fresh corn, shucked
- 1¼ teaspoons dry yeast (½ small packet)
- 2 tablespoons warm water (100°F, or around body temperature)
- ⅔ cup unbleached all-purpose flour
- 1 large egg
- 3 tablespoons butter, melted
- 1 tablespoon sugar
- ⅛ teaspoon nutmeg, preferably freshly grated
- ¼ teaspoon salt
- ⅛ teaspoon white or black pepper, preferably freshly ground
- 3 to 4 cups vegetable oil for frying

Following the instructions on page 522, prepare 2 ears of corn as pulp, making about ½ cup, and cut 1 to 2 ears into half kernels, making about ⅔ cup. Set aside.

Mix yeast and warm water in a 2-quart mixing bowl and set aside until the yeast is completely dissolved, 5 minutes or longer. Beat in corn pulp and kernels and all other ingredients except oil, mixing well. Cover bowl with plastic wrap and let rise in a warm place until doubled, 1 to 1½ hours.

Just before frying, preheat oven to "warm" (about 150°F) and place a baking sheet, lined with a triple thickness of paper towels, inside.

Pour about 1 inch of oil into a deep 10-inch skillet and heat over moderate flame until it shimmers, indicating that it is very hot. (If you are using a deep-fry thermometer, the correct temperature is around 375°F.) Scoop 2-tablespoon gobs of the fritter batter into the hot oil, adding only as many at one time as will fit comfortably. Fry about 1½ minutes, turning once with tongs or slotted spoon, then remove to the paper towel-lined baking sheet in the oven to keep warm while you prepare the rest.

CUCUMBERS

Too often watery and lacking in flavor, the large dark green cucumbers sold at the supermarket are certainly a second choice to garden cucumbers, but they make acceptable eating, especially when cooked. Select the smallest ones you can find—the monsters are mostly water and hard, tough seeds—and squeeze to make sure they are not soft (particularly at the ends) or pocked with watery dimples. Unfortunately the skins are often waxed to preserve freshness and should not be eaten.

Kirby cucumbers are available at some vegetable specialty markets. About the size of dill pickles, with whitish green skins, kirbys are more expensive than the supermarket giants, but far tastier. *English cucumbers,* often over a foot long, are crisp, thin-skinned, and virtually seedless. They are slightly less flavorful than kirbys, but still superior to the supermarket variety.

Bitter Cucumbers: Bitter cucumbers can usually be cooked, because the preliminary salting that is used to rid cucumbers of excess moisture also serves to remove the bitterness. Unfortunately, there is no way to salvage a bitter cucumber that was destined for the salad bowl.

MASTER RECIPE

Sautéed Cucumbers

4 servings

❦ *If you've never eaten cooked cucumbers before, you don't know what you've been missing. They are my vegetable of choice with poached or wine-sauced fish and are also good with veal, beef, and lamb.*

Sautéed cucumbers take well to quite a number of herbs and spices. Fresh parsley, chives, or dill are obvious choices; tarragon, fresh or dried, is also interesting. Ground or minced caraway, anise, or fennel seeds are also possibilities.

Step 1: Trimming and Salting the Cucumbers

2½ pounds cucumbers: 5 to 9 large or 15 to 20 small kirby
1½ teaspoons salt

Peel cucumbers with a knife or swivel-blade vegetable peeler and cut in half lengthwise. Scoop out seeds from both halves using a teaspoon. Cut halves into crescent-shaped slices about ¼ inch thick.

Turn cucumber slices into colander and toss with salt. Allow to drain over a sink or bowl for about 1 hour. A handful at a time, squeeze cucumbers firmly to remove additional moisture; the pieces should look ice green and translucent. Pat dry with paper toweling.

STEP 2: SAUTÉING THE CUCUMBERS

4 tablespoons butter
White pepper, preferably freshly ground, to taste

Heat butter in a 10- to 12-inch skillet until sizzling, add cucumbers, and cook over moderately high heat, stirring frequently, for 5 to 7 minutes, or until tender but still slightly crunchy. Season with white pepper and serve.

AHEAD OF TIME: Sautéed cucumbers are at their best when served fairly promptly, within an hour or so of cooking. However, you may hold them in a covered container in the refrigerator for a day or two and reheat them in a skillet just before serving.

Variation: CUCUMBERS IN HEAVY CREAM

4 servings

❦ *This goes well with virtually any simply prepared fish, poultry, or meat dish.*

Sautéed Cucumbers, cooked only 3 to 4 minutes
1 cup heavy cream
2 teaspoons snipped fresh chives or 1 teaspoon dried
1 teaspoon cornstarch mixed to a smooth paste with 1 tablespoon milk or cream
Salt and white pepper, preferably freshly ground, to taste
Fresh lemon juice

Add cream and chives to slightly undercooked cucumbers and simmer rapidly until reduced by about ⅓ and slightly thickened. Beat in cornstarch paste and simmer, stirring, 30 seconds longer. Season with salt, white pepper, and drops of fresh lemon juice.

Variation: SAUTÉED CUCUMBERS IN SOUR CREAM AND DILL

4 servings

❦ *Particularly good with pot roast.*

Sautéed Cucumbers
¾ cup sour cream
1 tablespoon chopped fresh dill (feathery leaves only) or 1 teaspoon dried dillweed
Salt and white pepper, preferably freshly ground, to taste
Sugar, if needed

Remove cucumbers from heat and blend in sour cream. Place over a low flame and heat, stirring, just long enough to warm the cream; if it comes near the simmer it will curdle. Remove skillet from heat and fold in chopped fresh dill or dried dillweed. Season to taste with salt, white pepper, and, if needed, pinches of sugar. Serve at once.

Variation: CRUMBED CUCUMBERS

4 servings

❦ *Serve with steaks, chops, and broiled fish or chicken.*

Sautéed Cucumbers, slightly undercooked
2 tablespoons minced shallots or scallions (white part only)
½ teaspoon anchovy paste or mashed drained anchovies, dissolved in 1 teaspoon hot water
½ cup Fine Fresh Bread Crumbs (see page 60)
Salt and pepper, preferably freshly ground, to taste
2 tablespoons minced fresh parsley

Stir shallots or scallions into cucumbers and sauté for about 30 seconds over moderately high heat. Add dissolved anchovy and allow water to boil off. Add crumbs, tossing to coat the cucumbers as evenly as possible, and sauté 1 to 2 minutes longer, or until crumbs brown very lightly. Season to taste with salt and pepper, toss with parsley, and serve at once.

EGGPLANT

An eggplant should feel firm and heavy in the hand, and its skin should be shiny and tight, without soft spots, withered patches, or blemishes of decay. Old eggplant is apt to taste bitter, even slightly metallic, and to have a mushy, slimy texture when cooked. Select medium-sized eggplants weighing 1½ pounds or less, as bigger ones tend to have large, hard seeds and dry, pithy flesh. Highly perishable, eggplant should be consumed soon after purchasing.

Eggplant must be either blanched or salted before being sautéed, or it will taste bitter, have a mushy texture, and absorb an ungodly quantity of oil. Though blanching is the quicker of the two precooking methods, salting better preserves the flavor and texture of the vegetable.

MASTER RECIPE

Sautéed Eggplant

4 servings

Sautéed eggplant has a particular affinity for lamb and is also good with broiled or roast chicken. Though delicious seasoned only with salt and pepper, it is perhaps even better when flavored with ½ teaspoon or so of minced fresh garlic, added a minute before the eggplant is taken off the heat, and sprinkled just before serving with several tablespoons of minced fresh parsley

STEP 1: PEELING AND SALTING THE EGGPLANT

2 eggplants, weighing about 2 pounds altogether
2 teaspoons salt

Pull off green caps and stems and cut about ½ inch off the tops of the eggplants; discard (this part of the eggplant tends to be bitter, tough, and dry). Cut off a thin slice from the blossom ends. Using a sharp knife, strip off skin from top to bottom (the skin is edible only if the eggplant is cooked for a prolonged time, as in moussaka). Cut the eggplants crosswise into ½-inch-thick slices, then cut slices into strips ½ inch wide and 1 inch long. You should have 5 to 6 cups.

Turn eggplant into a colander and toss with salt. Place colander over a sink or bowl and let eggplant drain for at least 40 minutes, tossing occasionally; an hour or more is even better. A small handful at a time, firmly press eggplant between sheets of paper toweling, squeezing out as much moisture as you can without mashing the flesh. When you are through, the eggplant should look limp, moist, greenish-brown, and almost translucent.

STEP 2: SAUTÉING THE EGGPLANT

3 tablespoons butter
2 tablespoons neutral vegetable oil
Salt and pepper, preferably freshly ground, to taste

Heat butter and oil in a 10- to 12-inch skillet until the butter foam subsides and the mixture is just beginning to color. Add eggplant and toss with a wooden spoon over high heat for about 5 minutes, or until tender and beginning to brown; if eggplant browns too quickly, lower heat. Remove skillet from heat and add salt and pepper as necessary. (Even though a great deal of salt is used in macerating the eggplant, most of this drips away as the vegetable drains, and more salt will probably be needed.) Serve sautéed eggplant as soon as possible, for it becomes mushy if it sits.

Variation: EGGPLANT IN HEAVY CREAM AND PARMESAN CHEESE

4 servings

❦*A delicious side dish with roasts, chops, or steaks, and especially good when teamed with green beans.*

Sautéed Eggplant, slightly undercooked
1 cup heavy cream
3 to 4 tablespoons (about 1 ounce) freshly grated Parmesan cheese
Salt and pepper, preferably freshly ground, to taste
Fresh lemon juice
2 tablespoons minced fresh parsley (optional)

Add cream to eggplant and boil down rapidly until reduced by about ⅓ and lightly thickened. Remove from heat, add cheese, and stir until cheese is melted. Season to taste with salt, pepper, and drops of lemon juice, fold in parsley, and serve at once.

Variation: CRUMBED EGGPLANT WITH BASIL AND GARLIC

4 servings

❦ *Serve with lamb or chicken.*

Sautéed Eggplant

SUBSTITUTE: 4 tablespoons olive oil for butter and neutral vegetable oil

ADD: ½ teaspoon mashed, pressed, or very finely minced garlic
½ cup Fine Fresh Bread Crumbs (see page 60)
1 tablespoon finely chopped fresh basil or 1 teaspoon dried

Prepare eggplant according to the Master Recipe, but use olive oil rather than butter and vegetable oil. When the eggplant is almost tender, stir in the garlic, then the bread crumbs, and toss over moderately high heat until the crumbs have colored lightly. Remove from heat and toss with basil. Season to taste with salt and pepper and serve immediately.

Variation: EGGPLANT IN TOMATO SAUCE

4 servings

Sautéed Eggplant

SUBSTITUTE: 4 tablespoons olive oil for butter and neutral vegetable oil

ADD: ½ teaspoon mashed, pressed, or very finely minced garlic (optional)
¾ to 1 cup thick tomato sauce, preferably homemade, page 183

Prepare eggplant according to the Master Recipe, but use olive oil instead of butter and neutral vegetable oil and sauté only 3 to 4 minutes, or until partially tender. Stir in optional garlic and tomato sauce and simmer slowly for 2 to 3 minutes, or until eggplant is completely cooked. Taste and adjust seasoning and serve at once.

BROILED EGGPLANT SLICES

4 servings

❦ *This is a very simple, straightforward way of preparing eggplant that allows the vegetable's subtle taste and texture to come through. Broiled eggplant can accompany lamb or chicken or, with a tossed green salad on the side, can be the mainstay of a light lunch or supper.*

PRELIMINARIES

1. Set broiler rack about 2 inches below heating element.
2. Preheat broiler 10 minutes before broiling.
3. Select a large rimmed baking sheet.

2 eggplants, each weighing about 1 pound
2 teaspoons salt
3 to 4 tablespoons olive oil
Salt and pepper, preferably freshly ground, to taste

Pull off green caps and stems and cut about ½ inch off the tops of the eggplants; discard. Cut off a thin slice from the blossom ends. Using a sharp knife, strip off skin from top to bottom. Cut eggplants crosswise into ½-inch-thick slices. Sprinkle slices on both sides with salt. Place a triple thickness of paper toweling on a large baking sheet and arrange eggplant slices in a single layer on the toweling. Let drain for 40 minutes or longer. When ready to cook eggplant, press it firmly between fresh sheets of paper toweling. Rinse and dry baking sheet.

Coat baking sheet with 3 tablespoons olive oil. Lay in eggplant slices, turning them once to coat thoroughly with oil; add a bit more oil if necessary. Broil eggplant 2 to 3 minutes on a side, or until lightly browned, turning with a spatula. Season to taste with salt and pepper and serve at once.

MASTER RECIPE

Breaded Fried Eggplant

4 servings

Serve fried eggplant as a first course, with lemon wedges on the side, or as an accompaniment to steaks, chops, or pasta. Cooled to room temperature, it also makes a delightful summer lunch with a tossed green or tomato salad.

2 eggplants, each weighing about 1 pound
1/3 cup all-purpose flour
2 large eggs beaten to blend with 1 tablespoon olive oil
1 1/3 cups Fine Fresh Bread Crumbs (see page 60) *or* 1 cup fresh bread crumbs and 1/3 cup (about 1 1/2 ounces) freshly grated Parmesan cheese
1/4 cup olive oil, more if needed
Salt and pepper, preferably freshly ground, to taste

Pare, cut, salt, drain, and dry eggplants as outlined in the recipe for broiled eggplant, above. Dredge slices first in flour, shaking off excess, then in egg, and then in crumbs. Arrange coated eggplant slices on a rack and let dry for 10 to 30 minutes.

Pour oil into a 10- to 12-inch skillet (or divide between two smaller skillets) and heat until it shimmers. Lay eggplant slices in the skillet(s) and cook over moderately high heat 4 to 5 minutes on each side, turning with a spatula. If you are unable to fry all of the eggplant in one batch, keep cooked eggplant warm in 150°F oven while you prepare more. You may have to add more oil to the skillet if you fry the eggplant in two batches. Season to taste with salt and pepper. Serve immediately or let cool to room temperature.

Variation: EGGPLANT PARMIGIANA

3 to 4 main-dish or 6 side-dish servings

❦ *The classic Italian-American eggplant dish.*

PRELIMINARIES

1. Set rack in the upper third of oven.
2. Preheat oven to 425°F 20 minutes before baking.
3. Select a 17×11-inch rimmed baking sheet; coat lightly with olive oil.

Breaded Fried Eggplant, using bread crumbs only as the coating
2 teaspoons oregano
¼ teaspoon pepper, preferably freshly ground
1½ cups (about 6 ounces) shredded whole-milk mozzarella
⅔ cup (about 3 ounces) freshly grated Parmesan cheese
2 tablespoons olive oil
1 to 1½ cups tomato sauce, preferably homemade, page 183

Arrange fried eggplant slices in a single layer on baking sheet and sprinkle with oregano and pepper. Mix mozzarella and Parmesan cheese. Cover eggplant slices with cheese mixture; drizzle with 2 tablespoons olive oil. Bake for about 10 minutes, or until cheese is melted and bubbly. Serve at once, with tomato sauce on the side.

BAKED STUFFED EGGPLANT WITH LAMB

4 main-dish or 8 side-dish servings

❦ *Stuffed eggplant makes a fine lunch or supper main course accompanied by French bread, a tossed salad, and a chilled white wine.*

PRELIMINARIES

1. Set rack in the upper third of oven.
2. Preheat oven to 375°F 20 minutes before baking.
3. Select a baking dish just large enough to hold the 4 eggplant halves. Lightly oil the dish.

Step 1: Salting and Precooking the Eggplants

2 eggplants, 12 ounces each
2 teaspoons salt
2 tablespoons olive oil

Pull off stems and green caps of the eggplants, but do not slice off any part of the tops or bottoms. Halve the eggplants lengthwise. Using the point of a small, sharp knife, cross-hatch the flesh of the eggplants at ¾-inch intervals, penetrating to within ½ inch or so of the skin. You want to score the eggplant deeply, but take care not to puncture the skin at any point. Rub ½ teaspoon salt into each of the eggplant halves and let stand skin side down for 1 hour. Holding eggplant halves upside down over the sink, squeeze them firmly to extract the bitter juices. Blot the flesh side of the eggplant halves with paper toweling.

Arrange eggplant skin side down in lightly oiled baking dish and rub ½ tablespoon olive oil into the cut surface of each half. Cover baking dish with lid or foil and bake eggplant in a preheated 375°F oven for 35 to 40 minutes, or until the flesh is quite soft but the eggplants still hold their shape firmly. Remove from oven, uncover, and let stand until cool enough to handle. Using a soup spoon, carefully scrape most of the flesh out of each eggplant half, leaving a ½-inch-thick wall on all sides. Chop flesh into 1-inch cubes and reserve.

Step 2: Stuffing and Baking the Eggplants

⅔ cup (about 6 ounces) ground lamb
1 cup finely chopped onions
5 tablespoons olive oil
½ cup cooked rice
¼ cup finely chopped fresh parsley
¼ cup (1 ounce) sliced or slivered almonds, toasted
1 tablespoon mashed, pressed, or very finely minced garlic
1 tablespoon chopped fresh basil or 1 teaspoon dried
⅔ cup heavy cream
6 tablespoons (1½ ounces) freshly grated Parmesan or Romano cheese
¼ to ½ teaspoon salt
⅛ teaspoon pepper, preferably freshly ground
2 tablespoons fresh or dry bread crumbs
1½ tablespoons butter or additional olive oil

Crumble lamb into a 10-inch skillet and cook over moderate heat, stirring, just long enough for lamb to cook through and render its fat. Spoon meat into small mixing bowl and pour off fat from skillet. Combine onions and 3 tablespoons olive oil in skillet and cook over low heat for 8 to 10 minutes, or until onions are very tender but not brown. Scrape onions into mixing bowl with lamb. Pour remaining 2 tablespoons olive oil into skillet and heat until it shimmers. Add eggplant cubes reserved from Step 1 and cook over moderately high heat, tossing gently, for 2 to 3 minutes to dry out and slightly brown the eggplant. Return lamb and onions to skillet; add rice, parsley, nuts, garlic and basil. Pour cream over all, mix well, and bring to a simmer. Cook slowly, stirring, for 3 to 5 minutes, or until the mixture is thick enough to hold its shape softly on the spoon. Remove skillet from heat and stir in 4 tablespoons grated cheese. Season with salt and pepper.

Arrange scooped-out eggplant halves in prepared baking dish. Divide stuffing among the eggplant halves, mounding it slightly in the center. Sprinkle tops with remaining 2 tablespoons grated cheese and 2 tablespoons bread crumbs; dot with 1½ tablespoons butter or drizzle with an equal amount of olive oil. Pour ⅛ inch water into the bottom of the baking dish and set the dish, uncovered, in preheated 375°F oven. Bake for 40 minutes, or until eggplant is hot and nicely browned on top. Allow eggplant to cool for about 5 minutes before serving.

Endive

Although endive is a leafy vegetable and is botanically related to chicory, it does not look anything like most greens. It grows in tight, cream-colored, spear-shaped heads that have a few tinges of purple at the edges and tips of the leaves. Endive is usually imported and always expensive. Choose heads that feel firm and show no signs of dryness or shriveling. Though most often used raw in a salad, endive is also delicious cooked.

BRAISED ENDIVE

4 servings

❦ *With its bitter-buttery taste and silky-crunchy texture, cooked endive makes a vegetable side dish of great distinction that particularly complements roast veal.*

6 tablespoons butter
8 small or 4 large heads endive
½ teaspoon salt
¼ teaspoon pepper, preferably freshly ground
½ teaspoon sugar
2 tablespoons strained fresh lemon juice

Pull off and discard any withered outer leaves and wipe the endives with damp paper toweling.

Select a heavy lidded skillet or pot that is 10 inches in diameter, or large enough to hold the endives in one layer, and made of or lined with a noncorroding material. Place butter in skillet or pot and set over moderate heat. When the butter has melted and ceased to foam, indicating that it is hot, add the endives, turn once to coat with butter, and sprinkle with salt and pepper. Regulating the heat so that the butter remains hot but does not begin to color, cook the endives for 5 to 10 minutes, turning frequently, or until they have absorbed most of the butter and turned a deep golden yellow. They should not brown. Sprinkle with sugar and lemon juice and add enough water to cover the the bottom of the skillet or pot to a depth of about 1/4 inch. Lay a sheet of buttered waxed paper over the endives, cover, and simmer very slowly for 40 minutes to 1 hour, turning 2 or 3 times and adding a bit more water if necessary. The endives are done when they feel tender when pierced with a fork. Remove waxed paper and gently boil off the liquid, turning the endives to coat with the glaze.

AHEAD OF TIME: Endives may be prepared 2 or 3 days in advance and kept in a covered container in the refrigerator. To reheat, place in a lightly buttered dish, add a few tablespoons water, cover, and bake at 325°F for 15 to 20 minutes, or until hot.

FENNEL (ANISE)

Florence fennel, the kind sold at supermarkets, looks similar to celery, except that its stalks form a bulbous knot at the bottom of the bunch and its leaves are soft and feathery, resembling dill. The slender upper portion of the stalk is tough and stringy and is discarded. The bulbous root end, which has a celerylike texture and a mild licorice taste, is most frequently cut up and served raw, either plain or in a salad, though it may also be cooked. In abundance at the market between Thanksgiving and New Year's, fennel is best when fairly young and small, measuring no more than 3 inches across at the thickest part. Large mature bunches tend to be pithy, flavorless, and full of tough strings.

WILD FENNEL FOR GRILLING: Florence fennel is not to be confused with wild fennel, a tall, bushy plant that grows in the western United States and in southern Europe. The dried stalks of wild fennel, which are available in gourmet food shops, can be placed on a grill over hot coals to give a fennel flavor to grilled fish and poultry. I have found that fresh stalks of Florence fennel, placed directly on hot coals, can be used as a substitute for dried wild fennel.

Although the moistness of fresh fennel will dampen the fire and slow the cooking process, it imparts a very pleasing flavor to grilled foods—sweet, smoky, and rich.

BRAISED FENNEL

4 servings

❦ *An unusual and provocative dish, braised fennel is particularly nice with pork, veal, or turkey.*

STEP 1: TRIMMING THE FENNEL

4 medium (about 3 inches across) or 8 small (about 2 inches across) heads fennel

Pull away and discard any outer ribs that appear dry, tough, blemished, or especially stringy. Cut off and discard the slender, dark green upper portion of the stalks and slice off a thin disk from the root end. Cut the heads in half lengthwise (that is, through the root end) and rinse.

STEP 2: BRAISING THE FENNEL

4 tablespoons butter
½ teaspoon salt
¼ teaspoon pepper, preferably freshly ground

Melt butter over moderate heat in a lidded skillet or pot large enough to hold the fennel in a single jumbled layer (do not use an unlined cast iron skillet or pot). Add fennel, stir to coat with butter, and sprinkle with salt and pepper. Cover and cook slowly for about 5 minutes, stirring several times. Add about ½ inch of water, cover, and cook fennel at a brisk simmer for 10 to 20 minutes, or until tender when pierced with a fork. Remove fennel to a plate and boil down the cooking liquid until reduced to a syrupy glaze. Return fennel to skillet or pot and stir gently over low heat for several minutes to coat with glaze.

AHEAD OF TIME: Fennel may be prepared several days in advance and kept in a covered container in the refrigerator. To reheat, arrange in a single layer, cut sides down, in a lightly buttered dish, add a few tablespoons water, cover, and bake at 325°F for 15 to 20 minutes, or until hot.

Jerusalem Artichokes (Sunchokes)

Jerusalem artichokes are knobby tubers with pale brown skin, somewhat suggesting ginger roots. Large, roundish specimens are easier to peel than small, irregularly shaped ones. Jerusalem artichokes should be hard to the touch, never spongy. The vegetable may be eaten either raw or cooked. Raw, it is reminiscent of water chestnuts; cooked, it suggests a slightly sweet, slightly crunchy white potato.

Jerusalem artichokes, by the way, do not come from Jerusalem, and botanically speaking they are no more closely related to true artichokes than they are to green beans. Rather, they are the tuber of a type of sunflower plant, and their name derives from the Italian word for sunflower, *girasole.*

Rescuing Overcooked Jerusalem Artichokes: Jerusalem artichokes are easy to overcook but not so easy to rescue. If they are not too far gone, you might try puréeing them, though unless you add a cooked potato or a cupful of cooked beans, the purée will be rather thin. Perhaps a wiser course would be to liquefy the Jerusalem artichokes with 2 cups or so of chicken broth and ½ cup heavy cream, making a delicious soup. Season the soup with chopped parsley and drops of fresh lemon juice.

MASTER RECIPE

Boiled Jerusalem Artichokes

4 servings

❦ *You will find that the lemon juice and salt used in cooking will have seasoned the vegetable nicely. Add plenty of soft butter, freshly ground pepper, and, if you wish, some chopped fresh parsley. Serve with beef, lamb, or pork.*

Step 1: Peeling and Trimming the Jerusalem Artichokes

2 quarts cold water
3 tablespoons fresh lemon juice
3 tablespoons salt
1½ pounds Jerusalem artichokes

Mix 2 quarts water, lemon juice, and salt in a 4-quart saucepan or pot made of or lined with a noncorroding material. Scrub Jerusalem artichokes well with a brush under running water. Peel the artichokes with a vegetable peeler; dig out any skin that remains lodged in the crevices with the point of a paring knife. Drop each artichoke as it is peeled into the acidulated water to prevent discoloration. When all of the artichokes have been peeled, cut any large ones into pieces the same size as the rest to insure even cooking.

STEP 2: COOKING THE JERUSALEM ARTICHOKES Bring the Jerusalem artichokes to a simmer in the acidulated water. Cook slowly, uncovered, for about 10 minutes if artichokes are small and for 20, 30, or even 40 minutes if large, adding boiling water to the saucepan as necessary. Watch the artichokes carefully as they cook. They do not become tender gradually; instead, they remain crisp and quite hard during most of the cooking time, and then will suddenly relent and become tender. You want them to be about as tender as a boiled new potato; that is, they should be pierceable with a fork but should give some resistance. If cooked after reaching tenderness, they will quickly turn to mush. Drain the artichokes in a colander. They are best served immediately, as they tend to discolor and pick up an off taste if they wait.

Variation: CURRIED GRATIN OF JERUSALEM ARTICHOKES

4 to 6 servings

❦ *Combining two different but complementary kinds of sweetness, that of the coconut-scented curry sauce and that of the Jerusalem artichokes, this dish is sublime with rare-roasted beef or lamb.*

PRELIMINARIES

1. Set broiler rack about 3 inches below heating element.
2. Preheat broiler 10 minutes before broiling.
3. Select a heat-proof serving platter or shallow oven-to-table dish large enough to hold the Jerusalem artichokes in one jumbled layer. Butter platter or dish lightly.

Boiled Jerusalem Artichokes
Curried Cream Sauce, page 39, thinned to serving consistency
2 tablespoons butter

Slice Jerusalem artichokes thickly and fold into cream sauce. Bring to a simmer on top of the stove, then spread in buttered platter or dish and dot with butter. Run under broiler for 1 to 3 minutes, or until lightly browned. Serve at once.

SAUTÉED JERUSALEM ARTICHOKES

4 servings

❦ *Sautéing is arguably a better cooking method than boiling for Jerusalem artichokes, as it accentuates the vegetable's sweet, nutlike flavor and preserves its soft yet crunchy texture. Take care that the outside of the Jerusalem artichokes does not brown before the inside has time to become tender.*

1½ pounds Jerusalem artichokes, peeled and dropped into acidulated water according to Step 1 of Boiled Jerusalem Artichokes, page 542
3 to 4 tablespoons olive oil or neutral vegetable oil
½ teaspoon mashed, pressed, or very finely minced garlic (optional)
2 tablespoons minced fresh parsley
Salt and pepper, preferably freshly ground, to taste
Nutmeg, preferably freshly grated
Fresh lemon juice

One at a time, remove peeled Jerusalem artichokes from acidulated water and cut into ¼-inch-thick slices. Return to water while you slice remaining Jerusalem artichokes. When all are sliced, drain (discarding water) and pat slices dry with paper toweling.

Pour 3 tablespoons oil into a 10- to 12-inch heavy-bottomed skillet. Add Jerusalem artichoke slices and stir to coat with oil. Cook over moderately low heat, tossing frequently with a spatula, until Jerusalem artichokes are golden brown and tender, about 15 to 20 minutes. If at any time a noise louder than a quiet sizzle issues from the skillet, turn the heat down. Add garlic and cook, stirring, for a minute or two. Remove skillet from heat, stir in parsley, and season to taste with salt, pepper, a pinch of nutmeg, and drops of lemon juice. Serve immediately.

KALE

A leafy vegetable related to cabbage, kale has thick, crinkly, dark green leaves with a distinctive misty sheen. When young and very fresh, the vegetable is delicious served raw in a salad. Ordinarily, however, kale is cooked as for collard greens.

Kohlrabi

Kohlrabi consists of a long tap root, a green bulb that grows just above ground, and a number of leafy stems that sprout from the bulb. It is the bulb that is eaten. The vegetable is generally sold whole at the supermarket, tied in bunches of four or five plants. Look for young, small specimens, as the bulbs of older plants are often woody or hollow. Though generally cooked, kohlrabi may also be peeled, sliced, and served raw with a sour cream- or mayonnaise-based dip.

STEAMED KOHLRABI

4 servings

❦ *Cooked kohlrabi may be dressed with butter, salt, pepper, and drops of fresh lemon juice or may be prepared according to any of the variation recipes given for broccoli, which it somewhat resembles in taste.*

2 to 2½ pounds whole kohlrabi or 1½ to 2 pounds kohlrabi bulbs

Cut off and discard the roots (if still attached) and the stems and leaves; only the bulbs of the plant are eaten. Using a sharp paring knife, peel the bulbs deeply to expose the pale ice green flesh. Halve or quarter the bulbs, depending on their size. Arrange on a 9-inch steaming basket or rack, place over 1 inch of simmering water, cover, and steam for 6 to 10 minutes, or until crisp-tender.

Ahead of Time: Kohlrabi may be prepared a day in advance and kept in a covered container in the refrigerator. Reheat with several tablespoons butter in a skillet.

Leeks

Leeks look like wildly overgrown scallions. The white root end, 1 to 2 inches in diameter and 4 to 6 inches long, is the edible part; the green top is discarded. Although in Europe they are referred to as the "poor man's asparagus," in the United States leeks are expensive and sometimes hard to come by. Oniony in flavor and very sweet, leeks are an essential ingredient in vichyssoise and in a number of meat and game pies and are also delicious braised and served as a side dish. For braising, it is preferable to choose leeks measuring an inch or less across at the root end, as larger specimens are apt to be tough and stringy.

MASTER RECIPE

Braised Leeks

4 servings

❦ *One of my favorite vegetable dishes, braised leeks go well with virtually any sort of roast, steaks, or chops.*

STEP 1: TRIMMING THE LEEKS

12 leeks, each measuring 1 inch or less across at the root end

Slice off the roots; cut off and discard the green tops. Leeks are apt to be sandy, especially at the leaf end. To wash, cut a cross in the leaf end going halfway down toward the root end, then hold leeks under running water and spread the layers with your fingers so that any grit will be rinsed away.

STEP 2: BRAISING THE LEEKS

4 tablespoons butter
½ teaspoon sugar
1 teaspoon salt
¼ teaspoon pepper, preferably freshly ground

Arrange the leeks in a single layer in a 10- to 12-inch lidded skillet or pot and add enough water to come halfway up their sides. Cut butter into pats and strew over the top; sprinkle with sugar, salt, and pepper. Cover and simmer leeks briskly for 15 to 25 minutes, turning several times. Leeks are done when they feel tender when pierced with a fork. Be careful not to overcook or they will turn mushy and disintegrate. Uncover skillet or pot, raise heat to high, and boil down cooking liquid to a syrupy glaze that coats the leeks.

AHEAD OF TIME: Leeks may be prepared 2 days ahead and kept in covered container in the refrigerator. Reheat in a skillet over gentle flame, adding a few tablespoons of water.

Variation: LEEKS IN HEAVY CREAM

4 servings

Braised Leeks, slightly undercooked
1 cup heavy cream
Salt and pepper, preferably freshly ground, to taste

Prepare the Master Recipe, but boil down the cooking liquid to a glaze while the leeks are still slightly undercooked. Add cream and cook down over high heat until reduced by half and thickened. Season to taste with salt and pepper.

LETTUCE

Since lettuce is generally thought of as a salad green, the various types are discussed at length in the salad chapter of this book. Boston and Bibb lettuce may also be cooked, a clever thing to do when your lettuce is no longer quite fresh enough to go into a salad.

BRAISED LETTUCE

4 servings

❦ *With its slightly bitter flavor and soft yet mildly chewy texture, cooked lettuce goes particularly well with roast turkey, chicken, or veal.*

STEP 1: TRIMMING AND BLANCHING THE LETTUCE

4 large heads Boston or Bibb lettuce
5 to 6 quarts water
2 tablespoons salt

Remove any floppy or crepey outer leaves and rinse the lettuce well under cold running water, spreading the leaves to wash away lurking grit but being careful not to break the leaves off the core. Bring 5 to 6 quarts salted water to a rapid boil, drop in washed lettuce heads, and blanch for 30 seconds, or just long enough to wilt the leaves. Using tongs, remove lettuce and place upside down on a rack to drain. When they are cool enough to handle, cut the heads of lettuce in half lengthwise, that is, through the core. Gently press out as much additional water as possible. Fold the lettuce halves into 8 neat little packages by smoothing the outer leaves and tucking their edges under the core side of the packages.

STEP 2: BRAISING THE LETTUCE

3 tablespoons butter
1 slice bacon, cut into ¼-inch pieces
2 tablespoons minced shallots or scallions (white part only)
1 to 1½ cups Chicken Stock, page 26, or canned broth
2 teaspoons fresh lemon juice
¼ teaspoon salt
¼ teaspoon pepper, preferably freshly ground

Melt butter in a 10- to 12-inch lidded skillet or pot made of or lined with a noncorroding material. Add bacon pieces and sauté over low heat until the bacon turns translucent and has begun to render its fat. Add shallots or scallions and sauté 1 minute longer. Arrange blanched lettuce core side down in a single layer in the skillet or pot. Add enough stock or broth to come halfway up the sides of the lettuce and sprinkle with lemon juice, salt, and pepper. Cover and simmer very slowly for 30 to 40 minutes, or until lettuce feels tender when pierced at the stem ends with a fork. Remove lettuce to a plate and boil down cooking liquid until reduced to about ½ cup of syrupy glaze. Return lettuce to skillet or pot and spoon glaze over it to coat.

AHEAD OF TIME: Lettuce may be prepared several days in advance and stored in a covered container in the refrigerator. To reheat, arrange core side down in a single layer in a buttered dish, sprinkle with several tablespoons water, cover, and bake at 325°F for 15 to 20 minutes, or until hot.

MUSHROOMS (INCLUDING WILD MUSHROOMS AND TRUFFLES)

CULTIVATED MUSHROOMS: Very fresh—or "green"—cultivated mushrooms are firm and dry to the touch, slightly earthy in scent, and creamy white (unless they are "brown" mushrooms, which, though they cost more, taste very much like the standard cultivated type). The caps of very fresh mushrooms are round and folded on the underside, nearly meeting the stems and thus concealing the crepey gills that lie on the underside of the caps.

As mushrooms age—or "ripen"—they become dark and soft, and the caps flatten and lift away from the stems to expose the gills underneath. Consumers in this country have always preferred to buy very fresh mushrooms, but in England and elsewhere in Europe ripe mushrooms are preferred because, while a bit bedraggled in appearance, they have a more pronounced and pungent flavor and a meatier, drier texture than green mushrooms. You might want to do a little experimenting on your own. Of course, mushrooms that are very soggy and obviously on the verge of rotting should be tossed out.

WILD MUSHROOMS: Some specialty food stores are now stocking wild mushrooms of various kinds, including oyster mushrooms, wide brown shiitakes, cèpes, chanterelles, and occasionally the classic morels. Wild mushrooms all have, of course, their own distinctive tastes, but as a group they may be said to be firmer, meatier, and more pungent than ordinary cultivated mushrooms. Fun to experiment with, wild mushrooms may be used in place of ordinary cultivated ones in any recipe, but don't buy them—especially at the exorbitant prices they generally command—if they are torn up, or shriveled, or look dried up with age.

Truffles are a specialized type of European wild mushroom. They are spherical and covered with a tough, crinkly skin, usually black. When fresh, truffles are incredibly pungent and aromatic. They have resisted attempts at cultivation and must be harvested by specially trained dogs or pigs who scent them out at the base of oak trees, where they grow. Naturally they are very expensive, and the recipes that call for them are generally of the haute cuisine type—*Filet de Bœuf Richelieu,* this or that under glass, breast of partridge truffé, and so on. Fresh truffles are worth their weight in gold, but unless you are in France during truffle season (late fall and early winter), the only truffles you are likely to find are those that come in cans, and canned truffles, which cost as much as $30 an ounce, have little more taste than California black olives. In fact, if it's just the black color that you want, olives will do fine as a substitute.

CLEANING MUSHROOMS: Since mushrooms readily absorb liquid, they should never be drenched with water or allowed to soak. Usually it is sufficient to wipe the caps with a damp paper or cloth towel to remove grit. If your mushrooms happen to be extremely dirty, place them a handful at a time in a colander, and quickly dunk two or three times into a sink filled with water before proceeding to wipe them clean. Never clean mushrooms by stripping off their skins, as the skins hold in flavorful juices during cooking.

RESCUING CANNED MUSHROOMS: For every 6 ounces or so of canned mushrooms, melt 1½ tablespoons butter in a small saucepan and briefly sauté a tablespoon of finely chopped shallot or scallion. Add mushrooms and their canning liquid along with ½ teaspoon fresh lemon juice, 2 teaspoons Sherry, a sprig of parsley, a pinch of dried thyme, and a few grindings of pepper. Cover saucepan and stew mushrooms for about 5 minutes over low heat. Uncover, raise heat, and boil off liquid to coat mushrooms with a light glaze. Much of the canned taste will have vanished.

Dried Mushrooms: Dried wild mushrooms of various types are imported from Europe and Asia. Perhaps the most sought-after variety is flavorful, aromatic cèpes, also called by their Latin name, *Boletus edulis*, or their Italian name, porcini. To prepare dried mushrooms for cooking, rinse them quickly under cold water to remove grit, then cover with warm water and soak for 30 minutes. Always use the flavorful soaking water—strained, to remove dirt and sand—as part of the liquid called for in your recipe.

To substitute dried wild mushrooms for fresh in recipes, use a packet of dried mushrooms weighing between 3/4 ounce (often written 6/8 ounce on the label) and 1 ounce for every 4 ounces fresh mushrooms.

MASTER RECIPE

Sautéed Mushrooms

4 servings

Improperly sautéed mushrooms steam in their own juice and become watery, shriveled, and tough; properly sautéed mushrooms retain their juices and come to the table lightly browned, plump, and meltingly tender. To achieve the desired effect, you must sauté the mushrooms over very high heat and you must not crowd too many in the skillet. Careful preparation makes all the difference.

To my mind, sautéed mushrooms are best when served simply, with just a sprinkling of chopped fresh parsley (and even that is far from necessary). They are a classic accompaniment to London broil and are also good with chicken and egg dishes.

Step 1: Cleaning and Trimming the Mushrooms

1½ to 2 pounds mushrooms

Since mushrooms readily absorb water, it is best to clean them by wiping off any clinging soil or debris with damp paper toweling. However, if the mushrooms are too dirty to be wiped clean, place them in a colander (you will probably have to do this in two or three batches) and dip them quickly into a sink filled with cold water. The dirt will loosen and can then be wiped away with toweling.

Once the mushrooms have been cleaned, shave a 1/16-inch slice from the bottoms of the stems and quarter or halve any especially large mushrooms lengthwise, making all roughly equal in size.

Step 2: Sautéing the Mushrooms

4 tablespoons butter
2 tablespoons neutral vegetable oil
Salt and freshly ground pepper, to taste

Heat half the butter and oil in a heavy-bottomed 10- to 12-inch skillet until butter is fragrant and beginning to color. Add half the mushrooms and immediately begin tossing them about with a wooden spoon. Keeping the heat very high, sauté mushrooms for 5 to 7 minutes, tossing continuously. At first the fat in the pan will seem to disappear, but in 3 or 4 minutes it will reemerge in small beads on the surface of the mushrooms, and the mushrooms will begin to brown. Continue cooking until nicely browned, another 2 minutes.

Turn finished batch of mushrooms onto plate or platter and repeat procedure with remaining mushrooms. When second batch is finished, return first batch to the skillet and toss briefly over high heat to warm through.

Ahead of Time: Mushrooms can become tough and weep their juices if they sit for longer than 15 or 20 minutes after cooking. If you must make them ahead, spread them out in a single well-spaced layer on a plate or platter so that they won't become soggy in their own steam. Reheat by tossing in a hot skillet.

Variation: CREAMED MUSHROOMS

4 servings

❦ *Serve either as an accompaniment to poultry, veal, or pork, or as a lunch dish on buttered toast.*

Sautéed Mushrooms
1 cup heavy cream
1½ teaspoons cornstarch
1 tablespoon medium-dry Sherry, preferably Manzanilla, or Madeira
Fresh lemon juice
Salt and pepper, preferably freshly ground, to taste

Add cream to the finished mushrooms and bring to a simmer. Mix 1½ teaspoons cornstarch to a smooth paste with Sherry or Madeira and blend into the mushrooms; cook only until the sauce thickens. Season with additional Sherry or Madeira and drops of fresh lemon juice; add salt and pepper to taste. Serve at once.

STUFFED MUSHROOMS

2 to 3 main-course or 4 to 5 side-dish servings

❦ *Stuffed mushrooms may be served hot or at room temperature. Accompany with a tossed green salad and a chilled white wine if the mushrooms are a main course.*

PRELIMINARIES

1. Set rack in upper third of oven.
2. Preheat oven to 375°F 20 minutes before baking.
3. Select a shallow baking dish just large enough to hold the mushrooms without crowding. Grease dish with 1 tablespoon soft butter.

16 large, unblemished mushrooms
1 cup (double recipe) Mushroom Stuffing, page 553, prepared with the stems of the 16 mushrooms above plus 12 ounces additional mushrooms
5 tablespoons Fine Fresh Bread Crumbs (see page 60)
¼ cup (1 ounce) freshly grated Parmesan cheese
2 tablespoons finely chopped fresh parsley
¼ teaspoon mashed, pressed, or very finely minced garlic
Salt and pepper, preferably freshly ground, to taste
Fresh lemon juice
Sherry or Madeira
1½ tablespoons butter

Clean mushrooms as outlined in Step 1 of Sautéed Mushrooms, page 550. Carefully snap off stems where they join the caps; use stems to prepare the stuffing. Turn mushroom stuffing into a bowl and add to it 3 tablespoons of the bread crumbs, 2 tablespoons of the Parmesan cheese, parsley, and garlic. Season to taste with salt, pepper, and drops of lemon juice and wine. Mound this mixture in mushroom caps and arrange in the prepared baking dish. Sprinkle stuffed mushrooms with 2 tablespoons each bread crumbs and Parmesan cheese and dot with butter. Bake for about 20 minutes, or until caps are cooked and stuffing is piping hot.

❦

MUSHROOM STUFFING

Makes about ½ cup

❦ *Mushroom stuffing, also called duxelles, is a flavorful and extremely handy item that can be mixed into scrambled eggs or omelets, slathered onto cooked chicken breasts or veal chops, spooned into pastry shells, and so on. Mushroom stuffing can be made ahead and refrigerated or frozen, so it may be worthwhile to make a double or triple batch.*

8 ounces mushrooms
1½ tablespoons butter
1 tablespoon neutral vegetable oil
2 tablespoons very finely minced shallots or scallions (white part only)
1 tablespoon dry Sherry, preferably Fino
Ground thyme
¼ teaspoon salt
Pepper, preferably freshly ground

Clean mushrooms as outlined in Step 1 of Sautéed Mushrooms, page 550. The mushrooms must be chopped very fine or until they resemble coarse sand. You can use a food processor, but be careful not to overprocess and render the mushrooms pastelike. If you do not have a processor, chop mushrooms with a chef's knife. Wrap chopped mushrooms, about ¼ cup at a time, in dampened cheesecloth or in a thin cotton towel and wring them very hard to extract their reddish juice (save the juice for soups or sauces if you like). If you have wrung the mushrooms forcefully enough, they will emerge from the cloth matted together in a solid lump. Unfortunately there is no way of omitting this rather tedious step; the stuffing will not brown properly or have the right flavor if the mushrooms are damp.

Heat butter and oil together in a 10-inch skillet until foam subsides. Add shallots or scallions and cook briefly. Add mushrooms and cook over moderately high heat, stirring frequently, until they have unclumped and begun to brown; this will take 5 to 6 minutes. Sprinkle in Sherry and cook until it evaporates completely. Season with a pinch of thyme, salt, and pepper.

STORAGE: Kept in a tightly covered container, mushroom stuffing can be refrigerated for 10 days or frozen for several months.

Mustard Greens

Though the seeds of the mustard plant are what we most frequently use, the green leaves and stems also have a place in the kitchen. Mustard greens are unpredictable; they may be quite hot and mustardy-tasting or very bland. Bite off a small piece before using the greens so you'll know what you are dealing with. Lettucelike in appearance and texture, mustard greens make an intriguing addition to a tossed green salad. An excellent if odd-sounding sandwich can be made of good homemade bread, peanut butter, hot, crisp bacon, and raw mustard greens.

Cooking Mustard Greens: The Chinese stir-fry young, tender mustard greens in sesame oil, adding salt and a bit of sugar. The traditional American treatment for mustard greens is to simmer them with bacon as for collards, or to braise them with pork hocks and other greens.

Okra

These green, grooved, pointy pods look as though they might contain some sort of surprise, and indeed they do—a clear sap with the consistency of warm corn syrup. It is this sap that thickens the famous Southern gumbo—gumbo is in fact a Creole word for okra. Select solidly green, firm pods, not those with spots, puckers, or signs of browning. Pods measuring 1 ½ inches or less in length and ½ inch or less in diameter at the stem end are preferable to larger ones, which will be tough and contain gritty, overly mature seeds.

BOILED OKRA

4 servings

❦*I had always found boiled okra slimy and generally unappealing until one day at a restaurant I was served small okra pods that had been left whole and boiled just to the point of crisp-tenderness. These were delicious and not slimy at all.*

Dressed with butter and drops of vinegar or lemon juice, okra can be served with practically anything, but it is particularly good, I think, with chicken or fish. Boiled okra can also be simmered briefly in a spicy, garlicky tomato sauce and served with beef or lamb.

1½ pounds okra, the pods preferably measuring 1½ inches or less in length
5 to 6 quarts water
2 tablespoons salt

Using a sharp paring knife, trim off the okra stems flush with the caps on top of the pods, taking care not to penetrate the pods themselves. Wash well, rubbing the okra between the palms of your hands under a stream of water; dirt and pesticides tend to cling to the slightly fuzzy skin.

Bring 5 to 6 quarts water and salt to a fast boil in a large pot and add the okra. Cook uncovered for 1 to 3 minutes after the water has returned to the boil; the pods should turn bright green, firmly retain their shape, and taste distinctly crunchy. Drain in a colander and serve at once.

Onions (Including Scallions, Shallots, Chives, and Garlic)

Cultivated since very early times, onions are among the most ubiquitous and essential of all culinary ingredients. Various types of onions are discussed below, followed by some onion tips.

Often sold in red mesh bags at the supermarket, *yellow globe onions* are the ones to choose for general cooking purposes. They may also be baked whole in their skins, separated into rings and french-fried, or hollowed out and baked with a stuffing. Globe onions are generally the size of a small apple, but some varieties can grow as large as grapefruits. It has been my experience that the very large specimens are often watery and lacking in flavor.

White onions hold their shape well during cooking, and their small size and snow-white color make a handsome sight on the serving platter. Thus these onions are usually chosen for braising and creaming. Large white onions, often referred to as *Bermuda onions,* are good in salads; very small ones, or *pearl onions,* are often pickled.

Because they are usually mild and sweet, *red onions* are often put into salads and sandwiches. But watch out: Some red onions are quite hot. Since their pigment fades when heated, red onions may be substituted for yellow-skinned ones in general cooking, though red onions are a bit milder and tend to be softer than yellow onions when cooked.

Leeks, scallions, shallots, and chives are also members of the onion family. Information on *leeks,* including cooking instructions, appears on pages 545–47. *Scallions,* the small green onions sold in bunches with the green tops attached, are immature white onions. Scallions are usually used raw in salads, cocktail dips and the like, but they may also be cooked as for asparagus. The white bulbs are often substituted for shallots, and the tender parts of their green tops may be used in place of chives. *Shallots,* an important ingredient in many French sauces and stuffings, are small clove-divided bulbs covered with dry, brown, papery skin. Though expensive, they are worth seeking out for their pungent, garlicky flavor. At the supermarket, shallots are often packaged in small mesh bags or in little boxes like the ones garlic is sold in. *Chives* are frequently sold as potted plants at the supermarket. When harvesting chives from the pot, cut the leaves at the base rather than snipping them at the top, for leaves snipped at the top will wither and die. Provided the pot is placed in a sunny window, chives will regenerate after being cut. Dried chives, sold along with other herbs and spices at the market, do not have the flavor of fresh, though they'll do when fresh chives are unavailable.

Garlic is known to everyone, but too many cooks continue to rely on garlic powder, which has a bitter and entirely unauthentic taste. This is a shame, since fresh garlic is so easy to prepare. To peel garlic, simply place the clove on your work surface and press down on it firmly with the side of a knife. The skin will then slide off easily. Trim off the root end, then either mash the garlic with the tines of a fork or mince it fine. A garlic press also makes quick work of fresh garlic.

PURCHASING AND STORAGE: Onions, including shallots and garlic, should be very hard to the touch and without green sprouts at the top when you buy them. Onions that are past their prime will have an unpleasant taste or no taste at all. Store onions in a cool, dry, dark place—not in the refrigerator. A mesh bag that allows air to circulate is the best kind of storage container, and if you plan to keep them for a while, it is a good idea to elevate onions on a rack.

TEARING: Tearing is caused by the contact of the irritating onion vapors with the membranes of the eyes, nose, and throat. Onions (and shallots and garlic too) may be peeled easily and without tears if dropped briefly into boiling water and then refreshed under cold water. But it's a nuisance to get a pot of water boiling for a single onion, and, in any case, one is still left with the chopping or slicing part of the task. I have never had any luck with any of the other supposed remedies (putting a piece of bread in the mouth while peeling; peeling onions under running water; and so on), but I half believe that after dealing with many onions over a period of years one gradually builds up a partial immunity—or perhaps it's simply a tolerance. The simplest advice is probably the best: Avert your eyes as much as possible, breathe shallowly, and work quickly. By the way, chopping onions in the food processor is not the solution. The machine bashes them up and makes them taste very bitter, even when cooked. It also causes them to exude moisture.

RESCUING OVERCOOKED ONIONS: If whole onions have been cooked to the point that they are watery mush, the only thing to do is save them for soup.

However, if they are merely a bit too soft and shapeless to serve as is, you might combine them with curried cream sauce and bake as a gratin.

Rescuing Canned Onions: Drain canned onions and simmer them in an inch or so of chicken broth flavored with bay leaf, fresh parsley, a pinch of dried thyme, and a few grindings of pepper. When the onions are fully tender, in 10 minutes or so, uncover the saucepan and boil down the cooking liquid until it has reduced to a glaze. The canned taste should be just about gone.

MASTER RECIPE

Braised Onions

4 to 5 servings

❦ *Braised onions may be sprinkled with minced parsley, dill, tarragon, basil, or virtually any other fresh herb just before serving; they go particularly well with roasts.*

Step 1: Peeling and Trimming the Onions

16 white onions about 1¼ inches in diameter
2 quarts water

Using a sharp paring knife, shave a thin disc off the root ends of the onions, taking care not to cut into the bulbs, and cut off the stems ¼ inch from the bulbs. Bring 2 quarts water to a fast boil, drop in the onions, remove from heat, and let stand 2 minutes. Drain in a colander and run under cold water until cool enough to handle. Pinch off the skins with your fingers.

Step 2: Braising the Onions

4 tablespoons butter
¼ teaspoon salt
¼ teaspoon pepper, preferably freshly ground
½ cup Chicken Stock, page 26, or canned broth
½ cup water
¼ cup dry white wine
2 large parsley sprigs
1 bay leaf, broken in half
⅛ teaspoon ground thyme

Melt butter in a 10-inch skillet made of or lined with a noncorroding material. Add the onions, stir once to coat with butter, and sprinkle with salt and pepper. Cover and cook onions over very low heat, stirring frequently, for about 10 minutes, or until they begin to turn a pale golden. Add all remaining ingredients—the liquid should come about halfway up the sides of the onions—bring to a very gentle simmer, and cover. Turning every 20 minutes, cook onions for about 1½ hours, or until very tender but not mushy. Remove onions to a plate with a slotted spoon, discard parsley and bay leaf, and boil down the cooking liquid to about ⅓ cup of syrupy glaze. Return onions to skillet and gently shake skillet by the handle to coat onions with glaze.

AHEAD OF TIME: Onions may be prepared 3 days in advance and kept in a covered container in the refrigerator. Reheat in a covered skillet over low heat, adding a few tablespoons of water to prevent scorching.

Variation: CREAMED ONIONS

4 to 6 servings

❦ *These are a classic accompaniment to roast turkey.*

Braised Onions
1½ cups Basic Cream Sauce, page 34, made with milk and unthinned
3 to 6 tablespoons milk
Salt and pepper, preferably freshly ground, to taste
Fresh lemon juice
1 tablespoon butter (optional; only if you are browning the onions under broiler)

Boil down the onion cooking liquid as indicated in the Master Recipe and beat in the cream sauce with a wire whip. Carefully fold in the onions and simmer very gently for 3 minutes. Thin as necessary with milk—the sauce should be thick enough to coat the onions but should not seem pasty—and season to taste with salt, pepper, and drops of lemon juice. Serve onions from a bowl or arrange in a single close layer in a lightly buttered dish, dot with butter, and run under a hot broiler for 1 to 2 minutes, or just long enough to brown the top lightly.

Variation: CURRIED ONION GRATIN

4 to 6 servings

❦ *Excellent with roast beef or lamb.*

PRELIMINARIES

1. Set rack in the upper third of oven.
2. Preheat oven to 425°F 20 minutes before baking.
3. Select a shallow 9- to 10-inch oven-to-table dish that holds the onions in one tight layer. Butter the dish lightly.

Braised Onions
Curried Cream Sauce, page 39, a bit thicker than serving consistency
1½ tablespoons butter

Boil down onion cooking liquid to a glaze as indicated in the Master Recipe, beat in the sauce, and bring to a simmer. Ladle a thin layer of sauce into prepared baking dish, arrange the onions on top, and mask with remaining sauce. Dot with butter and bake about 20 minutes, or until lightly browned. Serve at once.

Variation: GLAZED ONIONS

4 to 8 servings

❦ *These are usually served in combination with other vegetables—glazed carrots, sautéed mushrooms, and green beans, for example—as a garniture for a roast.*

Braised Onions
SUBSTITUTE: Beef Stock, page 24, or canned broth for chicken stock or broth

Proceed according to the Master Recipe, but let the onions brown lightly during their initial cooking in butter—simply cook over moderate rather than low heat, stirring frequently—and substitute beef stock or broth for chicken.

Variation: GRATINÉED ONIONS WITH CHEESE

4 to 5 servings

❦ *Good with chops and steaks.*

PRELIMINARIES

1. Set broiler rack 3 to 4 inches from heating element.
2. Preheat broiler 10 minutes before proceeding.
3. Select a heat-proof platter or shallow oven-to-table dish just wide enough to hold the onions in a single uncrowded layer. Butter lightly.

Braised Onions
⅓ cup Fine Fresh Bread Crumbs (page 60)
⅓ cup (1½ ounces) freshly grated Parmesan cheese
2 tablespoons butter

Arrange hot onions, glazed with their boiled-down cooking liquid, in a single layer in prepared dish. Cover evenly with crumbs and cheese, mixed together, and dot with butter. Run under broiler for 2 to 3 minutes, or until lightly browned. Serve at once.

BATTER-DIPPED DEEP-FRIED ONION RINGS

4 to 6 servings

❦ *A batter coating is usual for deep-fried onion rings, but a coating of bound breading, page 62, using white cornmeal, is equally good. Tempura batter, page 64, is also a possibility. For full information, consult the chapter on deep-frying, pages 59–66; do note that fritter batter is best if allowed to rest at least 2 hours before egg whites are folded in.*

3 large yellow globe onions (about 1½ pounds)
For fritter batter and deep-frying:
- 2 large eggs, separated
- ¾ cup beer
- 2 tablespoons neutral vegetable oil
- 1 cup unbleached all-purpose flour
- 1 teaspoon salt
- ¼ teaspoon pepper, preferably freshly ground
- 3 quarts very fresh vegetable oil

Cut onions into crosswise slices about 1/4 inch thick; separate them into rings. Save small rings for another use. Place larger onion rings in 4-quart mixing bowl, cover with ice water, and soak for 2 to 3 hours in the refrigerator. Soaking will make the onions juicy and will tame their bite. Prepare fritter batter according to the instructions on page 63 and let rest while onions soak.

Drain onions and pat thoroughly dry with paper toweling; batter will not adhere if onions are wet. Fold rings into prepared batter and, following the procedure for deep-frying outlined in Step 2 of the Master Technique for deep-frying, page 64, fry in 3 quarts oil heated to 375°F. Fry only a few rings at a time, or they will stick together; the rings will need 2 to 3 minutes in the oil to become properly crisp and golden brown. Drain on paper toweling and place in a warm (150°F) oven while you fry the rest. Serve promptly.

BAKED STUFFED ONIONS WITH SAUSAGE

4 servings

❦ *These can easily be the mainstay of a luncheon or light supper if accompanied by mashed potatoes and sliced tomatoes or a tossed salad.*

PRELIMINARIES

1. Set rack in the center of oven.
2. Preheat oven to 375°F 20 minutes before baking.
3. Select a baking dish just large enough to hold the onions comfortably. Butter generously.

STEP 1: PREPARING ONIONS FOR STUFFING

4 large yellow globe onions (about 2½ pounds)
Salt

Slit skin from top to bottom with the point of a sharp paring knife and peel onions by unwrapping the skin with your fingers. Do not cut off either the stem or the root ends. (Peeling the onions in this manner helps them remain intact during and after cooking.) Place onions in 4-quart saucepan and cover with salted water. Bring to a moderate simmer and cook, partially covered, for 20 to 25 minutes, or until onions are tender enough to be pierced by a cake needle or skewer but still feel crunchy and slightly resistant; be careful not to overcook or onions will fall apart or split when you attempt to hollow them out. Remove onions from the saucepan with skimmer and set root ends down on a flat baking dish. Let cool for at least 20 minutes, or until they are comfortable to handle.

To hollow out the onions, first slice off the top fourth of each onion at the stem end, reserving the tops. Using a small, pointed knife, make several cuts into the center of the onion, going about ⅔ of the way down to the bottom and cutting to within three or four of the outermost layers. When center of onion has been well scored and interior layers feel loose, hollow out the center with a small fork or teaspoon, leaving a wall three layers (about ¼ inch) thick. Coarsely chop the centers along with reserved onion tops.

Note: If there is a hole in the wall of an onion, simply cover it over with a piece scraped from the middle. If the wall of an onion tears, brace onion with your fingers when stuffing it; the onion may emerge from the oven slightly lopsided, but the stuffing will remain inside and the whole thing should stick together.

STEP 2: STUFFING AND BAKING ONIONS

½ cup (about 4 ounces) well-seasoned sausage meat
¼ recipe Steamed Spinach, page 590, squeezed to remove liquid and chopped fine (½ cup) or 10 ounces frozen spinach, thawed, squeezed, and chopped fine
⅔ cup heavy cream
5 to 6 tablespoons Fine Fresh Bread Crumbs (see page 60)
⅛ teaspoon ground sage (optional)
⅛ teaspoon nutmeg, preferably freshly grated
Salt and pepper, preferably freshly ground, to taste
1 tablespoon butter

Crumble sausage meat into skillet and brown well over moderate heat. Without draining off fat, add chopped onion tops and centers and cook over moderate heat for about 10 minutes, stirring, or until onion is golden and very soft. Add spinach and cook slowly for 5 minutes. Pour in cream and cook 1 minute longer; mixture should be quite thick. Remove from heat and stir in 3 to 4 tablespoons bread crumbs, or enough to make the stuffing stiff enough to hold its shape on the spoon. Stir in optional sage and nutmeg; taste and adjust seasoning with salt and pepper.

Arrange the scooped-out onions in a well-buttered baking dish. Pile in sausage stuffing, mounding it in the center. Sprinkle onions with 2 tablespoons bread crumbs and dot with butter. Bake in preheated oven for 20 to 25 minutes, or until lightly browned on top. Remove onions from oven and let cool for a few minutes before serving.

BAKED ONIONS

4 servings

❦ *Easy to prepare, baked onions are delectable with beef steaks and roasts.*

PRELIMINARIES

1. Set rack in center of oven.
2. Preheat oven to 350°F 20 minutes before baking.
3. Select a rimmed baking sheet just large enough to hold the onions comfortably. Cover bottom and sides with aluminum foil (the onions release a gooey, caramel-like syrup as they bake).

4 very large yellow globe onions (2½ to 3 pounds)
3 to 4 tablespoons butter
Salt and freshly ground pepper

Slice off just enough of the root ends of the onions to allow them to stand upright; do not penetrate into interior of the bulbs. Do not peel or cut off stems. Pierce onions in three places with the point of a paring knife to prevent them from bursting in the oven, and arrange them root ends down on baking sheet. Bake for 1½ to 2 hours, or until onions are tender enough to be pierced easily with the paring knife. Transfer to a serving dish and slash a cross in the top of each with a serrated knife. Gently squeeze onions around their middles to push the flesh up through the opening. Place a goodly lump of butter in the center of each onion and sprinkle lightly with salt and pepper. Offer additional butter at the table.

HEARTS OF PALM

The source of this vegetable is the Sabal palmetto, a palm tree that grows abundantly both in the southern United States and in parts of Latin America. The heart is obtained by cutting down the tree and stripping off both the fronds and the exterior layers of the trunk until the edible center of the trunk is exposed. Unless you live in an area where the Sabal palmetto grows, you will have to be content with canned hearts of palm, which, because of the heavy acidulation required to keep them white, retain little of the vegetable's natural taste. Canned artichoke hearts are a perfectly acceptable substitute for canned hearts of palm in salad recipes.

Parsnips

A delightful but strangely underappreciated vegetable, parsnips taste a bit like carrots, though parsnips are spicier and more earthy, and have a texture reminiscent of sweet potatoes. They look very much like slightly oversize carrots, except that their skin is beige, and they are often sold like carrots at the supermarket, either in plastic bags or tied together in small bunches. Their peak season is fall and winter. Choose parsnips that are hard to the touch and uniform in color. Avoid large or bulging parsnips, as these are apt to be woody and overpowering in taste.

Rescuing Overcooked Parsnips: Purée according to the variation on page 565, decreasing or omitting the milk or cream, depending on how much moisture the parsnips have absorbed.

MASTER RECIPE

Glazed Parsnips

4 to 6 servings

Generally served as a starchy vegetable in place of potatoes or rice, parsnips go particularly well with rich or strongly flavored dishes such as roast duck or goose, pork, or game.

Step 1: Trimming the Parsnips

1½ pounds parsnips

Strip off the skins with a swivel-blade vegetable peeler and trim the root and stem ends. Cut the parsnips in half widthwise and cut the stem-end halves lengthwise down the middle. If the core in the stem-end pieces is wider than ½ inch or woody-looking and very dark yellow, pry it out with the tip of a knife; this will not usually be necessary, unless the parsnips are large and overmature. If not cooking them immediately, cover parsnips with ice water to prevent discoloration; do not let stand for more than 1 hour.

STEP 2: COOKING THE PARSNIPS

2 cups water
3 tablespoons butter
2 teaspoons sugar
1 teaspoon salt
¼ teaspoon white pepper, preferably freshly ground

Combine parsnips and all above ingredients in a 10-inch skillet and bring to a slow boil. Cover and cook over moderate heat for 10 to 12 minutes, or until parsnips are tender; they should suggest a thoroughly cooked sweet potato in texture. Uncover skillet, raise heat to high, and boil cooking liquid down to a syrupy glaze that coats the parsnips, stirring frequently. Be careful not to scorch.

AHEAD OF TIME: Parsnips may be prepared several days ahead and kept in a tightly closed container in the refrigerator; they seem actually to improve in flavor after standing. Reheat slowly in a covered skillet or saucepan, adding a tablespoon of water to prevent scorching and stirring often.

Variation: MAPLE-GLAZED PARSNIPS

4 to 6 servings

❦ *Marvelous with duck or pork.*

Glazed Parsnips
3 tablespoons pure maple syrup
Nutmeg, preferably freshly grated

Add maple syrup to parsnips after boiling down the cooking liquid to a glaze. Continue to cook for about 1 minute longer, stirring gently, or until parsnips are nicely coated with the syrup. Add a bit of nutmeg.

Variation: PARSNIP PURÉE WITH SHERRY OR MADEIRA

4 servings

❦ *This is sublime with roast pork. For an interesting twist, substitute cut-up carrots for half the parsnips in preparing the Master Recipe, then purée as indicated below, decreasing the wine by half.*

Glazed Parsnips

4 tablespoons soft butter
2 to 3 tablespoons medium-dry Sherry, preferably Manzanilla, or Madeira
2 to 6 tablespoons hot milk or cream
Salt and pepper, preferably freshly ground, to taste
Fresh lemon juice

Turn parsnips and their reduced cooking liquid into the jar of a food processor or blender and purée thoroughly; if you use a blender, you will have to perform this step in several batches. Turn purée into a heavy 2-quart saucepan, place over low heat, and gradually beat in the soft butter. Remove from heat, add Sherry or Madeira to taste, and beat in enough milk or cream to give the purée the consistency of mashed potatoes. Season to taste with salt, pepper, and just a few drops of fresh lemon juice.

PEAS

Pick over fresh peas to find small, unspotted, bright green, moist-looking pods. It's a good idea to open a few of the pods and check on the peas inside: If they are bigger than the frozen kind, or if they appear dull, pale, or wrinkly, they are not a good buy. Unfortunately, this is too often the case.

If you can find them at the market, and if you are willing to pay their higher price, *Chinese peas,* also known as *snow peas* or *mangetouts,* are a delightful substitute for ordinary peas. These thin, flat pods are eaten in their entirety, with just the ends snapped off and the central string pulled off prior to cooking. Steam or stir-fry for no longer than a minute or so, or you will overcook them and destroy their crisp texture. *Sugar snap peas* are a relatively new variety that has just recently begun to show up in markets. These look much like regular peas, but, like snow peas, they are completely edible, pod and all. To prepare sugar snap peas for cooking, snap off the ends and pull off strings along the central groove. Stir-fry or steam for 3 to 4 minutes.

RESCUING FROZEN PEAS: Frozen peas are much more reliable than the fresh and they taste remarkably good. But disregard the cooking instructions on the package, which will lead to ruination. Instead, cook the peas in a small amount of boiling water just until they are warmed through, or stir-fry them quickly.

RESCUING STARCHY AND/OR TOUGH-SKINNED PEAS: Prepare the minted puree of peas on page 568. Add some extra cream or butter if the purée seems too stiff. A purée made from overmature peas will benefit from pinches of sugar.

MASTER RECIPE

Skillet-braised Peas

4 servings

Season with lots of butter, salt, and pepper. Add also pinches of sugar if the peas seem to need sweetening. A traditional flavoring for peas is finely chopped fresh mint.

Step 1: Shelling the Peas

3 to 4 pounds peas in the pod

To shell peas, hold each pod over a bowl and pry it open along the center groove with your thumbs. Run your thumb or a finger along inside of pod to loosen the peas so that they drop into the bowl. This operation is simple but rather time-consuming, so don't put off shelling the peas until just before dinner. You can hold shelled peas in a covered bowl in the refrigerator for several hours before cooking.

Step 2: Cooking the Peas

1 teaspoon sugar

Pour ¼ inch water into a 10-inch skillet and stir in sugar. Do not add salt, which will toughen the peas. Bring water to a rapid simmer; add peas and cover. Maintaining a gentle simmer, cook the peas from 4 to 12 minutes, depending on their size, or until they are tender and no longer have a starchy taste. Test frequently, adding more water if necessary. Drain in a colander and serve at once; peas will shrivel and toughen if they have to wait.

Variation: PEAS COOKED IN HEAVY CREAM

4 servings

❦ *This is best when prepared with very young, tender, sweet peas. Serve with beef or lamb.*

Skillet-braised Peas
SUBSTITUTE: 1 to 1½ cups heavy cream for water
ADD: Salt and white pepper, preferably freshly ground, to taste

Proceed according to the Master Recipe, but cook peas in ¼ inch cream rather than water; when the peas are nearly tender, uncover skillet, raise heat to high, and boil hard for 1 to 2 minutes, to thicken the cream slightly. Season with salt and white pepper and serve at once.

Variation: MINTED PURÉE OF PEAS

4 to 6 servings

❦ *The only time I enjoy mint with roast lamb is when the mint is in this marvelous purée. Team puréed peas with glazed carrots; a starch is not essential, but if you want one choose rice.*

Skillet-braised Peas
4 tablespoons soft butter
1 to 4 tablespoons milk or cream, if needed
1½ teaspoons minced fresh mint
Salt and pepper, preferably freshly ground
Sugar, if needed

Purée peas in a food processor or blender, leaving the mixture slightly coarse; if you use a blender, you will have to do this in several batches. Turn purée into a heavy saucepan, place over low heat, and gradually beat in the butter. The purée should be just stiff enough to hold its shape very softly on a fork; thin, if necessary, with spoonfuls of milk or cream. Remove from heat, stir in the mint, and season to taste with salt, pepper, and, if needed, pinches of sugar. Serve immediately.

Variation: COLD PEA SALAD

4 to 6 servings

❦ *Serve this as a side dish with cold fish, poultry, or meat and accompany with buttered black bread. Cooked frozen peas (about 3 cups) can be used successfully here.*

Skillet-braised Peas
⅔ cup mayonnaise, preferably homemade, page 51
1 tablespoon minced scallion (white part only)
1 tablespoon minced fresh parsley
⅛ teaspoon crushed dried tarragon
½ to 2 teaspoons white wine vinegar
Salt and pepper, preferably freshly ground, to taste

Fold mayonnaise, scallion, parsley, and tarragon into the peas; cover and refrigerate for about 30 minutes. Just before serving, taste and adjust seasoning with vinegar, salt, and pepper.

PEPPERS

The type of pepper most readily available at the supermarket is the *bell pepper,* which is green when immature and red when ripe. The green specimens are less expensive and keep better in the refrigerator, but red peppers are fatter and much sweeter. Some specialty markets also carry bell peppers that are bright yellow or purple black in color. These taste very much like red bell peppers, but are nice to use in combination to produce a decorative effect. In addition to the bell pepper, there is the elongated, pale green *Italian pepper,* often used for frying.

When purchasing peppers, check to make sure there are no soft or watery spots lurking in hidden places (in crevices or near the bottom, for example). Pass over any that seem wrinkly or soft. Peppers don't much like the cold temperature of the home refrigerator, so buy only as many as you can use within a couple of days.

There are many types of *chili peppers.* With the exception of the *ancho,* all are hot—some very hot. *Jalapeños,* small, bright green, and shaped like large bullets, are the chilis most often called for in American recipes. If you can't find fresh jalapeños, you are better off substituting either fresh oriental-type chilis (available at Asian grocery stores) or dried red chilis than using canned jalapeños, which have a steamy canned flavor.

Red chilis are not necessarily hotter than green ones—in fact, usually the opposite is true—and, strangely enough, individual chilis of the same species vary greatly in their potency. Thus, when I want to make a fiery dish I always buy a big batch of chilis on the assumption that some of them will prove to be too mild and will have to be put to some other use.

TIP: To test chilis for heat, pierce each one with a toothpick and hold the toothpick against your tongue; if the chili is hot, the toothpick will feel hot against your tongue.

After working with chilis be sure to wash your hands thoroughly with warm sudsy water and avoid touching your eyes (or putting in your contact lenses) for several hours afterward. Alternatively, wear rubber gloves when you handle chilis.

PEELING PEPPERS: Peppers prepared according to the Master Recipe below become loosened from their skins during cooking and are easy to peel. But if you want to fry peppers or marinate them raw for use in a salad, you will have to put them through a special peeling process. The first step is to char the skins until they become blackened and blistered. This can be accomplished either by spearing the peppers with a long-handled fork and turning them over a high gas flame or by placing them under a hot broiler, turning them to char uniformly. Transfer the charred peppers to a paper or plastic bag, close the bag, and let the peppers stand about 10 minutes or until lukewarm (the steam they release will loosen the skins). Holding the peppers under cool running water, strip off the skins.

MASTER RECIPE

Oil-Braised Peppers

6 to 8 first-course or 4 to 6 side-dish servings

This is one of the tastiest ways I know of preparing peppers. Braised peppers are excellent served warm as a first course with French bread and soft goat cheese or strips of mozzarella or Monterey Jack. They are also good as a vegetable side dish with roast chicken, fish, or a braised meat, in which case you may wish to sprinkle them with minced fresh parsley or basil. By the way, this dish is particularly handsome when made with peppers of various colors, though it is sweetest when made with red peppers alone.

Preliminaries

1. Set rack in center of oven.
2. Preheat oven to 300°F 20 minutes before baking.
3. Select a 9×12-inch shallow baking dish or other dish large enough to hold the peppers in a single snug layer.

Step 1: The Preliminary Braising

5 to 6 large or 8 medium bell peppers (about 3 pounds), either all red or a combination of half red and half green, yellow, and/or black peppers
⅓ cup olive oil
1 teaspoon mashed, pressed, or very finely minced garlic

Wash peppers and dry them thoroughly with towels. Leaving them whole and with stems still attached, arrange peppers in the baking dish and drizzle with olive oil, turning them until completely coated. Sprinkle on garlic. Bake the peppers, uncovered, for about an hour, or until they have softened and collapsed and the skin has blistered. Remove peppers from the oven and let cool for only a few minutes; they must be warm when peeled. Leave oven on for the next step.

Step 2: Peeling and Cleaning the Peppers; Reducing the Cooking Liquid

Salt and pepper, preferably freshly ground

Work with only one pepper at a time, leaving the rest in the baking dish so they will stay warm. Transfer pepper to a plate and pinch off the skin with your fingers; it should come off easily. Use a paring knive to scrape off any stubborn bits of skin. (If a pepper seems hard to peel, return it to the oven for a few more minutes.) Slit peeled pepper lengthwise, pull out the stem, and carefully scrape out seeds with a spoon. Turn the pepper and all of the juices in the plate into a mixing bowl, and repeat with remaining peppers.

Pour the braising liquid in the baking dish and the juices accumulated around the peppers into a noncoroding 10-inch skillet and simmer over moderate heat until reduced by half and slightly thickened. Add the cooked peppers, heat until warmed through, and season with salt and pepper.

Storage: Packed in their reduced braising liquid in a tightly covered container and refrigerated, the peppers will keep for 4 or 5 days at least.

Variation: PEPPERS WITH BASIL AND WALNUTS

6 to 8 first-course servings

❦ *Serve these peppers at room temperature as a first course, perhaps on lettuce, accompanied by either soft goat cheese or hard-cooked egg halves.*

Oil-braised peppers
SUBSTITUTE: Walnut oil for olive oil
3 tablespoons finely shredded fresh basil
⅓ cup (about 1½ ounces) coarsely chopped walnuts

Braise the peppers in walnut oil instead of the olive oil indicated in the Master Recipe. Fold in fresh basil—dried basil just won't do here—and chopped walnuts.

Variation: PEPPERS IN MEAT GLAZE

4 to 6 servings

❦ *This is best served hot with roasts, steaks, or chops.*

Oil-braised Peppers, prepared through the first part of Step 2
1½ cups Beef Stock, page 24, or canned broth
Freshly ground black pepper to taste
2 to 3 tablespoons minced fresh parsley

Simmer beef stock or broth in a 10-inch skillet until reduced to 3 to 4 tablespoons of syrupy glaze. Add the braising liquid and juices from the peppers, and reduce the mixture over moderate heat until a thick, syrupy sauce is formed. Add peppers to the skillet and simmer for several minutes over a gentle flame to heat them through and blend the flavors. Season highly with pepper and dust with fresh parsley.

Variation: PEPPER SALAD

4 main-course or 6 to 8 first-course servings

❦*Accompanied by hard rolls, this dish could be the main course of a light lunch or supper.*

Oil-braised Peppers, preferably all red
¼ cup minced fresh parsley
½ teaspoon mashed, pressed, or very finely minced garlic
1 to 2 teaspoons wine vinegar
Salt and pepper, preferably freshly ground, to taste
Lettuce leaves
2 to 4 hard-cooked eggs

Prepare peppers according to the Master Recipe and let cool to room temperature. Stir in parsley, garlic, and vinegar and salt and pepper to taste. Serve the peppers at room temperature or chilled on a bed of lettuce, garnished with hard-cooked egg quarters.

Variation: PURÉE OF RED PEPPERS

4 to 6 servings

❦*Serve with fish, fowl, or meat.*

Oil-braised Peppers, using red peppers
Salt and pepper, preferably freshly ground, to taste

Prepare red peppers according to the Master Recipe, but do not add peppers to skillet after cooking liquid is boiled down. Using a food mill, processor, or blender, purée the peppers until smooth. Turn the purée into a small saucepan, place over gentle heat, and beat in as much of the reduced cooking liquid as the peppers will absorb without thinning out too much—the purée should be thick enough to hold its shape softly on a fork. Season to taste with salt and freshly ground pepper.

CHILI-STUFFED GREEN PEPPERS

4 main-dish servings

❦ *These are spicy and delicious, a good change from the usual sort of stuffed peppers. Children may be satisfied with just half a pepper, as the stuffing is rich and filling. Accompany with a tossed salad.*

PRELIMINARIES

1. Set rack in center of oven.
2. Preheat oven to 375°F 20 minutes before baking.
3. Select either a deep saucepan or flameproof baking dish large enough to hold the peppers snugly but without squeezing. It is preferable that the pan or dish have a tight-fitting lid, but you may also use aluminum foil to cover.

4 very large green bell peppers (about 2 pounds)
1 cup (about 8 ounces) spicy sausage meat
1 tablespoon olive oil
1 cup chopped onions
2½ cups cooked red kidney beans, lightly mashed with a fork (canned beans, well drained, will do nicely here)
1 cup (about 8 ounces) ground lean beef or lamb
¾ cup thick canned tomato purée
2 tablespoons dry red or white wine (optional but recommended)
2 to 3 tablespoons chili powder, to taste
1 teaspoon mashed, pressed, or very finely minced garlic
1 teaspoon oregano
1 teaspoon ground cumin
¼ to ½ teaspoon salt
⅛ to ¼ teaspoon pepper, preferably freshly ground
2 cups peeled, seeded, diced tomatoes, fresh or canned (see page 607)

Slice off tops of the peppers; remove seeds and scrape off the whitish ribs from interior walls with a spoon. Drop peppers into 4 quarts rapidly boiling water and simmer for 4 to 5 minutes, or just until the color is beginning to fade; be sure not to overcook the peppers, or they will collapse when you stuff them. Turn blanched peppers upside down on the counter to drain. Pierce a ½-inch slit in the bottom of each lobe with the point of a paring knife; this will allow the peppers to drain during cooking.

Combine crumbled sausage meat and olive oil in 10-inch skillet and cook over moderate heat until sausage loses all traces of pink. Without draining off fat, add onions and cook over moderately high heat, tossing, until they begin to brown. Scrape contents of skillet, including the fat, into mixing bowl. Blend in beans, ground meat, 1/4 cup of the tomato purée, wine, chili powder, garlic, oregano, and cumin. Taste and add salt and pepper as necessary. Pack stuffing into the peppers.

Arrange stuffed peppers in saucepan or flameproof baking dish. Pour around them the remaining 1/2 cup tomato purée and the chopped tomatoes. (The tomato mixture should come at least 1/3 of the way up the sides of the peppers; if it does not, extend it with additional tomato purée, chopped tomatoes, tomato juice, or water.) Bring peppers to a rapid simmer on top of the stove, then cover tightly and bake for about 40 minutes, or until peppers are completely tender and the stuffing feels hot and firm when pressed. (You can test the stuffing using a meat thermometer, which should register at least 165°F, or you can insert a knife in the stuffing, wait a moment, and then touch the blade; if it feels hot, the stuffing should be cooked through.)

Transfer peppers to serving platter and let stand 5 minutes or so before bringing to the table. Serve peppers with the tomato sauce they cooked in; if the sauce seems thin, boil it down a bit before serving.

Plantains

Plantains look like large, slightly angular bananas, but unlike bananas, they must be cooked. Plantains may be either green or yellow in skin color. The unripe, green-skinned fruit tastes something like chestnuts, with slight banana overtones; the yellow-skinned fruit, which is fully ripened, is very soft when cooked and tastes much like banana. Plantains are usually used as a starchy vegetable to accompany meat or poultry.

Cooking plantains: Peel and remove any fibrous strings. Either cut the plantains into rough chunks and simmer until tender in well-salted water to cover, or slice and fry 3 to 4 minutes in deep fat heated to about 360°F.

Potatoes

There are countless varieties of potatoes on the market, but the old distinction between baking and boiling potatoes is still useful as a general guide. *Baking potatoes,* among them the russet Burbank or Idaho, tend to be large and elongated and to have rough, fairly thick brown or reddish brown skins. These potatoes are starch-laden and mealy and thus tend to disintegrate when cooked in a sauce or used in a salad. When subjected to dry heat, however, they become flaky—or crumbly—which is why they are preferred for baking. They may also be boiled and mashed, and some people like to french-fry them.

Boiling potatoes, many of which are grown in Maine or Long Island, are rounder and smaller than baking potatoes and their skins are thinner and smoother, ranging in color from brown to red to waxy yellow. (So-called "new potatoes" are immature and recently harvested boiling potatoes, typically but not necessarily a red-skinned variety.) Boiling potatoes are firm and moist, and thus are used when the potato flesh must hold its shape, as in potato salad or creamed potatoes. They may also be mashed or french-fried.

Finally, *all-purpose potatoes,* brown-skinned and medium-sized, supposedly combine the characteristics of bakers and boilers, but it's impossible to know just what an all-purpose potato will do in a recipe unless you are familiar with the particular hybrid. Most all-purpose potatoes are too wet or dense for successful baking.

PURCHASING AND STORAGE: Choose potatoes that are without soft or rotten spots and that feel hard when squeezed in the hand. Avoid potatoes that are tinged with green, the result of exposure to light, for the green parts are mildly toxic. Potatoes that have begun to sprout should also be passed over, as they will have lost much of their flavor. Keep potatoes in a cool, dry, dark place—for example, on a shelf under the counter—and don't refrigerate them.

RESCUING OVERCOOKED BOILED POTATOES: Slightly overcooked boiled potatoes are prime candidates for mashing. Follow the recipe on page 578, but decrease the milk or cream by half (or more) to compensate for the water that the potatoes have absorbed. If the damage is severe and the potatoes have nearly disintegrated, don't try to serve them mashed—the final product will taste watery. Instead, mash the potatoes with a fork (or put them through a food mill) and thin to soup consistency with the cooking water. Add a cup (or 2 or 3) of chopped onions or leeks and simmer soup until onions are soft. Enrich with heavy cream, season with salt, pepper (preferably white) and perhaps a hint of sage and nutmeg, and you've got delicious potato soup.

RESCUING LEFTOVER POTATOES: Whether boiled or baked, leftover potatoes can be used to make hash brown potatoes. The hash browns will be best if the potatoes are neither too soft nor too old.

MASTER RECIPE

Boiled Potatoes

4 to 6 servings

Boiled potatoes are most commonly served with pot roasts, stews, sautés, and other dishes that contain a gravy or sauce, or with fish. When used as an accompaniment to a sauced food, they need no dressing or seasoning, though butter, salt, and pepper may be added. When served with fish, they are frequently dusted with minced fresh parsley and sprinkled with drops of lemon juice.

For serving as a side dish, it is preferable to choose "new potatoes" or mature boiling potatoes of the red-skinned or waxy yellow-skinned type. Brown-skinned boiling potatoes and all-purpose potatoes may be boiled and then creamed, scalloped, roasted, or used as hash browns; boiled baking potatoes are excellent mashed.

2 pounds potatoes, all of a similar size to ensure even cooking
1 tablespoon salt

"New potatoes" (boiling potatoes measuring less than 2 inches around): Wash potatoes under running water. Using a paring knife or swivel-blade vegetable peeler, remove a ¼-inch band of skin around the circumference of each potato; this prevents the skin from bursting during cooking. Place potatoes in a pot, cover with water, add salt, and bring to the boil over high heat. Turn heat down to moderate and simmer potatoes, uncovered, for 8 to 12 minutes, or until just tender enough to be pierced easily with a fork. New potatoes become mushy if cooked just a minute or two too long, so watch carefully. Drain in a colander. Red-skinned new potatoes are always served with their skins on, but other varieties may be peeled with a paring knife if you wish, your hands protected with a towel.

Boiling potatoes measuring over 2 inches around, "all-purpose" potatoes, and baking potatoes: Scrub the potatoes with a brush under running water. Place in a pot, cover with water, stir in salt, and bring to a boil over high heat. Turn heat down to moderate, cover, and simmer the potatoes slowly for 15 to 45 minutes, depending on their size, or until tender when pierced with a fork. If you have any doubt the potatoes are done, remove one from the pot and cut in half. The interior should appear uniformly smooth and waxy; if the center is mealy-looking, give the potatoes a few more minutes. Drain in a colander, let cool briefly, then peel, holding the potato with a towel or pot holder. If large, potatoes may be halved or quartered before serving.

Note: To avoid the discomfort of handling hot potatoes, you can peel potatoes prior to boiling. To speed the cooking time, they may also be cut up. However, both strategies, particularly the latter, tend to make potatoes watery and crumbly. This is especially undesirable when you are preparing baked potatoes that are to be mashed.

Variation: POTATOES IN CREAM SAUCE

4 to 6 servings

Boiled Potatoes, using boiling or all-purpose potatoes
Bacon-Horseradish Cream Sauce (page 35), Cheese Sauce (page 37), Cream Sauce with Hard-cooked Eggs and Fresh Herbs (page 38), Dilled or Parsleyed Cream Sauce (page 41), or Sour Cream Sauce (page 44)

Cut peeled potatoes in cubes or slices, fold into hot sauce, and serve at once.

Variation: MASHED POTATOES

4 servings

❦ *Mashed potatoes are one of those simple yet elegant dishes that require attention to detail if they are to be first-rate. Above all, keep in mind that potatoes will be lumpy and heavy, no matter how long or hard they are beaten, unless put through a ricer or sieve before being mashed. By the way, mashed potatoes made in the food processor (I tried this once) turn into something that looks and tastes like wallpaper paste. Don't do it!*

I prefer to make mashed potatoes with baking rather than boiling potatoes. Baking potatoes produce a fluffy, light, yet earthy final result; mashed potatoes made with boiling potatoes often turn out heavy and a bit on the gluey side.

You can top a bowlful of hot mashed potatoes with a pat of butter or fold in any of the following: 3 tablespoons finely chopped fresh parsley or 1 tablespoon fresh dill; 1/3 cup or so freshly grated Parmesan cheese; 1/2 cup or more chopped onions sautéed in butter until golden; a dozen or more peeled cloves of garlic cooked very slowly in butter for 20 minutes, then mashed. Try also adding a tablespoon of dried rosemary to the water at the outset of cooking. Be sure, though, not to let any needles of rosemary end up in the finished mashed potatoes.

Boiled Potatoes, preferably using baking potatoes
8 tablespoons (1 stick) butter
½ cup cream or milk
½ to 1 teaspoon salt
¼ teaspoon white pepper, preferably freshly ground

Drain potatoes, reserving ½ cup or so of their cooking water. Dry out the pot in which potatoes were cooked; rice the potatoes or force through a sieve with the back of a spoon directly into the pot.

Cut butter into small pieces, combine with cream or milk in small saucepan, and bring almost to the boil. Set potatoes over the lowest possible flame and gradually add the butter mixture, gently beating all the while with a wire whip. Beat in by tablespoons as much of the potato cooking water as is necessary to bring mashed potatoes to the proper consistency; they should not seem pasty or heavy but must hold their shape quite firmly on a spoon. Beat steadily for 1 minute to fluff, season with salt and pepper, then cover the pot and let potatoes stand over a very low flame for exactly 3 minutes, which makes them lighter.

AHEAD OF TIME: The sooner mashed potatoes are served, the better. If there is an unavoidable delay in serving, set the mashed potatoes, uncovered, over almost-simmering water. Hold no longer than 20 minutes.

Variation: HASH BROWN POTATOES

4 to 6 servings

Boiled Potatoes; use boiling or all-purpose potatoes and undercook slightly (potatoes may be cooked a day in advance and stored, covered, in the refrigerator)
5 tablespoons butter
2 to 3 tablespoons neutral vegetable oil
Salt and pepper, preferably freshly ground, to taste

Peel potatoes and cut into rough ¾-inch cubes. Combine butter and 2 tablespoons oil in 12-inch skillet and place over moderately high heat. When fat is very hot and beginning to color slightly, distribute the cubed potatoes evenly over the bottom of the skillet and press down hard with a spatula to weld into a cake. Turning down the heat if the potatoes begin to scorch, cook potato cake until it turns crusty and nut brown on the bottom, pressing down occasionally with the spatula. Divide cake into quarters or thirds with the spatula and flip the pieces over. Brown the second side, adding a bit more oil to the skillet if the potatoes look dry. Season with salt and pepper to taste and serve immediately.

BAKED POTATOES

4 servings

❦ *The perfect baked potato is soft, dry, and very flaky. In order to achieve this result, you must start with large, mature, starch-laden baking potatoes, preferably the elongated variety known as Idaho potatoes, and you must never wrap the potatoes in foil or oil the skins, which will cause the potatoes to retain moisture.*

Baked potatoes are a classic accompaniment to roasts and steaks, and they also make an excellent light lunch or supper. To my mind, they are best when served only with soft butter, salt, and freshly ground pepper. (Well, I will submit to a big spoonful of caviar too!) Whatever you put on baked potatoes—sour cream, yogurt, crumbled bleu cheese, or other toppings—should be at room temperature, not chilled.

PRELIMINARIES

1. Set rack in the center of oven.
2. Preheat oven to 425°F 20 minutes before baking.

4 large baking potatoes, each weighing 8 to 12 ounces

Scrub potatoes thoroughly with a brush under running water and prick each one with a fork in 10 to 15 places to allow steam to escape. Place potatoes directly on the oven rack, spaced well apart, and bake for 1 to 1½ hours, or until they feel very soft when pierced deeply with a fork. (It is almost impossible to overcook baked potatoes. They simply become drier and drier, their skins crustier and crustier.) As soon as the potatoes are done, cut a lengthwise gash down the center to allow steam to escape. Serve at once.

STUFFED BAKED POTATOES

4 servings

❦ *Almost any flavoring—finely chopped ham, salami, or anchovies, patted-dry capers, mushroom stuffing, snipped chives, flaked crabmeat, and so on—can be used in addition to or in place of the Parmesan cheese in the following recipe.*

2 large baking potatoes, baked according to the recipe above
8 tablespoons (1 stick) soft butter
6 tablespoons (1½ ounces) freshly grated Parmesan cheese
¼ teaspoon mashed, pressed, or very finely minced garlic (optional)
Nutmeg, preferably freshly grated
⅛ to ¼ teaspoon salt
¼ teaspoon white or black pepper, preferably freshly ground
¼ cup Fine Fresh Bread Crumbs (see page 60)

Remove baked potatoes from oven, leaving the temperature at 425°F and resetting the rack in upper third of oven. Using a pot holder or other suitable insulator to protect your hands, halve the potatoes lengthwise with a paring knife, then scoop most of the flesh into a mixing bowl with a teaspoon; take care not to tear or puncture the skin. Add 7 tablespoons of the butter, the Parmesan cheese, garlic, and a pinch or two of nutmeg to the potato flesh and mix gently with a fork, lightly breaking up the potato into crumbly chunks. Taste and season with salt and pepper.

Lightly oil a baking pan large enough to hold the potato halves without touching. Arrange scooped-out potato skins in pan and fill with stuffing, mounding it slightly in the center. Sprinkle each half with 1 tablespoon bread crumbs and dot potatoes with remaining 1 tablespoon butter. Bake for about 15 minutes, or until stuffing is lightly browned on top. Serve at once.

SCALLOPED POTATOES WITH CHEESE

4 to 6 servings

Preliminaries

1. Set rack in lower third of oven.
2. Preheat oven to 375°F 20 minutes before baking.
3. Select a 9-inch round cake pan or other baking dish with sides 1½ to 2 inches deep. Grease with 1 tablespoon soft butter.

2 cups (8 ounces) shredded Swiss or Cheddar cheese, or a combination
¼ cup very finely minced onion
2 tablespoons all-purpose flour
⅛ teaspoon nutmeg, preferably freshly grated
½ teaspoon salt
¼ teaspoon white or black pepper, preferably freshly ground
1½ pounds boiling potatoes
3 tablespoons cold butter, cut into very thin pats
1½ cups milk

Place 1½ cups of the cheese in a 3-quart mixing bowl and set remaining ½ cup cheese aside. To the cheese in the bowl add the onion, flour, nutmeg, salt, and pepper; toss to blend. Peel potatoes and cut them into slices ⅛ inch thick or less (you will have about 5 cups). Arrange ⅓ of the sliced potatoes on the bottom of the buttered baking dish. Strew over them half of the cheese mixture in the bowl and ⅓ of the butter pats. Make a second layer, using a second third of the potatoes, all of the remaining cheese mixture in the bowl, and a second third of the butter pats. Cover top with all remaining potatoes. Heat milk almost to boiling in a small saucepan and pour evenly over potatoes. Mask the top with reserved ½ cup shredded cheese and dot with remaining butter. Bake for 45 to 55 minutes, or until top is lightly browned and potatoes feel fully tender when a knife is inserted in the center. Remove from oven and let rest a few moments before serving.

ROASTED POTATOES RUBINSTEIN

4 to 6 servings

❦ *The instructions given in this recipe assume that the potatoes will have to share the oven with a roast that requires a moderate temperature. Should your oven be free, you can bake the potatoes in the upper third of a preheated 425°F oven for about 30 minutes.*

- 2 pounds potatoes, preferably "new potatoes," though boiling or all-purpose potatoes may be used
- 1 tablespoon salt
- 3 tablespoons butter
- 3 tablespoons neutral vegetable oil
- ¼ teaspoon pepper, preferably freshly ground

Peel the potatoes. Leave new potatoes whole but halve or quarter larger potatoes to make pieces about 1½ inches in diameter. Place potatoes in a pot, cover with water, add 2½ teaspoons salt, and simmer new potatoes about 5 minutes, cut-up larger potatoes 10 to 12 minutes, or until about ⅔ tender. Gently tip into a colander, being careful not to break potatoes up, and let stand until all moisture evaporates.

Combine butter and oil in a small saucepan and place over low heat until the butter melts. Pour mixture into a shallow baking pan large enough to hold the potatoes with room to spare. Add potatoes and turn to coat completely with fat. Season with remaining ½ teaspoon salt and with pepper.

During the last 30 minutes of the estimated cooking time for your roast, bake the potatoes in the bottom level of the oven, underneath the roast, gently stirring them up and basting them twice with the fat in the pan. As soon as the roast is removed from the oven, turn the temperature up to 475°F and transfer potatoes to the upper third of oven. Stirring and basting two or three times, brown the potatoes for 15 to 20 minutes while the roast rests and is carved. Serve at once.

AHEAD OF TIME: After being parboiled, the potatoes may be turned into the butter and oil in the baking pan and set aside at room temperature, loosely covered, for several hours before being roasted.

LACY POTATO PANCAKES

4 servings

❦ *Containing only grated potatoes, these are the most elemental and, in my view, the loveliest of all potato pancakes. They may be served plain as a side dish with meat, or accompanied by applesauce and/or sour cream to make the main course of a modest supper.*

4 small to medium boiling potatoes (about 1 pound)
4 tablespoons butter
2 tablespoons neutral vegetable oil
Salt and freshly ground pepper to taste

Place serving platter in a 150°F oven. Peel the potatoes and submerge in cold water.

Using either a hand-held grater or a food processor fitted with the coarse shredding disc, shred one or two potatoes, depending on how many pancakes you will be cooking at one time. (Do not shred potatoes until you are ready to use them, for they will discolor if they sit.) Select one or two heavy-bottomed 8- to 9-inch skillets, preferably with a nonstick coating, and heat 1 tablespoon butter and ½ tablespoon oil in each. When fat is just beginning to color, drop in the shredded potato and quickly distribute it evenly over the entire bottom of the skillet by pushing it with a spatula. The pancake should have a lacy appearance, with small gaps throughout. Regulating heat so that the pancake sizzles actively but does not scorch, cook until it is a deep golden brown, about 5 minutes. Flip the pancake over and cook an additional 5 minutes or so, or until the fat, which will initially have been absorbed by the potato, re-emerges into the skillet. The second side of the pancake will not brown as prettily as the first. Place pancakes, preferably in a single layer, on the warm serving platter and keep in the oven while you make the rest. As soon as all the pancakes are done, sprinkle liberally with salt and pepper and serve.

FRENCH-FRIED POTATOES

4 to 6 servings

❦ *I always make french fries with boiling potatoes, as baking potatoes too often produce fries that are tough and knobby on the outside and dry and mealy within. There are no shortcuts to success here. The potatoes must have two fryings, the first at a low temperature to soften them, and the second at a high temperature to brown and crisp them.*

3 quarts vegetable oil
1½ pounds potatoes, preferably red-skinned or waxy yellow-skinned boiling potatoes
Salt

SPECIAL EQUIPMENT: A candy/deep-fry thermometer; a deep-frying basket about 8 inches wide and 5 inches deep (or a sieve of similar dimensions with a handle of a nonmelting material)

Pour oil into a heavy 6-quart pot approximately 10 inches wide and 5 inches deep. Place deep-fry basket in oil and insert thermometer. Set pot over moderate flame and heat oil to 300°F.

Peel potatoes and cut them into ½-inch-thick strips. Rinse quickly under cold water and pat with paper toweling to blot up excess moisture. When the oil in the pot has reached 300°F, lift basket out and place the potatoes in the basket. *Slowly* lower potatoes into the oil. If it bubbles up and threatens to overflow the lip of the pot, quickly pull up the basket, wait a moment, and then slowly reintroduce the potatoes. You may have to perform this maneuver several times, depending on the moisture content of the potatoes. (It is the water in the potatoes, released as steam, that causes the bubbling.) When at last the potatoes are resting in the fat, begin to stir them very gently with the spatula for a minute or two to prevent them from sticking together. Fry the potatoes for 5 to 6 minutes, or until all sputtering has ceased, indicating that they are cooked through; the potatoes should have colored hardly at all. Lift basket over pot and *gently* shake, being sure not to drop any fat on the stove burner. Scatter potatoes in a single layer on a baking sheet lined with a triple thickness of paper toweling. Let potatoes rest uncovered for no less than 20 minutes and no longer than 3 hours before proceeding to fry a second time.

For the second frying—which should be performed just before the potatoes are served—heat the oil to 385°F. Turn precooked potatoes into the frying basket and lower into hot oil. Immediately begin stirring potatoes very gently with a spatula to keep them from sticking together. Stop stirring as soon as the french fries begin to color, in about 45 seconds. Fry potatoes 2 to 4 minutes altogether, depending on how brown you like them. Lift potatoes out of oil, gently shake basket over pot to shake off excess oil, and spread french fries out on the baking sheet, lined with fresh paper toweling. Sprinkle with salt and serve at once in a cloth-lined basket or bowl. *Never* cover french fries, even with a napkin, or they will turn soggy.

Sweet Potatoes

Two kinds of sweet potatoes are commonly found in the supermarket: the small, roundish type, which has mealy, yellow flesh and tastes something like a cross between a potato and an acorn squash; and the long, irregularly shaped sweet potato with dense, smooth, very sweet flesh. The latter potato, the one chosen for "candying," is often called a yam but in fact is not. A true yam is a light-skinned, light-fleshed tuber, only slightly sweet in taste, that rarely makes its way to American markets.

Both round and long types of sweet potatoes should be firm to the touch and free of sprouts or dark, wrinkly patches. Store loosely wrapped in a dark, cool place, but do not refrigerate.

CANDIED SWEET POTATOES

4 to 5 servings

❦ *This classic American favorite is particularly popular at holiday time, for it is a perfect complement to roast turkey or baked ham.*

2 pounds yam-type sweet potatoes
⅔ cup sugar
5 tablespoons butter
2 tablespoons water or orange juice
4 teaspoons strained fresh lemon juice
¼ teaspoon nutmeg, preferably freshly grated
¼ teaspoon salt

Peel sweet potatoes deeply, exposing the dark orange flesh of the interior, and cut into halves or thirds. Place in a pot, cover with water, and boil slowly for 15 to 25 minutes, or until tender when pierced with a fork but still firm enough to hold their shape. Drain in a colander.

Combine all remaining ingredients in a 10-inch skillet made of or lined with a noncorroding material. Bring to a simmer and cook for 1 minute, stirring constantly. Add cooked sweet potatoes and gently turn in the glaze mixture to coat on all sides. Reduce heat to very low, cover skillet, and simmer for about

30 minutes, turning sweet potatoes every 6 to 7 minutes. They are done when most of the sugar glaze has been absorbed.

AHEAD OF TIME: Sweet potatoes may be prepared several days ahead and stored in a covered container in the refrigerator. To reheat, place in a skillet with several tablespoons water and warm over very gentle flame, turning frequently.

MASHED SWEET POTATOES

4 servings

❦ *Especially good with turkey, pork, or ham, mashed sweet potatoes may be garnished with chopped walnuts, preferably black, and/or minced candied ginger.*

2 pounds yam-type sweet potatoes
6 tablespoons butter
⅓ cup heavy cream
¼ to ½ cup pineapple or orange juice
Nutmeg, preferably freshly grated
Salt and pepper, preferably freshly ground, to taste

Peel sweet potatoes deeply, exposing the dark orange flesh of the interior, and cut into halves or thirds. Place potatoes in a pot, cover with water, and boil slowly for 15 to 25 minutes, or until they feel very tender but not mushy when pierced with a fork. Drain in a colander, turn into a 4-quart bowl, and mash with a large fork or potato masher; it's okay to leave a few lumps. Heat butter and cream together in a saucepan until the butter melts, then add gradually to the sweet potatoes, beating constantly with a wire whip. Warm juice in saucepan and beat in just enough to give the potatoes a soft, light consistency. Season with a pinch or two of nutmeg, salt, and pepper.

AHEAD OF TIME: These are best when served immediately but may be made a day in advance and stored, covered, in the refrigerator. Reheat in a double boiler over simmering water.

BAKED SWEET POTATOES

4 servings

❦ *I prefer to use the yam-type sweet potato for baking; the round variety seems to come out mealy. Whether served with roast pork or baked ham or eaten on their own as a snack or light supper, baked sweet potatoes are at their best when slathered with unconscionable quantities of soft butter.*

PRELIMINARIES

1. Set rack in the center of oven.
2. Preheat oven to 400°F 20 minutes before baking.
3. Select a baking dish large enough to hold the sweet potatoes comfortably. Line the inside of the dish with aluminum foil and fit with a cake rack.

4 large sweet potatoes, preferably the yam type

Scrub potatoes with a brush under running water. Prick each one in several places with a fork and arrange on the rack in the baking dish. Bake 45 minutes to 1 hour, or until very tender when pierced with a fork; sweet potatoes shrink, dry out, and toughen if cooked too long, so don't overdo it. As soon as they are baked, cut a gash down the middle of the potatoes to let the steam escape and press the sides lightly to force the flesh up. Serve at once.

FRENCH-FRIED SWEET POTATOES

4 to 6 servings

❦ *These are a very special treat with fried chicken.*

French-fried potatoes, page 584
SUBSTITUTE: 2 pounds sweet potatoes, preferably the yam-type, for white potatoes

If you are using yam-type sweet potatoes, peel them deeply to expose the dark orange interior flesh; round sweet potatoes may be peeled like white potatoes, with a swivel-blade vegetable peeler. Proceed according to the recipe for french-fried white potatoes, substituting the sweet potatoes.

Radishes

In addition to the familiar round, red-skinned radishes there are several other types that are worth experimenting with if you are lucky enough to find them at your market. Icicle radishes, white-skinned and finger-shaped, are juicier and much milder than ordinary radishes and make an attractive addition to an hors d'oeuvre tray. They should be peeled before serving. There are also the giant radish species, both white- and black-skinned, which are most frequently used as garnishes. After peeling, they may be sliced or, in the Asian manner, elaborately carved into roses, shellfish, or even large baskets.

Regardless of the type, all radishes should be firm and unblemished when purchased. When radishes are packed in plastic bags, check to make sure they have not become slimy and rotten. Trim the green tops of radishes and place them in a plastic bag before storing them in the refrigerator.

Cooked radishes: Radishes are rarely cooked, but there is no reason why they shouldn't be. Shave off stems and roots; cut very large radishes in half lengthwise. Sauté in butter or oil for several minutes, just enough to soften slightly. Cooked radishes taste a bit like sautéed turnips.

Rutabagas—See Turnips

Salsify (Oyster Plant)

Salsify is a long, thin root vegetable that very much resembles a stick of wood. There are both light- and dark-skinned varieties; aficionados say the dark-skinned kind is better. Fresh salsify is rare at the market and always quite expensive. The vegetable is also available in cans. Some people think that salsify tastes remotely like oysters—hence the vegetable's informal name, oyster plant—though I confess that the similarity eludes me. I think it more suggestive of parsnips.

COOKING SALSIFY: Cook salsify as for Jerusalem artichokes, peeling the roots deeply with a knife and then dropping them immediately into acidulated water. Salsify may be simmered until just tender, about 10 minutes, or it may be cooked until quite soft, 15 to 20 minutes, which is the way I prefer it. It may be served with a cream sauce, but I think it is at its best dressed with melted butter, chopped fresh parsley, and lemon juice, if needed.

Sorrel

Sometimes called sourgrass, sorrel is a leafy green with large, pointed, dark green leaves and a distinctive pungent, citrusy flavor. It is hard to find sorrel in the United States, but Europeans consume quantities of it both as a flavoring for cream sauces and as a vegetable in its own right. Sorrel may be added sparingly to tossed salads, used as the base for a cream soup, or cooked as for spinach.

Spinach

When buying loose spinach, look for young plants with small leaves and thin, smooth stems. The larger and older the spinach, the tougher the leaves and the stringier the stems. When spinach is sold in sealed cellophane bags it is hard to judge its quality. Check first of all for any signs of softness or sliminess visible through the cellophane, and for the presence of yellowed leaves. Do not buy any spinach that exhibits these symptoms of deterioration, for the vegetable is likely to be malodorous and beyond even the most skilled cook's powers of redemption.

Frozen Spinach: Frozen spinach is useful in preparing stuffings, sauces, and egg dishes. Defrost the spinach at room temperature or thaw by steaming slowly in a few spoonfuls of water in a covered pot. Let cool, then squeeze quite dry between your hands and chop fine with a knife. A 10-ounce package of frozen spinach should yield about ½ cup after squeezing and chopping.

Rescuing Gritty Cooked Spinach: Drop the spinach into a large kettle of rapidly boiling salted water and boil hard for 1 minute after water returns to the boil. Remove kettle from heat and let spinach stand undisturbed for 2 minutes. Gently skim spinach off the surface of the water with a strainer; most of the grit should have sunk to the bottom of the pot.

MASTER RECIPE

Steamed Spinach

4 servings

❦ *The simplest dressing is one of the best: 3 to 4 tablespoons soft butter, plus salt, pepper, and drops of fresh lemon juice to taste. Olive oil may be used in place of the butter if the rest of your meal has Mediterranean overtones. Dried rosemary (ground or minced fine) and nutmeg (preferably freshly grated) are particularly good flavorings for spinach.*

Spinach shrinks alarmingly in volume when cooked, a whole pound of raw spinach producing only a cup or so cooked.

STEP 1: TRIMMING AND WASHING THE SPINACH

2 pounds fresh spinach

If the spinach is still attached to the roots, cut them off about an inch below the leaves. Pick through the spinach, plucking off at the base of the leaves any stems that seem overly large or that have a hollow, stringy, or pale look. If the stems are very large and tough, do not pluck but rather pull up through the center of the leaves and discard.

Place the spinach in a sink filled with tepid water. Swish the leaves around to loosen grit, let the spinach stand for half a minute, then skim it from the water and set aside. If there is sand at the bottom of the sink, repeat the procedure. Wash the spinach as many times as is necessary to remove all the sand. (The old rule of thumb was that spinach and other greens needed to be washed seven times.)

STEP 2: STEAMING THE SPINACH Gather bunches of the trimmed, washed spinach between your hands, shake lightly, and turn into a 5- to 6-quart pot (the interior of the pot should not be unlined aluminum or cast iron, which will impart a metallic taste to the spinach). Adding no water or other liquid, stir over moderately high heat, using a long-handled fork, until spinach has wilted. Lower heat, cover the pot, and let spinach stew slowly for about 3 minutes. Taste, and if the spinach is still tough, let it cook a few minutes longer.

Remove spinach from heat. Using the fork, push spinach to one side of the pot. Tilt the pot so that the side holding the spinach is raised and press spinach firmly with the fork to extract excess water. Still tilting the pot, lift the spinach by forkfuls into a serving bowl.

Preparing Spinach for Stuffings, Spinach Beds, Egg Dishes, etc.: Spinach needs to be extra dry when used for these purposes. Prepare the spinach as above, let cool, then press firmly between your hands to wring out final drops of juice. (You might save the juice for a sauce, soup, or stew.) Alternatively you can turn the spinach into a colander or sieve and press it firmly with the back of a large spoon.

AHEAD OF TIME: Spread spinach out on a dinner plate and let cool to room temperature. Pack into a sealed container and refrigerate for a day or two. Reheat by tossing in a skillet with several tablespoons of butter.

Variation: CREAMED SPINACH

4 servings

❦ *Heavenly with lamb chops, roasts, and well-aged steaks.*

Steamed Spinach
2 tablespoons butter
2 teaspoons all-purpose flour
½ to ¾ cup heavy cream
½ teaspoon salt
White pepper, preferably freshly ground, to taste
Fresh lemon juice
Nutmeg, preferably freshly grated

Remove cooked spinach from pot and discard the cooking water. Melt butter in the pot, add the spinach, and toss with a fork until the leaves are coated. Sprinkle flour over the spinach and cook, stirring, over low heat for 1 minute. Pour in heavy cream and simmer over moderately low heat for about 5 minutes, or until the mixture thickens just enough to hold its shape loosely on a fork. Season with salt, white pepper, drops of lemon juice, and pinches of nutmeg.

Variation: SPINACH PURÉE

4 servings

Prepare creamed spinach above, cooking the mixture until quite thick. Purée using blender, food processor, or food mill.

Variation: OLD-FASHIONED BUTTER-BRAISED SPINACH

4 servings

❦ *This is the way that spinach was often cooked before tastes swung toward briefly cooked vegetables. Prepared in this manner, spinach takes on a very rich, nutlike flavor that particularly complements veal and roast chicken.*

Steamed Spinach
6 tablespoons butter
2 tablespoons finely chopped shallots or scallions (white part only)
Salt and white pepper, preferably freshly ground, to taste
Fresh lemon juice
Nutmeg, preferably freshly grated

Remove cooked spinach from pot and discard the cooking water. Add butter to the pot, stir in shallots or scallions, and sauté slowly until tender, about 2 minutes. Add the spinach, toss to coat with butter, and partially cover the pot. Stew the spinach slowly, stirring occasionally, for 30 minutes or longer, or until the spinach is so tender that it almost melts on the tongue. Season with salt, white pepper, lemon juice, and nutmeg to taste.

Variation: SPINACH SAUTÉ WITH GARLIC

4 servings

❦ *Excellent with broiled chicken, broiled or fried fish, or poached or fried eggs.*

Steamed Spinach
4 to 6 tablespoons olive oil
1 teaspoon mashed, pressed, or very finely minced garlic
½ teaspoon salt
Pepper, preferably freshly ground, to taste
Fresh lemon juice

Remove spinach from pot and discard the cooking water. Add to the pot 4 to 6 tablespoons olive oil and heat until it looks shimmery, then add the spinach along with garlic. Toss over moderately high heat for a couple of minutes. Season with salt, pepper to taste, and drops of fresh lemon juice.

Variation: SPINACH SAUTÉ WITH BACON AND HARD-COOKED EGG

4 servings

❦*I like to eat this with noodles as a light lunch or supper.*

Steamed Spinach
4 to 5 slices bacon, chopped
Salt and pepper, preferably freshly ground, to taste
Vinegar
2 hard-cooked eggs

Remove spinach from pot and discard the cooking water. Add chopped bacon to the pot and cook over moderate heat until the bits are brown and crisp and the fat is rendered. Add spinach and toss with a fork for a minute or two, or until heated through. Season to taste with salt, pepper, and drops of vinegar. Turn into a serving bowl and toss lightly with hard-cooked eggs, cut into quarters.

Variation: CHINESE-STYLE SPINACH SAUTÉ

4 servings

❦*Serve this provocative dish with chicken, lamb, or broiled fish.*

Steamed Spinach
3 tablespoons neutral vegetable oil
2 teaspoons dark sesame oil
1 teaspoon grated or very finely minced fresh ginger
½ teaspoon mashed, pressed, or very finely minced garlic
2 teaspoons dark soy sauce
¼ teaspoon sugar
Salt and cayenne pepper, to taste
2 to 3 tablespoons sesame seeds, lightly toasted (optional)

Remove spinach from pot and discard the cooking water. Add vegetable oil and dark sesame oil to the pot and heat over moderately high flame until shimmery. Stir in ginger and garlic, cook 15 seconds, then add the spinach and toss until heated through. Add soy sauce and sugar and cook 1 minute longer. Season with salt and cayenne pepper to taste. If you wish, toss spinach with sesame seeds just before serving.

SUMMER SQUASH

The summer squashes most frequently seen at the market are *zucchini* and *straightneck yellow squash; crookneck yellow squash* and the pale green, scallop-edged *pattypan squash,* also called *cymling squash,* are somewhat less common but can usually be found at a green grocer's. Summer squashes are quite similar in taste and texture, though zucchini is arguably a bit firmer and more flavorful than the others.

The thing to remember when shopping for summer squash is to buy *small.* Summer squash should weigh no more than 5 or 6 ounces apiece, and they are better when smaller still. Zucchini and yellow squash should be no more than 6 inches long; pattypans should be small enough to fit in the palm of your hand. Overmature squash have hard-shelled seeds and tough skins, and they tend to be either watery or pithy.

Summer squash are highly perishable, and unfortunately many of those one sees at the market are already long past their prime. Fresh squash have glossy skin and are very firm when squeezed. Avoid those that are limp, as well as any that exhibit signs of decay such as soft spots, wrinkles, puckers, or discoloration; these will be slightly bitter and off-tasting no matter how you cook them. Since summer squash are so perishable, it is a good idea to cook any first-rate specimens that you chance to find on the same day you buy them.

RESCUING OVERMATURE SUMMER SQUASH: If you somehow get stuck with a monster squash, peel it, cut it in half lengthwise, and scoop out and discard the seeds. Dice the squash and let it stand in 1 teaspoon salt per pound of squash for 30 minutes or longer. Gently squeeze between your hands and pat dry with paper toweling. Proceed to cook according to recipe.

MASTER RECIPE

Sautéed Summer Squash

4 servings

Although steamed summer squash is delicious and very low in calories, sautéing seems to me to give squash a firmer texture and to better accentuate its subtle nutlike flavor. Just before serving, season squash with salt, freshly ground pepper, and drops of fresh lemon juice, and, if you wish, sprinkle with minced fresh parsley or basil. Sautéed summer squash can be served with practically anything but is particularly good with eggs, fish, and chicken.

Step 1: Washing and Cutting up the Squash

2 pounds zucchini, yellow squash, or pattypan squash, preferably 6 or more small squash

Scrub squash thoroughly under warm running water with a brush or paper toweling. There are tiny, nearly invisible hairs on the skins of some summer squash that trap particles of grit.

Cut off stems and trim a bit off the blossom ends of the squash. Cut squash into ½-inch chunks.

Step 2: Sautéing the Squash

2 tablespoons butter
2 tablespoons olive oil or neutral vegetable oil

Over moderately high heat, melt butter and oil together in a 10- to 12-inch skillet. When butter stops foaming and mixture is mildly fragrant, add squash and cook 6 to 10 minutes, tossing frequently with a spatula, until squash is fully tender and just beginning to color. Season and serve immediately. The squash will turn mushy if it sits.

Variation: SUMMER SQUASH IN HEAVY CREAM WITH GARLIC AND BASIL

4 servings

❦ *This dish is particularly good with lamb.*

Sautéed Summer Squash, preferably zucchini
½ teaspoon mashed, pressed, or very finely minced garlic
1 cup heavy cream
1½ teaspoons cornstarch mixed to a smooth paste with 1 tablespoon milk or cream
1½ tablespoons finely chopped fresh basil
⅜ to ½ teaspoon salt
Pepper, preferably freshly ground
Fresh lemon juice

Proceed according to the Master Recipe. When squash is nearly cooked, stir in garlic and cream. Bring to a simmer and cook slowly for several minutes. Stir cornstarch paste and basil into the simmering squash; cook another minute. Season with salt, pepper, and drops of fresh lemon juice.

Variation: SAUTÉED SUMMER SQUASH WITH GARLIC AND CRUMBS

4 servings

❦ *Especially good with broiled fish or chicken.*

Sautéed Summer Squash
½ to 1 teaspoon mashed, pressed, or very finely minced garlic
½ cup Fine Fresh Bread Crumbs (see page 60)
Salt and pepper, preferably freshly ground, to taste
2 tablespoons finely chopped fresh parsley (optional)

Proceed according to Master Recipe. About 2 minutes before you estimate that the squash will be fully cooked, add garlic and bread crumbs to the skillet and toss with a spatula until crumbs brown lightly. Season with salt and pepper, and sprinkle, if you wish, with parsley.

Variation: SUMMER SQUASH WITH PARMESAN CHEESE, ONIONS, AND HERBS

4 servings

❦ *A variant of a recipe my mother clipped years ago from a home gardening magazine, this is delicious with chicken.*

Sautéed Summer Squash
ADD: 2 medium-large onions, peeled, thinly sliced, and separated into rings
½ cup (2 ounces) freshly grated Parmesan cheese
2 tablespoons finely chopped fresh parsley or basil
Salt and pepper, preferably freshly ground, to taste
Fresh lemon juice

Sauté onions along with squash in the Master Recipe, covering the skillet during the last 2 minutes of cooking. When squash is cooked, remove from heat and toss with Parmesan cheese and parsley or basil. Season with salt, pepper, and drops of lemon juice. Serve at once.

Variation: SUMMER SQUASH IN TOMATO SAUCE

4 servings

Sautéed Summer Squash
SUBSTITUTE: 4 tablespoons olive oil for butter and oil
½ teaspoon mashed, pressed, or very finely minced garlic
1 cup tomato sauce, preferably homemade, page 183

Proceed according to the Master Recipe, substituting olive oil for butter and oil. When squash is nearly tender stir in the garlic, then the tomato sauce, lower heat, and simmer slowly for 3 minutes.

Variation: SAUTÉED ZUCCHINI WITH WALNUTS

4 servings

❦ *Zucchini and walnuts are astonishingly complementary in flavor, and you can further accentuate the overall nutty savor of the dish if you sauté the squash in walnut oil. This is excellent with broiled fish or chicken.*

Sautéed Summer Squash, using zucchini
SUBSTITUTE: Walnut oil for olive oil or neutral vegetable oil (optional)
½ cup (2 ounces) coarsely chopped walnuts or black walnuts
¼ to ½ teaspoon salt
Pepper, preferably freshly ground, to taste
Fresh lemon juice

Sauté zucchini according to the Master Recipe, substituting walnut oil for olive oil or neutral vegetable oil, if you wish. When squash is nearly cooked, gently stir in walnuts. Remove from heat and season to taste with salt, pepper, and drops of lemon juice.

STEAMED SUMMER SQUASH

4 to 5 servings

2 pounds zucchini, yellow squash, or pattypan squash, preferably 6 or more small squash
1 tablespoon butter (optional)
Salt and pepper, preferably freshly ground, to taste
Fresh lemon juice

Scrub squash thoroughly under warm running water with a brush or paper toweling. Cut off stems and trim a bit off the blossom ends. Zucchini and yellow squash 1 inch or less in diameter may be left whole; cut larger squash lengthwise in halves or quarters. Unless they are tiny, cut pattypans in halves or quarters.

Bring ½ inch of water to a rapid boil in saucepan or pot that is at least 10 inches wide and 3 inches deep. Arrange squash cut side up in a 9-inch steaming basket, overlapping as necessary. Lower basket into saucepan, cover, and steam over moderately high heat for 7 minutes. Test by spearing with a fork; the squash should be just soft enough to yield readily. Steam a few minutes longer if necessary. (Whole squash will take longer to cook than cut-up squash.)

Arrange squash on serving dish.

Dress sparingly with butter, if you wish, and season to taste with salt, pepper, and drops of lemon juice. Serve immediately.

TIP: Spear optional butter with a fork and pass it over the pieces of squash as though you were buttering an ear of corn. A little butter goes a long way with squash.

STUFFED SUMMER SQUASH WITH BEEF OR LAMB

4 main-dish or 8 side-dish servings

❦ *Stuffed summer squash may be served hot, at room temperature, or slightly chilled. Crusty bread and a tossed green salad or sliced fresh tomatoes are good accompaniments.*

PRELIMINARIES

1. Set rack in center of oven.
2. Preheat oven to 375°F 20 minutes before baking.
3. Select a baking dish large enough to hold the squash comfortably; remember that the squash will be cut in half lengthwise. Grease the dish with 1 to 2 tablespoons olive oil.

4 medium-small summer squash, preferably zucchini, weighing 5 to 6 ounces each
6 to 8 quarts water
½ cup minced onion
3 tablespoons olive oil, plus some for topping if you wish
1 cup (about 8 ounces) ground lean beef or lamb
½ cup cooked rice, buckwheat groats (kasha), or barley
3 ounces cream cheese, softened
6 tablespoons (1½ ounces) freshly grated Parmesan cheese
3 to 4 tablespoons chopped walnuts (optional)
2 tablespoons strained fresh lemon juice
1½ tablespoons chopped fresh basil or 1½ teaspoons dried
½ teaspoon mashed, pressed, or very finely minced garlic
½ teaspoon salt
¼ teaspoon pepper, preferably freshly ground
3 tablespoons fresh or dry bread crumbs

Scrub the squash thoroughly under warm running water with a brush or paper toweling. Cut off stems and trim a bit off the blossom ends. Drop squash into a large pot containing 6 to 8 quarts rapidly boiling water. Cook for exactly 2 minutes after water returns to the boil. Remove squash from water and let cool until comfortable to handle. Slit the squash lengthwise and scoop out seeds and pulp with a teaspoon, being sure to leave a wall of flesh at least ¼ inch thick on all sides. Chop the scooped-out seeds and pulp coarsely.

Slowly sauté onion in olive oil in large skillet for 3 minutes. Add chopped squash pulp and cook slowly, stirring occasionally, for 10 minutes or more, or until squash is very soft and looks fairly dry. Scrape contents of skillet into mixing bowl and add ground beef or lamb, rice, cream cheese, 3 tablespoons Parmesan cheese, walnuts, lemon juice, basil, garlic, salt, and pepper. Blend thoroughly and taste for seasoning. The mixture should be well flavored at this point; if it seems bland, add more lemon juice, basil, garlic, salt, or pepper as necessary.

Arrange squash shells in oiled baking dish and pile the stuffing mixture into them, mounding it in the center. Sprinkle with remaining 3 tablespoons Parmesan cheese mixed with bread crumbs. Drizzle a little olive oil on top, if you wish. Bake for 25 to 35 minutes, or until squash is tender and stuffing feels firm and hot to the touch. Let stand at room temperature for a few minutes before serving.

Winter Squash

Between the months of October and February, when the winter squash are in their peak season, a well-stocked supermarket may carry a half dozen different varieties. Choosing among these is not so daunting a task as it might first appear, for with the exceptions of acorn squash, spaghetti squash, and chayote, all winter squash are similar to *butternut squash,* the ubiquitous favorite, in taste, texture, and cooking reactions. Butternut, of course, is the tan-skinned, pestle-shaped squash that runs anywhere from a quarter of a pound to several pounds in weight. Related squashes include the yellow-skinned *banana squash,* the scallop-edged, green-skinned *turban* (or *buttercup*) *squash,* and the gigantic grayish-blue-skinned *Hubbard squash,* which, because of its size, is usually offered in cellophane-wrapped pieces at the supermarket. Also affiliated with this group is the *pumpkin,* though pumpkin is a bit moister and paler in flesh than the other squash in this category. For cooking purposes, varieties of the small, brownish sugar pumpkin are preferable to large, orange-yellow jack-o'-lantern type pumpkins.

Acorn Squash: A small, handsome, green-and-orange-skinned squash resembling a large furrowed acorn, acorn squash has pale and vaguely crunchy flesh when cooked; in taste it is less sweet and rich than butternut-type squash, nearly suggesting a mature summer squash. Its shape, so conducive to stuffing, is surely one of the reasons for its popularity.

Spaghetti Squash: Yellow-skinned and shaped like a torpedo, this squash yields astonishing spaghettilike strands when cooked, but contains only a fifth of the calories of genuine pasta. In fact, spaghetti squash is often dressed as for pasta, either simply with butter and grated Parmesan cheese, or with tomato sauce, white clam sauce, and so on.

Cooking spaghetti squash: To prepare spaghetti squash, pierce it in four or five places with the point of a very sharp, sturdy knife (the rind is extraordinarily hard) and bake it in a dish in the center of a preheated 350°F oven. A 1-pound spaghetti squash will require about an hour of cooking; larger squash will take longer. Cut the squash in half lengthwise, scoop out and discard the seeds, and release the flesh with a spoon, scraping from end to end. Allow about 1 pound of spaghetti squash per person.

Chayote: Except in parts of the southern United States, where it has long been popular, this squash, also known as *mirliton, christophène,* or *vegetable pear,* is a relative newcomer to American supermarkets. There are different varieties of chayote, some with smooth and some with spiny skins. All are small and pear-shaped and have a single large seed in the center; both skin and flesh are pale green. Fresh-tasting, firm-textured, and dripping with juice, chayote is an appealing vegetable.

Cooking chayote: To prepare, halve chayotes and steam in a basket in a covered pot for about half an hour; serve with butter and grated Parmesan cheese. Allow 1 small or ½ large chayote per person.

PURCHASING AND STORAGE: All winter squashes should be rock-hard to the touch. When buying cut-up squash packaged in cellophane, check to make sure that the flesh is uniformly moist and bright, with no signs of molding or soft spots and no appearance of sliminess. Cut-up winter squash should be kept under refrigeration and cooked within a few days of purchase. Whole winter squash may be kept for several weeks—or even longer if they are fresh—in a cool dark place, such as a cellar cupboard.

MASTER RECIPE

Purée of Winter Squash

4 servings

Puréed winter squash goes well with broiled or roasted poultry or meat; it is usually served in place of potatoes, rice, or other starch. Winter squash may also be served in pieces rather than puréed, in which case I prefer to bake rather than steam it as required here; a recipe for baked squash appears on page 604.

The question always arises whether it is easier to peel winter squash before or after cooking. Since the rinds of most winter squash are extraordinarily tough, I prefer to peel after steaming, despite the difficulty of handling hot squash.

STEP 1: PREPARING THE SQUASH

2 pounds butternut or similar winter squash

Wipe rind of squash with damp paper toweling. If the squash is whole, cut it in half lengthwise through the stem with a sharp, sturdy utility knife and scrape out all seeds and stringy pulp with a spoon. Proceed to hack the squash into pieces 3 inches across and no more than 1½ inches thick for cooking. This may be easier said than done—some squash are very hard!

TIP: The seeds of winter squash are edible. Scrub them between your hands under running water to remove most of the clinging pulp; pat dry with paper toweling. Spread seeds in a single layer on an oiled baking sheet and toast in a 350°F oven for 8 to 12 minutes, stirring several times. Remove from oven when golden brown; salt well. The seeds may also be toasted in oil in a skillet.

Step 2: Steaming and Puréeing the Squash

6 tablespoons soft butter
½ to 1 teaspoon salt
White or black pepper, preferably freshly ground, to taste
White or brown sugar, if needed
Fresh lemon juice, if needed

Bring ½ inch of water to a boil in saucepan or pot that is at least 10 inches across and 3 inches deep. Arrange squash cut side up in a 9-inch steaming basket, overlapping the pieces as necessary. Lower basket into saucepan, cover, and steam the squash over moderate heat for 15 to 25 minutes, depending on maturity and type. When fully cooked, the squash will mash easily when pressed with the tines of a fork and the flesh will have darkened somewhat.

Scrape the flesh off the skin with a spoon, turn flesh into a fine sieve, and press through the sieve into a 3-quart mixing bowl with the back of a wooden spoon. (Squash can also be put through a ricer or food mill, but avoid using a blender or food processor, as the squash tends to get watery when puréed in a machine.) Add butter, and beat with a wire whip until fluffy. Season with salt, pepper, and, if needed, pinches of sugar and/or drops of lemon juice.

Ahead of Time: Squash can be made ahead without suffering any damage. Beat the squash with half the butter called for and refrigerate in a covered container for up to 3 days. When ready to serve, reheat squash in a heavy saucepan over a very low flame (or over simmering water in a double boiler), beating in the remaining butter along with seasonings.

Variation: PURÉE OF WINTER SQUASH WITH BACON

4 servings

Purée of Winter Squash
4 to 6 slices bacon

Fry bacon until crisp. Drain, crumble, and beat into squash just before serving.

Variation: PURÉE OF WINTER SQUASH WITH CHIVES

4 servings

Purée of Winter Squash
2 to 3 tablespoons snipped fresh chives

Prepare purée, beating in fresh chives just before serving.

Variation: PURÉE OF WINTER SQUASH WITH GINGER, MAPLE SYRUP, AND WALNUTS

4 servings

❦ *This is extremely nice with the Thanksgiving bird.*

Purée of Winter Squash
2 to 4 teaspoons ground ginger, or to taste
1 tablespoon pure maple syrup
1 teaspoon medium-dry Sherry, preferably Manzanilla
½ cup (2 ounces) coarsely chopped walnuts or black walnuts

Prepare purée. Just before serving, beat in ground ginger, maple syrup, Sherry, and nuts. Taste carefully and adjust seasoning as necessary.

Variation: PURÉE OF WINTER SQUASH WITH PARMESAN CHEESE

4 servings

❦ *Less sweet than most winter squash preparations, this dish goes well with veal, ham, and poultry.*

Purée of Winter Squash
OMIT: Salt
½ cup (2 ounces) freshly grated Parmesan cheese
1 tablespoon dry vermouth
½ teaspoon fresh lemon juice

Prepare a purée of winter squash as outlined in the Master Recipe, but omit the salt. Beat in Parmesan cheese, vermouth, and lemon juice. Taste carefully and adjust seasoning.

Variation: SPICED PURÉE OF WINTER SQUASH

4 servings

Purée of Winter Squash
¼ teaspoon ground cloves
¼ teaspoon cinnamon
¼ teaspoon nutmeg, preferably freshly grated
White or brown sugar

Prepare squash purée and beat in spices. Sweeten to taste with pinches of white or brown sugar.

BAKED WINTER SQUASH

4 to 6 servings

❦ *Winter squash develops a special sweetness and richness when baked. It is particularly delicious with a roast and may be baked along with the roast and basted with the drippings.*

Preliminaries

1. Set rack in center or bottom of oven.
2. Preheat oven to 350°F 20 minutes before baking.
3. Select a baking dish large enough to hold the squash comfortably. Oil the dish lightly.

2 pounds winter squash: 2 small acorn or butternut squash, 1 banana or turban squash, or a section of Hubbard squash
6 tablespoons soft butter, bacon fat, or drippings from a beef or pork roast
2 tablespoons packed dark brown sugar
⅛ teaspoon cinnamon
¼ teaspoon salt
⅛ teaspoon pepper, preferably freshly ground

Wipe squash rinds with damp paper toweling. Cut whole squash in half lengthwise and scoop out seeds and pulp. Divide Hubbard squash into serving pieces. Arrange squash halves or pieces cut side up in baking dish. Cream together all remaining ingredients in a small mixing bowl. Coat the flesh sides of the squash thickly with fat mixture and put a dollop of the mixture into the cavities of halved squash. Basting once or twice with pan juices, bake until very tender, 45 minutes to 1¼ hours, depending on the size of the pieces. Cut halves of banana or turban squash in two before serving.

BAKED BUTTERNUT SQUASH STUFFED WITH SAUSAGE AND APPLES

4 main-course servings

❦ *This dish is rich and filling and needs only a tossed green salad to become a full meal.*

Preliminaries

1. Set rack in center of oven.
2. Preheat oven to 375°F 20 minutes before baking.
3. Select a baking dish large enough to hold the squash halves in one layer. Oil the dish lightly.

2 butternut squash, about 1 pound each
1 tablespoon neutral vegetable oil
1 cup (about 8 ounces) well-seasoned sausage meat
1 large tart green apple, peeled, cored, and cut into ¼-inch cubes (about 1 cup)
3 tablespoons butter
2 tablespoons packed dark brown sugar
¼ teaspoon ground sage
Salt and freshly ground pepper to taste

Wipe squash with damp paper toweling, cut in half lengthwise through the stem, and scoop out seeds and pulp. Arrange squash cut side up in baking dish and brush lightly with oil. Cover with lid or aluminum foil and bake for 30 to 40 minutes, or until almost tender. Do not turn off oven.

While squash is baking, crumble sausage into skillet and cook over moderate heat until the meat loses all traces of pink. Without draining off fat, add apple and sauté for several minutes, or just until crisp-tender. Remove skillet from heat. When the squash is cooked, let it cool slightly, then scoop out most of the flesh, leaving a ⅜-inch wall on all sides. Lightly mix squash flesh into the sausage mixture, breaking up squash as little as possible. Mix in 2 tablespoons butter, 1 tablespoon brown sugar, the sage, and salt and pepper. Pile mixture into the squash halves, dot with remaining butter, and sprinkle with remaining brown sugar. Bake uncovered for an additional 20 to 25 minutes, or until piping hot and brown and crusty on top. Let cool a few minutes before serving.

Swiss Chard

Swiss chard is two delicious vegetables in one. Its leaves, which may be 4 or 5 inches wide and up to a foot long, taste like spinach, while its long stems suggest asparagus. The part of the stem that extends into the center of the leaf should be removed with the rest of the stem; use a paring knife to cut it out. Cook the leaves as for spinach and the stems as for asparagus. The stems are particularly good served with grated Parmesan cheese.

Tomatoes

The hothouse tomato has come to be emblematic of all that is wrong with the producing, shipping, and marketing of fresh fruits and vegetables in present-day America. Bred for its convenience to the grower and trucker, the hothouse tomato is a pale, hard, mealy, acid-tasting thing that is useful only for broiling—and even then it isn't great. Don't be misled by advertising. "Vine-ripened" hothouse tomatoes are no more flavorful than others, and "hard-ripe," a label frequently seen in supermarket windows, is a contradiction in terms.

Fortunately, there are acceptable substitutes for hothouse tomatoes. Cherry tomatoes can be used in salads—in fact, some people prefer them to large tomatoes, for they can be left whole and thus will not water down the dressing. Cherry tomatoes may also be cooked, either baked or quickly sautéed in butter or olive oil. Plum tomatoes, so named because their size and elongated teardrop shape suggest the fruit, are meatier than ordinary tomatoes, and are usually used to make tomato sauce. But there is no reason why ripe plum tomatoes should not be used in salads, where their relative lack of juice is an advantage, and they are also very good stewed. Last, there are canned tomatoes, perhaps the most useful of all canned vegetables. Hothouse tomatoes are virtually useless for making tomato sauce or for flavoring soups and gravies, but canned tomatoes can work quite well. Generally speaking, the Italian imports are the best.

The best substitutes of all for hothouse tomatoes are, of course, "real" tomatoes—that is, locally grown garden tomatoes that taste as tomatoes should. When buying local tomatoes, select those that are firm but not hard and that have a pronounced tomatoey bouquet. Some varieties are a deep scarlet when ripe, while others are bright orange red. Softened, darkened, or dented areas indicate interior rot; black dimples are also a bad sign. But don't reject a tomato simply because it has a few dark scars, furrows, or welts around the stem. Some tomatoes just grow this way.

HOW TO PEEL AND SEED FRESH TOMATOES: Bring at least 3 quarts water to boil in a large saucepan. Two or three at a time, lower the tomatoes into the boiling water and let stand for exactly 10 seconds. Remove with a slotted spoon and rinse under cold running water. The skins will now slip off quite easily.

Cut the tomatoes in half crosswise. Squeeze each half gently but firmly, flicking your wrist as you squeeze, to remove both seeds and juice. If necessary, run a fingertip through cavities to dislodge seeds. When all the tomatoes have been seeded, cut out the stem cores with a sharp paring knife. Tomatoes are now ready to be cut up as directed in recipes.

HOW TO SEED CANNED TOMATOES: Buy canned whole tomatoes, not tomato pieces. Drain tomatoes, saving liquid for some other purpose. With your finger open the cavities along the side of each tomato, gently pushing out the seeds. The tomatoes are now ready to be cut up as directed in recipe.

RESCUING UNRIPE TOMATOES: No tomato can be ripened once it has been chilled, so don't try to ripen the hothouse variety, which are refrigerated almost from the moment of harvest. To ripen a home-grown tomato place it in a paper bag for a day or two. The tomato must be pinkish to start with to ripen with complete success.

STEWED TOMATOES

4 servings

❦ *Stewed tomatoes are best served separately in small bowls. They are a classic accompaniment to macaroni and cheese and are also good with fish, chicken, or lamb. They are excellent seasoned with minced fresh parsley, basil, or tarragon, or with freshly grated Parmesan cheese.*

- 3 to 4 tablespoons butter or olive oil
- 6 to 8 medium-large tomatoes (about 3½ pounds), peeled and seeded (see page 607) and left in halves
- Salt and pepper, preferably freshly ground, to taste

Over moderate flame, heat butter or oil in a 3- to 4-quart heavy-bottomed saucepan made of or lined with a noncorroding material. Add tomatoes, stir, and bring to a simmer. Cover and cook tomatoes slowly for 6 to 8 minutes, or until they are soft but still retain their shape. Season to taste with salt and pepper.

AHEAD OF TIME: Stewed tomatoes taste freshest when served at once but can be prepared 2 or 3 days in advance, covered, and refrigerated. Reheat slowly.

CHERRY TOMATOES SAUTÉED IN BUTTER

4 servings

❦ *It is something of a chore to peel cherry tomatoes, and this step may be omitted if you're feeling lazy, though not without some detriment to the final result. With their vivid color and sprightly taste, sautéed cherry tomatoes are especially nice with fish and may also accompany chicken or lamb.*

- 24 cherry tomatoes
- 4 tablespoons butter
- 2 tablespoons finely chopped fresh parsley or basil (optional)
- ½ teaspoon salt
- ¼ teaspoon pepper, preferably freshly ground

Bring several quarts of water to boil in a large saucepan. A small handful at a time, drop in cherry tomatoes, let stand exactly 5 seconds, then remove with a slotted spoon. Slit the skin of each cherry tomato with the point of a paring knife—be sure not to penetrate the flesh—then slip the skin off with your fingers.

Melt butter in a skillet over moderate heat. Add tomatoes and cook over a gentle flame for just a minute or two, swirling them in the butter by gently shaking the skillet by the handle. (Stirring with a spoon would break the tomatoes apart.) Do not cook the tomatoes past the point when they are just warmed through, or they will turn soggy and burst. As soon as they are done, sprinkle tomatoes with parsley or basil, salt, and pepper and tilt into a serving dish. Serve at once.

Ahead of Time: After peeling, you may arrange the tomatoes in a single layer in a large dish, cover, and refrigerate for half a day or so before cooking.

BROILED TOMATOES

4 servings

❦ *These are classic with grilled or broiled fish, chicken, chops, or steaks.*

Preliminaries

1. Set broiler rack about 6 inches beneath heating element.
2. Preheat broiler for 10 minutes before broiling.
3. Select a shallow baking dish large enough to hold the tomatoes comfortably.

2 large tomatoes weighing 8 to 10 ounces each
1/3 cup Fine Fresh Bread Crumbs (see page 60)
1 1/2 tablespoons finely chopped fresh basil or 2 teaspoons dried
1 teaspoon mashed, pressed, or very finely minced garlic
1/2 teaspoon salt
1/4 teaspoon pepper, preferably freshly ground
3 tablespoons olive oil

Cut tomatoes in half crosswise. One half at a time, lightly squeeze tomato halves to press out some of the seeds and juice; don't aim to be too thorough here. Cut out the stem core, but don't penetrate the tomato too deeply or it may fall apart when cooked. Arrange tomato halves cut side up on prepared baking dish. Blend crumbs, basil, garlic, salt, and pepper in mixing bowl and press lightly onto tops of tomatoes. Drizzle with olive oil. Broil tomatoes for 8 to 10 minutes, or until heated through and lightly browned on top, watching carefully to make sure they don't burn. Transfer tomatoes to a serving dish with a spatula. Serve immediately.

CHEDDAR-STUFFED TOMATOES

4 main-course or 6 to 8 side-dish servings

❦ *These delicious tomatoes are excellent with ham or pork. They may also be the main course of a light supper or luncheon. A pasta or rice salad makes a very agreeable accompaniment.*

PRELIMINARIES

1. Set rack in center of oven.
2. Preheat oven to 425°F 20 minutes before baking.
3. Select a shallow baking dish just large enough to hold the tomatoes. Oil the dish lightly.

4 medium or 6 to 8 smaller tomatoes (1½ to 2 pounds)
½ teaspoon salt
6 tablespoons butter
¼ cup minced onion
¼ cup minced green bell pepper
¼ cup minced boiled ham
6 tablespoons fine cracker crumbs
1 cup (about 4 ounces) shredded sharp Cheddar cheese
Salt to taste
¼ teaspoon pepper, preferably freshly ground

Cut off the top of each tomato, slicing just deeply enough to remove all of the stem callus. Scoop out pulp (including seeds) with a teaspoon, leaving a wall a good ¼ inch thick all around the tomato; reserve pulp. Sprinkle insides of the scooped-out tomatoes with ½ teaspoon salt and turn upside down on a triple thickness of paper toweling. Let drain for 15 to 20 minutes.

Melt butter in a small skillet over moderate heat and add onion, green pepper, and ham. Cook mixture very slowly, stirring occasionally, for about 7 minutes, or until vegetables are soft but not brown. Chop reserved tomato pulp into small pieces and add it to the skillet. Raise heat to high and, stirring constantly, cook until mixture is thick and no longer looks juicy. Scrape contents of skillet into mixing bowl and let cool for a few minutes. Stir in 3 tablespoons cracker crumbs, the cheese, salt to taste, and pepper. Stir lightly to blend.

Sprinkle insides of tomatoes with 1½ tablespoons cracker crumbs and arrange in oiled baking dish. Spoon stuffing mixture into the tomatoes and sprinkle with remaining 1½ tablespoons cracker crumbs. Bake for about 20 minutes, or until tomatoes look cooked and are lightly browned on top. Let tomatoes stand for 5 minutes to firm the stuffing. Transfer to a serving plate with a spatula and serve immediately.

Turnips (and Rutabagas)

The turnips available at most supermarkets are of two kinds: the ordinary white globe turnip, often sold in bunches, and the larger reddish-brown-skinned rutabaga. Both kinds are perfectly delicious, and it bewilders me that so many people shun turnips and rutabagas as a matter of course. Turnips can be used in place of a starchy vegetable or other starch, yet they have only half the calories of potatoes and a quarter the calories of noodles.

With white turnips it's the smaller ones, preferably not much bigger than golf balls, that have the most delicate and subtle flavor. Choose white turnips carefully; they often turn out to be soft, pithy, or woody. You can partially test for quality by pressing the turnips with your fingers to see if they are rock-hard, as they should be. Perhaps a better piece of advice is to buy turnips only during the peak of their season, late summer through early winter.

Rutabagas are more reliable in quality than white turnips, and they are available nearly year-round at the supermarket. Unless you are cooking for a crowd, it is more practical to buy small rutabagas, but grapefruit-size specimens, which taste just fine, can be cut up and stored for a week at least in the refrigerator if wrapped in plastic and then in foil.

MASTER RECIPE

Glazed Turnips or Rutabagas

4 to 6 servings

Turnips are especially good with duck or pork and may also be served with beef or lamb.

Step 1: Trimming the Turnips or Rutabagas

2 pounds white turnips or rutabagas

Peel white turnips with paring knife or vegetable peeler and cut lengthwise in halves or quarters, depending on size. The skin of rutabagas is quite tough and thick. Using a sharp, sturdy utility knife, cut off skin and root ends and peel the skin deeply, exposing the dark golden flesh of the interior. Cut rutabaga into ½-inch cubes.

STEP 2: COOKING THE TURNIPS OR RUTABAGAS

2 cups water
3 tablespoons butter
2 teaspoons sugar
1 teaspoon salt
⅛ teaspoon pepper, perferably white and freshly ground

Combine prepared turnips or rutabagas with all ingredients in a 10-inch skillet and bring to a slow boil. Cover and cook over moderate heat for 10 to 15 minutes, or until turnips or rutabagas are almost tender. Uncover skillet, raise heat to high, and boil down the cooking liquid to a syrupy glaze, stirring frequently.

AHEAD OF TIME: Turnips or rutabagas may be prepared 2 or 3 days ahead and refrigerated in a tightly closed container. Reheat slowly in a covered skillet or saucepan, adding a tablespoon of water to prevent scorching, and stirring often.

Variation: RUTABAGA PURÉE WITH MUSHROOMS

4 to 5 servings

❦ *This unusual and stunningly fine purée is excellent with duck, turkey, or pork.*

Glazed Turnips or Rutabagas; use rutabagas and cook very soft
4 tablespoons soft butter
Mushroom Stuffing, page 553
Salt and pepper, preferably freshly ground, to taste
Sherry
Fresh lemon juice

Cook rutabagas until very soft—25 minutes or longer—before proceeding to boil down cooking liquid to a glaze. Turn into a bowl, add soft butter, and beat hard with a wire whip to form a lumpy purée. Beat in mushroom stuffing and season to taste with salt, pepper, Sherry, and lemon juice.

Variation: GLAZED TURNIPS OR RUTABAGAS IN MEAT STOCK

4 to 5 servings

❦ *Cooking turnips or rutabagas in meat stock helps to disguise the overly strong taste these vegetables sometimes acquire when large and mature. Serve in place of potatoes with a roast.*

Glazed Turnips or Rutabagas

SUBSTITUTE: Beef Stock, page 24, or canned broth for water
OMIT: Salt
ADD: 2 tablespoons minced fresh parsley

Proceed according to the Master Recipe, substituting stock or broth for water and omitting salt. If you should accidentally reduce the cooking liquid too much, causing it to separate, add 1 or 2 tablespoons water, remove skillet from heat, and shake skillet until glaze is reconstituted. Fold in parsley, adjust seasoning, and serve.

WATERCRESS

Watercress adds a delicious, peppery bite to salads and sandwiches. Trim off and discard any large stems, as these are likely to be tough or stringy and very hot. Watercress may be added to a potato soup or used as the star ingredient in a delicious cream soup. It may also be stir-fried or prepared as for spinach.

For years I wondered why my watercress wilted and yellowed so quickly once I brought it home—until I began to notice how smart vegetable dealers stored it at the market. They placed it upside down in a couple of inches of water, and if you store it this way at home (in the refrigerator, of course), it will last for at least 2 days and sometimes longer. Watercress grows underwater, so it makes sense that it likes to be stored this way too.

RICE and DRIED BEANS and PEAS

In the traditional American diet, rice and dried beans and peas, or legumes, have been cast in a supporting role as accompaniments for the true stars of a meal—meat, poultry, or fish. This practice, however, is changing. As we have become increasingly concerned about the calories and saturated fats contained in meat, we have begun to experiment with new ways of eating in which carbohydrates play a more central role. Many people now consider a large portion of rice flavored with a bit of meat and a good sauce a delicious and satisfying dinner, especially if accompanied by well-prepared fresh vegetables. In the rice-dependent cultures of the Far East, where rice-based meals are eaten daily, some of the most common serious diseases of the West, including obesity, are relatively rare. The legumes may also be used as meat extenders, or, if they are teamed with cheese or sour cream, as is typical in Mexican cooking, they may substitute for meat altogether. In addition to their high carbohydrate value, legumes contain a great deal of good-quality protein, and with the exception of soybeans, they are very low in fat.

Most of the rice and legume dishes in this chapter can be served either as accompaniments or, with the use of a little imagination, as meal mainstays. An added advantage of rice and legumes is their very low cost.

RICE

There are many methods of cooking rice, and they work equally well; I have chosen steaming as the Master Recipe because it seems to me the simplest. Before proceeding, read the recipe through, especially if you are inclined to be a bit nervous about rice cookery. All cooks want more or less the same sort of rice: fluffy, separate grains that are thoroughly tender but not gummy, mushy, or watery. However, personal preferences vary with respect to texture and consistency; the notes following the recipe title tell you how you can control rice cookery and get the kind of rice you like best.

Raw rice varies considerably in starch and moisture content. Therefore, sometimes your rice will be on the soft and creamy side, while at other times the grains will be drier and quite al dente. Don't expect it to turn out the same way every time.

TYPES OF RICE: The most commonly available rice is *long-grain white rice* (sometimes called "extra" long-grain). If properly made, long-grain white rice is very fluffy, the grains dry and separate. It may be used in virtually any recipe calling for rice. *Short-grain white rice* is similar to long-grain, but it tends to be creamier and to compact itself more than does the long-grain variety. For this reason, short-grain rice is often used for croquettes, rice rings, and other dishes in which it is important that the rice cohere; you may, however, use long-grain rice, which is easier to find at the supermarket, for these dishes too. Italian *Arborio rice,* available at specialty shops and some supermarkets, is a short-grain and very plump rice. It is the rice of choice for the famous Italian risotto, but other forms of white rice make a good risotto also. *Converted rice* has been pressure-steamed prior to being polished. The steaming serves to lock in some of the nutrients that are otherwise lost when hull and bran are removed during polishing. Converted rice retains its shape very well during cooking and just about never becomes sticky or gummy. For these reasons, many cooks prefer it over ordinary white rice. *Brown rice* differs from white rice in that most of the bran covering the grains is retained during processing; thus brown rice is more nutritious than white. Brown rice has a nutty and slightly bitter flavor that goes well with some foods and not so well with others. It cannot be used successfully in all recipes calling for rice. Last, there's *wild rice,* which is not a true rice at all but is rather the seed of a grass that grows in the American Great Lakes. Wild rice has a rich, musty flavor, making it a wonderful addition to stuffings and casseroles. Because it is harvested by hand, wild rice is always very expensive. Prepare wild rice according to the directions on the package. Typically it is combined with ordinary rice or some other ingredient.

Rescuing Overcooked Rice: Using a fork—not a spoon—stir in as much soft butter or olive oil as is necessary to give the rice a creamy, rather than gummy, appearance. Serve immediately, for it will quickly get sticky again.

Rescuing Undercooked Rice: Add a few tablespoons of boiling water to the rice in the saucepan and cook gently for 1 minute. Remove from heat and let stand 5 minutes, or for as long as it takes for the rice to become tender.

MASTER RECIPE

Steamed Rice

Makes 3 cups, serving 3 to 4

There are two distinct phases in the cooking of steamed rice. First the rice is simmered in water or some other liquid; then it is removed from the heat and allowed to stand for 5 to 15 minutes, during which time the grains swell and become completely tender. The most common cause of rice failure, I believe, is the mistaken practice—promoted by the instructions on many packages of rice—of cooking rice by simmering alone. If this practice is followed, an excessive quantity of liquid must be added in order to prevent scorching, and this causes the rice to become mushy and clumped together, and gives the ends of the grains a frayed, exploded look.

Instructions for steaming brown rice appear at the end of this recipe.

Increasing and Decreasing the Recipe: As a rule, the smaller the amount of raw rice you start with, the greater the proportion of liquid to rice that you should use. If you are cooking only ½ cup of raw rice (about 2 servings), you should add a full cup of liquid to make cooked rice of average consistency and texture. Conversely, if you are making 2 cups of raw rice (6 to 8 servings), use only 3 to 3¼ cups of liquid (or 1½ cups water per cup of rice). No matter how much rice you prepare, however, never use less than 1½ cups liquid per cup of raw rice.

When cooking over 3 cups of raw rice it is wise to use a wide skillet or casserole rather than a narrow, deep saucepan. If piled to a depth of more than 4 inches, cooked rice tends to pack down and clump together.

1 cup long- or short-grain white rice
1¾ cups water*
½ teaspoon salt
2 tablespoons soft butter

Measure rice, water, and salt into a heavy-bottomed 2-quart saucepan or casserole with a tight-fitting lid. Swirl pan gently by the handle to combine ingredients, then set over moderately high heat. As soon as the water is bubbling hard around the edges of the pan, stir up rice quickly with a fork, cover tightly, and turn heat down to the lowest point possible. *Without lifting the lid,* simmer rice for exactly 15 minutes, timing from the point you cover the pan.

Slide rice off heat and, still without lifting the lid, let stand exactly 5 minutes. Quickly sneak out a forkful of rice to taste, immediately covering the pan again. If the rice is not quite tender enough, let stand, covered, an additional 3 to 10 minutes. (If the rice is very hard, or if it has become overcooked, see rescues on page 617.) Add soft butter and toss very lightly with a fork—never stir rice with a spoon, or you will mash the grains and make them stick together—then gently scrape with a fork into a serving bowl.

AHEAD OF TIME: Provided your saucepan is heavy and retains heat well, you can extend the rest period up to 30 minutes. The rice will be a bit soft but otherwise fine. Add butter just before serving. Leftover rice may be refrigerated in a covered container for several days. To reheat, turn into a heavy pan, sprinkle with a few tablespoons water, and place over a very low flame for a few minutes.

PREPARING BROWN RICE ACCORDING TO THE MASTER RECIPE: Use 2½ cups water and simmer for 40 minutes. Lift the lid and taste. If the rice is nearly tender, remove from heat and let stand 10 minutes, covered. If the rice is still quite hard, simmer an additional 5 to 10 minutes, adding a few tablespoons boiling water if the rice seems in danger of scorching. Remove from heat and let rest 5 minutes.

*The amount of liquid added determines the texture and consistency of rice. If you like rice with very firm, small grains, use only 1½ cups liquid. For moist, rather soft rice with large swollen grains, use 2 cups liquid and extend the rest period to 10 minutes.

Variation: CURRIED RICE

Makes 4 servings

Steamed Rice, using white or brown rice

ADD:
- 1/4 cup finely chopped green bell pepper
- 1/4 cup finely chopped onion
- 1 1/2 teaspoons mild curry powder or 1 teaspoon hot (Madras) curry powder
- 1/4 teaspoon ground ginger
- 1/4 teaspoon ground allspice

SUBSTITUTE: Chicken Stock, page 26, or canned broth for water

OMIT: Salt

In the same saucepan in which you plan to cook the rice, sauté pepper and onion in the 2 tablespoons butter called for in the Master Recipe over moderate heat for about 5 minutes, or until partially softened but not brown. Stir in curry powder, ginger, and allspice, and cook slowly, stirring, about 1 minute longer. Add rice and chicken stock or broth but do not add salt. Cook according to the Master Recipe.

Variation: FRUITED RICE

Makes 4 servings

❦ *This is excellent with pork.*

Steamed Rice, using white or brown rice

SUBSTITUTE: Strained fresh orange juice for all or part of the water

ADD:
- 1/4 cup dried currants or chopped raisins
- 1/4 cup chopped dried apricots
- 1/8 teaspoon nutmeg, preferably freshly grated
- 1/3 cup (about 1 1/2 ounces) slivered almonds, toasted, or coarsely chopped walnuts or pecans

Proceed according to the Master Recipe, substituting orange juice for all or part of the water and adding raisins or currants, apricots, and nutmeg at the outset of cooking. Toss rice with nuts when you add the butter.

Variation: MIDDLE EASTERN RICE

Makes 4 servings

❦ *Good with chicken, pork, beef, and lamb.*

Steamed Rice, using white or brown rice
SUBSTITUTE: Beef Stock, page 24, or canned broth for water
OMIT: Salt
ADD: ½ cup raisins
½ teaspoon cinnamon
⅛ teaspoon ground allspice
⅓ cup (about 1½ ounces) slivered almonds, toasted, or pine nuts

Proceed according to the Master Recipe, substituting stock or broth for water, omitting salt, and adding raisins, cinnamon, and allspice at the outset of cooking. Toss rice with nuts when you add the butter.

Variation: PARSLEYED RICE

Makes 3 to 4 servings

❦ *This is particularly nice with broiled or poached fish.*

Steamed Rice, using white or brown rice
ADD: ¼ cup finely chopped parsley

Proceed according to the Master Recipe, adding parsley when you toss the rice with butter.

Variation: RICE WITH CHEESE

Makes 4 servings

❦ *This is excellent when prepared with brown rice. Serve with rare beef or lamb.*

Steamed Rice, using white or brown rice
½ cup (2 ounces) freshly grated Parmesan cheese
Freshly ground pepper
⅓ cup (about 1½ ounces) slivered almonds, toasted (optional)
1 to 2 tablespoons additional butter (optional)

Prepare rice according to the Master Recipe. After tossing with 2 tablespoons soft butter, sprinkle with 1/4 cup of the cheese and a few grindings of pepper. Toss briefly. Add remaining cheese and a bit more pepper and toss again. The idea here is to blend the rice and cheese quickly and gently so as to keep the rice grains separate and light; if you overblend the rice and cheese, the dish will turn out gummy. Top, if you wish, with nuts and additional soft butter.

Variation: RICE WITH MUSHROOMS

Makes 4 servings

❦ *This is very good with chicken, turkey, or veal.*

Steamed Rice, using white or brown rice
Mushroom Stuffing, page 553
2 tablespoons finely chopped fresh parsley

Prepare rice according to the Master Recipe. Add hot mushroom stuffing, toss quickly with a fork, sprinkle with parsley, and serve.

Variation: RICE WITH ALMONDS OR PINE NUTS

Makes 4 servings

Steamed Rice, using white or brown rice
INCREASE: Butter to 4 tablespoons
ADD: 3/4 cup (3 ounces) slivered almonds, toasted, or pine nuts
3 tablespoons finely chopped fresh parsley

Proceed according to the Master Recipe, but increase soft butter to 4 tablespoons and toss also with nuts and parsley.

Variation: SAFFRON RICE

Makes 4 servings

❦ *This is traditionally served with shellfish and red meats. A half teaspoon saffron is definitely better than 1/4 teaspoon, but then saffron is extremely expensive.*

Steamed Rice, using white rice

ADD: 1/4 to 1/2 teaspoon loosely packed saffron threads
1 1/2 tablespoons finely chopped fresh parsley (optional)

Crush the saffron threads in a mortar or with the back of a spoon. Proceed according to the Master Recipe, adding saffron at the outset of cooking and, if you wish, tossing the rice with parsley when you add the butter.

Variation: RICE PILAF

Makes 4 servings

❦ *Unlike other steamed rice variation recipes, rice pilaf involves both changes in ingredients and an additional cooking procedure, the sautéing of the rice, which gives the dish its characteristic brown color and special texture. Serve rice pilaf with any poultry or meat.*

Steamed Rice, using white rice

ADD: 2 tablespoons olive oil
1/4 cup finely chopped onion

SUBSTITUTE: 1/4 cup dry white wine and 1 1/2 cups Chicken Stock, page 26, or canned broth for water

DECREASE: Salt to 1/4 teaspoon

ADD: Freshly ground pepper

In the same saucepan in which you plan to cook the rice, sauté the onion in olive oil over moderate heat for 5 to 7 minutes, or just until the onion begins to color slightly around the edges. Add rice and sauté, stirring constantly, for 2 to 3 minutes longer, or until rice is covered with golden-brown speckles. Add wine, stock or broth, and 1/4 teaspoon salt and cook according to the Master Recipe, seasoning with fresh pepper when you toss with butter.

DRIED BEANS AND PEAS (DRIED LEGUMES)

There are numerous varieties of beans and peas, or "legumes," that become starch-laden when fully mature and may then be shelled and dried. Among the more popular kinds of legumes are soybeans, red kidney beans, pinkish pinto beans, the various white beans (pea, navy, Great Northern), black beans, dried lima beans, chickpeas, split peas, flageolets, lentils, and black-eyed peas (cowpeas). Each differs with respect to size, color, thickness of skin, texture, and taste, but all share a certain earthiness. If you are an experimenting type, you might enjoy making substitutions—kidney or pinto beans in black bean soup (the soup will then be red), lentils in a recipe for chili beans, chickpeas instead of white beans in a recipe for baked beans. You will likely have to adjust cooking times, seasonings, and other factors, but you are just about guaranteed to come up with a very good dish.

Soaking or Parboiling: Except for certain split peas, all dried legumes must either be soaked overnight in cold water or boiled briefly and allowed to stand in the hot water before being cooked. There is general agreement that the water in which legumes have been soaked or preliminarily boiled should be discarded, as it may contain traces of dirt or pesticides lifted from the legumes. Moreover, when you discard the soaking water you are also getting rid of many of the gas-producing components of the beans, because they are water-soluble.

Acidic foods such as tomato sauce, vinegar, and molasses should be added to legumes only in the final stages of cooking, as they inhibit the legumes from becoming tender. Salt has a similar, if less pronounced, effect. Out of curiosity, I once prepared baked beans without precooking the beans to near tenderness in a nonacidic medium. I learned my lesson. Even after a full 10 hours in the oven, the beans were not completely tender!

Canned Dried Peas and Beans: These are convenient, but they are invariably mushy and slightly off in taste, and their canning liquid is distinctly slimy. Rinse before using. The legumes will benefit from a stewing in butter or olive oil, with some garlic added as a flavoring.

Rescuing Overcooked Dried Peas and Beans: Turn the legumes into a purée following the instructions given on page 625.

MASTER RECIPE

Boiled White Beans or Other Dried Beans or Peas

Makes 6 to 8 servings

❦ *If you are serving the beans or peas plain as a side dish, dress them with a goodly quantity of butter, olive oil, or bacon fat and sprinkle liberally with salt (you may want a full teaspoon or more) and freshly ground black or white pepper. Crumbled bacon, freshly grated Parmesan cheese, or minced fresh parsley may be folded in. Dried beans, particularly flageolets, white beans, and lima beans, are a traditional—and excellent—accompaniment for roast lamb and are also good with beef.*

Step 1: Washing and Soaking

1 pound (2 to 2½ cups) white beans or other dried beans or peas
1½ quarts water

Turn the beans into a colander and carefully sort through them, picking out any pebbles or bits of dried vegetation that may be mixed in. Rinse under a hard stream of very warm water.

Place beans in saucepan or pot and cover with water. If you are in no hurry to cook them, cover and soak the beans for 10 hours, or overnight. To cook them quickly, bring to a boil and boil rapidly for 2 minutes. Remove from heat, cover the saucepan or pot tightly, and let stand 1 hour.

Step 2: Cooking

4 cups water
1 large onion, peeled and stuck with 1 whole clove
1 to 2 garlic cloves, peeled
1 bay leaf
¼ teaspoon whole dried thyme

Drain soaked beans and rinse well. Return to saucepan and add 4 cups fresh water. Add all remaining ingredients, cover, and cook the beans at a gentle simmer until tender, 1 to 2 hours depending on their type and condition. Drain in a colander, discarding onion and bay leaf (the garlic will have melted away) but reserving some or all of the cooking liquid if it is required for a variation recipe.

STORAGE: Beans will keep 3 or 4 days. Turn them into a storage container and stir in a tablespoon or so of oil. Cover tightly and refrigerate.

Variation: PURÉE OF DRIED BEANS

Makes 8 servings

❦ *Puréed beans are a classic accompaniment to roast lamb and are also good with beef roasts and steaks.*

Boiled White Beans or Other Dried Beans or Peas, using white or lima beans or flageolets
4 tablespoons soft butter
1 to 1½ teaspoons salt, to taste
¼ to ½ teaspoon pepper, preferably white and freshly ground, to taste
Fresh lemon juice and/or dry Sherry
2 to 3 tablespoons minced fresh parsley (optional)

Prepare beans according to the Master Recipe, but reserve the onion (discard clove) and the cooking water. Purée beans and onion in blender or food processor, leaving a few small unblended bits. (If using a blender, purée beans in batches and add spoonfuls of the cooking water to get the mixture moving.) Turn beans into a heavy-bottomed saucepan and set over low heat. Gradually beat in butter plus enough cooking water to make the purée just thick enough to hold its shape softly on a fork. It must be neither pasty nor soupy. Season with salt, pepper, and drops of lemon juice and/or Sherry. Just before serving, fold in parsley if you wish.

Variation: CHICKPEA OR WHITE BEAN SALAD

Makes 8 servings

❦ *This is usually served with cold poultry or meat, with wedges of hard-cooked eggs and ripe tomatoes on the side.*

Boiled White Beans or Other Dried Beans or Peas, using chickpeas or white beans
1 cup (double recipe) Vinaigrette Dressing, page 117, made with garlic
1 large onion, cut in shreds ½ inch long and ⅛ inch thick
1 large rib celery, cut in shreds ½ inch long and ⅛ inch thick
¼ cup chopped fresh parsley
Olive oil and vinegar, if needed
Fresh lemon juice, salt, and pepper, preferably freshly ground

Turn hot, drained chickpeas or white beans into a 4-quart bowl, fold in dressing, and let stand at room temperature for about 20 minutes, stirring several times. Cover and chill at least 1 hour, or overnight. About 15 minutes before serving, add onion, celery, parsley, and, if the beans seem dry, spoonfuls of olive oil and a few drops of vinegar. Let stand at room temperature, then correct the seasoning with lemon juice and, if needed, salt and pepper.

Variation: WHITE BEANS NIÇOISE

Makes 6 to 8 servings

❦ *This can be made several days in advance and refrigerated—it will improve in flavor upon standing—but should be served at room temperature or slightly warm. It is an excellent accompaniment for cold meat, particularly turkey, pork, ham, and lamb, and is thus a good dish to consider for a buffet or picnic.*

2 cups chopped onions
½ cup olive oil
Boiled White Beans or Other Dried Beans or Peas, using white beans
3 cups peeled, seeded, diced tomatoes, fresh or canned (see page 607; reserve juice if using canned tomatoes)
¼ cup chopped pitted oil-cured black olives
2 teaspoons mashed, pressed, or very finely minced garlic
2 to 4 minced, well-drained anchovy fillets (optional)

¼ teaspoon dried orange peel or ½ teaspoon freshly grated orange zest
Salt and pepper, preferably freshly ground, to taste
⅓ cup minced fresh parsley

Sauté onions in olive oil over low heat until soft but not brown, about 8 minutes. Add beans and all other ingredients except salt, pepper, and parsley. Cover and simmer over low heat for 30 minutes, adding a bit of water or tomato juice if the mixture threatens to scorch. Taste and add salt and pepper as necessary; the olives may have made the dish sufficiently salty. Stir in parsley just before serving.

Variation: CHILI BEANS

Makes 4 to 6 main-course or 8 side-dish servings

❦*Accompanied by corn bread and a tossed salad or cole slaw and topped, if you wish, with grated sharp Cheddar cheese, this makes a good meatless main dish. It may also be served as a side dish with fried eggs, sausages, or hamburgers.*

6 slices bacon, diced
2 cups chopped onions
1 cup chopped green bell peppers
Boiled White Beans or Other Dried Beans or Peas, using red kidney or pinto beans
1 quart liquid: bean cooking water plus tomato juice or water
2 cups thick canned tomato purée
2 to 3 tablespoons chili powder, to taste
2 tablespoons cider vinegar
2 teaspoons oregano
1 teaspoon ground cumin
1½ teaspoons mashed, pressed, or very finely minced garlic
1 large bay leaf
1½ teaspoons salt

Sauté bacon until crisp in 3½- to 4-quart saucepan. Add onions and green peppers and cook over moderately high heat, stirring frequently, until onions begin to color around the edges. Add beans and all other ingredients, and simmer, partially covered, for 30 to 40 minutes. Taste for seasoning, adding more chili powder if you wish. Discard bay leaf.

Variation: FRIED BEANS WITH SAUSAGE AND ONIONS

Makes 4 to 6 servings

❦ *Serve this with eggs in place of hash brown potatoes.*

1½ cups (about 12 ounces) sausage meat
3 tablespoons neutral vegetable oil or bacon fat
3 cups chopped onions
½ recipe ***Boiled White Beans or Other Dried Beans or Peas***, using red or black beans (about 3 cups cooked)
Salt and pepper, preferably freshly ground, to taste
2 to 3 tablespoons finely chopped fresh parsley (optional)

Crumble sausage meat into a heavy-bottomed 10- to 12-inch skillet, stir in oil, and cook over moderately high heat, stirring, until sausage is no longer pink. Add onions and cook until both onions and sausage are lightly browned. Spread beans evenly over sausage mixture and press with metal spatula to mash a bit. Cook without stirring for several minutes, or until beans begin to crust at the edges. Break up the beans with the spatula, then press into a new cake on the bottom of the skillet. Again let beans become crusty. Repeat this procedure two or three times more, or until the whole mass looks slightly browned and dry. Season with salt and pepper and sprinkle with optional parsley. Serve immediately.

Variation: BAKED BEANS

Makes 6 to 8 servings

❦ *This recipe does not pretend to authenticity with respect to tradition but it is delicious indeed.*

PRELIMINARIES

1. Set rack in center of oven.
2. Preheat oven to 275°F 20 minutes before baking.
3. Select a 3-quart bean crock or heavy, lidded pot.

Boiled White Beans or Other Dried Beans or Peas; use small white beans, cook only 45 to 60 minutes, or until not quite tender, and reserve cooking liquid

8 ounces salt pork (including rind), diced

1 cup chopped onions

½ cup dark molasses

½ cup packed dark brown sugar

3 to 4 cups liquid: bean cooking liquid plus water

1 tablespoon dry mustard

½ teaspoon ground cloves

2 teaspoons salt

½ to 1 teaspoon pepper, preferably freshly ground

Drain partially cooked beans, reserving cooking liquid. Turn beans into crock or pot and mix in salt pork, onions, molasses, and sugar. Add just enough of the bean cooking liquid (and water, if necessary) to come to top of beans. Stir in seasonings. Cover the crock or pot and bake for 4 to 5 hours, or until beans are very tender. If you wish, uncover the crock during the last 30 minutes of cooking so that the beans can form a slight crust on top.

THE HONEST LOAF: YEAST BREADS

Even though they may agree that, by and large, commercially available bread is just plain awful, many people continue to rely on store-bought loaves because they find it too much trouble to make bread at home. To get people out of this bind, I have tried in this chapter to provide an approach to bread-making that is uncomplicated, virtually fail-proof, and time-efficient. There are just three Master Recipes here, but, with their variations, they make nearly all of the yeast breads commonly consumed in American homes—including even such treats as raised doughnuts and pizza. Best of all, the Master Recipes themselves are so simple and so similar to one another that they can easily be learned by heart. There is no reason why everyone cannot bring the same confident, nonchalant attitude to bread-baking that nineteenth-century New England housewives did. They, according to the diaries and other records they left behind, routinely baked up to 20 loaves of bread every week.

Because bread-baking differs in important respects from the other culinary arts, this chapter contains several unusual features, all intended to instill a sense of confidence and to give flexibility. The Master Recipe for basic white bread is intentionally very detailed so that it can be used as an instructional text by a novice baker. The Master Recipes for egg bread and hard rolls are keyed to the white bread teaching recipe so that you can readily turn back to that detailed recipe if you encounter any problems in the middle of making a bread. Two tables appear at the end of the chapter. The first shows how bread-making can be slowed or temporarily arrested at several points by refrigerating or freezing the dough, thus allowing a busy person to prepare bread over a period of several days. The second table lists rescues for common bread-making problems, including the most feared disaster—a nonrising dough.

Notes on Bread Ingredients

As soon as you've acquired a feel for bread-making you may want to vary the Master Recipes in special ways of your own. The following list of typical bread ingredients is intended to provide basic information for the neophyte and to suggest, for the experienced baker, where the boundaries of safe experimentation lie.

YEAST: Yeast can be purchased in either of two forms: Granulated dry yeast comes in little packets; and moist compressed yeast is sold in cakes weighing from 0.6 ounce to several ounces. One 2½-teaspoon package of dry yeast and one 0.6-ounce yeast cake are equivalent in their leavening action. In terms of final results it makes no difference whether you use granulated or cake yeast. However, dry yeast will keep, with or without refrigeration, for a year or more (note the expiration date stamped on the package), while cake yeast, which must be refrigerated, lasts only a couple of weeks before developing spots of mold.

SUGAR AND OTHER SWEETENERS: Any bread may be sweetened or not, as you wish. A small amount of sugar flavors the bread without making it noticeably sweet and somewhat speeds the rising process. Doughnuts or other sweet breads, of course, contain significant amounts of sugar or of some other sweetener. A quarter cup or so of sugar per 4 cups of flour will noticeably speed the rise and make the baked loaf light and puffy. However, more than ½ cup sweetener per 4 cups flour will make the dough sticky and hard to handle, and slow the rising to a crawl.

SALT: In addition to giving flavor to bread, salt has the effect of slowing the growth of yeast. This latter function is crucial to successful bread-making, for if the yeast multiplies at a rampant pace, thereby speeding up the first rise of the bread, the baked loaf will be dull in flavor and texture. If for any reason you must omit or diminish the salt called for in the following recipes, let the bread rise in a cool place. This will also slow the growth of the yeast.

WATER, MILK, AND MILK PRODUCTS: With the exception of breads that are crusty and chewy, for example, hard rolls and bagels, most breads contain milk or a milk product like buttermilk or yogurt. Milk imparts a soft, dense, cakelike texture. Cultured milk products such as buttermilk and yogurt give bread body and a springy texture that I much favor.

BUTTER AND SHORTENING: Fats make bread tender and rich. This is why egg breads are made with a great deal of fat, while hard rolls, which should be crusty and chewy, contain none at all. Except in small quantities, butter and shortening act as yeast inhibitors, and adding too much of either to a bread dough can result in a dense loaf.

EGGS: While eggs tend to slow the rising of bread doughs outside the oven, they make breads rise dramatically during baking, resulting in a light, tender, puffy loaf. Thus a loaf of egg bread made with 25 percent less flour than a loaf of white bread will be just as large as the white loaf.

FLOUR: Loaves made with bread flour, which is especially high in gluten (the elastic protein that is activated by kneading and that makes bread chewy), may rise a bit more in the oven than those based on all-purpose flour. However, all-purpose flour, preferably unbleached, also makes delicious bread. Determined connoisseurs may enjoy experimenting with different *brands* of flour, either all-purpose or bread. Since each brand will be blended of a slightly different proportion of hard (high-gluten) and soft (low-gluten) wheats, each will yield—to the discerning palate—a slightly different loaf.

FOOD PROCESSOR NOTES:

Any of the yeast doughs in this chapter may be prepared using a food processor. Just be sure that your machine is strong enough to do the job. If it has balked in the past when asked to grind meat or do some other kind of heavy labor, it is not capable of mixing and kneading bread dough. Fit the machine with the blade recommended by the manufacturer for bread dough (usually the metal chopping blade) and modify the first four steps of any of the bread recipes as follows:

STEP 1: Add water to container; sprinkle on sugar and dry yeast (or cake yeast cut into cubes). Let dissolve and proof. Process 1 second.

STEP 2: Add liquid, salt, and any additional sugar; process 5 seconds.

STEPS 3 AND 4: Add first part of the flour; process 10 seconds. Add any shortening required; process 5 seconds. Add the rest of the flour (including flour reserved for kneading) and process for 20 seconds; the dough should detach itself from the sides of the container and wad around the blade. Be careful not to overprocess the dough or you will make it hot and kill the yeast. Let dough rest for 3 minutes, then knead for a minute or two by hand.

Proceed according to the recipe.

MASTER RECIPE

Basic American White Bread

Makes 1 large or 2 smaller loaves

❦ *This recipe produces a loaf like the one my Grandmother Rosalind used to make—yeasty, wheaty, and unsweet in flavor, light and yet quite chewy to the bite. Alas, I never got the recipe for her wonderful bread, which we visiting Easterners used to spread with honey my grandfather harvested from his hives in back of the house, but I like to think that this loaf would have pleased my grandmother, whose cooking, born of the turn-of-the-century Midwest, was simple and honest.*

Step 1: Dissolving and Proofing the Yeast

⅓ cup warm water
1 package (2½ teaspoons) dry yeast or 1 cake (0.6 ounce) compressed yeast
1½ teaspoons sugar

Yeast is a living thing, a fungus microorganism. If it is alive and healthy to begin with, and if it is handled with care, it will feed on the flour in bread dough, multiplying rapidly and "breathing out" bubbles of carbon dioxide gas as it grows. The gas bubbles lighten the dough and cause it to rise, much the same way that air causes a balloon to inflate. The first step of the Master Recipe is to dissolve the yeast in water, adding also a bit of sugar to feed the yeast and get its growth started (to "activate" it).

Measure ⅓ cup of warm water into a fairly deep, steep-sided 3- to 4-quart mixing bowl. "Warm," in this context, means a temperature just slightly higher than body temperature.

TIP: One funny-looking but very accurate way of gauging the water temperature is to put the forefinger of one hand into the water and the forefinger of your other hand into your mouth; the two fingers should be registering roughly the same degree of warmth. A thermometer may also be used as long as it registers temperatures as low as 100°.

The reason that bread dough is made with warm ingredients and allowed to rise in a warm place is that warmth speeds the reproduction of the yeast and therefore the rising of the dough. But if the temperature gets too hot—and, to be absolutely safe, any temperature over 100°F should be considered dangerously high, especially for compressed yeasts—the yeast dies. Cold and cool temperatures, by contrast, only slow down the growth of yeast, without killing it. Thus, if you doubt your ability to gauge temperatures, it is always wiser to dissolve yeast in tepid water than in water that is too hot. I suspect that the cause of nearly all failed bread-making ventures is yeast death brought on by the dissolving of the yeast in excessively warm water.

Once the water is measured into the bowl, sprinkle the dry yeast over it or mash the cake yeast into it with the back of the spoon. Stir 1½ teaspoons sugar into the yeast mixture and set it aside in a slightly warm (not over 100°F), draft-free place (an unlit oven or a cupboard is ideal). After about 10 minutes you should see frothy bubbles around the edge of the bowl; they indicate that the yeast is indeed alive and "breathing." If not, give the yeast another 10 minutes—perhaps the room is cold and the yeast is slow to get going. If after 20 minutes there is still no sign of activity, the yeast is probably dead. Throw the mixture out and start again with fresh yeast.

STEP 2: ADDING THE LIQUID AND SALT

Either 1½ cups buttermilk *or* 1 cup yogurt (preferably made without gelatin, starch, or other thickeners) and ½ cup milk
2½ teaspoons salt (2 teaspoons if you use buttermilk that contains added salt)

If the buttermilk (or yogurt plus milk) is cold, stir it over low heat until it has warmed slightly. Remember once again that body temperature is quite warm enough. (If the milk products are at room temperature, they need not be heated.) Pour the buttermilk or yogurt plus milk into the yeast mixture, add salt, and stir to blend thoroughly.

STEP 3: ADDING THE FLOUR

3½ to 4 cups unbleached all-purpose flour (measure by scooping cup into large container of flour and sweeping off excess with the back of a knife)

Add 2 cups of the flour to the yeast mixture and beat vigorously with a wooden spoon for a minute or two, or until the batter is smooth and elastic. Add 1½ cups additional flour, reserving ½ cup for use during kneading (Step 4). Stir flour into the dough, being sure to incorporate all loose bits and flakes at the sides and bottom of the bowl. The dough will look lumpy and unmixed at this point. This is all right—it will smooth out when kneaded.

Using some of the reserved flour, lightly flour your work surface (be sure to give yourself enough room, at least a two-foot square), turn the dough out onto it, and lightly dust the top of the dough with a bit of additional flour. Let dough rest a minute or two to give it a chance to absorb the liquid ingredients.

STEP 4: KNEADING THE DOUGH

The purpose of kneading is both to combine the ingredients in the dough and, more crucially, to activate the flour's gluten molecules, which become resilient after a thorough kneading. Many people have the impression that kneading is hard work but in fact you do not have to bear down hard on the dough as you work it. Furthermore, you can work at whatever pace suits you and stop whenever you want to rest.

Kneading consists of two motions. First, bear down on the dough with the heels of your hands, spreading it outward; then, gather up the outer edge of the dough with your fingertips and fold the dough in half again. Each time or every other time you perform these two movements, rotate the dough 45° on the work surface. In the beginning the dough will be soft and sticky and you will have to sprinkle both it and your hands with small amounts of the reserved flour. Within a few minutes, however, the dough will feel smooth and will no longer adhere to your hands or to the work surface; at this point you should stop working in flour even if you have not used the entire ½ cup. The amount of flour the dough will absorb depends on the moisture content of the flour, the humidity of the day, and other factors. Too much flour can make the loaf heavy and dry.

How long you will have to knead the dough depends on how efficient your movements are. You can assume that it will take at least 10 minutes and perhaps as long as 15; if you are not an experienced bread-maker, time yourself on a clock. When you are through, the dough should be elastic, smooth, and satiny, resembling very thick taffy. It is better to knead too much rather than too little; insufficiently kneaded dough will bake into a sticky, heavy, squat loaf with large holes.

Note: Recipe may be slowed at this point by refrigerating the dough; see page 657.

Step 5: The First and Second Rise

Form the dough into a ball. Place it in a clean, dry 3- to 4-quart bowl, and cover tightly with plastic wrap. Place the dough in a draft-free place where the temperature is between 80°F and 90°F. On a hot summer day, simply let the dough rise in a cool part of your kitchen (in a cupboard, for example); on a winter day, set the dough in a draft-free spot that is several feet from a radiator. (Never set dough on a radiator or you will kill the yeast.) Allow the dough to rise until it has slightly more than doubled in size and feels light and spongy when pressed with the fingers. This will take about 2 hours. Resist the temptation to cut short the rise or to speed things up by placing the dough in a very warm place; if the rise is rushed, the baked bread will not have the proper texture and will have little flavor.

At this point you can proceed to form the loaf (next step), but your bread will be more flavorful and better-textured if you let the dough rise a second time. Flatten the dough with your fist and reshape it into a ball. Return it to the bowl, cover, and let double a second time, which will take about an hour.

Note: Recipe may be slowed or temporarily arrested after the first rise by refrigerating or freezing the dough; see page 657.

Step 6: Forming the Loaf

1 tablespoon soft butter or vegetable shortening

To produce an evenly textured, professional-looking loaf, you must shape the raw bread dough rather than simply plopping it into the bread pan. I find the following method consistently reliable. (The instructions given below are for a single large loaf, but the same general procedures apply to the forming of two smaller loaves.)

- Select either one 7½-cup loaf pan measuring about 9×5×2½ inches, or two smaller loaf pans with a capacity of 4 to 5½ cups each. Grease the pan(s) with soft butter or vegetable shortening and set aside.
- Invert bowl and let risen dough fall upside down onto an *unfloured* work surface, pressing it lightly to deflate. (The work surface must be unfloured because if flour is incorporated into the dough during forming, the loaf may not stick together and may have gaps inside when baked.)
- Pat the dough into a rectangle about 6 inches wide and 8 inches long, with a short side facing you. Don't worry if the dough sticks to the work surface (1).

- Starting with the short side nearest you, roll the dough lengthwise into the tightest cylinder possible (2).
- The dough will widen when rolled, and interior layers may push out at the ends. Poke any protruding layers back into the cylinder, then bring the top layer of the loaf over the protruding folds to cover them (3) (4).
- With the sides of your hands, lightly jab along the bottom of the cylinder, both at the ends and the sides, to tuck the dough underneath loaf and stretch the top of the loaf tightly (5). Give the dough a few light slaps, particularly at the sides, to make sure that it is well stuck together; then press the sides of the loaf at the ends between your palms to make them taper slightly (6). When you are through, the loaf should resemble a mammoth grain of rice.
- Lift the formed loaf between your hands and place it, seam side down, in the center of the greased bread pan. If the loaf has been formed correctly, it will touch the ends of the pan, but not the sides. Don't worry if the loaf is slightly too long for the pan, and therefore wrinkles or crumples in the center: it will puff up as it rises (7).

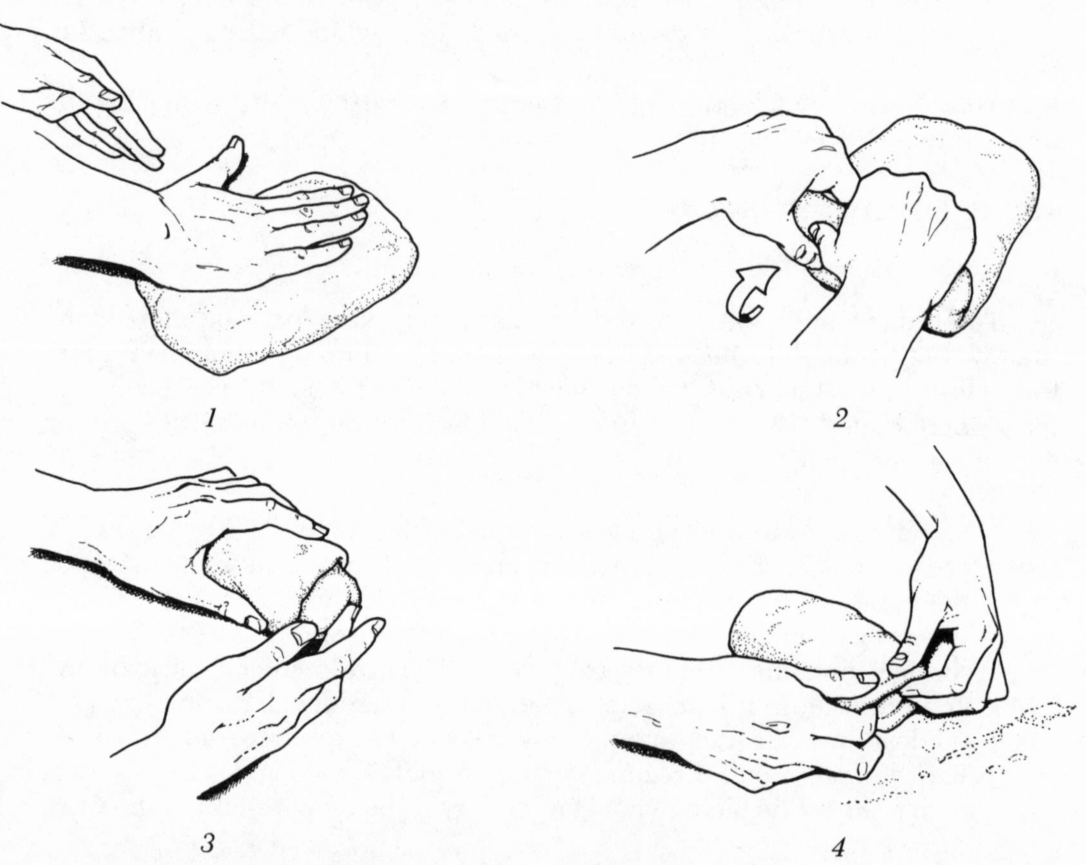

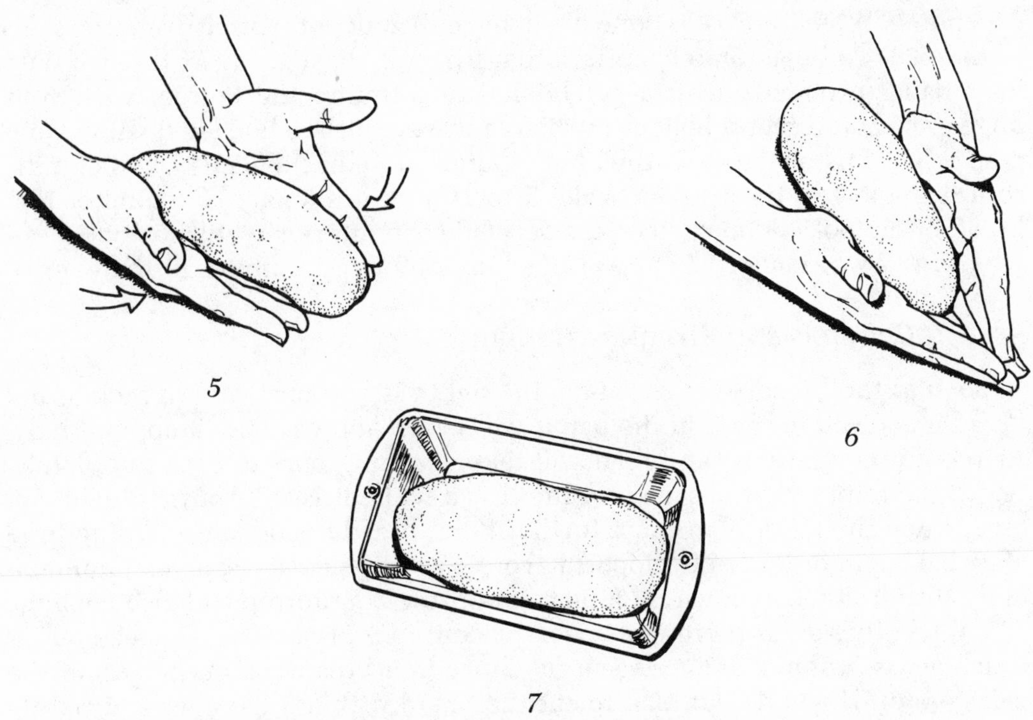

Note: Recipe may be slowed or temporarily arrested at this point by refrigerating or freezing the loaf; see page 657.

STEP 7: FINAL RISE OF THE FORMED LOAF; PREHEATING THE OVEN

Loosely drape a piece of plastic wrap over the bread pan. (If the day is humid, lightly flour the wrap to prevent the dough from sticking.) Place the dough in a draft-free place where the temperature is between 80°F and 90°F. Allow dough to rise for about an hour or until it has doubled in size; if you are using a 7½-cup loaf pan, the dough should fill the pan and puff slightly higher than the rim of the pan at the center. Avoid letting the dough rise too much, or a large bubble may form just beneath the top of the loaf, causing the loaf to flatten—rather than puff—as it bakes.

About 20 minutes before the end of the rising time, set rack in the center of the oven and preheat to 400°F.

Note: Recipe may be temporarily arrested at this point by freezing the risen loaf; see page 657.

STEP 8: BAKING THE BREAD

Place risen loaf in preheated oven and bake for about 45 minutes. Avoid opening the oven door during the first 20 minutes of baking, while the bread is expanding. When the loaf is done it will have shrunk perceptibly from the sides of the pan. To be absolutely certain that it is fully baked, invert the loaf onto your hand (protected with a pot holder) and thump the bottom with your finger—it should sound hollow, as though it were a shoe box filled with crumpled wads of tissue paper. If the bread sounds more like a filled carton of milk, return the loaf to the pan and bake 5 to 10 minutes longer. Remember that bread often looks done on the outside while the interior is still sticky.

Note: Two smaller loaves will need only 30 to 35 minutes in the oven.

Step 9: Cooling and Storing the Bread

As soon as the bread is done, unmold it right side up onto a wire rack; if hot bread is allowed to stand in the pan it will soften and wrinkle disappointingly. At room temperature, the bread will take about 2 hours to cool completely. Avoid the temptation to slice into the bread while it is still warm. Steam will escape and the loaf will dry out; furthermore, bread needs some settling time after baking in order to develop its flavor. If you do slice a warm loaf, immediately turn it cut side down on a plate or on the countertop to finish cooling.

When the loaf is thoroughly cool, place it in a plastic bag, squeeze out as much air as possible, and tie securely. Store in a bread box or, better, in the refrigerator. If you do not plan to eat the bread within 3 days, wrap it tightly in foil, place in a plastic bag, seal the bag airtight, and freeze. The bread will keep nicely for several months in the freezer, but it should be consumed soon after thawing since bread that has been frozen tends to go stale quickly.

Variation: CHEDDAR CHEESE BREAD

Makes 1 large or 2 smaller loaves

❦ *Make this bread either with all-purpose flour exclusively or with a mixture of all-purpose and whole wheat flours (see the variation for whole wheat bread, page 643). Cheddar cheese bread is delicious toasted and spread with strawberry preserves or apple butter.*

Basic American White Bread

DECREASE: Salt to 2 teaspoons (1½ teaspoons if you use buttermilk that contains added salt)

ADD: 2 cups (about 8 ounces) shredded extra-sharp Cheddar cheese

Decrease salt called for in Master Recipe to compensate for the salt in the cheese. In Step 3, add the initial 2 cups flour, beat until smooth, then stir in cheese. Add remaining 1½ cups flour and proceed with recipe. The risings may be slightly slower than usual.

Variation: HERB BREAD

Makes 1 large or 2 smaller loaves

❦ *This is good to eat plain with butter. Sliced thin and topped with cream cheese and smoked salmon or with chicken, crab, or egg salad, it also makes delicious canapés.*

Basic American White Bread

ADD: ½ cup finely chopped fresh parsley or ¼ cup *each* finely chopped fresh parsley and fresh dill (feathery leaves only)
⅓ cup finely snipped fresh chives or finely chopped scallions (including tender green parts)

In Step 3 of the Master Recipe, add the initial 2 cups flour, beat until smooth, then incorporate the herbs. Add remaining 1½ cups flour and proceed with recipe.

Variation: PULLMAN LOAF (BUTTERED WHITE BREAD)

Makes 1 large or 2 smaller loaves

❦ *The addition of butter to white bread dough makes a moist, soft, close-grained bread with a slightly cakelike texture. This bread keeps well. Sliced very thin and dried in a 200°F oven for 20 to 30 minutes, it makes excellent melba toast.*

Basic American White Bread

ADD: 4 or 5 tablespoons very soft butter

In Step 3 of the Master Recipe, add the initial 2 cups flour, beat until smooth, then thoroughly incorporate 4 tablespoons of the butter. Add remaining flour and proceed according to the recipe. The dough will feel a little soft when you first begin to knead it, and the risings may be a bit slower than usual.

If you wish a soft, opalescent crust, brush the top of the baked loaf with 1 additional tablespoon of soft butter as soon as it comes out of the oven.

Variation: RAISIN BREAD

Makes 1 large or 2 smaller loaves

❦ *This loaf may be sweetened and spiced or not, as you prefer.*

Basic American White Bread
ADD: 1½ cups (about 9 ounces) raisins
3 tablespoons sugar (optional)
¾ teaspoon cinnamon (optional)
1 tablespoon soft butter (optional)

Place the raisins in a heat-proof 1-quart mixing bowl and cover with boiling water. Let stand 10 minutes, drain, and press firmly between sheets of paper towels to blot excess moisture. Set aside.

Proceed according to the Master Recipe, adding sugar and cinnamon with the buttermilk (or yogurt plus milk) and salt. Knead the plumped raisins into the dough at the end of the kneading period.

If you want a soft crust, brush the top of the bread with soft butter as soon as it comes out of the oven.

Variation: LIGHT OR DARK RYE BREAD

Makes 1 large or 2 smaller loaves

❦ *Light rye flour is ground from degermed rye, just as ordinary all-purpose flour is produced from degermed wheat. By contrast, dark rye flour is made from whole-grain rye, just as whole wheat flour is produced from whole-grain wheat. Light rye flour bakes into a pale beige loaf with a subtle rye flavor; dark rye flour makes a brown, slightly dense bread with a pronounced rye taste. Although it is commercially produced by at least two national mills, light rye flour is not carried by some supermarkets and must be bought at specialty food shops. Dark rye flour is generally available only at health-food stores. Pumpernickel flour, by the way, is dark rye flour that has been ground very coarse.*

Basic American White Bread
SUBSTITUTE: Light or dark rye flour for *half* the all-purpose flour called for in Master Recipe
ADD: 1 to 2 tablespoons caraway seeds (optional)

Follow the Master Recipe, but use light or dark rye flour for half the all-purpose flour called for, always adding both flours in equal proportions. (Thus you will beat in 1 cup *each* rye and all-purpose flour to make the initial batter, stir in another 3/4 cup *each* rye and all-purpose flour to form the dough, and use up to 1/4 cup *each* rye and all-purpose flour during kneading.) If you want to flavor the bread with caraway seeds, add them toward the end of the kneading period. The dough will be slightly slow to rise if made with dark rye flour.

Variation: WHOLE WHEAT BREAD

Makes 1 large or 2 smaller loaves

❦ *Because it is a whole-grain flour containing the oil-rich germ of the wheat, whole wheat flour quickly becomes rancid under ordinary storage conditions. It is wise, therefore, to buy only as much as you will use within a couple of months and to keep unused flour in a lidded container in the freezer.*

It is customary to flavor whole wheat bread with honey, molasses, or maple syrup, though such sweetening is by no means essential.

Basic American White Bread

ADD: 2 tablespoons honey, molasses, or maple syrup (optional)

SUBSTITUTE: Whole wheat flour for *half* the all-purpose flour called for in Master Recipe

If you want to sweeten the loaf, add honey, molasses, or maple syrup along with the buttermilk or yogurt plus milk. Otherwise, follow the Master Recipe, but use whole wheat flour for half of the all-purpose flour called for, always adding both flours in equal proportions. (Thus you will beat in 1 cup *each* whole wheat and all-purpose flour to make the initial batter, stir in another 3/4 cup *each* whole wheat and all-purpose flour to form the dough, and reserve 1/4 cup *each* whole wheat and all-purpose flour for kneading. You will probably not have to add much of the reserved 1/2 cup flour during kneading, as the dough will be quite stiff.)

Variation: CLOVERLEAF DINNER ROLLS

Makes 24 rolls

❦ *You may use the dough from the Master Recipe or any of the variations in making these rolls, but you will be closest to tradition if you use the buttered dough for Pullman loaf, page 641.*

The dough for ***Basic American White Bread*** or one of its variations, pages 634–43
6 tablespoons butter, melted

Prepare the Master Recipe or any of the variation recipes through the second rise (Step 5 of the Master Recipe).

Invert dough onto lightly floured work surface and roll into rectangle 12 inches long and 6 inches wide. Cut the rectangle in half lengthwise, then cut the dough crosswise into 12 equal strips. You now have 24 strips of dough measuring approximately 3×1 inches. Cut each strip into three equal pieces, then roll each piece between the palms of your hands to form a ball. When you are through you will have 72 balls of dough.

Brush insides of two 12-cup muffin tins generously with melted butter and place 3 balls of dough in each cup. Brush tops with remaining melted butter. Cover the pans with plastic wrap and set in a warm place until the rolls have doubled in size, 30 to 45 minutes.

Remove plastic and bake rolls in the center of a preheated 425°F oven for 12 to 15 minutes, or until tops are nicely browned. Serve at once or turn out onto racks to cool. These rolls turn stale quickly, so freeze any that you do not plan to eat within a day or two.

STORAGE: Place rolls in a plastic bag, squeezing as much air as possible out of the bag before sealing. Refrigerate for up to 2 days or freeze several months. Take frozen rolls directly from freezer, warm for 3 to 5 minutes on a baking sheet in a 350°F oven, and serve immediately.

MASTER RECIPE

Egg Bread (Sally Lunn)

Makes 1 large or 2 smaller loaves

This recipe produces a high-rising, feather-light, slightly sweet loaf. Its texture is decidedly breadlike, not soft and cakelike like some egg breads. In the South, where it is often baked in a Bundt pan and served warm with butter and preserves, the loaf is known as Sally Lunn. Toasted or plain, this bread is lovely at breakfast or at tea, and the basic dough is readily transformed into a host of delicious variations.

If you are not an experienced bread-baker, read through the Master Recipe for basic white bread on pages 634–40 before embarking on this recipe. The instructions given below are numbered to correspond to the steps of the Master Recipe for easy reference. This recipe may be slowed or temporarily arrested at a number of points by refrigerating or freezing the dough. The table on page 658 tells you how to do this.

¼ cup warm water (around body temperature)
1 package (2½ teaspoons) dry yeast or 1 cake (0.6 ounce) compressed yeast
1½ teaspoons sugar
¼ cup milk
2 large eggs
2½ tablespoons sugar
1 teaspoon salt
2¾ to 3 cups unbleached all-purpose flour (measure by scooping cup into large container of flour and sweeping off excess with the back of a knife)
6 tablespoons very soft butter
1 tablespoon soft butter or vegetable shortening for greasing pans
1 egg beaten to blend with 1 teaspoon milk (optional)

1. Measure warm water into a fairly deep and steep-sided 3- to 4-quart mixing bowl. If you are using dry yeast, sprinkle it over the water; if you are using cake yeast, mash it into the water with the back of a wooden spoon. Stir 1½ teaspoons sugar into yeast and set mixture aside in a warm place for 10 minutes. In that time, the yeast should begin to bubble and froth, indicating that it is healthy and active. Five to 10 minutes longer may be required if the room is chilly. If there is still no sign of activity after 20 minutes, throw the mixture out and start again with new yeast.

2. If the milk and eggs are cold, beat them together in a 1½-quart bowl with a wire whip, set the bowl in a sink or larger bowl filled with warm water, and stir the mixture until slightly warm. (If milk and eggs are at room temperature, this step is not necessary; just add directly to the proofed yeast.) Pour milk and eggs into the yeast mixture, add the additional 2½ tablespoons sugar and 1 teaspoon salt, and beat with a wire whip to blend thoroughly.

3. Add 1½ cups flour to the yeast mixture and beat vigorously with a wooden spoon until the batter is smooth and elastic. Add 6 tablespoons soft butter and beat to blend well. Add 1¼ cups more flour, reserving ¼ cup for use during kneading, and stir flour into the dough until all flour is moistened and dough has gathered into a ball. Using some of reserved flour, lightly flour your work surface, turn the dough out onto it, and dust dough with flour. Let the dough rest for a minute or two.

4. Begin kneading the soft dough by giving it light, quick jabs with the heel of your hand and gathering it up with your fingertips. During this initial period, do not sprinkle any additional flour over the dough unless it is sticking to your hands so much that you can't handle it. In a few minutes, the dough will firm up and you can knead more forcefully, incorporating more of the reserved 1/4 cup flour if necessary. The dough should not be sticky but it will remain quite soft; it is important not to add more flour than is needed. Knead dough for 10 to 15 minutes altogether, or until it is smooth and satiny and resembles putty or thick taffy.

5. Form dough into a ball, place it in a clean, dry 3-quart mixing bowl, and cover bowl tightly with plastic wrap. Set dough in a warm, draft-free place and let rise until it has a little more than doubled in size, about 2 hours. At this point you can proceed to form the loaf but the bread will have more flavor and a better texture if the dough is allowed to rise a second time. Flatten the dough with your fist, reshape it into a ball, and let rise in the mixing bowl, covered, until doubled, about 1 hour.

6. Select either one 7 1/2-cup loaf pan measuring about 9×5×2 1/2 inches or two smaller loaf pans with a capacity of 4 to 5 1/2 cups each. Grease pan(s) with soft butter or vegetable shortening and set aside. Invert bowl and scoop out risen dough, letting it fall upside down onto an *unfloured* work surface. Pat the dough into a rectangle about 6 inches wide and 8 inches long, with a short side facing you. Starting with this short side, roll dough into a tight cylinder. Tuck in ends and sides, making the top of the loaf smooth and tight, and press and slap the loaf to make sure it is well stuck together. Press the sides of loaf at the ends to make them taper slightly. Place the formed loaf seam side down in the center of the greased bread pan.

7. Loosely drape plastic wrap over the pan. Let dough rise in a warm place until doubled in size, about 1 hour; dough should fill a 7 1/2-cup bread pan and be domed in the center. About 20 minutes before the end of the rising time, set rack in the center of the oven and preheat to 400°F. If you wish the bread to have a crisp, shiny crust, as is traditional for egg breads, just before putting the loaf in the oven brush the top with the egg-milk mixture; try not to let the egg dribble down the sides of the loaf, as this may cause bread to burn or stick to the pan.

8. Bake large loaf for about 40 minutes, smaller loaves for about 25 minutes. Check bread after 20 minutes and cover loosely with a sheet of foil if it is browning too quickly. The bread is done when it has shrunk slightly from the sides of the pan and sounds hollow when tapped on the bottom. Bake an additional 5 to 10 minutes if necessary.

9. Remove bread from pan at once and cool right side up on a wire rack for 2 hours before wrapping for storage. Egg bread goes stale very quickly. If you plan to consume the entire loaf within 36 hours of baking, wrap it in an airtight plastic bag and store in the refrigerator; bring to room temperature

before serving. Otherwise, seal the loaf in an airtight plastic bag and freeze it, cutting slices as you need them.

Variation: BRIOCHE-SHAPE BREAKFAST ROLLS

Makes 12 rolls

❦ *While not true brioches—brioche dough is, by weight, close to half butter and eggs—these rolls are delicious, especially when served with butter and preserves or marmalade.*

The dough for ***Egg Bread (Sally Lunn)***
2 tablespoons butter for greasing the molds
1 egg beaten to blend with 1 teaspoon milk

SPECIAL EQUIPMENT: 12 fluted brioche molds (or a 12-cup muffin tin with deep depressions)

Prepare the Master Recipe through the second rise (Step 5).

Invert dough onto an *unfloured* work surface and pat into a rectangle about 6 inches long and 4 to 5 inches wide. Cut the rectangle crosswise into 6 equal strips, then divide the strips in half. You should have 12 pieces of dough.

Form each roll as follows: Take one strip of dough and pinch off a ½-inch piece. Roll both the larger part of the dough strip and the pinched-off piece into balls between the palms of your hands. Make a dent with your index finger in the center of the large ball of dough and set the small ball in the depression.

Butter 12 muffin cups or brioche molds very generously; if you are using a muffin tin, butter not only the depressions but also the top of the tin *between* the depressions, as the rolls are likely to rise beyond the cups. Fill molds with formed dough, cover loosely with plastic wrap, and let rise in a warm place until doubled, about 1 hour. Twenty minutes before end of the rising time, set rack in the center of the oven and preheat to 425°F. Just before putting the rolls in the oven, brush them lightly with egg wash; do not let egg dribble down the sides of the rolls.

Bake rolls about 12 minutes, or until puffed and nicely browned. Cool on a rack. Since these rolls go stale quickly, freeze any that you do not plan to eat within 24 hours of baking.

STORAGE: Place rolls in a plastic bag, squeezing as much air as possible out of the bag before sealing. Refrigerate for 1 day or freeze for several months. To use frozen rolls, take them directly from the freezer, arrange on a baking sheet, and warm for about 5 minutes in a 350°F oven; serve immediately.

Variation: BRAIDED EGG LOAF

Makes 1 large loaf

❦ *To make a festive, slightly sweet braided loaf of the sort often served at Easter, flavor the dough as for Gugelhopf, page 649.*

The dough for ***Egg Bread (Sally Lunn)***
1 tablespoon butter for greasing baking sheet
1 egg beaten to blend with 1 teaspoon milk

Prepare Master Recipe through the second rise (Step 5). Invert dough onto an *unfloured* work surface and press lightly to deflate. Break off ⅓ of the dough and roll it over the work surface with the palms and spread fingers of your hands to form a rope about 15 inches long. Roll remaining dough into a rope about 30 inches long and set it on a well-buttered baking sheet, shaping it like a horseshoe. Now take the shorter length of dough and place it down the center of the horseshoe, with one end overlapping the horseshoe's curved top. Proceed to braid the loaf tightly. Press and pinch both ends of the loaf to seal, and, if necessary, gently push and pat the loaf into shape.

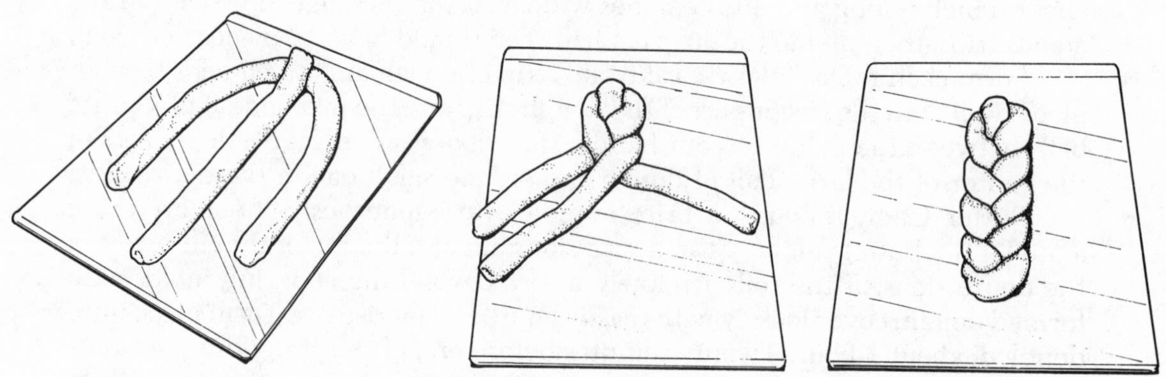

Cover dough loosely with plastic wrap and let rise in a warm place until doubled, about 1 hour. Twenty minutes before end of rising time, set rack in center of oven and preheat to 400°F. Just before putting bread in the oven, brush the top and sides lightly with egg wash. Do not let egg drip down onto baking sheet. Bake the loaf for about 30 minutes, or until nicely browned. Slide onto a wire rack to cool.

STORAGE: Wrap bread airtight in a plastic bag and refrigerate for up to 2 days or freeze for several months.

Variation: CHALLAH

Makes 1 large braided loaf

❦ *This light and very high-rising bread was once available only in Jewish delicatessens and bakeries, but its popularity has led nonethnic bakeries throughout the country to offer it to their customers.*

The dough for ***Egg Bread (Sally Lunn)***
SUBSTITUTE: 1/4 cup water for milk
3 tablespoons vegetable shortening for butter
1 tablespoon additional vegetable shortening for greasing baking sheet
1 egg beaten to blend with 1 teaspoon milk
2 to 3 tablespoons poppy seeds

Prepare Master Recipe through the second rise (Step 5), substituting water for milk and 3 tablespoons vegetable shortening for butter. Proceed to form and bake loaf as for braided egg loaf (preceding variation recipe), but set it on a baking sheet greased with vegetable shortening and sprinkle with poppy seeds just after brushing with egg wash.

Variation: RAISIN EGG BREAD

Makes 1 large or 2 smaller loaves

Egg Bread (Sally Lunn)
ADD: 1 1/2 cups (about 9 ounces) raisins

Place raisins in a heat-proof 1-quart mixing bowl and cover with boiling water. Let stand 10 minutes, drain, and press firmly between sheets of paper toweling to remove excess moisture. Proceed according to the Master Recipe, kneading in the plumped raisins at the end of the kneading period.

Variation: GUGELHOPF (RAISIN AND ALMOND COFFEECAKE)

Makes 1 coffeecake

❦ *You may bake this delicious coffeecake in any 8- to 10-cup mold—a regular bread pan or a brioche tin, for example—but it will have a more uniform texture and a more festive look if you bake it, as is traditional, in a Bundt pan or some other fancy ring-shaped mold of the requisite capacity.*

The dough for ***Egg Bread (Sally Lunn)***

INCREASE: Sugar to ⅓ cup (in Step 2)

ADD: 1¼ cups (about 7 ounces) dried currants
⅔ cup (about 2½ ounces) sliced almonds
⅓ cup (about 2½ ounces) finely chopped candied lemon or orange peel

1½ tablespoons soft butter for greasing mold

SPECIAL EQUIPMENT: A ring mold with an 8- to 10-cup capacity, preferably with fluted sides and bottom

Place currants in a heat-proof 1-quart bowl and cover with boiling water. Let stand 10 minutes, drain in a sieve, and press firmly between sheets of paper toweling to blot excess moisture. Dry out mixing bowl, return currants to it, and mix in almonds and citrus peel. Set aside.

Prepare Master Recipe, increasing the 2½ tablespoons sugar called for in Step 2 to ⅓ cup. Add the currant mixture to dough toward the end of the kneading period. Proceed to let dough rise twice in the bowl (end of Step 5); because of the extra sugar and other ingredients, the rises will take somewhat longer.

Invert risen dough onto an *unfloured* work surface and press to deflate. Roll dough into a rope and place in a thoroughly buttered ring mold. Press the ends of the rope together to seal. Press the dough firmly against the bottom of the mold to make sure it fills the mold's shape. Cover bread loosely with a towel and set in a warm place until doubled in size, about 1½ hours. Twenty minutes before end of rising time, set rack in center of oven and preheat to 400°F.

Bake coffeecake for about 30 minutes, or until it is nicely browned and has shrunk slightly from sides of mold. Remove from pan at once and cool upside down on a wire rack.

STORAGE: Wrapped in foil, coffee cake may be refrigerated for up to 2 days. To serve, warm coffeecake, still wrapped in foil, in a 250°F oven for about 10 minutes. For longer storage, seal foil-wrapped coffee cake airtight in a plastic bag and freeze. When you are ready to serve the frozen coffeecake, place it, still wrapped in foil, in a 250°F oven for 15 to 20 minutes, or until warmed through.

Variation: CINNAMON-NUT BUNS

Makes 18 buns

❦ *Thin persons of an experimental bent can make these already irresistible buns richer and sweeter by increasing the melted butter and brown sugar called for by as much as half.*

The dough for ***Egg Bread (Sally Lunn)***
8 tablespoons (1 stick) butter, melted and slightly cooled
2 cups (about 8 ounces) coarsely chopped walnuts or pecans
⅔ cup packed dark brown sugar
2 teaspoons cinnamon

Prepare the Master Recipe through the second rise (Step 5). The dough will be easier to handle if you deflate it, wrap it in plastic, and refrigerate it for half an hour or so, but this is not essential.

On a floured work surface, roll dough into a neat rectangle 18 inches long and 9 inches wide. Brush on about 3 tablespoons of the melted butter, then sprinkle dough with 1⅓ cups of the nuts, ⅓ cup of the brown sugar, and all of the cinnamon, distributing these ingredients evenly out to the very edges of the dough rectangle. To be sure that nuts and sugar adhere, pass a rolling pin lightly over the dough several times.

Beginning at a long side, roll up the dough tightly as though it were a jelly roll, then set the roll on your work surface with the seam side on the bottom. Press the whole length of the roll firmly with your hands to make it stick together, then let rest 4 minutes. Using a very sharp knife, cut roll crosswise into eighteen 1-inch-thick slices.

Brush two 8-inch round cake pans liberally with 2 tablespoons of the melted butter and arrange 9 slices in each pan, 6 around the edge of the pan and 3 in the middle. The slices probably won't touch, but this doesn't matter; the pan will fill out once the buns have risen and baked. Brush buns with the remaining 3 tablespoons melted butter and sprinkle with remaining nuts and sugar.

Cover buns with plastic wrap and let rise in a warm place until light, puffy, and doubled in size, 45 to 60 minutes. Twenty minutes before the end of the rising time, set rack in center of oven and preheat to 425°F. Bake buns for about 15 minutes or until nicely browned. Place pans on wire racks and let buns cool slightly before serving.

STORAGE: When buns are thoroughly cool, the pans may be covered securely with foil and refrigerated for 2 days or frozen for several months. Before serving, warm refrigerated buns, still covered with foil, in a 350°F oven for about 5 minutes; warm frozen buns in the same manner, giving them about 10 minutes.

Variation: RAISED DOUGHNUTS AND RAISED JELLY DOUGHNUTS

Makes about eighteen 3-inch doughnuts

❦ *These light, yeasty, eggy doughnuts will melt in your mouth. They make a superlative treat for brunch guests, and because the doughnuts can be fried ahead of time, frozen, and then warmed in the oven just before serving, there are no logistical problems in serving them on a Sunday morning.*

Like all doughnuts, these require frying in deep fat (or "boiling" in fat, as early Americans used to say and some New Englanders still do). If deep-fat frying is unfamiliar or intimidating territory to you, read through the chapter on deep-frying, which begins on page 59.

The dough for ***Egg Bread (Sally Lunn)***
INCREASE: sugar to 1/3 cup
About 1/3 cup raspberry, strawberry, apricot, or black currant jam or preserves (optional: for raised jelly doughnuts only)
1 1/2 to 2 quarts *very fresh* vegetable oil for deep-frying
About 1/4 cup confectioner's sugar
2 teaspoons cinnamon mixed with 1/8 teaspoon freshly grated nutmeg (optional)

SPECIAL EQUIPMENT: A 3-inch doughnut cutter or a 3-inch cookie cutter plus a 3/4-inch canapé/miniature biscuit cutter (or substitute a 3/4-inch bottle top); a deep-frying thermometer (optional but convenient)

To prepare the basic dough, follow the Master Recipe for egg bread dough through the second rise (Step 5), adding 1/3 cup (instead of 2 1/2 tablespoons) sugar along with milk and salt. The added sugar will make the dough a bit softer and stickier than usual—work in sprinklings of flour if necessary during kneading—and will slow the rise somewhat.

To make raised doughnuts: After dough has completed its second rise, invert it onto a well-floured work surface. Working as quickly as possible so that you do not overactivate the gluten and make the dough difficult to handle, roll dough into a 14-inch circle about 1/4 inch thick. Loosen dough from work surface; if it contracts, roll it out again to achieve the correct measurement. (If the doughnuts shrink up after they are cut, they will end up tall and fat.)

Keeping the cutter or cutters well floured as you go, cut out 16 to 18 doughnuts and holes. Knead scraps together, roll out, and cut 1 or 2 more doughnuts. (If the scraps are too soft or too rubbery to roll out, fashion them as best as you can into 1 or 2 twisted crullers.)

To make raised jelly doughnuts: After dough has completed its second rise, invert it onto well-floured work surface and divide it in half. Working as quickly as possible so that you do not overactivate the gluten and make the dough difficult to handle, roll half the dough into a 14-inch circle about 1/8 inch thick. Loosen dough from work surface; if it contracts, roll it out again to achieve the correct measurement. Using a 3-inch round cookie cutter, cut out 16 circles, flouring the cutter frequently. Push dough circles and scraps to a corner of your work surface and roll out and cut second half of dough in the same fashion as the first. Gather, roll out, and cut the scraps from the two halves of the dough, making 2 to 4 additional circles; or, if the scraps prove too rubbery to roll out, twist them into crullers. You will have at least 32 rounds, more if you managed to roll out the scraps.

Line up half the dough circles in front of you and drop 1 teaspoon jam or preserves in the center of each. Completing one doughnut at a time, lightly moisten with water all exposed dough around the dab of jam (your finger is the best tool here). Set an unfilled circle of dough on top. Lightly pat center of doughnut (where the jam is) to push out any air pockets, then press edges firmly to seal the two rounds of dough together.

Rising and frying: Cover 2 large baking sheets with aluminum foil and dust foil heavily with flour. Transfer half the doughnuts (and holes, if any) to each baking sheet, sprinkle lightly with flour, cover loosely with cloth towels, and let rise in a warm place until light, puffy, and doubled in size. This may take as long as 1 1/2 hours.

In preparation for frying the doughnuts, cover a third baking sheet with a triple thickness of paper toweling. Pour enough oil into a deep 10- to 12-inch skillet or sauté pan to reach a depth of 1 1/2 inches and heat oil to 360°F. Be sure the oil is not too hot or the outside of the doughnuts will be dark and tough.

Using a slotted spatula dipped in hot oil (the oil prevents doughnuts from sticking), transfer doughnuts one at a time to hot oil, frying no more than four or five at once. Fry doughnuts about 1 minute on each side, or until golden brown. A chopstick (or the handle of a wooden spoon) is a good tool for flipping doughnuts over; stand back a bit when turning doughnuts so that you will not be splattered. When doughnuts are done, transfer them to the paper towel-lined baking sheet, turning so that excess oil will be blotted from both sides. Continue until you have fried all the doughnuts, then fry the holes in one or two batches (the holes will need about 20 seconds).

Just before serving, place doughnuts, two or three at a time, in a plastic or sturdy paper bag containing about 1/4 cup confectioner's sugar and, if you wish, cinnamon and nutmeg. (Personally, I don't think the added spices are necessary or even desirable if doughnuts are filled with jam.) Gently shake doughnuts in the bag to coat with sugar mixture.

STORAGE: If doughnuts are not to be eaten on the same day they are made, seal them in plastic bags and freeze. Frozen doughnuts will keep well for about three months. To serve, arrange doughnuts, still frozen, on a baking sheet and place in a 350°F oven for 4 to 8 minutes, or until warmed through. Cover with fresh confectioner's sugar (and spice) and serve at once.

MASTER RECIPE

Hard Rolls

Makes 12 hard rolls

This is an exceedingly easy recipe. The dough, which can be used to make hard rolls, hamburger buns, hero rolls, or even pizza crust, contains just yeast, water, salt, and flour. If flavored with ham and cheese or with ripe olives and garlic, the rolls become practically meals in themselves.

The instructions given below are numbered to correspond with the steps of the Master Recipe for basic white bread starting on page 634. If you run into any problems, consult that more fully detailed recipe. This recipe may be slowed or temporarily arrested at a number of points by refrigerating or freezing the dough. The table on page 658 tells you how to do this.

1/3 cup warm water (around body temperature)
1 package (2 1/2 teaspoons) dry yeast or 1 cake (0.6 ounce) compressed yeast
1/8 teaspoon sugar (optional)
1 cup warm water
2 teaspoons salt
3 1/2 to 4 cups unbleached all-purpose flour (measure by scooping cup into large container of flour and sweeping off excess with the back of a knife)
Solid vegetable shortening for greasing the baking sheet

1. Measure 1/3 cup warm water into a deep, steep-sided 3- to 4-quart mixing bowl. If you are using dry yeast, sprinkle it over the water; if you are using cake yeast, mash it into the water with the back of a wooden spoon. Wait 3 to 5 minutes, or until the yeast is dissolved, and then proceed to the next step

of the recipe. (The yeast will not bubble or show any other signs of activity because you have not given it any sugar to feed on. If you have reason to doubt the health of the yeast, stir 1/8 teaspoon sugar into the yeast-water mixture and set aside in a warm place. In 12 to 15 minutes, bubbles should appear on the surface of the mixture, indicating that the yeast is active. If bubbles do not appear within 20 minutes, throw the mixture out and start again with fresh yeast.)

2. Stir the additional 1 cup warm water and salt into the yeast mixture.

3. Add 2 cups flour to the yeast mixture and beat vigorously with a wooden spoon until a smooth, elastic batter results. Add 1 1/2 cups more flour, reserving 1/2 cup for use during kneading, and stir into the dough. Using some of the reserved flour, lightly flour your work surface, turn dough out onto it, and dust dough with flour. Let dough rest for a minute or two.

4. Knead dough until it is smooth, satiny, and elastic and resembles putty or very thick taffy; this will take 10 to 15 minutes. Knead in only as much of the reserved flour as is necessary to prevent the dough from sticking to your hands and to the work surface.

5. Form the dough into a neat, compact ball, place it in a clean 3- to 4-quart mixing bowl, and cover the bowl tightly with a sheet of plastic wrap. Set dough in a warm, draft-free place, and let rise until doubled in bulk, about 2 hours. At this point you can proceed to form the rolls, but the bread will have a better flavor if you flatten the dough, reshape it into a ball, and let it double a second time, about 1 hour, in the covered mixing bowl.

6. Grease baking sheet with vegetable shortening and set aside. Invert the bowl and scoop out risen dough, letting it fall upside down onto an *unfloured* work surface.

To form hard rolls, pat dough into a rectangle about 12 inches long and 6 inches wide. Cut the rectangle crosswise into six 2-inch-wide slices, then divide the slices in half, making 12 pieces altogether. The object now is to form the rolls in such a way that they will retain a round shape rather than flattening out during rising and baking. To form each roll, shape one of the 12 pieces of dough into a ball between the palms of your hands, then flatten the ball into a rough circle about 3 1/2 inches in diameter. Fold the circle in quarters (that is, fold it in half, then fold the half onto itself) to form a fan shape. The smooth side of the fan—the side without open folds—is to become the top of the roll. Squeeze and stretch the smooth side to expand its surface, all the while tucking the other two sides of the fan into a dimple on the underside of the roll. As you proceed, coax the dough into an increasingly rounded shape. Arrange rolls seam side down on greased baking sheet.

7. Sprinkle rolls lightly with flour and drape with a dish towel. Let rise in a warm place until doubled in size, which will take about 1 hour. Twenty minutes before end of rising time, set rack in upper third of oven and preheat to 425°F. Just before putting rolls in the oven, spray or brush them with cold

water. Wait a moment, then spray or brush again. This will help give the rolls a hard crust.

8. Bake rolls about 18 minutes, lowering oven temperature to 400°F if the bread appears to be browning too quickly. The rolls are done when they sound hollow if tapped on the bottom.

9. Let rolls cool a minute or two on the baking sheet, then set them right side up on a wire rack to cool completely. Store rolls in an airtight plastic bag in the refrigerator; freeze if you do not plan to eat them within a day. Thaw frozen rolls for an hour at room temperature or for 5 minutes or so in a 350°F oven.

Variation: HAMBURGER BUNS

Makes 8 hamburger buns

Hard Rolls

In Step 6, after patting the dough into a rectangle 12 inches long and 6 inches wide, cut the rectangle into four 3-inch-wide pieces, then divide the pieces in half, making 8 altogether. Form hamburger buns according to the same procedure used to make hard rolls, but flatten each ball of dough into a circle roughly 5 inches in diameter (instead of 3½ inches) before proceeding to fold into a fan and shape into a bun. Arrange buns seam side down on greased baking sheet. Proceed with Master Recipe, baking buns 20 to 25 minutes.

Variation: HERO ROLLS

Makes four 10-inch hero rolls

Hard Rolls

In Step 6, after patting the dough into a rectangle 12 inches long and 6 inches wide, proceed to form hero rolls as follows: Cut the dough rectangle in half both lengthwise and crosswise to make 4 pieces. Starting at a longer side, roll each rectangle into a tight cylinder as though it were a jelly roll. Roll the cylinder back and forth on the work surface under the palms and outspread fingers of your hands until it is about 10 inches long. Smooth the surface with your fingers, if necessary, and tuck in the ends. Arrange rolls seam side down on greased baking sheet. Proceed with Steps 7 through 9 of the Master Recipe, baking the rolls 20 to 25 minutes.

Variation: HAM AND SWISS ROLLS

Makes 12 rolls

Hard Rolls

ADD: 1 cup finely diced boiled or baked ham
1 cup (about 4 ounces) shredded imported Swiss cheese

In Step 3, add the initial 2 cups flour, beat until smooth, then blend in ham and cheese. Add remaining 1½ cups flour and proceed with the Master Recipe. The risings may be slightly slower than usual.

Variation: OLIVE AND GARLIC ROLLS

Makes 12 rolls

Hard Rolls

ADD: ¾ cup chopped pitted oil-cured black olives (one 6½-ounce jar with pits)
1½ tablespoons mashed, pressed, or very finely minced garlic
1 teaspoon freshly ground pepper

In Step 3, add the initial 2 cups flour, beat until smooth, then stir in olives, garlic, and pepper. Add remaining 1½ cups flour and proceed with recipe.

HOW TO SLOW OR TEMPORARILY ARREST BREAD-MAKING: The table that follows below gives detailed instructions on how to slow or temporarily halt the bread-making process at several points, and how to resume the recipe when you are ready. Although refrigeration and freezing of raw bread dough is not as tricky a procedure as you might suppose—yeast, after all, is a hardy little creature—do keep the following guidelines in mind when working with the delay table:

- To be sure that the yeast remains active, don't refrigerate dough more than twice. The total length of time dough is held in the refrigerator should not exceed 2 days.
- Refrigerating dough sometimes causes it to become sour. This is not necessarily a catastrophe in white bread or hard rolls, but you would not want it in dinner rolls or doughnuts. Doughs made with a large amount of sugar seem particularly prone to souring.

- The longer doughs are frozen, the more likely they are not to rise. If you freeze doughs for longer than a week you are pressing your luck.
- Doughs that have been refrigerated or frozen after having risen in the bread pan may not rise to optimal heights when baked.

DELAY TABLE FOR BREAD DOUGHS

STEP 4 OF MASTER RECIPES:

TO SLOW THE FIRST RISE (UP TO 8 HOURS): Form dough into a compact ball, flour well, and place in a lidded container with a capacity of no less than 1½ and no more than 2½ quarts. If the lid of the container does not screw or clamp on, place a 5-pound object on *top* of the container—a heavy cutting board, for example. The weight will prevent the rising dough from popping out. Refrigerate. The dough may now be left for up to 8 hours, during which time it will rise to double or nearly triple (which is okay). *To resume the recipe,* knead dough for a minute or two to warm dough, then proceed to give it the second rise. The second rise will take up to 3 hours if the dough is very chilled.

STEP 5 OF MASTER RECIPES:

TO SLOW THE SECOND RISE (UP TO 3 HOURS): After the first rise, deflate dough, form it into a ball, return it to the bowl, and cover tightly with plastic wrap. Refrigerate for up to 3 hours. The dough will rise to double or triple. *To resume the recipe,* knead the dough for a minute or two to warm it, then proceed to form into a loaf or other desired shape. The final rise in the bread pan may take as long as 3 hours if the dough is very cold.

TO ARREST AFTER FIRST OR SECOND RISE (UP TO 2 DAYS): Flatten the dough into a square and flour it well. Wrap the dough in plastic and place it in a plastic bag. Squeeze as much air as possible out of the bag and tie securely. (A heavy-gauge, self-zipping storage bag works well here.) Place a 5-pound weight on top of the dough—a heavy cutting board is ideal. Refrigerate. Hold dough no more than 2 days. *To resume the recipe,* knead the dough for a minute or two to warm it, then either let rise the second time or form it and give it its final rise. Either rise may take as long as 3 hours if the dough is very cold. (Don't bother with a second rise in the mixing bowl if the dough has already risen once; it will have matured sufficiently in the refrigerator.)

TO ARREST AFTER THE SECOND RISE (UP TO 7 DAYS): Wrap dough in plastic, place in an airtight plastic bag, and freeze (at a maximum temperature of 20°F) for no longer than a week. *To resume the recipe,* thaw dough, still wrapped, at room temperature for 3 to 6 hours, or until completely defrosted. Form dough into a loaf (or whatever) and let rise until doubled, which may take as long as 3 hours.

STEP 6 OF MASTER RECIPES:

TO SLOW THE FINAL RISE (1 TO 3 HOURS): Allow dough to complete final rise in the refrigerator. White and hard-roll doughs will double in size and be ready for baking within 2 to 3 hours. Egg doughs (including cinnamon buns, coffeecakes, and doughnuts) will take longer and may not fully double under refrigeration; if this is the case, transfer the bread to a warm place and let it finish the rise. *To resume the recipe,* bake the bread, allowing 5 to 10 minutes' extra baking time for loaves, a minute or two extra for rolls and buns.

TO ARREST THE FINAL RISE (UP TO 7 DAYS): Cover formed, unrisen dough with plastic wrap and freeze until solid; remove from pan, wrap in foil, and seal airtight in a plastic bag; use within one week. *To resume the recipe,* unwrap dough, place in greased pan, and cover with plastic wrap. Let bread rise in a warm place until doubled, which may take as long as 6 hours.

STEP 7 OF MASTER RECIPES:

TO ARREST BEFORE BAKING (UP TO 7 DAYS): Remove plastic wrap or towel from formed and fully risen dough and sprinkle with flour. Freeze dough until solid, remove from bread pans, wrap in foil, and seal airtight in a plastic bag. Thaw and bake within a week. *To resume the recipe,* unwrap dough, place in greased pan, brush on any required wash, and bake at once, while still frozen. Give loaves an extra 5 to 10 minutes' baking time, rolls and buns an extra minute or two.

BREAD PROBLEMS: DIAGNOSES AND RESCUES

IF YOU LEAVE SOMETHING OUT: If you have left out one or more of the liquid ingredients—eggs, water, or milk—the dough will be hard and dry after you add the flour. To fix, simply cut and stir omitted liquid into the dough with a wooden spoon. The dough will look lumpy and messy, but it will smooth out during kneading.

If you realize during kneading that you have left out butter, sugar, or salt, simply incorporate these ingredients into the dough as you knead. If you do not discover your mistake until after the dough had its first rise, pat dough into a 14-inch square, sprinkle with sugar and/or salt or smear with softened butter, and knead thoroughly (at least 3 minutes) to incorporate the omitted ingredients. Ideally, you should allow the dough to rise again but you may proceed to form the dough at this point.

IF THE DOUGH WON'T RISE: The yeast may have been old and dead to start with, or it may have been killed because it was dissolved in excessively hot water or because the dough was set to rise in too warm a place. To remedy the problem, stir 1½ packages (3¾ teaspoons) dry yeast (or 1½ cakes compressed yeast) and 1 teaspoon sugar into ¼ cup warm water. Set mixture aside to dissolve and proof. Beat into the yeast mixture ½ to ⅔ cup all-purpose flour, or enough to make a soft dough. Thoroughly knead (5 minutes at least) this yeast mixture into the bread dough, then let the dough rise until doubled.

If the Dough is Rising Very Slowly: Either the room is cold or else too much salt, a yeast inhibitor, was added to the dough.

To get cold dough moving, set bowl in a sink filled with warm water (up to 110°F). If you suspect that salt is the problem, taste the dough. If it is not so salty as to be inedible, simply be patient; it will eventually rise to the desired bulk.

If the Baked Loaf is Gluey, Wet, or Grayish in Color: It is possible that too little flour was added to the dough. Next time, keep careful track of how many cupfuls of flour you measure into the dough and, if it feels very sticky while you knead (a telltale sign that the flour-to-liquid proportions are askew), incorporate extra flour.

Underbaking is a more likely cause of stickiness and wetness. Try the following rescue. Protect the cut end of the loaf with foil and return the bread to a 400°F oven for 15 to 30 minutes—the more underbaked and/or more thoroughly cooled the loaf is, the more time it will need in the oven. If this does not produce acceptable results, turn the loaf into bread crumbs or use to make bread pudding.

If the Bread Has Little Flavor: Part or all of the sugar or salt may have been left out, but more likely the first and second rises were terminated before the dough had fully doubled, and thus the yeast did not have sufficient time to develop and to flavor the loaf.

If the Bread Tastes Sour, "Alcoholic": This sometimes happens when a bread recipe is held too long in the refrigerator (sweet breads seem to be especially susceptible).

If the Bread is Dense and Doughy: Either the dough was not kneaded enough, or the loaf was put into the oven before it had had a chance to double in the bread pan.

If the Bread is Dry: Most likely too much flour was incorporated during kneading.

If the Crumb is Uneven, with Big Holes in the Middle of the Loaf and Under the Top Crust: There are two possible causes. First, the dough may not have become wholly integrated when it was formed. Next time, be sure to roll the dough into a tight cylinder and to slap, jab, squeeze, and press it into shape before setting it in the bread mold to rise. Second, the dough may have overrisen in the bread pan, causing large gas bubbles to form, especially beneath the top crust. Don't let the dough rise as much next time—or if it does, punch it down, reshape the loaf, and let it rise again, keeping a careful eye on it.

IF THE LOAF COLLAPSED OR LEVELED IN THE CENTER DURING BAKING: This is always due to the bread's having overrisen before being put in the oven.

QUICK BREADS and PANCAKES

Early American cookbooks are chock full of recipes for tea loaves, muffins, corn bread, biscuits, popovers, and pancakes, proving that quick breads and pancakes have long been a fundamental part of home baking. Even today we tend to associate certain quick breads and griddle cakes with famous times and places out of the American past—brown bread with Puritan Boston; pancakes with the frontier West; biscuits and corn bread with the old South; muffins with Pennsylvania Dutch farming country; and so on. It has become customary, however, to make quick breads from mixes or to buy them ready-made at the supermarket. This is a shame, because not only are the homemade versions infinitely more delicious, they are nearly as quick and easy to make as their packaged counterparts. Called "quick" because they are chemically leavened and do not require kneading or rising as yeast breads do, these breads can be made from scratch in about the same time it takes to open a box of mix and add to it whatever the instructions require. In addition, these breads are nearly failproof so long as you remember to mix the batter lightly, thus ensuring a tender crumb. Finally, variation possibilities for these breads are endless. There are, for example, 19 variations on the Master Recipe for muffins suggested in this chapter—and I bet you'll come up with a few more of your own.

MASTER RECIPE

Spiced Raisin-Nut Bread

Makes 2 medium loaves

❦ *People have different notions about what this kind of quick bread—variations of which include such American classics as banana, cranberry, and pumpkin—should be like. If your preference is for a light and cakelike loaf, similar to the usual store-bought or bakery kind, don't look here. This recipe and its variations produce rich, moist, and rather dense breads with a texture not at all like cake. Nice both for breakfast and for late afternoon tea, these breads can be served either warm or at room temperature, with or without cream cheese or butter. They keep fairly well, and may be reheated.*

PRELIMINARIES

1. Bring all ingredients to room temperature.
2. Set rack in the middle of the oven.
3. Preheat oven to 350°F 20 minutes before baking—325°F if using glass pans.
4. Select two medium-sized loaf pans (5- to 6-cup capacity each). Grease generously with 2 tablespoons soft butter or vegetable shortening.

STEP 1: BLENDING DRY INGREDIENTS

2 cups unbleached all-purpose flour (measure by scooping cup into large container of flour and sweeping off excess with the back of a knife)
¾ cup sugar
½ cup wheat germ
2 teaspoons baking powder
2 teaspoons cinnamon
1½ teaspoons nutmeg, preferably freshly grated
½ teaspoon ground cloves
½ teaspoon salt
1 cup (about 6 ounces) raisins
1 cup (about 4 ounces) walnuts or pecans, chopped into ¼-inch pieces

Combine flour, sugar, wheat germ, baking powder, spices, and salt in a 3- to 4-quart mixing bowl and stir thoroughly to mix. The baking powder must be distributed evenly within the dry ingredients if the bread is to rise properly.

Add the raisins and nuts and blend with your fingertips until raisins and nuts are separated and coated with flour mixture.

STEP 2: BLENDING LIQUID INGREDIENTS; MIXING BATTER; BAKING

4 large eggs
1½ cups milk
½ cup vegetable oil

Beat eggs in a 3-quart mixing bowl with wire whip until foamy. Then blend in the milk and oil. Pour egg mixture over the dry ingredients and stir with a wooden spoon just enough to moisten all the flour. Do not overbeat; the batter should look lumpy.

Turn batter into prepared pans and smooth the top. Bake 40 to 50 minutes, or until a knife inserted in the center comes out oily-looking, with a crumb or two adhering; the bread will have shrunk very slightly from the sides of the pan. Avoid overbaking, or the bread will be dry.

Let bread rest a few minutes in the pan(s) after being removed from the oven, then unmold onto a rack, top side up. Cool at least 30 minutes before serving; the bread will be sticky and bland-tasting if eaten too hot.

STORAGE: When completely cooled, bread can be wrapped in foil and refrigerated; it will keep for several days. Before serving, bring to room temperature or reheat, still wrapped in foil, in a 300°F oven for about 15 minutes. For longer storage bread may be frozen, but frozen bread has a tendency to become soft and sticky when thawed and a pronounced taste of baking powder emerges.

Variation: APPLESAUCE-RAISIN BREAD

Makes 2 medium loaves

Spiced Raisin-nut Bread
SUBSTITUTE: 2 cups *unsweetened* applesauce for milk

Proceed according to the Master Recipe, but substitute applesauce for milk.

Variation: BANANA BREAD

Makes 2 medium loaves

Spiced Raisin-nut Bread

OMIT: Cinnamon, nutmeg, and cloves
Raisins

SUBSTITUTE: 2 cups puréed *very ripe* bananas (about 5 medium) for milk

Proceed according to the Master Recipe, but omit spices and raisins and substitute puréed bananas for milk.

Variation: CARROT BREAD

Makes 2 medium loaves

Spiced Raisin-nut Bread

ADD: 1 cup lightly packed shredded carrots (2 to 3 medium)

Proceed according to the Master Recipe, but add the carrots along with the raisins and nuts.

Variation: CRANBERRY BREAD

Makes 2 medium loaves

Spiced Raisin-nut Bread

OMIT: Cinnamon, nutmeg, and cloves

SUBSTITUTE: 1 cup coarsely chopped raw cranberries for raisins
1¼ cups fresh orange juice for milk

ADD: Grated zest of 1 orange

Omit the spices and substitute chopped cranberries for the raisins called for in Step 1 of Master Recipe. (Since cranberries tend to bounce and roll off a chopping board, it is easiest to chop them in a food processor.) In Step 2, substitute orange juice for the milk called for and add grated zest along with the juice to the beaten eggs. Proceed with the Master Recipe.

Variation: DATE- OR PRUNE-NUT BREAD

Makes 2 medium loaves

Spiced Raisin-nut Bread
SUBSTITUTE: 1 cup chopped or snipped moist dates or prunes for raisins

Proceed according to the Master Recipe, but substitute dates or prunes for raisins.

Variation: ORANGE BREAD

Makes 2 medium loaves

Spiced Raisin-nut Bread
OMIT: Cinnamon, nutmeg, and cloves
SUBSTITUTE: ½ cup diced candied orange peel for raisins
1½ cups fresh orange juice for milk
ADD: Grated zest of 2 oranges

Proceed according to the Master Recipe, but omit the spices, substitute candied orange peel for the raisins and orange juice for the milk, and add grated orange zest along with the juice.

Variation: PUMPKIN BREAD

Makes 2 medium loaves

❦*Rich, moist, and fragrant, this is my personal favorite of all the quick tea loaves.*

Spiced Raisin-nut Bread
INCREASE: Sugar to 1 cup
OMIT: Raisins
SUBSTITUTE: 2 cups mashed cooked or canned unsweetened pumpkin (a 14- to 16-ounce can) for milk

Proceed according to the Master Recipe, but increase the sugar to 1 cup, omit the raisins, and substitute pumpkin for milk.

Variation: ZUCCHINI BREAD

Makes 2 medium loaves

Spiced Raisin-nut Bread

SUBSTITUTE: 1 cup lightly packed shredded zucchini (2 small or about 8 ounces) for raisins

DECREASE: Milk to 1¼ cups

Proceed according to the Master Recipe, but substitute zucchini for raisins and decrease milk to 1¼ cups.

MASTER RECIPE

Corn Bread

Makes 1 medium loaf

❦ *This sumptuously moist corn bread is best when made with stone-ground cornmeal, which contains the flavorful germ of the kernel. You should be able to find stone-ground cornmeal at your supermarket; if not, try a health-food store.*

PRELIMINARIES

1. Bring all ingredients to room temperature.
2. Set rack in the middle of oven.
3. Preheat oven to 425°F 20 minutes before baking—400°F if using a glass pan.
4. Select either a 10×6×2-inch or an 8×8×2-inch pan. Grease generously with 1 tablespoon soft butter.

12 tablespoons (1½ sticks) butter
4 large eggs
1 cup milk
1⅓ cups white or yellow cornmeal, preferably stone-ground
⅔ cup unbleached all-purpose flour (measure by scooping cup into large container of flour and sweeping off excess with the back of a knife)
1 tablespoon sugar
1 tablespoon baking powder
¼ teaspoon salt

Melt butter in a small saucepan over low heat. Remove from heat and set aside to cool briefly. Using a wire whip, beat the eggs in a 3-quart bowl until frothy. Beat in the milk, then the melted butter.

Combine cornmeal, flour, sugar, baking powder, and salt in a 4-quart mixing bowl and blend well with a fork to distribute the baking powder evenly. Make a well in the center of the dry ingredients, pour in the egg/butter mixture, and beat just until the dry ingredients are moistened; the batter should look lumpy. Turn batter into prepared pan and bake 20 to 25 minutes, or until the top cracks and a needle inserted in the center comes out clean. Let bread rest 5 minutes before serving, directly from the pan.

STORAGE: Corn bread is best when served fresh from the oven. However, leftovers can be removed from the pan when cooled, wrapped in foil, and refrigerated for several days. To serve, reheat, still wrapped in foil, in a 400°F oven for about 10 minutes.

Variation: CORN MUFFINS

Makes 12 muffins

Batter for ***Corn Bread***

Generously butter a 12-cup muffin tin (cups should measure about 3½ inches across the top and hold about ½ cup). Fill each cup ⅔ full with corn bread batter and bake in center of a 425°F oven for 18 to 20 minutes.

Variation: CORN STICKS

Makes 12 to 14 corn sticks

Batter for ***Corn Bread***

SPECIAL EQUIPMENT: two 6- to 7-mold corn stick pan.

Generously butter the pans and spoon an equal quantity of corn bread batter into each mold. Bake in center of a 425°F oven for 12 to 15 minutes, or until sticks are a deep golden brown.

Variation: SKILLET CORN BREAD

Makes 1 round loaf

Batter for ***Corn Bread***

Place a 9-inch round cast iron skillet over a high flame for a minute or two, or until the skillet is very hot. Using a pastry brush, coat sides and bottom of skillet with 1½ tablespoons of vegetable shortening. *Immediately* pour in corn bread batter and set skillet in the middle of a preheated 425°F oven. Bake for 20 to 25 minutes, or until bread is nicely browned and crusty around the edges. Serve immediately, straight from the skillet.

Variation: CRACKLING CORN BREAD

Makes 1 round loaf

❦ *This classic American favorite is delicious indeed, but it is not for those trying to cut down on cholesterol! Serve crackling corn bread for breakfast—it is virtually a meal in itself—or with pork hocks and greens.*

Step 1: Preparing Cracklings

8 ounces salt pork or fresh pork fatback, trimmed of any rind

If you are using salt pork, rinse it briefly under tepid water and pat dry with paper toweling.

Cut salt pork or pork fat into ¼-inch dice and fry in a 9-inch cast iron skillet over medium-low heat until pieces are very brown and have rendered their fat. Transfer pork pieces to a plate with a slotted spoon and set aside. Pour off the rendered fat into a measuring cup. Return 2 tablespoons fat to the skillet, reserving ¾ cup drippings in the measure.

Step 2: Baking the Bread

Batter for ***Corn Bread***

SUBSTITUTE: ¾ cup pork fat drippings (from Step 1) for butter

ADD: Fried pork bits (from Step 1)

Prepare corn bread batter according to Master Recipe, but substitute ¾ cup of rendered pork fat for the butter, and stir in fried pork bits. Set the skillet containing the pork fat over high heat for a minute or two, or until the fat smokes. Immediately pour in corn bread batter and set in middle of a preheated 425°F oven. Bake for 20 to 25 minutes, or until bread is nicely browned and crusty around the edges. Serve immediately, straight from the skillet.

MASTER RECIPE

Baking Powder Biscuits

Makes sixteen to eighteen 2-inch biscuits

Some people insist that baking powder biscuits should be flaky, like croissants or pastry crust. Others like them tender and fluffy, like fine cake. Still others prefer them slightly resistant to the bite, like bread. Obviously, no biscuit can be all things to all people. The biscuits produced by this recipe are very flaky, and, if the dough is kneaded briefly, slightly breadlike. For biscuits that are very fluffy and not at all flaky, try dropped biscuits.

As when making a pie dough, it is better to underblend than to overblend the fat and flour. The coarser the blend, the lighter and flakier the biscuits. Biscuits are flakier and fresher tasting when made with unsalted than with salted butter. The difference is quite remarkable.

Preliminaries

1. Set rack in the middle or lower-middle level of the oven.
2. Preheat oven to 425°F 20 minutes before baking.
3. Select a large baking sheet (16×13 inches, for example); do *not* grease.

Step 1: Preparing the Dough

2 cups unbleached all-purpose flour (measure by scooping cup into large container of flour and sweeping off excess with the back of a knife)
1 tablespoon baking powder
¾ teaspoon salt (½ teaspoon if you are using salted butter)
5 tablespoons *very cold* butter, preferably unsalted
2 tablespoons *very cold* vegetable shortening
¾ cup milk

Place flour, baking powder, and salt in a 3-quart bowl and toss thoroughly with a fork to distribute baking powder evenly.

Cut the butter into ⅛-inch pats and the shortening into ¼-inch pieces and toss with dry mixture. Using a pastry blender, two knives, or your fingertips, quickly cut or pinch the fat into the flour mixture. Underblend rather than overblend; the mixture should look like coarse oatmeal when you're done, and it's perfectly okay if there are some large lumps.

Pour in milk and stir 5 to 8 quick strokes with a wooden spoon, just enough to moisten dry ingredients and to bind the mixture into a rough-looking dough. Let dough rest for a moment or two in the bowl.

STEP 2: ROLLING AND CUTTING THE BISCUITS; BAKING

2 to 4 tablespoons butter, melted (optional)

You now have a choice: either proceed directly to roll out the biscuits, in which case they will have an extremely tender, almost crumbly texture, or knead them briefly before rolling, in which case your biscuits will be slightly chewy. If you decide to knead, proceed as follows: Scoop dough out of the bowl onto a lightly floured work surface and sprinkle very lightly with flour. Dust your hands with flour as well. Now, very gently jab and slap at the dough—think of a cat playing with a ball of yarn—for just *10 to 15 seconds,* or until you can feel the dough barely begin to gather and to firm up, indicating that the gluten molecules have been activated. Don't knead beyond this point or the biscuits will be tough.

On a lightly floured work surface, roll dough out to a thickness of about ½ inch, using just a few quick, deft strokes of the rolling pin. Press a 2-inch cutter into the dough with one neat, decisive punch, dipping cutter into flour before cutting each biscuit. Don't twist the cutter or you will pull the dough layers out of shape and cause the biscuits to rise unevenly. Combine leftover scraps of dough by pressing them together briefly, then roll out and cut.

Space the biscuits at least 1½ inches apart on an ungreased baking sheet. If you wish, brush tops of biscuits with melted butter just before putting them in the oven. Bake in preheated oven for about 12 minutes, or until pale brown on top. Serve immediately.

AHEAD OF TIME: Cut biscuits may be placed on the baking sheet, covered with plastic wrap, and refrigerated for several hours before baking.

TIP: For an informal meal, you can simply pat the biscuit dough into an 8-inch rectangle and cut it into sixteen 2-inch squares with a very sharp, well-floured knife. Be sure to handle the dough as gently and as little as possible. Biscuits formed in this way are never as pretty or quite as tender as cut-out biscuits, but then again you don't have to dirty up a rolling pin and there are no scraps to reroll.

Variation: DROPPED BISCUITS

Makes 18 small biscuits

❦*If you like your biscuits very fluffy, tender, and cakelike, and if you don't mind their having a freeform, dumplingesque shape, these are the ones to make. The added advantage here, of course, is that neither kneading nor rolling is necessary.*

Note: By increasing the liquid measure and following the procedure outlined below, any of the biscuit variation recipes that follow may also be dropped.

Baking Powder Biscuits
INCREASE: Milk to 1 cup

Add milk and give the batter 5 to 10 firm strokes with the wooden spoon, just enough to make it cohere and begin to draw away from sides of bowl. Do not knead or roll as outlined in the Master Recipe, but instead drop 2-tablespoon gobs of batter 2 inches apart onto baking sheet.

Variation: BUTTERMILK BISCUITS

Makes 16 to 18 biscuits

❦*Buttermilk makes very tender, rich, fine-textured biscuits with a slightly tangy taste. Buttermilk biscuits are not, however, as flaky as those made with whole milk.*

Baking Powder Biscuits
SUBSTITUTE: ¾ cup buttermilk for milk (to make dropped buttermilk biscuits, use 1 cup plus 2 tablespoons buttermilk)

Proceed according to Master Recipe, but substitute buttermilk for whole milk.

Variation: BACON-CHIVE BISCUITS

Makes 16 to 18 biscuits

Baking Powder Biscuits
ADD: 6 slices bacon, cooked very crisp and crumbled
2 tablespoons snipped fresh chives or 1 tablespoon dried

After blending fat and flour, add bacon and chives and toss. Add milk and proceed according to the Master Recipe.

Variation: CHEDDAR BISCUITS

Makes 16 to 18 biscuits

❦ *Try these biscuits with strawberry jam for brunch.*

Baking Powder Biscuits
DECREASE: Butter to 3 tablespoons
ADD: 1 cup (about 4 ounces) shredded extra-sharp Cheddar cheese

After blending fat and flour, add cheese and toss lightly. Add milk and proceed according to Master Recipe.

Variation: GARDEN HERB BISCUITS

Makes 16 to 18 biscuits

❦ *Terrific with a creamy chicken stew.*

Baking Powder Biscuits
ADD: 3 tablespoons finely chopped fresh parsley or 2 tablespoons finely chopped fresh dill (feathery leaves only)
2 tablespoons snipped fresh chives or 1 tablespoon dried

After blending fat and flour, add herbs and toss to blend. Add milk and proceed according to the Master Recipe.

Variation: LITTLE ITALY SAVORY BISCUITS

Makes 16 to 18 biscuits

❦ *The blend of herbs and spices used here gives these extraordinarily good biscuits an Italian taste. They are especially good with fried or scrambled eggs and spicy sausages.*

Baking Powder Biscuits
ADD: 2 teaspoons ground thyme
2 teaspoons rubbed or ground sage
3/4 teaspoon freshly ground pepper
6 tablespoons yellow cornmeal

Prepare biscuit dough according to Step 1 of the Master Recipe, but toss thyme, sage, and pepper with other dry ingredients until thoroughly combined, then blend in fat.

In Step 2, use 4 tablespoons of the cornmeal instead of flour to dust work surface before rolling out biscuits. Sprinkle the rolled-out dough with the additional 2 tablespoons cornmeal and lightly pass over with the rolling pin to make the cornmeal adhere. Cut and bake according to Master Recipe.

Variation: VIRGINIA HAM BISCUITS

Makes 16 to 18 biscuits

❦ *Split and buttered, these make wonderful tea sandwiches.*

Baking Powder Biscuits

ADD: 1 teaspoon dry mustard and/or ¼ teaspoon celery seed (optional)
½ cup (about 4 ounces) minced cooked smoked ham

Toss optional mustard and celery seed with other dry ingredients until thoroughly combined, then blend in fat. Add ham and toss again. Pour in milk and proceed according to the Master Recipe.

Variation: SCONES

Makes 18 scones

❦ *My sister Leah introduced me to these marvelous British tea pastries, which should always be offered hot with butter and jam.*

Baking Powder Biscuits

ADD: 1 tablespoon sugar
2 large eggs

SUBSTITUTE: ⅔ cup heavy cream for milk
1 egg yolk beaten with ½ teaspoon cream for melted butter

Blend the sugar with the other dry ingredients called for in Step 1 of the Master Recipe. Beat the eggs in a small bowl until foamy, stir in the heavy cream, then substitute the egg/cream mixture for milk.

Instead of kneading, rolling, and cutting the dough (Step 2), proceed as follows: On a floured work surface pat the dough into a 9-inch square. Using a very sharp knife and flouring the knife before each cut, trim the edges of the square to make it even, then cut the square down and across at 3-inch intervals, making 9 small squares. Cut each square in half diagonally to make 18 triangles.

Arrange scones on ungreased baking sheet and brush the tops with egg yolk glaze. Bake 10 to 14 minutes, or until the scones are nicely browned and feel firm when pressed with a fingertip.

Variation: SHORTCAKE

Makes one 8-inch, four 4-inch, or six 3-inch shortcakes

Baking Powder Biscuits

ADD: 1 tablespoon sugar

INCREASE: Butter to 12 tablespoons (1½ sticks)

In Step 1 of Master Recipe blend sugar with other dry ingredients called for and increase the butter to 12 tablespoons.

In Step 2, knead dough briefly, then roll out about ¾ inch thick and cut into the size shortcake(s) you desire. Brush with 4 tablespoons melted butter before baking. Bake small shortcakes 12 to 15 minutes, single large shortcake 14 to 17 minutes, or until the top is nicely browned and feels firm when pressed. To serve, split the warm shortcakes horizontally, fill with lightly sugared cut-up fruit, and top with heavy cream or whipped cream.

Variation: STREUSEL COFFEECAKE

Makes one 9-inch coffeecake serving 6 to 8

PRELIMINARIES

1. Set rack in the middle of the oven.
2. Preheat oven to 375°F 20 minutes before baking.
3. Select either a 9-inch round cake pan with sides at least 1½ inches deep or a 9-inch springform pan. Grease the pan with 1½ tablespoons soft butter.

The dough for ***Baking Powder Biscuits***

ADD: 1 to 2 tablespoons sugar (optional)

INCREASE: Milk to 1 cup

6 tablespoons cold butter

⅓ cup all-purpose flour

⅔ cup sugar

2 tablespoons packed dark brown sugar
½ cup (about 2 ounces) chopped walnuts or pecans (optional)
2 teaspoons cinnamon

Prepare the biscuit dough according to Step 1 of the Master Recipe, but toss optional sugar with dry ingredients, and increase milk to 1 cup, making a heavy batter. Drop batter evenly into prepared 9-inch pan and level it by pressing with lightly floured fingertips. Again using your fingertips, press dimples going about halfway down into the dough, giving the dough a cratered look. Set aside.

Cut cold butter into ¼-inch pieces and place in a 2-quart bowl. Add flour and sugars and cut with two knives or a pastry blender until mixture resembles coarse crumbs. Add nuts and the cinnamon and toss briefly with a fork to combine. Scrape streusel topping onto dough and distribute it evenly over the top with a fork.

Bake coffeecake in preheated oven for 25 to 30 minutes, or until it is risen and puffed, with perhaps just a small depression in the center. Let cool about 10 minutes before serving, with or without butter.

Variation: CINNAMON-NUT SNAILS

Makes 18 snails

Cinnamon-nut buns, page 651
SUBSTITUTE: The dough for ***Baking Powder Biscuits*** for the egg bread (Sally Lunn) dough

To make these irresistible sticky buns prepare the Master Recipe for biscuit dough and refrigerate dough 1 hour, wrapped in plastic, to firm it. Follow the recipe for cinnamon-nut buns, substituting biscuit dough for the egg-bread dough called for in the recipe. Except for the fact that biscuit dough does not require rising, all steps outlined in the recipe are exactly the same.

MASTER RECIPE

Muffins

Makes 12 medium muffins

Muffins are perhaps the simplest of all quick breads to make, and they lend themselves to almost endless variation. To throw a muffin party, make up a double or triple batch of muffin batter, divide the batter into two or three—or even more—equal parts, and flavor each part in a different manner, using the variation recipes or perhaps your own ideas. Muffin batter, by the way, may be held in a covered bowl for up to an hour if you don't have enough muffin tins or oven space to bake all of the muffins at once.

There is nothing remotely tricky about making muffins. Just remember to mix the batter as little as possible—too much mixing makes for tough, coarse-textured muffins—and to make sure the oven is thoroughly preheated before putting the muffins in.

PRELIMINARIES

1. Bring all ingredients to room temperature.
2. Set rack in the lower-middle level of the oven. (Muffins need a good, strong push of heat from the bottom to rise properly.)
3. Preheat oven to 400°F 20 minutes before baking.
4. Using 2 tablespoons soft butter, generously grease inside surfaces of a muffin tin having twelve cups. (For highest rise, do not use paper liners.)

2 cups unbleached all-purpose flour (measure by scooping cup into large container of flour and sweeping off excess with the back of a knife)
3 tablespoons sugar
1 tablespoon baking powder
¼ teaspoon salt
4 tablespoons butter
1 large egg
1 cup milk

Place flour, sugar, baking powder, and salt in a 3-quart mixing bowl and toss thoroughly with a fork to distribute baking powder evenly. Set aside.

Melt butter and set aside to cool. Using a wire whip, beat the egg in 2-quart bowl until frothy and very light. Add milk and cooled melted butter and blend thoroughly.

Make a well in center of the dry ingredients and pour in the milk mixture. With just a few strong, swift strokes of a rubber spatula, mix the ingredients just enough to moisten the flour (this should take only a few seconds); the batter should be lumpy and have the consistency of thick oatmeal.

Divide batter evenly among prepared muffin cups. Bake 20 to 25 minutes, or until muffins have risen to a point in the center, are lightly browned, and have shrunk slightly from the edges of the cups. Muffins are at their best eaten hot from the oven, but they may also be cooled on a rack and served later.

STORAGE: If sealed airtight in a plastic bag, muffins can be refrigerated for several days; freezing makes them soggy and is not recommended. To reheat, wrap muffins loosely in foil and place in a 450°F oven for about 5 minutes.

Variation: APPLE-CINNAMON MUFFINS

Makes 12 muffins

Muffins

ADD: 1 teaspoon cinnamon
1 cup lightly packed shredded peeled tart apple (1 medium-large)

Proceed according to Master Recipe, but toss cinnamon with the flour and other dry ingredients, then add the apple along with the milk mixture.

Variation: APRICOT-WALNUT MUFFINS

Makes 12 muffins

Muffins

ADD: ½ cup finely diced moist dried apricots
½ cup (about 2 ounces) chopped walnuts or black walnuts

Proceed according to the Master Recipe, but add apricots and walnuts to dry ingredients along with the milk mixture.

Variation: BACON MUFFINS

Makes 12 muffins

Muffins

ADD: 5 slices bacon

Fry bacon until very crisp, drain on paper toweling, and crumble. Proceed according to the Master Recipe, but add crumbled bacon to dry ingredients along with the milk mixture.

Variation: BANANA MUFFINS

Makes 12 muffins

Muffins

ADD: 1 cup finely diced (not mashed) ripe but firm bananas

Proceed according to Master Recipe, but add bananas to dry ingredients along with the milk mixture.

Variation: BLUEBERRY MUFFINS

Makes 12 muffins

Muffins

ADD: 1 cup blueberries

Wash blueberries, and roll on paper towels to dry. Remove any remaining small stems. Proceed according to the Master Recipe, but add berries to dry ingredients along with the milk mixture.

Variation: BRAN MUFFINS

Makes 12 muffins

Muffins

DECREASE: Flour to 1 cup
ADD: 1 cup 100% bran cereal
½ cup dried currants or chopped raisins, dates, prunes, or figs

Mix dry ingredients as indicated in the Master recipe, but use only 1 cup flour. Set aside.

Mix together egg, milk, and melted butter as indicated in the Master Recipe, then add bran, stirring well to moisten. Let stand for 10 minutes. Add this plus the dried fruit to the flour mixture and proceed according to the Master Recipe.

Variation: CHEESE MUFFINS

Makes 12 muffins

Muffins

OMIT: Sugar

ADD: ¾ cup (about 3 ounces) shredded extra-sharp Cheddar cheese

Proceed according to Master Recipe, but omit the sugar and add cheese to dry ingredients along with the milk mixture.

Variation: CHOCOLATE CHIP MUFFINS

Makes 12 muffins

Muffins

ADD: ⅔ cup (4 ounces) miniature or chopped regular-size chocolate chips

Proceed according to Master Recipe, but add chocolate chips to dry ingredients along with the milk mixture.

Variation: CRANBERRY MUFFINS

Makes 12 muffins

Muffins

INCREASE: Sugar to ⅓ cup

ADD: 1 cup chopped raw cranberries
Grated zest of 1 orange

Proceed according to the Master Recipe, but increase the sugar called for to ⅓ cup and add cranberries and orange zest to the dry ingredients along with the milk mixture.

Variation: DATE-NUT MUFFINS

Makes 12 muffins

Muffins

ADD: ⅔ cup finely diced moist dates
½ cup (about 2 ounces) chopped walnuts, black walnuts, or pecans

Proceed according to the Master Recipe, but add dates and nuts to the dry ingredients along with the milk mixture.

Variation: MAPLE-HAM MUFFINS

Makes 12 muffins

❦ *These are especially delicious with eggs.*

Muffins

SUBSTITUTE: 2 tablespoons pure maple syrup for sugar
ADD: ½ cup (about 4 ounces) minced cooked ham, preferably smoked

Proceed according to Master Recipe, but omit the sugar, and stir maple syrup and ham into the milk mixture before blending with the dry ingredients.

Variation: OATMEAL-RAISIN MUFFINS

Makes 12 muffins

Muffins

ADD: 1 teaspoon cinnamon (optional)
DECREASE: Flour to 1 cup
ADD: 1 cup rolled oats
⅔ cup dried currants or coarsely chopped raisins

Mix dry ingredients as indicated in the Master Recipe, but add cinnamon, if you wish, and substitute rolled oats for 1 cup of the flour. Stir in currants or raisins along with the milk mixture, and proceed according to the Master Recipe.

Variation: ORANGE MUFFINS

Makes 12 muffins

Muffins

ADD: Grated zest of 2 oranges

Proceed according to the Master Recipe, but add orange zest to the milk mixture.

Variation: PEANUT BUTTER (AND JAM) MUFFINS

Makes 12 muffins

Muffins

ADD: 1/4 cup peanut butter
2 tablespoons strawberry or black currant jam (optional)

Prepare muffin batter according to the Master Recipe. Distribute half of the batter among 12 prepared muffin cups. Place about 1 teaspoon peanut butter and, if you wish, 1/2 teaspoon jam in each cup and cover with remaining batter. Bake according to Master Recipe.

Variation: PINEAPPLE-WALNUT MUFFINS

Makes 12 muffins

❦ *These are very nice with cream cheese.*

Muffins

ADD: 2/3 cup drained crushed canned pineapple, preferably juice-packed
1/2 cup (about 2 ounces) chopped walnuts or black walnuts

Drain pineapple in a sieve, pressing firmly with the back of a spoon to remove as much moisture as possible. Proceed according to the Master Recipe, but add pineapple and walnuts to the dry ingredients along with the milk mixture.

Variation: PUMPKIN MUFFINS

Makes 12 muffins

Muffins

ADD: 1 teaspoon cinnamon
½ teaspoon nutmeg, preferably freshly grated
½ teaspoon ground cloves
1 cup mashed cooked or canned unsweetened pumpkin

Proceed according to the Master Recipe, but add spices to the flour and other dry ingredients and beat pumpkin into the milk mixture before mixing the batter.

Variation: SOUR CREAM MUFFINS

Makes 12 muffins

❦ *Tender, rich, and tangy, these muffins lend themselves to many additions—chocolate chips, apples and cinnamon, pineapple, and so on. See the preceding variations for ideas or experiment with your own.*

Muffins

OMIT: Butter
Milk

ADD: 1½ cups (12 ounces) sour cream

Omitting the butter and milk, add sour cream to beaten egg and beat until very thoroughly blended. Add this mixture to dry ingredients and proceed according to the Master Recipe.

Variation: SPICE MUFFINS

Makes 12 muffins

❦ *This recipe can be considered a jumping-off point for further experimentation.*

Muffins

ADD: 1 teaspoon cinnamon
1 teaspoon nutmeg, preferably freshly grated
½ teaspoon ground cloves
3 to 6 tablespoons very finely minced candied ginger (optional)

Proceed according to Master Recipe, but toss spices with the flour and other dry ingredients, and if you are using candied ginger, blend it into the dry ingredients along with the milk mixture.

Variation: WHOLE WHEAT MUFFINS

Makes 12 muffins

Any of the fresh, cooked, or dried fruits suggested in the other muffin variation recipes—cranberries, apples, pineapple, dates, and so on—can be added here.

Muffins

DECREASE: All-purpose flour to 1 cup
ADD: 3/4 cup whole wheat flour

Proceed according to Master Recipe, but decrease all-purpose flour to 1 cup and add whole wheat flour.

Popovers

Makes 10 to 12 popovers

For best results, use an 11-cup cast-iron popover pan rather than a muffin tin or porcelain cups, neither of which holds heat as well. Although it is customary to heat the popover pan before adding the batter, I find that this practice encourages popovers to sink in the middle.

PRELIMINARIES

1. Bring all ingredients to room temperature.
2. Set rack in lower level of the oven.
3. Preheat oven to 450°F 20 minutes before baking.
4. Select an 11-cup cast iron popover pan or substitute a muffin tin or 10 to 12 porcelain molds set on a baking tray if you do not have a popover pan. Brush inside surfaces with 2 tablespoons very soft butter.

4 tablespoons butter
2 large eggs
1 cup milk
¾ cup unbleached all-purpose flour (measure by scooping cup into large container of flour and sweeping off excess with the back of a knife)
¼ teaspoon salt

Melt butter and set aside to cool slightly.

Beat eggs just until blended in a 3-quart bowl. Using a wire whip, beat in milk and melted butter, then add the flour all at once and beat until the batter is smooth.

Pour batter into prepared pan or molds; be sure that each cup is no more than ⅔ full or the popovers will be heavy and may spill over. Immediately place in preheated oven. Without opening the oven door, bake at 450°F for 20 minutes, then lower oven temperature to 375°F and bake 10 minutes longer. Pierce the sides of the popovers with a sharp knife (this allows steam to escape, giving you very crispy, very sturdy popovers) and bake another 5 to 10 minutes. The popovers are done when they are brown and crusty-looking and have loosened from the sides of the pan; if removed from the oven too soon, the popovers will be undercooked inside and will collapse.

Popovers are best eaten as soon as they come out of the oven. Either serve them with jam and butter or use them as cases for scrambled eggs, creamed seafood, or creamed chicken.

Variation: YORKSHIRE PUDDING

Makes 6 to 8 servings

❦ *This is the classic accompaniment to roast beef; it is delicious, and fun to make, too.*

Batter for ***Popovers***
SUBSTITUTE: Roast beef drippings for butter

Select a 9-inch cast iron frying pan or heavy porcelain baking dish instead of a popover pan. Instead of greasing pan with butter use 2 to 4 tablespoons beef drippings.

Prepare batter according to Master Recipe, substituting ¼ cup drippings for the melted butter. Pour batter into greased pan and bake for 20 minutes at 450°F and 10 to 15 minutes longer at 375°F. Serve at once. Sprinkle with coarsely ground pepper if you wish.

MASTER RECIPE

Pancakes

Makes sixteen to eighteen 4-inch pancakes

❦ *I will record here my unshakable prejudice: These buttery, delicate pancakes must be eaten with a fine, 100 percent pure maple syrup, or perhaps with good honey or a homemade fruit sauce.*

STEP 1: PREPARING THE BATTER

- 4 tablespoons butter
- 4 large eggs, at room temperature
- 1½ cups milk
- ½ cup yogurt
- ¼ teaspoon cream of tartar
- 2 cups unbleached all-purpose flour (measure by scooping cup into large container of flour and sweeping off excess with the back of a knife)
- 1½ teaspoons baking powder
- 1 teaspoon baking soda
- ¼ teaspoon salt

Melt butter in a small saucepan over low heat. Remove from heat and set aside to cool slightly.

Separate eggs, placing whites in a 3-quart mixing bowl and yolks in a 1½-quart bowl. Add milk and yogurt to yolks and beat with a wire whip to blend.

Place flour, baking powder, baking soda, and salt in a 4-quart bowl and blend thoroughly with a fork. Make a well in the center of the dry ingredients and pour in milk mixture. Stir 3 or 4 strokes, add melted butter, then beat just long enough to moisten the flour—there will be lots of lumps, but this is okay. Set aside.

Beat egg whites at low speed with an electric mixer (or with a wire whip) until they foam, then add cream of tartar; gradually increasing the mixing speed, beat the whites until they form stiff peaks. Fold beaten egg whites into the batter with a rubber spatula.

STEP 2: COOKING THE PANCAKES Set 10-inch cast iron or nonstick skillet over high heat—do not grease the skillet—and heat until drops of water sputter and dance when dropped on the skillet. Reduce heat slightly, ladle in two 4-inch pancakes—you'll need about 1/4 cup batter per pancake—and cook until the bubbles bursting on the top leave dry craters. This will take just a minute or two. Flip pancakes with spatula and cook another minute or so. As you proceed, regulate the heat so that the skillet does not smoke; if it does begin to smoke, remove from heat at once and wait a few moments before returning it to the burner.

If you are not serving the pancakes immediately, arrange them on a baking sheet and set uncovered in a warm oven (about 150°F). Serve as soon as possible with warmed maple syrup, honey, or fruit sauce.

Variation: BANANA PANCAKES

Makes about twenty 4-inch pancakes

❦ *Banana pancakes served with warm maple syrup have always been a great favorite of mine.*

Pancakes

ADD: 1 cup diced ripe but firm bananas

Proceed according to the Master Recipe, folding bananas into the batter along with the beaten egg whites.

Variation: BERRY PANCAKES

Makes about twenty 4-inch pancakes

Pancakes

ADD: 1 cup blueberries, raspberries, or sliced strawberries

Proceed according to the Master Recipe, folding berries into the batter along with the beaten egg whites.

Variation: BUCKWHEAT PANCAKES

Makes sixteen to eighteen 4-inch pancakes

Pancakes

DECREASE: Flour to 1 cup
ADD: 1 cup buckwheat flour (available at health-food stores)
1 tablespoon sugar

Proceed according to the Master Recipe, but decrease all-purpose flour to 1 cup and combine it with buckwheat flour and sugar, along with the other dry ingredients.

Variation: BUTTERMILK PANCAKES

Makes sixteen to eighteen 4-inch pancakes

Pancakes

SUBSTITUTE: 2 cups buttermilk for milk and yogurt

Proceed according to Master Recipe, but substitute buttermilk for both the milk and yogurt.

Variation: CORNMEAL PANCAKES WITH BACON

Makes sixteen to eighteen 4-inch pancakes

❦ *These make a terrific winter-night Sunday supper.*

Pancakes

OMIT:	Butter
ADD:	5 or 6 slices bacon
DECREASE:	Flour to 1⅓ cups
ADD:	⅔ cup yellow cornmeal, preferably stone-ground
	1 tablespoon sugar

Fry bacon until very crisp, drain on paper towels, and crumble. Reserve bacon and ¼ cup of the drippings.

Mix dry ingredients as indicated in the Master Recipe, but decrease the flour to 1⅓ cups and add cornmeal and sugar. After adding the milk mixture to the dry ingredients, stir in the bacon and bacon drippings in lieu of melted butter, then proceed according to the Master Recipe.

Variation: WAFFLES

Makes 8 to 12 waffles, depending on size

❦ *There is absolutely no comparison between fresh, buttery homemade waffles and the frozen pop-'em-in-the-toaster kind. If you don't already own a waffle iron, be sure to buy one with deeply indented grids so that your waffles will have lots of crispy surface area as well as deep craters for holding maple syrup, honey, or other topping. Many of today's waffle irons are constructed to do double duty as sandwich grills and so on, and their grids are too shallow to produce first-rate waffles.*

Unfortunately for the calorie-conscious, perfect crisp, tender, delicate waffles can only be achieved by adding lots of butter to the batter (or by using heavy cream in place of milk). You will still get waffles, however, if you use the pancake batter in the Master Recipe without modification—they just won't be quite as good.

The batter for ***Pancakes***
INCREASE: Butter to 12 to 16 tablespoons (1½ to 2 sticks)

Prepare pancake batter according to Master Recipe, simply increasing the butter specified to 1½ to 2 sticks. Bake waffles in a thoroughly preheated waffle iron according to the manufacturer's instructions. Be sure to cook them until they are nicely browned and very crisp. They are best served at once, but may be kept warm for a while in a 150°F oven.

CRÊPES

Makes about thirty 6-inch or twenty 8-inch crêpes

❦ *When crêpes became popular some years ago they were considered a fancy French borrowing. But in fact crêpes have been enjoyed in this country since Colonial times, when, typically, they were stacked with sprinklings of maple sugar and served in wedges like cake.*

Crêpes can be very good, or they can be dreadful. If you want to make good ones, you must use a very thin, runny batter that makes thin—but easily torn—crêpes.

Crêpes may be served either as a savory hors d'oeuvre or entrée or as a sweet dessert, depending on what they are filled and/or sauced with.

Serving Ideas for Crêpes

Savory Crêpes: To serve 6 as a main course, prepare 1 recipe of Basic Cream Sauce or one of its variations, pages 34–46, and fold into the sauce 3 to 4 cups of diced cooked poultry, seafood, vegetables, etc. The casserole combinations listed in the chart on page 202 can be adapted for crêpes; simply replace the pasta with additional meat or vegetables. Distribute 3 to 5 tablespoons of the filling (depending on the size of the crêpe) on each crêpe, and either roll up cigarwise or fold into an envelope. The crêpes can be served as is, or you can give them more elegance by masking them with an additional cup of cream sauce, sprinkling them with cheese, and browning the stuffed crêpes quickly under a hot broiler.

Dessert crêpes: The simplest kind of dessert crêpes are just sprinkled with sugar (white, brown, or maple) or spread with jam or applesauce. You can roll or fold such crêpes, or stack them into a cake with the filling in between and cut the cake into wedges.

More elaborate desserts can be made by stuffing crêpes with warm pastry cream, page 855, enriched with crushed macaroons or toasted nuts; sautéed, flambeed fruit, page 870; or warmed cottage cheese slightly sweetened and flavored with cinnamon and grated orange zest or minced candied orange peel. Two to 3 cups of any of these fillings are enough for 30 small or 20 large crêpes, to serve 8.

Step 1: Mixing the Batter

1½ cups milk
1¼ cups water
1 large egg
2 large egg yolks
1½ cups unbleached all-purpose flour (measure by scooping cup into large container of flour and sweeping off excess with the back of a knife)
6 tablespoons butter, melted
For dessert crêpes only:
1 tablespoon sugar
½ teaspoon vanilla extract

Using a wire whip, beat together milk, water, egg, and yolks in a 4-quart bowl. Add the flour all at once and beat until the batter is completely smooth. Stir in the melted butter and, if you are making dessert crêpes, the sugar and vanilla extract. Cover the bowl with plastic wrap and refrigerate for at least 2 hours—or overnight—to relax the gluten in the flour and make crêpes tender.

STEP 2: COOKING THE CRÊPES

¼ teaspoon vegetable oil (unnecessary if you are using a nonstick skillet)

Gently stir up crêpe batter if it has separated, and bring it to room temperature. (If you are in a hurry, set bowl of chilled batter in sink filled with hot water to warm.)

Select a 6- to 8-inch heavy skillet, preferably one with a nonstick lining, though an ordinary skillet may also be used. Spread oil in skillet (unless it has a nonstick coating), then wipe with a paper towel, leaving only a thin film. Set skillet over high heat until drops of water sputter when dropped on the skillet.

Form each crêpe as follows: Grasp the handle of skillet with one hand. Ladle batter into center of skillet—about 3½ tablespoons for 8-inch crêpes, 2½ tablespoons for 6-inch crêpes—and immediately swirl skillet to spread batter out to the edges of the pan. (The more quickly and deftly this motion is accomplished, the thinner and shapelier your crêpe will be. The first few times you try it, you will probably end up with some holes and rough edges in your crêpes, which may be patched with a bit of extra batter.) Let crêpe cook for 1 to 2 minutes, or until it appears dry on top. Turn down the heat a bit if the edges are becoming frazzled. Lift up an edge of the crêpe with the spatula; if the bottom is brown, it is ready to turn. Either flip crêpe with a spatula as you would a pancake, or quickly grasp an edge with your fingers, peel the crêpe off the pan, and flip it onto its opposite side. Let crêpe cook about 30 seconds on the second side, or until brown speckles appear, then invert skillet over a baking sheet to flip crêpe out. Stack cooked crêpes between sheets of waxed paper to prevent sticking.

STORAGE: Crêpes freeze very well. Wrap the stack in foil and seal airtight in a plastic bag. They will keep for several months. Thaw them completely before filling.

BROWN BREAD

Makes 1 loaf serving 6 to 8

❦*An old New England specialty, brown bread is delicious not only with the traditional dinner of franks and beans, but also as a tea loaf, spread with cream cheese. The success of this very easy recipe hinges on using an appropriate mold for steaming the bread. The mold must be just about one quart in capacity—the bread will have a hole in the middle if the mold is too large and may explode if the mold is too small—and it must have a tight-fitting lid so that the bread won't pop out and get soggy during cooking.*

Preliminaries

1. Select a 1-quart mold with a tight lid. A covered bread pan or hinged melon mold is ideal. You can also use a 1-pound coffee can with a plastic lid, but you will have to tie the lid on with twine to prevent the bread from popping out; it is also a good idea to weight the lid with a brick or other heavy object.
2. Grease both the mold and the inside of the lid with 1 tablespoon soft vegetable shortening.
3. Select a lidded cooking pot tall enough to hold the mold upright. Bring several quarts water to the simmer while you prepare the batter.

½ cup cornmeal, preferably stone-ground
½ cup whole wheat flour
½ cup light or dark rye flour (available at health-food stores)
1 teaspoon baking soda
½ teaspoon salt
1 cup yogurt
½ cup dark molasses
½ to ⅔ cup dried currants or chopped raisins
Grated zest of 1 orange (optional but delicious)

Combine cornmeal, whole wheat and rye flours, baking soda, and salt in a 3-quart mixing bowl and stir with a wooden spoon to blend thoroughly. Add yogurt, molasses, currants or raisins, and orange zest and beat just until smooth. Immediately pour batter into prepared mold—the batter will begin to foam as the baking soda, molasses, and yogurt interact—and attach the lid. Place mold in the kettle, add enough simmering water to come halfway up the sides, and cover the kettle. Steam for 3 hours, keeping water at a slow simmer. Don't rush things; unless the bread steams for a full 3 hours it will be gooey and sticky inside. As soon as the bread is done, turn the mold onto its side on a baking sheet and carefully withdraw the mold from around the bread while gently shaking. Let rest uncovered for about 10 minutes at room temperature before serving.

Storage: Brown bread may be wrapped in foil and refrigerated for up to a week or frozen for several months. Reheat, still wrapped in foil, in a 300°F oven for 10 to 20 minutes.

ABOUT CHOCOLATE, COCONUT, and VARIOUS NUTS

CHOCOLATE

Chocolate-flavored desserts can only be as good as the chocolate that goes into them. The major American brands of bitter (or "baking") chocolate are quite satisfactory, but you must shop carefully for both semisweet (often labeled "bittersweet") chocolate and cocoa. Semisweet chocolate morsels ("chocolate chips") are highly flavored with imitation vanilla extract, or vanillin, which imbues desserts with the scent of dimestore perfume if they are used in any quantity. Furthermore, chocolate morsels are typically loaded with thickeners, emulsifiers, and extenders, which make mousses and cake and pie fillings gummy. A better but more expensive alternative is semisweet baking chocolate in bars or squares, which does not contain artificial flavorings and has a minimal amount of additives. For very refined desserts—chocolate mousse, for example—the best choice is a fine, imported European eating chocolate; it is smoother on the tongue than semisweet baking chocolate. (Be sure to check the label, because many imported eating chocolates, even the more expensive ones, also contain imitation flavorings; Lindt is an especially good brand.) As for cocoa, make sure that you buy the real thing, not a "chocolate flavored drink mix" adulterated with dried milk solids, carob powder or other extenders, and imitation flavorings.

KINDS OF CHOCOLATE: All chocolate (except for so-called "white chocolate") is made from cocoa beans that have been roasted, cracked, husked, degermed, and then crushed between steel rollers until the cocoa butter melts and blends with the chocolate solids to form a thick dark paste known as chocolate liquor. Unsweetened *baking chocolate* consists solely of chocolate liquor in solid form. *Cocoa* is chocolate liquor from which about ⅓ of the natural cocoa butter has been extracted, making a hard cake that is then pulverized. *Semisweet chocolate,* both eating chocolate and baking chocolate, requires more elaborate manufacturing procedures. Chocolate liquor is combined with sugar, flavorings, and often additional cocoa butter, and then passed through a series of vertically mounted rollers until it becomes a very fine paste. Finally this paste is "conched," that is, heated in huge vats and beaten back and forth by broad paddles until it becomes satiny smooth. The differences in quality between various semisweet chocolates are accounted for by the quality of the cocoa beans and other ingredients, and by the care taken by the manufacturer in processing the chocolate. *Milk chocolate* is semisweet chocolate to which dried milk and extra sugar have been added. It is rarely used in cooking because its chocolate taste is rather faint. The final member of the chocolate family is *"white chocolate."* This consists of cocoa butter mixed with sugar, milk solids, and vanilla; it is technically not chocolate at all because it contains no chocolate liquor. Nowadays, many domestic versions of the confection are made with hardened vegetable fat and have no relation to chocolate other than a common name, but fine imported white chocolates are still made with cocoa butter.

MELTING CHOCOLATE: Chocolate can be melted in the top of a double boiler over very gently simmering water or in a bowl set in a pan of almost-simmering water. Stir until chocolate is glistening and smooth, then remove from heat. Be careful not to splash in even a drop of water during the melting process, or the chocolate may stiffen, becoming hard and gritty-looking. If this should happen, you can almost always rescue it by beating in a teaspoon of solid vegetable shortening (not butter, which contains water) for each ounce of chocolate.

It is not a good idea to melt chocolate in a saucepan over direct heat since it scorches and hardens easily.

SUBSTITUTING ONE FORM OF CHOCOLATE FOR ANOTHER: As a general rule, the smaller the amount of chocolate called for in a recipe, the better a substitution is likely to work. Substitutions are most reliable in sauces and icings, least reliable in baked goods. In cake recipes calling for cocoa you should not use other forms of chocolate, since the cocoa acts both as a flavoring and a flour substitute. Table 1 contains an approximation of the ingredients in one ounce of each of the three major forms of chocolate. Table 2 gives proportions for substitutions based on the approximations in Table 1.

TABLE 1:
ESTIMATED CONTENTS OF 1 OUNCE COCOA, UNSWEETENED CHOCOLATE, AND SEMISWEET CHOCOLATE

1 OUNCE COCOA	1 OUNCE UNSWEETENED CHOCOLATE	1 OUNCE SEMISWEET CHOCOLATE
2/3 ounce chocolate	1/2 ounce chocolate	1/3 ounce chocolate
1/3 ounce cocoa butter	1/2 ounce cocoa butter	1/3 ounce cocoa butter
		1/3 ounce sugar

TABLE 2:
PROPORTIONS FOR SUBSTITUTING ONE TYPE OF CHOCOLATE FOR ANOTHER

FOR 1 OUNCE OF UNSWEETENED CHOCOLATE, SUBSTITUTE:

a) 3 tablespoons cocoa and 1/2 tablespoon butter or shortening
OR
b) 1 1/2 ounces semisweet chocolate, then decrease the sugar called for in the recipe by 1 tablespoon

FOR 1 OUNCE OF SEMISWEET CHOCOLATE, SUBSTITUTE:

a) 2/3 ounce unsweetened chocolate and 2 teaspoons sugar
OR
b) 2 tablespoons cocoa and 2 teaspoons sugar and 1 teaspoon butter or shortening

FOR 1 OUNCE OF COCOA SUBSTITUTE:

1 1/3 ounces unsweetened chocolate, then decrease the butter or other fat called for in the recipe by 2 teaspoons

COCONUT

When choosing a fresh coconut, be sure that there are no cracks or soft spots on the shell and that the three small dimples (often called "eyes") at the pointed end of the nut are dry and free of mold. Shake the coconut next to your ear. If you can hear liquid sloshing around inside, the coconut is probably fine; if there is no sound, it may be rancid.

A coconut can be stored in the refrigerator for a week or more, depending on its freshness.

HOW TO PREPARE FRESH COCONUT MEAT

1. Pierce the three eyes with a hammer and nail and drain out the coconut water, which may be drunk or used in preparing coconut milk (see below).

2. Place the coconut in a 350°F oven for exactly 15 minutes (but no longer, or the nut may begin to cook and both its flavor and texture will be ruined). This causes the flesh of the coconut to shrink from the shell and inner skin, making cracking and peeling easier. The coconut sometimes cracks while in the oven—this is okay.

3. Wrap the coconut in a plastic bag, then slip into a heavy brown grocery bag. Strike several times with the broad side of a hammer or some other flat, heavy object. Look inside the bag, and if you see any pieces of shell that are more than 3 or 4 inches across, rain down a few more blows.

4. Pry the meat loose from the shell pieces with a small, sturdy knife. Using either a vegetable peeler or a very sharp paring knife, remove all traces of the brown skin that adheres to the white meat. This is the most arduous task involved in preparing fresh coconut. It will go more smoothly if you can get to all the pieces of coconut while they are still warm from the oven.

5. The easiest way to grate coconut meat is in the food processor, using the fine or coarse shredding disks. To grate coconut in a blender, chop the meat in small pieces and add a small handful at a time, flicking the motor on and off until the desired consistency is reached. It is also possible to grate coconut using the large-hole side of a hand-held grater, but this is a chore, since the pieces are small and difficult to hold on to.

Note: Shelled coconut meat is highly perishable. It may be refrigerated in a covered container for about a day but should be frozen for longer storage.

Preparing Coconut Milk and Cream: The liquid inside a mature coconut is coconut water, not coconut milk. To prepare coconut milk, place the grated meat of 1 medium coconut (2 to 3 cups) in a food processor or blender, cover with an equal amount of boiling water, boiling milk, or either one combined with the coconut water, and process at highest speed for 2 minutes. (You will probably have to do this in two or more batches, especially if you are using a blender.) Let this mash steep for 10 minutes, then pour it into a strainer or potato ricer lined with a triple thickness of rinsed cheesecloth and set over a 3-quart bowl. Squeeze ricer firmly or press coconut against strainer with the back of a spoon. To extract the final drops of coconut milk, wad the coconut into a ball inside the cheesecloth and twist the cloth hard.

When the milk is allowed to stand for about half an hour, the fat—or "cream"—will float to the surface. If you wish to remove the cream, refrigerate the coconut milk until the cream hardens and can be scraped off.

Once coconut meat has been used to make coconut milk, it is leached of most of its taste. However, it makes a pleasant topping for puddings and other desserts if toasted.

Note: Coconut milk and cream should be refrigerated if not used immediately, and frozen if not used within 12 hours.

TOASTING COCONUT: Toss grated coconut in a heavy skillet over moderately high heat for 3 to 5 minutes, or until nicely browned.

PROCESSED COCONUT of the kind sold in supermarkets has been soaked in liquid, encrusted with sugar, doused with preservatives, and hyped up with artificial taste enhancers; it only faintly suggests the freshly prepared article.

NUTS

Most nuts are available shelled or unshelled. In my experience, nuts in the shell, whether bought in cellophane bags or in bulk, nearly always contain a number of rancid specimens. By contrast, shelled nuts, including those that have been sliced, chopped, or ground, are generally in very good condition provided they have been packaged in vacuum-sealed jars, cans, or plastic bags. Shelled nuts bought loose at vegetable markets and health-food stores are a risky proposition, though they are often seductively reasonable in price. Try to taste before making a purchase.

STORING NUTS: Nuts are highly prone to rancidity. Shelled nuts, especially those that have been sliced, chopped, or ground, must be stored in a tightly covered container in the freezer once the package has been opened. They should keep for several months; but to be safe, taste before adding to a recipe.

GRINDING NUTS: The goal in grinding nuts is to reduce the nuts to a uniform, meal-like powder without turning them oily or pasty. A rotary grinder, which also grinds coffee and spices, does an especially fine job, but a blender or food processor can be used as well. If you are grinding nuts in a blender, do them in ½-cup batches; use a fairly slow speed and turn the machine on and off at 2-second intervals so that the nuts will be ground evenly. If you are using a food processor, fit the machine with the metal chopping blade and grind 1 to 2 cups of nuts at a time (depending on the capacity of the machine), turning the machine on and off at 2-second intervals.

SLICING AND SLIVERING NUTS: Cover shelled nuts with a quantity of boiling water and allow to stand for 10 to 15 minutes, or until they are soft enough to work with. Removing only a few nuts at a time from the hot water, cut with a very sharp, thin knife into thin, even pieces. Spread sliced or slivered nuts in a single layer on a baking sheet and dry in a 200°F oven for about 15 minutes before using.

TOASTING NUTS: Spread shelled nuts out in a single layer on a rimmed baking sheet and place in the middle of an oven preheated to 350°F. Toast for 5 to 7 minutes, or until the nuts become light brown, stirring frequently with a wooden spoon so that they color evenly. Take care not to leave them in the oven too long, as nuts burn very easily.

BLANCHING (AND SKINNING) NUTS: Before being used in a recipe, shelled nuts are sometimes blanched (that is, scalded) or baked to remove the thin, bitter skin that surrounds the meat. It is unnecessary and quite difficult to remove the skins of some nuts such as walnuts and pecans. Instructions for blanching almonds, Brazil nuts, and pistachios and for skinning hazelnuts appear below under the individual headings for these nuts.

ALMONDS: Among the most versatile of all nuts, almonds may be bought unshelled or shelled, unblanched or blanched, whole, sliced, slivered, chopped, or ground. To blanch almonds, drop them into boiling water, immediately remove from heat, and let stand in the water until cool enough to handle. Pinch off the brown skins—they will slip off easily—and dry the nuts in a 200°F oven for about 10 minutes, taking care that they do not color.

Almond extract is made from bitter almonds, which are unavailable commercially in the United States because they are poisonous if consumed in any quantity. Almond extract is generally used along with—not in place of—almonds to intensify the almond flavor of a dish. It is very potent, so use it sparingly.

Almond paste, which is used as a filling for pastries and cakes and is the main ingredient of marzipan, is a mixture of more or less equal parts of very finely ground blanched almonds and sugar. It is not difficult to make at home. Grind 12 ounces blanched almonds to an oily paste in a food processor. With the motor still running, slowly pour in the hot sugar syrup from the recipe for meringue frosting, page 844, then add ½ teaspoon almond extract. Turn off machine, let paste cool, then pack into a sealed storage container and set in a cupboard for 1 to 3 weeks to age. Acceptable brands of commercial almond paste are sold at specialty food shops and at some supermarkets. Be sure to read labels when buying almond paste and reject any brands that contain peach pits, starches, or gums.

BRAZIL NUTS: Although they are most familiar as a component of a nut bowl, Brazil nuts, with their crisp texture and fine, pungent taste, are certainly suitable for use in any recipe that calls for nuts. Shelled Brazil nuts can be hard to locate, and if you must shell them yourself, you can make the task less arduous if you boil the nuts for 3 minutes or soak them overnight in cold water before going at them with a cracker. To blanch shelled Brazil nuts, simmer them for 3 minutes, then remove the pot from the heat; a few at a time, skim the nuts from the water and rub off their skins in a towel.

CASHEWS: These delicious nuts are sold shelled, either raw or roasted, unsalted or salted. Because they are sweet, soft, and rather mealy, cashews are rarely used in cooking, except in certain Asian dishes. However, they make a superb nut butter. Due to their high fat content, cashews are very perishable, especially if they have been roasted and salted, and they should be frozen if not consumed immediately.

CHESTNUTS: See pages 518–20.

FILBERTS/HAZELNUTS: The filbert tree is a modern hybrid of the hazel tree; the nuts of the two plants are virtually indistinguishable, and the terms filbert and hazelnut are used interchangeably. With their deep, rich, woody taste, hazelnuts are an indispensable ingredient in a number of fine European cakes, pastries, and confections. They are available both unshelled and shelled.

Hazelnuts are always skinned and lightly toasted before being used in baking. Place the shelled nuts in a single layer on a rimmed baking sheet in a 350°F oven for 10 minutes, or until the skins begin to look flaky. A small handful at a time, rub the nuts in a towel to remove the skins; a few shreds of skin will stubbornly cling to the nuts, but these may be disregarded. If necessary, return nuts to the oven a few minutes longer to finish toasting.

MACADAMIA NUTS: Macadamia nuts are delightful in stuffings, breads, sauces, and ice cream, but they are so costly that most people would rather reserve them for eating out of hand. If you have never sampled macadamia nuts, you have been missing a special eating experience; the nuts have a unique crunchy-tender texture and a flavor that suggests both Brazil nuts and hazelnuts. Macadamias are generally sold lightly toasted and salted, packed in glass jars.

PEANUTS: Peanuts are a legume, not a true nut. They are available unshelled and shelled, raw and roasted, unsalted and salted. There are numerous varieties. Defatted peanuts are a wonderful product that has only recently appeared on the market; they have only about half the calories of ordinary peanuts, but are quite delicious nonetheless. I have found, however, that they are unsuitable for cooking since they become limp when added to a dough or batter or any liquid.

Peanut butter varies a great deal from brand to brand, depending on how darkly the peanuts have been roasted, how finely the nuts have been ground, and how much oil, sugar, and flavorings have been added. I must confess that I prefer a particularly smooth, rich, dark-roasted commercial brand of peanut butter over homemade or health-food kinds, which tend to be heavy and gritty. To make your own peanut butter, simply grind skinless dark-roasted peanuts to a paste in a blender or food processor, adding some neutral vegetable oil and/or salt if you like.

PECANS: A native American nut, pecans have a sweet, rich, oily taste and soft texture that complement poultry stuffings, sweet potato dishes, pies, cakes, and candies. Pecans are available both in the shell and out; shelled pecans may be bought in halves or chopped.

PINE NUTS: Pine nuts are the fruit of pine trees. There are several species, which vary in size, shape, and taste. Most of the pine nuts appearing in American markets are a small, mildly flavored type called pignolias, which are imported from Europe. These are sold shelled, often in little glass jars. Pine nuts are expensive, but their rich and slightly resinous taste makes them worth their price. They are most often used in sweet baked goods but are also delicious in meat loaves, stuffings, casseroles, and rice and vegetable dishes.

PISTACHIO NUTS: Pistachios are prized both for their bright green color and their fine, sweet flavor. They are added to a wide range of dishes, including soups, sauces, pâtés, stuffings, cakes, candies, and ice cream. Pistachios are generally available only in the shells, which are often dyed red. Most pistachio shells are split and can be easily pried apart with your fingernails; sometimes, though, you must resort to cracking the shells. To skin pistachios, drop 1/4 cup of shelled nuts at a time into boiling water; remove from heat and let stand 1 minute. A few at a time, skim nuts from the water and pinch the skins off. Place blanched pistachios in a 200°F oven for 10 minutes to dry. Do not try to blanch more than 1/4 cup of nuts at a time, as the pistachios will fade if soaked in hot water for a prolonged period.

WALNUTS: There are two types of walnuts. The usual one is the so-called English walnut, actually a native of Persia, which is available unshelled and shelled, in halves or chopped. It has a wide range of uses—in salads, meat loaves, stuffings, pastas, and baked goods. The American black walnut is a much rarer nut, available only at specialty food shops. Very pungent in flavor, it is generally reserved for use in cakes and cookies. Most commercially shelled walnuts have been sprayed with an antirancidity preservative and thus have a longer shelf life than other nuts. Still, they should be kept in the freezer once the package is opened.

PUDDINGS, CHILLED DESSERTS, and SWEET SOUFFLÉS

The desserts in this chapter vary widely in the impression they make. Rice and Indian pudding and cup custard are homey and informal. Flan is soothingly bland and refreshing, yet a touch exotic. Cheesecake, chocolate mousse cake, and charlotte russe are very rich, almost meals unto themselves, while the elegant Bavarian creams and dessert soufflés are so light as to literally melt on the tongue. But different though they are, all the desserts here share the common bond of being based on eggs, milk, or cream—most are indeed a custard of one type or other—rather than on flour. For this reason, all are welcomed after a meal—even a rich one, if the dessert portions are small—while cakes and pastries often are not.

RICE PUDDING

Serves 4 to 6

❦ *Some rice puddings resemble baked custards, which is fine, but this one is decidedly creamy and puddinglike. This is what I want on those days when I crave the simple solace of this dessert.*

1 cup short- or long-grain white rice
2¼ cups water
Grated zest of ½ lemon
½ teaspoon salt
1 cup milk
3 tablespoons sugar
1 cup light cream or half-and-half
½ cup raisins (optional)
2 large egg yolks
¼ teaspoon vanilla extract
Cinnamon

Combine the rice, water, lemon zest, and salt in a heavy 3-quart saucepan. Bring to a simmer, stir once, and cover. Turn heat down to its lowest point and cook until the rice is dry, about 15 minutes. Stir in milk and sugar, cover, and simmer very gently for about 10 minutes, or until the milk is nearly absorbed. Add cream and raisins, cover and simmer about 10 minutes longer, stirring once or twice, or until most of the cream has been absorbed and the mixture looks thick. Remove from heat. Beat the egg yolks in a 2-quart bowl until light and lemon-colored, then beat in about 1 cup of the pudding, 1 tablespoon at a time; it is important to add the pudding slowly at first, beating constantly, or the heat of the pudding may cause the yolks to scramble. Stir mixture into the pudding remaining in the saucepan and blend thoroughly. Place saucepan over very low heat and, stirring constantly, heat just until the pudding thickens, being careful not to reach the simmer. Remove from heat and add vanilla extract. Serve warm or chilled, generously sprinkled with cinnamon and accompanied, if you wish, with cream or lightly sweetened whipped cream.

STORAGE: Rice pudding can be kept for 4 days in a covered container in the refrigerator.

INDIAN PUDDING

Serves 5 to 6

❦ *The key to success in making Indian pudding is long, slow baking, which transforms the cornmeal into a smooth, caramel-tasting cream. Serve this very warm with vanilla ice cream.*

PRELIMINARIES

1. Place rack in the center of oven.
2. Preheat oven to 250°F 20 minutes before baking.
3. Select an 8- to 12-cup lidded ceramic or enameled casserole. Grease with 1½ tablespoons soft butter.

⅓ cup stone-ground yellow cornmeal or ½ cup degerminated yellow cornmeal
1 quart milk
¼ cup sugar
¼ cup packed dark brown sugar
2 tablespoons pure maple syrup or dark molasses
1 teaspoon ground ginger
1 teaspoon salt
1½ cups light cream

Place cornmeal in a 3-quart saucepan. Dribble in 1 cup of the milk a little at a time, stirring constantly, to form a thick, smooth paste. Add the remaining milk, sugar, brown sugar, maple syrup or molasses, ginger, and salt. Stirring constantly with a wire whip, bring mixture to a boil over high heat, then turn heat down to low and simmer for 5 minutes, stirring frequently. The mixture should resemble a very thick soup. Pour into prepared baking dish.

Cover and bake 1 hour. Pour 1 cup of the cream over the top and partially stir in with wire whip, reaching to within ½ inch of—but not touching—the sides and bottom of the dish with the whip; if you scrape the pan, the pudding will stick. Replace lid and bake the pudding 3 hours longer. Add remaining ½ cup cream and stir as before. Uncover the pan and bake an additional 30 minutes, or until the center of the pudding is very softly set, rather than liquid. Let cool a few minutes before serving.

STORAGE: Leftover pudding can be refrigerated for several days in the baking dish, covered. Place in a 250°F oven for about 15 minutes to reheat.

BREAD PUDDING

Makes 4 to 6 servings

❦ *In addition to being soul-satisfying and delicious, bread pudding is an excellent dish for using up bread that did not turn out well or that has gone stale. You can prepare bread pudding with any bread or combination of breads, as long as they are yeast-based.*

PRELIMINARIES

1. Set rack in center of oven.
2. Preheat oven to 325°F.
3. Select an 8-cup baking dish; smear inside of dish with 1 tablespoon soft butter.

⅔ cup raisins
⅓ cup brandy or dark rum, preferably Jamaican
2 cups milk
1 cup light cream
4 to 5 cups (12 to 14 ounces) lightly packed crustless ½-inch cubes of bread
2 large eggs
¾ cup sugar
1½ teaspoons freshly grated nutmeg
¼ teaspoon salt
2 tablespoons butter

Cover raisins with liquor and set aside.

Heat milk and cream until steaming (watch carefully to prevent boiling over) and pour into a 3-quart mixing bowl. Fold in the bread cubes and let stand 30 minutes. Whisk together the eggs, sugar, nutmeg, and salt until light. Fold egg mixture and raisins and liquor into the bread.

Pour pudding into the buttered baking dish and dot with 2 tablespoons butter. Bake in preheated oven for about 60 minutes, or until the pudding has puffed about 1 inch and the center feels firm when touched with a finger. Serve warm or chilled, accompanied by heavy cream if you wish.

STORAGE: Leftover pudding can be refrigerated for several days in the baking dish, covered. Place in a 250°F oven for about 15 minutes to reheat.

MASTER RECIPE

Caramel Custard (Flan)

Serves 8

❦ *Often called by its Spanish name, flan, this dessert is made by baking egg custard in a mold or individual cups lined with caramel. The smooth, sweet custard and the sharp, bittersweet caramel make one of the most beautiful unions in all of cuisine, and the dessert is perfect following any heavy or spicy main course.*

PRELIMINARIES

1. Set rack in middle or lower-middle level of oven.
2. Preheat oven to 375°F 20 minutes before baking.
3. Select one of the following: a 9-inch round pan 1½ to 2 inches deep; a ring mold with a capacity of 6 to 8 cups; 8 individual heat-proof cups with a capacity of about ¾ cup each.
4. Select a roasting pan or other baking pan at least 2 inches deep and large enough to hold the mold or molds without crowding.
5. Have ready several quarts of simmering water.

STEP 1: LINING THE MOLD(S) WITH CARAMEL

1¼ cups sugar
⅓ cup water

Place the sugar in a heavy-bottomed 1½-quart saucepan, pour the water over it, and set over moderately high heat. Holding it by the handle, rotate pan over the heat so that the sugar solution travels in a slow circular wave around the inside wall of the pan. When the solution comes to a full boil and becomes a completely clear syrup, cover the saucepan and boil the syrup hard for 1 minute. Uncover and, rotating the pan as before, cook the syrup until it thickens and then darkens, or caramelizes, turning a deep amber color. (The syrup will continue to cook and darken after it is removed from the heat and poured into the molds, so be careful not to overcook it at this point.)

Immediately pour hot caramel into the mold or divide it evenly among the individual cups. Let the caramel cool for a minute or two, or until it is the consistency of thick maple syrup. Then, protecting your hands with potholders, tilt the mold(s) in all directions to coat the sides and bottom evenly with caramel. Continue to tilt the mold(s) until the caramel is so stiff that it will no longer flow. (If you are working with individual cups, swirl each one briefly, put it down, and then swirl the next. Repeat this procedure until the caramel sets, going back to each cup and reswirling it several times.)

STEP 2: PREPARING CUSTARD; FILLING THE MOLDS AND BAKING

3 large eggs
3 large egg yolks
¾ cup sugar
2 teaspoons vanilla extract
Generous pinch salt
2 cups milk
1 cup light cream

Combine the whole eggs, yolks, sugar, vanilla, and salt in a 3-quart mixing bowl and beat with a wire whip just until blended. (Do not overbeat, or bubbles may form in the custard.) Pour milk and cream into a 2-quart saucepan and heat over moderate flame until liquid feels distinctly hot to your fingertip but has not yet begun to steam (about 150°F on a thermometer); if the mixture gets too hot, it may scramble the eggs. Slowly pour warmed milk/cream into the egg mixture, beating continuously.

Set mold(s) in the roasting pan and fill with the custard mixture. Transfer roasting pan to the pulled-out rack of the preheated oven and pour enough water into the pan to come halfway up the sides of the mold(s) (the water insulates the custard and prevents it from separating or developing bubbles). Bake a single 9-inch round custard for 30 to 40 minutes, a ring custard for 25 to 35 minutes, and individual cup custards for about 20 minutes. The custard is done when a knife inserted midway between the rim of the mold and the center comes out clean. The center of the custard will still be a little undercooked and soft at this point, but it will firm up as the custard stands after baking. Do not overbake custard, or it may curdle, separate, and become watery.

Let custard stand at room temperature until completely cooled, then refrigerate for several hours or overnight. Just before serving, dip mold(s) for several seconds into very hot water, then invert custard(s) onto platter, letting last drops of caramel drizzle over the top.

AHEAD OF TIME: Caramel custard can be covered with foil and refrigerated for 2 days before being served. Do not freeze.

Variation: CUP CUSTARDS

Makes 8 servings

❦*Any of the custard pie fillings—plain, coconut, fruit, or orange—can also be baked in cups.*

Caramel Custard
ADD: Cinnamon

Proceed according to the Master Recipe, but skip Step 1 and lightly butter 8 individual custard cups instead of lining them with caramel; generously sprinkle the tops of the custards with cinnamon just before baking. Serve slightly warm or chilled. If chilled, the custards may be unmolded and served with berry sauce, page 860.

MASTER RECIPE

Vanilla Cream Cup Custards

Makes 4 servings

❦*Rich and sensuously smooth, these cup custards are known in France as* pots de crème. *They are a most sophisticated change from the usual cornstarch pudding but are not much more difficult to make.*

PRELIMINARIES

1. Set rack in the middle or lower-middle level of oven.
2. Preheat oven to 325°F 20 minutes before baking.
3. Select 4 individual heat-proof cups with a capacity of about 3/4 cup each; butter lightly. Arrange cups in a baking pan about 2 inches deep and just large enough to hold them.
4. Have ready about 1 quart simmering water.

3 large egg yolks
2 tablespoons sugar
Generous pinch of salt
1 1/2 cups heavy cream
2 teaspoons vanilla extract

Place yolks, sugar, and salt in a 3-quart mixing bowl and beat with a wire whip for about 15 seconds, or just until the mixture thickens very slightly and a few tiny air bubbles appear around the edges. Heat the cream to just below the simmer in a small saucepan. Beating constantly, slowly dribble about ½ cup of the cream into the egg yolks, then add the rest of the cream in two or three pours. Add vanilla and stir a moment to blend ingredients.

Pour custard into prepared cups and set the pan containing the cups on a pulled-out oven rack. Pour enough simmering water into the baking pan to reach ½ way up the sides of the cups. Bake 25 to 30 minutes, or until the rims of the custards have just begun to rise and the custards quiver like soft jelly when lightly jostled. They are not supposed to be firmly set at this point, so don't test with a cake needle or knife; they will finish cooking outside the oven. Do not overbake, or the custards will become grainy.

Remove from oven and let stand in the water bath for 1 hour, then transfer to a rack and let cool completely. Chill for 4 hours, or until very cold.

AHEAD OF TIME: Dessert may be made 2 days in advance of serving; cover the cups with foil.

Variation: CHOCOLATE CREAM CUP CUSTARDS

Makes 4 servings

Vanilla Cream Cup Custards

ADD: 3 ounces (3 squares) semisweet baking chocolate, grated or chopped very fine

Immediately after adding hot cream and vanilla to yolks, stir in the chocolate and beat with a wire whip until the chocolate has melted completely and the mixture is smooth. Bake 30 minutes, or slightly longer.

Variation: PRALINE CREAM CUP CUSTARDS

Makes 4 servings

Vanilla Cream Cup Custards

ADD: ⅓ to ½ cup Praline Powder, page 860

Proceed according to the Master Recipe, sprinkling the tops of the custards with a ¼-inch layer of praline about 10 minutes before removing them from the oven.

Variation: CRÈME BRÛLÉE

Makes 4 servings

❦*Justifiably renowned, this dessert entails covering vanilla custards with a layer of brown sugar and caramelizing the sugar under a broiler into a thin, brittle crust. Even if the sugar burns or ignites—the procedure is admittedly a bit tricky—the dessert will still be excellent.*

PRELIMINARIES

1. Arrange broiler rack so that the top of the custards will be about 1½ inches away from the heating element. (Elevate the custards on an inverted pan if the rack can't be set high enough.)
2. Preheat broiler at its highest setting 10 minutes before proceeding.

Vanilla Cream Cup Custards, very thoroughly chilled
⅓ cup packed dark brown sugar

Set custards on a strip of waxed paper and cover the top of each with an even layer of brown sugar, forcing the sugar through a sieve with your fingertips. Transfer custards to a baking sheet and place in preheated broiler. Watching very closely, broil 45 to 60 seconds, or until the sugar has melted and just begun to blacken in spots. Should the sugar ignite, simply blow the flames out. Serve immediately.

MASTER RECIPE

Cheesecake

Makes one 9½- to 10-inch cheesecake serving 10 to 14

❦*This cheesecake is smooth, rich, and very creamy. It can be topped with lightly sugared blueberries or hulled and sliced strawberries, but it really doesn't need them.*

PRELIMINARIES

1. Bring all ingredients, particularly the cream cheese, to room temperature.
2. Set rack in the center of oven.

3. Preheat oven to 250°F 20 minutes before baking.
4. Select a springform pan about 10 inches wide and 2½ to 3 inches deep. Coat inside of pan with 1½ tablespoons soft butter and sprinkle with ½ cup fine graham cracker crumbs or dry bread crumbs; roll crumbs inside pan to cover completely, then tap out excess. Set pan on a shallow-rimmed baking sheet or pizza pan to catch any possible leaks.

2 pounds cream cheese, preferably without added gums or thickeners (available at health-food stores and specialty food shops)
1¼ cups sugar
2 cups sour cream
1 cup heavy cream
6 large eggs
1 teaspoon vanilla extract

Place cream cheese and sugar in a 4- to 5-quart mixing bowl and beat at high speed with an electric mixer until completely smooth. Beat in the sour cream and cream, then the eggs, two at a time, and finally the vanilla. Continue to beat, scraping the sides of the bowl with a rubber spatula, until mixture is completely smooth. Pour into prepared pan and bake in preheated oven for 1 hour (1 hour and 10 minutes if your oven is poorly insulated or might conceivably be slow). Turn off oven but leave cheesecake inside for 2 hours longer, during which time it will finish baking. Avoid opening the oven door during this period.

Remove cheesecake from oven, place on a rack, and let stand at room temperature for 3 hours, or until completely cooled. (Never put a warm cheesecake in the refrigerator; steam may condense inside it and turn it watery.) Refrigerate cooled cheesecake for 12 hours or longer. Just before serving, carefully remove the rim of the pan and set the cheesecake on a serving platter.

STORAGE: Covered with foil, cheesecake will keep 3 to 4 days in the refrigerator or may be frozen for several weeks.

Variation: DAVE'S CHOCOLATE CHEESECAKE

Makes one 9½- to 10-inch cheesecake serving 10 to 14

❦ *This is extremely rich.*

Cheesecake

ADD: 12 ounces (12 squares) semisweet baking chocolate
½ cup freshly brewed very strong coffee

Chop or grate chocolate, then melt it in a heat-proof bowl set in a pan of almost-simmering water or in the top of a double boiler over very gently simmering water. Remove from heat and set aside.

Prepare cheesecake according to the Master Recipe, but beat in chocolate and coffee along with the vanilla, and add 5 minutes to the baking time.

Variation: HAZELNUT CHEESECAKE

Makes one 9½- to 10-inch cheesecake serving 10 to 14

Cheesecake

INCREASE: sugar to 1¾ cups

ADD: 1½ cups (about 6 ounces) hazelnuts, skinned and toasted (see page 701), then ground very fine

Proceed according to the Master Recipe, increasing the sugar and beating in nuts along with the vanilla.

Variation: LEMON CHEESECAKE

Makes one 9½- to 10-inch cheesecake serving 10 to 14

❦ *This is my favorite cheesecake. The subtle, sprightly lemon flavor cuts the richness of the other ingredients.*

Cheesecake

SUBSTITUTE: Grated zest of 1 large lemon and 3 tablespoons strained fresh lemon juice for vanilla extract

Proceed according to the Master Recipe, but substitute lemon zest and juice for vanilla.

Variation: LITTLE ITALY CHEESECAKE WITH CANDIED ORANGE PEEL

Makes one 9½- to 10-inch cheesecake serving 10 to 14

❦ *This cheesecake is similar to one served in a pastry shop in New York's Little Italy. It is a bit drier and firmer than the other cheesecakes listed here and is brightened by the typically Italianate flavoring combination of orange and almond.*

Cheesecake

SUBSTITUTE: 1 pound whole-milk "cream style" cottage cheese (large or small curd) or 1 pound ricotta cheese, forced through a sieve with the back of a spoon, for half of the cream cheese

ADD: ⅔ cup finely chopped candied orange peel
Grated zest of 1 orange
½ teaspoon almond extract

Proceed according to the Master Recipe, but use sieved cottage cheese or ricotta in place of half of the cream cheese and beat in candied peel, zest, and almond extract along with the vanilla.

MASTER RECIPE

Chocolate Mousse

Makes 8 to 12 servings

Chocolate mousses vary considerably in taste, texture, and intensity of flavor. This one is extremely chocolaty and rich, and it is smooth and unusually soft on the tongue, very much like a chocolate truffle candy. It can be served in individual cups or as an unmolded dessert.

Filling for ***Rum Cream Pie,*** page 776

ADD: 12 ounces semisweet chocolate, preferably fine, imported eating chocolate
¾ cup freshly brewed espresso or very strong coffee

SUBSTITUTE: 6 large egg whites and ¼ cup sugar for heavy cream

¾ to 1 cup heavy cream, whipped stiff and, if you wish, sweetened and flavored with vanilla extract or rum (see page 857)

Place chocolate, chopped or broken up, and coffee in a heat-proof bowl set in a pan of almost-simmering water or in the top of a double boiler set over very gently simmering water. Wait a few minutes for the chocolate to soften, then stir vigorously until the mixture is perfectly smooth. Remove from heat and set aside to cool to room temperature. Prepare pie filling according to the recipe through the beating of the butter into the egg yolk mixture; beat in the cooled chocolate mixture with a whip.

Using an electric mixer set at medium speed, beat egg whites, brought to room temperature, in a 4-quart bowl until they form soft peaks, then gradually sprinkle on the ¼ cup sugar. Increase mixer speed to high and continue to beat whites until stiff and glossy, being careful not to overbeat. Fold the beaten egg whites into the chocolate mixture, omitting the whipped cream called for in the pie filling recipe.

Turn mousse into 8 to 12 individual cups with a capacity of ½ to ¾ cup each or into a lightly oiled 6-cup ring-shaped or cylindrical mold (a soufflé dish works fine here). Cut a sheet of waxed paper to fit dimensions of cups or molds, and place it directly on top of the mousse. Chill small cups at least 2 hours, a single mold at least 4. Just before serving, put a dollop of whipped cream on the top of cup mousses. Unmold a large mousse by dipping the dish into very hot water for several seconds and inverting onto a platter. An unmolded mousse can be decorated with whipped cream piped through a pastry bag fitted with a ½- or ¾-inch star tip, or the cream may be passed separately.

AHEAD OF TIME: Mousse may be kept in the refrigerator for 2 days; unmold just before serving.

Variation: CHOCOLATE MOUSSE CAKE

Makes 10 to 12 servings

❦ *People seem always to be searching for the ultimate chocolate dessert to serve to chocolate-obsessed friends. I suggest this cake, which borders on the deadly.*

Chocolate Mousse
Sponge Cake, page 826, or the chocolate-flavored sponge cake from Chocolate Ganache Cake, page 832, baked in a 9×2-inch round pan
1½ tablespoons sugar
1½ tablespoons boiling water
3 tablespoons dark rum, preferably Jamaican
1½ cups (1½ recipes) Chocolate Glaze, page 851
¾ to 1 cup heavy cream, whipped stiff but not sweetened (see page 857)

Pack the mousse into a lightly oiled 9-inch round cake pan that has a capacity of at least 6 cups; chill 4 hours, or until very firm.

Set sponge cake on a baking tray and brush with warm liquor syrup made by dissolving the sugar in the boiling water and stirring in rum.

Dip the pan holding the mousse into very hot water, then invert the mousse directly over the sponge cake. If necessary, trim edges of cake or smooth sides of mousse with a spatula so that cake and mousse are flush. If the surface of the mousse has begun to liquefy, smooth it with a spatula. Refrigerate for at least 30 minutes to firm the mousse in preparation for glazing.

Prepare chocolate glaze and let cool to tepid. Pour glaze over the top and sides of chilled mousse cake, smoothing it quickly with a spatula, as necessary. Refrigerate for at least 1 hour to set the glaze. Just before serving, transfer cake to a serving platter by slipping two long spatulas or long, wide knives underneath it. Let mousse cake stand at room temperature for about 15 minutes before serving; serve with whipped cream.

AHEAD OF TIME: The completed mousse cake can be covered with an inverted bowl and refrigerated for up to 2 days.

CHARLOTTE RUSSE

Serves 8

❦ *Dessert-loving American hostesses have been whipping up charlottes since the nineteenth century. The term "charlotte russe" may be applied to any dessert cream that is molded in a dish lined with ladyfingers or strips of sponge cake. The flavoring combination suggested here, dark rum and strawberries, is one of my favorites.*

18 to 24 ladyfingers, or Sponge Roll Cake, page 835, not rolled up
2 tablespoons sugar
3 tablespoons boiling water
1/3 cup dark rum, preferably Jamaican
The filling for Rum Cream Pie, page 776
1 pint ripe but firm strawberries, hulled and halved lengthwise
Berry Sauce, page 860, made with strawberries

Select an 8-cup cylindrical mold with straight or slightly outward-sloping sides; a soufflé dish works fine. Line the bottom and sides of the mold with ladyfingers or strips of cake, trimming them as necessary with a knife. Arrange leftover scraps in a single layer on a plate.

Place the sugar in a small bowl, add boiling water, and stir until dissolved; stir in rum. Brush mixture liberally over ladyfingers or cake in the mold, making them quite moist but not saturated and mushy. Brush the scraps with liquor syrup, as well.

Turn 1/3 of the cream filling into the mold and cover with 1/2 of the berries and 1/3 of the scraps, pressing them in lightly. Make a second layer, using 1/3 of the filling, remaining berries, and 1/3 of the scraps. Add remaining filling, and, if it does not quite fill the mold, bend the protruding ends of the lady fingers or cake strips over it. Lightly press remaining scraps into the top of the filling, making it more or less even. Refrigerate for at least 6 hours, or overnight. To serve, invert dish onto a plate to unmold and pass with berry sauce.

AHEAD OF TIME: Filled mold may be covered with foil and refrigerated for 1 to 2 days; unmold just before serving.

ORANGE, STRAWBERRY, OR RASPBERRY BAVARIAN CREAM

6 servings

❦ *This is a light, refreshing dessert. A strawberry or raspberry Bavarian cream might be prepared in a heart mold if it is intended for someone special, or for Valentine's Day.*

Filling for Orange Chiffon Pie, page 780, or the strawberry or raspberry variations, page 783
½ cup cold heavy cream
2 tablespoons confectioner's sugar, sieved or sifted if lumpy
2 teaspoons orange liqueur or ¼ teaspoon pure orange extract
Custard Sauce, page 856, or Berry Sauce, page 860

Select any 6- to 8-cup mold (cylinder, ring, heart-shaped, etc.) and, just before filling, rinse with cold water, shaking out the excess. Scoop the pie filling into mold, smoothing the top, and refrigerate for 3 to 4 hours, or until set.

Just before serving, dip mold into very hot water for several seconds, then invert it onto a plate to unmold. Referring if necessary to the recipe on page 857, whip cream until stiff but not grainy, adding confectioner's sugar and liqueur or extract. Decorate the dessert by piping whipped cream through a pastry bag fitted with a ½-inch star tip (or, less elaborately, by dropping cream from a teaspoon). Cover the bottom of the serving plate with a thin layer of sauce—custard for orange cream, berry for strawberry or raspberry—and serve at once, passing remaining sauce separately.

MASTER RECIPE

Vanilla-Rum Soufflé

Makes 4 to 6 servings

❦*A hot dessert of any kind is always a treat, and when that dessert is a soufflé, you can count on cries of astonished delight from all assembled. Serve this soufflé with custard sauce or lightly sweetened whipped cream plus, if you wish, fresh blueberries, raspberries, or hulled strawberries that have been briefly macerated in a few tablespoons of sugar and a splash of rum. A chilled Sauterne may be offered as well.*

For information on egg whites, soufflé baking dishes, making larger soufflés, preparing soufflés ahead of time, and rescuing botched soufflés, consult the notes on pages 168–71. Recipe sleuths will note with interest that this and all other dessert soufflés are variations on cheese soufflé, with sugar and other sweet flavorings used in lieu of cheese, salt, and pepper.

PRELIMINARIES

1. Set rack in the lowest level of the oven, removing the upper rack so that the soufflé will have room to rise.
2. Preheat oven to 375°F 20 minutes before baking.
3. Select a 6-cup porcelain soufflé mold or other tall, deep, straight-sided baking dish with a capacity of 6 to 7 cups. Coat the inside with 1 tablespoon soft butter and roll with 1 tablespoon sugar, spilling out any excess. Set the prepared mold on a shallow-rimmed baking sheet.

1 cup milk
4 tablespoons butter
¼ cup all-purpose flour
½ cup sugar
2 tablespoons vanilla extract
2 tablespoons dark rum, preferably Jamaican
4 large eggs, at room temperature
1 large egg white, at room temperature
¼ teaspoon cream of tartar

Warm the milk to the verge of simmering over low heat. Melt the butter in a heavy-bottomed 1½-quart saucepan, remove from heat, and stir in the flour with a wire whip, beating until smooth. Gradually add the hot milk, beating constantly; scrape the corners of the saucepan with a spatula and beat until perfectly smooth. Place over moderate heat and, stirring constantly, bring to a full boil; the sauce will be as thick as paste. Turn heat down to low and continue to cook for 1 minute, stirring. Remove from heat, add the sugar, and beat until the sugar melts and the sauce is satiny and glistening. Beat in the vanilla extract and rum.

Separate the eggs, placing the yolks in a 4-quart mixing bowl and the whites, including the extra white, in a clean 3-quart mixing bowl. (Be sure not to get any yolk or other form of grease in the whites, or they will not mount properly when beaten.) Break up the yolks a bit with a wire whip, and gradually add the hot sauce base, beating constantly. Set aside. Beat the egg whites at low speed with an electric mixer until they look foamy, then add the cream of tartar and increase the mixer speed to medium. When the whites have turned frothy and opaque and retain furrows made by the beaters, increase mixer speed to high and beat until the whites are firm and glossy, resembling aerosol shaving cream. Do not overbeat, or the whites will break down and become dry and grainy.

Stir ¼ of the beaten whites into the sauce base to lighten it, then gently fold in the remaining whites. Turn batter into the prepared baking dish, gently smoothing the top with a rubber spatula. There should be at least ½ inch between the top of the batter and the rim of the dish; leave out a spoonful or two of batter if it won't fit.

Bake in preheated oven 30 to 35 minutes, or until the soufflé has puffed 3 to 4 inches beyond the rim of the dish and a cake tester comes out clean when inserted into the side of the puff and down toward the bottom of the dish. Do not overbake, or the soufflé will be dry and may collapse. Serve immediately.

Variation: APRICOT SOUFFLÉ

Makes 4 to 6 servings

❦ *Serve this lovely dessert with lightly sweetened whipped cream or custard sauce.*

Vanilla-rum Soufflé

ADD: ⅓ cup loosely packed dried apricots

SUBSTITUTE: 1 teaspoon almond extract and 1 tablespoon orange liqueur for vanilla extract and rum

Turn apricots into a 1-cup measure, fill measure with *boiling* water, and soak exactly 1 hour. Drain. Squeeze apricots between the palms of your hands to extract liquid. Turn apricots onto a chopping board, sprinkle with the ½ cup sugar called for in the Master Recipe, and, using a large chef's knife, chop very, very fine, until virtually puréed.

Proceed according to the Master Recipe, beating the apricot purée into the sauce base and adding almond extract and orange liqueur in lieu of vanilla extract and rum.

Variation: BANANA SOUFFLÉ

Makes 4 to 6 servings

❦ *Serve this unusual soufflé with lightly sweetened whipped cream.*

Vanilla-rum Soufflé
ADD: 1 cup puréed ripe bananas (3 to 4 medium)

Proceed according to the Master Recipe, adding the puréed bananas after beating in the sugar. This soufflé will rise only an inch or two beyond the rim of a 6-cup soufflé dish.

Variation: CHOCOLATE SOUFFLÉ

Makes 4 to 6 servings

❦ *For the very best chocolate soufflé, use semisweet baking chocolate rather than chocolate chips. Lightly sweetened whipped cream is almost mandatory here. For an especially grand dessert, serve the soufflé with berry sauce and whipped cream.*

Vanilla-rum Soufflé
DECREASE: Flour to 1½ tablespoons
ADD: 3 ounces semisweet chocolate and 1 ounce (1 square) unsweetened baking chocolate
DECREASE: Vanilla extract and rum to 1 tablespoon each

Prepare sauce base as in Master Recipe but use only 1½ tablespoons flour; the sauce will be fairly thin. Chop the chocolate into ¼-inch pieces, add to the hot sauce along with the sugar, and beat until the chocolate has completely melted. If necessary, return the mixture to very low heat briefly in order to melt the chocolate completely. Add the vanilla and rum, decreased by half, and proceed according to the Master Recipe. The soufflé may need an extra minute or two in the oven, but don't overbake, or it will be dry.

Variation: COCONUT SOUFFLÉ

Makes 4 to 6 servings

❦ *Accompanied by warm chocolate sauce, this soufflé will put you in mind of a certain famous American candy bar. It is equally good served with berry sauce, preferably made with raspberries.*

Vanilla-rum Soufflé

ADD: ½ cup desiccated coconut (available at health-food stores)

SUBSTITUTE: Grated zest of 1 lemon and 2 tablespoons crème de cacao, preferably white, for vanilla extract and rum

Proceed according to the Master Recipe, adding the coconut, grated lemon zest, and crème de cacao to the sauce base after beating in the sugar, and omitting the vanilla and rum. This soufflé will rise only an inch or two beyond the rim of a 6-cup soufflé dish.

Variation: ESPRESSO SOUFFLÉ

Makes 4 to 6 servings

❦ *Serve this assertively flavored coffee soufflé with whipped cream that has been sweetened, spiked with anise liqueur, and sprinkled with a tablespoon or two of finely chopped candied fruits.*

Vanilla-rum Soufflé

SUBSTITUTE: ½ cup freshly brewed espresso (or very strong coffee) and ½ cup half-and-half for milk

DECREASE: Vanilla extract to 1 tablespoon

OMIT: Rum

Proceed according to the Master Recipe, but substitute espresso and half-and-half for the milk, decrease the vanilla by half, and omit the rum.

❦

Variation: GRAND MARNIER SOUFFLÉ

Makes 4 to 6 servings

❦ *A classic dessert. A sauce is not essential here, but custard sauce, flavored with 2 tablespoons Grand Marnier rather than vanilla, certainly doesn't hurt things.*

Vanilla-rum Soufflé

SUBSTITUTE: Grated zest of 1 orange and 1/4 cup Grand Marnier for vanilla extract and rum

Proceed according to the Master Recipe, substituting grated orange zest and Grand Marnier for the vanilla and rum.

Variation: LEMON SOUFFLÉ

Makes 4 to 6 servings

❦ *This deliciously tart soufflé is a refreshing finale to a heavy meal. Accompany, if you wish, with lightly sweetened whipped cream.*

Vanilla-rum Soufflé

SUBSTITUTE: Grated zest of 2 lemons and 3 tablespoons strained fresh lemon juice for vanilla extract and rum

ADD: 1 more egg yolk

Flavor the sauce base with grated lemon zest and lemon juice instead of vanilla extract and rum, then blend with 5, rather than 4, egg yolks. Proceed according to the Master Recipe.

Variation: PRALINE SOUFFLÉ

Makes 4 to 6 servings

❦ *This soufflé has a marvelous toasted-nut flavor. Serve with custard sauce flavored with 2 tablespoons dark dark rum instead of vanilla.*

Vanilla-rum Soufflé

ADD: 1/2 cup Praline Powder, page 860

DECREASE: Sugar to 1/4 cup

SUBSTITUTE: 1/2 teaspoon almond extract for vanilla extract

Add the praline powder along with the sugar, decreased by half, to the sauce base, beating until the praline melts partially and the sauce base becomes glistening. Add the almond extract and the rum, then proceed according to the Master Recipe.

BARS and COOKIES

Compared to other kinds of baked goods, cookies are child's play to make, so there's really no need to rely on prepackaged doughs and mixes. The three Master Recipes in this chapter produce over two dozen different bars and cookies, including all of the classic American favorites such as brownies (both blond and chocolate), sugar cookies, chocolate chip cookies, oatmeal cookies, and peanut butter cookies. Unlike cake recipes, which must be followed to the letter, cookie formulas can be modified to suit the tastes of the baker. Some tips on how to vary the moistness, crispness, and chewiness of cookies appear following each recipe title. But do trust your own intuitions too.

NOTES ON COOKIE SHEETS: Cookie sheets are rimless on the two long sides (or on all four), allowing the baked cookies to be slid easily from sheet to rack. The standard cookie sheet measures approximately 14×17 inches and accommodates 12 to 16 cookies. Smaller cookie sheets suitable for small ovens are also available. If you don't have a cookie sheet, you may use a shallow-rimmed baking sheet—for example, a jelly roll pan—or an inverted roasting pan or cake pan. (Roasting pans must be inverted because their high sides reflect heat and would cause the cookies to bake unevenly.)

NOTES ON BAKING COOKIES IN A SMALL OVEN: If you are working with a small apartment-size oven, it is a good idea to take the following precautions:

1. If possible, use cookie sheets that are small enough to leave at least 2 inches of space between the edges of the sheets and the walls of the oven. Otherwise, there will not be room in the oven for hot air to circulate, and the cookies may bake unevenly.

2. Do not place cookies close to the edge of the baking sheet—especially if you must use a large sheet that barely fits into the oven—as these cookies are likely to get burned by the heat reflected from the oven walls.

3. Bake only one sheet of cookies at a time, setting it in the middle or upper-middle level of the oven. If you bake two sheets at once, the cookies on the top sheet are likely to burn, while the ones on the bottom may not brown at all.

BAR AND COOKIE RESCUE NOTES Unless they contain dried fruits, chocolate chips, candy bits, or jam, bars and cookies that have not turned out right or that have gone stale may be used to make one or more crumb pie crusts. If the bars or cookies have burnt, scrape off the blackened parts. Unless the bars or cookies are already crisp and dry as a bone, crumble them onto a large baking sheet and let them dry out for half an hour or more in a 200°F oven. Let cool, then pulverize in a blender or food processor. Substitute the cookie crumbs for graham cracker crumbs in the recipe on page 760. If you do not have quite enough cookie crumbs, make up the difference with ground nuts, cake crumbs, or graham cracker crumbs. If you have more cookie crumbs than you need, either sprinkle the leftovers on top of a cream pie or freeze them and combine at a later date with additional crumbs to make another pie shell.

MASTER RECIPE

Butterscotch Bars or Brownies (Blondies)

Makes sixteen 2-inch bars

Bar cookies are about as easy to make as anything could be. Be sure to use an 8-inch square pan; a smaller pan will make the bars cakelike rather than chewy, while a larger pan will produce crumbly, dry bars. And remember not to overbake the bars, or they will be dry.

Preliminaries

1. Bring all ingredients to room temperature.
2. Set rack in middle or lower-middle level of oven.
3. Preheat oven to 350°F 20 minutes before baking—325°F if using a glass pan.
4. Select an 8-inch square pan with sides 1½ to 2 inches deep. Grease pan generously with soft butter, line bottom of pan with a square of waxed paper, then lightly butter the paper.

6 tablespoons butter
1 cup packed dark brown sugar
1 large egg
1 teaspoon vanilla extract
¾ cup unbleached all-purpose flour (measure by scooping cup into large container of flour and sweeping off excess with the back of a knife)
½ teaspoon baking powder
¼ teaspoon salt
½ to ¾ cup (about 2 to 3 ounces) broken or coarsely chopped walnuts or pecans

Place butter, sugar, egg, and vanilla in a 3-quart bowl and beat with electric mixer at high speed for about 1 minute, or until smooth and creamy and just beginning to lighten in color and texture.

Combine flour, baking powder, and salt in a 1-quart bowl and blend thoroughly with a fork. Sprinkle over butter mixture and blend at low speed just until all flour is moistened, about 15 seconds; don't overblend, or the bars may be cakelike. Using a rubber spatula, scrape off beater blades and stir in nuts.

Spread batter evenly in prepared pan with spatula. Bake for 25 to 30 minutes, or until top is dry to the touch and edges look wrinkly. If in doubt, take pan out; better a bit underdone than overdone. Let bars cool in the pan. Invert onto a work surface, peel off waxed paper, and cut into sixteen 2-inch bars.

Storage: Bars are at their best if eaten within a day or so of being made. If you are not serving them at once, leave them uncut in the pan, cover the pan with foil, and store at room temperature. To freeze bars, pry the whole thing out of the pan uncut, wrap in foil, and seal in a plastic bag. Freeze for no longer than a month.

Variation: APPLESAUCE BARS

Makes sixteen 2-inch bars

❦ *Spicy and soft rather than chewy.*

Butterscotch Bars or Brownies (Blondies)

ADD: 1 teaspoon cinnamon and 1/4 teaspoon nutmeg, preferably freshly grated

INCREASE: Flour to 1 cup

ADD: 1/2 cup unsweetened applesauce

Proceed according to the Master Recipe, but add spices along with vanilla, increase flour to 1 cup, and add applesauce when flour mixture is about half blended into the batter. Continue beating until applesauce is absorbed.

Variation: APRICOT BARS

Makes sixteen 2-inch bars

Butterscotch Bars or Brownies (Blondies)

ADD: Grated zest of 1 orange
1/2 cup chopped dried apricots

Proceed according to the Master Recipe, adding orange zest along with vanilla and stirring in apricots with the nuts.

Variation: CHOCOLATE BROWNIES

Makes sixteen 2-inch bars

❦ *These brownies are moist, soft, intensely chocolaty, and a bit more cakelike and delicate than brownies usually are. If you prefer a chewier brownie, decrease the flour by 1/4 cup. The butter may be increased by several tablespoons to make very rich brownies.*

Butterscotch Bars or Brownies (Blondies)

ADD: 3 ounces (3 squares) unsweetened baking chocolate
1 more egg

Chop, grate, or break up the chocolate, then melt it in a heat-proof bowl set in a pan of almost-simmering water or in the top of a double boiler over very gently simmering water. Remove from heat and set aside until cooled to barely tepid.

Proceed according to the Master Recipe, adding an extra egg and beating the cooled chocolate into the creamed butter-sugar mixture just before incorporating dry ingredients.

Variation: CHOCOLATE CHIP BLONDIES

Makes sixteen 2-inch bars

Butterscotch Bars or Brownies (Blondies)
ADD: 1 cup (6 ounces) chocolate chips

Proceed according to the Master Recipe, adding chocolate chips along with the nuts.

Variation: DATE-NUT BARS

Makes sixteen 2-inch bars

Butterscotch Bars or Brownies (Blondies)
ADD: ¾ cup chopped or snipped dates

Proceed according to the Master Recipe, adding dates along with the nuts.

Variation: HERMIT BARS

Makes sixteen 2-inch bars

❦ *These are guaranteed to appeal to any hermit fan, and they are a lot simpler to make than the usual hermit cookie.*

Butterscotch Bars or Brownies (Blondies)
SUBSTITUTE: ½ cup granulated sugar and ½ cup dark molasses for brown sugar
ADD: 1 teaspoon cinnamon, ½ teaspoon ground cloves, and ½ teaspoon nutmeg, preferably freshly grated
INCREASE: Flour to 1 cup

Substituting granulated sugar and molasses for dark brown sugar, prepare creamed mixture as indicated in the Master Recipe; the mixture may look more liquid than creamy after beating, especially if the day is warm, but this won't matter. Combine spices with flour, increased to 1 cup, and other dry ingredients, then proceed with Master Recipe.

Variation: HONEY-GINGER BARS

Makes sixteen 2-inch bars

❦ *Don't be deceived by the simplicity of this recipe: these bars are truly special. Dust them with confectioner's sugar for an elegant touch.*

Butterscotch Bars or Brownies (Blondies)

SUBSTITUTE: ½ cup granulated sugar and ½ cup honey for brown sugar
ADD: 1 tablespoon ground ginger
INCREASE: Flour to 1 cup

Substituting granulated sugar and honey for dark brown sugar, prepare creamed mixture as indicated in the Master Recipe; the mixture may look more liquid than creamy after beating, especially if the day is warm, but this won't matter. Increase the flour to 1 cup, combine with ginger and other dry ingredients, and proceed according to the Master Recipe.

Variation: PEANUT BUTTER BROWNIES

Makes sixteen 2-inch bars

Butterscotch Bars or Brownies (Blondies)

ADD: ½ cup peanut butter
SUBSTITUTE: Skinned unsalted peanuts for walnuts or pecans

When butter-sugar mixture from the Master Recipe looks creamy, beat in the peanut butter. Add flour mixture, stirring with a spoon if the batter is too heavy for your mixer, then add the peanuts. The batter will be too thick to spread with a spatula, so press it evenly into prepared pan with your hands.

Variation: RAISIN-NUT BARS

Makes sixteen 2-inch bars

Butterscotch Bars or Brownies (Blondies)

ADD: ¾ cup raisins

Proceed according to the Master Recipe, stirring in raisins along with the nuts.

MASTER RECIPE

Butter Cookies

Makes 2 dozen 2-inch cookies

Butter cookies and their many delightful variations are all based on an extremely simple dough consisting of butter, sugar, egg yolks, and flour. Butter cookies may be formed in several different ways, depending on the look you wish to achieve, and their taste and texture may be altered to suit your preference by making minor changes in the dough formula. This Master Recipe produces crunchy cookies.

TIPS:

- To make cookies with a slightly chewy center, bake only until the edges of the cookies turn golden, 8 to 10 minutes.
- To make crisp cookies, flatten or roll the dough to a thickness of 1/8 inch.
- To make crumbly and very rich cookies of the sort that are often formed using a cookie press, decrease flour to 1 cup.
- To make sweet and chewy cookies, increase both butter and sugar by half and underbake the cookies slightly.

If you do experiment, it is a good idea to test-bake a couple of cookies to see how they come out. If you aren't happy with the results, add more sugar, flour, and so on, and rerun the test. If an experimental dough is too soft to handle, refrigerate it briefly to firm it.

PRELIMINARIES

1. Bring all ingredients to room temperature.
2. Set racks in lower-middle and upper-middle levels of oven.
3. Preheat oven to 350°F 20 minutes before baking.
4. Select two 14×17-inch cookie sheets. Grease lightly with solid vegetable shortening.

Step 1: Making the Dough

8 tablespoons (1 stick) butter
½ cup sugar
2 large egg yolks
1 teaspoon vanilla extract
1½ cups unbleached all-purpose flour (measure by scooping cup into large container of flour and sweeping off excess with the back of a knife)

Place butter, sugar, egg yolks, and vanilla in 3-quart mixing bowl. Beat with electric mixer at high speed for about 1 minute, or until the mixture is smooth and creamy and just beginning to lighten. Sprinkle flour on top and blend at low speed for about 20 seconds, or until all flour is incorporated. Proceed to form cookies according to Step 2a, 2b, or 2c.

Step 2a: To Form the Cookies with Your Hands

½ teaspoon soft butter
Sugar

Pinch off pieces of dough and roll between the palms of your hands to form ¾-inch balls. Set the balls at least 2 inches apart on prepared baking sheets. Lightly butter the bottom of a drinking glass, dip in sugar, and flatten the balls of dough into disks about 2 inches wide and 3⁄16 inch thick. Redip the drinking glass in sugar as necessary.

Step 2b: To Roll Out and Cut the Cookies

All-purpose flour
3 tablespoons sugar, crushed hard candies, or finely chopped nuts (optional)

Chill the dough briefly if it seems too soft to roll. Sprinkle work surface lightly with flour (if you use too much flour, the cookies will be hard and dry) and roll out dough to a thickness of 3⁄16-inch. If you wish, sprinkle the dough with sugar, crushed hard candies, or chopped nuts and press the topping lightly with the rolling pin to make it adhere. Cut dough with floured cookie cutters or a drinking glass and transfer the cookies to prepared cookie sheets with a spatula, spacing at least an inch apart. Gently knead scraps together, reroll, and cut out.

Step 2c: To Prepare Refrigerator Cookies

3 tablespoons sugar, crushed hard candies, or finely chopped nuts (optional)

Shape the dough into a rough oblong, encircle with a sheet of waxed paper, and roll dough to form a cylinder about 2 inches wide and 5 to 6 inches long. Seal waxed paper at the ends to enclose dough completely and chill for at least an hour; the dough may also be given an outer wrapping of aluminum foil and held in the refrigerator for several days before baking. To form the cookies, unwrap dough, roll the cylinder in sugar, crushed candies, or chopped nuts, if you wish, and slice dough into disks about 3⁄16 inch thick using a very sharp knife. Transfer the cookies to prepared cookie sheets, spacing them at least an inch apart.

STEP 3: BAKING THE COOKIES
Place the cookie sheets in a staggered fashion—this helps to promote air circulation—on the racks in the oven. Bake 11 to 15 minutes, or until cookies are pale brown around the edges and toasty brown on the bottom, switching positions of cookie sheets during the last third of baking. Using a spatula, transfer cookies to racks to cool.

STORAGE: Butter cookies are at their best if eaten within a few hours of baking, but they may be stored for several days at room temperature or frozen for several months if sealed airtight in a covered tin or plastic bag.

Variation: ALMOND CRESCENTS

Makes 2½ to 3 dozen 3-inch cookies

❦ *These are special—and very rich.*

PRELIMINARIES:

Follow those in the Master Recipe, but preheat the oven to only 300°F.

Butter Cookies, prepared through Step 1
ADD: 1⅓ cups (about 7 ounces) unblanched whole almonds
INCREASE: Butter to 16 tablespoons (2 sticks)
ADD: ½ teaspoon almond extract

Grind almonds a handful at a time in a blender or rotary grinder or all at once in a food processor. The nuts should be finely ground, but not oily and compacted.

Prepare dough according to Step 1 of the Master Recipe, doubling the butter, adding almond extract along with the vanilla, and incorporating ground almonds with the flour.

To form crescents, roll pieces of dough between your hands into 1½-inch balls, then roll the balls into ropes about 4 inches long, with slightly tapering ends. Place rope shapes about 3 inches apart on prepared baking sheets and curve the ends inward to form crescents measuring about 2½ inches across from tip to tip. Bake 20 to 25 minutes, or until cookies are just beginning to color, switching the position of the cookie sheets halfway through baking.

Variation: BUTTERCRUNCH COOKIES

Makes 2½ dozen 3-inch cookies

❦ *This recipe is a bit involved, but the cookies are a great deal of fun to make and absolutely wonderful to eat.*

Butter Cookies, prepared through Step 1
1 cup packed dark brown sugar
6 tablespoons butter
1 tablespoon distilled or cider vinegar
¼ teaspoon salt

SPECIAL EQUIPMENT: A candy thermometer (optional but helpful)

Prepare butter cookie dough according to Step 1 of the Master Recipe; wrap dough in plastic and refrigerate while you prepare the crunch.

Thickly butter an 8-inch round or square metal cake pan and have it ready to receive the molten candy. Place brown sugar, butter, vinegar, and salt in a heavy-bottomed 1½-quart saucepan and stir over low heat until thoroughly combined and smooth. Raise heat to moderately high, and cook candy for 4 to 5 minutes, stirring constantly, until it is thick and gummy-looking and you can distinctly smell smoke (a candy thermometer will register about 280°F at this point). Immediately pour candy into prepared pan and let stand at room temperature for about 20 minutes, or until cool and rock-hard. Pry candy out of pan and place in plastic bag. Crush with rolling pin or the bottom of a heavy bottle to form rough ¼-inch pieces. (The blender and food processor do not perform this task successfully; they tend to reduce much of the buttercrunch to powder.) Knead broken-up candy into prepared butter cookie dough.

Place 1½-inch balls of dough on well-greased baking sheets. Leave at least 3 inches between balls, as cookies will spread; flatten balls lightly with fingers or with the back of a fork. Switching the positions of the cookie sheets midway through baking, bake cookies for 10 to 13 minutes, or until edges are light brown. The buttercrunch will melt and the cookies will widen to about 3 inches. Let cookies rest on baking sheets for about 5 minutes after they have been removed from the oven so that candy will resolidify. (Do not leave cookies longer than 5 minutes, or candy chunks will stick.) Transfer cookies to wire racks to cool completely before storing.

Variation: BUTTER WAFERS (MELTAWAYS)

Makes about 3 dozen 3-inch cookies

❦ *These delicate, paper-thin cookies with lovely brown edges are the perfect accompaniment to homemade sherbet or ice cream.*

PRELIMINARIES

Follow those in the Master Recipe, but preheat oven to only 300°F.

Butter Cookies, prepared through Step 1
SUBSTITUTE: 2 large whole eggs for egg yolks
DECREASE: Flour to ½ cup

Prepare the dough—which will really be more like a thick batter—according to Step 1 of the Master Recipe, substituting whole eggs for yolks and decreasing flour to ½ cup.

Drop batter by teaspoonfuls 3 full inches apart on well-greased baking sheets; since you will be able to fit 12 cookies at most on each sheet, you will have to bake the cookies in two batches. Switching the position of the sheets about halfway through baking, bake cookies 16 to 20 minutes, or until edges are pale brown. Let cool slightly on the baking sheets before carefully transferring cookies to wire racks with a spatula.

Variation: BUTTERSCOTCH-NUT COOKIES

Makes about 2½ dozen 2½-inch cookies

❦ *These are chewy.*

Butter Cookies
INCREASE: Butter to 12 tablespoons (1½ sticks)
ADD: ½ cup packed dark brown sugar
1 cup (4 ounces) chopped walnuts or pecans

Prepare dough according to Step 1 of the Master Recipe, increasing butter to ¾ cup, adding brown sugar along with granulated sugar, and incorporating nuts along with the flour. Form cookies with your hands (Step 2a) or prepare as refrigerator cookies (Step 2c); bake according to the Master Recipe.

Variation: CURRANT COOKIES

Makes about 2½ dozen 2½-inch cookies

Butter cookies
ADD: 1 cup dried currants

Prepare dough according to Step 1 of the Master Recipe, adding currants along with the flour. Form the cookies with your hands (Step 2a); bake according to the Master Recipe.

Variation: JAM POCKETS

Makes about 2½ dozen

Butter Cookies, prepared through Step 1
About 3 tablespoons apricot or strawberry jam (finely mince any large pieces of fruit)

Prepare dough according to Step 1 of the Master Recipe. Roll out about ⅛ inch thick and cut into 2½-inch circles with a cookie cutter; reroll and cut out scraps. Place a heaping ¼ teaspoon jam in the center of each dough circle. To form cookies, very lightly moisten the edges of each circle with your finger dipped in water, fold the circle in half, and firmly press joined edges with the tines of a fork to seal into a half-circle shape. Place cookies 1½ inches apart on prepared baking sheets. Bake for about 15 minutes, or until cookies are lightly browned.

Variation: PECAN OR WALNUT BALLS

Makes about 32

❦ *These irresistibly rich cookies are traditional at holiday time. They can be served with vanilla ice cream, and they are also delicious with a glass of sweet marsala or Port, or cream Sherry.*

PRELIMINARIES
Follow those in Master Recipe, but preheat oven to only 300°F.

Butter Cookies, prepared through Step 1
ADD: 1½ cups (about 6 ounces) pecans or walnuts
INCREASE: Butter to 12 tablespoons (1½ sticks)
ADD: Confectioner's sugar for dusting (optional)

Grind nuts a handful at a time in a blender or rotary grinder or all at once in a food processor (you will have about 1¼ cups ground). They should be finely ground but not oily and compacted.

Prepare cookie dough according to Step 1 of the Master Recipe, increasing butter to ¾ cup and sprinkling in ground nuts along with the flour. To form cookies, roll pieces of dough between the palms of your hands into 1½-inch balls; do not flatten. Place cookies about 1 inch apart on prepared baking sheets. Switching the position of the sheets about halfway through baking, bake about 30 minutes, or until cookies have colored lightly. Do not underbake; the cookies must be thoroughly dry inside.

Just before serving, thickly powder the cookies with confectioner's sugar if you wish.

Variation: POPPYSEED COOKIES

Makes about 2 dozen 2-inch cookies

Butter Cookies
ADD: Grated zest of 1 orange
3 to 4 tablespoons poppyseeds

Prepare butter cookie dough according to Step 1 of the Master Recipe, adding orange zest along with vanilla. Follow instructions for forming cookies with your hands (Step 2a), rolling the balls of dough in poppyseeds before transferring to baking sheets and flattening with a drinking glass. Bake according to the Master Recipe.

Variation: SESAME SEED WAFERS

Makes about 2½ dozen 1¾-inch cookies

❦ *Sesame seed has a long history in American cooking, having been brought to the Carolinas by African slaves. In some parts of the South the seed is still known by its African name, benne. These cookies are rich, crumbly, and full of sesame taste. For best results, be sure your sesame seeds are very fresh.*

Butter Cookies, prepared through Step 1
SUBSTITUTE: 2 teaspoons dark sesame oil for vanilla (optional)
DECREASE: Flour to ⅔ cup
ADD: ¾ cup sesame seeds

Prepare cookie dough according to Step 1 of the Master Recipe, substituting sesame oil for vanilla if you wish, decreasing flour to ⅔ cup, and incorporating sesame seeds along with the flour. You will have a very thick batter rather than a dough.

Drop 2-teaspoon-size gobs of the batter 3 inches apart on prepared baking sheets; the cookies will spread. Bake for 8 to 10 minutes, or until they just begin to color. Let cool very briefly on the baking sheets, then carefully transfer cookies to racks with a spatula.

Variation: SUGAR COOKIES

Makes about 2 dozen 2½-inch cookies

❦ *These are the old-fashioned crunchy, dry kind of sugar cookies.*

Butter Cookies

SUBSTITUTE: 2 tablespoons water for egg yolks

ADD: 1 teaspoon baking powder and ¼ teaspoon salt
Sugar

Proceed according to the Master Recipe, substituting water for egg yolks and thoroughly combining flour with the baking powder and salt before sprinkling it over the creamed butter mixture (toss the dry ingredients together in a small bowl with a fork). Form cookies according to any of the three methods outlined in the Master Recipe, being sure to top with sugar if you prepare rolled or refrigerator cookies. Bake according to the Master Recipe.

MASTER RECIPE

Walnut or Pecan Cookies

Makes about 5 dozen 2½-inch cookies

❦ *This cookie and its variations—chocolate chip, oatmeal, and peanut butter—are among the most popular American cookies. This recipe makes crispy cookies with a slight chewiness in the center. You can get a different texture by changing the dough formula slightly.*

TIP:

- To make crisper cookies, add ½ teaspoon water along with the vanilla.
- To make chewier cookies, reverse the proportions of white and brown sugar.
- To make crispy, thin, and very rich cookies, add an extra 6 tablespoons butter, reverse the proportions of white and brown sugar, and use only 1 egg.
- To make chewy-soft and very rich cookies, proceed as for crispy, thin cookies (above) but do not flatten cookies after dropping them onto sheet, and bake the cookies only about 10 minutes, or until they appear dry on top.

PRELIMINARIES

1. Bring all ingredients to room temperature.
2. Set racks in lower-middle and upper-middle levels of oven.
3. Preheat oven to 350°F 20 minutes before baking.
4. Select two 14×17-inch cookie sheets. Grease lightly with solid vegetable shortening.

16 tablespoons (2 sticks) butter
1 cup sugar
½ cup packed dark brown sugar
2 large eggs
1 teaspoon vanilla extract
2 cups unbleached all-purpose flour (measure by scooping cup into large container of flour and sweeping off excess with the back of a knife)
1 teaspoon baking soda
½ teaspoon salt
1 to 1½ cups (about 4 to 6 ounces) broken or coarsely chopped walnuts or pecans

Place butter, white and brown sugar, eggs, and vanilla in 4-quart mixing bowl and beat at high speed with electric mixer for about 2 minutes, or until the mixture is perfectly smooth and creamy and has lightened somewhat in color.

Combine flour, baking soda, and salt in 2-quart bowl and blend thoroughly with fork. Sprinkle dry ingredients over butter mixture. Mix at low speed for about 45 seconds, or until all the flour is moistened. Stir in nuts.

Drop heaping tablespoons of batter about 2½ inches apart on prepared baking sheets. Flatten dough slightly with the back of a fork dipped in water. Place the cookie sheets in a staggered fashion—this helps to promote air circulation—on adjusted racks in oven. Bake 12 to 15 minutes, or until tops of cookies have begun to brown, switching the positions of the cookie sheets during the last third of baking. Let stand 2 minutes on sheets, then transfer cookies to racks to cool using a spatula. Regrease the sheets before baking more cookies.

STORAGE: These cookies are at their best if eaten within a few hours of baking, but they may be sealed airtight in a covered tin or plastic bag and stored for several days at room temperature or frozen for several months.

Variation: CHOCOLATE CHIP COOKIES

Makes about 6 dozen 2½-inch cookies

Walnut or Pecan Cookies
ADD: 1½ to 2 cups (9 to 12 ounces) chocolate chips

Proceed according to the Master Recipe, adding chocolate chips along with the nuts.

Variation: COCONUT CHOCOLATE CHIP COOKIES

Makes about 6 dozen 2½-inch cookies

❦ *Crisp, delicate, and delicious, these cookies should be eaten soon after baking as they do not keep well.*

Walnut or Pecan Cookies
SUBSTITUTE: 1 to 1½ cups grated fresh coconut (see page 697) for nuts
ADD: 1½ cups (9 ounces) chocolate chips

Proceed according to Master Recipe, adding grated fresh coconut and chocolate chips in place of nuts.

Variation: OATMEAL COOKIES

Makes about 6 dozen 2½-inch cookies

❦ *These can be made with nuts, as indicated in the Master Recipe, or with raisins, dried currants, or snipped dates.*

Walnut or Pecan Cookies

ADD:	½ teaspoon cinnamon, ¼ teaspoon ground cloves, and ¼ teaspoon nutmeg, preferably freshly grated
DECREASE:	Flour to 1 cup
ADD:	2½ cups regular or quick-cooking rolled oats

Proceed according to the Master Recipe, blending the spices with the flour (decreased to 1 cup) and other dry ingredients, and incorporating the oats into the batter along with the dry ingredients.

Variation: PEANUT BUTTER COOKIES

Makes about 6 dozen 2½-inch cookies

❦ *One of the fondest of my early food memories is the peanut butter cookies that a grade-school classmate used to bring to school in his lunch box and share with me. The recipe that follows produces cookies that are almost as rich, sandy-textured, and peanut-buttery as those I remember.*

Walnut or Pecan Cookies

INCREASE:	Brown sugar to 1 cup
ADD:	2 cups (one 18-ounce jar) peanut butter
OMIT:	Nuts

Prepare dough according to the Master Recipe, increasing brown sugar to 1 cup, beating in peanut butter when the butter mixture has become smooth and creamy, and omitting nuts.

Do not form cookies according to Master Recipe. Instead drop tablespoon-sized gobs of dough onto prepared cookie sheets and flatten into circles 2½ inches wide and 3/16 inch thick with the back of a wet fork. Cookies may be placed fairly close together on the sheets. Bake 12 to 16 minutes, switching the positions of the cookie sheets midway through baking; the cookies are done when they look dry and tea-colored; the edges should be lightly browned. Let stand 2 minutes on baking sheet, then remove to racks to cool.

MACAROONS

Makes eighteen to twenty 2-inch cookies

❦ *For a while during the creation of this book, it seemed as though the only thing I ever talked about with my editor was macaroons, or, more specifically, why the macaroons that she and I tried to make always failed. After several experiments I discovered that macaroons are not difficult, but one must have the right equipment. The medieval nuns who invented this confection ground the almonds and sugar together to a paste in a mortar and pestle. If you have leathern palms and a whole day to kill, you can do the same thing; otherwise, you can use a food processor. The processor must be a high-quality, efficient model that is capable of truly pulverizing the nuts; unless the almonds are very finely ground, the macaroons will spread out when baked. Another* essential *item is parchment paper (available at specialty cookware shops), which is used to line the baking sheet. Macaroons stick to an ungreased baking sheet, and they flatten and spread out if baked on a greased sheet. By the way, macaroons are less prone to difficulties if baked on a cool, dry day.*

PRELIMINARIES

1. Set rack in upper-middle level of oven.
2. Preheat oven to 325°F 20 minutes before baking.
3. Select a 15×9-inch baking sheet and line it with a piece of parchment paper.

1⅔ cups (about 8 ounces) blanched whole almonds
1 cup sugar
About ¼ cup egg whites (about 2 large)
½ teaspoon almond extract

SPECIAL EQUIPMENT: A pastry bag fitted with a ½-inch star tip (a tablespoon can be substituted)

Place almonds and sugar in food processor and grind for 3 to 4 minutes, or until a very fine meal results. Add ¼ cup of egg whites and the almond extract and process 30 seconds longer, or until dough wads around the blade of the machine. If the dough refuses to gather, add an extra teaspoon or two of egg whites and process another few seconds.

Either drop tablespoon-sized gobs of dough onto parchment-lined baking sheet or pipe dough onto parchment using a pastry bag fitted with a ½-inch star tip. Macaroons may be placed within an inch of one another on the baking sheet, as they should not expand at all. Bake for 18 to 20 minutes, or until cookies are lightly browned around the edges and look dry; do not overbake, or the macaroons will be hard and tough. Let cool completely before peeling off parchment paper.

STORAGE: Macaroons may be placed in an airtight tin or sealed in a plastic bag and stored at room temperature for several days or frozen for 3 months.

GINGERSNAPS

Makes about 5 dozen 2-inch cookies

PRELIMINARIES

1. Bring all ingredients to room temperature.
2. Set racks in lower-middle and upper-middle levels of oven.
3. Preheat oven to 325°F 20 minutes before baking.
4. Select two 14×17-inch cookie sheets. Grease lightly with solid vegetable shortening.

8 tablespoons (1 stick) butter
¾ cup sugar
¼ cup dark molasses
1 large egg
1 tablespoon cider vinegar
1 to 2 tablespoons ground ginger (1 tablespoon will produce cookies of a conventional pungency)
½ teaspoon cinnamon
¼ teaspoon ground cloves
2 cups unbleached all-purpose flour (measure by scooping cup into large container of flour and sweeping off excess with the back of a knife)
1 teaspoon baking soda
Sugar for dredging

Place butter, sugar, molasses, egg, vinegar, and spices in 4-quart mixing bowl and beat with electric mixer at high speed for about 1 minute, or until perfectly smooth. Combine flour and baking soda in 1-quart bowl and blend thoroughly with fork. Sprinkle dry ingredients over butter mixture and blend at low speed for about 45 seconds, or until all the flour is moistened. Scoop dough onto a sheet of plastic wrap, wrap securely, and chill for at least 3 hours.

Roll pieces of chilled dough between the palms of your hands to form ¾-inch balls. Dredge the balls in sugar and arrange about 2½ inches apart on prepared baking sheets. Place the baking sheets in a staggered fashion in the preheated oven. Bake 16 to 20 minutes, or until tops of gingersnaps are crinkly and look dry, switching the positions of the baking sheets during the last third of baking. Using a spatula, transfer cookies to racks to cool.

STORAGE: Gingersnaps keep well. Store them for up to a week in a covered tin or cookie jar, or freeze in a sealed plastic bag for up to 3 months.

OATMEAL LACE COOKIES

Makes about 4 dozen 2½-inch cookies

❦ *These are more tender and delicate than lace cookies often are, and no cookie could be easier to make.*

PRELIMINARIES

1. Set rack in upper-middle level of oven.
2. Preheat oven to 350°F 20 minutes before baking.
3. Select two 14×17-inch cookie sheets. Grease lightly with butter.

16 tablespoons (2 sticks) butter
¾ cup sugar (use half dark brown sugar, packed, if you wish)
1 large egg
1 tablespoon all-purpose flour
2 cups regular or quick-cooking rolled oats

Melt butter in a 2-quart saucepan over low heat. Remove from heat and beat in first the sugar, then the egg and flour. Stir in oats.

Drop slightly heaped teaspoons of batter at least 2½ inches apart onto prepared baking sheets; flatten mounds of batter slightly with your finger. Bake in preheated oven, *one sheet at a time,* for 8 to 10 minutes, or until cookies have spread out and browned nicely around the rims. Let cookies cool for a minute on baking sheet after removing them from the oven, then carefully transfer with a spatula to parchment paper or a folded brown paper bag to cool. Plan to eat lace cookies promptly, as they quickly lose their just-baked quality.

GRANDMOTHER ROSALIND'S SNICKERDOODLES

Makes about 5 dozen 2-inch cookies

❦*I loved these crisp-crunchy cookies as a child, so I was terribly excited to discover my grandmother's recipe on an old shortening-smudged notecard. I assumed, of course, that the recipe was my grandmother's alone, but when I examined it closely it turned out to be disappointingly similar to other snickerdoodle formulas. Still, these are fine cookies, even if they are not as unique as I once thought.*

PRELIMINARIES

1. Bring all ingredients to room temperature.
2. Set racks in lower-middle and upper-middle levels of the oven.
3. Preheat oven to 400°F 20 minutes before baking.
4. Select two 14×17-inch cookie sheets. Do not grease baking sheets, or the cookies will spread out too much.

8 tablespoons (1 stick) butter
½ cup lard or vegetable shortening
1½ cups sugar
2 large eggs
2¾ cups unbleached all-purpose flour (measure by scooping cup into large container of flour and sweeping off excess with the back of a knife)
2 teaspoons cream of tartar
1 teaspoon baking soda
½ teaspoon salt
2 tablespoons sugar
2 teaspoons cinnamon

Place butter, lard or shortening, 1½ cups sugar, and eggs in 4-quart mixing bowl and beat with electric mixer at high speed for about 2 minutes, or until mixture is smoothly blended and just starting to become fluffy.

Combine flour, cream of tartar, baking soda, and salt in a 2-quart bowl and blend thoroughly with a fork. Sprinkle dry ingredients over creamed mixture and blend at low speed for about 1 minute, or until all the flour is incorporated. Wrap dough in plastic and chill about 1 hour to firm.

Toss 2 tablespoons sugar and cinnamon together on plate. Roll pieces of dough into 1-inch balls between your palms, then dredge in the cinnamon mixture. Place balls 2 inches apart on baking sheets. Place the cookie sheets in a staggered fashion in the preheated oven and, switching the positions of the sheets during the last third of baking, bake cookies for 8 to 10 minutes, or until tops are slightly crinkly and pale gold in color. Remove from sheets with a spatula and transfer to racks to cool.

STORAGE: Snickerdoodles may be kept for several days in a cookie jar or sealed tin or frozen for 3 months in an airtight plastic bag.

PIES and OTHER PASTRIES

The idea of encasing fruits, custards, and other foods in pastry has appealed to virtually all cultures since the beginning of recorded culinary history. Originally, the pastry enclosure may have been intended to keep foods from spoiling quickly or to allow foods to be transported easily. But it must soon have been discovered that filled pastries are a particularly delicious type of food.

The centerpiece of this chapter is old-fashioned butter pie crust. Tender, full of flaky ledges, and rich with the taste of fresh butter, a perfectly executed pie crust is, to my mind, one of the crowning culinary achievements. Our grandmothers knew how to make a proper pie crust, but most of us have forgotten, and our anxiety about the whole matter seems to have risen to fantastic heights. To relieve some of this anxiety and to educate the prospective pastry chef, I have been especially thorough in detailing every step of the pie crust-making process.

Preparing the basic dough and rolling it out and forming it into pie and pastry crusts are two separate acts, each with its own special procedures and possible pitfalls. Hence, I have provided a recipe for making the dough, with proportions for two different quantities, and a separate Master Technique plus variations for rolling out, forming, and baking the dough into pie shells, large tart shells, individual tart shells, and tartlet shells. Before setting out, be sure to read through both recipes carefully to get your bearings. Remember that, as in all arts, practice makes perfect.

ABOUT BUTTER PIE CRUST DOUGH: To start you out on the right track, here are 5 notes on the dough-making process:

NOTE 1: TEMPERATURE: The colder your ingredients, your equipment, and your kitchen, the better. If the butter and shortening are sufficiently cold and hard, they will remain in relatively large pieces after being blended with the flour, and your crust will be properly light and flaky. If the butter and shortening are too soft, they blend with the flour into a pasty goo, making for a tough crust. Don't attempt to make pie crust in an unairconditioned kitchen in the middle of an August heatwave—even an expert would run into trouble. In warm weather, use the smaller amount of butter specified for each quantity of dough and, as a final safeguard, after measuring the flour and salt into the mixing bowl slip the bowl into the freezer for half an hour or so. Butter and shortening may be put briefly into the freezer too.

NOTE 2: THE FLOUR: Unbleached all-purpose flour makes excellent pie crusts. Bleached flour is considerably less satisfactory, for it produces a somewhat tough and brittle crust. A pie crust made with pastry flour has a special kind of tenderness, but you are not likely to find pastry flour at the supermarket. Whole wheat pastry flour, available at health-food stores, gives pie crusts a nice nutty taste, but whole wheat crusts are never as light and flaky as crusts made with unbleached all-purpose flour. Regular whole wheat flour produces a tough, heavy crust and I do not recommend its use.

Be sure to measure the flour accurately; too little flour produces a short and crumbly crust, and too much flour makes the crust tough and dry.

NOTE 3: THE BUTTER AND VEGETABLE SHORTENING OR LARD: Because it has a low moisture content and tends to be very fresh, unsalted butter is better than salted butter in pie crusts. However, unsalted—also called "sweet" butter—is hard to find in some parts of the country, and salted butter may be used instead.

Buy a good-quality butter. Some brands, particularly the cheaper ones, taste rancid or tainted and tend to be soft and watery. This means that no matter how skillful you are the dough is likely to turn out pasty and to bake into a tough, greasy crust.

Vegetable shortening and lard are used in pie crusts along with butter to help to make them tender. Do not substitute additional butter except in an emergency.

NOTE 4: FLOUR TO FAT PROPORTIONS: Using roughly equal amounts of flour and fat in your pie dough will give you the tenderest and flakiest crust possible, but it can also result in a dough that is difficult to handle. The recipe gives flexible proportions of butter for each quantity of dough. Use the larger amount of butter if you are an experienced pastry-maker, the smaller amount if you are a beginner.

NOTE 5: SUGAR: You can make a delicious sweet pie crust by adding 2 to 3 tablespoons of sugar to the dough. Be forewarned, however, that a sweetened dough may become sticky and break apart during rolling, and that sweetened pie crusts have to be watched very carefully in the oven lest they burn.

MAKING THE DOUGH IN A FOOD PROCESSOR: Many say that pie crusts made from machine-blended doughs are every bit as good as those made from doughs blended by hand, but I cannot agree. No matter how briefly the processor is run, it overblends the fat and flour, and the final pie crust never has the optimal flakiness. That said, I have to admit that a food processor certainly saves time and effort, and it makes outright failure almost impossible.

To adapt the recipe for use with the food processor, proceed as follows:

Place the flour, salt, and optional sugar in the container of a processor fitted with the metal chopping blade and blend for 3 seconds. Add the cold butter bits and the cold shortening or lard and process for exactly 3 seconds longer. The mixture should look like crushed pebbles. If you think it is slightly too coarse, process another second or two, but no longer. Sprinkle 4 tablespoons ice water (6 tablespoons for dough made with 2½ cups flour) evenly over the flour mixture and blend for 3 to 5 seconds, or just until the dough has begun to gather in ½-inch lumps. Press the dough into a rough ball, then wrap and chill.

BUTTER PIE CRUST DOUGH

To make one 9-inch pie shell; one 9-inch tart shell; eight 3-inch tart shells; or 18 to 22 tartlet shells:

1½ cups unbleached all-purpose flour (measure by scooping cup into large container of flour and sweeping off excess with the back of a knife)
2 to 3 tablespoons sugar (optional: for dessert pastries only)
¾ teaspoon salt (if you are using unsalted butter) or ¼ teaspoon salt (if you are using salted butter)
7 to 9 tablespoons (1 stick, give or take a tablespoon) *very cold* butter, preferably unsalted
2 tablespoons *very cold* vegetable shortening or lard
3½ to 5 tablespoons ice water

To make one 9-inch 2-crust pie; a 12-inch tart shell; about fourteen 3-inch tart shells; or 30 to 36 tartlet shells:

- 2½ cups unbleached all-purpose flour (measure by scooping cup into large container of flour and sweeping off excess with the back of a knife)
- 3 to 5 tablespoons sugar (optional, for dessert pastries only)
- 1¼ teaspoons salt (if you are using unsalted butter) or heaping ½ teaspoon salt (if you are using salted butter)
- 12 to 15 tablespoons (1½ to 1⅞ sticks) *very cold* butter, preferably unsalted
- 3 tablespoons *very cold* vegetable shortening or lard
- 5½ to 7 tablespoons ice water

STEP 1: COMBINING INGREDIENTS: Measure flour, optional sugar, and salt into 3-quart mixing bowl and toss with your fingers to blend thoroughly. Cut the cold butter lengthwise into quarters, then cut the quarters crosswise into ¼-inch bits; cut cold shortening or lard also into ¼-inch bits. Turn butter and shortening into flour mixture and quickly toss with your fingers or a spoon to distribute the ingredients.

STEP 2: BLENDING THE FLOUR AND FAT: This is the step that will spell success or failure for your pie crust. The object is to blend the flour and fat together just enough to allow a cohesive dough to form when water is added. As the crust bakes, the particles of fat melt and release air and steam, forming little pockets that make the crust flaky and light. If the fat softens and amalgamates with the flour into a paste during blending, no pockets will form and the pastry will be tough and greasy. Work quickly and don't try to be too thorough. If the fat begins to soften before blending is completed, put the bowl in the freezer for a few minutes, then start again.

There are two ways to perform the flour-and-fat blending—with a pastry blender (or two knives) or with your fingertips. Working with your fingertips will give you the better crust because your fingers flatten the fat into large thin flakes rather than merely chopping it up. However, you must work quickly lest the heat of your fingers cause the fat to soften excessively. For beginners, it may be better to work with a tool.

To blend the flour and fat with a pastry blender or two knives, simply cut the fat into the flour until the mixture resembles crushed pebbles.

To blend the flour and fat with your fingertips, use both hands and pinch the pieces of butter and shortening or lard between fingertips and thumb and then quickly release them, thus flattening the pieces of fat into flakes and smearing them with flour. Reach to the bottom of the bowl periodically and bring unblended flour to the top. The whole process should not take you longer than 2 or 3 minutes. The mixture should look dry and crumbly—like crumbled cake or very coarse meal; it will appear messy and lumpy in consistency, not uniform.

STEP 3: ADDING WATER AND GATHERING THE DOUGH INTO A BALL: Immediately sprinkle the *minimum* amount of ice water given in the ingredients list evenly over the flour and fat mixture, and, using a spoon or fork, rapidly stir the dough until it gathers into clumps. If the dough is reluctant to gather and remains crumbly, dry, and floury-looking, sprinkle it with an additional tablespoon or so of ice water and stir a moment longer. It is better that the dough be slightly too moist than too dry, as dry dough tends to crack when rolled and to bake up tough. Press the clumps of dough together to form a ball, handling the dough only enough to make it cohere. The dough will look very rough at this point.

STEP 4: WRAPPING; CHILLING: Wrap the dough first in plastic, then in foil, and refrigerate for at least 2 hours. During this rest the fat will firm up and the gluten in the flour will relax, making it easier to roll out and form the dough without its tearing or shrinking. For the flakiest and tenderest crust possible, allow the dough to rest a full 24 hours in the refrigerator before forming and baking.

AHEAD OF TIME: Pie crust dough may be refrigerated for 3 days or wrapped airtight in a plastic bag and frozen for several months (at least).

9-inch Pie Shell

Makes 1 shell

PRELIMINARY PREPARATIONS
In undertaking to roll out pastry dough, start with a cool kitchen and a clear, relaxed mind. Have ready the equipment you will need: a rolling pin, either a heavy one at least 12 inches long with ball-bearing handles or a handleless wooden pin, plus a pastry scraper or metal spatula, in case the dough should stick. A clean, unobstructed patch of formica countertop about 2 feet square is an ideal surface on which to roll out a pie crust. You may also use a large pastry board made of unvarnished wood—the advantage of the board is that pastry

dough rarely sticks when rolled out on it—or, if you are lucky enough to have one, a large marble slab. In truth, the work surface is of less importance than is commonly thought. What really counts is the skill with which the dough is made and rolled out.

PROBLEMS

- If the circle of dough splits around the edges as you roll, it is still too hard and cold. Let the dough stand a few minutes longer at room temperature before continuing.
- If the dough crumbles when you attempt to roll it, it is probably too dry. Try to proceed, but if the dough simply will not cohere, chop it into small pieces, sprinkle it with a tablespoon or two of water, *gently* knead it into a rough ball, wrap in plastic, and refrigerate for several hours before trying again.
- If the dough shrinks back, refusing to expand into a large circle, the gluten in the flour is overactivated. Wrap the dough and allow it to rest for an hour or more in the refrigerator before proceeding.
- If the dough softens to the point of becoming difficult to handle, slide a rimless baking sheet under it, cover it with plastic wrap, and refrigerate it for a few minutes to firm the butter and shortening.
- If the dough tears, join the edges of the tear, overlapping them by about ¼ inch. Press to seal, and then roll the pin clockwise and counter-clockwise—but not diagonally—over the rip. The tear probably occurred because the dough was rolled out unevenly; the upward and downward arc-sweeps of the pin over the tear should help to equalize the tension within the sheet of dough and thus prevent the tear from reopening.
- If lumps of butter keep breaking through the dough, causing the dough to stick to the work surface and to the pin, flour the work surface a bit more liberally and tamp pinches of flour into any butter breakthroughs that occur on the top of the dough. (This problem is common and not at all serious. In fact, the messiest-looking doughs generally bake into the flakiest and lightest crusts.)

SELECTING A PIE PAN: Pie pans are annoyingly nonuniform in their contours, dimensions, and capacities. What you want here is a pan that measures roughly 9 inches across between the inner edges of the rim and about 1½ inches deep. Filled to the brim, it should hold 4 to 4½ cups water, so that the baked shell with its raised rim will have a capacity of about 5 cups. I prefer pie pans made of plain or black-finished aluminum; glass pans sometimes cause pie crusts to brown unevenly or to burn.

Step 1: Rolling Out the Dough

Butter Pie Crust Dough, made with 1½ cups flour
3 to 6 tablespoons unbleached all-purpose flour

Let the chilled dough soften at room temperature, still wrapped in plastic, until it is malleable but firm, rather like stiff clay. If the dough has only been in the refrigerator for a couple of hours, it should be soft enough roll in 10 to 15 minutes, but dough that has been refrigerated for 12 hours or more will have to stand 20 minutes or longer. If the dough is too hard and cold, it will crack around the edges when you roll it out.

Sprinkle a 1-foot square of the work surface with about 2 tablespoons flour. Unwrap the dough, flour it lightly, and then briefly roll the dough over the work surface with the palm of your hand to form it into a fairly even sphere. Using the heel of your hand, flatten the sphere into a disk about 6 inches wide. Dust both sides of the dough lightly with flour, sprinkle a bit of additional flour on the work surface, and rub the rolling pin with flour.

TIP: In order to avoid stretching the dough, which may cause it to tear during handling or to buckle out of shape as it bakes, try to exert sideways rather than downward pressure on the pin as you roll, leaning the weight of your body forward and backward rather than bearing down on the pin.

Using short, quick, firm, even strokes, and always starting at the center of the dough, roll the dough out in all directions—that is, pass the pin one or two strokes over the far side, away from you, one or two strokes over the near side, toward you, several strokes to the left, and then several strokes to the right. Your object is to get the dough circle to expand in all directions equally. Each time you complete a full set of strokes, gently loosen the entire sheet of dough from the work surface; if it is sticking at any point, sprinkle a bit of flour underneath it, but don't use any more than is absolutely necessary, or the baked crust will be tough. In the beginning of the rolling-out process, when the dough sheet is still small and maneuverable, periodically give the dough a quarter- or half-turn when you loosen it; this will further insure an evenly rolled-out crust (1).

Stop rolling the dough when it has reached a thickness of just under ⅛ inch; if rolled thinner, the dough is liable to tear during handling or to develop scorched spots as it bakes, and the finished crust will be brittle and crumbly rather than flaky. When rolled to the proper thinness, the circle of dough will be about 14 inches across. To be doubly sure that the dough is the necessary circumference, invert the pie pan over the center of the sheet and see that the dough extends at least 2 inches beyond the rim of the pan at all points.

Step 2: Lining the Pie Pan with the Dough; Forming the Pie Shell

Gently fold the circle of dough in half, then fold the half-circle of dough in half, making a quarter-circle wedge. Transfer the wedge of dough to the pie pan, placing the tip of the wedge in the center of the pan (2). Carefully unfold the dough to cover the bottom and sides of the pan. Using floured fingers, firmly press the dough against the sides and bottom of the pan without stretching.

With kitchen shears or a sharp paring knife, trim the dough that hangs over the outside edge of the pie pan to an even 3/4 inch (3). (If the dough is too short in one place or another, or if it tears, moisten one of the trimmed-off scraps lightly with water and press it firmly over the tear or short spot.) Tuck the overhanging dough under to make the edge of the pie crust 2 layers thick and flush with the rim of the pie pan. Lightly press together the two layers of the pie shell edge to seal, then bend the edge slightly upward. Flute the edge by propping it on the outside with the thumb and forefinger of one hand while poking it from within with the index finger of your other hand (4). Finally, prick the bottom, sides, and corners of the shell at 1/4-inch intervals with a fork. Carefully slip the shell into a plastic bag and refrigerate for at least 20 minutes before baking.

Ahead of time: The shell may be kept in the refrigerator, in its plastic bag, for several hours before baking. It may also be frozen for several months. To prepare for freezing, place the shell in the freezer until frozen solid, then pry out of pan, wrap tightly in foil, seal in a plastic bag, and return to the freezer. To bake, unwrap, return to pie pan, and bake at once, still frozen (add a few extra minutes to the baking time if necessary).

Step 3: Baking the Shell Partially or Fully

1 large egg yolk thoroughly beaten with 1/8 teaspoon water

About 20 minutes before you wish to bake the shell, set rack in the middle of the oven and preheat to 375°F (350°F if you are using a glass pie pan).

The shell must be weighted during the initial phase of baking to keep it from shrinking. Press a sheet of aluminum foil about 16 inches long against the sides and bottom of the pie shell, leaving an overhang of several inches at both ends to serve as handles, and fill the foil-lined shell to the top of the fluted rim with metal pellets (sold for this purpose in housewares shops), clean pebbles, dried beans, or raw rice. (You will need 5 to 5½ cups of weights altogether, depending on the capacity of the shell. Dried beans or rice, by the way, can be stored in an airtight container and used again as pie weights.) (5)

Bake the shell for 8 minutes, then remove from the oven and quickly lift out the weights by grasping the foil at each end. Proceed as follows:

To make a partially baked shell: Return the shell to the oven and bake for 3 to 5 minutes longer, or until it is just beginning to color. If the bottom of the

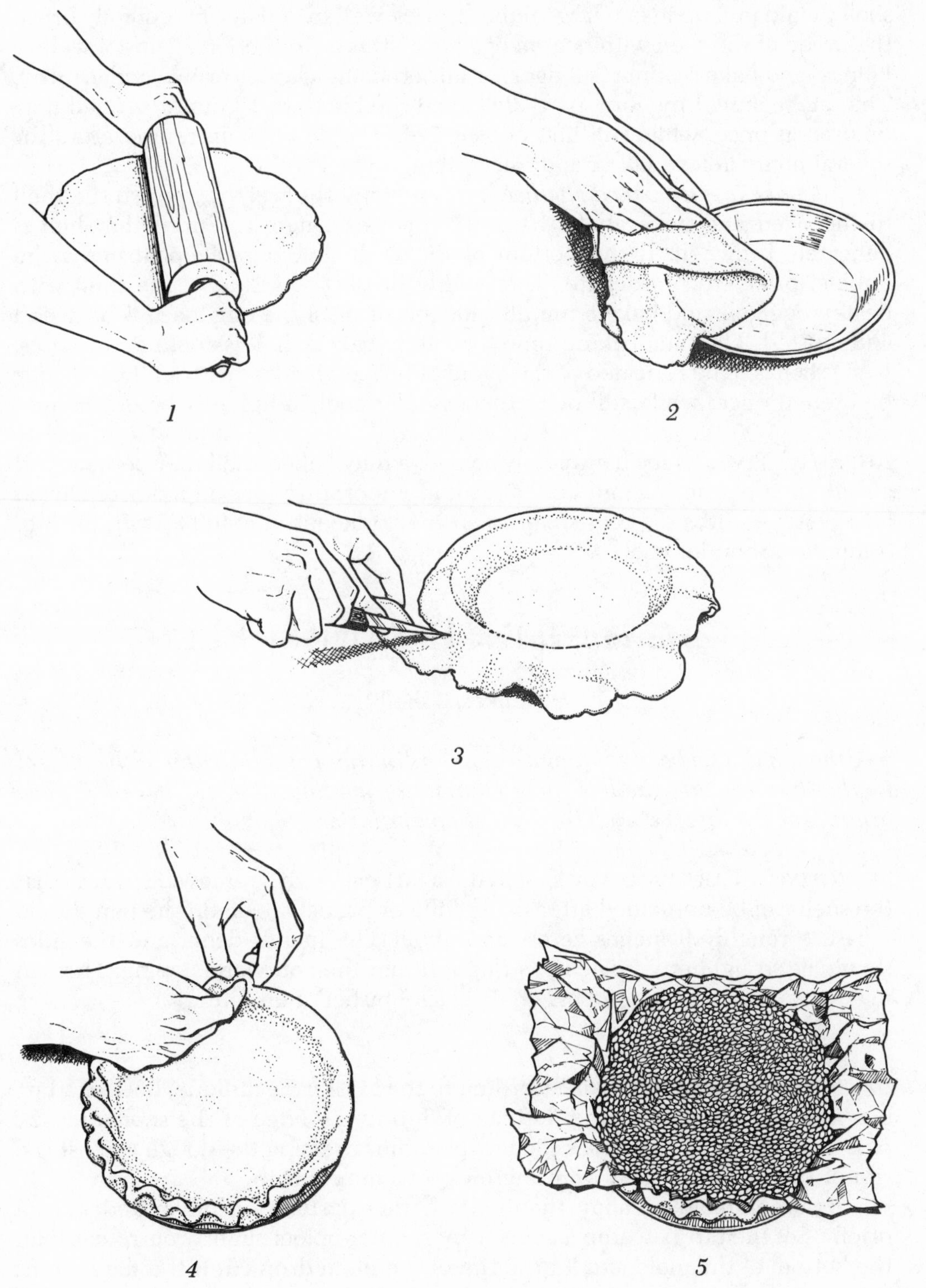

shell should puff up in one large bubble, prick well to deflate. Thoroughly brush the inside of the shell with beaten egg yolk—this is protection against a watery filling—and bake 5 minutes longer, or until the egg glaze is brown and crusted. The total baking time for a partially baked shell is 16 to 18 minutes. Shell may be used at once, while still hot, or may be set aside at room temperature for several hours before filling and final baking.

To make a fully baked shell: After removing the weights, return the shell to the oven and bake about 10 to 12 minutes longer, or until the shell is delicately browned. If the bottom of the shell should puff up in one large bubble, prick well to deflate. Thoroughly brush the inside of the shell with beaten egg yolk and bake 5 minutes longer, or until the egg glaze is browned and crusted. The total baking time for a fully baked shell is about 25 minutes. If the shell is to be returned to the oven and baked further with a filling, it may be used at once, while still hot; otherwise, let cool completely before filling.

AHEAD OF TIME: Once completely cooled, a fully baked shell may be wrapped airtight in a plastic bag and kept at room temperature for half a day or frozen for several months. To recrisp a frozen shell, place it in a 400°F oven for 3 to 5 minutes, then let cool.

Variation: 9-INCH TART SHELL

Makes 1 shell

❦ *Although it may be used in place of an ordinary pie shell in any of the recipes in this book, a tart shell is more commonly employed in recipes of French origin, such as quiche and fresh fruit cream tarts.*

SELECTING A TART PAN: You should use a tart pan with a removable rim so that the shell can be unmolded after being fully or partially baked. The pan should measure roughly 9 inches across and about 1½ inches deep, and the sides should be straight or very nearly straight rather than outward-sloping. The pan may be made of plain, embossed, or black-finished aluminum.

9-inch Pie Shell

Form and bake the shell according to the Master Technique, but use a tart pan instead of a pie pan and, instead of fluting the edge of the shell (Step 2), pass the rolling pin once over the tart pan, thus pressing the dough against the rim of the pan and cleanly cutting off protruding dough.

Before unmolding, allow the shell, whether partially or fully baked, to cool briefly. Set the tart pan atop a coffee can or other object slightly narrower than the bottom of the mold and let the rim of the mold drop off. If the shell seems fragile, leave the bottom of the pan attached as support; otherwise, carefully lift shell from the bottom of the tart pan using two large metal spatulas. Transfer the shell to a serving platter or, if it is to be filled and baked further, to a baking sheet.

Variation: 3-INCH TART SHELLS

Makes about 8 shells

❦ *Tart shells are marvelous receptacles for creamed foods and scrambled eggs, and they may be used in place of a single 9-inch shell in any of the pie or tart recipes in this book.*

SELECTING TART MOLDS: Choose 8 tart molds 3 to 3½ inches wide and about 1 inch deep, with a capacity of about ½ cup each. Molds that are wider and shallower may be used instead, provided they hold ½ cup.

9-inch Pie Shell

Following Step 1 of the Master Technique, roll out dough into a circle just under ⅛ inch thick. Using a sharp knife, cut out at least 8 rounds of dough about 1¼ inches wider than your molds; the scraps may be pressed together and rerolled to make more tarts, if you wish, but the shells made from the rerolled pastry will be slightly tough.

Form and bake tart shells according to Steps 2 and 3 of the Master Technique. You may either flute the rims of the shells—which is pretty and gives shells made in slightly small molds a bit of added room—or you may pass the rolling pin over the molds to cut off the excess dough cleanly. The tart shells may not need to bake quite as long after the removal of the foil and weights as a large pie shell.

Let the baked tart shells cool briefly, then ease them out of the molds with a blunt-tipped knife.

Variation: TARTLET SHELLS

Makes about 18 to 22 shells

❦ *Tartlet shells are typically used to make miniature quiches and various other sorts of hors d'oeuvre. If you find yourself in frequent need of them, you might consider making a big batch and storing them in a plastic bag in the freezer. (Start with butter crust pie dough made with 2½ cups of flour; roll out and cut only half the dough at a time.)*

SELECTING TARTLET MOLDS: Choose tartlet molds 1½ to 1¾ inches wide across the top and ¾ to 1 inch deep, with a capacity of about 1 tablespoon. Baking the tartlets in successive batches, you can get by with as few as 8 molds, but obviously your task will be easier if you have more.

9-inch Pie Shell

OMIT: Egg yolk beaten with water (Step 3)

Following Step 1 of the Master Technique, roll out dough into a circle just under ⅛ inch thick. Using a round cookie cutter or biscuit cutter about ¾ inch wider than your molds, cut out as many rounds of dough as you can, then press the scraps together, reroll, and cut out more. Refrigerate the rounds of dough that you will not be forming and baking at once.

Tartlet shells are formed and baked in a different manner from other pastry shells, so skip over Steps 2 and 3 of the Master Technique and instead proceed as follows:

Firmly press dough circles into tartlet molds with floured fingers, trimming the edges of the dough by pressing it against the rim of the molds with your thumbs to cut it off cleanly. Prick the shells very thoroughly with a small fork or cake tester. To keep the shells from shrinking during baking, you may fit each with a large glass marble or tightly crumpled ball of aluminum foil; or you may take your chances and bake the shells without weights. Arrange shells on a baking sheet and bake in the middle level of a 400°F oven for 15 to 20 minutes, or until nicely browned. Remove the weights, if used, midway during baking, and check on the shells periodically, pricking with fork or cake tester any that are puffing away from the sides or bottom of the molds. Remove from oven, let cool briefly, then carefully pry shells out of molds with the tip of a small knife. Let emptied molds cool completely before lining with fresh rounds of dough.

MASTER RECIPE

Graham Cracker Crumb Pie Crust

Makes one 9-inch pie shell

Delicious and a breeze to make, crumb crusts may be used with any filling that does not require baking after it is turned into the pie shell. Cream fillings are traditional favorites with a crumb crust but fruit fillings are equally tasty.

PRELIMINARIES

1. Set rack in middle or upper-middle level of oven.
2. Preheat oven to 350°F 20 minutes before baking.
3. Select a pie pan measuring 9 inches across between the inner edges of the rim and approximately 1½ inches deep.

6 tablespoons butter
1½ cups very fine graham cracker crumbs (10 to 12 double graham crackers; whirl in blender or food processor, or crush in plastic bag with rolling pin)
2 to 4 tablespoons sugar

Melt butter in small saucepan and set aside to cool briefly. Pour crumbs into pie pan and toss with sugar to taste. Drizzle on melted butter and stir with your fingers until mixture is thoroughly combined. Press evenly into bottom and sides of pie pan. Bake in preheated oven for 10 to 12 minutes, or until crust just begins to brown. Let cool to room temperature before filling.

Variation: CHOCOLATE CRUMB PIE CRUST

Makes one 9-inch pie shell

❦ *Try this with a cream pie filling flavored with rum, banana, coconut, coffee, orange, or vanilla.*

Graham Cracker Crumb Pie Crust
SUBSTITUTE: 1½ cups very fine dry chocolate wafer crumbs (about 30 2¼-inch wafers) for graham cracker crumbs

Proceed according to the Master Recipe, using chocolate wafer crumbs.

Variation: COCONUT CRUMB PIE CRUST

Makes one 9-inch pie shell

Graham Cracker Crumb Pie Crust
DECREASE: Butter to 4 tablespoons
Graham cracker crumbs to ¾ cup
ADD: ¾ cup desiccated coconut (available at health-food stores)

Proceed according to the Master Recipe, decreasing butter to 4 tablespoons and graham cracker crumbs to ¾ cup, and adding coconut to the pie pan along with the crumbs.

Variation: GINGER CRUMB PIE CRUST

Makes one 9-inch pie shell

Graham Cracker Crumb Pie Crust
SUBSTITUTE: 1½ cups very fine gingersnap crumbs (about 48 1½-inch cookies) for graham cracker crumbs

Proceed according to the Master Recipe, using gingersnap crumbs.

Variation: PECAN CRUMB PIE CRUST

Makes one 9-inch pie shell

Graham Cracker Crumb Pie Crust
DECREASE: Butter to 3 tablespoons
Graham cracker crumbs to ¾ cup
ADD: ¾ cup (about 3 ounces) pecans, ground fine

Proceed according to the Master Recipe, decreasing butter to 3 tablespoons and graham cracker crumbs to ¾ cup, and adding pecans to the pie pan along with the crumbs.

Variation: VANILLA CRUMB PIE CRUST

Makes one 9-inch shell

Graham Cracker Crumb Pie Crust
SUBSTITUTE: 1½ cups very fine dry vanilla wafer crumbs (about 36 1½-inch cookies) for graham cracker crumbs

Proceed according to the Master Recipe, using vanilla wafer crumbs.

MASTER TECHNIQUE

Double-Crust (Covered) Fruit Pie

Makes one 9-inch pie serving 6

❦ *Perennial favorites, fruit pies are delicious either warm or at room temperature, with or without vanilla ice cream.*

CHOOSING A FRUIT FILLING FOR A COVERED FRUIT PIE: The chart on page 771 lists fruits and other ingredients needed to make various fruit fillings. Choose any filling that appeals to you.

PRELIMINARIES

1. Set rack in the middle level of oven.
2. Preheat oven to 400°F 20 minutes before baking.
3. Select a pie pan measuring 9 inches across between the inside edges of the rim and about 1½ inches deep, and a shallow-rimmed baking sheet or pizza pan large enough to hold the pie pan.

A fruit filling (see chart, page 771)
Butter pie crust dough, page 751, made with 2½ cups flour
1½ tablespoons fine dry bread crumbs
1½ teaspoons cream or milk
1 tablespoon sugar

Squeeze the lemon juice called for in the fruit filling chart into a 4-quart mixing bowl. Prepare fruit as directed in the chart, adding it to the mixing bowl and tossing with the lemon juice. Add sugar, cornstarch, and flavoring and toss with a wooden spoon until cornstarch is dissolved and completely smooth. Set the fruit mixture aside. Cut the butter called for in the chart into small pieces or pats and set aside.

Cut off about ⅓ of the pie crust and set aside. Following the first step of the Master Technique, page 755, roll out the remaining ⅔ of the dough into a circle 14 inches wide and just under ⅛ inch thick. Following the first paragraph of Step 2, line the pie pan with dough, letting the excess hang over the rim of the pan without trimming it. Roll out the reserved ⅓ of the dough into a circle about 11 inches in diameter. Flour the surface lightly and fold into quarters.

Sprinkle the bottom of the pie shell evenly with bread crumbs. Turn the reserved fruit mixture into the shell, mounding it slightly in the center if there is more fruit than is necessary to fill shell evenly to the top. Distribute the reserved pieces of butter over the fruit.

Transfer folded dough circle to the top of the pie and unfold it to cover the filling. Trim edges of both the top and bottom crusts so that they do not hang more than 3/4 inch beyond the rim of the pan. Tuck in edges of both crusts, making the edge of the pie, now composed of four folded layers of dough, flush with the outside rim of the pan. Press the rim of the crust firmly with your fingers to seal, then either flute (see Step 2 of the Master Technique) or press with the tines of a fork. Using a sharp paring knife, cut four 1 1/2-inch slits in the top crust, making a cross that radiates outward from the center of the pie but that does not intersect at the center. Brush top crust with cream or milk and sprinkle evenly with sugar.

Set the pie on a baking sheet (in case it should drip) and bake in the preheated oven for 45 to 50 minutes. The pie is done when you can insert a knife deeply through one of the slits in the crust without resistance. At this point, juices from the filling should be bubbling enthusiastically through the vents in the top crust. Let pie cool on a wire rack for at least an hour before serving.

AHEAD OF TIME/STORAGE: When thoroughly cooled—in about 3 hours—the pie may be sealed airtight in a plastic bag and stored for 2 to 3 days at room temperature or in the refrigerator. Remember that the longer you keep the pie, the softer the crust will become. For longer storage, freeze the pie until hard, then remove from the pan, wrap tightly in foil, and seal airtight in a plastic bag. A frozen pie will keep for several months at least. To thaw, return pie to pan and let stand at room temperature for 6 to 8 hours or bake in a 300°F oven for 45 minutes to an hour, covering the top with foil if it should become too brown.

MASTER TECHNIQUE

Streusel Crumb Fruit Pie or Tart

Makes one 9-inch pie serving 6

Here a fruit filling is baked in a casserole dish until partially cooked, turned into a baked pie shell, covered with a buttery, crunchy crumb topping, then returned to the oven so that the fruit can finish cooking and the crumbs can brown. This is an especially delicious pie, not only because the crumbs and fruit go so well together, but also because the crust comes out so light and crisp.

CHOOSING A FRUIT FILLING FOR A STREUSEL CRUMB PIE: The chart on page 771 lists fruits and other ingredients needed to make various fruit fillings. Choose any filling that appeals to you.

PRELIMINARIES

1. Have ready a *fully baked* 9-inch pie shell (page 753) or a *fully baked* 9-inch tart shell (page 758). Set the shell on a baking sheet (for tart shell, preferably one that is rimless on two sides so that the baked tart may be slid from sheet to serving tray).
2. Set rack in middle level of oven.
3. Preheat oven to 400°F 20 minutes before baking.
4. Select a 9- to 10-inch covered casserole at least 4 inches deep. Grease with 1 tablespoon butter.

STEP 1: PREPARING THE FILLING

A fruit filling (see chart, page 771)

Squeeze the lemon juice called for in the fruit pie filling chart into a 4-quart mixing bowl. Prepare fruit as directed in the chart, adding it to the bowl and tossing with the lemon juice as it is peeled and cut. Add sugar, cornstarch, and flavoring and toss with a wooden spoon until cornstarch is dissolved and completely smooth. Turn fruit mixture into the buttered casserole. Cut the butter called for in the chart into small pieces or pats and scatter it over the fruit. Cover the casserole and bake in preheated oven for about 20 minutes, or until the mixture is thickened and bubbling and a piece of the fruit seems about half cooked.

STEP 2: FILLING, TOPPING, BAKING, AND STORING THE PIE

¾ cup (about 3 ounces) pecans or walnuts, ground coarse
6 tablespoons cold butter
½ cup all-purpose flour
⅔ cup sugar
2 tablespoons packed dark brown sugar
2 teaspoons cinnamon

Sprinkle 2 tablespoons of the ground nuts over bottom of baked pie or tart shell, then turn the hot fruit filling into the shell, smoothing the top.

Cut cold butter into ¼-inch bits and place in a 2-quart mixing bowl. Add remaining ground nuts, flour, and sugars, and cut with two knives or a pastry blender until mixture resembles moistened crumbs. Add cinnamon and toss crumb mixture briefly with a fork to blend.

Cover the hot fruit filling evenly with the crumb mixture and set the pie or tart, placed on a baking sheet, in the 400°F oven. Bake about 25 minutes, or until the filling bubbles and the fruit offers no resistance when a knife is inserted deeply into the pie. Let pie cool on a wire rack at least 1 hour before serving.

AHEAD OF TIME/STORAGE: The sooner you eat the pie, the crunchier the streusel and the crisper the crust will be. However, when thoroughly cooled—in about 3 hours—the pie may be sealed airtight in a plastic bag and stored for 2 to 3 days at room temperature or in the refrigerator. For longer storage, freeze until hard, then remove from the pan, wrap tightly in foil, and seal airtight in a plastic bag. A frozen pie will keep for several months at least. To thaw, return pie to pan and let stand at room temperature for 6 to 8 hours or bake in a 300°F oven for 45 minutes to an hour, covering the crumbs with foil if they should begin to darken too much.

MASTER TECHNIQUE

Fruit Pie in a Crumb Pie Crust

Makes one 9-inch pie serving 6

This is a perfect recipe for people who love fruit pies but hate to work with pastry dough. Either the Master Recipe for a graham cracker crumb pie crust or the pecan crumb crust variation recipe may be used with any fruit filling. A ginger crumb crust is especially good with a peach, pear, or nectarine filling, and a chocolate crumb crust is spectacular with cherries.

CHOOSING A FRUIT FILLING TO USE WITH A CRUMB PIE CRUST: The chart on page 771 lists fruits and other ingredients needed to make various fruit fillings. Choose any filling that appeals to you other than green tomato.

PRELIMINARIES

1. Have ready a crumb pie crust, either the Master Recipe on page 760 or one of its variations.
2. Set rack in middle level of oven.
3. Preheat oven to 400°F 20 minutes before baking.
4. Select a 9- to 10-inch covered casserole at least 4 inches deep. Grease with 1 tablespoon soft butter.

A fruit filling (see chart, page 771)
2 tablespoons crumbs made from the crackers or cookies used in the pie crust or 2 tablespoons of the crust mixture itself (reserve when making the crust; you will still have plenty to cover the pie pan)

Squeeze the lemon juice called for in the fruit filling chart into a 4-quart mixing bowl. Prepare fruit as directed in the chart, adding it to the bowl and tossing with the lemon juice as it is peeled and cut. Add sugar, cornstarch, and flavoring and toss with a wooden spoon until cornstarch is dissolved and completely smooth. Turn fruit mixture into the buttered casserole. Cut the butter called for in the chart into small pieces or pats and scatter it over the fruit. Cover the casserole and bake in preheated oven until fruit is tender and fully cooked, about 35 to 45 minutes. Spoon baked fruit mixture into prepared pie shell and top with crumbs. Let the pie cool to room temperature before serving.

AHEAD OF TIME/STORAGE: The sooner the pie is eaten, the better it will be. However, when thoroughly cooled—in about 2 hours—the pie may be sealed airtight in a plastic bag and stored for 2 to 3 days at room temperature or in the refrigerator. For longer storage, freeze until hard, then remove from the pan, wrap tightly in foil, and seal airtight in a plastic bag. A frozen pie will keep for several months at least. To thaw, return pie to the pan and let stand at room temperature for about 6 hours or cover with foil and bake in a 300°F oven for about 45 minutes.

MASTER TECHNIQUE

Fruit Cobbler

Makes 1 cobbler serving 6 to 8

❦ *A cobbler is a lightly thickened, tart cooked-fruit mixture baked under a topping of rich biscuit dough. It is best served warm and accompanied by either thick fresh cream or vanilla ice cream.*

CHOOSING A FRUIT FILLING FOR A COBBLER: The chart on page 771 lists fruits and other ingredients needed to make various fruit fillings. The best known cobblers are made with blackberries, blueberries, cherries, peaches, and rhubarb, but any of the fruits listed in the chart, with the exception of green tomatoes, may be used.

Preliminaries

1. Set rack in the middle level of oven.
2. Preheat oven to 400°F 20 minutes before baking—375°F if using a glass dish.
3. Select a baking dish measuring about 9 inches wide, 13 inches long, and 2 to 3 inches deep. Grease with 2 tablespoons soft butter. If the dish does not have a lid, have ready a sheet of aluminum foil large enough to cover it.

Step 1: Preparing the Fruit Mixture

A fruit filling (see chart, page 771)
DECREASE: The minimum amount of cornstarch called for in the chart by half

Squeeze the lemon juice called for in the fruit filling chart into a 4-quart mixing bowl. Prepare fruit as directed in the chart, adding it to the bowl and tossing with the lemon juice as it is peeled and cut. Add just enough sugar to make the mixture tart-sweet (the minimum amount suggested in the chart, or even a bit less), *half* of the minimum amount of the cornstarch called for in the chart, and the flavoring; toss with a wooden spoon until cornstarch is dissolved and completely smooth. Turn mixture into the buttered baking dish. Cut the butter called for in the chart into small pieces or pats and scatter it over the fruit. Cover tightly with lid or aluminum foil and bake in preheated oven for 15 to 20 minutes or until the mixture is bubbling-hot and a piece of fruit seems about half cooked.

Step 2: Topping the Cobbler and Completing Baking

Dough for ***Baking Powder Biscuits,*** page 671
ADD: 1 to 2 tablespoons sugar
SUBSTITUTE: 1 cup heavy cream for milk
4 tablespoons butter, melted

While the fruit is baking, proceed to prepare biscuit topping. Follow Step 1 of the biscuit recipe, but add sugar with the dry ingredients, and substitute 1 cup of heavy cream for the milk; give the batter 5 to 10 firm strokes with the spoon, just enough to make it cohere and begin to draw away from the sides of the bowl. Disregard remainder of biscuit recipe.

As soon as fruit mixture is ready, remove it from the oven and drop prepared biscuit dough in 12 or 16 evenly spaced mounds over the hot fruit. (It is crucial that the fruit be hot from the oven when the biscuit dough is dropped on; otherwise the topping will be soft and doughy.) Drizzle the biscuits with melted butter (cobblers should be quite rich). Return to the oven, uncovered, and bake about 20 minutes longer, or until biscuits are risen and lightly browned and a piece of fruit taken from beneath the topping tastes completely cooked. Let cobbler cool about 10 minutes before serving.

STORAGE: Leftover cobbler may be covered with foil and stored at room temperature for a day or so, but it's best to eat all of the cobbler shortly after baking.

MASTER TECHNIQUE

Fruit Tart

Makes one 9-inch tart serving 6

An open-faced fruit tart is as pretty to look at as it is delicious to eat. Use prime quality, ripe but firm fruit.

CHOOSING FRUIT FOR TARTS: The listing on page 770 gives instructions on how to prepare specific fruits suitable for tarts.

PRELIMINARIES

1. Have ready a *partially baked* 9-inch tart shell (page 758), unmolded and transferred to a baking sheet that is rimless on two sides so that the baked tart can be slid from sheet to serving tray.
2. Set oven rack in the middle or upper-middle level of oven.
3. Preheat oven to 400°F 20 minutes before baking.

1½ tablespoons dry bread crumbs or ground nuts
4 to 6 tablespoons sugar, depending on tartness of fruit
The prepared fruit (see page 770)
2 tablespoons strained fresh lemon juice
3 tablespoons butter
¾ cup apricot jam

Combine bread crumbs or nuts and 2 tablespoons sugar and sprinkle evenly over bottom of pastry shell. Prepare fruit and arrange in shell according to the instructions in listing. Brush fruit with lemon juice, sprinkle with remaining sugar, and dot with the butter, cut into small pieces or thin pats. Bake the tart for 25 to 35 minutes or until the juices are thick and bubbly and the fruit offers no resistance when pierced with a knife.

Force the jam through a sieve into a saucepan, bring to a boil over moderately high heat, and cook, stirring, for 20 seconds. Spoon jam over the tart, covering the fruit and the spaces between it, but not the crust. Serve the tart warm or at room temperature, accompanied, if you wish, by sour cream or crème fraîche.

AHEAD OF TIME: The tart may be covered with foil and stored in the refrigerator or at room temperature for a couple of days, though it is at its best when eaten promptly after baking. Freezing is not a good idea.

FRUITS FOR FRUIT TARTS

Apples: Peel 4 to 5 medium-size tart, hard apples (about 1½ pounds), cut them in half lengthwise, and remove the cores. One at a time, transfer the apple halves cored side down to a cutting board and cut crosswise into 3/16-inch slices, being sure to keep the slices in their original sequence. Slide a knife underneath the sliced apple halves and arrange them cored side down in a tight circle around the edge of the tart shell, with one or two halves in the center. Lightly press on the halves with your fingers to make them fan out slightly.

Apricots: Drop 12 to 15 fresh apricots (about 1¼ pounds) into boiling water for about 30 seconds, rinse under cold water, and strip off the skins. Halve apricots lengthwise and remove pits. Arrange the halves pitted side down in tight concentric circles in the tart shell.

Peaches: Drop 4 to 5 medium-large peaches (about 2 pounds) in boiling water for 40 to 60 seconds, rinse under cold water, and strip off the skins. Halve peaches lengthwise and remove the pits. Arrange 6 to 8 peach halves pitted side down in a tight circle around the outside of the tart shell and place 1 or 2 halves in the center.

Pears: Peel 5 ripe but firm medium-size Bosc pears (about 2 pounds) halve them lengthwise, and remove the cores. One at a time, transfer the pear halves cored side down to a cutting board and cut crosswise into ¼-inch slices, being sure to keep the slices in their original sequence. Slide a knife underneath the sliced pear halves and arrange the pear halves cored side down in a tight circle around the outside of the tart shell, with the tops facing inward. If necessary, place part of a sliced pear half in the center of tart.

Plums: Cut 6 to 7 large greengage plums (about 1½ pounds) or 16 to 20 prune plums (about 1 pound) in half lengthwise and remove the pits. Arrange the plums pitted side down in tight concentric circles in the tart shell.

FRUIT FILLING CHART

	FRUIT[1]	PREPARATION[2]	STRAINED FRESH LEMON JUICE	SUGAR[3]	CORNSTARCH[4]	FLAVORING	BUTTER
Apple	2 pounds (6 medium) tart, hard apples (5 cups prepared)	Peel, core, and slice thinly, tossing in lemon juice as you go	3 T	½ to ⅔ cup	½ to 1 T	1 t cinnamon, ½ t freshly grated nutmeg, and ⅛ t cloves	3 T
Cranberry/apple	1½ pounds (about 4 medium) apples (as above) and 1½ cups raw cranberries	Prepare apples as above; leave berries whole	2 T	⅔ to ¾ cup	½ to 1 T	1 t cinnamon and grated zest of ½ orange	3 T
Apricot	2½ pounds (24 to 30) ripe apricots (5 cups prepared)	Drop in boiling water 30 seconds, then rinse under cold water; peel, pit, and cut in quarters, tossing in lemon juice as you go	2 T	⅔ to 1 cup	2 to 3 T	¼ t almond extract	4 T
Blackberry	1 quart ripe berries	Wash, pat dry	1 T	⅔ to 1 cup	2 to 3 T	½ t vanilla extract (optional)	3 T

	FRUIT[1]	PREPARATION[2]	STRAINED FRESH LEMON JUICE	SUGAR[3]	CORNSTARCH[4]	FLAVORING	BUTTER
Blueberry	1 quart ripe berries	Wash, pat dry, remove small stems	3 T	⅔ to ¾ cup	2½ to 3 T	Grated zest of ½ orange	3 T
Cherry	5 cups (about 2 pounds) sour ("pie") cherries	Wash, pit, pat dry	1½ T	1 to 1¼ cups	2½ to 3 T	¼ t almond extract	3 T
Green tomato	2 pounds (4 to 5 medium-large) completely green tomatoes (4 cups prepared)	Drop in boiling water 60 seconds, then rinse under cold water; peel, core, and slice thinly	3 T	1¼ cups	2½ to 3½ T	1 t cinnamon and ½ t ground allspice or cloves	3 T
Peach or nectarine	2½ pounds (8 to 10 medium) ripe peaches or nectarines (5 cups prepared)	Drop in boiling water 40 to 60 seconds, then rinse under cold water; peel, pit, and slice, tossing in lemon juice as you go	3 T	½ to ¾ cup	2 to 3 T	⅛ t almond extract and either ½ t cinnamon or 2 t ground ginger	3 T
Pear	2½ pounds (5 to 7 medium) ripe but firm pears (5 cups prepared)	Peel, core and slice, tossing in lemon juice as you go	2 T	½ to ⅔ cup	2 to 3 T	1 t cinnamon, 1 t ground ginger, and ⅛ t cloves	3 T

Pineapple	1 large, ripe pineapple (about 4 to 5 cups prepared)	Cut off top, cut lengthwise into 8 wedges, shave core from each wedge, scrape flesh from skin, cut into ½-inch chunks	2 T	½ to 1 cup	2 to 3 T	½ cup dried currants or raisins soaked for 20 minutes in 2 T dark rum	3 T
Plum	2½ pounds (about 10 medium) greengage plums (5 cups prepared)	Peel, pit, and cut in eighths lengthwise	3 T	⅔ to 1 cup	2 to 3 T	½ t cinnamon	4 T
Rhubarb	1½ to 2 pounds young, tender rhubarb (about 4½ cups prepared)	Remove any leaves; peel any stalks wider than ¾ inch; cut into ½-inch pieces	1 T	1½ cups	2 to 2½ T	Grated zest of 1 orange	3 T
Strawberry/ rhubarb	1 pound rhubarb (about 2½ cups prepared; see above) and 1 pint strawberries	Prepare rhubarb as above. Wash, pat dry, and hull strawberries	2 T	1 to 1¼ cups	2½ T	Grated zest of ½ orange	3 T

[1,2]For more information on how to shop for fruit and how to prepare it for cooking, see the chapter that begins on page 863.
[3]Adjust the quantity of sugar according to the sweetness of the fruit—pineapples, for example, vary widely in their sweetness—and according to your taste.
[4]Use the lesser amount of cornstarch when a range of proportions is given, unless the fruit strikes you as unusually juicy or you have used the maximum amount of sugar. Decide also which you would rather risk—a filling that is slightly too thick and gooey or a filling that is slightly runny.

MASTER TECHNIQUE

Fresh Fruit Cream Tart or Pie

Makes one 9-inch tart or pie serving 6

In this recipe, pastry cream is spooned into a tart or pie shell or a crumb pie crust, and covered with fresh, raw fruit; then a shimmering glaze made of red currant jelly is applied. The dessert is sophisticated in appearance and, because the fruit is uncooked, delightfully subtle and fresh in taste.

CHOOSING FRUIT FOR CREAM TART: The listing on page 775 gives instructions for preparing specific fresh fruits suitable for this tart. By the way, it is also possible to use poached fruit such as apples, quinces, or pears, or even canned fruit, in making this dessert.

PRELIMINARIES:

Have ready any of the following: (1) a fully baked 9-inch tart shell (page 758), unmolded and set on a rimless baking sheet so that, when filled, it can be slid onto a serving plate; (2) a fully baked 9-inch pie shell (page 753); or (3) a 9-inch crumb pie crust, either the Master Recipe on page 760 or the variation recipe with pecans on page 762.

3/4 cup red currant jelly
2 tablespoons sugar
Pastry Cream, page 855
The prepared fruit (see page 775)

Combine currant jelly and sugar in small saucepan. Set over moderately high heat and bring to boil, stirring constantly. Cook for about 1 minute, or until glaze thickens enough to coat the spoon lightly; do not overcook, or the glaze will be rubbery when it hardens.

Brush inside of pastry shell with 3 tablespoons glaze. Let it set for several minutes, then spoon in the pastry cream. Prepare fruit and arrange it over the pastry cream according to instructions given in the listing. If necessary, warm remaining glaze over low heat until it is thin and liquidy. Spoon glaze over the fruit and the spaces between it, but not over the crust.

Chill the tart for an hour or two before serving.

AHEAD OF TIME: The tart will keep for several hours under refrigeration, but the sooner it is eaten, the better.

FRUITS FOR A FRESH FRUIT CREAM TART OR PIE

Bananas and berries: You will need 3 large ripe bananas and 1½ cups raspberries or blueberries. If necessary, wash blueberries quickly and pat dry; remove the small stems. Press about half of the berries into the pastry cream, crushing them as little as possible. Peel the bananas, halve them crosswise, and then cut the halves lengthwise down the middle. Arrange the banana pieces so that they radiate out from the center of the pie like the spokes of a wheel. Fill the spaces between the bananas with the remaining berries.

Blueberries: If necessary, wash and pat dry 2½ to 3 cups blueberries; remove small stems. Gently press 1 cup of the blueberries into the pastry cream, crushing them as little as possible. Either scatter the remaining berries over the top of the tart or, if you have the patience, arrange the berries in tight concentric circles.

Cherries: Wash and dry 3 to 4 cups dark, sweet cherries, then pit. Gently press about 1 cup of the cherries into the pastry cream, crushing them as little as possible. Arrange remaining cherries, pitted sides down, in tight concentric rings over the top of the tart.

Grapes: Use about 3 cups seedless white grapes, washed and well dried. Strip off the skins if you wish, but this is not essential. Gently press about 1 cup of the grapes into the pastry cream. Arrange remaining grapes in tight concentric rings over the top of the tart.

Kiwis: Peel 6 soft, ripe kiwis and cut into crosswise slices about 3⁄16 inch thick. Arrange in overlapping concentric circles over the top of the tart.

Peaches/nectarines: Drop 4 fragrant, ripe, juicy peaches or nectarines into boiling water for 40 to 60 seconds, then rinse under cold water and peel. Cut in half and remove the pits. Either slice the peaches or nectarines and arrange the slices in overlapping concentric circles over the top of the tart, or arrange 6 or 7 unsliced halves pitted side down in a tight circle around the outside of the tart and place 1 or 2 halves in the center.

Pineapple: If you can't find a very ripe pineapple, you are better off using canned pineapple for this. Following the instructions on page 895, peel and core the pineapple and cut it into rings about ¼ inch thick. Drain canned pineapple rings thoroughly. Cut the rings in half and arrange them in overlapping concentric circles over the top of the tart.

Raspberries: You will need about 3 cups raspberries. Gently press about 1 cup of the berries into the pastry cream, crushing them as little as possible. Arrange remaining berries upside down in a tight-fitting series of concentric circles over the top of the tart.

Strawberries: For this classic, you will need 3 to 4 cups of red, ripe berries. If necessary, wash the berries and gently pat them dry. Hull the berries and arrange them point sides up in a tight-fitting series of concentric circles over the top of the tart, placing the largest strawberries in the center.

MASTER RECIPE

Rum Cream Pie

Makes one 9-inch pie serving 8

❦*Sumptuously rich with egg yolks, butter, and cream, this dessert and its variations are definitely not for the calorie-conscious.*

PRELIMINARIES

Have ready a *fully baked* 9-inch pie shell (page 753) or a 9-inch crumb pie crust (pages 760–62).

6 large egg yolks
½ cup sugar
2 tablespoons dark rum, preferably Jamaican
⅛ teaspoon salt
¾ teaspoon vanilla extract
8 tablespoons (1 stick) unsalted butter, softened but still firm and slightly chilled
1⅓ cups cold heavy cream

In a heat-proof 4-quart mixing bowl, beat egg yolks and sugar with a wire whip or electric mixer until the mixture is pale yellow and thick enough to form a slowly dissolving ribbon when dropped from the whip or beaters. Beat in rum and salt.

Fill a deep 10-inch skillet about halfway with water and heat to just below the simmer. Set the mixing bowl in the skillet and, using the whip or electric mixer, beat the yolk mixture constantly for about 7 minutes, or until the mixture begins to come away from the sides of the bowl and to wad around the whip or beaters. You must cook the egg yolks to this point if the pie filling is to be stiff enough to hold its shape; but stop the cooking if the mixture begins to look dull or grainy.

Remove egg yolk mixture from heat and set the mixing bowl in a sink or larger bowl filled with cold water. Add vanilla and beat steadily for several minutes, or until mixture is cool to the touch and extremely thick. Remove the mixing bowl from the water and beat in butter a tablespoon at a time; you will now have a thick, shiny, perfectly smooth sauce resembling soft mayonnaise. (If the butter is a bit too firm and resists blending in smoothly, simply set mixture aside for a few minutes and beat again; if the butter is too soft and the mixture turns sticky and soupy, again set bowl in cold water and beat until thickened.)

Using a clean whip or beaters, beat the cream in a 3-quart mixing bowl until just stiff enough to form very soft, rounded peaks; do not beat beyond this point, or the dessert will have a grainy texture and a buttery taste. Using a rubber spatula, gently fold whipped cream into the egg yolk mixture.

Turn filling into the prepared pie shell, mounding it in the center. Refrigerate the pie for at least 4 hours before serving to firm the filling. Decorate the pie with sweetened whipped cream if you wish.

AHEAD OF TIME/STORAGE: Covered with plastic wrap, the pie will keep for several days under refrigeration, though it is best when eaten within a day of being made. For longer storage, freeze until frozen solid, then remove from the pan, wrap in plastic, seal in a plastic bag, and return to the freezer. Frozen pie will keep for about a month. You can serve the pie frozen—it's delicious—or you can return it to the pan and leave it overnight in the refrigerator to thaw.

Variation: BANANA CREAM PIE

Makes one 9-inch pie serving 8

Rum Cream Pie

ADD: 2 to 3 medium-size ripe bananas, cut crosswise into 3⁄16-inch slices

Proceed according to the Master Recipe, folding bananas into the filling along with the whipped cream. Serve the pie within 24 hours, lest the bananas begin to discolor.

Variation: BUTTERSCOTCH-NUT CREAM PIE

Makes one 9-inch pie serving 8

Rum Cream Pie

SUBSTITUTE: ½ cup packed dark brown sugar for granulated sugar

ADD: ½ cup (about 2 ounces) slivered or sliced almonds, lightly toasted, or hazelnuts, skinned (see page 701)

Proceed according to the Master Recipe, substituting dark brown sugar for granulated sugar and folding in nuts along with the whipped cream.

Variation: CHOCOLATE CREAM PIE

Makes one 9-inch pie serving 8

❦ *Fine-quality imported semisweet eating chocolate flavored with real vanilla makes the best pie, but semisweet baking chocolate may also be used. The pie is excellent when made with a chocolate crumb crust (page 761); coffee liqueur, orange liqueur, or crème de cacao may all be used in place of dark rum.*

Rum Cream Pie

ADD: 6 ounces semisweet chocolate
DECREASE: Butter to 5 tablespoons

Break chocolate into small pieces, turn into a small heat-proof mixing bowl, and set bowl in the same pan of almost-simmering water that is required in the Master Recipe. Being careful not to splash in even a drop of water, stir the chocolate until it is melted and completely smooth, then remove from heat and cool to room temperature. Proceed according to the Master Recipe, adding melted and cooled chocolate and then butter, decreased to 5 tablespoons, to the cooled egg yolk mixture.

Variation: COCONUT CREAM PIE

Makes one 9-inch pie serving 8

Rum Cream Pie

ADD: 1 cup grated fresh coconut (see page 697)

Proceed according to the Master Recipe, folding in the coconut along with the whipped cream.

Variation: MAPLE-WALNUT CREAM PIE

Makes one 9-inch pie serving 8

Rum Cream Pie

DECREASE: Sugar to 1/4 cup
SUBSTITUTE: 1/3 cup pure maple syrup for rum
ADD: 1/2 cup walnuts (about 2 ounces), chopped coarse

Halving the sugar and using maple syrup in place of rum, proceed according to the Master Recipe, folding in chopped nuts along with the whipped cream.

Variation: MOCHA CREAM PIE

Makes one 9-inch pie serving 8

Rum Cream Pie
SUBSTITUTE: 1½ tablespoons instant coffee, preferably instant espresso, and, if you wish, 2 tablespoons coffee liqueur or crème de cacao for rum

Dissolve instant coffee in 1 tablespoon warm water and add with optional liqueur to the beaten egg yolks in place of the rum called for in the Master Recipe.

Variation: ORANGE CREAM PIE

Makes one 9-inch pie serving 8

Rum Cream Pie
SUBSTITUTE: 2 tablespoons strained orange juice, preferably fresh, or 2 tablespoons orange liqueur for rum
ADD: Grated zest of 1 orange

Proceed according to the Master Recipe, substituting orange juice or liqueur for rum and beating in grated orange zest along with the juice or liqueur.

Variation: PRALINE CREAM PIE

Makes one 9-inch pie serving 8

Rum Cream Pie
ADD: ⅔ cup Praline Powder, page 860

Proceed according to the Master Recipe, folding in praline powder along with the whipped cream.

Variation: VANILLA CREAM PIE

Makes one 9-inch pie serving 8

Rum Cream Pie

SUBSTITUTE: 2 tablespoons water for rum
INCREASE: Vanilla extract to 1½ tablespoons

Proceed according to the Master Recipe, substituting water for rum and increasing vanilla to 1½ tablespoons.

MASTER RECIPE

Orange Chiffon Pie

Makes one 9-inch pie serving 6

❦ *Refreshing and gossamer-light, a chiffon pie makes a delightful ending to a heavy meal.*

PRELIMINARIES

Have ready a *fully baked* 9-inch pie shell (page 753) or a 9-inch crumb pie crust (pages 760–62).

½ cup strained fresh orange juice
1 tablespoon strained fresh lemon juice
1 tablespoon grated orange zest
1 envelope (2¼ teaspoons) unflavored gelatin
5 large eggs
⅔ cup sugar
¼ teaspoon cream of tartar
Salt
⅓ cup cold heavy cream

Combine orange juice, lemon juice, and grated zest in a heat-proof 4-quart mixing bowl and sprinkle evenly with gelatin. Let stand about 5 minutes, or until gelatin is softened and the mixture resembles a thick soup. Separate eggs, adding the yolks to the gelatin mixture and turning the whites into a very clean glass or metal 3-quart mixing bowl. Set egg whites aside. Beat sugar into the yolk mixture, blending thoroughly with whip or electric mixer.

Fill a skillet about halfway with water and heat to just below the simmer.

Set bowl containing the yolk mixture in the skillet, and using a wire whip or electric mixer, beat constantly for about 7 minutes, or until mixture becomes thick—it will much resemble hollandaise sauce—and coats the whip or beaters very heavily. Remove from heat and, beating occasionally, let stand at room temperature for about 15 minutes, or until cool to the touch and extremely thick.

Using clean, dry beaters, beat egg whites with the mixer set at low speed until they look foamy, then add cream of tartar and a generous pinch of salt and increase speed to medium. When egg whites have turned frothy and opaque and retain furrows made by the beaters, turn mixer to high speed and work the whites until they are thick and glossy and stand firmly at the end of the uplifted beaters or whip. Do not overbeat the whites, or they will become dry and grainy. Set beaten egg whites aside.

Using a wire whip or clean, dry beaters, beat the cream in a 2-quart mixing bowl until just stiff enough to form very soft, rounded peaks; do not beat the cream beyond this point, or the dessert will have a buttery rather than creamy-light taste.

Scoop beaten egg whites over the gelatin mixture and gently fold in using a rubber spatula. When nearly incorporated, fold in the whipped cream, which will deflate the mixture somewhat. Immediately—the gelatin must not be allowed to set at this point—turn filling into the prepared pie shell, mounding it slightly in the center. Refrigerate the pie for 2 to 3 hours, or until filling is firm, before serving. Decorate with sweetened whipped cream if you wish.

AHEAD OF TIME/STORAGE: Covered with plastic wrap, the pie will keep nicely for several days in the refrigerator, though it is at its very best when served within a day or so. For longer storage, freeze the pie until solid, then pry out of the pan, wrap in plastic, seal in a plastic bag, and return to the freezer. Frozen pie will keep for about a month. Let thaw overnight in the refrigerator before serving.

Variation: CHOCOLATE CHIFFON PIE

Makes one 9-inch pie serving 6

❦ *This recipe calls for black coffee as a flavoring, but an equally delicious pie may be made using the orange juice and zest that are specified in the Master Recipe.*

Orange Chiffon Pie

SUBSTITUTE: ½ cup very strong freshly brewed cold coffee (or espresso) for orange juice, lemon juice, and grated zest

ADD: 4 ounces semisweet chocolate, finely chopped or grated

Proceed according to the Master Recipe, but soften gelatin in cold coffee instead of in the juice/zest mixture. Immediately after removing yolk mixture from heat, add the chopped or grated chocolate; beat until the chocolate is melted and completely smooth.

Variation: COFFEE CHIFFON PIE

Makes one 9-inch pie serving 6

Orange Chiffon Pie
SUBSTITUTE: ½ cup freshly brewed very strong coffee, cooled to room temperature, for orange juice, lemon juice, and grated zest

Proceed according to the Master Recipe, but soften gelatin in coffee instead of in juice/zest mixture.

Variation: CRANBERRY CHIFFON PIE

Makes one 9-inch pie serving 6

Orange Chiffon Pie
ADD: 2 cups (about 6 ounces) raw cranberries
An extra ⅓ cup sugar

Chop the cranberries fairly finely in a blender or food processor and combine with ⅓ cup sugar in a heavy-bottomed 2-quart saucepan. Stirring often, simmer slowly for 5 to 7 minutes, or until thick and jamlike. Remove cranberry mixture from heat and let cool to tepid.

Proceed according to the Master Recipe, beating cranberry purée into the yolk/gelatin mixture after it has been removed from the pan of water.

Variation: LEMON CHIFFON PIE

Makes one 9-inch pie serving 6

Orange Chiffon Pie
SUBSTITUTE: ¼ cup water for orange juice
INCREASE: Lemon juice to ¼ cup
SUBSTITUTE: Grated lemon zest for grated orange zest

Proceed according to the Master Recipe, softening gelatin in water, lemon juice, and lemon zest instead of in orange juice and zest.

Variation: LIME CHIFFON PIE

Makes one 9-inch pie serving 6

Orange Chiffon Pie

SUBSTITUTE: ¼ cup strained fresh lime juice *and* ¼ cup water for orange juice

OMIT: Lemon juice

SUBSTITUTE: Grated lime zest for grated orange zest

Proceed according to the Master Recipe, softening gelatin in water, lime juice, and lime zest instead of in orange juice, lemon juice, and orange zest.

Variation: STRAWBERRY OR RASPBERRY CHIFFON PIE

Makes one 9-inch pie serving 6

Orange Chiffon Pie

ADD: 1 pint fresh strawberries or raspberries or two 10-ounce packages unsweetened frozen berries

OMIT: Grated orange zest

INCREASE: Sugar to 1 cup

Wash, dry, and hull fresh berries as necessary; thaw frozen berries thoroughly, turn into a sieve, and shake to drain well. Purée fresh or frozen berries in a blender or food processor, using enough berries to make a generous cup of purée. Strain through a very fine mesh sieve to remove the seeds. If the purée feels cold, turn it into a small bowl and stir it over warm water until it reaches room temperature.

Proceed according to the Master Recipe, omitting grated orange zest, increasing the sugar to 1 cup, and folding the berry purée into the filling along with the whipped cream.

MASTER RECIPE

Custard Pie

Makes one 9-inch pie serving 6 to 8

❦ *Made with light cream and egg yolks as well as milk and whole eggs, this custard pie is rich, eggy, smooth, and tender.*

CUSTARD PIE CAUTIONS: The dreaded pitfalls of custard pie are a soggy crust and a watery, separated filling, but these disasters are easily averted if you remember the following points:

1. Use a *fully baked* pie shell glazed with beaten egg. Since custard pie requires a short baking time, the crust will not burn after being returned to the oven.
2. In preparing the filling, be sure to warm the milk and cream and to have the eggs and other ingredients at room temperature. The warmer the filling is to begin with, the more quickly it will set once it is poured into the shell and baked, and the less chance there will be for the crust to become waterlogged.
3. Do not overbake the pie, as overbaking will cause the eggs to curdle and the filling to become watery. Take the pie out of the oven as soon as a knife inserted near the outer edge of the filling comes out clean. At this point the center of the custard will still be quite soft, but the heat stored in the pie will firm the custard as it stands.
4. Do not refrigerate the pie until it is thoroughly cooled to room temperature. Condensation will occur if a hot or warm pie is put in a cold refrigerator, softening the crust and possibly thinning the custard.

PRELIMINARIES

1. Have ready a *fully baked* 9-inch pie shell (page 753). Set pie shell on a shallow-rimmed baking sheet.
2. Bring all ingredients to room temperature.
3. Set rack in lower-middle level of oven.
4. Preheat oven to 400°F 20 minutes before baking.

3 large eggs
3 large egg yolks
¾ cup sugar
¾ teaspoon vanilla extract
¾ teaspoon freshly grated nutmeg
¼ teaspoon salt
2 cups milk
1 cup light cream

Combine whole eggs, egg yolks, sugar, vanilla, nutmeg, and salt in a 3-quart mixing bowl and beat with a wire whip just until blended. Do not overbeat; overbeating may cause bubbles to form in the custard. Heat milk and cream in a 2-quart saucepan over a moderate flame until it feels distinctly hot to your fingertip but has not yet begun to steam (about 150°F on a thermometer); if too hot, the mixture may scramble the eggs. Slowly pour warmed milk/cream into the egg mixture, beating constantly.

Place the shell, set on a baking sheet, on the pulled-out rack of the preheated oven and ladle in enough of the filling to come nearly to the top of the rim of the pie shell. There may be a few tablespoons of filling left over. Gently push in oven rack, close the oven door, and bake the pie for 25 to 30 minutes, or until outer edge of filling—but not the center—is puffed up and a knife inserted into the filling 1½ inches from the rim comes out clean. At this point, the pie will still quiver noticeably if shaken, and if you pry up a small piece in the center, the filling will be moist and only very softly set, like soft scrambled eggs. The custard will finish cooking as the pie stands.

Set pie on a rack and let stand undisturbed at room temperature for 3 hours. Cover with foil and refrigerate the pie for at least 3 hours, but for best flavor leave the pie at room temperature for 30 minutes before serving.

STORAGE: Covered with foil, the pie will keep for 1 to 2 days in the refrigerator, though the sooner it is eaten, the crisper the crust will be. Do not freeze.

Variation: COCONUT CUSTARD PIE

Makes one 9-inch pie serving 6 to 8

❦ *Using grated fresh coconut makes all the difference here; unsweetened desiccated coconut, available at health-food stores, is a second-best but acceptable alternative.*

Custard Pie

DECREASE: *All* ingredients in custard pie filling by 1/3

ADD: 1 1/2 cups grated fresh coconut (see page 697) or 1 1/4 cups desiccated coconut

Prepare custard pie filling in Master Recipe, decreasing all ingredients by 1/3 (use 2 eggs, 2 egg yolks, 1/2 cup sugar, 1/2 teaspoon vanilla, 1/2 teaspoon nutmeg, heaping 1/8 teaspoon salt, 1 1/3 cups milk and 2/3 cup cream) and stirring in coconut after adding the cream. Bake according to Master Recipe.

Variation: LEAH'S CUSTARD PIE WITH DRIED FRUITS

Makes one 9-inch pie serving 6 to 8

❦ *For my sister Leah, one of the best things about living in California was unquestionably the abundance and inexpensiveness of prime-quality dried apricots. Once, when Leah was ill, I made a dried-fruit-flavored custard to cheer her up, and thus I name this pie in her honor. I am, of course, by no means the first person to imagine baking dried fruits and a nutmeg-flavored custard in a pie shell. The early American colonists made many kinds of pies containing dried fruits, eggs, milk, and sometimes meat or poultry, and these pies were but versions of other custard-filled pastries that had been standard fare in England since the Middle Ages.*

Custard Pie

ADD: 2/3 cup loosely packed soft dried apricots
2/3 cup loosely packed soft pitted prunes

DECREASE: *All* ingredients in custard pie filling by 1/3

Snip or cut the fruits into 1/4-inch tidbits and combine with the milk, decreased to 1 1/3 cups, and light cream, decreased to 2/3 cup, in the saucepan. Watching the mixture carefully lest it boil over, heat to just below the simmer. Remove from heat and let stand until the milk/cream is no longer hot enough to steam. Proceed according to Master Recipe, decreasing all remaining ingredients by 1/3 (use 2 eggs, 2 egg yolks, 1/2 cup sugar, 1/2 teaspoon vanilla, 1/2 teaspoon nutmeg, and a heaping 1/8 teaspoon salt), and beating the warm milk/cream and fruit into the egg mixture.

Variation: ORANGE CUSTARD PIE

Makes one 9-inch pie serving 6 to 8

Custard Pie

ADD: Grated zest of 2 oranges

SUBSTITUTE: 2 tablespoons orange liqueur or ½ teaspoon pure orange extract for nutmeg

DECREASE: Salt to a generous pinch

Combine grated zest, milk, and cream in the saucepan and, watching carefully lest the mixture boil over, heat to just below the simmer. Remove from heat and let stand until milk/cream is no longer hot enough to steam. Strain milk/cream into a measure with a pour spout, discarding the zest in the sieve. Proceed according to Master Recipe, substituting liqueur or orange extract for nutmeg, decreasing the salt to a large pinch, and beating the warm milk/cream into the egg mixture.

LEMON MERINGUE PIE

Makes one 9-inch pie serving 6 to 8

❦ *This is an intensely lemony and somewhat tart interpretation of the classic American recipe.*

MERINGUE NOTES: The following meringue is guaranteed not to shrink, weep, toughen, or do any of the other nasty things that cooks so fear—so long as you observe the following:

1. Use confectioner's sugar. Confectioner's sugar dissolves quickly and completely in the egg whites, whereas ordinary sugar sometimes remains partially undissolved and forms tiny sticky droplets in the meringue.
2. Never add more than 2 tablespoons of confectioner's sugar per large egg white, as a sugar-laden meringue is likely to weep.
3. Never use more than 5 large egg whites for one 9-inch pie. If there is too much meringue, the outside will become brown before the inside is cooked and set and the meringue will be soft and unstable.
4. Always spread meringue on a *warm* pie filling. If the filling is too hot, a layer of condensed steam will form between the filling and the meringue, and thus the meringue will begin to deflate and dissolve as it

bakes. If the filling is cold, the bottom of the meringue will not get cooked through.

5. Always spread meringue so that it touches the pie shell at all points; if it is anchored to the shell, it will not shrink back.
6. Always bake a meringue in a 350°F oven for *exactly* 5 minutes per egg white used—or 25 minutes altogether for a 5-egg-white meringue.

Preliminaries

1. Have ready a *fully baked* 9-inch pie shell, preferably slightly sweetened (page 753). Do not use a crumb crust, as the meringue will not anchor to it.
2. Set rack in center of oven.
3. Preheat oven to 350°F 20 minutes before baking.

Step 1: Preparing the Lemon Custard

5 large eggs, at room temperature
1 cup sugar
3 to 5 large lemons
⅓ cup cornstarch
¼ teaspoon salt
1½ cups water
4 tablespoons butter, cut into pats

Separate the eggs, placing the yolks and whites in separate 3-quart mixing bowls (do not use a plastic bowl for whites). Set yolks and whites aside.

Place sugar in heavy-bottomed 1½-quart saucepan. One at a time, rub 2 lemons into the sugar (or rub sugar into the lemons, whichever is easier for you) until the sugar looks noticeably crumbly and translucent, indicating that it is saturated with flavorful lemon oil. (This trick allows you to omit grated lemon zest, which would make the custard slightly gritty.) Add cornstarch and salt to lemon sugar and mix with a wire whip. Gradually add about ¼ cup water, beating until a smooth paste forms. Beat in the remaining water and stir in butter pieces. Set mixture aside for a moment while you squeeze as many lemons as necessary to make ⅔ cup strained juice. Beat juice into reserved egg yolks.

Set saucepan containing cornstarch mixture over moderate heat and bring to a slow boil, beating constantly with a wire whip. If lumps start to form in the mixture, remove pan from heat and beat hard to smooth out. Reduce heat to low and simmer for 2 minutes, stirring constantly. The mixture will be very thick.

Beating constantly with the wire whip, slowly pour the hot cornstarch mixture over the egg yolks and lemon juice, scraping saucepan clean with a wooden spoon or spatula. Return mixture to saucepan and set over moderately low heat. Stirring constantly, bring custard just to the simmer; it will thicken perceptibly. Pour custard back into mixing bowl. Stirring occasionally, let custard cool until you can hold your finger in it for 2 seconds without discomfort (about 140°F). Pour into prepared pie shell and immediately proceed to prepare the meringue.

Step 2: Preparing and Baking the Meringue

5 egg whites (from Step 1)
½ teaspoon cream of tartar
⅛ teaspoon salt
⅔ cup confectioner's sugar (measure by spooning unsifted sugar into cup until overflowing, then tapping sharply several times and leveling off the excess with the back of a knife; sieve or sift sugar if lumpy)

Beat egg whites with electric mixer at low speed until foamy. Add cream of tartar and salt, increase speed to medium, and beat until whites stand in soft peaks. Set mixer at high speed. Sprinkling in sugar 2 tablespoons at a time, beat egg whites until they form stiff, glossy peaks and are nearly as thick as marshmallow. (This is one of those rare instances when it is better to err on the side of overbeating to insure that the sugar is completely dissolved.)

Immediately pile meringue onto warm pie filling. Using a spatula, spoon, or knife, mound the meringue slightly in the center of the pie, then spread it outward in a thick layer until it touches the rim of the pie crust at all points. Meringue will shrink if it is not anchored to the crust.

Bake pie in preheated oven for exactly 25 minutes. Meringue will become a deep café au lait color; a few tiny peaks may blacken. Let pie cool on a wire rack. Do not refrigerate until it reaches room temperature—2 hours or longer—or moisture is likely to condense between the filling and the meringue. Chill at least 1 hour before serving.

Ahead of Time/Storage: Lemon meringue pie may be stored uncovered in the refrigerator or 2 or 3 days. Do not freeze; the meringue will turn rubbery and watery.

PUMPKIN PIE

Makes one 9-inch pie serving 6 to 8

❦*A rich, creamy, gingery version of the holiday classic. I prefer it served slightly warm.*

PRELIMINARIES

1. Have ready a *partially baked* 9-inch pie shell (page 753).
2. Set rack in middle or lower-middle level of oven.
3. Preheat oven to 400°F 20 minutes before baking.

1¾ to 2 cups puréed cooked pumpkin (one 16- to 18-ounce can)
3 large eggs
1 cup packed dark brown sugar
1 cup heavy cream
2 teaspoons cinnamon
2 teaspoons ground ginger or, for a real treat, 3 to 6 tablespoons finely chopped crystallized ginger
1 teaspoon freshly grated nutmeg
¼ teaspoon ground cloves
½ teaspoon salt

Beat pumpkin and eggs to blend in a 2-quart mixing bowl, then add remaining ingredients and beat until smooth. Pour mixture into prepared pie shell and bake in preheated oven for 40 to 45 minutes, or until edge of filling has puffed about an inch and cracked slightly. The pie will quiver like gelatin when shaken, but it will flatten and firm as it cools. Let baked pie cool several hours on wire rack at room temperature before refrigerating.

STORAGE: Covered with plastic wrap, pumpkin pie will keep for several days in the refrigerator. For longer storage, freeze until hard, then remove from the pan, wrap tightly in foil, and seal airtight in a plastic bag. A frozen pie will keep for about two months, but it will not have quite the same rich, smooth texture when thawed.

❦

PECAN PIE

Makes one 9-inch pie serving 6 to 8

❦ *Made entirely with corn syrup rather than with a combination of corn syrup and sugar, as is customary, this is less sweet than pecan pies usually are. If you want to cut the sweetness even more, use lightly salted nuts or add pinches of salt. This pie can also be made with walnut halves, skinned peanuts, or macadamia nuts.*

PRELIMINARIES

1. Have ready a *partially baked* 9-inch pie shell (page 753).
2. Set rack in middle or lower-middle level of oven.
3. Preheat oven to 400°F 20 minutes before baking.

4 tablespoons butter
4 large eggs
2 cups (one 16-ounce bottle) dark corn syrup
2 tablespoons dark rum or bourbon or 2 teaspoons vanilla extract
1½ cups (about 6 ounces) pecan halves
Cinnamon and/or salt (optional)

Melt butter and set aside to cool briefly. Beat eggs to blend in a 3-quart mixing bowl, add corn syrup, and beat just until smooth. Stir in butter, liquor or vanilla, and nuts. Adjust flavor with pinches of cinnamon and salt.

Pour mixture into prepared pie shell and bake in preheated oven for 35 to 45 minutes, or until edge of filling has puffed about an inch and cracked slightly. Pie will quiver slightly when shaken, but it will become firm as it cools.

Allow baked pie to cool on a rack for at least 30 minutes before serving. Pecan pie should be served warm; unsweetened whipped cream makes a good foil for the rich, sweet filling.

AHEAD OF TIME/STORAGE: Covered with aluminum foil, pecan pie keeps quite nicely for several days at room temperature or in the refrigerator. To reheat the pie, set it in a 300°F oven for 10 to 20 minutes, or until a knife inserted in the center of the pie for a few seconds feels warm when held against your fingertips. Freezing is not recommended, as the filling may separate.

MASTER RECIPE

Meringue Nests

Makes six 4-inch-diameter nests

❦ *Meringue nests are delicious crunchy dessert shells made of a meringue paste that is dried in a very slow oven until it becomes crisp throughout. Fill the nests with vanilla ice cream (about 1 quart), then top with sautéed, flambéed fruit, sliced and sugared fresh fruit, warm chocolate sauce, or berry sauce. Meringue desserts, by the way, are often served with both fork and spoon. The fork is used to cut through the meringue, then the dessert is eaten with the spoon.*

If you are inexperienced in working with egg whites, read through the guidelines on the beating and folding of egg whites that appear on pages 133–36.

Preliminaries

1. Set oven rack in middle or lower-middle level of oven.
2. Preheat oven to 200°F 20 minutes before baking. (If you suspect your oven may be fast, set it at an even lower temperature; if the oven is too hot, the meringues will turn sticky rather than becoming crisp.)
3. Select a 14×17-inch baking sheet. Grease with 1 tablespoon soft butter and dust with 2 tablespoons flour, tapping off excess.

4 large egg whites, at room temperature
¼ teaspoon cream of tartar
Salt
1 cup sugar, preferably superfine
1 teaspoon vanilla extract
½ teaspoon almond extract

Beat egg whites in a 4-quart mixing bowl (do not use a plastic bowl) with electric mixer at low speed. When the whites are loose and foamy, add cream of tartar and a pinch of salt, increase mixer speed to medium, and beat until the egg whites stand in soft, frothy peaks. Turn speed to high and add ⅔ cup of the sugar 1 tablespoon at a time, beating for 5 seconds after each addition before making the next. (It is important that the egg whites be beaten to the soft-peak stage before you begin adding sugar, or the meringues will come out soft and chewy rather than crisp.) When the entire ⅔ cup sugar has been added to the meringue paste, continue to beat for about a minute (the mixture will become very stiff and glistening), then beat in vanilla and almond extracts. Withdraw beaters from the meringue paste, scraping them clean, then sprinkle remaining ⅓ cup sugar evenly over top of paste and fold in with a rubber spatula (this makes for a tender meringue).

Drop meringue paste in six equal, evenly spaced portions on prepared baking sheet. Using the back of a large spoon, flatten each dollop into a circle about 3 inches wide, then make a deep depression in the center of each circle to form a nest about 4 inches in diameter. Set nests in the preheated oven for 2 hours. The meringue nests should neither color nor change shape in the slightest; they are simply drying out, not baking.

Turn off the oven and either let the meringues remain in the oven until completely cooled—leave them overnight, if you wish—or remove them from the turned-off oven after 30 minutes to finish cooling at room temperature. When meringues are thoroughly cooled, detach them from the baking sheet by pushing them firmly but gently with your finger.

STORAGE: If placed in an airtight tin, meringues will keep quite well for up to a month at room temperature, or they may be frozen for 4 months or longer. To recrisp meringues that have become softened—due either to exposure to air or freezing—dry them in a 200°F oven for 30 minutes, then turn off oven and let meringues stand in the oven until completely cooled. Serve filled meringues immediately, lest they begin to soften.

Variation: CLOUD BERRY PIE

Serves 6 to 8

❦ *Here, the meringue paste from the Master Recipe is formed into a pie shell instead of into individual nests. The shell can be filled with ice cream and served with fruit or a sauce, as suggested for meringue nests, or it can be piled high with whipped cream and fresh berries as outlined here.*

Paste for ***Meringue Nests***
2 cups cold heavy cream
½ cup confectioner's sugar, sieved or sifted if lumpy
1 teaspoon vanilla extract or 1 tablespoon orange liqueur
1 pint raspberries, blueberries, or hulled and sliced strawberries

Line a 9- or 10-inch pie pan with foil, crimping the foil around the edges of the pan to make it adhere. Butter the foil lightly and sprinkle with flour, turning the pan to dust evenly and completely; invert pan and tap lightly to knock out excess flour. Spread the meringue paste evenly in pan and bake according to the Master Recipe (2 hours in a 200°F oven). Let cool completely.

Just before serving, carefully peel foil off the shell and return shell to pie pan. Referring if necessary to the recipe on page 857, whip cream until stiff in a 4-quart bowl, adding confectioner's sugar and vanilla or liqueur. Gently fold in all but a small handful of the berries and mound mixture in shell. Decorate with reserved berries and serve at once.

Variation: NUTTED MERINGUE FINGERS

Makes 40 to 48 fingers

❦ *When you fold ground nuts into a meringue paste and pipe it through a pastry bag to form finger shapes (or any other shapes you wish), you end up with delicious crunchy cookies that may be served with ice cream or sherbet.*

Paste for ***Meringue Nests***

ADD: 1 cup (about 5 ounces) whole blanched almonds, 1 cup (about 4 ounces) hazelnuts, skinned (see page 701), or 1 cup (about 4 ounces) walnuts

1 tablespoon cornstarch

SPECIAL EQUIPMENT: A pastry bag fitted with a 3/4-inch plain or star tip (a teaspoon can be substituted)

Grind nuts a handful at a time in a blender or all at once in a food processor. Be sure not to overgrind the nuts, which will make them oily and compacted. Turn nuts into a small bowl, add cornstarch, and toss with your fingers until mixture is free of lumps. Proceed to make meringue paste according to the Master Recipe, folding in nut mixture along with the final 1/3 cup sugar. The paste may deflate slightly when it comes into contact with the oil from the nuts.

Scoop the nutted meringue paste into a large pastry bag fitted with a plain or star tip about 3/4-inch in diameter. Holding pastry bag almost perpendicular to the buttered and floured baking sheet so that the meringue paste will widen as it is squeezed out, form fingers about 3 1/2 inches long and just over an inch wide. Since the fingers will not spread or otherwise change shape in the oven, you may place them quite close together. (If you do not have a pastry bag, form the fingers with a spoon. The cookies will not have the neat and uniform appearance of those formed with the bag, but they will still be good.)

Bake the fingers according to the Master Recipe. They may color slightly due to the toasting of the nuts.

MASTER RECIPE

Miniature Cream Puffs

Makes about 24 1½-inch puffs serving 6

❦*I have chosen to feature miniature cream puffs in this Master Recipe and to make large cream puffs a variation, because small puffs do double duty as hors d'oeuvre and dessert shells, while large puffs are generally reserved for desserts only. Cream puffs and their variations, which include éclairs, are among the most delicious and grand-looking of all pastries, and yet they are all based on an extremely simple-to-make dough, called a choux paste.*

DOUBLING THE RECIPE: When making a large batch, you can turn the cooked flour-water mixture into a food processor fitted with the metal chopping blade and, with the motor running, add the eggs one at a time. Of course, you can also beat in the eggs by hand. Use two baking sheets set in lower and upper thirds of oven and switch their positions during the last third of baking.

PRELIMINARIES

1. Set rack in center of oven.
2. Preheat oven to 425°F 20 minutes before baking.
3. Select a large baking sheet; grease the sheet very lightly with vegetable shortening.

STEP 1: PREPARING THE PASTRY SHELLS

½ cup water
4 tablespoons butter, cut into pats
½ teaspoon sugar (substitute ¼ teaspoon salt if making cocktail puffs)
6 tablespoons unbleached all-purpose flour (measure by scooping tablespoons into large container of flour and sweeping off excess with the back of a knife)
2 large eggs
1 egg beaten to blend with ½ teaspoon water

SPECIAL EQUIPMENT: A pastry bag fitted with a ½-inch plain tip (a teaspoon can be substituted)

Combine water, butter, and sugar or salt in a 2-quart saucepan and set over moderately high heat. Meanwhile, measure flour into a small bowl. When water has come to a boil and the butter has melted, remove mixture from heat and add the flour all at once, beating until a smooth paste forms. Return mixture to moderate heat and beat vigorously for 5 to 10 seconds, or until the paste wads into a firm, doughy ball that detaches itself from the walls of the saucepan and clings to the spoon. Do not overcook, or the paste will not puff properly.

Turn dough into a 2-quart bowl, form a depression in the center, drop in an egg, and beat until completely smooth. Work in the second egg, beating until mixture is satiny smooth.

Using pastry bag or teaspoon, form 2-teaspoon mounds of the paste about 1½ inches apart on prepared baking sheet. Brush puffs sparingly with egg beaten with water, avoiding dripping any egg onto the baking sheet. Bake in preheated oven for about 17 minutes, or until puffs are doubled in size, nicely browned, and firm to the touch. Remove puffs from the oven and pierce the side of each with the point of a knife to let steam escape. Turn off oven, return puffs, and allow the puffs to dry out for 20 minutes. Let puffs cool thoroughly on a rack before filling or storing.

STEP 2: FILLING THE PUFFS; STORAGE

Pastry Cream, page 855, or 1 cup cold heavy cream whipped stiff with 3 tablespoons confectioner's sugar and ½ teaspoon vanilla extract (see page 857)

Chocolate Glaze, page 851, or confectioner's sugar in a sieve or shaker

SPECIAL EQUIPMENT: A pastry bag fitted with a ¼-inch plain tip (a teaspoon may be substituted)

Shortly before serving, either pipe pastry cream or whipped cream through a small slit in the side of the puffs, using a pastry bag fitted with a ¼-inch plain tip, or cut puffs in half crosswise with a serrated knife and spoon in the filling. If you wish, dip tops of puffs in chocolate glaze and refrigerate briefly to set; otherwise, dust with confectioner's sugar. Once filled, puffs should be served within 30 minutes, or the pastry will soften.

STORAGE: Sealed in an airtight container, unfilled puffs will keep for 1 to 2 days, though they will lose some of their fresh taste. They may also be placed in a plastic bag and frozen for a month or so. Thaw and recrisp in a 300°F oven for about 10 minutes.

Variation: CHOCOLATE OR STRAWBERRY PROFITEROLES

6 servings

❦ *Technically speaking, the word "profiterole" refers to any miniature cream puff shell, whether it is filled with a savory or sweet mixture and whether or not it is accompanied by a sauce. In common usage, however, the word profiterole has come to denote a miniature shell that has been filled with ice cream or whipped cream and is served with a dessert sauce.*

Miniature Cream Puffs, prepared through Step 1
1 pint softened vanilla ice cream or 1 cup cold heavy cream whipped stiff with 3 tablespoons confectioner's sugar and ½ teaspoon vanilla extract (see page 857)
Chocolate Sauce, page 852, or Berry Sauce, page 860, made with strawberries

Cut puffs in half lengthwise with a serrated knife and fill with ice cream or whipped cream. Spoon several tablespoons very warm chocolate sauce or berry sauce into each of 6 dessert plates and arrange filled puffs on top. Serve at once.

Variation: CROQUEMBOUCHE

6 servings

❦ *This elaborate-looking dessert from classic haute cuisine turns out to be quite easy to make. An even more dramatic pastry cone can be fashioned by doubling the number of filled puffs and all other ingredients.*

Miniature Cream Puffs, prepared through Step 1
Pastry Cream, page 855
DECREASE: Vanilla extract to 1 teaspoon
ADD: 1 tablespoon orange liqueur or ½ teaspoon orange flower water
¾ cup sugar
3 tablespoons water
Strips of candied orange peel

SPECIAL EQUIPMENT: A pastry bag fitted with a ¼-inch plain tip

Prepare puffs and pastry cream, decreasing vanilla and adding orange liqueur or flower water in making the cream. Cut a small slit in the side of each puff and pipe pastry cream into puffs using a pastry bag. Set aside in a cool place.

Place sugar in a heavy-bottomed 1½-quart saucepan, pour water over it, and set over moderately high heat. Holding the saucepan by the handle, swirl pan over heat so that the sugar solution rotates in a slow wave around the inside wall of the pan. When solution comes to a full boil and becomes a clear syrup, cover tightly and boil hard for 2 minutes. Uncover and, swirling the pan as before, cook the syrup until it thickens and then finally darkens—or caramelizes—to a deep amber color. Immediately remove from heat to prevent further cooking and let syrup cool for a few minutes, or until it is about as thick as warm molasses.

Being careful not to burn your fingers, dip 8 filled puffs into the hot caramel syrup one at a time and arrange them in a solid circle, caramel side down, on a serving platter. Wait a few moments for caramel to solidify and anchor the puffs, then proceed to build a second layer of puffs over the first, this time using only 6 caramel-dipped puffs. Finally, add several more layers of puffs, composed of 4, then 3, then 2, then just 1 puff, fashioning the pastry into a haphazard cone. When all the puffs have been stuck together, drizzle any remaining caramel over the top of the cone and attach strips of candied orange peel. If you are serving the pastry within an hour or two—which is the best idea—simply leave it in a cool place; if there is a wait of longer than 2 hours, refrigerate the croquembouche. Serve the croquembouche by pulling it asunder with two forks.

Note: If the caramel syrup in the saucepan begins to harden before you are finished assembling the croquembouche, simply place it over very low heat and stir until it reliquefies.

Variation: CREAM PUFFS

6 servings

Paste for ***Miniature Cream Puffs***
1 cup cold heavy cream whipped stiff with 3 tablespoons confectioner's sugar and ½ teaspoon vanilla extract (see page 857)
Additional confectioner's sugar in a sieve or shaker

Prepare the basic paste according to Step 1 of the Master Recipe, but make the following changes in forming and baking the puffs. Instead of forming 2-teaspoon puffs using a pastry bag fitted with a ½-inch tip, form 6 puffs about 2½ inches wide, ¾ inch high, and slightly domed in the center, using a pastry bag fitted with a ¾-inch plain tip (or, less desirably, a teaspoon); space mounds at least 3 inches apart on baking sheet to allow for expansion. Glaze with beaten egg. Bake at 425°F for 20 minutes, then at 350°F for 20 minutes longer. Remove puffs from oven, slit crosswise with a serrated knife, and carefully scrape out soft, uncooked dough from the inside. Turn oven off and let puffs dry out in oven, the door ajar, for 20 minutes, then transfer to a rack and let cool completely.

Just before serving, spoon whipped cream into puffs and dust heavily with confectioner's sugar.

Variation: ÉCLAIRS

6 servings

Paste for ***Miniature Cream Puffs***
Pastry Cream, page 855
ADD: 2 tablespoons instant espresso or instant coffee
DECREASE: Vanilla to 1 teaspoon
½ cup (½ recipe) Chocolate Glaze, page 851

Prepare the basic paste according to Step 1 of the Master Recipe, but make the following changes in forming and baking the éclair shells. Instead of forming 2-teaspoon puffs using a pastry bag fitted with a ½-inch tip, form 6 strips of paste about 4 inches long and 1¼ inches wide, using a pastry bag fitted with a ¾-inch plain tip (or, less desirably, a teaspoon); space strips at least 3 inches apart on baking sheet to allow for expansion. Glaze with beaten egg. Bake at 425°F for 20 minutes, then at 350°F for 20 minutes longer. Remove shells from oven, slit crosswise with a serrated knife, and carefully scrape out soft, uncooked dough from the inside. Turn oven off and let shells dry out in oven, the door ajar, for 20 minutes, then transfer to rack and let cool completely.

Prepare pastry cream according to the recipe, but dissolve instant coffee in hot milk and decrease vanilla to 1 teaspoon. Shortly before serving, spoon pastry cream into éclair shells and coat the tops of the shells with chocolate glaze. Refrigerate about 15 minutes to set glaze, then serve.

THE CLASSIC AMERICAN SWEET: CAKES

The saying has it that something is "as American as apple pie," but when I try to conjure up a vision of the quintessential American sweet, images of cakes always come to mind. From colonial New England came Boston cream pie, pineapple upside-down cake, and gingerbread. Southern cooks have created over a period of at least two centuries such dessert classics as Lane cake, Key West lemon cake, Lady Baltimore cake, and Robert E. Lee cake, all grand and showy creations consisting of multiple cake layers sandwiched together with rich fillings, swathed with snowy meringue or butter cream icings, and thickly encrusted with grated fresh coconut, chopped nuts, or crushed candies. Generations of housewives throughout the country have been virtually obsessed with making ever bigger, ever moister, ever tastier, and ever more novel layer cakes. You see the often stupendous results of their efforts—and sometimes those of their cake-baking husbands—at bake sales and county fairs, on picnic tables and beach blankets, at family dinners and on formal buffet tables. According to John and Karen Hess in their provocative book *The Taste of America,* it was the introduction of baking powder and the new availability of highly refined machine-milled flour in the decades immediately following the Civil War that started Americans on their baking spree (which, by the way, the Hesses see as a development of dubious value). Whatever the cause, the bake-off continues to this day, not only, I'd conjecture, because people like to eat cake, but also because cakes are so satisfying to create.

Because I am aware that many people today are intimidated by the thought of making a cake from scratch, I have made every effort to streamline and simplify the recipes as much as possible while also being explicit and detailed in outlining the procedures that cannot be eliminated or abbreviated. If you are a beginner, before embarking on your cake-making adventure, read through the tips that follow below as well as the filling and frosting notes. Recipes for cake fillings and frostings appear in a separate chapter that begins on page 843.

Tips on Pleasurable and Successful Cake-baking

1. *Be methodical and pay attention to detail.* This is the most important piece of advice that can be given about the whole process. Read the recipe through before beginning. Lay out all your ingredients and equipment beforehand. Perform even the simplest steps, such as buttering and flouring the cake pan, with care. Don't rush, don't dispense with any of the steps, and don't estimate any of the measurements. In short, proceed with a Swiss watchmaker's care and precision.

2. *Use the right cake pan.* Most cake recipes can be baked in pans of several different sizes and shapes. Information on appropriate pans is supplied in the recipes, and the charts here and on page 807 go into still further detail on this matter. But only a certain degree of latitude is permissible before trouble results. If the pan is too small, the cake will overflow. If the pan is too large, the cake will not rise well and it will likely dry out and toughen. If the pan is narrow and deep, the cake is likely to collapse in the middle into a sticky-wet mass. And if the design of the pan is too intricate, the cake may burn around the extremities and stick when you attempt to unmold it.

Equipping yourself with workable cake pans need by no means be an expensive proposition. Nearly all of the cake recipes in this chapter can be prepared in *two round cake pans measuring 9 inches across and 2 inches deep.* If you also invest in a 16-cup tube pan you can make angel food cake too, the one cake included here that cannot be done in a shallow round pan. The following chart provides guidelines for making pan substitutions:

CAKE PAN SUBSTITUTION CHART

	USUALLY BAKED IN	BUT MAY BE BAKED IN
Yellow cake and variations	Three 9×1½-inch round pans	Two 9×2-inch round pans
Pound cake and variations	One 9×5×3-inch loaf pan	One 9×2-inch round pan
Sponge cake and variations	Two 8×1½-inch round pans OR one 15×10×1½-inch jelly roll pan	One 9×2-inch round pan
Gingerbread	One 8×2-inch square pan	One 9×2-inch round pan

3. *For the best results use cake flour,* a soft (that is, low-gluten), finely milled flour that produces tender, fine-textured cakes. Cake flour generally comes packaged in cardboard boxes. Read the label carefully, and be sure you are buying plain cake flour, not so-called "self-rising" flour, which contains baking powder and salt and is obviously useless for cake recipes that do not require chemical leavening. If you cannot find cake flour, you can substitute ⅞ cup of all-purpose flour for each cup of cake flour, but the resulting cake will be noticeably coarse, flat, dry, and heavy.

4. *Do not sift the flour before measuring.* The recipes in this chapter are based on flour that is not sifted before measuring. (If you do sift the flour you will get a measurement that is off by some 30 percent.) Measure the flour as follows: Scoop a dry measuring cup into your bag or canister of flour, dredge up a heaping cupful, and, without tapping the cup or tamping down the flour, sweep off the excess flour with the back of a knife, leaving remainder level with the lip of the cup.

Does this mean that you can throw away your sifter? If you are content to make only yellow cake and its variations, you can indeed. But in preparing the slightly more temperamental air-leavened cakes—pound cakes, sponge cakes, and angel food cakes—it is a good idea to sift the dry ingredients over the batter before folding them in. Sifting insures that there will not be any lumps of unmoistened flour in the finished cake.

5. *Use an electric mixer.* Most cake batters require heavy-duty beating at several steps along the way, and it is hard work to try to do it all by hand. You'll end up exhausting yourself, and you'll probably not be able to do the beating efficiently enough to get a properly light and fine-textured cake. In addition, an

electric mixer streamlines the mixing process. For example, you need not cream the butter separately before gradually adding sugar and eggs, as old-fashioned recipes direct. If you are backed by the power of a machine you can combine all of the ingredients at once and cream them together.

You do not, by the way, need a fancy mixer to make a good cake. A small hand-held model does a fine job of creaming the butter, sugar, and egg yolks and of blending the batter, and I think it does even a better job of beating the egg whites than does a standard stationary mixer.

FILLING AND FROSTING NOTES:

The "filling" of a cake is what is spread between the layers; the "frosting" (or "icing") is whatever is used to cover the top and sides. When the cake is both filled and covered with the same preparation—as has become the common contemporary practice—that mixture is simply known as frosting.

Cake fillings are always rich and intensely flavored. The simplest and most old-fashioned filling is plain jam, usually apricot, raspberry, or strawberry. Other cake fillings include the traditional American custard types, which may be flavored with lemon, rum, coconut, or nuts; the famous French whipped chocolate filling known as ganache; and the Sherry-soaked dried fruit and nut filling that is used to make Lady Baltimore cake.

American cake frostings are primarily of two types, the so-called "boiled icings," which consist of cooked meringue plus a flavoring, and the standard all-purpose icings, which are based on raw confectioner's sugar and butter and are often referred to as butter cream frostings. The boiled icings are fluffy and puffy, suggestive of marshmallow—unless they contain, as they certainly may, butter; then they, too, are called butter creams. The confectioner's sugar frostings are sweet and substantial; they are easier to make and work with than the boiled icings, and they keep better.

Yellow cake and its many variations are nearly always both filled and frosted to produce the classic American layer cake—spice, chocolate, banana, or what have you. On the other hand, pound cake and its variations are seldom filled and almost never frosted, for these cakes are by themselves quite rich and substantial. Finally, sponge cakes and angel cakes may be served plain, or only filled, or both filled and frosted, depending on the kind of dessert you wish to achieve.

All of the cake recipes in this chapter include filling and frosting suggestions, but you should feel free, in the Master Recipe spirit, to experiment or choose your own.

HOW TO FILL AND FROST A CAKE: As in all things, practice makes perfect and the more cakes you make, the more professional-looking will be your results. Here's the procedure:

1. Start with a thoroughly cool cake. If the cake is still warm, the filling and frosting will thin out, become runny, and soak into the cake, and you'll have a full-blown disaster on your hands.

2. To fill a single cake layer, slice it horizontally into 2 or 3 layers as follows. Place the cake on waxed paper or foil on a flat work surface. Cut one or two even bands (depending on the number of slices you are making) ½ inch deep all around the circumference of the cake to outline the slices. Then, with your hand spread open-fingered on the cake to steady it, use a serrated knife (preferably one slightly longer than the cake is wide) to cut the cake crosswise, keeping the knife as level as possible and using the band to line up the knife's tip and handle ends. As each slice is cut, remove it with the outspread fingers of both hands to a sheet of waxed paper.

3. Place the bottom layer of the cake on a serving platter and slip small tabs of waxed paper beneath it around the edges. The paper will protect the platter from becoming smudged as you frost the cake. When the cake is fully filled, frosted, and decorated, pull the tabs free and discard.

4. Use about ⅓ of your icing to fill a cake. Reserve the rest for the top and sides.

5. If one of the layers has developed an unsightly hump during baking, stack it hump side down, which will help to flatten the hump. If the hump is very large, cut it off.

6. For a smooth surface, use a long-bladed frosting spatula, the implement favored by professionals, or, lacking such a spatula, either a large rubber spatula or a large knife. For a very smooth finish, particularly desirable if you plan to decorate the cake, give the icing a final going-over with the spatula or knife dipped in cold water. (But don't do this if you have used a meringue-type frosting, as the water will cause the frosting to crust over.) A swirl effect can be achieved by spreading the frosting with the back of a spoon.

7. A decorated cake is always a grand and festive sight. To make icing decorations, reserve about ⅔ cup of your frosting—the cake won't miss it—and pipe the reserved frosting over the cake through a pastry bag. The icing decorations will of course be more dramatic if they are tinted a different color from the frosting base. You may also decorate a cake—the sides, the top, or both—with such things as grated fresh coconut, chopped nuts, crushed hard candies, or candied fruits, and if your cake happens to be in any way lopsided or gouged, these finishing decorations can go a long way toward making it seem more nearly perfect.

INCREASING OR DECREASING CAKE RECIPES: Yellow cake and its variations may be made in ½ recipes, ¾ recipes, 1½ recipes, or double recipes, allowing you to produce cakes of various sizes and shapes. A recipe yield variation chart for yellow cake and a cake pan chart for smaller and larger yellow cakes appear on page 803. Remember also the following tips:

1. When increasing a recipe yield, make corresponding changes in the sizes of the mixing bowls that you use and keep in mind that it will take longer to complete each step of the recipe.

2. Since cake pans must be staggered in the oven to allow room for air to circulate, if you are baking two very large cakes or a number of small cakes you will likely have to bake them in two stages.

3. Small cakes will bake a bit more quickly than the usual 9-inch round layers. Large cakes—from 12 to 14 inches in diameter—will require a longer baking time. If you suspect that the outer rim of the cake is becoming dried out before the inside has finished cooking, lower the oven temperature to 325°F.

4. Even very large cakes can be split horizontally into two or three slices for filling. Split the cake with a long chef's knife, and to prevent the slices from breaking apart, lift them using a large rimless cookie sheet. Don't worry too much if a slice turns out uneven or cracks. Skillful frosting of the cake will cover over all errors.

5. Remember to decrease or increase filling and frosting recipes in proportion to the decrease or increase in the cake recipe. As a general rule, it is always better to prepare slightly more filling and frosting than you think you'll need, as the surface area of a cake does not necessarily decrease or increase proportionately to changes in the volume of the cake.

CAKE RESCUE NOTES: If the major problem with the cake is its *appearance*—that is, if it is lumpy, lopsided, flat, cracked, split in several pieces, gouged, or otherwise deformed—you can piece it all back together again and make it look perfect once frosted. Prepare 1½ recipes of meringue frosting, maple frosting, or toffee frosting, and use the frosting both as glue and as a covering for any disaster zones. A final coating of chopped nuts or grated coconut or chocolate can be applied over the frosted cake if more camouflage is needed, but the frosting will likely do the trick by itself.

If the cake didn't rise properly and is dense, tough, or wet, you must first decide just how bad the problem is. Slice a thin piece off the top of one layer and taste. Don't be too hard on yourself. Most likely the cake can be filled and frosted as planned and no one will even think of complaining. But if the cake really is seriously defective, slice and serve with warm chocolate sauce, warm custard sauce, or berry sauce.

RECIPE YIELD VARIATION CHART FOR YELLOW CAKE

	½ RECIPE	¾ RECIPE	1 RECIPE	1½ RECIPES	2 RECIPES
Eggs	2	3	4	6	8
Sugar	1 cup	1½ cups	2 cups	3 cups	4 cups
Butter	½ cup	¾ cup	1 cup	1½ cups	2 cups
Vanilla	1 t	1½ t	2 t	1 T	4 t
Cake flour	1 cup plus 2 tablespoons	1⅔ cups	2¼ cups	3⅓ cups	4½ cups
Baking powder	1½ t	2¼ t	1 T	4½ t	2 T
Milk	½ cup	¾ cup	1 cup	1½ cups	2 cups
Cream of tartar	⅛ t	¼ t	¼ t	½ t	½ t
Salt	Pinch	Pinch	Large pinch	Large pinch	⅛ t

CAKE PAN CHART FOR SMALLER AND LARGER YELLOW CAKES

VOL. OF RISEN CAKE	½ RECIPE 8 CUPS	¾ RECIPE 12 CUPS	1 RECIPE 16 CUPS	1½ RECIPES 24 CUPS	2 RECIPES 32 CUPS
8×1½-inch round pans (4 cups)	2 pans	3 pans	4 pans	6 pans	8 pans
8×2-inch square pans (7½ cups)	1 pan		2 pans	3 pans	4 pans
9×1½-inch round pans (6 cups)			3 pans		6 pans
9×2-inch round pans (8 cups)	1 pan		2 pans	3 pans	4 pans
9×2-inch heart pans (6 cups)			3 pans		6 pans
12×2-inch heart pans (12 cups)		1 pan		2 pans	
13×9-inch rectangular pans (12 cups)		1 pan		2 pans	
14×2-inch round pans (18 cups)			1 pan		2 pans

MASTER RECIPE

Yellow Cake

Makes three 9×1½-inch layers serving 8 to 12

❦ *Delicious in its own right, this simple-to-make cake is also the basis of over a dozen variation recipes. When filled and frosted these variations in turn become a dazzling assortment of layer cakes, most traditional but a few of my own devising.*

Before embarking on this recipe, be sure to read through all the preliminary cake-baking, filling, and frosting tips on pages 802–6.

PRELIMINARIES

1. Bring all ingredients to room temperature. If the ingredients are either chilled or warmed, they will not become aerated when beaten and they will not blend with one another in the proper manner.
2. Set racks in upper-middle and lower-middle levels of oven.
3. To bake the cake in three 9-inch layers, select three round pans measuring 9 inches across and 1½ inches deep. (To bake the cake in pans of other sizes and shapes, see charts on page 803 and page 807.)
4. There must be enough room in the oven for the cakes to be placed at least 2½ inches apart and 3 inches distant from the oven walls; otherwise, they will rise in a lopsided fashion. If you have a small oven, test the oven size with the empty pans. If there is not enough room, bake just two layers at a time, one on each rack. Set the third layer aside at room temperature, loosely covered, and bake when the other two are done.
5. Smear the bottom, sides, and corners of each pan with 2 teaspoons soft butter or vegetable shortening. Sprinkle 1½ tablespoons flour in each pan and shake and tap the pan so that the bottom and sides are completely dusted. Then invert pan over the sink and rap it sharply against the faucet to remove any excess flour. If you follow this procedure conscientiously, your cakes will never stick to the pans.
6. Preheat oven to 350°F 20 minutes before baking.

STEP 1: CREAMING BUTTER, SUGAR, AND EGG YOLKS

- 4 large eggs
- 2 cups sugar
- 16 tablespoons (2 sticks) butter

Separate eggs, placing yolks in 4-quart mixing bowl and whites in an absolutely grease-free 3-quart bowl (do not use a plastic bowl for whites). Set egg whites aside.

Add sugar and butter to yolks and beat at moderately high speed with an electric mixer, scraping down the sides of the bowl with a rubber spatula, until soft, off-white in color, and nearly as fluffy as stiff whipped cream. This will take 6 to 8 minutes, depending on the efficiency of your mixer. The purpose of this step is to incorporate air into the batter, so don't stint on the beating. On the other hand, don't overbeat the batter either, or it will turn grainy and curdled-looking and much of the air that you have beaten in will escape.

STEP 2: ADDING FLOUR, BAKING POWDER, MILK, AND VANILLA EXTRACT

- 2¼ cups unsifted cake flour (measure by scooping cup into large container of flour and sweeping off excess with the back of a knife)
- 1 tablespoon baking powder
- 1 cup milk
- 2 teaspoons vanilla extract

Measure flour and baking powder into a 2½-quart mixing bowl and toss with a fork or wire whip to blend thoroughly; the leavening must be well distributed within the flour or the baked cake will be riddled with large holes. Sprinkle ⅓ of the flour mixture evenly over top of creamed butter mixture. With electric mixer set at moderately low speed, beat for about 5 seconds, or until flour is partly incorporated. Pour ⅓ of the milk over the batter, again mixing about 5 seconds. Continue to add flour and milk alternately, by thirds, until both are used up, beating about 5 seconds after each addition; add the vanilla. With the mixer still set at low speed, beat the batter about 20 seconds longer, scraping the sides and bottom of the bowl with a rubber spatula. As soon as all the ingredients seem blended together and the batter looks smooth, raise mixer speed to moderate and beat for 20 to 30 seconds, or until the batter thickens perceptibly and takes on a satiny, creamy appearance. Do not beat beyond this point, or you will deflate the air bubbles and cause the baked cake to be low and excessively fine and crumbly.

STEP 3: BEATING EGG WHITES; COMPLETING THE BATTER

- 4 egg whites (from Step 1)
- ¼ teaspoon cream of tartar
- Salt

Wash beaters thoroughly in hot sudsy water and dry well; the slightest trace of grease will prevent egg whites from mounting properly.

Refer, if necessary, to the guidelines on beating and folding egg whites on pages 133–36. Beat egg whites at low speed with electric mixer until they look foamy, then add cream of tartar and a generous pinch of salt and increase speed to medium. When egg whites form soft, frothy peaks, increase speed to high and beat until the whites are thick, glossy, and stand firmly at the end of the uplifted beaters.

Using a rubber spatula, gently but thoroughly fold egg whites into cake batter.

STEP 4: BAKING, COOLING, AND FROSTING THE CAKE: Divide batter evenly between prepared pans. Then gently shake each one back and forth on a flat surface to level the batter and to burst any too-large air bubbles.

Set filled cake pans in the thoroughly preheated oven, being sure that pans are at least 2½ inches distant from each other and 3 inches from the oven walls and that they are staggered—rather than one right above the other—on the racks. Three 9×1½-inch layers will need to bake 20 to 25 minutes; other sizes will require proportionately longer or shorter baking times. To test for doneness, insert a cake tester or toothpick in the center of a layer; the needle should come out clean, with no liquid batter adhering. Another sign of doneness is the shrinking of the cake from the sides of the pan. You may also test for doneness by pressing the center of a layer with your finger; the cake will spring back if fully baked.

Place cakes on racks and let cool in the pans for about 10 minutes but no longer, or they may get soggy. One layer at a time, run a knife around inside of pan to loosen sides of cake, then shake the cake back and forth, *very gently,* to loosen the bottom. Invert a rack over top of cake and, gripping pan and rack, invert them both. Cake should immediately fall out onto rack; lift pan off cake. Invert a second rack over the bottom of the unmolded cake and, holding the cake between the racks, flip the layer over so that it rests on its bottom side. Remove rack from top of cake.

Allow cakes to cool thoroughly—at least 1 hour at room temperature—before wrapping or frosting. Frosting will become runny if spread on a cake that is even slightly warm, and warm cakes become sweaty and gummy when wrapped.

STORAGE: To store unfrosted cakes, wrap layers individually in foil and tie in a plastic bag. Cakes will keep well for several days under refrigeration or may be frozen for about 1 month. To store a frosted cake, protect under an inverted bowl or cake cover and refrigerate for up to 3 days. To freeze a frosted cake, place it in the freezer unwrapped until frozen hard, then wrap cake first in foil and then in a plastic bag and return to the freezer. Unwrap cake before thawing.

- *Classic Chocolate-frosted Layer Cake:* Fill and frost yellow cake layers with chocolate butter cream frosting, page 849; decorate cake with a single long-stemmed maraschino cherry placed in the center.
- *Jam Layer Cake:* Fill yellow cake layers with 1¼ cups raspberry jam, forced through a sieve to eliminate seeds, and frost with ⅔ recipe of butter cream frosting, page 848.

Variation: APPLESAUCE CAKE

Makes three 9×1½-inch layers serving 8 to 12

❦ *Spectacularly tender and moist.*

Yellow Cake

ADD:	½ teaspoon baking soda
	½ teaspoon cinnamon
SUBSTITUTE:	1½ cups *unsweetened* applesauce for milk

Proceed according to the Master Recipe, but add soda and cinnamon along with the baking powder and substitute applesauce for milk. The cakes may need to bake a few extra minutes.

- *Classic Applesauce Layer Cake:* Fill and frost cake layers with butter cream frosting, page 848.
- *Applesauce Layer Cake with Pecans and Raisins:* Fill cake layers with pecan-raisin cake filling, page 854, frost with ⅔ recipe of butter cream frosting, page 848, and decorate cake with pecan halves.

Variation: BANANA CAKE

Makes three 9×1½-inch layers serving 8 to 12

Yellow Cake

ADD:	½ teaspoon baking soda
SUBSTITUTE:	1½ cups well-puréed very ripe bananas (4 to 5 medium) for milk

Proceed according to the Master Recipe, adding soda along with the baking powder and substituting puréed bananas for milk.

- *Classic Banana Layer Cake:* Fill and frost cake layers with butter cream frosting, page 848, or meringue frosting, page 844.
- *Banana-Orange Layer Cake:* Fill cake layers with orange-butter cake filling, page 854, and frost with ⅔ recipe of butter cream frosting, page 848, or the orange-flavored variation, page 850.

Variation: CHOCOLATE CAKE

Makes three 9×1½-inch layers serving 8 to 12

❦ This is the standard American chocolate cake—rich but not cloying, crumbly, and not too sweet. For a sweeter, moister, chewier cake, try chocolate devil's food cake; for a very light chocolate cake with a melting texture, see chocolate wind cake; and for a dense, almost gooey chocolate cake, see chocolate brownie cake.

Yellow Cake

ADD:	6 ounces unsweetened baking chocolate
INCREASE:	Sugar to 2¼ cups
DECREASE:	Flour to 1¾ cups

Chop or grate chocolate, then melt it in a heat-proof bowl set in a pan of almost-simmering water or in the top of a double boiler over very gently simmering water. Remove from heat and let cool to tepid while you prepare the cake batter.

Proceed according to the Master Recipe, but cream the butter with an extra ¼ cup sugar, decrease flour to 1¾ cups, and add the melted and cooled chocolate along with the vanilla. When done, the cake will feel firm when pressed in the center and a cake tester will come out with an oily crumb adhering; do not overbake, or the cake will be dry.

- *Classic Chocolate Layer Cake:* Fill and frost cake layers with sour cream chocolate frosting, page 852, and decorate with walnut halves.
- *Chocolate-Mocha Layer Cake:* Fill and frost cake layers with mocha butter cream frosting, page 850; if you wish, sieve a bit of cocoa over the top.

Variation: CHOCOLATE DEVIL'S FOOD CAKE

Makes three 9×1½-inch layers serving 8 to 12

❦ *I am very fond of this cake, with its moist, chewy texture and fudgelike taste.*

Yellow Cake

ADD: 4 ounces unsweetened baking chocolate
DECREASE: Butter to 8 tablespoons (1 stick)
SUBSTITUTE: 2 teaspoons baking soda for baking powder
1½ cups buttermilk for milk

Chop or grate chocolate, then melt it in a heat-proof bowl set in a pan of almost-simmering water or in the top of a double boiler over very gently simmering water. Remove from heat and let cool to tepid while you prepare the cake batter.

Proceed according to the Master Recipe, but halve the butter, use baking soda instead of baking powder, substitute 1½ cups buttermilk for milk, and add melted and cooled chocolate along with the vanilla. The cake will rise quite high and, probably, flatten slightly in the center. Be very careful not to overbake.

- *Classic Devil's Food Layer Cake:* Fill and frost cake layers with sour cream chocolate frosting, page 852.

Variation: CHOCOLATE WIND CAKE

Makes three 9×1½-inch layers serving 8 to 12

❦ *As the name implies, this cake is so light that it melts on the tongue before it can be chewed; yet it is also very rich and chocolaty.*

Yellow Cake

ADD: 6 ounces unsweetened baking chocolate
INCREASE: Sugar to 2¼ cups
SUBSTITUTE: 1⅔ cups freshly brewed espresso or very strong coffee, cooled to room temperature, for milk

Chop or grate chocolate, then melt it in a heat-proof bowl set in a pan of almost-simmering water or in the top of a double boiler over very gently simmering water. Remove from heat and let cool to tepid while you prepare the cake batter.

Proceed according to the Master Recipe, but cream the butter with an extra 1/4 cup sugar, substitute 1 2/3 cups coffee for milk, and add melted and cooled chocolate along with the vanilla.

- *Classic White on Black Layer Cake:* Fill and frost cake layers with meringue frosting, page 844; if you wish, sieve a border of cocoa over the top of the cake.
- *Chocolate-Raspberry Layer Cake:* Fill cake with 1 1/4 cups raspberry jam, forced through a sieve to remove seeds, and frost with 2/3 recipe of meringue frosting, page 844.
- *Chocolate Whipped Cream Cake:* Just before serving, stiffly whip 2 cups cold heavy cream, adding 1/3 cup sifted confectioner's sugar, 1 teaspoon vanilla extract, and 1/4 teaspoon almond extract (see page 857). Fill and frost the cake layers with the whipped cream and decorate top and sides of the cake with 1/2 cup toasted sliced almonds.

Variation: CHOCOLATE BROWNIE CAKE

Makes three 9×1 1/2-inch layers serving 8 to 12

❦ *This cake is different from other layer cakes in that it is supposed to be quite dense and heavy, like a chocolate brownie. It makes a delightful surprise for children and cake-loving friends.*

Yellow Cake

DECREASE: Cake flour to 1 cup

ADD: 1 cup cocoa (measure by spooning unsifted cocoa into cup until overflowing, then tapping sharply several times and leveling off excess with the back of a knife)

INCREASE: Milk to 1 3/4 cups

Proceed according to the Master Recipe, but add cocoa, mixing it with the decreased quantity of flour and baking powder in bowl, and increase milk to 1 3/4 cups. The batter will be runny. Bake the cake a few extra minutes, but don't overbake. The cake is done when it has shrunk slightly and begun to pull away from the sides of the pan. A tester inserted in the center will come out with a few moist crumbs adhering; the top will feel delicately set—but not springy—when pressed with a finger.

- *Chocolate Brownie Layer Cake:* Fill and frost cake layers with butter cream frosting, page 848, to which has been added about 1 cup of very coarsely chopped walnuts.

Variation: CHOCOLATE CHIP COOKIE CAKE

Makes three 9×1½-inch layers serving 8 to 12

❦ *This cake tastes astonishingly like chocolate chip cookies, yet retains the light, fluffy texture of a layer cake. Kids adore it.*

Note: It is absolutely essential here to use miniature chocolate chips; ordinary chocolate chips will sink to the bottom of the cake layers.

Yellow Cake

DECREASE: Granulated sugar to 1½ cups

ADD: ½ cup packed dark brown sugar
1½ cups (9 ounces) *miniature* chocolate chips

Proceed according to the Master Recipe, but decrease granulated sugar to 1½ cups, add the brown sugar along with the white sugar, and fold chocolate chips into the batter when the beaten egg whites are about ⅔ incorporated.

- *Chocolate Chip Layer Cake:* Fill and frost cake layers with butter cream frosting, page 848, or the mocha butter cream variation, page 850. If you wish, decorate the top and sides with coarsely chopped walnuts and/or a handful of miniature chocolate chips.

Variation: COCONUT CAKE

Makes three 9×1½-inch layers serving 8 to 12

❦ *You really must use fresh grated coconut to make this very moist, special cake; neither desiccated coconut nor, certainly, processed supermarket coconut is an effective substitute.*

Yellow Cake

ADD: 1½ cups (about 6 ounces) fresh grated coconut (see page 697)

INCREASE: Vanilla extract to 1 tablespoon

If you prepared the coconut using the large-hole side of a hand grater or a food processor fitted with a large-hole grating disc, turn it out onto a chopping board and chop lightly, reducing the flakes to about 3/16 inch. Proceed according to the Master Recipe, but increase vanilla to 1 tablespoon and fold the coconut into the batter when the beaten egg whites are about ⅔ incorporated.

- *Classic Coconut-Lemon Layer Cake:* As sumptuous as it is famous. Fill cake layers with lemon-butter cake filling, page 853, and frost with ⅔ recipe of meringue frosting, page 844. Cover top and sides of cake with about 2 cups fresh grated coconut.
- *Coconut-Raspberry Layer Cake:* Force ½ cup raspberry jam through a sieve to eliminate seeds and spread over the tops of all three cake layers. Fill and frost with meringue frosting, page 844.

Variation: LEMON CAKE

Makes three 9×1½-inch layers serving 8 to 12

Yellow Cake

ADD:	Grated zest of 2 large lemons (about 1½ tablespoons)
SUBSTITUTE:	1 teaspoon pure lemon extract for vanilla extract

Proceed according to the Master Recipe, but add the grated zest to the butter and sugar at the outset of creaming and substitute lemon extract for vanilla.

- *Classic Lemon Layer Cake:* Fill and frost cake layers with lemon butter cream frosting, page 850.
- *Robert E. Lee Cake:* At least according to legend, this cake was much favored by the great Confederate general. Fill cake layers with lemon-butter cake filling, page 853, frost with ⅔ recipe of lemon butter cream frosting, page 850, and completely mask the top and sides of the cake with 2 cups fresh grated coconut meat (1 small-medium coconut; see page 697).

Variation: ORANGE CAKE

Makes three 9×1½-inch layers serving 8 to 12

❦ *Light as a feather and luciously orangy.*

Yellow Cake

ADD:	Grated zest of 1 large orange (about 1½ tablespoons)
	½ teaspoon baking soda
SUBSTITUTE:	1 cup strained orange juice, preferably fresh, for milk

Proceed according to the Master Recipe, but add the grated zest to the butter and sugar at the outset of creaming, mix baking soda into flour along with the baking powder, and substitute orange juice for milk.

- *Classic Orange Layer Cake:* Fill cake layers with orange-butter cake filling, page 854, and frost with a ⅔ recipe of orange butter cream frosting, page 850.
- *Orange-Chocolate Layer Cake:* Fill and frost cake layers with chocolate butter cream frosting, page 849; if you wish, decorate the cake with long, thin strips of candied orange peel.

Variation: PEANUT BUTTER CAKE

Makes three 9×1½-inch layers serving 8 to 12

❦ *While this makes an excellent surprise birthday cake for a youngster, it will also appeal to adults, as the taste is subtle and sophisticated.*

Yellow Cake

ADD: 1½ cups (about 6 ounces) skinned roasted peanuts, preferably unsalted
2 additional large eggs
1⅓ cups (12 ounces) peanut butter

If your peanuts are salted, turn them into a sieve and rinse quickly under cold running water; rub between sheets of paper toweling until thoroughly dried. Chop peanuts coarsely either by spinning briefly in a blender or food processor or by turning them into a sturdy plastic bag and crushing them with a rolling pin or wine bottle. Set aside.

After completing Step 1 of the Master Recipe, beat together the 2 whole eggs, the peanut butter, and the milk and vanilla required in Step 2 of the Master Recipe. Add this mixture alternately with the flour. The batter will deflate a bit and become quite thick.

Proceed from there according to the Master Recipe, folding in reserved chopped peanuts when beaten egg whites are about ⅔ incorporated into the batter (Step 3). The cake layers will need to bake an extra 5 to 10 minutes—or 25 to 30 minutes altogether—and will be high.

- *Peanut-Toffee Layer Cake:* This is a delicious cake that both children and grownups will enjoy. Fill and frost cake with toffee frosting or, better, toffee meringue butter cream, page 848. If you wish, decorate the sides of the cake either with a cup or so of coarsely chopped unsalted skinned peanuts or with crushed peanut brittle, page 860.
- *Peanut Butter and Jam Layer Cake:* Force ½ cup strawberry jam through a sieve and spread a very thin layer on the tops of all three cake layers. Fill and frost with butter cream frosting, page 848. This is for the small fry.

Variation: SPICE CAKE

Makes three 9×1½-inch layers serving 8 to 12

❦ *Moist, tender, and redolent with spices, this is perhaps my favorite cake of all. The spice proportions may seem rather large, but don't use less or you'll regret it. The nutmeg used here really must be freshly grated.*

Yellow Cake

SUBSTITUTE:	2 cups packed dark brown sugar for granulated sugar
ADD:	½ teaspoon baking soda
	4 teaspoons freshly grated nutmeg
	2 teaspoons ground ginger
	1 teaspoon ground cloves
SUBSTITUTE:	1¼ cups buttermilk for milk
OMIT:	Vanilla extract

Proceed according to the Master Recipe, but cream butter with brown rather than granulated sugar, beating until the mixture is very fluffy and the color of café au lait; mix baking soda and spices with flour and baking powder, substitute buttermilk for milk, and omit vanilla extract.

- *Classic Spice Layer Cake:* Fill and frost cake layers with any of the following: butter cream frosting, page 848, meringue frosting, page 844, or toffee frosting, page 848.

Variation: WALNUT CAKE

Makes three 9×1½-inch layers serving 8 to 12

Yellow Cake

ADD:	1½ cups (about 6 ounces) walnuts
INCREASE:	Vanilla extract to 4 teaspoons

The walnuts here must be coarsely chopped into about 3⁄16-inch pieces. Either chop by hand with a utility or large chef's knife or in a food processor fitted with the metal blade, flicking the motor on and off. Do *not* use a blender or rotary nut grinder, both of which tend to reduce some of the nuts to a powder; if the nuts are finely ground, the cake will be dry and heavy.

Proceed according to the Master Recipe, but double the vanilla extract and fold the nuts into the batter when the beaten egg whites are about ⅔ incorporated.

- *Maple-Walnut Layer Cake:* Fill and frost the cake with maple frosting or, better, maple meringue butter cream, page 847. Sprinkle top and sides of cake with additional coarsely chopped walnuts, if you wish.
- *Walnut-Orange Layer Cake:* Fill cake layers with orange-butter cake filling, page 854, and frost with ⅔ recipe of orange butter cream frosting, page 850.
- *Linzer Layer Cake:* Fill the cake layers with 1¼ cups raspberry jam, forced through a sieve to remove seeds, and frost with ⅔ recipe of chocolate butter cream frosting, page 849.

Variation: WHITE CAKE

Makes three 9×1½-inch layers serving 8 to 12

❦ *Though it conjures up images of Victorian weddings and other genteel scenes, white cake is truly soul-satisfying in both taste and texture.*

Yellow Cake

OMIT:	Egg yolks
INCREASE:	Flour to 2½ cups
SUBSTITUTE:	1 teaspoon almond extract for vanilla
INCREASE:	Egg whites to 8
	Cream of tartar to ½ teaspoon

Proceed according to the Master Recipe, but cream butter and sugar without egg yolks (the mixture should look almost white when you're through), increase flour to 2½ cups, substitute almond for vanilla extract, and double the egg whites and cream of tartar, beating whites in a 4- to 5-quart bowl.

- *Classic Black on White Layer Cake:* Fill and frost cake layers with chocolate butter cream frosting, page 849.
- *Classic White Layer Cake:* Fill and frost cake with meringue frosting, page 844. If you wish, decorate cake with 2 cups grated fresh coconut, page 697, 1 cup coarsely crushed nut brittle, page 860, or ⅔ cup crushed peppermint candies.
- *Lady Baltimore Cake:* A grand old American cake whose origins are hotly debated by food scholars, Lady Baltimore cake may be served as a dessert, but I think it is best reserved for afternoon tea.

  Chop ½ cup raisins, 8 large dried figs, and 1 cup walnuts or pecans into fairly fine pieces. Cover the fruits and nuts with ¾ cup medium-dry Sherry (Manzanilla or Amontillado) and let stand for at least an hour (overnight would be better), stirring the mixture up a couple of times. Prepare meringue frosting, page 844, flavoring it with ½ teaspoon almond extract instead of vanilla. Drain the fruit/nut mixture thoroughly in a sieve and combine with ⅓ of the frosting. Split each cake layer in half horizontally and fill the layers with the fruit/nut mixture. Cover top and sides of cake with the remaining plain frosting; decorate with pecan or walnut halves.

- *Lane Cake:* Another famous cake from the South. Fill the cake layers with pecan-raisin cake filling, page 854, and cover top and sides with ⅔ recipe meringue frosting, page 844. Decorate with pecan halves.

Variation: WHOLE WHEAT CAKE

Makes three 9×1½-inch layers serving 8 to 12

❦ *I offer this cake not because I suppose it to be healthful, but because it tastes so good.*

Yellow Cake

DECREASE:	Granulated sugar to 1 cup
ADD:	1 cup packed dark brown sugar
DECREASE:	Cake flour to 1 cup
ADD:	1 cup whole wheat flour (measure as for cake flour)
INCREASE:	Vanilla extract to 1 tablespoon

Proceed according to the Master Recipe, but cream butter with 1 cup each granulated and dark brown sugar; decrease cake flour and mix with whole wheat flour and baking powder in small bowl, and increase vanilla to 1 tablespoon.

- *Whole Wheat Jam Layer Cake:* Force ½ cup apricot or raspberry jam through a sieve and spread thinly on the tops of the cake layers. Fill and frost with butter cream frosting, page 848, and decorate, if you wish, with a handful of coarsely chopped walnuts or pecans.

MASTER RECIPE

Pound Cake

Makes one 9×5×3-inch loaf serving 10 to 12

Tender, fine-textured, rich, and fragrant with butter and other honest flavorings, this pound cake needs no adornment other than, perhaps, a sprinkling of confectioner's sugar, though it can also be split horizontally into three or four layers and filled with lemon-butter or orange-butter cake filling. Pound cake is traditional at tea and, unfilled, also makes an excellent dessert with sliced fresh peaches or strawberries.

As it contains no baking powder, pound cake depends entirely on the air you beat into it for leavening. Before beginning, read through the cake-baking tips that begin on page 802.

ABOUT PAN SIZES: Traditionally, pound cakes are baked in a 9×5×3-inch (7½-cup) loaf pan. However, this recipe may also be baked in any of the following pans:

1. Two 4-cup loaf pans
2. Two 8×1½-inch round pans
3. One 9×2-inch round pan
4. One 8- to 10-cup tube or Bundt pan

HALVING THE RECIPE: Simply decrease all ingredients by half and bake the cake in either a 4-cup loaf or an 8-inch round pan.

PRELIMINARIES

1. Bring all ingredients to room temperature.
2. Set rack in middle level of oven.
3. Preheat oven to 325°F 20 minutes before baking.
4. Grease a 9×5×3-inch loaf pan with 1½ tablespoons soft butter. Dust with 2 tablespoons flour, shake the pan to coat bottom and sides with flour, then invert over the sink and rap pan sharply against the faucet to remove excess flour.

Step 1: Preparing the Cake Batter

16 tablespoons (2 sticks) unsalted butter
½ teaspoon salt
2 cups confectioner's sugar (measure by spooning unsifted sugar into cup until overflowing, then tapping sharply several times and leveling off excess with the back of a knife)
3 large egg yolks
2 large eggs
1½ teaspoons vanilla extract
1½ cups unsifted cake flour (measure by scooping cup into large container of flour and sweeping off excess with the back of a knife)

Place butter and salt in a 4-quart bowl and beat at high speed with an electric mixer for 2 to 3 minutes, or until fluffy. Gradually add the confectioner's sugar, sifting or sieving it over the butter if it is lumpy. Continue to beat at high speed for at least 5 minutes longer, or until the mixture has quadrupled in volume and is nearly white. (Stop beating, though, if the mixture turns grainy or begins to deflate.) Turn mixer to low speed, add the yolks and eggs in rapid succession, then the vanilla, and beat just until the mixture is blended and smooth, about 15 seconds after the vanilla has gone in. Sieve or sift the flour over the top and gently but thoroughly fold in with a rubber spatula; the batter will be quite heavy.

Step 2: Baking and Cooling the Cake

Immediately turn batter into prepared pan, gently smoothing top with a rubber spatula. Set in the center of the rack in preheated oven and bake 55 to 65 minutes (40 to 45 minutes if you are using two smaller cake pans). The cake is done if the top springs back when pressed with your finger and a cake tester or toothpick inserted in the center comes out clean, with no trace of liquid batter.

Place cake on a rack and let cool in the pan for about 10 minutes. To unmold the loaf, run a knife around the edges of the cake and gently shake the pan until the cake is loose. Set cake on its side on the rack and ease the pan out from underneath it. Then quickly flip the cake upright with your hands. (If you have prepared the cake in a round pan, unmold following the instructions given for yellow cake on page 810.)

Let cake cool thoroughly—about 2 hours at room temperature—before either serving or wrapping for storage.

Storage: Wrapped in foil and sealed in an airtight plastic bag, pound cake may be kept for 4 or 5 days in the refrigerator or frozen for several months. Always bring a chilled pound cake to room temperature before serving.

Variation: PINEAPPLE UPSIDE-DOWN CAKE

Makes one 10-inch cake serving 8 to 10

❦ *The cake in an upside-down cake should be rich, moist, and flavorful to stand up to the buttery caramelized fruit on the bottom. A slightly modified pound cake fits the bill perfectly.*

Preliminaries

1. Set rack in middle level of oven.
2. Preheat oven to 325°F 20 minutes before baking.
3. Select a heavy oven-proof skillet measuring 9 to 10 inches across the bottom and 2½ inches deep. The skillet must have a capacity of at least 7½ cups. If in doubt, test by measuring water into it.

8 tablespoons (1 stick) butter
¾ cup packed dark brown sugar
7 to 8 slices canned pineapple, drained
7 to 8 candied cherries or drained maraschino cherries
1 cup (about 4 ounces) pecan or walnut halves
Batter for ½ recipe ***Pound Cake***

Melt butter in skillet over low heat, tilting skillet to grease sides. Off heat, stir in brown sugar. Arrange pineapple slices in a single layer over bottom of skillet; fill in the holes in the slices with cherries. Tuck nuts into the spaces between pieces of fruit; strew additional nuts over fruit, if you wish. Set aside.

Prepare a half recipe of pound cake batter, using 2 egg yolks. Pour cake batter evenly over fruit in the skillet. Bake in preheated oven for 35 to 40 minutes; cake is done when a toothpick or cake tester inserted in the center comes out clean. If cake seems to be browning too quickly, cover loosely with a sheet of aluminum foil.

Let upside-down cake rest in the skillet for 3 minutes after being removed from the oven. To unmold, run a knife around the edge of the cake to loosen it. Protecting your hand with pot holders, grasp the handle of the skillet in both hands and flip cake over onto a serving platter as though you were turning a giant pancake. (The platter should be at least 14 inches in diameter and flat and unbreakable.) Let skillet rest over cake for a few minutes so that any last drops of buttery caramel can drip down.

Serve upside-down cake slightly warm or at room temperature. If you want a real treat, accompany with unsweetened whipped cream. Store any leftovers in the refrigerator covered directly with plastic wrap; bring to room temperature before serving.

Variation: BOSTON CREAM PIE

Makes one 9-inch cake serving 8 to 12

Pound Cake, baked in a 9×2-inch round pan
Pastry Cream, page 855
SUBSTITUTE: 2 teaspoons rose water and 1/4 teaspoon cinnamon for vanilla extract, if you wish
1/2 cup (1/2 recipe) Chocolate Glaze, page 851

Split cake horizontally into three layers and fill with pastry cream, flavored, if you wish to be traditional, with rose water and cinnamon instead of vanilla. Let chocolate glaze cool until it is just thin enough to pour—you don't want it to dribble down the sides of the cake—and cover the top of the cake evenly and completely, smoothing the glaze with a frosting spatula or large knife. Store cake in the refrigerator, under an inverted bowl or cake cover, but let stand at room temperature for 1 hour before serving.

Variation: CHOCOLATE POUND CAKE

Makes one 9×5×3-inch loaf serving 10 to 12

❦*If you like pound cake and chocolate, this rich cake will appeal to you tremendously. A sprinkling of confectioner's sugar is all it really needs, but it may certainly be split into several horizontal layers and filled with orange-butter or rum-butter cake filling. I like to serve the cake with fresh cherries that have been soaked in brandy and lightly sweetened, with sweetened whipped cream on the side.*

Pound Cake
DECREASE: Cake flour to 1 1/4 cups
ADD: 1/2 cup cocoa (measure by spooning unsifted cocoa into cup until overflowing, then tapping sharply several times and leveling off excess with the back of a knife)

Proceed according to the Master Recipe, but decrease flour and add cocoa, sieving or sifting flour and cocoa together into the batter. Cake batter will be very heavy and will deflate somewhat during folding.

Variation: CITRUS POUND CAKE

Makes one 9×5×3-inch loaf serving 10 to 12

❦ *Grated orange and/or lemon zest are a traditional flavoring for pound cake, especially in England.*

Pound Cake

SUBSTITUTE: Grated zest of 1 large orange and grated zest of 1 large lemon for vanilla extract

Proceed according to the Master Recipe, substituting grated zests for vanilla.

Variation: HAZELNUT POUND CAKE

Makes one 9×5×3-inch loaf serving 10 to 12

❦ *Sprinkled with confectioner's sugar, this make a nice cake to serve when friends drop in at holiday time.*

Pound Cake

ADD: 1 cup (about 4 ounces) hazelnuts
INCREASE: Vanilla extract to 1 tablespoon

Skin the hazelnuts (see page 701), cool, and then chop or grind very coarse; the pieces should be the size of small pebbles. Proceed according to the Master Recipe, doubling the vanilla and folding in the nuts along with the flour.

Variation: GINGER POUND CAKE

Makes one 9×5×3-inch loaf serving 10 to 12

❦ *Smashing when served faintly warm with tea.*

Pound Cake

ADD: ½ cup (about 4 ounces) finely chopped crystallized ginger

Proceed according to the Master Recipe, folding in the ginger when the flour is nearly incorporated into the batter.

Variation: SPICED POUND CAKE

Makes one 9×5×3-inch loaf serving 10 to 12

Pound Cake
ADD: 2 teaspoons freshly grated nutmeg
1 teaspoon ground cardamom

Proceed according to the Master Recipe, but mix flour with spices before adding to cake.

Variation: SEED CAKE

Makes one 9×5×3-inch loaf serving 10 to 12

Pound Cake
ADD: 2 tablespoons anise seed or caraway seed, lightly crushed using a mortar and pestle or a heavy rolling pin
Grated zest of 1 large orange

Proceed according to the Master Recipe, adding seeds and grated zest along with the vanilla.

MASTER RECIPE

Sponge Cake

Makes two 8×1½-inch layers or one 9×2-inch layer serving 8

Light yet rich with the taste of eggs, sponge cake can be used as the basis for a number of desserts—American-type layer cakes, fancy European-type cakes, whipped cream cakes, and so on. Like the preceding pound cake, this contains no chemical leavening, and thus you must thoroughly beat the egg yolks and whites in order to incorporate enough air into the batter to make the cake light.

Before beginning, read through both the chapter introduction and the cake-baking, filling, and frosting tips, pages 802–5.

ABOUT PAN SIZES: This sponge cake recipe may also be baked in any of the following pans:

1. One 9×2-inch round pan
2. One 8- to 10-cup tube pan
3. One 15×10×½-inch jelly roll pan (for recipes such as the variation on page 835)

DOUBLING THE RECIPE: Double all ingredients, use double-size mixing bowls, and bake the cake in four 8-inch round pans, two 9×2-inch round pans, or a 16- to 18-cup tube pan. *Two caveats:* Do not try to bake a double recipe in a single large pan unless you use a tube pan; the cake will not rise properly. And do not bake the cake in four pans unless your oven is large enough to accommodate them all; this batter must be baked immediately, or it will begin to deflate.

PRELIMINARIES

1. Bring all ingredients, particularly eggs, to room temperature.
2. Set rack in middle of oven. (If your oven is too small to allow the two 8-inch pans to be placed 2½ inches apart and 3 inches distant from the oven walls, set two racks in the lower-middle and upper-middle levels of the oven.)
3. Preheat oven to 325°F 20 minutes before baking.
4. Select two 8×1½-inch round pans or one 9×2-inch round pan. Cut out two 8-inch circles or one 9-inch circle of waxed paper and use them to line bottom(s) of pan(s). *Do not grease the pan(s).* Sponge cake batter will slip down the sides of a greased pan as it bakes, and the cake will rise lopsidedly.

STEP 1: BEATING EGG YOLKS WITH SUGAR AND LIQUID

4 large eggs
⅔ cup sugar
2 teaspoons vanilla extract
2 tablespoons boiling water

Being careful not to get even a speck of yolk in the egg whites, separate the eggs, placing yolks in a 3-quart mixing bowl and whites in another bowl of the same size (do not use a plastic bowl for whites). Set egg whites aside.

Add sugar and vanilla to egg yolks and beat at low speed with an electric mixer for 1 minute. Raise mixer speed to high and, beating constantly, dribble in boiling water. Continue to beat for about 5 minutes longer, pushing beaters all around the bowl (or, if you are working with a stationary mixer, scraping the sides of the bowl frequently with a rubber spatula). When you are through, the yolk mixture should have increased at least 5 times in volume; it will be thick, glistening, and very pale, suggesting mayonnaise in appearance and consistency. The egg yolks *must* be beaten to this point if the sponge cake is to be light.

Step 2: Beating the Egg Whites; Folding in Egg Whites and Flour

- ⅔ cup unsifted cake flour (measure by scooping cup into large container of flour and sweeping off excess with the back of a knife)
- 4 egg whites (from Step 1)
- ¼ teaspoon cream of tartar
- Salt
- 4 tablespoons butter, melted and cooled

Measure flour into sifter or sieve set on a piece of waxed paper and set aside.

Wash the beaters in hot, sudsy water and rinse and dry well. Referring, if necessary, to the guidelines on beating and folding egg whites on pages 133–36, beat egg whites at low speed until foamy, then add cream of tartar and a pinch of salt. Increase speed to medium and beat until whites form soft peaks, then switch to high speed and beat whites until thick, glossy, and stiff enough to clump around the beaters.

Gently fold beaten whites into the yolk mixture, using a rubber spatula. When the whites are nearly incorporated, sift ½ of the flour on top of the batter and fold in. Sift on remaining flour and fold; when nearly incorporated, drizzle the butter over the batter and continue to fold just until all ingredients are blended.

Step 3: Baking the Cake

Spread batter in prepared cake pan(s), running it up the pan sides and smoothing top with rubber spatula. Rap pan(s) once against the countertop to rupture any large air bubbles, then immediately place in preheated oven. Bake two 8-inch layers 20 to 25 minutes, single 9-inch layer (or tube cake) 30 to 35 minutes. Sponge cake is done if the center springs back when lightly pressed with your finger or if a cake tester or toothpick comes out clean when inserted in the center.

Place sponge cake on cake rack and let stand in the pan about 5 minutes, or until cake pulls away from sides of pan. Detach completely from sides of pan with knife, then invert onto cake rack. Peel off waxed paper. Invert second rack over bottom of sponge cake and flip over so that cake is right side up. Let stand until thoroughly cooled.

Storage: Dust cake liberally with confectioner's sugar and tie airtight in a plastic bag. Keep in the refrigerator, but plan to serve within a day or two. Sponge cake may also be frozen for a month or so, but dries out quickly when defrosted. (The best uses for a defrosted sponge cake are English trifle and Italian rum cake.)

Variation: APRICOT SPONGE LAYER CAKE

Makes one 9-inch cake serving 8

Sponge Cake, baked in a 9×2-inch round pan
3½ tablespoons sugar
2 tablespoons boiling water
2 tablespoons dark rum
4 tablespoons unsalted butter, softened
⅔ cup confectioner's sugar, sieved or sifted if lumpy
¼ teaspoon vanilla extract
1¼ cups apricot jam
½ cup (2 ounces) sliced almonds (optional)

Split sponge cake horizontally into 2 layers. Place 1½ tablespoons of the granulated sugar in a small bowl, add boiling water, and stir until dissolved; add rum. Brush mixture over the cut sides of the cake layers.

In a small bowl, beat butter until fluffy with a wooden spoon or an electric mixer set at medium-high speed. Gradually add confectioner's sugar, beat about 1 minute longer, then blend in vanilla. Force the apricot jam through a fine sieve into a heavy-bottomed 1½-quart saucepan. Set aside. Scrape solids out of sieve, chop fine, and beat into confectioner's sugar mixture. Spread all this apricot icing on bottom layer of sponge cake, cover with top layer, and set cake on a rack.

Stir remaining 2 tablespoons granulated sugar into apricot jam, set over moderately high heat, and bring to a boil. Stirring constantly, cook about 1 minute, or until the glaze is sticky and coats the spoon heavily; be careful not to overcook, or the glaze will be rubbery when set. Let glaze cool for 3 minutes, or until it has thickened slightly but is still liquid, then slowly pour over the top and sides of the cake. If you wish, encrust the sides of the cake with almonds. Store cake in the refrigerator, under an inverted bowl or cake cover, but serve at room temperature.

Variation: ENGLISH TRIFLE (ZUPPA INGLESE)

Makes 8 to 12 servings

❦*A sumptuous dessert!*

Sponge Cake, baked in two 8×1½-inch round pans
¾ cup medium-dry Madeira or Sherry, preferably Manzanilla or Amontillado
Custard Sauce, page 856
About 3 cups fresh or defrosted and thoroughly drained frozen raspberries (a 10-ounce package yields about ⅔ cup drained fruit)
1 cup cold heavy cream
3 tablespoons confectioner's sugar
½ teaspoon vanilla extract
Fresh raspberries or crystallized violets for garnish (optional)

Select a glass bowl about 8 inches wide with fairly straight rather than outward-sloping sides. Slice each layer of sponge cake in half horizontally using a long serrated knife. Line bottom of serving bowl with one of the four cake layers, sprinkle with 3 tablespoons wine, ladle on about ⅔ cup custard sauce, and scatter about ⅓ of the raspberries over the top, pressing some of the berries against the side of the bowl so that they will make an attractive red layer when viewed from the side. Repeat this process twice, using up all of the custard sauce and raspberries. Finally, cover with the last slice of cake and sprinkle it with the last 3 tablespoons wine. Cover trifle with plastic wrap and refrigerate for several hours or overnight to blend the flavors.

Just before serving, turn cream into a 3-quart bowl and, referring if necessary to the recipe on page 857, whip until stiff, adding confectioner's sugar and vanilla. Pipe whipped cream decoratively over the trifle through a pastry bag fitted with a star tip, or simply drop the cream in mounds with a teaspoon. If you wish, you can further adorn the dessert with fresh raspberries or, in traditional fashion, with crystallized violets. Serve the trifle at once, while still very cold, cutting it with a knife but scooping out serving portions with a wide, shallow spoon.

Variation: FILLED ORANGE SPONGE CAKE

Makes one 9-inch cake serving 8

❦ *It has long been a popular practice to flavor sponge cake with orange.*

Sponge Cake, flavored, if you wish, with the grated zest of 1 orange and baked in a 9×2-inch round pan
2 tablespoons orange liqueur or strained fresh orange juice (optional)
1 cup (½ recipe) Orange-butter Cake Filling, page 854
Confectioner's sugar in a shaker or sieve

Prepare a 9×2-inch sponge cake, adding orange zest, if you wish, to the yolk/sugar mixture at the outset of beating. When thoroughly cooled, split cake in 2 or 3 horizontal layers, sprinkle with optional liqueur or juice, and fill with orange-butter cake filling. Refrigerate cake under an inverted bowl or cake cover for several hours or overnight, but let stand at room temperature for 1 hour before serving. Sprinkle the top with confectioner's sugar just before serving.

Variation: SPONGE LAYER CAKE WITH PRALINE BUTTER CREAM

Makes one 9-inch cake serving 8 to 10

❦ *This is the sort of cake that one might see in a fine European pastry shop.*

Sponge Cake, baked in a 9×2-inch round pan
1½ tablespoons sugar
2 tablespoons boiling water
2 tablespoons dark rum, preferably Jamaican
2 cups (⅔ recipe) Butter Cream Frosting, page 848
Praline Powder, page 860

Split sponge cake horizontally into 2 layers. Place sugar in a small bowl, add boiling water, and stir until dissolved; add rum. Brush mixture over the cut sides of the cake layers.

Combine about ⅔ cup of the butter cream and ⅓ cup of the praline powder in a small bowl. Spread mixture thickly on the bottom layer of sponge cake and cover with top layer. Mask top and sides of cake with remaining butter cream and encrust with remaining praline powder. Store cake in the refrigerator, under an inverted bowl or cake cover, but bring to room temperature before serving.

Variation: CHOCOLATE GANACHE CAKE

Makes one 9-inch cake serving 8 to 10

❦ *This is a European type of chocolate cake, extremely rich and sophisticated in taste and stunningly glamorous to behold. It consists of sponge cake filled and covered with a layer of whipped chocolate filling (or* ganache soufflée, *as it is often called) over which is poured a mirror-smooth chocolate glaze to finish. A bit of work is involved but the final results are well worth the effort. Anyone looking at your creation will swear it is the work of a Viennese pastry chef.*

STEP 1: PREPARING THE CAKE

Sponge Cake, baked in a 9×2-inch round pan; modify as follows if you wish

DECREASE: Cake flour to ½ cup

ADD: ½ cup cocoa (measure by spooning unsifted cocoa into cup until overflowing, then tapping sharply several times and leveling off the excess with the back of a knife)

OMIT: Butter

1½ tablespoons sugar
2 tablespoons boiling water
2 tablespoons freshly brewed coffee or dark rum, preferably Jamaican

Prepare a 9×2-inch sponge cake according to the Master Recipe. If you wish to flavor the cake with chocolate, decrease the flour, sieve or sift cocoa into the batter after the flour has gone in, and omit the butter.

Split thoroughly cooled cake horizontally into 2 layers. Place sugar in a small bowl, add boiling water, and stir until dissolved; add coffee or rum. Brush mixture over the cut sides of the cake layers. Set aside while you prepare the glaze and filling.

STEP 2: MAKING THE CHOCOLATE GLAZE AND WHIPPED FILLING; FILLING THE CAKE

2 cups (double recipe) Chocolate Glaze, page 851

Measure 1 cup of the chocolate glaze mixture into a 2-quart mixing bowl, reserving remainder in the saucepan. Refrigerate chocolate in mixing bowl for about 30 minutes, or until it is very thick and feels cool to the touch when you put your finger into it. (If the mixture becomes too cool and solidifies, let it stand at room temperature to soften.)

Using an electric mixer set at medium speed or a wire whip, beat the cooled chocolate for 2 to 3 minutes, or until it nearly doubles in volume and becomes fluffy and mocha-colored. Do not overbeat, or the cream will turn to butter and the filling will be hard and grainy.

Set bottom cake layer on baking sheet and evenly spread about ½ of the chocolate filling over it, using a frosting spatula or knife. Set the second cake layer on top and coat top and sides of cake with the remaining filling. When the cake has been completely masked with chocolate filling, make the surface as smooth as possible with the spatula or knife, dipped first in cold water. Refrigerate the cake for about 30 minutes to harden the filling in preparation for glazing.

STEP 3: GLAZING THE CAKE; DECORATING THE CAKE (OPTIONAL)

The remaining chocolate glaze mixture from Step 2

SPECIAL EQUIPMENT: A pastry bag fitted with a ¼-inch star tip (optional—only if you wish to decorate the cake)

Slide two metal spatulas under the chilled cake and transfer from the baking sheet to a cake rack. Remove any crumbs from baking sheet and set the rack holding the cake over it.

Place chocolate glaze over very low heat and, stirring constantly, warm the glaze until it is about as thick as molasses and feels barely tepid to the touch. (If the glaze should separate and turn oily when reheated, remove it from the stove and beat in water by ½ teaspoons until glaze is reconstituted and smooth.) Holding the saucepan in your nonwriting hand, slowly pour glaze over the center of the cake while using a frosting spatula or knife held in the other hand to spread glaze evenly over top and sides of cake. Ideally, by the time the last of the glaze has been drained from the saucepan the entire cake will be smoothly coated. If there are some bare or rough patches you may go over them with the spatula, but you must work quickly, as the glaze begins to set almost at once. Refrigerate the cake for at least an hour to firm the glaze, then carefully transfer to a serving plate using metal spatulas.

If you wish to decorate the cake, scrape glaze drippings in the baking sheet into a 1½-quart mixing bowl, let glaze stand at room temperature until softened, and then beat with a whip or electric mixer until fluffy and mocha-colored. Scoop the whipped chocolate into a pastry bag and pipe onto the thoroughly chilled cake through a small star tip, making rosettes, ribbons, or whatever else strikes your fancy. Store cake in refrigerator (see below) but allow to stand at room temperature for 1 hour before serving.

STORAGE: Cake will stay fresh in the refrigerator for several days; cover it with an inverted bowl or cake cover to protect it from food odors. For longer storage, freeze the cake until solid, then wrap in plastic and place in an airtight bag. The cake will keep for several months. Unwrap the cake and thaw under an inverted bowl.

Variation: ITALIAN RUM CAKE

Makes 8 to 12 servings

Sponge Cake, baked in two 8×1½-inch round pans
3 tablespoons granulated sugar
⅓ cup boiling water
⅓ cup dark rum, preferably Jamaican
Pastry Cream, page 855
1½ cups cold heavy cream
¼ cup confectioner's sugar, sieved or sifted if lumpy
2 additional tablespoons dark rum, preferably Jamaican
Any of the following decorations: ½ cup (2 ounces) lightly toasted slivered or sliced almonds or pine nuts; ⅓ cup slivered candied orange peel and 1 tablespoon lightly toasted aniseed; 1 ounce semisweet chocolate, grated
Additional confectioner's sugar in a sieve or shaker

Using a long serrated knife, slice each sponge layer in half horizontally. Stir granulated sugar and boiling water together in a small bowl until sugar dissolves, then stir in ⅓ cup rum. Place bottom slice of cake on a serving platter, brush with ¼ of the rum mixture, and mask with ⅓ of the pastry cream. Repeat this procedure twice, using up all of the cream, then cover dessert with the final slice of cake and brush with the last of the rum mixture. Cover cake with an inverted bowl or cake cover and refrigerate for at least 3 hours—12 to 24 hours is better—to firm the cake and allow the flavors to blend.

Just before serving, turn heavy cream into a 2-quart bowl and, referring if necessary to the recipe on page 857, whip until stiff, adding ¼ cup confectioner's sugar and 2 tablespoons rum. Pipe cream decoratively over top and sides of cake using a pastry bag fitted with a ½-inch star tip, or simply spread cream over the cake using a spatula. Decorate the cake with toasted nuts or whatever else sounds good to you and sprinkle lightly with additional confectioner's sugar to give the cake a snowy appearance. Serve immediately.

Variation: SPONGE ROLL CAKE

Makes one 10-inch roll cake serving 8 to 10

❦*Roll cakes are fun both to eat and to make, and may be filled with almost anything that strikes your fancy. Filling and frosting suggestions, some of them simple and some quite elaborate, appear immediately following the recipe.*

PRELIMINARIES

1. Set rack in center of oven.
2. Preheat oven to 325°F 20 minutes before baking.
3. Select a 15×10×½-inch jelly roll pan. Grease the pan thoroughly, using 1½ tablespoons vegetable shortening. Cut a sheet of waxed paper about 17 inches long, fit it into the bottom of the pan, and run your index finger all around the sides and corners to make paper fit snugly. Use scissors to trim paper so that it overhangs the edges of the pan by about ½ inch on all sides. Grease the waxed paper lining with an additional tablespoon of vegetable shortening, then sprinkle with 2 tablespoons flour, shake the pan to distribute flour evenly, then invert over the kitchen sink and tap excess flour out.

Batter for ***Sponge Cake***
⅓ cup confectioner's sugar in a sieve or shaker
Filling and additional confectioner's sugar or frosting (see pages 836–37)

Prepare sponge cake batter and pour into prepared pan, gently spreading as evenly as possible with rubber spatula and running batter up to the sides of the pan. Bake 10 to 12 minutes, or just until cake springs back when pressed with a finger. The cake will not brown. Do not overbake, or the cake will dry out and crack or crumble when you try to roll it.

Let baked cake rest exactly 3 minutes in pan. Sift a thin, even layer of confectioner's sugar on top. Place a lightweight dish towel (not a terry cloth dish towel) next to the cake and pan and flip pan over, as though it were a page in a book, so that cake unmolds upside down onto the towel. Slowly peel off the waxed paper liner, being careful not to tear the cake. If necessary, use a rubber spatula to help separate cake from paper (1). (A small rip or two will be hidden by confectioner's sugar or frosting.) Sprinkle exposed surface of cake evenly with confectioner's sugar. Starting at a short end of the cake, fold the end of the towel over the cake, then gently roll the cake up inside the towel (2). You must roll the cake while it is hot and soft; it will crack if rolled when cold. Let cake stand until completely cooled, about 1 hour.

To fill, unroll cake, spread evenly with the filling, and roll up again, gently separating cake from the towel (3) (4). (Use a knife or frosting spatula if necessary.) Pat cake into shape and cut off any uneven edges with a serrated knife. Transfer to serving platter by sliding a rimless cookie sheet underneath cake and using it like a giant spatula. Sprinkle with additional confectioner's sugar or frost (5).

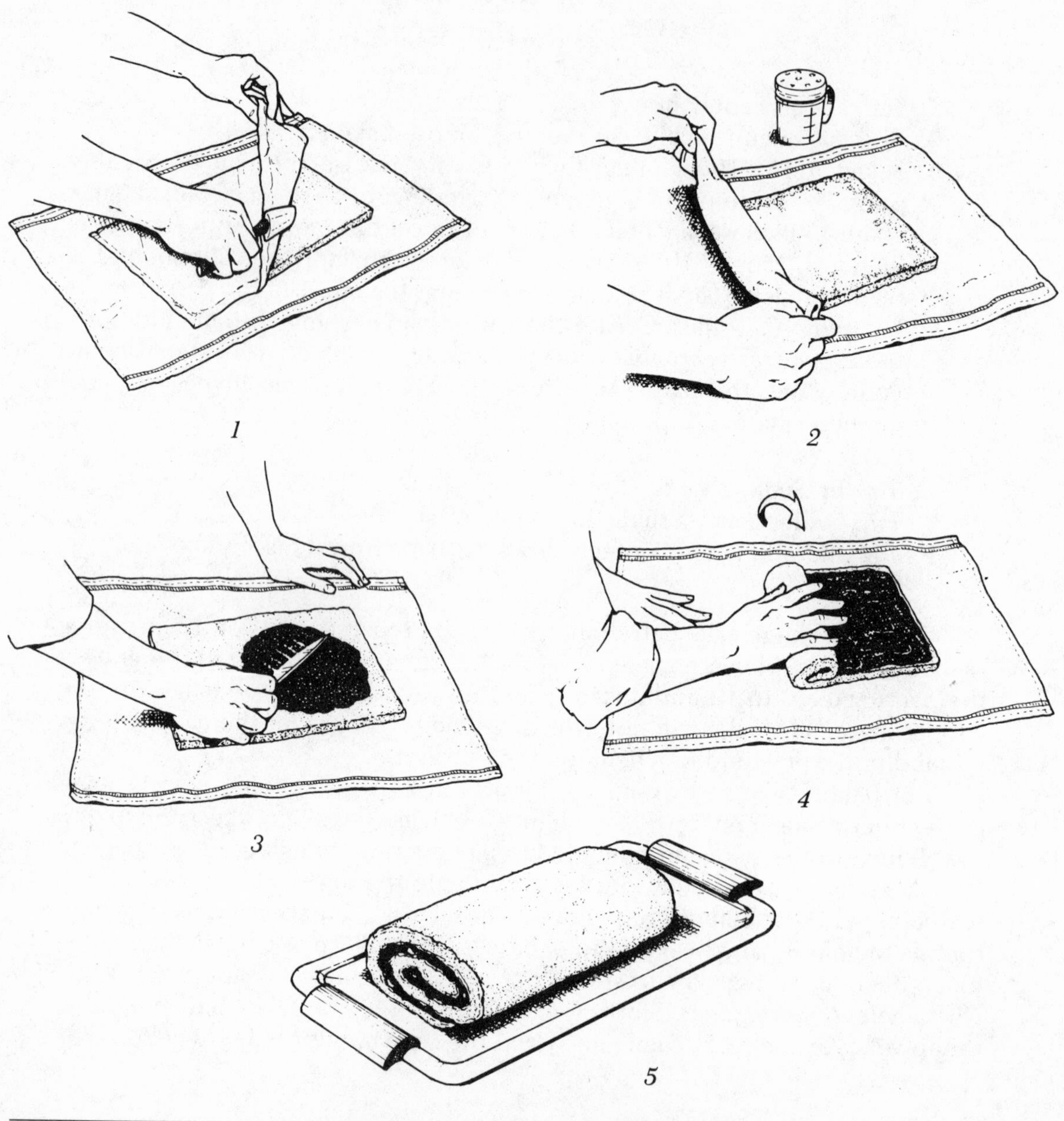

1 *2* *3* *4* *5*

- *Jelly roll:* Melt 1 cup raspberry, strawberry, or currant jelly over low heat. Remove from heat and set aside until the jelly has cooled to tepid and is on the verge of resetting. Immediately spread jelly evenly over cake and roll up. Dust liberally with confectioner's sugar.
- *Lemon or orange sponge roll:* Spread cake with lemon-butter cake filling, page 853, or the orange-flavored variation on page 854. Roll up and dust liberally with confectioner's sugar.
- *Cream sponge roll:* Spread cake with pastry cream, page 855, and roll up. Refrigerate for several hours or overnight and serve cold, dusting liberally with confectioner's sugar just before serving.
- *Pineapple Whipped Cream Roll:* Referring, if necessary, to the recipe on page 857, whip ⅔ cup heavy cream until fairly stiff, adding 2 tablespoons confectioner's sugar and ¼ teaspoon vanilla extract. Gently fold in ⅔ cup very thoroughly drained canned crushed pineapple. Spread mixture over cake and roll up. Serve immediately, dusting the top liberally with confectioner's sugar.
- *Bûche de Noël (Christmas log cake):* This cake is a lot of fun to make and serve, and it never fails to impress and please your guests. Classic recipes call for toadstools made out of meringue and "moss" confected of green-tinted spun sugar as decorations—so be as elaborate in setting the scene as you have the time or inclination to be.

  Prepare whipped chocolate filling, page 852, and ½ recipe of Meringue butter cream, page 844. Beat into the meringue butter cream ¾ cup cocoa (sieved or sifted if lumpy) after the last of the butter has gone in.

  To assemble cake, spread the roll with the whipped chocolate filling and roll up. Cut a 2-inch slice, slightly on the bias, from one end of the roll and set aside—this is to be stuck onto the top of the log in simulation of a branch stump. Transfer cake to a serving platter, using a rimless baking sheet as a giant spatula.

  Next, frost the top and sides only with the cocoa-flavored meringue butter cream (not the ends, whose "rings" you want to be visible). Attach the sliced-off "branch" asymmetrically to the top of the cake and frost the sides of the "branch" as well. You now have a log, complete with cut-off "branch," butter cream "bark" (striate "bark" with a knife for added verisimilitude), and "age rings" where the interior "wood" is exposed. Decorate the platter with sprigs of holly and dust both cake and holly very lightly with confectioner's sugar "snow." Invite the elves and gnomes and serve by starlight.

ANGEL FOOD CAKE

Makes one 10-inch cake serving 12

❦ *This is a classic American cake that summons forth images of county fair bake-offs, weekend evening picnics, and refined ladies' luncheons of former times. It can be split horizontally into 3 layers and filled and frosted with meringue frosting, but more usually it is left plain and served with warm or chilled custard sauce, warm chocolate sauce, berry sauce, or sliced and lightly sugared fresh berries or peaches. In addition to being delicious and versatile, angel cake provides an excellent means of using up egg whites that you have been storing in your freezer.*

CAUTIONARY NOTES: Angel cakes apparently give some bakers a great deal of trouble. I suspect that the two usual reasons for angel cake disasters are careless handling of the all-important egg whites and—I have done this myself—overbaking the cake. Since egg whites are such a crucial component, you might do well to read through the tips on beating and folding egg whites that start on page 133. Read also the cake-baking tips starting on page 802, and, if you wish to fill and/or frost the cake, the notes beginning on page 804.

CAKE PAN AND RECIPE-DECREASING NOTES: An angel cake will not rise properly unless it is baked in a tube pan. You may decrease this recipe by half—simply use a half measure of all the ingredients called for—and bake the cake in an 8- to 10-cup tube pan; the pan should be plain rather than fancy and fluted, or the cake will stick.

PRELIMINARIES

1. Bring all ingredients, particularly egg whites, to room temperature. Egg whites will not mount properly if chilled.
2. Set rack in middle or lower-middle level of oven.
3. Preheat oven to 325°F 20 minutes before baking.
4. Select a tube pan measuring about 10 inches across, with a capacity of about 16 cups. (A 2-piece tube pan—that is, a pan whose rim and bottom can be detached—makes for easier unmolding, but it is not essential.) *Do not grease the pan,* and be sure the pan is completely clean. An angel cake will not rise in the presence of grease.

STEP 1: PREPARING THE DRY INGREDIENTS

¾ cup unsifted cake flour (measure by scooping cup into large container of flour and sweeping off excess with the back of a knife)
½ cup sugar

Measure flour into sifter or sieve; add sugar. Sift onto waxed paper. Set sifter or sieve on a plate and return the dry ingredients to it. Set aside.

STEP 2: BEATING EGG WHITES; COMPLETING THE BATTER

1½ cups egg whites (about 12 large)
1 teaspoon vanilla extract
1 teaspoon almond extract
1½ teaspoons cream of tartar
½ teaspoon salt
1 cup sugar

With an electric mixer set at low speed, beat egg whites with vanilla and almond extracts in a 5- to 6-quart glass or stainless steel mixing bowl for about 1 minute, or until they have become a loose, foamy mass. Add cream of tartar and salt and increase mixer speed to medium. Pushing beaters aggressively through the egg whites (or moving the bowl of a stationary mixer around under the beaters), beat egg whites until they are frothy and stand in soft peaks. Increase mixer speed to high and add the 1 cup sugar gradually, taking about 1 minute to pour all of it in. Continue to beat egg whites for 10 to 30 seconds after the last of the sugar has gone in, or just long enough for the whites to look thick and glossy, like shaving lather. Do *not* overbeat the whites and make them dry. As soon as the beaters form deep furrows and the whites seem to shrink back, stop.

Sift dry ingredients from Step 1 ⅓ at a time over the egg whites, folding in each addition before sifting on the next. Do not overfold, or you will deflate the egg whites.

STEP 3: BAKING AND COOLING CAKE

Pour batter into ungreased tube pan. Smooth the top with a rubber spatula and gently shake the pan back and forth several times to settle the batter into the corners. Bake about 45 minutes, or until top of cake is brown and covered with cracks and the cake has shrunk slightly from around the central tube. *Do not overbake angel cake or it will toughen, deflate, and shrink,* just like an overdone soufflé.

After removing cake from the oven, place the hole in the center of the pan over the neck of a bottle and let the cake hang upside down until completely cooled. (If the rim of your pan has built-in feet to keep the cake elevated, you need not use the bottle; simply invert the pan over a heat-proof surface.) To unmold, run a long knife around inside of pan and around the tube. Rap the pan sharply against the countertop two or three times to loosen the cake from the bottom, then invert cake onto a serving plate; it should drop out at once.

STORAGE: Wrapped in an airtight plastic bag, angel cake will keep for 2 or 3 days at room temperature. Freezing makes the cake rubbery, but stale slices of angel cake may be toasted and/or served with warm custard sauce.

GINGERBREAD

Makes one 8-inch square, one 9-inch round, or one 9×7-inch cake serving 8

❦ *This is a gingerbread for adults—spicy, rich, and not too sweet. Serve it warm, with unsweetened whipped cream on top.*

PRELIMINARIES

1. Set rack in middle or upper-middle level of oven.
2. Preheat oven to 350°F 20 minutes before baking.
3. Select an 8×2-inch square pan, a 9×7×1½-inch rectangular pan, or a 9×2-inch round pan. Grease with 1 tablespoon soft butter or vegetable shortening.

½ cup molasses
⅓ cup sugar
8 tablespoons butter (1 stick), cut into pats
1 cup boiling water
1 large egg
1¾ cups unbleached all-purpose flour (measure by scooping cup into large container of flour and sweeping off excess with the back of a knife)
1 to 2 tablespoons ground ginger (the larger amount will make the cake quite spicy)
1 teaspoon cinnamon
½ teaspoon nutmeg, preferably freshly grated, or ground mace
¼ teaspoon ground cloves or allspice
1 teaspoon baking soda

Place molasses, sugar, and butter in a 3-quart mixing bowl. Cover with boiling water and stir until butter melts. Add egg and beat until all ingredients are thoroughly blended. Combine flour, spices, and baking soda in a small bowl, mix well, and then add to the molasses mixture, beating until batter is smooth.

Pour batter into prepared pan and bake for about 35 minutes, or until cake tester comes out clean when inserted in the center. Cake will be cracked around the edges and domed in the center. Let cool about 10 minutes in the pan, then unmold onto a plate. Serve while still warm with unsweetened whipped cream.

THE FINISHING TOUCH:

CAKE FILLINGS and FROSTINGS, PASTRY CREAMS, and DESSERT SAUCES

It is often the icing on a cake—or the filling in a pastry, or the sauce accompanying a custard or fruit dessert—that gives the dessert the finishing touch of glory. This being the case, try to divide the making of the dessert base (the cake, pastry shell, and so on) and the preparation of the filling, frosting, or sauce into two separate stages, allowing an ample rest period in between for rest and contemplation. You may decide—as I frequently do—that you would rather use some other filling, frosting, or sauce than you had originally planned, or that a different serving platter is in order, or that you would like to make fancy decorations by piping whipped cream or part of the frosting through a pastry bag or by adorning the dessert with crushed hard candies, grated chocolate or coconut, toasted nuts, or what have you.

MASTER RECIPE

Meringue Frosting (Boiled Icing) and Meringue Butter Cream

Makes about 5½ cups frosting or about 4 cups butter cream, enough to fill and frost a 9-inch 3-layer cake

❦ *Meringue frosting, also known as boiled icing when flavored with vanilla, is made by whipping hot sugar syrup into stiffly beaten egg whites. It is fluffy and smooth on the tongue, with a texture akin to soft marshmallows, and, at least as made here, it is considerably less sweet than standard cake frostings based on confectioner's sugar. A versatile confection, meringue frosting can be combined with soft butter to make a smooth, light butter cream of the type used in fancy European pastries such as* bûche de Noël. *It can also be made with maple syrup or brown sugar instead of with granulated sugar, to produce excellent maple- and toffee-flavored fluffy frostings and butter creams.*

TIP: Meringue frosting and its maple and toffee variations can be turned into delectable soft ice creams. Prepare frosting as indicated in the recipe, then fold in 1½ cups heavy cream, lightly whipped, and about 1 cup chopped pecans, walnuts, toasted almonds, or skinned hazelnuts. Turn into a 2-quart container, cover, and freeze until set (about 6 hours at 0°F)—or spread over and between sponge cake layers and freeze to make an ice cream cake.

RESCUING BOILED ICING THAT IS TOO THICK OR TOO THIN: An unspreadably thick frosting, resulting from overcooked sugar syrup, is easy to rescue. Simply beat in boiling water ¼ teaspoon at a time until the frosting is the proper consistency.

A thin, runny frosting is caused by undercooking the sugar syrup. To rescue, scoop the frosting into the top of a large double boiler and beat over gently simmering water until the frosting forms moderately stiff peaks; this may take 5 minutes or longer. Remove from heat and continue to beat until cooled and thickened.

DECREASING THE MERINGUE FROSTING RECIPE

Some of the recipes in this book require only ⅔ of a recipe of meringue frosting, or enough to frost the top and sides of—but not to fill—a 9-inch 3-layer cake. Other cake recipes require just a half recipe of meringue butter cream frosting, or enough to fill—but not to frost—the cake. The chart below gives the proportions of ingredients for ⅔ recipes and half recipes.

	1 RECIPE	⅔ RECIPE	½ RECIPE
Egg whites	4	3	2
Cream of tartar	¼ teaspoon	Scant ¼ teaspoon	⅛ teaspoon
Salt	Pinch	Pinch	Small pinch
Sugar	1½ cups	1 cup	¾ cup
Water	½ cup	⅓ cup	¼ cup
Vanilla	1 teaspoon	¾ teaspoon	½ teaspoon
For Meringue Butter Cream:			
Butter	2½ to 3 sticks (20 to 24 tablespoons)	1¾ to 2 sticks (14 to 16 tablespoons)	1¼ to 1½ sticks (10 to 12 tablespoons)
Vanilla	1 teaspoon	¾ teaspoon	½ teaspoon

4 large egg whites, absolutely free of grease or egg yolk, at room temperature
1/4 teaspoon cream of tartar
Salt
1 1/2 cups sugar
1/2 cup water
1 teaspoon vanilla extract

SPECIAL EQUIPMENT: A candy thermometer (optional but recommended)

Turn egg whites into a 4-quart heat-proof mixing bowl (do not use a plastic bowl) and beat with an electric mixer set at low speed until whites are loose and foamy. Add cream of tartar and a pinch of salt and switch mixer to medium speed. Beat whites until they form soft peaks, then switch to high speed and beat whites until they are thick and glossy and stand in stiff peaks. Set aside.

Immediately place sugar in 1 1/2- to 2-quart heavy-bottomed saucepan and add 1/2 cup water. Set over moderate heat, grasp pan by the handle, and swirl gently so that the sugar solution rotates in a slow wave inside the wall of the pan. When the mixture reaches a full boil and changes from a cloudy solution to a transparent syrup, raise heat to high, clamp on a tight-fitting lid, and let syrup boil undisturbed for 1 minute. Uncover the saucepan. If you are using one, clip a candy thermometer to the side of the pan, being sure that the stem does not touch the bottom of the pan; if necessary hold the saucepan at a tilt over the heating element in order to pool enough syrup around the thermometer stem to get an accurate reading. Boil syrup for about 2 minutes longer, or until it reaches a temperature of 238°F.

(Lacking a candy thermometer, you can test the syrup the old-fashioned way, which is inevitably a bit risky. As soon as the syrup thickens and the bubbles seem to shrink, begin dropping 1/8-teaspoonfuls of the syrup into a bowl of ice water. When the proper temperature has been reached, the little dabs of syrup will immediately clot, when the syrup hits the water, into soft shapeless balls that can be picked up and manipulated with the fingers.)

Immediately begin beating the thick, glossy egg whites with the mixer set at high speed, while at the same time pouring the hot syrup in a thin, steady stream directly in the path of the beaters. Do not take longer than 10 or 15 seconds to drain all the syrup from the saucepan. Beat the meringue mixture for 5 to 7 minutes, or until it has cooled to room temperature and become nearly as thick as marshmallow. Add 1 teaspoon vanilla and beat until blended in. Taste and add a bit more vanilla if needed (but only if the frosting is thick enough to withstand additional liquid) plus, perhaps, a tiny pinch or two of salt.

The meringue frosting is now ready to be spread on a cake or turned into meringue butter cream (see Step 2).

Ahead of Time: Since it is apt to crust over and turn grainy, especially in humid weather, the frosting is best used at once. However, it may be set aside at room temperature for several hours. Scrape the sides of the bowl with a rubber spatula and press a sheet of plastic wrap directly on the surface of the frosting. (Frosted cake should likewise be served promptly, preferably within 3 hours, to prevent crusting; however, it may be stored at room temperature for several days under an inverted bowl or cake cover.)

Step 2: Preparing Meringue Butter Cream (Optional)

20 to 24 tablespoons (2 1/2 to 3 sticks) unsalted butter, softened but still firm and slightly chilled
About 1 teaspoon vanilla extract
Salt, if needed

With mixer set at medium-high speed, beat butter into the thoroughly cooled meringue frosting 2 tablespoons at a time, waiting for one dollop to be smoothly blended in before adding the next. At first the meringue will deflate and thin out, but as more butter is added it will thicken and gain body. By the time you have added 2½ sticks of butter, the mixture should have become stiff enough to spread. If not, set the bottom of the bowl in cold water and beat in additional butter 1 tablespoon at a time until the butter cream reaches spreading consistency. (Take care not to add too much butter or over-beat the frosting; if you do either, the mixture will become too stiff and will deflate.)

Beat in about 1 teaspoon vanilla and, if needed, a little salt. The butter cream will likely have a dull sheen and look a bit grainy, indicating that the butter is still cold and has not been completely absorbed. Set aside at room temperature for 5 to 15 minutes, gently beating several times. As soon as the butter cream looks soft, glistening, and perfectly smooth, it is ready to spread.

AHEAD OF TIME: Unless the weather is hot, the butter cream may be set aside at room temperature for several hours, a sheet of plastic wrap pressed directly on the surface. The butter cream may also be stored in a covered container in the refrigerator for 2 days, but you must not touch it until it has returned to room temperature and become soft and glistening, or it will turn soupy. (Frosted cake should be stored in the refrigerator, under an inverted bowl; bring to room temperature before serving.)

Variation: MAPLE FROSTING AND MAPLE MERINGUE BUTTER CREAM

Makes about 5½ cups frosting or about 4 cups butter cream, enough to fill and frost a 9-inch 3-layer cake

Meringue Frosting (Boiled Icing) and Meringue Butter Cream

SUBSTITUTE: 2 cups pure maple syrup for sugar and water
Salt for vanilla extract

Proceed according to the Master Recipe, but substitute maple syrup for sugar and water and boil the syrup, uncovered, until it reaches a temperature of 230°F on the candy thermometer (or spins a 2½-inch thread when dropped from a spoon), stirring it down or lowering the heat slightly if it threatens to bubble over the lip of the pan. In making either maple frosting or maple butter cream, replace the vanilla indicated in the Master Recipe with pinches of salt.

Variation: TOFFEE FROSTING (SEAFOAM ICING) AND TOFFEE MERINGUE BUTTER CREAM

Makes about 5½ cups frosting or about 4 cups butter cream, enough to fill and frost a 9-inch 3-layer cake

❦ *No one would be likely to guess that the major flavoring ingredient in these delightful toffee-flavored confections is simple brown sugar.*

Meringue Frosting (Boiled Icing) and Meringue Butter Cream
SUBSTITUTE: 1½ cups packed dark brown sugar for granulated sugar

Proceed according to the Master Recipe, but substitute dark brown sugar for granulated sugar and make the following modifications. Swirl the pan gently until the syrup reaches the boil—the syrup will not clarify—and boil the syrup, uncovered, over moderate heat until it reaches 238°F on the candy thermometer (or forms a soft ball). Stir the syrup down if it threatens to overflow the saucepan.

MASTER RECIPE

Butter Cream Frosting

Makes about 3½ cups, enough to fill and frost a 9-inch 3-layer cake

❦ *Made with confectioner's sugar, this is the standard American type of butter cream frosting. Debased versions of this frosting have given it a bad name. However, if made with top-quality, very fresh unsalted butter and if beaten thoroughly, so as to become light and fluffy, this confection melts on the tongue.*

DECREASING THE RECIPE: In preparing cakes that require only a ⅔ recipe of butter cream, use the following proportions:

11 tablespoons butter (1 stick plus 3 tablespoons)
1 egg yolk
⅛ teaspoon salt
2⅔ cups confectioner's sugar
½ teaspoon vanilla extract
1 tablespoon plus 1 to 2 teaspoons milk

16 tablespoons (2 sticks) unsalted butter, at room temperature
2 large egg yolks
Scant 1/4 teaspoon salt
1 pound (4 cups) confectioner's sugar (if you are not using a single 1-pound box, measure out 4 cups by spooning unsifted sugar into cup until overflowing, then tapping sharply several times and leveling off excess with the back of a knife)
3/4 to 1 teaspoon vanilla extract
2 to 2 1/2 tablespoons cold milk

Sieve or sift the sugar if it is lumpy. Place butter, egg yolks, salt, and 1 cup of the sugar in a deep 4-quart mixing bowl and beat at high speed with an electric mixer for about 3 minutes, or until the mixture is very fluffy and almost white. Add 3/4 teaspoon vanilla and a second cup of sugar and beat 30 seconds longer. Add 1 tablespoon of the milk and a third cup of sugar; beat 30 seconds more. Add a second tablespoon milk and all remaining sugar and beat 1 minute. Taste and add a bit more vanilla, by drops, if needed. If the frosting is too thick, beat in a bit more milk.

AHEAD OF TIME: Butter cream frosting is best if used at once, but it may be refrigerated or frozen. Turn into a storage container, press a sheet of plastic wrap directly on the surface, and seal tightly; refrigerate for up to 3 days or freeze up to 1 month. Bring frosting to room temperature before beating or using; otherwise it will deflate, thin out, and become slick and pasty.

Variation: CHOCOLATE BUTTER CREAM FROSTING

Makes about 3 1/2 cups, enough to fill and frost a 9-inch 3-layer cake

❦ *This is an exceptionally dark and chocolaty version of the favorite butter cream. If preparing 2/3 recipe, use 5 1/2 ounces chocolate.*

Butter Cream Frosting
ADD: 8 ounces (8 squares) unsweetened baking chocolate

Chop or grate chocolate, then melt it in a heat-proof bowl set in a pan of almost-simmering water or in the top of a double boiler over very gently simmering water. Remove from heat and let cool to tepid.

Prepare frosting according to the Master Recipe, add the cooled chocolate, and beat until smooth.

Variation: LEMON BUTTER CREAM FROSTING

Makes about 3½ cups, enough to fill and frost a 9-inch 3-layer cake

Butter Cream Frosting

ADD: The grated zest of 1 large lemon
SUBSTITUTE: ¾ to 1 teaspoon strained fresh lemon juice for vanilla

Proceed according to the Master Recipe, but add grated zest along with the salt and use lemon juice in place of vanilla.

Variation: MOCHA BUTTER CREAM FROSTING

Makes about 3½ cups, enough to fill and frost a 9-inch 3-layer cake

Butter Cream Frosting

ADD: 1 tablespoon instant espresso or instant coffee
DECREASE: Vanilla to ¼ teaspoon
ADD: 1½ tablespoons cocoa, sieved or sifted if lumpy

Mix the 2½ tablespoons milk called for in the Master Recipe with coffee powder, stirring until coffee dissolves. Proceed according to the Master Recipe, using the coffee-flavored milk in place of regular milk, decreasing the vanilla, and adding cocoa with the last of the sugar.

Variation: ORANGE BUTTER CREAM FROSTING

Makes about 3½ cups, enough to fill and frost a 9-inch 3-layer cake

Butter Cream Frosting

ADD: The grated zest of 1 large orange
DECREASE: Vanilla to ¼ teaspoon
SUBSTITUTE: 2 to 2½ tablespoons strained orange juice for milk

Proceed according to the Master Recipe, but add grated zest along with the salt, decrease vanilla, and substitute orange juice for milk.

MASTER RECIPE

Chocolate Glaze

Makes about 1 cup, enough to glaze the top and sides of a 9-inch cake

This deliciously bittersweet chocolate glaze becomes a fluffy, rich filling when whipped or an irresistible chocolate sauce when thinned with coffee. This is one instance where you really must use good-quality semisweet chocolate, either semisweet baking chocolate or, better, a fine imported eating chocolate. Don't settle for chocolate chips, which are loaded with thickeners and emulsifiers, and don't buy any brand of eating chocolate, either imported or domestic, that contains artificial vanilla flavoring, which has an unpleasant and overpowering fragrance.

4 ounces semisweet chocolate
1 ounce (1 square) unsweetened baking chocolate
½ cup heavy cream
2 tablespoons freshly brewed, very strong coffee

Chop or break up both kinds of chocolate and combine with cream in 1½-quart heavy-bottomed saucepan. Place over moderate heat and, stirring constantly with a wooden spoon or spatula, bring mixture to a full boil. It may look lumpy, oily, and separated at this point. Remove from heat and add the coffee 1 tablespoon at a time, beating with a whip until the glaze is satiny smooth. (If mixture remains oily-looking after the last of the coffee has been added, set bottom of saucepan in a sink or large bowl filled with cold water and beat the mixture with the whip just until it recombines.) Let glaze cool to tepid, or until thickened but still pourable, then use as directed in the recipes. Should glaze solidify before you have a chance to use it, simply stir over low heat until reliquefied.

STORAGE: Glaze can be refrigerated in a tightly covered container for 1 week. Reheat over very low flame, stirring.

Variation: WHIPPED CHOCOLATE FILLING

Makes about 2 cups, enough to fill a 9-inch cake

❦ *This is* ganache soufflée, *one of the most widely used of all chocolate cake and pastry fillings. When you taste it, you'll know why.*

Chocolate Glaze

Turn chocolate glaze from the Master Recipe into a 2-quart mixing bowl and refrigerate for about 30 minutes, or until it is very thick and feels cool to the touch when you put your finger into it. (If the mixture becomes too cool and solidifies, let it stand at room temperature until softened.)

Using electric mixer set at medium speed, or a wire whip, beat chocolate for 2 to 3 minutes, or until it nearly doubles in volume and becomes fluffy and mocha-colored. Do not overbeat, or the cream will turn to butter and the filling will be hard and grainy.

If not used at once, the filling may be covered and set aside at room temperature for 30 minutes.

Variation: CHOCOLATE SAUCE

Makes about 1¼ cups

Chocolate Glaze
INCREASE: Coffee to 5 to 6 tablespoons

Prepare chocolate glaze according to the Master Recipe, then stir in enough additional coffee to make a liquid sauce; bear in mind that the sauce will thicken as it cools. Serve warm.

SOUR CREAM CHOCOLATE FROSTING

Makes about 3½ cups, enough to fill and frost a 9-inch 3-layer cake

❦ *No frosting could be easier to make than this one.*

20 ounces (20 squares) semisweet baking chocolate
1½ cups sour cream
½ teaspoon vanilla extract
⅛ teaspoon salt

Chop or grate chocolate, then melt it in a heat-proof 3-quart mixing bowl set in a pan of almost-simmering water or in the top of a large double boiler set over very gently simmering water. Remove from heat, add sour cream, vanilla, and salt, and beat with a wire whip until frosting is glistening and smooth. If too soft to spread, refrigerate for 5 to 10 minutes, beating several times, but be careful not to refrigerate too long, or frosting will become very thick and difficult to work with. Store frosted cake in the refrigerator, under an inverted bowl or cake cover, but bring to room temperature before serving.

MASTER RECIPE

Lemon-butter Cake Filling

Makes about 1½ cups, enough to fill a 9-inch 3-layer cake

This smooth, rich, piquantly lemony custard and its variations are among the traditional cake fillings that have given the American layer cake its proud reputation.

6 large egg yolks
⅓ cup strained fresh lemon juice
8 tablespoons (1 stick) butter, softened
1 cup sugar
2 teaspoons cornstarch
Generous pinch salt

Combine all ingredients in a heavy-bottomed 1½-quart saucepan and beat with a wire whip until fairly smooth. Place over low heat and, beating constantly with the whip, bring just to the simmer, at which point the filling will thicken. Immediately set the bottom of the saucepan in cold water and continue to beat the filling until cool and thick enough to spread.

AHEAD OF TIME: To refrigerate filling (for up to 3 days), turn into a storage container, press a sheet of plastic wrap directly on the surface, and cover. Bring to room temperature, beating occasionally, before using.

Variation: ORANGE-BUTTER CAKE FILLING

Makes about 1½ cups, or enough to fill a 9-inch 3-layer cake

Lemon-butter Cake Filling
SUBSTITUTE: ⅓ cup strained orange juice for lemon juice

Proceed according to the Master Recipe, substituting orange juice for lemon juice.

Variation: PECAN-RAISIN CAKE FILLING

Makes about 2 cups, enough to fill a 9-inch 3-layer cake

Lemon-butter Cake Filling
SUBSTITUTE: ⅓ cup bourbon for lemon juice
ADD: ½ cup (about 2 ounces) pecans, chopped coarse
ADD: ⅓ cup coarsely chopped raisins

Proceed according to the Master Recipe, substituting bourbon for lemon juice and beating pecans and raisins into the cooled and thickened filling.

Variation: RUM-BUTTER OR BRANDY-BUTTER CAKE FILLING

Makes about 1½ cups, enough to fill a 9-inch 3-layer cake

Lemon-butter Cake Filling
SUBSTITUTE: ⅓ cup dark rum, preferably Jamaican, or brandy for lemon juice

Proceed according to the Master Recipe, substituting rum or brandy for lemon juice.

MASTER RECIPE

Pastry Cream

Makes about 2 cups

❦*This egg-rich, lightly sweetened custard filling may be spread between cake layers, piped into cream puff shells, spooned over the bottom of a pie shell to make a fresh fruit tart, or used as a filling for dessert crêpes. Its uses are limited only by the bounds of your imagination. The custard may be flavored in a number of different ways as outlined in various recipes throughout this book, and, by omitting the flour and following a slightly modified procedure, you can transform this Master Recipe into a delicious dessert custard sauce.*

1½ cups milk
4 large egg yolks
½ cup sugar
⅓ cup all-purpose flour
1 tablespoon butter
1 tablespoon vanilla extract

Pour milk into heavy-bottomed 1½- to 2-quart saucepan and set over low heat. Combine egg yolks and sugar in 3-quart mixing bowl and beat with electric mixer or wire whip for 4 to 5 minutes, or until the mixture turns a pale yellow and becomes very thick and heavy. Now beat in the flour. When milk is on the verge of simmering—bubbles will form around inside of pan and a skin will form on top—pour it a few tablespoons at a time into egg yolk mixture, beating constantly. When about half the milk has gone in, add the remainder in two or three pours.

Pour mixture into the saucepan you used to warm the milk and set over a moderate flame. Beating constantly with the whip, cook the mixture until it becomes thick and lumpy; remove from the heat, scrape corners of the saucepan with a rubber spatula, and beat the custard hard to smooth it out. Return to heat and, beating constantly, simmer over moderate heat for 3 minutes.

Remove custard from heat, add butter and vanilla, and beat for about a minute, or until it looks smooth and glistening, like very thick mayonnaise. Dot custard with bits of butter or lay a sheet of plastic wrap directly on the surface to prevent a skin from forming on top. Set aside until cooled to room temperature before using in a recipe.

STORAGE: Turn custard into a storage container, lay plastic wrap directly on top, cover tightly, and refrigerate. The custard will keep for 3 or 4 days. It tends to become a bit grainy when frozen and thawed, but you can correct the problem by beating the thawed custard hard or whirring it in a blender.

Variation: CUSTARD SAUCE

Makes about 2 cups

❦*Known in some parts of this country as stirred custard, and called* crème anglaise *or "English cream" by the French, custard sauce may be served with a dessert soufflé, poached fruit (try pears), cake, or a Bavarian cream.*

TIP: Custard sauce is the basis for my favorite eggnog. To make eggnog, simply omit the butter, substitute the grated zests of half a lemon and half an orange and 1/4 teaspoon freshly grated nutmeg for the vanilla called for in the recipe, and stir about 3/4 cup light cream into the cooked custard. Cover and let stand in the refrigerator for a day or two to allow the flavors to blend, then strain (to remove the zests) into a pitcher (or, if you increase the recipe, a punch bowl). Pass with bourbon or dark rum plus whole nutmegs and a nutmeg grater.

CAUTIONARY NOTE: Custard sauce contains exactly the same ingredients as pastry cream, except that it is made without flour. Thus, while pastry cream requires boiling to cook the flour, custard sauce is heated just enough to thicken the egg yolks. If the sauce is overheated—that is, if it is brought near to simmering—the egg yolks, unprotected by flour or other starch, will scramble and the sauce will be lumpy.

RESCUING OVERHEATED SAUCE: If the lumps are soft and just beginning to form, simply immerse the bottom of the pan—at once—in cold water and beat the sauce hard. It should smooth out.

If the custard has been brought near to boiling and large, hard lumps have formed, beating will not help. Instead, strain the sauce, beat in 2 fresh egg yolks and 2 tablespoons sugar, and carefully reheat the sauce to thicken the newly added yolks.

Pastry Cream
OMIT: Flour

Make the initial custard mixture as outlined in the Master Recipe; beat yolks and sugar until thick and then, omitting the flour called for in the Master Recipe, gradually beat in hot milk.

To cook the custard sauce, proceed as follows. Have ready a bowl filled with very cold water (or fill the sink with cold water) so that, if the custard becomes overheated, you can immediately place the bottom of the saucepan in the cold water and beat the custard to cool it off.

Set saucepan over low heat. Stirring continuously with a rubber spatula, and reaching to all parts of the bottom of the pan, heat custard sauce until it is about as thick as cold heavy cream and has enough body to coat the spatula fairly heavily. At this point, a candy thermometer will register 165°F and the custard will have just begun to steam. Do not cook the custard sauce beyond this point or it will become lumpy.

Briefly set bottom of saucepan in cold water and stir the custard until it has cooled slightly. Add 1 tablespoon butter if you wish and stir in vanilla. Serve the sauce at once or cover and chill.

STORAGE: Custard sauce may be kept in a covered container in the refrigerator for 3 or 4 days, but do not freeze it. The safest way to warm a chilled custard sauce is by turning it into a saucepan or heat-proof bowl and setting it into a skillet filled with almost-simmering water. Stir the custard until it warms through.

WHIPPED CREAM

Makes about 2½ cups

❦ *Essential both as an ingredient in and an accompaniment to many desserts as well as a few savory dishes, whipped cream is not difficult to make, and it is far superior to aerosol whipped toppings, which are largely water, sugar, and other nondairy ingredients. The most important thing to remember is that everything must be cold—the cream itself, the bowl and beating equipment, and, most crucially, the room you are working in; otherwise, the butterfat will liquefy and the cream will refuse to mount, instead remaining soupy and then finally curdling as it is beaten. Cream can be whipped without special precautions at normal room temperature, that is, around 70°F. But if the temperature is nearing 75°F, the bowl should be set in a sink filled with cold water and a tray of ice cubes during whipping. As a beating implement, I much prefer a large wire whip, which, at a leisurely pace of about 2 strokes per second, whips cream in just 2 to 3 minutes. A hand-held mixer set at* low speed *can also be used, though it always produces a slightly grainy, heavy product. Do not use a stationary two-beater-type electric mixer, a blender, or a food processor, all of which fail to aerate cream properly.*

DECREASING AND INCREASING THE RECIPE: This recipe is for 1 cup cream. If the recipe you are working with calls for more or less cream, increase or decrease bowl size, sugar, flavorings, and, most importantly, beating times proportionately.

RESCUING OVERBEATEN WHIPPED CREAM: When you overbeat cream, the butterfat clots into largish grains and the liquid part of the cream separates from the fat. If this process has only just begun, it can be arrested by beating into the cream 3 to 4 tablespoons additional cold heavy cream or 2 tablespoons of cold milk. Beat only until the cream smooths out, and then serve at once. If the cream is seriously overwhipped and has taken on a curdled appearance, you might just as well make it into butter since whipped cream is now out of the question. Beat the failed cream hard for several minutes, or until it is clearly broken down into yellowish globs of fat floating in a watery liquid. Refrigerate for an hour or so, and then strain off the fat, discarding the liquid. The fat is butter.

CHOOSING CREAM FOR WHIPPING: Heavy cream, with a butterfat content of about 36 percent, works best; medium cream, about 25 percent fat, can also be used, though it produces watery and easily deflated whipped cream. Half-and-half (about 10 percent fat) and light cream (about 18 percent fat) will not whip.

Most of the heavy cream sold in supermarkets nowadays has been ultrapasteurized—that is, heated to a temperature higher than that used in ordinary pasteurization. This extends the shelf life of the cream to an incredible two or three months, but also destroys the nutlike savor of cream and imparts a cooked milk taste. If you shop around, you should be able to find a supermarket that stocks ordinary pasteurized heavy cream, much the better choice for whipping.

1 cup very cold heavy cream
3 tablespoons confectioner's sugar, sieved or sifted if lumpy (optional: for dessert whipped cream only)
½ teaspoon vanilla extract or 1½ tablespoons dark rum, brandy, or liqueur (optional: for dessert whipped cream only)

Choose a large (3- to 4-quart) bowl that is tall and deep (cream tends to splash during whipping), preferably made of metal, glass, or ceramic, which will take and hold a chill. Pour the cream into the bowl and set it, along with a large wire whip, in the freezer about 5 minutes before proceeding.

Using no more than 2 strokes per second and resting your arm briefly if necessary, beat the cream for about 2 minutes, or until it has become about as thick as stirred yogurt and has enough body to barely hold a soft shape on a spoon. If you are folding the cream into a recipe (mayonnaise, chiffon pie, cream pie, and so on) stop beating at this point; if beaten further, the cream will impart a buttery taste and a hard, butterlike texture to the dish it is being used in. If you are using the cream as a dessert filling or topping, add the confectioner's sugar and flavoring and continue to beat at 2 strokes per second for about 1 minute longer, or just until the cream is fluffy and stiff enough to hold a soft peak when dropped from a spoon. Should the cream begin to seem at all coarse or grainy, stop beating at once; you are on the verge of making butter.

STORING LEFTOVER WHIPPED CREAM: Whipped cream can be turned into a small sieve lined with a triple layer of cheesecloth, set over a bowl, covered with plastic wrap, and refrigerated for up to 24 hours. As it sits, it will drain into the bowl, becoming a bit dry and heavy, but, amazingly, it will stay whipped. For longer storage, drop mounds of whipped cream on a sheet of waxed paper, freeze solid, remove from the paper, and then store the frozen mounds in the freezer in a plastic bag. Arrange frozen mounds on top of your dessert, and allow to stand briefly until thawed.

CRÈME FRAÎCHE

Makes 1 to 1⅓ cups

❦ *Crème fraîche is made by introducing a bacterial culture into heavy cream, causing it to thicken and take on a tangy, slightly nutlike flavor. Richer and mellower than sour cream, crème fraîche is heavenly on berries and other fresh fruits and has a variety of other uses. It is expensive when bought at the store, but you can make your own by combining ordinary heavy cream, either pasteurized or ultrapasteurized, with sour cream or buttermilk and allowing the mixture to ferment. Crème fraîche made with sour cream has a somewhat lower butterfat content than heavy cream.*

1 cup heavy cream
⅓ cup sour cream or 1 tablespoon buttermilk

Combine cream and sour cream or buttermilk in a small storage container and blend thoroughly with a wire whip. Cover partially and set at room temperature, away from direct sunlight, for about 8 hours, or until nearly as thick as sour cream. Stir briefly, cover, and refrigerate.

STORAGE: Crème fraîche will keep in the refrigerator at least 10 days. (When all but a few tablespoons are used up, add 1 cup fresh cream, blend well, and let stand at room temperature until thickened, thus making a new batch of crème fraîche.)

BERRY SAUCE

Makes about 2 cups, serving 6 to 8

❦ *Berry sauce is one of my favorite dessert accompaniments—fresh-tasting and much lighter than either whipped cream or chocolate sauce. Luckily, it is a snap to make. Use fresh berries if possible; frozen berries, though, will do in a pinch.*

1 pint fresh strawberries, raspberries, or blackberries (or a 16-ounce box unsweetened frozen berries, thoroughly defrosted)
2 tablespoons fresh lemon juice
1⁄3 cup sugar

If necessary, quickly wash the berries; strawberries must be hulled.

Place fresh berries (or frozen berries with juice) in blender or food processor and purée thoroughly. With machine running, pour in lemon juice and then add sugar a little at a time. Continue to blend sauce at high speed for a minute or two after the last of the sugar has been added. The sauce will thicken and increase slightly in volume.

Strain sauce through a very fine sieve into a glass, ceramic, or stainless steel bowl, cover with plastic wrap, and chill for 2 to 5 hours before serving. Make the sauce on the same day you plan to serve it; it does not keep well.

PRALINE POWDER

Makes 1 to 1¼ cups

❦ *An indispensable ingredient in many kinds of cakes, pastries, and chilled desserts, praline powder is actually almond (or hazelnut) brittle, coarsely ground.*

TIP: To make peanut brittle candy, substitute skinned unsalted peanuts for almonds or hazelnuts, grinding 1⁄3 of the peanuts fine before adding them to the sugar syrup in order to make the brittle crunchy, rather than rock-hard. Add ¼ teaspoon salt to the sugar/water solution before cooking it.

3/4 cup blanched whole almonds (about 3½ ounces), lightly toasted, or
3/4 cup hazelnuts (about 3 ounces), skinned and toasted (see page 701)
3/4 cup sugar
3 tablespoons water

Lightly oil bottom and sides of a jelly roll pan or pizza pan. Have prepared nuts ready.

Place sugar in heavy-bottomed 1½-quart saucepan, pour water over it, and set over moderately high heat. Holding saucepan by the handle, swirl pan over the heat so that sugar solution rotates in a slow wave around the inside wall of the pan. When the solution comes to a full boil and becomes a completely clear syrup, cover tightly and boil hard for 2 minutes. Uncover and, swirling pan as before, cook the syrup until it thickens and then finally darkens—or caramelizes—to a deep amber color. Immediately stir in prepared nuts, then pour mixture into the prepared pan, tilting it in all directions to spread the mixture as thinly as possible. Let stand at room temperature until cooled, then break into pieces. Grind the pieces coarsely in a blender or food processor.

STORAGE: Placed in a tightly lidded container, nut brittle and praline powder may be stored at room temperature for several weeks or frozen for 3 months.

FRESH FRUITS and FRUIT DESSERTS

Modern techniques of producing, storing, and transporting fresh fruits have made more varieties available during a greater part of the year than was ever the case in the past. However, this abundance has exacted a price. Some fruits cannot easily withstand the new growing and handling procedures, so new and sturdier strains have been developed. But at least until quite recently, producers paid more attention to the prettiness of the new breeds than to their flavor.

Since the technology is here to stay, we might as well make the best of the fruits that we find at the market. In this spirit I offer in this chapter both tips on how to pick and choose the best fresh fruits and rescues for specimens that turn out to be less than topnotch. I have also given instructions on how to cook most fruits using one or more of the four Master Techniques that follow this introduction. Fruit desserts are delicious, and are among the simplest and quickest of all desserts to make, yet they are infrequently served; so it would be easy to become famous, at least among your friends, for your own fresh apple fritters, flambéed cherries over vanilla ice cream, or pineapple sherbet.

A NOTE ON RIPENING AND STORING FRUITS: Some fruits will ripen if held at room temperature and some will not; this information is included under the individual headings. Fruits, like all other living things, are subject to decay, and they will decay much more rapidly if kept in a fruit bowl in a warm room than if they are stored in the refrigerator. Provided they are not terribly ripe to begin with, certain fruits—particularly apples and pears—will keep for as long as a month in a very cold refrigerator.

About Poaching Fruit

There are many poaching syrup formulas for fruit—some using wine rather than water, others using greater or lesser amounts of sugar—but the moderately heavy syrup featured in the Master Recipe, flavored only with lemon zest and either cinnamon or vanilla, is the one I have always loved best. If sugar calories are of concern to you, you may, when poaching the firm fruits such as apples, pears, or pineapple, cut the sugar suggested by as much as half. Do not, however, decrease the sugar when poaching pulpy or delicate fruits such as cherries, gooseberries, peaches, or plums, as such fruits tend to disintegrate and lose their flavor when poached in a light syrup.

Choosing Fruit for Poaching: The listing on pages 866–69 gives instructions for poaching specific fruits. Almost any fruit can be poached, but I prefer to use firm, smooth-textured fruits rather than soft, pulpy ones such as strawberries or plums. Poaching is also an excellent rescue for blemished or hard, underripe fruits.

Serving Suggestions for Poached Fruits:

- *Poached fruit with custard sauce:* This is a classic dessert, especially nice when done with poached pears. Simply arrange drained poached fruit in shallow bowls or large dessert plates, baste with a few tablespoons of its syrup, and surround with custard sauce. I prefer both fruit and sauce warm, but they may be chilled. Serve with butter cookies if you wish.
- *Fruit compote:* Chill thoroughly one poached fruit or a combination of compatible fruits. Serve with some of the syrup and pass with heavy cream or crème fraîche.
- *Poached fruit with sponge cake:* Drizzle two layers of sponge cake with a bit of the warm poaching syrup. Stack the layers with some of the fruit in between and top with remaining fruit. Serve with lightly sweetened whipped cream.
- *Poached fruit shortcake:* Prepare either one large or several individual shortcakes. While they are still slightly warm, split and fill with warm cut-up poached fruit. Pass with cold heavy cream or crème fraîche.

- *Poached fruit with ice cream and meringues:* Prepare Meringue nests. Fill with vanilla ice cream, top with chilled poached fruit, and drizzle on a little of the poaching syrup. Decorate with sweetened whipped cream piped through a pastry bag fitted with a large star tip.

MASTER TECHNIQUE

Poached Fruit

4 to 6 servings

2½ cups water
1½ cups sugar
Zest (colored part only) of 1 lemon, removed with a swivel-blade vegetable peeler
Either a 3- to 4-inch cinnamon stick *or* 1 tablespoon vanilla extract
The prepared fruit (see listing, pages 866–69)

Combine water, sugar, lemon zest, and cinnamon or vanilla in an 8- to 9-inch saucepan made of or lined with a noncorroding material. Stirring occasionally, bring the mixture to a simmer over moderately high heat, then turn heat down to low, cover, and let the syrup simmer very slowly for 5 to 10 minutes while you prepare the fruit.

Add fruit to the syrup, raise heat to moderately high and bring to a simmer, then immediately turn heat down to the point where the liquid quivers and shudders but does not quite bubble. Cover partially and poach fruit for the length of time indicated in the listing. Since the fruit will float, exposing the top surface, turn it *very gently* several times during cooking, using a wooden spoon or spatula. The fruit is done as soon as it gives only slight resistance when pierced with a cake tester. Be very careful not to overcook, or the fruit will turn mushy and fall apart.

Remove fruit from heat. Unless it is very soft and in danger of falling apart, cover gently with a small plate to keep it completely submerged in the syrup. Let stand in the warm syrup for at least 30 minutes before using.

STORAGE: Poached fruit should be kept in its syrup until you are ready to use it, stored either in the covered saucepan or in a lidded storage container. It will keep for close to a week in the refrigerator and may be rewarmed over very gentle heat if you wish.

FRUITS FOR POACHING

APPLES: Shave off a band of skin 1/4 inch wide from the circumference of 4 to 6 small or 8 to 12 very small (plum-size) firm, tart apples, dropping the apples into a bowl containing 1 quart water and 2 tablespoons fresh lemon juice as you proceed. Poach 6 to 12 minutes, depending on size of apples, in syrup flavored with cinnamon. Serve warm or chilled, with custard sauce lightly scented with cinnamon.

APRICOTS: Halve and pit but do not peel 8 to 12 fresh apricots and poach 5 to 8 minutes in syrup flavored with vanilla and, if you wish, 1/8 teaspoon almond extract.

BANANAS: Choose 4 to 6 large bananas, underripe and firm but not tinged with green. Peel and cut in half. Using a vanilla-flavored syrup, poach 3 to 6 minutes, or until tender and translucent around the edges; be sure not to overcook the bananas and make them mushy. Serve chilled with heavy cream.

CHERRIES: Poach 1 1/2 pounds dark sweet cherries, pitted (see page 884), for 3 to 5 minutes, flavoring the syrup with vanilla and, if you wish, 2 tablespoons dark rum or brandy. Serve chilled with heavy cream or over ice cream or cake.

FIGS: Poach 8 to 12 small whole unpeeled fresh figs for 4 to 7 minutes, flavoring the syrup with vanilla. Often called fig compote, this should be served chilled, with heavy cream if you wish.

GOOSEBERRIES: Choose 1 pound firm, very green gooseberries. Using a vanilla-flavored syrup, poach 2 to 3 minutes, or just until the skins burst. Serve chilled with heavy cream.

Variation: GOOSEBERRY FOOL

4 to 6 servings

❦ *Serve this old-fashioned summer dessert with butter cookies.*

Poached Fruit, using gooseberries
1 cup heavy cream, whipped soft but not sweetened or flavored (see page 857)

Chill gooseberries thoroughly in their syrup, drain, and purée rather coarsely using a blender, food processor, or food mill. Gently fold in whipped cream, mixing only partially so that streaks of unblended purée and cream remain. Spoon into a 1½-quart glass bowl or individual parfait glasses and chill several hours.

GRAPES: Poach 1 pound green seedless grapes in a vanilla-flavored syrup for 2 to 3 minutes, or just until the skins burst. Serve chilled with heavy cream.

KUMQUATS: Poach 2 to 3 cups kumquats in vanilla-flavored syrup for 10 to 12 minutes, or until they are soft and have begun to look translucent. Cool to room temperature, then remove seeds by placing kumquats one at a time on a flat surface and pressing firmly with the back of a wooden spoon. Serve poached kumquats chilled as a condiment for pork, or drizzle their syrup over cake and serve with whipped cream or ice cream.

MELONS: Reserve poaching as a rescue technique for melons that turn out to be unacceptably underripe after they have been cut. Remove seeds of 1 medium-size melon and fashion flesh into balls or cut into chunks. Poach 3 to 5 minutes, or until soft and translucent but not mushy, in a vanilla-flavored syrup. Serve very cold, with butter cookies.

NECTARINES: Poach as for peaches, below.

PEACHES: Choose 4 medium slightly underripe peaches. Cut in half lengthwise, twisting the halves to separate them, and dig out the pits; do not peel. Poach 8 to 10 minutes in syrup flavored with vanilla or with cinnamon and, if you wish, 1 or 2 whole cloves. The skins are easily pinched off after the peaches are cooked.

Variation: PEACHES MELBA

8 servings

❦ *This rather grand dessert out of the French classic cuisine might conclude a formal dinner party featuring a roast. Serve with butter cookies, if you wish.*

Poached Fruit, using peaches
½ cup cold heavy cream
Custard Sauce, page 856, thoroughly chilled
Berry Sauce, page 860, made with raspberries and thoroughly chilled

Poach peaches as indicated above, using a vanilla-flavored syrup. Chill peaches thoroughly in their syrup, then drain and peel. Whip cream until it has barely enough body to hold its shape softly on a spoon; it should be more like a very thick sauce than like traditional whipped cream. Fold cream gently but thoroughly into custard sauce, then spoon mixture onto 8 chilled dessert plates or shallow soup plates. Arrange a peach half, pitted side down, in the center of each plate and mask with berry sauce. Serve at once.

PEARS: Choose 4 to 6 medium pears, preferably Bartlett or Bosc, that are hard and not yet ripe enough for eating out of hand. Leaving the stems attached, peel with swivel-blade vegetable peeler and shave off a thin piece on the bottom so that the pears will stand upright. As you peel each pear, drop it into a bowl containing 1 quart water and 2 tablespoons fresh lemon juice to prevent discoloration. Poach pears in a syrup flavored with cinnamon and, if you wish, 1 or 2 whole cloves for 6 to 15 minutes, or until tender but not mushy. Sublime with custard sauce.

Variation: PEARS IN RED WINE

4 servings

Poached Fruit, using pears
SUBSTITUTE: 2½ cups dry red wine for water
ADD: Zest of 1 orange, removed with swivel-blade vegetable peeler
Custard Sauce, page 856, thoroughly chilled
½ cup crushed macaroons

Poach pears as indicated above, but substitute red wine for water and add orange zest along with cinnamon to poaching syrup. Chill thoroughly in the syrup. Just before serving, spoon custard sauce onto 4 dessert plates or shallow soup plates and place a pear in the center of each. Drizzle each pear with spoonfuls of the poaching syrup and sprinkle with crushed macaroons.

Variation: PEARS HÉLÈNE (WITH ICE CREAM AND CHOCOLATE SAUCE)

4 servings

Poached Fruit, using pears
Chocolate Sauce, page 852, very warm
1 pint vanilla ice cream

Poach pears as indicated above and let cool until the syrup feels quite warm but not uncomfortable for your finger. (Alternatively, pears could be poached ahead of time and warmed over gentle flame in their syrup.) Remove pears from syrup, dab lightly with paper toweling, and arrange in the center of 4 dessert plates or shallow soup plates. Mask pears with chocolate sauce, spoon a bit of their syrup into the bottom of each plate, and place a scoop of vanilla ice cream on the side. Serve at once, with butter cookies if you wish.

PINEAPPLE: Cut 1 small pineapple into rings (see page 895). Poach in vanilla-flavored syrup for 5 to 7 minutes if ripe, 8 to 10 minutes if hard and unripe. Serve in the syrup, flavored lightly with dark rum or kirschwasser if you wish, or drain and serve with berry sauce made with raspberries.

QUINCES: Use 2 to 3 large or 4 small-medium quinces. Peel, cut in half lengthwise (or into quarters if very large), and core, dropping the pieces into a bowl containing 1 quart water and 2 tablespoons fresh lemon juice as you go. Poach in a cinnamon-flavored syrup until fully tender; this will take some time, perhaps 20 minutes or longer. Serve chilled in the syrup with heavy cream or crème fraîche.

Variation: QUINCES IN JELLY

4 servings

Poached Fruit, using quinces
1 cup heavy cream or crème fraîche, page 859
Cinnamon

The seeds of quinces are rich in pectin, the gelatinous substance that helps jellies and jams to jell. To make this dessert, poach quinces as indicated above, tying the seeds in a cheesecloth bag and simmering them in the poaching syrup along with the quinces. Remove quinces when tender to a shallow glass serving dish and cover directly with a sheet of plastic wrap. Continue to simmer the syrup, with the bag of seeds still in it, for 20 to 30 minutes, or until it is reduced in volume and almost as thick as honey. Pour syrup over the quinces, discarding seeds and other solids, and refrigerate until very cold. Serve topped with heavy cream or crème fraîche and a sprinkling of cinnamon. Pass butter cookies if you wish.

RHUBARB: Cut young, tender stalks of rhubarb into 1-inch pieces, making 3 to 4 cups altogether. Using a syrup flavored with cinnamon and orange zest instead of lemon, poach rhubarb for 6 to 10 minutes, being very careful not to overcook it and turn it mushy and stringy. Serve warm over vanilla ice cream or freshly made shortcakes or cold with heavy cream.

About Sautéed, Flambéed Fruit

Fruit sautéed in butter, sprinkled with sugar, and then flamed with dark rum or some other liquor or liqueur makes an easy, delicious, and dramatic dessert when served with cake, cookies, crêpes, or ice cream. If you choose sautéed, flambéed fruit to conclude a formal dinner party, you might consider preparing and flaming it in a chafing dish in front of your guests.

Note: If you don't like the idea of working with flaming liquor you may simply pour the liquor directly into the fruit and boil it off until the juices are thick and bubbly. Or you may omit liquor altogether, perhaps adding a dash of vanilla extract or the grated zest of an orange instead.

Choosing Fruit for Sautéing: The listing at the end of the Master Technique gives instructions on sautéing specific fruits. As you will note, firm fruits such as apples, peaches, and pineapple work best here. Sautéing is a good cooking method for blemished or underripe fruits but not for overripe or mealy fruits, which will tend to disintegrate.

Serving Suggestions for Sautéed, Flambéed Fruit

- *Sautéed, flambéed fruit with crêpes:* Fold or roll sautéed fruit inside 18 to 24 crêpes. If you wish, you may do this a few hours in advance and arrange the crêpes in a lightly buttered oven-to-table tray or platter; just before serving, reheat for 5 minutes or so in a 400°F oven.
- *Sautéed, flambéed fruit with cake:* Spoon the fruit over slices of sponge cake or pound cake. Serve with whipped cream if you wish.
- *Sautéed, flambéed fruit with ice cream:* This is a classic combination. Choose best-quality vanilla ice cream and spoon fruit on top. To make things even dressier, you might want to spoon the ice cream into meringue nests, or to serve the fruit and ice cream with butter cookies or nutted meringue fingers.

MASTER TECHNIQUE

Sautéed, Flambéed Fruit

4 to 6 servings

5 tablespoons unsalted butter
3 to 6 tablespoons sugar
2 to 3 tablespoons strained fresh lemon juice
The prepared fruit (see listing, pages 872–73)
1/3 cup dark rum, preferably Jamaican, or other liquor or liqueur (see listing)

Before beginning, you should have everything at the ready, as the sautéing process must move quickly. Place butter in a 10-inch skillet (not made of unlined cast iron; a nonstick skillet is best) or a chafing dish. Measure out 6 tablespoons sugar and 3 tablespoons lemon juice (though you may not need all of either of them). Pour rum or other liquor or liqueur into a small saucepan and have long wooden matches handy. Peel and pare the fruit last, just before you are ready to cook it, or it may dry out or discolor.

Heat butter in the skillet or chafing dish over moderately high heat until sizzling hot. Add prepared fruit and sauté, stirring constantly but gently, for just a minute or two, or until it begins to soften. Sprinkle 3 tablespoons sugar and 2 tablespoons lemon juice over fruit and continue to sauté, stirring gently, until the fruit is almost tender and pan juices are very thick and bubbly. Taste a small piece of the fruit and a little of the juice. If the fruit is not quite sweet enough, add 2 to 3 tablespoons more sugar; if it is too sweet or if it is bland, add another tablespoon lemon juice; if fruit is still a bit hard, cook a moment or two longer—but don't cook it so long as to make it fall apart.

Remove fruit from heat and place saucepan containing the liquor over the flame for *just a few seconds,* or long enough to warm the liquor to tepid (if the liquor is cold, it will not flame; if it is warmed too much, the alcohol will evaporate and it will not flame either). Turning your face away from the liquor, either ignite it with a long wooden match or, if you are using a chafing dish or a gas stove, tilt the liquor into the flame. The liquor should ignite at once. Immediately pour the flaming liquor over the sautéed fruit, return fruit to the heat, and, stirring, cook until the juices are as thick as molasses and coat the fruit heavily.

FRUITS FOR SAUTÉING AND FLAMBÉING

APPLES: Choose 3 or 4 medium-sized tart, firm apples, preferably Granny Smiths. Peel, core, and cut lengthwise into eighths, tossing the slices with 2 tablespoons of the lemon juice called for in the Master Technique as you proceed. The apples should be sautéed within 15 minutes of cutting, or they will discolor. Proceed according to the Master Technique, flaming the apples with dark rum, calvados, applejack, or Cognac; the total cooking time will be 6 to 8 minutes.

APRICOTS: Peel (see page 883), halve, and pit 8 to 12 fresh apricots. Sauté according to the Master Technique, flaming with rum; the total cooking time will be 3 to 5 minutes.

BANANAS: Peel and halve crosswise 4 to 6 ripe but firm bananas. Sauté in butter about 2 minutes, turning with two wooden spoons to cook as evenly as possible, then sprinkle on sugar and lemon juice and sauté only 1 minute longer before flaming with rum. Very good with vanilla ice cream.

CHERRIES: Pit 1½ pounds dark sweet cherries (see page 884), then sauté according to the Master Technique, flaming with rum; the total cooking time will be 3 to 4 minutes. This is an excellent version of Cherries Jubilee, the famous topping for vanilla ice cream.

NECTARINES: Proceed as for peaches, below.

PEACHES: Peel (see page 893) and slice lengthwise into quarters or eighths 4 large-medium firm but ripe peaches. Sauté according to the Master Technique, flaming the peaches with Cognac or brandy; the total cooking time will be 4 to 5 minutes. Delectable with vanilla ice cream and/or pound cake.

PEARS: Peel, core, and slice lengthwise into quarters or eighths 4 large firm but ripe pears. Sauté according to the Master Technique, flaming the pears with applejack or pear brandy; the total cooking time will be 5 to 7 minutes. Serve with vanilla ice cream.

PINEAPPLES: Following the instructions on page 894, peel and cut into chunks 1 very small or ½ medium-size pineapple, making about 3 cups fruit. Sauté according to the Master Technique, flaming the pineapple with dark rum; the total cooking time will be about 5 minutes. Excellent with vanilla ice cream.

PLUMS: Cut into quarters lengthwise and pit—but do not peel—6 large greengage plums. Following the Master Technique, sauté about 5 minutes altogether, flaming with brandy or Cognac. Serve over cake and/or ice cream.

MASTER TECHNIQUE

Fruit Fritters

4 to 6 servings

Here, chunks or slices of fruit are encased in a light batter and deep-fried, making a spectacular hot dessert that is generally served warm with custard sauce. Please note that this Master Technique is to be used in conjunction with the Master Technique for deep-frying, page 61. It is best to prepare the fritter batter several hours in advance.

CHOOSING FRUIT FOR FRITTERS: The listing at the end of this Master Technique gives instructions on using specific fruits to make fritters. As you will note, most of the fruits suggested are fairly firm types that can be cut into large pieces.

The prepared fruit (see page 874)
1/2 cup dark rum, preferably Jamaican (optional)
1/4 cup sugar (optional)
2/3 to 1 cup confectioner's sugar
1 cup fine cake crumbs
For fritter batter and deep-frying:
- 2 large eggs, separated
- 3/4 cup beer
- 2 tablespoons vegetable oil or melted butter
- 1 cup unbleached all-purpose flour
- 1 1/2 tablespoons sugar
- 1/8 teaspoon salt
- 3 quarts very fresh vegetable oil

Custard sauce, page 856, warm (optional)

Though not essential, it is nice to macerate fruit in rum and sugar before cooking, especially if it seems dry, hard, or lacking in flavor. Prepare fruit as indicated in listing and toss in a 9-inch glass or ceramic baking dish with rum and granulated sugar; cover and let stand 30 to 60 minutes, stirring up several times. Drain fruit well and, whether or not it has been soaked in rum, pat dry with paper toweling. Turn onto a sheet of waxed paper and toss with ½ cup sifted confectioner's sugar, or enough to make pieces sticky on all sides. Roll in crumbs until lightly but evenly coated, place on a rack, and let stand at least 10 to 15 minutes, or for as long as 3 hours.

Using the eggs, beer, 2 tablespoons oil or butter, flour, 1½ tablespoons sugar, and salt, prepare fritter batter as instructed on page 63.

Preheat oven to warm (150°F) and place a baking tray lined with a triple thickness of paper toweling inside.

Fold fruits gently into batter, mixing only until all pieces are completely coated. Heat oil to around 370°F and deep-fry (page 64) fruit a few pieces at a time for 3 to 4 minutes, or until nicely browned; as each batch is cooked, transfer it with a slotted spoon to the towel-lined baking tray in the oven and add more fruit to the pot. When all the fruit is cooked, sift a bit of additional confectioner's sugar over it and carefully transfer it to platter or individual plates. Serve immediately, with warm custard sauce if you wish.

FRUITS FOR FRITTERS

APPLES: Peel and core 3 large apples, preferably McIntosh, Rome Beauty, or another slightly soft and mealy variety, then cut into rings about ⅜ inch thick; save the small slices from the ends for some other purpose. Proceed according to the Master Technique; the rum maceration is highly desirable here, as it both softens and flavors the apples.

APRICOTS: Peel (see page 883), halve, and pit 8 to 10 fresh apricots and prepare according to the Master Technique.

BANANAS: Peel and halve crosswise 4 large or 6 small firm but ripe bananas and prepare according to the Master Technique.

FIGS: Peel but leave whole 8 ripe but firm small fresh figs. Proceed according to the Master Technique, but do not macerate in rum. Glaze generously with warm honey and sprinkle with coarsely chopped walnuts; warm custard sauce may also be passed.

NECTARINES: Proceed as for peaches below.

ORANGES: This sounds a bit strange but is very good. Carefully peel 3 large navel oranges, being sure not to bruise any of the sections. Break sections apart and pull away as much of the stringy white pith as possible, *but do not break the membrane* (save for some other purpose any sections that get punctured).

Proceed according to the Master Technique, but do not macerate in rum, toss with confectioner's sugar, or roll in crumbs.

PEACHES: Choose 3 large or 6 small-medium peaches. Peel (page 893); halve small peaches, or quarter large ones, removing the pits. Proceed according to the Master Technique, macerating the peaches in brandy, Cognac, Port, or dark rum, if you wish. These may be served with berry sauce (made with either strawberries or raspberries) in addition to or in place of custard sauce.

PEARS: Choose 3 to 4 medium-large pears that are quite soft and ripe but not mushy. Peel, core, and cut into quarters lengthwise. Omit the rum maceration, but otherwise proceed according to the Master Technique.

PINEAPPLES: Following the instructions on page 895, cut 8 rings about ½ inch thick from the center of a small pineapple. Proceed according to the Master Technique, being sure to macerate the pineapple in rum and sugar unless it is very ripe and sweet.

About Sherbet

The Master Technique that follows produces a French sort of sherbet, which is much smoother, denser, and more intensely fruit-flavored than are typical American store-bought sherbets. Because it contains a great deal of sugar, this sherbet is high in calories. But it is so rich that a ½-cup serving is more than sufficient, so weight-watchers need not deny themselves entirely.

Cautionary Notes

- The proportions in this formula must not be tampered with if you want good results. The fruit purée must be measured out exactly. If you decrease the sugar, the sherbet will be hard and full of grainy ice crystals; if you increase the sugar, the sherbet will not freeze at all. (Of course, you may cut the recipe in half, and so on, but you must always use a ratio of 1 cup plus 2 tablespoons sugar for every 2 cups of fruit purée.)
- Your freezer must maintain a temperature of 15°F or lower, or the sherbet will not become solid. Indeed, it is preferable to freeze the sherbet at a temperature of between 0°F and −15°F, for if the sherbet is rather soft when taken out of the freezer it will melt quickly when served.
- The sherbet should be consumed within a week of being made, and it is at its best when served within 2 days of preparation.

CHOOSING FRUIT FOR SHERBET: The listing at the end of this Master Technique gives instructions on using specific fruits to make sherbet. As you will note, a wide variety of fruits may be used, though the best sherbets are made from smooth-textured fruits, such as strawberries and peaches.

MASTER TECHNIQUE

Sherbet

Makes about 1 quart, or enough for 8 to 12 servings

The Prepared Fruit (see listing, pages 877–78)
4 to 6 tablespoons strained fresh lemon juice
2¼ cups sugar

Peel and pare the minimum amount of fruit indicated in the list, turn into a food processor fitted with the metal chopping blade, and add 4 tablespoons lemon juice. Purée thoroughly—1 minute or more, depending on the efficiency of your machine. Measure out *exactly* 1 quart purée. If there is not quite enough, prepare additional fruit, adding a small amount of lemon juice; if there is more than 1 quart, save excess to eat with yogurt.

Return purée to food processor, add sugar, and blend about 1 minute longer, or until the mixture is shiny and soupy. Taste a spoonful. If you can detect any undissolved sugar granules, blend 30 seconds longer. If the mixture seems too sweet, add a bit more lemon juice. (If you are working with a food processor that has a small container, you will have to perform this step in two batches.)

Pour purée back into bowl, cover, and freeze at a temperature no higher than 15°F until the sherbet has hardened on the outside and become slushy in the middle. This will take 1 to 3 hours, depending on the efficiency of your freezer. Remove from freezer and beat hard with an electric mixer or wire whip until uniformly smooth and roughly the consistency of a very thick pea soup; if you accidentally overfreeze the sherbet, simply let it stand at room temperature until soft enough to beat. Immediately pour sherbet into a wide, flat-bottomed 6-cup mold—a soufflé dish is perfect—that has been thoroughly chilled in the freezer. Cover with foil or a plate and freeze 4 to 6 hours, or until solid.

If the sherbet is very hard and unspoonable, let stand briefly at room temperature before serving. If you wish, pass nutted meringue fingers, butter cookies, or butter wafers with the sherbet.

FRUITS FOR SHERBET

APRICOTS: Proceed according to the Master Technique, using 1½ to 2 quarts fresh apricots, peeled (see page 883), halved, and pitted, and add ⅛ teaspoon almond extract, which accentuates the apricots' flavor.

BLACKBERRIES: Purée 2 quarts blackberries in food processor with 4 tablespoons lemon juice, then force through a very fine sieve to remove seeds. Measure out 1 quart, then return to processor and add sugar; proceed from there according to Master Technique.

BLUEBERRIES: Remove stems from 2 quarts blueberries, purée in food processor with 4 tablespoons lemon juice, then force through a very fine sieve to remove seeds and bits of skin. Measure out 1 quart, then return to processor and add sugar; proceed from there according to Master Technique.

CHERRIES: For this to be good, your cherries must be dark, sweet, and luciously ripe but not mushy; otherwise, the sherbet will lack flavor. Proceed according to the Master Technique, using 2½ to 3 pounds cherries, pitted (see page 885), and add ⅛ teaspoon almond extract to bring out the cherries' taste.

CRANBERRIES: Purée 2 quarts (two 12-ounce bags) fresh cranberries in food processor, but do not add lemon juice; force through a very fine sieve to remove seeds and bits of skin. Measure out 1 quart, then return to processor and add sugar; proceed from there according to the Master Technique.

GRAPEFRUITS: Proceed according to the Master Technique, using 4 to 5 large or 6 to 9 small-medium grapefruits, peeled and with all pith, membrane, and seeds removed from the sections (see instructions on page 887).

LEMONS: Peel 14 to 18 lemons and remove all membrane, pith, and seeds from the sections according to the instructions given for preparing orange segments, page 892. Omitting lemon juice called for in Master Technique, purée and measure out just 3 cups. Add water to make exactly 1 quart, then return to processor and combine with sugar; proceed from there according to the Master Technique.

LIMES: Proceed as for lemons, above.

MANGOES: Use 6 to 10 large or a dozen or more small very ripe mangoes. Remove skin and pit, cut flesh into chunks, and proceed according to Master Technique.

MELONS: Choose 2 to 3 cantaloupes or 1 to 1½ Persian melons; the melons must be exceedingly ripe, juicy, and aromatic if the sherbet is to be smooth and flavorful. Proceed according to the Master Technique, removing the rind and seeds from the melons, then cutting into chunks, before puréeing.

NECTARINES: Proceed as for peaches, below.

ORANGES: Proceed according to the Master Technique, using 8 to 12 large navel oranges, peeled and with all pith, membrane, and seeds removed from the sections (see instructions on page 892).

PEACHES: Peel (see page 893), halve, pit, and then slice 2½ to 3 pounds of ripe, juicy peaches—9 to 12 altogether—and proceed according to the Master Technique.

PEARS: Choose only very ripe, very juicy pears, preferably Comice, 2 to 2½ pounds. Peel, core, and slice, then proceed according to the Master Technique. One of my favorite ways to end a meal, pear sherbet is especially lovely when drizzled with ice-cold *eau de vie de poire.*

PINEAPPLES: You must use very ripe, flavorful pineapple here. Following the instructions on page 895, peel and cube 1 very large or 1½ to 2 smaller pineapples, being sure to remove all traces of the fibrous, brownish eyes. Proceed according to the Master Technique.

RASPBERRIES: This is one of the finest of all sherbets. Purée 2 quarts raspberries in food processor with 4 tablespoons lemon juice, then force through a very fine sieve to remove seeds. Measure out 1 quart, then return to processor and add sugar; proceed from there according to Master Technique.

STRAWBERRIES: Hull (see page 899) 2 quarts strawberries, purée in food processor with 4 tablespoons lemon juice, then force through an extremely fine-mesh sieve to remove the seeds, which are surprisingly annoying if left in. Measure out 1 quart and combine with sugar in food processor; proceed from there according to the Master Technique.

TANGERINES: Use 16 to 24 tangerines. Following the instructions for making orange segments, page 892, remove all skin, pith, membrane, and seeds from the sections, and proceed according to the Master Technique.

Fruit Glossary

Apples: There are many kinds of "baking" apples, including greening, Northern Spy, Cortland, and, one of the more common varieties, Rome Beauty, a large apple dappled with green and blushes of deep rose. But among all the apples suitable for baking, my first choice is Granny Smiths, smallish, solidly green-skinned, hard-fleshed, very tart apples that are grown around the world. Granny Smiths can be bought virtually all year round at most supermarkets, and they will keep for weeks and weeks in your refrigerator's vegetable bin. They are on the expensive side, but are very much worth the price.

The three most popular "eating" (or "dessert") apples are McIntosh, Red Delicious, and Golden Delicious. McIntosh apples are small, round, pale red, and are often packaged in plastic bags at the grocery store. Though excellent when very fresh, they become mealy and soft within a couple of days after picking. Red Delicious are solidly red, shiny-skinned, and shaped like an inverted bell. While somewhat bland in flavor, they are generally crisp and juicy, except perhaps at the end of summer, by which time they have been in storage for six or eight months. Golden Delicious apples are similar to Red Delicious in taste but are crisper in texture. They tend to be mealy unless very fresh.

An apple that is dry and/or brown around the core has been stored too long or at an excessively low temperature; unfortunately there is no way to know if an apple has such problems until you taste it. You can, however, guard against an apple with interior rot by checking to make sure there are no shallow, softened areas beneath the skin; gently prod the apple with your fingers, and look for any flabby, flattened patches. Apples should feel heavy in the hand. The skin should be firm and shiny if rubbed.

Rescuing bad apples: Both baking and eating apples can be turned into a delicious applesauce. Cut away and discard any rotted portions before proceeding.

APPLESAUCE

Makes about 1 quart

Grated zest and strained juice of 1 large lemon
3 pounds (about 8 medium) apples, preferably Granny Smith or another tart, firm variety
¼ to ½ cup sugar, depending on tartness of apples
1 to 2 tablespoons butter (optional)
Any or all of the following spices (optional): ½ teaspoon cinnamon; ½ teaspoon nutmeg, preferably freshly grated; ⅛ teaspoon ground cloves

Place lemon rind and juice in a heavy-bottomed 3- to 4-quart saucepan made of or lined with a noncorroding material. Peel, core, and coarsely chop one apple at a time, turning it into the saucepan and tossing with lemon juice to prevent discoloration. (Add a tablespoon or two of water if, as you add more apples, there doesn't seem to be enough lemon juice to moisten all the pieces.) When all apples have been prepared, cover saucepan and place over lowest heat possible. Stirring frequently to prevent scorching, cook apples very slowly for 20 to 30 minutes, or until they have become a kind of lumpy purée. Add sugar to taste, uncover saucepan, raise heat slightly, and let applesauce cook down for 10 to 30 minutes, or until it is just thick enough to mound softly on a spoon. Stir often; if you want a very smooth applesauce, beat vigorously every couple of minutes with a wire whip. Off heat, beat in butter and spices if you wish. Stir applesauce occasionally as it cools; refrigerate when it reaches room temperature.

AHEAD OF TIME: Applesauce can be refrigerated for at least a week or frozen for several months in a covered container.

Apple Crisp

8 servings

A wonderful luncheon dessert or snack, apple crisp is also portable for picnics.

PRELIMINARIES

1. Set rack in upper-middle level of oven.
2. Preheat oven to 375°F 20 minutes before baking—350°F if using a glass dish.
3. Select either an 8-inch square or a 9-inch round cake pan. Grease with 1½ tablespoons soft butter and sprinkle with 2 tablespoons sugar; tap pan against the palm of your hand to spread sugar evenly.

Step 1: Preparing the Apples

1½ pounds (about 4 medium) very tart, firm apples, such as Granny Smith
Grated zest and strained juice of 1 large lemon
3 to 4 tablespoons sugar
¼ teaspoon cinnamon
¼ teaspoon nutmeg, preferably freshly grated

Place lemon zest and juice in a 2-quart mixing bowl. Preparing one apple at a time and tossing it with lemon juice to prevent discoloration, peel and core the apples, then slice into ¼-inch crescents, making about 4 cups. Add sugar to taste and spices. Toss. Spread apples evenly in prepared baking dish.

Step 2: Preparing Topping; Baking

⅔ cup unbleached all-purpose flour
4 tablespoons cold butter, cut into ½-inch bits
⅓ cup sugar
⅓ cup packed dark brown sugar
1 teaspoon cinnamon
Salt

The topping for apple crisp is prepared with the same technique used to make pie crust. Your goal is to blend cold butter and flour only until the mixture is crumbly and resembles a very coarse meal; if you overwork the mixture, it will become soft and oily and the baked topping will be tough. Working quickly, either pinch flour and butter together with your fingertips or cut butter into flour using two knives or a pastry blender. Add the two sugars, cinnamon, and a generous pinch of salt; toss lightly with fork just until sugar is beginning to stick to the flour/butter crumbs. Immediately sprinkle mixture over the apples.

Bake for 25 to 35 minutes in preheated oven. Crisp is done when juices bubble around the edges of the dish and apples feel tender when pierced with a cake needle or table fork. Remove from oven and let cool 20 minutes or so before serving, accompanied by whipped cream, sour cream, yogurt, or vanilla ice cream, if desired.

Ahead of Time: Cover thoroughly cooled crisp with plastic wrap and refrigerate for up to 3 days. Dessert may also be covered with foil, placed in a plastic bag, and frozen for several months. Reheat refrigerated or thawed apple crisp uncovered in a 300°F oven for 15 minutes or so before serving.

BAKED APPLES

4 servings

PRELIMINARIES

1. Set rack in the center of oven.
2. Preheat oven to 300°F 20 minutes before baking.
3. Select a shallow glass or ceramic baking dish just large enough to hold the apples comfortably.

4 large baking apples, preferably Rome Beauty
6 to 8 tablespoons heavy cream
⅔ to ¾ cup sugar
Cinnamon
½ cup dry white wine or water
1 cup heavy cream, crème fraîche, sour cream, or yogurt

Using a sharp paring knife, dig a cone-shaped plug about 1 inch wide across the top out of the center of each apple, removing the stem and seeds but leaving about ½ inch of the core at the blossom end of the apple. With the point of a paring knife, make an incision 1/16-inch deep around the middle of each apple.

Place ⅔ cup of sugar on a large sheet of waxed paper. One at a time, brush apples lightly with cream, then roll in sugar, encrusting the outside completely. Arrange in baking dish and sprinkle inside and out with cinnamon. Fill the cores almost to the top with the sugar remaining on the waxed paper; use additional sugar if you don't have quite enough. Drizzle remaining cream over the sugar in the cores, using enough cream to saturate the sugar completely.

Pour wine or water into baking dish. Bake apples about 1½ hours, or until very tender when pierced with a fork, basting every 30 minutes. Serve warm or chilled with spoonfuls of their baking juice plus heavy cream, crème fraîche, sour cream, or yogurt.

AHEAD OF TIME: Baked apples can be covered and kept under refrigeration for 3 or 4 days before being served.

APRICOTS: Very likely you have had bad luck with fresh apricots. Because these fruits are fragile, they are picked when underripe, and as a result they are frequently pithy, dry, and flavorless. Of course they can—and should—be better than this, and my advice is to give them another try, choosing large fruits that are a deep orangish tan in skin color and that are quite soft to the touch. Fully ripened, good-quality apricots are meltingly tender on the tongue, juicy, very sweet, and intense in flavor.

To peel apricots: Drop apricots into boiling water for about 30 seconds, drain in a colander, and rinse under cold water. The skins will slip off easily.

Rescuing underripe, canned, and dried apricots: Although apricots will color and soften if held at room temperature for a day or more, they do not gain anything in flavor. Underripe apricots, however, do respond well to poaching in sugar syrup. Canned apricots, which can be pretty good if they are not packed in a cloyingly sweet syrup, will have a deeper, more apricotlike taste if allowed to stand for 30 minutes in their juice with 1/8 teaspoon almond extract for every 2 cups fruit and juice. Dried apricots vary tremendously in quality. Try to buy them loose or in a see-through container so you can choose those that are plump, moist, and soft. Dried apricots that turn out to be tough or shriveled can be steeped for 2 or 3 minutes in boiling water, then drained and patted dry. They may also be poached as for fresh fruit and served as part of a fruit compote.

AVOCADOS: see pages 478–79.

BANANAS: see also plantains, page 575.

The standard yellow-skinned banana found at the supermarket is actually but one of many varieties of this versatile, inexpensive, and nutritious fruit. Look also for miniature bananas, not much larger than fingers, which make an attractive dessert when baked, sautéed, or poached whole; also occasionally available are red-skinned bananas, a bit thicker and stubbier than the yellow kind and deliciously sweet. But take care, when experimenting with different kinds of bananas, that you don't accidentally pick up plantains, starchy bananas that are served as vegetables. Green plantains are easy to spot, but ripe plantains are yellow, just like regular bananas, and can only be differentiated by their slightly larger size and thicker, more fibrous-looking skins.

Rescuing underripe and overripe bananas: Underripe bananas will ripen in 1 to 5 days if held at room temperature away from direct sunlight. They are ready to eat when the skins turn dark yellow and develop brownish speckles and the fruits break easily from the bunch. The row of smaller bananas on the outside of the bunch usually ripens first. Overripe bananas may be puréed and used to make banana bread and banana cake.

BLACKBERRIES: A late-summer delight, blackberries should be glossy, plump, and blue-black from stem to stern. Before purchasing, check the bottom of the carton to make sure there are no signs of leakage that would indicate the presence of bruised or rotting berries somewhere in the box.

Rescuing underripe blackberries: A pint of hard, acrid, underripe blackberries will taste better if combined with 3 to 4 tablespoons sugar and 2 tablespoons liquor or liqueur (dark rum, crème de cassis, or orange liqueur) and refrigerated for several hours.

BLUEBERRIES: Look for plump, unwrinkled blueberries that are a deep purple-blue. The size of the berries is unimportant. Berries that are reddish or slightly green near the stem end, and those whose skins appear shiny or thin, have been picked before reaching full ripeness and will not be sweet. As with all berries, check the bottom of the carton to make sure there are no stains indicating leakage from damaged berries within.

Freezing blueberries: Frozen blueberries retain their taste remarkably well and are nice to have on hand during the winter. To prepare them, remove stems, rinse berries in a colander, spread out on paper toweling, and allow to dry completely. Handle the berries very gently so as not to bruise them; if bruised they will leak and stick together when frozen. Turn cleaned, dry berries into a plastic container or bag so that you can pour them out as needed, returning the remainder to the freezer. Add frozen blueberries to muffin and pancake batters without thawing first.

When buying frozen blueberries, choose those that have been packed dry, not in a syrup.

Rescuing dry, flavorless, underripe blueberries: Combine each pint berries with 1/4 cup sugar and 2 to 3 tablespoons orange liqueur; refrigerate for several hours or overnight, and serve chilled.

CACTUS PEARS: see prickly pears, page 897.

CHERRIES: Various kinds of "dessert" cherries appear at the supermarket. Bing cherries, the most popular, range in color from apple red to deep burgundy; the latter specimens are the riper, but they may be soft and pithy. When picking through a bin, be wary if the cherries seem sticky, for this is a sign that some are bruised or rotten and that the whole lot may be inferior. Pass over any cherries that are wrinkly, gouged, or blemished.

Often labeled "sour" cherries at the market, most pie cherries are smaller and paler than dessert cherries. The bulk of the crop of pie cherries is shipped to processing plants, so you may have to make do for baking with the rather bland sour cherries that come in cans.

Pitting cherries: Everyone has his own theory and practice of cherry pitting. I find that it works well to make an incision on one side of the cherry and to nudge the pit out with the point of the knife or with a thumbnail. There are also inexpensive cherry/olive pitters available in housewares shops. These gadgets, which work very well, use a small plunger to push the pit out of one end of the fruit, leaving the flesh intact. If you cook with cherries often, a pitter is worth the small investment.

CRANBERRIES: Cranberries have remarkable keeping properties, so it is unlikely that any you encounter at the supermarket will be bad. Obviously a bag full of small, shriveled, or bruised cranberries should be passed over. Because they are so amenable to being stored, you may buy cranberries several weeks in advance of your holiday feast, before the supermarket has a chance to run out, and keep them in the refrigerator in the plastic bag in which they were packed. You may also freeze cranberries, right in their plastic bag, for up to a year.

CRANBERRY-ORANGE RELISH

Makes about 2 cups

❦*A tangy accompaniment to roast pork as well as turkey.*

One 12-ounce bag (about 4 cups) fresh cranberries
⅔ cup sugar
Grated zest and juice of 1 large orange
⅓ cup water

Combine all ingredients in a 3- to 4-quart saucepan. Stirring occasionally, bring to a simmer over moderate heat and cook uncovered for 3 to 4 minutes, or just until cranberries burst and the mixture becomes thick. Do not overcook and turn the relish mushy. Let cool to room temperature, then chill for several hours before serving.

AHEAD OF TIME: Relish may be refrigerated for 3 or 4 days in a covered container.

CURRANTS: Fresh currants, which may be either black or red, look very much like large, bright beads of fish roe. They are delicious in cakes and puddings and may also be eaten raw with sugar and cream, but you are unlikely to come across them in the supermarket as they are perishable and difficult to transport; furthermore, their cultivation is discouraged in some states as the current bush is a carrier of a fungus deadly to the white pine tree. If you are lucky enough to find some, choose those that are plump and shiny and check the carton to make sure that none have been squashed.

Dried currants: Dried currants are actually not currants at all but rather a species of miniature grape. Their small size makes them ideal substitutes for raisins in cakes and breads. I do not find it necessary to remove the small stems before using currants in a recipe.

DATES: If you can't find loose dried dates (health-food stores often carry them), buy those in a see-through container. Check to make sure that they look shiny and plump rather than dull and shriveled, and that there are no signs of greenish or grayish mold. Packaged chopped dates rolled in sugar are very convenient for making muffins and breads.

Rescuing stale, dried-out dried dates: Cover dates with boiling water and let stand for a few minutes, but do not soak them too long or they will dissolve.

FIGS: The purple black figs on my grandfather's farm in Italy were as large as pears. Alas, such figs are not to be found in American supermarkets. Ours are smaller and some varieties have green rather than black skins. Figs should be soft to the touch, but not mushy. The skin near the stem end will be grooved, but if it looks puckered the fig is past its prime. Figs that have split open at the blossom end are overripe. To peel a fig, snip off the hard little piece at the stem end and peel back the skin in strips, as you would peel a banana. Eat plain or with heavy cream and a sprinkling of brown sugar.

Dried figs: Dried figs packaged in flat, traylike boxes and covered with cellophane are moister and more tender—if less picturesque—than those that have been strung on a piece of dried vine and tied in a loop. When cooking with dried figs, be sure to cut off the hard cap of stem in the middle of each fruit.

GOOSEBERRIES: Gooseberries are globe-shaped berries about the size of small marbles. Their green or pinkish green translucent skin is scored by faint lines running from top to bottom; at the blossom end of just-picked berries you will often find a ragged shred of dried bloom that is easily flicked away. Like currant bushes, gooseberry bushes harbor the destructive white pine fungus, so their cultivation is restricted in some states. If you do happen upon a box of gooseberries at the market, buy it only if the berries look perfectly round, plump, and firm. Pinkish berries are best for eating out of hand, but, if possible, choose greenish, underripe berries for poaching.

GRAPEFRUITS: Pinch grapefruits before purchasing. If the skin feels tight, leathery, and thin, the grapefruit is likely to be meaty and full of juice, but if the skin feels bloated, pithy, bumpy, or thick, the fruit may be shrunken or dried out. Pink- and red-fleshed grapefruits are thought by some people to be more attractive than the white-fleshed kind, but they are not sweeter or better flavored. Grapefruits purchased toward the end of winter, a friend from Florida tells me, are likely to be especially mature and therefore sweeter than usual.

Preparing grapefruit sections: First, peel off the outer rind as you would an orange. Break the grapefruit open. Working over a bowl to catch dripping juices, hold grapefruit in one hand while using the thumb and forefinger of your other hand to pinch and strip off the membrane, section by section. (The best place to get hold of the membrane is in the middle of the upper portion of the segments, near where the seeds are.) Once you have exposed one side of the segment, loosen the grapefruit from the opposite sheath of membrane with your forefinger. Flip the section—unbroken, you hope—into the bowl, scraping it free of the bottom (or outer) crescent of membrane as necessary with your forefinger. Remove any seeds. Strip off the empty shell of membrane and proceed to the next section.

GRAPES: Most grapes fall into one of three categories: table grapes, cooking grapes, and wine grapes. Mostly grown in California, table grapes are available through much of the year, though their peak is in the summer. Members of this group include the oval-shaped, green-skinned Thompson seedless that one often sees at the supermarket, Tokay grapes of various kinds ranging in color from deep blue to wine red, and the dramatic-looking, blue-black Ribier grapes. People sometimes think that blue grapes are automatically sweeter and more flavorful than the green-skinned types, but this isn't so. On the matter of seeds, I am told that there exist seedless strains of nearly all types of table grapes, but for some reason many grapes sold at the supermarket have seeds in them. Ask your grocer before making a purchase so as not to be unpleasantly surprised once you get the grapes home.

Cooking grapes have pulpy, flavorful flesh and thick skins that slip off easily. The best-known variety is Concord. These grapes are usually reserved for the making of pies, preserves, and jams, though they may certainly be eaten off the bunch as well. Most are grown in the East and are available from midsummer to late fall.

When buying grapes, check bunches to make sure that the berries are uniformly plump and heavy, their skins taut and unwrinkled. Green-skinned grapes that are very pale or very small are often immature and may be acrid or overly tart. Grapes detached from the bunch and sold loose in cartons are a real bargain if you plan to cook them, but they are not desirable for plain eating since some are certain to be bruised.

Raisins: Most—if not all—raisins sold these days are seedless. Muscat raisins have the most pungent flavor of all and are a delicious addition to curries and salads.

Peeling and seeding grapes: Whether or not to peel grapes before adding them to a fresh fruit salad, sauce, or other recipe is a question to which there is no absolute answer. A lot depends on how sensitive you are to the chewy texture and somewhat astringent taste of grape skin. Before resolving to peel, eat a few grapes from the bunch to determine how distracting you find the skins to be: table grapes, particularly Tokays, often have such thin skins that peeling is pointless (not to mention difficult!).

To peel grapes, you must simply strip off the skins, one grape at a time. To seed them, cut in half lengthwise and flick out the seeds with the point of a paring knife.

Frosting grapes: Dip unbruised grapes either in plain water or, for a heavier frosting, beaten egg white. Roll in regular or superfine granulated sugar. Let dry for 20 minutes on a cake rack and use to garnish fruit salads.

KIWIS: On the outside, kiwis look like large, brown, fuzzy eggs. Inside, their flesh is bright green, translucent, and studded with tiny black seeds that form an ornamental star pattern in crosswise slices of the fruit. In taste and texture, kiwis suggest a tart, soft pear, with overtones of honey. Besides being eaten out of hand and added to fruit salads, the most common use for kiwis is in a fresh fruit tart or pie.

When purchasing kiwis, choose plump fruits without pockmarks, dents, or scars. Prod kiwis gently with your finger to make sure they yield slightly to pressing, but don't squeeze hard or you will damage them.

KUMQUATS: Available at the supermarket in the late fall and early winter, fresh kumquats are generally sold still attached to their decorative leafy branches. Kumquats are roughly the size and shape of large grapes. The skins turn orange with a few patches of green when the fruits are fully ripe and ready to eat.

Though they are often thought of as platter decoration, kumquats have a sweet-sour, citrusy taste and are fun to eat raw, skin and all. They may also be poached in sugar syrup.

Canned Kumquats: Canned kumquats can be substituted for poached fresh kumquats in any recipe, but they can be mushy, bland, or terribly sweet. They need to be seeded before use.

LEMONS: Thin-skinned, rounded, smallish lemons usually have more juice than large, bumpy-skinned specimens. Before purchasing, squeeze lemons to make sure they are firm, and pass over any that are withered or pockmarked.

Preparing lemon juice and zest: To get the most juice out of a lemon, roll it over a flat surface with the palm of your hand while bearing down firmly. To extract juice, impale lemon halves through the core with a table fork and twist (or use a juicer). Lemon juice is generally poured through a fine strainer—a tea strainer, for example—to remove tiny seeds and fragments of flesh. Always use fresh lemon juice for best results in cooking since bottled lemon juice is highly acidic and can have a peculiar metallic undertaste.

When grating lemon peel, scrape off only the *colored* part of the rind, called the "zest," as the white pith underneath is bitter. Strips of lemon zest are best removed with a swivel-blade vegetable peeler, not a knife, because a knife will cut too deeply.

Lemon flavoring in recipes: If you wish to intensify the lemon flavoring in a recipe, add extra grated lemon zest rather than lemon juice. The zest contains more lemon flavor than the juice and will not affect the balance of the recipe's other ingredients. If you are making a smooth sauce, pie filling, or other recipe that might be made gritty by the addition of grated lemon zest, you may do one of three things. First, you can rub whole lemons in the sugar that the recipe calls for until the sugar becomes saturated with lemon oil. Second, you can heat whatever liquid is included in the recipe with strips of lemon zest and let the zest steep in the liquid for 20 minutes or longer, then strain. Third, you can add a small amount of *natural* lemon extract, which will impart a somewhat flowery taste.

LIMES: Limes should be thin-skinned, smallish, round, hard, and bright green. Avoid any that are soft or look puckered. Like lemon juice, lime juice suffers immensely when processed for bottling, so fresh juice is always preferable. Try, for example, making a gimlet cocktail with fresh lime and sugar, instead of with the presweetened bottled kind; the results are spectacular. Prepare lime juice and zest as for lemon juice and zest.

Key limes: Small and yellowish in skin color, Key limes have a pungent, spicy taste prized by many cooks, especially for the making of Key lime pie. Unfortunately, Key limes are rarely available, even in Florida, where the few remaining Key lime trees are located. Regular limes may be substituted for Key limes in any recipe; add a grating or two of fresh nutmeg to enhance the flavor.

LITCHIS: Fresh litchis, sometimes available at Chinese markets, are about the size of walnuts and are covered by a rough, parchmentlike, brown or reddish brown shell that is easily removed with fingers or a paring knife. Underneath the shell is a globe of juicy, icy-crisp, highly aromatic flesh surrounding a shiny black nut. To serve litchis, peel and place in a glass bowl; refrigerate until very cold.

Rescuing canned litchis: Canned litchis are often soft and overly sweet. To improve their flavor, add drops of lemon juice and almond extract and refrigerate in an uncovered bowl for several hours.

MANGOES: There are countless varieties of this oval-shaped semitropical fruit, which tastes something like a peach with spicy, resinous undertones. Mangoes that are orange, yellow, or red are not necessarily riper than those that are green; it is the feel of the fruit, not the color, that counts. Hold a mango in your hand and give it a firm squeeze; it should give slightly, like a ripe peach, but it should not feel soft or squashy. Avoid spotted fruits; they may be stringy.

Rescuing underripe and overripe mangoes: A too-hard mango will ripen if left at room temperature for two or three days. An overripe fruit will be stringy and wet and will fall apart when cut, but you can make use of it by puréeing it in a blender or food processor and stirring the pulp into applesauce. If you have several overripe mangoes on hand, you can turn them into a delicious sherbet.

MELONS: Everyone knows what a cantaloupe looks and tastes like, but other melons require, I think, some discussion. *Persian melons* are round and have reddish brown netted skin when fully mature; they look much like cantaloupes, except that Persians are usually about twice as large. In taste, Persian melons are also reminiscent of cantaloupes, though their dark orange flesh is more spicy and aromatic. *Cranshaws (or Crenshaws)* are large, teardrop-shaped melons whose skins turn deep beige when the fruits are mature. These melons, which have pale rose-orange flesh, are suggestive of cantaloupe in taste but softer in texture. *Casaba* melons much resemble Cranshaws in size and shape but have grooved, bumpy, bright yellow skins. The flesh of casaba melons is cream-colored and veritably dripping with extremely sweet juice. When overripe, casabas tend to be bland in flavor and slightly stringy, especially around the seed pocket. *Honeydew* melons, second in popularity to cantaloupes, are round and creamy-colored on the outside, while inside the flesh is a beautiful translucent chartreuse. Honeydews are sometimes bland even when fully ripe, though a squeeze of fresh lime or lemon juice can help to perk them up. And last but by no means least, there are those giants of the melon family, *watermelons.* If you are serving a small group, look for the sometimes available round watermelons, which are about ⅓ the size of their behemoth forebears.

Choosing a ripe melon: The man or woman who could set down on paper a foolproof method for determining the ripeness of melons would be one of the great heroes of Western culture. In lieu of such a method, I provide the following guidelines. Remember that melons of dubious ripeness will—usually—ripen if kept at room temperature, away from sunlight, for two or three days.

(a) With the exception of watermelons, all melons are at least slightly soft when ready to eat. You should be able to feel the fleshy wall give a bit, at the stem and blossom ends of the melon especially, when you squeeze with your fingers.

(b) The seeds of a fully mature melon will be large and loose and will make a sloshing sound when you shake the melon to your ear. However, it is rare that a melon of such ripeness and maturity will make it to the market, so don't flunk a melon on the basis of this test alone.

(c) Excepting watermelons and a few fairly rare varieties of Cranshaw-type melons such as Santa Claus melons, a suggestion of greenness in the rind is a bad sign—catastrophic in Persians and cantaloupes, where a green cast may indicate a melon picked so immature as to be permanently unripenable.

(d) Melons that are faintly aromatic but that show no signs of decay (soft spots or a general withered look) are likely to be at their prime. However, scentless melons may also be ripe. Strong-smelling melons are probably rotting.

(e) Soft spots, gouges, dents, or darkened patches indicate that melons are overripe or have been frostbitten or damaged during handling. Avoid such melons.

(f) Pass over any melon to which a dried piece of stem is attached. When a melon is picked at or near the point of ripeness, the fruit pulls away cleanly from the stem.

(g) The more textured and callused the skin of a melon, the more mature it is likely to have been when picked.

Rescuing underripe melons that have been cut: Cut the flesh into 1-inch dice or shape it into balls with a melon baller. Following the Master Technique, poach the melon slowly in vanilla-flavored syrup until it looks translucent. Serve very cold, either plain or over vanilla ice cream. Surprisingly good.

NECTARINES: Nectarines look and taste much like fuzzless peaches. Choose those that are blushed with auburn and that feel fairly soft to the touch. Unfortunately, nectarines do not respond well to home-ripening; they will soften if held at room temperature, but they will not become sweeter or juicier.

Peeling nectarines: Follow the procedure outlined for peaches.

Rescuing underripe nectarines: Poach in sugar syrup following the Master Technique.

ORANGES: The two most common types of "eating" oranges are temple oranges and navel oranges. Temples, a tangerine hybrid, are globe-shaped and have thin, rough skins. As their flesh is firm, they are particularly good for slicing into salads; sometimes they are a bit too dry for eating out of hand. Navels are slightly oblong, with thick, bright-orange skins that culminate in a bumpy, navel-like protuberance at the blossom end. Juicy and full of flavor when at their best, navels are the royalty of eating oranges.

Overwhelmed by the low price, many shoppers, I suspect, have inadvertently bought "juice" oranges when they wanted eating oranges, only to find that their bargain fruits were coarse-fleshed, membranous, and full of seeds.

Juice oranges, most of which are the kind called Valencias, are usually clearly labeled as such in the supermarket, but even if they are not marked, you can differentiate them from "eating" oranges by their pale, yellowish skin color and their small size.

Occasionally you will see at the market such specialty items as blood oranges and Seville oranges. As the name implies, the flesh of blood oranges is ruby red, and these fruits are a delightful surprise in a fruit salad. Seville oranges are slightly bitter. They are used in making marmalade and in flavoring tarts and pastry fillings.

All oranges should be firm and heavy; lightweights may be dried out or may contain more rind than flesh (this is particularly true of navels). Toward the end of the winter especially, check oranges to make sure they are not squashy, withered, or marred by broad, soft dents. Skin color is not a good indicator of quality. Many oranges, particularly juicers, are yellowish even at their prime; by contrast, navel oranges are almost always a perfect orange color regardless of their quality. Furthermore, oranges are sometimes gassed or dyed to enhance their color, though it is my impression that this practice is on the wane.

Preparing orange zest and juice; intensifying orange flavor in recipes: Follow the procedures outlined for lemons.

Store-bought orange juice: Orange juice made from frozen concentrate is a useful product, but it never tastes like the real thing, regardless of what the manufacturers promise. When buying orange juice in cartons, read the label carefully, as most cartoned orange juice (and all the bottled juice that I have ever run across) has been made from the same concentrate that you can buy for one-third the price at the freezer bin. Even those brands of orange juice that are not made from concentrate will not have as good a flavor as fresh juice, as they have been pasteurized.

Preparing orange sections: When serving oranges in salads or desserts, it is nice to present neat, wedge-shaped sections, without the slightest trace of pith or membrane adhering. To accomplish this, peel the orange; then, using a small serrated knife, slice a thin layer off the entire circumference of the orange, removing both pith and membrane. Once this is done, you will be able to see clearly the membranous divisions between the sections and you can proceed to cut out V-shaped wedges from between the membrane walls. Remember to flick out any seeds. Hold the orange over a bowl as you work to catch dripping juice. As each orange is gutted, squeeze the empty membrane sac in your hand to wring out remaining juice.

PAPAYAS: Papayas are yellowish gourd-shaped fruits, usually 6 to 8 inches long. Both in texture and in taste, papayas suggest a cross between a boiled sweet potato and a mango (if such a cross were possible). Papayas are often cut in halves or quarters and served with ham as a first course. They have a piny aftertaste that can be minimized by chilling and by sprinkling the fruit with lime juice. The black, peppery-tasting seeds in the center look like caviar; they may be used as a garnish or put into salads. The peel is discarded.

Choose papayas with uniformly yellow skins rather than those with greenish skins, a sign of underripeness. Papayas should be as soft as ripe avocados or peaches to the touch, but avoid any that feel squashy or look puffy.

PEACHES: Most of the peaches found at the supermarket are the yellow-fleshed freestone variety, meaning that the flesh separates easily from the pit. Hard peaches are definitely unripe; soft ones may be ripe, or they may be half rotten. Sad to say, you are probably better off buying bruised peaches than perfect-looking specimens, for a perfect appearance is a telltale sign of the peaches having been hard and unripe at the time of picking and shipping. Reddish peaches are not necessarily riper than tan or yellow ones, but peaches that are very pale or touched with green are a bad risk. If the peaches at your supermarket have no fragrance whatsoever, wait for another day to make a purchase. Fragrance is really the best clue of all.

Peeling peaches: Drop peaches into boiling water for 1 minute, then rinse under cold water. The skins will come off easily.

Canned peaches: Canned peaches can be used quite successfully in sauces and warmed desserts as they seem to gain in flavor when heated. If serving chilled, add a few drops of almond extract to syrup and refrigerate peaches for 30 minutes. In my view, canned peaches that have been processed with a minimal amount of sugar are brighter-tasting than those packed in heavy syrup.

Rescuing underripe or flavorless peaches: Alas, peaches do not ripen once off the tree, though holding them at room temperature for a day or so will sometimes help to soften them and make them more palatable. If this doesn't do the trick, poach the peaches in sugar syrup.

PEARS: I am exceedingly fond of pears, both cooked and raw, but especially raw, with a fine cheese such as a ripe Stilton, Roquefort, or Camembert or a sharp, crumbly Cheddar. The most familiar types are the *Bartlett* and its close cousin, the *Packam.* Both are teardrop-shaped, the Packam tending to be a bit bumpy at the base, and both are generally sold green, though the Bartlett especially is better when it is very ripe and its skin has turned pale, not dark, yellow. These are good all-purpose pears, tender, sweet, and juicy when at their best, though always a little bland no matter how fresh and ripe. Another common variety is the *Anjou.* Green-skinned and squatter than Bartletts and Packhams, the Anjou is rather sour and nonaromatic, and its texture is decidedly firm and dry. The Anjou is excellent poached and makes a fine sherbet, but it is not my choice for eating out of hand. *Bosc* pears are different in appearance from other varieties, having very long necks and papery brownish or yellow-brown skins. Bosc pears are quite hard even when ripe. Although they are juicier, sweeter, and more flowery-aromatic when soft enough to yield slightly to firm pressure, these pears may be eaten even when rock-hard, in which case their flesh has a crispy texture and slightly tart taste similar to that of a very fresh apple. The *Comice* pear and its several close relatives are large, round, lumpy fruits that hardly look like pears at all. These are too soft and juicy for cooking, but for eating out of hand they are unequaled, their intensely scented flesh having an almost sherbetlike consistency that tempts one to eat them with a spoon.

With the exception of Boscs, pears, when ripe, should be soft enough to retain a definite dent when pressed firmly with the thumb; however, should the skin break, the pear is overripe and will likely be mushy or mealy. Brown nicks in the skin indicate that the pear has been handled roughly, but it may be fine to eat anyway. A strong pear smell tinged with the scent of decay is a sign that the pears in a bin are past their prime, as is the annoying presence, in the fall, of swarms of yellowjackets.

Rescuing underripe and overripe pears: Hard pears will soften if held at room temperature in a paper bag for two or three days, but don't expect terrific results if the pears have been picked very immature. You might also consider poaching underripe pears in sugar syrup. Pears that have become soft, discolored, or grainy with age may be turned into a sherbet or a delicious pear purée. To make pear purée, follow the recipe for applesauce, substituting pears for some or all of the apples. If necessary, add some water or fruit juice as the pears cook to prevent scorching. You may wish to flavor the purée with ground or preserved ginger. Eat pear purée with wheat germ, yogurt, or heavy cream, either at breakfast or as a dessert.

PERSIMMONS: Available in the fall, persimmons are small fruits with smooth, glossy, orange rose skins. The two most commonly available kinds of persimmon are the inverted teardrop-shaped domestic type and the smaller, squatter oriental variety, which has a slightly drier and smoother texture. When choosing persimmons, it is better to err on the side of overripeness, picking fruits that are very soft and wrinkly near the stem; unripe persimmons are extremely astringent, and they taste on the tongue like particles of bitter wax. Persimmons will ripen if placed in a paper bag for several days. A cut fruit that turns out to be inedibly unripe must be discarded.

PINEAPPLES: Although a number of pineapple varieties are grown throughout the world, most of the pineapples currently available in American markets are of the kind known as smooth cayennes. Choosing a ripe pineapple is a decidedly tricky affair. Color is only a partially reliable indicator of quality. As they ripen, pineapples often take on a golden yellow hue, particularly near the bottom, but a pineapple that has become intensely and uniformly yellow may well be rotting. To complicate matters further, some ripe pineapples remain wholly green, and some nicely rose pineapples are unripe. A fully ripe pineapple should give very slightly if squeezed hard, but any fruit that is soft, either generally or in spots, has begun to rot. Check the bottom to make sure there is no leaking juice, a sure sign of decay. A pineappley aroma emanating from the bottom is a good omen, but some ripe pineapples are scentless. A strong fermented odor is a symptom of advanced deterioration. Whether or not a leaf can be pulled easily from the center of the crown is not an accurate test of ripeness, traditional belief notwithstanding. Avoid, though, any pineapple whose leafy crown is especially yellowed or dried out. Large and small pineapples of the same species taste equally good, so buy larger ones and get more fruit for your money.

Unless it has begun to ferment, a pineapple may be stored at room temperature for 1 or 2 days before being cut. A very ripe or partially fermented pineapple should be stored in the refrigerator to prevent rotting, but be advised that pineapple tends to become watery and fibrous if refrigerated for more than 12 hours.

Preparing a fresh pineapple: To make pineapple chunks, start by cutting off the top of the fruit just beneath the leafy crown, then cut pineapple lengthwise into 8 wedges. Running along the top of each wedge will be a sliver of the tough, whitish central core: shave this piece off and discard. Run the knife along the bottom curve of the flesh to separate flesh from shell. Do not cut too close to the skin, or you will pick up fibrous pieces—the eyes. Slice the pineapple into inch-wide chunks and either serve it on the wedge of shell or turn it into a serving bowl.

If you want to make pineapple rings, cut off the crown, stand pineapple on the work surface, and cut off the skin in strips, working from top to bottom. Peel fairly deeply so that eyes are removed with the skin; gouge out any eyes that remain in the flesh, using the point of the knife. Place peeled pineapple on its side and slice. Remove the circle of core from each slice with a small cookie cutter.

Pineapple and gelatin: Fresh uncooked pineapple contains an enzyme that keeps gelatin from thickening. However, this enzyme is destroyed by heat, so both cooked and canned pineapple can be added to gelatin mixtures.

Rescuing an unripe or fermented pineapple: While pineapples cease to ripen in the true sense of the word once they are picked, they will, if held at room temperature for 1 to 3 days, undergo a fermentation process that makes the flesh softer and more flavorful, though not sweeter. A cut pineapple that proves unpalatably hard and sour will be much improved if sliced into chunks and macerated for 4 to 5 hours in 2 tablespoons sugar and, if you wish, 1 tablespoon dark rum or kirschwasser per cup of fruit. Chill 1 to 2 hours before serving, but not longer, or the pineapple will wilt and become stringy. For exceedingly unripe pineapples, the best approach is to slice the fruit into rings and poach it in sugar syrup.

Provided they are not actually rotten, partially fermented pineapples, including the brownish parts, can make acceptable eating, though they are bound to have a slightly alcoholic flavor. A particularly good use for a fermented pineapple is pineapple fritters, which are, if anything, enhanced by the alcohol taste and which are not damaged by the discoloration of the fruit.

PLUMS: There are countless varieties of plums and all make delicious eating, either raw or cooked. Large, dark, purple-skinned plums and red plums, the most prevalent types, are delicate in taste and texture and, ideally, very juicy. Greengage and yellow plums, the latter somewhat resembling translucent-skinned nectarines, have fairly firm flesh and are therefore the ones chosen for baking and poaching. The miniature, dark blue "prune" plums are, as one would expect, the ones that are dried and made into prunes. When at their best, prune plums are sweet and tender-skinned and may be eaten out of hand like other plums.

The problem with plums is that they must be quite ripe to be worth eating, and it is not always easy to tell the ripe ones from the ones that will taste pithy and sour. Generally speaking, the softer the plum the better, though any that are wrinkled or shriveled should be passed over. Luckily, plums ripen quite successfully when placed in a paper bag, away from direct sunlight, for two to four days.

Rescuing canned plums and prunes: Canned plums are one of the least appealing of all canned fruits—pulpy, much too sweet, and close to tasteless. They can be somewhat improved if drained of their syrup and refrigerated overnight with 2 tablespoons fresh lemon juice and 1/4 cup dark rum per 2-pound can; recombine plums with some or all of the canning syrup and chill 2 hours before serving. Prunes that have become tough and dried out will soften if covered with boiling water and allowed to stand for a minute or two. Be careful not to leave them in their hot bath for too long, or they will turn mushy.

PLUM CRISP

8 servings

❦ *This is perhaps the best recipe I know for cooked plums.*

Apple Crisp, page 880
SUBSTITUTE: 2 pounds very firm greengage plums for apples

Slice plums in quarters or eighths, depending on size, and remove pits but do not peel. Proceed according to the Master Recipe for apple crisp, substituting the plums for apples.

Pomegranates: Pomegranates are a curious fruit indeed. Generally about the size of oranges, pomegranates are covered with a leathery, rose-colored skin that culminates in a small, jagged crown. Inside, the fruit is composed of hundreds of tiny, transparent, ruby-red beads, each enclosing a seed, held together by whorls of whitish membrane. Since the seeds are somewhat puckery-tasting and gritty, experienced pomegrante-eaters chew gently so as to break the tart-sweet pulp without crushing the seeds, which may be safely swallowed whole. Likewise, when preparing pomegranate juice (which is lovely when mixed with apple juice), the beads of the fruit should be pressed gently against a sieve with a wooden spoon—never crushed in a juicer or whirled in a blender.

Pomegranates should be uniformly rosy in color and feel firm, dry, and heavy in hand. A broad, softened dent in the fruit indicates a section of interior decay, but don't panic if you accidentally buy a dented fruit, for most of it will likely be salvageable.

Prickly Pears: Prickly pears, the fruit of a cactus, resemble stubby pine cones in size and shape. They are green and hard when unripe; when ready to eat, they turn orange red and become about as soft as a firm-ripe avocado. A prickly pear that is less than fully ripe will taste mealy and dry, and the presence of its hard, swallowable seeds will seem annoyingly pronounced. By contrast, a fully ripe prickly pear will be sweet and very juicy, suggestive of a cross between a pear and a tart peach in flavor and texture. Alas, prickly pears do not ripen after picking. As you might expect, prickly pears are covered with nearly invisible hairlike spines that are extremely hard to remove once they get lodged in your finger. Though the prickly pears sold at the supermarket have been defuzzed, I never take any chances, and I protect my hand with a plastic bag when prodding the fruits for ripeness.

To peel a prickly pear, lay the fruit on a cutting board, cut off thin slices at the top and bottom, make a lengthwise incision through the skin from stem to stern, and unwrap the flesh from the skin using a fork and knife or two forks. You need never touch the possibly prickly skin. Slice the fruit crosswise; serve slightly chilled. Rinse the cutting board under a strong stream of water before using it for any other purpose.

Quinces: Quinces were once widely used in American cooking, but they have become scarce and, in some quarters, virtually unknown today. Related to apples and in fact resembling Golden Delicious apples at first glance, quinces may be found in some specialty markets during the late autumn and early winter. They are likely to command a hefty price. Quinces are oddballs among the fruits, for they cannot be eaten raw. The usual cooking method is poaching in sugar syrup. Cooked quinces have an appley, flowery taste and a firm, rich, custardlike texture. They are really quite marvelous and worth a try if you can find them.

RASPBERRIES: Raspberries hull themselves when they are picked from the bush, leaving only the fragile, edible fruit. This is why fresh raspberries are so difficult to transport and to keep—and why they are so expensive. Choose dry, dark red berries, and pass over any that look slick or collapsed, as they have been bruised or are rotting. Make sure there are no signs of mold and that the bottom of the container is not sodden with juice.

The sooner you eat raspberries after purchasing the better. If you must store them for longer than 24 hours, gently scatter them over the countertop and pick out and discard any that are soft or moldy—they will contaminate the rest. Do not wash. Turn into a bowl or container, cover tightly, and refrigerate.

Frozen raspberries: Provided they have not been done in by too much added sugar, frozen raspberries have a very authentic taste. Thaw the berries partially at room temperature or in cold water, and serve them while they are still icy and firm. A 10-ounce container will yield about 1 cup of berries and berry juice; be forewarned that some brands contain as much juice as they do fruit. Dry-packed frozen raspberries can sometimes be found.

RHUBARB: In earlier eras rhubarb, which looks like a variety of celery, was called "pie plant." Look for firm, juicy stalks with a nice reddish sheen. Smaller stalks will be more tender and less stringy than large ones. Stalks thicker than 3/4 inch at the base usually need to be peeled. The leaves, by the way, are toxic if eaten in any quantity; throw them out. Rhubarb is always cooked before eating.

Variation: RHUBARB CRISP

8 servings

Apple Crisp, page 880

SUBSTITUTE: 3½ cups 1-inch pieces young, tender rhubarb stalks for apples

Grated zest and strained juice of ½ orange for lemon juice and zest

INCREASE: Sugar called for in Step 1 to 3/4 cup

Proceed according to the Master Recipe for apple crisp, but substitute rhubarb for apples and orange zest and juice for lemon, and increase the sugar called for in Step 1 to 3/4 cup.

STRAWBERRIES: Strawberries should be uniformly red, without white or greenish patches near the stem or tip. Truly ripe strawberries will give off a subtle but discernible scent when held close to the nose. Remember to pick up the box that the berries are packaged in and examine the bottom to see if any undesirables have been hidden there.

Hulling strawberries: To hull a strawberry means to pull out its stem and firm, whitish, cone-shaped core. If you are not sure what the core is, cut a large strawberry in half lengthwise and you will get a good view of the core. A tweezer-like hulling gadget is available at specialty cookware shops, but most people remove the core by digging it out with the nails of their thumb and forefinger or the tapered tip of a teaspoon.

Frozen strawberries: Buy frozen strawberries that have been dry-packed, not those packed in sugar syrup. Thaw partially at room temperature or in cold water, and serve the berries while still slightly icy in the center.

Rescuing unripe strawberries: Even red, perfect-looking strawberries often turn out to be crunchy, sour, and dry. To rescue such berries, hull them, cut them in half lengthwise (or in quarters if very large), and combine them with 3 tablespoons sugar per pint of berries. Refrigerate for at least 2 hours. The berries will taste much better, though they will also inevitably soften.

STRAWBERRY SHORTCAKE

4 to 6 servings

1½ pints strawberries
⅓ cup sugar
1 large, 4 medium, or 6 small shortcakes, page 676, freshly baked and still warm
1 to 1½ cups heavy cream, plain or whipped soft (see page 857)

Hull strawberries, cut in half lengthwise, and mix gently with sugar. Unless the strawberries are exceptionally ripe and fine, in which case they should be served immediately, cover strawberries and set aside at room temperature for about 1 hour, stirring up several times.

Split shortcakes in half and fill with berries and their juice, strewing remaining berries over the top. Let stand a few minutes to allow the shortcakes to absorb the flavor of the berries, then serve topped with heavy cream, whipped or not, as you prefer.

CHOCOLATE-DIPPED STRAWBERRIES

Makes 12 to 16 pieces, or enough for 6 to 8 servings

❦ *Chocolate-dipped strawberries are the height of elegant simplicity. One would think they would be quite simple to produce, but no confection that involves melted chocolate is ever foolproof. By the way, you may use banana chunks or unbruised, perfectly dry orange sections in place of strawberries.*

1 pint perfect strawberries (buy 2 pints; probably only half the berries will be perfect)
3 ounces semisweet chocolate (use a fine imported eating chocolate here)

Turn strawberries into a colander and wash under a gentle stream of tepid water, handling them as little as possible. Gently blot berries dry with paper towels, then scatter on a cake rack and let stand until completely dry, at least an hour. Do not hull them! Strawberries must be at room temperature when they are dipped, or the chocolate will thicken and lump.

Break up chocolate and place in a fairly narrow, short container: a drinking glass about 2 inches wide at the base, 3 or 4 inches tall, and 3 inches wide at the mouth is ideal. (You want to be able to dip the strawberries—not roll them—in the chocolate so that the finish will be smooth, and therefore the container should be small enough to hold the chocolate in a deep pool. At the same time, the container must be wide enough to allow you to insert your thumb and forefinger holding the berry.) Place the glass holding the chocolate in a pan of water just below the simmer. When chocolate is melted and smooth, remove from water bath and let stand for a few minutes at room temperature to thicken slightly.

One at a time, dip dry strawberries into the melted chocolate, covering them about ⅔ of the way up to the stem end. Do *not* dip any strawberries that are leaking; the leaking juice will make chocolate thicken immediately and you'll have to start all over again with fresh chocolate. If the day is cool and the chocolate becomes thick, set it briefly in warm water to reliquefy.

As each strawberry is dipped, place it on a tray covered with a sheet of waxed paper. Don't jostle the tray as you work or you may smear the strawberries. When all berries have been dipped, slide tray into the refrigerator and chill for 30 minutes to 4 hours. Be sure to bring the strawberries to room temperature before serving, in paper or foil candy cups if you wish.

TIP Strawberries that are allowed to harden on a baking tray, as above, will develop a flattened side. If you don't like this idea, you can perform the following clever—but tricky—procedure. Impale each strawberry through the hull on a flat-sided toothpick, dip it quickly into the melted chocolate, then stab the blunt end of the toothpick into a sheet of styrofoam so that the strawberry now hangs over the styrofoam, pointing upward. Refrigerate the berries still inverted on their picks. Most florists will give away small sheets of styrofoam free.

TANGERINES AND TANGELOS: Tangerines, of which there are many types, and their larger cousins, tangelos, should be bright orange, shiny, and heavy in the hand. Though their skins are naturally loose and puffy and their shapes a bit irregular (especially tangelos), the fruits should not feel squashy or look caved-in, signs of bruising or rot.

UGLI FRUITS: A cross between a grapefruit and a tangerine, an ugli fruit could easily be mistaken for a lumpy, misshapen grapefruit, except that, like a tangerine, its yellow skin is thin, loose, and usually rather bumpy. Uglis are the juiciest fruits one is ever likely to encounter, their sections mere sacklike swellings of grapefruit-tangerine nectar. Specimens that are heavy in the hand will have the most juice. Because of their fragility, ugli fruits are best peeled at the table, over a plate, and eaten out of hand.

INDEX

Acorn squash. *See* Squash, winter
Allspice, 16–17
Almonds
  about, 700
  blanching, 700
  crescents, 735–36
  in macaroons, 744–45
  in nutted meringue fingers, 794
  paste, making, 700
  in praline powder, 861
  soup; cream of, 80
Aluminum, cast. *See* Cookware
Aluminum, lightweight. *See* Cookware
Anchovies
  butter, 259
  jalapeño pizza, 195
  onion-olive pizza, 196–97
  pepper pizza, 197
  pizza, 195
  as salad addition, 112
Angel food cake, 838–40
Anglerfish. *See* Monkfish
Anise
  about, 17
  seed cake, 826
  see also Fennel
Appetizers. *See* Hors d'oeuvre
Apples
  about, 879
  applesauce, 879–80
  baked, 882
  and chestnuts; bread stuffing with, 363–64
  cinnamon muffins, 679
  cranberry filling, for pastry, 771
  and cream deglazing sauce, 410–11
  crisp (master recipe), 880–81
  filling, for pastry, 771
  fritters, 874
  for fruit tarts, 770
  omelet, 158
  poaching, 866
  and prunes; bread stuffing with, 363
  and sausage stuffing, for butternut squash, 606
  sautéing and flambéing, 872
Applesauce, 879–80
  bars, 730
  cake, 811
    classic layer, 811
    layer, with pecans and raisins, 811
  raisin bread, 665
Appliances, small, 12
Apricots
  about, 883
  bars, 730
  dried
    bread stuffing with, 364
    Leah's custard pie with, 786
  filling, for pastry, 771
  fritters, 874
  for fruit tarts, 770
  jam omelet, 158–59
  peeling, 883
  poaching, 866
  rescuing, 883
  sautéing and flambéing, 872
  sherbet, 877
  soufflé, 721–22
  sponge layer cake, 829
  walnut muffins, 679

Artichokes
about, 469
baked stuffed, 472–73
boiled (master recipe), 470–72
canned, 469
frittata with, 152
hearts, as salad addition, 112
overcooked, rescuing, 469
presenting and eating, 470
soup; cream of, 80
trimming, 470
Arugula, 109
Asparagus
about, 473–74
canned, 474
with crumbs and parmesan cheese, 477
frozen, 474
gratin, 476–77
leftover, rescuing, 474
overcooked, rescuing, 474
in pasta primavera, 188
peeling and trimming, 474, 475–76
presenting, 474
with sesame seeds (and hard-cooked egg), 478
skillet-boiled (master recipe), 475–76
soup; cream of, 80
Avocados
about, 478
guacamole, 479
as salad addition, 112–13

Bacon
chive biscuits, 673
in classic quiche Lorraine, 164–65
corn soufflé, 174
and cornmeal pancakes, 689
horseradish cream sauce, 35
muffins, 680
and onion scramble, 141
as salad addition, 113
spinach, and mushroom salad, 126–27
stuffing, for trout, 247
Baked apples, 882
Baked beans, 628–29
Baked butternut squash stuffed with sausage and apples, 605–6
Baked cod with tomato stuffing, 244
Baked glazed ham (and roasted fresh ham) master recipe, 376–77
Baked onions, 563
Baked potatoes, 580
Baked salmon with dill and cucumber stuffing, 245
Baked sole or flounder fillets with crabmeat stuffing, 246
Baked sole or flounder fillets with mushroom stuffing, 246
Baked stuffed artichokes, 472–73
Baked stuffed clams, 284–85
Baked stuffed eggplant with lamb, 537–39
Baked stuffed eggs, 147
Baked stuffed fish (master technique), 240–42
Baked stuffed fish chart, 243–44
Baked stuffed giant shrimp, 319
Baked stuffed onions with sausage, 561–62
Baked sweet potatoes, 587
Baked winter squash, 604–5
Baking equipment, 12–14
baking sheets, 14
molds
soufflé, 14
tart, French, 14
tartlet, 14
muffin tins, 14
pans
cake, 14, 802–3
jelly roll, 14
loaf, 13
pie, 13–14
springform, 14
pastry bags, 13
pastry blenders, 13
pastry brushes, 13
racks, 13
rolling pins, 12–13
sifters, 13
Baking powder biscuits (master recipe), 671–72
Baking sheets, 14
Balloon whips. *See* Wire whips
Balsamic vinegar, 117
Bananas
about, 883–84
and berries, for cream tart or pie, 775
bread, 666
cake, 811–12
classic layer, 812
orange layer, 812
cream pie, 777
fritters, 874
muffins, 680
pancakes, 688
poaching, 866
rescuing, 884
sautéing and flambéing, 872
soufflé, 722
see also Plantains
Bar cookies. *See* Cookies
Basic American white bread (master recipe), 634–40
Basic cream sauce (master recipe), 34–35
Basil
about, 17
pasta in cream with, 188
in pesto, 191
tomato cream sauce, 45
Bass. *See* Sea bass; Striped bass
Batter-dipped deep-fried onion rings, 560–61
Batters
fritter (master technique), 63–64

Batters *(Continued)*
pancake (master recipe), 687–88
tempura (master technique), 64
Bay leaf, 17
Beans and peas, dried
about, 615, 622–23
black beans
fried, with sausage and onions, 628
soup, 104–5
boiled (master recipe), 624–25
canned, 623
chickpea salad, 626
flageolets, purée of, 625
green split pea soup, 98–99
kidney, red, in chili beans, 627
lima beans, purée of, 625
navy bean soup, 104–5
overcooked, rescuing, 623
pinto beans, in chili beans, 627
red beans, fried, with sausage and onions, 628
soaking or parboiling, 623
washing and soaking, 624
white beans
baked, 628–29
niçoise, 626–27
purée of, 625
salad, 626
Beans, cranberry
about, 485
boiled (master recipe), 486
overcooked, rescuing, 485
purée of, 487
salad with bacon; warm, 488
Beans, fava
about, 485
boiled (master recipe), 486
overcooked, rescuing, 485
salad with bacon; warm, 488
Beans, green
about, 479–80
boiled (master recipe), 481–82
frozen, 480
in Greek-style tomato sauce, 483–84
in heavy cream, 482
with mushrooms; gratin of, 483
overcooked, rescuing, 480
in pasta primavera, 188
trimming, 481
in vegetable soup, 100
with vinegar and bacon; Grandmother Rosalind's, 484–85
Beans, lima
about, 485
boiled (master recipe), 486
canned, 485
frozen, 485
in heavy cream, 487
overcooked, rescuing, 485
purée of, 487
salad with bacon; warm, 488
see also Beans and peas; dried
Beans, shell, 485–88
about, 485
boiled (master recipe), 486
overcooked, rescuing, 485
Beans, wax
about, 479–80
boiled (master recipe), 481–82
frozen, 480
in Greek-style tomato sauce, 483–84
in heavy cream, 482
with mushrooms; gratin of, 483
overcooked, rescuing, 480
trimming, 481
with vinegar and bacon; Grandmother Rosalind's, 484–85
Béarnaise sauce, 48
Beef
broth; rescued canned, 28–29
choosing, 337–38
chuck steak
braised, Napa Valley, 450
braising, preparing for, 442–43
in chili, 449
with onions and beer; Flemish, 445–46
corned, in New England boiled dinner, 465
curried casserole, 202
doneness of, 340
goulash, 451
grades of, 336–37
ground
in chili-stuffed green peppers, 574–75
chuck, for hamburgers, 204
chuck, in mother's meat loaf, circa 1958, 205
in meat sauce, 185
round, in mother's meat loaf, circa 1958, 205
sirloin, for hamburgers, 204
in stuffing, for summer squash, 598–600
liver, calves
sautéed, with bacon and onions, 419–20
sautéing, choosing for, 419
London broil (master recipe), 390–91
mushroom-noodle soup, 92–93
pot roast
braised (master technique), 440–42
braised, Napa Valley, 450
braising, preparing for, 442
with ginger; Pennsylvania Dutch soured, 445
old-fashioned, 444
with onions and beer; Flemish, 445–46
Swedish-American, 448

Beef *(Continued)*
rib roast
about, 378
au jus (master recipe), 378–80
round steak
braised (master technique), 440–43
braised, Napa Valley, 450
braising, preparing for, 442–43
in chili, 449
with onions and beer; Flemish, 445–46
salad, 120
shank, in beef stock, 24–26
steak tartare, 206–7
steaks
broiled (including London broil) master recipe, 390–91
broiling, choosing for, 390
London broil, preparing, 390
sautéed, with cognac and cream, peppered, 415–16
sautéed (with cognac and parsley) master recipe, 412–13
sautéed, with colbert sauce, 415
sautéed, with mustard and green peppercorns, 414
sautéed, with red wine and mushrooms, 414
sautéing, choosing for, 412
stew meat
braised (master technique), 440–42
braised, Napa Valley, 450
braising, choosing for, 440
in chili, 449
curry, 447–48
in goulash, 451
mushroom-noodle soup, 92–93
old-fashioned, 443–44
with onions and beer; Flemish, 445–46
stock (master recipe), 24–26
tenderloin, for steak tartare, 206–7
top loin, preparing for roasting, 380–81
top round
roasting, preparing for, 381
rolls stuffed with sausage and eggs; Italian-style, 452–53
see also Veal
Beets
about, 488
boiled (master recipe), 489–90
canned, 488
greens, 488
Harvard (glazed beets), 490
pickled, 490
rescuing, 489
Russian, 491
trimming, 489
Benne seed *see* Sesame seed
Berries
and bananas, for cream tart or pie, 775
pancakes, 688
sauce, 860
see also individual names
Biscuits
bacon-chive, 673
baking powder (master recipe), 671–72
buttermilk, 673
cheddar, 674
dropped, 673
garden herb, 674
ham, Virginia, 675
for hors d'oeuvre, 68
Little Italy savory, 674–75
scones, 675–76
shortcake, 676
see also Coffeecakes; Muffins; Rolls and buns
Black beans. *See* Beans and peas, dried
Black on white layer cake, classic, 819
Black walnuts. *See* Walnuts
Blackberries
about, 883–84
filling, for pastry, 771
rescuing, 884
sherbet, 877
Blenders, 12
Bleu cheese
in cheese soufflé, 171–73
ham and parsley quiche, 165
hors d'oeuvre, 73–74
salad dressing, 119
Blowfish
about, 269
broiling, 225
oven-broiling, 231
pan-frying, 258
tails with rosemary; oven-broiled, 232
Blueberries
about, 884
and bananas, for cream tart or pie, 775
for cream tart or pie, 775
filling, for pastry, 772
freezing, 884
muffins, 680
pancakes, 688
rescuing, 884
sherbet, 877
Bluefish
about, 269–70
baked stuffed, 243
broiler-grilling, 228
broiling, 225
in fish salad, Ruth Hoberman's, 121
oven-broiling, 231
pan-frying, 258
teriyaki; broiler-grilled, 229
Boiled artichokes (master recipe), 470–72
Boiled beets (master recipe), 489–90

Boiled broccoli (master recipe), 492–93
Boiled brussels sprouts (master recipe), 497
Boiled celery root (master recipe), 516–17
Boiled green or wax beans (master recipe), 481–82
Boiled icing. *See* Meringue frosting
Boiled Jerusalem artichokes (master recipe), 542–43
Boiled lobsters, 296
Boiled okra, 554–55
Boiled potatoes (master recipe), 577–78
Boiled shell beans (master recipe), 486
Boiled white beans or other dried beans or peas (master recipe), 624–25
Bok choy
  about, 500
  stir-fried, 503
Boston cream pie, 824
Boullabaisse, 93–94
Bowls, 8
Braided egg loaf, 648
Braised beef stew meat (or lamb stew meat, or beef pot roast or round steak) master technique, 440–43
Braised celery (master recipe), 514–15
Braised chestnuts, 519–20
Braised chicken (or giblets or pork or veal stew meat, chops, or steaks) master technique, 426–28
Braised collards with bacon (master recipe), 520–21
Braised endive, 539–40
Braised fennel, 541
Braised fish with vegetables (master technique), 235–36
Braised leeks (master recipe), 546
Braised lettuce, 547–48
Braised onions (master recipe), 557–58
Braised red cabbage, 504–5
Braised trout with tarragon and cream, 239–40
Braising
  fish, 235–40
  meat, 425–28, 430–53
  poultry, 425–37, 438–40
Bran muffins, 680–81
Brandy butter cake filling, 854
Brazil nuts
  about, 700
  shelling and blanching, 700
Bread 631–61
  challah, 649
  cheddar cheese, 640
  dough
    kneading, 636
    slowing or arresting, 657–59
  egg (Sally Lunn) master recipe, 644–47
  egg loaf, braided, 648
  herb, 641
  ingredients, about, 632–33
  preparing with food processor, 633–34
  problems, 659–61
  pullman loaf (buttered white bread), 641
  raisin, 642
  raisin egg, 649
  rye, light or dark, 642–43
  white, basic American (master recipe), 634–40
  white, for hors d'oeuvre, 68
  whole wheat, 643
  see also Bread, quick; Coffeecakes; Corn bread; Doughnuts; Rolls and buns
Bread cases, for hors d'oeuvre, 72–73
Bread crumbs
  making, 60
  storing, 61
  toasting, 513
Bread pudding, 708
Bread, quick
  about, 663
  applesauce-raisin, 665
  banana, 666
  brown bread, 692–93
  carrot, 666
  cranberry, 666
  date-nut, 667
  orange, 667
  prune-nut, 667
  pumpkin, 667
  raisin-nut, spiced (master recipe), 664–65
  zucchini, 668
  see also Biscuits; Corn bread; Muffins; Popovers
Bread stuffing
  with apples and prunes, 363
  with chestnuts and apples, 363–64
  with dried fruits, 364
  with oysters (master recipe), 361–62
  with oysters and pecans, 364
  with sausage, 364–65
  with turkey and chicken livers, 365
  see also Stuffing
Breaded fried eggplant (master recipe), 536
Breaded sautéed chicken cutlets (with white wine sauce), 398
Breaded sautéed veal scallops or turkey breast scallops (with lemon-butter sauce), 403–4
Brioche-shape breakfast rolls, 647
Broccoli
  about, 491
  boiled (master recipe), 492–93

Broccoli *(Continued)*
with cheddar cheese; gratin of, 494
with crumbs, bacon, and garlic, 494–95
frozen, 491–92
in heavy cream, 493–94
overcooked, rescuing, 492
in pasta primavera, 188
peeling, 491, 492
purée of, 495
soup; cream of (master recipe), 78–79
trimming, 492
in vegetable soup, 100
Broccoli rabe
about, 495
with garlic; sautéed, 495–96
Broiled beef steaks (including London broil) master recipe, 390–91
Broiled chicken (master recipe), 384–85
Broiled chicken livers on skewers, 387–88
Broiled eggplant slices, 535
Broiled fish (master technique), 223–24
Broiled lamb chops, 391–92
Broiled scallops, 313–14
Broiled tomatoes, 609–10
Broiled veal chops (master recipe), 388–89
Broiled veal chops with cheese, garlic, and sage, 389
Broiler-grilled bluefish teriyaki, 229
Broiler-grilled fish (master technique), 226–27
Broiling
fish, 223–34
meat, 388–92
poultry, 384–88
Broiling pans, 7, 383
Broths. *See* Stocks
Brown bread, 692–93
Brown rice. *See* Rice
Brownies. *See* Cookies
Brussels sprouts
about, 496
boiled (master recipe), 497
frozen, 496
with onions and cheese; gratin of, 498
overcooked, rescuing, 496–97
in tomato sauce, 498
trimming, 497
with vinegar and garlic, 499
Bûche de Noël (Christmas log cake), 837
Buckwheat pancakes, 688–89
Buns: *see* Rolls and buns
Butter
anchovy, 259
browned, 512
clarified, 57
storing, 57
garlic, 303
Maître d' Hôtel, 258
spinach, 307–8
Butter cookies (master recipe), 733–35
Butter cream frosting (master recipe), 848–49
Butter pie crust dough, 750–55
Butter-poached shad roe, 275
Butter wafers (meltaways), 737
Buttercrunch cookies, 736–37
Butterfish
about, 270
baked stuffed, 243
broiler-grilling, 228
broiling, 225
oven-broiling, 231
pan-frying, 258
Buttermilk
biscuits, 673
dressing, 52
pancakes, 689
Butterscotch
bars or brownies (blondies), master recipe, 728–29
nut cookies, 737
nut cream pie, 777
Cabbage
about, 499
Bavarian puréed, Martha Abraham's, 503–4
cole slaw, 124
in heavy cream, 501
in New England boiled corned beef dinner, 465
potato soup, 94
cream of, 81
rolls in sweet-and-sour sauce; stuffed, 505–7
as salad addition, 113
scalloped, 502
skillet-braised (master recipe), 500–501
stir-fried, 503
trimming, 500
with vinegar and bacon, 502
see also Cabbage, Chinese; Cabbage, red
Cabbage, celery. *See* Bok choy
Cabbage, Chinese
about, 499–500
stir-fried, 503
Cabbage, red
about, 499
braised, 504–5
Cactus pears. *See* Prickly pears
Caesar salad, 127–29
Cake fillings
about, 804
brandy-butter, 854
chocolate, whipped, 852
lemon-butter (master recipe), 853
orange-butter, 854
pastry cream, 855–56
pecan-raisin, 854
rum-butter, 854
see also Frosting
Cake flour, 803
Cake pans, 14, 802–3
chart for smaller and larger yellow cakes, 807
substitution chart, 803

Cakes, 801–41
about, 801–4
angel food, 838–40
applesauce, 811
layer; classic, 811
layer with pecans and raisins, 811
apricot sponge layer, 829
baking tips, 802–4
banana, 811–12
layer; classic, 812
banana orange layer, 812
black on white layer, classic, 819
Boston cream pie, 824
Bûche de Noël, 837
chocolate, 812
layer; classic, 812
chocolate brownie, 814
layer, 814
chocolate chip cookie, 815
chocolate chip layer, 815
chocolate devil's food, 813
classic, 813
chocolate frosted layer, classic, 811
chocolate ganache, 832–34
chocolate mocha layer, 812
chocolate mousse, 717–18
chocolate pound, 824
chocolate raspberry layer, 814
chocolate whipped cream, 814
chocolate wind, 813–14
Christmas log, 837
citrus pound, 825
coconut, 815
coconut lemon, classic, 816
coconut raspberry layer, 816
cream sponge roll, 837
fill, how to, 804–5
frost, how to, 804–5
ginger pound, 825
gingerbread, 840–41
hazelnut pound, 825
increasing or decreasing recipes, 805–6
jam layer, 811
jelly roll, 837
Lady Baltimore, 819–20
Lane, 820
lemon, 816
layer; classic, 816
lemon sponge roll, 837
linzer layer, 819
maple-walnut layer, 819
orange, 816
layer; classic, 817
orange chocolate layer, 817
orange sponge, filled, 831
orange sponge roll, 837
peanut butter, 817
and jam layer, 817
peanut-toffee layer, 817
pineapple upside-down, 823–24
pineapple whipped cream roll, 837
pound (master recipe), 821–22
chocolate, 824
citrus, 825
ginger, 825
hazelnut, 825
spiced, 826
rescuing, 806
Robert E. Lee, 816
rum, Italian, 834
seed (anise or caraway), 826
spice, 818
layer; classic, 818
spiced pound, 826
sponge (master recipe), 826–28
layer, with praline butter cream, 831
sponge roll, 835–36
walnut, 818
walnut orange layer, 819
white, 819
layer; classic, 819
on black layer, classic, 814
whole wheat, 820
jam layer, 820
yellow (master recipe), 808–11
yield variation chart, 807
see also Cake fillings; Cheesecake; Coffeecakes; Frosting
California cream sauce with olives and almonds, 36
Candied sweet potatoes, 585–86
Candy, peanut brittle, 861
Cannibal balls, 71
Cantaloupe. *See* Melons
Caper
cream sauce, 36
mustard deglazing sauce, 210, 417–18
Capons. *See* Chicken
Caramel
coloring, 24–25
custard (flan) master recipe, 709–10
making, 709
Caraway seed
about, 17
cake, 826
Cardamom, 17
Carrots
about, 507
bread, 666
canned, 508
frozen, 508
glazed (master recipe), 508–9
in meat stock, 510
in heavy cream, 509
overcooked, rescuing, 508
purée, 509–10
as salad addition, 113
soup; cream of, 81
trimming, 508
in vegetable soup, 100
Cashews, 701
Casserole dishes, 7
Casseroles, 199–202
about, 199
basic (master technique), 200–201
chicken and olive, 202
curried beef, chicken, lamb, or pork, 202
day-after-Thanksgiving, 202
egg, 202

Casseroles *(Continued)*
fish, New England, 202
using leftovers in, 267
macaroni
and cheese, 202
and ham, 202
party, with grapes, 202
pork and caper, 202
shellfish, 202
spaghetti, 202
tuna-noodle, 202
variation chart, 202
Cast iron. *See* Cookware
Catfish
about, 270
baked stuffed, 243
braising, 237
broiling, 225
french-frying, 266
oven-broiling, 231
pan-frying, 258
poaching, 254
skinning, 270
southern-fried, 260
Cauliflower
about, 510
in browned butter with capers, 512
with cheddar cheese; gratin of, 512
frozen, 510
overcooked, rescuing, 511
soup; cream of, 81–82
steamed (master recipe), 511–12
in toasted crumbs, 513
trimming, 511
in vegetable soup, 100
Caviar and cream cheese scramble, 143
Cayenne pepper, 17
Celeriac. *See* Celery root
Celery
about, 513
braised (master recipe), 514–15
in heavy cream, 515
as salad addition, 113
soup; cream of, 82
trimming, 514
with walnuts; sherried, 515
wilted, rescuing, 513
Celery cabbage. *See* Bok choy
Celery root
about, 515–16
boiled (master recipe), 516–17
canned, rescuing, 516
peeling, 516
purée (with mushrooms or onions), 517
rémoulade, 517–18
soup; cream of, 82
Celery seed, 17
Cèpes mushrooms
sautéed veal chops with, 406
in wild mushroom scramble, 143–44
Challah, 649
Champagne cream sauce, 37
Chanterelles
sautéed veal chops with, 406
in wild mushroom scramble, 143–44
Charlotte russe, 718–19
Charts. *See* Tables and charts
Chayote. *See* Squash, winter
Cheddar cheese
biscuits, 674
bread, 640
in cheese omelet, 159
in cheese sauce, 37–38
in cheese scramble, 141
in cheese soufflé, 171–72
in ham and cheese soufflé, 175
hors d'oeuvre, 73–74
and jalapeño quiche, 163
in macaroni and cheese, 202
muffins, 681
stuffed tomatoes, 610–11
Cheese
blanketed fried eggs, 138
and ham soufflé, 175
hors d'oeuvre (master recipe), 73–74
muffins, 681
omelet, 159
pizza (master recipe), 193–94
as salad addition, 113
sauce, 37–38
with wine, 38
scramble, 141
soufflé (master recipe), 171–73
see also individual names
Cheesecake (master recipe), 713–14
with candied orange peel; little Italy, 715–16
chocolate, Dave's, 714–15
hazelnut, 715
lemon, 715
Cherries
about, 885
for cream tart or pie, 775
filling, for pastry, 772
pitting, 885
poaching, 866
sautéing and flambéing, 872
sherbet, 877
Cherry tomatoes sautéed in butter, 608–9
Chervil, 17
Chestnuts
about, 518
and apples; bread stuffing with, 363–64
braised, 519–20
peeling, 519
soup; cream of, 82–83
Chicken
à la king, 458–59
about, 329–30
braised (master technique), 426–27
breast cutlets
cutting and preparing, 335
sautéed, breaded (with white wine sauce), 398
sautéed, with cream and port, 399
sautéed (with white wine and herbs) master recipe, 397–98

Chicken *(Continued)*
sautéing, choosing for, 397
broiled (master recipe), 384–85
choosing, 384
marinated, with chili, soy sauce, or lemon, 385–87
broth; rescued canned, 28–29
cacciatore (hunter stew), 431
chowder, 103
country captain fricasse of, 428–29
in country pâté, 213–14
creamed
with olives and toasted almonds, 459–60
with white grapes (véronique), 460–61
in creamed omelet, 159–60
croquettes, 215–16
curried casserole, 202
cutting and preparing
breast cutlets, 335
parts, 330–34
split and quartered, 334–35
deep-frying, 424
doneness of, 339
fried (with cream gravy), 421–22
giblets
à la king, 458–59
about, 330
braised (master technique), 426–28
braising, preparing for, 427–28
country captain fricassee of, 428–29
mushroom fricassee of, 433
paprika fricassee of, 434
red wine fricassee of, 436
stew; creole, 429
stew with parsley dumplings, 462
stew with vegetables and cream gravy, old-fashioned (master recipe), 456–58
stew with vegetables; curried, 461
stewing, preparing for, 458
green pepper ragout of, 430–31
gumbo, 96
hors d'oeuvre (master recipe), 73–74
livers
about, 330
broiled, on skewers, 387–88
doneness of, 339
as hors d'oeuvre, 71
omelet, 159
pâté, 207–8
sautéed, with white wine and mustard, 400–401
sherried sautéed (master recipe), 399–400
and turkey livers; bread stuffing with, 365
marinades for, 386
mushroom fricassee of, 433
noodle soup with corn, 95
and olive casserole, 202
paprika fricassee of, 434
in party casserole with grapes, 202
pot pies, 463
quiche, 164
red wine fricassee of, 436
roast (master recipe), 346–48
about, 345–46
choosing, 346
with garlic and rosemary, 349
with giblet cream gravy, 348–49
roasting, for stock, 26
salad (master recipe), 119–20
sautéed
choosing for, 394
(with lemon) master recipe, 394–95
with lemon and garlic, 396
with vinegar, 396
with white wine, 396
soufflé, 174
soup with rice; curried, 97
stew
Creole, 429–30
with parsley dumplings, 462
with spices, fruits, and olives; Mexican-style, 432–33
with vegetables and cream gravy; old-fashioned (master recipe), 456–58
with vegetables; curried, 461
stewing hen
preparing, 457–58
for stock, 26
stock, 26
in Swedish meatballs, 211–12
tarragon and white wine fricassee of, 435
tetrazzini, 464–65
veal, and pork meatballs in parsley cream sauce, 210–11
veal, and pork patties (master recipe), 208–10
wings, deep-fried, as hors d'oeuvre, 70
see also Duck; Stuffing; Turkey
Chickpeas
salad, 626
as salad addition, 113
see also Beans and peas, dried
Chicory, 109
Chili
beans, 627
with beef or lamb stew, or beef steak, 449
marinade, 386
powder, 17

Chili *(Continued)*
stuffed green peppers, 574–75
Chinese chard. *See* Bok choy
Chinese parsley. *See* Coriander
Chinese peas. *See* Peas
Chinese shredded eggs, 161
Chinese-style spinach sauté, 593
Chives
about, 556
parsley omelet, 160
Chocolate
about, 695
brownie cake, 814
layer, 814
brownies, 730–31
butter cream frosting, 849
cake, 812
cheesecake; Dave's, 714–15
chiffon pie, 781–82
chip
blondies, 731
coconut cookies, 742
cookie cake, 815
cookies, 742
layer cake, 815
muffins, 681
cream cup custards, 712
cream pie, 778
crumb pie crust, 761
devil's food cake, 813
classic, 813
dipped strawberries, 900–901
estimated contents of table, 697
filling, whipped, 852
frosted layer cake; classic, 811
ganache cake, 832–34
glaze (master recipe), 851
kinds of, 696
layer cake; classic, 812
melting, how to, 696
mocha layer cake, 812
mousse (master recipe), 716–17
cake, 717–18
pound cake, 824
profiteroles, 797
raspberry layer cake, 814
sauce, 852
soufflé, 722
sour cream frosting, 852–53
substituting, 696
proportions tables, 697
whipped cream cake, 814
wind cake, 813–14
Chowders. *See* Soups
Cilantro. *See* Coriander
Cinnamon
about, 17
nut buns, 651–52
nut snails, 677
Citrus pound cake, 825
Clams
about, 280
baked stuffed, 284–85
broiled in garlic butter, 284
casino, 282–83
chowder, 102
Manhattan, 97–98
cleaning, 280
fried, 285
as hors d'oeuvre, 71
juice; rescued bottled, 29
mariner-style, 282
opening and shucking, 280–81
oreganato, 282–84
purchasing and storing, 280
quahogs
in clam chowder, 102
in Manhattan clam chowder, 97–98
raw, on the half-shell, 281
sauce; red, 186
steamed, 281–82
steamer, in bouillabaisse, 93–94
in stuffing, for cod, 245
Clarified butter, 57
Classic quiche Lorraine, 164–65
Cloud berry pie, 793–94
Cloverleaf dinner rolls, 643–44
Cloves, 18
Coatings
bound breading (master technique), 62–63
fritter batter (master technique), 63–64
simple breading (master technique), 61–62
tempura batter (master technique), 64
Cobblers
fruit (master technique), 767–69
filling chart for, 771–73
see also Pastry crusts, doughs, and shells; Pies; Tarts
Cocoa. *See* Chocolate
Coconut
about, 697
cake, 815
chocolate chip cookies, 742
cream pie, 778
crumb pie crust, 761
custard pie, 785–86
fresh meat, preparing, 697–98
fried shrimp; Leah's stuffed, 320–21
lemon layer cake; classic, 816
milk and cream, preparing, 698
milk; sea bass braised in, 238
processed, 699
raspberry layer cake, 816
soufflé, 723
toasting, 699
Cod
about, 270–71
baked stuffed, 243
New England, 245
with tomato stuffing, 244
braising, 237
Mediterranean, 238
broiling, 225
cakes, 267–69
croquettes, 267–69
in fish casserole, New England, 202

Cod *(Continued)*
in fish stock, 27–28
french-frying, 266
oven-broiling, 231
with mustard, 233
with parsley and garlic, 233
pan-frying, 258
poaching, 254
in white wine sauce, 251
see also Scrod
Coffee chiffon pie, 782
Coffeecakes
gugelhopf (raisin and almond), 649–50
streusel, 676–77
Cognac deglazing sauce, 413
Colanders, 11
Colbert sauce
sautéed beef steaks with, 415
sautéed lamb chops or steaks with, 419
Cold pea salad, 569
Cole slaw, 124
Collards
about, 520
braised, with bacon (master recipe), 520–21
in pork hocks and greens, 466
Consommé, 76–77
Cookie sheets, 727
Cookies, 727–48
almond crescents, 735–36
baking in small oven, 728
bar
applesauce, 730
apricot, 730
butterscotch (blondies)
master recipe, 728–29
chocolate brownies, 730–31
chocolate chip blondies, 731
date-nut, 731
hermit, 731
honey-ginger, 732
peanut butter brownies, 732
raisin-nut, 732
butter (master recipe), 733–35
wafers (meltaways), 737
buttercrunch, 736–37
butterscotch-nut, 737
chocolate chip, 742
coconut, 742
crumbs, making, 728
currant, 738
gingersnaps, 745–46
jam pockets, 738
macaroons, 744–45
oatmeal, 743
lace, 746
peanut butter, 743
pecan (master recipe), 740–42
balls, 738–39
poppyseed, 739
sesame seed wafers, 739–40
snickerdoodles, Grandmother Rosalind's, 747–48
sugar, 740
walnut (master recipe), 740–42
balls, 738–39
Cooking temperature table for poultry and meat, 344
Cookware, 5–7, 394
aluminum, cast, 6
aluminum, lightweight, 6
cast iron, 6
stainless steel, 6
Coriander, 18
Corn
about, 521–22
bacon soufflé, 174
canned, 522
chowder (master recipe), 101–2
cooking, on the cob, 522–23
creamed (master recipe), 523
with bacon, 523
with basil, 524
with parmesan cheese, 524
with peppers and onions, 525
custard, 526–27
fritters, 528
frozen, 522
kernels and pulp, preparing, 522
on the cob, cooking, 522–23
pudding, 526–27
quiche; Marilyn's Tex-Mex, 525–26
rescuing unsweet or flavorless, 522
shucking, 522
soup; cream of, 83
Corn bread (master recipe), 668–69
crackling, 670
muffins, 669
skillet, 670
sticks, 669
stuffing with oysters, 365–66
Corn muffins, 669
Corn sticks, 669
Corned beef boiled dinner; New England, 465
Cornmeal pancakes with bacon, 689
Counter space, 3
Country captain fricassee of chicken or giblets, 428–29
Country pâté, 213–14
Crabs and crabmeat
about, 286
blue, steamed, 287–88
cakes
as hors d'oeuvre, 70
Maryland, 290–91
canned, 286
cream sauce, 42–43
deviled, 291–92
as hors d'oeuvre, 71
fresh, 286–87
pasteurized, 287
frozen, 286
hors d'oeuvre, 73–74
Louis, 288–89
in pasta in cream with seafood, 190

Crabs *(Continued)*
quiche, 164
salad, 120–21
sautéed soft-shell, amandine or meunière, 289–90
scramble; curried, 141–42
in shellfish casserole, 202
shelling, 287
shells
in crab cream sauce, 42–43
in shellfish stock, 42
stuffing, for sole or flounder, 246
Crackling corn bread, 670
Cranberries
about, 885
apple filling, for pastry, 771
bread, 666
chiffon pie, 782
muffins, 681
orange relish, 885–86
sherbet, 877
Cranberry beans. *See* Beans, cranberry
Crawfish. *See* Crayfish
Crayfish
about, 292
preparing, 292–93
Cream
in crème fraîche, 859–60
deglazing sauce, 408
gravy, 457
made with basic cream sauce, 422
in pasta in cream, 186–87
whipped, 857–59
leftover, storing, 859
overbeaten, rescuing, 858
Cream cheese
in cheesecake, 713–14
and lox (or caviar) scramble, 143
Cream of almond soup, 80
Cream of artichoke soup, 80
Cream of asparagus soup, 80
Cream of broccoli soup (master recipe), 78–79
Cream of cabbage and potato soup, 81
Cream of carrot soup, 81
Cream of cauliflower soup, 81–82
Cream of celery root soup, 82
Cream of celery soup, 82
Cream of chestnut soup, 82–83
Cream of corn soup, 83
Cream of cucumber soup, 83
Cream of fennel soup, 84
Cream of green pea soup, 84
Cream of Jerusalem artichoke soup, 84
Cream of kohlrabi soup, 85
Cream of lettuce soup, 85
Cream of mushroom-potato soup with dill, 86
Cream of mushroom soup, 85
Cream of onion soup, 86
Cream of parsnip soup, 86
Cream of potato soup, 87
Cream of pumpkin soup, 90–91
Cream of rutabaga soup, 89
Cream of salsify soup, 87
Cream of sorrel soup, 87–88
Cream of spinach soup, 88
Cream of Swiss chard soup, 88
Cream of tartar, to stabilize egg whites, 134
Cream of tomato soup, 88–89
Cream of turnip soup, 89
Cream of watercress soup, 90
Cream of winter squash soup, 90–91
Cream of zucchini soup, 91
Cream puffs, 798–99
miniature (master recipe), 795–96
shells, bite-size, 72
see also Pastries
Cream sauces. *See* Sauces
Cream sponge roll, 837
Creamed chicken with olives and toasted almonds, 459–60
Creamed chicken or turkey with white grapes (chicken or turkey véronique), 460–61
Creamed corn (master recipe), 523
Creamed corn with bacon, 523
Creamed corn with basil, 524
Creamed corn with parmesan cheese, 524
Creamed corn with peppers and onions, 525
Creamed mushrooms, 551
Creamed omelet, 159–60
Creamed onions, 558
Creamed spinach, 591
Crème brûlée, 713
Crème fraîche, 859–60
Creole chicken or giblet stew, 429–30
Crêpes, 690–92
for hors d'oeuvre, 72
sautéed flambéed fruit with, 870
see also Pancakes
Croaker
about, 271
baked stuffed, 243
broiler-grilling, 228
broiling, 225
french-frying, 266
pan-frying, 258
Croquembouche, 797–98
Croquettes
chicken, 215–16
fish (master technique and rescue), 267–69
miniature, as hors d'oeuvre, 70
turkey, 215–16
Croutons
making, 127, 128
as salad addition, 113
Crumbed cucumbers, 531
Crumbed eggplant with basil and garlic, 534
Cucumbers
about, 528–29
crumbed, 531
and dill stuffing, for salmon, 245

Cucumbers *(Continued)*
- in heavy cream, 530
- mayonnaise, 53
- salad, 125
- as salad addition, 113
- salad dressing, 53
- sautéed (master recipe), 529–30
- soup; cream of, 83
- in sour cream and dill; sautéed, 531
- trimming and salting, 529–30

Cumin, 18
Cup custards, 711
Currants
- about, 886
- cookies, 738
- dried, 886

Curried casserole, 202
Curried chicken soup with rice, 97
Curried chicken, turkey, giblets, or veal stew with vegetables, 461
Curried crab scramble, 141–42
Curried cream sauce, 39–40
Curried gratin of Jerusalem artichokes, 543
Curried lobster, 298
Curried onion gratin, 559
Curried pan-fried smelts, 263
Curried rice, 619
Curried shrimp, 318
Curry, lamb or beef, 447–48
Curry powder, 18
Custard
- caramel (flan) master recipe, 709–10
- chocolate cream cup, 712
- corn, 526–27
- crème brûlée, 713
- cup, 711
- pie (master recipe), 784–85
- praline cream cup, 712
- sauce, 856–57
- vanilla cream cup (master recipe), 711–12
- *see also* Pudding; Timbales

Dandelion greens, 109
Dates
- about, 886
- nut bars, 731
- nut bread, 667
- nut muffins, 682
- rescuing, 886

Dave's chocolate cheesecake, 714–15
Day-after Thanksgiving casserole, 202
Deep-fried batter-dipped shrimp, 321–22
Deep-fried breaded scallops, 314–15
Deep-fried breaded shrimp, 320
Deep-frying, 59–66
- about, 59–60
- coatings for
  - bound breading (master technique), 62–63
  - fritter batter (master technique), 63–64
  - simple breading (master technique), 61–62
  - tempura batter (master technique), 64
- fish, 264–66
  - french-fried (master technique), 264–65
- master techniques, 64–66
- meat, 422–23
  - variation chart, 423
- poultry, 422–23
  - variation chart, 423

Deep-frying basket, 11
Desserts
- apple crisp (master recipe), 881–82
- baked apples, 882–83
- Bavarian cream, orange, strawberry, or raspberry, 719
- Charlotte russe, 718–19
- chocolate-dipped strawberries, 900–901
- chocolate mousse (master recipe), 716–17
- cobbler, fruit (master technique), 767–69
- English trifle (zuppa inglese), 830
- fritters, fruit (master technique), 873–75
- gooseberry fool, 866–67
- ice cream, soft, 844
- peaches melba, 867–68
- pears Hélène (with ice cream and chocolate sauce), 868–69
- pears in red wine, 868
- plum crisp, 896–97
- quinces in jelly, 869
- rhubarb crisp, 898–99
- sherbet, 876–79
- strawberry shortcake, 899–90
- *see also* Cakes; Cheesecake; Coffeecakes; Cookies; Custard; Fruits; Pastries; Pies; Pudding; Soufflés; Tarts

Deviled crab, 291–92
Deviled cream sauce, 40
Deviled eggs (master recipe), 146–47
Dill
- about, 18
- and cucumber stuffing, for salmon, 245
- in dilled cream sauce, 41
- in dilled hollandaise, 49

Dilled or parsleyed cream sauce, 41
Dilled stuffed veal or turkey rolls, 438–40
Double-crust fruit pie (master technique), 763–64
Doughnuts, raised, 652–54
- jelly, 652–54

Dressings. *See* Salad dressing; Sauces
Dropped biscuits, 673
Duck
- doneness of, 339
- in party casserole with grapes, 202
- roast
  - about, 349–50

Duck *(Continued)*
with cherries, 353
choosing, 350
with orange sauce (master recipe), 350–53
with peaches, 353
Dumplings, parsley, for stew, 462

Éclairs, 799
Egg bread (Sally Lunn) master recipe, 644–47
Egg noodles. *See* Pasta
Eggnog, 856
Eggplant
about, 532
baked stuffed, with lamb, 537–39
with basil and garlic; crumbed, 534
breaded fried (master recipe), 536
in heavy cream and parmesan cheese, 533
in "moussaka" pizza, 195–96
parmigiana, 537
peeling and salting, 532–33
pizza, 195
sautéed (master recipe), 532–33
slices; broiled, 535
in tomato sauce, 534
Eggs and egg dishes, 131–76
baked stuffed, 147
flavoring and saucing chart for, 148
as hors d'oeuvre, 69
Benedict, 149
"Benetine," 150
buying and storing, 132
casserole, 202
Chinese shredded, 161
deviled (master recipe), 146–47
for hors d'oeuvre, 69
Florentine, 150
freshness, testing for, 132
fried (master recipe), 137
with browned butter and capers, 138
cheese-blanketed, 138
with red peppers, 138–39
with zucchini, 139
hard-cooked (master recipe), 144–45
peeling and storing, 145
as salad addition, 113
timing chart for, 145
huevos rancheros (cowboy eggs), 151
peewee, as hors d'oeuvre, 69
poached (master recipe), 148–49
salad, party-type, for hors d'oeuvre, 68
scrambled (master recipe), 140
bacon and onion, 141
cheese, 141
curried crab, 141–42
with ham and green peppers; Georgia, 142
ham and Swiss, 142
herb, 142
lox (or caviar) and cream cheese, 143
wild mushroom, 143–44
separating, 133
sizes, 132
chart, 133
soft-cooked (master recipe), 144–45
peeling and storing, 145
timing chart for, 145
whites
beating, 133–36
folding in, 136
overbeaten, rescuing, 135
storing, 133
yolks, storing, 133
see also Frittatas; Omelets; Quiche; Soufflés; Timbales
Endive
about, 539
Belgian, 109
braised, 539–40
English trifle (zuppa inglese), 830
Escargots. *See* Snails
Escarole, 109–10
Espresso soufflé, 723

Fava beans. *See* Beans, fava
Fennel
about, 540
braised, 541
seed, 18–19
soup; cream of, 84
trimming, 541
wild and fresh, for grilling, 540–41
see also Anise
Fettuccini Alfredo, 187
Figs
about, 886
dried, 886
fritters, 874
poaching, 866
Filberts. *See* Hazelnuts
Filled orange sponge cake, 831
Fillings. *See* Cake fillings
Fines herbes, 19
Finnan haddie. *See* Haddock
Fish, 217–78
about, 217–23
baked stuffed (master technique), 240–42
chart, 243–44
in bouillabaisse, 93–94
braising
chart, 237
with vegetables (master technique), 235–36
broiling (master technique), 223–24
chart, 225–26
broiler-grilling (master technique), 226–27
chart, 228

Fish *(Continued)*
cakes (master technique and rescue), 267–69
casserole; New England, 202
using leftovers in, 267
chowder, 103
using leftovers in, 267
croquettes (master technique and rescue), 267–69
cuts of, 220
filleting, 221–23
flesh color, 219
french-frying (master technique), 264–65
chart, 266
freshness, checking for, 218–19
glossary, 269–78
leftover, rescuing, 267
oven-broiling (master technique), 230–31
chart, 231–32
pan-frying (master technique), 256–58
chart, 258–60
poaching (master technique), 252–54
chart, 254–56
salad; Ruth Hoberman's, 121
using leftovers in, 267
seafood soufflé, 175–76
stock, 27–28
stock substitute, 29
storing, 220–21
in white wine sauce (master technique), 248–51
chart, 251
see also individual names
Fish-Lovers' Cookbook, The (London), 277
Fish poacher, 7, 253
Flageolets
lamb stew with, 446–47
see also Beans and peas, dried
Flan. *See* Caramel custard
Flemish beef stew, pot roast, or steak with onions and beer, 445–46
Flounder
about, 275–76
baked stuffed, 244
fillets with crabmeat stuffing, 246
fillets with mushroom stuffing, 246
braising, 237
sweet-and-sour, 239
broiling, 226
fillets amandine; sautéed, 263–64
fillets stuffed with shrimp mousse, 252
in fish stock, 27–28
french-frying, 266
meunière, 264
oven-broiling, 232
pan-frying, 259
poaching, 255
in white wine sauce, 251
Flour, cake, 803
Food mills, 10
Food processors, 12
French-fried fish (master technique), 264–65
French-fried potatoes, 584–85
French-fried sweet potatoes, 587
French-frying. *See* Deep-frying
French omelet (master recipe), 155–57
Fresh fruit cream tart or pie (master technique), 774
Fricassee. *See* Stews
Fried beans with sausage and onions, 628
Fried chicken (with cream gravy), 421–22
Fried clams, 285
Fried eggs (master recipe), 137
Fried eggs with browned butter and capers, 138
Fried eggs with red peppers, 138–39
Fried eggs with zucchini, 139
Fried oysters, 309–10
Fried squid, 327
Frittatas
about, 151
with artichokes, 152
with green or red peppers, 153
with ham, 153
as hors d'oeuvre, 69
potato (master recipe), 151–52
with sausage, 153
with spinach, 154
with tomato, 154
with zucchini, 154
Fritters
apple, 874
apricot, 874
banana, 874
batter for (master technique), 63–64
corn, 528
fig, 874
fruit (master technique), 873–75
nectarine, 874
orange, 874–75
oyster, 310
peach, 875
pear, 875
pineapple, 875
Frosting
about, 804
butter cream (master recipe), 848–49
chocolate butter cream, 849
chocolate glaze (master recipe), 851
lemon butter cream, 850
maple, 847
maple meringue butter cream, 847
meringue (master recipe), 844–47
decreasing chart, 845
rescuing, 844
meringue butter cream (master recipe), 844–47

Frosting *(Continued)*
mocha butter cream, 850
orange butter cream, 850
seafoam icing, 848
sour cream chocolate, 852
toffee, 848
toffee meringue butter cream, 848
see also Cake fillings; Sauces
Fruited rice, 619
Fruits, 863–901
about, 863–64
cobbler (master technique), 767–69
compote, 864
filling chart, for pastry, 771–73
fresh, cream tart or pie, 774
fresh, for cream tarts and pies, 775
fritters (master technique), 873–75
for fritters, 874–75
glossary of, 879–901
pie
double-crust (master technique), 763–64
in a crumb pie crust (master technique), 766–67
streusel crumb, 764–66
poached (master technique), 865–69
compote, 864
with custard sauce, 864
with ice cream and meringue, 865
shortcake, 864
with sponge cake, 864
poaching, about, 864
for poaching, 866–69
sautéed, flambéed (master technique), 871–73
about, 870
with cake, 870
with crêpes, 870
with ice cream, 870
for sautéing and flambéing, 872–73
sherbet (master technique), 876–79
for sherbet, 877–78
tart (master technique), 769–70
streusel crumb, 764–66
for tarts, 770
see also individual names
Fruits, dried. *See* individual names
Frying. *See* Deep-frying
Frypans. *See* Skillets
Garden herb biscuits, 674
Garlic
about, 556
butter, 303
flavored oil, 127–28
and olive rolls, 657
peeling, 556
purchasing and storage, 556
Garlic presses, 10
Georgia scramble with ham and green peppers, 142
Georgia-style stuffed pork chops, 437–38
Giblets
à la king, 458–59
about, 330
braising (master technique), 426–28
preparing for, 427–28
country captain fricassee of, 428–29
gravy; roast turkey with, 360–61
mushroom fricassee of, 433
paprika fricassee of, 434
red wine fricassee of, 436
stew
Creole, 429
with parsley dumplings, 462
with vegetables and cream gravy, old-fashioned (master recipe), 456–58
with vegetables; curried, 461
stewing, preparing for, 458
Ginger
about, 19
bread, 840–41
pound cake, 825
snaps, 745–46
crumb pie crust, 762
Glazed carrots (master recipe), 508–9
Glazed carrots in meat stock, 510
Glazed onions, 559
Glazed parsnips (master recipe), 564–65
Glazed turnips or rutabagas (master recipe), 611–12
Glazed turnips or rutabagas in meat stock, 613
Glazes. *See* Frosting
Gooseberries
about, 886–87
fool, 866–67
poaching, 866
Gorgonzola cheese, cognac, and walnuts; pasta in cream with, 187–88
Gouda cheese blanketed fried eggs, 138
Goulash, 451
Graham cracker crumbs
making, 761
pie crust (master recipe), 760–61
Grand Marnier soufflé, 724
Grandmother Rosalind's green or wax beans with vinegar and bacon, 484–85
Grandmother Rosalind's snickerdoodles, 747–48
Grapefruit
about, 887
sections, preparing, 887
sherbet, 877
Grapes
about, 887–88
frosting, 888
peeling and seeding, 888

Grapes *(Continued)*
white
cream sauce with, 39
for cream tart or pie, 775
poaching, 867
Graters, 9–10
Gratin of broccoli with cheddar cheese, 494
Gratin of brussels sprouts with onions and cheese, 498
Gratin of cauliflower with cheddar cheese, 512
Gratin of green or wax beans with mushrooms, 483
Gratinéed onions with cheese, 560
Gravy
chicken, for roast chicken, 347–48
cream (master recipe), 457
for fried chicken, 422
giblet
cream, roast chicken with, 348–49
roast turkey with, 360–61
Green goddess mayonnaise and green goddess salad dressing, 53
Green mayonnaise. *See* Herb mayonnaise
Green or wax beans in Greek-style tomato sauce, 483–84
Green or wax beans in heavy cream, 482
Greens
beet, 488
collard
about, 520
braised, with bacon (master recipe), 520–21
in pork hocks and greens, 466
dandelion, 109
mustard
about, 554
cooking, 554
in pork hocks and greens, 466
turnip, in pork hocks and greens, 466
see also Salads; Spinach
Grilling, outdoor and indoor, 383
see also Broiling
Grouper
about, 271
baked stuffed, 243
braising, 237
broiling, 225
cakes, 267–69
croquettes, 267–69
french-frying, 266
oven-broiling, 231
pan-frying, 258
poaching, 254
in white wine sauce, 251
Guacamole, 479
Gumbo. *See* Soups

Haddock
about, 271
baked stuffed, 243
braising, 237
broiling, 225
cakes, 267–69
croquettes, 267–69
french-frying, 266
oven-broiling, 231
pan-frying, 258
poaching, 254
in white wine sauce, 251
Halibut
about, 271
baked stuffed, 243
broiling, 225
cakes, 267–69
croquettes, 267–69
in fish stock, 27
french-frying, 266
oven-broiling, 232
pan-frying, 258
poaching, 254
in white wine sauce, 251
Ham
about, 375
baked glazed (master recipe), 376–77
biscuits; Virginia, 675
bleu cheese and parsley quiche, 165
and cheese soufflé, 175
choosing, 375
in eggs Benedict, 149
in eggs "Benetine," 150
fresh
preparing, 177
roasted (master recipe), 376–77
frittata with, 153
and macaroni, 202
maple muffins, 682
in pork and caper casserole, 202
salad, 121
as salad addition, 114
steaks
choosing for sautéing, 409–10
sautéed (with apples and cream) master recipe, 409–11
sautéed, with apples, curry, and cream, 411
sautéed, with pineapple, 411–12
in stuffing, for cabbage rolls, 506
and Swiss quiche (master recipe), 162–63
and Swiss rolls, 657
and Swiss scramble, 142
see also Pork
Hamburgers
buns, 656
tips on making, 204
Hand-made egg noodles, 180–83
Hard-cooked eggs (master recipe), 144–45
Hard rolls (master recipe), 654–56
Harvard beets (glazed beets), 490
Hash brown potatoes, 579

Hazelnuts
about, 701
blanching and toasting, 701
cheesecake, 715
in nutted meringue fingers, 794
pound cake, 825
in praline powder, 861
Hearts of palm, 563
Hens. *See* Chicken
Herb biscuits; garden, 674
Herb bread, 641
Herb mayonnaise, 54
Herb scramble, 142
Herbs and spices, 15–22
about, 15–16
grinding, 16
as salad addition, 114
see also individual names
Hermit bars, 731
Hero rolls, 656
Hollandaise sauce. *See* Sauces
Honey-ginger bars, 732
Hors d'oeuvre, 67–74
about, 67
baked stuffed eggs, 69
bread cases for, 72–73
breads for, 68
cannibal balls, 71
cheese, hot (master recipe), 73–74
chicken, hot (master recipe), 73–74
chicken livers as, 71
chicken wings, deep-fried, 70
crab cakes, miniature, 70
cream puff shells, bite-size, 72
crêpes for, 72
croquettes, miniature, 70
deviled eggs, 69
frittatas as, 69
meatballs as, 71
potatoes, boiled new, 72
quiches as, 69
seafood, hot (master recipe), 73–74
shellfish as, 70–71
deep-fried, 70
spreads for, 68–69
tempura vegetables, 70
vegetable, 71–72
Horseradish
about, 19
bacon cream sauce, 35
cream sauce, 41
mayonnaise, 54
Huevos rancheros (cowboy eggs), 151
Hunter stew (chicken cacciatore and veal chasseur), 431

Ice cream, soft, 844
Icing. *See* Frosting
Indian pudding, 707
Italian parsley. *See* Parsley
Italian salad dressing, 118
Italian-style beef rolls stuffed with sausage and eggs, 452–53

Jalapeños. *See* Peppers, chili
Jam layer cake, 811
Jam pockets, 738
Jelly roll, 837
Jelly roll pans, 14
Jerusalem artichokes
about, 542
boiled (master recipe), 542–43
curried gratin of, 543
overcooked, rescuing, 542
peeling and trimming, 542–43
sautéed, 544
soup; cream of, 84
Juniper, 19

Kale
about, 544
in pork hocks and greens, 466
Key limes. *see* Limes
Kidney beans. *see* Beans and peas, dried
Kingfish. *See* Mackerel
Kitchens, 3–14
cookware, 5–7
counter space, 3
lighting, 3–4
storage space, 4
utensils, 5–14
Kiwis
about, 888
for cream tart or pie, 775
Knives, 8–9
Kohlrabi
about, 545
soup; cream of, 85
steamed, 545
Kumquats
about, 888
canned, 888
poaching, 867

Lacy potato pancakes, 583
Lady Baltimore cake, 819–20
Lamb
about, 338–39
chops
broiled, 391–92
broiling, choosing for, 391
sautéed, with colbert sauce, 419
sautéed, with madeira, 418
sautéed (with mustard and capers) master recipe, 416–18
sautéing, choosing for, 416
curried casserole, 202
doneness of, 340
ground
in chili-stuffed green peppers, 574–75

Lamb *(Continued)*
in meat sauce, 185
in "moussaka" pizza, 195–96
in stuffing, for eggplant, 538–39
in stuffing, for summer squash, 598–600
leg of
preparing, 381
roast au Jus (master recipe), 378–80
salad, 120
steaks
sautéed, with colbert sauce, 419
sautéed, with madeira, 418
sautéed (with mustard and capers) master recipe, 416–18
sautéing, choosing for, 416
stew meat
braised (master technique), 440–42
braised, Napa Valley, 450
braising, preparing for, 442
in chili, 449
curry, 447–48
with flageolets or lima beans, 446–47
in goulash, 451
old-fashioned stew, 443–44
Lane cake, 820
Lasagna, 192–93
Leah's custard pie with dried fruits, 786
Leah's stuffed coconut-fried shrimp, 320–21
Leeks
about, 545
braised (master recipe), 546
in heavy cream, 547
trimming, 546
Legumes, dried. *See* Beans and peas, dried
Lemons
about, 888–89
cake, 816
layer; classic, 816
butter cake filling (master recipe), 853
butter cream frosting, 850
butter deglazing sauce, 402
cheesecake, 715
chiffon pie, 782
cream sauce, 41–42
deglazing sauce, 395
flavoring, 889
juice and zest, preparing, 889
marinade, 386
meringue pie, 787–89
sherbet, 877
soufflé, 724
sponge roll, 837
tip about, 128
Lettuce
about cooking, 547
Bibb
about, 109
soup; cream of, 85
Boston
about, 109
soup; cream of, 85
braised, 547–48
iceberg, 110
leaf, 110
radicchio, 110
romaine, 110
trimming and blanching, 547
Light or dark rye bread, 642–43
Lighting, kitchen, 3–4
Lima beans. *See* Beans and peas, dried; Beans, lima
Limes
about, 889
chiffon pie, 783
sherbet, 877
Linzer layer cake, 819
Litchis
about, 889
rescuing canned, 889
Little Italy cheesecake with candied orange peel, 715–16
Little Italy savory biscuits, 674–75
Liver
calves'
choosing for sautéing, 419
sautéed, with bacon and onions, 419–20
chicken
about, 330
broiled, on skewers, 387–88
doneness of, 339
as hor d'oeuvre, 71
omelet, 159
pâté, 207–8
sautéed, with white wine and mustard, 400–401
sherried sautéed (master recipe), 399–400
and turkey livers; bread stuffing with, 365
turkey
and chicken livers; bread stuffing with, 365
doneness of, 339
Loaf pans, 13
Lobster
about, 293
baked in mustard crumbs, 299–300
baked stuffed, my mother's, 298–99
boiled, 296
broth, 294
cooked, storing, 297
cream sauce, 42–43
curried, 298
extracting meat from, 293–94
hors d'oeuvre, 73–74
Newburg (master recipe), 297–98
in pasta in cream with seafood, 190
purchasing, 293
quiche, 164
salad, 122

Lobster *(Continued)*
  in shellfish casserole, 202
  shells
    for broth, 294
    in fish stock, 27–28
    in lobster cream sauce, 42–43
    in shellfish stock, 42
  storing, 293
London broil. *See* Beef
Lotte. *See* Monkfish
Lox (or caviar) and cream cheese scramble, 143

Macadamia nuts, 701
Macaroni
  and cheese, 202
  and ham, 202
  see also Pasta
Macaroons, 744–45
Mace, 19
Mackeral
  about, 271–72
  baked stuffed, 243
  braising, 237
  broiler-grilling, 228
  broiling, 225
  pan-frying, 259
    with rosemary, 261
Maître d' Hôtel butter, 258
Mako shark. *See* Shark
Mangetouts. *See* Peas
Mangoes
  about, 890
  rescuing, 890
  sherbet, 877
Manhattan clam chowder, 97–98
Maple
  frosting, 847
  glazed parsnips, 565
  ham muffins, 682
  meringue butter cream, 847
  walnut cream pie, 778
  walnut layer cake, 819
Marilyn's Tex-Mex corn quiche, 525–26
Marinades
  chili, 386
  lemon, 386
  soy sauce, 386
  see also Sauces
Marinated broiled chicken with chili, soy sauce, or lemon, 385–87
Marjoram, 19
Marsala. *see* Wine
Martha Abraham's Bavarian puréed cabbage, 503–4
Maryland crab cakes, 290–91
Mashed potatoes, 578–79
Mashed sweet potatoes, 586
Mayonnaise (master recipe), 51–52
  about, 50–51
  blender or food processor method, 51
  cucumber, 53
  green goddess, 53
  herb, 54
  horseradish, 54
  mustard, 55
  storing, 52
  whipped cream, 56
  see also Sauces
Measures, 7–8
Meat
  about, 329–44
  braising, about, 425–26
  broiled, 388–92
  cooking, facts about, 341–42
  deep-frying, 422–23
    variation chart, 423
  ground, 203–16
    grinding with food processor, 203
    in spaghetti casserole, 202
    veal, chicken, and pork patties (master recipe), 208–10
  roast, 366–81
  sauce, 185
    bolognese, 185
  sautéing, 401–20
    about, 393–94
  stewing, 455–58, 461–62, 465–66
    about, 455
  temperature table for, 343
  temperature taking, 343
  see also individual names
Meat grinder, 10
Meat loaf, mother's, circa 1958, 205
Meat pies
  chicken, 463
  turkey, 463
Meat thermometers
  about, 11, 342
  accuracy, testing for, 342
  temperature taking with, 343
Meatballs
  as hors d'oeuvre, 71
  Swedish, 211–12
  veal, chicken, and pork, in parsley cream sauce, 210–11
Mediterranean braised cod or scrod, 238
Mediterranean broiler-grilled swordfish, 229
Melons
  about, 890–91
  poaching, 867
  rescuing, 891
  ripe, how to choose, 890–91
  sherbet, 878
Meringue, 787–88
  butter cream (master recipe), 844–47
  frosting (boiled icing)
    master recipe, 844–47
    decreasing chart, 845
    rescuing, 844
  nests (master recipe), 792–93
Mexican-style chicken or pork stew with spices, fruits, and olives, 432–33
Microwave ovens, 12
Middle Eastern rice, 620
Minestrone, 105–6

Miniature cream puffs (master recipe), 795–96
Mint, 19
Minted purée of peas, 568
Mixers, electric, 12
Mocha
butter cream frosting, 850
cream pie, 779
Molds
soufflé, 14
tart, French, 14
tartlet, 14
Monkfish
about, 272
baked stuffed, 243
braising, 237
broiling, 225
oven-broiling, 232
pan-frying, 259
poaching, 255
in white wine sauce, 251
Monterey Jack cheese
blanketed fried eggs, 138
in cheese scramble, 141
Morels, sautéed veal chops with, 406
Mortar and pestle, 10–11
Mother's meat loaf, circa 1958, 205
"Moussaka" pizza, 195–96
Mousse
chocolate (master recipe), 716–17
cake, 717–18
Mousseline sauce, 49
Muffin tins, 14
Muffins (master recipe), 678–79
apple-cinnamon, 679
apricot-walnut, 679
bacon, 680
banana, 680
blueberry, 680
bran, 680–81
cheese, 681
chocolate chip, 681
corn, 669
cranberry, 681
date-nut, 682
maple-ham, 682
oatmeal-raisin, 682
orange, 683
peanut butter (and jam), 683
pineapple-walnut, 683
pumpkin, 684
sour cream, 684
spice, 684–85
whole wheat, 685
see also Biscuits; Rolls and buns
Mushrooms
about, 548–49
beef-noodle soup, 92–93
canned, rescuing, 549
cleaning, 549
and trimming, 550
cream sauce, 43
creamed, 551
dried, 550
fricassee of chicken, giblets, pork, or veal, 433
marinating, 126
pizza, 196
potato soup with dill; cream of, 86
quiche, 165
and red wine sauce, for beef steaks, 414
as salad addition, 114
sautéed (master recipe), 550–51
smothered pork or veal chops or steaks, 433
soup; cream of, 85
spinach, and bacon salad, 126–27
stuffed, 552
stuffing, 553
for sole or flounder, 246
timbale, 167–68
Mushrooms, wild
about, 549
dried, 550
sautéed veal chops with, 406
scramble, 143–44
Mussels
about, 300
broiled in garlic butter (master recipe), 303
cleaning and soaking, 301
as hors d'oeuvre, 71
mariner-style (master recipe), 301
salad, 302
storing, 300
Mustard, 20
caper deglazing sauce
for lamb chops or steaks, 417–18
for veal, chicken, and pork patties, 210
hollandaise, 49
mayonnaise, 55
tarragon salad dressing, 118
Mustard greens
about, 554
cooking, 554
in pork hocks and greens, 466
My mother's baked stuffed lobster, 298–99
My mother's potato salad, 124–25

Napa Valley braised beef or lamb, 450
Navy bean or black bean soup, 104–5
Nectarines
about, 891
for cream tart or pie, 775
filling, for pastry, 772
fritters, 874
peeling, 891
poaching, 867
rescuing, 891
sautéing and flambéing, 872
sherbet, 878
New England baked stuffed whole cod, 245
New England boiled corned beef dinner, 465
New England fish casserole, 202
Noodles. *See* Pasta

Nutmeg, 20
Nutmeg graters, 10
Nuts, 699–703
  about, 699
  blanching and skinning, 700
  grinding, 699
  slicing and slivering, 699
  storing, 699
  toasting, 699–700
  see also individual names
Nutted meringue fingers, 794

Oatmeal
  cookies, 743
  lace cookies, 746
  raisin muffins, 682
Ocean perch
  about, 272–73
  baked stuffed, 243
  braising, 237
  broiling, 225
  french-frying, 266
  oven-broiling, 232
  pan-frying, 259
  poaching, 255
  in white wine sauce, 251
Oil
  about, 115–16
  braised peppers (master recipe), 570–71
  garlic-flavored, 127–28
  nut and seed, 116
  olive, 115–16
  reusing, 66
  vegetable, 115
  and vinegar salad dressing (master recipe), 117–18
Okra
  about, 554
  boiled, 554–55
  in chicken gumbo, 96
Old-fashioned beef or lamb stew, 443–44
Old-fashioned beef pot roast, 444
Old-fashioned butter-braised spinach, 592
Old-fashioned chicken (or turkey, giblet, or veal) stew with vegetables and cream gravy, (master recipe), 456–58
Olive oil. *See* Oil
Olives
  and garlic rolls, 657
  onion-anchovy pizza, 196–97
  as salad addition, 114
Omelets
  apple, 157
  apricot jam, 157–59
  cheese, 159
  chicken liver, 159
  Chinese shredded eggs, 161
  creamed, 159–60
  French (master recipe), 154–57
    about, 154
  parsley-chive, 160
  Spanish, 160–61
Onions
  about, 555
  anchovy-olive pizza, 196–97
  and bacon scramble, 141
  baked, 563
  baked stuffed, with sausage, 561–62
  braised (master recipe), 557–58
  canned, rescuing, 557
  with cheese; gratinéed, 560
  cream sauce, 43–44
  creamed, 558
  glazed, 559
  gratin; curried, 559
  overcooked, rescuing, 556–57
  peeling and trimming, 557
  pizza, 196
  purchasing and storage, 556
  in quiche Moira, 165–66
  rings; batter-dipped deep-fried, 560–61
  as salad addition, 114
  soup; cream of, 86
  and tearing, 556
Oranges
  about, 891–92
  Bavarian cream, 719
  bread, 667
  butter cake filling, 854
  butter cream frosting, 850
  cake, 816
  chiffon pie (master recipe), 780–81
  chocolate layer cake, 817
  cream pie, 779
  custard pie, 787
  fritters, 874–75
  juice
    preparing, 892
    store-bought, 892
  layer cake; classic, 817
  muffins, 683
  peel, 20
  sauce, for duck, 350–53
  sections, preparing, 892
  sherbet, 878
  sponge roll, 837
  zest, preparing, 892
Oregano, 20
Oven-broiled blowfish tails with rosemary, 232
Oven-broiled cod with mustard, 233
Oven-broiled cod with parsley and garlic, 233
Oven-broiled fish (master technique), 230–31
Oven-broiled salmon with dill, 233
Oven-broiled salmon with green peppercorns, 234
Oven-broiled salmon with lime butter, 234
Oven-broiled shad with anchovy butter, 234
Oyster plant. *See* Salsify
Oysters
  about, 304
  bread stuffing with, 361–62
  broiled in garlic butter, 308

Oysters *(Continued)*
cooking, 305
corn bread stuffing with, 365–66
fried, 309–10
fritters, 310
as hors d'oeuvre, 71
opening and shucking, 304–5
and pecans; bread stuffing with, 364
purchasing and storing, 304
raw, on the half-shell, 305
Rockefeller, 307–8
scalloped (master recipe), 308–9
steamed in soy and ginger, 305–6
stew, 306
in stuffing, for cod, 245
tempura, 311

Pan-fried fish (master technique), 256–58
Pan-fried mackerel with rosemary, 261
Pan-fried salmon steaks with tomato cream sauce, 262
Pancakes (master recipe), 687–88
banana, 688
berry, 688
buckwheat, 688–89
buttermilk, 689
cornmeal, with bacon, 689
see also Crêpes; Waffles
Papayas, 892–93
Paprika
about, 20
fricassee of chicken, giblets, pork, or veal, 434
smothered pork or veal chops or steaks, 434
Parmesan cheese
in cheese omelet, 159
in cheese scramble, 141
in cheese soufflé, 171–73
in creamed omelet, 159–60
in pizza soufflé, 175
Parsley
about, 20–21
chive omelet, 160
cream sauce, for meatballs, 210–11
dumplings, for stew, 462
ham and bleu cheese quiche, 165
in parsleyed cream sauce, 41
Parsley, Chinese. *See* Coriander
Parsley, Italian. *See* Parsley
Parsleyed rice, 620
Parsnips
about, 564
glazed (master recipe), 564–65
maple-glazed, 565
overcooked, rescuing, 564
purée with sherry or Madeira, 565–66
soup; cream of, 86
trimming, 564
Party casserole with grapes, 202
Pasta
about, 177–78
cooking, 178–79
in cream (master recipe), 186–87
with basil, 188
with garlic and walnuts, 187
with Gorgonzola, cognac, and walnuts, 187–88
with prosciutto or pepperoni and peas, 189
with sausage, 189
with seafood, 190
fettuccini Alfredo, 187
lasagna, 192–93
leftover, 179
making
by hand, 180–83
by machine, 179
primavera, 188
serving, 178
with vodka and hot pepper, 190
see also Sauces
Pasta machines, 179
Pasta rolling pins, 179–80
Pastries
cloud berry pie, 793–94
cream puffs, 798–99
miniature (master recipe), 795–96
croquembouche, 797–98
éclairs, 799
meringue nests (master recipe), 792–93
nutted meringue fingers, 794
profiteroles
chocolate, 797
strawberry, 797
see also Cobblers; Pies; Tarts
Pastry bags, 13
Pastry blenders, 13
Pastry brushes, 13
Pastry cream (master recipe), 855–56
Pastry crusts, doughs, and shells
about, 749
butter pie crust dough
about, 750–53
food processor method, 751
chocolate crumb pie crust, 761
coconut crumb pie crust, 761
cream puff shells, miniature, 795–96
ginger crumb pie crust, 762
graham cracker crumb pie crust, 760–61
pecan crumb pie crust, 762
pie shell, 9-inch (master recipe), 753–58
tart shells
3-inch, 759
9-inch, 758–59

Pastry crusts *(Continued)*
tartlet shells, 759–60
vanilla crumb pie crust, 762
Pâté
chicken liver, 207–208
country, 213–14
as hors d'oeuvre, 69
Patties, veal, chicken, and pork (master recipe), 208–10
Pattypan squash. *See* Squash, summer
Peaches
about, 893
canned, 893
for cream tart or pie, 775
filling, for pastry, 772
fritters, 875
for fruit tarts, 770
melba, 867–68
peeling, 893
poaching, 867
rescuing, 893
sautéing and flambéing, 872
sherbet, 878
Peanut butter
brownies, 732
cake, 817
cookies, 743
and jam layer cake, 817
(and jam) muffins, 683
making, 702
Peanuts
about, 701–2
brittle, 861
in peanut butter cake, 817
toffee layer cake, 817
Pears
about, 893–94
filling, for pastry, 772
fritters, 875
for fruit tarts, 770
Hélène (with ice cream and chocolate sauce), 868–69
poaching, 868
in red wine, 868
rescuing, 894
sautéing and flambéing, 872
sherbet, 878
Pears, prickly. *See* Prickly pears
Peas
about, 566
cooked in heavy cream, 568
frozen, rescuing, 566
minted purée of, 568
salad; cold, 569
shelling, 567
skillet-braised (master recipe), 567
soup
cream of green, 84
green split, 98–99
starchy and tough, rescuing, 566
in vegetable soup, 100
Peas, dried. *See* Beans and peas, dried
Pecans
about, 702
balls, 738–39
cookies (master recipe), 740–42
crumb pie crust, 762
in date-nut muffins, 682
and oysters; bread stuffing with, 364
pie, 791
raisin cake filling, 854
in raisin-nut bread, spiced, 664–65
Pennsylvania Dutch soured beef pot roast with ginger, 445
Pepper, 21
Pepper or pepper-anchovy pizza, 197
Peppered sautéed beef steaks with cognac and cream, 415–16
Peppermills, 10
Pepperoni
and peas; pasta in cream with, 189
pizza, 197
Peppers, bell
about, 569
with basil and walnuts, 572
green
chili-stuffed, 574–75
frittata with, 153
and ham; Georgia scramble with, 142
ragout of chicken, pork, or veal, 430–31
as salad addition, 114
in meat glaze, 572
oil-braised (master recipe), 570–71
peeling, 570
in pepper or pepper-anchovy pizza, 197
red
fried eggs with, 138–39
frittata with, 153
marinated, as salad addition, 114
purée of, 573
roasted, as salad addition, 114
salad, 573
as salad addition, 114
Peppers, chili
about, 569–70
anchovy pizza, 195
and cheddar quiche, 163
peeling, 570
pickled, as salad addition, 114
testing for heat, 570
Persimmons, 894
Pesto, 191
Pickled beets, 490
Pie pans, 13–14
Pies
about, 749
banana cream, 777
butterscotch-nut, 777
chocolate chiffon, 781–82
chocolate cream, 778
chocolate crumb crust, 761
cloud berry, 793–94
coconut cream, 778
coconut crumb crust, 761
coconut custard, 785–86

Pies *(Continued)*
coffee chiffon, 782
cranberry chiffon, 782
custard (master recipe), 784–85
with dried fruits, Leah's, 786
fruit cream, fresh (master technique), 774
fruit, in a crumb crust (master technique), 766–67
fruit, double crust (master technique), 763–64
fruit filling chart for, 771–73
fruit, streusel crumb (master technique), 764–66
fruits, fresh, for, 775
ginger crumb crust, 762
graham cracker crumb crust, 760–61
lemon chiffon, 782
lemon meringue, 787–89
lime chiffon, 783
maple-walnut cream, 778
mocha cream, 779
orange chiffon (master recipe), 780–81
orange cream, 779
orange custard, 787
pecan, 791
pecan crumb crust, 762
praline cream, 779
pumpkin, 790
raspberry chiffon, 783
rum cream (master recipe), 776–77
shells, 9-inch (master technique), 753–58
strawberry chiffon, 783
vanilla cream, 780
vanilla crumb crust, 762
see also Cobblers; Pastry crusts, doughs, and shells; Tarts
Pignolias. *See* Pine nuts
Pine nuts, 702
Pineapple
about, 894–96
for cream tart or pie, 775
filling, for pastry, 773
fresh, preparing, 895
fritters, 875
poaching, 869
rescuing, 895–96
sautéing and flambéing, 872
sherbet, 878
upside-down cake, 823–24
walnut muffins, 683
whipped cream roll, 837
Pinto beans. *See* Beans and peas, dried
Pistachio nuts
about, 702
blanching, 702
Pizza
anchovy, 195
anchovy-jalapeño, 195
cheese (master recipe), 193–94
eggplant, 195
"moussaka," 195–96
mushroom, 196
onion, 196
onion-anchovy-olive, 196–97
pepper, 197
pepper-anchovy, 197
pepperoni, 197
sausage, 198
soufflé, 175
Plantains
about, 575
cooking, 575
see also Bananas
Plums
about, 896
crisp, 896–97
filling, for pastry, 773
for fruit tarts, 770
rescuing canned, 896
sautéing and flambéing, 873
Poached eggs (master recipe), 148–49
Poached fish (master technique), 252–54
Poached fruit (master technique), 865–69
Pomegranates, 897
Pompano
about, 273
baked stuffed, 243
broiler-grilling, 228
broiling, 225
oven-broiling, 232
pan-frying, 259
in white wine sauce, 251
Popovers (master recipe), 685–86
Poppyseed
about, 21
cookies, 739
Porcini mushrooms. *See* Cèpes mushrooms
Porgy
about, 273
baked stuffed, 243
broiler-grilling, 228
broiling, 225
french-frying, 266
pan-frying, 259
sweet-and-sour, Southeast Asian style, 261–62
Pork
about, 338
braising, preparing for, 428
and caper casserole, 202
chops
braised (master technique), 426–28
mushroom smothered, 433
paprika smothered, 434
red wine smothered, 436
sautéed, with applejack and cream, 408
sautéed (with mustard, capers, and cream) master recipe, 406–8
sautéed with tomatoes and fresh herbs, 409
sautéing, choosing for, 407
stuffed, Georgia-style, 437–38
in country pâté, 213–14
curried casserole, 202
doneness of, 340

Pork *(Continued)*
fat, for pâté mold, 213
ground, in meat sauce, 185
hocks, and greens, 466
loin, deep-frying, 424
roast (master recipe), 367–69
about, 366
with apples, 370
with potatoes and onions, 371
provençal, 372–73
stuffed with wine-soaked dried fruits, 370–71
tonnato, 373–74
with turnips, 372
salad, 122
spareribs
choosing, 374
roasted, 374–75
steaks
braised (master technique) 426–28
mushroom smothered, 433
paprika smothered, 434
red wine smothered, 436
stew meat
braised (master technique), 426–28
green pepper ragout of, 430–31
mushroom fricassee of, 433
paprika fricassee of, 434
red wine fricassee of, 436
with spices, fruits, and olives; Mexican-style, 432–33
in Swedish meatballs, 211–12
veal, and chicken meatballs in parsley cream sauce, 210–11
veal, and chicken patties (master recipe), 208–10
see also Bacon; Ham
Pot pies. *See* Meat pies
Pot roast. *See* Beef
Potato ricers, 10
Potatoes
about, 575–76
baked, 580
boiled (master recipe), 577
as hors d'oeuvre, 72
cabbage soup, 94
cream of, 81
with cheese; scalloped, 581–82
in cream sauce, 578
french-fried, 584–85
frittatas (master recipe), 151–52
hash brown, 579
leftover, rescuing, 576
mashed, 578–79
mushroom soup with dill; cream of, 86
overcooked boiled, rescuing, 576
pancakes; lacy, 583
purchasing and storage, 576
roasted, Rubinstein, 582–83
salad; my mother's, 124–25
scalloped, with cheese, 581–82
soup; cream of, 87
soup from overcooked boiled potatoes, 576
stuffed baked, 580–81
in vichyssoise, 89–90
see also Sweet potatoes
Pots, 7
Poultry
about, 329–44
braising, about, 425–26
broiling, 384–88
cooking, facts about, 341–42
deep-frying, 422–23
variation chart, 423
livers, doneness of, 339
roast, 345–61
sautéing, 394–404
about, 393–94
stewing, 455–64
about, 455
stuffing, about, 361–62
temperature table for, 343
temperature taking, 343
see also Chicken; Duck; Turkey
Poultry seasoning, 21
Pound cakes. *See* Cakes
Praline
cream cup custards, 712
cream pie, 779
powder, 860–61
soufflé, 724–25
Prickly pears
about, 897
peeling, 897
Prosciutto and peas; pasta in cream with, 189
Provençal roast pork or veal, 372–73
Prunes
and apples; bread stuffing with, 363
dried
bread stuffing with, 364
Leah's custard pie with, 786
nut bread, 667
Pudding
bread, 708
corn, 526–27
Indian, 707
rice, 706
Yorkshire, 686
Pullman loaf (buttered white bread), 641
Pumpkin
bread, 667
muffins, 684
pie, 790
soup; cream of, 90–91
Purée of broccoli, 494
Purée of cranberry or lima beans, 487
Purée of dried beans, 625
Purée of red peppers, 573
Purée of winter squash (master recipe), 601–2
Purée of winter squash with bacon, 603
Purée of winter squash with chives, 603
Purée of winter squash with ginger, maple syrup, and walnuts, 603

Purée of winter squash with parmesan cheese, 604

Quiche
cheddar and jalapeño, 163
chicken, 164
corn, Marilyn's Tex-Mex, 525–26
crab, 164
ham, bleu cheese, and parsley, 165
ham and Swiss (master recipe), 162–63
as hors d'oeuvre, 69
lobster, 164
Lorraine, classic, 164–65
Moira (onion and cheese), 165–66
mushroom, 165
salmon, 166
shells, about, 161–62
shrimp-chili, 166
spinach, 167
turkey, 164
zucchini, 167
see also Timbales
Quinces
about, 897–98
in jelly, 869
poaching, 869

Racks, 13
Radishes
about, 588
cooking, 588
as salad addition, 114
Ragout. *See* Stews
Raised doughnuts and raised jelly doughnuts, 652–54
Raisins
about, 887
applesauce bread, 665
bread, 642
egg bread, 649
nut bars, 732
nut bread; spiced (master recipe), 644–65
oatmeal muffins, 682
Raspberries
about, 898
and bananas, for cream tart or pie, 775
Bavarian cream, 719
chiffon pie, 783
for cream tart or pie, 775
frozen, 898
pancakes, 688
sherbet, 878
Raw scallops rémoulade or vinaigrette, 312
Recipes, how to use, xiv
Red beans. *See* Beans and peas, dried
Red clam sauce, 186
Red pepper, crushed, 18
Red snapper
about, 273
baked stuffed, 243
braising, 237
broiling, 225
broiler-grilling, 228
in fish stock, 27–28
oven-broiling, 232
pan-frying, 259
poaching, 255
in white wine sauce, 251
Red wine fricassee of chicken, giblets, pork, or veal, or smothered pork or veal chops or steaks, 436
Relishes, cranberry-orange, 885–86
Rémoulade sauce, 55
raw scallops in, 312
Reschovsky, Helen, 143
Rescued bottled clam juice, 29
Rescued canned beef (or chicken) broth, 28–29
Rhubarb
about, 898
crisp, 898
filling, for pastry, 773
poaching, 869
strawberry filling, for pastry, 773
Rice
about, 615–16
with almonds or pine nuts, 621
with cheese, 620–21
curried, 619
fruited, 619
Middle Eastern, 620
with mushrooms, 621
overcooked, rescuing, 617
parsleyed, 620
pilaf, 622
pudding, 706
saffron, 621–22
steamed (master recipe), 617–18
tomato soup with dill, 99
types, 616
undercooked, rescuing, 617
see also Wild rice
Roast beef (or lamb) au jus (master recipe), 378–81
Roast chicken (master recipe), 346–48
Roast chicken with garlic and rosemary, 349
Roast chicken with giblet cream gravy, 348–49
Roast duck with cherries, 353
Roast duck with orange sauce (master recipe), 350–53
Roast duck with peaches, 353
Roast pork with apples, 370
Roast pork stuffed with wine-soaked dried fruits, 370–71
Roast pork with turnips, 372
Roast pork or veal with potatoes and onions, 371
Roast pork (or veal or turkey breast) master recipe, 367–69
Roast turkey with bread and oyster stuffing and giblet gravy, 356–61

Roasted potatoes Rubinstein, 582–83
Roasted spareribs, 374–75
Roasting
  meat, 366–81
  poultry, 345–61
Roasting pans, 7
Robert E. Lee cake, 816
Rock Cornish hens. *See* Chicken
Rocket. *See* Arugula
Rockfish. *See* Monkfish; Sea bass
Roe. *See* Shad roe
Rolling pins, 12–13
  pasta, 179–80
Rolls and buns
  brioche-shape breakfast rolls, 647
  cinnamon-nut buns, 651–52
  cinnamon-nut snails, 677
  cloverleaf dinner rolls, 643–44
  ham and Swiss rolls, 657
  hamburger buns, 656
  hard rolls (master recipe), 654–56
  for hors d'oeuvre, 68
  hero rolls, 656
  olive and garlic rolls, 657
  see also Biscuits; Muffins
Roquefort cheese
  hors d'oeuvre, 73–74
  salad dressing, 119
Rosemary, 21
Roux, 32
Rum
  butter cake filling, 854
  cake; Italian, 834
  cream pie (master recipe), 776–77
Russian beets, 491
Russian dressing and Russian salad dressing, 55–56
Rutabagas
  about, 611
  glazed (master recipe), 611–12
    in meat stock, 613
  purée with mushrooms, 612
  soup; cream of, 89
  trimming, 611–12
  in vegetable soup, 100
  see also Turnips
Ruth Hoberman's fish salad, 121

Saffron
  about, 22
  rice, 621–22
Sage, 22
Salad bowls, 111–12
Salad dressing
  about, 115
  bleu cheese, 119
  cucumber, 53
  green goddess, 53
  Italian, 118
  low-calorie, 117
  mustard-tarragon, 118
  oil and vinegar (master recipe), 117–18
  Roquefort cheese, 119
  Russian, 55–56
  sour cream, 119
  vinaigrette (master recipe), 117–18
  see also Mayonnaise; Sauces
Salads, 107–15, 119–29
  about, 107–8
  beef, 120
  Caesar, 127–29
  chicken (master recipe), 119–20
  chickpea or white bean, 626
  cole slaw, 124
  crab, 120–21
  cucumber, 125
  egg, party-type, for hors d'oeuvre, 68
  fish, Ruth Hoberman's, 121
    using leftovers in, 267
  greens, 108–12
    amounts to use, 109
    storing, 110–11
    tearing or cutting, 112
    varieties, 109–10
    washing and drying, 111
    wilted, rescuing, 111
  ham, 121
  lamb, 120
  lobster, 122
  mayonnaise, for hors d'oeuvre, 68
  mussel, 302
  nongreen additions to, 112–15
  pea, cold, 569
  pepper, 573
  pork, 122
  potato, my mother's, 124–25
  serving, 112
  shrimp, 122
  spinach, mushroom, and bacon, 126–27
  turkey, 123
  veal, 123
  warm shell bean, with bacon, 488
  and wine, 108
Sally Lunn. *See* Egg bread
Salmon
  about, 273–74
  baked stuffed, 243–44
    with dill and cucumber stuffing, 245
  broiler-grilling, 228
  broiling, 225
  cakes, 267–69
  croquettes, 267–69
  in fish casserole, New England, 202
  in fish salad, Ruth Hoberman's, 121
  oven-broiling, 232
    with dill, 233
    with green peppercorns, 234
    with lime butter, 234
  pan-frying, 259
    steaks with tomato cream sauce, 262
  poaching, 255
  quiche, 166

Salmon *(Continued)*
in seafood soufflé, 175–76
skin, removing, 274
smoked, in lox and cream cheese scramble, 143
in white wine sauce, 251
Salsify
about, 588
cooking, 588
soup; cream of, 87
Salt, 22
Saucepans, 6
Sauces, 31–57
about, 31–32
béarnaise, 48
buttermilk dressing, 52
cheese, 37–38
with wine, 38
cherry, for roast duck, 353
clarified butter, 57
colbert, 415, 419
cream
about, 32–34
bacon-horseradish, 35
basic (master recipe), 34–35
California, with olives and almonds, 36
caper, 36
champagne, 37
cheese, 37–38
cheese with wine, 38
crab, 42–43
curried, 39–40
deviled, 40
dilled, 41
with hard-cooked eggs and fresh herbs, 38–39
horseradish, 41
lemon, 41–42
lobster, 42–43
lumpy, rescuing, 33
milk-based, about, 34
mushroom, 43
onion, 43–44
parsley, for meatballs, 210–11
parsleyed, 41
scorched, rescuing, 33
sherried, 44
sour, 44
stock-based, about, 34
thin, rescuing, 33
tomato-basil, 45
with white grapes, 39
cream, for pasta (master recipe), 186–87
with basil, 188
with garlic, for fettuccine Alfredo, 187
with garlic and walnuts, 187
with Gorgonzola, cognac, and walnuts, 187–88
with prosciutto or pepperoni and peas, 189
with sausage, 189
with seafood, 190
with vegetables, for primavera, 188
with vodka and hot pepper, 190
deglazing
apple and cream, 410–11
applejack and cream, 408
apples, curry, and cream, 411
cognac, 413
cognac and cream, 415–16
cream, 408
cream and port, 399
lemon, 395
lemon-butter, 402
lemon and garlic, 396
lemon, garlic, and capers, 402–3
madeira, 418
madeira and cream, 405
marsala, 403
mustard-caper, for lamb chops or steaks, 417–18
mustard-caper, for meat patties, 210
mustard and green peppercorns, 414
red wine and mushrooms, 414
sherry, 400
tomatoes and fresh herbs, 409
vinegar, 396
white wine, for chicken cutlets, 398
white wine, for sautéed chicken, 396
white wine and mustard, 400–401
wild mushrooms, 406
wine and cream, 405
hollandaise (master recipe), 46–47
about, 45, 46
blender or food processor method, 45–46
dilled, 49
mustard, 49
seafood, 50
separated, rescuing, 45
meat, 185
bolognese, 185
Mousseline, 49
orange, for roast duck, 350–53
for pasta, about, 177–78
peach, for roast duck, 353
pesto, 191
red clam, 186
rémoulade, 55
Russian dressing, 55–56
sour cream, 44
sour cream dressing, 52
tartar, 56
tomato (master recipe), 183–84
storing, 184
tomato cream, for salmon steaks, 262
tomato with olives, for squid, 326–27
white wine, for fish, 248–51
yogurt dressing, 52
see also Marinades; Mayonnaise; Salad dressing; Sauces, dessert
Sauces, dessert
berry, 860–61
chocolate, 852

Sauces *(Continued)*
crème fraîche, 860
custard, 856–57
Sausage
and apples stuffing, for butternut squash, 605–6
bread stuffing with, 364–65
in chili-stuffed green peppers, 574–75
and eggs stuffing, for beef rolls, 452–53
frittata with, 153
in meat sauce, 185
and onions; fried beans with, 628
pasta in cream with, 189
pizza, 198
in stuffing, for cabbage rolls, 506
in stuffing, for onions, 562
Sautéed beef steaks (with cognac and parsley) master recipe, 412–13
Sautéed beef steaks with colbert sauce, 415
Sautéed beef steaks with mustard and green peppercorns, 414
Sautéed beef steaks with red wine and mushrooms, 414
Sautéed broccoli rabe with garlic, 495–96
Sautéed calves' liver with bacon and onions, 419–20
Sautéed chicken breast cutlets (with white wine and herbs) master recipe, 397–98
Sautéed chicken breasts with cream and port, 399
Sautéed chicken (with lemon) master recipe, 394–95
Sautéed chicken with lemon and garlic, 396
Sautéed chicken livers with white wine and mustard, 400–401
Sautéed chicken with vinegar, 396
Sautéed chicken with white wine, 396
Sautéed cucumbers (master recipe), 529–30
Sautéed cucumbers in sour cream and dill, 531
Sautéed eggplant (master recipe), 532–33
Sautéed, flambéed fruit (master technique), 871–73
Sautéed ham steaks (with apples and cream) master recipe, 409–11
Sautéed ham steaks with apples, curry, and cream, 411
Sautéed ham steaks with pineapple, 411–12
Sautéed Jerusalem artichokes, 544
Sautéed lamb chops or steaks with colbert sauce, 419
Sautéed lamb chops or steaks with madeira, 418
Sautéed lamb chops or steaks (with mustard and capers) master recipe, 416–18
Sautéed mushrooms (master recipe), 550–51
Sautéed pork chops with applejack and cream, 408
Sautéed pork chops (with mustard, capers, and cream) master recipe, 406–8
Sautéed pork chops with tomatoes and fresh herbs, 409
Sautéed soft-shell crabs amandine or meunière, 289–90
Sautéed sole or flounder fillets amandine, 263–64
Sautéed summer squash (master recipe), 594–95
Sautéed summer squash with garlic and crumbs, 596
Sautéed veal chops with madeira and cream, 405
Sautéed veal chops (with white wine and cream) master recipe, 404–5
Sautéed veal chops with wild mushrooms, 406
Sautéed veal scallops or turkey breast scallops (with lemon-butter sauce) master recipe, 401–2
Sautéed veal scallops or turkey breast scallops with lemon, garlic, and capers, 402–3
Sautéed veal scallops or turkey breast scallops with marsala, 403
Sautéed zucchini with walnuts, 597
Sautéing
meat, 393–94, 401–20
poultry, 393–404
skillets for, 394
Savory, 22
Scallions
about, 555–56
as salad addition, 114
Scalloped cabbage, 502
Scalloped oysters (master recipe), 308–9
Scalloped potatoes with cheese, 581–82
Scallops
about, 311
baked in garlic crumbs, 314
broiled, 313–14
cooking, 312
deep-fried breaded, 314–15
as hors d'oeuvre, 71
purchasing, 312
raw
rémoulade, 312
vinaigrette, 312

Scallops *(Continued)*
sautéed with garlic and lemon (master recipe), 312–13
Scones, 675–76
Scrambled eggs (master recipe), 140
Scrod
about, 270–71
baked stuffed, 243
with tomato stuffing, 244
braising, 237
Mediterranean, 238
broiling, 225
french-frying, 266
oven-broiling, 231
pan-frying, 258
poaching, 254
in white wine sauce, 251
see also Cod
Scup. *See* Porgy
Sea bass
about, 274
baked stuffed, 244
braising, 237
in coconut milk, 238
broiler-grilling, 228
broiling, 225
cakes, 267–69
croquettes, 267–69
in fish stock, 27–28
french-frying, 266
oven-broiling, 232
pan-frying, 259
poaching, 255
in white wine sauce, 251
see also Striped bass
Sea squab. *See* Blowfish
Sea trout. *See* Weakfish
Seafoam icing. *See* Toffee frosting
Seafood
hollandaise, 50
soufflé, 175–76
using leftovers in, 267
see also individual names
Seed cake, 826
Sesame seed
about, 22
wafers, 739–40
Shad
about, 274
baked stuffed, 244
braising, 237
broiling, 226
oven-broiling, 232
with anchovy butter, 234
pan-frying, 259
in white wine sauce, 251
Shad roe
about, 274
butter-poached, 275
Shallots
about, 556
purchasing and storage, 556
Shark
about, 275
broiler-grilling, 228
broiling, 226
pan-frying, 259
Shell beans. *See* Beans, shell
Shellfish, 279–327
about, 279–80
casserole, 202
deep-fried, as hors d'oeuvre, 70
as hors d'oeuvre, 70–71
stock, 42
see also individual names
Sherbet (master technique), 876–79
about, 875–76
apricot, 877
blackberry, 877
blueberry, 877
cherry, 877
cranberry, 877
grapefruit, 877
lemon, 877
lime, 877
mango, 877
melon, 878
nectarine, 878
orange, 878
peach, 878
pear, 878
pineapple, 878
raspberry, 878
strawberry, 878
tangerine, 878
Sherried celery with walnuts, 515
Sherried cream sauce, 44
Sherried sautéed chicken livers (master recipe), 399–400
Sherry
deglazing sauce, for chicken livers, 400
in sherried cream sauce, 44
Shiitake mushrooms. *See* Mushrooms, wild
Shortcake, 676
Shrimp
about, 315
baked in crumbs, Louisiana-style, 318–19
baked stuffed giant, 319
in bouillabaisse, 93–94
chili quiche, 166
cooking, 316
curried, 318
deep-fried
batter-dipped, 321–22
breaded, 320
freshness, checking for, 315
hors d'oeuvre, 73–74
as hors d'oeuvre, 71
mousse stuffing, for sole or flounder, 252
Newburg, 318
in pasta in cream with seafood, 190
peeling and deveining, 316
purchasing, 315
salad, 122
sautéed with garlic and lemon, 317
in shellfish casserole, 202
shells, in fish stock, 27–28
sizes and servings, 316
steaming, 317
stuffed coconut-fried, Leah's, 320–21
tempura, 322–23
Sifters, 13
Skillet-boiled asparagus (master recipe), 475–76

Skillet-braised cabbage (master recipe), 500–501
Skillet-braised peas (master recipe), 567
Skillet corn bread, 670
Skillets, 6–7
  for sautéing, 394
Smelts
  about, 275
  broiler-grilling, 228
  broiling, 226
  french-frying, 266
  pan-frying, 259
    curried, 263
Snails
  about, 323
  in garlic butter, 323–24
Snapper. *See* Red snapper
Snowpeas. *See* Peas
Soft-cooked eggs (master recipe), 144–45
Sole
  about, 275–76
  baked stuffed fillets, 244
    with crabmeat stuffing, 246
    with mushroom stuffing, 246
  braising, 237
    sweet-and-sour, 239
  broiling, 226
  fillets amandine; sautéed, 263–64
  fillets stuffed with shrimp mousse, 252
  in fish stock, 27–28
  french-frying, 266
  meunière, 264
  oven-broiling, 232
  pan-frying, 259
  poaching, 255
  in white wine sauce, 251
Sorrel
  about, 110, 589
  soup; cream of, 87–88
Soufflé molds, 14
Soufflés
  about, 168–71
  apricot, 721–22
  banana, 722
  cheese (master recipe), 171–72
  chicken, 174
  chocolate, 722
  coconut, 723
  corn-bacon, 174
  espresso, 723
  Grand Marnier, 724
  ham and cheese, 175
  ingredients chart, 170
  lemon, 724
  pizza, 175
  praline, 724–25
  rescuing, 169–70, 171
  seafood, 175–76
    using leftovers in, 267
  spinach, 176
  vanilla-rum (master recipe), 720–21
Soups, 75–106
  about, 75–76
  almond, cream of, 80
  artichoke, cream of, 80
  asparagus, cream of, 80
  beef-mushroom-noodle, 92–93
  black bean, 104–5
  bouillabaisse, 93–94
  broccoli, cream of (master recipe), 78–79
  cabbage-potato, 94
    cream of, 80
  carrot, cream of, 81
  cauliflower, cream of, 81–82
  celery, cream of, 82
  celery root, cream of, 82
  chestnut, cream of, 82–83
  chicken chowder, 103
  chicken gumbo, 96
  chicken noodle, with corn, 95
  chicken with rice, curried, 97
  clam chowder, 102
    Manhattan, 97
  consommé, 76–77
  corn chowder (master recipe), 101–2
  corn, cream of, 83
  cucumber, cream of, 83
  fennel, cream of, 84
  fish chowder, 103
    using leftovers in, 267
  home-style (master technique), 91–92
  Jerusalem artichoke, cream of, 84
  kohlrabi, cream of, 85
  lettuce, cream of, 85
  lobster broth, 294
  Manhattan clam chowder, 97
  minestrone, 105–6
  mushroom, cream of, 85
  mushroom-potato, with dill, cream of, 86
  Navy bean, 104–5
  onion, cream of, 86
  oyster stew, 306
  parsnip, cream of, 86
  pea, green, cream of, 84
  potato, cream of, 87
  potato, from overcooked boiled, 576
  pumpkin, cream of, 90–91
  rutabaga, cream of, 89
  salsify, cream of, 87
  sorrel, cream of, 87–88
  spinach, cream of, 88
  split pea, 98–99
  Swiss chard, cream of, 88
  tomato, cream of, 88–89
  tomato-rice, with dill, 99
  turnip, cream of, 89
  vegetable, 100
  vichyssoise, 89–90
  watercress, cream of, 90
  winter squash, cream of, 90–91
  zucchini, cream of, 91
  see also Stocks
Sour cream
  in cheesecake, 713–14
  chocolate frosting, 852–53
  dressing, 52
  muffins, 684
  salad dressing, 119
  sauce, 44
Sourgrass. *See* Sorrel
Southern-fried catfish, 260
Soy sauce marinade, 386

Spaghetti casserole, 202
Spaghetti squash. *See* Squash, winter
Spanish omelet, 160–61
Spareribs
  choosing, 374
  roasted, 374–75
Spatulas, 9
Spice cake, 818
Spice layer cake; classic, 818
Spice muffins, 684–85
Spiced pound cake, 826
Spiced purée of winter squash, 604
Spiced raisin-nut bread (master recipe), 664–65
Spices. *See* Herbs and spices; individual names
Spinach
  about, 110, 589
  butter, 307–8
  creamed, 591
  in eggs "Benetine," 150
  in eggs florentine, 150
  frittata with, 154
  frozen, 589
  gritty cooked, rescuing, 589
  mushroom, and bacon salad, 126–27
  old-fashioned butter-braised, 592
  purée, 591
  quiche, 167
  sauté
    with bacon and hard-cooked egg, 593
    Chinese-style, 593
    with garlic, 592
  soufflé, 176
  soup; cream of, 88
  steamed (master recipe), 590
  stuffings, preparing for, 591
  timbales, 167–68
  trimming and washing, 590
Split pea soup, 98–99
Sponge cake (master recipe), 826–28
Sponge layer cake with praline butter cream, 831
Sponge roll cake, 835–36
Spoons, 9
Spreads
  egg salad, party-type, 68
Springform pans, 14
Sprouts, as salad addition, 114
Squash, summer
  about, 594
  with garlic and crumbs, sautéed, 596
  in heavy cream with garlic and basil, 595
  overmature, rescuing, 594
  with parmesan cheese, onions, and herbs, 596
  sautéed (master recipe), 594–95
  steamed, 598
  stuffed with beef or lamb, 598–600
  in tomato sauce, 597
  washing and cutting, 595
  see also Squash, winter; Zucchini
Squash, winter
  about, 600–601
  with bacon; purée of, 603
  baked, 604–5
  butternut, stuffed with sausage and apples; baked, 605–6
  preparing, 601
  purchasing and storage, 601
  purée of (master recipe), 601–2
    with chives, 603
    with ginger, maple syrup, and walnuts, 603
    with parmesan cheese, 604
  spiced, 604
  seeds, toasting, 602
  soup; cream of, 90–91
  see also Squash, summer
Squid
  about, 324
  cleaning, 324
  fried, 327
  sautéed with garlic and lemon, 326
  in tomato sauce with olives, 326–27
Stainless steel. *See* Cookware
Steak tartare, 206–7
  cannibal balls from, 71
Steaks. *See* Beef; Ham; Lamb; Pork
Steamed blue crabs, 287–88
Steamed cauliflower (master recipe), 511–12
Steamed clams, 281–82
Steamed kohlrabi, 545
Steamed rice (master recipe), 617–18
Steamed shrimp, 317
Steamed spinach (master recipe), 590
Steamed summer squash, 598
Steaming basket, 11
Stewed tomatoes, 608
Stewing
  meat, 455–58, 461–62, 465–66
  poultry, 455–64
Stews
  beef
    braised, Napa Valley, 450
    chili, 449
    curry, 447–48
    goulash, 451
    old-fashioned, 443–44
    with onions and beer; Flemish, 445–46
    stew meat, braised (master technique), 440–42
  chicken
    à la king, 458–59
    cacciatore, 431
    country captain fricassee of, 428–29
    creamed, with olives and toasted almonds, 459–60

Stews *(Continued)*
creamed, with white grapes (véronique), 460–61
Creole, 429–30
curried, with vegetables, 461
green pepper ragout of, 430–31
mushroom fricassee of, 433
paprika fricassee of, 434
with parsley dumplings, 462
red wine fricassee of, 436
with spices, fruits and olives, Mexican-style, 432–33
tarragon and white wine fricassee of, 435
with vegetables and cream gravy; old-fashioned (master recipe), 456–58
chili, 449
giblet
country captain fricassee of, 428–29
Creole, 429–30
curried, with vegetables, 461
mushroom fricassee of, 433
paprika fricassee of, 434
with parsley dumplings, 462
red wine fricassee of, 436
with vegetables and cream gravy; old-fashioned (master recipe), 456–58
goulash, 451
hunter, 431
lamb
braised (master technique), 440–42
braised, Napa Valley, 450
chili, 449
curry, 447–48
with flageolets or lima beans, 446–47
goulash, 451
old-fashioned, 443–44
oyster, 306
pork
chops or steaks mushroom smothered, 433
chops or steaks paprika smothered, 434
chops or steaks red wine smothered, 436
green pepper ragout of, 430–31
mushroom fricassee of, 433
paprika fricassee of, 434
red wine fricassee of, 436
with spices, fruits, and olives, Mexican-style, 432–33
turkey
creamed, with white grapes, (véronique), 460
curried, with vegetables, 461
with parsley dumplings, 462
with vegetables and cream gravy, old-fashioned (master recipe), 456–58
veal
chasseur, 431
chops or steaks mushroom smothered, 433
chops or steaks paprika smothered, 434
chops or steaks red wine smothered, 436
chops or steaks tarragon and white wine smothered, 435
curried, with vegetables, 461
green pepper ragout of, 430–31
mushroom fricassee of, 433
paprika fricassee of, 434
with parsley dumplings, 462
red wine fricassee of, 436
tarragon and white wine fricassee of, 435
with vegetables and cream gravy; old-fashioned (master recipe), 456–58
Stir-fried Chinese cabbage, 503
Stocks, 23–29
beef (master recipe), 24–26
canned beef (or chicken) broth, rescued, 28–29
chicken, 26
clam juice, rescued bottled, 29
clarifying, 76–77
fish, 27–28
substitute for, 29
freezing, 26
reducing to glaze, 26
shellfish, 42
veal, 27
see also Soups
Storage
containers, 4
space, 4
Strainers, 11
Strawberries
about, 899
Bavarian cream, 719
chiffon pie, 783
chocolate-dipped, 900–901
for cream tart or pie, 775
frozen, 899
hulling, 899
pancakes, 688
profiteroles, 797
rescuing, 899
rhubarb filling, for pastry, 773
sherbet, 878
shortcake, 899–900

Streusel coffeecake, 676–77
Streusel crumb fruit pie or tart (master technique), 764–66
Striped bass
 about, 276
 baked stuffed, 244
 braising, 237
 broiler-grilling, 228
 broiling, 226
 in fish stock, 27–28
 oven-broiling, 232
 pan-frying, 259
 poaching, 255
 in white wine sauce, 251
 see also Sea bass
Stuffed baked potatoes, 580–81
Stuffed cabbage rolls in sweet-and-sour sauce, 505–7
Stuffed mushrooms, 552
Stuffed summer squash with beef or lamb, 598–600
Stuffing
 with bacon, for trout, 247
 with beef, for summer squash, 599
 bread
  with apples and prunes, 363
  with chestnuts and apples, 363–64
  with dried fruits, 364
  with oysters (master recipe), 361–62
  with oysters and pecans, 364
  with sausage, 364–65
  with turkey and chicken livers, 365
 with cheddar, for tomatoes, 610–11
 chili, for green peppers, 574–75
 corn bread, with oysters, 365–66
 crabmeat, for fish, 246
 dill and anchovy
  for turkey rolls, 439
  for veal rolls, 439
 dill and cucumber, for fish, 245
 dried fruit, for pork, 370–71
 with garlic and parmesan cheese, for clams, 284–85
 with ham, for pork chops, 437
 with ham and onion, for artichokes, 472–73
 with lamb
  for eggplant, 538–39
  for summer squash, 599
 for lobster, 298–99
 mushroom, 552, 553
  for sole or flounder, 246
 with onion and celery, for fish, 241
 with oysters or clams, for fish, 245
 with parmesan cheese and garlic, for potatoes, 581
 poultry, about, 361–62
 sausage
  for beef rolls, 452
  for onions, 562
 sausage and apple, for butternut squash, 606
 sausage and ham, for cabbage rolls, 506
 shrimp mousse, for sole or flounder, 252
 with shrimp and parsley, for shrimp, 319
 tomato, for fish, 244
Sugar cookies, 740
Sugar snap peas. *See* Peas
Summer squash. *See* Squash, summer
Sunchokes. *See* Jerusalem artichokes
Swedish-American beef pot roast, 448
Swedish meatballs, 211–12
Sweet-and-sour braised sole or flounder, 239
Sweet-and-sour fried porgy southeast Asian style, 261–62
Sweet potatoes
 about, 585
 baked, 587
 candied, 585–86
 french-fried, 587
 mashed, 586
Swiss chard
 about, 606
 soup; cream of, 88
Swiss cheese
 in cheese omelet, 159
 in cheese sauce, 37–38
 in cheese sauce with wine, 38
 in cheese scramble, 141
 in cheese soufflé, 171–73
 in ham and cheese soufflé, 175
 and ham quiche (master recipe), 162–63
 and ham rolls, 657
 and ham scramble, 142
 hors d'oeuvre, 73–74
 in pizza soufflé, 175
 in quiche moira, 165–66
Swordfish
 about, 276
 braising, 237
 broiler-grilling, 228
  Mediterranean, 229
 broiling, 226
 pan-frying, 259

Tables and charts
 cake pan chart for yellow cakes, 807
 cake pan substitution chart, 803
 casserole variation, 202
 chocolate
  estimated contents of, 697
  proportions for substituting, 697
 cooking temperatures, for poultry and meat, 344
 deep-fried poultry or meat variation, 424

Tables *(Continued)*
delay table for bread doughs, 658–59
egg sizes, 133
fish
baked stuffed, 243–44
braising, 237
broiler-grilling, 228
broiling, 225–26
french-frying, 266
oven-broiling, 231–32
pan-frying, 258–60
poaching, 254–56
in white wine sauce, 251
flavoring and saucing, for baked stuffed eggs, 148
fruit filling, for pastry, 771–73
meringue frosting, decreasing, 845
recipe yield variation chart for yellow cake, 807
soufflé ingredients, 170
timing-for six eggs, 145
Tangelos, 901
Tangerines
about, 901
sherbet, 878
Tarragon
about, 22
and white wine fricassee of chicken or veal, 435
and white wine smothered veal chops or steaks, 435
Tart molds, French, 14
Tartar sauce, 56
Tartlet molds, 14
Tartlet shells, 759–60
Tarts
fruit (master technique), 769–70
fruit cream, fresh (master technique), 774
fruit, streusel crumb (master technique), 764–66
fruits for, 770, 775
shells
3-inch, 759
9-inch, 758–59
tartlet, 759–60
see also Cobblers; Pastry crusts, doughs, and shells; Pies
Temperatures, cooking, 344
Tempura
batter (master technique), 64
oysters, 311
shrimp, 322–23
vegetables, as hors d'oeuvre, 70
Thermometers
candy/deep-fry, 11
meat
about, 11, 342
accuracy, testing for, 342
temperature taking with, 343
oven and freezer, 11
Thyme, 22
Tilefish
about, 276
baked stuffed, 244
braising, 237
broiling, 226
cakes, 267–69
croquettes, 267–69
in fish stock, 27–28
oven-broiling, 232
pan-frying, 260
poaching, 255
in white wine sauce, 251
Timbales
mushroom, 167–68
spinach, 167–68
zucchini, 167–68
see also Quiche
Toaster ovens, 12
Toffee
frosting (seafoam icing), 848
meringue butter cream, 848
Tomatoes
about, 606–7
basil cream sauce, 45
broiled, 609–10
canned, seeding, 607
cheddar-stuffed, 610–11
cherry, sautéed in butter, 608–9
cream sauce, for salmon steaks, 262
and fresh herb sauce, for pork chops, 409
frittata with, 154
green, as pastry filling, 772
peeling and seeding, 607
rice soup with dill, 99
as salad addition, 114–15
sauce (master recipe), 183–84
Greek-style, for green or wax beans, 483–84
storing, 184
seeding, 607
soup; cream of, 88–89
stewed, 608
stuffing, for cod, 244
unripe, rescuing, 607–8
in vegetable soup, 100
Tongs, 9
Trout
about, 277
baked stuffed, 244
whole, with bacon stuffing, 247
braising, 237
with tarragon and cream, 239–40
broiler-grilling, 228
broiling, 226
french-frying, 266
oven-broiling, 232
pan-frying, 260
poaching, 255
"au bleu," 256
in white wine sauce, 251
Truffles, 549
Tuna
about, 277
broiler-grilling, 228
noodle casserole, 202
pan-frying, 260
in seafood soufflé, 175–76
Turkey
à la king, 458–59
breast, roast (master recipe), 367–69

Turkey *(Continued)*
preparing, 369
tonnato, 373–74
breast rolls; dilled stuffed, 438–40
breast scallops
sautéed, breaded (with lemon-butter sauce), 403–4
sautéed (with lemon-butter sauce) master recipe, 401–2
sautéed, with lemon, garlic, and capers, 402–3
sautéed, with marsala, 403
sautéing, choosing for, 401
casserole, day-after-Thanksgiving, 202
creamed, with white grapes (véronique), 460–61
croquettes, 215–16
deep-frying, 424
doneness of, 339
giblets
à la king, 458–59
braised (master technique), 426–28
braising, preparing for, 427–28
country captain fricassee of, 428–29
gravy, 360–61
mushroom fricassee of, 433
paprika fricassee of, 434
red wine fricassee of, 436
stew; Creole, 429
stew with parsley dumplings, 462
stew with vegetables and cream gravy, old-fashioned (master recipe), 456–58
stew with vegetables; curried, 461
stewing, preparing for, 458
livers
and chicken livers; bread stuffing with, 365
doneness of, 339
pot pies, 463
quiche, 164
roast
about, 353–55
with bread and oyster stuffing and giblet gravy, 356–61
choosing, 355
salad, 123
stew
with parsley dumplings, 462
with vegetables and cream gravy; old-fashioned (master recipe), 456–58
with vegetables; curried, 461
stewing, preparing for, 458
tetrazzini, 464–65
veal, and pork patties (master recipe), 208–10
see also Chicken; Duck; Stuffing
Turmeric, 22
Turnips
about, 611
glazed (master recipe), 611–12
in meat stock, 613
greens, in pork hocks and greens, 466
soup; cream of, 89
trimming, 611–12
in vegetable soup, 100
see also Rutabagas

Ugli fruits, 901
Utensils, 5–14
appliances, small, 12
for baking, 12–14
baskets
deep-frying, 11
steaming, 11
bowls, 8
colanders, 11
cookware, 5–7, 394
food mills, 10
garlic presses, 10
graters, 9–10
knives, 8–9
measures, 7–8
meat grinders, 10
mortar and pestle, 10–11
nutmeg graters, 10
pasta machines, 179
pasta rolling pins, 179–80
peppermills, 10
potato ricers, 10
spatulas, 9
spoons, 9
strainers, 11
thermometers, 11, 342, 343
tongs, 9
wire whips, 9

Vanilla
cream cup custards (master recipe), 711–12
cream pie, 780
crumb pie crust, 762
rum soufflé (master recipe), 720–21
Veal
about, 336
braising, preparing for, 428
chicken, and pork meatballs in parsley cream sauce, 210–11
chicken and pork patties (master recipe), 208–10
chops
braised (master technique), 426–28
broiled (master recipe), 388–89
broiled, with cheese, garlic, and sage, 389
broiling, choosing for, 388

Veal *(Continued)*
mushroom smothered, 433
paprika smothered, 434
red wine smothered, 436
sautéed, with madeira and cream, 405
sautéed (with white wine and cream) master recipe, 404–5
sautéed, with wild mushrooms, 406
sautéing, choosing for, 404
tarragon and white wine smothered, 435
in country pâté, 213–14
doneness of, 340
ground, in meat sauce bolognese, 185
in party casserole with grapes, 202
roast (master recipe), 367–69
with potatoes and onions, 371
preparing, 369
Provençal, 372–73
tonnato, 373–74
salad, 123
scallops
about, 336
deep-frying, 424
rolls; dilled stuffed, 438–40
sautéed, breaded (with lemon-butter sauce), 403–4
sautéed (with lemon-butter sauce) master recipe, 401–2
sautéed, with lemon, garlic, and capers, 402–3
sautéed, with marsala, 403
sautéing, choosing for, 401
shoulder roast, for stock, 27
steaks
braised (master technique), 426–28
mushroom smothered, 433
paprika smothered, 434
red wine smothered, 436
tarragon and white wine smothered, 435
stew meat
in blanquette de veau (chicken à la king recipe), 458–59
braised (master technique), 426–28
chasseur (hunter stew), 431
green pepper ragout of, 430–31
mushroom fricasse of, 433
paprika fricassee of, 434
with parsley dumplings, 462
red wine fricasse of, 436
stewing, preparing for, 458
tarragon and white wine fricassee of, 435
with vegetables and cream gravy; old-fashioned (master recipe), 456–58
with vegetables; curried, 461
stock, 27
in Swedish meatballs, 211–12
Vegetables, 467–613
cooking, 467–69
times and doneness, 468–69
in minestrone, 105–6
raw, as hors d'oeuvre, 71–72
soup, 100
tempura, as hors d'oeuvre, 70
see also individual names
Vichyssoise, 89–90
Vinaigrette dressing (master recipe), 117–18
raw scallops in, 312
Vinegars
about, 116–17
flavored, about, 117
Virginia ham biscuits, 675

Waffles, 690
see also Pancakes
Walnuts
about, 702–3
apricot muffins, 679
balls, 738–39
cake, 818
cookies (master recipe), 740–42
in date-nut muffins, 682
maple cream pie, 778
maple layer cake, 819
in nutted meringue fingers, 794
orange layer cake, 819
pineapple muffins, 683
in raisin-nut bread; spiced, 664–65
Warm shell bean salad with bacon, 488
Watercress
about, 110, 613
soup; cream of, 90
storing, 613
Watermelons. *See* Melons
Wax beans. *See* Beans, wax
Weakfish
about, 277
broiler-grilling, 228
broiling, 226
pan-frying, 260
Whipped chocolate filling, 852
Whipped cream, 857–59
Whipped cream mayonnaise, 56
White beans. *See* Beans and peas, dried
White on black layer cake, classic, 814

White cake, 819
White layer cake, classic, 819
Whitefish
  about, 277
  baked stuffed, 244
  braising, 237
  broiling, 226
  oven-broiling, 232
  pan-frying, 260
  poaching, 255
Whiting
  about, 278
  baked stuffed, 244
  braising, 237
  broiling, 226
  oven-broiling, 232
  pan-frying, 260
  poaching, 256
Whole baked trout with bacon stuffing, 247
Whole wheat
  bread, 643
  cake, 820
  jam layer cake, 820
  muffins, 685
Wild mushrooms. *See* Mushrooms, wild
Wild rice, 616
Wine
  marsala deglazing sauce, for veal or turkey, 403
  and salad, 108
  white
    and cream deglazing sauce, 405
    deglazing sauce, 398
    sauce (master technique), 250–51
    and tarragon fricassee of chicken or veal, 435
    and tarragon smothered veal chops or steaks, 435
Wine vinegars. *See* Vinegars
Wire whips, 9
Wire whisks. *See* Wire whips
Yeast
  about, 632
  dissolving and proofing, 634–35
Yellow cake (master recipe), 808–11
Yellow squash. *See* Squash, summer
Yogurt dressing, 52
Yorkshire pudding, 686
Zucchini
  bread, 668
  fried eggs with, 139
  frittata with, 154
  quiche, 167
  soup; cream of, 91
  timbale, 167–68
  with walnuts; sautéed, 597
  see also Squash, summer